INDEX OF TITLES

CROWN COURT
INDEX 2012

CROWN COURT INDEX

THIRTY-SECOND EDITION

By

His Honour IAN McLEAN
Formerly a Circuit Judge

and

His Honour Judge
JOHN DIXON
A Circuit Judge

SWEET & MAXWELL  THOMSON REUTERS

First published 1964
Twentieth edition 2000
Twenty-First edition 2001
Twenty-Second edition 2002
Twenty-Third edition 2003
Twenty-Fourth edition 2004
Twenty-Fifth edition 2005
Twenty-Sixth Edition 2006
Twenty-Seventh Edition 2007
Twenty-Eighth Edition 2008
Twenty-Ninth Edition 2009
Thirtieth Edition 2010
Thirty-First Edition 2011
Thirty-Second Edition 2012

Published in 2012 by Sweet & Maxwell, 100 Avenue Road, London NW3 3PF
Part of Thomson Reuters (Professional) UK Limited
(Registered in England & Wales, Company No 1679046.
Registered Office and address for service:
Aldgate House, 33 Aldgate High Street, London EC3N 1DL)

For further information on our products and services, visit
www.sweetandmaxwell.co.uk

Typeset by Servis Filmsetting Ltd, Stockport, Cheshire
Printed and bound by CPI Group (UK) Ltd, Croydon, CR0 4Y

No natural forests were destroyed to make this product;
only farmed timber was used and replanted

A CIP catalogue record for this book is available from the British Library

ISBN 978-0-414-04771-6

PREFACE

THIS EDITION has been spared the usual outpourings of legislation, which has enabled the authors to attend to a number of cosmetic features. A real effort has been made to reduce its size. This has been achieved in a number of ways including the removal of material not immediately relevant to "An index of Common Penalties and Formalities", which has always been the volume's secondary title. Bearing in mind the purpose of the volume as an Index, it has long been thought unnecessary to have a lengthy subject index or "Tachiography" like a textbook, and the index at the rear of the volume has been returned to its original purpose, the listing of topics in "catch-all" titles. There are already quick guides in place in most of the titles and there is widespread cross-referencing.

Since 2003, at least the work has contained elements of enacted legislation, much of which has never come into force. The Legal Aid etc Bill 2011, now before Parliament, buries some of these topics, and the authors have taken the opportunity of removing them from the text.

Some titles contain explanations of the changes affected by legislation dating back to the 2003 Act, and material which applies to offences committed some six or even more years ago. This material has been severely pruned and reference is made to earlier editions of the work. An attempt has also been made to remove much of the patronising comment contained in the guidelines of the Sentencing Guidelines Council.

A number of cosmetic changes have been made in the order of titles. The authors, with hindsight, and a fresh eye, have considered one or two of the titles to be misleading, thus INDICATIONS ON SENTENCE has been changed into GOODYEAR INDICATION, CDS FUNDING which seems to have mystified many readers, has been returned to its original LEGAL AID; PUBLIC FUNDING. RT DISQUALIFICATION has been changed to DRIVING DISQUALIFICATIONS, which better identifies the width of the provisions; and RECOMMENDATION FOR DEPORTATION to plain DEPORTATION, which indicates the change of emphasis on this topic. CHALLENGING THE CROWN COURT has been changed to APPEALS FROM THE CROWN COURT, while APPEALS (i.e. to the Crown Court) has been altered to APPELLATE JURISDICTION. PARENTING ORDERS now form a separate title, and FORFEITURE, RESTITUTION AND AWARDS have been split into three separate titles. AGE OF OFFENDER has been returned to the tabular form which many readers missed. A new section has been added on applications to the Crown Court in relation to INDICTMENTS. There are other minor changes in the titles.

A number of sections have been widely re-structured. These include ABUSE OF PROCESS, APPEALS FROM THE CROWN COURT, Preparatory hearings in CASE MANAGEMENT, CONTEMPT OF COURT, DEALING WITH AN OFFENDER, DISCOUNTS ON SENTENCE, GUILTY PLEAS and, IMPRISONMENT.

Important changes will be made to COSTS, BAIL, COMMUNITY SENTENCES, DEFERRING SENTENCE, suspended sentences of IMPRISONMENT and YOUTH REHABILITATION ORDERS by the Legal Aid Etc Bill 2011 now before Parliament, but unlikely to be in force by the time this edition goes to print. Amendments tabled in the last days of October propose the repeal of the existing sentences for dangerous offenders and their replacement by new forms of sentence.

The authors have taken the opportunity to standardise case references throughout the volume, selecting as their first choice the Criminal Appeal Reports which is the series most widely available in the smaller locations of the Crown Court and in individual

PREFACE

private libraries. In second place, it may be necessary to refer to the Criminal Appeal (Sentencing) Reports. Cases may be referred to only in other sets of reports, but these are not so widely available, and some, such as Weekly Law Reports are frequently left unbound, tending to be lost or mislaid. Few courts still have an enthusiastic member of staff who extracts and files copy copies of *The Times* reports.

Market research show that this work is very much a book used by judges and court staff. Every attempt is made to make it a practical guide of use to advocates, probation officers and to others connected with the Crown Court, even to aspirants to the bench now faced with qualifying examinations.

The law is as stated on November 22, 2011.

TABLE OF ABBREVIATIONS

The following abbreviations appear in the text and refer to the respective enactments shown:

Statutes

ECHR	European Convention on Human Rights
CLA 1826	Criminal Law Act 1826
OAPA 1861	Offences Against the Person Act 1861
CPA 1865	Criminal Procedure Act 1865
BBEA 1879	Bankers' Books Evidence Act
ESA 1883	Explosive Substances Act 1883
POA 1907	Prohibition of Offenders Act 1907
AJ(MP)A 1933	Administration of Justice (Miscellaneous Provisions) Act 1933
CYPA 1933	Children and Young Persons Act 1933
ABOOA 1956	Magistrates' Courts (Appeals from Binding Over Orders) Act 1956
SOA 1956	Sexual Offences Act 1956
MHA 1959	Mental Health Act 1959
AJA 1960	Administration of Justice Act 1960
CYPA 1963	Children and Young Persons Act 1963
CP(I)A 1964	Criminal Procedure (Insanity) Act 1964
LA 1964	Licensing Act 1964
CP(AW)A 1965	Criminal Procedure (Attendance of Witnesses) Act 1965
M(ADP)A 1965	Murder (Abolition of Death Penalty Act) 1965
CJA 1967	Criminal Justice Act 1967
CLA 1967	Criminal Law Act 1967
CAA 1968	Criminal Appeal Act
FA 1968	Firearms Act 1968
JPA 1968	Justices of the Peace Act 1968
TA 1968	Theft Act 1968
CYPA 1969	Children and Young Persons Act 1969
AJA 1970	Administration of Justice Act 1970
CA 1971	Courts Act 1971
CDA 1971	Criminal Damage Act 1971
IA 1971	Immigration Act 1971
MDA 1971	Misuse of Drugs Act 1971
CJA 1972	Criminal Justice Act 1972
HSWA 1974	Health and Safety at Work Act 1974
JA 1974	Juries Act 1974
ROA 1974	Rehabilitation of Offenders Act 1974
BA 1976	Bail Act 1976
CLA 1977	Criminal Law Act 1977
IA 1978	Interpretation Act 1978
TA 1978	Theft Act 1978
CEMA 1979	Customs and Excise Management Act 1979
LP(E)A 1980	Licensed Premises (Exclusions of Certain Persons) Act 1980
MCA 1980	Magistrates' Courts Act 1980
CAA 1981	Criminal Attempts Act 1981

TABLE OF ABBREVIATIONS

CCA 1981	Contempt of Court Act 1981
SCA 1981	Supreme Court Act 1981
CJA 1982	Criminal Justice Act 1982
MH(A)A 1982	Mental Health (Amendment) Act 1982
MHA 1983	Mental Health Act 1983
PACE 1984	Police and Criminal Evidence Act 1984
RTRA 1984	Road Traffic Regulation Act 1984
POA 1985	Prosecution of Offenders Act 1985
CDDA 1986	Company Directors Disqualification Act 1986
DTOA 1986	Drug Trafficking Offences Act 1986
GA 1986	Gaming (Amendment) Act 1986
POrA 1986	Public Order Act 1986
CJA 1987	Criminal Justice Act 1987
CJA 1988	Criminal Justice Act 1988
LA 1988	Licensing Act 1988
RTA 1988	Road Traffic Act 1988
RTOA 1988	Road Traffic Offenders Act 1988
CA 1989	Children Act 1989
FSA 1989	Football Spectators Act 1989
CJ(IC)A 1990	Criminal Justice (International Co-operation) Act 1990
CLSA 1990	Courts and Legal Services Act 1990
CJA 1991	Criminal Justice Act 1991
CP(IUP)A 1991	Criminal Procedure (Insanity and Unfitness to Plead) Act 1991
RTA 1991	Road Traffic Act 1991
AVTA 1992	Aggravated Vehicle Taking Act 1992
B(A)A 1993	Bail (Amendment) Act 1993
CJA 1993	Criminal Justice Act 1993
PCP(S)A 1993	Prisoners and Criminal Proceedings (Scotland) Act 1993
CJPOA 1994	Criminal Justice and Public Order Act 1994
DTA 1994	Drug Trafficking Act 1994
CAA 1995	Criminal Appeals Act 1995
CEA 1995	Civil Evidence Act 1995
PCA 1995	Proceeds of Crime Act 1995
CPIA 1996	Criminal Procedure and Investigations Act 1996
CSA 1997	Crime (Sentences) Act 1997
F(A)A 1997	Firearms (Amendment) Act 1997
JPA 1997	Justices of the Peace Act 1997
PHA 1997	Protection from Harassment Act 1997
SOA 1997	Sex Offenders Act 1997
CDA 1998	Crime and Disorder Act 1998
HRA 1998	Human Rights Act 1998
AJA 1999	Access to Justice Act 1999
FOD 199	Football (Offences and Disorder) Act 1999
IAA 1999	Immigration and Asylum Act 1999
YJCEA 199	Youth Justice and Criminal Evidence Act 1999
CJCSA 2000	Criminal Justice and Court Services Act 200
FDA 200	Football Disorder Act 2000
IA 2000	Insolvency Act 2000
PCC(S)A 2000	Powers of Criminal Courts (Sentencing) Act 2000
RIPA 2000	Regulation of Investigatory Powers Act 2000
TerrA 2000	Terrorism Act 2000

CJPA 2001	Criminal Justice and Police Act 2001
POCA 2002	Proceeds of Crime Act 2002
PRA 2002	Police Reform Act 2002
ASBA 2003	Anti Social Behaviour Order Act 2003
CA 2003	Courts Act 2003
C(IC)A 2003	Crime (International Co-Operation) Act 2003
CJA 2003	Criminal Justice Act 2003
CJCSA 2003	Criminal Justice and Courts Services Act 2003
EA 2003	Extradition Act 2003
SOA 2003	Sexual Offences Act 2003
DVA 2004	Domestic Violence, Crime and Victims Act 2004
CRCA 2005	Commissioners for Revenue and Customs Act 2005
SOCPA 2005	Serious Organised Crime and Police Act 2005
CDSA 2006	Criminal Defence Services Act 2006
RHA 2006	Racial and Religious Hatred Act 2006
FrA 2006	Fraud Act 2006
PJA 2006	Police and Justice Act 2006
RSA 2006	Road Safety Act 2006
TerrA 2006	Terrorism Act 2006
VCRA 2006	Violent Crime Reduction Act 2006
CMCHA 2007	Corporate Manslaughter and Corporate Homicide Act 2007
MHA 2007	Mental Health Act 2007
OMA 2007	Offender Manager Act 2007
CE(WA)A 2008	Criminal Evidence (Witness Anonymity) Act 2008
CJIA 2008	Criminal Justice and Immigration Act
CTA 2008	Counter Terrorism Act 2008
PCrA 2009	Policing and Crime Act 2009
CorJA 2009	Coroners and Justice Act 2009
CSA 2010	Crime and Security Act 2010
LA EtcB 2011	Legal Aid ... and Punishment Bill 2011

Subordinate Legislation

R.	Criminal Procedure Rules 2011
ROA 2006	CDS (Representation Orders; Appeals Etc) Regulations, 2006
ROCR 2006	CDS (Representation Orders and Consequential Amendments) Regulations, 2006
COR 2009	CDS (Contribution Orders) Regulations, 2009
MC(F)R 1981	Magistrates' Courts (Forms) Rules 1981
GR 1986	Costs in Criminal Cases (General Regulations) 1986
GR(A)R 1991	Costs in Criminal Cases (General)(Amendment) Regulations 1981
CPR 1998	Civil Procedure Rules 1998
CVHCCR 2001	Criminal Defence Service (Choice in Very High Costs Cases) Regulations 2001
GR 2001	Criminal Defence Service (General) Regulations 2001
RDCOR 2001	Criminal Defence Service (Recovery of Defence Costs) Regulations 2001
ROAR 2001	Criminal Defence Service (Representation Order:Appeals) Regulations 2001
DTTO 2002	Drugs Testing and Treatment Order 2002
PCAO 2003	Proceeds of Crime Act 2002 (Appeals under Part 2) Order 2003
ROA 2006	CDS (Representation Orders; Appeals Etc) Regulations, 2006

TABLE OF ABBREVIATIONS

ROCR 2006	CDS (Representation Orders and Consequential Amendments) Regulations, 2006
COR 2009	CDS (Contribution Orders) Regulations, 2009
CPR 2011	Criminal Procedure Rules 2011
DTLR 2011	Criminal Procedure and Investigations Act 1996 (Defence Disclosure Time Limits) Regulations 2011

Miscellaneous

ASBO	Anti-social behaviour order
CACD	Court of Appeal (Criminal Division)
CCP 2004	Code for Crown Prosecutors 2004
CPS	Crown Prosecution Service
CTL Protocol	Custody time limits Protocol agreed between HMCS and CPS 17 March 2009
DRC	Director of Revenue and Customs
DSFO	Director of the Serious Fraud Office
EPE	Electronic presentation of evidence
Guide	Guide to Commencing Proceedings in CACD 2008
HO 1990	Home Office publication Sentence of the Court (1990)
ISO	Individual Support Order
JSB	Judicial Studies Board (Judicial College)
LSC	Legal Services Commission
PCMH	Plea and case management hearing
PDC 2010	Practice Direction (Costs in Criminal Cases) 2010
RCPO	Revenue and Customs Prosecution Office
RT	Road traffic
SAP	Sentencing Advisory Panel
SCEW	Sentencing Council for England and Wales (created by CorJA 2009)
SFO	Serious Fraud Office
SGC 1	Sentencing Guidelines Council, 'Reduction in sentence for a guilty plea'
SGC 2	Sentencing Guidelines Council, 'Overarching principles – seriousness'
SGC 3	Sentencing Guidelines Council, 'New sentences CJA 2003'
SGC 2010	Definitive Guidelines Corporate Manslaughter and Health and Safety Offences Causing Death 2010
SGC (Y)	SGC Guidelines Overarching Principles – Sentencing Youths
SOCA	Serious Organised Crime Agency
SOPO	Sexual Offences Prevention Order

TABLE OF CASES

TABLE OF CASES

TABLE OF CASES

TABLE OF CASES

TABLE OF CASES

TABLE OF CASES

TABLE OF CASES

TABLE OF CASES

TABLE OF CASES

TABLE OF CASES

TABLE OF CASES

TABLE OF CASES

TABLE OF CASES

TABLE OF CASES

TABLE OF STATUTES

TABLE OF STATUTES

TABLE OF STATUTES

TABLE OF STATUTES

Table of Statutes

Table of Statutes

Table of Statutes

Table of Statutes

TABLE OF STATUTES

TABLE OF STATUTORY INSTRUMENTS

TABLE OF STATUTORY INSTRUMENTS

Table of Statutory
Instruments

TABLE OF STATUTORY INSTRUMENTS

Table of Statutory
Instruments

Table of Statutory
Instruments

TABLE OF STATUTORY INSTRUMENTS

1. ABSENT AND UNREPRESENTED ACCUSED

1. Absent accused

Meaning of "absent"

1–001   An accused may be said to be "absent" from proceedings in
the Crown Court where:

(1) he fails to surrender to custody at the time and place fixed for the
proceedings, or having surrendered absents himself:
(2) though physically in the custody of the Crown Court:
   (a) through illness, he is unable; or
   (b) through his own free will he declines to participate in the
      proceedings; or
(3) by order of the judge he is removed from the proceedings for
misbehaviour or disruption.

He is not "absent" from specified proceedings where he is the subject
of a live link order (see LIVE LINKS).

Non-appearance

1–002   The non-appearance of the accused is a principal cause of
"cracked" trials. The reasons may be various; the culpability or negligence of the accused, or lack of communication between the accused
and his representatives. The fault may lie with the prosecutor or even
with the Prison Service.

Faced with the absence of the accused, the judge will need to make
enquiries of the advocates to identify the position, and to call upon
them where appropriate to make administrative arrangements for the
accused's attendance.

Where no satisfactory information is forthcoming, or no arrangements can be made, a bench warrant may be issued.

Bench warrant

1–003   A bench warrant may be issued for the arrest of a person: BA 1976,
s.7(1)(2)

(1) released on bail in criminal proceedings, and thus under a
duty to surrender to the custody of the court who;
(a) fails to surrender at the appointed time and place; or
(b) having surrendered, absents himself at any time and before
the court is ready to begin or resume the hearing of the proceedings, unless he is absent in accordance with leave given
by or on behalf of the court; or
(2) where an indictment has been signed but the person charged   SCA 1981,
has not been sent for trial, where a summons is inappropriate.   s.80(2)

A warrant may, in an appropriate case, be backed for bail.

There is no express requirement that a warrant for arrest issued
under BA 1976, s.7 following failure to surrender to bail, must state
on its face the statutory source of its authority. Lords Wilberforce and

Diplock in *IRC v Rossminster Ltd* [1980] A.C. 952, HL (suggesting that a warrant should state its statutory authority upon its face), were making a statement of what would be good practice in such circumstances; *R. (Bromley) v Secretary of State for Justice* [2010] EWHC 112 (Admin); [2010] A.C.D. 146, DC.

As to the terms and contents of a warrant, see CPR 2011, r.18.2. As to the information to be included in it, see ibid r.18.4.

A warrant that contains an error is not invalid, as long as it was issued in respect of a lawful decision by the court, and it contains enough information to identify that decision.

2. Absconding accused

Absconding accused; trial in absence

1–004 An accused has, in general, a right to be present at his trial and to be legally represented.

Where:

(1) he waives those rights, separately or together;
   (a) wholly, if, knowing when and where his trial is to take place, he deliberately and voluntarily absents himself, or withdraws his instructions from those representing him; or
   (b) partly, if, being present and represented at the outset, during the course of the trial he behaves in such a way as to obstruct the proper course of the proceedings and/or withdraws his instructions from those representing him; or
(2) he absents himself immediately before the trial, aware that the prosecutor intends to apply to amend the indictment to add a more serious charge, thus waiving his rights to an arraignment (*R. v Kepple* [2007] EWCA Crim 1339);

the trial judge has a discretion as to whether a trial should take place or continue in the absence of the accused and/or his legal representative. The overriding consideration is the overall fairness of the trial whether the charge is serious or relatively minor. The cases in which trial in absence is appropriate are likely to be rare, and confined to those where the interests of the other parties to the trial may be prejudiced by delay.

As to the factors to be considered before exercising this discretion, see below 1–007—1–008.

Unruly behaviour

1–005 Where the accused behaves in such an unruly manner in court as to make it impracticable for the trial to continue in his presence the trial judge may order his removal (*R. v Lee Kun* [1916] 1 K.B. 337). In such a case, the judge ought to warn the accused of his intention, and, where appropriate, give him the opportunity to return to court later provided he behaves.

Accused in custody refusing to attend

1–006   An accused in custody failing to attend, even when he is in the course of giving evidence, presents a special problem. It is important that the judge is satisfied the accused has deliberately absented himself (*R. v Amrouchi* [2007] EWCA Crim 3019; *R. v Hodges* [2008] EWCA Crim 620) before making a decision. His attendance should not be compelled by the use of force. The case may be adjourned and the accused warned that the case will continue. He may be dealt with for contempt if appropriate (*R. v Boyle* (1992) 92 Cr. App. R. 202).

Trial in absence; factors to be considered

1–007   The judge's discretion to proceed to trial in the absence of the accused needs to be exercised with care, and only in a rare case in favour of the trial taking place or continuing, particularly if the accused is unrepresented.

Fairness to the defence is of prime importance, but fairness to the prosecution must also be taken into account (*R. v Jones* [2002] UKHL 5; [2002] 2 Cr. App. R. 9; *R. v O'Hare* [2006] EWCA Crim 471; [2006] Crim. L.R. 950).

The judge must consider:

(1) the nature and circumstances of the accused's behaviour, in particular, whether his behaviour was deliberate, voluntary and such as plainly waived his right to appear;

(2) whether an adjournment might result in the accused being apprehended, or attending voluntarily and/or agreeing not to disrupt the proceedings, also the likely length of such an adjournment;

(3) whether the accused, though absent, is, or wishes to be, legally represented at the trial or whether he has, by his conduct, waived his right to representation;

(4) whether the legal representatives of the absent accused are able to receive instructions from him during the trial and the extent to which they are able to present his defence;

(5) the extent of the disadvantage to the accused in not being able to give his account of events, having regard to the nature of the evidence against him; and

(6) the risk of the jury, where there is one, reaching an improper conclusion about the absence of the accused.

The public interest

1–008   The judge will also need to consider:

(1) the general public interest; and

(2) the particular interests of the victims and witnesses that a trial should take place within a reasonable time of the events to which it relates, bearing in mind the effect of delay on the memories of witnesses; and

(3) where there is more than one accused, and not all are absent, the undesirability of separate trials and the prospects of a fair trial for those who are present.

The seriousness of the offence, though a relevant factor, is not an overriding consideration (*R. v O'Hare*, above).

Considerations of fairness.

1–009 A clear additional safeguard to the fairness of a trial is the presence of an advocate on behalf of the accused, who can ensure that all points which can be put forward in the absence of the accused's evidence are clearly before the jury (*R. v O'Hare*, above). The judge must be careful as to any restrictions he places on cross-examination (see *R. v Kepple*, above, and *R. v Pomfrett* [2009] EWCA Crim 1939, [2010] 2 Cr. App. R. 28.

Where the judge decides that the trial should take place, or should continue, in the absence of an unrepresented accused, he:

(1) is under a duty to ensure that the trial is as fair as circumstances permit;
(2) must take reasonable steps, both during the giving of the evidence and in his summing up, to expose any weaknesses in the prosecutor's case and to make such points on behalf of the accused as the evidence permits; and
(3) ought to warn the jury, if there is one, that absence is not an admission of guilt, and adds nothing to the case for the prosecution.

As to the warning to the jury under CJPOA 1994, s.35, see ACCUSED NOT GIVING EVIDENCE) and *R. v Gough* [2002] EWCA Crim 2545, [2002] Cr. App. R. 8.

Confiscation orders

1–010 As to the power to make a confiscation order under POCA 2002, in the absence of an absconding accused, see CONFISCATION ORDERS.

3.   Unrepresented accused

General

1–011 The judge's power to proceed in the absence of representation is dealt with in *R. v Smith (Henry Lee)* [2006] EWCA Crim 2307; [2007] Crim. L.R. 325 (where the accused, having been refused a transfer of representation, declined to co-operate with the court).

There is no obligation on an accused person to be represented in proceedings in the Crown Court: he may be unrepresented because:

(1) he chooses to be;
(2) he does not qualify for public funding (see LEGAL AID; PUBLIC FUNDING) and is not prepared to fund representation himself.

An unrepresented accused causes considerable difficulty for the parties to criminal proceedings. In particular the judge, in his duty to ensure that the proceedings are fair, will need to take such steps as are necessary to assist the accused, without prejudicing the interests of the prosecutor, the witnesses or the public at large.

He may need to:

(1) explain the meaning and content of the counts in the indictment;
(2) advise the accused of any special defences and how they may be established;
(3) indicate relevant rules of evidence. the burden of proof and the nature of any evidential traps into which the accused may fall, emphasising that the rules of evidence apply even-handedly to the prosecution and the defence;
(4) explain his right to cross-examine prosecution witnesses and, if necessary, assist in phrasing the questions the accused seeks to put;
(5) explain the rights and nature of conducting the defence, in particular his rights to give evidence and the consequences of not doing so (see ACCUSED NOT GIVING EVIDENCE)
(6) explain the accused's right to address the jury, if there is one, but not to introduce evidence in his speech;
(7) if there is a jury, explain the nature of the verdict;
(8) on sentence, extract from the offender such mitigation as is available.

Certain restrictions apply in relation to the cross-examination of witnesses by an accused in person, as to which see SPECIAL MEASURES DIRECTIONS. As to the judge's control over an unrepresented accused, particularly in regard to cross-examination of witnesses, see *R. v Brown* [1998] 2 Cr. App. R. 364.

Notes

2. ABUSE OF PROCESS

Quick guide

1.   General Principles

The underlying principle

2–001   "Abuse of process" has been defined as "something so unfair and wrong that the court should not allow a prosecutor to proceed with what is, in all other respects, a regular proceeding" *(R. v Hui Chi-Ming* 94 Cr. App. R. 236 PC).

It is well established that the court has the power to stay proceedings in two categories of case, namely:

(1) where it will be impossible to give the accused a fair trial, and
(2) where it offends the court's sense of justice and propriety to be asked to try the accused in the particular circumstances of the case.

In the first category of case, if the judge concludes that the accused cannot receive a fair trial, he will stay the proceedings without more. No question of the balancing of competing interests arises. In the second category of case, the focus is on whether the court's sense of justice and propriety is offended or public confidence in the criminal justice system would be undermined by the trial. That is not about fairness to the accused. The two categories are distinct and should be considered separately (*Maxwell* [2010] UKSC 48: per Lord Dyson at p.35, cited in *Warren v HM Attorney-General of the Bailiwick of Jersey* [2011] UKPC 10).

In the first category the Crown Court has jurisdiction to prevent abuse of its process, the discretionary power to stay an indictment (or part of an indictment—*R. v Munro* (1993) 97 Cr. App. R. 183) being conferred to ensure that there is a fair trial involving as it does fairness both to the accused and to the prosecutor. The right to a fair trial is guaranteed by ECHR, art.6.

In the second category it should be noted that:

(a) a stay should be granted where necessary to protect the integrity of the criminal justice system;

(b) a balancing of interests should be conducted in deciding whether a stay is required to fulfil this primary purpose;

(c) the public interest in ensuring that those that are charged with grave crimes should be tried will always weigh in the balance (*R. v Latif* [1996] 2 Cr. App. R. 92 per Lord Steyn);

(d) the 'but for' factor (i.e. where it can be shown that the accused would not have stood trial but for executive abuse of power) is merely one of various matters that will influence the decision;

(e) a stay should not be ordered for the purpose of punishing or disciplining prosecutorial or police misconduct.

Where abuse may arise

2–002   The cases show that there may be abuse of process where:

(1) the prosecution has manipulated or misused the process of the court so as to deprive an accused of a protection afforded by the law, or to take advantage of a technicality *(R. v Liverpool MC Ex p. Slade* [1998] 1 Cr. App. R. 147);

(2) the proceedings before the court have only been made possible by acts of agents of the state which offend the court's conscience as being contrary to the rule of law, or would otherwise bring the administration of justice into disrepute (e.g. *R. v Horseferry Rd MC Ex p. Bennett* 98 Cr. App. R. 114; *R. v Mullen* [1999] 2 Cr. App. R. 143, *R. (on the application of Hausschildt) v Highbury Corner MC* [2009] Crim. L.R. 512; cf. *R. v Mote* [2008] Crim. L.R. 193);

(3) illegal conduct by the police or the prosecutor is so grave as to threaten or undermine the rule of law itself *(R. v Grant* [2005] EWCA Crim 1089; [2005] 2 Cr. App. R. 28);

(4) on a balance of probabilities, the accused has been, or will be, prejudiced in the preparation or conduct of his defence by delay on the part of the prosecution which is unjustifiable, being not due, for example, to:

(a) the complexity of the enquiry and the preparation of the prosecution case;

(b) the action of the accused or one or more co-accused;

(c) genuine difficulties of service *(R. v Derby City Council Ex p. Brooks* (1985) 80 Cr. App. R. 164); or

(5) a prosecuting authority ignores or fails to comply with its own declared prosecuting criteria *(R. v Adaway* [2004] EWCA Crim 2831, 168 J.P. 645).

As to the position of non-state agents, see *Council for the Regulation of Health Care Professionals v CMC* [2007] A.C.D. 128/29 QB As to the approach to private prosecutions, see *R. (Dacre) v City of Westminster MC* [2008] EWHC 1667 (Admin); [2009] 1 Cr. App. R. 77.

As to the limited application of the doctrine of abuse in relation to the Council of Europe Convention on Trafficking in Human Beings, 2005, art.26, see *R. v LM* [2010] EWCA Crim 2327, [2011]1 Cr. App. R. 12.

Potential prejudice to the accused: a "fair trial"

2–003   An application to stay is, in effect, a plea in bar of trial and should not succeed where there are other methods of achieving a fair hearing of the case *(DPP v Hussain* (1994) 158 J.P.N. 570, DC). Once a decision has been taken to stay proceedings on grounds of abuse, that is the effective final determination of the case; it is inconceivable that it could be subsequently pursued *(Council for the Regulation of Health Care Professionals v CMC,* above). Abuse of process is an exceptional remedy and each case turns on its own facts. *R. v Abu Hamza* [2007]1 Cr. App. R. 27 does not lay down strict minimum requirements (*R. v Gripton* [2010] EWCA Crim 2260).

The crux of the matter is whether, in all the circumstances, the situation created by any apparent abuse is such as to make any trial unfair (see, e.g. *Tan v Cameron* (1993) 96 Cr. App. R. 172; *Att Gen of Hong Kong v Cheung Wai-bun* 98 Cr. App. R. 17).

Where there is no fault on the part of the police or the prosecutor, it will be very rare for a stay to be justified. Even where the judge finds that there has been an abuse of process in the conduct of the proceedings, whatever the category of abuse, in general, he:

(1) must consider as a "further and separate" question, whether there is potential prejudice to the accused;
(2) has a discretion, even where he finds abuse of process, to allow the trial to proceed, where he finds no prejudice to the accused *(R. v Gloucester City Council Ex p. Jackman* [1993] 12 C.L. 118); unless the unlawful acts by the police or the prosecutor are so great an affront to the integrity of the justice system and therefore to the rule of law, that the associated prosecution should not be countenanced by the courts, whether or not prejudice is caused to the accused *(R. v Grant* [2005] EWCA Crim 1089; [2005] 2 Cr. App. R. 28).

An indictment should be stayed only in exceptional circumstances *(DPP v B* [2008] EWHC 201 (Admin); [2008] Crim. L.R. 707, but see *R. v Hereworth* [2011] EWCA Crim 74 and should not be granted in the absence of prejudice to the accused so serious that no fair trial could be held. When assessing "serious prejudice" the judge needs to bear in mind, however, his control over the admission of evidence and the important fact that the trial process itself will ensure that all factual issues arising will be properly before the jury *(R. v S (Stephen Paul)* [2006] EWCA Crim 756; [2006] 3 Cr. App. R. 23).

Thus:

(a) it is important to distinguish between the sort of case in which the issues at the trial will depend upon the recollection of witnesses about some event, and a case which turns largely upon documents *(R. v Buzalek* [1991] Crim. L.R.115, 116);
(b) the complexities of the case and the difficulties of investigation are a factor to be considered; there may be cases where the case is so complex that, despite the diligent efforts of the Crown, the delay is such that a fair trial is impossible

(cf. *R .v Telford JJ. Ex p. Badham* (1991) 93 Cr. App. R. 171; *H v L* [1998] 1 W.L.R. 854).

Where confiscation proceedings are properly bought within POCA 2002, they should not be stayed as an abuse of process because the judge considers that they may have an oppressive result *(R. v Nelson* [2009] Crim. L.R. 811).

Whether a retrial, particularly a second retrial, is in the interests of justice (which require a fair trial in circumstances which are neither oppressive nor unjust) is ultimately a question for the trial judge *(R. v Bell* [2010] EWCA Crim 3; [2010] 1 Cr. App. R. 27).

2.   Investigative Methods

2–004   Action by the investigating body, luring persons into committing acts forbidden by law and then seeking to prosecute them for doing so, amounts to an abuse of the process of the court, and a judge has an inherent power and duty to prevent it. The boundary between acceptable and unacceptable behaviour will depend in each case on its own facts, but a useful guide to identifying the limits of the type of conduct which is acceptable, is to consider whether, in the particular circumstances, the investigators did no more than present the accused with an unexceptional opportunity to commit a crime. Thus:

(1) if the conduct of the investigators preceding the commission of the offence was no more than might have been expected from others in the circumstances, they are not to be regarded as having instigated or encouraged or assisted in the commission of the crime; or

(2) if they did no more than others might be expected to do, they were not creating crime artificially, but the investigatory technique of providing an opportunity to commit crime should not be applied in a random fashion or be used for wholesale virtue-testing without good reason; or

(3) a degree of active involvement by an undercover police officer will not necessarily amount to entrapment *(R. v M* [2011] EWCA Crim 648).

The greater the degree of intrusiveness, the closer will be the need for the judge to scrutinise the reason for using it.

While:

(a) the investigators must act in good faith, and having reasonable suspicion is one way in which such good faith might be established;

(b) reasonable suspicion of a particular individual will not always be necessary.

In deciding what is acceptable, the judge must have regard to the accused's circumstances, including his vulnerability *(R. v Loosely; Att Gen's Reference (No.3 of 2000)* [2001] UKHL 53; [2002] 1 Cr. App. R. 29).

The prosecution must disclose fully the role of any prosecution witness as a participating informant *(R. v Patel* [2001] EWCA Crim 2505; [2002] Crim. L.R. 304; see also *R. v Early* [2003] 1 Cr. App. R. 19).

3. Missing Exhibits

2–005   The absence of an exhibit does not, of itself, give rise to abuse of process *(R. v Beckford* [1996] 1 Cr. App. R. 94). In particular there is no general principle that mere speculation as to what a missing document contains must result in proceedings being stayed *(R. v MacKreth* [2009] EWCA Crim 1849; [2010] Crim. L.R. 226). A distinction needs to be drawn between the *deliberate destruction* of evidence *(R. v Birmingham* [1992] Crim. L.R. 117), and the *loss* of an exhibit *(R. v McNamara & McNamara* [1998] Crim. L.R. 278; *R. v Medwar* [2000] Crim. L.R. 415; *R. v T* [2000] Crim. L.R. 832; *R. v Feltham MC Ex p. Ebrahim* [2001] EWCA Admin 130; [2001] 2 Cr. App. R. 23; *R. v Boyd* [2002] EWCA Crim 2836; [2004] R.T.R. 7). The judge should:

(1) consider the nature of the investigator/prosecutor's duty to obtain and/or retain the evidence; if there was none before the defence first sought its retention, no question of a trial being unfair on that ground arises (see *R. v Parker* [2003] *Archbold News* 1);

(2) bear in mind, if the evidence was not obtained and/or retained in breach of the obligations set out in the Code of Practice (CPIA 1996, ss.22, 23 and 26) or under the Attorney-General's Guidelines on Disclosure (April 2005), that the ultimate objective is to ensure that there be a fair trial according to law and while this involves fairness both to the prosecutor and to the defence:

   (a) the trial process is equipped to deal with the examination of complaints, and there will be few cases in which the judge will be able to conclude that a trial would be unfair;

   (b) it is commonplace in criminal trials for the defence to rely on gaps in the prosecution case and if, in such a case, there is sufficient credible evidence which, if believed, would justify a safe conviction, then the trial may proceed, leaving the defence to seek to persuade the jury, if there is one, or the judge, not to convict owing to the un- avail ability, through no fault of their own, of the evidence in question;

(3) stay the proceedings, if the conduct of the prosecutor has been such that it would be unfair to put the accused on trial.

In *R. v Lamont* [2010] EWCA Crim 2144, CACD summarised the principles to be derived from *Ebrahim* (above) as:

   (a) Was the prosecutor in breach of duty?

   (b) Has the prosecutor acted in bad faith?

   (c) Is there serious prejudice to the accused?

   (d) Can the absence of evidence be dealt with by an appropriate direction in the trial process itself (as in most cases is likely)?

ABUSE OF PROCESS

The most useful test is to ask whether there has been bad faith, or at least some serious fault on the part of the investigating body or of the Crown (see *DPP v Ara* [2001] EWCA Admin 493; [2002] 1 Cr. App. R. 16 and see PD 2004, IV.36 at 2–011 and following.

See, as to missing video recordings, *DPP v S* 67 JCL 87; and as to gaps in video evidence, *R. v Brooks* [2004] EWCA Crim 3537, (2004) 148 S.J. 1031. As to the absence of CCTV evidence, see *Morris v DPP* [2008] EWHC 2788.

4. Delay

The principles

2–006 Delay is relevant to the right to a fair trial guaranteed by ECHR, art.6; it is normally taken to run from the date of charge or summons: *Att Gen's Reference (No. 2 of 2001)* [2001] UKHL 53; [2002] 1 Cr. App. R. 29. As to the situation where the fairness of the trial has not been nor would be compromised (See ibid), approved by the Privy Council in *Spiers (Procurator Fiscal) v Ruddy* [2007] UKPC D2; [2008] 2 W.L.R. 608.

Where the judge is considering an application to stay proceedings on the ground of prejudice resulting from delay in the institution of proceedings, the appropriate test is directly addressed and answered in *Att Gen's Reference (No 1 of 1990)* 95 Cr. App. R. 296 which continues to provide the benchmark.

Thus,

(1) a stay on grounds of delay is to be imposed only in exceptional circumstances even where the delay was unjustifiable, even more rarely in the absence of fault on the part of complainant or prosecution and never when the delay is due to the complexity of the case or the actions of the accused;

(2) no stay should be imposed unless the defence establishes that the accused will suffer serious prejudice because of the delay to the extent that no fair trial can be held. The judge should bear in mind his powers of the judge and the trial process itself to provide protection from prejudice.

Where delay in the proceedings is put forward as amounting to abuse, the judge must consider the reasons for the delay and the potential unfairness, if any, to the accused.

In considering the question of whether there is potential prejudice to the accused, the cases show that that relevant factors will be:

(a) the *length* of the delay;

(b) any *reasons* given by the prosecutor for that delay; and

(c) any *efforts* made by the accused to assert his rights.

The longer the delay the more likely it will be that the prosecution is at fault and that the delay has caused prejudice to the accused; the less the prosecution has to offer by way of explanation, the more easily can prejudice be inferred.

The approach

2–007   The above principles were re-emphasised in *R. v S (Stephen Paul)* [2006] 2 Cr. App. R. 23. CACD stated the discretionary decision, whether or not to grant a stay as an abuse of process because of delay, was an exercise in judicial assessment dependent on judgment rather than on any conclusion as to facts based on evidence.

It is therefore potentially misleading to apply to the exercise of that discretion the language of burden and standard of proof, which is more apt to an evidence-based fact-finding process. In the light of the authorities, CACD repeated the principles stated in *Att Gen's Reference (No. 1 of 1990)* (above), adding that when assessing possible serious prejudice, the judge should bear in mind his power to regulate the admissibility of evidence and the fact that the trial process itself should ensure that all relevant factual issues arising from delay will be placed before the jury for its consideration in accordance with appropriate directions from the judge. If, having considered all those factors, a judge's assessment is that a fair trial would be possible, a stay should not be granted

In *R. v F(S)*, [2011] EWCA Crim 726; [2011] 2 Cr. App. R. 13 *The Times*, July 25, 2011, (a five judge court presided over by the Lord Chief Justice) CACD said that where abuse of process submissions on the ground of delay were advanced, provided the principles articulated in *R. v Galbraith* (1981) 73 Cr. App. R. 124 and *Att Gen Reference (No. 1 of 1990)* (above) were clearly understood, it would no longer be necessary or appropriate for reference to be made to any of the decisions of CACD save for *R. v S (Stephen Paul)* and *R. v F(S)* itself. Those four authorities contained all the necessary discussion about the applicable principles.

Abuse of process and no case submission

2–008   An application to stay for abuse of process on the ground of delay and a submission of no case to answer are two distinct matters requiring distinct and separate consideration. An application to stay for abuse of process on the ground of delay cannot succeed unless, exceptionally, a fair trial is no longer possible owing to prejudice to the accused occasioned by the delay which cannot fairly be addressed in the normal trial process, whereas on a submission of no case the question is whether the evidence, viewed overall, is such that the jury can properly convict

In *R. v F(S)*, (above), at the close of the prosecution case, after the complainant in the course of his evidence had explained why the complaint was delayed, the basis for the judge's decision was the absence of any real satisfactory explanation for the complainant's failure to take advantage of several opportunities to report what had happened to him.

It was apparent that the argument, and perhaps in consequence the ruling, represented an amalgam of two distinct questions, namely should:

(1) the prosecution be stayed for abuse of process on the ground that the accused could not receive a fair trial?; or

(2) the case be withdrawn from the jury on the ground that the evidence was such that a conviction would be unsafe?

CACD noted that it was apparent that some of the jurisprudence about long delays in sexual complaint cases appeared to have elided the distinct concepts of abuse of process and withdrawal of the case from the jury on evidential grounds, and pointed out that the authority of *R. v Galbraith* (1981) 73 Cr. App. R. 124, with its emphasis on the responsibilities of the jury as the fact-finding body responsible for delivering the verdicts, is undiminished. The principles have not been modified or extended for the purposes of addressing trials which involved historic unreported sexual crimes.

In accordance with the second limb of *Galbraith* there would be cases where the state of the evidence called by the prosecution, and taken as a whole, is so unsatisfactory, contradictory, or so transparently unreliable, that no jury, properly directed, could convict. In such cases it is the judge's duty to direct the jury that there is no case to answer and to return a not guilty verdict. But in making that judgment the judge has to bear in mind the constitutional primacy of the jury, and not usurp its function. Judges would find it easier to ensure that submissions of no case concentrated on the correct principles if expressions such as "safe to convict" or "safely left to the jury" were avoided. If the jury convicts, and the conviction may be unsafe, it must be dealt with by CACD. Any suggestion that, on the basis of delay, the judge may be responsible for assessing whether, in advance of a conviction, the conviction would be unsafe, is based on a misunderstanding of the principles in both *Galbraith* and *Att Gen Reference (No. 1 of 1990)*.

Historic sex cases

2–009 In most historic sex allegations the reasons for the delayed complaint, and whether and how the delay is explained or justified, bears directly on the credibility of the complainant. They therefore form an essential part of the factual matrix on which the jury has to make its decision. That is the principal, and in the overwhelming majority of cases, the only relevance of the evidence on those issues.

In general, submissions as to whether the trial should proceed at all, should take place before the evidence is called but, as the authorities underline, it is only in exceptional cases, where a fair trial is not possible, that such applications are justified on the ground of delay.

The question whether the complainant's explanation for the delay in reporting the alleged offence is truthful is a matter capable of exploration at the trial. It does not provide any reason, on abuse of process grounds, for preventing the trial from taking place.

5. Serial prosecutions

2–010 There is a general rule of criminal procedure that:

(1) the prosecutor should join in one indictment all the charges that he wishes to prefer in respect of one incident, and
(2) he should not be permitted, *save in special or exceptional circumstances*, to bring a second set of proceedings arising out of the same incident as the first, after the first set of proceedings have been concluded, and

the judge has a discretion to stay the subsequent proceedings if to proceed would be oppressive or prejudicial and therefore an abuse of the process of the court.

The correct question in a case of this kind is whether the second set of proceedings arises out of the same, or substantially the same, facts as the first.

Consideration of whether or not the appellant can have a fair trial, which is material to an application to stay on grounds of delay (see *Att Gen's Reference (No 1 of 1990)* (above) is inappropriate. A stay on the ground of delay is an exceptional course, the burden being on the defence to show that, on the balance of probabilities, no fair trial can be held. The general rule in respect of a second prosecution is that there *should* be a stay, and it is for the prosecutor to show that there are special circumstances why there should not be a stay (See *R. v Phipps* [2005] EWCA Crim 33, where the authorities are reviewed; cf. *DPP v Alexander* [2010] EWHC 2255 (Admin).

6. Undertaking not to prosecute; agreement as to plea

2–011   There may be abuse of process where the prosecutor seeks to go back on:

(1) an unequivocal promise made to an accused that he will not be prosecuted; or

(2) a carefully prepared and agreed basis for plea approved by the court *(CPS v Mattu* [2010] Crim L.R. 220).

A prosecution undertaking ought to be relied on and it is not right to allow a prosecutor to proceed in such circumstances unless he can show affirmatively that the original decision was exclusively evidentially based and was clearly wrong *(R. (DPP) v Taylor* [2004] EWCA Crim 1554 (Admin); [2004] 7 *Archbold. News).*

There is a convention that if the prosecutor fails to secure a conviction on two occasions he will not seek a further retrial—*R. v Henworth* [2001] EWCA Crim 120; [2001] 2 Cr. App. R. 4; *DPP v Edgar* (2002) 164 J.P. 471). See also *R. v Bell* [2009] EWCA Crim 3; [2010] 1 Cr. App. R. 27.

In general, the circumstances of the case need to be exceptional (see, e.g. *R. v Croydon JJ. Ex p. Dean* [1994] 98 Cr. App. R. 76; *R. v Horseferry Rd MC Ex. p. Bennett* (1999) 98 Cr. App. R. 114; *R. v Slesinger* [1995] Crim. L.R. 137; *R. v Latif* [1996] 2 Cr. App. R. 92; *R. v Mullen* [1999] 2 Cr. App. R. 143. *R. v Townsend* [1997] 2 Cr. App. R. 540 makes it plain that breach of a promise not to prosecute does not necessarily give rise to abuse *(cf. R. v Bloomfield* [1997] 1 Cr. App. R. 235 where an assurance had been given to the judge that no evidence would be offered). See also R. v Killick [2011] EWCA Crim 1608.

Abuse of process is unlikely to arise unless:

(a) there has been an unequivocal representation by those with the conduct of the prosecution that the accused will not be prosecuted; and

(b) the accused has acted to his detriment on that representation.

Even then, proceedings may not be stayed if fresh material facts have come to light since the representation was made *(R. v Abu Hamza* [2006] UKHL 41; [2007] 1 Cr. App. R. 27).

Where the prosecutor has elected not to proceed against a co-accused, although such proceedings were possible, such a decision does not amount to an abuse of process *(R. v Forsyth* [1997] 2 Cr. App. R. 299). See also *Environment Agency v Stanford* [1999] Env. L.R. 286.

Where an offender admits an offence and, with his agreement, is formally cautioned by the police under CDA 1998 on their assurance that he will not be brought before a criminal court in connection with the matter, it is an abuse of the court's process to permit the victim subsequently to bring a private prosecution in respect of that offence *(Jones v Whalley* [2006] UKHL 41; [2007] 1 Cr. App. R. 2; cf. *R. v Gore* [2009] EWCA Crim 1424; [2009] W.L.R. (D) 240).

7. Failure to obey court orders

2–012   Orders made by judges must be obeyed; and the normal consequence of disobeying such an order, made in the interests of a fair trial, is either:

(1) the exclusion of the evidence to which the order relates, or
(2) in a case which is entirely dependent on the evidence in question, a stay of proceedings.

See *CPS v LR* [2010] EWCA Crim 924 in relation to charges of making indecent photographs of children, contrary to the Protection of Children Act 1978. The arrangements suggested by the prosecution to enable the accused and his legal advisers to examine the material had been wholly inadequate the judge having ordered the prosecution to supply the court and the defence with copies of the images, the prosecution refused to comply with that order.

8. Adverse publicity

2–013   As to a stay owing to the publicity surrounding a case, see *R. v Stone* [2001] EWCA Crim 297; [2001] Crim. LR. 465 and the Scots cases of *Montgomery v HMA, Coulter v HMA* [2003] 1 A.C.641. See also *R. v Hamza* [2007] Crim. L.R. 320; *R. v Abu Hamza* [2006] EWCA Crim 2918; [2007] 1 Cr. App. R. 27.

9. Procedure on application

Making the application

2–014   The following procedure applies where an accused proposes to make an application to stay an indictment on the grounds of abuse of process: PD 2004, IV.36.2

(1) written notice of application must be given to the prosecuting authority and to any co-accused not later than 14 days before the date fixed or warned for trial ("the relevant date"):
  (a) specifying the name of the case, and the indictment number;
  (b) stating the fixed date or the warned date for trial, as appropriate;

(c) specifying the nature of the application;

(d) setting out in numbered sub-paragraphs the grounds upon which the application is to be made; and

(e) being copied to the Chief Listing Officer at the court centre where the case is to be heard.

Any co-accused who wishes to make a like application must give a like notice not less than seven days before the relevant date, setting out any additional grounds relied upon;

(2) the following automatic directions apply:

PD 2004, IV.36.3

(a) the advocate for the applicant(s) must, not later than five clear working days before the date fixed or warned for trial ("the relevant date"), lodge with the court and serve on all other parties, a skeleton argument in support of the application and, if reference is to be made to any document not in the existing trial documents, a paginated and indexed bundle of such documents must be provided with the skeleton argument;

(b) the advocate for the prosecution must lodge with the court and serve on all other parties a responsive skeleton argument at least two clear working days before the relevant date together with a supplementary bundle if appropriate.

All skeleton arguments must specify any propositions of law to be advanced (together with the authorities relied on in support with page references to passages relied on), and where appropriate include a chronology of events and a list of the *dramatis personae*.

PD 2004, IV.36.4

In all instances where reference is made to a document, the reference in the trial documents or supplementary bundle must be given.

Time limits; plea and case management hearing

2–015 The above time limits are minimum time limits; in appropriate cases the court may order longer lead times. In all cases where defence advocates are, at the time of the PCMH, considering the possibility of an abuse of process application, this must be raised with the judge who will order a different timetable if appropriate, and may wish, in any event, to give additional directions about the conduct of the application.

PD 2004, IV.36.5

Spelling it out

2–016 In giving judgment on an application, a few sentences showing the judge's command of the law on the topic will usually suffice, followed by a summary of the reasons for granting or rejecting the application *(R. v Manchester City Council Ex p. Brockenbrow, The Times,* October 31, 1991, DC; *R. v Feltham Magistrates Court, Mouat v DPP* [2001] EWHC Admin 130; [2001] 2 Cr. App. R. 23).

Notes

3. ACCUSED NOT GIVING EVIDENCE

Accused's right to give or not to give evidence

3–001 At the conclusion of the evidence for the prosecution, in a trial on indictment with a jury, CJPOA 1994, s.35(2), (as amended by CJA 2003, s.331, Sch.36, Pt 4, para.62) requires the judge to satisfy himself that the accused is aware that the stage has been reached at which evidence can be given for the defence and that: PD 2004, IV.44.2, 3, 4

(1) if he wishes, he may give evidence; and,
(2) if he chooses not to give evidence, or having been sworn, without good cause refuses to answer any questions, it will be permissible for the jury to draw such inferences as appear proper from his failure to give evidence or his refusal, without good cause, to answer any question.

Accused legally represented

3–002 Where the accused's legal representative informs the judge in the presence of the jury, if there is one, that the accused: PD 2004, IV.44.1

(1) *will give evidence*, the case proceeds in the normal way;
(2) *does not intend to give evidence* (or the judge is not informed that he does), the judge must address the advocate as follows:

> *"Have you advised your client that the stage has now been reached at which he may give evidence and, if he chooses not to do so or, having been sworn, without good cause refuses to answer any question, the jury may draw such inferences as appear proper from his failure to do so?"*

If the representative replies that the accused has been so advised, the case will proceed in the normal way; if the judge is informed that the accused has not been so advised, then he will direct the representative to advise his client of the consequences set out in PD 2004 IV.44.3 and should adjourn briefly for this purpose before proceeding.

The advocate has a duty to make a record in writing, signed by the accused recording his client's decision not to give evidence: *R. v Bevan*, 98 Cr. App. R. 354; *R. v Chatroodi* [2001] 3 *Archbold News* 3, CA; *Ebanks (Kurt) v The Queen*, *The Times*, March 31, 2006, PC. See generally *R. v Anderson* [2010] EWCA Crim 2553.

Accused not legally represented

3–003 If the accused is not represented, the judge must, at the conclusion of the evidence for the prosecution and in the presence of the jury, if there is one, say to the accused: PD 2004, IV.44.5

> *"You have heard the evidence against you. Now is the time for you to make your defence. You may give evidence on oath, and be cross-examined like any other witness. If you do not give evidence or, having been sworn, without good cause refuse to answer any question, the jury may draw such inferences as appear proper. That means they may hold it against you. You may call any witness whom you have arranged to attend court. Afterwards you may also, if you wish, address the jury*

by arguing your case from the dock. But you cannot at that stage give evidence. Do you now intend to give evidence?"

Directions to jury

3–004 There will be cases where the judge will consider it necessary to discuss with the advocates in the absence of a jury, the form of his direction. In the ordinary case a suggested direction to a jury is as follows:

"The accused has not given evidence. That is his right. But, as he has been told, the law is that you may draw such inferences as appear proper from his failure to do so. Failure to give evidence on its own cannot prove guilt but depending on the circumstances, you may hold his failure against him when deciding whether he is guilty."

In a case where there is such evidence the judge may add:

"There is evidence before you on the basis of which counsel for the defence invites you not to hold it against the accused that he has not given evidence before you namely . . . If you think that because of this evidence you should not hold it against him that he has not given evidence, do not do so. But if the evidence he relies on presents no adequate explanation for his absence from the witness box then you may hold his failure to give evidence against him. You do not have to do so.

What proper inferences can you draw from his decision not to give evidence before you? If you conclude that there is a case for him to answer you may think that he would have gone into the witness box to give you an explanation for, or an answer to, the case against him. If the only sensible explanation for his decision not to give evidence is that he has no answer to the case against him, or none that could have stood up to cross-examination, then it would be open to you to hold against him his failure to give evidence. It is for you to decide whether it is fair to do so."

As to the position where the accused absconds and the trial proceeds in his absence, see *R. v Gough* [2002] EWCA Crim 2545; [2002] 2 Cr. App. R. 8. See also *R. v Hamidi* [2010] EWCA Crim 66, [2010] Crim. L.R. 578.

Basic essentials

3–005 *R. v Cowan* (1996) 1 Cr. App. R. 1, CACD highlighted certain essentials in relation to a trial with a jury.

The judge:

(1) must tell the jury that the burden of proof remains upon the prosecution throughout, and define the required standard;

(2) must make clear to the jury that the accused is entitled to remain silent; it is his right and his choice;

(3) must tell the jury that an inference from failure to give evidence cannot, on its own, prove guilt (it is expressly stated in CJPOA 1994, s.38(3)); therefore, they must be satisfied that the prosecution have established a case to answer before drawing any inferences from silence (see *R. v Alford's Transport and Others* (1997) 2 Cr. App. R. 326; *R. v Birchall* [1999] Crim. L.R. 311);

(4) may tell them that if, despite any evidence relied upon to explain his silence, or in the absence of any such evidence, they conclude that silence can only sensibly be attributed to

the accused's having no answer, or none that would stand up to cross-examination, they may draw an adverse inference.

3–006 It is not possible to anticipate all the circumstances in which a judge might think it right to direct or advise a jury against drawing an adverse inference. Adopting the reasoning of a Northern Ireland case (*R. v McLernon* [1992] N.I. 168) CACD said in *R. v Cowan* that:

> "... the [jury] has then a complete discretion as to whether inferences should be drawn or not. In these circumstances it is a matter for the [jury] in any criminal case (1) to decide whether to draw inferences or not; and (2) if it decides to draw inferences what their nature, extent and degree of adversity, if any, may be. It would be improper and indeed quite unwise for any court to set out the bounds of either steps (1) or (2). Their application will depend on factors peculiar to the individual case".

CACD accepted in *R. v Cowan* that:

(a) apart from the mandatory exceptions in CJPOA 1994 s.35(1), it will be open to a jury to decline to draw an adverse inference from silence at his trial and for a judge to direct or advise them against drawing such inference if the circumstances of the case justify such a course;

(b) there would, however, need either to be some evidential basis for doing so or some exceptional factors in the case, making that a fair course to take;

(c) the inferences permitted by the section are only such "as appear proper"; the use of that phrase was no doubt intended to leave a broad discretion to the trial judge to decide in all the circumstances whether any proper inference is capable of being drawn by the jury. If not, he should tell them so; otherwise it is for the jury to decide whether, in fact, an inference should properly be drawn.

The possession of a previous criminal record upon which an accused could be cross-examined (if he has attacked prosecution witnesses) is no good reason for directing a jury that they should not hold his silence against him (See *R. v Becouarn* [2005] UKHL 55; [2006] 1 Cr. App. R. 2).

Counsel is not entitled to give evidence dressed up as a submission; it cannot be proper for him to give to the jury reasons for his client's silence at trial in the absence of evidence to support such reasons.

Medical reasons

3–007 Where it is contended under s.35(1)(b) that the accused's physical or mental condition makes it undesirable for him to give evidence, that issue must be properly raised (see *R. v Friend* [1997] 2 Cr. App. R. 231; *R. v A* [1997] Crim. L.R. 883) and must be decided by the judge. If the judge decides in favour of the accused the jury must be directed not to draw any adverse inference. It is a matter for the judge whether he hears evidence on the *voir dire* (*R. v Chadwick* [1998] 7 *Archbold News* 3, CA).

If the judge considers that the accused's physical or mental state makes it undesirable for him to give evidence, s.35(3) does not apply, but if the accused is not suffering from such a condition at the trial,

ACCUSED NOT GIVING EVIDENCE

s. 35(3) permits the drawing of such inferences as appear proper (*R. v Barry* [2010] EWCA Crim 195; [2010] 1 Cr. App. R. 32 doubting the relevance of *R. v Bathurst* 52 Cr. App. R. 251, to the position under s.35).

4. AGE OF OFFENDER

4–001 In the TABLE below an x indicates where there is a statutory restriction of age, an * indicates where there is no such statutory restriction. Neither signifies that an order is appropriate in the case of an offender of that age. The bracketed numbers refer to the short notes appended below. These are followed by one or two statements of principle in determining the age of an offender at 4–003.

Sentence or order	under 14	14	15	16	17	18	19	20	21 & over
Action plan order	*(1)	*(1)	*(1)	*(1)	*(1)	x	x	x	x
Anti-social behaviour order	*(2)	*(2)	*(2)	*(2)	*(2)	*(2)	*(2)	*(2)	*(2)
Attendance centre	x	x	x	*(3)	*(3)	*(3)	*(3)	*(3)	*(3)
Bind over	*(4)	*(4)	*(4)	*(4)	*(4)	*	*	*	*
Committal for Contempt	x	x	x	x	*(5)	*	*	*	*
Community order	x(6)	x(6)	x(6)	x(6)	x(6)	*	*	*	*
Company officer's disqualification	*	*	*	*	*	*	*	*	*
Compensation order	*(7)	*(7)	*(7)	*(7)	*(7)	*	*	*	*
Confiscation order	*	*	*	*	*	*	*	*	*
Deportation recommendation	x	x	x	x	*	*	*	*	*
Deprivation order	*	*	*	*	*	*	*	*	*
Detention of juveniles Custody for life,	x	x	x	x	x	*(8)	*(8)	*(8)	x
Detention YOI	x	x	x	x	x	*	*	*	x
Detention HMP	*(9)	*(9)	*(9)	*(9)	*(9)	x	x	x	x
Sentence or order	under 14	14	15	16	17	18	19	20	21 & over

23

Sentence or order	under 14	14	15	16	17	18	19	20	21 & over
Detention for life	*(10)	*(10)	*(10)	*(10)	*(10)	x	x	x	x
Detention s.91	*(11)	*(11)	*(11)	*(11)	*(11)	x	x	x	x
Detention (public Protection)	*(12)	*(12)	*(12)	*(12)	*(12)	x	x	x	x
Detention & training order	*(13)	*(13)	*(13)	*(13)	*(13)	x	x	x	x
Discharge, absolute conditional	*(14)	*(14)	*(14)	*(14)	*(14)	*(14)	*(14)	*(14)	*(14))
Drinking banning order	x	x	x	*	*	*	*	*	*
Driving dis qualifica-tions	*	*	*	*	*	*	*	*	*
Extended sen tence	*(15)	*(15)	*(15)	*(15)	*(15)	*(15)	*(15)	*(15)	*(15)
Financial reporting order	*(16)	*(16)	*(16)	*(16)	*(16)	*(16)	*(16)	*(16)	*(16)
Fines, costs etc	*(7)	*(7)	*(7)	*(7)	*(7)	*	*	*	*
Football banning order	*(17)	*(17)	*(17)	*(17)	*(17)	*(17)	*(17)	*(17)	*(17)
Forfeiture	*	*	*	*	*	*	*	*	*
Guardianship order MHA	x	x	x	*	*	*	*	*	*
Hospital order MHA	*	*	*	*	*	*	*	*	*
Hospital & limitation direction	*	*	*	*	*	*	*	*	*
Imprisonment	x	x	x	x	x	x	x	x	*
IPP dangerous offenders	x	x	x	x	x	x	x	x	*
Individual support order (ISO)	*	*	*	*	*	x	x	x	x
Sentence or order	under 14	14	15	16	17	18	19	20	21 & over

Sentence or order	under 14	14	15	16	17	18	19	20	21 & over
Licensed premises exclusion order	*	*	*	*	*	*	*	*	*
Parenting order	*	*	*	*	*	x	x	x	x
Publicity order cor-porations only (18)									
Reparation	*	*	*	*	*	x	x	x	x
Restitution order	*	*	*	*	*	*	*	*	*
Remedial order corporations only (19)									
Restraining order	*	*	*	*	*	*	*	*	*
Restraint order	*	*	*	*	*	*	*	*	*
Restriction order MHA	*	*	*	*	*	*	*	*	*
Serious Crime Prevention order	x	x	x	x	x	*	*	*	*
Sex offences prevention order	*	*	*	*	*	*	*	*	*
Youth rehabilitation order	*	*	*	*	*	x	x	x	x
Sentence or order	under 14	14	15	16	17	18	19	20	21 & over

Notes
4–002

(1) **Action plan order** (PCC(S)A 2000, s.69), only in respect of offences committed Nov 30, 2009. Repealed CJIA 2008, s.6.

(2) **ASBO** (CDA 1998, s.3). Ancillary order, cannot stand alone. Conviction must be after December 2, 2002. See ANTI-SOCIAL BEHAVIOUR ORDERS. Note power to suspend order, also power to add individual support order (ISO).

(3) **Attendance centre order** (PCC(S)A 2000, s.60; repealed CJIA 2008, s.6) Now restricted to offenders (a) aged 18,19, or 20 in respect of offences punishable with imprisonment committed before Nov 30, 2009, (b) those 17–21 found in contempt of court. Limits

on hours in accordance with age. See generally COMMUNITY SENTENCES, YOUTH REHABILITATION ORDERS.

(4) **Bind over** Although both common law bind overs and bind overs under JPA 1968, s.3 are available in respect of persons under 18, that person must consent, and if he does not, the court is, in practice, powerless to compel him (see BIND OVERS). An attendance centre order may be appropriate in the case of a juvenile aged 17, but is more common in the case of offenders under 18 to bind over the subject's parent or guardian (see BIND OVERS).

(5) **Committal for contempt** Attendance centre order may be appropriate.

(6) **Community sentences** The appropriate order in this age-bracket is a youth rehabilitation order, (see YOUTH REHABILITATION ORDERS).

(7) **Compensation, also fines, costs** Since the means of the offender are an important factor in making compensation or other financial orders, it will be more appropriate in the case of offenders under 18 to order payment by a parent or guardian, see (COMPENSATION ORDERS, FINES).

(8) **Custody for life** (PCC(S)A 2000, s.93) Appropriate where persons 18-20 are convicted of offences other than murder.

(9) **Detention HMP** (PCC(S)A 2000, s.90) Applies to an offender convicted of murder who appears to have been under 18 at the time the offence was committed (notwithstanding anything in PCC(S)A 2000 or any other Act).

(10) **Detention for life** (CJA 2003, s.226(2), see DANGEROUS OFFENDERS; PROTECTIVE SENTENCES.

(11) **Detention s.91** (PCC(S)A 2000, s.91). Applies to an offender:
  (a) under 18 convicted of certain specified offences only, namely an offence:
    (i) punishable in the case of an offender aged 21 or over with 14 years' imprisonment, not being an offence for which the sentence is fixed by law; or
    (ii) under SOA 2003, s.3 (sexual assault); or
    (iii) under SOA 2003, s.13 (child sex offences committed by children or young persons); or
    (iv) under SOA 2003, s.25 (sexual activity with a child family member);
    (v) under SOA 2003, s.26 (inciting a child family member to Engage in activity);
  (b) aged at least 14 but under 18 convicted of certain specified offences, namely: (i) causing death by dangerous driving under RTA 1988, s.l; or (ii) causing death by careless driving while under the influence of drink or drugs; the sentence may not exceed the maximum term of imprisonment to which a person aged 21 or over would be liable.

(12) **Detention Public Protection** (CJA 2003, s. 226). Applies to an offender aged under 18 convicted of a serious offence where the court is of the opinion that there is a significant risk to members of the public of serious harm occasioned by his

commission of further specified offences, see DANGEROUS OFFENDERS; PROTECTIVE SENTENCES.

(13) Detention and training order (PCC(S)A 2000, s.100) Available in respect of any offender aged under 18 convicted of an offence punishable with imprisonment in the case of an offender aged 21 or over, but:

(a) in respect of offenders aged under 15 at the time of conviction, he must be, in the judge's opinion, a persistent offender; and

(b) in the case of an offender under the age of 12 at that time, the offence must have been committed after a date specified by the Secretary of state, and the judge must be of the opinion that only a custodial sentence would be adequate to protect the public from further offending by him; the term of the sentence must be for 4, 6, 8, 10, 12, 18 or 24 months and must not exceed the maximum term of imprisonment the judge could impose for the offence.

(14) Discharge, absolute or conditional (PCC(S)A 2000, s. 12) Available in the circumstances outlined in DISCHARGE, ABSOLUTE AND CONDITIONAL, but may not be made in the instances set out in 29-003. As to combining other orders, see 29–004. Order not to exceed three years.

(15) Extended sentence order (Applies to both detention in the case of offenders 18 CJA 2003, s.228) and to imprisonment in the case of those aged 18 or over (CJA 2003 s.227) where the offender is convicted of certain specified offences, and the judge considers that there is a significant risk to members of the public of serious harm occasioned by his commission of further specified offences and the term otherwise imposed would not be adequate for the purpose.

(16) Financial reporting order (SOCPA 2005, s. 76). Limits on length of order – where offender sentenced to life imprisonment 20 years; otherwise 15.

(17) Football banning order (FSA 1989, s.14A. Ancillary order only, cannot stand alone;

(18) Publicity orders are available in the case of corporate manslaughter only: Corporate Manslaughter and Corporate Homicide Act 2007, s.10. As to the use of such orders see the SGC Definitive Guidelines on Corporate Manslaughter & Health and Safety Offences Causing Death 2010, paras 30-32.

(19) Remedial orders are available both for corporate manslaughter under the Corporate Manslaughter and Corporate Homicide Act 2007, s.9, and under the Health and Safety at Work Act 1974, s.42. As to the use of such orders see the SGC Definitive Guidelines on Corporate Manslaughter & Health and Safety Offences Causing Death 2010, paras 33–36.

Determination of age

4–003 Where an available sentence depends upon the age of the offender:

(1) The starting point is the sentence which the offender would have been likely to receive if he had been sentenced on the date of his conviction of the offence (*R. v Ghafoor* [2003] 1 Cr. App. R(S) 84; *R. v Britton* [2007] 1 Cr. App. R(S) 21);

(2) for the purposes of liability to a custodial sentence, or to a community sentence, the relevant age is the age of the offender on the date of his conviction, whether he pleaded guilty or not (*R v Danga* (1992) 13 Cr. App. R (S) 408; *R. v Robson* [2007] EWCA Crim 1416; [2007] 1 Cr. App. R(S.) 54); *R. v Robinson* 98 Cr. App. R. 370);

(3) where the offender has crossed the age threshold into adulthood between the date of the commission of the offence and the date of his conviction, the judge is bound to have regard to CJA 2003, s.141(1) including deterrence (*R. v Bowker* [2007] EWCA Crim 1608).

here the offender's age is in doubt or in dispute, the judge should adjourn and obtain proper evidence of age before sentence.

For the purposes of the following orders the age of the offender is deemed to be, after considering any available evidence on the day of conviction, what it appears to the judge to be (again there are exceptions, as to which see below):

(a) imprisonment;
(b) detention in a young offender institution;
(c) detention under PCC(S)A 2000, s.91; and
(d) a detention and training order.

In *R. v Robson* [2007] 1 All E.R. 506, distinguishing *Ghafoor* (above) CACD held that as a matter of statutory construction, the age of the offender for the purpose of determining which of the statutory regimes under Ch.5 of Pt 12 of the 2003 Act applied was the offender's age at the date of conviction.

The sentencing regime under which the appellant is to be sentenced must be determined by what was contemplated by the provisions which created the new sentencing regime.

Committal for sentence; breaches

4–004   There are a number of exceptions to the general rules stated in 4–003 above, thus:

(1) an offender committed to the Crown Court for sentence under PCC(S)A 2000, ss.3, 4 or 6 must be sentenced on the basis of his age **on the day he appears before the Crown Court;**

(2) an offender subject to a community order who appears before the Crown Court for sentence, while the community order is in force, and where the judge revokes the community order and passes a further sentence for the offence, must be sentenced on the basis of his age **when he appears before the Crown Court;**

(3) an offender who is found to be in breach of community order and in whose case the order is revoked must be sentenced on the basis

of his age **when he appears before the court which revokes the order;**

(4) an offender who is subject to a community order under CJA 2003 and in **whose case the community order is revo**ked following a breach or subsequent conviction must be sentenced on the basis of his age **when the original order was made;**

(5) an offender subject to a conditional discharge convicted of a further offence during the operational period of the order, where the conditional discharge is revoked, any sentence imposed for the original offence must be based on the offender's age **when he is so sentenced** *(R. v Keelan* (1975) 61 Cr. App. R. 212).

Other exceptions

4–005   In addition to the cases set out above, note that:

(1) an offender convicted *at any age* of a murder committed when he was under 18 must be sentenced to be detained during HM Pleasure;

(2) the power to make an RT disqualification order depends upon the offender's age *when he committed the offence.*

Notes

5. ALLOCATION AND DISTRIBUTION OF CASES

1. Allocation of cases sent etc., for trial

SCA 1981, s.77

Case sent for trial; date of trial

5–001 The trial of a person whose case is sent to the Crown Court for trial must:

(1) not begin until the expiration of 14 days beginning with the date it was sent for trial, except with the consent of the person charged; and

(2) unless the Crown Court has otherwise ordered, begin no later than the expiration of eight weeks beginning with that date.

A trial is taken to "begin" for this purpose when the accused is arraigned.

The time limits were said in *Ex p. Scott* (1988) 85 Cr. App. R. 382 to be "directory only", but see the decisions of the House of Lords in *R. v Soneji* [2005] UKHL 40; [2006] 2 Cr. App. R. 20 and the decisions of CACD in *R. v Knights* [2006] UKHL 50; [2006] 2 Cr. App. R. (S.) 80 and *R. v Ashton* [2006] 2 Cr. App. R. 15, referred to at para.5–010, below.

CJPOA 1994 Sch.4, para.52(5) requires the judge to have regard to the desirability of avoiding prejudice to the welfare of any witness which may be occasioned by unnecessary delay.

Allocation of business

5–002 The cases, or classes of cases, in the Crown Court suitable for allocation respectively to a judge of the High Court and to a Circuit Judge or a Recorder, and all other matters relating to the distribution of Crown Court business, are determined in accordance with directions given by or on behalf of the Lord Chief Justice.

SCA 1981, s.75(1)(2)

The same applies to the cases or classes of cases suitable for allocation to a court comprising magistrates. The directions at present in force are those given in PD 2004, III.21 and following, as amended, set out below, and taking effect from June 6, 2005.

Classification

5–003 For the purposes of trial in the Crown Court, offences are classified as follows:

Class 1: (a) Misprision of treason and treason felony; (b) murder; (c) genocide; (d) torture, hostage-taking and offences under the War Crimes Act 1991; (e) an offence under the Official Secrets Acts; (f) manslaughter; (g) infanticide; (h) child destruction; (i) abortion (OAPA 1861 s.58); (j) sedition; (k) an offence under s.1 of the Geneva Conventions Act 1957; (l) mutiny; (m) piracy; (n) soliciting, incitement, attempt or conspiracy to commit any of the above offences.

Class 2: (a) rape; (b) sexual intercourse with a girl under 13; (c) incest with a girl under 13; (d) assault by penetration; (e) causing a person to engage in sexual activity; (f) rape of a child under 13; (g) assault of a child under 13 by penetration; (h) causing or inciting a child to engage in sexual activity, where penetration is involved; (i) sexual activity with a person with a mental disorder; (j) inducement to procure sexual activity with a mentally disordered person, where penetration is involved; (k) paying for sexual services of a child where child is under 13 and penetration is involved; (l) committing an offence with intent to commit a sexual offence, where the offence is kidnapping or false imprisonment; (m) soliciting, incitement, attempt or conspiracy to commit any of the above offences.

Class 3: All other offences not listed in classes 1 or 2.

Cases committed, transferred or sent for trial

5–004   A magistrates' court upon either committing a person for trial under MCA 1980, s.6 or sending a person for trial under CDA 1998, s.51, must:

(a) if the offence, or any of the offences, is included in Class 1, specify the most convenient location of the Crown Court where a High Court Judge, or where a Circuit Judge duly authorised by the Lord Chief Justice to try Class 1 cases, regularly sits;

(b) if the offence, or any of the offences, is included in Class 2, specify the most convenient location of the Crown Court where a judge duly authorised to try Class 2 cases, regularly sits; these courts on each Circuit will be identified by the Presiding Judges with the concurrence of the Lord Chief Justice, on each circuit;

(c) if an offence is in Class 3, specify the most convenient location of the Crown Court.

Where a case is transferred under CJA 1987, s.4 or CJA 1991, s.53, the authority must, in specifying the proposed place of trial in the notice of transfer, comply with the above provisions. *PD 2004, III.21.2*

In selecting the most convenient location of the Crown Court, the magistrates must have regard to the considerations referred to in MCA 1980, s.7 and CDA 1998, s.51(10), and to the location or locations of the Crown Court designated by a Presiding Judge as the location to which cases should normally be committed, from their petty sessions area. *PD 2004, III.21.3*

Where on one occasion a person is committed in respect of a number of offences, all the committals must be to the same location of the Crown Court and that location must be the one where a High Court Judge regularly sits if such a location is appropriate for any of the offences. *PD 2004, III.21.4*

As to Welsh language cases, see WELSH LANGUAGE CASES.

Committals following breach

5–005   Where, in the Crown Court, a community order or an order for conditional discharge has been made, or a suspended sentence has been passed, and the offender is subsequently found or alleged to be in breach *PD 2004, III.21.5* before a magistrates' court which decides to commit the offender to the Crown Court, he must be committed in accordance with paras III.21.6, III.21.7 or III.21.8. Thus:

PD 2004, III.21.6

(1) he must be committed to the location of the Crown Court where the order was made or the suspended sentence was passed, unless it is inconvenient, impracticable or inappropriate to do so in all the circumstances;

PD 2004, III.21.7

(2) if, for whatever reason, he is not so committed and the order was made by a High Court Judge he must be committed to the most convenient location of the Crown Court where a High Court Judge regularly sits;

PD 2004, III.21.8

(3) in all other cases he must be committed to the most convenient location of the Crown Court.

In selecting the most convenient location of the Crown Court, the magistrates must have regard to the locations of the Crown Court designated by a Presiding Judge as the locations to which cases should normally be committed from their court.

PD 2004, III.21.9

Serious or complex fraud cases
5–006   Where notice of transfer is served under CJA 1987, s.4 the proposed place of trial to be specified in the notice must be one of the Crown Court centres designated by the Senior Presiding Judge.

PD 2004, III.21.10

Child witness cases
5–007   Where a notice of transfer is served under CJA 1991, s.53 (child witness cases), the proposed place of trial to be specified in accordance with CJA 1991, Sch.6, para.1(1) must be a Crown Court centre which is equipped with live television link facilities.

PD 2004, III.21.11

Transfer between circuits
5–008   The distinction between transfers from one location to another on the same circuit, and transfers from one circuit to another has now been abolished, Resident Judges on different circuits may make such arrangements between them without needing to notify, or seek the concurrence of, the Presiding Judges and Regional Directors.

PD 2004, IV.31.1

Transfer of proceedings between locations of the Crown Court
5–009   Without prejudice to the provisions of SCA 1981, s.76 (committal for trial; alteration of place of trial), directions may be given for the transfer from one location of the Crown Court to another of:

PD 2004, IV.32.1–3

(a) appeals; and
(b) proceedings on committal for sentence, or to be dealt with.

Such directions may be given in a particular case by an officer of the Crown Court, or generally, in relation to a class or classes of case, by the Presiding Judge or a judge acting on his behalf.

If dissatisfied with such directions given by an officer of the Crown Court, any party to the proceedings may apply to a judge of the Crown Court who may hear the application in chambers.

Note that:

- Any case referred by a Presiding Judge under guidance issued by the Senior Presiding Judge may only be transferred to another court by or under the direction of a Presiding Judge, who will have the assistance of the regional listing coordinator.
- It may be necessary to transfer a specific case at shorter notice to a different but proximate court centre to enable a trial to go ahead on a fixed date, or within the trial window, or for some other similar reason. Every effort must be made to avoid transferring a case where the witnesses have had a pre-court visit for familiarisation with the court and courtroom, or where there are transport difficulties. The listing officer must consult the parties; if they do not agree to the change, then the case must be referred to the Resident Judge of the transferring court for his decision
- No block transfer, i.e. the planned movement of a significant volume of cases from one centre to another. should take place without the approval of the Presiding Judge(s) for the relevant circuit(s).

PD 2004, Annex F, 4.8.

Alteration of venue

5–010 Without prejudice to the above provisions, directions, or further directions, altering the place of any trial on indictment, whether by varying the decision of the magistrates' court under MCA 1980, s.7, (or CDA 1998, s.51 – *R. v Croydon CC Ex p. Britton* (2000) 164 J.P. 729) or by substituting some other place for the place specified in a notice of transfer or varying a previous decision of the Crown Court, may be given by or on behalf of the Crown Court by a Crown Court officer. Where a preparatory hearing has been ordered under CJA 1987, s.7, such directions may be given at any time before the jury is sworn (or would be sworn but for the making of an order under CJA 2003, Pt 7 (trial without jury)). SCA 1981, ss.8(1), 76(1)(2)

If dissatisfied with the place of trial as:

(1) fixed by the magistrates' court;
(2) specified in a transfer notice under CJA 1987, s.4 or CJA 1991, s.53; or
(3) fixed by the Crown Court,

a party may apply to the Crown Court for a direction, or a further direction, varying the place of trial, and the Crown Court must take the matter into consideration, and may comply with or refuse the application, or give a direction not in compliance with the application, as it thinks fit.

2. Allocation of business within the Crown Court

General

5–011 Cases in: PD 2004, IV.33.1

Class 1 may be tried only by:

(1) a High Court Judge; or

(2) a Circuit Judge, a Deputy High Court Judge or a Deputy Circuit Judge provided that:
   (a) in all cases save attempted murder such judge is authorised by the Lord Chief Justice to try murder cases, or in the case of attempted murder, to try murder or attempted murder; and
   (b) the Presiding Judge has released the case for trial by such a judge.

Class 2 may be tried by:

PD 2004, IV.33.2

(1) a High Court Judge;
(2) a Circuit Judge, a Deputy High Court Judge or Deputy Circuit Judge or a Recorder, provided that in all cases such judge is authorised to try Class 2 cases by the Lord Chief Justice and the case has been assigned to the judge by order under the direction of either the Presiding Judge or Resident Judge in accordance with guidance given by the Presiding Judges.

Class 3 may be tried by a High Court Judge or, in accordance with guidance given by the Presiding Judges, by a Circuit Judge, Deputy Circuit Judge or a Recorder. A Class 3 case must not be listed before a High Court Judge except with the consent of a Presiding Judge.

PD 2004, IV.33.3

Appeals from decisions of magistrates:

5–012   Appeals from decisions of magistrates must be heard by:

PD 2004, IV.33.45

(1) a Resident Judge; or
(2) a Circuit Judge who regularly sits at that Crown Court centre, nominated by the Resident Judge; or
(3) an experienced Recorder or Deputy Circuit Judge specifically approved by or under the direction of the Presiding Judges for the purpose; or
(4) where no Circuit Judge or Recorder satisfying the requirements above is available and it is not practicable to obtain the approval of the Presiding Judges, by a Circuit Judge, Recorder or Deputy Circuit Judge selected by the Resident Judge to hear a specific case or cases listed on a specific day.

The most satisfactory situation is for the Resident Judge to deal with appeals from magistrates' courts in the area, thus ensuring consistency and, and showing that local problems are being adequately considered. It is particularly inappropriate for such matters to be given to visiting or temporary judges or Recorders.

Plea and management hearings

5–013   With the exception of courts operating the management and directions scheme referred to in PD 2004 para.41.1, the following arrangements for **pre-trial proceedings** apply:

PD 2004, para.33.6

(1) to applications or matters arising before trial (including those relating to bail) should be listed where possible before the judge by whom the case is expected to be tried. Where a case is to be tried by a High Court Judge who is not available the application or matter should be listed before any other High Court Judge

35

then sitting at the Crown Court centre at which the matter has arisen; before a Presiding Judge; before the Resident Judge for the centre, or with the consent of the Presiding Judge, before a Circuit Judge nominated for the purpose;

(2) in other cases, if the Circuit Judge or Recorder who is expected to try the case is not available, the matter must be referred to the Resident Judge or, if he is not available, to any judge or Recorder then sitting at the centre.

Committals following breach

5–014 Committals following breach (such as a matter in which a community order has been made or a suspended sentence passed) should, where possible, be listed before the judge who originally dealt with the matter or, if not, before a judge of the same or a higher level.

PD 2004, IV.33.5.

Application for removal of a driving disqualification

5–015 Application should be made to the location of the Crown Court where the order of disqualification was made.

PD 2004, IV.33.6.

Listing

5–016 Listing is a judicial responsibility and function. The overall purpose is to ensure that, as far as possible, all cases are brought to a hearing or trial in accordance with the interests of justice, that the resources available for criminal justice are deployed as effectively as possible, and that, consistent with the needs of the victims, witnesses of the prosecution and the defence and defendants, cases are heard by an appropriate judge or bench with the minimum of delay. The Concordat (reached between the Lord Chief Justice and the Secretary of State for Constitutional Affairs and Lord Chancellor set out in his statement to the House of Lords on January 26, 2004) states that judges are responsible for deciding on the assignment of cases to particular courts and the listing of those cases before particular judges, working with HMCS.
Therefore:

PD 2004, Annex F,1

(1) The Presiding Judges of the circuit have the overall responsibility for listing on each circuit/region. As outlined at 5–020 below, certain cases in the Crown Court must be referred to the Presiding Judges for directions; the Presiding judges will be supported by a regional listing coordinator.

(2) In the Crown Court, subject to the supervision of the Presiding Judges, the Resident judge at each Crown Court is responsible for listing at his Crown Court centre; the Resident Judge is responsible (following guidance or directions issued by the Lord Chief Justice and by the Senior Presiding Judge and Presiding Judges (under PD 2004, IV 33) for determining the listing practice to be followed at that centre, for prioritising the needs of one case against another and deciding upon which date a case is listed and before which judge.

(3) The listing officer in the Crown Court is responsible for carrying out the day-to-day operation of listing practice under the direction of the Resident Judge. The listing officer at each

Crown Court centre has one of the most important functions at that Crown Court and makes a vital contribution to the efficient running of that Crown Court and to the efficient operation of the administration of criminal justice.

As to the principles governing listing generally, see *A-G's Reference No.3 of 1999* [2000] UKHL 63 [2001] 1 Cr. App. R. 34, *per* Lord Steyn. As to the principles to be observed in Crown Court listing, see PD 2004, Annex F, para.2.

A Resident Judge must appoint a deputy to exercise his functions when he is absent from his centre (PD 2004, IV.33.7).

Presiding Judges' guidance

5–017 For the just, speedy and economical disposal of the business of a circuit, the Senior Presiding Judge, or the Presiding Judges with his approval (PD 2004, IV.33.8), may issue guidance to Resident Judges in relation to the allocation and management of the work at their court.

With the approval of the Senior Presiding Judge, general directions may be given by the Presiding Judges of the South Eastern Circuit concerning the distribution and allocation of business of all classes (all cases or classes of cases) at the Central Criminal Court (PD 2004, IV.33.9).

3. Guidance for Resident Judges

General responsibilities

5–018 A Resident Judge has the general responsibility, subject to the guidance of the Presiding Judges, within his court centre for the allocation of criminal judicial work, to ensure the just and efficient despatch of the business of the court or group of courts. This includes the overseeing of the deployment of allocated judges at the court or group, including the distribution of work between all the judges allocated to that court.

The Resident Judge will set overall listing practice in his court in accordance with the objectives and considerations set out in PD 2004, Annex F and will consider representations made by local criminal justice agencies and representatives of the defence and witnesses, in the setting of the listing practice (PD 2004, Annex F, 3.1). Where difficulties arise, whether around listing generally or regarding specific cases, which cannot be resolved by the listing officer, the matter will be referred for consideration to the Resident Judge or the judge assigned to a specific case. Where resolution of disagreement, cannot be reached locally the issue should be referred without delay to the Presiding Judges or the Senior Presiding Judge (*ibid* 3.4).

Under PD 2004, IV.33. (see 5–017, above) the Senior Presiding Judge and the Presiding Judge's issued guidance (dated May 26, 2005 and taking effect on June 6, 2005) in relation to cases which must be referred to:

(1) a Presiding Judge for release; and
(2) the Resident Judge before being assigned to a judge or Recorder to hear.

ALLOCATION AND DISTRIBUTION OF CASES

It is applicable to all Crown Courts, but its application at certain Crown Courts may be modified by the Presiding Judges, with the approval of the Senior Presiding Judge, through the provision of further specific guidance applicable to such Crown Courts as are identified in the further guidance. Note that:

    (a) cases which do not come within (1) or (2) are not specifically covered by this Guidance, but are subject to the directions given to the Listing Officer by the Resident Judge at each centre;

    (b) this Guidance does not seek to prescribe the way in which the Resident Judge gives directions as to listing policy to the listing officer; its purpose is to ensure that there is appropriate judicial control over the listing of cases specified in this Guidance;

    (c) in view of the changes effected to this Guidance in respect of Class 2 cases, it is essential that a Resident Judge nominates a judge to act on his behalf and discharge his responsibilities when he is away.

Assignment of cases to judges

5–019   The responsibility for the assignment of a judge to a case is, subject to any general or specific direction or guidance of the Presiding Judge, that of the Resident Judge. The time at which a judge is assigned is a matter for the discretion of the Resident Judge. At larger court centres, the Resident Judge may delegate certain functions in relation to assignment to another judge. (PD 2004, Annex F, 4.4).

Cases to be referred to a Presiding Judge

5–020   The following cases must be referred to a Presiding Judge:

    (1) all Class I cases (see 5–003, above);

    (2) all cases expected to last four weeks or more. If there are serious fraud cases (as defined by the Lord Chief Justice in 1998) that are estimated to last less than this, they must also be referred;

    (3) all cases involving rape or other sexual offences which are of especial sensitivity or likely to attract publicity such as those involving well known persons or circumstances of particular difficulty or notoriety or serial cases. Paragraph 5–021 (below) sets out the procedure for assignment by the Resident Judge or the judge who is to try such cases without reference to the Presiding Judge;

    (4) terrorist and firearms cases;

    (5) cases involving explosives, terrorism or the actual discharge of firearms in the course of another crime; also the more serious cases of possession of firearms, especially where possession is in the context of robbery or other serious crime.

The form is attached as Annex A to the Guidance. Of particular importance when a release request is made are a case summary, which can be very brief in a standard sort of case, a clear recommendation by the Resident Judge about the judges available to try the case, and any brief comments or reasons he/she thinks helpful.

Cases to be referred to the Resident Judge

5–021   The following cases must be referred by listing officers to the Resident Judge:

(1) all cases under (1)–(5) of para.5–020 above which are required to be referred to a Presiding Judge must in the first instance be referred to the Resident Judge;

(2) all sexual offences (not merely those in Class 2, see 5–003, above); he may deal with them without reference to the Presiding Judge, save in the circumstances specified in 5–020 (above) at (3);

(3) all cases involving firearms or imitation firearms;

(4) cases involving causing death by dangerous or careless driving;

(5) arson;

(6) kidnapping and false imprisonment;

(7) cases where any accused is under 18;

(8) any case which appears to raise particularly complex, sensitive or serious issues.

Administrative arrangements

5–022   It is the Resident Judge's duty to arrange with the Listing Officer a satisfactory means of ensuring that all cases listed at their court are listed before judges or recorders of suitable seniority and experience, subject to the following:

(1) if a case is referred to the Presiding Judge, and the Presiding Judge does not assign the judge who is to try the case, the assignment of the judge must be made by the Resident Judge; the time at which the assignment is made is at his discretion;

(2) in all rape cases and other sexual offences falling within Class 2 (see 5–003, above), the judge who is to try the case must be assigned by or under the direction of the Resident Judge, the time at which the assignment is made being at his discretion. The judge assigned must have been authorised to try Class 2 cases. It is a condition of the authorisation that it does not take effect until the judge has attended the relevant JSB course; the Resident Judge should check in the case of newly authorised judges that they have attended the course;

(3) the following offences, save in exceptional circumstances specifically authorised by the Resident Judge, should also be tried by a judge authorised to try Class 2 cases who is assigned to try the case by the Resident Judge; **all serious sexual offences** including:

- cases of buggery with a person under 16;
- all cases of serious cases of indecent assault and indecency, especially those involving children or vulnerable complainants whether under the 2003 Act or otherwise;
- unlawful sexual intercourse with young girls; indictable-only offences under the 2003 Act—see ss.9 and 25;
- cases involving breach of trust—see ss.38–41;
- any other cases which are potentially sensitive;

(4) all cases specified in 5–021(3)–(8) must be assigned for trial to a judge by or under direction of the Resident Judge; the time at which the assignment is made being a matter for his discretion.

Notes

6. ANCILLARY ORDERS

General

6–001 A number of ancillary orders are available, which may be attached, in appropriate circumstances, to the principal sentence. Orders which form part of a community sentence are not included.

With the exception of a compensation order, which may stand alone, all other such orders depend upon their being a principal sentence. The "plea and sentence document" served on the court (see GUILTY PLEAS) should include a statement of any ancillary order for which the prosecution intends to apply.

The available orders are:

Name of order	Age restrictions	Section in text	Comment
Anti-Social Behaviour Order (ASBO)	none	7	Convicted after December 2, 2002; minimum period two years
Bind Over	under 18 only with consent	11	As to binding over parent or guardian of offender under 18, see 11–010 and following
Company Officer's Disqualification Order	none	17	
Compensation Order	none	18	Parent or guardian of under 16 must, of 16–18 may, be ordered to pay. As to local authorities see 14–021
Confiscation Order POCA 2002	none	19	Enforceable as a fine
Costs	none	21	Parent or guardian of under 16 must, of 16–18 may, be ordered to pay. As to local authorities see 14–021

ANCILLARY ORDERS

Name of order	Age restrictions	Section in text	Comment
Default Sentence (Financial Penalties)	–	36	
Deprivation Order (s.143)	none	38	
Disqualification from Driving	none	33	
Drinking Banning Order	16 or over	32	Not less than six months, not more than two years (not yet in force)
Drug Abstinence Order	18 and over	16	Only in respect of offence committed before April 4, 2005
Exclusion Order (licensed premises)	none	46	
Financial Circumstances Order	none	36	
Financial Reporting Order	none	35	
Football Banning Order	none	37	Certain offences only; prescribed periods
Forfeiture Order (MDA 1971)	none	38	
Hospital and Limitation Direction (MHA)	none	50	
Individual Support Order (ISO)	under 18	7	Period not exceeding six months; must be attached to ASBO

Name of order	Age restrictions	Section in text	Comment
Offences taken into consideration	over 17	25	
Parenting order	under 18	53	Obligatory under 16 unless reasons 20–023
Publicity order (under CMCHA 2007)	corporations only	4	See SGC 2010, paras 30-32
Recom- mendation for Deportation	none	27	
Reparation Order	none	14	(reparation other than money) restrictions apply in relation to offences committed before April 4, 2005
Remedial order (CMCHA 2007, HSWA 1974)	corporations only	4	See SGC 2010, paras 33-36
Restitution Order	none	57	
Restraining Order (Harassment)	none	58	Applies only in respect of offences committed under PHA 1999, ss.2,4
Restriction Order (MHA)	none	50	
Return to custody (s.116)	18 or over	41	
Sexual Offences Notification Requirement	none	64	
Serious Crime Prevention Order	18 and over	62	

Ancillary Orders

ANCILLARY ORDERS

Name of order	Age restrictions	Section in text	Comment
Sexual Offences Prevention Order	–	64	
Surcharge	none	36	Applies only to offenders dealt with on or after April 1, 2007
Suspended Sentence Supervision Order	–	41	Applies to imprisonment and detention YOI
Travel Restriction Order	none	68	Only in respect of offender convicted of drug trafficking offence on or after April 1, 2002

Machinery

6–002 In general, unless the statute otherwise permits (e.g. in the case of a confiscation order) all aspects of the sentence, i.e. the principal penalty and any ancillary order, ought to be imposed on the same occasion. In the case of RT disqualifications, however:

(1) there is nothing to prevent the judge from dealing with the substantive part of the sentence on the day of conviction and postponing ancillary questions of endorsement and disqualification until the licence is produced, and any other relevant information is to hand *(R. v Annesley* (1976) 62 Cr. App. R. 113);
(2) a judge who:
  (a) defers sentence in respect of an offence carrying obligatory or discretionary disqualification; or
  (b) adjourns after convicting an offender of such an offence, before dealing with him,

may order him to be disqualified until he has been dealt with for the offence.

Sheriff's awards under CLA 1826, ss.28, 29 and commendation(s) should be considered in appropriate cases (see FORFEITURE).

7. ANTI-SOCIAL BEHAVIOUR ORDERS

General

7–001   An anti-social behaviour order for a specified period of not less than two years may be made whether on application or otherwise, where:

(1) an offender is convicted of an offence committed after December 2, 2002; and   CDA 1998, s.1C
(2) the judge considers that:
   (a) the offender has acted, at any time since the above date, in an anti-social manner, that is to say in a manner that caused, or was likely to cause, harassment, alarm or distress to one or more persons not of the same household as himself; and
   (b) that such an order is necessary to protect persons in any place (in England and Wales) from an offence as described above, or from further anti-social acts by him.

An order is not appropriate to protect the wife of the offender where they are living under the same roof (*R. v Gowan* [2007] EWCA Crim 360; [2007] 1 Cr. App. R. (S.) 12).

The order is preventative in nature. It is designed for the protection of others and is not a penalty for an offence. The approach should be to sentence for the substantive offence, and then to consider whether an order should be made, albeit at the same hearing where that is appropriate.

An order may cover a multitude of matters but will commonly include harassment, noise nuisance, writing graffiti and verbal abuse. A guidance paper is available from the Judicial Studies Board.

Necessity is the test

7–002   The test for the making of an order is one of necessity, i.e. each separate order prohibiting the doing of a specified thing must be necessary to protect persons from further anti-social acts by the offender. The test requires judgment and evaluation; it does not require proof beyond a reasonable doubt that the order is necessary (*R. v Wadmore* [2006] Crim. L.R. 857). The order must be tailor-made for the individual offender, not designed on a word processor for use in every case (*R. (Lonergan) v Lewes CC*, [2005] 1 W.L.R. 2670; *R. v Boness* [2005] EWCA Crim 2395; [2006] 1 Cr. App. R. (S.) 120).

The judge is not required to consider what sentence he would have imposed (whether by way of curfew or otherwise), if he had been sentencing the same person for one or more of the same acts which justified the making of the order (*R. (McCann) v Manchester CC* [2002] UKHL 39, [2003] 1 Cr.App.R.27).

The order must be substantially, not just formally, prohibitory; a curfew order which imposes a restraint upon leaving or travelling between specified premises between particular times meets that test (*R. (Lonergan) v Lewes CC*, above).

Anti-Social Behaviour Orders

ANTI-SOCIAL BEHAVIOUR ORDERS

The judge must also consider making an ISO, see below at, 7–007 and following.

Procedure

7–003 An order cannot stand alone; it is an ancillary order which may be attached to any sentence imposed for an offence as described above, or to a conditional discharge. It may be initiated by the judge of his own motion, or on application. A warrant may be issued where the offender fails to appear on an adjourned hearing.

The procedure is prescribed by r.50 (Civil behaviour orders after verdict or finding) as follows;

Where:

(1) the prosecutor wants the judge to make an order if the accused is convicted (other than an interim order):   R.50.3

    (a) he must serve a notice of intention to apply for such an order, in the form provided in PD 2004, Annex D, on the Crown Court officer, the accused against whom the order is sought and any person on whom the order would be likely to have a significant adverse effect, as soon as practicable (without waiting for the verdict);

    (b) he must identify the evidence on which he relies in support, attach any written statement that he has not already served, and specify the order he wants the judge to make; and the accused must serve written notice of any evidence on which he relies, on the Crown Court officer and on the prosecutor (without waiting for the verdict) and in that notice identify the evidence and attach any written statement that has not already been served;

(2) the judge indicates that he may, on his own initiative, make an order, a party who wants the judge to take account of any particular evidence before making that order, must serve notice in writing on the Crown Court officer and every other party, as soon as practicable (without waiting for the verdict), attaching that evidence and any written statement that has not already been served.   R.50.4

As to hearsay evidence, see rr.50.6, 50.7 and 50.8.

Making an order

7–004 The judge must not make an order (except an interim order) unless the person to whom it is directed has had an opportunity to consider what is proposed, and why, and to make representations at the hearing (whether or not he attends).   R.50.2

In so far as an interim hearing is concerned, the order has no effect unless the person to whom it is directed is present when it is made and is handed a document recording the order not more than seven days after it is made.

The whole of the procedure should take place in the presence of the accused; also

(1) the terms of any order must be precise and capable of being understood by the accused, to whom they must be explained;

(2) the conditions in the order must be enforceable in the sense that they allow a breach to be readily identified;

(3) the findings of fact giving rise to the making of the order must be recorded;

(4) the exact terms of the order must be pronounced in open court, and explained to the offender, and the written order must accurately reflect the order as pronounced.

(*R. v Parkin* [2004] EWCA Crim 1480; [2004] Crim. L.R. 490; *R. v P (Shane Tony)* [2004] EWCA Crim 287; [2004] 2 Cr. App. R.(S) 65; *R. v Boness*, above.

Where an order is made at the time of the imposition of a prison sentence, the judge should have regard to the nature, length and likely effect of the sentence, the nature, length and actual effect of prior sentences, and the duration, conditions and likely effect of any period of licence (*R. v Barclay* [2011] L.S. Gazette, February 17, 18. See also *R. v P (Shane Tony)*, above).

As to reporting restrictions, see REPORTING AND ACCESS RESTRICTIONS.

Form of order

7–005   A form of order is set out in PD 2004, Annex D. As to forms of prohibition, see Thomas L.J.'s *ASBO Guidance for the Judiciary*, published by HM Court Service on their website.

In drawing up the order:

(1) the duration of the order ought to be for a determinate period: *R. v Vittles* [2004] EWCA Crim 1089; [2005] 1 Cr. App. R. (S.) 8 (where five years was substituted for an indeterminate period (see also *R. v Werner* [2004] EWCA Crim 2931);

(2) the judge must seek carefully to match the prohibitions in the order with the type of behaviour it is necessary to prohibit for the purposes in the Act (*CPS v T*, [2006] EWHC 728 (Admin); [2006] 3 All E.R. 471); to ban the offender from "committing any criminal offence" is too wide and is unenforceable (*W v DPP*, 1333 (Admin); 169 JP 435), as is a term "not to act in an antisocial manner in the City of Manchester" (*CPS v T*, above).

(3) It is not necessary that every condition imposed in the order run for the full term of the order; the test must be "what is necessary to deal with the particular anti-social behaviour", and "what is proportionate in the circumstances" (*R. v Boness*, above).

Where an order prohibits conduct which is also a distinct criminal offence care should be exercised in deciding whether to make an order. If an order is made:

(a) it must be justified with reference to CDA 1998, s.1C(2)(a) (b); and;

(b) should not be made simply for the purpose of increasing the sentence available on a breach beyond the maximum provided for that other offence.

As to variation and discharge, see BREACH, AMENDMENT AND REVOCATION. Appeal lies under CDA 1998, s.4.

Anti-Social Behaviour Orders

ANTI-SOCIAL BEHAVIOUR ORDERS

Suspended order; breach

7–006 An order takes effect on the day it is made, but s.1C(5) enables the judge to provide that any requirements of the order as he may specify be suspended until the offender is released from any period of custody during which he is detained.

Where a custodial offence of more than a few months is passed, the offender being liable to be released on licence, and subject to recall, the need for a suspended order taking effect on release, is limited, though there may be cases where, e.g. geographical restraints might conveniently supplement the licence conditions (*R. v Parkin*, above). **CDA 1998, s.1B(5)–(7);**

As to breach of an ASBO see BREACH, AMENDMENT AND REVOCATION, Pt G, below at 12–058.

Individual support orders (ISOs)

7–007 Where the judge makes an anti-social behaviour order in respect of a person under 18 he must consider whether the individual support conditions are made out. **CDA 1998, s.1AA**

These are that:

(1) an individual support order (ISO) would be desirable in the interests of preventing any repetition of the kind of behaviour which led to the making of the anti-social behaviour order;
(2) the offender is not already subject to an ISO; and
(3) the judge has been notified that arrangements for implementing such orders are available in the area in which it appears to it that the offender resides or will reside.

If the judge is satisfied that these conditions are fulfilled, he must make an order requiring the offender to comply:

(a) for a period not exceeding six months, with such requirements as are specified in the order; and
(b) with any directions given by the responsible officer with a view to the implementation of the requirements under (a).

If he is not satisfied that these conditions are fulfilled, he must state in open court that he is not so satisfied and why.

Preconditions to making of ISO

7–008 Before making an order, the judge must obtain a report from a social worker of a local authority social services department or a member of a youth offending team, and consider any information which he considers necessary in order to determine whether the individual support conditions are fulfilled, or to determine what requirements should be imposed by the order if made. **CDA 1998, s.1AA(9)**

"Responsible officer" in relation to an ISO means a social worker of a local authority a person nominated by a person appointed as Chief Education Officer under the Education Act 1996, s.532, or a member of a youth offending team.

The requirements of the order

7–009 The requirements that may be specified are any that the judge considers desirable in the interests of preventing any repetition of the **CDA 1998, s.1AA(5)–(8)**

kind of behaviour which led to the making of the anti-social behaviour order.

The requirements included in, and the directions given under such an order by the responsible officer, may require the offender to do all or any of the following things:

(1) to participate in activities specified in the requirements (or directions) at a specified time or times;
(2) to present himself to a specified person or persons at a place or places and at a time or times so specified;
(3) to comply with any specified arrangements for his education,

provided the requirements (or directions) do not require the offender to attend (whether at the same place or at different places) on more than two days in any week; and "week" here means a period of seven days beginning with a Sunday. The requirements must, as far as practicable, be such as to avoid any conflict with the offender's religious beliefs, and any interference with the times, if any, at which he normally works or attends school or any other educational establishment.

Spelling it out

7–010   Before making an order, the judge must explain to the offender in ordinary language:

CDA 1998, s.1B(1)(3)

(1) the effect of the order and of the requirements proposed to be included in it;
(2) the consequences which may follow if he fails to comply with any of those requirements; and
(3) that the judge has power (under s.1B(6)) to review the order on the application either of the offender or of the responsible officer.

The consequences of failing without reasonable excuse to comply with any requirement included in the order, are that the offender is guilty of an offence and liable on summary conviction to a fine, not exceeding, if he is aged 14 or over at the date of his conviction, £1,000 or if he is aged under 14, £250 (As to payment by parent or guardian, see CHILDREN AND YOUNG PERSONS).

Variation etc. of ISO

7–011   Both the offender and the responsible officer may apply to the court which made the order for a variation or discharge, and if the order is varied, the court varying it may, by further order, vary or discharge it.

CDA 1998, s.1B(5)–(7)

If the antisocial behaviour order, as a result of which the ISO was made, ceases to have effect, the ISO, if it has not previously ceased to have effect, ceases to have effect at the same time (CDA 1998, s.1B(5)–(7); CJA 2003, s.322). Appeal lies under CDA 1998, s.4 as amended by CJA 2003, s.323(2).

Variation etc. of ASBO

7–012   See BREACH, AMENDMENT AND REVOCATION, Part G.

CDA 1998, s.1C

Notes

8. APPEALS FROM THE CROWN COURT

Quick guide

Further appeal lies, with leave of CACD to the Supreme Court of the United Kingdom under the Constitutional Reform Act 2005, s.40 and Sch.9. Procedure is under the Supreme Court Rules 2009 (SI 2009/1603).

A.   Appeals to CACD

1.   About conviction and sentence

(1)   By the accused/offender

General

8–001   All the usual consequences following from a conviction, etc. on indictment, are susceptible to appeal to CACD:

(1) by a person convicted on indictment, against his conviction and/ or sentence (not being a sentence fixed by law);
(2) by a person convicted in the magistrates' court and sentenced on committal to the Crown Court in certain limited circumstances *(R. v Gatehouse* [2001] 2 Cr. App. R.(S.) 94);

(3) by a person in whose case a verdict of not guilty by reason of insanity has been returned—against that verdict;

(4) where there has been a determination under CP(I)A 1964, s.4 of the question of a person's fitness to be tried, and findings that he was under a disability and did the act or made the omission charged against him have been returned—against those findings;

(5) by a person arraigned on or after March 31, 2005, in whose case a hospital order or an interim hospital order is made by virtue of CP(I)A 1964, ss.5 or 5A, or a supervision order is made under s.5; and

(6) where, upon conviction, judgment is respited and the offender is bound over to come up for judgment when called upon to do so—against any sentence subsequently imposed *(R. v Smith* (1925) 89 J.P. 79).

An appeal lies to CACD at the instance of a defendant from any order or decision of the Crown Court in the exercise of its jurisdiction to punish for contempt of court (AJA 1960, s.13) (see 8–014 below), including an appeal against a refusal of bail made in the course of contempt proceedings *(R. v Serumaga* [2005] EWCA Crim. 370 [2005] 2 Cr. App. R. 12).

An offender upon whom a mandatory life sentence was imposed before December 18, 2003 and who has had his minimum term set or reviewed by a judge of the High Court may appeal to CACD. (CJA 2003, Sch.22, para.14) (see 8–011 below). See also CJA 2003 (Mandatory Life Sentences: Appeal in Transitional Cases) Order 2005, SI 2005/2798.

As to the right of appeal to CACD *after the* determination of an Attorney General's reference of an unduly lenient sentence, see *R. v Hughes* [2009] EWCA Crim. 841; [2010] 1 Cr. App. R. (S.) 25.

Pleas of guilty

8–002   CACD is entitled to allow an appeal against conviction *only* where the conviction is unsafe (see *R. v Chalkley* [1998] 2 Cr. App. R. 79: accused pleading guilty following judge's ruling). Where the accused pleads guilty *before* being put in charge of the jury, CACD has no power to substitute a conviction for another offence *(R. v Horsman* [1997] 2 Cr. App. R. 418).

Need for leave

8–003   Appeal to the CACD, save in respect of a contempt matter brought under AJA 1960, s 13, where appeal lies of right, lies only: CAA 1968, ss.1(2), 12, 15

(1) with the leave of the CACD; or

(2) in an exceptional case, if the judge of the trial court gives a certificate that the case is fit for appeal (see 8–025).

Absconding, etc. appellants

8–004   As to appeals by absconding appellants, see *R. v Charles* [2001] EWCA Crim 129; [2001] 2 Cr. App. R. 15; as to appellants who escape from custody before the hearing of their appeal, see *R. v Gooch*

[1998] 2 Cr. App. R. 130, also *R. v Flower* (1966) 50 Cr. App. R. 22, and *R. v Panayi* (1989) 88 Cr. App. R. 267.

As to appellants failing to answer their bail, see *R. v Whiting* (1987) 85 Cr. App. R. 78, and *R. v Carter* (1994) 98 Cr. App. R. 106.

Appeal in case of deceased appellant

8–005   In the case of a person since deceased:

CAA 1968, s. 44A

(1) any appeal under CAA 1968, ss.l, 9, 12, or 15, or under s.33, which might have been begun by him had he remained alive may be begun by a person approved by CACD (see, e.g. *R. v Whelan* [1997] Crim. L.R. 659); and

(2) where such an appeal was begun by him while he was alive or is begun in relation to his case by virtue of (1) or by a reference by the Criminal Cases Review Commission, any further step which might have been taken by him in connection with the appeal if he were alive, may be taken by a person so approved.

Approval for these purposes may only be given to a widow or widower of the deceased, or to certain personal representatives, or to a person appearing to the court, or a single judge, by reason of a family or similar relationship with the deceased, to have a substantial financial or other interest in the determination of the appeal.

CAA 1968, s. 44A(3)(6)

Except where the case is referred by the Criminal Cases Review Commission (see, e.g. *R. v Bentley* [2001] 1 Cr. App. R. 21; *R. v Hanratty,* (deceased) [2002] EWCA Crim 1141; [2002] Cr. App. R. 30) an application for approval must be made within a year beginning with the date of the death.

CAA 1968, s.44A(4)

Meaning of "sentence"

8–006   "Sentence", in terms of CAA 1968, means any order made by a court when dealing with an offender including, in particular:

CAA 1968, s. 50

(1) a hospital order under MHA 1983, Pt III with or without a restriction order;

(2) an interim hospital order under that Part;

(3) a hospital direction and a limitation direction under MHA 1983, Pt III;

(4) a confiscation order under POCA 2002, Pt 2;

(5) an order which varies a confiscation order made under POCA 2002, Pt 2, if the varying order is made under POCA 2002, ss.21, 22 or 29 (but not otherwise);

(6) a recommendation for deportation;

(7) a confiscation order under DTA 1994, other than one made in the High Court;

(8) a confiscation order under CJA 1988, Pt VI (proceeds of major crime);

(9) an order varying a confiscation order of a kind included in (7) or (8) above;

(10) an order made by the Crown Court varying a confiscation order made by the High Court by virtue of DTA 1994, s.19;

(11) an order which varies a confiscation order made under POCA

2002, if that variation is made under ss.21, 22 or 29 (but not where made under s.23 – *R. v Ward (Barry)* [2010] EWCA Crim. 1932, *The Times*, August 27, 2010)

(12)   a financial reporting order (*R. v Adams* [2008] EWCA Crim 914; [2008] 4 All E.R. 574).

A mandatory life sentence imposed on conviction for murder under M(ADP)A 1965, s.l(l) is a sentence fixed by law, and therefore excluded from appeal under CAA 1968, s.9(l), except in so far as a question of compatibility with ECHR arises: *R. v Lichniak* [2002] UKHL 47; [2003] 1 Cr. App. R. 33, or as to the minimum term imposed *(R. v Sullivan* [2004] EWCA Crim1762; [2005] 1 Cr. App. R. 3).

A sentence for contempt of court imposed upon an appellant, whether in respect of his conduct at the trial or for absconding from bail, is treated as a sentence for the purposes of appeal.

Where the judge has deferred passing sentence on an offender, the CACD will treat such an order as being a "sentence" within s.50 *(Att Gen's Reference (No.22 of 1992) (1994) 97 Cr. App. R. 275; R. v L (DEFERRED SENTENCE Etc) [1999] 2 Cr. App. R. (S.) 78.*

Single appeal; time for appeal

8–007   Generally CAA 1968 provides for a single appeal in respect of each case, but this does not preclude an appeal against a confiscation order under DTA 1994 made subsequent to sentence *(R. v Neal* [1999] 2 Cr. App. R.(S.) 352).

Generally, it will be inappropriate to seek to appeal against conviction until the Crown Court proceedings have been completed, which includes the passing of sentence. It is clear, however, that the word "conviction" in the Act may properly encompass the verdict of the jury, and there may be cases where the Court of Appeal will entertain an appeal short of that stage *(R. v Drew* (1985) 81 Cr. App. R. 190). The general rule is that time runs from the date of conviction – in the case of trial by jury from the date of verdict: *R. v Hawkins* [2010] 9 Archbold Review 1. There is no rule of practice or otherwise that an application for leave to appeal against conviction should await the imposition of sentence. As to appeal against conviction after a plea of guilty following the trial judge's direction, see *R. v Chalkley (*above*), R. v Jefferies* [1998] 2 Cr. App. R. 79.

(2)   Appeal following reference by CCRC

Reference

8–008   The Criminal Cases Review Commission, set up by CAA 1995, s.8 may refer to CACD the conviction or sentence (not being one fixed by law) of a person convicted on indictment, a verdict of not guilty by reason of insanity and a finding of disability, where a finding that he did the act or made the omission was returned. Its powers and functions are reviewed in *R. v Criminal Cases Review Commission Ex p. Pearson* [2000] 1 Cr. App. R. 141.

CAA 1995, s.9;

CAA 1995, s.14, as amended by CJA 2003, s.315, contains further provisions relating to such references.

Powers of CACD to order investigation

8–009 On an appeal against conviction, or an application for leave to appeal against conviction, CACD (not a single judge) may direct the Commission to investigate and report on any matter if it appears that:

CAA 1968, s.23A

(1) in the case of an appeal, the matter is relevant to the determination of the appeal, and ought, if possible, to be resolved before the appeal is determined;
(2) in the case of an application for permission to appeal, the matter is relevant to the determination of the application and ought, if possible, to be resolved before the application is determined;
(3) an investigation of the matter is likely to result in CACD being able to resolve it; and
(4) the matter cannot be resolved by CACD without an investigation by the Commission.

In due course the parties will be informed of the results, and the report and any statements, opinions and reports will be made available to them.

(3) Appeal by offender or specified prosecutor in respect of substituted sentence under SOCA 2005, s.74

8–010 Both:

SOCA 2005, s.74(8)(9)

(1) an offender in respect of whom a reference is made under SOCA 2005, s.74(3) (assistance by offenders); or
(2) the specified prosecutor who has made a reference to a judge of the Crown Court

may, with the leave of CACD, appeal to that court against the decision of the Crown Court, either to substitute, or not to substitute, a sentence under the provisions of the Act.

An appeal is initiated by serving Form NG(RD) on the Crown Court where sentence was reviewed

CAA 1968, s.33(3) (limitation on appeal from CACD) does not prevent a further appeal to the Supreme Court.

(4) Mandatory life sentences (Minimum Term)

8–011 An offender upon whom a mandatory life sentence was imposed before **Dec 18, 2003** and who has had his minimum term set or reviewed by a judge of the High Court may appeal to CACD.

CJA 2003, Sch.22, para.14

(See also SI 2005/2798 (CJA 2003 (Mandatory Life Sentences: Guide D5 Appeals in Transitional Cases Order 2005, Pt 2, para.8)).

The procedure is under r.68 and is initiated by a notice of appeal in Form NG(MT) not more than 28 days after the decision appealed against. Where the appellant also wishes to appeal against conviction, notice should be in Form NG. The Registrar may direct a respondent's notice in Form RN or the prosecutor may serve one if he wishes to make representations to the court. An application for a representation order may be made to the Registrar (AJA 1999, s.12(2)(b)).

Special provisions apply under CJA 2003, s, 274(3) an r. 68.1 to offenders sentenced to life imprisonment outside the United Kingdom, and transferred to serve the sentence in England and Wales.

(5)   Appeals in relation to serious crime prevention orders (SCA 2007, s 24)

8–012   An appeal against a decision of the Crown Court in relation to a serious crime prevention order (see generally SERIOUS CRIME PREVENTION ORDERS) may be made to the CACD by: SCA 2007, s. s.24(1)–(4))

(1) the person who is the subject of the order; or
(2) the relevant applicant authority.

In addition, an appeal may be made to the CACD in relation to a decision of the Crown Court:

(a) to make an order; or
(b) to vary, or not to vary, such an order;

by any person who was given an opportunity to make representations in the proceedings concerned by virtue of s. 9(4).

Appeal lies only:

(i)   with the leave of CACD, or
(ii) without such leave, where the judge who made the decision grants a certificate that the decision is fit for appeal.

Procedure: SI 2008/1868

8–013   A special form of procedure is set out in Pt 1 of the Serious Crimes Act 2007 (Appeals under s.24) Order 2008 (SI 2008/1868). Forms NG (SCPO) and RN (SCPO) are set out in PD 2004, Annex D.

Note, in particular, that:

(1) an appeal is limited to a review of the decision of the Crown Court unless CACD considers that in the circumstances of the appeal it would be in the interests of justice to hold a re-hearing;
(2) CACD will allow an appeal where the decision of the Crown Court was wrong or unjust because of a serious procedural or other irregularity in the proceedings in the Crown Court.
(3) CACD has all the powers of the Crown Court, and may:
    (a) make a serious crime prevention order;
    (b) affirm, set aside or vary any order or judgment made or given by the Crown Court;
    (c) refer any issue for determination by the Crown Court;

(d) order a new hearing in the Crown Court;
(e) make an order for costs;
(f) make an order for the payment of interest on those costs, in relation to the whole or part of an order of the Crown Court.

(6)   Contempt Cases

8–014   AJA 1960, s.13 gives an appeal as of right to the CACD to any person dealt with by the Crown Court for contempt. No permission is required. Most appeals concern persons wishing to appeal a sentence for failing to appear at the Crown Court, which is treated as if it were a contempt.

The procedure is governed by r.68. Proceedings are commenced by lodging form NG at the Crown Court not more than 28 days after the order to be appealed. The Registrar may direct a respondent's notice in Form RN, or the prosecutor may serve one if he wishes to make representations to the CACD.

An undischarged Crown Court representation order will cover advice and assistance on the merits of opposing the appeal and drafting the respondent's notice, otherwise an application for a representation order may be made to the Registrar (AJA 1999, ss.12(2)(b)).

Guide D4

(7)   Procedure

(a)   Initiating an appeal

8–015   In relation to appeals about conviction and sentence an offender wishing to appeal initiates the proceedings in accordance with:

R.68.1

*   CPR 2010, r 68,
*   PD 2004 Part II and
*   the Guide to Commencing Proceedings in the Court of Appeal Criminal Division, effective from October 1, 2008 (see http://www.gov.uk/docs/proc_pdf).

The procedure subsequent to giving notice is essentially in the hands of the Registrar of the CACD and the role of the Crown Court, and its officers is confined to the acceptance, collation and transmission of documents (see 8–029), and in exceptional cases; the giving of a certificate of fitness to appeal (see 8–026) and the granting of bail (see 8–027).

Service of appeal notice

8–016   An appeal is commenced, as a general rule, by the appellant serving an appeal notice on the Crown Court officer at the Crown Court centre where

R.68.2

(1) the conviction, verdict, or finding;
(2) the sentence; or
(3) the order, or failure to make an order,

about which the appellant wants to appeal, occurred, not more than 28 days after it occurred.

Where the trial was conducted without a jury under the provisions of CJA 2003, Pt 7, the date of conviction is the date of the judgment delivered by the court under s.48(5)(a) (CJA 2003, s.48(5)(b)).

Where:

(a) the appeal is against a minimum term review decision under CJA 2003, Sch.22, para.14; or

(b) the case is referred to the court by CCRC, the appellant must serve an appeal notice on the Registrar not more than 28 days after such a decision, or after the Registrar serves notice that the Commission has referred a sentence, or 56 days after the Registrar serves notice that the Commission has referred the conviction.

Service of appeal notice

8–017 (1) The general rule is that an appellant must serve an appeal notice   R.68.2

(1) on the Crown Court officer at the Crown Court centre where there occurred:

(a) the conviction, verdict, or finding;

(b) the sentence; or

(c) the order, or the failure to make an order about which the appellant wants to appeal; and

(2) not more than:

(a) 28 days after that occurred; or

(b) 21 days after the order, in a case in which the appellant appeals against a wasted or third party costs order, but an appellant must serve an appeal notice:

(i) on the Registrar instead where:

• the appeal is against a minimum term review decision under CJA 2003, s. 274(3) of, or Sch. 22, para.14, or

• the CCRC refers the case to the court; and

(ii) not more than 28 days after—

• the minimum term review decision about which the appellant wants to appeal, or

• the Registrar serves notice that the Commission has referred a conviction.

A confiscation order (whether made under CJA 1988, DTA 1994 or PCA 2002) is a sentence (CAA 1968, s.50).

Where sentences are passed in separate proceedings on different dates there may be two appeals against sentence, e.g. an appeal against the custodial part of a sentence and an appeal against a confiscation order (*R. v Neal* [1999] 2 Cr. App. R. (S.) 352).

In the case of a mandatory minimum sentence depending on one or more previous convictions (under CSA 1997, Pt I), if a relevant previous conviction is set aside by CACD, thus invalidating the mandatory sentence, notice of appeal against the latter may be given at any time within 28 days from the date on which the previous conviction was set aside.

As to extension of time, see 8–021 below; as to the duties of the Crown Court officer, where a party wants to appeal, see r.65.8 at 8–029 below.

Need for leave

8–018   It should be noted that leave to appeal is required in all cases except where:

(1) the trial judge or sentencing judge has certified that the case is fit, for appeal (see 8–025 below); or
(2) the case has been referred by the CCRC;
(3) the case is a "contempt" case under AJA 1960, s.13.

In (2) the appellant must obtain leave to pursue grounds not related to the Commission's reasons for referral (CAA 1995, s.14(4B)).

The grant of representation is a matter for the registrar. His practice is contained in the Guide.

Form NG and Grounds of Appeal

8–019   Where counsel has advised an appeal, solicitors should forward the forward the signed grounds of appeal to the Crown Court accompanied by Form NG and such other forms as may be appropriate. Note that: R.68.5(2)

(1) Form NG and grounds of appeal are required to be served within the relevant time limit in all cases, whether or not on a reference by CCRC, however,
(2) if no Form NG and grounds are served within the required period, the reference will be treated as the appeal notice.

Form NG is self-explanatory, and outlines the material required.

Grounds of appeal

8–020   Counsel should not settle grounds of appeal or support them with written advice unless they consider that they are properly arguable. Such grounds must be carefully drafted and properly particularised. Should leave be granted to amend the grounds it is most unlikely that further grounds will be considered. The sufficiency of the notice and the grounds is a matter for the Registrar. The requirements are set out in the Guide.   PD 2004, II.15.1

Note that, in respect of legal advice:

(1) a positive advice on appeal should always be incorporated into the same document as the grounds of appeal, thus enabling an assessment of the strength of the appeal to be made more easily;
(2) an adverse advice should never be lodged with the Registrar (so that if there is a new, personal, appeal, there will be nothing adverse in the file and the application can be considered entirely on its merits.

The Guide indicates where particular grounds of appeal, such those involving the calling of fresh evidence (A2.7.1), complaints about trial advocates (A2-7.2) or in sufficient weight being given for assistance to the prosecuting authority (A2-7.3) require a special approach.

Extension of time

8–021   CACD has power under r.65(3) to shorten a time limit or extend it (even after it has expired) unless that is inconsistent with other legislation (see the note to r.65.(3)). A person who wants an extension of time within which to serve a notice or make an application must apply for that extension when serving the notice or making the application, giving the reasons for his application for an extension of time (r.65.4).

An application for extension of the 28 day period in which to give notice of application for leave to appeal or notice of appeal must always be supported by reasons why the application for leave was not submitted in time. It is not enough merely to tick the relevant box on Form NG. Such an application should be submitted when the application for leave to appeal against either conviction or sentence is made and not in advance.

A person who wants an extension of time within which to serve a notice or make an application must: R.65.4

(1) apply for that extension of time when serving that notice or making that application; and
(2) give the reasons for the application for an extension of time.

(b)   Advice and assistance; representation

Action on conclusion of trial

8–022   Provision for advice or assistance on appeal is included in the   Guide A1.1
representation order effective for the first instance proceedings. Immediately following the conclusion of the case:

(1) the legal representatives should see the client and counsel should express orally his final view as to the prospects of a successful appeal (whether against conviction or sentence or both);
(2) if there are no reasonable grounds of appeal, that should be confirmed in writing and a copy provided to the client;
(3) if there are reasonable grounds of appeal they should be drafted, signed and sent as soon as possible to instructing solicitors who should immediately send a copy of the documents received from counsel to the client.

Further representation

8–023   Prior to the lodging of notice and grounds of appeal the   Guide A1.2
Registrar has no power to grant a representation order; the Crown Court may amend a representation order in favour of fresh legal representatives only if advice on appeal has not been given by the trial legal representatives and it is necessary and reasonable for another legal representative to be instructed.

Where advice on appeal has been given by the trial legal representatives, application for funding may be made only to the Legal Services Commission.

Once Form NG has been lodged, the Registrar is the authority for decisions about representation orders, in accordance with the principle that the court before which there are proceedings is the court with power to grant a right to representation (AJA 1999, Sch.3; GR 2001, reg.10).

Where, in order to settle grounds of appeal, work of an exceptional nature is contemplated or where the expense will be great, legal representatives should submit Form NG with provisional grounds of appeal and with a note to the Registrar requesting a representation order to cover the specific work considered necessary to enable proper grounds of appeal to be settled.

(c) Bail pending appeal

General

8–024 There is no statutory right to bail after conviction; CACD is reluctant to grant bail pending appeal. Bail will be granted pending appeal only where (subject to CJPOA 1994, s.25):

Guide A8

(1) it appears prima facie on cogent grounds that the appeal is likely to succeed, or
(2) where there is a risk that the sentence will have been served by the time the appeal is heard.

Even in short sentence cases, CACD is reluctant to grant bail, preferring to expedite the appeal and if necessary to list it at short notice (*R. v Walton* (1979) 68 Cr. App. R. 295; *R. v Shah*, unreported, August 13, 1978, CA).

In an appropriate case, bail may be granted by:

(a) a single judge or the CACD; or
(b) a trial or sentencing judge who has certified the case fit for appeal (see 8–027 below).

An application to CACD for bail must be supported by a completed Form B(CAO), whether or not the application is made at the same time as the notice and grounds are served.

Note that:

(i) if the form is served with Form NG it should be served on the Crown Court;
(ii) if it is served subsequently it should be sent to the Registrar;
(iii) where the defence consider that bail should be applied for as a matter of urgency, the application should normally be made in the first instance to the trial judge;

CACD may decline to treat an application as urgent if there is no good reason why the application was not made to the Crown Court.

The completed Form B(CAO) must be served on the court and on the prosecution at least 24 hours before any application is made to enable the prosecutor to make representations (either written or oral) about the application and any conditions.

It is not appropriate for an application to be made to a judge who also sits as a member of CACD, e.g. on circuit, until a formal application for permission to appeal has been made through the Registrar (*R. v Suggett* (1985) 81 Cr. App. R. 243).

As to bail with condition of surety in CACD, see r.68.9.

(d) Applying to the Crown Court for leave

Fitness for appeal; trial judge's certificate

8–025 Exceptionally, in a proper case, and within 28 days of the conviction, a certificate may be given:

CAA 1968. 11(1)
(2),12. 15(2)

(1) that a case is fit for appeal against conviction, etc., on a question of fact, or of mixed law and fact, by the trial judge;

(2) that a case is fit for appeal against sentence under s.9, by the trial judge;

(3) that a case is fit for appeal against sentence under s.10, by the judge who passed the sentence; or

(4) as a pre-condition to granting bail, that a case is fit for appeal on a ground involving a question of law alone, by the trial judge.

Only in exceptional circumstances should an appeal go before CACD on a certificate granted by the trial judge rather than by leave.

A certificate should normally be granted only if:

(a) there is a very clear reason for doing so, such as an unre-solved issue of law; or

(b) there are clear reasons for supposing that an appeal is likely to succeed (*R. v Harries* [2007 EWCA Crim. 820).

It should not be granted without seeking representations from the prosecutor.

In particular, the trial judge should not give his certificate merely in the light of mitigation to which he has, in his opinion, already given due weight *R v. Killeen* [19851 Crim. L.R. 331).

Where the judge has taken the view, in the course of the trial, that he has of necessity ruled on the interpretation of primary or subordinate legislation in a manner which is not compatible with any provision of the ECHR, it is anticipated that he will give a certificate in order to give the CACD the opportunity to make a declaration of incompatibility which the Crown Court has no power to make.

Applying for the judge's certificate

8–026 An appellant who wishes the Crown Court judge to certify that a case is fit for appeal must either:

CAA 1968. 11(1) (2),12. 15(2)

(1) apply orally, with reasons, immediately after;
    (a) the conviction, verdict or finding;
    (b) the sentence; or
    (c) the order, or the failure to make an order about which the appellant wishes to appeal; or
(2) apply in writing and serve the application on the Crown Court officer not more than 14 days after (a)-(c).

A written application must include the same information as that required in Form NG (see 8–019 above with the necessary adaptations).

The judge may well think it right to hear an oral application for a certificate in chambers with a shorthand writer or logger present, and to invite the accused's advocate to submit, before the hearing of the application, a draft of the grounds of appeal which he will ask the judge to certify. The advocate for the Crown will be better able to assist the judge at the hearing if the draft grounds are sent beforehand to him also.

The judge:

(a) must first decide whether there exists a particular and cogent ground of appeal; if there is no such ground there can be no certificate and if there is no certificate there can be no bail;

(b) should bear in mind that where he refuses a certificate, application may be made to CACD for leave to appeal and for bail;

(c) should bear in mind that the length of time which may elapse before the hearing of the appeal is not relevant to the grant of a certificate, but if he grants a certificate, it may be one factor in the decision whether or not to grant bail.

The judge ought not to grant bail without any prior enquiry of the Criminal Appeal Office as to the speed with which an appeal could be brought on. The ordinary course will be to take steps to ensure expedition (*R. v Harries* [2007] EWCA Crim. 820).

Bail on grant of certificate

8–027 The judge who tried the case, where the appeal is under CAA 1968, s.1 or s.9, or the judge who passed the sentence in the case of an appeal under s. 10 may, in exceptional circumstances grant bail, provided:

(1) the case is not one to which CJPOA 1994, s.25 (see BAIL) applies;

(2) the case is not one to which CAA 1968, s.12 (appeal against a verdict of not guilty by reason of insanity), ss. 15 or 16 A (appeal against a finding that the accused was under disability, or that he did the act or made the omission charged against him) apply; and

(3) the judge gives a certificate under CAA 1968, ss.l(2) (question of fact or mixed law and fact) and 11(1 A) (fit for appeal against sentence), or under SCA 1981, s. 81(lB) that the case is fit for appeal on a ground which involves a question of law alone;

(4) the appellant has not made un application to CACD for bail in respect of the offence or offences to which the appeal relates;

(5) he power is exercised within 28 days from the date of the conviction appealed against, or from the date the sentence was passed where the appeal is against sentence, or in the case of an order made or treated as made on conviction, from the date of the making of the order.

Where an appeal notice has not been served in accordance with CAA 1968, s.18(l),

it must be a condition of any bail granted at the Crown Court that:

(a) notice is lodged within the prescribed period; and

(b) not later than 14 days from the end of that period, the appellant lodge with the Crown Court the Registrar's certificate to that effect.

The Crown Court may direct the appellant to appear:

(i) if notice is lodged within time, at such time as the CACD requires; or

(ii) if notice is not lodged within the period, at such lime and place as the Crown Court may require.

The Registrar may vary any conditions of bail granted to the appellant by the Crown Court, (or by CACD) provided the respondent does not object. If the Registrar refuses to do so, the appellant is entitled to have the matter determined by a single judge.

See *R. v Ofori* (1994) 99 Cr. App. R. 219 in relation to recommendations for deportation.

Suspension of RT disqualification

8–028 Where a person disqualified from holding or obtaining a driving licence appeals, or applies for permission to appeal, against his conviction or sentence, the Crown Court judge (or CACD) may suspend the disqualification, if he thinks fit.

(8)   Duty of Crown Court officer

Duty of Crown Court officer

8–029 The Crown Court officer must provide the Registrar with any R.65.8 document, object or information for which the Registrar asks within such period as the Registrar may require. See generally *Guide to Commencing Proceedings in the Court of Appeal Criminal Division* effective from October 1, 2008 available at Crown Courts and on http://www.hmcourts-service.gov.uk/docs/proc_guide.pdf.

Unless the Crown Court otherwise directs, the Crown Court officer must, where:

(1) **someone may appeal to CACD**, arrange for
   (a) the recording of the proceedings in the Crown Court;
   (b) the transcription of such a recording if:
      (i) the Registrar wants such a transcript; or
      (ii) anyone else wants such a transcript (subject to the restrictions in r.65.9(2)); and
   (c) any document or object exhibited in the proceedings in the Crown Court to be kept there, or kept by some other appropriate person, until six weeks after the conclusion of those proceedings.
(2) CPR 2011, Pt 66 applies (**appeal to CACD against ruling at preparatory hearing**),as soon as practicable serve on the appellant a transcript or note of:
   (a) each order or ruling against which the appellant wants to appeal; and
   (b) the judge's decision on any application for permission to appeal.
(3) CPR 2011, Pt 67 applies (**appeal to CACD against ruling adverse to the prosecution**), as soon as practicable serve on the appellant a transcript or note of:
   (a) each ruling against which the appellant wants to appeal;
   (b) the judge's decision on any application for permission to appeal; and
   (c) the judge's decision on any request to expedite the appeal;
(4) CPR 2011, Pt 68 applies (**appeal to CACD about conviction or sentence**), as soon as practicable serve on the Registrar:
   (a) the appeal notice and any accompanying application that the appellant serves on the Crown Court officer;

    (b) the judge's certificate, if any, that the case is fit for appeal; the judge's decision on any application at the Crown Court centre for bail pending appeal;

    (c) such of the Crown Court case papers as the Registrar requires; and

    (d) such transcript of the Crown Court proceedings as the Registrar requires.

(5) CPR 2011, Pt 69 applies (**appeal to CACD regarding reporting or public access**) and an order is made restricting public access to a trial,

    (a) immediately notify the Registrar of that order, if the appellant has given advance notice of intention to appeal; and

    (b) as soon as practicable provide the applicant for that order with a transcript or note of the application.

(9) Subsequent Procedure

General

8–030   Subsequent procedure is within the jurisdiction of CACD, (see rr.65, 68.6, 9–14), as amended by S.I. 2007/2317, supervised by the single judge and the Registrar. Reference should be made to the *Guide to Commencing Proceedings in the Court of Appeal Criminal Division* effective from October 1, 2008 available at Crown Courts and on http://www.hmcourts-service.gov.uk/docs/proc_guide.pdf.

Transcript and notes of evidence

8–031   The position as to transcripts etc is this;   Guide A4-1,2.3

    (1) in conviction cases, transcripts of the summing-up and proceedings up to and including verdict are obtained as a matter of course;

    (2) similarly, the transcript of the prosecution opening of facts on a guilty plea, and the judge's sentencing remarks are usually obtained in sentence cases;

    (3) R.68.3(2) obliges counsel to identify any further transcript which he considers the court will need and to provide a note of names, dates and times to enable an order to be placed with the shorthand writers;

    (4) whether or not any further transcript is required is a matter for the judgment of the Registrar or his staff;

    (5) a transcript should be requested only if it is essential for the proper conduct of the appeal in the light of the grounds;

    (6) if the Registrar and counsel are unable to agree the extent of the transcript to be obtained, the Registrar may refer that matter to a judge; the Registrar may propose that counsel agree a note in place of transcript;

    (7) in certain circumstances the costs of unnecessary transcript may be ordered to be paid by the appellant. Where a transcript is

obtained otherwise than through the Registrar, he may disallow the cost on taxation of public funding.

Perfection of grounds of appeal

8–032   The purposes of perfection are:

(1) to save valuable judicial time by enabling the court to identify at once the relevant parts of the transcript; and
(2) to give counsel the opportunity to reconsider his original grounds in the light of the transcript.

They should consist of a fresh document which supersedes the original grounds of appeal and contains *inter alia* references by page number and letter (or paragraph number) to all relevant passages in the transcript.
In:

(a) conviction or confiscation cases, the Registrar will almost certainly invite counsel to perfect grounds in the light of the transcript obtained, to assist the single judge or the full court;
(b) sentence cases, where counsel indicates a wish to perfect grounds of appeal, the Registrar will invite perfection only where he considers it necessary for the assistance of the single judge or the court.

If

- perfection is appropriate, counsel will be sent a copy of the transcript and asked to perfect his grounds within 14 days;
- in the absence of any response from counsel, the existing notice and grounds of appeal will be placed before the single judge or the court without further notice;
- if counsel does not wish to perfect his grounds, the transcript should be returned with a note to that effect;
- having considered the transcript, counsel is of opinion that there are no valid grounds, he should set out his reasons in a further advice and send it to his instructing solicitors; he should inform the Registrar that he has done so, but should not send him a copy of that advice.

Solicitors should send a copy to the appellant and obtain instructions, at the same time explaining that if the appellant persists with his application the Court may consider whether to make a loss of time order.

Respondent's Notice

8–033   Under r.68.6(1) the Registrar:

(1) may serve the appeal notice on any party directly affected by the appeal (usually the prosecution); and
(2) must do so in a CCRC case.

That party may then serve a respondent's notice if it wishes to make representations and must do so if the Registrar so directs 68.6(2). That notice should be served within 14 days on the appellant, the Registrar and any other party on whom the Registrar served the appeal notice.

The notice must be in Form RN, in which a respondent should set out the grounds of opposition and which must include the information set out in r.68.6(6).

In practice, this procedure applies primarily prior to consideration of leave by the single judge in both conviction and sentence cases.

Agreement has been reached by the registrar with the principal prosecuting authorities as to the types of cases and/or issues where the Registrar should consider whether to serve an appeal notice and direct or invite a party to serve a respondent's notice before the consideration of leave by the single judge. Examples include cases where the grounds concern matters which were the subject of public interest immunity (Pll), allegations of jury irregularity, criticism of the conduct of the judge, and complex frauds, also, where appropriate homicide offences, serious sexual offences, cases with national profile or high media interest cases of domestic violence.

In conviction cases where leave has been granted or where the application for leave has been referred to the full court, the prosecutor is briefed to attend the hearing and required to submit a respondent's notice/skeleton argument. In relation to sentence cases where leave has been granted, referred or an appellant is represented on a renewed application, the sentence protocol set out in PD 2004, II.1 will apply. In those cases, a respondent's notice/skeleton argument will have to be served when the prosecutor indicates a wish to attend or when the Registrar invites or directs the prosecutor to attend.

Power to vary requirements

8–034   CACD or the Registrar may: R.65.3

(1) shorten a time limit or extend it (even after it has expired) unless that is inconsistent with other legislation;
(2) allow a party to vary any notice that that party has served;
(3) direct that a notice or application be served on any person;
(4) allow a notice or application to be in a different form, or presented orally.

Application to CACD for bail

8–035   A party wanting to make an application to CACD about bail   R.68.8
pending appeal or retrial must serve an application in the form set out in PD 2004, Annex D, on the Registrar, unless the application is with the appeal notice, and on the other party. CACD will not decide such an application without giving the other party an opportunity to make representations, including representations about any conditions or surety proposed by the applicant.

As to bail with condition of surety in CACD, see r.68.9; as to the forfeiture of recognisances in respect of failing to appear at CACD, see r.68.10.

Loss of time

8–036   Applicants need to be aware that both CACD and the single   PD 2004, II.16.1
judge have a discretionary power to direct that part of the time during
which the applicant is in custody after putting in his notice of application for per-mission to appeal should not count towards sentence.

Where an application devoid of merit has been refused by the single
judge and a direction for loss of time has been made, the full court,
on renewal of the application, may direct that additional time shall be
lost if it, once again, thinks it right to exercise its discretion in all the
circumstances of the case. Although the power has been very sparingly
used in recent years, *R. v Kulumba, The Times,* May 17, 2005 indicates
that CACD is prepared to use it in the case of unmeritorious appeals
and renewed applications.

Abandonment

8–037   Both an application for permission and an appeal may be
abandoned by giving notice in Form A, as may a ground of appeal
identified in a notice of appeal or in a respondent's notice. An abandoned application will be treated as if it had been refused, an abandoned appeal as if it had been dismissed.

2.   Interlocutory hearings

Quick guide

(1) Appeals against rulings at preparatory hearings CJA 1987, s.9
   (8–038)
(2) Public regarding reporting or public access restriction (8–045)
(3) Trials without a jury (8–049)

(1)   Appeals against rulings at preparatory hearings CJA 1987, s.9

8–038   An appeal lies by either side from an order or ruling made by   CJA 9(11)(12)
a judge of the Crown Court at, or for the purposes of, a preparatory
hearing in a serious fraud case (see CASE MANAGEMENT), on either:

(1) a question as to the admissibility of evidence; or
(2) any other question of law relating to the case; or
(3) any question as to the joinder or severance of charges,

(Re Gunarwardena, Harbutt & Banks (1990) 91 Cr. App. R. 55) but not
from the trial judge's ruling on a challenge to the prosecution case statement *(R. v Smithson* [1995] 1 Cr. App. R. 14) or from the judge's decision refusing to quash counts on the indictment *(R. v Hedworth* [1991]
1 Cr. App. R. 421) or to the judge's decision whether to order disclosure
(R. v H (Interlocutory application; Disclosure) [2007] UKHL7; [2007]
2 Cr. App. R. 6). Where the judge conducting a preparatory hearing
under the Act, simultaneously conducts a parallel hearing (see 13–027)
to exercise other powers, a right of interlocutory appeal arises under
s.9(11) only where the matters dealt with come within the scope of
s.9(3) *(R. v H (Interlocutory Application; Disclosure),* above).

Rule 65 applies, with necessary modifications, to appeals under CJA 2003, s.217 (discharge of jury following tampering) (r.65(ll); S.I. 2006/353). Appeal lies only with the leave of the trial judge or of CACD.

CPIA 1996, ss.35, 36
8–039 An appeal lies from a ruling of the judge under CPIA 1996, s.31(3) (see CASE MANAGEMENT) but only with his leave or that of CACD.

The preparatory hearing may be continued notwithstanding the grant of permission to appeal but the jury will not be sworn until the appeal has been abandoned or determined.

Initiating an appeal
8–040 Where a party ("the appellant") wants to appeal under: `R.66.1(1)-(3)`

(1) CJA 1987, s.9(ll) or CPIA 1996, s.35(l); or
(2) CJA 2003, s.47(l)

he must serve an appeal notice in Form NG (Prep) on the Crown Court officer, the Registrar and every party directly affected by the order or ruling against which he wants to appeal, not more than five business days after the order or ruling which he wants to appeal or the Crown Court judge gives or refuses permission to appeal.

"Business day" means any day except Sunday, Christmas Day, `R.2.2(10)` Boxing Day, Good Friday, Easter Monday or a bank holiday.

If time limits are not adhered to CACD has power to grant an extension, but cogent reasons in support will be required.

Form NG (Prep) must:

(a) state the grounds of appeal; and `Guide B 7`
(b) where leave has been granted by the trial judge, state that fact and the grounds on which leave was granted; and

must comply with the provisions of r.66.3(2) including any application for leave to appeal, if required, extension of time to serve the appeal notice, and to attend the hearing. Where the trial date is imminent and the application urgent, the Registrar should be notified by telephone so that he may be consider referring the application directly to the full court and make arrangements for listing.

Judge's leave to appeal
8–041 An appellant who wants the Crown Court judge to give permission to appeal must apply either:

(1) orally, with reasons, immediately after the order or ruling against which he wants to appeal; or
(2) in writing, serving the application on the Crown Court officer, and every party directly affected by the order or ruling not more than two business days after that order or ruling.

A written application must include the same information (with the nec- `R.66.6` essary adaptations) as an appeal notice (see above 18–020). A judge of CACD may give leave to appeal.

Respondent's notice

8–042 A party on whom an appellant serves an appeal notice may R.66.5(1)
serve a respondent's notice in Form RN (Prep) and must do so, if, he
wants to make representations to the court; or the court so directs.

He must serve the respondent's notice on the appellant, the Crown
Court officer; the Registrar, and any other party on whom the appellant
served the appeal notice.

Such notice must be not more than five business days after the appellant serves the appeal notice, or a direction to do so.

The respondent's notice must:

(1) outline each argument in support, identifying the ground of
appeal to which each argument relates; and
(2) comply with r.66(5),

including or attaching any application for, with reasons, an extension
of time within which to serve the notice, or a direction to attend in
person any hearing that the respondent could attend by live link, if the
respondent is in custody.

CDS funding of appeal; costs

8–043 Defence representation is usually covered by the Crown Court Guide B6
representation order if one is still in force.

As to costs, see POA 1985, ss.6(4A), 18(2); CJA 2003, s.312.

Abandoning an appeal

8–044 An appeal under these provisions may be abandoned in the R.65.13, 14
same way as an appeal against conviction (see 18 037 above), as may
a ground of appeal or of opposition, by service on the Registrar of Form
A (Prep).

(2) Appeals regarding reporting or public access restriction

General

8–045 A person aggrieved may appeal to CACD, if the court gives CJA 1988, s.159
leave, against:

(1) an order under CCA 1981, s.4 (reporting by media) or s. 11 (permanent ban on reporting certain matters), made in relation to trial
on indictment;
(2) an order restricting the access of the public to the whole or any
part of a trial on indictment or to any proceedings ancillary to
such a trial;
(3) an order restricting the publication of a report of the whole or any
part of a trial on indictment or any such ancillary proceedings; and
(4) an order made by the Crown Court under s.58(7) or (8) of CPIA
1996 (derogatory assertions in mitigation), in a case where the
court has convicted a person on trial on indictment.

Persons who may be aggrieved include both media representatives
and the accused (*Re A* [2006] 1 W.L.R. 1351).

This form of appeal does not extend to proceedings in the magistrates' courts and therefore is not available in respect of proceedings in the Crown Court on appeal from such courts (see *R. v Malvern JJ Ex parte Evans* (1988) 87 Cr. App. R. 19).

Note also that applications for leave, and appeals in relation to: Rr.65.6(1), (3)

(a) reporting restrictions *may* be heard in private; and
(b) restricting public access *must* be determined without a hearing.

The procedure is governed by R.69. CACD may make such order as to costs as it thinks fit (CJA 1988, s.159(5) (c)) but not out of central funds (*Holden v CPS* (1993) 97 Cr. App. R. 376).

Service and form of appeal notice

8–046 A person wanting to appeal against one of the orders set out in Rr.69.2, 3
18–045 must serve an appeal notice on the Crown Court officer, the Registrar, the parties and any other person directly affected by the order against which the appellant wants to appeal, not later than:

(1) the next business day (see 18–040 above) after an order restricting public access to the trial; or
(2) 10 business days after an order restricting reporting of the trial.

The notice must be Form NG (159), and in addition to setting out the general matters referred to in r.69(3) must include, with reasons, an application for leave to appeal, and, where relevant, an application for an extension of time within which to serve the notice, and any applications in relation to attendance at the hearing or the introduction of evidence.

Order restricting public access; advance notice

8–047 Where an appellant wants to appeal against an order restricting Rr.69.4, 5
public access to a trial, he may serve advance written notice of an intention to appeal against any such order that may be made, on the Crown Court officer, the Registrar, the parties and any other person who will be directly affected by the order against which he intends to appeal, if it is made, not more than five business days (see 8–040 above) after the Crown Court officer displays notice of the application for the order. The notice must give the same information (with any necessary adaptations) as the appeal notice. If the order is made, the court will treat the advance notice as the appeal notice.

Where an appellant wants to appeal against an order restricting public access, it is the duty of the party who applied for the order, to serve on the Registrar a transcript or note of the application for the order and any other document or thing which that party thinks CACD will need to decide the appeal, as soon as practicable after the appellant serves an appeal notice or, after the order, where the appellant served advance notice of intention to appeal.

Appeal against reporting restrictions; respondent's notice

8–048 Where an appellant wants to appeal against an order restricting R.69.6
the reporting of a trial, a person on whom an appellant serves an appeal

notice may, and must if that person wants to make representations to CACD or if CACD directs, serve on the appellant and the persons referred to in 8–046, within three business days, a notice in Form RN (159) containing those matters set out in r.69.6(6), in particular summarising any relevant facts not already summarised in the appeal notice.

(3)   Trials without a jury

8–049   Where the provisions of CJA 2003 relating to trials without a jury are in force (see TRIALS WITHOUT A JURY) appeal lies to CACD in accordance with the procedure set out in r.66 in relation to appeals from preparatory hearings (see 8–038 above)). The leave of the Crown Court judge, the single judge or CACD is required Guide D12, D13, D14

Form NG (Prep) must be served on the Crown Court, the Registrar and any party directly affected, not more than five business days (see 19–040 above) after the order, or the judge of the Crown Court granting or refusing leave.

A respondent's notice in Form RN (Prep) may be served if the court directs, or the prosecutor or any party affected wants to make representations to the court.

Defence representation is usually covered by the Crown Court representation order if one is in force (AJA 1999, Sch.3, para.2(2)).

3.   Appeals by prosecutors against judges' rulings under CJA 2003, Pt 9

8–050   CJA 2003, Pt 9, gives to a prosecutor a right of appeal to the CACD:

(1) generally, in regard to rulings made by the judge in relation to a trial on indictment (s.58), ("terminatory rulings"); and

(2) against certain evidentiary rulings made by the judge in the course of such a trial (s.62) excepting that the prosecutor has no right of appeal under these provisions against: a ruling:

    (a) that the jury be discharged; or

    (b) from which an appeal lies to CACD by virtue of any other enactment, e.g. an appeal from a preparatory hearing against a ruling on the admissibility of evidence (evidentiary rulings).

The first of these is in force in relation to criminal proceedings committed, transferred or sent for trial, or where a voluntary bill was preferred, after April 4, 2005.

The second is not yet in force, although there will be evidentiary rulings which will be susceptible of appeal under s.58 *(Prosecutor's Appeal (No. 2 of 2008) R. v Y* [2008] EWCA Crim 10 [2008] 1 Cr. App. R. 34). See *R. v N Ltd* [2008] EWCA Crim 1223, [2007] 1 Cr. App. R. 3 (appeal against improper ruling of no case to answer); *R. v B* [2008] EWCA Crim 1997, [2009] 1 Cr. App. R. 19 (issue of separate trials where two of three accused were unfit to be tried).

An appeal under these provisions may be brought only with the leave of the judge who made the ruling. CJA 2003, s.57(4)

Right of appeal

8–051 The prosecutor may appeal, in respect of a ruling made by the judge in relation to one or more offences included in the indictment at any time

CJA 2003, ss.57, 58(1)(2) (13)(14)

(1) whether before or after the commencement of the trial;
(2) before the judge starts his summing-up; or
(3) would start his summing-up but for the making of an order under CJA 2006, Pt 7 (trial without a jury).

Note that:

(a) "Ruling" here includes any decision, determination, direction, finding, notice, order, refusal, rejection or requirement;
(b) the procedure covers the case both of a ruling which formally terminates a trial and a ruling which is in practice terminatory, since, in the absence of a right of appeal, the prosecutor would offer no further evidence.

A case management decision refusing to order an adjournment before trial or indeed at any time before the start of the summing-up may constitute a "terminatory" ruling against which a prosecutor may appeal *R. v Clarke* [2007] EWCA Crim 2532, [2008] 1 Cr. App. R. 33).

The procedure under s.58 does not give the prosecutor a right of appeal from the dismissal of a charge or the quashing of a count in an indictment under the procedure provided by CDA 1998, s.51, Sch.3, para.2, see SENDING ETC FOR TRIAL *(R. v Thompson* [2006] EWCA Crim 2849; [2007] 1 Cr. App. R. 15).

Although such rulings have come to be known as "terminatory," this expression does not appear in s.58, and there is no requirement that the prosecution case should be dealt a fatal blow by the ruling.

What matters is the "acquittal agreement" (see 8–052, below), i.e. the critical condition that the prosecutor accepts that if the appeal fails, the accused must be acquitted. That is the price the prosecutor has to pay for bringing the appeal *(Prosecutor's Appeal (No.2 of 2008) R. v Y)* (above).

The judge's ruling has no effect whilst the prosecutor is able to take any steps under s.58(4), below.

Prosecutor seeking to appeal

8–052 Following the ruling, the prosecutor must, if he is to appeal in respect of it:

CJA 2003, s.58(4)(5); R.67.2

(1) inform the judge, immediately after the ruling against which he wants to appeal, of his decision; or
(2) immediately after the ruling, request an adjournment to consider whether to appeal; and
(3) following that adjournment, if granted, inform the judge that he intends to appeal.

The duty under s.58(4) is to inform the court immediately after the ruling is given or after any period of adjournment allowed *(R. v Arnold* [2008] EWCA Crim 1084; [2008] 2 Cr. App. R. 37). Section 57 gives both the Crown Court judge and CACD power to give leave to appeal, but applications should ordinarily be made to the trial judge. A suspicion that the judge was likely to be hostile to the application is not a good reason; nor is the belief that application to the CACD was less likely to succeed if the trial judge refuses leave (*R. v F* [2009] EWCA Crim 1639).

As a general rule the judge should not require the prosecutor to decide there and then but should allow him until the next business day.

Where the ruling:

>   (a) relates to two or more offences,
>> (i) any one or more of those offences may be the subject of an appeal; and
>> (ii) in informing the judge that he intends to appeal, the prosecutor must, at the same time, inform him of the offence or offences which he seeks to make the subject of the appeal;
>   (b) is a ruling that there is no case to answer, the prosecutor may, at the same time nominate one or more other rulings which relate to the offence(s) the subject of the appeal, and those other rulings will be treated as the subject of the appeal.

The "acquittal agreement". If the prosecutor is to seek leave to appeal under s.58 he must at the time, or before, he informs the judge of his intention to appeal, undertake in open court that an acquittal will follow in respect of those offences that are the subject of the appeal, where either he fails to obtain permission to appeal or he abandons the appeal before it is determined by CACD. *(See R. v N(T)* [2010] Crim. L.R. 411; [2010] W.L.R. (D) 93; also *Prosecutor's Appeal (No. 2 of 2008) R. v Y* (above)*; R. v Arnold,* (above) , (a decision in respect of the comparable procedure under the Services Acts).

Application to the judge; judge's leave to appeal

8–053   A prosecutor who wants the Crown Court judge to give leave   R.67.5(1)
to appeal must apply:

>   (1) orally, with reasons, immediately after the ruling against which he wants to appeal;
>   (2) in writing, and serve the application on the Crown Court officer and every accused directly affected by the ruling, on the expiry of the time allowed to decide whether to appeal.

The written application under (2) must include the same information (with any necessary adaptations) as an appeal notice, as to which see 8–019, 8–020 above.

Except in the case of an appeal against a Pt II ruling (see DISCLOSURE), the judge must allow every accused directly affected by the ruling an opportunity to make representations.

The general rule is that the judge should decide whether or not to give leave to appeal on the day that the application is made to him, but he may adjourn for longer where there is a real reason for doing so (*R. v H* [2008] EWCA Crim 483).

Leave should be granted only where the judge considers that there is a real prospect of success, not in an attempt to speed up the hearing of the appeal (*R. v Gilbert* [2006] EWCA Crim. 3276).

Effect on ruling; continuation of proceedings

8–054   The judge's ruling effectively acquitting the accused or otherwise terminating the trial, will not take effect in relation to the offence or offences which are the subject of the appeal whilst the appeal is pursued, and:

CJA 2003, s.
58(10)-(12)

(1) any consequences of it have no effect;
(2) the judge may not take any steps in consequence of it; and
(3) if he does, any such steps will be of no effect.

Where the trial involves more than one offence, or more than one accused, but the appeal does not apply to all the offences or all the accused, proceedings in respect of any offence which is or any accused who is, not the subject of an appeal may, at the discretion of the judge, be continued. See again (*R. v SH* [2010] EWCA Crim. 1931.

The judge has no power to carry on regardless.

Expedited and non-expedited appeals

8–055   The Act places a mandatory obligation on the judge to consider the issue of expedition. The provision is not discretionary. A decision has to be made (which in a long trial may have serious repercussions) whether to await any decision of CACD or to abandon the trial with the risk that, if the appeal succeeds, the trial will have to start again (*R. v SH*, above). At the time he informs the judge that he intends to seek leave to appeal against a ruling, the prosecutor must also make oral representations as to whether or not that appeal should be expedited under CJA 2003, s.59(1).

CJA 2003,
SS.59, 60

Before deciding whether or not the appeal should be expedited, he judge must allow every accused directly affected by the ruling an opportunity to make representations.

The court officer will provide a copy of the reasons given by the judge, for his decision to the prosecutor, the accused and all interested parties.

The judge may reverse his decision that the appeal should be expedited at any time before notice of appeal or application for leave to appeal is served on the Crown Court under r.67.3(1) providing reasons for that reversal in writing to the prosecutor, the accused and all interested parties. A judge of the CACD may revoke the judge's decision to expedite an appeal.

Where the judge decides:

(1) to expedite the appeal, he may adjourn the trial;
(2) not to expedite the trial, he may either adjourn the trial or discharge the jury, if one has been sworn.

Appeal to CACD

8–056   Where leave to appeal is refused by the trial judge, application may be made to CACD, where it may be granted by the single judge or by the court. The prosecutor must serve an appeal notice in Form NG (Pros) on the Crown Court officer, the Registrar and every accused directly affected by the ruling against which he wants to appeal, not later than:

R.67.3

(1) the next business day (see 8–040 above) after telling the judge of the decision to appeal, if the judge expedites the appeal; or

    (2) five business days after telling the judge of that decision, if the judge does not expedite the appeal.

The must include those matters set out in r.67.4(2), and in particular, include or attach any application (with reasons) for:

    (a) permission to appeal, if the court's permission is needed;

    (b) extension of time within which to serve the notice; or

    (c) expedition of the appeal, or revocation of the judge's direction expediting the appeal,

and attaching any form of respondent's notice for an accused served with the appeal notice, who wants to complete one (see 8–057 below).

Respondent's notice

8–057 An accused on whom an appellant prosecutor serves an appeal notice may serve a respondent's notice in Form RN (Pros), and must do so if: R.67.7

    (1) he wants to make representations to the court; or

    (2) the court so directs.

He must serve his notice on the prosecutor, the Crown Court officer, the Registrar and any other accused on whom the prosecutor served the appeal notice, and he must serve the notice:

    (a) not later than the next business day (see 8–040 above) after:

        (i) the prosecutor serves the appeal notice, or

        (ii) a direction to do so, if the Crown Court judge expedites the appeal; or

    (b) not more than five business days after:

        (i) the prosecutor serves the appeal notice, or

        (ii) a direction to do so, if the Crown Court judge does not expedite the appeal.

The notice must state the matters set out in r.67.7(5). Any application for the following, for instance an extension of time within which to serve the notice, or a direction to attend in person any hearing that the respondent could attend by live link, if the respondent is in custody, with reasons, must be attached.

    Defence representation is ordinarily covered by the representation order if one is in force.

Public interest rulings

8–058 Where the prosecutor wants to appeal against a public interest ruling he must not serve on any accused directly affected by the ruling: R.67.8

    (1) any written application to the Crown Court judge for permission to appeal; or

    (2) an appeal notice if he thinks that to do so in effect would reveal something that he thinks ought not be disclosed, nor may he include in an appeal notice:

        (a) the material that was the subject of the ruling; or

        (b) any indication of what sort of material it is if he thinks that to do so would reveal something that he thinks ought not be disclosed.

In such cases the prosecutor must serve on the Registrar with the appeal notice an Annex marked to show that its contents are only for CACD and the Registrar, containing whatever he has omitted from the appeal notice, with reasons, and if relevant, explaining why he has not served the appeal notice.

In such cases, rr.67.5(3) and 67.6(2) (as to representations by the accused) do not apply.

Contacting CACD

8–059 Expedition does not impose time limits on the Registrar or CACD. However, if leave has not been granted by the trial judge, the application may be referred to the full court by the Registrar to enable the application and the appeal to be heard together to ensure that the matter is dealt with quickly.

Guide C6

The Registrar endeavours to list prosecution appeals where a jury has not been discharged as quickly as possible. He is unlikely to be able to list an appeal in less than a week from the ruling because it is necessary for the prosecution to obtain transcripts, papers to be copied and the judges to read their papers. If it is anticipated that there is to be an appeal against a ruling where the jury has not been discharged, a telephone call should be made to the Registrar or CAO General Office (020 7947 6011) notifying the office even before the appeal notice is sent, so that the List Office may be put on notice.

Guide C7

Abandoning an appeal

8–060 An appeal under these provisions may be abandoned in the same way as an appeal against conviction (see 8–037 above), as may a ground of appeal or of opposition, by service on the Registrar of Form A (Pros).

Rr.65.13, 14

Determination of appeal

8–061 On an appeal under s.58, CACD may confirm, reverse or vary any ruling to which the appeal relates, and where it does so must make it clear how the case is to proceed. Thus where the appeal relates to:

CJA 2003, ss. 56(1), 62(1)–(5)

(1) a single ruling, and CACD:
   (a) confirms the ruling, it must, in respect of the offence (or each offence which is the subject of the appeal), order that the accused in relation to that offence be acquitted of that offence;
   (b) reverses or varies the ruling, it must, in respect of the offence (or each offence which is the subject of the appeal) order that:
      (i)   proceedings for that offence be resumed in the Crown Court;
      (ii) a fresh trial take place in the Crown Court; or
      (iii) the accused in relation to the offence be acquitted of the offence, but it may not make an order under (b)(i) or (ii) above unless it considers it necessary in the interests of justice;

(2) a ruling that there is no case to answer and one or more other rulings, and CACD:

    (a) confirms the ruling that there is no case to answer, it must, in respect of the offence (or each offence which is the subject of the appeal), order that the accused in relation to that offence be acquitted of that offence;

    (b) reverses or varies the ruling that there is no case to answer, it must, in respect of the offence (or each offence which is the subject of the appeal), make any of the orders under (1) (b) above, and subject to the same proviso.

Effect on time limits

8–062 Any period during which proceedings for an offence are adjourned pending the determination of an appeal under Pt 9, is disregarded so far as the offence is concerned, for the purposes of the overall time limit or the custody time limit (under POA 1985, s.22) which applies to the stage which the proceedings have reached when they are adjourned. *CJA 2003, s.70*

Costs

8–063 Where CACD reverses or varies a ruling on an appeal under the provisions, it may make such order as to the costs to be paid by the accused, to such person as may be named in the order as it considers just and reasonable. *POA 1985, s. 18(2A)*

Reporting restrictions

8–064 CJA 2003, ss.71 and 72 provide for restrictions on reporting anything of the proceedings associated with the appeal until after the conclusion of the trial, and create offences in respect of infringements of those proceedings.

Retrials

8–065 Special rules under CJA 2003, s.84, govern the retrial of an accused person on an indictment preferred by CACD (see RETRIALS).

B. References to the Court of Appeal by the Attorney-General

1. On a point of law

8–066 Where a person tried on indictment has been acquit-ted (whether in respect of the whole or part of the indictment) the Attorney-General may, if he desires the opinion of CACD on a point of law which has arisen in the case, refer that point to the court for consideration and their opinion. In such a case, the court may hear argument: *CJA 1972, s.36*

    (1) by, or by an advocate for, the Attorney-General;

    (2) if the acquitted person desires to present argument, by an advocate on his behalf or, with leave, by the acquitted person himself.

If the court thinks fit, it may refer the matter to the Supreme Court.

The acquittal at the trial is not affected by the proceedings and steps are taken to protect the anonymity of the acquitted person.

2. Lenient sentences

General

8–067 Where it appears to the Attorney-General that in the case of an offence:

(1) of a description specified by the Home Secretary; or
(2) in which sentence is passed on a person for an offence triable only on indictment; or
(3) of a description presently specified in SI 2006/1116 that:
  (a) the sentencing judge in a proceeding in the Crown Court has been unduly lenient; or
  (b) the trial judge has:
    (i) erred in law as to his powers of sentencing; or
    (ii) failed to impose a sentence required to be passed under FA 1968, s.51A(2), PCC(S)A 2000,ss.l09 (where still appropriate), ss.110(2) or 111(2), any of CJA 2003, ss.225(2) and 226(2) (dangerous offender) or VCRA 2006, s.29(4) or (6),

the case may be referred to CACD. The leave of that court is required. Note that:

(a) "sentence" has the same meaning as in CAA 1969 save that it does not include an interim hospital order;
(b) "offence triable only on indictment" means an offence punishable only on conviction on indictment;
(c) any two or more sentences are to be treated as passed in the same proceedings if they would be treated as such for the purposes of CAA 1968, s.10.

A reference lies in respect of the specification of the minimum term in relation to a life sentence (*R. v Sullivan* The Times, July 14 2004).

As to certain transitional cases under CJA 2003, see SI 2007/1762.

Conduct of prosecutor

8–068 Where the prosecutor has been party to a bargain with the defence, or has acquiesced in a bargain between the court and the defence (see GOODYEAR INDICATION), it may be an abuse of the process to refer a resulting sentence to CACD, albeit that it was too lenient (see, e.g. *Att-Gen.'s References (Nos 80 and 81 of 1999) (R. v Thompson)* [2000] 2 Cr. App. R.(S.) 138, CA; *Att-Gen's Reference (No. 44 of 2000) (R. v Peverret)* [2001] 1 Cr. App. R. 27, CA; *Att Gen's References (Nos 86 and 87 of 1999) (R. v Webb and Simpson)* [2001] 1 Cr. App. R. 141).

CJA 1988, ss. 35(3)(9), 36(1); CJIA 2008, s.148, Sch.26, Pt 22, para.23

CJA 1988, s.35(9)

CJA 1988, s.36(3)

3. Procedure

The application

8–069 Where the Attorney-General refers either a point of law under CJA 1972, s.36, or a sentencing case under CJA 1988, s.36, although r.70(3) implies that there is a specific form to commence such proceedings, in practice he will:

Guide D6, 7

(1) send to the Registrar a standard letter with supporting documents, stating the matters set out in r.70.3(1) and including, in a sentencing case, an application for leave;
(2) in a reference on a point of law, give the Registrar details of the accused affected, the date and place of the relevant Crown Court decision and the relevant verdict and sentence;
(3) send the letter referred to in (1), together with the application for leave to refer a sentencing case, not later than 28 days after the last of the sentences in that case (there is no limit of time in cases referring a point of law).

Where CACD gives the Attorney-General permission to refer a sentencing case, it may treat the application for leave as the notice of reference.

R.70.3(5)

Registrar's notice to accused/offender

8–070 The Registrar will serve on the accused/offender the notice of reference and any application for leave to refer a sentencing case.

R.70.4(1)

Where the Attorney-General refers a point of law, the Registrar will give the accused/offender notice that the outcome of the reference will not make any difference to the outcome of the trial; and he is entitled to serve a respondent's notice. No particular form is prescribed. Where the Attorney-General applies for leave to refer a sentencing case, the Registrar will give the accused/ offender notice that the outcome of the reference may make a difference to that sentencing, and in particular may result in a more severe sentence, and telling him that he may serve a respondent's notice.

Respondent's notice

8–071 An accused/offender on whom the Registrar serves a reference or an application for leave to refer a sentencing case may serve a respondent's notice, and must do so if either he wants to make representations to CACD, or if CACD so directs, he must serve any respondent's notice on the Attorney-General and on the Registrar. No particular form is prescribed.

R.70.5(1)

The respondent's notice must be served, where the Attorney-General:

(1) refers a point of law, not more than 28 days after either the Registrar serves the reference, or any direction to do so;
(2) applies for leave to refer a sentencing case, not more than 14 days after the Registrar serves the application, or a direction to do so.

Where the Attorney-General:

(a) refers a point of law, the respondent's notice must comply with r.70.5(4), including inter alia any application (with reasons) for an extension of time within which to serve his notice, leave to attend a hearing that he does not have a right to attend, or a direction to attend in person a hearing that the respondent could attend by live link, if he in custody;

(b) applies for leave to refer a sentencing case, the respondent's notice must comply with r.70.5(5), including such applications as are mentioned in (a).

Representation orders are not issued to respond to an Attorney General's reference but a defendant who appears by counsel is entitled to his reasonable costs from central funds. The cost of instructing leading counsel in addition to or instead of junior counsel is generally not considered reasonable unless there is a compelling reason. It is advisable to consult with the Registrar before leading counsel is instructed. `Guide D7`

Variation/withdrawal of notice or application

8–072 Where the Attorney-General wants to vary or with draw a notice of reference or an application for leave to refer a sentencing case, he may vary or withdraw the notice or application without the leave of CACD by serving notice on the Registrar and the accused/offender before any hearing of the reference or application; but, at any such hearing, he may only vary or withdraw that notice or application with the court's leave. `R.70.6(1)`

Right to attend hearing

8–073 A respondent who is in custody has a right to attend a hearing in public unless it is a hearing preliminary or incidental to a reference, including the hearing of an application for permission to refer a sentencing case. The court or the Registrar may direct that such a respondent is to attend a hearing by live link. `R.70.7(1)`

Anonymity of defendant on reference of point of law

8–074 Where the Attorney-General refers a point of law, CACD will not allow anyone to identify the accused/offender during the proceedings unless the latter gives permission. `R.70.8`

C. Appeal by way of case stated

8–075 Any order, judgment or other decision of the Crown Court, *other than a judgment or other decision relating to trial on indictment,* or certain matters under the Betting and Gaming legislation, may be questioned by any party to the proceedings, on the ground that:

(1) it is wrong in law; or
(2) in excess of jurisdiction,

by applying to the Crown Court to state a case for the opinion of the High Court.

As a matter of practice this means that this procedure will apply essentially to the Crown Court's appellate jurisdiction.

"Decision" means "final decision" and the High Court will not entertain such an appeal unless the Crown Court has reached a final determination *(Loade v DPP* (1990) 90 Cr. App. R. 162).

Appeals by way of case stated are not usually an appropriate procedure for appealing against sentence: *Allen v W Yorks Probation Service* [2001] EWHC (Admin) 2.

Making the application

8–076   An application under SCA 1981, s.28 to the Crown Court to state a case for the opinion of the High Court must be made in writing to the Crown Court officer within 21 days after the date of the decision in respect of which the application is made, stating the ground on which the decision is questioned, a copy being sent to any other party to the proceedings.   Rr.64.6(1)-(3)

On receipt of the application the Crown Court officer will forthwith send it to the judge who presided at the proceedings in which the decision was made and the judge:

(1) will inform the Crown Court officer whether or not he has decided to state a case, and that officer will give notice in writing to the applicant of the judge's decision;
(2) if he considers the application to be frivolous may refuse to state a case and, if the applicant so requires, will cause a certificate stating the reasons for refusal to be given to him.

If he decides to state a case, the procedure under rr.64.6(8)-(12) will be followed.

Procedure

8–077   If the judge decides to state a case:

(1) the applicant must, within 21 days of receiving notice of that decision, draft the case and send a copy of it both to the Crown Court officer and to the other parties to the proceedings;   Rr.64.6(8)-(10),
(2) each party to the proceedings in the Crown Court must then, within 21 days of receiving a copy of the draft case:
   (a) give notice in writing to the applicant and to the Crown Court officer that he does not intend to take part in the proceedings in the High Court; or
   (b) indicate in writing on a copy of the draft case that he agrees with it, and send a copy to a court officer; or
   (c) draw up an alternative case and send it, together with the copy of the applicant's case, to the Crown Court officer;
(3) the judge will then consider the applicant's draft case and any alternative draft case sent to the Crown Court officer under (2) (c) above and will state and sign the case within 14 days after either:
   (a) receipt of all the documents required to be sent to the court; or
   (b) the expiration of the 21 days referred to in (1) above, whichever is the sooner.

As to the position where the judge has given a reasoned judgment, see *R. v Blackfriars CC Ex p. Sun World Ltd* [2000] Crim. L.R. 593.

Extension of time

8–078 Any of the time limits referred to in the Rules may be extended, either before or after it expires, by the Crown Court.   R.64.6(14)

The use of the term "Crown Court" as distinct from "judge" in r.26(11), (14) of the previous Rules, dealing with recognisances and extension of time, was held not to require the participation of the magistrates in the decision, but to reflect the possibility that a judge, other than the judge who heard the original application, might consider the application for an extension *(DPP v Coleman* [1998] 2 Cr. App. R. 7).

If the prosecutor applies for an extension of time, the acquitted appellant ought to have an opportunity to make representations.

Rule 64.6(15) makes certain adjustments in r.64.6 where a case is stated in accordance with a mandatory order of the High Court.

Form of case: ancillary orders

8–079 A case stated by the Crown Court must state: R.64.6(13)

(1) the facts found by the Crown Court;
(2) the submissions of the parties, including any authorities relied on by them during the course of those submissions;
(3) the decision of the Crown Court in respect of which the application is made; and
(4) the question on which the opinion of the High Court is sought.

It should be bourne in mind that on an appeal by way of case stated the court is concerned with the facts as stated "within the four corners of the case". There is no right to refer to other evidence, not stated in the case, without the agreement of the parties or on an application under SCA 1981, s.28A(2) to amend the case *(M v DPP* [2009] EWHC 752 (Admin.); [2009] 2 Cr. App. R. 12).

The Crown Court, in dealing with such an appeal:

(a) may order the applicant, before the case is stated and delivered to him, to enter into a recognisance before the Crown Court officer, with or without sureties, and in such sums as the court thinks proper having regard to his means, conditioned to prosecute the appeal without delay;
(b) may grant the applicant bail (as may the High Court); may not (but the High Court may) suspend an RT disqualification pending appeal;
(c) may not grant public funding. The representation order in force in the Crown Court is authority for counsel and solicitor assigned to advise on reasonable grounds of appeal and to make the application for a case to be stated; thereafter an applicant will need to apply to the Commission under AJA 1999, s.12.

Withdrawal of appeal

8–080   An appellant is entitled to withdraw an appeal by case stated without leave of the court *(Collett v Bromsgrove DC* (1996) 160 J.P. 593).

D.   Judicial review

8–081   In relation to the jurisdiction of the Crown Court *other than its jurisdiction in relation to trial on indictment,* the High Court has all such jurisdiction to make: SCA 1981, s.29

(1) a mandatory order (CPR 1998, r.54.1), to compel the Crown Court to exercise its proper jurisdiction;
(2) a prohibiting order, to restrain it from proceeding improperly; and
(3) a quashing order, to quash any order which has been made improperly.

In *R. (CPS) v Guildford CC* [2007] EWHC 1798 (Admin), [2007] 1 W.L.R. 2886, a Divisional Court refused to quash the sentence imposed at the Crown Court holding that such a matter plainly fell within SCA 1981, s.29(3) as a matter "relating to trial on indictment". The Lord Chief Justice declined to accept that *R. v Maidstone CC Exp. Harrow LBC* [2000] 1 Cr. App. R. 117; *R. (Kenneally) v Snaresbrook CC* [2001] EWHC Admin 968, [2002] 2 W.L.R 1430 created a general legitimate principle that where an order is jurisdictionally flawed, the High Court may intervene despite the fact that the order relates to a trial on indictment.

A judge's decision refusing to recuse himself from proceedings is amenable to judicial review *(R. (on the application of B) v X CC* [2010] Crim. L.R. 145).

Nature of judicial review

8–082   While judicial review provides a speedy and effective remedy in a proper case, it is a discretionary remedy (see *R. v Peterborough MC Ex p. Dowler* [1996] 2 Cr. App. R. 561; *R. v Hereford MC Ex p. Rowlands* [1997] 2 Cr. App. R. 340). Its ambit is restricted; in particular:

(1) the issue of these orders is reserved for simple and straightforward cases; the High Court will not attempt to resolve direct conflicts of evidence on material facts;
(2) the jurisdiction is confined essentially to matters of jurisdiction, thus the proper exercise of a discretion to admit or reject evidence in committal proceedings is not subject to control;
(3) the High Court will not permit the machinery of judicial review to be used as a means of appeal.

It is an abuse of process to attack a finding of fact which has been the basis of a judgment in the Crown Court by means of judicial review *(R. v Knightsbridge CC Ex p. Quinlan, The Times,* December 13, 1988).

Application for permission

8–083   Procedure for judicial review is under CPR 1998, r.54. The permission of the High Court must be obtained before a claim for judicial review is made.

A claim is made by filing a claim form:

(1) promptly; and
(2) in any event not later than three months after the grounds to make the claim first arose (unless any other enactment specifies a shorter time limit), and this time limit may not be extended by agreement between the parties.

Where the decision of the Crown Court to dismiss an appeal is quashed, it is necessary for the case to be relisted before the Crown Court where it will be for a differently constituted court to determine the matter *de novo (R. v Leeds CC Ex p. Barlow* [1989] R.T.R. 246).

Applications for judicial review are not usually an appropriate procedure for appealing against sentence: *Allen v W Yorks Probation Service* [2001] EWHC (Admin) 2, but see below, 8–095.

Bail; RT disqualification; public funding

8–084   In relation to such proceedings, the Crown Court:

(1) may grant bail to a person who has applied for *certiorari,* or who has applied for leave (so may the High Court);
(2) may not remove an RT disqualification pending the decision of the High Court (but the High Court may);
(3) does not deal with public funding; application must be made to the Legal Services Commission under AJA 1999, s.12.

Jurisdiction; "relating to trial on indictment"

8–085   The following matters are **not** matters relating to trial on indictment, and are, therefore, susceptible to judicial review;

(1) an order as to defence public funding made under AJA 1999, s.17, (SCA 1981, s.29(6));
(2) an order for costs made on entering a finding of not guilty under CJA 1967, s.17 *(R. v Wood Green CC Ex p. DPP* [1993] 2 All E.R. 656; *R. v Leicester CC Ex p. CC & E,* [2001] EWHC (Admin) 33);
(3) while an application to a judge under CJA 1987, s.6(l) for dismissal of transferred charges is not a matter relating to trial on indictment, being analogous to proceedings for the transfer of a case from the magistrates' court for trial in the Crown Court, the jurisdiction to review such an order is likely to be exercised only in exceptional circumstances *(R. v CCC Ex p. Director of SFO* (1993) 96 Cr. App. R. 248);

The following matters **are within the exclusive jurisdiction of the Crown Court:**

(a) the decision to revoke a previous order discharging a representation order *(R. v Isleworth CC Ex p. Willington* [1993] 2 All E.R. 390);

85

(b) an order refusing to amend a representation order so as to provide for leading counsel (*R. v Liverpool CC, The Times,* February 13, 2001);

(c) an order staying a trial on the ground of abuse of process *(R v Manchester CC ex p. DPP* (1993) 97 Cr. App. R. 203);

(d) an order deciding which of two or more indictments should be tried first (*R. v Southwark CC Ex p. Ward* [1996] Crim.L.R.123);

(e) arraignment and the conduct of a plea and directions hearing *(R. v Leeds CC Ex p. Hussain* [1995] 3 All E.R. 527);

(f) an order as to disclosure relates to trial on indictment *(R. v Chester CC Ex p. Cheshire CC* [1996] Crim. L.R. 336);

(g) an order detaining a witness for the purpose of his giving evidence *(R. (H) v Wood Green CC* [2007] Crim. L.R. 727).

An order under CYPA 1933, s.39 (protecting the anonymity of a child or young person) may, or may not be, a matter relating to trial on indictment, depending on the circumstances (see *R. v Manchester CC Exp. H & D* [2000] 1 Cr. App. R. 262);

No right to judicial review arises in (a) – (g) above unless, perhaps, the judge acts in a way which was clearly contrary to the statutory provisions *(R. v Maidstone CC Ex p. Harrow LBC* [2000] 1 Cr. App. R. 117, *R. (Kenneally) v Snaresbrook CC* [2001] EWHC Admin 969; [2002] 2 W.L.R 1430, *cf. R. v Leicester CC Ex p. Commissioners of Customs & Excise,* [2001] EWHC (Admin) 33.

As to orders in relation to costs, for example, see *In re Sampson* (1987) 84 Cr. App. R. 376.

The position is not affected by ECHR, see *R. v Canterbury CC Ex p. Regentford Ltd, The Times,* February 6, 2001 and also *R. v Leicester CC,* above.

Suspension of RT disqualification

8–086 Where a person ordered to be disqualified applies to the High Court for a quashing order to remove proceedings in the Crown Court, being proceedings in, or in consequence of which, he was convicted or his sentence was passed, or applies for leave to make such an application, the High Court may, if it thinks fit, suspend the disqualification on such terms as it thinks fit.

RTOA 1988, s.40(1)(5)(7)

E.   Tainted acquittals

General

8–087 Under CPIA 1996, s.54 provision is made for a form of judicial review in a case where one person has been acquitted of an offence, and another person has been convicted of perverting the course of justice, intimidating witnesses, jurors, etc., under CJPOA 1994, s.51(l) or aiding, abetting, counselling, procuring, suborning or inciting the committing of an offence under s.l of the Perjury Act 1911, involving interference or intimidation of a juror or a witness (or potential witness) in any proceedings which led to the acquittal.

Need for certificate

8–088   Where it appears to the court before which the person was convicted that there was a real possibility that, but for the interference or intimidation, the acquitted person would not have been acquitted, and that there is no doubt, because of lapse of time or any other reason, that it would not be contrary to the interests of justice to take proceedings against the acquitted person for the offence of which he was acquitted, the court must certify that fact.

CPIA 1996, s.54(1)(2)(5)

Certification

8–089   The certification referred to in s.54(2) must be made in the form set out in the PD 2004, Annex D at any time following conviction but no later than:

R.40.1, 2

(1) immediately after the court sentences, or otherwise deals with, that person in respect of the offence;
(2) where the court, being a magistrates' court, commits that person to the Crown Court, or remits him to another magistrates' court, to be dealt with in respect of the offence, immediately after he is so committed or remitted, as the case may be; or
(3) where that person is a child or young person and a judge of the Crown Court, remits him to a youth court to be dealt with in respect of the offence, immediately after he is so remitted.

Subsequent procedure

8–090   The court officer will then, as soon as practicable after the drawing up of the form, serve (as to which see CPR 2011, Pt 4) a copy on:

(1) the acquitted person referred to in the certification;
(2) the prosecutor in the proceedings which led to the acquittal; and,
(3) where the acquittal has taken place before a court other than, or at a different place to, the court where the certification has been made, on the clerk of the magistrates' court before which the acquittal has taken place; or the Crown Court officer at the place where the acquittal has taken place.

The court officer of the court before which an acquittal has taken place will after receipt of a copy of a form recording a certification under s.54(2) relating to the acquittal, enter in the register or record a note:

(a) that the certification has been made;
(b) the date of the certification;
(c) the name of the court which has made the certification;
(d) the name of the person whose conviction occasioned the making of the certification; and
(e) a description of the offence of which that person has been convicted.

Where the certification has been made by the same court as the court before which the acquittal has occurred, sitting at the same place, the entry must be made as soon as practicable after the making of the certification.

R.40.5

Where a court makes such a certification, the court officer will, as soon as practicable after the drawing up of the form, display a copy at a prominent place within court premises to which place the public has access, for at least 28 days from the day on which the certification was made, or, as the case may be, the day on which the copy form was received at the court. If the acquittal has taken place before a court other than, or at a different place to, the court which has made the certification, the court officer at the court where the acquittal has taken place must do the same. R.40.6

Application to High Court

8–091 Where a court so certifies, it will be possible to make an application to the High Court for an order quashing the acquittal, and if such an order is made, it will be possible to take proceedings against the acquitted person for the offence of which he was acquitted. CPIA 1996, s.54(3)(4)

See also *Practice Statement (Administrative Court: annual statement)* [2002] 1 W.L.R. 810.

Conditions precedent to order

8–092 The High Court will not be empowered to make such an order unless four conditions are fulfilled. If it appears to the High Court, taking into account all the information before it but ignoring the possibility of new factors coming to light, that: CPIA 1996, ss.54(3), 55

(1) but for the interference or intimidation, the acquitted person would not have been acquitted;
(2) because of lapse of time or for any other reason it would not be contrary to the interest of justice to take proceedings against the acquitted person for the offence of which he was acquitted;
(3) the acquitted person has been given a reasonable opportunity to make written representations to the court; and
(4) the conviction for the administration of justice offence will stand,

the High Court will not make an order if, for instance, the time for giving notice of appeal has not expired or an appeal is pending.

Time limits

8–093 Where an order is made quashing an acquittal and it is proposed to take proceedings against the acquitted person, any time limits within which, by statute, a prosecution must be commenced will run from the making of the order. CPIA 1996, s.56

Entry in records; display of notice

8–094 The court officer at the court:

(1) where an acquittal has taken place will, on receipt from the Administrative Court Office of notice of an order made under CPIA 1996, s.54(3) quashing the acquittal, or of a decision not to make such an order, enter in the records a note of the fact that the acquittal has been quashed, or that a decision has been made not to make such an order, as the case may be;

(2) which has made a certification under s.54(2) will, on receipt from the Administrative Court Office of notice of an order made under s.54(3) quashing the acquittal referred to in the certification, or of a decision not to make such an order, enter in the records, in relation to the conviction which occasioned the certification, a note that the acquittal has been quashed by the said order, or that a decision has been made not to make such an order, as the case may be.

Where the court officer of a court which has made a certification under s.54(2), or before which an acquittal has occurred to which such a certification refers, receives from the Administrative Court Office notice of an order quashing the acquittal concerned, or notice of a decision not to make such an order, he will, as soon as practicable after receiving the notice, display a copy of it at a prominent place within court premises to which place the public has access. This copy must continue to be displayed at least until the expiry of 28 days from the day on which the notice was received at the court.

F. Powers of High Court to vary sentence

8–095 Where a person who has been sentenced for an offence by the Crown Court:

(1) after being convicted of an offence by a magistrates' court and committed for sentence; or
(2) on appeal against conviction or sentence,

applies to the High Court for a quashing order, then if the High Court determines that the Crown Court had no power to pass that sentence it may, instead of quashing the conviction, amend it by substituting any sentence which the magistrates' court in a case under (2) or the Crown Court in a case under (1) above, had power to impose.

The High Court will, in an exceptional case, quash a sentence imposed by the Crown Court:

(a) where it is plainly demonstrated that in the process of sentencing an error of law has been perpetrated *(R. v Liverpool CC Ex p. Baird* (1985) 7 Cr. App. R.(S.) 437);
(b) which is harsh and oppressive and so far outside the normal sentence imposed for the offence as necessarily to involve an error of law *(R. v St Albans CC Ex p. Cinnamond* [1980] 2 Cr. App. R.(S.) 235; *cf. R. v Croydon CC Ex p. Miller* (1987) 85 Cr. App. R. 152; *R. (Sogbesan) v ILCC* [2002] EWHC 1581 (Admin), [2003] 1 Cr. App. R.(S.) 79);
(c) which is irrational and truly astonishing *(R. v Acton CC Ex p. Bewley* (1988) 10 Cr. App. R.(S.) 105; *R. v Chelmsford CC Ex p. Birchall* (1989) 11 Cr. App. R.(S.) 510); and
(d) where the sentence imposed is "outside the broad area of the lower court's jurisdiction" *[sic]: (R. v Truro CC Ex p. Adair[1997]* C.O.D. 296, DC; *R. v Southwark CC Ex p. Smith* [2001] 2 Cr. App. R.(S.) 35).

Such sentence begins to run, unless the High Court directs otherwise, from the time when it would have started to run if passed in those proceedings, disregarding any time during which the offender was released on bail pending his application.

Where, on judicial review, the decision of the Crown Court to dismiss an appeal is quashed, it is necessary for the case to be relisted before the Crown Court, where it will be for a differently constituted court to determine the matter *de novo* (*R. v Leeds CC Ex p. Barlow* [1989] R.T.R. 246).

G. References by and to the Criminal Cases Review Commission

8–096 The Criminal Cases Review Commission, set up by CAA 1995, s.8 may refer to CACD the conviction or sentence (not being one fixed by law) of a person convicted on indictment, a verdict of not guilty by reason of insanity and a finding of disability, where a finding that he did the act or made the omission was returned (CAA 1995, s.9; DVA 2004, s.58(1), Sch.10, para.31). Its powers and functions are reviewed in *R. v Criminal Cases Review Commission Ex p. Pearson* [2000] 1 Cr. App. R. 141 and *R. (DRCP) v CCRC* [2006] EWHC 3064 (Admin); [2007] 1 Cr. App. R. 30. CAA 1995, s.14, as amended by CJA 2003, s.31, contains further provisions relating to such references.

Powers of CACD to order investigation

8–097 On an appeal against conviction, or an application for leave to appeal against conviction, CACD (not a single judge) may direct the Commission to investigate and report on any matter if it appears that:

(1) in the case of an appeal, the matter is relevant to the determination of the appeal, and ought, if possible, to be resolved before the appeal is determined;

(2) in the case of an application for leave to appeal, the matter is relevant to the determination of the application and ought, if possible, to be resolved before the application is determined;

(3) an investigation of the matter is likely to result in the CACD being able to resolve it; and

(4) the matter cannot be resolved by CACD without an investigation by the Commission.

In due course the parties will be informed of the results, and the report and any statements, opinions and reports will be made available to them.

H. Appeals to CACD under POCA 2002

Quick guide

(1) Prosecutor's appeal; regarding confiscation (8–098)
(2) Restraint orders (8–102)
(3) Appointment etc of receiver (8–104)
(4) Procedure (8–105)

(1) Prosecutor's appeal regarding confiscation

Appeal by prosecutor

8–098 The prosecutor may appeal to CACD where a judge of the Crown Court:

POCA 2002, ss.31, 32(1)(4)

(1) makes a confiscation order under POCA 2002, in respect of the order; or
(2) decides not to make a confiscation order, against that decision,

except in the case of an order or decision made by virtue of ss.19,20 (reconsideration), 27 or 28 (convicted and unconvicted absconders).

The 2002 Act does not create a retrospective right for the prosecutor to appeal in respect of a decision under 1988 Act (*R. v Moulden* [2008] EWCA Crim 2648; [2009] 1 Cr. App. R. 27.

The *Explanatory Notes* published by TSO state that only an appeal on a point of law lies under this section. The post-conviction procedures being mandatory there is no scope for an appeal on the merits; it is otherwise in revaluation cases.

An appeal requires the permission of CACD. Further appeal lies to the Supreme Court under s.33.

As to appeals to CACD in respect of orders made by the Crown Court in relation to external requests or orders, see POCA 2002 (External Requests and Orders) Order 2005 (SI 2005/3181), Pt 2, or, in regard to the former law, see CJ(IC)A 1990 (Enforcement of Overseas Forfeiture Orders) Order 2005 (SI 2005/3180).

Prosecutor's notice of appeal

8–099 Where the prosecutor seeks to apply to CACD for leave to appeal under POCA 2002, s.31, he must serve a notice of appeal in Form POCA 1 on the Crown Court officer and on the accused within 28 days of the making of the ruling. Where an extension of time is required, reasons must be given (POCA 2002 (Appeals under Pt 2) Order 2003, SI 2003/82). As to further procedure in CACD see arts 5–10.

Rr.72.1(1), 2 3

The notice of appeal served upon the accused must be accompanied by a Notice of Opposition in Form POCA 2 for him to complete:

(1) informing him that the result of the appeal could be that CACD would increase a confiscation order already imposed on him, make a confiscation order itself, or direct the Crown Court to hold a fresh hearing;
(2) informing him of his right under art.6 of the above Order to be present at the hearing, even though he is in custody; and
(3) inviting him to serve notice on the Registrar if he wishes to apply for leave to be present, or to present any argument on the hearing of the application, and whether he wishes to present it in person or by means of a legal representative.

The notice will also draw to his attention r.71.4 (supply of documentary and other exhibits) and advise the defendant to consult a solicitor as soon as possible.

The appellant must provide a Crown Court officer with a certificate of service stating that he has served the notice of appeal on the

91

defendant in accordance with the Rules, or explaining why he has been unable to effect service.

Respondent's notice

8–100   Where an accused is served with a notice of appeal under r.72.1, and wishes to oppose the application for leave to appeal, he must, not later than 14 days after the date on which he received the notice of appeal in Form POCA 1, serve on the Registrar and on the appellant notice in Form POCA 2:

R.72.2

(1) stating the date on which he received the notice of appeal;
(2) summarising his response to the arguments of the appellant; and
(3) specifying the authorities which he intends to cite.

The time for giving notice may be extended by the Registrar, a single judge or by CACD. If the Registrar refuses an extension of time, the defendant is entitled to have his application determined by a single judge; if the single judge refuses the extension the defendant is entitled to have his application determined by the court.

An undischarged Crown Court representation order will cover advice and assistance on the merits of opposing the appeal and drafting the respondent's notice, otherwise an application for a representation order can be made to the Registrar (AJA 1999, ss.12(2)(b), 26). In any event, where an application for a representation order is made on POCA 2, the Registrar will consider a representation order for the hearing.

Guide D1

Amendment and abandonment of appeal

8–101   The appellant may amend a notice of appeal served under r.72.1 or abandon an appeal under POCA 2002, s.31:

R.73.3

(1) without the leave of CACD at any time before the hearing of the appeal has begun; and
(2) with the permission of CACD after the hearing of the appeal has begun,

by serving notice in writing on the Registrar, and where the appellant abandons an appeal under (1) above he must send a copy of the notice to the defendant, a court officer of the court of trial and the magistrates' court responsible for enforcing any confiscation order which the Crown Court has made.

Where the appellant serves a notice amending a notice of appeal he must send a copy of it to the defendant.

Where an appeal is abandoned the application for leave to appeal or appeal will be treated, for the purposes of POCA 2002, s.85 (conclusion of proceedings), as having been refused or dismissed by CACD.

(2)   Appeal in relation to restraint orders

General

8–102   There is no appeal against the making of a restraint order. A person dissatisfied with the making of an order must apply to the Crown Court for its variation or discharge.

POCA 2002, ss.43, 44; Guide D2

Appeal does, however, lie to CACD by:

(1) the prosecutor or an accredited financial investigator from a refusal by the Crown Court to make an order, against that decision;
(2) the person who applied for an order or any person affected by who applies to the Crown Court to vary or discharge it, against the judge's decision,

and CACD may either confirm the order or make such order as it believes appropriate.

Leave is required, and leave will be given only where CACD considers that the appeal would have a real prospect of success or there is some other compelling reason why the appeal should be heard. An order giving leave may limit the issues to be heard and may be made subject to conditions.

As to procedure, see 8–105, below. As to appeals to CACD in respect of orders made by the Crown Court in relation to external requests or orders, see POCA 2002 (External Requests and Orders) Order 2005 (SI 20057 3181), Pt 2, or, in regard to the former law, see CJ(IC)A 1990 (Enforcement of Overseas Forfeiture Orders) Order 2005 (SI 2005/3180).

Effect of appeal

8–103 Unless CACD or the Crown Court orders otherwise, an appeal under s.43 will not operate as a stay of any order or decision of the Crown Court.

Futher appeal lies to the Supreme Court under POCA 2002, s.44.

(3) Appeals in relation to the appointment etc of receivers

8–104 Appeal lies to CACD where:

(1) on an application for an order under any of ss.48 to 51 or s.53 the Crown Court decides not to appoint a receiver, by the person who applied for the order, against the decision;

POCA 2002, s.65; Guide D3

(2) the Crown Court appoints a receiver under any of ss.48 to 51 or s.53, by the person who applied for the order or any person affected by it, against the court's decision;
(3) on an application for an order under s.62 the Crown Court decides not to make a direction, one, by the person, who applied for the order, against that decision;
(4) the Crown Court makes an order under s.62, giving directions to a receiver, by the person who applied for the order, any person affected it and the receiver; in respect of the court's decision;
(5) against a decision of the Crown Court on an application under s.63, to vary or discharge a receivership order, by the person who applied for the order in respect of which the application was made, any person affected by the court's decision or the receiver.

The procedure for initiating an appeal is the same as that in the case of an appeal under s.43, as to which see 8–105 above.

APPEALS FROM THE CROWN COURT

On such an appeal CACD may confirm the decision, or make such order as it believes is appropriate. Further appeal lies to the Supreme Court.

As to appeals to CACD in respect of orders made by the Crown Court in relation to external requests or orders, see POCA 2002 (External Requests and Orders) Order 2005 (SI 2005/3181), Pt 2, or, in regard to the former law, see CJ(IC)A 1990 (Enforcement of Overseas Forfeiture Orders) Order 2005 (SI 2005/3180).

(4) Procedure

Notice of appeal

8–105   Where a person wishes to apply to the CACD for leave to appeal under any of the provisions of POCA 2002, s.43 or s.65 as set out above, he must serve notice of application in Form POCA 3 on the Crown Court officer within 14 days of the decision being appealed being given. R.73.2; Guide D3

Unless the Registrar, a single judge or CACD directs other-wise, the applicant must serve the notice, accompanied by a respondent's notice in Form POCA 4 for the respondent to complete, within seven days after the form is lodged at the Crown Court, on:

(1) each respondent;
(2) any person who holds realisable property to which the appeal relates; and
(3) any other person affected by the appeal.

The documents which are to be served with POCA 3 are set out in R.73.2(3).Where it is not possible to serve all of these documents the appellant must indicate which documents have not yet been served and the reasons why they are not currently available.

The appellant must provide a Crown Court officer with a certificate of service stating that he has served the notice of appeal on each respondent in accordance with para.(2) and including full details of each respondent or explaining why he has been unable to effect service.

Respondent's notice

8–106   A respondent who wishes to ask the CACD to uphold the decision of the Crown Court for reasons different from or additional to those given by the Crown Court, must serve a respondent's notice on the Registrar, in Form POCA 4, and where he seeks leave to appeal to CACD he must request it in the notice. R.73.3

The notice must be served on the Registrar not later than 14 days after:

(1) the date the respondent is served with notification that CACD has given the appellant leave to appeal; or
(2) the date the respondent is served with notification that the application for leave to appeal and the appeal itself are to be heard together.

Unless the Registrar, a single judge or CACD directs otherwise, the respondent serving a respondent's notice must serve the notice on the appellant and any other respondent:

(a) as soon as practicable; and
(b) in any event not later than seven days, after it is served on
the Registrar.

Representation

8–107   Where:

Guide D3

(1) a defendant has been charged with a criminal offence connected to a receivership order then the receivership proceedings are regarded as incidental to the criminal proceedings and are
treated as criminal proceedings for funding purposes (Reg.3(3)
(c) Criminal Defence Service (General)(No.2) Regulations
2001) and the Registrar may grant a representation order if a
defendant appeals a decision relating to a receivership order;
(2) a management receivership order or an application for such an
order is made in the Crown Court before a criminal offence has
been charged and a person affected by the order (including the
proposed defendant) wishes to appeal a decision then civil legal
aid may be available as these proceedings fall within AJA 1999,
Sch.2, para.3, and the Legal Services Commission should be contacted for funding within the Community Legal Service scheme.

Public funding

8–108   An application for a restraint order may be made as soon as a
criminal investigation has begun. The proposed defendant may not have
been charged: POCA 2002, s.40. This affects the type of public funding
available to him. Thus if:

(1) a defendant has been charged with a criminal offence connected
to the restraint order, the restraint proceedings are regarded as
incidental to the criminal proceedings and are treated as criminal
proceedings for funding purposes (GR 2001, reg.3(3)(c)) and the
Registrar may grant a representation order if a defendant appeals a
decision on an application to vary or discharge the restraint order;
(2) the prosecution apply for a restraint order in the Crown Court
before the subject of the restraint order has been charged with a
criminal offence and the subject of that order wishes to appeal
a decision on an application to vary or discharge the restraint
order, civil legal aid may be available as these proceedings fall
within AJA 1999, Sch.2, para.3.

Similarly, a person affected by the order who wishes to appeal a decision on an application to vary or discharge the restraint order should
apply to the Legal Services Commission for funding within the
Community Legal Service scheme).

Amendment and abandonment of appeal

8–109   The appellant may amend his notice of appeal or abandon his
appeal without the leave of CACD at any time *before* CACD has begun
hearing the appeal; and *with* its leave after the hearing of the appeal has
begun, by serving notice in writing on the Registrar. He must give
notice to each respondent.

R.73.4

Notes

9. APPELLATE JURISDICTION

Quick guide

1. Introduction

9–001 The Crown Court exercises all appellate and other jurisdiction conferred on it by order under the provisions of the SCA 1981, or exercisable by it immediately before the commencement of that Act (SCA 1981, s.45(1)). CA 1971, s.8, Sch.1 vested in the Crown Court all jurisdiction formerly conferred on courts of quarter session, or any committee of the same. Rights of appeal to the Crown Court are governed by MCA 1980, ss.108–110 and the Criminal Procedure Rules 2011, r.63. The 2008 statistics, the most recently available, show a receipt of 6,447 appeals against finding, and 6,838 against sentence.

MCA 1980, s.108(1)

2. Rights of appeal

General

9–002 A general right of appeal to the Crown Court is given to a person convicted in a magistrates' court where he pleaded:

MCA 1980, s.108(3)

(1) guilty, against his sentence;
(2) not guilty, against his conviction and sentence.

Subject to the rare exceptional case (see 9–024, below), a plea of guilty in the magistrates' court is a bar to an appeal against conviction to the Crown Court (*R. v Birmingham CC Ex p. Sharma* [1988] Crim. L.R. 741).

"Sentence" includes any "order made on conviction" by a magistrates' court except an order:

(a) for the payment of costs (*R. v Tottenham JJ. Ex p. Joshi* (1982) 75 Cr. App. R. 72);
(b) under the Protection of Animals Act 1911, s.2 (which enables a court to order the destruction of an animal); or
(c) made in pursuance of an enactment under which the court has no discretion as to the making of the order or its terms;

and also includes a declaration of relevance under FSA 1989.

Note that (c) above does not prevent an appeal against a surcharge imposed under CJA 2003, s.161A (MCA 1980, s.108(3)(d); DVA 2004, s.58(1), Sch.10, para.10).

An invalid sentence does not nullify the conviction on which it is based, which remains a "conviction" entitling the Crown Court to entertain an appeal (*R. v Birmingham JJ. Ex p. Wyatt* (1975) 61 Cr. App. R. 306).

"Orders made on conviction"

9–003 An "order made on conviction" is an order made as a consequence of the conviction for the particular offence of which the appellant was convicted. In consequence the following do not qualify:

(1) an order which does not depend upon the fact of conviction (*R. v Hayden* (1975) 60 Cr. App. R. 304—a legal aid contribution order);

(2) an order sending a case to the Crown Court for trial (see (*R. v London Sessions Appeals Committee Ex p. Beaumont* [1951] 1 K.B. 557)); or

(3) an order committing an accused to the Crown Court for sentence under PCC(S)A 2000, s.3.

By statute the following may be appealed:

(a) a recommendation for deportation (which is treated as a "sentence" (IA 1971, s.6(5)(a));

(b) a guardianship or hospital order (MHA 1983, s.70);

(c) an RT disqualification under RTOA 1988, s.34 or s.35.

Other specific cases

9–004 Appeal also lies to the Crown Court from a magistrates' court: [MCA 1980, s.108(2) CJA 2003, s.179, Sch.8, para.21(4)]

(1) by an offender sentenced for an offence in respect of which a conditional discharge was previously made;

(2) by an offender sentenced for breach of the requirements of a community order;

(3) by a juvenile sentenced in respect of the breach of an attendance centre order, or the rules of the centre; [PCC(S)A 2000, s.61, Sch.5, paras 2(6), 4(4)]

(4) by a person ordered, under JPA 1968 or otherwise to enter into a recognisance, with or without sureties, to keep the peace; [ABOOA 1956, s.1]

(5) by a person, or the parent or guardian of a juvenile, on the making of a hospital or guardianship order without proceeding to conviction; [MHA 1983, s.45(1)]

(6) by a parent or guardian ordered to pay a fine, compensation or costs in respect of a juvenile; [PCC(S)A 2000, s.137(7)]

(7) by a parent or guardian ordered to enter into recognisances to ensure payment of outstanding sums owed by a juvenile offender; [PCC(S)A 2000, s.150(8)]

(8) by a parent or guardian ordered to enter into recognisances to take proper care and exercise proper control of a relevant minor; [PCC(S)A 2000, s.150(8)]

(9) against the extension or further extension of a custody time limit, or the giving of a direction by the court under POA 1985, s.6A; [POA 1985, s.22(8)]

(10) by a person aggrieved by the making of an order under FSA 1989, s.22(7);
FOD 1999, s.7

(11) against an order making or dispensing with, or refusing to dispense with reporting restrictions in the case of -juveniles;
YJCEA 1999, s.44(11) CJ(IC)A 1990, s.24A

(12) by party to any proceedings in which the forfeiture of cash is made by a magistrates court under CJ(IC)A 1990, s.26;

(13) against the making of an anti-social behaviour order, or an individual support order (ISO);
CDA 1998, s.4(1), (2)

(14) by a parent or guardian against the making of a parenting order;
CDA 1998, s.10(1)

(15) by a juvenile offender dealt with for an offence on the revocation of a referral order made under PCC(S)A 2000, ss.16–32;
PCC(S)A 2000, s.32

(16) by a person against whom a forfeiture order has been made under TerrA 2000, s.23(5);
Terr A 2000, s.29

(17) by a person in whose case a notification order under SOA 2003, s.97, or an interim order under s.100 has been made;
SOA 2003, s.101

(18) by a person against whom a sexual offences prevention order (SOPO) under SOA 2003, s.104, has been made or an interim order under s.109;
SOA 2003, s.110

(19) by a person against whom a foreign travel order under SOA 2003, s.114 or an order making or refusing an order under s.118;
SOA 2003, s.119

(20) by a person against whom a risk of sexual harm order (RSHO) under SOA 2003, s.123, or an interim order under s.126 has been made;
SOA 2003, s.127

(21) by the Security Industry Authority or the individual against the grant or refusal of a licence under the Private Security Industry Act 2001;
Private Security Industry Act 2001, s.11(4)

(22) by a person against whom a third party costs order is made in the magistrates' court (POA 1985, s.19B);
SI 2004/2408, reg.7

(23) against the making of an anti-social behaviour order in the magistrates' court;
CDA 1998, s.4(1)

(24) against the making of a parental compensation order;
CDA 1998, s.13D

(25) against a financial reporting order;

(26) against seizure or forfeiture of cash, see CONFISCATION ORDERS;

(27) against the making of a drinking banning order under VCRA 2006.
VCRA 2006, s.10

(28) by an individual whose application for the grant of a representation order in respect of an appeal to the Crown Court has been refused;
ROA 2006; S.I. 2009/3329

(29) by the applicant, where a justice of the peace refuses an application for an investigation anonymity order;
Cor JA 2009, s. 79

As to appeals against refusal to excuse, etc. from jury service, see JURY MANAGEMENT.
SOCA 2005, ss.76

Contempt of court

9–005 The effect of MCA 1980, s.108, combined with the CCA 1981, s.12(5), seems to give a right of appeal to a person sentenced in a magistrates' court for contempt, against the sentence imposed and against the finding (*Haw v Westminster MC* [2007] EWHC 2960, (Admin); [2008] 2 All E.R. 326).

The unsuccessful prosecutor

9–006 An unsuccessful prosecutor:

(1) has no right of appeal to the Crown Court against the dismissal of an information or an acquittal in the magistrates' court, unless conferred by statute, e.g. Commissioners for Revenue & Excise under CEMA 1979, s.147(2).

(2) has, by statute, a right of appeal to the Crown Court:

    (a) against the refusal to extend, or further extend, the overall custody time limits, or a refusal to give a (direction under POA 1985, s.22 and see CUSTODY TIME LIMITS); and *POA 1985, s.22(8)*

    (b) against the grant of bail, where B(A)A 1993 applies (see BAIL). *B(A)A 1993, s.1*

Reference by Criminal Cases Review Commission

9–007 Where a person has been convicted of an offence by a magistrates' court the Commission may refer to the Crown Court: *CAA 1995, s.11*

(1) the conviction; and

(2) (whether or not it refers the conviction), any sentence imposed on, or in subsequent proceedings relating to, the conviction.

A reference of the:

    (a) conviction is treated for all purposes as an appeal by the offender under MCA 1980, s.108(1) (whether or not he pleaded guilty); and

    (b) sentence is treated for all purposes as an appeal by the offender under MCA 1980, s.108(1) against the sentence, and any other sentence imposed on, or in subsequent proceedings relating to, the conviction or to any related conviction.

On a reference of this nature, whether of the conviction or sentence, the Crown Court may not award any punishment more severe than that awarded by the court whose decision is referred.

3. Procedure of application

Application of CPR 2011, R 63

9–008 CPR R 63 applies where: *R.63.1*

(1) a defendant wants to appeal under;

    (a) MCA 1980, s.109;

    (b) MHA 1983, s.45;

    (c) PCC(S) A 2000, Sch.3, para.10;

    (d) VRCRA 2006, s.10;

    (e) CTA 2008, s.42;

(2) the Criminal Cases Review Commission refers a defendant's case to the Crown Court under CCA 1995, s.11;

(3) a prosecutor wants to appeal under:

    (a) FSA 1989, s.14A(5A); or

    (b) C&EMA 1979, s.147(3); or

(4) a person wants to appeal under:
  - (a) ABOOA 1965;
  - (b) CCA 1981, s.12(5);
  - (c) GR 1986, regs 3C or 3H;
  - (d) FSA 1989, s.22

Note that the Crown Court may, under R 63:   R.63.9

- shorten or extend (even after it has expired) a time limit
- allow an appellant to vary an appeal notice that he has served
- direct that an appeal notice be served on any person
- allow an appeal notice or a notice of abandonment to be in a different form to one set out in PD 2004, Annex D, or to be presented orally.

Service of appeal notice
9–009 An appellant must serve an appeal notice on: R.63.2

(1) the magistrates' court office; and
(2) every other party.

He must serve the appeal notice:

  - (a) as soon after the decision appealed against as he wants; but
  - (b) not more than 21 days after:
    - (i) sentence, or the date sentence is deferred, whichever is earlier, if the appeal is against conviction or against a finding of guilt;
    - (ii) sentence, if the appeal is against sentence; or
    - (iii) the order or failure to make an order about which the appellant wants to appeal, in any other case; and

he must serve with the appeal notice any application for an extension of time, and in that application explain why the appeal notice is late.

The applicant has no right to an oral hearing in relation to an application for extension of time, though in a rare case the judge may, in his discretion, grant one *(R. v Croydon CC Ex p. Smith* (1983) 77 Cr. App. R. 277). The judge need give no reasons for his decision; he may grant an extension in respect of sentence only, if that is appropriate.

If the judge grants an extension, notice will be given to the parties and to the magistrates' court, see 9–017, below.

Form of appeal notice
9–010 The appeal notice must be in writing and must: R.63.3

(1) specify:
  - (a) the conviction or finding of guilt;
  - (b) the sentence; or
  - (c) the order, or the failure to make an order, about which the appellant wants to appeal;
(2) summarise the issues;
(3) in an appeal against conviction:

(a) identify the prosecution witnesses whom the appellant will want to question if they are called to give evidence; and

(b) say how long the trial lasted in the magistrates' court and how long the appeal is likely to last in the Crown Court;

(c) in an appeal against a finding that the appellant insulted someone or interrupted proceedings in the magistrates' court, attach:

  (i) the magistrates' court's written findings of fact, and

  (ii) the appellant's response to those findings;

(4) say whether the appellant has asked the magistrates' court to reconsider the case (under MCA 1980, s.142); and

(5) include a list of those on whom the appellant has served the appeal notice.

A specimen form is to be found in PD 2004, Annex D, but see 9–009, above.

Documents; exhibits

9–011 The magistrates' court officer will;
      Rr.63.4; 63.5

(1) forward to the Crown Court the appeal notice and any accompanying application served by the appellant, details of the parties, including their addresses, a copy of each entry in the register relating to the decision under appeal, and to any application for bail pending appeal;

(2) keep any documents or objects exhibited in the proceedings for a specified period, or arrange for them to be kept by some other party; and

(3) provide the Crown Court with any document, object or information for which the Crown Court officer asks.

Any person who under any arrangement with the magistrates' court keeps any exhibit, etc must provide it to the Crown Court when required.

CDS Contribution orders

9–012 The circumstances in which a contribution order must be made, and the calculations of any relevant amount, in relation to appeals to the Crown Court in criminal proceedings against;

(1) conviction;

(2) sentence or an order (under GR 2001, reg.3(2)); or

(3) conviction and sentence,

are dealt with in Pt 3 of CORJA 2009 (see LEGAL AID; PUBLIC FUNDING)

Reference by CCRC

9–013 A reference by the Criminal Cases Review Commission must be served as soon as practicable by the Crown Court officer, on:
      R.63.4.5

(1) the appellant;

(2) every other party; and

(3) the magistrates' court officer,

and the appellant may serve an appeal notice on the Crown Court officer and every other party not more than 21 days later.

If the appellant does not serve an appeal notice, the Crown Court will treat the reference as the appeal notice.

Bail

9–014   A judge of the Crown Court may grant bail:

SCA 1981, s.81(1)(b)

(1) to a person giving notice of appeal (as may the magistrates' court); and

(2) to a person whose conviction or sentence is referred to it by the Criminal Cases Review Commission.

The judge may alternatively find it expedient, following the practice of CACD, to expedite the appeal hearing instead of granting bail.

Any time during which such a person is released on bail does not count towards sentence.

Suspension of RT disqualification

9–015   If a person convicted of an offence and disqualified from holding or obtaining a driving licence appeals to the Crown Court, either:

RTOA 1988, ss.39(1), 40(1), (2), (6)

(1) the magistrates' court; or

(2) the Crown Court,

may suspend the disqualification pending the appeal, on such terms as the court thinks fit.

Interim hospital order

9–016   The fact that an appeal to the Crown Court is pending does not affect the power of the magistrates' court which has made an interim hospital order to:

SCA 1981, s.48(7)

(1) renew or terminate the order; or

(2) deal with the accused on its termination.

4.   Hearings and decision

Public hearings; notice

9–017   The Crown Court must, as a general rule, hear any appeal or reference to which 63 applies (see 9–009, above) in public, but:

R.63.7

(1) may order any hearing to be in private; and

(2) where a hearing is about a public interest ruling, must hold the hearing in private.

The Crown Court officer will:

(a) give as much notice as is reasonably practicable of every hearing, to the parties, any party's custodian and any other person whom the Crown Court requires to be notified;

(b) serve every decision on the parties, or on any other person whom the Crown Court requires to be served; and

(c) where the decision determines a appeal, on the magistrates' court officer and the party's custodian, save that where a hearing or decision is about a public interest ruling, he will not give notice of that hearing, or serve that decision, on anyone other than the prosecutor who applied for that ruling unless the court otherwise directs.

Where there is both an appeal against conviction and also a committal for sentence the Crown Court officer should ensure that the appellant/offender is informed of both hearings in one document: *R. (Bromley) v Secretary of State for Justice* [2010] A.C.D. 146(43), DC.

Non-appearance
9–018 Where neither party appears, either personally or by advocate, an appeal may be struck out. If the appellant fails to appear one of several courses may be adopted:

(1) if neither appellant nor his advocate appears, and notice of hearing is proved, the appeal should be dismissed (*R. v Spoke Ex p. Buckley* (W12) 76 J.P. 354; *R. v Croydon CC Ex p. Clair* (1986) 83 Cr. App. R. 202), it should not be treated as impliedly abandoned (*R. (Hayes) v Chelmsford CC* [2003] EWHC 73, [2003] Crim L.R. 400);
(2) if notice of appeal has been given, has not been withdrawn and no application to abandon is made, the appeal may be heard in the appellant's absence (*R. v Guildford CC Ex p. Brewer* (1988) 87 Cr. App. R. 265);
(3) if an advocate appears on his behalf, the appeal may go on (*R. v Croydon CC Ex p. Clair (above)*).

The judge should not take it upon himself to conduct the respondent's case where an advocate fails to appear: *R. v Wood Green CC Ex p. Taylor* [1995] Crim. L.R. 879. If the respondent does not appear, either personally or by advocate, and service of the notice, etc. is proved, any conviction or sentence appealed may be quashed (*R. v Croydon CC Ex p. Clair*, above), but before taking such a step, the judge ought to consider the position of any victim who may be deprived of compensation (*R. (CPS) v Portsmouth CC* [2003] EWHC 1079 (Admin); [2004] Crim. L.R. 224).

Nothing prevents the court from setting aside its own order, and hearing the appeal if this is an appropriate course (R. v London QS Appeals Ex p. Rossi [1956] 1 Q.B. 682).

The magistrates as respondents
9–019 The prosecutor in the case below invariably takes upon himself the conduct of the respondent's case on the appeal.

The magistrates have an absolute right to appear, instruct counsel and call evidence in support of their decision. They seldom do, but:

(1) they may need to where the "other party" has no interest in defending the appeal;
(2) if they do, they appear as amicus curiae, and should not enter into disputes, or make themselves a party to the appeal; in which case,

(3) no costs may be awarded against them.

(*R. v Kent JJ Ex p. MPC* [1936] 1 K.B. 547; *R. v Preston CC Ex p. Pamplin* [1981] Crim. L.R. 338).

Abandoning an appeal; bail; costs

9–020   An appellant:

> (1) may abandon an appeal without the Crown Court's permission   R.63.8
>   by serving a notice of abandonment, see PD 2004, Annex D (but
>   see 9–018, above) on:
>   (a) the magistrates' court officer;
>   (b) the Crown Court officer; and
>   (c) every other party before the hearing of the appeal begins;
> (2) may only abandon the appeal after the hearing begins, with the
>   leave of the Crown Court (see 9–023, below).

A notice of abandonment must be signed by or on behalf of the appellant. Note that:

> (1) where an appellant is allowed to abandon an appeal, the court
>   has no power to increase the sentence (*R. v Gloucester CC Ex
>   p. Betteridge* [1998] Crim L.R. 218); the judge has a discretion
>   whether to make an order for costs on dismissing the appeal
>   (R.76.1).
> (2) failure to appear when bailed to do so is not to be treated as an
>   implied abandonment; provided service of the notice of hearing
>   is proved the ease may be treated as one of non-appearance (see
>   9-018, above);
> (3) an appellant who has been on bail pending appeal, and who
>   abandons his appeal must surrender to custody as directed by the
>   magistrates' court officer; any conditions of bail applying until
>   then.

Notice of abandonment, deliberately given, was, under the previous rules regarded as final; it could not be afterwards withdrawn. It might be treated as a nullity only if the Crown Court found, after investigation, that it was given under a mistake or as a result of fraudulent inducement, so that there had been no real abandonment. No other jurisdiction to relist the appeal was recognised (*R. v Essex Q.S. Ex p. Larkin* [1961] 3 All E.R. 930; *R. v Knightsbridge CC Ex p. C.&E Commrs* [1986] Crim. L.R. 324).

Constitution of the court

9–021   On the hearing of an appeal: R.63.10

> (1) the general rule is that the Crown Court must comprise:
>   (a) a judge of the High Court, a Circuit Judge or a Recorder; and
>   (b) no less than two nor more than four justices of the peace,
>   none of whom took part in the decision under appeal;
> (2) if the appeal is from a youth court:
>   (a) each justice of the peace must be qualified to sit as a member
>   of a youth court; and
>   (b) the Crown Court must include a man and a woman; but

(3) the Crown Court may include only one justice of the peace and need not include both a man and a woman if:
  (a) the judge decides that otherwise the start of the appeal hearing will be delayed unreasonably; or
  (b) one or more of the justices of the peace who started hearing the appeal is absent.

If the court conducts a hearing with only one justice, problems are likely to arise if the justice and the judge are unable to agree.

Objection to the constitution of the court needs to be taken not later than the time the proceedings are entered upon, or when the irregularity begins. SCA 1981, ss.8(2)74(6)

Special provisions apply to appeals under the Licensing Act 1964, the Betting, Gaming and Lotteries Act 1963, and the Gaming Act 1968, and the licensing Act 2003.

The judge must sit without justices in an appeal in relation to an investigation anonymity order under CorJA 2009, s.79, see r 6.25 and following.

Status of lay magistrates
9–022 Where a judge, Recorder or District Judge (Magistrates' Courts) sits with lay magistrates, he presides, and:

(1) the decision of the court may be by a majority; and
(2) if the members are equally divided, the judge, District Judge or Recorder has a second and casting vote;
(3) interlocutory decisions are taken by the court as a whole, though on questions of law the lay magistrates are likely to defer to the judge's views (*R. v Orpin* (1974) 59 Cr. App. R. 231);
(4) where the exercise of discretion arises, as where the admissibility of a confession is in issue (*R. v Orpin*, above), or otherwise, the discretion falls to be exercised by the whole court, but where, as a matter of law, the discretion can only be exercised in one way, the lay magistrates are bound by the judge's decision (*Cook v DPP* [2001] Crim. L.R. 321).

Abandonment after hearing begins; lapse
9–023 An appellant who has not abandoned his appeal before the hearing begins (see r.63.8 at 9–020 above) may still apply to the court after the hearing has begun, to abandon his appeal, but in such circumstances:

(1) the court has a discretion whether to permit him to do so or not; and
(2) he has no immunity from costs. Under the previous rules it was said that only in the most exceptional circumstances would the court:
  (a) refuse the application if it was made before the hearing of the appeal had begun; or
  (b) grant the application, once the hearing had begun.

(*R. v Manchester CC Ex p. Welby* (1981)73 Cr. App. R. 248; *R. v Knightsbridge CC Ex p. C.E.C.* [1986] Crim. L.R. 324).

The hearing begins, not when it is called on and the appellant is identified, but rather once the prosecution has opened the facts to the court (*R. (Goumane) v Canterbury CC* [2009] EWHC 1711, [2010] Crim. L.R. 46).

The appellant does not abandon his appeal merely by failing to appear or to instruct counsel, so obliging the court to dismiss it *(R. v Guildford CC Ex p. Brewer* (1988) 87 Cr. App. R. 265).

The proceedings will ordinarily lapse on the death of the appellant; not on the death of the informant *(R. v Jefferies* (1968) 52 Cr. App. R. 654).

Equivocal plea

9–024   An appellant may contend that he has a right of appeal against conviction because his plea of guilty in the magistrates' court was an equivocal one. To be "equivocal" the appellant must have added to his plea a qualification which, if substantiated, might show that he was not guilty of the offence (*Foster (Haulage) Ltd v Roberts* (1978) 67 Cr. App. R. 305). It is an issue that the Crown Court must determine as a preliminary point (*R. v Durham Q.S. Ex p. Virgo* [1952] 1 All E.R. 466).

The procedure to be followed is as follows (*R. v Marylebone JJ. Ex p. Westminster City Council* [1971] 1 All E.R. 1025; *R. v Rochdale JJ. Ex p. Allwork* (1981) 73 Cr. App. R. 319):

(1) evidence must be heard from or on behalf of the appellant as to the basis of the plea;

(2) if that evidence casts no doubt on the validity of the plea, or falls short of establishing "equivocality", the issue is resolved and the court proceeds to hear any appeal against sentence;

(3) if the evidence for the appellant does disclose *prima facie* that the plea in the magistrates' court was equivocal, help should be sought from the court below as to what happened at the hearing;

(4) the magistrate, chairman or legal adviser should be called upon to swear an affidavit as to what happened, and only after considering that evidence should the court determine the issue (and see *R. v Coventry CC Ex p. Manson* (1978) 67 Cr. App. R. 315);

(5) in appropriate circumstances, the case may be remitted to the magistrates for a fresh hearing.

Provided the Crown Court has made a proper enquiry before determining the issue, the remittal for a fresh hearing must be complied with by the court below (*R. v Plymouth JJ. Ex p. Hart* (1986) 83 Cr. App. R. 81). If a dispute arises as to whether there was a proper enquiry, the issue can only be resolved by the High Court on judicial review. SCA 1981, s.48(2)(b)

The fact that an unequivocal plea was entered below does not prevent an appellant putting forward a plea of *autrefois convict* or *autrefois acquit* at the hearing of the appeal (*Cooper v New Forest DC* [1972] Crim. L. R. 877). In exceptional circumstances an appellant may be permitted to appeal against conviction, even though his plea of guilty was unequivocal, where his plea was entered under duress (*R. v Huntingdon CC Ex p. Jordan* (1981) 73 Cr. App. R. 194).

Form of hearing

9–025 An appeal to the Crown Court is by way of rehearing; the customary practice and procedure with respect to appeals to Quarter Sessions is continued by SCA 1981. In an appeal against:

(1) *conviction*:
   (a) the party seeking an order or conviction proves his case again;
   (b) there is no obligation on the prosecution to put its case in the same way as in the court below (*Hingley-Smith v DPP* [1998] 1 Arch. News 2, DC);
   (c) evidence is heard afresh;
   (d) the Crown Court does not "review" the decision of the lower court; it takes the place of the magistrates, forming its own view and substituting its opinion for that of the court below, in regard to conviction and/or sentence (*Drover v Rugman* [1950] 2 All E.R. 575; *Sagnata Ltd v Norwich Corpn* [1971] 2 All E.R. 1441; *R. v Swindon CC Ex p. Murray* (1998) 162 J.P. 36; *Hingley-Smith v DPP,* above); and
   (e) it may find the case proved on a different basis from that found in the lower court (*Hingley-Smith v DPP,* above);

(2) *sentence*:
   (a) there is a rehearing from conviction onwards;
   (b) the Crown Court is not limited to considering whether the sentence imposed by the lower court was within its jurisdiction. The court goes through the sentencing process afresh, including, where appropriate, the inspection of driving licences, etc. (*Dyson v Ellison* (1974) 60 Cr. App. R. 191; *R. v Knutsford CC Ex p. Jones* (1985) 7 Cr. App. R. (S.) 448), and the examination of any suggested "special reasons" for not disqualifying (*DPP v O'Connor* (1992) 95 Cr. App. R. 135);

(3) *binding over order*:
   (a) there is a rehearing; and
   (b) unless the appellant is prepared to admit the evidence which was before the magistrates, the facts must be proved by sworn evidence (*Shaw v Hamilton* (1982) 75 Cr. App. R. 288);
   (c) the issue is whether or not the court below was justified in making the order, *not* whether the appellant is likely to repeat the conduct (*Hughes v Holley* (1988) 86 Cr. App. R. 130);

(4) *refusal of a firearms certificate* (see 9–034, below):
   (a) there is a rehearing;
   (b) the views of the police being only one of the factors to be taken into consideration (*Cliff v MPC* (1973) 117 S.J. 855).

Special considerations govern appeals against local government decisions, see, e.g. *Stepney B.C. v Joffe* [1949] 1 All E.R. 256; *Northern Ireland Trailers Ltd v Preston Corp* [1972] 1 All E.R. 260.

The Crown Court is empowered to determine an appeal on a factual basis which differs from that adopted by the magistrates' court (see

Hingley-Smith v DPP [1998] Arch. News 2). Any such question is determined in precisely the same way as on a plea to an indictment. The court is not bound by any finding of fact made in the magistrates' court which might limit its power of sentence.

If the Crown Court decides not to accept the express view of the court below, it should explain that to the appellant: *Bussey v DPP* [1999] 1 Cr. App. R.(S.) 125.

5. Powers

In the course of the hearing
9–026 In the course of the hearing, the court may:

(1) correct any error or mistake in the order or judgment incorporating the decision which is the subject of the appeal; but

(2) *not* purport to amend the substance of the information on which the appellant was tried below (*Meek v Powell* [1952] 1 All E.R. 347; *Garfield v Maddocks* (1973) 57 Cr. App. R. 372; *Fairgrieve v Newman* (1986) 82 Cr. App. R. 60; *R. v Swansea CC Ex p. Stacey* [1990] RTR 183; *R. v Norwich CC Ex p. Russell* [1993] Crim.L.R. 518);

(3) hear the appeal on the basis of the unamended information and may exercise the same jurisdiction as the court below, e.g. in the use of MCA 1980, s.123 (*R. v Swansea CC Ex p. Stacey* [1990] R.T.R. 183).

On the termination of the hearing
9–027 On the termination of the hearing of an appeal the court may

SCA 1981, s.48(2), (3)

(1) *decision*:
  (a) confirm, reverse or vary any part of the decision appealed against, including a determination not to impose a separate penalty; or
  (b) remit the matter with its opinion thereon to the authority whose decision is appealed against; or
  (c) make such order in the matter as it thinks just, and by such order exercise any power which that authority might have exercised, subject to any enactment which expressly restricts or limits its powers;

(2) *sentence*, whether the appeal was against conviction or sentence:

SCA 1981, s.48(4)

  (a) award any punishment, whether more or less severe than that awarded by the magistrates whose decision is appealed, provided it is a punishment which those magistrates might have awarded at the time the appellant was sentenced by them (*R. v Portsmouth CC Ex p. Ballard* (1990) 154 J.P. 109) save where the appeal is referred to the court by the Criminal Cases Review Commission (see 9–007 above);
  (b) if the appeal is against one of several convictions on the same occasion, vary the sentences imposed for all the offences (*Dutta v Westcott* (1987) 84 Cr. App. R. 103).

The Crown Court should not increase sentence without giving a clear warning of its intention (see, e.g. *R. (Tottman) v DPP* [2004] EWHC 258 (Admin)).

SCA 1981, s.48(6)

"Sentence" includes any order made by a court when dealing with an offender, including a hospital order, and a recommendation for deportation.

Interim hospital order

9–028 If, on the termination of an appeal, the Crown Court:

SCA 1981, s.48(7)

(1) quashes an interim hospital order made by the magistrates, but does not pass any sentence or make any other order, it may direct the appellant to be kept in custody or released on bail pending his being dealt with by the magistrates;

(2) makes an interim hospital order, the court below:
   (a) has the power to renew or terminate the order, and to deal with the accused on its termination;
   (b) is to be treated for the purposes of absconding offenders (MHA 1983, s.31(8)) as the court which made the order.

Recommendation for deportation

9–029 Where the appellant appeals against a recommendation for deportation made by the magistrates, or the conviction in respect of which it is made, the court may direct his release in accordance with the Act, without setting aside the recommendation (See also *R. v Ofori* (1994) 99 Cr. App. R. 219).

IA 1971, Sch.3

Forfeiture of cash under POCA 2002, s.298

9–030 An appeal by a party to proceedings in which a cash forfeiture order is made under POCA 2002, s.298, is by way of rehearing. The Crown Court may make any order it thinks appropriate, and if it upholds the appeal may order the release of the cash.

POCA 2002, s.299

Anti-social behaviour; sex offenders; parenting orders

9–031 Where the appellant appeals against the making of an anti-social behaviour order, parenting order or sex offender order, the Crown Court may:

CDA 1998, s.4(1), (2), (3)

(a) make such orders as may be necessary to give effect to its determination of the appeal; and
(b) make such incidental or consequential orders as appear to it to be just.

Any order, other than one directing a rehearing by a magistrates' court, is treated as an order of the court from which the appeal was brought, not of the Crown Court.

Reasons for decision

9–032 The judge presiding in the Crown Court is obliged to give reasons for the decision of the court, at least sufficient to demonstrate that the court has identified the main issues in the case and how it has resolved them (*R. v Harrow CC Ex p. Dave* (1994) 99 Cr. App. R.

114) and so that an appellant can know the reasons for the decision as soon as is reasonably possible, understand the nature of the criminality found and consider whether to appeal (*R. v ILCC Ex p. Lambeth LBC* [2000] Crim. L.R. 303). Failure to do so may vitiate the decision, unless the reasons are obvious, the case is simple or the subject matter of the appeal unimportant: *R. v Kingston CC Ex p. Bell* 164 J.P. 633. Reasons should be given contemporaneously with the decision (*R. v Snaresbrook CC Ex p. Input Management Ltd* (1999) 163 J.P. 533; *R. v ILCC Ex p. Lambeth LBC* [2000] Crim. L.R. 303).

6.   Costs and assessment

9–033   See COSTS AND ASSESSMENT

7.   Appeals under the Firearms Act 1968

9–034   An appeal against a decision of a chief officer of police under FA 1968, ss.28A, 29, 30A, 30B, 30C, 34, 36, 37 or 38 lies to the Crown Court. It is determined on the merits and not by way of review.   FA 1968, s.44

The procedure for initiating the appeal is similar to that for other appeals to the Crown Court, thus:

(1) notice of appeal must be given within 21 days after the date on which the appellant received notice of the decision of the chief officer of police by which he is aggrieved;
(2) the notice must be given both to the designated officer of the magistrates' court and to the chief officer, and must state the general grounds of his appeal;
(3) the Crown Court officer will give notice of the date and place of the hearing both to the appellant and to the chief officer, who is entitled to appear and be heard on the appeal;
(4) the appellant may abandon his appeal at any time, not less than two clear days before the date fixed for the hearing, by giving notice in writing to the magistrates' court and to the chief officer.

On the hearing of the appeal, the Crown Court may either dismiss the appeal or give the chief officer such directions as it thinks fit as respects the certificate or the register which is the subject of the appeal.

Notes

10. BAIL

Quick guide

1. Granting bail

Jurisdiction

10–001 Bail may be granted in the Crown Court, subject to CJPOA 1994 s.25 (see 10–007, below), to any person: *SCA 1981, s.83(1)*

(1) who has been sent in custody to the Crown Court for trial under CDA 1998, s.51 or s.51A;

(2) who is in custody pursuant to a sentence imposed by a magistrates' court and has appealed to the Crown Court against his conviction or sentence;

(3) who is in the custody of the Crown Court pending the disposal of his case by that court;

(4) who, after the decision of his case by the Crown Court, has applied to the court for a case to be stated for the opinion of the High Court on that decision or is seeking a quashing order in respect of that decision;

(5) to whom a judge of the Crown Court has granted a certificate under CAA 1968 ss.1(2) or 11(1A), or SCA 1981, s.81(1B) that a case is fit for appeal (see APPEALS FROM THE CROWN COURT);

(6) to any person charged with murder, the magistrates' court having no such jurisdiction (10–008).

Where an accused is sent for trial to the Crown Court, the magistrates' bail ceases when he surrenders to the Crown Court, whether for arraignment or otherwise, and a judge, if releasing him again on bail, must consider afresh the appropriateness of any conditions afresh, including the position of any surety (*R. v Kent CC Ex p. Jodka* (1997) 161 J.P. 638).

As to granting bail during the trial, see 10–014, below. As to granting bail on application for leave to appeal to the CACD see APPEALS FROM THE CROWN COURT.

It should always be made to clear to an accused granted bail that if he fails to attend his trial, the consequences may be that it will proceed in his absence and without legal representation (*R. v O'Hare* [2006] EWCA Crim 471, [2006] Crim. L.R. 950).

Where a young person is charged with a serious offence the judge ought to show that he has given sufficient and appropriate consideration to any suggested potential safeguards and the question of whether they provide sufficient protection against absconding or failing to surrender *(R. (on the application of Bailey) v CCC* [2010] Crim. L.R. 733).

If the Legal Aid Etc Bill 2011, now going through Parliament, is enacted in its present form, it will make substantial changes to this section.

Challenging a Crown Court decision

10–002 CJA 2003, s.17 abolishes the inherent power of the High Court to entertain an application in relation to bail where a judge has determined such an application under:

(1) BA 1976, s.3(8); or
(2) SCA 1981, s.81(1)(a), (b), (c) or (g),

though this does not affect that court's jurisdiction to grant bail in other matters (such as a case stated), or in *habeas corpus* applications. The High Court, however, retains the jurisdiction to entertain an application for judicial review of a refusal of bail based on the *Wednesbury* principles "robustly applied", at any time before the start of his trial at the Crown Court *(R. (Shergill) v Harrow CC* [2005] EWHC 648 (Admin)). See also *(R. (on the application of M) v Isleworth CC* [2005] EWHC 363 (Admin.); *R. (on the application of Fergus) v Southampton CC* [2008] EWHC 3273).

A reference to an "application in relation to bail" includes an application for:

(a) bail to be granted;
(b) bail to be withheld;
(c) conditions of bail to be varied.

A reference to the withholding of bail includes a reference to the revocation of bail.

Right to bail before conviction

10–003 Under the general provisions of BA 1976, **but subject to CJPOA 1994, s.25** (see 10–007 below) a person who: BA 1976, s.4;

(1) appears or is brought before the Crown Court in the course of, or in connection with, proceedings for an offence, or applies to the Crown Court for bail in connection with the proceedings; or
(2) has been convicted of an offence and whose case is adjourned for reports before sentence;
(3) has been convicted of an offence and appears before the Crown Court under:
  (a) PCC(S)A 2000, Sch.1 (referral orders: referral back to appropriate court);
  (b) PCC(S)A 2000, Sch.8 (breach of reparation order);
  (c) CJIA 2008, Sch.2, (breach, revocation or amendment of youth rehabilitation orders); or
  (d) CJA 2003, Sch.8, Pt 2 (breach of requirements of a community order),

has a right to bail unless one of the exceptions under BA 1976, Sch.1(see 10–004) is made out, and the judge exercises his discretion to refuse bail.

As to bail during the trial, see 10–014, below; as to bail on the expiry of a time limit under POA 1985 and the Regulations made thereunder see CUSTODY TIME LIMITS. As to bail on a retrial under CJA 2003, Pt 10, see RETRIALS.

Refusing bail; indictable and either way imprisonable offence

10–004   Quite apart from CJPOA 1995, s. 25, (10–007) the judge may refuse to grant bail to an accused (subject to expiry of the custody time limits) where, in the case of an **imprisonable offence**, triable on indictment or either way: BA 1976, Sch.1

(1) there exist substantial grounds for the belief (*R. v Slough JJ. Ex p. Duncan* (1982) 75 Cr. App. R. 354, cf. *R. v Mansfield JJ. Ex p. Sharkey* [1985] 1 All ER 193) that if released on bail, whether with sureties or not, he will:
  (a) fail to surrender;
  (b) commit an offence while on bail; or
  (c) interfere with witnesses or otherwise obstruct the course of justice, whether in relation to himself or any other person;
(2) it appears he was on bail in criminal proceedings on the date of the offence (10–010), unless the judge is satisfied that there is no significant risk of his committing an offence while on bail, whether subject to conditions or not;
(3) he is satisfied that the accused should be kept in custody for his own protection (or welfare in the case of a juvenile);
(4) the accused is already in custody in pursuance of the sentence of a court or of any authority acting under the Services Acts; or
(5) he is satisfied that it has not been practicable to obtain sufficient information for the purpose of taking the decisions in (1)–(3) above for want of time since the institution of proceedings against him.

In deciding whether he is satisfied that there are substantial grounds for believing that the accused, if released on bail, whether subject to conditions or not, would commit an offence while on bail, **the judge must give particular weight to the fact if it be the case that he was on bail in criminal proceedings on the date of the offence.**

BA 1976, Sch.1, Pt 1A, inserted by CJIA 2008, applies in relation to summary imprisonable offences.

Exercise of discretion

10–005   Before the discretion to refuse bail arises:

(1) the judge must be satisfied that one of the five conditions in 10–004 above obtains; with regard to (1) it is the existence of substantial grounds for the belief, not the belief itself, which is the crucial factor (*R. v Slough JJ. Ex p. Duncan* above);

(2) in deciding whether substantial grounds exist, the judge must act compatibly with ECHR, art.5(3) which limits pre-trial custody; he must take into account *all* relevant considerations, including those relating to the character of the person involved, his morals, his home, his occupation, his assets, his family ties and all kinds of links with his community and country (*Letellier v France* (1992) 14 E.H.R.R. 83 R);

(3) there should be evidence to support objections to bail, but it seems that the strict rules of evidence need not apply; evidence upon which the prosecution intend to rely in opposing bail should be disclosed (*Lamy v Belgium* (1989) 11 E.H.R.R. 529).

The seriousness of the offence is not to be treated as a conclusive reason for withholding bail from an unconvicted suspect. (*Hurnam v State of Mauritius* [2005] UKPC 49, [2006] 1 W.L.R. 857, per Lord Bingham of Cornhill).

In *Gault v UK* [2008] Crim. L.R. 476, *The Times* November 28, 2007 ECHR regarded the fact that the prosecution did not object to bail as a "significant factor"; but see *R. (Burns) v Woolwich CC etc* [2010] *LS Gazette*, January 28, 35 where it was made clear that decisions as to the grant of bail are a matter for the courts, not for the prosecutor.

Non-imprisonable offences

10–006 Where the accused faces, or is convicted of, a non-imprisonable offence, bail need not be granted where:

BA 1976, Sch.1, Pt II, paras 2-5

(1) having been previously granted bail in criminal proceedings, it appears that he has failed to surrender to custody in accordance with his obligation; and

(2) the judge believes, in view of that failure, that the accused, if released on bail (whether subject to conditions or not), would fail to surrender to custody, and

the judge is satisfied that:

(a) the accused should be kept in custody for his own protection or, if he is a child or young person, for his own welfare;

(b) he is in custody in pursuance of the sentence of a court or of any authority acting under any of the Services Acts; or

(c) if:

    (i) having been released on bail in or in connection with the proceedings for the offence, he has been arrested in pursuance of BA 1976, s.7; and

    (ii) the judge is satisfied that there are substantial grounds for believing that if released on bail, (whether subject to conditions or not), he would fail to surrender to custody, commit an offence on bail or interfere with witnesses or otherwise obstruct the course of justice (whether in relation to himself or any other person).

There is nothing to prevent conditions being imposed in such a case (*R. v Bournemouth MC Ex p. Cross* (1989) 89 Cr. App. R. 90).

Previous conviction for certain serious offences

10–007 In the case of certain prescribed serious offences, namely:

CJPOA 1994, s.25

(1) murder;

(2) attempted murder;

(3) manslaughter;

(4) rape under the law of Scotland or Northern Ireland;

(5) an offence under SOA 1956, s.1 (rape);

(6) an offence under SOA 2003, s.1 (rape);

(7) an offence under SOA 2003, s.2 (assault by penetration);

(8) an offence under SOA 2003, s.4 (causing a person to engage in sexual activity without consent) where the activity involved penetration within s.4(4)(a)–(d);

(9) an offence under SOA 2003, s.5 (rape of a child under 13);

(10) an offence under SOA 2003, s.6 (assault of a child under 13 by penetration);

(11) an offence under SOA 2003, s.8 (causing or inciting a child under 13 to engage in sexual activity);

(12) an offence under SOA 2003, s.30 (sexual activity with a person with a mental disorder impeding choice) where the touching involved penetration within s.30(3)(a)–(d);

(13) an offence under SOA 2003, s.31 (causing or inciting a person with a mental disorder impeding choice to engage in sexual activity) where an activity involving penetration within s.31(3)(a)–(d) was caused; and

(14) an attempt to commit an offence within any of the paras (4) to (13) above involving penetration within s.8(3)(a)–(d).

A person charged with, or convicted of, any of the above offences, who:

(a) has been previously convicted in any part of the United Kingdom of such an offence; or

(b) in the case of a previous conviction for manslaughter or culpable homicide, was then a child or young person and was sentenced to long term detention,

may be granted bail in those proceedings **only if the judge is satisfied that there are exceptional circumstances which justify it.**

If a person to whom s.25 applies, if granted bail, is likely to fail to surrender, to offend on bail or to interfere with witnesses or otherwise obstruct the course of justice, bail should not be granted. If, however, taking all the circumstances into consideration the accused does not create such an unacceptable risk, he is an exception to the norm and should be granted bail (*R. (O) v Harrow CC [2006] UKHL 42,* [2007] 1 Cr. App. R. 9). Note that the section does not breach ECHR, art.5 (*R. (O) v Harrow CC*, above).

CorJA 2009, s.115

Special cases: (1) murder

10–008 A person charged with murder (and this includes a person charged with murder and one or more other offences) may not be granted bail except by order of a judge of the Crown Court.

Where a person appears or is brought before a magistrates' court charged with murder, a judge of the Crown Court will make a decision about bail in respect of that person:

(1) as soon as reasonably practicable; and

(2) in any event, within the period of 48 hours beginning with the day after the day on which the person appears or is brought before the magistrates' court.

BA 1976, Sch.1, para. 6ZA

In calculating the period of 48 hours referred to above, Saturdays, Sundays, Christmas Day, Good Friday and bank holidays are to be excluded.

The magistrates' court will, if necessary for these purposes, commit the person to custody to be brought before a judge. It is immaterial whether the lower court sends the person to the Crown Court for trial, or adjourns proceedings under CDA 1998, s.37, or remands him.

Where an accused is charged with murder, he may not be granted bail unless the judge is of the opinion that there is no significant risk of his committing, while on bail, an offence that would, or would be likely to, cause physical or mental injury to any person other than the accused.

Special cases: (2) drug users

10–009 There is a presumption against bail in the case of a person aged 18 or over, where that person is

BA 1976, Sch.1, Pt 1, paras 6A-6C

(1) charged with an imprisonable offence; and

(2) under arrangements in force in the court's area;,
    (a) he tests positive for a specified (CJCSA 2000, Pt 3) Class A drug; and
    (b) he does not consent to:
        (i) undergo an assessment as to his dependency or propensity to use drugs; or
        (ii) following assessment, any relevant follow up action recommended,

unless the judge is satisfied that there is no significant risk of that person committing another offence while on bail.

Before this provision applies, however, a sample (taken under PACE 1984, s.63B in connection with the offence, or under CJA 2003, s.161 after conviction and before sentence) must have revealed the presence in that person's body of a specified Class A drug, and either:

- the offence must be one under MDA 1971, s.5(2) or 5(3), and relate to a specified Class A drug; or
- the judge must be satisfied that there are substantial grounds for believing that misuse by the accused of a specified Class A drug caused or contributed to the offence; or, even if it did not, the offence was motivated wholly or partly by his intended misuse of such a drug; and

if an assessment or a follow-up is proposed and agreed to, it must be a condition of bail that it be undertaken. See HO Circular 22/2004.

Special Cases: (3) breach of existing bail

10–010 Where the accused is aged 18 or over, and it appears that:

BA 1976, Sch.1, Pt 1, para.2A(1), 6(1)-(3)

(1) he was on bail in criminal proceedings on the date of the offence; or

(2) having been released on bail in or in connection with the proceedings for the offence, he failed to surrender to custody,

he may not be granted bail unless the judge is satisfied that there is no significant risk of his committing an offence while on bail (whether subject to conditions or not), or failing to surrender to custody.

Where it appears that the accused had reasonable cause for his failure to surrender to custody, (2) above does not apply unless it also appears that he failed to surrender to custody at the appointed place as soon as reasonably practicable after the appointed time.

In the case of an accused under 18, the judge must give particular weight to the fact that he has failed to surrender to bail in assessing the risk of future offending.

Special cases: (4) extradition

10–011 Where the Home Secretary has given an undertaking in connection with a person's extradition to the United Kingdom which includes terms that that person be kept in custody until the conclusion of any proceedings against him for an offence, a judge may grant bail only if he considers that there are exceptional circumstances which justify it.

EA 2003, s.154

Bail

Statutory considerations

10–012 In taking the decision whether to grant, withhold or vary bail in the case of a person accused or convicted of an **imprisonable offence,** the judge is bound to have regard to such of the following considerations as appear to be relevant, that is to say:

BA 1976, s.4(1), Sch.1, Pt 1

(1) the nature and seriousness of the offence (or default) and the probable method of dealing with the accused for it (though see 10–005 above);
(2) the character, antecedents, associations and communities of the accused;
(3) the accused's record as respects the fulfilment of his obligations under previous grants of bail in criminal proceedings; and
(4) except in the case of an accused whose case is adjourned for enquiries or a report, the strength of the evidence of his having committed the offence (or having defaulted),

as well as to any others which appear to be relevant.

If the judge is satisfied that there are substantial grounds for believing that the accused, if released on bail (whether subject to conditions or not), would commit an offence while on bail, the risk that he may do so by engaging in conduct that would, or would be likely to, cause physical or mental injury to any person other than the accused, bail should not be granted.

In making the decision, the considerations to which the judge must have regard, include, so far as is relevant, any misuse of controlled drugs by the accused (BA 1976, s.4(9); CJCSA 2000, s.58).

BAIL

Common sense approach

10–013   It is common sense that:

(1) the presumption of innocence which, is clearly a factor, is one which does not exclude competing factors which may be more formidable in the circumstances of the case;

(2) previous convictions *per se* should not be regarded as an automatic reason for refusing bail, but if there is a significance in the record and the nature of the charges, protection of the public needs to be considered;

(3) the allegation that at the time of the alleged commission of the offence the accused was in a position of trust to behave as a good citizen and not breach the law is an important factor; this may arise where, e.g. he is on bail in respect of another offence, subject to a community sentence, on licence or parole; or subject to a deferred sentence or a suspended sentence when, unless there are cogent reasons for deciding otherwise, bail ought to be refused;

(4) vague or unspecified arguments that the police are still, after the case has been sent to the Crown Court for trial, making enquiries are hardly a good ground for refusing bail, but it is otherwise where the prosecutor can prove that it is in the interests of the public administration of justice that the accused be detained while those enquiries are made.

Bail during the trial

10–014   Once a trial has begun, the further grant of bail, subject to BA 1976, (especially s.4 at 10–003), whether during the short adjournment or overnight, is in the discretion of the trial judge.

In particular:

(1) an accused who was on bail while on remand should not be refused overnight bail during the trial unless in the judge's opinion there are positive reasons to justify the refusal; such reasons are likely to be that:

   (a) a point has been reached where there is a real danger that the accused will abscond, either because the case is going badly for him, or for any other reason;

   (b) there is a real danger that he may interfere with witnesses or jurors;

(2) there is no universal rule of practice that bail should not be renewed once the summing-up has begun; each case must be decided in the light of its own circumstances and having regard to the judge's assessment from time to time of the risks involved;

(3) once the jury has returned a verdict a further renewal of bail should be decided in the light of the gravity of the offence and the likely sentence to be passed in all the circumstances of the case;

(4) it may be a proper exercise of that discretion to insist on the accused surrendering earlier and being released later than the times during which other persons are present, particularly in courts where no proper segregated refreshment facilities for jurors and witnesses are available (*Burgess v S of S* [2001] 1 W.L.R. 93).

Bail on remand for inquiries or reports

10–015 Where an offender's case is adjourned for enquiries or reports and the offence, or one of the offences, of which he is convicted in the proceedings is punishable with imprisonment, he need not be granted bail if it appears that it would be impracticable to complete the inquiries or make the report without keeping him in custody (e.g. the obvious case of the offender who has a history of non-co-operation).

BA 1976, ss.1(6),4(5), Sch.1, Pt 1

Prior to the passing of CJA 1991 it could be said that:

(1) where an offender had never been to prison before; or
(2) where the judge, in order to impose a custodial sentence, had to be satisfied, after considering reports, that a custodial sentence was the only proper disposal,

very good reasons were required to justify refusing bail pending reports being obtained (BA 1976, Sch.1, Pt II). Whether that principle can be maintained now that reports are mandatory, even in the case of an offender who must inevitably receive a custodial sentence for what is a grave, though an either-way, offence, is doubtful.

2. Conditions and requirements

Imposing conditions

10–016 Bail in criminal proceedings is either;

BA 1976, ss.1(6),4(5), Sch.1, Pt 1

(1) unconditional; or
(2) subject to conditions.

A condition must not be imposed unless it appears to the judge necessary to do so for the purpose of:

(a) preventing a person's:
   (i) failure to surrender,
   (ii) commission of offences while on bail, or interference with witnesses or obstruction of the course of justice;
(b) the accused's own protection, or, if he is a child or young person, for his own welfare or in his own interests; or
(c) an accused, in an appropriate case, making himself available for the purpose of enabling enquiries or a report to be made, and, in this case, only where it is necessary.

Surety, security and requirements

10–017 As a general rule no security for his surrender is to be taken from an accused, nor is he required to provide a surety, nor is any other requirement to be imposed upon him as a condition of bail.

Nevertheless, he may be required:

BA 1976, ss.3(3)-(6)

(1) provide a **surety o**r sureties or
(2) give **security**, which may be given by himself or on his behalf,

before being released, for his surrender (though neither of these provisions applies in the case of an accused granted bail on the expiry of a time limit under POA 1985, s.22); and he may also be required, before release on bail, or later, to comply with such **requirements** as appear to be necessary to secure the matters listed at (a) to (c) in 10–016 or before the time appointed for him to surrender to custody, he attends an interview with an authorised advocate or authorised litigator, as defined by CLSA 1990, s.119(1).

As to the nature of the security envisaged by the Act, see *R. (Stevens) v Truro MC* [2001] EWHC Admin 558 [2002] 1 W.L.R. 144. As to drug users, see 10–024, below; as to murder cases, see 10–023, below. As to procedure for "taking" the surety, see 10–020.

Suitability of surety

10–018 In considering the suitability of any surety required, the judge needs to have regard, amongst other things, to the surety's:

BA 1976, s.8(1) (2)

(1) financial resources;
(2) character and previous convictions, if any; and
(3) proximity, whether in point of kinship, place of residence or otherwise, to the person for whom he seeks to stand surety.

In considering "financial resources":

(a) it is the resources of the surety, rather than of the principal, that are relevant;
(b) in relation to the spouse of the principal, it is important to consider whether he/she has sufficient means to discharge the liability out of his/her separate property, and no account should be taken of any joint property or of the matrimonial home (*R. v Southampton JJ. Ex p. Green* [1975] 2 All E.R. 1073).

There will be cases where a token investigation into the resources of the proposed surety will suffice; in appropriate cases it will be sensible to insist on examining bank accounts, building society books and other documents. "Jewellery" will seldom fetch the value suggested, nor is there likely to be an opportunity to sell a house or other immovable property.

A surety is not to be equated with a guarantor; a surety is not discharged from his/her recognisance by operation of law where the judge changes other conditions of bail (*R. v Bow Street MC Ex p. Hall* (1986) 136 N.L.J. 1111).

Parent or guardian

10–019 Where the parent or guardian of a child or young person consents to be a surety for him, that person may be required to secure that the juvenile comply with any requirement of bail imposed upon him (under BA 1976, s.3(6) or (6A)), save that:

BA 1976, s.3(7)

(1) no requirement may be imposed on that person where it appears that the juvenile will attain the age of 17 before the time appointed for him to surrender to custody;
(2) the parent or guardian may not be required to secure compliance with a requirement to which he does not agree; and

BA 1976, s.8(3)

(3) the parent or guardian must not, in respect of the requirements to which he does agree, be bound in a sum greater than £50.

"Taking" the surety

10–020 The recognisance of any surety may be taken;

BA 1976, s.8(3)(4); R.19.22

(1) forthwith, after enquiry into his suitability, or
(2) subsequently.

Where the accused cannot be released because no surety, or no suitable surety, is available, the judge must fix the amount of the surety, which may then be taken subsequently, in accordance with BA 1976, ss.3(4), (5) and (6).

BA 1976, s.8(3)(6)

In such circumstances the recognisance may be entered into before an officer of the Crown Court; the governor or keeper of any prison or other place of detention in which the person granted bail is held, or those other persons specified in BA 1976, s.8(4).

In a case where the proposed surety resides in Scotland, the judge may, if satisfied of the suitability of the proposed surety, direct that arrangements be made for the surety to be entered into there, before a constable having charge at any police office or station there.

BA 1976, s.8(50)

Where a surety seeks to enter into a recognisance before one of those persons specified in BA 1976, s.8(4), and that person declines to take it because he is not satisfied of the surety's suitability, the proposed surety may apply:

(a) to the court which fixed the amount in which the surety was to be bound; or
(b) to a magistrates' court for the local justice area in which he resides,

for that court to take his recognisance, and that court will do so if satisfied of his suitability.

Where a recognisance is entered into before a court other than that which fixed the amount of the recognisance, the same consequences follow as if it had been entered into before the original court.

"Bail as before"

10–021 A judge granting "bail as before" needs to be careful with the procedure. Bail granted on a previous occasion ceases on the surrender of the accused, or offender, so that where the judge:

(1) contemplates granting bail on the same conditions as it was granted previously; and
(2) a surety was required on the previous occasion,

then, unless he proposes to remove the requirement of a surety he must consider the surety's position (*R. v Maidstone CC Ex p. Jodka* (1997) 161 J.P. 638) and see *R. v Dimond* [2000] 1 Cr. App. R. 21.

Other requirements of bail

10–022 There can be no closed list of requirements which may be imposed, but common requirements are those as to residence, including sleeping every night at a named address, reporting periodically at a named police station between specified hours on specified days, observing a curfew between specified hours, residing in a specified hostel,

Bail

surrender of passport and restrictions on entering or leaving certain defined areas, or approaching named persons.

Special conditions apply to bail pending appeal to the CACD (see APPEALS FROM THE CROWN COURT).

A requirement may be added that:

(1) before the time appointed for surrender to custody, the accused attend an interview with an advocate or authorised litigator as defined by CLSA 1990, s.119(1);   *BA 1986, s.3(6)(e)*

(2) where bail is granted pending reports, the offender attend on an officer of a probation provider or a medical practitioner, as directed;

(3) where one of the conditions imposed is residence in a bail or probation hostel, he comply with the rules of the hostel;   *BA 1976, 3(6ZA)*

(4) subject to s.3AA (see 10–025) in the case of a child or young person, s.3AB (see 10–026) in the case of other persons, and s.3AC (10–027) 3(6ZAA) in all cases, he be subject to electronic monitoring requirements for the purpose of securing his compliance with any other requirement imposed on him as a condition of bail;   *BA 1976, ss.3(6ZAB)*

(5) "not to drive", but before imposing such a requirement, the judge ought to consider whether it may have possibly unjust results (*R. v Kwame* (1975) 60 Cr. App. R. 64); there is power to impose an interim disqualification under RTA 1991, on remanding an accused (see DRIVING DISQUALIFICATIONS).

Where the judge imposes a requirement to be complied with before a person's release on bail, he may give directions as to the manner in which, and the person or persons before whom, the requirement is to be complied with.   *R.19.22(2)(3)*

If released on bail with a condition of residence, the accused must notify the prosecutor of the address at which he will reside, as soon as practicable: *R.19.25*

(a) after the institution of proceedings, unless already done; and
(b) after any change of address.

The court is entitled to expect the help of the prosecutor in assessing the suitability of any address proposed.

The duties of the Crown Court officer where the judge imposes as a condition of bail that the accused reside in accommodation provided for the purpose by or on behalf of a local authority, or receive bail support provided by or on behalf of such an authority, are set out in r. 19.27.

Murder cases; medical reports

10–023   Where the judge grants bail to a person accused of murder, he must, unless he considers that satisfactory reports on his mental condition have already been obtained, impose as a condition of bail, a requirement that the accused: *BA 1976, s.3(5A)(6B)*

(1) is examined by two medical practitioners for the purpose of enabling reports to be prepared; and
(2) attend such institution or place as the judge directs, and comply

with such other directions as may be given to him for the purpose by either of those medical practitioners.

Of those medical practitioners, at least one must be a practitioner approved for the purposes of MHA 1983, s.12 (see MENTALLY DISORDERED OFFENDERS). Failure to impose such a requirement renders the grant of bail a nullity (*R. v CCC Ex p. Porter* [1992] Crim. L.R. 121).

Drug users; assessment and follow-up

10–024   In relation to an accused to whom BA 1976, Sch.1 para.6B(1) (a) and (b) apply), (see 10–009 above) and the court has been notified that arrangements for conducting a relevant assessment, or, as the case may be, providing relevant follow-up, have been made for the local justice area in which it appears that the relevant accused would reside if granted bail (and the notice has not been withdrawn), then if:

BA 1976, s.3(6C)-(6E)

(1) after analysis, he has been offered a relevant assessment or, if a relevant assessment has been carried out, has had relevant follow-up proposed to him; and
(2) he has agreed to undergo the relevant assessment or, as the case may be, to participate in the relevant follow-up,

a condition **must** be imposed, if bail is granted, that he both undergo the relevant assessment and participate in any relevant follow-up proposed to him or, if a relevant assessment has been carried out, that he participate in the follow-up.

In this provision:

(a) "relevant assessment" means an assessment conducted by a suitably qualified person of whether that person is dependent upon or has a propensity to misuse, any specified Class A drugs;
(b) "relevant follow-up" means, in a case where the person who conducted the relevant assessment believes the accused to have such a dependency or propensity, such further assessment, and such assistance or treatment in connection with the dependency or propensity, as the person who conducted the relevant assessment (or conducts any later assessment) considers to be appropriate in his case.

In para.(a) above "Class A drug" and "misuse" have the same meaning as in MDA 1971, and "specified" (in relation to a Class A drug) has the same meaning as in CJCSA 2000, Pt 3, as to both of which, see 10–009, above.

Electronic monitoring requirement; (1) juveniles

10–025   An electronic monitoring requirement may not be imposed on a child or young person unless each of the following conditions is met, namely that:

BA 1976, s.3AA

(1) he has attained the age of 12 years;
(2) he is charged with, or has been convicted of:
    (a) a violent or sexual offence; or
    (b) an offence punishable in the case of an adult with imprisonment for 14 years or more; or

(c) one or more imprisonable offences which, together with any other imprisonable offences of which he has been convicted in any proceedings, amount, or would amount, if he were convicted of the offences with which he is charged, to a recent history of repeatedly committing imprisonable offences while remanded on bail or to local authority accommodation;

(3) the judge is satisfied that the necessary provision for dealing with the person concerned can be made under arrangements for the electronic monitoring of persons released on bail that are currently available in each relevant local justice area.

The requirement must include a provision making a person responsible for the monitoring.

The duties of the Crown Court officer in relation to the grant of bail on such a condition are set out in CPR 2011, r.19.26.

Electronic monitoring requirement: (2) other persons

10–026   An electronic monitoring requirement may not be imposed on a person who has attained the age of 17 unless each of the following conditions is met:

BA 1976, s.3AB

(1) the judge is satisfied that without the electronic monitoring requirement the person would not be granted bail.

(2) the judge is satisfied that the necessary provision for dealing with the person concerned can be made under arrangements for the electronic monitoring of persons released on bail that are currently available in each relevant local justice area.

(3) if the person is aged 17, a youth offending team has informed the judge that in its opinion the imposition of an electronic monitoring requirement will be suitable in his case.

Electronic monitoring requirement: (3) responsible monitor

10–027   Where an electronic monitoring requirement is imposed as a condition of bail, it must include provision for making a person responsible for the monitoring.

BA 1976, s.3AC;CJIA 2008, s.51, Sch.11, para.4

A person may not be made responsible for the electronic monitoring of a person on bail unless he is of a description specified in an order made by the Secretary of State.

For the purposes of ss.3AA or 3AB a local justice area is a "relevant area" in relation to a proposed electronic monitoring requirement if the court considers that it will not be practicable to secure the electronic monitoring in question unless electronic monitoring arrangements are available in that area.

3.   Applications to the Crown Court

Applications before trial

10–028   Where an application in relation to bail is made to the Crown Court otherwise than during the hearing of proceedings, notice in writing of the intention to make such application must be given (in the

R.19.18(1) (2) (4)

form set out in PD 2004, Annex D), at least 24 hours before the application is made:

(1) to the prosecutor; and
(2) if the prosecution is being carried on by the CPS, to the appropriate Crown Prosecutor; or
(3) if the application is to be made by the prosecutor or a constable under BA 1976, s.3(8), to the person to whom bail was granted,

and the applicant must give a copy of the notice to the Crown Court officer.

A person making such an application must inform the court of any earlier application to the High Court, or to the Crown Court, relating to bail in the course of the same proceedings (r.19.18(10)). R.19.18(3)

On receiving the notice, the prosecutor, or the appropriate Crown Prosecutor or, as the case may be, the person to whom bail was granted, must notify the Crown Court officer, and the applicant, either that

(a) he wishes to be represented at the hearing of the application, or that he does not oppose it; or
(b) give to the Crown Court officer, for the consideration of the court, a written statement of his reasons for opposing the application, sending a copy, at the same time, to the applicant.

Special provisions apply in the case of bail granted on the expiry of a custody time limit under POA 1985, s.22 (see CUSTODY TIME LIMITS).

As to methods of service, see r.4.7.

Assignment of Official Solicitor

10–029 It is unlikely that the need will arise, in the Crown Court at any rate, preceding the trial, for the Official Solicitor to be assigned to an applicant, since any representation order granted in the magistrates' court will cover such an application. R.19.8(6)(7)

Where, however, the necessity arises (as where the representation order has been revoked), a person in custody, or on bail, who desires to make an application in relation to bail and who has been unable to instruct a solicitor to apply on his behalf, may give notice in writing to the Crown Court of his desire to make an application requesting that the Official Solicitor act for him, and the court may, if it thinks fit:

(1) assign the Official Solicitor to act for him; and, if it does so;
(2) dispense with the requirements of giving notice in advance of the application; and
(3) deal with the application in a summary manner.

Chambers hearing versus open justice

10–030 Applications for bail otherwise than during the proceedings may be, and traditionally have been, heard in chambers. In *R. (on the application of Malik) v CCC [2006] EWHC 1539 (Admin); [2006] 4 All E.R. 1141*, the High Court said that;

(1) while there is nothing objectionable in listing such applications on the provisional assumption that the interests of justice will call for a closed hearing;

(2) if an application to sit in public is made the judge must approach it on the footing that it must be acceded to unless there is a sound reason for excluding the public;

(3) the judge has an obligation to consider whether it is necessary to depart from the ordinary rule of open justice in the interests of justice itself; that might be at the instance of a party or on his own initiative in the interests of third parties.

His decision is an exercise not of discretion, which implies a judicial choice between two or more equally proper courses, but of judgment as to whether a departure from the norm is justified. Any decision must start from the fundamental presumption in favour of open justice.

Hearing the applications

10–031 Wherever possible an application will be listed before the judge by whom the case is expected to be tried, or before the Resident Judge.

PD 2002, para.33.6 (not reproduced in PD 2004) provided that where a case:

(1) is to be tried by a High Court Judge who is not available, the application should be listed before any other High Court Judge then sitting at the Crown Court centre at which the application has arisen, before a Presiding Judge, before the Resident Judge for the centre, or, with the consent of a Presiding Judge, before a Circuit Judge nominated for the purpose;

(2) does not fall within (1) and the Circuit Judge or Recorder who is expected to try the case is not available, the matter must be referred to the Resident Judge, or, if he is not available, to any judge or Recorder then sitting at the centre. R.19.18(5)

Except where an application is made by the prosecutor or a constable under BA 1976, s.3(8), an applicant is not entitled to be present on the hearing of the application unless the judge gives leave (r.19.18(5)).

The jurisdiction to grant bail is that of the court, not the individual judges of the court; applications are not to be made, simultaneously or immediately consecutively, to more than one judge of the court (*R. v Reading CC Ex p. Malik* (1981) 72 Cr. App. R. 146).

Reconsideration; subsequent applications

10–032 If a judge does not grant bail to an applicant, it is his duty to consider, at each subsequent hearing, while a person to whom the presumption under BA 1976, s.4 (see 10–003) applies and remains in custody, whether he ought to be granted bail: BA 1976, Sch.1, Pt.IIA

(1) at the first hearing after that at which the judge decided not to grant bail, the applicant may support his application with any argument as to fact or law which he desires, whether or not he has advanced that argument previously;

(2) at subsequent hearings the judge need not hear arguments as to fact or law which he has heard previously.

A decision based on BA 1976, Sch.1, para.5 (not practicable to have sufficient information) is not a decision for these purposes (*R. v Calder JJ. Ex p. Kennedy* (1992) 156 J.P. 716).

Where the judge, in reconsidering bail, refuses to withhold bail after hearing representations from the prosecution in favour of withholding bail, he must give reasons for refusing to withhold bail, and include a note of those reasons in the record of his decision, providing a copy to the prosecution if requested.

4. Record, variation and breach

Reasons and record; notification of recognisance, etc.
10–033 A judge:

BA 1976, ss.5(3)-(5)

(1) granting or withholding bail; or
(2) varying conditions,

in relation to a person to whom the right to bail before conviction (10–003) applies, must, with a view to enabling that person to consider applying to another court, give his reasons, though he need not do so, where that person is represented by a solicitor or advocate , unless asked to do so.

BA 1976, s.5(1)

His reasons will be entered on the court file and a copy of the note will be given to the person in relation to whom the decision was taken, unless his representative does not ask for it.

Where a recognisance is entered into, or a requirement is complied with, before any person, that recognisance, or a statement of the requirement, must be transmitted forthwith to the Crown Court officer, a copy being sent at the same time to the governor or keeper of any prison or place of detention in which the person named is detained, unless, of course, the recognisance was entered into, or the requirement was complied with, before that person.

R,19.22(4)

Variation of conditions
10–034 On an application by, or on behalf of, a person to whom bail was granted, or by the prosecutor or a constable, a judge of the Crown Court may:

BA 1976, s.5(10)

(1) if that court has granted bail; or
(2) a magistrates' court has committed a person to it for trial or to be sentenced or otherwise to be dealt with, or has sent that person for trial under CDA 1998, s.51 (see *R. v Lincoln MC Ex p. Mawer* (1996) 160 J.P. 219),

vary any conditions of bail or impose conditions in respect of bail granted unconditionally.

Breach of condition or requirement
10–035 A person arrested under BA 1976, s.7(2) as being likely to abscond or to breach his conditions, or as having breached a condition

of his bail (even where that bail was granted by the Crown Court) must be brought before a justice of the peace for the local justice area in which he is arrested (and not before the Crown Court). That justice may remand him, or commit him to custody, or grant him bail on the same or different conditions. He has no power to send him to the Crown Court to be dealt with for the breach. See *Re Teesside MC Ex p. Elliott, The Times*, February 20, 2000.

A recorder of the Crown Court is not a justice for this purpose (*Re Marshall* [1994] Crim. L.R. 915).

Unlike failure to surrender, which is a contempt of court and may be dealt with as such, breach of a bail condition is not, and should be dealt with under BA 1976 (*R. v Ashley* [2003] EWCA Crim 2571; [2004] 1 Cr App. R 23).

"Withdrawal" of surety

10–036   A surety, believing that his principal is about to abscond or has already absconded, has no right to "withdraw" his recognisance, unless the principal is before the court. He is, however, entitled to make an application in writing at a police station, stating that the principal is unlikely to surrender, which empowers an officer to arrest the accused without warrant (*R. v Wood Green CC Ex p. Howe* (1991) 93 Cr. App. R. 213).

5.   Failure to appear; Absconding

Effect of failure to surrender

10–037   A person granted bail in criminal proceedings has a duty to surrender himself into the custody of the appropriate court at the time and place for the time being appointed for him to do so.   BA 1976, ss.2(2),3(1)(2), 6(1)

The failure of an accused to comply with the terms of his bail by not surrendering may undermine the administration of justice; it may disrupt proceedings. The resulting delays impact on victims, witnesses and other court users and also waste costs. Failure to surrender affects not only the case with which the accused is concerned, but also the courts' ability to administer justice more generally by damaging the confidence of victims, witnesses and the public in the effectiveness of the court system and the judiciary.

It is most important, therefore, that accused persons who are granted bail appreciate the significance of the obligation to surrender to custody in accordance with the terms of their bail and that judges take appropriate action if they fail to do so.

The judge may consider at least three courses of action:

(1) imposing a penalty for the failure to surrender;
(2) revoking bail or imposing more stringent bail conditions; and
(3) conducting the trial in the absence of the accused (see ABSENT AND UNREPRESENTED ACCUSED).

In the case of offences which cannot, or are unlikely to result in a custodial sentence, trial in the absence of the accused may be a pragmatic sensible response to the situation (see ABSENT AND UNREPRESENTED ACCUSED). A penalty may also be imposed for the bail offence.

Absconding; a bail offence

10–038   A person granted bail in criminal proceedings, who: BA 1976, s.6(1) (2) (5) (7)

(1) fails, without reasonable cause, to surrender to the appropriate court at the time and place for the time being appointed for him to do so; or

(2) having reasonable cause for such failure he has failed to surrender, and then fails to surrender to custody at the appointed place as soon after the appointed time as is reasonably practicable,

commits an offence, which in the Crown Court is punishable as if it were a criminal contempt of court, and the offender is liable to imprisonment for up to 12 months or to a fine or both (see also *R. v Reader* (1987) 84 Cr. App. R. 294).

An offender who fails to appear in answer to a summons issued as a result of an alleged failure to comply with a community order, but is not otherwise on bail, does not commit an offence under s.6 (*R. v Noble* [2008] EWCA Crim 1473; *The Times*, 2008, July 21).

Breach of bail by failing to surrender to the magistrates' court is not indictable; it may be dealt with in the Crown Court only where the magistrates commit the offender for sentence under BA 1976, s.6(6) (see COMMITTALS FOR SENTENCE).

What amounts to "surrender"

10–039   "Court" in this context includes an official of the court where the accused has followed the procedure he is directed to follow (*DPP v Richards* (1989) 88 Cr. App. R. 97). A person "surrenders" to custody when he complies with the procedure of the court at which he is due to appear, directing him to report to a particular office or particular official; it is not sufficient for him simply to attend the courthouse; he must report and comply with the procedure and thereafter, though not physically restrained, he is in the custody of the court and should be instructed not to leave the building without consent (*DPP v Richards* above).

Where an accused is arraigned he surrenders to custody if he has not done so at an earlier stage (*R. v CCC Ex p. Guney* [1996] 2 Cr. App. R. 352).

Absconding as a contempt of court

10–040   The fact that such an offence is to be treated as if it were a criminal contempt does not alter the fact that it is an offence, and therefore:

(1) a person convicted in the magistrates' court of absconding and committed under BA 1976, s.6(6) to the Crown Court for sentence is liable to the same penalties;

(2) an offender must be dealt with in respect of any suspended sentence on the ordinary principles; and

(3) as in the case of any other offence, the *de minimis* principle may be applied.

An accused who commits a bail offence, commits an offence that stands apart from the proceedings in respect of which bail was granted. The seriousness of the offence may be reflected by an appropriate penalty being imposed for the bail offence. Thus:

(a) the fact that the accused is acquitted of the substantive offence for which he is being tried or dealt with or the indictment is not proceeded with does not preclude the court, in a proper case, from imposing an immediate custodial sentence for the offence of absconding (*R. v Kohli* (1983) 5 Cr. App. R.(S.)175, *R. v Cockburn-Smith* [2009] 2 Cr. App. R.(S.) 20);

(b) whilst the seriousness of the substantive offence does not of itself aggravate or mitigate the seriousness of the bail offence, its nature may be relevant in assessing the likelihood of harm caused by the failure to surrender;

(c) acquittal of the substantive offence does not mitigate the bail offence;

(d) the fact that a fine is imposed on the substantive offence does not prevent a custodial sentence being imposed on the bail offence (*R. v Uddin* (1992) 13 Cr. App. R.(S.) 114).

Dealing with the offence

10–041 The judge dealing with a bail offence, should do so as soon as is practicable, taking into account:

(1) when the proceedings in respect of which bail was granted are expected to conclude;

(2) the seriousness of the offence for which the accused is already being prosecuted;

(3) the type of penalty that might be imposed for the bail offence and the original offence; as well as

(4) any other relevant circumstances.

At whatever stage the bail offence is dealt with, it should be noted that:

(a) the fact that it has proved possible to conclude the substantive proceedings in the absence of the accused has no bearing on his culpability for the bail offence, but may be relevant to the assessment of the harm caused;

(b) fleeing the jurisdiction is to be regarded as an aggravating feature (*R. v CC* [2011] EWCA Crim 524);

(c) where, at the same time, determinate custodial sentences are imposed, both for the substantive offence and for the bail offence, the normal approach is for the sentences to be consecutive.

SGC has issued a definitive guideline on dealing with adults failing to surrender to bail (BA 1976, ss.6(1) and (2), which seeks to give guidance on the assessment of culpability, and the sentencing range.

The fact that it has proved possible to conclude proceedings in the absence of the accused has no bearing on his culpability for the bail offence, but may be relevant to the assessment of harm caused.

Execution of warrant; venue

10–042 Where a person granted bail by a court subsequently fails to surrender to custody, he should normally, on arrest, be brought as soon as appropriate before the court at which the proceedings in respect of which bail was granted are to be heard.

Where he has committed another offence outside the jurisdiction of the bail court, the bail offence should, where practicable, be dealt with by the new court at the same time as the new offence. If impracticable, the accused may, if this is appropriate, be released formally on bail by the new court so that the warrant may be executed for his attendance before the first court in respect of the substantive and the bail offences.

Institution of proceedings

10–043 It is neither necessary nor desirable that a formal charge or indictment should be laid in order to commence proceedings for a bail offence. The judge should initiate the proceedings his own motion or he may be invited to do so by the prosecutor, where the latter considers proceedings are appropriate.

As to procedure:

(1) where the judge is invited to take proceedings by the prosecutor, the prosecutor will conduct the proceedings, and, if the matter is contested, will call the evidence; absconding is a criminal charge which must be proved following the correct procedure (*R. v Davies* (1986) 8 Cr. App. R.(S.) 97; *R. v Woods* (1989) 11 Cr. App. R.(S.) 551; *R. v O'Boyle* (1991) Cr. App. R. 202).
(2) where the judge initiates proceedings without such an invitation, the same role may be played by the prosecutor at the request of the judge, where this is practicable;
(3) the burden of proof is on the accused to prove that he had reasonable cause for his failure to surrender (BA 1976, s.6(3));
(4) the judge must give the accused the opportunity to explain himself; and invite submissions from the advocates; and *BA 1976, s.6(8)*
(5) the judge must make a finding of guilt or otherwise as the case may be.

A document purporting to be a copy of the prescribed record which relates to the time and place appointed for the accused to surrender to custody, and duly certified to be a true copy, is evidence of the time and place appointed for that person to surrender.

6.   Estreatment and forfeiture

Estreatment of recognisance

10–044 Where it appears to a judge of the Crown Court that a default *R.19.23,24*
has been made in performing the conditions of a surety's recognisance, then where:

(1) the recognisance was conditioned for the appearance of the accused at the Crown Court, and the accused fails to appear in accordance with the condition, the judge *must* declare the recognisance to be estreated; and

    (2) the default is other than by failing to appear at the Crown Court in accordance with such condition, the judge *may* order the recognisance to be estreated.

In either case, before the recognisance is actually estreated or forfeited, a notice under r.19.23(2) or a summons under r.19.24(2) must be given to the person by whom the recognisance was entered into, to enable him to show cause why it should not be estreated.

At the time specified in the summons, the judge may proceed in the absence of the person by whom the recognisance was entered into, if satisfied that the summons has been served.

Approach to estreatment

10–045   Where an accused for whose attendance a person has stood surety fails to appear:

    (1) the full recognisance of the surety should be forfeited unless it appears fair and just that a lesser sum should be forfeited or none at all;

    (2) the burden of satisfying the judge that the full sum should not be forfeited rests on the surety and is a heavy one; it is for him to lay before the court the evidence of want of culpability and of means on which he relies;

    (3) where a surety is unrepresented the judge should assist him by explaining the principles in ordinary language, and giving him an opportunity to call evidence and advance argument in relation to them;

    (4) lack of culpability on the surety's part, or even a commendable diligence, is not of itself a reason for reducing or setting aside the obligation into which he has freely entered, but the judge has a broad discretion as to whether and to what extent it would be fair to remit some or all of the recognisance The basis of forfeiture is not culpability; it is non-attendance.

(*R. v Uxbridge Justices Ex p. Heward-Mills* [1983] 1 All E.R. 530; *R. v Maidstone CC Ex p. Lever* [1996] 1 Cr App R 524).

What is reasonable in any given case depends on the circumstances of that case (*R. v York Crown Court Ex p. Coleman* (1988) 86 Cr. App. R. 151). The judge should, look at the conduct of the surety to see whether there are mitigating circumstances (*R. v ILCC Ex p. Springall* (1987) 85 Cr. App. R. 214; *R. v Reading CC Ex p. Bello* (1991) 92 Cr App R 303; *R. v Wood Green CC Ex p. Howe* (1991) 93 Cr. App. R. 213).

Where a wife's recognisance is estreated, the proceeds should come out of her own property and not out of her husband's, nor out of their joint property or the matrimonial home (*R. v Southampton JJ. Ex p. Green* [1975] 2 All E.R. 1073).

Enforcement of estreated recognisances

10–046   A judge estreating a surety's recognisance:

PCC(S)A 2000 s.139(2)

    (1) *must* make an order fixing a term of imprisonment in default if any sum which the surety is liable to pay is not duly paid or recovered; in which case:

(a) the maximum default term is that set out in the table applicable to fines (see FINES AND ENFORCEMENT); and

(b) the restrictions as to immediate imprisonment or detention apply as they do in the case of a fine (see FINES AND ENFORCEMENT); CJA 2003, s.16(3)-(6)

(2) *may* make an order: PCC(S)A 2000, ss.139(1), R.14,2

(a) in the case of a person before the court, that he be searched, and any money found on him be applied, unless otherwise directed, to the payment of the recognisance;

(b) allowing time for payment of the amount due under the recognisance;

(c) directing payment of the amount by instalments of such amounts and on such dates as may be specified in the order; BA 1976, s.5(7)(8); R.19. 21(5)

(d) discharging the recognisance or reducing the amount thereunder.

Forfeiture of security (s.3(5))
10–047   Where;

(1) an accused has given security (under BA 1976, s.3(5)), before his release on bail; and BA 1976, s.5(8A)(9)

(2) the judge is satisfied that he has failed to surrender to custody, then, unless it appears that he had reasonable cause for failure, the judge may order the forfeiture of the security, or such amount less than the its full value as he thinks fit.

Such order, unless previously revoked, takes effect at the end of 21 days beginning with the day on which it is made. If the security consists of money it is accounted for and paid in the same way as a fine imposed by the Crown Court. If it does not, it is enforced by such magistrates' court as is specified in the order. BA 1976, s.5(8B)(8C)(9A)

The Crown Court officer will give notice of the decision to the person before whom security was given.

If the judge is subsequently satisfied on an application made by or on behalf of the person who gave security that he did, after all, have reasonable cause for his failure to surrender, he may:

(a) remit the forfeiture; or

(b) declare that the forfeiture extend to such an amount less than the full value as he sees fit to order.

An order for remission may be made before or after the original order has taken effect, but an application is not to be entertained unless the judge is satisfied that the prosecutor was given reasonable notice of the applicant's intention to make it.

Where an order for remission is made after the order for forfeiture has taken effect, any balance due to the person concerned will be repaid.

Where security is provided to the accused by a third person, that person has no right to demand its return where the accused fails to appear (*R. (Stevens) v Truro MC* [2001] EWHC (Admin) 558; [2002] 1 W.L.R.144).

7. Bail appeals from magistrates' courts

Appeal by accused

10–048 Apart from its jurisdiction to grant bail to an accused in its custody, the Crown Court may entertain an appeal by the person concerned in relation to certain specified situations where a case is still proceeding in the magistrates court:, as where the magistrates' court: *(BA 1976, s.5(6A))*

(1) adjourns a case under :
  (a) MCA 1980, s.10;
  (b) MCA 1980, s.17C (intention as to plea);
  (c) MCA 1980, s.18 (initial procedure on information against an adult for an offence triable either way);
  (d) MCA 1980, s.24C (intention to plead by child or young person);
  (e) CDA 1998, s.52(5) (cases sent for trial s.51); or
  (f) PCC(S)A 2000, s.11 (remand for medical examination); and
(2) the magistrates' court:
  (a) refuses to grant bail; or
  (b) refuses to entertain an application by the accused for a rehearing; or
  (c) grants bail subject to the specified conditions set out below.

In such circumstances the Crown Court must have a certificate in the prescribed form (MC(F)R 1981, Form 151A), issued by the magistrates;' court and stating that it has heard full argument on the application before refusing it. *(BA 1976, s.5(6A))*

Bail granted with conditions

10–049 Where the magistrates' court grants bail to a person on adjourning the proceedings in one of the situations set out in 10–048 above, the person concerned may appeal against any requirement:

(1) that he resides away from a particular place or area;
(2) that he resides at a particular place other than a bail hostel;
(3) for the provision of a surety or sureties or the giving of security;
(4) that he remains indoors between certain hours; or
(5) imposed under BA 1976, s.3(6ZAA) (requirements with respect to electronic monitoring); or
(6) that he make no contact with another person, provided that such appeal may not be brought unless the application to the magistrates' court under:
  (a) BA 1976, s.3(8)(a); or
  (b) BA 1976, s.3(8)(b) (application by constable or prosecutor), or
  (c) BA 1976, s.5B(1) (application by prosecutor), was made and determined before the appeal was brought.

The judge, under this provision, may vary the conditions of bail, and where he determines such an appeal the person concerned may not bring a further appeal under the section in respect of the conditions of bail, unless an application or a further application to the magistrates' court under BA 1976, s.3(8)(a) is made and determined after the appeal. *(CJA 2003, s.16(7)(8))*

Appeal by prosecutor

10–050 Where a magistrates' court grants bail to a person who is charged with, or convicted of, an offence punishable by imprisonment, the prosecution, in a case conducted:

B(A)A 1993, s.1(1)(2)(10)

(1) by or on behalf of the DPP; or

(2) by or on behalf of a prescribed person (see S.I. 1994/1438, as amended by S.I. 2001/1149, and S.I. 2005/1129), may appeal to a judge of the Crown Court against the granting of bail, provided that such an appeal lies only where:

    (a) in relation to offences punishable with less than a term of five years or more, the case was committed, transferred or sent, or a voluntary bill was preferred after April 4, 2005 (SI 2005/ 950);

    (b) the prosecution made representations that bail should not be granted; and

    (c) such representations were made before it was granted.

As far as the prosecutor is concerned, oral notice of appeal must be given to the magistrates' court and to the person concerned at the conclusion of the proceedings in which such bail was granted, and before the release of the person concerned. The magistrates will remand the person concerned in custody (or in local authority accommodation in the case of a juvenile) until the appeal is determined or otherwise disposed of.

B(A)A 1993, s.1(4) (5)(7) (10)(b); R.19. 16(1)-(9)

Oral notice must be followed by written notice within two hours of the conclusion of the proceedings, otherwise the appeal will be deemed to have been disposed of if, having given oral notice of appeal, the prosecutor fails to serve written notice within the appropriate period, the person concerned will be released.

Where written notice of appeal is served on the magistrates' court, the Crown Court officer will, as soon as is practicable, be provided with a copy, the notes of argument made under the Rules, and a note of the date or dates when the person concerned is next due to appear in the magistrates' court.

R.19.6(1)

Procedure in the Crown Court:

10–051 The written notice of appeal required by B(A)A 1993, s.1(5) must be;

(1) in the form set out in PD 2004, Annex D; and

R.19.17

(2) served on the magistrates' court officer, and the person concerned (within the meaning of B(A)A 1993, s.1).

As to methods of service, see r.4.7 and SERVICE OF DOCUMENTS.

The Crown Court officer will enter the appeal and give notice of the time and place of the hearing to the prosecutor, the person concerned or his legal representative and the magistrates' court officer.

The person concerned is entitled to be present at the hearing of the appeal (he is treated as so where he attends by a live link: CDA 1998, ss.57A, 57B).

See also *Allen v UK* [2011] Crim L.R, 147. Where a person concerned has not been able to instruct a solicitor to represent him at the appeal:

(a) he may give notice to the Crown Court requesting that the Official Solicitor represent him at the appeal; and

(b) the court may, if it thinks fit, assign the Official Solicitor to act for him.

At any time after the service of written notice of appeal, the prosecution may abandon the appeal by giving notice in writing in the form set out in PD 2004, Annex D and served on the person concerned or his legal representative, the magistrates' court officer and the Crown Court officer.

The appeal hearing must begin within 48 hours, excluding weekends and public holidays (construed as "two working days", see *R. v Middlesex Guildhall Crown Court Ex p. Okoli* [2001] 1 Cr. App. R. 1; see also *R. (Jeffrey) v Warwick CC* [2003] Crim. L.R. 190).

Under B(A)A 1993, s.1, the appellate proceedings are expressly stated to be a rehearing, the judge having power to remand in custody or to release on bail on such conditions as he thinks fit. If the judge upholds the prosecutor's appeal, he must fix a date on which the accused is to appear before the magistrates in accordance with the magistrates' powers under MCA 1980, ss.128, 128A and 129 (as amended by CJA 2003, ss.41, 304, 337, Sch.3, para.51(7), Sch.37, Pt 4) otherwise the accused will be unlawfully detained once the eight days of the remand have expired (*Szakal Re* [2001] 1 Cr. App. R. 248; *Remice v Belmarsh Prison Governor* [2007] Crim. L.R. 796).

Administrative provisions; record

10–052 Any record required by BA 1976, s.5 (together with any note R.19.17(8) of reasons required by s.5(4) to be included) is made by way of an entry in the file relating to the case in question and the record will include the following particulars, namely:

(1) the effect of the decision;

(2) a statement of any condition imposed in respect of bail, indicating whether it is to be complied with before or after release on bail; and

(3) where bail is withheld, a statement of the relevant exception to the right to bail (as provided in Sch.1 to the 1976 Act) on which the decision is based.

The Crown Court officer will, as soon as practicable after the hearing of the appeal, give notice of the decision and of the matters required by the preceding paragraph to be recorded to the person concerned or his legal representative, the prosecutor, the police, the magistrates' officer and the governor of the prison or person responsible for the establishment where the person concerned is being held.

In addition to the methods of service permitted by r.4.3 (see SERVICE OF DOCUMENTS), the notices required by r.19.17(3), (5), (7) and (9) may be sent by way of facsimile transmission and the notice required by r.19.17(3) may be given by telephone.

11. BIND OVER

General
11–001   A "bind over" requires a person to consent to enter into a recognisance, and, where appropriate, to provide a surety, for refraining from a specified conduct or activity, for a specified period.

That conduct or activity must be spelled out in the order; it is no longer appropriate to require recognisances for "good behaviour" or "to keep the peace" (PD 2004, III.31 (inserted by Amendment No. 15 in the light of the judgments of the ECHR in *Steel v United Kingdom* (1999) 28 E.H.R.R. 603, [1998] Crim. L.R. 893 and *Hashman v United Kingdom* (2000) 30 EHRR 241 [2000] Crim. L.R. 185)).

The court's jurisdiction may be exercised over:

(1) an offender, at common law or under statute, principally JPA 1968;
(2) any other person under JPA 1968;
(3) the parent or guardian of a convicted juvenile, under PCC(S)A 2000, s.150(1)(2).

Since there are technical distinctions applicable to the form of each order, it is important in making an order to specify which jurisdiction is being exercised (thus avoiding the difficulties arising in *R. v Finch* (1962) 41 Cr. App. R. 58 and *R. v Ayu* (1959) 43 Cr. App. R. 31).

As to binding over the parents or guardians of juveniles, see 11–010, below.

Note that:

(a) an offender must consent to the making of an order, and that consent is not vitiated by the fact that a custodial sentence is the only realistic alternative (*R. v Williams* (1982) 75 Cr. App. R. 378);
(b) the court cannot force a person to enter into recognisances, or treat him as bound where he declines to be; the remedy, where such person is over the age of 18 to commit him to prison until he agrees (*Veater v Glennon* (1981) 72 Cr. App. R. 331); but.
(c) the court is powerless in respect of a person under 18 (*Veater v Glennon* (above); *Rowley v Oxford* (1985) 81 Cr. App. R. 246; *Surrey Chief Constable v Ridley* [1985] Crim. L.R. 725; unless that person consents (*Conlan v Oxford* (1984) 79 Cr. App. R. 157).

A.   Common law bind over; respited judgment

11–002   Where judgment is pending, an appeal is pending, or in any other case where the circumstances make it expedient in the interests of justice, an offender may be required:

BIND OVER

(1) to enter into recognisances, with or without sureties, in a specific amount or amounts;

(2) to come up for judgment within a reasonable, specified period, if called upon to do so; and

(3) meanwhile to comply with certain stated conditions,

SCA 1981, s.79(2)(b); PD 2004, III. 31.16

and the order needs to be carefully couched in these very terms.

Distinctive features

11–003 A common law bind over differs from one under JPA 1968 in that:

(1) a common law bind over ranks as a penalty, not as an ancillary order, and cannot therefore be combined with any other penalty such as fine or imprisonment (*R. v Ayu* (1959) 43 Cr. App. R. 31);

(2) an offender called upon to come up for judgment is liable to be sentenced for the original offence, not merely to estreatment of recognisances;

(3) a common law bind over ranks as a conviction, and even where no sentence is subsequently passed for the offence, appeal lies to the Court of Appeal (*R. v Abrahams* (1952) 36 Cr. App. R. 147; *R. v Williams* (1982) 75 Cr. App. R. 378).

Condition to leave jurisdiction

11–004 It may be a condition of a common law bind over (but not of an order under JPA 1968), provided the offender consents, that he leave the jurisdiction and not return for a specified period. The CACD has said that the power should be used very sparingly. Thus, in the following cases, the conditions listed below were imposed:

(1) *R. v Ayu* (above) "to return to Nigeria forthwith and not to return to Great Britain during the period of the recognisance";

(2) *R. v Flaherty* [1958] Crim. L.R. 556 "to return to Ireland and not land again in this country for at least three years";

(3) *R. v Hodges* (1967) 51 Cr. App. R. 361 to attend a Carmelite organisation in the Republic of Ireland, which was prepared to accept the offender, and "not to return to England for ten years".

Only in exceptional circumstances should it be used to return an offender to a country of which he is not a citizen, and in which he does not habitually reside (*R. v Williams* (1982) 75 Cr. App. R. 378).

Appearing for judgment

11–005 An offender may be called upon to come up for judgment for something less than the commission of a further offence (*R. v McGarry* (1945) 30 Cr. App. R. 187). When he appears:

(1) the facts of any breach must be proved as if they were allegations of an offence;

(2) he must be given an opportunity to give evidence or call witnesses;

(3) if the matter of complaint is his failure to leave the country, the judge should enquire into whether that failure was a deliberate one (*R. v Philbert* [1973] Crim. L.R. 129);

(4) he may be dealt with for the original offence; the judge is not limited to estreating any recognisances.

B.   Justices of the Peace Act 1968, s.l

General

11–006   A bind over under the Act is not dependent on conviction and, in a proper case, an acquitted accused may be bound over (*R. v ILCC Ex p. Benjamin* (1987) 85 Cr. App. R. 267), as where no evidence is offered.

JPA 1968, s.l(7); PD 2004, III. 31.

Jurisdiction extends beyond the offender, to any person who, or whose case, is before the court, requiring that person:

(1) to enter into recognisances, with or without sureties, in a specific sum;
(2) to refrain from some specific conduct or activity, for a specified period, which should not generally exceed 12 months; or
(3) in the case of an adult to go to prison if he does not comply.

PD 2004, III.31.2, 3, 4

For the distinctions between such a bind over and one at common law, see 11–001, above.

Before imposing a bind over, the judge:

(a) must be satisfied that a breach of the peace involving violence or an imminent threat of violence has occurred, or that there is a real risk of violence in the future;
(b) should identify the specific conduct or activity from which the individual must refrain, and the details of that conduct or those activities should be specified in a written order served on the relevant parties; and
(c) should state his reasons for:
  (i) the making of the order,
  (ii) its length, and
  (iii) the amount of the recognisance.

The length of the order should be proportionate lo the harm sought to be avoided and should not generally exceed 12 months.

The violence referred to in (a) may be perpetrated by the individual who will be subject to the order or by a third party as a natural consequence of that individual's conduct.

"Persons before the court"

11–007   RHOA 1974, s.7(5) excludes from a person's antecedents any order of the court "with respect to any person otherwise than on conviction". A "person before the court":

(1) includes a witness who gives evidence, whether for the Crown or for the accused (*Sheldon v Bromfield* [1964] 2 All E.R. 131);
(2) does not include a person who is not a party and is not called as a witness (*R. v Swindon CC Ex p. Singh* (1984) 79 Cr. App. R. 137; *R. v Kingston CC Ex p. Guarino* [1986] Crim. L.R. 325; *R. v Lincoln CC Ex p. Jones, The Times*, June 16, 1989).

PD 2004, III.31.5

BIND OVER

Evidence and procedure; burden of proof

11–008 Where the judge considers making an order, he should, in effect, apply the procedure prescribed for a magistrates' court under MCA 1980, ss.51 to 57, which include a requirement (s.53) to hear evidence and representations before making an order.

PD 2004, III.31.8, 10

Thus, the judge should (even where there is an admission sufficient to found an order, and the person concerned consents to its being made):

(1) give:
    (a) the person who would be the subject of the order; and
    (b) the prosecutor, the opportunity to make representations, both as to the making of the order and as to its terms; and
(2) hear any admissible evidence the parties may wish to call (and which has not already been heard in the proceedings),

so as to satisfy himself that an order is appropriate in all the circumstances, and to be clear as to its terms.

The judge should be satisfied:

(a) of the matters complained of, the burden of proof being on the prosecutor; and
(b) on the merits of the case, that an order is appropriate

and should announce his decision before considering the amount of the recognisance.

PD 2004, III.31.11

The person made subject to the order should be told that he has a right of appeal

In fixing the amount of any recognisance, the judge should have regard to the person's financial resources and should hear representations either from him or his legal representatives, as to them.

Enforcement and estreatment

11–009 If there is any possibility that a person will refuse to enter into a recognisance;

PD 2004, III.31.9, 12, 13, 14

(1) the judge should consider whether there are any appropriate alternatives to a binding over order (for example, continuing with the prosecution);
(2) where there are no appropriate alternatives and the person concerned continues to refuse to enter into the recognisance, the judge may use his common law power to commit that person to custody.

A recognisance may be enforced only by estreatment (see BAIL), and committal to prison in default of payment. The judge must make such enquiries as are required before estreating the recognisance of a surety for bail *(R. v Marlow JJ Ex p. O'Sullivan* (1984) 78 Cr. App. R. 13).

Where there is an allegation of a breach of recognisance:

(a) the judge should be satisfied beyond a reasonable doubt that a breach has occurred before making an order for estreatment, the burden of proof resting on the prosecutor;
(b) before such person is committed to custody, he must be given the opportunity to consult a legal representative and be

represented in the proceedings if he so wishes; public funding should generally be granted to cover such representation; and.

(c) in the event that the person does not take the opportunity to seek legal advice, the judge must give him a final opportunity to comply with the request and must explain the consequences of a failure to do so.

C.   Parents and guardians of juvenile offenders

11–010   Where a person under 18 is convicted of an offence, the judge:

PCC(S)A 2000, ss.150(1), (2); PD 2004, III.31.17

(1) *may*; and
(2) where the offender is under 16 when sentenced, *must*, if satisfied having regard to the circumstances of the case that it would be desirable in the interest of preventing the commission by him of further offences,

with the consent of that person, order the parent or guardian to enter into a recognisance to take proper care of him and exercise proper control over him, specifying the actions which the parent or guardian is to take and

(a) if the parent or guardian refuses consent, and the judge considers that refusal unreasonable, order that person to pay a fine not exceeding £1,000; and
(b) where the judge has passed on the offender a sentence which consists of or includes a youth rehabilitation order, he may include in the recognisance a provision that the parent or guardian ensure that the offender complies with the requirements of the sentence.

Where he does not exercise his duty under (2) above, the judge must state in open court that he is not satisfied as mentioned in that paragraph, and why.

PCC(S)A 2000, ss.150(3), (7)

Amount and period of recognisances
11–011   In fixing the amount of a recognisance under these provisions, the court must take into account, among other things, the means of the parent or guardian so far as they appear or are known to him, and an order shall not require him to enter into a recognisance:

(1) for an amount exceeding £1,000; or
(2) for a period exceeding three years or where the young person will attain the age of 18 in a shorter period, for a period exceeding that shorter period.

PCC(S)A 2000, ss.150(9), (10)

A parent or guardian may appeal to the CACD against the making of such an order, as if he had been convicted on indictment and the order were a sentence passed on his conviction. The court may vary or revoke an order made by it if, on the application of the parent or guardian, it appears, having regard to any change in circumstances since the order was made, to be in the interests of justice to do so.

Bind Over

Notes

12. BREACH, AMENDMENT AND REVOCATION OF ORDERS

Quick guide

12–001 A judge of the Crown Court may be required to deal with the breach of sentencing orders made by the Crown Court, or, in certain circumstances, on appeal, by the magistrates' courts. As far as amendment and revocation of community orders and requirements is concerned, the judge will need, in making any order to direct expressly that amendment, etc. be left to the appropriate magistrates' court; if he does not, amendments, etc. will be referred to the Crown Court.

There is no uniform code for dealing with these matters, and it is necessary to consider each separately.

A. Deferred sentences; CJA 2003, Sch.23

Breach of undertaking(s)

12–002 A court which has deferred passing sentence on an offender under PCC(S)A 2000, s.1 (see DEFERRING SENTENCE) may, whether the offence for which sentence was deferred was committed before or after April 4, 2005, deal with him before the end of the period of deferment where:

> PCC(S)A 2000, s.1B

(1) sentence was deferred;
(2) the offender undertook to comply with one or more requirements imposed under s.1(3)(b) in connection with the deferment; and
(3) a supervisor in relation to the offender has reported to the court that the offender has failed to comply with one or more of those requirements; and
(4) he appears or is brought before the Crown Court, and the judge is satisfied that he has failed to comply with one or more requirements imposed in connection with the deferment.

To bring the offender before the court, the Crown Court may issue:

> (a) a summons requiring him to appear before the court at a time and place specified in the summons; or

> PCC(S)A 2005, s.1C: CJA 2003, s.278, Sch.23, para.1

145

(b) a warrant to arrest him and bring him before the court at a
time and place specified in the warrant.

Conviction of further offence

12–003   A court which has deferred passing sentence on an offender
may deal with him before the end of the period of deferment if during
that period he is convicted in Great Britain, whether before or after
April 4, 2005, of any offence.

Where a court has, under PCC(S)A 2000, s.1, deferred passing sentence on an offender in respect of one or more offences and:

(1) during the period of deferment the offender is convicted in
England or Wales of any offence ("the later offence"); then,

(2) whether or not the offender is sentenced for the later offence
during the period of deferment, the court which passes sentence
on him for the later offence may also, if this has not already been
done, deal with him for the offence or offences for which passing
of sentence has been deferred; except that

(a) this power must not be exercised by a magistrates' court if
the court which deferred passing sentence was the Crown
Court; and

(b) a judge of the Crown Court, in exercising that power in a case in
which the court which deferred passing sentence was a magistrates' court, must not pass any sentence which could not have
been passed by a magistrates' court in exercising that power.

Where a court which has deferred passing sentence on an offender
proposes to deal with him under these provisions before the end of the
period of deferment, it may issue a summons requiring him to appear
at a time and place specified, or a warrant to arrest him and bring him
before the court at a time and place specified.

Powers on due date

12–004   Where the passing of sentence on an offender has been
deferred, the power of the judge to deal with the offender at the end of
the period of deferment and any power in relation to the breach of an
undertaking (s.1B(1)) or a further conviction (s.1C(1)) or of any other
court which deals with him (s.1C(3)): PCC(S)A 2000, s.1D

(1) is a power to deal with him, in respect of the offence for which
passing of sentence has been deferred, in any way in which the
original court could have dealt with him if it had not deferred
passing sentence; and

(2) where:

(a) the passing of sentence on an offender in respect of one or
more offences has been deferred under s.1; and

(b) a magistrates' court deals with him in respect of the offence
or any of the offences by committing him to the Crown
Court under PCC(S)A 2000, s.3 the power of the Crown
Court to deal with him includes the same power to defer
passing sentence on him as if he had just been convicted of
the offence or offences on indictment before the court.

It should be noted that under the former legislation:

   (i)   it was not necessary that the offender be dealt with exactly on the date originally specified; there was nothing to prevent the court adjourning or postponing the hearing of the matter, provided there is no further deferment (*R. v Ingle* (1974) 59 Cr. App. R. 306); but

  (ii) if sentence was deferred to a date after the expiry of the six-month period, the court was deprived of its jurisdiction (*R. v W London Stipendiary Magistrate, Ex p. Watts, The Times*, May 30, 1987);

 (iii) it was desirable that the judge who passed sentence should be the same as the judge who deferred sentence in the first place, but if that was not possible the second judge should be fully apprised of the first judge's views (*R. v Gurney* [1974] Crim. L.R. 472);

 (iv) the advocate who represented the offender on the earlier occasion should, if possible, appear for him on the date when sentence is to be passed (*R. v Ryan* [1976] Crim. L.R. 508).

Purpose of deferment

12–005   The judge needs to ascertain the purpose of the deferment, and to determine whether the offender has substantially conformed, or attempted to conform, with the proper expectations of the judge who made the order.

If the offender:

(1) has done so, he may legitimately expect that an immediate custodial sentence will *not* be imposed;

(2) has not done so, the judge should be careful to state precisely in what respects he has failed.

(*R. v George* (1984) 79 Cr.App.R.26).

He should not be influenced by proceedings which are pending but incomplete (*R. v Aquarius* (1989) 11 Cr. App. R.(S.) 431).

Nature of sentence on deferred date

12–006   On the day on which the sentence originally deferred is dealt with, the judge is bound to approach the matter on a fair consideration of the offender's progress, if any, during the period of deferment. Thus:

(1) it is wrong to imprison the offender if he has fulfilled that which was required of him (*R. v Gilby* (1975) 61 Cr. App. R. 112; *R. v Head* (1976) 63 Cr. App. R. 157; *R. v Smith* (1979) 1 Cr. App. R. (S.) 339); and

(2) if the report made to the court is not unfavourable, a substantial custodial sentence is probably not appropriate.

B.   Community orders

12–007   CJA 2003, Sch.8 deals with the breach, revocation and amendment of community orders made under CJA 2003 on or after April 4, 2005 in respect of offenders aged 18 or over. The persons not coming within the above provisions fall to be dealt with under PCC(S)A.

The following topics need to be considered:

1. Breach of requirement (12–008);
2. Revocation with or without re-sentencing (12–012);
3. Amendment of order (12–014);
4. Amendment of requirements (12–016);
5. Powers following subsequent conviction (12–020); and
6. Administrative provisions (12–025).

If the Legal Aid etc Bill 2011, now going through Parliament, is enacted in its present form, it will make substantial changes to this section.

1. Breach of requirement

Process

12–008 If a community order made by the Crown Court does not include a direction that failure to comply with the requirements is to be dealt with by a magistrates' court, then if, at any time, it appears to a judge of the Crown Court that the offender has failed to comply with any of the requirements of the order, a summons may be issued, or if the information is on oath, a warrant, to bring him before the court. If he does not appear on a summons, a warrant may be issued.

CJA 2003, s.179, Sch.8, para.8

Any question whether the offender has failed to comply with the requirements of the order is to be determined by the judge and not by the verdict of a jury; the ordinary rules as to the presentation of the prosecution case apply (*R. v Gainsborough JJ. Ex p. Green* (1983) 78 Cr. App. R. 9).

CJA 2003, s.179, Sch.8, para.10(6)

The bare fact that an appeal has been lodged against conviction or sentence does not afford a reasonable excuse for failure to comply with the requirements of an order (*W. Midlands Probation Service v Sadler Sutton Coldfield MC* [2008] EWHC 15 (Admin); [2008] 3 All E.R. 1193).

Powers of Crown Court

12–009 Where it is proved to the judge's satisfaction that an offender aged 18 or over has failed without reasonable excuse to comply with any of the requirements of the order, the judge may deal with him in respect of that failure in any one of the following ways, taking into account the extent to which the offender has complied with any of the requirements, namely:

CJA 2003, s.179, Sch.8, para.10(1)–(5)

(1) by **amending** the terms of the order so as to impose more onerous requirements which he could impose if he were then making the order;
(2) by **dealing with the offender** for the offence in respect of which the order was made in any way in which he could deal with him if he had just been convicted before the Crown Court of the offence; and revoking the order if it is still in force;
(3) in the case of an offender who has wilfully and persistently failed to comply, by imposing a **custodial sentence**, and, if the order was made in respect of an offence punishable with imprisonment,

a sentence of imprisonment may be passed notwithstanding the restrictions imposed on community sentences by CJA 2003, s.152(2) (see DEALING WITH AN OFFENDER);

In dealing with an offender under (1) above, the judge may extend the duration of particular requirements (subject to any limit in respect of individual requirements imposed by CJA 2003, Pt 12, Ch.4) but may not extend the period beyond the maximum of three years specified under ibid. s.177(5).

Approach to breach

12–010   The primary objective must be to ensure that the requirements of the original sentence are completed. A custodial sentence should be the last resort, where all reasonable efforts to ensure that an offender complete a community sentence have failed. If a custodial sentence is imposed, without adequate consideration being given to alternatives, the purposes identified originally as being important, may be undermined (SGC 2, 2.1.46).

In approaching the alternatives set out in 12–009, the judge should take account of:

(1) the extent to which the offender has complied with the requirements of the order;
(2) the reasons for the breach; and
(3) the point at which the breach has occurred.

Where a breach takes place towards the end of the operational period, and the judge is satisfied that the offender's appearance before the court is likely to be sufficient in itself to ensure future compliance, he should sentence in a way that enables the original order to be completed properly, for example, by a differently constructed community sentence that aims to secure compliance with the purposes of the original sentence.

Where he decides to increase the onerousness of the order, he ought to:

(a) give careful consideration (with advice from the probation service), to the offender's ability to comply; and
(b) consider the impact on the offender's ability to comply and the possibility of precipitating a custodial sentence for a further breach,

and may consider:

(i)   extending the supervision or operational periods will be more sensible; or
(ii) in other cases adding punitive or rehabilitative requirements instead, being mindful, however, of the legislative restrictions on the overall length of community sentences (see 12–009) and on the supervision and operational periods allowed for each type of requirement.

In dealing with an offender for breach of a requirement, as opposed to dealing with him in respect of a new offence, non-compliance is not to be taken as an aggravation of the original offence; he must be sentenced on the facts upon which the original order was made (*R. v Clarke* [1997] 2 Cr. App. R.(S.) 163). If a driving disqualification was imposed at the time the relevant order was made, there is no power to impose a further disqualification when the order is revoked and the offender is re-sentenced: (*R. v Coy* (1992) 13 Cr. App. R(S.) 619).

Treatment cases

12–011   An offender who is required by any of the following require-ments of a community order:

(1) "a mental health treatment requirement";
(2) "a drug rehabilitation requirement"; or
(3) "an alcohol treatment requirement",

CJA 2003,
s.179, Sch.8,
para.11

to submit to treatment for his mental condition, or his dependency on, or propensity to misuse, drugs or alcohol, is not to be treated for these purposes as having failed to comply with that requirement on the ground only that he had refused to undergo any surgical, electrical or other treatment if, in the judge's opinion, his refusal was reasonable having regard to all the circumstances.

The judge may not, under these provisions, amend a mental health treatment requirement, a drug rehabilitation requirement or an alcohol treatment requirement unless the offender expresses his willingness to comply with the requirement as amended.

2.   Revocation with or without re-sentencing

General

12–012   Where a community order is made by the Crown Court it will generally (12-001) include a direction that any failure to comply with the order be dealt with by a magistrates' court; but where:

CJA 2003,
s.179, Sch.8,
para.14

(1) an order, still in force, does not include such a direction; and
(2) the offender, or the responsible officer, applies to the Crown Court for the order or for the offender to be dealt with in some other way for the offence in respect of which the order was made, the judge may, it is appears to him to be in the interests of justice to do so, having regard to circumstances which have arisen since the order was made;
(a) **revoke** the order; or
(b) both **revoke** the order, **and deal with the offender** for the offence in respect of which the order was made, in any way in which the court could deal with him if he had just been convicted of that offence by or before the court which made the order.

Note that:

- The circumstances in which an order may be revoked include the offender's making good progress or his responding satisfactorily to supervision or treatment, as the case requires.
- In dealing with an offender under this provision the judge must

take into account the extent to which the offender has complied with the requirements of the order.

- Where the judge proposes to exercise his powers under this paragraph otherwise than on the application of the offender, he must be summoned to appear before the court and, if he does not appear in answer to the summons, a warrant may be issued for his arrest.

Illness or disability

12–013   Where revocation is on the ground that the offender is unable to comply by reason of illness or disability, the imposition of a custodial sentence depends on the circumstances. Thus, under the previous legislation it was held that:

(1) in general it should not be imposed (*R. v Fielding* (1993) 14 Cr. App. R.(S.) 494); particularly
(2) where the offender made it clear from the outset that there might be difficulties (*R. v Johnson* [2000] Cr. App. R.(S.) 405); but
(3) it may well be appropriate where the offender failed to disclose any difficulties at the time (*R. v Hammon* [1998] 2 Cr. App. R.(S.) 202).

If the application is based on grounds which amount, in effect, to an alleged breach of the order, the judge should satisfy himself as to the grounds for revocation by hearing evidence, as if on a breach (*R. v Jackson* [1984] Crim. L.R. 573).

3.   Amendment of order

General: summons or warrant

12–014   The appropriate magistrates' court has wide powers of amendment of community orders, even those made by the Crown Court, and the Crown Court order will generally include a direction that failure to comply with any requirements is to be dealt with by the magistrates' court. This will, however, not always be the case.

Where no such direction has been included, and the judge proposes to exercise his powers of amendment, save for an order: CJA 2003, s.179, Sch.8, para.25

(1) cancelling a requirement;
(2) reducing the period of any requirement; or
(3) substituting a new local justice area, or a new place for the one specified in the order,

the offender must be summoned to appear, and if he does not appear in answer to the summons a warrant may be issued.

Change of residence

12–015   Again, where an order made by the Crown Court which does not include a direction that failure to comply with any of the requirements of the order be dealt with by the magistrates' court, a judge of the Crown Court, if he is satisfied that the offender proposes to change, or has changed, his residence from the local justice area concerned to another such area: CJA 2003, s.179, Sch.8, paras 16(1)–(5), 24(1)

(1) may and,

(2) on the application of the responsible officer *must*,

amend the order by substituting the other area for the area specified in the order, but he may not do so where;

(a) the order contains requirements which, in his opinion, cannot be complied with unless the offender continues to reside in the local justice area concerned unless, in accordance with para.17, he either cancels those requirements or substitutes for those requirements other requirements which can be complied with if the offender ceases to reside in that area;

(b) an order imposes a programme requirement, unless it appears that the accredited programme specified in the requirement is available in the other local justice area; or

(c) while an appeal against the order is pending.

The judge has the same powers in relation to a drug rehabilitation requirement which is subject to review made by the Crown Court (see 16–036).

4. Amendment of requirements

General

12–016 In relation to an order made by the Crown Court which does not include a direction that any failure to comply with any of the requirements of the order be dealt with by the magistrates' court, the judge may, on the application of the offender or the responsible officer, amend an order:

CJA 2003, s.179, Sch.8, paras.17, 24(1), (2)

(1) by cancelling any of the requirements of the order; or

(2) by replacing any of those requirements with a requirement of the same kind, which the judge could include if he were then making the order,

provided that he may *not* amend under this paragraph a mental health treatment, a drug rehabilitation or an alcohol treatment requirement unless the offender consents to the requirement as amended.

Note that:

(a) no application may be made while an appeal against the community order is pending except in a case where it relates to a "mental health", "drug rehabilitation" or "alcohol treatment requirement", and the offender consents to comply with the requirement as amended;

(b) the judge has the same powers in respect of a drug rehabilitation requirement (see 12–018) which is subject to review, imposed by the Crown Court; and

(c) if the offender fails to consent to the proposed amended requirement, the judge may:

(i) revoke the community order; and

(ii) deal with the offender or the offence in respect of which the order was made, in any way in which he

152

could deal with him if he had just been convicted in the Crown Court of the offence,

taking into account the extent to which the offender has complied with the requirements of the order.

Where the order was made in respect of an offence punishable with imprisonment a custodial sentence may be imposed notwithstanding the restrictions imposed by CJA 2003, s.152(2) (see DEALING WITH AN OFFENDER).

Amendment of treatment requirements

12–017   Where the medical practitioner or other person by whom, or under whose direction, an offender is, in pursuance of:

CJA 2003, s.179, Sch.8, para.18

(1) "a mental health treatment requirement";
(2) "a drug rehabilitation requirement"; or
(3) "an alcohol treatment requirement",

being treated for his mental condition or his dependency on or propensity to misuse drugs or alcohol:

  (a) is of the opinion:
    (i) that the treatment of the offender should be continued beyond the period specified in that behalf in the order;
    (ii) that the offender needs different treatment;
    (iii) that the offender is not susceptible to treatment; or
    (iv) that the offender does not require further treatment, or
  (b) is for any reason unwilling to continue to treat or direct the treatment of the offender,

he must make a report in writing to that effect to the responsible officer and that officer must apply to the appropriate court for the variation or cancellation of the requirement.

Review of drug rehabilitation requirement

12–018   Where the responsible officer is of the opinion that a community order imposing a drug rehabilitation requirement which is subject to review should be so amended as to provide for each subsequent periodic review (required by CJA 2003, s.191) to be made without a hearing instead of at a review hearing, or vice versa, he must apply to the court responsible for the order for the variation of the order.

CJA 2003, s.179, Sch.8, para.19

Extension of unpaid work requirement

12–019   Where, in relation to any community order made by the Crown Court which does not include a direction that any failure to comply with any of the requirements of the order be dealt with by the magistrates' court, an unpaid work requirement is in force and, on the application of the offender or the responsible officer it appears to the judge that it would be in the interests of justice to do so, having regard to circumstances which have arisen since the order was made, he may extend the period beyond the 12 months specified in CJA 2003, s.200(2).

CJA 2003, s.179, Sch.8, paras 20, 24(1)

5.   Powers following subsequent conviction

Process

12–020   Where a judge of the Crown Court proposes to exercise the above powers otherwise than on the offender's application:

CJA 2003,
s.179, Sch.8,
para.25

(1) the offender must be summoned to appear; and
(2) if he does not appear in answer to the summons, a warrant may be issued for his arrest.

Revocation and fresh sentence

12–021   Where an offender in respect of whom a community order is in force is:

CJA 2003,
s.179, Sch.8,
para.23

(1) convicted of an offence in the Crown Court; or
(2) brought or appears before the Crown Court having been committed by a magistrates' court for sentence, and

it appears to the judge that it would be in the interests of justice to exercise his powers under this provision, having regard to circumstances which have arisen since the community order was made, he may:

(a) revoke the order, or
(b) both:
    (i)   revoke the order; and
    (ii) deal with the offender for the offence in respect of which the order was made, in any way in which the court which made the order could deal with him if he had just been convicted of that offence by or before the court which made the order,

taking into account under (b)(ii) the extent to which the offender has complied with the requirements of the community order.

Sentence on the breach

12–022   The fact that an offence committed during the currency of a relevant order is different in character from that or those for which the community order was passed, does not prevent the court revoking the order and dealing with the offender by imposing, for instance, a custodial sentence (*R. v Fleming* (1989) 11 Cr. App. R.(S.) 137).

There is no binding principle that it can never be right to impose a consecutive term for an offence committed before offences for which a community sentence was passed; it depends in each case on what the interests of justice require (*R. v Newton* [1999] 2 Cr. App. R.(S.) 172).

In an appropriate case, the sentence passed on a breach may be a substantial one (*R. v Barresi* [1981] Crim. L.R. 268) though:

(1) some discount ought to be given for: any hours worked under an unpaid work requirement (*R. v Baines* (1983) 5 Cr. App. R.(S.) 264; *R. v Whittingham* (1986) 8 Cr. App. R.(S.) 116; *R. v Williams* (1986) 8 Cr. App. R.(S.) 230); and
(2) credit for time spent on remand for the offence before the community order was made, should be given, under the provisions of CJA 2003, ss 140, 140A (see IMPRISONMENT),

though such credit may be denied if the judge made clear when the original sentence was imposed, that he had taken that time into account (*R. v Bodman* [2011] 3 Archbold Review 4, C.A).

The fact that a community sentence was originally imposed does not mean that the offence was not one qualifying for a custodial sentence. If the commission of a further offence destroys any mitigation there may have been, a custodial sentence may be appropriate. An offender cannot tie the hands of the court by seeking to complete, e.g. the specified hours of unpaid work, once breach proceedings have begun (*R. v Tebbutt* (1989) 10 Cr.App.R.(S.) 88).

There is no obligation to take into account time spent in custody before the order was made (*R. v Broomfield* [2004] Crim. L.R. 672).

Offence committed prior to order

12–023 Where a person is sentenced in the Crown Court for an offence committed before a current community sentence was imposed, it is uncertain whether the Crown Court should revoke the earlier community sentence and re-sentence for the earlier offence (*R. v Neville* [1993]14 Cr. App. R.(S.) 765; *R. v Cawley* (1993) 15 Cr. App. R.(S.) 209; *R. v Kenny* [1996] 1 Cr. App. R.(S.) 397; *R. v Saphier* [1997] 1 Cr. App. R.(S.) 235; *R. v Day* [1997] 2 Cr. App. R.(S.) 328; *R. v Newton* [1993] 2 Cr. App. R.(S.) 172; *R. v Reid* [1998] 2 Cr. App. R.(S.) 40; *R. v Brighton* [1999] 2 Cr. App. R.(S.) 196).

Magistrates' courts orders

12–024 Different divisions of CACD have had difficulty in interpreting the provisions of the former legislation (CJA 1991, Sch.2, para.8(2)(b)), in relation to the sentencing powers of the Crown Court where a judge revokes a community order made by a magistrates' court:

(1) in *R. v Mackness* (1994) 16 Cr. App. R.(S.) 549 and in *R. v Doyle* [1996] 1 Cr. App. R.(S.) 239 it was held that the judge's powers on indictment applied;
(2) in *R. v Kosser* (1994) 16 Cr. App. R.(S.) 737 and in *R. v Hewitt* [1996] 2 Cr. App. R.(S.) 14 it was held that the judge was restricted to magistrates' sentencing powers;
(3) in *R. v Ogden* [1996] 2 Cr. App. R.(S.) 387 CACD followed (2).

6.   Administrative Provisions

12–025 On the making of an order revoking or amending a community order, the Crown Court officer must:

CJA 2003, s.179, Sch.8, para.27

(1) provide copies of the revoking or amending order to the offender and the responsible officer;
(2) in the case of an amending order which substitutes a new local justice area, provide a copy of the amending order to:
   (a) the relevant provider of probation services, and
   (b) the magistrates' court acting for that area, and
(3) in the case of an amending order which imposes or amends a requirement specified in the first column of CJA 2003, Sch.14,

provide a copy of so much of the amending order as relates to that requirement to the person specified in relation to it in the second column of that Schedule;

(4) where the proper officer of the court provides a copy of an amending order to a magistrates' court acting for a different area, he must also provide to the court such documents and information relating to the case as he considers likely to be of assistance to a court acting for that area in the exercise of its functions in relation to the order.

C.   Youth Rehabilitation Orders

The following topics are relevant:

1. Breach of order (12–026)
2. Revocation of order (12–030)
3. Amendment of the order (12–031)
4. Powers following subsequent conviction (12–036)
5. Administrative provisions (12–038)

1.   Breach of order

Powers of Crown Court

12–026   Where:

CJIA 2008, Sch.2, Pt 1, para.8

(1) an offender appears or is brought before the Crown Court (whether under Sch.2, para.5, or by virtue of committal under para.7(2)), and
(2) it is proved to the judge's satisfaction that the offender has failed without reasonable excuse to comply with the youth rehabilitation order,

the judge is not obliged to make any order, and may allow the youth rehabilitation order to continue as imposed, nor is there any obligation to make an order more onerous, but if the judge determines that a sanction is necessary, he may deal with the offender:

(a) by ordering the offender to pay a fine of an amount not exceeding;
   (i) £250, if the offender is aged under 14; or
   (ii) £1,000, in any other case;
(b) by amending the terms of the order so as to impose any requirement which could have been included in the order when it was made, in addition to, or in substitution for, any requirement or requirements already imposed by the order, provided that an extended activity requirement, or a fostering requirement, may not be imposed if the order does not already impose such a requirement;
(c) by dealing with the offender, for the offence in respect of which the order was made, in any way in which the Crown Court could have dealt with the offender for that offence, and revoking the original order if it is still in force, taking

into account the extent to which the offender has complied with the order.

Any requirement imposed under (b) must be capable of being complied with before the date specified under para.32(1) of Sch.1.

SGC(Y) (10.37) suggests that where the failure arises primarily from non-compliance with reporting or other similar obligations and a sanction is necessary, the most appropriate order is likely to be the inclusion of (or increase in) a primarily punitive requirement such as the curfew, unpaid work, exclusion and prohibited activity requirements, or in the imposition of a fine. However, continuing failure to comply with the order is likely to lead to revocation of the order and re-sentencing for the original offence.

Where the judge is dealing with the offender under (b) above and the order does not contain an unpaid work requirement, para.10(2) of Sch.1. applies in relation to the inclusion of such a requirement as if for "40" (hours) there were substituted "20" (hours).

Any question whether the offender has failed to comply with the order must be determined by the judge and not by a jury.

Fostering requirement

12–027   Where;

(1) the order imposes a fostering requirement (the "original requirement"), and

(2) under sub-para.(b) in the preceding section the judge proposes to substitute a new fostering requirement ("the substitute requirement") for the original requirement,

Paragraph 18(2) of Sch.1 applies in relation to the substitute requirement as if the reference to the period of 12 months beginning with the date on which the original requirement first had effect were a reference to the period of 18 months beginning with that date.

CJIA 2008, Sch.2, Pt 2, para.8(9)

Persistent offenders

12–028   Where:

(1) an offender has wilfully and persistently failed to comply with an order; and

(2) the judge is dealing with the offender under (c) in 12–026, above, additional powers include:

   (a) the making of a youth rehabilitation order with intensive supervision and surveillance, even though the offence is not imprisonable or a custodial sentence would not have been imposed if the order had not been available; and

   (b) even though the offence is not imprisonable, the imposition of a detention and training order for 4 months for breach of a youth rehabilitation order with intensive supervision and surveillance, imposed following wilful and persistent breach of an order made for a non-imprisonable offence.

CJIA 2008, Sch.2, Pt 2, paras.8(12–14)

In considering whether the failure to comply is "persistent", account should be taken of the principles set out at 28–010.

SGC(Y) (10.42) suggests that the primary objective when sentencing for breach of an order is to ensure that the offender completes the requirements imposed by the court.

Thus:

- Where the failure arises primarily from non-compliance with reporting or other similar obligations, and a sanction is necessary, the most appropriate is likely to be the inclusion of (or increase in) a primarily punitive requirement.
- The judge ought to ensure that he has sufficient information to enable him to understand why the order has been breached and to satisfy himself that all steps have been taken by the youth offending team and other local authority services to give the offender appropriate opportunity and support; this will be particularly important if the judge is considering imposing a custodial sentence as a result of the breach.
- Where the judge is determining whether the offender has "wilfully and persistently" breached an order, he should apply the same approach as when determining whether an offender is a "persistent offender".
- In particular, almost certainly an offender will have "persistently" breached a youth rehabilitation order where there have been three breaches (each resulting in an appearance before a court) demonstrating a lack of willingness to comply with the order.

Restriction of powers where treatment required

12–029   Where a youth rehabilitation order imposes in respect of an offender either a mental health treatment requirement, a drug treatment requirement, or an intoxicating substance treatment requirement, the offender is not to be treated as having failed to comply with the order on the ground only that he has refused to undergo any surgical or electrical treatment if, in the judge's opinion, the refusal was reasonable having regard to all the circumstances.

CJIA 2008, Sch.2, Pt 2, para.9

2.   Revocation of order

Crown Court's powers

12–030   The revocation of a youth rehabilitation order will generally be a matter for a magistrates' court acting under CJIA 2008, Sch.2, Pt 3, but where:

CJIA 2008, Sch.2, Pt 3, para.12

(1) a youth rehabilitation order is in force in respect of an offender;

(2) the order was made by the Crown Court, and does not contain a direction under para.36 of Sch.1; and

(3) the offender or the responsible officer makes an application to the Crown Court,

and it appears to a judge of the Crown Court to be in the interests of justice to do so, having regard to circumstances which have arisen since the order was made, he may either:

    (a) revoke the order, or

    (b) both:

        (i) revoke the order, and

        (ii) deal with the offender, for the offence in respect of which the order was made, in any way in which the Crown Court could have dealt with the offender for that offence.

The circumstances in which a youth rehabilitation order may be revoked include the offender's making good progress or responding satisfactorily to supervision or treatment (as the case requires).

In dealing with an offender under (b)(ii) the judge must take into account the extent to which the offender has complied with the order.

No application may be made by the offender while an appeal against the youth rehabilitation order is pending.

If an application for revocation is dismissed, then during the period of three months beginning with the date on which it was dismissed no further such application may be made in relation to the order by any person except with the consent of the Crown Court.

3.   Amendment of the order

General

12–031 In the majority of cases, amendments to the order will be made in the appropriate magistrates' court, but where an order is in force which was made by the Crown Court and which does not contain a direction under Sch.1, para.36, any application to amend may be made to the Crown Court by either the offender or the responsible officer.

CJIA 2008, Sch.2, Pt 4 para.16(1)

If the judge is satisfied that the offender proposes to reside, or is residing, in a local justice area ("the new local justice area") other than the local justice area for the time being specified in the order, he;

    (1) must, if the application is made by the responsible officer; or

    (2) may, amend the order by substituting the new local justice area for the area specified in the order.

The judge may also amend the order:

    (a) by cancelling any of the requirements; or

    (b) by replacing any of those requirements with requirement of the same kind which could have been included in the order when it was made.

Any such requirement must be capable of being complied with before the date specified under para.31(1) of Sch.1.

Specific area requirements; programme requirements

12–032 "Specific area requirement", in relation to an order, means a requirement contained in it which, in the judge's opinion, cannot be complied with unless the offender continues to reside in the local justice area specified in the order.

CJIA 2008, Sch.2, Pt 4 para.15

An order which contains specific area requirements may not be amended unless, either;

(1) those requirements are cancelled; or
(2) other requirements are substituted which can be complied with if the offender resides in the new local justice area.

If:

(a) the application to amend is made by the responsible officer; and
(b) the order contains specific area requirements,

the judge must, unless he considers it inappropriate, so exercise his powers that he is not prevented by sub-para.(2) from amending the order.

A programme requirement may not be amended unless the judge is satisfied that a programme which:

(i) corresponds as nearly as practicable to the programme specified in the order for the purposes of that requirement; and
(ii) is suitable for the offender, is available in the new local justice area.

Fostering requirement

12–033 Where—

CJIA 2008, Sch.2, Pt 4, para.16

(1) an order imposes a fostering requirement (the "original requirement"), and
(2) the judge proposes to substitute a new fostering requirement ("the substitute requirement")

para.18(2) of Sch.1 applies in relation to the substitute requirement as if the reference to the period of 12 months beginning with the date on which the original requirement first had effect were a reference to the period of 18 months beginning with that date.

Mental health and drug treatment

12–034 Where the offender is aged 14 or over:

CJIA 2008, Sch.2, Pt 4 para.16

(1) a mental health treatment requirement,
(2) a drug treatment requirement, or
(3) a drug testing requirement

may not be imposed unless the offender has expressed willingness to comply with the requirement. If an offender who is aged 14 or over fails to express willingness to comply with any of the above which the court proposes to impose, the judge may:

(a) revoke the youth rehabilitation order, and
(b) deal with the offender, for the offence in respect of which the order was made, in any way in which the court could have dealt with him for that offence (had he been before that court to be dealt with for it),

provided that in dealing with the offender under (b), the judge must take into account the extent to which the offender has complied with the order.

Extension of unpaid work requirement

12–035 Where:

(1) an order imposing an unpaid work requirement is in force in respect of an offender, and

(2) on the application of the offender or the responsible officer, it appears to the appropriate court that it would be in the interests of justice to do so having regard to circumstances which have arisen since the order was made,

the judge may, in relation to the order, extend the period of 12 months specified in para.10(6) of Sch.1.

CJIA 2008, Sch.2, Pt 4, para.17

4. Powers following subsequent conviction

General

12–036 Where:

(1) a youth rehabilitation order is in force in respect of an offender, and

(2) the offender;

    (a) is convicted by the Crown Court of an offence, or

    (b) is brought or appears before the Crown Court by virtue of Sch.2 paras 18(9) or (11) or having been committed by the magistrates' court to the Crown Court for sentence,

the judge may revoke the order and, where he considers that it would be in the interests of justice to do so, may deal with the offender for the offence in respect of which the order was made, in any way in which the court which made the order could have dealt with the offender for that offence, having regard to circumstances which have arisen since the order was made, taking into account the extent to which the offender has complied with the order.

CJIA 2008, Sch.2, Pt 5 para.19

Appearance of offender; process

12–037 Where, otherwise than on the application of the offender, a judge of the Crown Court proposes to exercise his powers in relation to the breach, amendment or revocation of a youth rehabilitation order, except where the where the order is one:

(1) revoking the order

(2) cancelling or reducing the duration of a requirement, or

(3) substituting a new local justice area or place for one specified in the order,

the offender must be summoned to appear before the court, and if he does not appear in answer to the summons, a warrant may be issued for his arrest.

CJIA 2008, Sch.2, Pt 6, para.20

5. Administrative provisions

12–038 Where an order is made under Sch.2 revoking or amending a youth rehabilitation order, the proper officer of the court must forthwith:

CJIA 2008, Sch.2, Pt 6, para.24

(1) provide copies of the revoking or amending order to the offender and, if the offender is aged under 14, to his parent or guardian;

(2) provide a copy of the revoking or amending order to the responsible officer;

(3) in the case of an amending order which substitutes a new local justice area, provide copies of the amending order to;

    (a) the local probation board acting for that area; and

    (b) the magistrates' court acting in that area;

(4) in the case of an amending order which imposes or cancels a requirement specified in the first column of the Table in para.33(6) of Sch.1, provide a copy of so much of the amending order as relates to that requirement to the person specified in relation to that requirement in the second column of that Table,

(5) in the case of an order which revokes a requirement specified in the first column of that Table, provide a copy of the revoking order to the person specified in relation to that requirement in the second column; and

where the Crown Court officer provides a copy of an amending order to a magistrates' court acting in a different area the officer must also provide to that court such documents and information relating to the case as appear likely to be of assistance to a court acting in that area in the exercise of its functions in relation to the order.

D.   Reparation Orders

12–039   Where an offender in respect of whom a reparation order made by the Crown Court is in force:

    PCC(S)A 2000, Sch.8, paras, 2, 4, 5, 7

(1) is brought before the Crown Court: and

(2) it is proved to the judge's satisfaction that he has failed to comply with the requirement in question,

he may be dealt with for the offence in respect of which the order was made, in any way in which he could have been dealt with if the order had not been made, taking into account the extent to which the term of the order have been complied with, and the judge may revoke the order.

E.   Suspended sentence orders

1.   Procedure

Issue of summons or warrant by Crown Court

12–040   If at any time while a suspended sentence order made by the Crown Court (save one where a direction was included that failure to comply with the community requirements of it be dealt with by a magistrates' court) is in force in respect of an offender it appears on information that the offender has failed to comply with any of the community requirements of the order, the Crown Court may:

    CJA 2003, s.193, Sch.12, para.7(2)

(1) issue a summons requiring the offender to appear at the place and time specified in it; or

(2) if the information is in writing and on oath, issue a warrant for his arrest.

Where the summons requires the offender to appear before the Crown Court and the offender does not appear in answer to it, a judge may issue a warrant for his arrest.

Powers on the breach

12–041   Where it is proved:

CJA 2003 s.193, Sch. 12, para.8

(1) that the offender has failed, without reasonable excuse, to comply with any of the community requirements of the suspended sentence order; or
(2) the offender is convicted of an offence committed during the operational period of a suspended sentence (other than one which has already taken effect),

the judge before whom he is brought must consider the case and deal with him.
He may:

(a) order that the suspended sentence take effect with the original term and custodial period unchanged;
(b) order that the suspended sentence take effect with the substitution of a lesser term (of not less than 28 weeks); or
(c) amend the order by imposing more onerous community requirements or extending the supervision period (for not less than 6 months nor more than two years) or the operational period.

He may not, however, increase the length of the original sentence by converting it into an immediate term (*R. v Cassidy* [2011] 2 Cr. App. R.(S.) 240(40).Any activated term under (2) above will ordinary be made consecutive to any sentence imposed for the further offence.

Where the judge deals with an offender in respect of a suspended sentence, the Crown Court officer will notify the appropriate officer of the court which passed the sentence of the order made.

If the Legal Aid etc Bill 2011, now going through Parliament, is enacted in its present form, it will make changes to this section.

Obligation to activate sentence

12–042   The judge must make an order under (a) or (b) of 12–041 unless he considers that, in all the circumstances it would be unjust to do so, taking into account, in particular:

(1) the extent to which the offender has complied with the community requirements of the order (*R. v Zeca* [2009] EWCA Crim 133 [2009] 2 Cr. App. R.(S.) 65); and
(2) the facts of the any subsequent offence in the case of para.(2) of 12–041.

R.42

When the judge decides not to order, where he could, that a suspended sentence of imprisonment is to take effect, he must explain why he has not done so, when he explains the sentence that it has passed.

Guidelines

12–043   Guidelines issued (SGC 2, 3.2.18–21) suggest that where:

(1) the further offence is of a less serious nature than the offence for which the suspended sentence was imposed, it may justify activating the sentence with a reduced term or amending the terms of the order under (c) of 12–044;

(2) the offender, near the end of the operational period, has complied with the requirements imposed, but commits a further offence, it may be more appropriate to amend the order (under (c)) than to activate the sentence;

(3) the judge decides to amend the original order rather than to activate the sentence he should give serious consideration to extending the operational or supervision periods, within the statutory limits, rather than making the community requirements more onerous;

(4) the further offence is non-imprisonable, the judge ought to consider whether it is appropriate to activate the suspended sentence at all.

Further provisions as to order that suspended sentence is to take effect

12–044   When making an order that a sentence is to take effect (with or without any variation of the original term and custodial period), the judge may order that the sentence is to take effect immediately or that the term of that sentence is to commence on the expiry of another term of imprisonment passed on the offender by him or by another court, subject, in the case of (2) to CJA 2003, s.265 (restriction on consecutive sentences for released prisoners, for which see IMPRISONMENT).   CJA 2003, s.193. Sch.12, para.9

In proceedings for dealing with an offender in respect of a suspended sentence which take place before the Crown Court, any question whether the offender has been convicted of an offence committed during the operational period of the suspended sentence is to be determined by the judge and not by the verdict of a jury.

For the purpose of any enactment conferring rights of appeal in criminal cases, an order made is to be treated as a "sentence" passed on the offender by that court for the offence for which the suspended sentence was passed.

Restrictions where treatment required

12–045   An offender who is required by any of the following community requirements of a suspended sentence order: CJA 2003, s.193, Sch.12, para.10

(1) a mental health treatment requirement;
(2) a drug rehabilitation requirement; or
(3) an alcohol treatment requirement,

to submit to treatment for his mental condition, or his dependency on or propensity to misuse drugs or alcohol, is not to be treated as having failed to comply with that requirement on the ground only that he had refused to undergo any surgical, electrical or other treatment if, in the opinion of the court, his refusal was reasonable having regard to all the circumstances.

A judge may not amend the requirements (1)–(3) above unless the offender consents to the amended requirement.

Court by which suspended sentence may be dealt with on conviction for a further offence

12–046 An offender may be dealt with in respect of a suspended sentence by the Crown Court or, where the sentence was passed by a magistrates' court, by any magistrates' court before which he appears or is brought.

CJA 2003, s.193, Sch.12, para.11

Where an offender is convicted by a magistrates' court of any offence and the court is satisfied that the offence was committed during the operational period of a suspended sentence passed by the Crown Court:

(1) the court may, if it thinks fit, commit him to the Crown Court; and
(2) if it does not, must give written notice of the conviction to the Crown Court officer.

For these purposes, a suspended sentence passed on an offender on appeal is to be treated as having been passed by the court by which he was originally sentenced.

Conviction of further offence; judge not dealing with suspended sentence

12–047 If it appears to the judge where the Crown Court has jurisdiction or to a magistrate having jurisdiction:

CCJA 2003, s.193, Sch.12, para.12

(1) an offender has been convicted in the United Kingdom of an offence committed during the operational period of a suspended sentence; and
(2) that he has not been dealt with in respect of the suspended sentence,

that court or magistrate may issue a summons requiring the offender to appear at the place and time specified in it, or a warrant for his arrest.

Jurisdiction may be exercised:

(a) if the suspended sentence was passed by the Crown Court, by a judge of that court;
(b) if it was passed by a magistrates' court, by a magistrate acting for the area for which that court acted.

Where:

(i) an offender is convicted in Scotland or Northern Ireland of an offence, and
(ii) the judge is informed that the offence was committed

> during the operational period of a suspended sentence passed in England or Wales,

that court must give written notice of the conviction to the appropriate officer of the court by which the suspended sentence was passed.

2.   Amendment of suspended sentence order

Cancellation of community requirements

12–048   Where at any time while a suspended sentence order is in force, it appears to the Crown Court that:

CJA 2003, s.193, Sch.12, para.13

(1) in the case of an order which is subject to review, the Crown Court is responsible for the order; or
(2) the order was made by the Crown Court,

then, on the application of the offender or the responsible officer that, having regard to the circumstances which have arisen since the order was made, it would be in the interests of justice to do so, a judge may cancel the community requirements of the suspended sentence order.

The circumstances in which he may exercise this power in these circumstances include the offender's making good progress or his responding satisfactorily to supervision.

No application may be made by the offender while an appeal against the suspended sentence is pending.

Change of residence

12–049   Where, at any time while a suspended sentence is in force, the Crown Court, as the appropriate court (see 12–040, above), is satisfied that the offender proposes to change, or has changed, his residence from the local justice area concerned to another, a judge may, and on the application of the responsible officer must, amend the suspended sentence order by substituting the other local justice area for the area specified in the order, unless:

CJA 2003, s.193, Sch.12, para.14

(1) the suspended sentence order contains requirements which, in his opinion, cannot be complied with unless the offender resides in the local justice area concerned unless he either cancels those requirements, or substitutes for them other requirements which can be complied with if the offender does not reside in that area; or
(2) where the order imposes a programme requirement, unless it appears to him that the accredited programme specified in the requirement is available in the other local justice area.

Amendment of community requirements

12–050   At any time during the supervision period, a judge of the Crown Court, as the appropriate court (see 12–040, above) may, on the application of the offender or the responsible officer, by order amend any community requirement of a suspended sentence order, by

CJA 2003, s.193, Sch.12, para.15

cancelling it, or by replacing it with a requirement of the same kind, which he could include if he were then making the order, but:

(1) he may not under this paragraph amend a mental health treatment requirement, a drug rehabilitation requirement or an alcohol treatment requirement unless the offender consents to the amended requirement; and

(2) if the offender fails to consent to comply any of the proposed amended requirements, specified in (1) above, the judge may:

    (a) revoke the suspended order and the suspended sentence to which it relates, and

    (b) deal with him, for the offence in respect of which the suspended sentence was imposed, in any way in which it could deal with him if he had just been convicted by or before the court of the offence.

In dealing with the offender under (b), the judge must take into account the extent to which the offender has complied with the requirements of the order.

    Note that:

      (i) a requirement is of the same kind as another if it falls within the same paragraph of CJA 2003, s.190(1), (setting out the requirements which may be imposed (see IMPRISONMENT);

      (ii) an electronic monitoring requirement is a requirement of the same kind as any requirement falling within s.190(1) to which it relates.

Amendment of treatment requirements on practitioner's report

12–051 Where the medical practitioner or other person by whom, or under whose direction, an offender is, in pursuance of any requirement, being treated for his mental condition or his dependency on or propensity to misuse drugs or alcohol:

CJA 2003, s.193, Sch.12, para.16

(1) is of opinion that:

    (a) the treatment of the offender should be continued beyond the period specified in that behalf in the order;

    (b) the offender needs different treatment;

    (c) the offender is not susceptible to treatment; or

    (d) the offender does not require further treatment, or

(2) is for any reason unwilling to continue to treat or direct the treatment of the offender, he must make a report in writing to that effect to the responsible officer and that officer must apply to the appropriate court for the variation or cancellation of the requirement.

Review of drug rehabilitation requirement

12–052 Where the responsible officer is of the opinion that a suspended sentence order imposing a drug rehabilitation requirement which is subject to review should be amended as to provide or each periodic review (required by CJA 2003, s.191) to be made without a

CJA 2003, s.193, Sch.12, para.17

hearing instead of at a review hearing, or vice versa, he must apply to the court responsible for the order for a variation of the order.

Appeal pending

12–053 No application may be made under Sch.8 paras 12, 14 or 17, and no order may be made under ibid. para.13, while an appeal against the suspended sentence is pending.

CJA 2003,
s.193, Sch.12,
para.19(1)

Process

12–054 Where a judge of the Crown Court proposes to exercise his powers to amend a community requirement otherwise than on the application of the offender, and apart from an order cancelling a community requirement, the offender must be summoned to appear, and if he does not appear in answer to the summons, a warrant may be issued for his arrest.

CJA 2003,
s.193, Sch.12,
para.20

Administrative matters

12–055 On the making of an order amending a suspended sentence order, the Crown Court officer must provide:

CJA 2003,
s.193, Sch.12,
para.22

(1) copies of the amending order to the offender and the responsible officer,
(2) in the case of an amending order which substitutes a new local justice area, a copy of the amending order to:
   (a) the appropriate provider of probation services and
   (b) the magistrates' court acting for that area, and

in the case of an amending order which imposes or amends a requirement specified in the first column of Sch.14, provide a copy of so much of the amending order as relates to that requirement to the person specified in relation to that requirement in the second column of that Schedule.

Where the proper officer provides a copy of an amending order to a magistrates' court acting for a different area, he must also provide to that court such documents and information relating to the case as he considers likely to be of assistance to a court acting for that area in the exercise of its functions in relation to the order.

F.   Sexual offences prevention orders under SOA 2003, s.104

Breach of order

12–056 A person commits an offence punishable with a maximum of 5 years imprisonment if he breaches a sexual offences prevention order.

SOA 2003,
s.113.

Significant sentences are necessary in respect of serious breaches (see *R. v Byrne* [2010] 1 Cr. App. R(S.) 433 where the authorities are reviewed).

It is not open to the judge to impose a conditional discharge (see DISCHARGE; ABSOLUTE AND CONDITIONAL).

Amendment, variation and discharge

12–057 In relation to a sexual offences prevention order (see SEX OFFENDER ORDERS) made by the Crown Court or CACD the offender, the chief officer of police for the area in which he resides, or a chief officer of police who believes that the offender is in, or is intending to come to, his police area, may apply to the Crown Court for an order varying, renewing or discharging the order. *(SOA 2003, s.108(1)–(3), (7), (8))*

On application, the judge, after hearing the applicant and (if they wish to be heard), the other persons mentioned above, may make any order, varying, renewing or discharging the order, that he considers appropriate.

An order may be renewed, or varied, by imposing additional prohibitions on the accused, only if it is necessary to do so for the purpose of protecting the public, or any particular members of the public, from serious sexual harm from him, and any renewed or varied order may contain only such prohibitions as are necessary for this purpose. *(SOA 2003, s.108(6))*

The judge must not discharge an order before the end of five years beginning with the day on which it was made, without the consent of the accused and:

(a) where the application is made by a chief officer of police, that chief officer; or

(b) in any other case, the chief officer of police for the area in which the accused resides.

G. Anti-social behaviour orders

Breach of order

12–058 An offender in breach of an order commits an offence punishable on indictment with five years imprisonment. In *R. v Thomas* [2005] 1 Cr. App. R.(S.) 35 and *R. v Braxton* [2005] 1 Cr. App. R.(S.) 167, CACD upheld terms of 18 months and three and a half years respectively. *(CDA 1998, s.10C)*

Where the conduct constituting the breach also amounts to a distinct criminal offence the maximum sentence for which is prescribed by statute, while this should be borne in mind in the interests of proportionality, the sentence in respect of the breach is not limited to the statutory maximum for that offence, and the sentence should be commensurate with the breach (*R. v Lamb* [2005] EWCA Crim 3000; [2006] 2 Cr. App. R. (S.) ll; *R. v H* [2006] EWCA Crim 255 [2006] 2 Cr. App. R. (S.) 68).

Once CSA 2010, s.40 comes into force, a person under the age of 16 convicted of an offence under CDA 1998, s.l (10) (breach of an ASBO) must be made the subject of a parenting order (see PARENTING ORDERS).

In so far as procedure and evidence is concerned, note that;

(1) a copy of the original order, certified as such by the proper officer of the court which made it, is admissible as evidence of its having been made and of its contents to the same extent that oral evidence of those things is admissible in those proceedings;

(2) whether or not the accused is in breach of the specific terms of the order is a question of fact (*R. v Doughan* [2007] EWCA Crim 598, 171 J.P. 397);

(3) while questions as to the validity of the original order cannot found a defence, lack of clarity may be taken into account both in relation to reasonable excuse and to penalty (*CPS v T* [2006] EWHC 728 (Admin), [2006] 3 All E.R. 471);

(4) where the accused is charged with breaching the terms of an order prohibiting him from engaging in behaviour "without reasonable excuse", the burden of proving absence of reasonable excuse, if it is raised, is on the prosecutor (*R. v Charles*, [2009] EWCA Crim 1570, [2010] 1 Cr. App. R. 2). See also *R. v Hunt* (1987) 84 Cr.App.R.163; *R. v Evans* [2005] 1 W.L.R. 1435, *R. v Nicholson* [2006] EWCA Crim 1518, [2006] 2 Cr. App. R. 30.

As to the position where a condition is included in an interim order but not replicated in the final order see *Parker v DPP*, *The Times*, June 20, 2005.

Variation and discharge

12–059 An offender subject to an anti-social behaviour order made in the Crown Court may apply to the court that made it for it to be varied or discharged, but not before the end of the period of two years beginning with the date on which the order took effect.   CDA 1998, s.1C(6), (8)

The person designated by r.50.5 must apply in writing as soon as practicable after becoming aware of the grounds for doing so: R.50.5

(1) explaining what material circumstances have changed since the order was made, and why the order should be varied or revoked as a result; and

(2) serve the application on the court officer and, as appropriate, the prosecutor or accused, and any other person designated in r.51.5 (1)(b), if the court so directs.

A party who wants the judge to take account of any particular evidence before making its decision must, as soon as practicable, serve notice in writing on the same persons identifying in that notice the evidence and attaching any written statement that has not already been served.

The judge may decide such an application with or without a hearing, but must not;

(a) dismiss an application unless the applicant has had an opportunity to make representations at a hearing (whether or not the applicant in fact attends); or

(b) allow an application unless everyone required to be served, by this rule or by the court, has had at least 14 days in which to make representations, including representations about whether there should be a hearing.

The Crown Court officer will serve the application on any person, if the court so directs; and give notice of any hearing to the applicant, and to any person required to be served, by this rule or by the court.

H. Parenting orders

Review
12–060   On the application of the responsible officer, or a parent or guardian, a judge may, if he considers it appropriate, discharge any order in force, or vary it by:

CDA 1998, s.8A(5)(6), 9(5) CSA 2010, s.40

(1) cancelling it; or
(2) inserting into it (either in addition to or in substitution for any of its provisions) any provision which could have been included in the order, if he had then the power to make, and was exercising that power.

Variation and discharge of parenting order
12–061 If, while an order is in force, it appears to the court which made the order, on the application either of the responsible officer or the parent, that it is appropriate to do so, a judge may:

CDA 1998, s.8A(6); CSA 2010,s.40 2010,s.40

(1) discharge the order; or
(2) vary it by cancelling any provision in it, by inserting, whether in addition to or in substitution for any of its provisions, any provision which could have been included in the order if the court then had power to make it and was executing the power.

Where an application under s.10(5) for the discharge of an order is dismissed, no further application for its discharge may be made by any person except by consent of the court that made the order.

Procedure on revocation and discharge is governed by r.50.5 as amended by SI 2010/1921, as to which see under Anti-Social Behaviour Orders.

Notes

13. CASE MANAGEMENT

Quick guide

A. Introduction

Legislation and rules, etc.

13–001 Case management in the Crown Court is governed by CPR 2011, PD 2004 and the Criminal Cases Management Framework (CCMF). Forms are set out in Annex D to PD 2004. The overriding objective of the Rules is (r.1.1) that criminal cases be dealt with justly (see *SL (A Juvenile v DPP* [2001] EWHC (Admin.) 882; [2002] 1 Cr. App. R. 32). This includes, in so far as case management is concerned (r.3.2), dealing with a case efficiently and expeditiously while:

(1) dealing with the prosecution and the defence fairly;
(2) recognising the rights of the accused, particularly those under ECHR, art.6; and
(3) respecting the interests of witnesses, victims and jurors, and keeping them informed of the progress of the case.

The Rules impose duties and burdens on all the participants in a criminal trial, including the judge, and the preparation and conduct of criminal trials is dependent on, and subject to, the Rules *(R. v K* [2006] Crim. L.R. 1012). Each participant, in the conduct of a criminal case (and that includes anyone involved in any way with the case) has a duty actively to assist the court in fulfilling its duty under r.3.2 without, or if necessary with, a direction; and to apply for any direction if to further the overriding objective and is under a duty to:

(a) prepare and conduct the case in accordance with the overriding objective;
(b) comply with the Rules, practice directions and directions made by the court; and
(c) at once inform the court and all parties of any significant failure (whether or not that participant is responsible for that failure) to take any procedural step required by the Rules, any practice direction or any direction of the court. A failure is significant if it might hinder the court in furthering the overriding objective.

CASE MANAGEMENT

In a number of cases (see e.g. *R. v Phillips* [2007] EWCA Crim 1042) CACD has emphasised the need for judges to be robust in case management decisions, for parties ordered to take steps, to take them, and for case progression staff to ensure compliance with management orders.

Civil matters in the Crown Court continue to be governed by the Crown Court Rules 1982, recently amended in relation to case management by S.I. 2009/3361.

Case progression officers

13–002 From the beginning of the case, unless the court other-wise directs each party must nominate a case progression officer (CPO), informing all other parties and the court who that person is and how to contact him. The court will, in fulfilling its duty under r.3.2, where appropriate, nominate a court officer responsible for progressing the case.   R.3.4

A CPO's duties are to:

(a) monitor compliance with any directions; and
(b) ensure that the court is kept informed of events that may affect the progress of that case.

He must ensure that he can be contacted promptly about the case during ordinary business hours, act promptly and reasonably in response to communications about the case and if he will be unavailable, appoint a substitute to fulfil his duties and inform the other case progression officers.

The Crown Court CPO will be under a general duty to liaise closely with the parties' CPOs to ensure that the case is ready for trial on the date set. At or as soon as possible after the PCMH, the parties will be supplied with a copy of the directions made. Although it is the primary duty of the parties to comply with the directions made, it is the function of the Crown Court case progression officer to monitor compliance with the directions made and to ensure that any failures that cannot be remedied, and which may affect the readiness of the case and the date for trial, are brought to the attention of the judge assigned to the case (if there is one) or to the Resident Judge (PD 2004, Annex F, 6.1).   PD 2004, Annex F, 6.1

As to the use of a case progression form to prove an admission, see *R. (on the application of Firth) v Epping Magistrates Court* [2011] EWHC 388 (Admin); [2011] 1 W.L.R. 1818; [2011] Crim. L.R. 717.

Case management; the Judge's duty

13–003 The Judge has a duty to further the overriding objective by actively managing the case. Such active case management includes: R.3.2(2)

(1) the early identification of the real issues;
(2) the early identification of the needs of witnesses;
(3) achieving certainty as to what must be done, by whom, and when, in particular by the early setting of a timetable for the progress of the case;
(4) monitoring the progress of the case and compliance with directions;
(5) ensuring that evidence, whether disputed or not, is presented in the shortest and clearest way;

(6) discouraging delay, dealing with as many aspects of the case as possible on the same occasion, and avoiding unnecessary hearings;

(7) encouraging the participants to co-operate in the progression of the case; and

(8) making use of technology.

The Judge must actively manage the case by giving any direction appropriate to the needs of that case as early as possible.

The rules as to case management do not, however, override the general principles of the criminal law. "Stopping" a case, quashing an indictment or otherwise preventing continuation of the trial, is not an exercise of the power to manage a case. Quashing an indictment brings a case to its end. Provided a judge does so appropriately he is perfectly entitled to express his views of a case and to encourage the prosecutor to reconsider the public interest He must bear in mind, however, that pursuant to POA 1985 the decision to institute or continue criminal proceedings is vested in the CPS (*R. v FB, AJ, JC* [2010] EWCA Crim. 1857; [2010] 2 Cr. App. R. 35) For a consideration of the duties of the CPS, and the judge's power to stop a case, see *R. v SH* [2010] EWCA Crim 1931 1 Cr. App. R. H.

He is responsible for the management of the trial, and has to strike a balance between the needs of everyone involved in the case and the need for justice to be done swiftly. He should e.g. refuse an adjournment unless satisfied that it is necessary and justified. He is also responsible for controlling the timetable of the trial and may exercise his powers to ensure that the trial ends by a certain date, see, *R. v Chaaban (Khodr)* [2003] EWCA Crim 1012; [2003] Crim. L.R. 658. As to his power impose time limits on cross-examination, see *R. v B (Ejaz)* [2005] EWCA Crim 805; [2006] Crim. L.R. 54.

Listing; PD 2004, Annex F

13–004   PD 2004, Annex F, inserted in July 2010, sets out the principles applicable to listing in the Crown Court. It supports CPR 2011 which introduces new principles of case management to criminal cases. The changes made emphasise the fact that:

(1) judges will be required to make firm arrangements for the listing of cases at the PCMH (or earlier);

(2) parties must comply with the directions and timetable then set so that cases are ready to be heard in accordance with that timetable;

(3) cases commence promptly at the appointed hour in accordance with that timetable.

It sets out the new arrangements for the assignment of judges to cases, and emphasises the importance, recently stressed by the CACD, of ensuring that no short hearings in other cases interrupt the prompt commencement or continuation of trials each day at the time appointed.

The court's case management powers

13–005   In fulfilling its duty under r.3.2, the court may give any direction and take any step actively to manage a case unless, of course, that   R.3.5

direction or step would be inconsistent with legislation, including the Rules, (but see *R. (Kelly) v Warley MC* [2008] Crim. L.R. 643 in relation to legal privilege).

In particular, it may:

(1) nominate a judge to manage the case;
(2) give a direction on its own initiative or on application by a party;
(3) ask or allow a party to propose a direction;
(4) for the purpose of giving directions, receive applications and representations by letter, by telephone or by any other means of electronic communication, and conduct a hearing by such means;
(5) give a direction without a hearing;
(6) fix, postpone, bring forward, extend or cancel a hearing;
(7) shorten or extend (even after it has expired) a time limit fixed by a direction;
(8) require that issues in the case should be determined separately, and decide in what order they will be determined; and
(9) specify the consequences of failing to comply with a direction.

The above powers enable the judge to deal with preliminary matters exclusively by reference to written submissions limited to a length specified by him if he thinks it right to do so. He is not bound to allow oral submissions, but if he does so he is entitled to put a time limit on them. The necessary public element of any hearing will be sufficiently achieved if the accused and representatives of the media in court are supplied with copies of written submissions if they wish to see them. No particular method of approach is prescribed, as case management decisions are case specific *(R. v K* [2006] EWCA Crim 724; [2006] 2 All E. R (Note)). R.3.5.(3)(4)

A magistrates' court may give a direction that will apply in the Crown Court if the case is to continue there, and conversely, the Crown Court may give a direction that will apply in a magistrates' court if the case is to continue there.

Application to vary a direction
13–006 The power to give a direction under these provisions includes a power to vary or revoke that direction. A party may apply to vary a direction (r.3.6(l)) if: R.3.5(5)

(1) the court gave it without a hearing;
(2) the court gave it at a hearing in his absence; or
(3) circumstances have changed.

The party who applies to vary a direction must apply as soon as practicable after he becomes aware of the grounds for doing so; and give as much notice to the other parties as the nature and urgency of his application permits. R.3.6

Agreement to vary a time limit fixed by a direction
13–007 The parties may agree to vary a time limit fixed by a direction, but only if: R.3.7

(1) the variation will not:
    (a) affect the date of any hearing that has been fixed; or
    (b) significantly affect the progress of the case in any other way;
(2) the court has not prohibited variation by agreement; and
(3) the court's case progression officer is promptly informed.

The court's case progression officer must refer the agreement to the court if he doubts the conditions in (1)(a) and (b) are satisfied.

Case preparation and progression

13–008 At every hearing: R.3.8(1)

(1) if a case cannot be concluded there and then, the court must give directions so that it can be concluded at the next hearing or as soon as possible after that;
(2) the court must, where relevant:
    (a) if the accused is absent, decide whether to proceed nonetheless;
    (b) take the accused's plea (unless already done) or if no plea   R.3.8(2) can be taken find out whether the accused is likely to plead guilty or not guilty;
    (c) set, follow or revise a timetable for the progress of the case, which may include a timetable for any hearing including the trial or the appeal;
    (d) in giving directions, ensure continuity in relation to the court and to the parties' representatives where that is appropriate and practicable; and
    (e) where a direction has not been complied with, find out why, identify who was responsible, and take appropriate action.
(3) in order to prepare for a trial in the Crown Court a judge must conduct a plea and management hearing unless the circumstances make that unnecessary;
(4) in order to prepare for the trial, the court must take every reason-   R.3.11 able step to facilitate the attendance of witnesses when they are needed.

The case management forms set out in the Practice Direction must be used, and where there is no form then no specific formality is required. The court will make available to the parties a record of any directions given.

Readiness for trial or appeal

13–009 In relation to a party's preparation for trial or appeal, (and in   R.3.9 this rule and r.3.10 trial includes any hearing at which evidence will be introduced) each party must, in fulfilling his duty under r.3.3, above:

(1) comply with directions given by the court;
(2) take every reasonable step to make sure his witnesses will attend when they are needed;
(3) make appropriate arrangements to present any written or other material; and
(4) promptly inform the court and the other parties of anything that may:

(a) affect the date or duration of the trial or appeal; or

(b) significantly affect the progress of the case in any other way.

The court may require a party to give a certificate of readiness.

Conduct of trial or an appeal

13–010   In order to manage a trial or an appeal, the judge: R.3.10; I.

(1) must establish, with the active assistance of the parties, what are the disputed issues;

(2) must consider setting a timetable that:
   (a) takes account of those issues and of any timetable proposed by a party; and
   (b) may limit the duration of any stage of the hearing;

(3) may require a party to identify:
   (a) which witnesses that party wants to give evidence in person;
   (b) the order in which he intends those witnesses to give their evidence;
   (c) whether he requires an order compelling the attendance of a witness;
   (d) what arrangements, if any, he proposes to facilitate the giving of evidence by a witness;
   (e) what arrangements, if any, he proposes to facilitate the participation of any other person, including the accused;
   (f) what written evidence he intends to introduce;
   (g) what other material, if any, he intends to make available to the court in the presentation of the case;
   (h) whether he intends to raise any point of law that could affect the conduct of the trial or appeal; and

(4) may limit:
   (a) the examination, cross-examination or re-examination of a witness; and
   (b) the duration of any stage of the hearing.

The approach to procedural defects

13–011   The prevailing approach is to avoid determining cases on technicalities when they do not result in real prejudice and injustice but instead to ensure that they are decided fairly on their merits. This approach is reflected in the Rules and, in particular, in the overriding objective.

Accordingly, where a judge is confronted with procedural failure in the progress of an accused's case through the courts he should:

(1) first ask himself whether the intention of the legislature was that any act done following that procedural failure should be invalid;

(2) if the answer to that question is "no", go on to consider the interests of justice generally, and most particularly whether there is a real possibility that either the prosecution or the defence may suffer prejudice on account of the procedural failure; if there is such a risk, he must decide whether it is just to allow the proceedings to continue;

(3) unless there is a clear indication that Parliament intended jurisdiction automatically to be removed following procedural failure, base his decision on a wide assessment of the interests of

justice, with particular focus on whether there is a real possibility that the prosecution or the accused may suffer prejudice. If that risk is present, the judge should then decide whether it is just to permit the proceedings to continue.

A procedural failure should result in a lack of jurisdiction only if this is necessary to ensure that the criminal justice system serves the interests of justice and thus the public, or where there is at least a real possibility of the accused suffering prejudice as a consequence of that procedural failure. It is otherwise, of course, where a court acts without jurisdiction, in those circumstances the proceedings will usually be invalid. (*R. v Soneji* [2005] UKHL 49; [2006] 2 Cr. App. R. 20; *R. v Knights* [2005] UKHL 50; [2006] 1 Cr. App. R. (S.) 80; *R. v Ashton* [2006] EWCA Crim 794; [2006] 2 Cr. App. R. 15; *R. Clarke* [2008] UKHL 8; [2008] 2 Cr. App. R. 2; *R. (Bromley) v S of S for Justice* [2010] EWHC 112 (Admin); [2010] A.C.D. 43).

As to a judge rectifying defects by assuming the powers of a District Judge (Magistrates' Courts) under CA 2003, s.66, see JURISDICTION.

B. Case Management Hearings

1. Plea and Case Management Hearings (PCMH)

General

13–012   PD 2004, IV.41, as amended, applies to the sending, committal or transfer of cases by magistrates' courts for trial in the Crown Court.

Active case management at plea and case management hearings are intended to reduce the number of ineffective and disrupted trials.

A magistrates' court committing, transferring or sending a case for trial to the Crown Court:

(1) must order a plea and case management hearing at the Crown Court in every case; and
(2) may, where it considers it necessary, order a pre-trial hearing.

The date of such hearing will be fixed by arrangement with the Crown Court.

For cases:

(a) committed to the Crown Court for trial under MCA 1980, s.6 the case progression form to be used in the magistrates' court is set out in Annex E with guidance notes. A plea and case management should be ordered by the magistrates court in every case, to be held within about seven weeks after committal;
(b) transferred to the Crown Court for trial under CJA 1987, s.14(1) or under CJA 1991, s.53(1) the directions contained in the case progression form used in cases for committal for trial applies as if the case had been committed on the date of the notice of transfer. A plea and case management hearing should be listed by the Crown Court to be held **within about seven weeks after transfer**.

PD 2004, IV.45.1.6

PD 2004, IV.41.7

CASE MANAGEMENT

Where both hearings are ordered, both dates should be fixed at the same time.

Management of cases to be heard in the Crown Court

13–013   Part IV.41 supplements the rules in CPR 2011, Pt 3 as they apply to the management of cases to be heard in the Crown Court. Note that:

PD 2004, IV.41.1.2

(1) where time limits or other directions in PD 2004 appear inconsistent with this section, the directions in this section take precedence;
(2) the case details form set out in Annex E should be completed by the Crown Court case progression officer in all cases to be tried on indictment.

As to the control and management of heavy fraud and other complex criminal cases, see 13–043 and following, below.

As to live links, see LIVE LINKS.

Necessity for preliminary hearing

13–014   A preliminary hearing is not required in every case sent for trial under CDA 1998, s.51 (see r.12.2, which alters the Crown Court rule from which it is derived).

PD 2004, IV.41.3–5

A preliminary hearing should be ordered subject to any directions by the Resident Judge only where (according to the guidance notes):

(1) there are case management issues which call for such a hearing;
(2) the case is likely to last for more than four weeks;
(3) it is desirable to set an early trial date;
(4) the accused is a child or young person;
(5) there is likely to be a guilty plea and the accused could be sentenced at the preliminary hearing; or
(6) it seems that it is a case suitable for a preparatory hearing in the Crown Court (see below).

The preliminary hearing form to be used in the Crown Court is set out in Annex E with guidance notes. A preliminary hearing, if there is one, should be held about 14 days after sending.

It will not normally be appropriate to order that the PCMH be held on a date before the expiry of at least four weeks from the date on which the prosecutor expects to serve the prosecution case papers, to allow the defence a proper opportunity to consider them. To order that a PCMH be held before the parties have had a reasonable opportunity to complete their preparation in accordance with the CPR 2010, risks compromising the effectiveness of this most important pre-trial hearing and risks wasting their time and that of the court.

Plea and case management hearing

13–015   The effectiveness of a plea and case management hearing in a contested case depends in large measure upon preparation by all concerned and upon the presence of the trial advocate or an advocate who is able to make decisions and give the court the assistance which the trial advocate could be expected to give.

PD 2004, IV.41, 8, 9

Special provisions apply in the case of heavy fraud and other complex criminal cases, see 13–043 and following, below. Resident judges in setting the listing policy should ensure that listing officers fix cases as far as possible to enable the trial advocate to conduct the plea and case management hearing and the trial.

In Class 1 and Class 2 cases, and in all cases involving a serious sexual offence against a child, the plea and case management hearing must be conducted:

(1) by a High Court judge, by a Circuit Judge or by a Recorder to whom the case had been assigned in accordance with para.33 of Pt IV (allocation of business within the Crown Court) (see ALLOCATION AND DISTRIBUTION OF BUSINESS); or

(2) by a judge authorised by the Presiding Judges to conduct such hearings.

In the event of a guilty plea in such a case before an authorised judge, the case must be adjourned for sentencing by a High Court Judge or by a Circuit Judge or Recorder to whom the case had been assigned.

The form

13–016   The form on which the hearing takes place is self-explanatory. Copies are provided at the court. Notes for Guidance are attached to it.

The parties must complete only one copy of the form and make it available to the judge at or before the hearing (if there are more than five defendants, a further form should be filled in only so far as necessary). Local practice will determine how the form should be completed and by whom and whether electronically or not. The directions must be easily understood by, and made available to, the CPOs. Time limits should normally be expressed by reference to a particular date rather than by the number of days allowed, to make the task of the CPO easier.

The court may make rulings (see 13–040—13–042, below) which have binding effect (subject to being discharged or varied) under CPIA 1996, s.40 as to:

"(a) any question as to the admissibility of evidence;
(b) any other question of law relating to the case concerned."

The extent to which courts exercise the power to make these rulings at this hearing is a matter for the judge after considering representations.

Except where otherwise required, a direction to "serve" material means serve on the other parties and file with the Crown Court.

Where a direction requires a party to respond to a proposal (e.g. a proposed edited interview) the party responding will be expected to suggest a counter-proposal.

It is essential that the issues in a case are carefully examined and identified at the plea and case management hearing. Where, at a later stage, it occurs to counsel that he has failed to do so (in this case, counsel realised during the course of cross-examination), it is his duty to alert the judge before continuing, and ask how to proceed; compliance with CPR 2011 is a necessity; it is no longer possible to attempt to ambush the prosecution at half-time with a submission of no case to answer *(cf. R. (D.P.P.) v Chorley JJ. and another*, unreported, June 8, 2006, DC. *R. v Penner* [2010] EWCA Crim 1155, [2010] Crim. L. R. 936).

CASE MANAGEMENT

Further pre-trial hearings after the plea and case management hearing

13–017 Additional pre-trial hearings should be held only if needed for some compelling reason. Where necessary the power to give, vary or revoke a direction without a hearing should be used.

Abuse of process

13–018 Where the defence are considering making an abuse of process application, the matter should be raised at the plea and case management hearing (see ABUSE OF PROCESS).

Children and young persons

13–019 Where a young person is indicted jointly with an adult accused, the judge should, at the plea and case management hearing:

PD 2004, IV.39.4, 5

(1) consider whether the young accused should be tried on his own, and should ordinarily so order unless of opinion that a joint trial would be in the interests of justice and would not be unduly prejudicial to his welfare; if he is to be tried jointly with an adult, the ordinary procedures will apply subject to such modifications, if any, as the judge may see fit to order;

(2) consider and so far as practicable give directions on the matters covered by PD 2004, IV.39, 9–15.

PD 2004, Annex F, 5.1

Cases will be listed for trial depending on the circumstances of each particular case, in accordance with the listing practice determined by the Resident Judge.

Under the regime set out in CPR 2011, the parties will be expected to provide an accurate estimate of the length of trial at the PCMH (or earlier) and accurate information about the availability of witnesses. Accurate information is essential. Experience has shown that dates on which an expert witness is available to attend the trial sometimes is the cause of difficulty. Although the provision of accurate information is the responsibility of the prosecution and defence, the listing officer or the CPO should try and ensure that this issue is addressed prior to the PCMH. A trial date or trial window will generally be fixed at or immediately after the PCMH, or at a preliminary hearing if appropriate.

PD 2004, Annex F, 4.3

Fixing trial dates; custody time limits

13–020 Cases will be listed for trial depending on the circumstances of each particular case, in accordance with the listing practice determined by the Resident Judge.

PD 2004, Annex F, 5.1

Judge's approach

13–021 Experience from the operation of the former PDHs discloses a number of points:

(1) the directions judge needs to have a very firm control of the proceedings, and having studied the papers, needs to be very aware of the issues involved and the nature of the evidence to be adduced by the Crown;

(2) since two of the objects of the procedure are to concentrate the minds of both sides on the issues involved and the requirements as to witnesses, at a very early stage, to avoid the situation where witnesses at the trial are sent away as superfluous, the attention of counsel must be concentrated on all the issues relevant to the hearing;

(3) if any relevant matter is unresolved, the case should not be released until it has been or, if that is not practicable, an adjourned hearing should be fixed; and

(4) only in the most exceptional circumstances should there be no arraignment—one of the principal purposes of the hearing is to establish the plea; this is done by arraignment, not by vague indications of pleas that will eventually be entered at the trial.

As to the control and management of heavy fraud and other complex criminal cases, see 13–043 and following, below.

B. Preparatory hearings

(1) General

Statutory provisions

13–022 Statute provides for a preparatory hearing being ordered, either on application by the prosecutor or an accused, or on the judge's own initiative, in two distinct types of case, namely in:

CJA 1987, s.7

(1) **serious and complex fraud cases**, where, before the time when the jury are sworn it appears to the judge that the evidence on the indictment reveals a case of fraud of such seriousness or complexity that substantial benefits are likely to accrue from such a hearing; or

(2) **cases other than serious fraud**, where, in relation to an offence:

CPIA 1996, ss.28,29

(a) an accused is committed for trial, or sent for trial under under CDA 1998, s.51 for the offence concerned; or

(b) proceedings for trial on the charge concerned are trans-transferred to the Crown Court (or when CJA 2003, Sch.3 comes into force the subject of a notice under CDA 1998, s.51C); or

(c) a voluntary bill of indictment is preferred, and

(d) a case of such complexity, or of such seriousness, is revealed, or a case whose trial is likely to be of such a length that substantial benefits are likely to accrue from a preparatory hearing before the time the jury are sworn.

The reference to the time the jury are sworn is to be read, in the case of a trial without a jury, as a reference to the time when, if the trial were conducted with a jury, the jury would be sworn.

CJA 1987, s.7(2B); CPIA 1996, s.29(5)

Special provisions apply to terrorist cases, see CPIA 1996, ss.29(1B). As to complex health and safety cases, see the observations of CACD in *R. v EGS Ltd* [2009] EWCA Crim 1942.

In *R. v I (C)* [2009] W.L.R. (D) 286 CACD pointed out that for all practical purposes a judge of the Crown Court now has exactly the same powers of case management in a non-preparatory hearing as in one where a direction for a statutory preparatory hearing is given. Given the co-extensive powers of case management outside the preparatory hearing regime, judges ought to be very cautious about directing formal preparatory hearings under CPIA 1996 or CJA 1987. In *R. v CH* [2010] Crim. L.R. 312 CACD suggested that virtually the only reason for holding one is if the judge is going to give a ruling which ought to be the subject of an interlocutory appeal (13–039). Such rulings are likely to be few and far between.

The desire of one party to test a ruling by interlocutory appeal is not a good enough reason for doing so, unless the point is one of the few which are genuinely suitable for such procedure and there is a real prospect of such appeal being both capable of resolution in the absence of evidence and avoiding significant wastage of time at the trial (*R. v I (C)*, above).

Statutory purposes
13–023 The purposes of such hearings are laid down by statute, thus:

(1) identifying issues which are likely to be material to the determinations and findings which are likely to be required during the trial; CJA 1987, s.7(1)

(2) if there is a jury, assisting their comprehension of those issues and expediting the proceedings before them;

(3) determining an application for trial without a jury (see TRIAL WITOUT A JURY);

(4) assisting the judge's management of the trial; and

(5) considering questions as to the severance or joinder of charges.

A judge who is considering whether to hold such a hearing needs only to ask himself whether exercising any of his power under s.9 (13–026) below) at such a hearing, rather than at the trial when a jury has been sworn, is likely to result in substantial benefits. If so, he may order a preparatory hearing and exercise those of his powers under s.9 which he thinks likely to achieve those benefits (*R. v H (Interlocutory Application; Disclosure)* [2007] UKHL7; [2007] 2 Cr. App. R. 6).

"Expediting the proceedings" includes dealing with issues of evidence, and those questions which typically arise under PACE 1984, s.78 (*R. v Claydon* [2001] EWCA Crim 1359; [2004] 1 Cr. App. R. 36).

The judge who is to conduct the hearing should be, save in the most exceptional cases, the judge who is to conduct the trial (*R. v Southwark CC Ex p. Commrs of C & E* (1993) EWCA Crim 3436, and 13–046 below).

Restriction to statutory purposes
13–024 A preparatory hearing may be held only where the statutory provisions set out in 13–023 above are fulfilled (not e.g. *merely* to allow points of law to be decided and then tested by interlocutory appeal: *R. v Pennine Acute Hospital NHS Trust, etc* [2003] EWCA Crim 3436 (2003) 147 S.J. 1426).

A statutory preparatory hearing:

(1) needs to be distinguished from an informal pre-trial review (*Re Gunawardena* (1990) 91 Cr. App. R. 55); it is to be used only for the purposes specified in the statute, and for no others (*ibid*);

(2) is concerned with matters which will facilitate the trial, not with applications to prevent the trial taking place (*R. v Hedworth* [1997] 1 Cr. App. R. 421).

A ruling as to the scope of the indictment is a ruling as to its construction (*R. v G* [2002] Crim. L.R. 59). As to the issue of separate trials where two of three accused were unfit to be tried, see *R. v B* [2009] 1 Cr. App. R. 19.

For preparatory hearings relating to decisions as to whether a particular defence may be advanced at the trial, see *R. v Quayle* [2003] 2 Cr. App. R. 34, *R. v S Ltd* [2009] 2 Cr. App. R.11. As to consideration of evidence and issues under PACE 1984, s.78, see *R. v Claydon,* above.

In relation to (2) in 13–022 (i.e. cases other than serious fraud) there must be a case of such complexity, a case of such seriousness, or a case whose trial is likely to be of such a length that a preparatory hearing would be beneficial, as where, e.g.:

(a) the process of proper disclosure can be conducted;
(b) the marshalling of evidence can be prepared with direct reference to the live issues in the case;
(c) issues as to the proper interpretation of the relevant legislation, and as to the directions to be given to the jury may be resolved, but it is important for the judge to bear in mind that his power to make rulings on questions of law is confined to questions of law "relating to the case" (*R. v Shayler* [2002] UKHL 11 [2002] 2 All E.R. 477). An application for disclosure under CPIA 1996, s.8 is not question of law "relating to the case" and does not therefore fall to be decided within the scope of a preparatory hearing; under CPIA 1996, s.8(2) a judge may determine such an application at any time, and nothing prevents him from dealing with it in parallel proceedings (see 13–026) on the same occasion as he holds a preparatory hearing, though no interlocutory appeal lies under CJA 1987, s.9(11) (*R. v H (Interlocutory Application; Disclosure)*, above).

The hearing

13–025 If a statutory preparatory hearing is ordered:

(1) for purposes connected with the hearing the trial starts with that hearing (*R. v PGH* [2006] 1 Cr. App. R. 14), and arraignment takes place at the start of the hearing, if it has not taken place already;
(2) the judge needs, therefore, to bear in mind the effect on the custody time limits of the decision to hold such a hearing (*Re Kanaris* [2003] UKHL 2; [2003] 2 Cr. App. R. 1);
(3) in most cases, the decision to hold a hearing should be in respect of all accused joined in the same indictment (*Re Kanaris* above);
(4) any matter dealt with before the jury is sworn is to be treated as forming part of the hearing, provided that the purpose of dealing with it at that stage is one of the objects set out in the statute (*R. v Jennings* (1994) 98 Cr. App. R. 308).

CJA 1987, s.9(4); CPIA 1996, s.31(4) (5)

CASE MANAGEMENT

As to reporting restrictions, see REPORTING AND ACCESS RESTRICTIONS.

Rulings and orders; parallel proceedings

13–026   At the hearing, the judge may determine: CJA 1987, s.9;
                                                                          CPIA

(1) any question arising under CJA 1993, s.6 (relevance of external law to certain charges of conspiracy, attempt and incitement);
(2) any question as to the admissibility of evidence; and
(3) any other questions of law relating to the case,

but note that:

   (a) he may not give a ruling which is tantamount to an order granting a stay or quashing the indictment (*R. v Hoogstraten*, [2003] EWCA Crim 3642; [2004] Crim L.R. 498);
   (b) any ruling he gives has effect throughout the trial unless it appears to him, on application, that the interests of justice require him to vary or discharge it;
   (c) he must be prepared to vary his rulings where required (*R. v Shayler* [2002] UKHL 11; [2002] All E. R. 477).

He may adjourn the hearing from time to time.

Parallel proceedings

13–027   While the only powers which the judge may exercise in a   CJA 1987,
statutory preparatory hearing are those set out above,   s.9(10); CPIA
                                                                          1996, s.31(11)

(1) where there is a parallel hearing going on at the same time, the judge may in that other hearing exercise his other common law and statutory powers, although a right of interlocutory appeal arises under s.9(11) only where the matters come within s.9(3); and
(2) there is no reason in principle why the two hearings should not take place on the same occasion provided that the distinctions between the two hearings and the issues which the judge may determine in each, is kept clearly in mind (*R. v H (Interlocutory Application; Disclosure)* above).

In relation to cases under CPIA 1996, there will be those where the judge decides that orders under s.30(4)–(7) should be made before the hearing. In such a case he may make an order either before or at the hearing, and the above provisions apply accordingly (*ibid,* s.32).

An order or ruling made by the judge has effect during the trial unless it appears to the judge, on an application made to him during the trial, that the interests of justice require him to discharge it.

Disclosure by prosecutor

13–028   The judge may order the prosecutor   CJA 1987,
                                                                          s.9(10),CPIA
                                                                          1996, s.31(11)

(1) to supply the court and each accused with a written "case statement", of the following, namely:
   (a) the principal facts of the prosecution case;
   (b) the witnesses who will speak to those facts;

(c) any exhibits relevant to those facts;

(d) any propositions of law on which the prosecutor intends to rely; and

(e) the consequences in relation to any of the counts in the indictment which appear to him to flow from the matters stated in (a)–(d);

(2) to prepare his evidence and other explanatory material in such form as appears likely to aid the comprehension of a jury and to supply it in that form to the court and to each accused;

(3) to give the court and each accused notice of documents, the truth   R.15.1
of the contents of which ought, in the prosecutor's view, to be admitted, and of any other matters which ought to be agreed; and

(4) to make any amendments to any case statement supplied that appear to the judge to be appropriate, having regard to any objections made by any accused.

The judge may specify the time within which any requirements are to be complied with.

Disclosure by accused

13–029   Where the judge has ordered the prosecution to supply a case   CJA 1987,
statement and the prosecutor has complied, the judge may order each   s.9(5)
accused to:

(1) give the court and the prosecutor notice of any objections that he has to the case statement; and

(2) inform the court and the prosecution of any point of law (including points as to the admissibility of evidence) which he wishes to take, and any authority on which he intends to rely for that purpose; and

in addition to the general provisions as to compulsory disclosure in   CJA 1987, s.9A;
criminal cases as to which see DISCLOSURE.   CPIA 1996,
Sch.3, para.4
Note that the judge:

(a) if he considers the reasons inadequate, will inform the party concerned and has the power to require further or better reasons.

(b) if he decides that any order which could be made at the hearing should be made *before* the hearing, he may act accordingly.

(c) may specify the time within which any requirement contained in it is to be complied with.

Orders under s.9(5) should be clear, comprising short questions   CJA 1987, s.9(9)
identifying matters upon which the prosecutor requires the accused's agreement. In the case of several accused each one's case should be the subject of individual orders (*Case Statements made under CJA 1987, s.9* (1993) 97 Cr. App. R. 417).

Certain consequences may flow from failure to comply with such orders (see 13–031 below), and the judge will need to warn each accused of them. In making an order he must warn the accused of the possible consequences of not complying with it; if it appears to him that the reasons given in pursuance of s.9(5)(iv) are inadequate, he will inform the person giving them, and may require him to give further or better reasons.

Case statements of no evidential value

13–030 It was said in *R. v Mayhew*, unreported, November 18, 1991 that neither the prosecutor's case statement nor the defence statement has any evidential value, nor do they limit the respective parties in the evidence they may call.   CJA 1987, s.9(7); CPIA 1997, s.31(6)

The object of ordering a case statement is to:

(1) inform the other side of the case that is intended to be put forward;
(2) facilitate preparation for trial, and to avoid surprise; and
(3) enable comment to be made under CJA 1987, s.10 where there is a significant departure from the statement.

The judge should not permit a case statement to be put before the jury as a matter of course, as if it were particulars of the indictment.

Departure from the case at trial

13–031 A party may depart from the case he disclosed in pursuance of a requirement under s.9 or s.31 respectively but where he: CJA 1987, ss.9(7) (9), 9A,10

(1) does so; or
(2) fails to comply with the requirement to disclose,

the judge, or with his leave, any other party, may make such comment as appears appropriate, and the jury, or in the case of a trial without a jury, the judge, will be able to draw such inferences as appear proper, though no part of the case statement or any other information relating to the accused may be disclosed after the jury have been sworn without the consent of the accused concerned.

The judge, in doing anything under this provision, or in deciding whether to do anything under it, may have regard to such matters as the extent of any departure or failure and whether it is justified.

(2)   Procedure

Application for preparatory hearing;

13–032 A party who wants the court to order a preparatory hearing under CJA 1987, s.7(2) or under CPIA 1996, s.29(4) must: CPIA 1996, ss.31(6)(7)(9), 34, Sch.3, paras 3, 4, 5

(1) apply in the form set out in PD 2004, Annex D;
(2) include a short explanation of the reasons for applying; and
(3) serve the application on the court officer and all other parties.

A prosecutor who wants the court to order that: R.15.2

(a) the trial be conducted without a jury under CJA 2003, ss.43 or 44; or
(b) the trial of some of the counts included in the indictment be conducted without a jury under DVA 2004, s.17,

must apply under r.15 for a preparatory hearing, whether or not the accused has applied for one.

Time for applying
13–033 A party who applies under r.15.1 must do so not more than 28 days after:

(1) the committal of the accused;
(2) the consent to the preferment of a bill of indictment in relation to the case;
(3) the service of a notice of transfer; or
(4) where a person is sent for trial, the service of copies of the documents containing the evidence on which the charge or charges are based.

A prosecutor who applies under r.15.1 because he wants the court to order a trial without a jury under CJA 2003, s.44 (jury tampering) must do so as soon as reasonably practicable where the reasons do not arise until after that time limit has expired. The court may extend the time limit, even after it has expired.

A form of application is set out in PD 2004, Annex D; specifying the grounds of the application which must be served on the Crown Court officer, a copy of the application being served at the same time on any other party.

Representations concerning an application
13–034 A party who wants to make written representations concerning an application made under r.15.1 must: R.15.3

(1) do so within seven days of receiving a copy of that application; and
(2) serve those representations on the court officer and all other parties.

An accused who wants to oppose an application for an order that the trial be conducted without a jury under CJA 2003, ss.43 or 44 must serve written representations under this rule including a short explanation of the reasons for opposing that application.

Determination of application
13–035 Where an application has been made under r.15.1(2) the court   R.15.4
must hold a preparatory hearing; other applications made under r.15.1 should normally be determined without a hearing.

The court officer will serve on the parties in the case, in the form set out in PD 2004, Annex D:

(a) notice of the determination of an application made under r.15.1; and
(b) an order for a preparatory hearing made by the court of its own initiative, including one that the court is required to make.

Orders for disclosure
13–036 Any disclosure order under CJA 1987, s.9, or CPIA 1996,   R.15.5
s.31, must identify any documents that are required to be prepared and served by the prosecutor under that order.

A disclosure order under either of those sections does not require an accused to disclose who will give evidence, except to the extent that disclosure is required by:

(1) CPIA 1996, s.6A(2) (disclosure of alibi); or
(2) CPR 2010, Pt 24 (disclosure of expert evidence).

The court officer will serve notice of the order, in the relevant form set out in PD 2004, Annex D, on the parties.

Service of documents, etc.
13–037 The service of notices or other documents is covered by r.15.6.

CJA 1987, s.9(11), (12)

(3)   Reporting restrictions
13–038   See REPORTING AND ACCESS RESTRICTIONS

D.   Interlocutory appeals
Right of appeal
13–039   Appeal lies, but only with leave from that court, to the CACD, from:

CJA 1987, s.9(13), (14)

(1) any order or ruling of a judge;
(2) made within the ambit of a preparatory hearing as defined in CJA 1987, s.7(1), or as the case may be, CPIA 1996, s.31(3); and
(3) involving a question of law within CJA 1987, s.9(3)(b) or (c) (see APPEALS FROM THE CROWN COURT).

As to defence costs, see POA 1985, s.16(4A); CJA 2003, s.257.

The judge may continue the preparatory hearing notwithstanding that leave has been granted to appeal, but the preparatory hearing is not to be concluded until the appeal has been determined or abandoned (see *R. v Y* [2001] Crim.L.R. 389).

CACD may confirm, vary or reverse the judge's decision.

E.   Preliminary hearings; pre-trial rulings
Definitions
13–040   A pre-trial hearing is one which relates to a trial on indictment and takes place:

CPIA 1996, s.39, 71

(1) after the accused has been sent for trial for the offence; or
(2) after a voluntary bill of indictment has been preferred; and
(3) before the start of the trial.

The "start" of a trial on indictment (s.39(3)) occurs at the time when a jury are sworn or, if the court accepts a plea of guilty *at* the time when a jury is sworn, when that plea is accepted (subject to s.30, and to CJA 1987 in relation to preparatory hearings).

The reference to the time the jury are sworn is to be read, in the case of a trial without a jury, is a reference to the time when, if the trial were conducted with a jury, the jury would be sworn. CDA 1998, s.57 permits the use of TV links at such a hearing where such facilities exist, and the accused is in custody.

Effect of pre-trial ruling

13–041   At such a hearing, the judge may, either on application by a party or of his own motion, make a ruling:

CPIA 1996, s.39

(1) as to the admissibility of evidence; or
(2) on any question of law in the case.

That ruling has (subject to CPIA 1996, s.40(4)) immediate effect from the time it is made until the case against the accused is disposed of by acquittal or conviction or by the prosecutor deciding not to proceed (ibid s.40).

It is desirable, where the judge is asked to decide whether the facts support a charge, for the facts on which the ruling is sought to be recorded (*R. v Marshall* [1998] 2 Cr. App. R. 282).

Under s.40(4) a judge, whether or not the judge who made the ruling, may, either on application or of his own motion, discharge, vary, or further vary it, if it appears to him to be in the interests of justice so to do, where there has been a change of circumstances since the ruling or the last application was made.

Reporting restrictions

13–042   Reporting restrictions apply to proceedings and rulings under the section but the judge may lift the restrictions in certain circumstances.

CPIA 1996, ss.41.42

A ruling made under s.40(1) is not binding for the purposes of a re-trial where the first jury disagreed. A judge may discharge or vary any ruling of his own motion if it appears to be in the interests of justice to do so.

F.   Protocol for the control and management of heavy fraud and other complex criminal cases [2005] 2 All E.R. 429

1.   Introduction

General

13–043   This protocol supplements CPR 2011, and summarises good practice which experience has shown may assist in bringing about some reduction in the length of trials of fraud and other crimes that result in complex trials. Flexibility of application of this protocol according to the needs of each case is essential; it is designed to inform but not to prescribe.

The protocol:

(1) is primarily directed towards cases which are likely to last eight weeks or longer; but
(2) should also be followed in all cases estimated to last more than four weeks;

(3) applies to trials by jury, but many of the principles will be applicable if trials without a jury are permitted under CJA 2003, s.43.

The best handling technique for a long case is continuous management by an experienced judge nominated for the purpose.

2. The investigation

Prosecution and defence teams

13–044 The judge will treat:

(1) the lead advocate for the prosecution
  (a) as having the responsibility for taking all necessary decisions in the presentation and general conduct of the prosecution case in court, although
  (b) in relation to "policy decisions", the advocate must not give an indication or undertaking which binds the prosecution without first discussing the issue with the director of the prosecuting authority or other senior officer.
(2) the lead advocate for the defence as having responsibility to the court for the presentation and general conduct of the defence case.

"Policy" decisions (in (1(b)) should be understood as referring to non-evidential decisions on: such matters as:

  (i) the acceptance of pleas of guilty to lesser counts or groups of counts or *available* alternatives;
  (ii) offering no evidence on particular counts;
  (iii) consideration of a retrial, whether to lodge an appeal; certification of a point of law; and
  (iv) the withdrawal of the prosecution as a whole.

(For further information see the "Farquharson Guidelines" on the role and responsibilities of the prosecution advocate).

Note that, in each case;

- a CPO must be assigned by the court, prosecution and defence from the time of the first hearing when directions are given until the conclusion of the trial.
- where there are multiple accused, the Legal Services Commission (LSC) will need to consider carefully the extent and level of representation necessary.

Length of case; initial consideration

13–045 If the prosecutor in charge of the case or the lead advocate for the prosecution consider that the case as formulated is likely to last more than eight weeks, the case should be referred in accordance with arrangements made by the prosecuting authority to a more senior prosecutor. The senior prosecutor will consider whether it is desirable for the case to be prosecuted in that way or whether some steps might be taken to reduce its likely length, whilst at the same time ensuring that the public interest is served.

Any case likely to last six months or more must be referred to the director of the prosecuting authority.

Special arrangements will be put in place for the early notification by the CPS and other prosecuting authorities, to the LSC and to a single designated officer of the court in each region of any case which the CPS or other prosecuting authority consider likely to last over eight weeks.

The court will allocate such cases and other complex cases likely to last four weeks or more to a specific venue suitable for the trial in question, taking into account the convenience to witnesses, the parties, the availability of time at that location, and all other relevant considerations.

3. Designation of trial judge

Continuity of judge

13–046 In any complex case which is expected to last more than four weeks the trial judge will be assigned under the direction of the Presiding Judges at the earliest possible moment.

In *R. v EGS Ltd* [2009] EWCA Crim 1942, CACD suggested that in health and safety prosecutions at the Crown Court, at all events when the matter is not the subject of an early plea, a judge may need to be appointed at an early stage to manage the case to trial. This should be done in all cases involving death or very serious injury and in any other cases where there is potential complexity.

Note that:

(1) the ordinary rule that the judge who has had conduct of the preparatory hearing should also conduct the trial, may not be departed from without compelling reason *(R. v I (C)* [2009] W.L.R. (D) 286 CACD);
(2) active steps need to be taken in the planning of court business and judicial commitments to avoid wherever possible the necessity for a judge to find himself having to consider leaving a complex case between a case management/preparatory hearing and trial.

A judge faced with a direct clash of commitments, which can only be resolved by disengaging from one case or uprooting the carefully planned timetable of another, is entitled to take such a course. Such reason while it is "administrative" is not comparable to the mere "operational convenience" under consideration in *R. v Southwark CC, Ex p C & E Commrs* (1993) 97 Cr. App. 266 which would not suffice. It does not help to apply the label "exceptional" to the circumstances which will justify such a course, save that:

(a) a decision not to conduct the trial is the exception to the general rule;
(b) there must be a sufficiently compelling cause to depart from the norm, stated above;
(c) the decision must be made by the judge, not, for example, by the listing officer;
(d) the decision must be made only after a hearing at which all parties have had an opportunity to make representations; and

(e) before departing from the norm, the judge, if not himself the court's Resident Judge, ought to consult that judge; and

(f) all judges should consult one of the circuit's Presiding Judges and, of course, respect any directions or advice given.

If, unusually, that necessity should arise in a preparatory hearing, the question to be resolved is not "a matter of law" but of judgment for the judge, and CACD will not interfere unless his decision is at which no reasonable judge could arrive.

See also *R. v GH* [2010] Crim. L.R. 312.

4. Case management

Objectives

13–047 The number, length and organisation of case management hearings will depend critically on the circumstances and complexity of the individual case. However, thorough, well-prepared and extended case management hearings will save court time and costs overall.

Effective case management of heavy fraud and other complex criminal cases requires the judge to have a much more detailed grasp of the case than may be necessary for many other plea and case management hearings.

A case management decision refusing to order an adjournment before trial or indeed at any time before the start of the summing-up may constitute a "terminatory" ruling against which a prosecutor may appeal (*R. v Clark,* unreported, October 9, 2007, CACD).

Fixing the trial date

13–048 Although it is important that the trial date should be fixed as early as possible, this may not always be the right course. There are two principal alternatives. The trial date should:

(1) be fixed at the first opportunity, i.e. at the first (and usually short) directions hearing, from then on:
   (a) everyone must work to that date;
   (b) all orders and pre-trial steps will be timetabled to fit in with that date; and
   (c) all advocates and the judge should take note of this date, in the expectation that the trial will proceed on the date determined; or
(2) not be fixed until the issues have been explored at a full case management hearing, after the advocates on both sides have done some serious work on the case. Only then can the length of the trial be estimated.

Which procedure is apposite must depend on the circumstances of each case, but the earlier it is possible to fix a trial date, by reference to a proper estimate and a timetable set by reference to the trial date, the better.

It is generally to be expected that once a trial is fixed on the basis of the estimate provided, that it will be *increased* if, and only if, the party seeking to extend the *time* justifies why the original estimate is no longer appropriate.

The first hearing for the giving of initial directions

13–049   At the first opportunity the assigned judge should hold a short hearing to give initial directions. The directions on this occasion might well include:

(1) that there should be a full case management hearing on, or commencing on, a specified future date by which time the parties will be properly prepared for a meaningful hearing and the defence will have full instructions;

(2) that the prosecution should provide an outline written statement of the prosecution case at least one week in advance of that case management hearing, outlining in simple terms:

(a) the key facts on which it relies;

(b) the key evidence by which the prosecution seeks to prove the facts. The statement must be sufficient to permit the judge to understand the case and for the defence to appreciate the basic elements of its case against each defendant. The prosecution may be invited to highlight the key points of the case orally at the case management hearing by way of a short mini-opening. The outline statement should not be considered binding, but it will serve the essential purpose in telling the judge, and everyone else, what the case is really about and identifying the key issues;

(3) that a core reading list and core bundle for the case management hearing should be delivered at least one week in advance;

(4) preliminary directions about disclosure.

The first case management hearing

13–050   At the first case management hearing:

(1) the prosecution advocate should be given the opportunity to highlight any points from the prosecution outline statement of case (which will have been delivered at least a week in advance), and

(2) each defence advocate should be asked to outline the defence.

If the defence advocate is not in a position to say what is, and what is not, in issue, then the hearing may be adjourned for a short and limited time and to a fixed date to enable the advocate to take instructions.

Such an adjournment should only be necessary in exceptional circumstances, since:

(a) the defence advocate should be properly instructed by the time of the first case management hearing; and

(b) in any event he is under an obligation to take sufficient instructions to fulfil the obligations contained in CJA 2003, ss.33–39.

Nature of hearing

13–051   At the hearing there should be a real dialogue between the judge and all advocates for the purpose of identifying:

(1) the focus of the prosecution case;
(2) any common ground; and
(3) the real issues in the case (see CPR 2011, r.3.2).

As to the issues in health and safety cases, see *R. v. EGS Ltd (above)*. The judge will try to generate a spirit of cooperation between the court and the advocates on all sides.

It may be noted that:

(a) the expeditious conduct of the trial and a focusing on the real issues must be in the interests of all parties;
(b) it cannot be in the interests of any accused for his good points to become lost in a welter of uncontroversial or irrelevant evidence;
(c) in many fraud cases the primary facts are not seriously disputed; the real issue being what each accused knew and whether that accused was dishonest.

Once the judge has identified what is, and what is not, in dispute, he is in a position to discuss with the advocate:

(i)   how the trial should be structured;
(ii)   what can be dealt with by admissions or agreed facts;
(iii) what uncontroversial matters should be proved by concise oral evidence;
(iv)   what timetabling can be required under CPR 2010, r.3.10; and
(v)   other directions.

It is important that proper defence case statements be provided as required by CPR 2011; judges will use the powers contained in CPIA 1996, ss.28–34 (and the corresponding provisions of CJA 1987, ss.33 and following) and CPR 2011 to ensure that realistic defence case statements are provided.

This objective may also be achieved by requiring the prosecution to serve draft admissions by a specified date and by requiring the defence to respond within a specified number of weeks.

The date of the next case management hearing should be fixed at the conclusion of the hearing so that there is no delay in fixing the date.

Further case management hearings; length of trial

13–052 Even intensive case management on the lines referred to above may still be insufficient to reduce a potentially long trial to a manageable length. Generally a trial of three months should be the target, but there will be cases where a duration of six months or, in exceptional circumstances, even longer may be inevitable. If the trial is not estimated to be within a manageable length, it will be necessary for the judge to consider what steps should be taken to reduce the length of the trial, whilst still ensuring that the prosecutor has the opportunity of placing the full criminality before the court.

To assist the judge in this task:

(1) the lead advocate for the prosecution should be asked to explain

why the prosecution have rejected a shorter way of proceeding; they may also be asked:

(a) to divide the case into sections of evidence;

(b) to explain the scope of, and the need for, each section;

(2) the lead advocates for the prosecution and for the defence should be prepared:

(a) to put forward, in writing, if requested, ways in which a case estimated to last more than three months can be shortened, and

(b) to consider possible severance of counts or accused, exclusion of sections of the case or of evidence or areas of the case where admissions can be made.

The judge may consider pruning the indictment by omitting certain charges and/or by omitting certain accused.

The judge's powers (1) abandonment, severance

13–053   CPR 2011 require the judge to take a more active part in case management. Nevertheless these salutary provisions do not have to be exercised on every occasion. The judge must not usurp the function of the prosecution; in pruning the indictment, he ought bear in mind that he will, at the outset, know less about the case than the advocates. The aim is to achieve fairness to all parties.

The judge does, however, have two methods of pruning available for use in appropriate circumstances:

(1) persuading the prosecutor that it is not worthwhile pursuing certain charges and/or certain accused;

(2) severing the indictment.

Severance for reasons of case management alone is perfectly proper, although the judge should have regard to any representations made by the prosecutor that severance would weaken his case. Before using what may be seen as a blunt instrument, however, the judge should insist on seeing full defence statements of all affected accused.

Severance may be unfair to the prosecutor if, for example, there is a cut-throat defence in prospect. For example, the defence of the principal accused may be that he relied on the advice of his accountant or solicitor that what was happening was acceptable. The defence of the professional may be that he gave no such advice. Against such a background, it might be unfair to the prosecutor to order separate trials of the two accused.

The judge's powers (2) evidence and charges

13–054   Where the advocates have done their job properly, by narrowing the issues, pruning the evidence and so forth, it may be quite inappropriate for the judge to "weigh in" and start cutting out more evidence or more charges of his own volition. The judge should make a careful assessment of the degree of judicial intervention which is warranted in each case.

In particular, in respect of:

(1) **expert evidence**

(a) identification of the subject matter of expert evidence to be adduced by the prosecutor and the defence should be made as early as possible, preferably at the directions hearing;

(b) following the exchange of expert evidence, any areas of disagreement should be identified and a direction should generally be made requiring the experts to meet and prepare, after discussion, a joint statement identifying points of agreement and contention and areas where the prosecutor is put to proof on matters of which a positive case to the contrary is not advanced by the defence;

(c) after the statement has been prepared it should be served on the court, the prosecutor and the defence; in some cases, it might be appropriate to provide that to the jury;

(2) **surveillance evidence** where:

(a) a prosecution is based upon many months of' observation or surveillance evidence; and

(b) it appears that it is capable of effective presentation based on a shorter period,

The advocate should be required to justify the evidence of such observations before it is permitted to be adduced, either substantially or in its entirety; schedules should be provided to cover as much of the evidence as possible and admissions sought.

Disclosure: (1) fraud cases

13–055   In fraud cases the volume of documentation obtained by the prosecutor is liable to be immense. The problems of disclosure are intractable and have the potential to disrupt the entire trial process. As to non-fraud cases, see 13–056 below.

The prosecution lawyer (and the prosecution advocate if different) brought in at the outset, have each a continuing responsibility to discharge the prosecution's duty of disclosure, either personally or by delegation, in accordance with the A-G's Guidelines on Disclosure. The prosecution should disclose only those documents which are relevant (i.e. likely to assist the defence or undermine the prosecution (CPIA 1996, s.3(1) and CJA 2003).

In considering questions of disclosure it is almost always undesirable to give the "warehouse key" to the defence, since this amounts to an abrogation of the prosecutor's responsibility and the defence solicitors may spend a disproportionate amount of time and incur disproportionate costs trawling through a morass of documents.

The judge should:

(1) try to ensure that disclosure is limited to what is likely to assist the defence or undermine the prosecution;

(2) at the outset set a timetable for dealing with disclosure issues; he should fix a date by which all defence applications for specific disclosure must be made;

(3) at the outset (and before the cut-off date for specific disclosure applications) ask the defence to indicate what documents they are interested in and from what source; a general list is not an acceptable response to this request;

(4) insist upon a list which is specific, manageable and realistic; he may also require justification of any request;

Disclosure (2) non-fraud cases

13–056 In non-fraud cases, the same considerations as set out in 13–055 apply but some may be different:

Thus:

(1) it is not possible to approach many non-fraud cases on the basis that the accused knows what is there or what the defence are looking for; but on the other hand
  (a) this should not be turned into an excuse for a "fishing expedition"; and
  (b) the judge should insist on knowing the issue to which any request for disclosure applies;
(2) if the *bona fides* of the investigation is called into question, the judge will be concerned to see that:
  (a) there has been independent and effective appraisal of the documents contained in the disclosure schedule; and
  (b) and that its contents are adequate.

In an appropriate case where this issue has arisen and there are grounds which show there is a real issue, consideration should be given to receiving evidence on oath from the senior investigating officer at an early case management hearing.

Abuse of process

13–057 Applications to stay or dismiss for abuse of process have become a normal feature of heavy and complex cases. Such applications may be based upon delay and the health of defendants. See *R. v Howell* [2003] EWCA Crim 486. It should be noted that abuse of process is not there to discipline the prosecution or the police. Where the issue arises:

(1) the arguments on both sides must be reduced to writing;
(2) oral evidence is seldom relevant;
(3) the judge should direct full written submissions (rather than "skeleton arguments") on any abuse application in accordance with a timetable set by him; these should identify any element of prejudice the defendant is alleged to have suffered.

And see ABUSE OF PROCESS.

5.   The trial

Case management at the trial

13–058 The Protocol recognises that a heavy fraud or other complex trial has the potential to lose direction and focus:

(1) the jury may lose track of the evidence, thereby prejudicing both prosecution and defence;
(2) the burden on the accused, the judge and indeed all involved may become intolerable; and

(3) scarce public resources will be wasted.

In this situation, the judge needs to exercise firm control over the conduct of the trial at all stages; his role in a heavy fraud or other complex criminal case is different from his role in a "conventional" criminal trial.

So far as possible, he should be freed from other duties and burdens, so that he can give the high degree of commitment which a heavy fraud trial requires.

Schedules, timetabling, taking stock

13–059 The protocol suggests that:

(1) by the outset of the trial at the latest (and in most cases very much earlier) the judge be provided with a **schedule,** showing the sequence of prosecution (and in an appropriate case defence) witnesses and the dates upon which they are expected to be called;

(2) this schedule should be kept under **review** by the judge and by the parties; if a case is running behind or ahead of schedule, each witness affected must be advised by the party who is calling him at the earliest opportunity;

(3) if an **excessive amount of time** is allowed for any witness, the judge may ask why; he may probe with the advocates whether the time envisaged for the evidence-in-chief or cross-examination (as the case may be) of a particular witness is really necessary;

(4) there should be periodic case **management sessions,** during which the judge engages the advocates upon a stock-taking exercise: asking, amongst other questions, "where are we going?" and "what is the relevance of the next three witnesses?"; this will be a valuable means of keeping the case on track (CPR 2011, r.3.10 will again assist the judge;

(5) "**case management notes**" from the judge to the advocates, setting out the judge's tentative view on where the trial may be going off track, which areas of future evidence are relevant and which may have become irrelevant (e.g. because of concessions, admissions in cross-examination and so forth) together with written responses may, if cautiously used, provide a valuable focus for debate during the periodic case management reviews held during the course of the trial;

(6) setting rigid **time limits** in advance **for cross-examination** is rarely appropriate, but the judge can and should indicate when cross-examination is irrelevant, unnecessary or time wasting, the judge may limit the time for further cross-examination of a particular witness;

EPE, graphics, self-serving statements

13–060 There is potential for saving time in fraud and other complex criminal trials, by:

(1) electronic presentation of evidence (EPE), which should be used more widely; there should still be a core bundle of those

documents to which frequent reference will be made during the trial;

(2) greater use of other modern forms of graphical presentations, wherever possible;

(3) the judge considering the extensive editing of self-serving interviews, even when the defence want the jury to hear them in their entirety; such interviews are not evidence of the truth of their contents but merely of the accused's reaction to the allegations.

Problems have arisen when the LSC have declined to allow advocates or solicitors to do certain work; on occasions the matter has been raised with the judge managing or trying the case. The LSC has provided guidance to judges on how they can obtain information from the LSC as to the reasons for their decisions; further information in relation to this can be obtained from the Complex Crime Unit, Legal Services Commission, 29–37 Red Lion Street, London, WC1R 4PP.

G. Records; transcripts

Duty to make records

13–061 For each case, as appropriate, the Crown court officer will record, by such means as the Lord Chancellor directs: R. 5.4.

(1) each charge or indictment against the accused;

(2) the accused's plea to each charge or count;

(3) each acquittal, conviction, sentence, determination, direction or order;

(4) each decision about bail;

(5) the power exercised where the court commits or adjourns the case to another court:

(a) for sentence, or

(b) for the offender to be dealt with for breach of a community order, a deferred sentence, a conditional discharge, or a suspended sentence of imprisonment, imposed by that other court;

(6) the court's reasons for a decision, where legislation requires those reasons to be recorded;

(7) any appeal;

(8) each party's presence or absence at each hearing;

(9) any consent that legislation requires before the court can proceed with the case, or proceed to a decision.

As to arrangements for recording and transcription of proceedings where appeal may be brought to CACD, see r.5.5. See as to the custody of case materials, r. 5.6.

Notes

14. CHILDREN AND YOUNG PERSONS

14–001   A number of topics are relevant here as affecting children and young persons, in particular:

Quick guide

1. Juveniles defined (14–002)
2. Juveniles as accused persons (14–003)
3. Trial of juveniles (14–004)
4. Remand of juveniles (14–005)
5. Remittal to youth court (14–012)
6. Penalties on conviction (14–015)
7. Evidence of children (14–025)
8. Reparation orders (14–032)
9. Youth offender panels (14–039)

1.   Juveniles defined

14–002   Young persons under 18 are commonly known as juveniles though the law distinguishes for some purposes between "children" (under 14) and "young persons" (14 to 18). Section 44 (1) of CYPA 1933 provides that every court dealing with a child or young person brought before it, whether as an offender or otherwise, must have regard to the welfare of the child or young person who is brought before it, and shall, in a proper case, take steps for removing him from undesirable surroundings and seeing that proper provision is made for his education and training.

CYPA 1933, ss.44(1), 107(1)

2.   Juveniles as accused persons

Jurisdiction

14–003   A juvenile appears in the Crown Court where:

(1) he is charged with an offence of homicide; or
(2) each of the requirements of FA 1968, s.51A(1) would be satisfied with respect to:
   (a) the offence; and
   (b) the person charged with it, if he were convicted of the offence;
(3) a minimum sentence under VCRA 2006, s.29(3) would apply if he were convicted of the offence;
(4) the offence is a "grave crime" such as is mentioned in PCC(S)A 2000, s.91(1) and the magistrates' court considers that, if found guilty, it ought to be possible to sentence him in pursuance of that section, or where a sentence under the "dangerous offender" provisions is likely to be required;
(5) he is charged jointly with an adult and the magistrates' court considers it necessary in the interests of justice to commit the

cases of both for trial, or to send the case or transfer the case to the Crown Court for trial; or

(6) he is charged jointly with an adult; or

(7) (a) the charge arises out of circumstances connected with an offence with which an adult is charged; or

(b) an adult is charged with aiding and abetting or procuring an offence by a juvenile; or

(c) a juvenile is charged with aiding and abetting or procuring an offence by an adult; otherwise he will be tried in the youth court.

In (6) and (7) there is a discretion and it is for the lower court to determine whether the trial should be in the adult court or the youth court.

As to the manner in which juveniles are brought before the Crown Court, see SENDING ETC FOR TRIAL.

Juveniles may be remitted to the youth court from the Crown Court, see 14–012 below.

3.   Trial of juveniles

14–004   In addition to the differences in the purposes of sentencing (14-002), juvenile offenders are generally dealt with in the youth court. Where they are tried on indictment there is no "juvenile assize court". They are tried in the Crown Court, generally where the juvenile is being tried with an adult; or where, due to the gravity of the offence it can only be tried at the Crown Court. A juvenile may be committed to the Crown Court for sentence (see COMMITTALS FOR SENTENCE). As to procedure etc see VULNERABLE ACCUSED.

4.   Remand of juveniles

If the Legal Aid Etc Bill 201, now going through Parliament, is enacted in its present form, it will make substantial changes to this section.

14–005   The court remanding a child or young person charged with or convicted of one or more offences, sending his case to the Crown Court for trial, or committing him for sentence, which does not release him on bail, must remand or commit him to local authority accommodation (and in the following provisions reference to a "remand" is to be construed as reference to a committal).   CYPA 1969, s.23(1)

"Young person" here means a person who has attained the age of 14 years and is under the age of 17.

The court remanding such a person to local authority accommodation must designate the local authority which is to receive him, and that authority must be:

(1) in the case of a person who is being looked after by a local authority, that authority; and

(2) in any other case, the local authority in whose area it appears to the court that he resides or that one of the offences was committed.

Where a juvenile is so remanded with conditions, and a constable has reasonable grounds for suspecting that he has broken any of those conditions, he may be arrested and taken before a magistrate in a manner similar to that applying in breach of bail (CYPA 1969, s.23A; CJPOA,1994, s.23), see BAIL.

Remand with security requirement

14–006 Where a person is remanded to local authority accommodation, it is lawful for any person acting on behalf of the designated authority to detain him.

CYPA 1969, ss.23(3), (4), (5)

The judge remanding him may, after consultation with the designated authority, require that authority to comply with a security requirement, that is to say, a requirement that the person in question be placed and kept in secure accommodation, though such a requirement is not to be imposed unless that young person:

(1) has attained the age of 12 or is a young person of a description prescribed under CDA 1998, s.97(2) (yet to be prescribed); and

(2) is charged with or has been convicted of a violent or sexual offence, (as listed in CJA 2003, Sch.15, Pts 1 and 2 respectively) or an offence punishable in the case of an adult with imprisonment for 14 years or more; or

(3) has a recent history of absconding when remanded to local accommodation, and is charged or has been convicted of an imprisonable offence alleged or found to have been committed while he was so remanded,

and, in the case of (2) or (3) above, the judge is of the opinion that only such a requirement would be adequate to protect the public from serious harm from him.

CYPA 1969, ss.23(4), (5A)

If the young person is aged 15 or 16, then the Judge may remand to a remand centre if no local authority secure accommodation is available, provided the court has been notified that such a centre is available, or to a prison if neither secure accommodation nor a remand centre is available. This is unless the judge is of the opinion that, by reason of his physical or emotional immaturity, or a propensity to harm himself, it would be undesirable for him to be remanded to a remand centre or a prison.

CYPA 1969, s.7A

The local authority is empowered to detain the accused in a secure training centre.

Definitions

14–007 "Secure accommodation" means accommodation which is provided in a community home, a voluntary home or a registered children's home for the purpose of restricting liberty and is approved for that purpose by the Secretary of State.

CYPA 1969, ss.23(1), (4)

The judge may require the local authority to keep a child or young person in secure accommodation if it has been notified that such accommodation is available for him.

"Sexual offence" and "violent offence" are defined in CJA 2003, Sch.15.

Legal representation

14–008 The judge may not impose a security requirement in respect of a child or young person, nor declare him to be a person eligible for remand centre or prison, if he is not legally represented, unless:

CYPA 1969, s.23(5A)

(1) he was granted a right to representation funded by the CDS but the right has been withdrawn because of his conduct, or because it appeared that his financial resources were such that he was not eligible to be granted such a right; or

(2) having been informed of his right to apply for a representation order and having had the opportunity to do so, he refused or failed to apply; or

(3) he applied for such representation and the application was refused because it appeared that his financial resources were such that he was not eligible to be granted a right to it.

Explanation in open court

14–009 When imposing a security requirement, the judge must:

(1) state in open court that he is of the opinion set out above; and

(2) explain to the person remanded or committed in open court and in ordinary language why he is of that opinion.

CYPA 1969, s.23(6)

Remand without security requirement

14–010 A judge remanding a person to local authority accommodation without imposing a security requirement may, after consultation with the designated authority:

CYPA 1969, ss.23(7), (7A), (8), (9)

(1) subject to CYPA 1969, s.23AA (electronic monitoring), require the person to comply with:

   (a) any conditions as could be imposed under BA 1976, s.3(6) (see BAIL) if he were then being granted bail; and

   (b) any conditions imposed for the purpose of securing the electronic monitoring of his compliance with any other condition imposed; and

where such conditions are being imposed, must explain in open court and in ordinary language why they are being imposed; and

(2) impose on the authority requirements for securing compliance with any of the above bail conditions, or stipulating that he must not be placed with a named person.

CYPA 1969, ss.23(9), (10), (11)

Where a person is remanded to such accommodation, a "relevant court" may:

   (i) on the application of the designated authority impose on that person any such conditions as might be imposed under BA 1976, s.3(6);

   (ii) impose on the authority any requirements for securing compliance with the conditions imposed; and

   (iii) on the application of the authority or the person remanded, vary or revoke any such conditions.

A "relevant court" for these purposes means the court by which such person was remanded or any magistrates' court having jurisdiction over the place where he is for the time being (CYPA 1969, s.23(12)).

Electronic monitoring

14–011 The judge must not impose an electronic monitoring condition under CYPA 1969, s.23(7)(b) unless the accused:

CYPA 1969, s.23AA

(1) has attained the age of 12 years;
(2) is charged with, or has been convicted of:
  (a) a violent or sexual offence;
  (b) an offence punishable in the case of an adult with imprisonment for 14 years or more; or
  (c) one or more imprisonable offences which, together with any other imprisonable offences of which he has been convicted in any proceedings, amount, or would amount if he were convicted of the offences with which he is charged, to a recent history of repeatedly committing imprisonable offences while remanded on bail or to local authority accommodation; and provided that:
    (i) such arrangements are currently available, and the necessary provision can be made; and
    (ii) a youth offending team has informed the judge that in its opinion the imposition of such a requirement is suitable in the case of the accused.

The requirement must include a provision making a person responsible for the monitoring.

5. Remittal to youth court

14–012 Special provisions apply to juveniles in relation to punishment on conviction. As to the approach to sentencing juveniles, see SGC Guidelines Overarching Principles – Sentencing Youths, and DEALING WITH OFFENDERS. Custodial sentences are dealt with under DETENTION OF YOUNG OFFENDERS; Community sentences are dealt with under YOUTH REHABILITATION ORDERS.

PCC(S)A 2000, s.8(1)(2)(8)

Remittal to youth court

14–013 Where a person under 18 is convicted in the Crown Court of an offence other than homicide, the judge, unless he is of opinion that the case is one which can properly be dealt with by:

(1) an absolute or conditional discharge;
(2) a fine; or
(3) an order under PCC(S)A 2000, s.150, requiring his parent or guardian to enter into recognisances,

is required to remit him to a youth court for sentence. This is unless the judge is satisfied that it would be undesirable to do so.
The appropriate youth court will be:

(a) if the offender was sent to the Crown Court under CDA 1998, s.51 or s.51A, a youth court acting for the place where he sent to the Crown Court for trial; or

(b) in any other case, a youth court acting either for the same place as the Crown Court or for the place where the offender habitually resides.

The judge may, subject to CJPOA 1994, s.25 (restrictions on granting bail), give such directions as appear to be necessary with respect to the offender's custody or release on bail until he can be brought before the youth court. The appropriate certificate will be sent to the justices' chief executive (PCC(S)A 2000, s.8(4)).

An offender has no right of appeal against the order of remittal (*ibid.* s.8(5)).

PCC(S)A 2000, s.8(1)(2)(8)

"Undesirable" to remit
14–014   Clearly, it may be "undesirable" to remit an offender to the youth court, where, for example:

(1) the judge who has presided over the trial is likely to be better informed as to the facts and circumstances of the case;

(2) there will be a risk of disparity in sentencing if co–accused are sentenced in different courts on different occasions;

(3) there is the risk of delay, duplication of proceedings and fruitless expense in such a procedure; or

(4) difficulties may be caused in seeking to challenge the proceedings, appeal from the conviction lying to CACD, and against sentence to the Crown Court.

It may be desirable to remit where a report has been sought and the trial judge is likely to be unavailable when it is completed, though this situation can always be avoided by the magistrates who transfer the case to the Crown Court for trial giving directions for the preparation of reports (*R. v Lewis* (1984) 79 Cr. App. R. 94, per the Lord Chief Justice). A modern example of the approach is to be found in *R. v Akehurst* [2010] EWCA Crim 206.

It is suggested that the only occasion when remittal to a youth court is merited is where the judge has in mind the making of a supervision order, in which circumstances the magistrates may have a more complete knowledge of the local situation.

6.   Penalties on conviction
Purposes, etc. of sentencing: offenders under 18
14-015 Where a judge is dealing with an offender aged under 18 in respect of an offence, he must have regard to:

(1) the principal aim of the youth justice system (which is to prevent offending (or re-offending) by persons aged under 18, see CDA 1998, s.37(1));

(2) in accordance with CYPA 1933, s.44, the welfare of the offender; and

(3) the purposes of sentencing mentioned below; namely
  (a) the punishment of offenders;
  (b) the reform and rehabilitation of offenders;
  (c) the protection of the public; and
  (d) the making of reparation by offenders to persons affected by their offences;

save that this provision does not apply;

  (i) to an offence the sentence for which is fixed by law;
  (ii) to an offence the sentence for which falls to be imposed under;

  • FA 1968, s.51A(2) (minimum sentence for certain firearms offences);
  • VCRA 2006, s.29(6) (minimum sentences in certain cases of using someone to mind a weapon); or
  • CJA 2003, s.226(2) (detention for life for certain dangerous offenders), or
  • in relation to the making under MHA 1983, Pt 3 of a hospital order (with or without a restriction order); an interim hospital order, a hospital direction or a limitation direction.

Children and young persons

14–016 A judge, in dealing with a child or young person who is brought before him, either as an offender or otherwise, must have regard to the welfare of the child or young person, and must, in a proper case, take steps for removing him from undesirable surroundings, and for securing that proper provisions is made for his education and training.

This provision must be read with CJA 2003, s.142A which require a court dealing with an offender aged under 18 also to have regard to the principal aim of the youth justice system and the specified purposes of sentencing.

Accordingly in determining, in the case of an offender, whether he should take such steps as are mentioned above, the judge must also have regard to the matters mentioned in those paragraphs.

SGC(Y) (4.9) suggests that the proper approach when sentencing a young offender is for the judge, within a sentence that is no more restrictive on liberty than is proportionate to the seriousness of the offence(s), to seek to impose a sentence that takes proper account of the matters to which a court must have regard by:

  (a) confronting the offender with the consequences of his offending and helping him to develop a sense of personal responsibility;
  (b) tackling the particular factors (personal, family, social, educational or health) that put him at risk of offending;
  (c) strengthening those factors that reduce the risk that he will continue to offend;
  (d) encouraging reparation to victims; and
  (e) defining, agreeing and reinforcing the responsibilities of parents.

CHILDREN AND YOUNG PERSONS

Financial penalties: (1) general

14–017 While fines, compensation and orders to pay costs may be made against juveniles in much the same way as against adults (see FINES AND ENFORCEMENT), certain differences need to be noticed: MCA 1980, s.36

(1) there is no statutory limit on the amount of a fine that may be imposed on a juvenile in the Crown Court, but where the court is limited to magistrates' court powers, the maxima are:
   (a) in the case of a young person under 18, £1,000; and
   (b) in the case of a child, £250, unless the maximum fine in the case of an adult is less, when that maximum applies;
(2) a juvenile may not be committed to prison in default of payment of a fine or compensation, though a magistrates' court enforcing a Crown Court fine may order him to attend at an attendance centre.

Financial penalties: (2) responsibility of parent or guardian

14–018 Since few juveniles are likely to have the money available to pay fines, compensation or costs, where a person aged under 18 is convicted of an offence for which a fine, surcharge or an order for costs may be imposed or a compensation order made, and the judge is of the opinion that the case would best be met by such an order, whether or without any other punishment, the judge: PCC(S)A 2000, ss.137(1), (3), (4), (5) CJIA 2008, s.149, Sch.28, Pt 1, s.6, Sch.4, Pt 1, para.58

(1) must, in the case of an offender under 16; and
(2) may, in the case of an offender aged 16–17;

order the fine, surcharge, compensation or costs to be paid by the offender's parent or guardian unless:

   (a) that person cannot be found; or
   (b) it would be unreasonable, having regard to the circumstances, to make such an order.

This provision is extended to cover a case in which the judge would otherwise order a child or young person to pay a surcharge under CJA 2003, s.161A.

A similar provision applies in a case where the judge is minded to impose a fine in respect of the breach of certain community and other orders (ibid s.173(3)).

An order should not be made unless the parent or guardian has been given an opportunity of being heard, or has been required to attend and has failed to do so.

Financial penalties: (3) purpose of section 137

14–019 In considering whether to make an order under these provisions, the judge should have regard to the purpose of the section, which is that:

(1) parents should take some responsibility for their children's activities and they should take their duties seriously; though
(2) they cannot be held vicariously liable for every act of their child (*Lenihan v West Yorkshire Met Police* (1981) 3 Cr. App. R.(S.) 42); and

(3) it is unreasonable to make an order where a parent has done the best he or she can to keep their child from criminal ways (*R. v Sheffield CC Ex p. Clarkson* (1986) 8 Cr. App. R.(S.) 454) and is in no position to control it (*TA v DPP* [1997] 1 Cr. App. R.(S.) 1).

If the judge observes the principle that compensation orders should be made only in simple and straightforward cases, orders are likely to be rare: see the complications outlined in *Bedfordshire CC v DPP* [1996] 1 Cr. App. R.(S.) 322.

Financial penalties: (4) local authority as "parent or guardian"

14–020 References to a parent or guardian are to be construed as references to a local authority where the child or young person is: *PCC(S)A 2000, s.137*

(1) one for whom that authority has parental authority; and
(2) in their care; or
(3) provided with accommodation by them in the exercise of any function (in particular those under CA 1989) which stands referred to their social services committee under the Local Authority Social Services Act 1970.

An order remanding a young person into local authority accommodation does not confer parental responsibility (*North Yorkshire County Council v Selby Youth Court JJ* [1994] 1 All E.R. 991).

Financial penalties: (5) orders against local authorities

14–021 The power of a local authority to restrain an offender in its care might be less than that of a parent. It has the same right to assert the unreasonableness of an order as has the parent.

Where the authority has done everything it reasonably and properly can to protect the public from the offender, it is unreasonable to make an order against it (*D v DPP* (1995) 16 Cr. App. R.(S.) 1040).

Where the authority stands *in loco parentis* and the accused juvenile is acquitted, the authority is entitled to a defendant's costs order, where it would be appropriate in the case of the accused: *R. v Preston CC Ex p. Lancashire CC* [1998] 3 All E.R. 765.

Financial penalties: (6) fixing the quantum

14–022 Similar provisions apply to an order against a parent or guardian as apply to financial orders in respect of offenders, and a parent or guardian, other than a local authority, may be required to comply with a financial circumstances enquiry. *PCC(S)A 2000, s.138*

Financial penalties: (7) parents, etc. as appellants

14–023 A parent or guardian may appeal to CACD against an order made in the Crown Court as if he had been convicted on indictment and the order was a sentence passed on his conviction. *PCC(S)A 2000, s.137(7)*

Paragentive Order

14–024 See PARAGENTIVE ORDER *CDA 1998, s.8(1)(c),(2)(3); CSA 2010, s.40*

7. Evidence of children

Competency

14–025 A child, of whatever age, is, like all other persons competent to give evidence in criminal proceedings unless it appears to the judge that he is not a person who is able to:

YJCEA 1999, s.53

(1) understand questions put to him as a witness; and
(2) give answers to them which can be understood.

This section applies without the need for any gloss. Previous conceptions regarding children and their capacity to understand the nature and purpose of an oath and to give truthful and accurate evidence no longer apply and have no relevance (*R. v Barker* [2010] EWCA Crim 4; *The Times*, February 5, 2010).
Note that:

(a) the questions are entirely "witness-specific;"
(b) there are no presumptions or preconceptions;
(c) the witness need not understand the special importance of telling the truth,
(d) need not understand every question or give a readily understood answer to every question,

Many competent adult witnesses would fail such a test. Provided the witness can understand the questions put to him and can give understandable answers, he is competent (*ibid*).
There is no minimum age for competence. The age of the child is not the test, but whether the above two conditions are satisfied (see *R. v Malicki* [2009] EWCA Crim 365).
It is for the judge to determine whether the child witness is competent, approaching the matter as set out in 14–026 below. It is a matter well within his capacity and he requires no expert evidence on the matter, though the Act provides for it if required.

Judge's approach

14–026 The judge's task in assessing the competence of the witness is to determine whether the child fulfils the conditions set out in 14–025. It may be said that:

YJCE 1999 s.54.

(1) the enquiry should take the form of hearing evidence on the *voir dire* in the absence of the jury from the witness and any other relevant witness;
(2) any questioning the witness if considered necessary, should be conducted by the judge;
(3) the burden of establishing competence lies on the party calling the witness, on a balance of probabilities;
(4) that enquiry should ordinarily take place at the commencement of the trial (*R. v MacPherson* [2005] EWCA Crim 3605; [2006] 1 Cr.App.R.30); although
(5) there may be cases where evidence emerges in the course of the trial which causes the judge to change his mind.

Where, as is frequently the case, the assessment is based, at least in part on the content of pre-recorded video interviews with the witness, it is important to bear in mind that it is the competence of the child at the time of the trial that is in issue, so that if the position has changed when his evidence is looked at as a whole, the question of competence should be reconsidered (*R. v Powell* [2006] EWCA Crim 3; [2006] 1 Cr. App. R 3). See also *R. v M* [2008] EWCA Crim 2751.

Warning as to very young children

14–027　There is no longer any rule of law requiring corroboration of the unsworn evidence of a child, or any rule of practice to warn of the danger of convicting on such evidence, but it may be appropriate to warn the jury, if there is one, to take particular care with the evidence of a very young child.

Evidence through TV link and by means of video recording

14–028　The special protection for child witnesses is dealt with in SPECIAL MEASURES DIRECTIONS.

YJCEA 1999, s.35(1), (2); SOA 2003, Sch.6, para.4

Restrictions on accused cross-examining in person

14–029　No person charged with an offence as is mentioned below may cross-examine in person a witness who:

YJCEA 1999, ss.38(1), (2), (3); r.31

(1) is alleged to be the person against whom the offence was committed or a witness to the offence; and

(2) is a child, or is to be cross-examined after giving evidence in chief by means of a video recording made or in any other way when he was a child.

Section 35 applies to any offence under SOA 1956, ss.33–36, SOA 2003, Pt 1, or any relevant or superseded enactment (as to which see CJIA 2008, s.148, Sch.26, Pt 2, para.37) kidnapping, false imprisonment, or an offence under the Child Abduction Act 1984, ss.1, 2, any offence under CYPA 1933, s.1 or any other offence which involves an assault on, or injury to, any person.

The prohibition applies not only to the offence to which s.35 applies, but also to any other offence of whatever nature with which that person is charged in the proceedings.

These restrictions should be explained to the accused by the judge as early in the proceedings as reasonably practicable.

Trial judge's duty

14–030　Where, under this restriction, an accused is prevented from cross-examining a witness in person, the judge must:

YJCEA 1999, ss.38(1), (2), (3); r.31

(1) invite the accused to arrange for a legal representative to act for him for the purpose of cross-examining the witness; and

(2) require the accused to notify the court within seven days as to whether a legal representative is to act for him for that purpose and the details of that representative. The court is required to notify all parties of these details.

If the accused declines to be represented or fails to notify the court as required, the judge must consider whether it is necessary in the interests of justice to appoint a legal representative. If he does so, the court will notify all parties of the details of the appointment.

Where under this restriction the accused is prevented from cross-examining a witness in person, the judge must give an appropriate warning to the jury, if there is one, to ensure the accused is not prejudiced:

(a) by any inferences that might be drawn from the fact that the accused has been prevented from cross-examining the witness in person;

(b) where the witness has been cross-examined by a legal representative appointed by the court, by the fact that this has happened rather than the witness being cross-examined by a person acting as the accused's own legal representative.

As to procedure, see generally r.31, and SPECIAL MEASURES DIRECTIONS.

Restrictions on publication
14–031 See REPORTING RESTRICTIONS ACCESS.

YJCEA 1999, s.39(1)

8. Reparation orders

Making an order
14–032 "Reparation" here means an order to make reparation otherwise than by the payment of compensation.

PCC(S)A 2000, s.73(1), (2), (3), (4), (6) CJIA 2008, s.6, Sch.4, Pt 1, para.53

Where a child or young person is convicted of an offence other than one for which the sentence is fixed by law, the judge may make a reparation order requiring the offender to make reparation as specified in the order, to a specified person or persons identified as a victim of the offence, or a person otherwise affected by it, provided that:

(1) he does not pass upon him a custodial sentence, or make in respect of him a youth rehabilitation order or a referral order;

(2) the person to whom reparation is to be made consents; and

(3) the court has been notified by the Secretary of State that arrangements for implementing such orders are available in the area proposed to be named in the order.

The judge must not make a reparation order in respect of the offender at a time when a youth rehabilitation order is in force in respect of him unless when he makes the reparation order he revokes the youth rehabilitation order.

R.42

Where the judge could but does not make a reparation order (unless he passes a custodial or a community sentence), he must explain why he has not so when he explains the sentence he has passed.

Before making an order the judge must obtain and consider a written report by a probation officer or a local authority social worker or a member of a youth offending team indicating the type of work suitable to the offender, and the attitude of the victim or victims to the requirements proposed to be included in the order.

Requirements of the order

14–033 The requirements specified in the order must be such as are in the judge's opinion, commensurate with the seriousness of the offence, or the combination of that offence and one or more offences associated with it, and must, so far as is practicable, be such as to avoid any conflict with the offender's religious beliefs or any interference with the times, if any, at which the offender normally works or attends school or any other educational establishment; and the order must not require the offender:

(a) to work for more than 24 hours in aggregate; or
(b) to make reparation to any person without the consent of that person.

PCC(S)A 2000, s.74(1), (2), (8) CJIA 2008, ss.6, 149, Sch.4, Pt 1, para.54, 28, Pt 1

The order will name the local justice area in which it appears that the offender resides, or will reside, and any reparation required by the order will be made under the supervision of the responsible officer, and within a period of three months from the date the order is made.

Failure to comply with the order

14–034 Schedule 8 has effect for dealing with the discharge, revocation and amendment of reparation orders. The appropriate court for dealing with these matters is the youth court acting for the local justice area for the time being named in the order.

Where a reparation order is in force, and it is proved to the satisfaction of that court.

PCC(S)A 2000, s.75, Sch.8, paras 2, 4, 5; CJIA 2008, s.6, Sch.4, Pt 1, para.55

(1) that an offender has failed to comply with any requirement included in an order; and
(2) that the order was made by the Crown Court,

it may commit him in custody or release him on bail until he can be brought or appear before the Crown Court.

Where such offender is brought before the Crown Court, and it is proved to the judge's satisfaction that he has failed to comply with the requirement in question, he may revoke the order, and deal with him for the offence in respect of which the order was made in any manner in which he could have dealt with him for that offence if the order had not been made, taking into account the extent to which the offender has complied with the order. He may do so, notwithstanding the offender has reached the age of 18 before coming before the court.

The offender must be present in court unless the judge decides to take no action other than to:

(a) revoke the reparation; or
(b) cancel a requirement included in the order; or
(c) alter in the order the name of any area; or
(d) change the responsible officer.

9.   Youth offender panels

14–035   The power to refer a juvenile to a youth offender panel under PCC(S)A 2000, s.16, is reserved to the magistrates' courts. Jurisdiction will arise in the Crown Court only on appeal, or where an offender is subject to such an order at the time he was convicted in the Crown Court.

PCC(S)A 2000, Sch.1, para.14(3)

15. COMMITTALS FOR SENTENCE

Quick guide

1. Jurisdiction and powers

Magistrates' powers

15–001 The powers of a magistrates' court to impose a sentence of imprisonment are presently restricted to the imposition of a sentence of: MCA 1980, s.12

(1) 6 months for a single either-way offence, or
(2) totalling 12 months for two or more such offences imposed consecutively.

Increases in that jurisdiction, projected by the CJA 2003, s.283, have not come into force.

Special provisions apply to "schedule offences" i.e. those offences contained in MCA 1980, Sch.2 (i.e. criminal damage under CDA 1971, s.1, and aggravated vehicle taking under TA 1968, s.12A where no allegation is made other than damage, or where the damage involved does not exceed the prescribed limit).

As to fines, see MCA 1980, ss.24, 32, CJA 1982, s.37(2), PCCA 2000, s.135. The maximum fine available to a magistrates' court, save where statute provides otherwise is £5,000.

A magistrates'' court may commit an offender to the Crown Court for sentence, or to be dealt with, where it considers that a sentence in excess of its powers is required, under the statutory framework.

The Crown Court, in hearing an appeal from a magistrates' court, has no power to commit the appellant to itself for sentence under PCC(S) A 2000,s.3 in order to obtain enlarged powers of sentence, *R. v Bullock* (1963) 47 Cr. App. R. 288 (a decision on earlier legislation), but see *R. v Ashton* [2006] EWCA Crim 794, [2006] 2 Cr. App. R.15.

As to the information to be provided to the Crown Court on committal, see r.42.10.

Crown Court jurisdiction; procedure

15–002 The powers of the Crown Court will vary according to the statute under which the committal is made. Jurisdiction is, exercisable by a judge of the Crown Court sitting alone. A judge hearing an appeal with justices should ensure, if there is a committal for sentence in the same case, that he sits alone when he comes to deal with it (SCA 1981, s.73(1)): *R. (Bromley) v Secretary of State for Justice* [2010] A.C.D. 146(43), B.C.

The Crown Court has no jurisdiction to hear an appeal from the offender as to his committal, though a case may be remitted to the magistrates where the committal is clearly invalid. Otherwise the committal will need to be challenged by judicial review (*R. v Sheffield CC, ex p DPP* (1994) 15 Cr. App. R(S.) 768). Judicial review is dealt with in APPEALS FROM THE CROWN COURT.

Note that:

- the offender should be called on to admit his identity and the fact of conviction and committal;
- formal evidence of the conviction and committal should also be given (*R. v Jeffries* [1963] Crim.L.R.559);
- it is sensible before embarking on committal proceedings to ensure that there is no appeal against the conviction on which the committal is based; if there is, the committal proceeding should be adjourned until the appeal has been determined (*R. v Faithful* 34 Cr. App. R. 220);
- the proceedings then follow those applicable on a plea of guilty on indictment;
- care should be taken as to the age of the offender, since the statutory framework makes a sharp distinction between those under and over 18 years of age; the age at the date of conviction governs the *issue* (*R. v Robson* [2006] EWCA Crim 1414, [2007] 1 Cr. App. R.(S.) 54.

Advocates should always check the section under which the committal was made to identify the court's sentencing powers: *R. v Qayum* [2010] EWCA Crim 2237.

Disputes as to the facts

15–003 It is the duty of the committing magistrates to ensure that the Crown Court is informed of the facts found, and the judge should sentence on the facts found below and should not normally allow any dispute as to the facts to be reopened. Where:

(1) an issue arises for the first time before the Crown Court, the judge should normally determine the issue on any necessary and available evidence; but

(2) the offender claims to have raised the matter before the lower court, where the magistrates did not attempt to decide the issue, the judge will need to decide upon the course to be followed, taking into account all the circumstances, including:

    (a) the facts of the offence(s) as alleged by each party;

    (b) whether, on a balance of probabilities, he is satisfied that the offender raised the issue before the lower court;

    (c) the fact that the offender was committed because his record was considered serious enough to justify such a course; and

(d) the delay which remittal to the magistrates' court will cause *(Munroe v DPP* [1988] Crim LR 823).

The judge has a discretion to hold a Newton hearing (see GUILTY PLEAS) or further Newton hearing if there was one before the court below. In *R (Gillan) v DPP* [2007] 2 Cr. App. R.12 it was suggested that where there had been a Newton hearing at the magistrates' court, another should not be held at the Crown Court unless the offender could point to a significant new development.

See r. 42.10 as to the material to be transmitted from the lower court to the Crown court.

Limitation of powers

15–004   The judge's powers vary, according to whether the offender is committed under PCC(S)A 2000, ss.3 or 4A or under, ibid, s.6. He may deal with an offender on a committal:

(1) under **ss.3** and **4,** in any way in which he could have dealt with him if he had just been convicted of the offence, on indictment, but may not remit him to the magistrates' court (*R.* v *Isleworth CC Ex p. Buda* [2000] 1 Cr. App. R.(S.) 538); *PCC(S)A 2000, s.5*

(2) under ss.**3B, 3C and 4A,** in any way in which he could have dealt with him if he had just been convicted of the offence, on indictment; *PCC(S)A 2000, s.5A*

(3) under **s.6,** in any way in which the magistrates' court could deal with him if it had just convicted him of the offence, save that; *PCC(S)A 2000, s.6*

    (a) if the offender is committed in respect of a suspended sentence, the powers in CJA 2003, Sch.12, paras 8 and 9 are exercisable; and

    (b) where the offender is committed in respect of an offence triable only on indictment in the case of an adult, but which was tried summarily because the offender was under 18 years of age, the judge's powers are to:

        (i) impose a fine not exceeding £5,000; or

        (ii) deal with the offender in respect of the offence in any in which the magistrates' court could have dealt with him if it had just convicted him of an offence punishable with a term of imprisonment not exceeding six months.

Any duty or power which would, apart from these provisions, fall to be discharged or exercised by the magistrates, must not be exercised, but instead, will be discharged or exercised by the judge of the Crown Court.

Ancillary orders; interim RT disqualification

15–005   Since committal to the Crown Court is an alternative to dealing with the offender, the magistrates' court is not empowered on committal to make any ancillary orders, save that where the magistrates' court: *RTOA 1988, s.26(1),(4),(10)*

(1) commits an offender under s.6 or any enactment to which that section applies; and

(2) does not exercise its power or duty to disqualify under RTOA 1988, ss.34, 35 or 36,

it may order him to be disqualified until the Crown Court has dealt with him in respect of the offence.

If the offender is not sentenced within six months of the date of committal, that disqualification lapses. On dealing with the offender, a judge of the Crown Court, if he imposes a disqualification, must reduce the period by the length of the interim disqualification.

2. General power; conviction of either-way offence (s.3)

15–006 Magistrates may commit a person aged 18 or over convicted of an offence triable either-way (unless excluded by MCA 1980, s.17D "schedule" offences) where they are of opinion that: PCC(S)a 2000,S.3

(1) the offence or the combination of the offence and one or more offences associated with it is so serious;

(2) the Crown Court should, in the magistrates' opinion, have the power to deal with the offender in any way it could deal with him if he had been convicted on indictment.

Committal may be in custody or on bail to the Crown Court for sentence in accordance with PCC(S)A 200, s.5(l), and committal may be also in respect of certain other ancillary offences (see 15-013 below).

The power may be exercised where the magistrates consider that a financial penalty in excess of their powers (£5,000) ought to be imposed (R. v N Essex JJ. Ex p. Lloyd [2001] 2 Cr. App. R.(S.) 15), where it was suggested that in such a case the magistrates' should inform the Crown Court of their reasons for committal, While the judge would not be bound by their statement, it would be extremely valuable for him to know why the committal was made.

The magistrates may also commit where they are of opinion that a restriction order under MHA 1983 is required; see MHA 1983, s.43(4); CJA 2003, s.41, Sch.3, para.55(2).

A convicted corporation is treated as an individual aged 18 or over, but the custody and bail provisions do not apply.

If, on appearance before the Crown Court, it appears that the appellant pleaded guilty under a material mistake of fact, the court has a discretion to allow him to change his plea, and if, as a consequence, he pleads not guilty, he may be remitted to the magistrates' court: *R. v Isleworth CC Exp. Buda* (above).

3. Juvenile's indication of guilty plea (s.3B)

15–007 A magistrates' court may commit: PCC(S)A 2000,s.3B

(1) a person under 18 brought before them on an information charging him with an offence mentioned in PCC(S)A 2000, s.91; where

(2) he or his representative indicates under MCA 1980, S.24A or, as the case may be, S.24B, that he would plead guilty if the offence were to proceed to trial; and

(3) proceeding as if MCA 1980, s.9(l) were complied with and

he pleaded guilty under it, the magistrates convict him of the offence, and

the magistrates are of opinion that the offence or the combination of the offence and one or more offences associated with it is so serious that the Crown Court should, in their opinion have the power to deal with the offender as if the provisions of PCC(S)A 2000, s.91(3) (detention for grave crimes) applied.

In such circumstances the offender may be committed:

(a) in custody or on bail to the Crown Court for sentence in accordance with PCC(S)A 200, s.5A(l); and

(b) in respect of certain other ancillary offences (see 15-013, below).

As to the power to commit where magistrates are of the opinion that a restriction order under MHA 1983 is required, see MHA 1983, s.43(4); CJA 2003, s.41, Sch.3, para.55(2).

4. Dangerous young offender (s.3C)

15–008 magistrates' court may commit a person under 18 where: PCC(S)A: 2000, s.3C

(1) he is convicted on summary trial of one of those offences specified in CJA 2003, s.224, and

(2) it appears to the magistrates' court, in relation to the offence, that the criteria for the imposition of a sentence under CJA 2003, s.225(3) or s.227(2) would be met (see DANGEROUS OFFENDERS; PROTECTIVE SENTENCES).

The offender:

(a) must be committed in custody or on bail to the Crown Court for sentence in accordance with PCC(S)A 2000, s.5A(l); and

(b) may also be committed in respect of certain other ancillary offences (see 15-013,below),

though nothing prevents the court from committing a specified offence to the Crown Court for sentence under s.3 (above) if the provisions of that section are satisfied. See as to the problems raised by conflicting legislation in this area *R. (CPS) v S. E. Surrey Youth Court, Ex p. G* [2005] EWHC (Admin); [2006] 2 Cr. App. R. (S.) 26.

5. Adult's indication of guilty plea (s.4)

15–009 The magistrates' court may commit a person aged 18 or over where: PCC(S)A 2000, a.4

(1) he appears or is brought before it on an information charging him with an offence triable either way (other than a "schedule offence"); and

(2) he, or, where applicable, his representative, indicates under MCA 1980, ss.17A, 17B or 20(7) that he would plead guilty if the offence were to proceed to trial; and

(3) the magistrates court, proceeding under MCA 1980, s.91 convicts him of that offence.

Where:

(a) the magistrates have committed him to the Crown Court for one or more offences which, in their opinion are related to the offence, they may commit him in custody or on bail to the Crown Court, to be dealt with in respect of the offence in accordance with s.5(1); or

(b) that power is not exercisable but the court is still to determine whether to send the offender for trial under CDA 1998, s.51 or s.51 A for one or more related offences:

  (i) it must adjourn the proceedings relating to the offence until after it has made those determinations; and

  (ii) if it sends the offender to the Crown Court for trial for one or more related offences, may then exercise that power.

15–010 In reaching their decision, or taking any step, under this provision:

(1) the magistrates' court is not bound by any indication of sentence given in respect of the offence under MCA 1980, s.20 (mode of trial proceedings); and

(2) nothing the court does under this section may be challenged, or be the subject of any appeal in any court on the ground that it is not consistent with an indication of sentence.

If the power conferred above is not exercisable, but the court still has to determine whether to, send the offender for trial under CDA 1998, s.51 or S.51A (see SENDING ETC FOR TRIAL) for one or more related offences, it must adjourn the proceedings until after it has made those determinations, and then, if it sends the offender to the Crown Court for trial for one or more related offences, may exercise this power.

If the magistrates' court does not, in committing under s.4, state that it has, in its opinion, power also to commit him under s.3(2) or, as the case may be, s.3A(2), the Crown Court may act in accordance with s.5(1) unless he is convicted before it of one or more of the related offences

6. Juvenile's indication of guilty plea; related ancillary offences (s.4A)

15–011 Where:

PCC(S)A 2000, s.4A

(1) a person under 18 appears or is brought before a magistrates' court on an information charging him with an offence mentioned in s.91(1); and

(2) he or his representative indicates under MCA 1980, s.24A, or as the case may be, s.24B, that he would plead guilty if the offence were to proceed to trial; and

(3) proceeding as if MCA 1980, s.9(1) were complied with and he pleaded guilty under it, the magistrates convict him of the offence,

then

    (a) if the magistrates have committed him to the Crown Court for one or more offences which, in their opinion are related to the offence, they may commit him in custody or on bail to the Crown Court, to be dealt with in respect of the offence in accordance with s.5(l); or

    (b) if that power is not exercisable but the court is still to determine whether to send the offender for trial under CDA 1998, s.51 or 51A for one or more related offences:

        (i) it must adjourn the proceedings relating to the offence until after it has made those determinations; and

       (ii) if it sends the offender to the Crown Court for trial for one or more related offences, may then exercise that power.

Where the court under (a) above commits the offender to the Crown Court to be dealt with in respect of the offence, and does not state that, in its opinion, it also has power to commit him under s.3B(2), or as the case may be, ss.3C(2), s.5A(l) will not apply unless he is convicted before the Crown Court of one or more of the related offences. Where s.5A(l) does not apply, the Crown Court may deal with the offender in respect of the offence in any manner in which the magistrates' court could have dealt with him if it had just convicted him of the offence.

Where the magistrates' court commits a person in accordance with PCC(S)A 2000, s.4A(2), it may also commit him in respect of certain other ancillary offences under s.6.

7. Proceeds of Crime Act 2002

15–012 Where an offender is convicted of an offence by a magistrates' court, and the prosecutor asks the court to commit him to the Crown Court with a view to a to a confiscation order being considered under POCA 2002, s.6, the magistrates' court must commit him to the Crown Court in respect of the offence, and may commit him in respect of any other offence where: POCA 2002,s.70

    (1) the offender has been convicted of it by the magistrates' court or any other court; and

    (2) the magistrates' court has power to deal with him in respect of it.

If a committal is made under this section in respect of an offence or offences, POCA 2002, s.6 applies accordingly, and the committal operates as a committal of the offender to be dealt with at the Crown Court in accordance with POCA 2002, s.71.

If a committal is made under this section in respect of an offence for which (apart from this section) the magistrates' court could have committed the offender for sentence under PCC(S)A 2000, s.3(2) (above) the court must state whether it would have done so.

A committal under this section may be in custody or on bail.

Where an offender is committed to the Crown Court under s.70 in respect of an offence or offences, then (whether or not the court proceeds under s.6): POCA 2002,s.71

    (a) in the case of an offence in respect of which the magistrates' court has stated under s.70(5) that it would have committed the offender for sentence, the judge at the Crown Court must inquire into the circumstances of the case, and may deal with the offender in any way in which he could deal with him if he had just been convicted of the offence on indictment before it; or

    (b) in the case of any other offence the judge must inquire into the circumstances of the case, and may deal with the offender in any way in which the magistrates' court could deal with him if it had just convicted him of the offence.

8. Ancillary matters (s.6)

15–013 Where magistrates commit an offender to the Crown Court under:

    (1) the Vagrancy Act 1824 (as amended by SOA 2003, Sch.6, paras 1,2);

    (2) PCC(S)A 2000, ss.3 to 4A (above);

    (3) PCC(S)A 2000, s.1 3(5) (conditionally discharged offender convicted of further offence),

to be sentenced or otherwise dealt with in respect of an offence, then, if the relevant offence is:

    (a) an indictable offence, they may also commit him in respect of any other offence, in respect of which they have power to deal with him (being an offence of which he has been convicted by them or any other court); and

    (b) a summary offence, they may commit him in respect of any other offence of which they have convicted him, being either one punishable with imprisonment, or one in respect of which they have a power or a duty to disqualify him under RTOA 1988, ss.34, 35 or 36, or any suspended sentence in respect of which they have power to deal with him (under CJA 2003, Sch.12, para.ll(l)).

15–014 **TABLE.** The Table below seeks to identify the powers of the Crown Court in committals under differing provisions.

Committal Powers	Category of Offender	Sentencing Powers	Sentencing Authority
(1) PCC(S)A 2000, s.3	Offender aged 18 or over indicating plea guilty to either-way offence committed because offence(s) so serious as to require Crown Court powers on indictment. A corporation may be committed for sentence and is treated as an individual of not less than 18. Bail/custody does not apply (MCA 1980, s.38(4); CJA 1991, s.25(1)(2)).	Powers on indictment	PCC(S)A 2000, s.5(1)

PCC(S)A 2000, s.6

Committal Powers		Category of Offender	Sentencing Powers	Sentencing Authority
(2)	PCC(S)A 2000, s.3B	Offender under 18 indicating plea of guilty to either-way offence committed because offence(s) so serious as to require Crown Court powers on indictment	Powers on indictment	PCC(S)A 2000, s.5A(1)
(3)	PCC(S)A 2000, s.3C	Offender under 18 convicted summarily of an offence and categorised as a "dangerous young offender" under CJA 2003, s.226(3) or s.228(2)	Powers on indictment	PCC(S)A 2000, s.5A(1)
(4)	PCC(S)A 2000, s.4	Accused not less than 18, charged with offence triable either way, indicating plea of guilty if committed for trial, and accordingly convicted by magistrates, and committed for sentence	Powers on indictment where magistrates certify power to commit under s.3 otherwise magistrates' powers	PCC(S)A 2000, ss.4(5), 5
(5)	PCC(S)A 2000, s.4A	Accused under 18, charged with either way offence and indicating plea of guilty, committed in respect "related offences"	Powers on indictment where magistrates certify power to commit under s.3 otherwise magistrates' powers	PCC(S)A 2000, s.6
(6)	CJA 2003, s.179, Sch.8 para.9(6)	Offender found by magistrates to be in breach of requirement of community order made by Crown Court	May (a) add more onerous requirements; (b) powers on indictment; (c) in case of persistent failure by 18+ to comply in case of non-imprisonable offence, up to 51 weeks.If (b) – revocation	CJA 2003, s.179, Sch.8, paras10(1), 10(1) (6)
(7)	PCC(S)A 2000, Sch.3, para.4(4)	Offender found by magistrates to be in breach of relevant youth community order made by the Crown Court	Choice between (a) £1,000 fine; (b) making an attendance centre order; (c) making a curfew order; and (d) revocation and "as if order not made"	PCC(S)A 2000, Sch.3, para.5(1)
(8)	PCC(S)A 2000, Sch.3, para.13(3)	Offender in respect of whom a relevant Crown Court youth community order is in force, committed with a view to its revocation	Revocation	PCC(S)A 2000, Sch.3, para.14

Committals for Sentence

COMMITTALS FOR SENTENCE

Committal Powers	Category of Offender	Sentencing Powers	Sentencing Authority
(9) PCC(S)A 2000, Sch.3, para.11(1), (2)	Offender committed for sentence during currency of relevant youth community order	Choice between (a) a simple revocation; and (b) "powers on indictment"	PCC(S)A 2000, Sch.3, para.11(2)
(10) PCC(S)A 2000, s.6	Offender committed in respect of (1)–(6) and (17) also in respect of other joined offences	Magistrates' powers in respect of ancillary cases	PCC(S)A 2000, s.7
(11) MHA 1983, s.43(1)	Offender 14 or over committed with a view to a restriction order being made under MHA 1983, s.41	Choice between (a) making a restriction order; and (b) "magistrates' powers"	MHA 1983, s.43(2)
(12) PCC(S)A 2000, s.61 Sch.5, para.2(1) (c)	Juvenile offender committed for failure to attend at, or breach of rules at, attendance centre	Revocation and "as if order not made"	PCC(S)A 2000, s.61, Sch.5, para.3
(13) PCC(S)A 2000, s.66, Sch.7, para.2(1) (c)	Juvenile offender committed in respect of breach of supervision order	Revoke the order and "as if not made"	PCC(S) A 2000, s.66, Sch.7, para.2(4)
(14) PCC(S)A 2000, s.72, Sch.8	Juvenile offender committed by the youth court for breach of action plan or reparation order	Revocation of the order and "as if not made"	PCC(S) A 2000, s.72, Sch.8, para.2(4), (5)
(15) BA 1976, s.6(6)	Bail absconder committed because greater punishment required; or more appropriate	Imprisonment for not more than 12 months and/or a fine	BA 1976, s.6(7)
(16) POCA 2002, s.70	Offender committed with a view to a confiscation order being made	Powers on indictment	POCA 2002, s.71
(17) PCC(S)A 2000, s.13 (5)	Offender committed for breach of Crown Court condtional discharge	Powers on indictment	PCC(S)A 2000, s.13(6)

16. COMMUNITY SENTENCES

Quick guide

A. INTRODUCTION

1. General provisions

Power to make order

16–001 Where a person aged 18 or over is convicted of an offence, the judge may:

(right margin: CJA 2003, ss.177(1)(2) 150A, 178(5);)

(1) where the sentence is not one prescribed by law (see 16-003); and
(2) none of the general restrictions on the making of such orders (16-004) applies,

pass upon him a single generic "community order", imposing on him any one of the requirements set out in 16-002 below. Such orders, together with a youth rehabilitation order for an offender under 18 (seen YOUTH REHABILITION ORDERS), constitute "community sentences".

As to the threshold for such an order, see 16-004 below.

The order must specify a date, not more than three years after the date of the order by which all the requirements in it must have been complied with; an order which imposes two or more requirements may also specify an earlier date or dates in relation to compliance with any one or more of them.

As to the breach, revocation or amendment of orders, see BREACH,

(vertical right margin: Community Sentences)

COMMUNITY SENTENCES

AMENDMENT AND REVOCATION; as to the transfer of orders to Scotland and Northern Ireland, see CJA 2003, Sch.9.

The available requirements

16–002 The requirements which may be attached to a community order are:

(1) an unpaid work requirement (as defined by s.199), see 16–023, below;

(2) an activity requirement (as defined by s.201), see 16–025 below;

(3) a programme requirement (as defined by s.202), see 16–026, below;

(4) a prohibited activity requirement (as defined by s.203), see 16–027, below;

(5) a curfew requirement (as defined by s.204), see 16–028, below;

(6) an exclusion requirement (as defined by s.205), see 16–029, below;

(7) a residence requirement (as defined by s.206), see 16–030, below;

(8) a mental health treatment requirement (as defined by s.207), see 16–031, below;

(9) a drug rehabilitation requirement (as defined by s.209), see 16–033, below;

(10) an alcohol treatment requirement (as defined by s.212), see 16–038, below;

(11) a supervision requirement (as defined by s.213), see 16–039, below; and

(12) in a case where an offender is under 25, an attendance centre requirement (as defined by s.214), see 16–040; and

(13) in a case where an offender is under 25, an electronic monitoring requirement (as defined by s.215), see 16–041, below,

though these provisions are subject to CJA 2003, ss.150 (not available where sentence fixed by law) and 218,(availability of arrangements in local areas) and to the following provisions of CJA 2003, Ch.4 relating to particular requirements, namely:

(a) s.199(3) (unpaid work requirement);

(b) s.201(3)(4) (activity requirement);

(c) s.202(4)(5) (programme requirement);

(d) s.203(2) (prohibited activity requirement);

(e) s.207(3) (mental health requirement);

(f) s.209(2) (drug rehabilitation requirement); and

(g) s.212(2)(3) (alcohol treatment requirement).

Sentence fixed by law, etc.

16–003 Neither a community order nor a youth rehabilitation order   CJA 2003, s.150 may be made in respect of an offence for which the sentence:

(1) is fixed by law;

(2) falls to be imposed under FA 1968, s.5IA (required sentences for certain firearms offences);

(3) falls to be imposed under PCC(S)A 2000, s.110(2) or s.111(2) (required sentences for certain repeated offences committed by offenders aged 18 or over,(see IMPRISONMENT);

(4) falls to be imposed under CJA 2003, ss.225(2), 226 (2) (requirement to impose imprisonment or detention for life) (see DANGEROUS OFFENDERS; PROTECTIVE SENTENCES); or

(5) falls to be imposed under VCRA 2006, s.29(4) or (6) (required custodial sentence in certain cases of using someone to mind a weapon).

In the case of an offender aged 18 or over, no community order under CJA 2003 may be made in respect of an offence committed before April, 2005.

General restrictions on imposing community sentence

16–004   There is a general restriction on imposing a community sentence on an offender unless the judge is of opinion that the offence, or the combination of the offence and one or more offences associated with it, is serious enough to warrant such a sentence, and where he does pass such a sentence: *CJA 2003, s.148*

(1) the particular order or orders comprising or forming part of the sentence must be such as in his opinion is, or taken together are, the most suitable for the offender; and

(2) the restrictions on liberty imposed by the order or orders must be such as in his opinion are commensurate with the seriousness of the offence, or the combination of the offence and the one or more offences associated with it.

Before making an order imposing two or more different requirements, the judge must consider whether, in the circumstances of the case, the requirements are compatible with each other. *CJA 2003, s.178(6)*

As far as practicable, any requirement imposed by a relevant order should be such as to avoid: *CJA 2003, s.217*

(a) any conflict with the offender's religious beliefs or with the requirements of any other relevant order to which he may be subject; and

(b) any interference with the times, if any, at which he normally works or attends school or any other educational establishment.

Approach to community order

16–005   Having decided that a community sentence is justified, the judge must decide which requirements should be included in the community order. These will have the effect of restricting the offender's liberty, whilst providing punishment in the community, rehabilitation for the offender, and/or ensuring that the offender engages in reparative activities.

SGC identifies the key issues as being: *SGC 3*

- which requirements to impose; 1.1.11
- how to make allowance for time spent on remand; and
- how to deal with breaches.

The judge will need to have the possibility of a breach firmly in mind when passing sentence for the original offence. If he is to reflect the seriousness of an offence, there is little value in setting requirements as part of a community sentence that are not demanding enough for the offender; there is equally, on the other hand, little value in imposing requirements that would "set an offender up to fail" and almost inevitably lead to sanctions for a breach.

Seriousness; the initial factor

16–006 The guiding principles, in community sentences, are proportionality and suitability. Once the judge has decided that:

SGC 3,
1.1.13, 1.1.14

(1) the offence has crossed the community sentence threshold; and
(2) a community sentence is justified,

the initial factor in defining which requirements to include in the order should be the seriousness of the offence(s) committed.
   In the view of the SGC:

(a) "seriousness" is an important factor in deciding the range of sentence (see 16–009); but
(b) having taken that decision, selection of the content of the order within the range needs to be determined by a much wider range of factors.

Account needs to be taken: of:

(i) the suitability of the offender;
(ii) his ability to comply with particular requirements; and
(iii) their availability in the local area.

The justification for imposing a community sentence in response to persistent petty offending is the persistence of the offending behaviour rather than the seriousness of the offences being committed. The requirements imposed should ensure that the restriction on liberty is proportionate to the seriousness of the offending, to reflect the fact that the offences, of themselves, are not sufficiently serious to merit a community sentence.
   The primary purpose of a prohibited activity requirement or an exclusion requirement being not to punish the offender, but to prevent, or at least reduce, the risk of further offending, any such requirement must be proportionate to the risk of further offending (*R. v J* [2008] EWCA Crim 2002, 172 JP 518).

Reports

16-007 A pre-sentence report may be pivotal in helping the judge to decide whether to impose:

SGC 3, 1.1.15

(1) a custodial sentence; or
(2) a community sentence; and if so, whether

(3) particular requirements, or a combination of requirements, are suitable for an individual offender,

but the judge must always ensure, especially where there are multiple requirements, that the:

- restriction on liberty placed on the offender is proportionate to the seriousness of the offence committed; and
- the likely effect of one requirement on another and
- that they do not place conflicting demands upon the offender.

If he reaches the provisional view that a community sentence is the most appropriate disposal, the judge should request a pre-sentence report, indicating:

(a) which of the three sentencing ranges is relevant; and
(b) the purpose(s) of sentencing that the package of requirements is required to fulfil.

It may be helpful for the judge to produce a written note for the report writer, copied on the court file, though if it is known that the same judge and the same defence advocate will be present on the day of sentence and a probation officer is present in court when the request is made, it may not be necessary to commit details of the request to writing. However, it is good practice to ensure that there is a clear record of the judge's request. SGC 3, 1.1.13

There will be occasions when a report may be unnecessary, though this is likely to be infrequent. The judge might consider dispensing with the need to obtain a pre-sentence report for adult offenders, e.g. where:

(i) the offence falls within the *low* range of seriousness; and
(ii) where he is minded to impose a single requirement, such as an exclusion requirement (where the circumstances of the case show that this would be an appropriate disposal without electronic monitoring); and
(iii) the sentence will not require the involvement of the probation authorities.

High, medium and low ranges of sentence

16–008 While the judge has a statutory obligation to pass a sentence commensurate with the seriousness of the offence, within the range of sentences justified, he may quite properly consider factors which heighten the risk of the offender committing further offences or causing further harm, with a view to lessening that risk. The extent to which requirements are imposed must be capable of being varied to ensure that the restriction on liberty is commensurate with the seriousness of the offence. SGC 3, 1.1.18

SGC identifies three sentencing ranges within the community sentence band, Based upon seriousness:

(1) low, for those offenders whose offence is relatively minor within the community service band, including persistent petty offenders whose offences only merit a community sentence by virtue of failing to respond to the previous imposition of fines—such SGC 3, 1.1.19-25

offenders would merit a "light touch" approach, for example, normally a single requirement such as a short period of unpaid work, or a curfew, or a prohibited activity requirement or an exclusion requirement (where the circumstances of the case mean that this would be an appropriate disposal without electronic monitoring);

(2) medium; and

(3) high, for those offenders who have only just fallen short of a custodial sentence and for those who have passed the custody threshold but for whom a community sentence would be deemed appropriate.

It is not intended that the offender necessarily progress 'from one range to the next on each sentencing occasion. The decision as to the appropriate range each time is based upon the seriousness of the new offence(s).

Nature and severity of the requirements

16–009   The decision on the nature and severity of the requirements to be included in a community sentence should be guided by: SGC 3, 1.1.23,24

(1) the assessment of offence seriousness (low, medium or high);

(2) the purpose(s) of sentencing the judge wishes to achieve;

(3) the risk of re-offending;

(4) the ability of the offender to comply; and

(5) the availability of requirements in the local area.

The resulting restriction on liberty must be a proportionate response to the offence that was committed.

It falls to the judge to ensure that the sentence strikes the right balance between proportionality and suitability. When passing sentence in any one of the three ranges, the judge should consider whether a rehabilitative intervention such as a programme requirement, or a restorative justice intervention might be suitable as an additional or alternative part of the sentence.

Where the judge seeks to impose an electronic monitoring requirement (it is mandatory in some circumstances) he should bear in mind that it should be used with the primary purpose of promoting and monitoring compliance with other requirements, in circumstances where the punishment of the offender and/or the need to safeguard the public and prevent re-offending are the most important concerns (SGC 3, 1.1.33).

Recording the sentence

16–010   The judge, in imposing sentence will wish to be clear about the "purposes" that the community sentence is designed to achieve when setting the requirements "sharing" those purposes with the offender and the probation authorities will enable them to be clear about the goals that are to be achieved. SGC 3, 1.1.34,35

Note that:

(1) if he does not include in the order an express direction that any failure to comply with the requirements of the order is to CJA 2003, s.179,Sch.8,

be dealt with by a magistrates' court, the responsible officer will bring the; breach proceedings in the Crown Court; and

(2) any judge dealing with the matter thereafter will need to have full information about the requirements which were inserted into the previous community sentence imposed on the offender (including whether it was a low/medium/high level order), and about the offender's response.

(3) this information will enable the subsequent judge to consider the merits of imposing the same or different requirements as part of another community sentence.

(4) the requirements should be recorded in such a way as to ensure that they can be made available to another court if another offence is committed.

SGC 3, 1.1.35

When an offender is required to serve a community sentence, the court records should be clearly annotated to show which particular requirements have been imposed.

Time spent on remand

16–011   If the judge is considering a community order in the case of an offender who has served time on remand, he must consider not just the punishment of the offender (including that already undergone by virtue of his period on remand) but also his rehabilitation and public protection (see CJA 2003, s142(1). Further, CJA 2003, s.149 says that the judge imposing a community order 'may have regard to any period' served on remand (that section being differently phrased from the entitlement normally arising from s.240). While a judge passing a community order will usually have regard to time spent by the offender on remand, the value of the community order in rehabilitative or public protective terms may still make such an order, even one with substantial restrictions, appropriate *(R. v Rakib* [2011] EWCA Crim 870; [2011] Crim L. R. 570).

SGC 3, 1.1.37, 38

Where an offender has spent a period of time in custody on remand, there will be occasions where a custodial sentence is warranted but the length of the sentence justified by the seriousness of the offence would mean that the offender would be released immediately.

Under the present framework it may be more appropriate:

SGC 3, 1.1.39, 40

(a) to pass a community sentence since that will ensure supervision on release; or

(b) where the custodial sentence would be for 12 months or more, to pass a custodial sentence in the knowledge that licence requirements will be imposed on release from custody; this will ensure that the sentence imposed properly reflects the seriousness of the offence.

Recommendations made by the judge at the point of sentence will be of particular importance in influencing the content of the licence. This will properly reflect the gravity of the offence.

Adding an electronic monitoring requirement

16–012   Where the judge makes an order imposing:

CJA 2003, s.177(3)

(1) a curfew requirement, or an exclusion requirement on a person aged 18 or over, he must also impose an electronic monitoring requirement (as defined by s.215), unless either he is prevented from doing so by the non-consent of the proposed supervisor or the unavailability of facilities (s.218(4)), or in the particular circumstances of the case, he considers it inappropriate to do so;

(2) a requirement under (1)–(4), or (7)–(12) (See 16–002) above, he may also impose an electronic monitoring requirement unless either he is prevented from doing so by s.215(2) or s.218(4), referred to in (1) or in the particular circumstances of the case, he considers it inappropriate to do so. CJA 2003, s.177(4)

If the judge imposes an electronic monitoring requirement, the monitor of which is not the responsible officer, the Crown Court officer will notify; R.42.2(3)

(a) the offender and, where the offender is under 16, an appropriate adult, of the monitor's name, and the means by which the monitor may be contacted; and

(b) the monitor of the offender's name, address and telephone number (if available), the offence or offences of which the offender was convicted, the place or places at which the offender's presence must be monitored, the period or periods during which the offender's presence there must be monitored, and the responsible officer's name, and the means by which that officer may be contacted.

2.   Administrative

"Relevant orders"

16–013   Certain general provisions, as set out below, apply to "relevant orders" which expression includes both community orders and suspended sentence orders (see IMPRISONMENT). They are set out below. CJA 2003, s.220

Duties of responsible officer

16–014   Where a relevant order has effect, it is the duty of the responsible officer (as defined in s.197, except in relation to s.197(1)(a)): CJA 2003, s.198

(1) to make any arrangements that are necessary in connection with the requirements imposed by the order;

(2) to promote the offender's compliance with those requirements; and

(3) where appropriate, to take steps to enforce those -requirements.

Local justice area to be specified

16–015   A community order or suspended sentence order must specify the local justice area in which the offender resides or will reside. CJA 2003, s.216

Availability of arrangements in local area

16–016   The judge must not include: CJA 2003, s.218

(1) an unpaid work requirement in a relevant order unless he is satisfied that provision for the offender to work under such a requirement can be made under the arrangements which exist in the local justice area in which he resides or will reside;
(2) an activity requirement unless he is satisfied that provision for the offender to participate in the activities proposed to be specified can be made under the arrangements which exist in the local justice area in which he resides or will reside;
(3) an attendance centre requirement in respect of an offender unless the court has been notified by the Secretary of State that an attendance centre is available for persons of his description.

CJA 2003, s.205

In subs.(5) "place", in relation to an exclusion requirement, includes an area.

Copies of relevant orders

16–017 The court by which any relevant order is made must forthwith provide copies of the order:

CJA 2003, s.219

(1) to the offender;
(2) if the offender is aged 18 or over, to a probation officer assigned to the court;
(3) where the order specifies a local justice area for which the court making the order does not act, to the appropriate provider of probation services acting for that area.

Where a relevant order imposes any requirement specified in the first column of CJA 2003, Sch.14, the court by which the order is made must also forthwith provide the person specified in relation to that requirement in the second column of that Schedule with a copy of so much of the order as relates to that requirement.

Where a relevant order specifies a local justice area for which the court making the order does not act, the court making the order must provide to the magistrates' court acting for that area, a copy of the order, and such documents and information relating to the case as it considers likely to be of assistance to a court acting for that area in the exercise of its functions in relation to the order.

Duty of offender to keep in touch with responsible officer

16–018 An offender in respect of whom a community order or a suspended sentence order is in force must keep in touch with the responsible officer in accordance with such instructions as he may from time to time be given by that officer, and must notify him of any change of address. The obligation is enforceable as if it were a requirement imposed by the order.

Duty of court officer

16–019 The Crown Court officer will notify:

R.42.2

(1) the offender of:
    (a) the requirement or requirements imposed; and
    (b) the name of the responsible officer or supervisor, and the means by which that person may be contacted; and

(2) the responsible officer or supervisor, of:
  (a) the offender's name, address and telephone number (if available);
  (b) the offence or offences of which the offender was convicted; and
  (c) the requirement or requirements imposed.

Breach, amendment and revocation

16–020 Action on the breach, amendment and revocation of orders is dealt with at BREACH, AMENDMENT AND REVOCATION.

B. Requirements available in case of all offenders

16–021 CJA 2003, ss.199–214 describes in detail the requirements available in relation to a community order. They are also available in respect of a suspended sentence order (see IMPRISONMENT).

If the Legal Aid Etc Bill 2011, now going through Parliament, is enacted in its present form, it will make some changes to this section.

1. Unpaid work requirement

General

16–022 Under this requirement, the offender is required to perform unpaid work in accordance with s.200 for the number of hours specified in the relevant order, being in the aggregate: CJA 2003, s.199(1), (2), (5)

(1) not less than 40;
(2) not more than 300.

Where orders are made in respect of two or more offences of which the offender has been convicted on the same occasion, and each includes such a requirement, the judge may direct that the hours of work specified be concurrent with, or in addition to, those specified in any other of those orders, provided the number of hours which are not concurrent does not exceed 300.

Under the previous legislation it was held that there was nothing to prevent different courts, on different occasions, from imposing orders which would, in effect, exceed the maximum, but that it was undesirable *(R. v Siha* (1992) 13 Cr. App. R.(S.) 588; cf. *R. v Anderson* (1989) 11 Cr. App. R.(S.) 417).

Such a requirement is not to be included in a community order unless, after hearing a probation officer, a provider of probation services; the judge is satisfied that the offender is a suitable person to perform work under such a requirement.

Under such a requirement, the offender must perform for the number of hours specified such work at such times as he may be instructed by the responsible officer. CJA 2003, s.189(1), (2), (3)

Subject to Sch.8, para.20 and the power in Sch.12, para.18 to extend the period, the work must be performed within 12 months, but until it is revoked the order remains in force until the work has been performed under it.

Suspended sentences

16–023 Where a requirement is imposed by a suspended sentence order, the supervision period as defined by s.189(1)(a) continues until the offender has worked under the order for the number of hours specified, but does not continue beyond the end of the operational period as defined by s.189(1)(b)(ii).

CJA 2003, s.199(5)

2.   Activity requirement

16–024 Such a requirement requires the offender to do either or both of the following:

CJA 2003, s.201(1)(2)(3) (4)(5)

(1) to present himself to a person or persons specified in the order at a place or places specified on such number of days as may be specified;
(2) to participate in such activities specified in the order, on such number of days (not exceeding 60) as may be so specified,

such activities including, in particular, activities having a reparative purpose, but the judge must not include such a requirement in an order unless:

(a) he has consulted a probation officer; and
(b) is satisfied that it is feasible to secure compliance with the requirement.

Such a requirement may not be included in an order if compliance with it would involve the co-operation of a person other than the offender and the offender's responsible officer, unless that other person consents to the inclusion.

CJA 2003, ss.201(6)–(10)

A requirement of this nature operates to require the offender:

(i) in relation to (1) above, in accordance with instructions from his responsible officer, to present himself at a place or places, being a community rehabilitation centre or other approved place, on the number of days specified in the order and while there, to comply with instructions given by, or under the authority of the person in charge;
(ii) where (2) above is concerned, in accordance with instructions to participate in activities on the number of days specified and, while doing so, to comply with instructions given by, or under the authority of, the person in charge.

3.   Programme requirement

16–025 Such a requirement requires the offender to participate in an accredited programme, that is, a systematic set of activities specified in the order at a specified place on a specified number of days.

CJA 2003, ss.202(1)–(5)

A requirement of this sort must not be included in an order unless:

(1) the accredited programme which the judge proposes to specify

    has been recommended to him as being suitable for the offender, by a probation officer and;

(2) the judge is satisfied that the programme will be available at the place proposed to be specified.

A requirement may not be included in an order if compliance with it would involve the co-operation of a person other than the offender and the offender's responsible officer, unless that other person consents to the inclusion. CJA 2003, s.202(6)(7)

    Under such a requirement, the offender is required:

    (a) in accordance with instructions from his responsible officer, to participate in the accredited programme at the place specified in the order on the number of days specified in the order; and

    (b) while there, to comply with instructions given by, or under the authority of the person in charge.

4.   Prohibited activity requirement

16–026 A "prohibited activity requirement", in relation to a relevant order, is a requirement that the offender refrain from participating in activities specified in the order on a specified day or days, or during a specified period. CJA 2003, s.203

    The judge may not include a "prohibited activity requirement" in a relevant order unless he has consulted a probation officer.

    The requirements that may, by virtue of this provision, be included in a relevant order include a requirement that the offender does not possess, use or carry a firearm within the meaning of FA 1968.

5.   Curfew requirement

16–027 A "curfew requirement", in relation to a relevant order, means a requirement that the offender remain, for periods specified in the order, at a place so specified. The order may specify different places or different periods for different days, but may not specify periods which amount to less than two hours or more than 12 hours in any day, and note that a community order or a suspended sentence order (see 41–051) which imposes a curfew requirement must not specify periods falling outside the period of six months beginning with the day on which it is made. CJA 2003, s.204

    Before making an order imposing a curfew requirement, the judge must obtain and consider information about the place proposed to be specified in the order (including information as to the attitude of persons likely to be affected by the enforced presence there of the offender).

6.   Exclusion requirement

16–028 An exclusion requirement, in relation to a relevant order, means a provision prohibiting the offender from entering a place (or CJA 2003, s.205

area) specified in the order for a period so specified. Where the order is a community order, the period specified must not be more than two years.

An "exclusion requirement" may:

(1) provide for the prohibition to operate only during the periods specified in the order; and
(2) specify different places for different periods or days.

7. Residence requirement

16–029 A residence requirement, in relation to a community order or a suspended sentence order, means a requirement that, during a period specified in the relevant order, the offender reside at a place specified in the order. If the order so provides, a residence requirement does not prohibit the offender from residing, with the prior approval of the responsible officer, at a place other than that specified in the order.

CJA 2003, s.206

Before making a community order or suspended sentence order containing a residence requirement, the judge must consider the offender's home surroundings.

The requirement may not specify a hostel or other institution as the place where an offender must reside, except on the recommendation of an officer of a provider of probation services.

8. Mental health treatment requirement

16–030 A mental health treatment requirement, in relation to a relevant order, is a requirement that the offender submit, during a period or periods specified in the order, to treatment by or under the direction of a registered medical practitioner or a chartered psychologist (or both, for different periods) with a view to the improvement of the offender's mental condition.

CJA 2003, s.207(1)(2)

The treatment required must be one of the following kinds of treatment, specified in the order:

(1) treatment as a resident patient in an independent hospital or care home within the meaning of the Care Standards Act 2000, or a hospital within the meaning of MHA 1983, but not in hospital premises where high security psychiatric services within the meaning of that Act are provided;
(2) treatment as a non-resident patient at such institution or place as may be specified in the order;
(3) treatment by or under the direction of such registered medical practitioner or chartered psychologist (or both) as may be so specified,

but the nature of the treatment is not to be specified in the order except as mentioned above.

CJA 2003, s.207(3)

16–031 The judge may *not*, by virtue of this provision include a mental health treatment requirement in a relevant order unless;

(a) he is satisfied, on the evidence of a registered medical practitioner approved for the purposes of MHA 1983, s.12, that the mental condition of the offender;

    (i) is such as requires and may be susceptible to treatment; but

    (ii) is not such as to warrant the making of a hospital order or a guardianship order within the meaning of MHA 1983;

(b) he is also satisfied that arrangements have been, or can be, made for the treatment intended to be specified in the order (including arrangements for the reception of the offender where he is to be required to submit to treatment as a resident patient); and

(c) the offender has consented to such a requirement.

CJA 2003, s.207(4)

While the offender is under treatment as a resident patient in pursuance of a "mental health requirement" of a relevant order, the responsible officer will carry out supervision only to such extent as may be necessary for the purpose of the revocation or amendment of the order.

Note that:

CJA 2003, s.207(5)(6)

    (i) MHA 1983, s.54(2)(3) has effect with respect to proof for, the purposes of subs.(3)(a) of an offender's mental condition as they have effect with respect to proof of an offender's mental condition for the purposes of MHA 1983, s.37(2)(a);

    (ii) "chartered psychologist" means a person for the time being listed in the British Psychological Society's Register of Chartered Psychologists.

Treatment at place other than that specified in order

16–032 Where the medical practitioner or chartered psychologist by whom or under whose direction an offender is being treated for his mental condition in pursuance of a "mental health treatment requirement" is of the opinion that part of the treatment can be better or more conveniently given in or at an institution or place which:

CJA 2003, s.208

(1) is not specified in the relevant order; and

(2) is one in or at which the treatment of the offender will be given by or under the direction of a registered medical practitioner or chartered psychologist,

he may, where the offender consents, make arrangements for him to be treated accordingly.

Such arrangements as are mentioned may provide for the offender to receive part of his treatment as a resident patient in an institution or place notwithstanding that the institution or place is not one which could have been specified for that purpose in the relevant order.

9. Drug rehabilitation requirement

General

16–033 A "drug rehabilitation requirement", in relation to a community order or suspended sentence order, means a requirement that during a period specified in the order ("the treatment and testing period") the offender must:

CJA 2003, s.209(1)(2)(7)

(1) submit to treatment by or under the direction of a specified person having the necessary qualifications or experience, with a view to the reduction or elimination of the offender's dependency on or propensity to misuse drugs; and

(2) for the purpose of ascertaining whether he has any drug in his body during that period, provide samples of such description as may be so determined, at such times or in such circumstances as may (subject to the provisions of the order) be determined by the responsible officer or by the person specified as the person by or under whose direction the treatment is to be provided.

"Drug" here means a controlled drug as defined by MDA 1971, s.2.

CJA 2003, s.209(2)

(CJA 2003, Sch.37 repeals PCC(S)A 2000, s.51 thus abolishing the drug treatment and testing order.)

The judge may *not* impose a "drug rehabilitation requirement" unless:

(a) he is satisfied:
   (i) that the offender is dependent on, or has a propensity to misuse, drugs; and
   (ii) that his dependency or propensity is such as requires and may be susceptible to treatment;

(b) he is also satisfied that arrangements have been or can be made for the treatment intended to be specified in the order (including arrangements for the reception of the offender where he is to be required to submit to treatment as a resident);

(c) the requirement has been recommended to the court as being suitable for the offender:
   (i) in the case of an offender aged 18 or over, by an officer of a provider of probation services or
   (ii) in the case of an offender aged under 18, either by an officer of a provider of probation services or by a member of a youth offending team; and

(d) the offender consents to comply with the requirement.

The treatment and testing period must be at least six months, and the required treatment for any particular period must be treatment as a resident in such institution or place as may be specified in the order, or treatment as a non-resident in or at such institution or place, and at such intervals, as may be so specified, but the nature of the treatment is not to be more precisely specified in the order except in the above -provisions.

CJA 2003, s.209(3)(4)(6)

A community order or a suspended sentence order imposing a "drug rehabilitation requirement" must provide that the results of tests carried out on any samples provided by the offender in pursuance of the requirement to a person other than the responsible officer are to be communicated to the responsible officer.

Drug abstinence order

16–034 Note that a drug abstinence order under PCC(S)A 2000, ss.58A and 58B (inserted as from July 2, 2001 by CJCSA 2000, s.47) applies only to offences committed before April 4, 2005. Although s.58A was repealed as from April 4, 2005 (see CJA 2003, s.332, Sch.37), the repeal does not affect offences committed before that date: see SI 2005/950.

Provision for review by court

16–035 A community order or a suspended sentence order imposing a drug rehabilitation requirement may, and must if the treatment and testing period is more than 12 months:

CJA 2003, s.210(1)(2)(4)

(1) provide for the requirement to be reviewed periodically at intervals of *not less than one month*;
(2) provide for each review of the requirement to be made, subject to s.211(6) (whereby the offender is excused attendance), at a hearing held for the purpose by the court responsible for the order (a "review hearing");
(3) require the offender to attend each review hearing;
(4) provide for the responsible officer to make to the court responsible for the order, before each review, a report in writing on the offender's progress under the requirement; and
(5) provide for each such report to include the test results communicated to the responsible officer under s.209(6) or otherwise and the views of the treatment provider as to the treatment and testing of the offender;
(6) provide for each such report to include the test results communicated to the responsible officer under s.209(6) or otherwise and the views of the treatment provider as to the treatment and testing of the offender.

References to the court responsible for a community order or suspended sentence order imposing a "drug rehabilitation requirement" are references, in so far as the Crown Court is concerned, to the court by which the order is made.

Where a community order or suspended sentence order imposing a "drug rehabilitation requirement" has been made on an appeal brought from the Crown Court or from CACD, for the purposes of this provision it is taken to have been made by the Crown Court.

Periodic reviews

16–036 At a review hearing (as defined in s.210(l)) the judge may, after considering the responsible officer's report, amend the community order or suspended sentence order, so far as it relates to the drug rehabilitation requirement, but may *not* amend:

CJA 2003, s.211(1)(2)(9)

(1) the "drug rehabilitation requirement" unless the offender consents to comply with the requirement as amended;

(2) any provision of the order so as to reduce the period for which the drug rehabilitation requirement has effect below the minimum, i.e. not less than six months, specified in s.209(3); and

(3) except with the offender's consent, any requirement or provision of the order while an appeal against the order is pending.

If the offender fails to consent to the "drug rehabilitation requirement" as proposed to be amended, the judge may:

CJA 2003, s.211(3)(4)(9)

(a) revoke the community order, or the suspended sentence order and the suspended sentence to which it relates; and

(b) deal with him, for the offence in respect of which the order was made, in any way in which it could deal with him if he had just been convicted by the court of the offence, and

in relation to (2) after taking into account the extent to which the offender has complied with the requirements of the order, the judge may impose a custodial sentence (where the order was made in respect of an offence punishable with such a sentence) notwithstanding anything in s.152(2).

Effect of progress

16–037 If at a review:

CJA 2003, s.211(6)(7)(8) (9)

(1) *hearing* (see s.210(1)(b)) the judge, after considering the responsible officer's report, is of the opinion that the offender's progress under the requirement is satisfactory, the judge may so amend the order as to provide for each subsequent review to be made by the court without a hearing;

(2) *without a hearing*, the judge, after considering the responsible officer's report, is of the opinion that the offender's progress under the requirement is no longer satisfactory, he may require the offender to attend a hearing at a specified time and place.

At that hearing the judge, after considering the report, may either:

(a) exercise the powers conferred by the section as if the hearing were a review hearing; and

(b) so amend the order as to provide for each subsequent review to be made at a review hearing.

10. Alcohol treatment requirement

16–038 An "alcohol treatment requirement" in relation to a relevant order is a requirement that the offender submit during a period specified in the order to treatment by or under the direction of a specified person having the necessary qualifications or experience, with a view to the reduction or elimination of the offender's dependency on alcohol.

CJA 2003, s.212

Such a requirement may *not* be imposed unless the judge is satisfied:

(1) that the offender is dependent on alcohol; and

(2) that his dependency is such as requires and may be susceptible to treatment; and

Community Sentences

(3) the offender consents to its requirements.

The period for which the "alcohol treatment requirement" has effect must be for not less than six months, and must be -treatment:

(a) as a resident in such institution or place as may be specified in the order;

(b) as a non-resident in or at such institution or place, and at such intervals, as may be so specified; or

(c) by or under the direction of such person having the necessary qualification or experience as may be specified,

but the nature of the treatment must not be more precisely specified in the order.

11. Supervision requirement

16–039 A "supervision requirement", in relation to a relevant order requires the offender during the relevant period, to attend appointments with the responsible officer or another person determined by him, at such time and place as may be determined. The purpose of the require-ment is to promote the offender's rehabilitation.   CJA 2003, s.213

"The relevant period" means, in relation to:

(1) a community order, the period for which the community order remains in force; and

(2) a suspended sentence order (41–044), the supervision period (as defined by s.189(1)(a)).

C. Requirements available in the case of offenders aged under 25

12. Attendance centre requirement

16–040 The original attendance centre order under PCC(S)A 2000, s.60 became, as a result of CJA 2003, a requirement which might be inserted in a community order. Under the present legislation it appears to be confined to offenders:

(1) between the ages of 16 and 18 who are convicted of offences for which an adult might be imprisoned, or who has failed to comply with a court order, committed before November 30, 2009; and

(2) under the age of 21 who are convicted of offences committed before April 4, 2005.

The requirement is expressly saved by CJIA 2008 in relation to young offenders made the subject of youth rehabilitation orders (see YOUTH REHABILITATION ORDERS).

The requirement is unlikely to be of much significance under present legislation, but the detailed provisions are to be found in CJA 2003, s.214.

The main purpose of the requirement was to put a restriction on young offenders' leisure time. The order might last up to 36 hours.

13. Electronic monitoring requirement

16–041 An electronic monitoring requirement, in relation to a relevant order, is a requirement for securing the electronic monitoring of the offender's compliance with other requirements imposed by the order during a period specified in the order, or determined by the responsible officer in accordance with the relevant order.

CJA 2003, s.215

Electronic monitoring should be used with the primary purpose of promoting and monitoring compliance with other requirements, in circumstances where the punishment of the offender and/or the need to safeguard the public and prevent reoffending are the most important concerns.

SGC 2, 2.1.34

The responsible officer will, before the beginning of the period, notify the offender, the person responsible for the monitoring, and any person falling within (2) above, of the time when the period is to begin.

The judge may not include such a requirement in a relevant order unless the court has been notified by the Secretary of State that electronic monitoring arrangements are available in each relevant area; and is satisfied that the necessary provision for dealing with the offender can be made under the arrangements currently available.

Where:

(1) it is proposed to include in a relevant order such a requirement; but
(2) there is a person (other than the offender) without whose co-operation it will not be practicable to secure that the monitoring takes place, the requirement may *not* be included in the order without that person's consent.

A relevant order which includes an electronic monitoring requirement must include provision for making a person responsible for the monitoring.

Consent of person other than accused

16–042 An electronic monitoring requirement, in relation to a relevant order, is to secure by the electronic monitoring, the offender's compliance with other requirements imposed by the order during a period specified in the order, or determined by the responsible officer in accordance with the relevant order.

CJA 2003, s.215

Where:

(1) it is proposed to include in a relevant order a requirement for securing electronic monitoring; but
(2) there is a person (other than the offender) without whose co-operation it will not be practicable to secure the monitoring,

the requirement may *not* be included in the order without that person's consent.

SGC 2.2.3.34

Electronic monitoring should be used with the primary purpose of promoting and monitoring compliance with other requirements, in circumstances where the punishment of the offender and/or the need to safeguard the public and prevent reoffending are the most important concerns.

COMMUNITY SENTENCES

A relevant order which includes an "electronic monitoring requirement" must include provision for making a person responsible for the monitoring.

The responsible officer will, before the beginning of the period, notify the offender, the person responsible for the monitoring, and any person falling within (2) above, of the time when the period is to begin.

D. Youth Rehabilitation Orders

16–043   see YOUTH REHABILITATION ORDERS

17. COMPANY OFFICER'S DISQUALIFICATION

General

17–001 An offender convicted before the Crown Court of:

(1) an indictable offence (IA 1978, Sch.1);
(2) in connection with the promotion, formation, management or liquidation of a company; or
(3) with the receivership or management of a company's property, may be disqualified from being:
   (a) a director, liquidator or manager of a company;
   (b) a receiver or manager of a company's property; or,
   (c) in any way, whether directly or indirectly, concerned, or taking part in, the promotion, formation or management of a company, without leave of the court, and may not act as an insolvency practitioner.

There is no jurisdiction to limit a disqualification to the holding of a directorship in a public company. The judge should make it clear that the order applies to *all* the categories (a)–(c) (*R. v Ward* [2001] EWCA Crim 1648, *The Times* August 10, 2001).

Rationale behind disqualification

17–002 The rationale behind such an order is to protect the public from persons who, whether for reasons of dishonesty, naivety or incompetence, use or abuse their role as a company director to the detriment of the public (*R. v Millard* (1994) 15 Cr. App. R. (S.) 445; *R. v Edwards* (1998) 2 Cr. App. R. (S.) 213; *R. v Victory* (1999) 2 Cr. App. R. (S.) 102).

"Management of the company" defined

17–003 The words "management of the company" refer to the management of the company's affairs. There is no reason to differentiate between internal and external affairs (*R. v Corbin* (1984) 6 Cr. App. R. (S.) 17; *R. v Austen* (1985) 7 Cr. App. R. (S.) 214; *R. v Georgiou* (1988) 87 Cr. App. R. 207).

The correct test, in deciding whether an offence is in connection with the management of a company, is to decide:

(a) whether the offence has some relevant factual connection with the management;
(b) *not* whether it "relates to the management" *nor* whether it was committed "in the course of managing the company".

(See *R. v Goodman* (1993) 97 Cr. App. R. 210).

Terms and length of disqualification

17–004 The order must contain a prohibition in respect of *all* the functions referred to in the section (*R. v Cole* [1998] B.C.L.C. 87). Periods of disqualification of:

(1) over 10 years should be reserved for particularly serious cases, which may include those where there has been a previous disqualification;

(2) between six and 10 years should be reserved for intermediate cases, and

(3) between two to five years may be imposed in cases which are not particularly serious.

(*R. v Millard* (1994) 15 Cr. App. R. (S.) 445; *R v Sheikh* [2010] EWCA Crim 921, [2011] 1 Cr. App. R. (S.) 12).

A person acting in contravention of such an order is liable on conviction on indictment, to imprisonment for not more than two years or to a fine, or both. The period of disqualification should reflect the level of risk to the public.

Compensation; confiscation

17–005   While the ordinary powers of the Crown Court to order compensation apply, where there are complex financial issues involved, it is probably undesirable to couple such an order with a disqualification of this kind (*R. v Holmes* (1992) 13 Cr. App. R. (S.) 29).

If an offender has been convicted of an offence of contravening an order under the Act, the questions to be asked in connection with confiscation are no different from those for any other offence. There is nothing in CDDA 1986, or in the confiscation legislation that suggests any different approach (*R. v Blatch* [2009] EWCA Crim 1303, [2010] 1 Cr. App. R. (S.) 60).

18. COMPENSATION

This section deals not only with the general provisions for compensation in criminal cases, under PCC(S)A 2000, s.130, but also the specialised provisions of compensation under POCA 2002, s. 72 in respect of serious default in the execution of procedures under that Act (18–027 and following).

1.   PCC(S)A 2000, s.130

General
18–001   A judge of the Crown Court may order the payment of compensation in a criminal case, **as a convenient and rapid means of avoiding the expense of civil litigation** in the High Court or the county court; provided the offender has the means to pay *(R. v Inwood* (1974) 60 Cr. App. R. 70). The last statistics available (for 2008) show 5,800 offenders ordered to pay compensation at the Crown Court. There is no limit on the amount.

In a case where an issue of compensation arises the judge is expected to make an order; PCC(S)A 2000, s.130(2) requires him to give reasons for not doing so where he has that power.

The judge is expected to follow a common sense course, he should not make an order where there is any:

(1) doubt as to the liability to compensate; or
(2) real doubt as to whether the offender can find the compensation.

A line of authorities seeking to confine such orders to the "plainest and most straightforward situations" were reconsidered in *R. v Pola* [2009] EWCA Crim 655, [2010] 1 Cr. App. R. (S.) 6, where, upholding an order for compensation for personal injuries amounting to £90,000, CACD noted that the courts had now developed expertise in financial matters as a result of experience of proceedings under POCA 2002. The judge had had the necessary evidence before him and had considered the JSB's *Guidelines for the Assessment of General Damages in Personal Injuries Cases.*

As to compensation in cases of corporate manslaughter and health and safety offences causing death, see the Definitive Guidelines at SGC 2010, paras 27, 28. The view of SGC (para.21) that the assessment of compensation in cases of death will usually be complex and "will involve the payment of sums well beyond the powers of a criminal court" hardly bears consideration when compared with the observations of CACD in *R. v Pola* (above).

Sentence may be deferred (see DEFERRING SENTENCE) with a view to the making of reparation, without any formal order for compensation being made.

COMPENSATION

Power to make order

18–002 Where a person is convicted of an offence, the judge may, whether on application or otherwise, and subject to certain restrictions (as to which see 18–013 below), make an order requiring him to: PCC(S)A 2000, s.130(1)(2)

(1) pay compensation for any *personal injury, loss or damage* resulting from the offence, or any offence taken into consideration on sentence; or
(2) make payments for funeral expenses or bereavement in respect of a death resulting from any such offence, other than a death due to an accident arising out of the presence of a motor vehicle on a road; and

that order may be made:

(a) in addition to, or R.42.1
(b) in a case where the sentence is not fixed by law, or falls to be imposed under PCC(S)A 2000, s.109 where appropriate, or ss.110(2) or 111(2), FA 1968, s.51A(2), CJA 2003, ss.225, 226, 227 or 228 or VCRA 2006, s.29(4) or (6), instead of dealing with him in any other way.

Where the judge could but does not make a compensation order (unless he passes a custodial or a community sentence) he must explain why he has not done so when he explains the sentence he has passed.

"Personal injury" or "damage" include shock and anxiety directly occasioned by the offence (*Bond v Chief Constable of Kent* (1982) 4 Cr. App. R. (S.) 314). "Loss" includes the loss suffered by an innocent purchaser of stolen goods (*R. v Howell* (1978) 66 Cr. App. R. 179).

Offences taken into consideration; specimen charges

18–003 Where an offender is convicted on specimen charges, the amount of compensation which may be ordered is limited to that set out in the specimen charges (*R. v Crutchley* (1994) 15 Cr. App. R. (S.) 627). The fact that an offender freely admits to having made away with a certain sum does not alter the position, and does not, without the proper procedure being followed (see 25–042), mean that those offences are being taken into consideration for that purpose (*R. v Hose* (1995) 16 Cr. App. R. (S.) 682, applying *DPP v Anderson* (1978) 67 Cr. App. R. 185).

Damage: Theft Act and Fraud Act cases

18–004 In the case of an offence under TA 1968 or FrA 2006, where the property: PCC(S)A 2000. s.130(5)

(1) is recovered, any damage to it occurring while it was out of the owner's possession is treated as having resulted from the offence, however and by whomsoever it was caused; but
(2) is not recovered, that presumption does not apply (*R. v Ahmad* (1992) 13 Cr. App. R. (S.) 212).

In a case of dishonest handling, where the goods are recovered, no order may be made in respect of their permanent loss (*R. v Tyce* (1994) 15 Cr. App. R. (S.) 415).

Road accidents

PCC(S)A 2000,
s.130(6)(7)(8)

18–005 An order may only be made in respect of injury or loss or damage (other than that suffered by a person's dependants in consequence of his death) which was due to an accident arising out of the presence of a motor vehicle on a road, if it is in respect of:

(1) damage which is treated under s.130(5) as resulting from an offence under the TA 1968; or
(2) loss or damage for which:
   (a) the offender is uninsured in relation to the use of the vehicle (see *McDermott v DPP* [1997] R.T.R. 474); and
   (b) compensation is not payable under any arrangements to which the Secretary of State is a party.

Where an order is made in respect of such injury, loss or damage, the amount to be paid may include an amount representing the whole or part of any loss of, or reduction in, preferential rates of insurance attributable to the accident.

Where sums are payable by the Motor Insurers' Bureau (MIB), the compensation payable is limited to the amount payable by MIB—i.e. £175 (*DPP v Scott* (1995) 16 Cr. App. R. (S.) 292).

A vehicle exempted from insurance under RTA 1988, s.144, is not "uninsured" for this purpose, nor is a driver uninsured who merely refuses to produce details, but is, in fact, covered (*McDermott v DPP*, above).

Funeral expenses

PCC(S)A 2000,
s.130(9)(10)

18–006 Where an order is made in respect of funeral expenses, it may be made for the benefit of any person who incurred the expense, but an order in respect of bereavement may be made only for the benefit of a person for whose benefit a claim for damages for bereavement could be made under the Fatal Accidents Act 1976, s.1A.

The amount of compensation must not exceed that specified in s.1A(3) of that Act, namely, £3,500.

Compensation from Criminal Injuries Compensation Board no bar

18–007 The fact that the victim may be able to get compensation from the Criminal Injuries Compensation Board under CJA 1988, Pt VII should not prevent the judge making an order under s.130 in a proper case.

Compensation ordered by a criminal court is different from that which victims of crime may receive from the Board. Victims may apply to the Board and receive compensation whether or not the offender is detected or convicted. No award is made by the Board unless the appropriate amount exceeds £1,000.

Guidelines have been prepared by the Board on the range of compensation which might be payable, and are attached to Home Office Circular 85/1988, but they have not been approved by the Lord Chief Justice.

Approach to making an order

18–008 Before making an order, the judge must:

COMPENSATION

(1) satisfy himself that injury, loss or damage has resulted from the offence of which the offender has been convicted or is having taken into consideration on sentence;

(2) settle the amount of the injury, loss or damage which the offender may be required to pay; and

(3) consider the means of the offender, giving him or his counsel the opportunity to be heard.

General principles

18–009　The general principles to be followed in making an order were restated in *R. v Miller* (1976) 68 Cr. App. R. 56. Those still relevant are:

(1) first and foremost, that an order should be made only where the legal position is clear (See 18–010 and 18–011 below);

(2) the order must be precisely drawn and must be related to an offence of which the offender has been convicted, or which he has agreed to have taken into consideration;

(3) the judge must have regard to the offender's means (see 18–013);

(4) the order ought not to be oppressive (see 18–014); and

(5) the fact that the victim to whom compensation is payable has since died does not mean that an order is inappropriate (*Holt v DPP* (1996) 2 Cr. App. R. (S.) 314).

Causation

18–010　There must be a causal connection between the offence committed and the damage done or injury caused. The existence of civil liability is not a prerequisite to making an order in criminal proceedings (*R. v Chappell* (1984) 6 Cr. App. R. (S.) 342). The judge needs to ask himself whether loss or damage can fairly be said to have resulted to anyone from the offence (*R. v Rowiston* (1982) 4 Cr. App. R. (S.) 85, and see *R. v Taylor* (1994) 14 Cr. App. R. (S.) 276; *R. v Guertjens* (1992) 14 Cr. App. R. (S.) 280; *R. v Denness* [1996] 1 Cr. App. R. (S.) 159).

Real issue as to liability

18–011　Where there is a real issue as to the offender's liability to pay compensation, whether in respect of specific offences or specific victims:

(1) the question cannot be determined by argument;

(2) the judge will need to hear evidence; and

(3) it is for the prosecutor put forward evidence, so that the offender may have an opportunity to test the basis on which the order is to be made (*R. v Horsham JJ. Ex p. Richards* (1985) 7 Cr. App. R. (S.) 158; *R. v Halliwell* (1991) 12 Cr. App. R. (S.) 692).

Where issues may be unclear, as where, e.g.:

(a) up-to-date medical reports, photographs, etc., need to be provided (*R. v Cooper* (1982) Cr. App. R. (S.) 55);

(b) questions of loss of use arise, which in civil cases are "notoriously open to argument" (*R. v Donovan* (1981) 3 Cr. App. R. (S.) 192); or

(c) matters of set-off and contribution arise in social security benefit frauds (*Hyde v Emery* (1984) 6 Cr. App. R.(S.) 206),

such cases should generally be left to the civil courts or to the executive to deal with.

Amount of compensation payable; interest

18–012 The amount of compensation ordered to be paid under s. 130 must be such as the judge considers appropriate, having regard to the evidence, and to any representations made by, or on behalf of, the offender or the prosecutor. An order is not intended to be a precise evaluation of loss, such as takes place in a civil court when damages are awarded. The power to award compensation is a fairly blunt instrument. The remedy for the victim is intended to be speedy, efficacious and cost free (*R. v Williams* [2001] Cr. App. R. (S.) 500).

Note that:

(1) the precise extent of the injury, loss or damage does not need to be established by evidence; but
(2) there should be some basis of evidence on which the judge can determine what sum is appropriate; and
(3) where no sufficient information is available, or the evidence is unclear, the judge may adjourn until that information is to hand.

The amount ought, in general, to be limited to the judge's assessment of the amount that might have been recovered in a civil action (*R. v Gateway Foodmarkets Ltd* [1997] 2 Cr. App. R. 40).

See the JSB's *Guidelines on the Assessment of General Damages in Personal Injury Cases*. As to guidance offered by the Criminal Injuries Compensation Board, see 18–007 above.

A sum may be added by way of interest equivalent to what the victim would be likely to recover if he proved his claim in the civil courts (*R. v Schofield* (1978) 67 Cr. App. R. 282).

Offender's means

18–013 In deciding whether to make an order, and in what amount, the judge is restricted by the overriding provisions of:

(1) PCC(S)A 2000, s.130(11) which require him to have regard to the means of the offender, in so far as they are known to him; and
(2) the principle set out in *R. v Webb* (1979) 1 Cr. App. R. (S.) 16 that an order should not be made in such an amount that the offender will have no prospect of paying it within the foreseeable future (*R. v Bradburn* (1973) 57 Cr. App. R. 948; *R. v Bagga* (1989) 11 Cr. App. R. (S.) 497; *R. v Olliver* (1989) 11 Cr. App. R. (S.) 10; *R. v Hewitt* (1990–91) 12 Cr. App. R. (S.) 466; *R. v Yehou* [1997] 2 Cr. App. R. (S.) 48).

PCC(S)A 2000, s.137

Difficulties can be avoided if the judge indicates a provisional figure, and asks the defence advocate to provide information as to the offender's means (*R. v Phillips* [1988] 10 Cr. App. R. (S.) 419).

Note that:

COMPENSATION

- (a) It is the offender's duty to put information as to his means before the court (any attempt to mislead entitles the judge to infer that he has assets (*R. v Bolden* (1987) 9 Cr. App. R. (S.) 83));
- (b) it is the duty of his representatives to verify the accuracy of any statements (*R. v Roberts* (1987) 9 Cr. App. R. (S.) 275); and
- (c) if he offender fraudulently claims to have means to pay, he has only himself to blame if an order is made (*R. v Dando* [1996] 1 Cr. App. R. (S.) 155).

Where the offender gives no evidence on the matter, and explanations given through counsel are "utterly unconvincing", the judge is entitled to act on the basis of any material put before him by the prosecutor drawing appropriate inferences (*R. v Maisey* [2001] 1 Cr. App. R. (S.) 98).

Offender without means
18–014 Where an offender is clearly without means, a compensation order should not be made on the basis of:

- (1) a promise to pay; or
- (2) offers by friends and relatives to pay (*R. v Hunt* [1983] Crim. L.R. 250; *R. v Webb* [1979] 1 Cr. App. R. (S.) 16); or
- (3) the proposed future sale of the matrimonial home (*R. v Harrison* (1980) 2 Cr. App. R. (S.) 313; *R. v Blackmore* (1984) 6 Cr. App. R. (S.) 244; *R. v Butt* (1986) 8 Cr. App. R. (S.) 216; *R. v Hackett* (1988) 10 Cr. App. R. (S.) 388), but

it is not unreasonable to require the offender to sell other items of property to enable him to pay the compensation (*R. v Workman* (1981) 3 Cr. App. R. (S.) 318), provided the judge takes steps to ascertain their value (*R. v Chambers* (1981) 3 Cr. App. R. (S.) 318).

Offender sentenced to custodial sentence
18–015 If a victim is entitled to compensation, an order obviates the necessity for civil proceedings. There is no principle that an order should *not* be made against a person upon whom a custodial sentence is imposed, provided that the judge bears in mind that:

- (1) a custodial sentence will deprive the offender of his earning power; and
- (2) it may make it difficult for him to find work when he is released; and
- (3) by the time he came out he might be in financial difficulty; but

if the offender has sufficient assets, or will have earning capacity upon his release it will often be appropriate to make an order in such a case (*R. v Love* [1999] 1 Cr. App. R. (S.) 75, *R. v Jorge* [1999] 2 Cr. App. R. (S.) 1).

Compensation preferred to fine
18–016 Where the judge considers it appropriate both:

- (1) to impose a fine; and
- (2) to make a compensation order; but
- (3) the offender has insufficient means to satisfy both an appropriate fine and appropriate compensation,

preference must be given to compensation, although a fine may be imposed as well.

Compensation has priority over confiscation

18–017 While there is no objection to the judge imposing both a confiscation order (see CONFISCATION ORDERS) and a compensation order under this section where the amount that may be realised is sufficient, the courts should always be at pains to ensure that so far as possible the victim is compensated, and compensation should be the first priority: *R. v Mitchell* [2001] 2 Cr. App. R. (S.) 29.

Payment by parent or guardian

18–018 Where the offender is a juvenile, the judge *must* order his parent or guardian to pay the order, unless he is satisfied that: PCC(S)A 2000, s.130(12)

(1) the parent or guardian cannot be found; or
(2) it would be unreasonable to so order, having regard to the circumstances of the case.

Where the offender has reached the age of 16, this provision has effect as if, instead of imposing a duty on a parent or guardian to pay, it confers a power on the court to make an order. In such a procedure it is the parent or guardian's means which need to be taken into account, not those of the juvenile (see further CHILDREN AND YOUNG PERSONS).

Form of order: (1) joint orders

18–019 Where an offender is convicted of a number of offences:

(1) and a number of different victims are involved, a separate order must be made in respect of each offence, in respect of each amount (*R. v Oddy* (1974) 59 Cr. App. R. 66; *R. v Inwood* (1974) 60 Cr. App. R. 70);
(2) where there is only one victim, but several offences, one compendious order covering all the amounts, while not desirable, is not objectionable (*R. v Wharton* [1976] Crim. L.R. 320);
(3) where the offender's means are insufficient to meet claims by a number of victims, the amount of any compensation ordered should generally be apportioned *pro rata* among them, but there may be cases where there are good reasons for departing from this general rule (*R. v Amey* (1983) 76 Cr. App. R. 206);
(4) it is technically permissible, though undesirable, to make a joint order against two or more offenders; a separate order should be made in respect of each offender.

Form of order: (2) joint orders; several offenders

18–020 An order is not an additional penalty, which gives rise to adjustment of sentence or to claims of disparity. An order may be made against one or more co-offenders who have assets, and yet not against a third who has none (*R. v Love* [1999] 1 Cr. App. R. (S.) 75).

Where two or more offenders are charged jointly and one claimant establishes a claim against them with regard to one item, each ought, in general, to be ordered to pay in equal proportions, unless one of them

COMPENSATION

is shown to be more directly responsible for the offence, or their ability to pay is markedly different (*R. v Grundy* [1974] 1 All E.R. 292, [1974] Crim. L.R. 128).

Order made on appeal

18–021 Where an order is made on appeal, it is deemed, if it was made on an appeal brought from magistrates' court to have been made by that court, and if it was made on appeal from the Crown Court or the CACD, to have been made by the Crown Court.

PCC(S)A 2000, s.133(5)

Enforcement of orders

18–022 In general, compensation is treated in the same way, for the purposes of enforcement, as a fine (see FINES AND ENFORCEMENT). As with fines and other money payments due to the court, there is power to allow time for payment, or to order payment by instalments.

The superior courts have said that:

(1) an order ought to be sharp in its effect and not protracted by small amounts over a long period (*R. v Bradhurn* (1973) 57 Cr. App. R. 948; *R. v Daly* (1974) 58 Cr. App. R. 333);
(2) where the offender is sentenced at the same time to a custodial term, the judge should direct the first of any instalments to be paid within a specified time of his release (*R. v Bradburn* (1973) 57 Cr. App. R. 948).

Despite a number of decisions to the contrary, CACD said in *R. v Olliver* (1989) 11 Cr. App. R. (S.) 10, that there is no reason in principle why an order to pay a fine by instalments should not extend beyond a period of 12 months, even to a period of two or three years.

No default sentence

18–023 The Crown Court, while it may allow time to pay, and payment of compensation by instalments, has no power to impose a default sentence unless:

AJA 1970, s.41(8), Sch.9

(1) the order is for an amount of £20,000 or more; and
(2) the judge considers that the maximum default term of 12 months available to the collecting magistrates' court (under MCA 1980, Sch.4) is inadequate,

in which case he may order a longer period up to the maximum default term for a fine in the equivalent amount.

Payment under order

18–024 The person in whose favour a compensation order is made is not entitled to receive any sum(s) due to him until the possibility of an appeal on which the order could be varied or set aside has expired, though the power of the Crown Court to give leave to appeal out of time is to be disregarded.

PCC(S)A 2000, s.132(1)(3)(5)

Where an order is made in respect of an offence taken into consideration on sentence, that order ceases to have effect if the offender successfully appeals against his conviction for the substantive offence(s), or if the CACD annuls the order.

An offender may appeal against an order as if it were part of the sentence imposed in respect of the offence(s) of which he was convicted.

Compensation out of forfeited property

18–025   Where the court makes an order under PCC(S)A 2000, s.143 (see FORFEITURE ORDERS) in a case where:

PCC(S)A 2000, s.145

(1) the offender has been convicted of an offence which has resulted in a person suffering personal injury, loss or damage; or

(2) any such offence is taken into consideration on sentence; and

(3) the judge is satisfied that, but for the inadequacy of the offender's means, it would have made a compensation order under which he would have been required to pay compensation of an amount not less than a specified amount,

he may also order that any proceeds which arise from the disposal of the property, and which do not exceed the sum specified, be paid to that person.

Such an order will not be effective:

(a) before the expiration of six months from the date on which the forfeiture order was made; or

(b) if a successful application is made under s.1(1) of the Police (Property) Act 1897.

As to the position in relation to a confiscation order made under POCA 2002, Pt 1, see CONFISCATION ORDERS.

Review of order

18–026   At any time before the offender has paid into court the whole amount of any order made, and once there is no further possibility of an appeal, the court responsible for enforcing the order may, on the application of the offender, either discharge or reduce the amount remaining to be paid under the order if it appears that:

PCC(S)A 2000, s.133

(1) the injury, loss or damage in respect of which it was made has been held in civil proceedings to be less than it was taken to be for the purposes of the order; or

(2) where the order is in respect of the loss of property, the property has been recovered by the victim; or

(3) the offender's means are insufficient to satisfy in full the compensation order and any confiscation order made in the same proceedings; or

(4) the offender has suffered a substantial reduction in his means which was not expected at the time the order was made, and that they are unlikely to increase for a considerable period (*R. v Palmer* (1994) 15 Cr. App. R. (S.) 550),

provided the consent of a judge of the Crown Court has been obtained (which will be unlikely to be withheld if the offender is unable to pay (*R. v Favell* [2010] EWCA Crim 2948)).

R.42.5

A copy of any application made by an offender to the enforcing magistrates' court, containing the information specified by r.42.5 will be served on the Crown Court officer, who will serve a copy on the person for whose benefit the compensation order was made. The magistrates' court must not vary or discharge the compensation order unless the offender and the person for whose benefit it was made, have each had an opportunity to make representations at a hearing (whether or not either in fact attends); and where the order was made in the Crown Court, the Crown Court has notified its consent.

2. Compensation for serious default: POCA 2002

18–027 POCA 2002 provides for compensation to be paid to a person whose property has been affected by the enforcement of the confiscation legislation. POCA 2002, ss.72(1)–(8)

A judge of the Crown Court may order the payment of such compensation as he believes just:

(1) where, but only where:
   (a) a criminal investigation has been started with regard to an offence and proceedings are not started for the offence; or
   (b) proceedings for an offence are started against a person and:
      (i) they do not result in his conviction for the offence; or
      (ii) he is convicted of the offence but the conviction is quashed or he is pardoned in respect of it; and
(2) where (1)(a), above, applies:
   (a) in the criminal investigation there has been a serious default by a person mentioned in subs.(9); and
   (b) the investigation would not have continued if the default had not occurred; and
(3) where (1)(b), above, applies, and:
   (a) in the criminal investigation with regard to the offence or in its prosecution there has been a serious default by a person who is mentioned in subs.(9); and
   (b) the proceedings would not have been started or continued if the default had not occurred; and
(4) an application is made by a person who held realisable property and has suffered loss in consequence of anything done in relation to it by or in pursuance of an order under Pt 2 of the Act.

Note that the offence referred to: R.58.10

   (i) in (1) above may be one of a number of offences with regard to which the investigation is started;
   (ii) in (2) above may be one of a number of offences for which the proceedings are started.

Application is made in writing and may be supported by a witness statement. It must be lodged in the Crown Court, and served on both the person alleged to be in default and the person by whom the compensation would be payable under s.72(9)(a) (below), or if the compensation is payable out of a police fund under s.72(9)(a), the chief officer of the force concerned.

Source of payment

18–028   Compensation is payable to the applicant as follows. If the person in default was:

POCA 2002, s.72(9)

(1) a member, or was acting as a member, of a police force, the compensation is payable out of the police fund from which the expenses of that force are met;

(2) a member of the CPS or was acting on its behalf, the compensation is payable by the DPP;

(3) a member of the SFO, the compensation is payable by the Director of that Office;

(4) a member of, or acting on behalf of, the Revenue and Customs Prosecution Office, the compensation is payable by the DRCP.

Compensation on variation or discharge

18–029   Where the court varies a confiscation order under s.29 or discharges one under s.30, an application may be made to the Crown Court by a person who held realisable property and has suffered loss as a result of the making of the order, and the judge may order the payment of such compensation as it believes is just, to the applicant, by the Lord Chancellor.

POCA 2002, s.73

The application must be in writing, supported by a witness statement giving details of the order made under s.28, the variation or discharge under s.29 or s.30, the realisable property to which the application relates and the loss suffered by the applicant as a result of the making of the order.

These documents must be lodged with the Crown Court, and must be served on the prosecutor where he is appointed the enforcement authority, at least seven days before the date fixed for the hearing unless the Crown Court specifies a shorter period.

R.58.11

Compensation

Notes

19. CONFISCATION ORDERS

Quick guide

1.   General

The orders under POCA 2002

19–001   In respect of an offence committed after March 24, 2003 a judge of the Crown Court may make:

(1) **a confiscation order** (s.6) for the purpose of recovering from an offender:
   (a) having a "criminal lifestyle" the benefit of his "general criminal conduct"(see 19–017); and
   (b) who has been convicted of particular offences, the benefit of his "particular criminal" conduct, (see 19–019); and
(2) **a restraint order** (s.41), prohibiting the dealing with property, where
   (a) a criminal investigation has been started with regard to an offence; and
   (b) there is reasonable cause to believe that the alleged offender has benefited from his "criminal conduct".

He may also appoint a **receiver** to realise any property, and to apply the proceeds to discharging any sum due under a confiscation order (see RESTRAINT ORDERS; RECEIVERS.

Under POCA 2002 Pt 8 Ch. 2 a judge also has powers to make a number of orders in connection with confiscation investigations (see PRODUCTION AND ACCESS ORDERS; SEARCH WARRANTS. As to travel restriction orders under CJPOA 2001 see TRAVEL RESTRICTION ORDERS.

Jurisdiction

19–002   Where an offender is, in relation to offences committed on or after March 24, 2003:

CONFISCATION ORDERS

   (1) convicted of an offence or offences in proceedings (see *R. v Moulden* [2008] EWCA Crim 3561, [2009] 1 Cr. App. R. 27 before the Crown Court; or

   (2) committed to the Crown Court for sentence; or

   (3) committed to the Crown Court in respect of an offence or offences under POCA 2002, s.70 (committal with a view to a confiscation order being made;

and either:

   (a) the prosecutor asks the court to proceed under this provision; or

   (b) the judge believes it is appropriate to do so,

the judge must proceed to hold a "section 6 enquiry" for the purpose of investigating and deciding the matters set out in 19–016 below.

Paragraphs (1)–(3) above are not satisfied if the accused absconds, but in such a case POCA 2002, s.27 (see 19–051) may apply.

Date is of the essence; the provisions of POCA 2002 in relation to confiscation orders have no effect where the offence(s) were committed before March 24, 2003. If the prosecutor does not rely on a pre-commencement offence for the purpose of the confiscation proceedings, POCA 2002 applies (*R. v Aslam* [2005] 1 Cr. App. R. (S.) 116). There may be cases, as where there is more than one indictment, where more than one framework, i.e. under the 1988 Act and POCA 2002 apply (see e.g. *R. v Moulden* [2008] EWCA Crim 2561, [2009] 1 Cr. App. R. 27).

An offence committed over a period of two or more days (or during a period of days) is to be taken to have been committed on the first day. There is no limitation on the date of the commission of offences to be taken into consideration.

A confiscation order, since it is punitive in nature, may not be made in respect of an offence which the offender was conditionally discharged (*R. v Clarke* [2009] EWCA Crim 1074, [2010] 1 Cr. App. R. (S.) 48; *R. v Magro* EWCA Crim 2575, [2010] 2 Cr. App. R. 25).

As to previous legislation see the 2003 edition of this work under the heading DRUG TRAFFICKING OFFENCES.

Nature of order

19–003 The provisions of POCA 2002 though draconian, are not penal in nature; their purpose is to deprive an offender of that which is not rightfully his.

The legislation is intended to deprive an accused, within his available means, of the benefit he has gained from relevant criminal conduct, whether or not he has retained such benefit. It does not provide for confiscation in the sense understood by school children and others, but nor does it operate by way of fine. The benefit gained is the total value of the property or advantage obtained, not the net profit after deduction of expenses or any amount payable to co-conspirators (*R. v May* [2008] UKHL 28, [2008] 2 Cr. App. R. 28).

It is open for the prosecutor and the offender to agree a figure for realisable assets, but, consistent with his obligations to make a confiscation order under s.6, the judge cannot simply accept that figure without the offender disclosing and the prosecutor accepting the assets that make up the agreed valuation. Where there are 'hidden assets' it is not open to the prosecutor and the offender to settle the amount to pay (*Telli v RCPO* [2007] EWCA Crim 1385, (2008) 2 Cr. App. R. (S.) 48).

See also *Jennings v CPS* [2008] UKHL 29, [2008] 2 Cr. App. R. 29; *R. v Green* [2008] UKHL 30, [2009] 1 Cr. App. R. 30; *R. v Silvram* [2008] Crim. L.R. 989.

2.   Obligation to hold s.6 enquiry

Prosecutor's duty

19–004   Section 6 does not make confiscation proceedings automatic in every case where some benefit has been obtained by criminal conduct.
The prosecutor has a duty to decide in each case;

(1) whether to ask the judge to apply the provisions of s.6; and
(2) on what basis to put his claim, if he makes one.

Although s 6 gives the judge power to invoke the procedure of his own initiative, the responsibility for deciding whether to seek an order is effectively vested in the prosecutor. The judge lacks any corresponding discretion to interfere with that decision if made in accordance with the statute.
It is open to the judge;

(a) to permit confiscation proceedings to be withdrawn at any stage, or to permit them to be compromised; or
(b) as in any other criminal proceedings, to stay them where they amount to an abuse of the court's process, but,

the power under (b) may be exercised where it would be oppressive to seek confiscation, or oppressive in the circumstances of the case, but that "oppression" must be real and the proceedings ought not to be stayed merely because the judge disagrees with the prosecutor's decision to seek confiscation (*R. v Shabir* [2008] EWCA Crim 1809, [2009] 1 Cr. App. R. (S.) 84). Abuse of process cannot be founded on the basis that the proper application of the legislative structure might produce an "oppressive" result with which the judge is unhappy; to conclude that proceedings taken in accordance with the statute constitute an abuse of process is tantamount to asserting a power to dispense with the statute, which, as a matter of principle, is impermissible (*CPS v Nelson* [2009] EWCA Crim 1573, [2010] 1 Cr. App. R. (S.) 82).

The judge's options

19–005   Where the issue is raised by the prosecutor, or where the judge himself invokes the process, the judge has two options. He may either:

(1) proceed under s.6 **before he passes sentence** on the offender (s.14(1)(a)); or
(2) proceed to sentence, **postponing proceedings** under s.6 (s.14(1)(b)), for a specified period where, e.g. he requires further information before proceeding.

263

CONFISCATION ORDERS

The specified period referred to in (2) above, must not exceed two years from the date of conviction.

If the judge "postpones" the proceedings in any way, it is important that he indicate whether he is doing so under s.14(1)(a) or s.14(1)(b) (to avoid the sort of problems which arose in *CPS v Gilleeney* [2009] EWCA Crim 193, [2009] 2 Cr. App. R. (S.) 80). An adjournment *sine die* amounts to a decision not to proceed under s.6 and confers a right of appeal on the prosecutor (*ibid.*).

Where he makes an order **before** sentence the judge must take account of it before imposing:

(a) a fine, or making any order involving payment by the offender, other than a compensation order under PCC(S)A 2000, s.130; or

(b) a forfeiture order under MDA 1971, s.27; a deprivation order under PCC(S)A 2000, s.143; or a forfeiture order under TerrA 2000, s.23.

"Payment by the offender" includes an order for costs to be paid by the offender (*R. v Constantine* [2010] EWCA Crim 2406, [2011] 1 Cr. App. R. (S.) 124).

Subject to the above, the judge may leave the confiscation order out of account in deciding the appropriate sentence for the offender.

He may make both a confiscation order and a compensation order, and may leave the amount of the former out of account in making the latter. Where he makes both a **confiscation order and a compensation order** under PCC(S)A 2000, s.130 against the same offender in the same proceedings; and, considers that the offender will not have sufficient means to satisfy both the orders in full:

(a) he must direct that so much of the compensation as he specifies is to be paid out of any sums recovered under the confiscation order;

(b) the specified amount being that amount he believes will not be recoverable because of the insufficiency of the person's means.

A confiscation order may not be combined with a conditional discharge on the same count of an indictment (*R. v Clarke* [2009] EWCA Crim 1074, [2010] 1 Cr. App. R. (S.) 48).

A sentence already imposed may be **varied** within 28 days of the last day of the postponement period (as set out in s.15(3)).

As to the **subsequent reconsideration** of an order, see 19–035, below.

The offender cannot rely in mitigation on the fact that a confiscation order has been made or will be made against him.

Where the judge gives the offender an unequivocal representation (to which the prosecutor does not object) that confiscation proceedings will not proceed if the offender repays the benefit obtained from his criminal conduct and the offender has done so, it is an abuse of process for the court to proceed with the application. For the court to give an offender an inducement and then renege on its indication after he has acted on that inducement to his disadvantage would damage the integrity of the process of criminal justice. See *R. (Secretary of State for Work and*

Pensions) v Croydon Crown Court [2010] EWHC 805 (Admin), [2011] 1 Cr. App. R.(S.) 1. See also *R. v LM* [2010] EWCA Crim 2327, [2011] 1 Cr. App. R. 12.

Postponement of the enquiry

19–006   The judge may either:

(1) proceed under s.6 before he sentences the offender (s.14(1)(a)); or

(2) postpone proceedings under s.6 for a specified period (s.14(1)(b)), where, e.g. he requires further information before proceeding,

and is important if he "postpones" the proceedings in any way, that he indicate whether he is doing so under s.14(1)(a) or s.14(1)(b), to avoid the sort of problems which arose in *CPS Swansea v Gilleeney* [2009] EWCA Crim 193; [2009] 2 Cr. App. R. (S.). Whether it is described as an adjournment or a relisting, a decision to put the hearing back to a later date constitutes a postponement (*R. v Neish* [2010] EWCA Crim 1011; [2011] 1 Cr. App. R. (S.) 33 where the judge gave instructions to the listing officer and the listing officer carried out those instructions). An adjournment *sine die* amounts to a decision not to proceed under s.6 and confers a right of appeal on the prosecutor (*ibid.*).

The specified period referred to in (2) above, must not exceed two years from the date of conviction.   PD 2004, Annex F, 9.1

It is important that confiscation hearings take place in good time after the defendant is convicted or sentenced. Where possible, the judge who conducted the trial or passed sentence should be the judge who conducts confiscation proceedings (see *R. v Knagg* [2009] EWCA Crim 1363, [2010] 1 Cr. App. R. (S.) 75).

When listing confiscation and related matters, court staff should consider the potential for such matters to encounter delay, and should take steps to ensure their swift listing and progression, and in particular have regard to the reasonable time requirement under ECHR, art.6 which requires the total length of proceedings to be considered, not simply the time that elapses between hearings.

Where he proceeds under s.14(1)(a):

(a) he must not, as part of that sentence, include a fine, a financial order other than a compensation order under PCC(S)A 2000, s.130, or any of the forfeiture orders set out in the following paragraphs, although,

(b) if the offender is sentenced during the postponement period, the sentence may be varied by adding one of the prohibited orders, within 28 days starting with the last day of the period of postponement.

For the purpose of time limits relating to appeal, sentence is regarded as having been passed on the date of the variation.

19–007   Where the judge proceeds under s.14(1)(a) (see 19–005 above, at sub-para.(1)):

(1) he must not, as part of that sentence include a fine, a financial order (other than a compensation order under PCC(S)A 2000,

CONFISCATION ORDERS

s.l30), or any of the forfeiture orders set out in 19–004 at sub-para.(b); although,

(2) if the offender is sentenced during the postponement period, the sentence may be varied by adding one of the prohibited orders, within 28 days starting with the last day of the period of postponement.

For the purpose of time limits relating to appeal, sentence is regarded as having been passed on the date of the variation. If he knows that he will be carrying out fact-finding exercises in relation to the same offender at a later stage, the judge will need to take care, in his sentencing remarks not to express himself in a manner that may sensibly be perceived to show that he is unlikely to believe anything the offender is likely to tell him. If remarks of that nature are pertinent to explaining his sentence, the judge will need to recuse himself from conducting any subsequent fact-finding exercise (*R. v Odewale* [2005] EWCA Crim 709, [2005] 2 Cr. App. R. (S.) 202).

Relationship between order and sentence

19–008   The judge may pass sentence for the offence(s) of which the offender has been convicted either **before** making an order, as where he postpones his duty to conduct a s.6 enquiry (see 19–006 above), or **after** making an order.

The offender cannot rely in mitigation on the fact a confiscation order had been made or will be made against him.

Where an order is made **before** sentence the judge must take account of it before imposing:

POCA 2002, ss.l3(l)–(4)

(1) a fine, or making any order involving payment by the offender, other than a compensation order under PCC(S)A 2000, s.130; or
(2) a forfeiture order under MDA 1971, s.27; a deprivation order under PCC(S)A 2000, s.143; or a forfeiture order under TerrA 2000, s.23.

Subject to the above, the judge may leave the confiscation order out of account in deciding the appropriate sentence for the offender; he may make both a confiscation order and a compensation order. He may leave the amount of the former out of account in making the latter.

POCA 2002, s.13(5)(6)

Where the judge:

(a) makes both a confiscation order and a compensation order under PCC(S)A 2000, s.130 against the same offender in the same proceedings; and,
(b) considers that the offender will not have sufficient means to satisfy both the orders in full,

he must direct that so much of the compensation as he specifies is to be paid out of any sums recovered under the confiscation order, the specified amount being that amount he believes will not be recoverable because of the insufficiency of the person's means.

A confiscation order may not be combined with a conditional discharge on the same count of an indictment (*R. v Clarke* [2009] EWCA Crim 1074, [2010] 1 Cr. App. R. (S.) 48; *R. v Magro* [2010] EWCA

Crim 1575; [2010] 2 Cr. App. R. 25; cf. *R. v Wilkinson* [2009] EWCA Crim 2733.

A sentence already imposed may be **varied** within 28 days of the last day of the postponement period (as set out in s.15(3)).

As to the **subsequent reconsideration** of an order, see 19–035, below.

3. Enforcement of order

Time for payment; interest

19–009   The amount ordered to be paid must ordinarily be paid on the making of the order. If the offender asks for time to pay, the judge may:

POCA 2002, s.11

(1) allow time for payment within a specified period not exceeding six months from the date on which the order is made; or
(2) where, on the offender's application, he accepts that there are exceptional circumstances, the judge may extend the period to a maximum of 12 months from the date of the order.

An application under (2) may be made after the expiry of the date originally specified, but not after the expiry of the 12 months from the date the order was made.

No extension may be granted unless the prosecutor is given an opportunity to make representations.

The period of time allowed for payment runs from the date the order is made, not from the determination of an appeal against the order. It would be wrong as a matter of principle for offenders to be encouraged to believe that the bringing of an appeal would be likely to lengthen the time allowed for payment *(R. v May* [2008] UKHL 28, [2008] 2 Cr. App. R. 28).

Where the amount required to be paid under the order is not paid when it is required to be paid, interest falls to be paid for the period for which it remains unpaid (at the rate for the time being specified in the Judgments Act 1838, s.17, in relation to civil debts), unless:

POCA 2002, s.12(3)(4)

(a) an application has been made under s.11(4) for an extension of time,
(b) that application has not been determined by the court, and
(c) the period of 12 months starting with the day on which the order was made has not ended.

The amount of the interest is to be treated as part of the amount to be paid under the confiscation order.

Fixing default sentence

19–010   The judge **must** fix a term of imprisonment to be served in default of payment, in terms of the Table set out in PCC(S)A 2000, s.139(4) (see FINES AND ENFORCEMENT).

POCA 2002, s.35

The default term imposed should be within the permitted maximum so as to make clear to the offender that he has nothing to gain by failing to comply with the order (see *R. v Szrajber* (1994) 15 Cr. App. R. (S.) 821; *R. v French* (1995) 16 Cr. App. R. (S.) 841; *R. v Smith* [2003] EWCA Crim

344; *R. v Qema* [2006] EWCA Crim 1736; *R. v Liscott* [2007] EWCA Crim 1706; *R. v Howard* [2007] EWCA Crim 1489 considered in *R. v Pigott* [2009] EWCA Crim 2292, [2010] 2 Cr. App. R. (S.) 16). The judge has a discretion up to the maximum period in the Table; he is not bound to follow any arithmetical approach, but should consider the circumstances, bearing in mind that the purpose of the default sentence is to secure payment of the amount ordered (*R. v Pigott, above,* where the legislation is considered). The imposing of the sentence for the offence and the fixing of the default sentence are thus two separate exercises and the judge is not restrained by the "totality principle" (see 41–014) in respect of the two terms, see *R. v Price* [2009] EWCA Crim 2918, [2010] 2 Cr. App. R. (S.) 44; *R. v Cukovic* [1996] 1 Cr. App. R. (S.) 131, CA, not followed.

Enforcement is as for a fine imposed by the Crown Court (i.e. PCC(S)A 2000, ss.139(2)–(4) and (9), and ss.140(1)–(4) apply), with modifications disapplying MCA 1980, s.75 (allowing time to pay – see *CPS v Greenacre* [2007] EWHC 1193 (Admin)), s.81 (young offenders), s.85 (remittal) and s.87 (means enquiry).

The provisions of PCC(S)A 2000, s.139(3) prevent immediate committal to prison. *POCA 2002, s.38*

If the offender serves a term of imprisonment or detention in default of paying any amount due under a confiscation order, his serving that term does not prevent the confiscation order from continuing to have effect so far as any other method of enforcement is concerned.

Enforcement as fine; receivers
19–011   Where a confiscation order is made the court's functions as to fines and their enforcement (PCC(S)A 2000, ss.139(2)–(4), 140(1)-(4)) apply as if the amount ordered to be paid were a fine imposed on the offender by the court making the order. *POCA 2002, s.35(1)*

In addition the judge:

(1) may, on the application of the prosecutor, appoint an enforcement receiver, where a confiscation is made and not satisfied (and is not subject to appeal) and confer on him the powers in s.51; and *POCA 2002, s.50*

(2) must, where a management receiver has been appointed under any restraint order, order him to transfer any property held by him to the enforcement receiver.

4.   Section 6 enquiry: procedure

Enquiry a precondition
19–012   A s.6 enquiry is a mandatory precondition to the making of a confiscation order. The judge may sentence an offender before making a confiscation order, but in relation to offences committed:

(1) **on or before March 23, 2003,** if he proceeds to sentence without ruling on whether or not there should be an enquiry, he may not make a confiscation order (*R. v Ross* [2001] Crim. L.R. 405);

(2) **on or after March 24, 2003,** he *should consider* whether to make an order or hold an enquiry before moving to sentence, and

he *must* do so before he is entitled to impose a fine, compensation, forfeiture or deprivation of property.

Confiscation proceedings are not a criminal trial to which the presumption of innocence applies but part of the sentencing process in respect of a convicted offender, (see *R. v Gavin* [2010] EWCA Crim 2727, [2011] 1 Cr. App. R. (S.) 126; *R. v Bhanji* [2011] EWCA Crim 1198). Where an offender is absent from confiscation proceedings, otherwise than where he has absconded (as to which, see POCA 2002, ss.6(8), 27 and 28), the judge has a discretion to proceed in his absence, even where the absence is involuntary (*R. v Jones (Anthony)* [2002] UKHL 5, [2002] Cr. App. R. 9).

As to his powers of postponement, see 19–033 below.

As to the compatibility of the procedure under the previous legislation with ECHR, art.6, see *R. v Benjafield* [2002] UKHL 2, [2002] 2 Cr. App. R. 3.

These proceedings are an extension of the sentencing hearing and are therefore criminal in nature. In *R. v Clipston* [2011] EWCA Crim 446, [2011] 2 Cr. App. R. (S.) 101 CACD opined that hearsay evidence is admissible, stating that where admissibility is contested, having regard to the nature of the proceedings and the need for fairness to both sides, the statutory provisions of CJA 2003 are the appropriate framework, not the provisions of CEA 1995.

Statement of information

19–013 Where the judge is to proceed under s.6 in a case where: POCA 2002, s.16

(1) asked by the prosecutor to do so, he will be given a statement of information within such period as he orders;
(2) he proceeds of his own motion he will order the prosecutor to give him a statement of information, and the prosecutor must do so within such period as the judge orders.

Where the prosecutor:

(a) believes the offender has a "criminal lifestyle", that statement will be a statement of the matters he believes are relevant in connection with deciding whether the offender has a criminal lifestyle, whether he has benefited from his general criminal conduct and his benefit from the conduct, and will include such information as he believes is relevant in connection with the making by the judge of any required assumption under s.10, (see 19–027, below) and for the purpose of enabling him to decide if the circumstances are such that he must not make such an assumption;
(b) does not believe that the offender has a criminal lifestyle, the statement will be a statement of matters he believes are relevant in connection with deciding whether the offender has benefited from his "particular criminal conduct," and the benefit from the conduct.

Such a statement must also contain the information prescribed in r.58.1 (2) and in the Crown Court (Confiscation, Restraint and Receivership) Rules (SI 2003/421) which must be served upon the offender.

CONFISCATION ORDERS

If the prosecutor gives the court a statement, he may at any time give a further statement, and must do so if the judge so orders, and within the period ordered.

If the judge makes an order under this section he may at any time vary it by making another.

Offender's response to statement

19–014 Where a statement of information is given to the judge and a copy is served on the offender, the judge may order him: POCA 2002, s.17

- (1) to indicate, within the period ordered, the extent to which he accepts each allegation in it; and
- (2) so far as he does not accept an allegation, to give particulars of any matters he proposes to rely on.

If the offender:

- (a) accepts to any extent an allegation in the statement the judge may treat his acceptance as conclusive of the matters to which it relates for the purpose of deciding the issues referred to in ss.16(3) or (5), (above), as the case may be;
- (b) fails in any respect to comply with such an order he may be treated as accepting every allegation in the statement apart from:
  - (i) any allegation in respect of which he has complied with the requirement; or
  - (ii) any allegation that he has benefited from his general or particular criminal conduct, and

no acceptance under this section that the offender has benefited from conduct is admissible in evidence in proceedings for an offence.

Rule 58.1(3) requires such information be given in writing to the prosecutor and a copy be given to the court.

An allegation may be accepted or particulars may be given in a manner ordered by the judge. If he makes an order under this provision he may at any time vary it by making another.

An offender who pleads guilty without challenging in any way the evidence for the prosecution, is not debarred thereby from challenging the prosecution evidence for the purposes of the s.6 hearing (*R. v Knaggs* [2007] EWCA Crim. 1363, [2010] 1 Cr. App. R. (S.) 75).

Offender providing information

19–015 Where the judge is proceeding under s.6 in a case where: POCA 2002, s.18

- (1) he has been asked by the prosecutor to do so; or
- (2) he proceeds of his own motion, or he is considering whether to proceed,

he may, for the purpose of obtaining information to help him in carrying out his functions, at any time, order the offender to give him specified information, and such an order may require all, or a specified part, of the information to be given in a specified manner and before a specified date, provided no information given which amounts to an admission by the defendant that he has benefited from criminal conduct is admissible in evidence in proceedings for an offence.

R.58.1(4)

Such information must be given in writing, and a copy must be sent to the prosecutor.

Where:

POCA 2002, s.18(5)(6)

(a) the offender fails, without reasonable excuse, to comply with an order, the judge, quite apart from any power he may have to deal with him in respect of a failure to comply with an order under this section, may draw such inference as he believes to be appropriate;

(b) the prosecutor accepts to any extent an allegation made by the offender in giving information required by the judge's order, or in any other statement given to the court in relation to any matter relevant to deciding the available amount under s.9, the judge may treat the acceptance as conclusive of the matters to which it relates.

An allegation may be accepted in any manner the judge may order.

If the judge makes an order under these provisions he may at any time vary it by making another.

Aims of the enquiry

19–016   Confiscation under POCA 2002 is by reference:

POCA 2002, s.6

(1) to the offender's benefit from his "general criminal conduct" where he is shown on conviction to have a "criminal lifestyle"; or

(2) where he does not have such a lifestyle, to his benefit from his "particular criminal conduct".

The judge must therefore investigate and decide:

(a) whether the offender has "a criminal lifestyle" (within the meaning of s.75 as to which see below); and

(b) if he decides that he has, whether he has "benefited" (see 19–021) from his "general criminal conduct" (19–019, below); and

(c) if he does *not* have a "criminal lifestyle" whether he has benefited from his "particular criminal conduct" (see 19–019); and

(d) finally, if he has benefited, what is recoverable from him (the "recoverable amount") as to which (see 19–030),

unless the judge is satisfied either that:

(i) the offender has repaid the victim; or

(ii) a victim of any relevant criminal conduct has instituted, or intends to institute, civil proceedings against the offender in respect of loss, injury or damage sustained in connection with the conduct (*R. v Morgan* [2008] EWCA Crim 1323, [2009]1 Cr. App. R. (S.) 60), in which case the judge has a discretion whether or not to make an order.

Confiscation Orders

CONFISCATION ORDERS

These are separate questions calling for separate answers.

In addressing them the judge has first to establish the facts as best he can on the material available, relying, as appropriate, on the assumptions required to be made by the Act. Considering similar provisions, HL pointed out in *R. v Briggs-Price* [2009] UKHL 19; [2009] 4 All E.R. 594, that the judge was not restricted to the mandatory application of the statutory assumptions, but might instead rely on the evidence given at the trial. In many cases the factual findings made will be decisive. In addressing them he needs to focus on the language of the statutory provision in question. Any judicial gloss or exegesis needs to be viewed with caution (*R. v May* [2008] UKHL 28; [2008] 2 Cr. App. R. 28). POCA 2002, s.6(7)

The judge must decide any question arising under (1) and (2) above on a balance of probabilities.

"Criminal lifestyle"

19–017 An offender has a criminal lifestyle for the purposes of the Act, if the offence, or any of the offences of which he is convicted: POCA 2002, s.75(1)–(6)

(1) is a "lifestyle offence" specified in Sch.2;
(2) constitutes conduct forming part of a **course of criminal activity**;
(3) is an offence committed over a period of at least six months and the offender has **benefited** from the conduct which constitutes the offence.

The condition that an offence must be "committed over a period of at least six months" relates to the particular accused's part in an offence; where, therefore, the prosecutor fails to prove that he the part played by the particular accused in a conspiracy lasted at least six months, even though the conspiracy itself lasted at least six, he cannot be said to have had a "criminal lifestyle" within s.75, *R. v Bajwa*, unreported, May 6, 2011, CA.

Where the offender has benefited from conduct which constitutes the offence (committed **after March 24, 2003**), such conduct forms part of a course of criminal activity in two circumstances, namely if where:

(a) in the proceedings in which he was convicted, he was also convicted of three or more other offences (i.e. at least four offences in the same proceeding), each of the three or more of them constituting conduct from which he has also benefited, committed **after March 24, 2003** (SI 2003/333, art.7(4)); or

(b) in the period of six years ending with the day when those proceedings were started (or, if there is more than one such day, the earliest day), he was convicted on at least **two separate occasions** of an offence constituting conduct from which he has benefited notwithstanding that any of those offences were committed before **March 24, 2003** (SI 2003/333, art.7(5));

and in either case the offender obtained "relevant benefit" of not less than £5,000.

272

Benefit from "general criminal conduct"

19–018 Once the judge has decided that the offender has a criminal lifestyle the next step is to decide whether he benefited from his general criminal conduct.

Relevant benefit is benefit from:

(1) conduct which constitutes the offence;
(2) any other conduct which forms part of the course of criminal activity and which constitutes an offence of which the offender has been convicted; or
(3) conduct which constitutes an offence which has been or will be taken into consideration by the judge (see TICs) in sentencing the offender for an offence mentioned in (a) or (b) of the preceding paragraph.

For the purposes of (3) above it is benefit from:

(a) conduct which constitutes the offence; or
(b) conduct which constitutes an offence which has been or will be taken into consideration by the judge in sentencing the offender for the offence mentioned in (a) or (b) of the preceding paragraph,

SI 2003/333, art.7(3)

provided that the judge must not take into account benefit from conduct constituting an offence committed **before March 24, 2003**.

As to the assumptions to be made where a criminal lifestyle is proved, see s.10 at 19–027, below.

Definitions

19–019 "Criminal conduct" is defined (in s.76) as conduct which constitutes an offence in England and Wales, or would constitute such an offence if it occurred in England and Wales. The **"general criminal conduct"** of an offender is *all* his criminal conduct, and it is immaterial whether:

POCA 2002, s.76(1)–(3)

(1) that conduct occurred before or after the passing of POCA 2002;
(2) property constituting a benefit from that conduct was obtained before or after the passing of the Act; or
(3) it formed the subject of criminal proceedings.

The **"particular criminal conduct"** of the offender is his criminal conduct which constitutes:

(a) the offence or offences concerned;
(b) offences of which he was convicted in the same proceedings as those in which he was convicted of the offence or offences concerned; or
(c) offences which the judge will be taking into consideration in deciding his sentence for the offence or offences concerned,

but conduct which constitutes an offence which was committed **before March 24, 2003,** is not particular criminal conduct under ss.76(3) or 224(3) (SI 2003/333).

273

CONFISCATION ORDERS

Assessing the offender's benefit

19–020   In deciding whether the offender has "benefited" (see below) from conduct, and in deciding the benefit from that conduct, the judge must take account of: POCA 2002, s.8(1)–(3)

(1) conduct occurring up to the time he makes his decision; and
(2) property (see 19–022 and following) obtained up to that time.

Where:

(a) the conduct concerned is general criminal conduct; or
(b) a confiscation order has at an earlier time been made against the offender, and his benefit for the purposes of that previous order was benefit from his general criminal conduct,

then his benefit found at the time the last confiscation order (mentioned in (b) above) was made against him must be taken for the purposes of this section to be his benefit from his general criminal conduct at that time.

Definition of "benefit"

19–021   A person "benefits" from conduct if he obtains property as a result of or in connection with the conduct. If he obtains a pecuniary advantage as a result of or in connection with conduct, he is to be taken to obtain as a result of or in connection with the conduct a sum of money equal to the value of the pecuniary advantage.

References to "property" or a "pecuniary advantage obtained in connection with conduct" include references to property or a pecuniary advantage obtained both in that connection and some other.

It is important to bear in mind that:

(1) The purpose of the order is to deprive an offender of the product of his crime, not to operate by way of fine;
(2) the question whether an offender has obtained an interest in property is not determined merely by the fact of temporary possession nor is an offender to be deprived of what he never actually obtained but merely helped others to obtain (*Jennings v CPS* [2008] UKHL 29, [2008] 2 Cr. App. R. 29).

The exercise of the confiscation jurisdiction involves no departure from familiar rules governing entitlement and ownership. An offender ordinarily obtains property if in law he owns it, whether alone or jointly, which will ordinarily connote a power of disposition or control, as where a person directs a payment or conveyance of property to someone else. Mere couriers or custodians or other very minor contributors to an offence, rewarded by a specific fee and having no interest in the property or the proceeds of sale, are unlikely to be found to have obtained that property. Where co-accused jointly receive property as a result of criminal activity, each is liable to receive a confiscation order representing the entire value, as if he had acted alone, provided he has sufficient assets to meet the order (*R. v May,* above).

An offender "obtains" property for the purposes of s.76(4) if he assumes possession of it, which includes collecting it for another, regardless of whether he is aware of its true value and of whether he retains it for any length of time (*ibid.*). Section 84(2)(b) is concerned only with situations where the offender has not had physical possession of the property *(R. v Stanley* [2007] EWCA Crim 2857, [2008] 2 Cr. App. R.(S) 119).

If a person benefits from conduct, his benefit is the value of the property obtained. In the case of an offender benefiting from particular criminal conduct, that value is the market value of his interest in the property. As to:

(a) the market value of property obtained by a thief or handler (*CPS v Rose* [2008] EWCA Crim 239, [2008] 2 Cr. App. R. 15);

(b) liability in respect of unpaid tax (*R. v Dimsey* [2000] 1 Cr. App. R. (S.) 497);

(c) the liability of smugglers evading duty on importation, see *R. v Bakewell* [2006] EWCA Crim 2, [2006] 2 Cr. App. R. (S.) 42 following *R. v Smith (David Cadnam)* [2002] 1 Cr. App. R. 35; see also *R. v White, Dennard* [2010] EWCA Crim 978;

(d) the 'black market' value of drugs, *R. v Islam* [2009] UKHL 30, [2010] 1 Cr. App. R. (S.) 42;

(e) counterfeit goods, the value is to be assessed as if they were genuine, *R. v Varsani* [2010] EWCA Crim 1938, [2011] 1 Cr. App. R. (S.) 96;

(f) dishonest mortgage applications, *T v Waya* [2010] EWCA Crim 412, [2011] 1 Cr. App. R. (S.) 4.

Section 76(4) provides that a person benefits from conduct if he obtains property as a result of or in connection with the conduct. Section 76(7) provides that if a person benefits from conduct his benefit is the value of the property obtained. It is necessary to look at the property coming to an offender which is his, and not what happens to the property subsequently. The judge is concerned with what the offender has obtained "so as to own it, whether alone or jointly, which will ordinarily connote a power of disposition or control" (*R. v May*, above, *Jennings v CPS*, above). Profit (viz. turnover less expenses) is not the test. "The offender's benefit is the property which he obtains from his criminal conduct even though he may then dispose of it for legitimate purposes" (*R. v del Basso* [2010] EWCA Crim 119, [2011] 1 Cr. App. R. (S.) 268(41)).

While in certain circumstances the judge may make the assumption that drugs were purchased with the proceeds of earlier crimes, for the purposes of confiscation under POCA 2002 the "market value" should not include the value of drugs found in the possession of the offender (*R. v Islam*, above).

Under the previous legislation it was said in relation to DTA 1994, s.2(3) that a person's "proceeds" are his gross receipts rather than his net profits (see, e.g. *R. v Banks* [1997] 2 Cr. App. R. (S.) 110; *R. v Fadden, The Times,* January 26, 1998).

"Property"; general provisions

19–022   "Property" is all property wherever situated and includes:

POCA 2002, s.150

(1) money;

(2) all forms of real or personal property; and

(3) things in action and other intangible or incorporeal property (as

to inheritance and damages received from civil action, see *Maye v DPP Northern Ireland* [2008] UKHL 9, [2008] 1 W.L.R. 315).

The following rules apply in relation to property:

(a) property is held by a person if he holds an interest in it;
(b) property is obtained by a person if he obtains an interest in it;
(c) property is transferred by one person to another if the first one transfers or grants an interest in it to the second;
(d) references to property held by a person include references to property vested in his trustee in bankruptcy, (*R. v Shahid* [2009] EWCA Crim 831; [2009] 2 Cr. App. R. (S.) 105) permanent or interim trustee (within the meaning of the Bankruptcy (Scotland) Act 1985) or liquidator;
(e) references to an interest held by a person beneficially in property include references to an interest which would be held by him beneficially if the property were not so vested;
(f) references to an interest, in relation to land in England and Wales or Northern Ireland, are to any legal estate or equitable interest or power;
(g) references to an interest, in relation to land in Scotland, are to any estate, interest, servitude or other heritable right in or over land, including a heritable security;
(h) references to an interest, in relation to property other than land, include references to a right (including a right to possession).

"Criminal property" is defined in POCA 2002, s.340, see *R. v Loizou* [2005] EWCA Crim 1579, [2005] 2 Cr. App. R. 37; *R. v Amir* [2011] EWCA Crim 146, [2011] 1 Cr. App. R. 37.

"Free" property

19–023 Property is free unless an order is in force in respect of it under:

(a) MDA 1971, s.27;
(b) Criminal Justice (Northern Ireland) Order 1994 (SI 19947/2795 (N.I. 15)) art.ll, (deprivation orders);
(c) Proceeds of Crime (Scotland) Act 1995, Pt 2 (forfeiture of property used in crime);
(d) PCC(S)A 2000, s.143;
(e) Terr A 2000, s.23 or s.111 (forfeiture orders);
(f) POCA 2002, ss.246, 266, 295(2) or 298(2).

An offender's vested life interest in possession in one third of a trust fund set up by his grandfather, giving him power to receive income from it, is 'free' property (*R. v Walker* [2011] 3 Archbold Review 3).

"Realisable" property

19–024 Realisable property is any free property held by the accused, and any "free" property (see above) held by the recipient of a "tainted gift" (see 19–026 below).

POCA 2002, s.83

Gifts and their recipients

19–025   Where the defender transfers property to another person for a consideration whose value is significantly less than the value of the property at the time of the transfer, he is to be treated as making a gift, and the property given is to be treated as such share in the property transferred as is represented by the fraction whose:

POCA 2002, s.78

(1) numerator is the difference between the two values mentioned above; and
(2) denominator is the value of the property at the time of the transfer.

References to a recipient of a "tainted gift" are to a person to whom the defendant has made the gift.

The "gift" provisions (of DTA 1994) have no bearing on a wife's share of the matrimonial home, for which she has given consideration by bringing up her children and looking after the family home, even though she has guilty knowledge of the source of her husband's wealth (*Gibson v RCPO* [2008] EWCA Civ 645; [2009] 2 W.L.R. 171, cf. *C&E Commrs v A* [2003] Fam. 55, *CPS v Richard* [2006] 2 F.L.R. 1220).

"Tainted gifts"

19–026   Where:

POCA 2002, ss.77(1)–(5)

(1) a decision has *not* been made as to whether the accused has a criminal lifestyle or a court has decided that he has such a lifestyle, a gift is said to *be tainted*:
  (a) where it was made by him at any time after "the relevant day"; and
  (b) if it was made by him at any time and was of property:
    (i) which was obtained by him as a result of or in connection with his general criminal conduct, or
    (ii) which (in whole or part and whether directly or indirectly) represented in his hands property obtained by him as a result of or in connection with his general criminal conduct;
(2) a court has decided that the accused does *not* have a criminal lifestyle, a gift is said to be "tainted" if it was made by him at any time after:
  (a) the date on which the offence concerned was committed; or
  (b) if his particular criminal conduct consists of two or more offences and they were committed on different dates, the date of the earliest.

An offence which is a continuing offence is committed on the first occasion when it is committed. For the purposes of (2)(b) in the preceding paragraph, the accused's "particular criminal conduct" includes any conduct which constitutes offences which the court has taken into consideration in deciding his sentence for the offence or offences concerned.

POCA 2002, ss.77(6)–(9)

A gift may be a "tainted gift" whether it was made before or after the passing of the Act.

Confiscation Orders

The "relevant day" referred to in (1)(a) in the preceding paragraph, is the first day of the period of six years ending with:

(a) the day when proceedings for the offence concerned were started against the accused, or

(b) if there are two or more offences and proceedings for them were started on different days, the earliest of those days.

Assumptions to be made in case of "criminal lifestyle"

19–027 Where the judge decides that the offender has a "criminal lifestyle" he *must* make the following four assumptions for the purpose both of deciding:

POCA 2002, ss.10(1)–(7)

(1) whether the offender has benefited from his "general criminal conduct" (see 19–018, 19–019, above), and;

(2) his benefit from that conduct namely:

(a) **any property transferred** to the offender at any time after the "relevant day" is assumed to have been obtained by him:
(i) as a result of his "general criminal conduct"; and
(ii) at the earliest time he appears to have held it;

(b) **any property held** by the offender at any time after the date of conviction is assumed to have been obtained by him:
(i) as a result of his "general criminal conduct"; and
(ii) at the earliest time he appears to have held it;

(c) **any expenditure incurred** by the offender at any time after "the relevant day" was met from property obtained by him as a result of his "general criminal conduct";

(d) for the purpose of valuing any **property obtained** (or assumed to have been obtained) by the offender, it is assumed that he obtained it free of any other interests in it;

unless that assumption is shown to be incorrect, or if there would be a "serious risk of injustice if the assumption were made."

Note that this latter phrase in s.10(6)(b):

(i) does not mean hardship to the offender by virtue of the order;

(ii) is not to provide for the exercise of a discretion by the judge in determining whether it is fair to make an order; but

(iii) is to ensure a sensible calculation of the benefit and to ensure that the assumptions are not so unreason-able or unjust in respect of the particular offender that they should not be made

(CPS v Jones [2006] W.L.R.(D) 174). The judge is not restricted to relying on the assumptions and may, instead, rely on the evidence given at the trial *(R. v Briggs-Price* [2009] UKHL 19, [2009] 4 All E.R. 594 (a decision on the similar provisions in DTA 1994, s.4).

Where the judge does not make one or more of the required assumptions he must state his reasons; he must still decide whether the offender has benefited from his general criminal conduct and determine the recoverable amount, albeit without the assistance of those assumptions.

POCA 2002, s.9

Note that the "relevant day" is the first day of the period of six years ending with,

- the day when proceedings for the offence concerned were started against the accused; or
- if there are two or more offences, and proceedings for them were started on different days, the earliest of those days,

but if a confiscation order mentioned in s.8(3)(c) has been made against the accused at any time during the period mentioned in subs.(8), then the "relevant day" is the day when the offender's benefit was calculated for the purposes of the last such confiscation order, and assumption (b) does not apply to any property which was held by him on or before the relevant day.

The "date of conviction" is the date on which the offender was convicted of the offence concerned, or if there are two or more offences and the convictions were on different dates, the date of the latest.

Offender having no criminal lifestyle

19–028   Where the judge decides that the offender does not have a "criminal lifestyle" he must go on to decide whether the offender has benefited from his "particular criminal conduct", defined at 19–019, above. Conduct which constitutes an offence committed **on or before March 23, 2003** does not come within the definition.

SI 2003/333

Assessment of benefit

19–029   For the purpose of deciding the value at any time of property then held by a person, its value is the market value of the property at that time, but if at that time another person holds an interest in the property its value, in relation to such person is the market value of his interest at that time, ignoring any previous charging order made under the enactments referred to in POCA 2002, ss.79–81.

POCA 2002, ss.8(1)–(4)

Special rules apply to the valuation of property obtained from conduct (s.80), and to "tainted gifts" (see 19–026 above).

Where the conduct concerned is general criminal conduct, the judge must, in order to avoid double counting, deduct the aggregate of the any amounts ordered to be paid under those orders made under the enactments listed in s.8(7) unless an amount has been taken into account for the purposes of a deduction under this provision on an earlier occasion.

POCA 2002, ss.8(5)–(8)

Where an offender is convicted of importing drugs, the value of the drugs should be included in the calculation of the value of his benefit (*R. v Islam* [2009] UKHL 30, [2010] 1 Cr. App. R. (S.) 42).

Deciding the "recoverable amount"

19–030   Once the judge has assessed the amount of the offender's benefit, he must make a confiscation order in that amount, unless:

POCA 2002, s.7

(1) the offender shows that the "available amount" is less than that assessed benefit; in which case the amount subject to confiscation (the "recoverable amount") is the "available amount" (see 19–031, below), or a nominal amount, if the available amount is nil, but

(2) a victim of the offender's conduct has started or intends to start civil proceedings (s.6(6)), in which case the amount subject to

Confiscation Orders

confiscation is such amount as the judge believes is just, and which does not exceed the assessed benefit.

In calculating the offender's benefit from the conduct concerned, any property in respect of which:

> (a) a recovery order is in force under POCA 2002, s.266, or
> (b) a forfeiture order is in force under PCC(S)A 2000, s.298(2), must be ignored.

Where the judge decides the available amount, he must include in the confiscation order a statement of his findings as to the matters relevant for deciding that amount.

"The available amount"
19–031 The "available amount" is the aggregate of:

(1) the total of the values (at the time the confiscation order is made) of all the **"free property"** (see 19–023, above) then held by the offender;
(2) deducting the total amount payable in pursuance of **obligations** which then have priority; and
(3) adding the total of the values (at that time) of all "tainted gifts" (see 19–026, above).

An obligation "has priority" if the offender has an obligation to pay:

> (a) an amount due in respect of a fine or other order of a court which was imposed or made on conviction of an offence and at any time before the time the confiscation order is made, or
> (b) a sum which would be included among the preferential debts (within the meaning of the Insolvency Act 1986, s.385) if the defendant's bankruptcy had commenced on the date of the confiscation order or his winding up had been ordered on that date.

As to the value of a pension policy, see *R. v Chen* [2009] EWCA Crim 2669, [2010] 2 Cr. App. R. (S.) 34. As to assessing the value of a life interest in trust property, see *R. v Walker* [2011] EWCA Crim 103, [2011] 2 Cr. App. R. (S.) 54.

Expert evidence
19–032 A party to proceedings POCA 2002, Pt 2 (confiscation orders) who wishes to adduce expert evidence (whether of fact or opinion) in the proceedings must, as soon as practicable: R.57.9

(1) serve on the other parties a statement in writing of any finding or opinion which he proposes to adduce by way of such evidence; and
(2) serve on any party who requests it in writing, a copy of (or if it appears to the party proposing to adduce the evidence to be more practicable, a reasonable opportunity to examine):
> (a) the record of any observation, test, calculation or other procedure on which the finding or opinion is based, and
> (b) any document or other thing or substance in respect of which the observation, test, calculation or other procedure has been carried out.

A party may serve notice in writing waiving his right to be served with any of those matters and, in particular, may agree that the statement mentioned in (1) may be given to him orally and not served in writing.

If a party who wishes to adduce expert evidence in such proceedings fails to comply with this rules he may not adduce that evidence in those proceedings without the leave of the court, except where r.57.10 below applies.

Where a party has reasonable grounds for believing that the disclosure of any evidence in compliance with r.57.9 might lead:

(i) to the intimidation, or attempted intimidation, of any person on whose evidence he intends to rely in the proceedings, or

(ii) otherwise to the course of justice being interfered with, he is not obliged to comply with the above requirements in relation to that evidence, unless a judge of the Crown Court orders otherwise.

Where such a party considers that he is not obliged to comply with the requirements of r.57.9 with regard to any evidence in relation to any other party, he must serve notice in writing on that party stating that the evidence is being withheld, and the reason for so doing.

CPR 2010, Pt 57 applies with necessary modifications to the POCA 2002 (External Requests and Orders) order 2005 (SI 2005/3181) in the same way as it applies to the corresponding provisions of POCA 2002 (SI 2005/353).

5. Postponement of making order

The act of postponement

19–033   Instead of proceeding under s.6 **before** sentencing the offender for his offence(s), the judge may, on the application of the offender or of the prosecutor, or indeed of his own motion (*R. v Zelzele* [2001] EWCA Crim 1763, [2001] 1 Cr. App. R. (S.) 62), postpone the s.6 proceeding, on one or more occasions for up to "the permitted period", i.e.:

POCA 2002, ss.14(1)–(7)

(1) a total of two years from the offender's conviction; or

(2) three months from the date on which any appeal against conviction is disposed of, if the three months ends more than two years after the date of conviction.

There is no limit to what may amount to exceptional circumstances (see, e.g. *R. v Jagdev* [2002] EWCA Crim 1326; [2003] 11 Cr. App. R. 2).

If two or more offences are involved, and they were on different dates, the date of the offender's conviction is the later of the latest.

A postponement may be granted without a hearing (r.58). (*R. v Neish* [2010] EWCA Crim 1011, [2011] 1 Cr. App. R. (S.) 335.)

It is not enough for the judge to adjourn the proceedings, he must postpone the confiscation hearing in terms. Though:

(a) it is not necessary to specify the very date on which the substantive hearing is to begin, still less the day on which any order will be made;

Confiscation Orders

(b) it is sufficient if he gives directions for the service of statements and specifies a date on which the proceedings will next be listed, whether for disposal or for such other directions as may be necessary, or for its disposal (*R. v Knights* [2005] UKHL 50, [2006] 1 Cr App R (S) 80).

POCA 2002, s.14(8)

The period of postponement may be extended provided the whole period ends before the expiry of the permitted period, unless there are exceptional circumstances. Where the application is made before the permitted period ends, it may be granted even after it ends.

Effect of postponement

19–034   If the judge postpones s.6 proceedings, he may proceed to sentence the offender for the offence (or any of the offences) concerned, provided that he does not in respect of those offences:

POCA 2002, s.15

(1) impose a fine on him;
(2) make one of those orders enumerated in s.13(3) (19–009); or
(3) make a compensation order under PCC(S)A 2000, s.130.

He must take care, in his sentencing remarks, if he knows that he will be carrying out fact finding exercises in relation to the same offender at a later stage, not to express himself in a manner that may sensibly be perceived to show that he is unlikely to believe anything the offender is likely to tell him. If remarks of that nature are pertinent to explaining his sentence, he will need to recuse himself from conducting any subsequent fact-finding exercise (*R. v Odewale* [2005] EWCA Crim 709, [2006] 2 Cr. App. R.(S.) 102).

If he sentences the offender for the offence (or any of the offences) concerned in the postponement period after that period ends, he may vary the sentence by:

(a) imposing a fine on him;
(b) making an order falling within s.13(3) (19–008); or
(c) making a compensation order under PCC(S)A 2000, s.130,

but only within the period of 28 days which starts with the last day of the postponement period. (See under the previous legislation *R. v Davies* [2001] EWCA Crim 2902, [2002] 2 Cr. App. R. 23, where the judge had only specified a timetable for exchange of information and had not specified a period of postponement, or adopted the statutory period.)

For the purposes of the time limit for notice of appeal or of application for leave to appeal to CACD, and the time limit for notice of application for leave to refer a case under CJA 1988, s.36 (Attorney-General's reference) sentence is to be regarded as imposed or made on the day on which it was varied.

6.   Subsequent reconsideration

General

19–035   The question of making a confiscation order may fall to be considered subsequently as where, for example:

(1) the judge at the original proceedings decided not to enquire under s.6, and it is sought to reconsider the case;

(2) the judge at the original proceedings decided that there was no relevant benefit to the offender, and it is sought to lead evidence which was not available at the time;

(3) an order was made at the time, but it is sought to lead fresh evidence as to the amount of the benefit;

(4) an order was made at the time, but it is sought to lead fresh evidence as to the available amount; or

(5) the available amount calculated at the time is inadequate to satisfy the order.

An application by the prosecutor for reconsideration under ss.19, 20 or 21 is made in writing, giving, amongst other detail, the grounds for the application and an indication of the evidence available to support it. It must be lodged with the Crown Court, and must be served on the offender at least seven days before the date fixed for the hearing of the application.

Statement of information

19–036 Where the judge holds a s.6 enquiry, in reconsidering an earlier order (ss.19, 20), or the prosecutor applies for a reconsideration of the benefit calculated under the original order (s.21):

POCA 2002, s.26

(1) the prosecutor will give the court a statement of information (see 19–013, above) within the period the judge orders;

(2) s.l6 as to such statements (see 19–013, above) will apply accordingly (with appropriate modifications where the prosecutor applies under s.21);

(3) s.17 as to the offender's response (see 19–014, above) will apply accordingly; and

(4) s.18 as to the offender providing information (see 19–015, above) will apply as it applies in the circumstances mentioned in s.l8(1).

Case (1): no s.6 enquiry originally; fresh evidence

19–037 Where an offender was before the Crown Court in the circumstances obtaining under s.6(2) (19–012, above) but no judge has proceeded to hold an enquiry under that section, and:

POCA 2002, ss.19(1)(2)

(1) there is evidence which was not available to the prosecutor on the relevant date, and

(2) before the end of the period of six years starting with the date of conviction the prosecutor applies to a judge of the Crown Court to consider the evidence, and

(3) after considering the evidence the judge believes it is appropriate to proceed under s.6, he must proceed to hold a confiscation enquiry ("a section 19 enquiry").

Modifications appropriate to s.19 enquiry

19–038 Where the judge embarks upon a s.19 enquiry, the provisions of the Act are modified, thus:

POCA 2002, ss.19(3)–(8)

R.58.3

CONFISCATION ORDERS

(1) if the offender has already been sentenced for the offence, (or any of the offences) concerned, s.6 has effect as if his "particular criminal conduct" (see 19–019, above) included conduct which constitutes offences which the judge has taken into consideration in deciding his sentence for the offence or offences concerned;

(2) s.8(2) in relation to calculating the offender's "benefit" (see 19–020 and 19–021, above) does not apply; instead the judge must take account of:

    (a) conduct occurring before the "relevant date" (see below);

    (b) property obtained before that date;

    (c) property obtained on or after that date if it was obtained as a result of, or in connection with, conduct occurring before that date.

(3) in relation to s.10 (assumptions) (see 19–027, above):

    (a) assumptions (a) and (b) do not apply with regard to property first held by the offender on or after the relevant date;

    (b) assumption (c) does not apply with regard to expenditure incurred by him on or after that date;

    (c) assumption (d) does not apply with regard to property obtained (or assumed to have been obtained) by him on or after that date.

(4) "the recoverable amount" for the purposes of s.6 is such amount as the judge believes is just, but does not exceed the amount found under s.7 (see 19–030, above);

(5) in arriving at the just amount the judge must have regard in particular to:

    (a) the amount found under s.7;

    (b) any fine imposed on the offender in respect of the offence (or any of the offences) concerned;

    (c) any order which falls within s.13(3) (see 19–008) and has been made against him in respect of the offence (or any of the offences) concerned and has not already been taken into account by the judge in deciding what is the free property held by him for the purposes of s.9; and

    (d) any compensation order which has been made against him in respect of the offence (or any of the offences) concerned under PCC(S)A 2000, s.130;

(6) if a compensation order under s.130 has been made against the offender in respect of the offence or offences concerned, ss.13(5) and (6) do not apply.

Note that:

    (i) the "relevant date" is, if the judge made a decision not to proceed under s.6, the date of the decision, and if he did not make such a decision, the date of conviction;   POCA 2002, s.19(10)

    (ii) the "date of conviction" is the date on which the offender was convicted of the offence concerned, or if there are two or more offences and the convictions were on different dates, the date of the latest.

Case (2): no benefit found originally; fresh evidence

19–039 Where, in the original s.6 enquiry the judge decided either, that the offender had a criminal lifestyle but had not benefited from his general criminal conduct, or that he did not have a criminal lifestyle and had not benefited from his particular criminal conduct then, if the judge proceeded under s.6 because:
POCA 2002, ss.20(1)–(5)

(1) there is evidence which was not available to the prosecutor when the court decided that the offender had not benefited from his general or particular criminal conduct; and

(2) before the end of the period of six years starting with the date of conviction the prosecutor applies to the Crown Court to consider the evidence; and

(3) after considering the evidence the judge concludes that he would have decided that the offender had benefited from his general or particular criminal conduct (as the case may be) if the evidence had been available to him,

he must make a fresh decision under ss.6(4)(b) or (c) whether the offender has benefited from his general or particular criminal conduct (as the case may be), and may make a confiscation order under that section.

Modifications appropriate to s.20 enquiry

19–040 Where the judge then proceeds under s.6, if the offender has already been sentenced for the offence (or any of the offences) concerned, s.6 has effect as if his particular criminal conduct included conduct which constitutes offences which the court has taken into consideration in deciding his sentence for the offence or offences concerned. The following modifications also apply:
POCA 2002, ss.20(6)–(9)

(1) s.8(2) in relation to calculating the offender's benefit (see 19–018—19–029, above) will not apply, and instead the judge must take account of:

  (a) conduct occurring before the date of the original decision that the offender had not benefited from his general or particular criminal conduct;

  (b) property obtained before that date;

  (c) property obtained on or after that date if it was obtained as a result of or in connection with conduct occurring before that date.

(2) in relation to s.10 (assumptions) (see 19–027, above):

  (a) assumptions (1) and (2) do not apply with regard to property first held by the defendant on or after the date of the original decision that he had not benefited from his general or particular conduct;

  (b) assumption (3) does not apply with regard to expenditure incurred by him on or after that date;

  (c) assumption (4) does not apply with regard to property obtained (or assumed to have been obtained) by him on or after that date.

CONFISCATION ORDERS

"Recoverable amount": s.20

19–041 "The recoverable amount" (see 19–030, above) for the purposes of a s.6 enquiry conducted under s.20 will be such amount as:

POCA 2002,
s.20(10)–(13)

   (1) the court believes is just, but

   (2) does not exceed the amount found under s.7.

In arriving at the just amount the court must have regard in particular to:

   (a) the amount found under s.7;

   (b) any fine imposed on the defendant in respect of the offence
      (or any of the offences) concerned;

   (c) any order which falls within s.13(3) and has been made
      against him in respect of the offence (or any of the offences)
      concerned and has not already been taken into account by
      the court in deciding what is the free property held by him
      for the purposes of s.9 (see 19–023, above);

   (d) any compensation order which has been made against him
      in respect of the offence (or any of the offences) concerned
      under PCC(S)A 2000, s.130.

If a compensation order under s.130 has been made against the defendant in respect of the offence or offences concerned, s.13(5) and (6)
above do not apply.

The date of conviction is the date found by applying s.19(10)
(19–038, above).

Case (3): benefit calculated originally: fresh evidence as to amount

19–042 Where the judge did make a confiscation order at the time, but
there is evidence which was not available to the prosecutor at the relevant time, and the prosecutor believes that if the court were to find the
amount of the offender's benefit in pursuance of this section it would
exceed the relevant amount, then where:

POCA 2002,
s.21(1)–(2)

   (1) before the end of the period of six years starting with the date of
      conviction the prosecutor applies to a judge of the Crown Court
      to consider the evidence; and

   (2) after considering the evidence the judge believes it is appropriate
      for him to proceed under this provision,

he must make a new calculation of the offender's benefit from the
conduct concerned.

Modifications appropriate to s.21 enquiry

19–043 Where the judge holds a s.6 enquiry in accordance with s.21,
the following modifications apply:

   (1) if the offender has already been sentenced for the offence (or any
      of the offences) concerned, s.6 has effect as if his particular
      criminal conduct included conduct which constitutes offences
      which the judge has taken into consideration in deciding his
      sentence for the offence or offences concerned;

POCA 2002,
s.21(4)–(6)

   (2) s.8(2) in relation to calculating the offender's benefit (see

19–020—19–029, above) does not apply, and the rules applying instead are that the judge must take account of:

   (a) conduct occurring up to the time it decided the offender's benefit for the purposes of the confiscation order;

   (b) property obtained up to that time;

   (c) property obtained after that time if it was obtained as a result of or in connection with conduct occurring before that time;

(3) in applying s.8(5) as to aggregate (see 19–029, above) the confiscation order must be ignored;

(4) in relation to s.10 (assumptions) (see 19–027, above):

   (a) assumptions (1) and (2) will not apply with regard to property first held by the defendant after the time the court decided his benefit for the purposes of the confiscation order;

   (b) assumption (3) will not apply with regard to expenditure incurred by him after that time;

   (c) assumption (4) will not apply with regard to property obtained (or assumed to have been obtained) by him after that time.

Position where benefit exceeds relevant amount

19–044   If the amount found under the new calculation of the offender's benefit exceeds:

POCA 2002,
s.21(7)–(10)

(1) the relevant amount, the judge must make a new calculation of the recoverable amount for the purposes of s.6; and

(2) the amount required to be paid under the confiscation order, the judge may vary the order by substituting for the amount required to be paid such amount as he believes is just.

In applying (1) above, the judge must:

   (a) take the new calculation of the offender's benefit; and

   (b) apply s.9 (available amount, 19–031, above) as if references to the time the confiscation order is made were to the time of the new calculation of the recoverable amount and as if references to the date of the confiscation order were to the date of that new calculation.

In applying (2) above, the judge must have regard in particular to:

   (i) any fine imposed on the offender for the offence (or any of the offences) concerned;

   (ii) any order which falls within s.13(3) (see 19–008, above) and has been made against him in respect of the offence (or any of the offences) concerned, and has not already been taken into account by the judge in deciding what is the free property held by the defendant for the purposes of s.9;

   (iii) any compensation order which has been made against him in respect of the offence (or any of the offences), concerned under PCC(S)A 2000, s.130,

but in applying subs.(2) above the judge must not have regard to an order falling within (c) above if a court has made a direction under

Confiscation Orders

CONFISCATION ORDERS

s.13(6) (19–008, above) that payment be made out of the confiscation order.

Supplementary provisions
19–045   Note that:

POCA 2002, s.21(11)–(14)

(1) in deciding under this section whether one amount exceeds another the judge must take account of any change in the value of money;
(2) the relevant time is, when the court calculated the offender's benefit for the purposes of the confiscation order, if this section has not applied previously, or when the court last calculated his benefit in pursuance of this section, if this section has applied previously;
(3) the relevant amount is the amount found as the offender's benefit for the purposes of the confiscation order, if this section has not applied previously, or the amount last found as his benefit in pursuance of this section, if this section has applied previously;
(4) the date of conviction is the date found by applying s.19(10) (19–038, above).

Case (4): order made: reconsideration of available amount
19–046   Where a court has made a confiscation order, and the amount required to be paid was the "available amount" as assessed under s.7(2) (see 19–030 and following, above), the prosecutor or a receiver appointed under s.50 may apply to the Crown Court to make a new calculation of the available amount.

POCA 2002, s.22(1)–(4)

The application must be in writing, and may be supported by a witness statement. These must be lodged with the Crown Court, and must be served on the offender, on the receiver if the prosecutor is making the application, and a receiver has been appointed under s.50, and if the receiver is making the application, on the prosecutor, at least seven days before the date fixed for the hearing unless the Crown Court specifies a shorter period.

On the hearing the judge must:

(1) make the new calculation, and in doing so,
(2) apply s.9, in relation to the available amount, as if references to the time the confiscation order is made were a reference to the time of the new calculation and as if references to the date of the confiscation order were to the date of the new calculation.

If the amount found under the new calculation exceeds the relevant amount the judge may vary the order by substituting for the amount required to be paid such amount as he believes is just, but does not exceed the amount found as the defendant's benefit from the conduct concerned.

POCA 2002, s.22(5)–(6)

In deciding what is just he must have regard in particular to:

(a) any fine imposed on the offender for the offence (or any of the offences) concerned;
(b) any order which falls within s.13(3) (19–008, above) and has been made against him in respect of the offence (or any of the offences) concerned and has not already been taken into

account in deciding what is the free property held by him for the purposes of s.9 (19–023, above); and

(c) any compensation order which has been made against him in respect of the offence (or any of the offences) concerned under PCC(S)A 2000, s.130), but

in deciding what is just regard must not be paid to an order falling within s.22(5)(c) if a court has made a direction under s.13(6) (see 19–008 above) that it be paid from the confiscation order.

Note that:

POCA 2002, s.22(7)–(9)

    (i) in deciding under this section whether one amount exceeds another the judge must take account of any change in the value of money;

   (ii) the "relevant amount" is the amount found as the available amount for the purposes of the confiscation order if this section has not been applied previously, or the amount last found as the available amount in pursuance of this section, if it has been applied previously;

  (iii) the amount found as the defendant's benefit from the conduct concerned is the amount so found when the confiscation order was made, or, if one or more new calculations of his benefit have been made under s.21 (above), the amount found on the occasion of the last such calculation.

Case (5): inadequacy of "available amount": variation of order

19–047 Where a judge has made a confiscation order, the offender, or a receiver appointed under s.50, may apply to a judge of the Crown Court to vary the order by substituting a lesser sum.

POCA 2002, s.23

The application must be in writing, and may be supported by a witness statement. These must be lodged with the Crown Court, and must be served on the prosecutor, the offender, if the receiver is making the application, and the receiver if the offender is making the application, at least seven days before the date fixed for the hearing unless the Crown Court specifies a shorter period.

On such an application, the judge:

(1) must calculate the available amount, and in doing so he must apply s.9 (19–031, above) as if references to the time the confiscation order is made were to the time of the calculation and as if references to the date of the order were to the date of the calculation; and

(2) if he finds that the available amount (so calculated) is inadequate for the payment of any amount remaining to be paid under the order, he may vary the order by substituting for the amount required to be paid, such smaller amount as he believes is just; but

(3) may not determine, as a preliminary matter, that the application is bound to fail because it required an investigation of the facts (*Glaves v CPS* [2011] EWCA Civ 69, *The Times*, February 22, 2011).

CONFISCATION ORDERS

If a person has been adjudged bankrupt or his estate has been seques-trated, or if an order for the winding up of a company has been made, the judge must take into account the extent to which realisable property held by that person or that company may be distributed among creditors.

The judge may disregard any inadequacy which he believes is attributable (wholly or partly) to anything done by the offender for the purpose of preserving property held by the recipient of a tainted gift (19–026, above) from any risk of realisation under Pt 2 of the Act.

CACD has no jurisdiction to hear an appeal against a refusal by a Crown Court judge, on an application under POCA 2002, s.23 to vary a confisca-tion order. An order made under s.23 varying a confiscation order is not included in the definition of "sentence" in CAA 1968, s.50(1) as amended, (*R. v Ward (Barry)* [2010] EWCA Crim 1932, *The Times*, August 27, 2010).

"Company" above, means any company which may be wound up under the Insolvency Act 1986 or the Insolvency (Northern Ireland) Order 1989 (SI 1989/2405 (NI19)).

Inadequacy of available amount: discharge of order

19–048   Where a judge has made a confiscation order, the designated officer of a magistrates' court may apply to a judge of the Crown Court for the discharge of the order, the amount remaining to be paid under the order being less than £1,000.

POCA 2002, s.24

The application must be in writing and must give details of the amount outstanding under the order and the grounds for the application. It must be served on the offender, the prosecutor and any receiver appointed under s.50. The judge may determine the application without a hearing unless one of those persons named above indicates, within seven days after the application was served on him, that he would like to make representations.

R.58.6

In dealing with the matter, the judge:

(1) must calculate the available amount, and in doing so it must apply s.9 (19–031, above) as if references to the time the confis-cation order is made were to the time of the calculation and as if references to the date of the confiscation order were to the date of the calculation; and

(2) if he finds that the available amount (as so calculated) is inad-equate to meet the amount remaining to be paid, and is satisfied that the inadequacy is due wholly to a specified reason or a com-bination of specified reasons as set out below, he may discharge the confiscation order.

The specified reasons are:

(a) in a case where any of the realisable property consists of money in a currency other than sterling, that fluctuations in currency exchange rates have occurred; and

(b) any reason specified by the Secretary of State.

Reconsideration etc: variation of prison term

19–049   Where a judge varies a confiscation order under ss.21, 22, 23, 29, 32 or 33, the effect of the variation is to vary the maximum

POCA 2002, s.39

period applicable in relation to the order under PCC(S)A 2000, s.139(4) and:

(1) the result is that that maximum period is less than the term of imprisonment or detention fixed in respect of the order under PCC(S)A 2000, s.139(2), the judge must fix a reduced term of imprisonment or detention in respect of the confiscation order under s.139(2) in place of the term previously fixed; or

(2) if (1) is not the case, the judge may amend the term of imprisonment or detention fixed in respect of the confiscation order under PCC(S)A 2000, s.139(2).

If the effect of s.12 is to increase the maximum period applicable in relation to a confiscation order under PCC(S)A 2000, s.139(4), the prosecutor may apply to a judge of the Crown Court to amend the term of imprisonment or detention fixed in respect of the order under s.139(2).

Application is made in writing giving the grounds for the application and details of the enforcement measures taken if any. On receipt of the application the court must at once send to the offender and the magistrates' court responsible for enforcing the order, a copy of the application; and fix a date, time and place for the hearing and notify the same to the applicant and the offender.   R.58.9

If the judge makes an order increasing the default term, the court must, at once, send a copy of the order to the applicant, the offender, and the enforcing magistrates' court, and, if the offender is in custody at the time of the making of the order, the person having custody of him.

Small amount outstanding: discharge of order

19–050 Where a court has made a confiscation order, and a justices' chief executive applies to the Crown Court for the discharge of the order, the amount remaining to be paid under the order being £50 or less, the judge may discharge the order.   POCA 2002, s.25

7.   Offender absconding; s.27

Offender convicted or committed

19–051 Where the offender absconds after:

(1) (a) he is convicted of an offence or offences in proceedings before the Crown Court;   POCA 2002, s.27(1)–(4)

   (b) he is committed to the Crown Court for sentence in respect of an offence or offences under PCC(S)A 2000, ss.3, 4 or 6; or

   (c) he is committed to the Crown Court in respect of an offence or offences under s.70 below (committal with a view to a confiscation order being considered); and

(2) the prosecutor applies to the Crown Court to proceed under this section, and the judge believes it is appropriate for him to do so,

the judge must proceed under s.6 in the same way as he must proceed if the two conditions above are satisfied POCA 2002, ss.27(1)–(4), but if he proceeds under s.6 as applied by this section, Pt 2 has effect with these modifications: POCA 2002, s.27(5)

    (i)   any person the judge believes is likely to be affected by an order under s.6 is entitled to appear before him and make representations;

    (ii) the judge must not make an order under s.6 unless the prosecutor has taken reasonable steps to contact the defendant;

    (iii) s.6(9) as to the offences concerned applies as if the reference to subs.(2) were to subs.(2) of this section;

    (iv) ss.10 (assumptions), 16(4), 17 and 18 (as to statements of information) are to be ignored; and

    (v) ss.19, 20 and 21 in regard to subsequent applications are to be ignored while the defendant is still an absconder.

An offender is not an "absconder" when he is deported by an act of the State (*R. v Gavin* [2010] EWCA Crim 2727; [2011] 1 Cr. App. R. (S.) 126); it is otherwise where he is removed at his own request to serve his sentence elsewhere (*ibid.*). *[POCA 2002, s.27(7)]*

Once the defendant ceases to be an absconder, s.19 in relation to the reconsideration of his case has effect as if subs.(1)(a) read "(a) at a time when the first condition in s.27 was satisfied the court did not proceed under s.6".

If the judge does not believe it is appropriate for him to proceed under this section, once the defendant ceases to be an absconder s.19 has effect as if subs.(1)(b) read: "(b) there is evidence which was not available to the prosecutor on the relevant date".

Defendant neither convicted nor acquitted
19–052   Where:

(1) proceedings for an offence or offences are started against a defendant but are not concluded; and *[POCA 2002, s.28(1)–(5)]*

(2) he absconds; and

(3) the period of two years (starting with the day the judge believes he absconded) has ended; and

(4) the prosecutor applies to a judge of the Crown Court to proceed under this section; and

(5) the judge believes it is appropriate for him to do so,

he must proceed under s.6 in the same way as he is required to proceed if the two conditions mentioned in 19–044, above are satisfied, but if he does so, Pt 2 has effect with these modifications:

    (a) any person the judge believes is likely to be affected by an order under s.6 is entitled to appear before him and make representations;

    (b) the judge must not make an order under s.6 unless the prosecutor has taken reasonable steps to contact the defendant;

    (c) s.6(9) as to offences applies as if the reference to subs.(2) were to subs.(2) of this section;

    (d) ss.10 (assumptions), 16(4), 17 and 18 (statements of information) and 19 and 20 (reconsideration of case) are to be ignored;

    (e) s.21 (reconsideration of benefit) must be ignored while the defendant is still an absconder.

Once the defendant has ceased to be an absconder s.21 has effect as if references to the date of conviction were to:

POCA 2002, s.29(1)(2)

(i) the day when proceedings for the offence concerned were started against him; or

(ii) if there are two or more offences and proceedings for them were started on different days, the earliest of those days.

If the judge makes an order under s.6 as applied by this section, and the defendant is later convicted in proceedings before the Crown Court of the offence (or any of the offences) concerned, s.6 does not apply so far as that conviction is concerned.

Variation of order

19–053 Where the judge makes a confiscation order under s.6 as applied by s.28, and the defendant ceases to be an absconder, then, if he is convicted of an offence (or any of the offences) mentioned in the last paragraph, the offender:

R.58.7

(1) if he believes that the amount required to be paid was too large (taking the circumstances prevailing when the amount was found for the purposes of the order);

(2) may, before the end of the relevant period, apply to the Crown Court to consider the evidence on which his belief is based.

Application must be made in writing and must be supported by a witness statement, giving details of the order made against him, the circumstances in which he ceased to be an absconder, his conviction of the offence or offences concerned and the reason why he believes the amount required to be paid under the order was too large.

The application and the statement must be lodged with the Crown Court and must be served on the prosecutor, at least seven days before the date fixed for the hearing unless the Crown Court specifies a shorter period.

If the judge, after considering the evidence concludes that the defendant's belief is well founded, he:

(a) must find the amount which should have been the amount required to be paid (taking the circumstances prevailing when the amount was found for the purposes of the order); and

(b) may vary the order by substituting for the amount required to be paid such amount as it believes is just.

The "relevant period" is the period of 28 days starting with:

POCA 2002, s.29(3)(4)

(i) the date on which the defendant was convicted of the offence mentioned in s.28(2)(a); or

(ii) if there are two or more offences and the convictions were on different dates, the date of the latest.

But in a case where s.28(2)(a) applies to more than one offence the court must not make an order under this section unless it is satisfied that there is no possibility of any further proceedings being taken in relation to any such offence in respect of which the defendant has not been convicted.

Discharge of order

19–054 Where the judge makes a confiscation order under s.6 as applied by s.28, and the defendant is later tried for the offence or offences concerned and acquitted on all counts, he may apply to the Crown Court to discharge the order, and in such a case the judge must discharge the order. POCA 2002, s.30(1)(2)

Application is made in writing and must be supported by a witness statement giving details of the order made against him, the date on which he ceased to be an absconder, his acquittal, if he has been acquitted of the offence concerned, and if he has not been acquitted of the offence concerned:

(1) the date on which he ceased to be an absconder;
(2) the date on which the proceedings taken against him were instituted and a summary of the steps taken in the proceedings; and R.58.8
(3) any indication by the prosecutor that he does not intend to proceed against him.

The application and the statement must be lodged with the Crown Court and must be served on the prosecutor at least seven days before the date fixed for the hearing unless the Crown Court specifies a shorter period. POCA 2002, s.30(3)(4)

If a confiscation order under s.6 as applied by s.28, was made and the defendant ceased to be an absconder, but was not tried and acquitted on all counts, then, if he applies to the Crown Court to discharge the order, the judge may discharge it only if he finds that:

(a) there has been undue delay in continuing the proceedings mentioned in s.28(2); or POCA 2002, s.30(5)
(b) the prosecutor does not intend to proceed with the prosecution.

If the judge discharges a confiscation order under this section he may make such a consequential or incidental order as he believes is appropriate. R.58.8(5)

If the judge orders the discharge of the order, the court must serve notice on the magistrates' court responsible for its enforcement.

8.   Appeals; fresh proceedings

Appeal by prosecutor
19–055   See APPEALS FROM THE CROWN COURT.

Crown Court proceeding afresh after appeal
19–056   Where CACD orders the Crown Court to proceed afresh, a judge of the Crown Court must comply with any directions CACD makes, and if he makes or varies a confiscation order under this section or in pursuance of a direction under this section he must have regard to any:

(1) fine imposed on the accused in respect of the offence (or any of the offences) concerned;

(2) order which falls within s.13(3) (see 19–008) and has been made against him in respect of the offence (or any of the offences) concerned, unless the order has already been taken into account by a court in deciding what is the free property held by the accused for the purposes of s.9.

Ancillary provisions

19–057   Where the Crown Court proceeds afresh under that section in pursuance of a direction by the CACD:

POCA 2002, s.32(5)(11)

(1) if a court has already sentenced the defendant for the offence (or any of the offences) concerned, s.6 will have effect as if his particular criminal conduct included conduct which constitutes offences which the court has taken into consideration in deciding his sentence for the offence or offences concerned;

(2) if a compensation order has been made against the defendant in respect of the offence (or any of the offences) concerned under PCC(S)A 2000, s.130, the judge must have regard to it, and s.13(5) and (6) (19–008, above) do not apply;

(3) s.8(2) in relation to benefit (19–020, above) does not apply, and the rules applying instead are that the judge must take account of:

   (a) conduct occurring before the relevant date;

   (b) property obtained before that date;

   (c) property obtained on or after that date if it was obtained as a result of or in connection with conduct occurring before that date;

(4) in s.10 (assumptions, see 19–027, above):

   (a) assumptions (1) and (2) do not apply with regard to property first held by the defendant on or after the relevant date;

   (b) assumption (3) does not apply with regard to expenditure incurred by him on or after that date; and

   (c) assumption (4) does not apply with regard to property obtained (or assumed to have been obtained) by him on or after that date;

(5) s.26 (statement of information) applies as it applies in the circumstances mentioned in subs.(l) of that section.

The relevant date is the date on which the Crown Court decided not to make a confiscation order.

POCA 2002, s.23

Further appeal lies to the Supreme Court where similar provision in respect of a fresh order by a judge of the Crown Court apply.

9.   Commencement and conclusion of proceedings

Proceedings for an offence

POCA 2002, s.85

19–058   Proceedings for an offence are **started** when:

(1) a magistrate issues a summons or warrant under MCA 1980, s.l in respect of the offence;

(2) a person is charged with an offence after being taken into custody without a warrant;

(3) a voluntary bill of indictment is preferred under AJ(MP)A 1933, s.2 in a case falling within subs.(2)(b) of that section (preferment by CACD or a High Court judge).

If more than one time is found under the subsection in relation to proceedings they are started at the earliest of them.

Proceedings are **concluded:**

(1) if the defendant is acquitted on all counts in proceedings for an offence, when he is acquitted;

(2) if the defendant is convicted in proceedings for an offence and the conviction is quashed or the defendant is pardoned before a confiscation order is made, when the conviction is quashed or the defendant is pardoned;

(3) if a confiscation order is made against the defendant in proceedings for an offence (whether the order is made by the Crown Court or CACD):
   (a) when the order is satisfied or discharged; or
   (b) when the order is quashed and there is no further possibility of an appeal against the decision to quash the order;

(4) if the defendant is convicted in proceedings for an offence but the judge decides not to make a confiscation order against him:
   (a) if an application for leave to appeal under s.31(2) is refused, when the decision to refuse is made;
   (b) if the time for applying for leave to appeal under s.31(2) expires without an application being made, when the time expires;
   (c) if on appeal under s.31(2) CACD confirms the judge's decision and an application for leave to appeal under s.33 is refused, when the decision to refuse is made;
   (d) if on appeal under s.31(2) CACD confirms the judge's decision and the time for applying for leave to appeal under s.33 expires without an application being made, when the time expires;
   (e) if on appeal under s.31(2) CACD confirms the judge's decision and on appeal under s.33 the Supreme Court confirms CACD's decision, when the latter confirms the decision;
   (f) if on appeal under s.31(2) CACD directs the Crown Court to reconsider the case, and on reconsideration the judge decides not to make a confiscation order against the defendant, when he makes that decision;
   (g) if on appeal under s.33 the Supreme Court directs the Crown Court to reconsider the case, and on reconsideration the judge decides not to make a confiscation order against the defendant, when he makes that decision.

In applying any one of the above provisions any power to extend the time for making an application for leave to appeal is to be ignored, as must the fact that a court may postpone making a confiscation order.

Conclusion of applications

19–059 Applications are concluded as follows:

(1) under ss.19, 20, 27 or 28 in a case where:

    (a) the judge decides not to make a confiscation order against the defendant, when he makes the decision;

    (b) a confiscation order is made against him as a result of the application, when the order is satisfied or discharged, or when the order is quashed and there is no further possibility of an appeal against the decision to quash the order;

    (c) the application is withdrawn, when the person who made the application notifies the withdrawal to the court to which the application was made;

(2) under s.21 or s.22:

    (a) in a case where the judge decides not to vary the confiscation order concerned, when he makes the decision;

    (b) in a case where the judge varies the confiscation order as a result of the application, when the order is satisfied or discharged, or when the order is quashed and there is no further possibility of an appeal against the decision to quash the order;

    (c) in a case where the application is withdrawn, when the person who made the application notifies the withdrawal to the court to which the application was made.

POCA 2002, s.86

Other interpretative provisions

19–060 A reference to "the offence (or offences)" concerned must be construed in accordance with s.6(9).

A "criminal investigation" is an investigation which police officers or other persons have a duty to conduct with a view to it being ascertained whether a person should be charged with an offence.

A "defendant" is a person against whom proceedings for an offence have been started (whether or not he has been convicted).

A reference to "sentencing the defendant for an offence" includes a reference to dealing with him otherwise in respect of the offence.

POCA 2002, s.88

10.   Seizure and forfeiture of cash

Detention of cash

19–061 POCA 2002 empowers an officer of revenue and customs, an accredited financial investigator or a constable to seize any cash if he has reasonable grounds for suspecting it to be:

(1) recoverable property; or

(2) intended by any person for use in unlawful conduct

or part of it, if it is reasonably practicable to seize only that part, provided, in either case, the cash to which his suspicion relates, exceeds the minimum amount, i.e. £5,000 (SI 2004/420).

There is nothing to prevent seizure under s.295 of money which has already been seized under, for instance, PACE 1984, s.19 (*Merseyside Chief Constable v Hickman* [2006] EWHC 451 (Admin), *The Times,* April 7, 2006).

POCA 2002, ss.294, 295, 297

CONFISCATION ORDERS

As to the meaning of "recoverable property", see POCA 2002, s.304(1), as to "unlawful conduct" see ibid. ss.241, 316(1).

While the officer of revenue and customs, accredited financial investigator or constable continues to have reasonable grounds for his suspicions, the cash may be detained initially for a period of 48 hours (calculated in accordance with s.295(1A)(1B)). The period may be extended on application, by any magistrates' court (SI 2003/638), or a single justice, but not beyond the period of three months beginning with the date of the order, or, in the case of any further order, not beyond a period of two years from the date of the first, provided that, in relation to any cash to be further detained, there are reasonable grounds for suspecting that the cash is:

    (a) **recoverable property; or**
    (b) **intended to be used in unlawful conduct,** and in either case:
        (i) its continued detention is justified while its derivation is further investigated or consideration is given to bringing proceedings (in the United Kingdom or elsewhere) against any person for an offence with which the cash is connected; or
        (ii) the proceedings against any person for an offence with which the cash is connected have been started and have not be concluded.

Persons affected by the order must be notified of its making.

If, on application by the person from whom the cash was seized, a magistrates' court, is satisfied that the conditions in s.295 for the detention of the cash are no longer met, it may order it to be released. A constable, an officer of revenue and customs or an accredited financial investigator, after notifying the magistrates' court, may release the whole or any part of the cash if satisfied that its detention is no longer justified. Unless the cash, or part of it, is required as evidence, it must be paid into an interest-bearing account and any interest on it will be added to it on forfeiture or release.

POCA 2002, s.296

Forfeiture

19–062 While cash is detained under s.295, an application for the forfeiture of the whole or any part it may be made to the magistrates' court by HM Revenue and Customs, a constable or an accredited financial investigator under s.298 and the court may order forfeiture of the cash or any part of it if satisfied that it is recoverable property or is intended by any person for use in unlawful conduct. Special provisions apply in relation to recoverable property belonging to joint tenants.

POCA 2002, s.298

Procedure in the magistrates' court is governed by the Magistrates' Courts (Detention and Forfeiture of Cash) Rules 2002 (SI 2002/2998).

Where an application for forfeiture is made, there is no power to release the cash until the proceedings (including any appeal) have been concluded.

Appeal against forfeiture

19–063   An appeal lies to the Crown Court *by any party to proceed-*
ings for an order for forfeiture of cash under s.298 who is aggrieved by
an order made or a decision not to make such an order. The appeal must
be made before the end of the period of 30 days starting with the day on
which the court made its order or decision.

POCA 2002,
s.209

The Crown Court may make any order it thinks appropriate, and if it
upholds the appeal, may order the release of the cash.

The proceedings are civil in nature and by way of rehearing.

11.   External Requests; cross-border enforcement

The legislation

19–064   Foreign requests and orders are received by the Secretary
of State and forwarded to the appropriate authority, the CPS, DARA.
RCPO or SFO to take court action. Those bodies have a discretion
whether or not to proceed. Procedure is under POCA 2002 (External
Requests and Orders) Order 2005 (SI 2005/3181), Pt 2, or, in regard
to the former law, under the CJ(IC)A 1990 (Enforcement of Overseas
Forfeiture Orders) Order 2005 (SI 2005/3180).

The scheme

19–065   The procedure under both orders is similar. It provides for the
registration of external forfeiture orders:

(1) arising from a criminal conviction in the country from which the
order is sent; and
(2) concerning relevant property in England and Wales.

Such an order must be an order made by a court in a designated country for
the forfeiture and destruction, or the forfeiture and disposal of anything:

(a) in respect of which a "relevant offence" has been committed; or
(b) which was used or intended for use in connection with the
commission of such an offence.

A "relevant offence" is defined as one that corresponds to or is similar
to an offence under the law of England and Wales.

Such a request is channelled through the Secretary of State to the
"relevant Director", being the DPP or DRC, or in certain circumstances
the DSFO.

An application by a relevant Director to a judge of the Crown Court
must include a request to appoint the Director as the enforcement
authority, and may be made to a judge in chambers without giving
notice to the other party.

The judge's role

19–066   The judge must give effect to an external forfeiture order by
registering it where he is satisfied that:

(1) the order was made consequent on the conviction of the person
named in the order and no appeal is outstanding in respect of that
conviction;

(2) the order is in force and no appeal is outstanding in respect of it;
(3) giving effect to the order would not be incompatible with any of the Convention rights of any persons affected by it; and
(4) the property whose confiscation is specified is not subject to a charge.

Where the judge decides to give effect to an external forfeiture order he must:

(a) register the order in that court; provide for notice to be given to any person affected by it; and
(b) appoint the relevant Director as the enforcement authority for the order.

Only an order registered in the Crown Court may be implemented under the legislation.

There are provisions for cancelling or varying the order, appealing to CACD and the Supreme Court and the appointment of enforcement receivers.

An order is satisfied when the property specified in it has been forfeited or disposed in accordance with the legislation.

Procedure
19–067   CPR 2011, rr.59–61 and 71 apply with the necessary modifications to proceedings under SI 2005/3181 as they apply to corresponding proceedings under POCA 2002 (r.57.15 inserted by SI 2006/353).

Cross-border enforcement
19–068   The enforcement in England and Wales of confiscation orders made under the Proceeds of Crime (Scotland) Act 1995, is governed by SI 2001/953.

As to the enforcement in England and Wales of restraint and receivership proceedings from Scotland and Northern Ireland, see SI 2002/3133 and RESTRAINT ORDERS; RECEIVERS.

12.   Production etc orders; search and access

19–069   As to production etc orders, and search and access under POCA 2002, see PRODUCTION AND ACCESS ORDERS; SEARCH WARRANTS, Part B.

20. CONTEMPT OF COURT

Quick guide

1.   General

20–001   Generally, contempt of court may arise in three situations:

(1) where proceedings are affected by obstructive, disruptive, insulting or intimidating conduct on the part of the accused or, others, in the courtroom or its vicinity or otherwise affecting the proceedings (see 20–002, below);
(2) where there is disobedience to an order or direction of the court or other unlawful conduct (see 20–007 below);
(3) infringements of statutory prohibitions under CCA 1981 (see below and REPORTING AND ACCESS RESTRICTIONS).

Contempt is punishable by imprisonment of up to two years or a fine or, (if appropriate) orders available in cases of mentally disordered offenders (see 20–024 below).   *CCA 1981 s.14*

Apart from a person who commits a bail offence (*R. v Tyson* (1979) 68 Cr. App. R. 314), a person adjudged guilty of contempt of court has not been "convicted of an offence" (*R. v Selby M.C. Ex p. Frame* (1990) 12 Cr. App. R. (S.) 434).

Proof of contempt is according to the criminal standard – beyond reasonable doubt.

CPR r.62 now regulates the procedure to be adopted where contempt is alleged.

2.   Forms of contempt

(1) Contempt in the face of the court

General
20–002   A judge has power to punish summarily for: "contempt in the face of the court" where that contempt is committed:

(1) in the courtroom, witnessed by the judge;
(2) in the courtroom and reported to the judge;
(3) beyond the courtroom, and even beyond the precincts of the court; where it
    (a) it is reported to the judge; and
    (b) relates to proceedings then in progress, or pending before the court.

The process by which the judge deals with such a matter is usually described as "summary", but two circumstances need to be clearly distinguished.

    (i) proceedings where the investigation is truly summary (see 20–010—20–012 below);
    (ii) cases where the judge defers dealing with the matter until the conclusion of the trial where a formal procedure is followed as in *R. v Santiago* [2005] EWCA Crim 556; [2005] 2 Cr. App. R. 24; *R. v S* [2008] EWCA Crim 138; [2008] Crim. L.R. 716 (see 20–015 below).

The procedures to be followed in both situations are now set out in r.62 (see 20–009 below).

Disruptive, insulting or intimidating conduct

20–003 Where the contempt consists of abuse or vilification of the judge personally, it should be referred by him to another judge (see *Kyprianou v Cyprus (No.2)* [2007] 44 E.H.R.R. 44). An intention to disrupt the proceedings is not an essential element of contempt (*R. v Huggins* [2007] EWCA Crim 132; [2007] 2 Cr. App. R. 8).

Where the contempt proceedings arise in the course of a trial, the judge should ask the jury to withdraw before, e.g., having a witness arrested in court (*R. v Maguire* [1997] 1 Cr. App. R. 61).

Where a contempt is alleged to have taken place out with the presence of the judge, he has no power to remand the alleged contemnor into custody before the contempt is proved. Where he wishes to ensure restrict his liberty during the further course of the trial he will have either to adjourn the trial and proceed to deal with the alleged contempt, or arrange for another judge to hear the allegation (*R. v Stevens, The Independent*, June, 1997, QBD).

Where the accused disrupts the proceedings (*R. v Aquarius* (1974) 59 Cr. App. R. 165), or stages an outburst after sentence (*R. v Logan* [1974] Crim. L.R. 609), or abuses the trial judge (*R. v Hill* [1986] Crim. L.R. 457; *R. v McDaniel* (1990–91) 12 Cr. App. R. (S.) 45), the appropriate course is to pass a sentence for contempt consecutive to that for the substantive offence, and not attempt to include a contempt element in the sentence for the substantive offence.

Intimidation of witnesses

20–004 The most common situations are where witnesses are victimised or threatened, or attempts are made to influence or intimidate jurors. Here there is a "real need" for the judge to intervene, not only to safeguard the dignity of the court, but in the latter case to reassure other jurors waiting their call to court; this sort of contempt is prevalent and calls for a deterrent sentence (*R. v Goult* (1983) 76 Cr. App. R. 140; *R. v Mulvaney* (1982) 4 Cr. App. R. (S.) 106; *R. v Maloney* (1986) 8 Cr. App. R. (S.) 123; *R. v Pittendrigh* (1985) 7 Cr. App. R. (S.) 221; *R. v Edmonds* [1999] 1 Cr. App. R. (S.) 476; *R. v Smith* [2001] 1 Cr. App. R. (S.) 66; *R. v Rogers* [2002] 1 Cr. App. R. (S.) 272).

Recalcitrant witnesses
20–005 A number of potential situations may occur here:

(1) failure to attend may be dealt with by warrant (WITNESS SUMMONSES AND WARRANT);
(2) disobedience to a witness summons is governed by r.62.5 (see 20–007 below).
(3) in the case of a witness who attends but declines to testify, it will be a question for the judge whether some positive action is called for in the circumstances. Refusal to answer a question may be dealt with by mere admonition, unless the answer to it is vital;

The judge ought to approach (2) only after reflection. Unless there is good reason for dealing with the matter speedily, sentence should be adjourned to the end of the trial, or at least to the end of the prosecution case (*R. v Moran* (1985) 7 Cr. App. R.(S.) 101; *R. v Lewis* (1993) 96 Cr. App. R. 412), so that the witness has a chance to reconsider his position (*R. v Phillips* (1984) 78 Cr. App. R. 88; *R. v Moran* (1985) 81 Cr. App. R. 51; *R. v Leonard* (1984) 6 Cr. App. R. (S.) 279; *R. v Jardine* (1987) 9 Cr. App. R. (S.) 41; *R. v Montgomery* [1995] 2 Cr. App. R. 23; *R. v MacLeod* [2001] Crim. L.R. 589; *R. v Huggins* [2007] EWCA Crim 132; [2007] 2 Cr. App. R. 8; *R. v Tedjame-Mortty* [2011] EWCA Crim 950, [2011] Crim. L.R. 676).

Conduct of legal practitioners
20–006 For the conduct of a legal practitioner to amount to contempt, it will need to be scandalous; bad manners, incompetence or discourtesy do not amount to contempt (*Weston v CCC Courts Administrator* [1976] 2 All E.R. 875).

(2)   Contempt of court orders

20–007 A judge of the Crown Court has power to punish for contempt of court any person who:

(1) disobeys an order of the court (SCA 1981, s.45);
(2) uses disclosed prosecution material in contravention of CPIA 1996, s.17 (see DISCLOSURE);
(3) disobeys certain investigative orders (see PRODUCTION AND ACCESS ORDERS; SEARCH WARRANTS);
(4) disobeys a restraint order (see RESTRAINT ORDERS).

Where a person is accused in the Crown Court of such conduct ("the respondent"), the judge must not exercise his power to punish for contempt in his absence unless the has respondent has had at least 14 days in which to make representations and introduce any evidence.

(3)   Statutory contempts

20–008   A judge of the Crown Court has power to punish as a contempt:

(1) breaches of reporting restrictions under CCA 1981, ss.4 and 11 (see REPORTING AND ACCESS RESTRICTIONS);
(2) failure of a juror to answer a summons to attend court (JA 1974, s.20(1);
(3) disclosures relating to jury deliberations (CCA 1981, s.8);
(4) misuse of sound recorders in court (CCA 1981, s.9);
(5) refusal to disclose sources of information (CCA 1981, s.10) (see REPORTING AND ACCESS RESTRICTIONS);
(6) publication relating to proceedings in private (CCA 1981, s.12) (see REPORTING AND ACCESS RESTRICTIONS);
(7) photography and sketching in court (CJA 1925, s.41) (see REPORTING AND ACCESS RESTRICTIONS);
(8) publication of any material relating to proceedings which is prejudicial to the administration of justice (see REPORTING AND ACCESS RESTRICTIONS);
(9) electronic communications from court other than in accordance with *Practice Guidance (Court Proceedings: Live Text-based Communications)* [2011] 1 W.L.R. 61 (see REPORTING AND ACCESS RESTRICTIONS).

3. Procedure

(1)   General

20–009   CPR 2011, Pt 62 applies where the court has jurisdiction to deal with a person ('the respondent') for conduct, either in contempt of court or in contravention of the legislation to which r.62.5 (obstructing proceedings) or r.62.9 (failure to comply with court orders) refers.

A judge must determine at a hearing;   R.62.2

(1) any enquiry under r.62.8 (below);
(2) any allegation under r.62.9 (below); and must not proceed in the respondent's absence unless:
   (a) the respondent's behaviour makes it impracticable to proceed otherwise; or
   (b) the respondent has had at least 14 days' notice of the hearing, or was present when it was arranged.

If the judge hears part of an enquiry or allegation in private, he must announce at a hearing in public, the respondent's name, in general terms the nature of any conduct that the respondent admits, or the court finds proved; and any punishment imposed.

(2)   Summary procedure

Initial procedure on obstruction, disruption, etc.   R.62.5
20–010   Where the judge observes, or someone reports to him:

(1) obstructive, disruptive, insulting or intimidating conduct, in the courtroom or in its vicinity, or otherwise, immediately affecting the proceedings; or

(2) a contravention of:
    (a) CP(AW)A 1965, s.3 (disobeying a witness summons);
    (b) JA 1974, s.20 (disobeying a jury summons);
    (c) CCA 1981, s.8 (obtaining details of a jury's deliberations, etc.);
    (d) CCA 1981, s.9 (without the court's permission, recording the proceedings, etc); or

(3) any other conduct with which the court can deal as, or as if it were, a criminal contempt of court, (except failure to surrender to bail under BA 1976, s.6 (see BAIL),

Rule 62.5 prescribes the following procedure:

Unless the respondent's behaviour makes it impracticable to do so, the judge must explain, in terms the respondent can understand (with help, if necessary):

- the conduct that is in question;
- that the judge may impose imprisonment, or a fine, or both, for such conduct;
- (where relevant) that the judge has power to order the respondent's immediate temporary detention, if in his opinion that is required;
- that the respondent is entitled to explain the conduct;
- that the respondent may apologise, if he so wishes, and that this may persuade the judge to take no further action; and
- that the respondent is entitled to take legal advice; and

he must allow the respondent a reasonable opportunity to reflect, take advice, explain and, if he so wishes, apologise.

The judge may then:

    (i) take no further action in respect of that conduct;
    (ii) enquire into the conduct there and then; or
    (iii) postpone that enquiry.

Review after temporary detention
R.62.6

20–011 In a case where the judge has ordered the respondent's immediate temporary detention for conduct to which r.62.5 (above) applies, he judge must review the case no later than the next business day, and on that review, must, unless the respondent is absent, repeat the explanations required by r.62.5(2)(a) (above) and allow the respondent a reasonable opportunity to reflect, take advice, explain and, if he so wishes, apologise.

The judge may then:

(1) take no further action in respect of the conduct; or
(2) enquire into the conduct there and then; or
(3) postpone the enquiry, and order the respondent's release from such detention in the meantime.

Postponement of enquiry

20–012   Where the judge postpones the enquiry: R.62.7

(1) the court must arrange for the preparation of a written statement containing such particulars of the conduct in question as to make clear what the respondent appears to have done; and

(2) the court officer must serve on the respondent:
   (a) that written statement;
   (b) notice of where and when the postponed enquiry will take place; and
   (c) a notice that:
      (i) reminds the respondent that the court may impose imprisonment, or a fine, or both, for contempt of court; and
      (ii) warns him that the court may pursue the postponed enquiry in his absence, if he does not attend.

(3)   Procedure at r.62 enquiry

20–013   At the enquiry, the judge must: R.62.8

(1) ensure that the respondent understands (with help, if necessary) what is alleged, if the enquiry has been postponed from a previous occasion;

(2) explain what the procedure will be; and

(3) ask whether the respondent admits the conduct in question.

If the respondent admits the conduct, the judge need not receive evidence; if he does not admit the conduct, the judge will receive any statement served under r.62.7, any other evidence of the conduct, and any evidence introduced by the respondent. He will also receive any representations by the respondent about the conduct.

If the respondent admits the conduct, or the judge finds it proved, the judge must:

   (a) before imposing any punishment for contempt, give the respondent an opportunity to make representations relevant to punishment;

   (b) explain, in terms the respondent can understand (with help, if necessary):
      (i) the reasons for his decision, including his findings of fact; and
      (ii) the punishment he imposes, and its effect.

The need for immediate action (1) assessment

20–014   The judge must make his own assessment of the need for taking immediate action to deal with an alleged contempt (*R. v Goult* (1983) 76 Cr. App. R. 140). He will need to distinguish between conduct which:

(1) involves disruption of the court, or threats to witnesses or jurors, which should be visited by immediate arrest; and

(2) is not likely to disturb the trial or affect the verdict or judgment,

as this can be dealt with at a later stage of the trial, under RSC Ord.52, r.5 (CPR 1998, Sch.1) or on indictment at the instance of the Attorney-General (although procedure on indictment was ruled inappropriate in *R. v D* (1984) 79 Cr. App. R. 313.

The "urgency to act immediately" expressed in *Balogh v St Albans CC* [1974] 3 All E.R. 283 has been tempered by *Wilkinson v The Official Solicitor* [2003] EWCA Civ 95; [2003] 1 W.L.R. 1254. See also *Rooney v Snaresbrook CC* (1979) 68 Cr. App. R. 78; *R. v Grififin* (1989) 88 Cr. App. R. 63.

As to the need not to act too hastily, and to give the contemnor an opportunity to apologise and to offer mitigation, see *R. v Phelps* [2009] EWCA Crim 2308; [2010] 2 Cr. App. R. (S.) 1.

The need for immediate action (2) procedure sui generis

20–015 The procedure described in *R. v S* [2008] EWCA Crim 138; [2008] Crim. L.R. 716 as "truly summary" is a procedure *sui generis* (*R. v Griffin* (1989) 88 Cr. App. R. 63, per Mustill, L.J.). Thus:

- there is no prosecutor;
- there is no requirement that the prosecutor or an injured party initiate the proceedings, no summons or indictment;
- there is no mandatory requirement for any written account of the accusation;
- there is no preliminary procedure; and
- the proceedings are not adversarial.

The relevant principles which should ordinarily be observed when dealing with summary contempt cases (*R. v Moran* (1985) 81 Cr. App. R. 51, *R. v Grant* [2010] EWCA Crim 215) include that:

(1) a judge has the power to order the immediate arrest and detention of the suspected offender;
(2) the decision to try a suspected offender summarily should be taken only when it is necessary to do so to preserve the integrity of the trial or the dignity of the court;
(3) such a decision should never be taken too quickly and that time should always be allowed for reflection, if necessary overnight;
(4) the suspected offender must be distinctly and clearly told what acts or conduct are alleged against him;
(5) he should be allowed the opportunity of legal representation; and should be allowed a reasonable opportunity properly to investigate the circumstances; and
(6) the contemnor should be given an opportunity to apologise, which in an appropriate case might obviate the need for further action.

No-one should be convicted of contempt unless he distinctly admits it or, if he does not, unless it be proved against him beyond reasonable doubt. The judge should enquire from the suspected contemnor whether he admits the conduct alleged against him and the fact that the conduct amounts to contempt of court.

The need for immediate action (3) speed, publicity

20–016   By its nature the summary process needs to be used quickly or not at all omitting, as it does, many of the safeguards to which the accused is ordinarily entitled (*R. v S* [2008] EWCA Crim 138; [2008] Crim. L.R. 716; *Wilkinson v S* [2003] EWCA Civ 95; [2003] 1 W.L.R. 1254). In *R. v Serumaga* [2005] EWCA Crim 370; [2005] 2 Cr. App. R. 12 CACD found no material to justify a remand of seven days.

There is nothing in AJA 1960, s.13(l) to prohibit the grant of bail to an alleged contemnor (*ibid.*).

Where the contempt proceedings touch upon a trial in session, they must be in open court, and the defence advocate cannot be excluded (*R. v Cooledge* [1996] Crim. L.R. 749). The matter should not, however, be dealt with in the presence of the jury, nor should a recalcitrant witness be detained in their presence.

(4)   Rule 26(9) application

Initial procedure (1) by party

20–017   Rule 26.9 applies in cases where: R.62.9

   (1) a party, or other person directly affected, alleges:
   - (a) a failure to comply with an order to which rr. 6.13, 6.22 (certain investigation orders), or 59.6 (restraint orders), applies;
   - (b) any other conduct with which the court may deal as a civil contempt of court; or
   - (c) there is unauthorised use of disclosed prosecution material under CPIA 1996, s.17 (see below);
   (2) the judge deals on his own initiative with conduct to which (1) applies.

Such party or person as in mentioned in (1) must:

   - (a) apply in writing and serve the application on the court officer; and
   - (b) serve on the respondent such application, and notice of where and when the judge will consider the allegation (not less than 14 days after service).

The application must:

   - identify the respondent;
   - explain that it is an application for the respondent to be dealt with for contempt of court;
   - contain such particulars of the conduct in question as to make clear what is alleged against him; and
   - include a notice warning him that the court may impose imprisonment, or a fine, or both, for contempt, and may deal with the application in his absence, if he does not attend the hearing.

Initial procedure (2) judge acting on his own initiative

20–018   A judge who acts on his own initiative under paragraph (1)(b)   R.62.9(4)
must:

(1) arrange for the preparation of a written statement containing the same information as in an application by a party (20–017); and

(2) arrange for the service on the respondent of that written statement, and notice of where and when the judge will consider the allegation (not less than 14 days after service).

Stay or adjournment
20–019   Where:

(1) there is an application to commit a person for contempt of court because he is in breach of a court order; and,

(2) at the same time, a criminal trial is pending against the person accused of contempt,

the judge has a power to stay or adjourn the contempt proceedings until after the completion of the accused's criminal trial (*Harris v Crisp The Times*, August 12, 1992), but the power to stay or adjourn should only be exercised **exceptionally,** where there is a "real risk of serious prejudice which may lead to injustice": or, as it was put in *R. v Payton* [2006] EWCA Crim 1226, [2006] Crim. L.R. 997, "the issue was whether the fair trial of an [accused] would be prejudiced" (by the cash forfeiture proceedings in that case going ahead before the principal criminal trial).

If an application to stay or adjourn the contempt proceedings to await the outcome of a criminal trial is made, the judge must consider the issues that will arise on the contempt application and those that appear likely to arise at the criminal trial in the light of the prosecution case and the accused's case, so far as it is known at the time of the application (*R. v AA* [2010] EWCA Crim 2805).

He will have to consider also what evidence an accused might wish to give in the contempt hearing. He must form a judgment on whether, in holding the contempt hearing in which an accused may decide to give evidence, that would give rise to a real risk of serious prejudice to the accused in relation to his criminal trial which could thereby lead to injustice.

In forming that judgment, the judge must take account of all relevant factors and must disregard all those that are irrelevant.

Procedure on hearing
R.62.10

20–020   At the hearing of an allegation under r.62.9, the judge must:

(1) ensure that the respondent understands (with help, if necessary) what is alleged;

(2) explain what the procedure at the hearing will be; and

(3) ask whether the respondent admits the conduct in question.

If the respondent admits the conduct, the court need not receive evidence; if the respondent does not admit the conduct, the court will receive:

(a) the application or written statement served under r.62.9;

(b) any other evidence of the conduct;

(c) any evidence introduced by the respondent; and

(d) any representations by the respondent about the conduct.

If the respondent admits the conduct, or the judge finds it proved, the judge must, before imposing any punishment for contempt, give the respondent an opportunity to make representations relevant to punishment and must explain, in terms the respondent can understand (with help, if necessary) the reasons for his decision, including his findings of fact, and the punishment he imposes, and its effect.

Evidence: written witness statements or other hearsay

20–021   Where r.62.9 (above) applies, an applicant or respondent who   R.62.11
wishes to introduce in evidence the written statement of a witness, or other hearsay, must:

(1) serve a copy of the statement or notice of other hearsay;
   (a) on the court officer, and the other party; and
   (b) serve the copy or notice:
(2) do so when serving the application under r.62.9, in the case of an applicant, or not more than 7 days after service of that application or of the court's written statement, in the case of the respondent.

Such service is notice of that party's intention to introduce in evidence that written witness statement, or other hearsay, unless he otherwise indicates when serving it.
   Note that:

   (a) a party entitled to receive such notice may waive that   R.62.12
       entitlement;
   (b) a written witness statement served under r.62.11. must
       contain a declaration by the person making it that it is true
       to the best of that person's knowledge and belief;
   (c) notice of hearsay, other than a written witness statement,   R.62.13
       served under r.62.11(2) must set out the evidence, or attach
       the document that contains it; and identify the person who
       made the statement that is hearsay.

Cross-examination of maker of written witness statement or other hearsay

20–022   Where a party wants the judge's permission to cross-examine   R.62.14
a person who made a statement which another party wants to introduce as hearsay, then:

(1) the party who wants to cross-examine that person must:
   (a) apply in writing, with reasons; and
   (b) serve the application on the court officer and on the party
       who served the hearsay;
(2) a respondent who wants to cross-examine such a person must
    apply to do so not more than seven days after service of the
    hearsay by the applicant.

The judge may decide an application under this rule without a hearing, but must not dismiss such an application unless the person making it has had an opportunity to make representations at a hearing.

Credibility and consistency of maker of written witness statement or other hearsay

20–023 Where a party wants to challenge the credibility or consist-   R.62.15
ency of a person who made a statement which another party wants to
introduce as hearsay, then:.

(1) The party who wants to challenge the credibility or consistency
of that person must–
  (a) serve a written notice of intention to do so on the the court
  officer, and the party who served the hearsay; and
  (b) in that notice, identify any statement or other material on
  which that party relies.

A respondent who wants to challenge such a person's credibility or
consistency must serve such a notice not more than 7 days after service
of the hearsay by the applicant, and must serve such a notice not more
than 3 days after service of the hearsay by the respondent.

The party who served the hearsay may call that person to give oral
evidence instead, and if so, must serve a notice of intention to do so on
the court officer, and the other party, as soon as practicable after service
of the notice under (1)(a).

Court's power to vary requirements of service

20–024 The judge may shorten or extend (even after it has expired) a   R.62.17
time limit under r.62.11, 62.14 or 62.15.

A person who wants an extension of time must apply when serving
the statement, notice or application for which it is needed, and explain
the delay.

"Summary" procedure contrasted with that under r.62

20–025 The procedure followed before the amendment to r.62 is
exemplified in *R. v Santiago* [2005] EWCA Crim 556; [2005] 2 Cr.
App. R. 24. Where the judge defers dealing with the matter until the
conclusion of the trial, though properly classified as a "summary" the
process is very different from the procedure described in 20–013 above.
It involves the calling of witnesses by a prosecutor, the opportunity of
examining them, the opportunity for the accused to give evidence and
call his own witnesses, and the giving of a reasoned judgment. It is little
different from a hearing in a magistrates' court (*R. v S*, above).

In general, the judge should invite the alleged contemnor, but cannot
compel him, to be legally represented. This ensures that the judge has the
assistance of an advocate in considering his powers in the circumstances
of the case (*R. v Tyne Tees TV Ltd, The Times*, October 20, 1997).

4.   Punishment

The judge's powers

20–026 Penalties for contempt are governed by CCA 1981, s.14. The
judge may:

(1) impose a term of imprisonment which must be for a fixed term
and may not exceed two years;

(2) impose a fine of an unlimited amount (see FINES AND ENFORCEMENT);
(3) in cases of a mentally disordered offender make any order available as if he had been convicted of an offence (see MENTALLY DISORDERED OFFENDERS).

Different considerations apply on the case of young persons (see 20–031 below).

Sentence: (1) nature and length
20–027   The authorities are usefully summarised in *R. v Montgomery* (1995) 16 Cr. App. R. (S.) 274. The following general principles emerge:

(1) an immediate term of imprisonment is the only appropriate sentence to impose on a person aged 18 or over who interferes with the administration of justice, unless the circumstances are wholly exceptional (*R. v Owen* (1976) 63 Cr. App. R. 199);
(2) where victims of, or witnesses to, serious crime refuse to do their duty or succumb to fear of reprisals by refusing to give evidence, there is a failure of law and order. When this occurs it is usually necessary to impose a custodial sentence to mark the gravity of the matter and to stiffen the resolve of other potential witnesses who may similarly be minded to default (*R. v Montgomery*, above);
(3) while interference with jurors is often visited with higher sentences than refusal to give evidence, there is no rule or established practice to that effect. In the case of a recalcitrant witness, while it is legitimate to have regard to the fact that the maximum sentence for failing to comply with a witness order is three months, this need not inhibit the judge from imposing a substantially longer sentence for a blatant contempt by a witness in the face of the court (*R. v Phillips* (1984) 78 Cr. App. R. 88 and *R. v Jardine* (1987) 9 Cr. App. R. (S.) 41; *R. v Samuda* (1989) 11 Cr. App. R. (S.) 471); in most cases, however a moderate term will suffice (*R. v Montgomery*, above);
(4) Where the same conduct can amount to a contempt and to a specific statutory offence the court must have some regard to the maximum for the offence but is not bound by it (*R. v Montgomery*, above).

The judge may order the sentence for contempt to run consecutively to another term, even to a term imposed in a civil court (*R. v Anomo* [1998] 2 Cr. App. R. (S.) 269).

Sentence: (2) principal factors affecting length of sentence
20–028   The principal factors affecting sentence are set out in the guideline case of *R. v Montgomery* above, affirmed in *R. v Richardson* [2004] EWCA Crim 758.
They are:

(1) the gravity of the offence being tried;
(2) the effect upon the trial;
(3) the contemnor's reasons for e.g. refusing to give evidence;

(4) whether the contempt is aggravated by impertinent defiance of the judge (as opposed to a simple refusal (*R. v Leonard* (1984) 6 Cr. App. R. (S.) 279));

(5) the scale of sentences in similar cases;

(6) the antecedents and personal circumstances of the contemnor (*R. v Palmer* (1992) 13 Cr. App. R. (S.) 595); and

(7) whether, for instance, a special deterrent is needed, as where at the beginning of a series of trials it is becoming clear that witnesses are being threatened, or where there is a developing pattern of refusal in relation to certain types of offences or in particular parts of the country.

In the case of a witness refusing to testify, the importance of his evidence ought to be taken into account (*R. v Phillips* (1983) 5 Cr. App. R. (S.) 297).

Notice of suspension of imprisonment

20–029   Where a judge exercises his power under SCA 1981 to suspend an order of imprisonment for contempt (whether on condition or for a period or both), and the respondent is absent when the court does so, the respondent must be served with notice of the terms of the court's order; R.62.3

(1) by any applicant under r.62.9; or

(2) by the court officer, in any other case.

Application to discharge an order for imprisonment

20–030   Where the judge has jurisdiction (by reason of SCA 1981, ss.15 and 45) to discharge an order for a respondent's imprisonment for contempt, and a respondent wants the court to discharge such an order, he must: R.62.4

(1) apply in writing, unless the court otherwise directs, and serve any written application on: the court officer, and on any applicant under r.62.9 on whose application the respondent was imprisoned;

(2) in the application explain why it is appropriate for the order for imprisonment to be discharged, and give details of any appeal, and its outcome, and ask for a hearing, if the respondent wants one.

Young persons

20–031   In relation to young contemnors:

(1) imprisonment is available only for those aged 21 and over (*R. v Byas* (1995) 16 Cr. App. R. (S.) 869);

(2) for those aged between 18 and 20 detention may be ordered, if appropriate, under PCC(S)A, s.108;

(3) in the case of those under 16, a fine is probably the only appropriate penalty, though an attendance centre order may be appropriate (CCA 1981, s.14(2A));

(4) it seems doubtful whether there is power to make a community order (see *R. v Palmer* [1992] 1 W.L.R. 568: community rehabilitation order).

313

5.   Text-based messages etc. from court

20–032   In an *Interim Practice Guidance* on the use of text-based forms of communication (including Twitter) from court (see [2010] All E.R. (D) 228), the Lord Chief Justice stated that, subject to further consultation with interested parties, contemporaneous live communication of text-based communication by a mobile telephone or laptop from a court was permissible so long as there was no interference with the administration of justice and subject to the discretion of the judge. Similar guidance has been given in relation to proceedings in the Supreme Court (*Policy on the use of live text-based communications from court*, unreported, February 3, 2011).

6.   Appeals

20–033   See APPEALS FROM THE CROWN COURT.

21. COSTS AND ASSESSMENT

Quick guide

1. Introduction

General

21–001 The powers enabling a judge to award costs in criminal proceedings are primarily contained in POA 1985, ss.16, 17 and 18, AJA 1999 in relation to funded clients, and in the Regulations made under those Acts, including GR 1986 (SI 1986/1335) as amended. The current approach to the award of costs in the Crown Court is to be found in PDC 2010. Procedure is governed by r.76.

PDC 2010, 4.2.2

The judge has a much greater and more direct responsibility for costs in criminal proceedings than in civil and should keep the question of costs in the fore-front of his mind at every stage of the case and ought to be prepared to take the initiative himself without any prompting from the parties. His only concern should be to serve the public interest in the administration of justice (*Hurley v McDonald (New Zealand)* [2001] UKPC 18, [2001] 2 W.L.R. 1749 PC).

Principal power to award costs

21–002 POA 1985, by virtue of:

(1) s.16 makes provision for the award *of defence* costs out of central funds;
(2) s.17 provides for an award of costs *to private* prosecutors out of central funds;

(3) s.18 empowers the judge to order a convicted offender, or unsuccessful appellant, to pay costs to the prosecutor;

(4) s.9(l) and GR 1986, reg.3 provide for the award of costs between parties;

(5) s.19A provides for the court to disallow, or order a legal or other representative of a party to the proceedings to meet, wasted costs;

(6) s.19B provides for the court to make a "third party costs order" where there has been serious misconduct by a third party.

"Costs" in r.76 means:

(a) the fees payable to a legal representative;

(b) the disbursements paid by a legal representative; and

(c) any other expenses incurred in connection with the case.

In addition, a judge of the Crown Court, as part of the Senior Courts (formerly the Supreme Court), has power under its inherent jurisdiction over officers of the court, to order a solicitor personally to pay costs thrown away.

The judge has the same powers under ss.17 and 18 in relation to the award of costs on committals for sentence, and under s.16 for failure to comply with the conditions of a recognisance, as he has in relation to trials on indictment.

He may also give directions relating to publicly-funded costs and make Recovery of Defence Costs Orders (21–040).

Other powers governed by r.76

21–003 The procedural provisions of r.76 govern these and certain other powers, such as awards of costs under:

(1) MCA 1980, s.109, SCA 1981 s.52 and r.76.6, for the payment by an appellant of a respondent's costs on abandoning an appeal to the Crown Court (see r.76.6);

(2) SCA 1981, s.52 and r.76.6, for the payment by a party of another party's costs on an appeal to the Crown Court in any case not covered by the above (see r.76.6);

(3) BBEA 1879, for the payment of costs by a party or by the bank against which an application for an order is made (see r.76.7);

(4) CP(AW)A 1965, s.2C(8), for the payment by the applicant for a witness summons of the costs of a party who applies successfully under r.28.7 to have it withdrawn (see r.76.7);

(5) FSA 1989, s.14H(5), for the payment by a defendant of another person's costs on an application to terminate a football banning order (see r.76.7);

(6) The Serious Crime Act 2007 (Appeals under Section 24) Order 2008, arts 14 (see r.76.4); 15 (see r.76.6), 16, (see r.76.8); 17 (see r.76.9), or 18 (see r.76.10).

General rules: (1) making the order

21–004 The judge must not make an order about costs unless each party and any other person directly affected is present; or has had an

R.76.2

opportunity to attend, or to make representations. It may make an order about costs at a hearing in public or in private; or without a hearing. In deciding what order, if any, to make about costs, the court must have regard to all the circumstances, including the conduct of all the parties; and any costs order already made. If the court makes an order:

(1) about costs, it must specify who must, or must not, pay what, to whom, and must identify the legislation under which the order is made, where there is a choice of powers, giving reasons if it refuses an application for an order or rejects representations opposing an order;

(2) for the payment of costs the general rule is that it will be for an amount that is sufficient reasonably to compensate the recipient for costs actually, reasonably and properly incurred, and reasonable in amount; but the court may order the payment of:
(a) a proportion of that amount,
(b) a stated amount less than that amount,
(c) costs from or until a certain date only,
(d) costs relating only to particular steps taken, or
(e) costs relating only to a distinct part of the case.

An order for the payment of costs takes effect when the amount is assessed, unless the court exercises any power it has to order otherwise.

As to a parent or guardian liable to pay the costs of a child under PCC(S)A 2000, s.171, see *R. v Preston Ex p. Lancashire CC* [1998] 3 All E.R. 765 and see *ibid* as to a local authority standing in *loco parentis* under PCC(S)A 2000, s.130.

General rules: (2) assessment

21–005 On an assessment of the amount of costs, relevant factors include: R.76.2

(1) the conduct of all the parties;
(2) the particular complexity of the matter or the difficulty or novelty of the questions raised;
(3) the skill, effort, specialised knowledge and responsibility involved;
(4) the time spent on the case;
(5) the place where and the circumstances in which work or any part of it was done; and
(6) any direction or observations by the court that made the costs order.

If the judge orders a party to pay costs to be assessed under r.76.11, he may order that party to pay an amount on account.

Power to vary requirements

21–006 The court may: R.76.3

(1) extend a time limit for serving an application or representations under ss.2, 3 or 4 even after it has expired; and
(2) consider an application:
(a) made in a different form to one set out in the Practice Direction, or

(b) made orally instead of in writing.

A person wanting an extension of time must apply when serving the application or representations for which it is needed; explaining the delay.

Amount of costs to be paid

21–007   Except where the judge has directed in an order for costs out of central funds that only a specified sum be paid, the amount of costs to be paid being assessed by the Crown Court officer.

The judge may, however:

(1) order the disallowance of costs out of central funds not properly incurred; or
(2) direct the Crown Court officer to consider whether or not specific items have been properly incurred; and may also
(3) make observations regarding CDS funded costs (see 21–035 below).

Where the court orders an offender to pay costs to the prosecutor, orders one party to pay costs to another, disallows or orders a legal or other representative to meet wasted costs, the order for costs must specify the sum to be paid or disallowed.

Where the judge is required to specify the amount of costs to be paid, he cannot delegate the decision. He may, however, require the Crown Court officer to make enquiries and inform him of the costs incurred, and may adjourn, if necessary, for enquiries to be made.

Special provisions apply in relation to recovery of defence costs orders (see 21–040, below). (As to the extent of the investigation by POA 1985, s.16 and SI 1986/1335, see *R. (Brewer) v Supreme Courts Costs Office* [2006] EWHC 1955 (Admin); [2007] 1 Costs L.R. 20.)

2.   Costs out of central funds

If the Legal Aid etc. Bill 2011, now going through Parliament, is enacted in its present form, it will make substantial changes to this section.

Defence costs from central funds

21–008   The judge may make a "defendant's costs order" where an accused: PDC 2010, 2.2.1

(1) is not tried for an offence for which he has been indicted in respect of which proceedings against him have been sent or transferred for trial; or
(2) has been acquitted on any count in the indictment.

Note that:

(a) an order should normally be made whether or not an order for costs between parties is made, unless there are positive reasons for not doing so, (see below);

(b) a refusal must be based on independent evidence and not simply prosecution evidence that the allegations have been withdrawn *(Mooney v Cardiff JJ* (2000) 164 J.P. 220); and

(c) when declining to make a costs order, the judge should explain in open court that the reason for not making it does not involve any suggestion that the accused is guilty of any criminal conduct, but that the order is refused because of a positive reason, which should be identified.

Extent of costs from central funds

21–009   Where the court may order the payment of costs out of central funds costs include:

R.76.4

(1) on an appeal, costs incurred in the court that made the decision under appeal; and

(2) at a retrial, costs incurred at the initial trial and on any appeal; but do not include costs funded by the Legal Services Commission (see LEGAL AID; PUBLIC FUNDING).

The court may make an order on application by the person who incurred the costs or on its own initiative. A person wanting the court to make an order must apply as soon as practicable, outlining the type of costs and the amount claimed, if he wants the court to direct an assessment, or specifying the amount claimed, if he wants the court to assess the amount itself.

The general rule is that an order will be made, but the court may decline to make:

(a) a defendant's costs order if, for example:
    (i) the defendant is convicted of at least one offence; or
    (ii) the defendant's conduct led the prosecutor reasonably to think the prosecution case stronger than it was; and

(b) a prosecutor's costs order if, for example, the prosecution was started or continued unreasonably.

Where an accused is convicted of some counts in the indictment but acquitted on others the judge may exercise his discretion to make a defendant's costs order; but may order that only part of the costs incurred be paid. He should make whatever order seems just having regard to the relative importance of the charges and the conduct of the parties generally. If he considers it inappropriate that the defendant recover all of the costs properly incurred, specify the amount in the order.

PDC 2010, 2.2.2

A judge may make a defendant's costs order in favour of a successful appellant in an appeal to the Crown Court (see APPELLATE JURISDICTION).

PDC 2010, 2.2.2

Further considerations

21–010   Note that:

• the judge is entitled to take note of the fact that the accused elected trial on indictment, and if, in his opinion, such election was extravagant and unreasonable, he is entitled to take that fact

into consideration in exercising his discretion *(R. v Dawood* [1974] Crim. L. R. 486);
- it is not incompatible with the presumption of innocence for the judge to refuse to make an order because he considers that the accused brought suspicion on himself and misled the prosecutor into believing that the case against him was stronger than it was in reality; such is also the case where the accused brought the prosecution on himself because he availed himself of the right to silence *(Ashenden v UK, The Times,* September 22, 2011);
- the fact that he disagrees with the verdict of a jury is not a ground for refusing costs out of central funds *(Practice Direction* (1959) 43 Cr. App. R. 419);
- where the prosecutor does not proceed because a witness is unavailable an application for costs should normally succeed *(R. v Preston CC* [2001] EWHC Admin 599 (unreported, July 16, 2001));

In relation to the second bulleted point, ECHR looks to whether, in refusing to make an order the judge's reasons indicate a reliance on suspicions as to the innocence of the accused after he has been acquitted (ibid.).

It does not necessarily follow that because a solicitor has claimed costs under a defendant's costs order that his client cannot make a claim for costs which he, the client, has incurred *(R. v Bedlington MC Ex p Wilkinson* (2000) 164 J.P. 156).

Assessment of costs

21–011   If the judge makes an order for costs out of central funds, he may either:

(1) direct an assessment under GR 1986, regs 4–12, or under SOCA 2007 (Appeals under Section 24) Order 2008, regs 21–28, whichever is applicable; or
(2) assess the amount himself, if the recipient agrees.

He must assess the amount himself, in a case in which he decides not to allow an amount that is reasonably sufficient to compensate the recipient for expenses properly incurred in the proceedings.

Where the party who obtains the order is publicly funded (see LEGAL AID; PUBLIC FUNDING) he will only recover his personal costs (see POA 1985, s.21(4A)(a)).

PDC 2010, Sch (see 21–055) sets out the extent of the availability of costs from central funds and the relevant statutory authority.

Private prosecutor's costs

21–012   There is no power to order the payment out of central funds of any prosecutor who is a public authority, a person acting on behalf of a public authority or acting as an official appointed by a public authority as defined in the Act.   PDC 2010, 2.6.1

In the limited number of cases in which a prosecutor's costs may be awarded out of central funds an application must be made by the prosecutor in each case and:

(1) an order should be made, save where there is good reason for not doing so, as where proceedings have been instituted or continued without good cause; and

(2) the procedure applies to proceedings in respect of an indictable offence, or proceedings before the Administrative Court in respect of a summary offence;

(3) GR 1986, reg.4(1) extends the provision to certain committals from a magistrates' court.

Where the judge is of the opinion that there are circumstances which make it inappropriate to award the full amount of costs out of central funds, he must assess whatwould in his opinion be just and reasonable and specify that amount in the order. Subject to that, the amount to be paid out of central funds will either be specified in the order where the judge considers it appropriate to do so, and the prosecutor agrees the amount, or, in any other case, be determined in accordance with the Regulations. PDC 2010, 2.6.2

For the purposes of an order under s.17 the costs of the prosecutor are taken to include the expense of compensating any witness for the expenses, travel and loss of time properly incurred in or incidental to his attendance. PDC 2010, 2.6.3

If there has been misconduct a private prosecutor should not be awarded costs out of Central Funds. PDC 2010, 2.6.4

Where the conduct of a private prosecution is taken over by the CPS the power to order payment of prosecution costs out of central funds extends only to the period prior to the intervention of the CPS. Rule 76.4, and the general rules in CPR 2011, r.76, s.1 apply to the exercise of the court's powers to award costs out of central funds. PDC 2010, 2.6.5

Witness, interpreter or medical evidence

21–013 The costs of the attendance of: PDC 2010, 2.5.1

(1) a witness required by the accused, a private prosecutor or the court; or

(2) an interpreter required because of the accused's lack of English; or

(3) an intermediary required under YJCEA 1999, s.29 (see SPECIAL MEASURES DIRECTIONS);

(4) an *oral* report by a medical practitioner, are allowed out of central funds unless the judge otherwise directs (POA 1985, s.20(3), GR 1986, reg.6(1)). If, and only if, the court makes such a direction can the expense of the witness be claimed as a disbursement out of CDS funds.

A "witness" includes any person properly attending to give evidence, whether or not he gives evidence or is called, but it does not include a character witness unless the judge has certified that the interests of justice require his attendance.

The court may also order the payment out of central funds of such sums as appear to it to be reasonably sufficient to compensate any medical practitioner for the expenses, trouble, or loss of time properly incurred in preparing and making a report on the mental condition of a person accused of murder (see MH(A)A 1982, s.34(5)). PDC 2010, 2.5.2

COSTS AND ASSESSMENT

Disallowance of items out of central funds

21–014   Where the judge makes an order for costs out of central funds, he:

(1) *must* direct the Crown Court officer to disallow the costs incurred in respect of any items if it is plain that those costs were not properly incurred (such costs are not payable under POA 1985, ss.6(6), 17(1));

(2) *may* direct the Crown Court officer to consider or to investigate on assessment any items which may have been improperly incurred.

Costs not properly incurred include costs in respect of work unreasonably done, e.g. if the case has been conducted unreasonably so as to incur unjustified expense, or costs have been wasted by failure to conduct proceedings with reasonable competence and expedition. In a plain case it will usually be more appropriate to make a wasted costs order under POA 1985, s.19A (see below). The precise terms of the order for costs and of any direction must be entered on the court record.

The word "improper" in POA 1985, s.19 and GR 1986, reg.3(l) does not denote some grave impropriety but is intended to cover an act or omission which would not have occurred if the party concerned had conducted his case properly *(DPP v Denning* 94 Cr. App. R. 272).

Where the judge is minded to give a direction in accordance with (1) or (2), above, he;

(a) must inform any party whose costs might be affected, or his legal representative, of its precise terms; and

(b) must, in the case of a direction under (1), give a reasonable opportunity to show cause why no direction should be given; and

(c) should, in the case of a direction under (2), inform the party concerned of his rights to make representations to the Crown Court officer.

The Crown Court officer may consult the judge on any matter touching the allowance or disallowance of costs, but it is not appropriate for the judge to make a direction under (1) above when so consulted.

'The judge is entitled to rely on the CPS scale of average costs when fixing the amount of costs to be paid *(R. v Dickinson* [2010] EWCA Crim 2143, [2011] 1 Cr. App. R, (S.) 93).

3.   Awards of cost against accused persons

Award against offenders and appellants

21–015   A judge may make an order for costs against: PDC 2010, 3.1.9

(1) a person convicted before him; or

(2) in dealing with a person in respect of certain orders as to sentence specified in GR 1986, reg.14; or

(3) a person committed by a magistrates' court in respect of the proceedings specified in reg.4(1) and (2).

Where he is satisfied that the offender or appellant has the means and ability to pay he may make such order payable to the prosecutor as he considers just and reasonable (POA 1985, s.8(1); the amount must be specified in the order).

The judge has a duty to consider the offender's means (see e.g. *R. v Mountain* (1979) 68 Cr. App. R. 4) and, if he allows time for payment he must ensure that the length of time would not be oppressive (*R. v Nuthoo* [2011] Costs L.R. 87).

An order under s.18 includes LSC funded costs (POA 1985, s.21(4A) (b) as to which see LEGAL AID; PUBLIC FUNDING).

An order:

PDC 2010, 3.4.5

- should be made where the judge is satisfied that the accused or appellant has the means and the ability to pay;
- is not intended to be in the nature of a penalty which can only be satisfied on the offender's release from prison;
- should not be made on the assumption that a third party might pay.

Whilst the court should take into account any debt of the appellant or offender, where the greater part of those debts relates to the offence itself, the judge may still make an order for costs.

Where there are multiple accused the judge may make joint and several orders, but the costs ordered to be paid by an individual should be related to the costs in or about the prosecution of that individual. In a multi-handed case where some accused have insufficient means to pay their share of the costs, it is not right for that share to be divided among the other defenders. Where co-accused are husband and wife, the couple's means should not be taken together.

In exceptional circumstances costs may be awarded against a non-party (*H Leverton Ltd v Crawford Offshore (Exploration) Services Ltd (in liquidation), The Times,* November 22, 1996).

Accused electing trial on indictment
21–016 In relation to an accused who elects trial on indictment:

(1) while it is wrong to penalise him merely because he has taken advantage of his constitutional right, nevertheless if he elects and the case is one in which the prosecution costs should fall on him, it is perfectly right that he should suffer a higher penalty as a result of going to the Crown Court (*R. v Hoyden* (1974) 60 Cr. App. R. 304, *R. v Yoxall* (1973) 57 Cr. App. R. 263);

(2) in a case which could conveniently have been tried summarily he may be ordered to pay costs on a Crown Court basis (*R. v Bushel* (1980) 2 Cr. App. R. (S.) 77; *R. v Boyle* [1995] 16 Cr. App. R. (S.) 92); it is otherwise where the offender pleads guilty at the Crown Court to a lesser offence which could have been tried by the magistrates (*R. v Sentonco* [1996] 1 Cr. App. R. (S.) 174);

(3) it is wrong in principle to make an order for the whole of the prosecution costs against an offender who is convicted on e.g. three, out of a total of 17, counts (*R. v Splain* [2010] EWCA Crim 49, [2010] Costs L.R. 465, CA); it is not necessary to take a mathematical approach, but the judge should take an overall view considering fairness and proportionality.

The fact that the amount of costs is disproportionate to any fines imposed is not the crucial factor; there may well be cases in which, in the totality of the sentencing process, the judge is justified in weighting the penalty on to the costs more than on to the fine (*ibid.*).

The principles were reviewed in *R. v Northallerton MC Ex p. Dove* [2000] 1 Cr. App. R. (S.) 136 and *Neville v Gardner Merchant* [1983] 5 Cr. App. R. (S.) 349, DC.

Procedure

21–017 The judge may make an order under 21–015 above on application by the prosecutor or on his own initiative. Where the prosecutor wants him to make an order he must apply as soon as practicable, and specify the amount claimed. R.76.5

In so far as procedure is concerned:

- the prosecution should serve upon the defence, at the earliest time, full details of its costs so as to give the accused a proper opportunity to make representations upon them if appropriate; PDC 2010, 3.6
- if an offender wishes to dispute all or any of the prosecution's claim for costs, he should, if possible, give proper notice to the prosecution of the objections proposed to be made or at least make it plain to the court precisely what those objections are;
- there is no provision for assessment of prosecution costs in a criminal case, such disputes have to be resolved by the court, which must specify the amount to be paid (*R. v Associated Octel Ltd* [1996] EWCA Crim 1327, [1996] 4 All E.R. 846);
- the general rule is that the court will make an order if it is satisfied that the accused can pay; but it may decline to do so.

The judge, when awarding prosecution costs, may award costs in respect of time spent in bringing the offences to light, even if the necessary investigation was carried out, for example, by an environmental health official. Only in very limited circumstances may the CPS recover particular costs associated with the investigation incurred by the police. PDC 2010, 3.7

The Divisional Court has held that there is a requirement that any sum ordered to be paid by way of costs should not ordinarily be greatly at variance with any fine imposed.

Where substantial research is required in order to counter possible defences, the court may also award costs in respect of that work if it considers it to be justified.

Costs on appeal

21–018   CPR 2011, r.76.6:   R.76.6

(1) applies where the Crown Court may order a party to pay another person's costs on an appeal; and

(2) authorises the Crown Court, in addition to its other powers, to order a party to pay another party's costs on an appeal to that court, except on an appeal under MCA 1980, s.108 or MHA 1983, s.45.

In this rule, "costs" include costs incurred in the court that made the decision under appeal; and costs funded by the Legal Services Commission.

The court may make an order on application by the person who incurred the costs or on its own initiative. A person wanting the court to make an order must apply as soon as practicable, notifying each other party and specifying the amount claimed, and against whom.

Where:

(a) an appellant abandons an appeal by serving a notice of abandonment, he must apply in writing not more than 14 days later, and serve the application on the appellant and on the Crown Court officer;

(b) a party wants to oppose an order, he must make representations as soon as practicable, and where the application was under (a) serve written representations on the applicant, and on the Crown Court officer, not more than seven days after it was served.

Where the application was under (a) above the Crown Court officer will submit it to the Crown Court; or serve it on the magistrates' court officer, for submission to the magistrates' court.

Where:

(i) the appellant abandons an appeal to the Crown Court;

(ii) the Crown Court decides an appeal, (except an appeal under MCA 1980, s.108, or MHA 1983, s.45);

the court if it makes an order, may direct an assessment under r.76.11, or assess the amount itself.

If the court makes an order in any other case, it must assess the amount itself.

Bank records, football banning orders, witness summonses

21–019   Where the judge may order a party to pay another person's   R.76.7
costs in a case in which:

(1) he decides an application for the production in evidence of a copy of a bank record;

(2) he decides an application to terminate a football banning order; or

(3) he allows an application to withdraw a witness summons,

he may make an order either on application by the person who incurred the costs or on his own initiative.

A person wanting the court to make an order must apply as soon as practicable notifying each other party and specifying:

COSTS AND ASSESSMENT

    (a) the amount claimed; and
    (b) against whom.

A party who wants to oppose an order must make representations as soon as practicable.

If the judge makes an order, he may direct an assessment under r.76.11, or assess the amount himself.

4. Other costs orders

(1) Costs incurred as a result of unnecessary or improper act or omission

Costs resulting from unnecessary or improper act, etc.

21–020 A judge may order the payment of any costs incurred as a result of any unnecessary or improper act or omission by or on behalf of any party to the proceedings as distinct from his legal representative (POA 1985, s.19, and GR 1986, reg.3).

The judge may find it helpful to adopt a three stage approach:

(1) Has there been an unnecessary or improper, act or omission?
(2) As a result have any costs been incurred by another party?
(3) If the answers to (1) and (2) are "yes", should he exercise hisdis-cretion to order the party responsible to meet the whole or any part of the relevant costs, and if so what specific sum is involved?

Such an order is appropriate only where the failure is that of the prosecutor or, the accused; where the failure is that of a legal representative, paras 4.2 and 4.3 (21–022 and following) may be more suitable.

Procedure

21–021 The judge may make an order on application by the party who incurred such costs or on his own initiative. A party wanting the judge to make an order must apply in writing as soon as practicable after becoming aware of the grounds for doing so, serving the application on the Crown Court officer and each other party, specifying:

- the party by whom costs should be paid,
- the relevant act or omission,
- the reasons why that act or omission meets the criteria for making an order,
- the amount claimed, and
- those on whom the application has been served.

The judge will hear the parties and may then order that all or part of the costs so incurred by one party shall be paid to him by the other party.

Before making such an order the judge may take into account any other order as to costs and the order must specify the amount of the costs to be paid. He is entitled to take such an order into account when making any other order as to costs in the proceedings (GR 1986, regs3(2)–(4)).

The order can extend to LSC costs incurred on behalf of any party.

Where the judge considers making an order on his own initiative, he must identify the party against whom he proposes making the order; and specify:

PDC 2010, 4.1.5

R.76.8

PDC 2010, 4.1.2

PDC 2010, 4.1.3

POA1985, s.21(4A)(b)

(a) the relevant act or omission;

(b) the reasons why that act or omission meets the criteria for making an order; and

(c) with the assistance of the party who incurred the costs, the amount involved.

A party wanting to oppose an order must make representations as soon as practicable and in reply to an application, serve written representations on the applicant and on the Crown Court officer not more than seven days after it was served.

If the judge makes an order, he must assess the amount itself.

(2) Costs against a legal representative—wasted costs

General

21–022 POA 1985, s.19A allows a judge to disallow or order the legal or other representative to meet the whole or any part of wasted costs. The order may be made against any person exercising a right of audience or a right to conduct litigation (in the sense of acting for a party to the proceedings). PDC 2010, 4.2.1

"Wasted costs" are costs incurred by a party (which includes a publicly funded party):

* as a result of any improper, unreasonable or negligent act or omission on the part of any representative or his employee; or
* which, in the light of any such act or omission occurring after they were incurred, the judge considers it unreasonable to expect that party to pay.

(POA 1985, s.9A(3), PCA 2002, s.89(8)).

GR 1986, reg.3B requires the judge to specify the amount of the wasted costs and before making the order to allow the legal or other representative and any party to the proceedings to make representations. In making the order the judge may take into account any other orders for costs and may take the wasted costs order into account when making any other order as to costs. The judge should give reasons for making the order and any interested party (which includes the CDS fund and Central Funds determining authorities) must be informed of the order and of the amount. PDA 2010, 4.2.3

There has to be proved improper, unreasonable or negligent conduct (*Ridehalgh v Horsefield* [1994] Ch. 205; *Re Hickman and Rose, The Times,* May 3, 2000). Counsel is responsible for his clerk's errors, in, e.g. not getting him to court, or missing the case in the list *(R. v Rodney (Wasted Costs Order* [1997] 1 Arch. News 2)).

As to the approach where the accused fails to appear and solicitor and advocate withdraw, see *Re Boodhoo* [2007] EWCA Crim 14, [2007] 1 Cr. App. R. 32.

Procedure

21–023 The judge may make an order on application by the party who incurred such costs; or on his own initiative. A form of application is set out in PDC 2010, Sch.5. R.76.9

COSTS AND ASSESSMENT

A party who wants the judge to make an order must apply in writing as soon as practicable after becoming aware of the grounds for doing so, serving the application on:

(1) the Crown Court officer;
(2) the representative responsible;
(3) each other party; and
(4) any other person directly affected,

specifying:

- the representative responsible;
- the relevant act or omission;
- the reasons why that act or omission meets the criteria for making an order;
- he amount claimed; and
- those on whom the application has been served.

Where the judge considers making an order on his own initiative, he will identify the representative against whom he proposes making the order; and will specify:

(a) the relevant act or omission;
(b) the reasons why that act or omission meets the criteria for making an order; and
(c) with the assistance of the party who incurred the costs, the amount involved.

A representative wanting to oppose an order must make representations as soon as practicable; and in reply to an application, serve written representations on the applicant and on the Crown Court officer not more than seven days after it was served.

Before making an order the judge must allow the legal or other representative and any party to the proceedings to make representations (*R. v Wiseman Lee (Solicitors) (Wasted Costs Order) (No.5 of 2000)* [2001] EWCA Crim 707). He will assess the amount himself, taking into account, where appropriate, any other order for costs, and notifying any interested party (which includes the CDS fund and central funds determining authorities) of the order and the amount.

In a case where a party's costs are funded by the Legal Services Commission (see LEGAL AID; PUBLIC FUNDING), or are to be paid out of central funds, or there is to be an assessment under r.76.11, the judge may, instead of making an order, make adverse observations about the representative's conduct for use in an assessment.

If he makes an order, the general rule is that he will do so without waiting until the end of the case, but he may postpone making the order. *Film Lab Systems International v Pennington* [1994] 4 All E.R. 673 and *Medcalf v Mardell* [2002] 3 All E.R. 721, both indicate the importance (at least in civil cases) of the judge dealing with the matter at the end of the case, avoiding the position where an advocate's conduct of the case is influenced by his self-interest.

The hearing

21–024 A judge contemplating making a wasted costs order should bear in mind the guidance given in *Re A Barrister (Wasted Costs Order)* PDC 2010, 4.2.4

328

(No. 1 of 1991) (1992) 95 Cr. App. R. 288, which should be considered together with all the statutory and other rules and recommendations set out by Parliament and in this practice direction.

Thus:

(1) There is a clear need for the judge intending to exercise the wasted costs jurisdiction to formulate carefully and concisely the complaint and grounds upon which such an order may be sought; these measures are draconian and, as in contempt proceedings, the grounds must be clear and particular;

(2) where necessary, a transcript of the relevant part of the proceedings under discussion should be available and in accordancewith the rules a transcript of any wasted cost hearing must be made.

An accused involved in a case where such proceedings are contemplated should be present if, after discussion with an advocate, it is thought that his interest may be affected and he should certainly be present and represented if the matter might affect the course of his trial. Rule 76.2(l) requires that the judge must not make a costs order unless each party, and any other person affected, (a) is present, or (b) has had an opportunity to attend or to make representations.

A three stage approach

21–025   The same three stage test or approach advocated at 21–020 is recommended when a wasted costs order is contemplated (see also *R. (B) v X CC* [2009] EWHC 1149 (Admin), [2010] Crim. L.R.145).   PDC 2010, 4.2.4

It is inappropriate to propose any settlement that the representative might forgo fees. The complaint should be formally stated by the judge and the representative invited to make his own comments. After any other party has been heard the judge should give his formal ruling. Discursive conversations may be unfair and should certainly not take place.

The judge must specify the sum to be allowed or ordered. Alternatively the relevant available procedure should be substituted should it be impossible to fix the sum: see 4.2.7.

Though the judge cannot delegate his decision to the appropriate authority, he may require the appropriate officer of the court to make enquiries and inform him as to the likely amount of costs incurred. By r.76.9(5) the judge is entitled to the assistance in this respect of the party who incurred the costs concerned.   PDC 2010, 4.2.6

He may postpone the making of a wasted costs order to the end of the case if it appears more appropriate to do so, for example, because the likely amount is not readily available, there is a possibility of conflict between the legal representatives as to the apportionment of blame, or the legal representative concerned is unable to make full representations because of a possible conflict with the duty to the client.   PDC 2010, 4.2.5

CACD Guidelines

21–026   In *Re P (A Barrister)* [2001] EWCA Crim 1728; [2002] 1 Cr. App. R. 207, CACD gave the following guidance: PDC 2010, 4.2.5

(1) the primary object is not to punish but to compensate, albeit as the order is sought against a non party, it can from that perspective be regarded as penal;

(2) the jurisdiction is a summary jurisdiction to be exercised by the court which has "tried the case in the course of which the misconduct was committed";

(3) fairness is assured if the lawyer alleged to be at fault has sufficient notice of the complaint made against him and a proper opportunity to respond to it;

(4) because of the penal element a mere mistake is not sufficient to justify an order: there must be a more serious error;

(5) although the trial judge can decline to consider an application in respect of costs, for example on the ground that he is personally embarrassed by an appearance of bias, it will only be in exceptional circumstances that it will be appropriate to pass the matter to another judge, and the fact that, in the proper exercise of his judicial function, a judge has expressed views in relation to the conduct of a lawyer against whom an order is sought, does not of itself normally constitute bias or the appearance of bias so as to necessitate a transfer;

(6) the normal civil standard of proof applies but if the allegation is one of serious misconduct or crime clear evidence will be required to meet that standard.

Relevance of public funding

21–027   A wasted costs order should normally be made regardless of the fact that the client of the legal representative concerned is CDS funded (see LEGAL AID; PUBLIC FUNDING). However where the judge is minded to disallow substantial costs out of the CDS fund, he may, instead of making a wasted costs order, make observations to the determining authority that work may have been unreasonably done: see 21–028 below. This practice should only be adopted where the extent and amount of the costs wasted is not entirely clear.

Disallowance of publicly funded costs

21–028   Where it appears to the judge, sitting in proceedings for which public funding has been granted (see LEGAL AID; PUBLIC FUNDING) that work may have been unreasonably done, e.g. if the publicly funded person's case may have been conducted unreasonably so as to incur unjustifiable expense, or costs may have been wasted by failure to conduct the proceedings with reasonable competence or expedition, he may make observations to that effect for the attention of the appropriate authority. `PDC 2010, 4.3.1`

He should specify as precisely as possible the item, or items, which the determining officer should consider or investigate on the determination of the costs payable pursuant to the representation order. The precise terms of the observations must be entered in the court record.

The Criminal Defence Service (Funding) Order 2007: `PDC 2010, 4.7.2`

- art.27 permits the appropriate officer to reduce any fee which 4.7.2 would otherwise be payable by such proportion as the officer considers reasonable in the light of any adverse comments made by the judge; the power to make adverse comments co-exists with the power to disallow fees when making a wasted costs order;

- art.28 allows the determining officer to disallow the amount of the wasted costs order from the amount otherwise payable to the litigator or advocate and allows for deduction of a greater amount if appropriate.

Where the judge has in mind making such observations the litigator or advocate whose fees or expenses might be affected must be informed of the precise terms thereof and of his right to make representations to the appropriate authority and be given a reasonable opportunity to show cause why the observations or direction should not be made, and where such observations or directions are made the appropriate authority must afford an opportunity to the litigator or advocate whose fees might be affected to make representations in relation to them.

PDC 2010, 4.3.3, 4

Whether or not observations under 4.3.1 above have been made the appropriate authority may consult the judge or the court on any matter touching the allowance or disallowance of fees and expenses, but if the observations then made are to the effect mentioned in 4.3.1, the appropriate authority should afford an opportunity to the litigator or advocate concerned to make representations in relation to them.

PDC 2010, 4.3.5

Very high cost cases

21–029 In proceedings which are classified as a very high cost case ("VHCC") as defined by the Criminal Defence Service (General) (No.2) Regulations 2001, reg.2, (see LEGAL AID; PUBLIC FUNDING):

PDC 2010, 4.4.1

- The representative of the funded person should be asked, at the earliest opportunity whether the LSC has been informed of the case in accordance with reg.23.
- If they have not been, the representative should be warned that they may not be able to recover his costs.
- Further, the representative should be informed that the case can only be conducted by a firm approved by the LSC to carry out VHCC work and firms and advocates instructed by such firms may not be able to recover their costs (save in those cases which are governed by the regulations relating to VHCCs prior to January 14, 2008 CDS General (No.2) Regulations; amended by SI 2007/3550, reg.13(2)).

Appeals against wasted costs orders

21–030 A party against whom a wasted costs order has been made may appeal against that order. In the case of an order made at first instance by the Crown Court, the appeal is to CACD and the procedure is set out in r.68. The time limit for appeal is 21 days from the date of the order. Having heard the submissions, the appeal court may affirm, vary or revoke the order as it thinks fit and must notify its decision to the appellant, any interested party and the court which made the order.

PDC 2010, 4.2.9, 10

(3) Award of costs against third parties

Power to make order
21–031 Where:

(1) there has been serious misconduct (whether or not constituting contempt of court) by a person who is not a party ("the third party"); and PDC 2010, 4.7.1

(2) the judge considers it appropriate having regard to that misconduct, to make such an order against him, he may make a third party costs order against him, which is an order for the payment of costs incurred by a party to criminal proceedings by a person who is not a party to those proceedings (POA 1985, s.19B, GR 1986, regs 3E to 31). Rule 76.10 sets out the procedure.

Note that:

the judge may make an order at any time during or after the proceedings, but should only make an order during the proceedings if he decides that there are good reasons to do so; PDC 2010, 4.7.2

- the court must notify the parties and the third party of those reasons and allow any of them to make representations; PDC 2010, 4.7.3
- an order may be made on the application of any party, or on the judge's own initiative, but not in any other circumstances; before making an order the judge must allow the third party, and any other party, to make representations and may hear evidence; PDC 2010, 4.7.4
- when the judge makes an order, he may take into account any other order as to costs in respect of the proceedings, and may take the third party costs order into account when making any other order for costs in respect of those proceedings; PDC 2010, 4.7.5
- the order must specify the amount of costs to be paid, and the court must notify the third party and any interested party of the order and the amount ordered to be paid; PDC 2010, 4.7.6
- if the judge is considering making an order on his own initiative, the appropriate officer should serve notice in writing on the third party and any other parties; PDC 2010, 4.7.7
- where a party applies for such an order the application must must be in writing, and contain the names and addresses of the applicant, the other parties and the third party against whom the order is sought, together with a summary of the facts upon which the applicant intends to rely, including in particular details of the alleged misconduct of the third party; PDC 2010, 4.7.8
- at the hearing of the application the judge may proceed in the absence of the third party, and of any other party, if satisfied that that party has been duly served with the notice by the appropriate officer, and with a copy of the application. PDC 2010, 4.7.9

The power to make an order extends to making such an order against a Government Department where there has been serious misconduct, including deliberate or negligent failure to attend to one's duties, or falling below a proper standard in that regard, but there is a higher threshold for liability than for a wasted costs order *(R. v Ahmati (Agron) (Order for Costs)* [2006] EWCA Crim 1826).

Appeal by third party

21–032   A third party against whom the judge makes a third party costs order at first instance may appeal to CACD: SI 2004/ 2408, reg.7

(1) subject to an extension being granted, within 21 days of the order being made;
(2) by the appellant giving notice in writing to the court which made the order;
(3) stating the grounds of appeal; and
(4) serving a copy of the notice of appeal and grounds, including any application for extension of time in which to appeal, on any interested party (as defined in the regulations).

The time limit within which an appeal may be instituted may, for good reason, be extended before or after it expires by a judge of the High Court or Court of Appeal, or by the Registrar. CACD will give notice of the extension to the appellant, to the court which made the order and to any interested party, and will give notice of the hearing date to the same persons, and will allow the interested party to make representations which may be made orally or in writing. The order may be affirmed, varied or revoked as CACD thinks fit.

Recovery of sums due under a third party costs order

21–033 Where the person required to make a payment in respect of sums due under a third party costs order fails to do so, the payment may be recovered summarily as a sum adjudged to be paid as a civil debt by order of a magistrates' court by the party benefiting from the order, save that where he was receiving services funded for him as part of the Criminal Defence Service (see LEGAL AID; PUBLIC FUNDING) or an order for the payment of costs out of central funds was made in his favour, the power to recover is exercisable by the Lord Chancellor.

(4) Solicitors; Crown Court's inherent jurisdiction

21–034 In addition to the power under:

PDC 2010, 4.6.1–4.6.3

(1) GR 1986, reg.3 to order that costs improperly incurred be paid by a party to the proceedings; and
(2) POA 1985, s.19A, to make wasted costs orders,

a judge of the Crown Court, a judge of one of the Senior Courts (formerly part of the Supreme Court) may, in the exercise of his inherent jurisdiction over officers of the court, order a solicitor personally to pay costs thrown away by reason of a serious dereliction of his duty to the court, but:

(a) this power should be used only in exceptional circumstances not covered by the statutory power; *R. v Smith* [1974] 1 All E.R. 651 and *Shaw Thew v Reeves (No.2)* [1982] 3 All E.R. 1086 emphasise that an order should be made only where the conduct of the solicitor is inexcusable and such as to merit reproof, not where mere mistake, error of judgment or negligence is disclosed; and
(b) no order may be made unless reasonable notice has been given to the solicitor of the matter alleged against him and he is given a reasonable opportunity of being heard in reply.

If the judge considers it necessary to hold such a hearing in chambers, a shorthand note should be kept.

5.   Assessment of costs

Assessment of defence costs out of central funds

21–035   Where a publicly funded accused (see LEGAL AID; PUBLIC FUNDING) wishes to claim out of pocket expenses or costs for work which has not been done under the representation order, the assessment of those costs should be carried out at the same time as the assessment of his solicitor's costs under the representation order and the solicitors should ensure that the two claims are submitted together for assessment (*R. v Supreme Court Costs Office Exp. Brewer* [2006] EWHC 1955 (Admin) [2007] Crim. L.R. 20).

PDC 2010, 5.1.1

Procedure following assessment

21–036   Where the judge directs an assessment under:

R.76.11

(1) r.61.20 (POCA 2002 – rules applicable to restraint and receiver ship proceedings, assessment of costs);
(2) r.76.6 (costs on appeal); or
(3) r.76.7 (costs on an application),

the assessment will be carried out by the relevant assessing authority, namely, where the direction was given by a judge of the Crown Court, the Crown Court officer.

The party in whose favour the court made the costs order ("the applicant") must:

(a) apply for an assessment, in writing, in any form required by the assessing authority, and not more than three months after the costs order; and
(b) serve the application on the assessing authority and the party against whom the court made the costs order ("the respondent").

The applicant must summarise the work done, specifying:

(i) each item of work done, giving the date, time taken and amount claimed;
(ii) any disbursements or expenses, including the fees of any advocate; and
(iii) any circumstances of which the applicant wants the assessing authority to take particular account; and

supplying receipts or other evidence of the amount claimed, and any other information or document for which the assessing authority asks, within such period as that authority may require.

A respondent wanting to make representations about the amount claimed must do so in writing, serving the representations on the assessing authority, and on the applicant.

The assessing authority will, if it seems likely to help with the assessment, obtain any other information or document, will resolve in favour of the respondent any doubt about what should be allowed, and serve the assessment on the parties.

Re-assessment

21–037   Where either party wants the amount allowed re-assessed he must;

R.76.11(7)(8)

(1) apply to the assessing authority, in writing and in any form required by that authority;
(2) serve the application on the assessing authority, and on the other party, not more than 21 days after service of the assessment,

explaining the objections to the assessment, supplying any additional supporting information or document, and asking for a hearing, if he wants one.

A party wanting to make representations about an application for re-assessment must do so in writing, serving the representations on the assessing authority, and on the other party, not more than 21 days after service of the application, and asking for a hearing, if he wants one.

The assessing authority:

- will arrange a hearing, in public or in private, if either party asks for one;
- subject to that, may re-assess the amount allowed with or without a hearing; will reassess the amount allowed on the initial assessment;
- taking into account the reasons for disagreement with that amount and any other representations;
- may maintain, increase or decrease the amount allowed on the assessment;
- will serve the re-assessment on the parties; and
- will serve written reasons on the parties, if not more than 21 days later either party asks for such reasons.

Any time limit under this rule may be extended even after it has expired, by the assessing authority, or by the Senior Costs Judge, if the assessing authority declines to do so.

As to appeal to a Costs Judge see r.76.12, and to a High Court Judge, see r.76.13.

Appeals to a costs judge

21–038   A party dissatisfied with a costs assessment may apply to the relevant authority for a review of the assessment (GR 1986, reg.9 or CPR 2011 r.76.11(7)). An appeal against a decision on such a review lies to the Senior Costs Judge of the Supreme Court Costs Office (r.76.12). Written notice in the form set out in the Schedule to PDC 2010 (adapted where appropriate) must be given within 21 days of receipt of the reasons for the assessment, or such longer time as the Costs Judge directs.

PDC 2010, 5.2–5.5

6. Contribution orders and recovery of defence costs orders

(1) Legally aided costs

Contribution orders

21–039 In proceedings to which the CDS (Contribution Orders Regulations 2009 apply (see LEGAL AID; PUBLIC FUNDING) the funded accused may be liable to make payments under an income contribution order. If he is convicted, or if the representation order is withdrawn, he may be required to pay the whole or part of the cost of the representation under a capital contribution order. *PDC 2010, 6.1.1*

If the trial judge considers that there are exceptional reasons, an accused who is acquitted may nevertheless be required to pay the whole or part, of the costs of the representation in the Crown Court (reg.11). A contribution order must not be made for the costs of his representation to the extent that those costs are already the subject of an Recovery of Defence Costs Order (as to which, see 21–040 below). *PDC 2010, 6.1.2*

Where an accused is convicted of one or more, but not all, offences he may apply in writing to the trial judge (or a judge nominated for that purpose by the Resident Judge) for an order that he pay a proportion only of the costs of the representation in the Crown Court on the ground that it would be manifestly unreasonable that he pay the whole amount. An application must be made within 21 days of the date on which the individual is dealt with. The judge may refuse the application or make an order specifying the proportion of costs which the defendant must pay. *PDC 2010, 6.1.3*

(2) Recovery of defence costs orders

General

21–040 Recovery of defence costs orders ("RDCOs") are created and regulated by RDCOR 2001 (as amended) made under AJA 1999, s.17 An RDCO must not be made where an assessment has been made under reg. 6(1) of the CDS (Contribution Orders) Regulations 2009 (see LEGAL AID; PUBLIC FUNDING). *PDC 2010, 6.2.1*

Where a person receives representation in respect of criminal proceedings funded as part of the criminal defence service the judge before whom the proceedings are heard must make an order requiring him to pay some or all of the costs of any representation, except for the following, namely where a funded accused: *PDC 2010, 6.2.2*

- is committed for sentence to the Crown Court;
- has been acquitted, other than in exceptional circumstances; or
- is not financially liable; or
- is in receipt of a passported benefit; or
- is under the age of 18.

(RDCOR 2001, reg.4.)

Other than in circumstances where an order for the full costs must be made, the judge must not make an order where he is satisfied that it would not be reasonable to do so. He will make this decision based on the information or evidence made available to the court or where he considers that the payment of an order would involve undue financial hardship due to the exceptional circumstances of the case. Where the judge exercises his discretion in these circumstances he must give his reasons for reaching that decision: (regs 4 and 11).

Further provisions

21–041   Note that:

(1) it should be borne in mind that in proceedings to which the 2009 Regulations apply a funded accused may be liable to make payments under an income contribution order;   PDC 2010, 6.2.3

(2) if he is convicted, if the representation order is withdrawn or if the judge orders that there are exceptional reasons why the accused (although acquitted) should be liable to make payments under a contribution order, the accused may be required to reimburse the whole or part of the costs of the representation through a capital contribution order;

(3) a contribution order must not be made for the costs of an accused's representation in the Crown Court to the extent that those costs are already the subject of an RDCO; similarly an order must not be made where an assessment has been made under reg.6(1) of the 2009 Regulations;

(4) an RDCO may be made up to the maximum of the full costs of the representation in any court under the representation order and may provide for the payment to be made forthwith or in specified instalments (reg.5) this includes the cost of representation in the magistrates' court;   PDC 2010, 6.2.4

(5) subject to the exceptions set out above, the judge must make an RDCO (reg.11); he must give reasons for the terms of the order;   PDC 2010, 6.2.5

(6) where a funded accused has been acquitted, the judge must consider whether it is reasonable in all the circumstances to make such an order; where he makes an order following acquittal he must give reasons for his decision (reg.11);   PDC 2010, 6.2.6

(7) where a person of modest means properly brings an appeal against conviction or sentence it should be borne in mind that it will not usually be desirable or appropriate for the court to make an RDCO for a significant amount, if to do so would inhibit an appellant from bringing an appeal.   PDC 2010, 6.2.7

Amount and value of income and capital

21–042   The judge must consider the amount or value of every source of income and capital available to the accused. The amount or value of every source of income and every resource of a capital nature available to the accused's partner must be taken into consideration unless the partner has a contrary interest in the criminal proceeding.   PDC 2010, 6.2.8

Other than in exceptional circumstances, the judge must not take into account:

- the first £3,000 of available capital;
- the first £100,000 of equity in the principal residence; or
- his income where his gross annual income is less than £22,235: (reg.9).

COSTS AND ASSESSMENT

The judge may ask the accused's litigator to provide an estimate of the total costs which are likely to be incurred under the representation order.

PDC 2010, 6.2.9

It should be borne in mind that whilst the litigator may have little difficulty in producing an estimate of the costs incurred up until the point of request, this estimate may not be accurate. In a very high cost case (see LEGAL AID; PUBLIC FUNDING) which has been managed under contract, the litigator will be able to provide accurate figures of all costs incurred to date and to say what costs have been agreed as reasonable for the next stage of the case.

Where an RDCO is made based on this estimate the defendant's litigator must inform the Legal Services Commission (LSC) if it subsequently transpires that the costs incurred were lower than the amount ordered to be paid under an RDCO. In these circumstances, where the defendant has paid the amount ordered, the balance will be repaid to him: (reg.14).

An RDCO for full costs may be made at the end of the proceedings. The appropriate authority will tax the costs incurred under the representation order. The accused will be notified of the amount of the RDCO once this figure is known.

Referral to SIU

21–043 Where a representation order has been made or is being considered, the appropriate officer or the judge may refer the financial resources of the funded accused to the Special Investigations Unit ("SIU") at the LSC for a report, where:

PDC 2010, 6.2.10

- the accused is being prosecuted by HMRC, the SFO, or the Department for Business, Innovation and Skills or CPS HQ;
- the accused is deemed to be high risk – for example, has a wealthy lifestyle, has assets abroad or assets which are subject to a freezing order; or
- other factors are present, for example press interest, alleged terrorist activity, nature of the offence, local knowledge (where facts about the accused or linked individuals are known to the court staff), or negative disposable income.

The referral is made using a Certificate of Referral to SIU (Form C of Annex C "New Guidance to Courts on Grant of Representation and Recovery of Defence Costs Orders").

The SIU will produce a report for the judge to consider at the end of the case in the same way that the court will provide the judge with a summary of the accused's means. This report is made to support the role of the court, and is not an application for costs.

During the proceedings, the judge may refer the matter to the LSC/SIU for investigation where further information has come to light which had previously not been disclosed by the accused to the court. The SIU may investigate the financial resources of the funded accused and require him to provide further information or evidence as required.

PDC 2010, 6.2.11

Adjournment; further information

21–044   At the end of the case where the judge is considering whether, to make an order or what order to make, he may adjourn the making of the order and direct that any further information which is required should be provided (reg.7A). This power may be used where further information has come to light during the case about the accused's means.

PDC 2010, 6.2.12

Accused's obligation to provide information

21–045   The accused is obliged to provide details of his means or evidence as is required by the court or the LSC (reg.6). Arrangements are in place to ensure that a summary of the means information is available for the judge at the first hearing, or details as to whether or not the accused has provided any information. Where the funded defendant does not provide this information, the judge may order him to do so.

PDC 2010, 6.2.13–6.2.16

Where information required under the Regulations is not provided the judge must make an RDCO for the full cost of the representation incurred under the representation order (reg.13).

Where it appears to the judge that the funded accused has:

- directly or indirectly transferred any resources to another person or deprived himself of any resources or expectations;
- another person is or has been maintaining him in any proceedings; or any of the resources of another person are or have been made available to him,

the value of the resources or expectations that the accused has deprived himself of or the resources of that other person may be assessed or estimated and may be treated as those of the funded accused. In this context "person" includes a company, partnership, body of trustees and any body of persons, whether corporate or not corporate (reg.8).

The judge may make an order prohibiting any individual who is required to furnish information or evidence from dealing with property where:

- information has failed to be provided in accordance with the Regulations;
- he considers that there is a real risk that relevant property will be disposed of; or
- at the conclusion of the case, the assessment of costs incurred under the representation order or of the financial resources of the accused has not yet been completed (reg.15).

7.   Costs in restraint, confiscation or receivership proceedings

The order for costs

21–046   Special provisions apply where a judge is deciding whether to make an order for costs in relation to restraint or receivership proceedings brought under POCA 2002 (confiscation proceedings are treated for costs purposes as part of the trial).

PDC 2010, 7.1.1

The judge has a discretion as to: whether costs are payable by one party to another; the amount of those costs; and, when they are to be paid. The general rule is that if the judge decides to make an order about costs the unsuccessful party will be ordered to pay the costs of the successful party but the judge may make a different order: CPR 2011, r. 61.19(3)

Attention is drawn to the fact that in receivership proceedings the Rules provide that the Crown Court may make orders in respect of security to be given by a receiver to cover his liability for his acts and omissions as a receiver: r.60.5. The judge may also make orders in relation to determining the remuneration of the receiver: r.60.6. (See 21–048 below.) PDC 2010, 7.1.2

In deciding what if any order to make about costs the judge is required to have regard to all the circumstances including the conduct of all the parties and whether a party has succeeded on part of an application, even if that party has not been wholly successful. PDC 2010, 7.1.3–7.1.6

The Rules set out the type of order which the court may make (the list is not exclusive):

- (a) a proportion of another party's costs;
- (b) a stated amount in respect of another party's costs;
- (c) costs from or until a certain date only;
- (d) costs incurred before proceedings have begun;
- (e) costs relating to particular steps taken in the proceedings;
- (f) costs relating only to a distinct part of the proceedings; and
- (g) interest on costs from or until a certain date including a date before the making of an order.

The judge is required, where it is practicable, to award a proportion (e.g., a percentage) of the costs, or costs between certain dates, rather than making an order relating only to a distinct part or issue in the proceedings. The latter type of order makes it extremely difficult for the costs to be assessed. Where the judge orders a party to pay costs he may, in addition, order an amount to be paid on account by one party to another before the costs are assessed. Where he makes such an order, the order should state the amount to be paid and the date on or before which payment is to be made.

Assessment of costs

21–047 Where the judge makes an order for costs in restraint, or receivership, proceedings he may make an assessment of the costs itself there and then (a summary assessment), or order assessment of the costs under r.76.11 (r.61.20(1)). If the judge neither makes an assessment of the costs nor orders assessment as specified above, the order for costs will be treated as an order for the amount of costs to be decided by assessment under r.76.11 unless the order otherwise provides. Whenever the judge awards costs to be assessed he should consider whether to exercise the power to order the paying party to pay such sum of money as he thinks just, on account of those costs. PDC 2010, 7.2.1–7.2.2

In carrying out the assessment of costs the judge or the assessing authority is required to allow only costs which are proportionate to the matters in issue, and to resolve any doubt which he may have, as to whether the costs were reasonably incurred or were reasonable and proportionate in amount, in favour of the paying party. PDC 2010, 7.2.3

The judge or assessing authority carrying out the assessment should have regard to all the circumstances in deciding whether costs were proportionately or reasonably incurred or proportionate and reasonable in amount. Effect must be given to any orders for costs which have already been made. PDC 2010, 7.2.4

The judge or the assessing authority should also have regard to:

(a) the conduct of all the parties, including in particular conduct before as well as during the proceedings;
(b) the amount or value of any property involved;
(c) the importance of the matter to all the parties;
(d) the particular complexity of the matter or the difficulty or novelty of the questions raised;
(e) the skill, effort, specialised knowledge and responsibility involved;
(f) the time spent on the case; and
(g) the place where and the circumstances in which work or any part of it was done.

In applying the test of proportionality regard should be had to the objective of dealing with cases justly. Dealing with a case justly includes, so far as practicable, dealing with it in ways which are proportionate to: PDC 2010, 7.2.5–7.2.7

- the amount of money involved;
- the importance of the case;
- the complexity of the issues; and
- the financial position of each party.

The relationship between the total of the costs incurred and the financial value of the claim may not be a reliable guide.

In any proceedings there will be costs which will inevitably be incurred and which are necessary for the successful conduct of the case. Litigators are not required to conduct litigation at rates which are uneconomic, thus in a modest claim the proportion of costs is likely to be higher than in a large claim and may even equal or possibly exceed the amount in dispute. Where a hearing takes place, the time taken by the court in dealing with a particular issue may not be an accurate guide to the amount of time properly spent by the legal or other representatives in preparing for the trial of that issue.

CPR 2011 do not apply to the assessment of costs in proceedings to the extent that AJA 1999, s.11 (costs in funded cases) applies and statutory instruments made under that Act make different provision (in this regard attention is drawn to the guidance notes issued by the Senior Costs Judge: Costs Orders Against an LSC Funded Client and against the LSC under AJA 1999, s.11(l)). PDC 2010, 7.2.8

Remuneration of a receiver

21–048 A receiver may only charge for his services if the Crown Court so directs and specifies the basis on which the receiver is to be remunerated (r.60.6(2)). The Crown Court (unless it orders otherwise) is required to award such sum as is reasonable and proportionate in all the circumstances. In arriving at the figure for remuneration the judge should take into account: PDC 2010, 7.3.1

- the time properly given by the receiver and his staff to the receivership
- the complexity of the receivership;
- any responsibility of an exceptional kind or degree which falls on the receiver in consequence of the receivership;
- the effectiveness with which the receiver appears to be carrying out or to have carried out his duties; and
- the value and nature of the subject matter of the receivership.

The Crown Court may instead of determining the receiver's remuneration itself refer it to be ascertained by the assessing authority of the Crown Court.   PDC 2010, 7.3.2

In these circumstances rr.76.11 to 76.13 (which deal with review by the assessing authority, further review by a Costs Judge and appeal to a High Court Judge) have effect.

Procedure on appeal to CACD

21–049   The costs of, and incidental to, all proceedings on an appeal CACD against orders made in restraint proceedings, or appeals against or relating to the making of receivership orders, are in the discretion of the court (POCA 2002, s.89(4)). The court has full power to determine by whom and to what extent the costs are to be paid.   PDC 2010, 7.4.1

In any such proceedings the court may disallow or (as the case may be) order the legal or other representative concerned to meet the whole of any wasted costs or such part of them as may be determined in accordance with CPR 2011.   PDC 2010, 7.4.2

(As to wasted costs orders see 21–022 above.)

8.   Advice on appeal to CACD

21–050   In all cases the procedure set out in "A Guide to Proceedings in the Court of Appeal (Criminal Division)" published by the Criminal Appeal Office with the approval of the Lord Chief Justice should be followed, together with PDC 2010, Pt 8.

9.   VAT

21–051   Every taxable person as defined by the VATA 1994 must be registered and in general terms (subject to the exceptions set out in the 1994 Act) whenever a taxable person supplies goods or services in the United Kingdom in the course of business a liability to VAT arises. See PDC 2010, Pt 9.

10.   Enforcement and challenge

Search; time to pay; instalments

21–052   The enforcement of costs is a matter for the appropriate magistrates' court, but where a judge of the Crown Court makes an order against an accused for the payment of costs, he may: AJA 1970, s.41(1)(2)

(1) if the person against whom the costs have been awarded is present in court, order him to be searched and, unless the court otherwise directs, any money found on him will be applied towards payment of the costs;

(2) allow time to pay the sum due under the order; or

(3) direct payment by instalments of such amounts and on such dates as he may specify.

Payment by parent or guardian

21–053   Where a young person is found guilty of an offence, the court must order any costs awarded to be paid by the parent or guardian (see CHILDREN AND YOUNG PERSONS).

Appeal against award of costs

21–054   An appeal lies to CACD by an offender convicted on indictment and ordered to contribute towards the costs of the prosecution; no appeal lies by an accused tried on indictment and ordered to contribute towards the costs of his publicly funded defence (*R. v Hayden* (1974) 60 Cr. App. R. 304).

An order for costs made in relation to proceedings on indictment may not be challenged by a quashing order in the High Court.

11.   Costs from Central Funds and relevant Statutory Authorities: PDC 2010, Sch.2

21–055

Proceedings	Court	Extent of Availability	Authority
Information not proceeded with	Magistrates'	Defendant	S.16(1)(a) POA 1985
Decision not to commit for trial	Magistrates'	Defendant	S.16(1)(b) POA 1985
Dismissal of information	Magistrates'	Defendant	S.16(1)(c) POA 1985
Person indicted or committed for trial but not tried	Crown	Defendant	S.16(2)(a) POA 1985
Notice of transfer given but person not tried	Crown	Defendant	S.16(2)(aa) POA 1985
Acquittal on indictment	Crown	Defendant	S.16(2)(b) POA 1985
Successful appeal to the Crown Court against conviction or sentence	Crown	Appellant	S.16(3) POA 1985
Successful appeal to CACD against conviction or sentence or insanity/disability finding	CACD	Appellant	S.16(4) POA 1985
Appeal against order or ruling at preparatory hearing	CACD	Appellant	S.16(4A) POA 1985
Application for leave to appeal to Supreme Court	CACD	Appellant	S.16(5)(c) POA 1985
Attorney General reference to CACD on point of law following acquittal	CACD, Supreme Court	Acquitted Defendant	S.36(5) CJA 1972

Attorney-General reference under s.36 CJA 1988 (lenient sentence appeals)	CACD	Sch.3 para.11 CJA 1988
Determination of proceedings in a criminal cause or matter in Divisional Court	Divisional Court	S.16(5)(a) POA 1985
Determination of appeal or application for leave to appeal from CACD or DC	Supreme Court	S.16(5)(b) and (c) POA 1985
Proceedings in respect of an indictable offence	Magistrates' and Crown	S.17(1)(a) POA 1985
Proceedings before DC or Supreme Court (following summary offence)	Divisional Court and Supreme Court	S.17(1)(b) POA 1985
Criminal cause or matter	All	S.19(3) POA 1985 – there are restrictions on what may be paid (see regs 18, 19, 20, 21, 24 and 25 CCC (General) Regulations 1986.
Murder case	Crown	S.34(5) MH(A)A 1982
Criminal Procedure (Insanity) Act proceedings	Crown	S.19(3)(d) POA 1985
Cross examination of vulnerable witnesses	Magistrates' and Crown	S.19(3)(e) POA 1985
Compensation where a court refuses an application for a banning order	Magistrates' and Crown Court (on appeal where compensation refused by the magistrates' court).	S.21D Football Spectators Act 1989
Compensation where loss results from closure notice or order or Part 1A closure notice or order	Magistrates' court and Crown Court on appeal	SS.10 and 11J Anti Social Behaviour Act 2003
Costs where discharge ordered	Magistrates' court, High Court, Supreme Court	S.62 Extradition Act 2003

Notes

22. COURT SECURITY OFFICERS

General

22–001   Court security officers may be appointed and designated   CA 2003, s.51
by the Lord Chancellor. An officer must be readily identifiable as
such (whether by means of his uniform or badge or otherwise),
otherwise he is not to be regarded as acting in the execution of his
duty.

It is an offence (s.57) to assault (fine on level 5), resist or wilfully
obstruct (a fine on level 3) a court security officer acting in the execution of his duty.

Powers of search

22–002   A court security officer, acting in the execution of his duty   CA 2003, s.52
may search:

(1) any person who is in, or is seeking to enter, a court building;
    and
(2) any article in the possession of such a person,

such power does not authorise him to require a person to remove
any of his clothing other than a coat, jacket, headgear, gloves or
footwear.

"Court building," here, means *any* building where the business of
any of the courts referred to in CA 2003, s.1, which includes the Senior
Courts (formerly the Supreme Court), of which the Crown Court is one,
carried on, and to which the public has access.

Powers to exclude, remove or restrain persons

22–003   An officer acting in the execution of his duty may exclude or   CA 2003, s.53
remove from a court building, or a part of a court building, any person
who refuses:

(1) to permit a search under s.52(1); or
(2) to surrender an article in his possession when asked to do so
    under s.54(1) (below); and may also:
    (a) restrain any person who is in a court building; or
    (b) exclude or remove any person from a court building, or a
        part of a court building,

if it is reasonably necessary to do so to:

    (i)   enable court business to be carried on without interfer-
        ence or delay;
    (ii) maintain order; or
    (iii) secure the safety of any person in the court building.

An officer acting in the execution of his duty may remove any person
from a courtroom at the request of the court.

These powers include a power to use reasonable force, where
necessary.

COURT SECURITY OFFICERS

Surrender and seizure of articles

22–004 An officer acting in the execution of his duty, and reasonably CA 2003, s.54 believing that an article in the possession of a person who is in, or seeking to enter, a court building, ought to be surrendered on the ground that it may:

(1) jeopardise the maintenance of order in the court building (or a part of it); or
(2) put the safety of any person in the court building at risk; or
(3) be evidence of, or in relation to, an offence,

must ask the person to surrender the article; if that person refuses to surrender the article, the officer may seize it.

Powers to retain articles surrendered or seized

22–005 An officer may retain an article which was: CA 2003, s.55

(1) surrendered in response to a request under s.54(1); or
(2) seized under s.54(2),

until the time when the person who surrendered it, or from whom it was seized, is leaving the court building, but if he reasonably believes that the article may be evidence of, or in relation to, an offence, he may retain it until the time when the person who surrendered it, or from whom it was seized, is leaving the court building, or the end of the permitted period, whichever is later.

The "permitted period" is such period, not exceeding 24 hours from the time the article was surrendered or seized, as will enable the court security officer to draw the article to the attention of a constable.

23. CUSTODY TIME LIMITS

General

23–001   POA 1985 and the regulations made thereunder (SI 1987/299 amended by SI 1999/2744, SI 1999/2743) prescribe time limits during which an accused may be held in custody before being invited to tender pleas. The Regulations also limit the time during which the accused can be kept in custody. "Custody" includes remand, or committal to local authority accommodation) of the magistrates' court or of the Crown Court, in relation to specified stages of the proceedings.

Subject to CJPOA 1994, s.25 (which disapplies these regulations—*R. (O) v Harrow CC* [2006] UKHL 42, [2007] 1 Cr. App. R. 9) an accused is entitled to be released on bail where a custody time limit and any extension to it, expires, but his release requires an order of the court. As to the duties of the prosecution (see SI 1987/299, reg.6). Where the prosecution fails to act, the accused will need to apply for bail to the Crown Court or go to the High Court by way of judicial review (*Olotu v Home Office* [1997] All E.R. 385).

Note that the expiry of a time limit does not necessarily give rise to a breach of ECHR, art 5(3) in relation to trial within a reasonable time (*R. (O) v Harrow CC* [2003] EWHC 868 (Admin), [2003] 1 W.L.R. 2756).

Objectives

23–002   The objectives of the legislation are threefold, to:

(1) ensure that any periods during which an unconvicted person is held in custody awaiting trial are as short as is reasonably and practicably possible;
(2) oblige the prosecution to prepare its case for trial with all due diligence and expedition; and
(3) invest the court with the power and duty to control any extension of the maximum period under the regulations for which such a person may be held in custody awaiting trial.

These are very important objectives, and a judge making a decision on the extension of custody time-limits (see 23–009 below) must be careful to give full weight to all three (*R. v Manchester CC Ex p. McDonald* [1999] 1 Cr. App. R. 409). See further under CASE MANAGEMENT.

The court has a statutory duty to ensure that:

(a) trials involving unconvicted accused held in custody take place promptly and wherever possible within the original limit, and
(b) that a person is not detained beyond the expiry of the original limit unless it has been properly extended.

In order to help meet the challenges faced by criminal justice agencies in dealing with cases that have custody time limits, a joint HMCS

CUSTODY TIME LIMITS

CPS Protocol has been developed for the handling of these cases. The protocol took effect from April 1, 2009.

Crown Court limits

23–003 Although the Regulations set a uniform 112 day limit between the last hearing at the magistrates' court and the start of the trial in the Crown Court, the way in which the time is calculated is slightly different depending upon the type of case.

PD 2004, Annex F

In relation to each of the following circumstances, each offence charged for each accused attracts its own time limit. If an indictment contains two offences charged which were sent separately, then both offences charged will have differing custody time limit dates:

(1) the maximum period for which the accused can be held in custody when committed for trial to the Crown Court is 112 days (reg.5(3)(a));

(2) the maximum period an accused can be held in the custody of the magistrates' courts in relation to an indictable only offence is 70 days (reg.4(2) and (4));

(3) where an indictable only case is sent for trial under CDA 1998, s.51, the maximum period of custody the maximum period of custody between being sent to the Crown Court is 182 days less any period previously spent in the custody of the magistrates' court for the relevant offence;

(4) where a voluntary bill is preferred, the 112 day time period runs from the date of preferment of the indictment (reg.5(3)(b));

(5) cases transferred from the magistrates' to the Crown Court have a custody time limit of 112 days;

(6) cases transferred between Crown Court centres retain the original custody time limit date; and,

(7) in cases where a retrial is ordered by CACD the custody time limit is 112 days starting from the date that the new indictment is preferred, i.e. from the date that the indictment is delivered to the Crown Court.

Where a case has been sent for trial and the indictment contains counts:

(a) alleging offences which were sent on different occasions—the time limit applies to each count separately;

(b) which were not included in the case sent for trial—the maximum period between the preferment of the bill of indictment, or the addition of the count, and the offender's arraignment is 112 days, less the aggregate of any periods during which, since he was sent for trial, he has been in the custody of the Crown Court in relation to an offence for which he was sent for trial.

The "maximum period" laid down does not include the day on which custody commenced, and a custody time limit which would otherwise expire on a Saturday, Sunday, Christmas Day, Good Friday or a bank holiday, is treated as expiring on the nearest preceding day which is not one of those days.

350

The prosecutor may apply to the judge before expiry for an extension to the custody time limit period (see 23–009 below).

The "start of the trial"

23–004 The "start of a trial" on indictment is taken to occur (subject to CJA 1988, s.8 and CPIA 1996, s.28 (preparatory hearings)) when: POA 1985, 22(11)(11A)(11B)

(1) a jury is sworn and the accused is put in the charge of the jury;
(2) when a jury would have been sworn but for the making of an order under CJA 2003, Pt 7 (trials without a jury); or
(3) the judge accepts a guilty plea.

When the court is to consider fitness to plead, the trial starts when a jury is sworn, and not at the time when the court first begins to hear evidence.

If a preparatory hearing is ordered under CJA 1988, s.8, or CPIA 1996, s.28, the trial is deemed to start with that hearing, and arraignment takes place then if it has not taken place before (CJA 1988, s.8, CPIA 1996, s.31).

The custody time limits still run when young offenders are remanded to the care of the local authority and in the case of transfers and remands under MHA ss.35 and 36.

The start of a trial on indictment occurs:

(1) subject to CJA 1988, s.8 and CPIA 1996, s.28 (in relation to preparatory hearings) at the time when a jury is sworn to consider the issue of guilt or fitness to plead or, if the judge accepts a plea before the time when a jury is sworn, when that plea is accepted;
(2) if a preparatory hearing is ordered under: CJA 1988, s.8, or CPIA 1996, s.28 (see CASE MANAGEMENT), the trial starts with that hearing, and arraignment takes place then if it has not taken place before (CJA 1988, s.8, CPIA 1996, s.31);
(3) in the case of a trial without a jury when a jury would be sworn but for the making of an order under CJA 2003, Pt 7.

In the event of a trial being aborted, the judge should be vigilant to take steps in fixing a speedy retrial, or, if there are difficulties about such a course, considering the grant of bail or, in an appropriate case, staying the prosecution as an abuse of process (*R. v Leeds CC Ex p. Whitehead* (2000) 164 J.P. 102).

When DVA 2003 abolished trial by jury of an issue of unfitness to plead raised on arraignment it seems that POA 1985, s.22(11A), in respect of the start of a trial on indictment, was not amended.

Where the limits do not apply

23–005 Where a person: POA 1985, s.22(5)(6)

(1) escapes from the custody of a magistrates' court or the Crown Court before the expiry of a limit which applies in his case; or
(2) having been released on bail in consequence of the expiry of a custody time limit (see 23–015 below), fails to surrender at the appointed time, or is arrested for breach of bail,

and is accordingly at large, the following periods, namely:

(a) the period for which the person is unlawfully at large; and
(b) such additional period (if any) as the court may direct, having
    regard to the disruption of the prosecution occasioned by:
    (i) that person's escape or failure to surrender; and
    (ii) the length of the period mentioned in (i), above.

must be disregarded so far as the offence in question is concerned for
the purposes of the overall time-limit which applies in his case in relation to the stage which the proceedings have reached at the time of the
escape or, as the case may be, at the appointed time.

The fact that the accused is in custody for other matters does not
prevent the time-limit running (*R. v Peterborough CC Ex p. L* [2000]
Crim. L.R. 470). *POA 1985, s.22(6A)*

Where, following the initial charge(s) on which the accused first
appeared before the magistrates, another charge is added, then irrespective of its nature, or when it was added, subject only to the accused
being able to show abuse of process, a new custody time-limit is
created (*R. v Leeds CC Ex p. Wardle* [2001] UKHL 12, [2001] 2 Cr.
App. R. 20).

In relation to prosecution appeals (under CJA 2003, Pt 9) any
period during which proceedings for an offence are adjourned
pending the determination of an appeal will be disregarded so far as
the offence is concerned, for the purpose of the custody time limit
which applies to the stage where proceedings have reached when
they are adjourned.

Expiry of time limit

SI 1987/299, reg.6(6)

23–006 On being notified that:

(1) an accused who is in custody pending trial;
(2) has the benefit of a custody time limit under reg.5; and
(3) the time limit is about to expire,

a judge of the Crown Court must grant that person bail in accordance
with BA 1976 as modified for the purpose (see BAIL), with effect from
the expiry of the limit, subject to a duty to appear before the Crown
Court for trial. Where this situation arises, the prosecution will need to
decide *before* the expiry of the limit, whether:

(a) to apply for an extension, or further extension, of the time
    limit; or
(b) to apply for conditions to be attached to the bail granted to
    the accused.

Application for extension

SI 1987/299, reg.7

23–007 An application by the prosecution for the extension, or further
extension, of a time limit may be made orally or in writing:

(1) *before* the relevant time-limit has expired (*R. v Peterborough CC
    Ex p. L*, see above);
(2) by giving, not less than five days before making the application,
    notice in writing to the accused or his representative, and to the

Crown Court officer of his intention to make the application; unless

(3) the accused or his representative informs the Crown that he does not require such notice; or

(4) a judge is satisfied on a balance of probabilities (*Re Craig* (1991) 91 Cr. App. R. 7) that it is not practicable for the prosecution to comply and directs either that the Crown need not comply, or specifies a lesser minimum period.

In the case of an application based on the length and complexity of the case, though reg.7 does not require it, it is good practice to give the grounds in the notice (*R. v CCC Ex p. Marotta* [1998] 10 Arch. News 2). Bail Act considerations have no place under these provisions (*R. (Eliot) v Reading CC* [2001] EWHC 464 (Admin), [2002] 1 Cr. App. R. 3).

Successive applications

23–008 It is not:

(1) normally permissible, when an application is refused, for an application to be made to a second judge on the same grounds, but see *R. v Bradford CC Ex p. Crossling* [2000] 1 Cr. App. R. 463 (where the first judge may have acted on misleading information);

(2) permissible, where the High Court has reviewed a judge's decision, for a further application to be made to a judge of the Crown Court.

(*R. v Peterborough CC Ex p. L*, above; cf. *R. v Leeds CC Ex p. Wandle*, above.)

Grounds for extension of period

23–009 A time limit may be extended or further extended by a judge of the Crown Court, *at any time before* its expiry (*R. v Croydon CC Ex p. Commrs of Customs & Excise* [1997] 8 Arch. News 1, DC), but not unless he is satisfied on the balance of probabilities:

(1) that the need for the extension is due to:
   (a) the illness or absence of the accused, a necessary witness, or a judge;
   (b) a postponement which is occasioned by the ordering by the court of separate trials in the case of two or more accused or two or more offences; or
   (c) some other good and sufficient cause; and

(2) that the prosecution has acted with all due diligence and expedition (*R. v Norwich CC Ex p. Parker and Ward* (1993) 96 Cr. App. R. 68; *R. v CCC Ex p. Behbehani* [1994] Crim. L.R. 352; *R. v CCC Ex p. Belle Lane* [1994] Crim. L.R. 352; *R. v Leeds CC Ex p. Briggs (Ronald) (No.2)* [1998] 2 Cr. App. R. 424).

"Good and sufficient cause", and "due diligence and expedition" are two distinct issues, and require both separate consideration and a separate ruling. "Good cause" will not avail the Crown, if they have not acted with "due expedition" (*R. v CCC Ex p. Bennett*, *The Times*, January 25, 1999).

"Good and sufficient cause" interpreted

23–010   The words are not susceptible of a precise definition (*R. v Norwich CC Ex p. Ricketts* [1990] Crim. L.R. 715). It will be a matter of fact in each case (*McKay White v DPP* [1989] Crim. L.R. 375). See also *R. v Norwich CC Ex p. Cox* (1993) 97 Cr. App. R. 145; cf. *R. v Maidstone CC Ex p. Schultz* (1993) 157 J.P. 601; *R. v Governor of Belmarsh Prison Ex p. Gilligan* [2000] 1 All E.R. 113, HL. Thus:

(1) an almost infinite number of matters may, depending on the facts, constitute such cause, though: e.g.:
   (a) the seriousness of the offence; or
   (b) the need to protect the public; or
   (c) the fact that the extension sought is only a short one, are not amongst them (*R. v Manchester CC Ex p. McDonald* [1999] 1 Cr. App. R. 409); and
(2) matters relevant to the granting or refusing of bail cannot of themselves provide good and sufficient cause for extending a time limit (*R. v Sheffield CC Ex p. Headley* [2000] 2 Cr. App. R. 1).

The unavailability of a suitable judge or court-room, may, in special cases and on appropriate facts, amount to such a cause, see 23–012 below under "listing difficulties."

"Due diligence and expedition"

23–011   "Due diligence" is not the same as "due expedition". To fulfil the test of "due expedition" it is not enough to show that the prosecuting authorities "are doing their best." The test needs to be measured against some yardstick, or the object of the Act is defeated (*R. v Southampton CC Ex p. Roddie* (1991) 93 Cr. App. R. 190; *R. v Sheffield MC Ex p. Turner* (1991) 93 Cr. App. R. 180. See also *R. v CCC Ex p. Behbehani* [1994] Crim. L.R. 352).

"All due expedition" requires the diligence and expedition which would be shown by a competent prosecutor conscious of his duty to bring the case to trial as quickly and fairly as possible (*R. v Manchester CC Ex p. McDonald etc.*, above).

Note that:

(1) delay on the part of an independent third party, such as a forensic laboratory (*R. v CCC Ex p Johnson* [1999] 2 Cr. App. R. 51) or an expert witness (*R. (on the application of Hadfield) v Manchester CC* [2007] EWHC 2408 (Admin); *R. (on the application of Alexander) v Isleworth CC* [2009] Crim. L.R. 583) is not directly relevant to the question whether the prosecutor has acted with "due expedition", though he should take every possible step to ensure that any relevant evidence was available on time *R. (on the application of Clarke) v Lewes CC* [2009] EWHC 805 (Admin);
(2) the reference to the Crown having acted "with all due expedition" refers to the time up to the making of the application to extend the limit, not to the issue of whether future delay may be

caused by acceding to the application (*R. v Woolwich CC Ex p. Gilligan* (above));

(3) lack of due diligence and expedition will not be fatal if it has no causal connection with the need for an extension (*R. (Gibson) v Winchester CC* [2004] EWHC 361 (Admin); [2004] 2 Cr. App. R. 14).

Listing difficulties

23–012 The superior courts have held (see *R. v CCC Ex p. Abu-Wardeh* [1999] 1 Cr. App. R. 43; *R. v Manchester CC*, above; *R. v Winchester CC*, above; *Kalonji v Wood Green CC* [2007] EWHC 2804 (Admin)) that the unavailability of a suitable judge, or a suitable courtroom in which to try an accused in custody, is capable, in special cases, and on appropriate facts, of amounting to a "good and sufficient cause" for extending the time limits though any such application should be rigorously examined.

In such circumstances:

(1) the judge should approach such grounds with great caution, as there is obviously a danger that the purposes of the statute will be undermined by too readily granting extensions on this basis;
(2) the fact that witnesses are professional investigators does not make their convenience, particularly with regard to other duties, irrelevant;
(3) where the application is made on the basis that the case clashes with another, the prosecutor will need to show why the other case requires priority (*R. v Stoke-on-Trent CC Ex p. Marden* [1999] 1 Arch. News 2; *R. v Croydon YC Ex p. C* [2001] Crim. L.R. 40);
(4) many of the problems which arise in this area can be obviated by fixing an early date for the trial.

Clearly before a court is prepared to grant an extension because of the lack of availability of a courtroom, or a particular judge required to try the case, it should go to considerable endeavours to avoid having to postpone the trial to a date beyond the custody time limits. However, it has to be remembered that the availability of a particular category of judge can be important for the achievement of justice in particular cases, e.g. where a High Court judge is required. While expedition is important, so is the quality of the justice which will be provided at the trial. In these circumstances it is necessary for a judge considering an application for an extension of custody time limits to evaluate the importance of the judge of the required calibre being available. (*R. (Gibson) v Winchester Crown Court* [2004] EWHC 361 (Admin), [2004] 2 Cr. App. R. 14).

The courts cannot ignore the fact that available resources are limited. They cannot ignore the fact that occasions will occur when pressures on the court will be more intense than they usually are. In such a situation it is important that the courts and the parties strive to overcome any difficulties that occur.

CUSTODY TIME LIMITS

Fixing a date

23–013 In *R. v Worcester CC Ex p. Norman* [2000] 2 Cr. App. R. 33, it was said that there is a joint duty on the prosecutor and on the court to make early arrangements for the fixing of a trial date within the custody time limits:

(1) ideally, the date should be fixed at the PCMH with the directions then being tailored to the date that has been fixed;
(2) if it is impossible to fix a date at the PCMH the judge should direct that the date be fixed on a date before the expiration of the custody time limit and that the matter should be re-listed in the event of a failure to agree such a date;
(3) if the fixing of a date within the custody time limit is impossible, this should be appreciated at an early date and an application to extend made sooner rather than later, thereby enhancing the prospect of a date being fixed as soon as possible after the expiry of the limit;
(4) if the court fails to take the initiative, it is for the prosecutor to press for a date within the time limit, the duty on the defence being to provide the names of witnesses required so that their availability can be ascertained.

As legal argument may delay the swearing in of a jury, it is desirable to extend custody time limits to a date later than the first day of the trial.

The hearing of the application to extend

23–014 Bearing in mind the overriding purposes of the legislation (see 23–002, above) a judge, invested with the power and duty of controlling any extension:

(1) needs to be satisfied, on a balance of probabilities, that both the conditions in s.22(3) are made out, before exercising his discretion;
(2) must not abdicate his responsibility to address the issues by granting the application on the nod, because the parties agree, or because there is no objection to this course (*R. v Manchester CC*, above);
(3) should consider all matters directly and genuinely bearing on the preparation of the case for trial, bearing in mind that:
  (a) the time limit is a maximum not a target; and
  (b) the prosecutor is not required to show that every stage has been completed as quickly and efficiently as is humanly possible, though
  (c) no attention should be paid to excuses such as staff shortages, sickness, etc.;
(4) may need to hear evidence or may, according to the circumstances of the case, be able to rely on information supplied by the advocates. It is for the prosecutor to decide which witnesses to call on the application, and the defence are not entitled to require specific witnesses to be called (*R. v Chelmsford CC* [2001] EWHC 1115 (Admin), [2002] Crim. L.R. 485);

(5) may, if, but only if, he is so satisfied, exercise his discretion to extend the time-limit. If he is not satisfied he may not, but, if he is satisfied he may, but need not, extend the time limit (*R. v Manchester CC*, above), and

(6) must give brief reasons for his ruling, indicating the way in which he has reached his conclusions (*R. v Leeds CC Ex p. Briggs* [1998] 2 Cr. App. R. 424).

Where the judge is considering a *further* extension, he has to consider those matters giving rise to that *further* extension. In relation to delay prior to an earlier extension, while it may relied on by the accused in any challenge, needs to be relied on as the root cause of the need to seek a *further* extension. (*R. (Thomas) v CCC* [2006] EWHC 2138 (Admin), [2007] 1 Cr. App. R. 7). SI 1987/299, reg.6(1), (2), (3), (4), (5)

There may be cases where, even though there has been avoidable delay, an extension will not be refused.

Conditions of bail

23–015 An application by the prosecution for conditions to be attached to the bail granted to an accused where the time limits have expired is made:

(1) by giving notice in writing not less than five days before the expiry of the time limit, to the appropriate Crown Court officer and to the accused or his representative;

(2) stating whether or not it intends to ask the Crown Court to impose conditions, and, if it does, the nature of the conditions sought; and

(3) making arrangements for the accused to be brought before the Crown Court within the period of two days preceding the expiry of the time limit.

The prosecutor need not comply with (1) above if it has given notice of its intention to apply for an extension, or further extension, of the limit; it need not comply with (2) if the judge so directs. If the judge is satisfied that it is not practicable, in all the circumstances, for the prosecution to comply with (1) he may so direct, or specify a lesser minimum period.

On receiving notice that the prosecution intends to ask the court to impose conditions on the grant of bail, the accused or his representative must:

(a) give notice in writing to the Crown Court officer and to the prosecution, that the accused wishes to be represented at the hearing of the application; or

(b) give notice to the appropriate officer, and to the prosecution, stating that the accused does not wish to oppose the application; or

(c) give to the appropriate officer, for the consideration of the Crown Court a written statement of the accused's reasons for opposing the application, sending a copy of the statement, at the same time, to the prosecution.

Custody Time Limits

357

Appeal to the Crown Court from the magistrates' court

23–016 An appeal brought:

(1) by an accused under POA 1985, s.22(7) against a decision of the R.20.1(1)(2)
magistrates' court to extend, or further extend, a time limit
imposed by the 1987 Regulations; or

(2) by the prosecution under POA 1985, s.22(8) against a decision
refusing to extend or further extend such a time limit,

is commenced by the appellant's giving notice in writing of appeal:

(a) to the designated officer of the magistrates' court which took R.20.1(3)
the decision;

(b) if the appeal is brought by the accused, to the prosecutor,
and if the prosecution is being carried on by the CPS, to the
appropriate Crown Prosecutor;

(c) if the appeal is brought by the prosecution, to the accused;
and

(d) to the Crown Court officer.

23–017 The notice of appeal must state: R.20.1(5)

(1) the date on which the time limit applicable to the case is due to
expire; and

(2) if the appeal is brought by the accused under POA 1985, s.22(7),
the date on which the time limit would have expired had the
magistrates' court decided not to extend, or further extend, the
time limit.

On receiving the notice of appeal, the Crown Court officer will enter the R.20.1(5)
appeal, and give notice of the time and place of the hearing to the appellant, the other party to the appeal and the clerk to the magistrates' court
which took the decision.

Without prejudice to the power of the Crown Court to give leave for
an appeal to be abandoned (see APPEALLATE JURISDICTION), an
appellant may abandon an appeal under these provisions by giving
notice in writing to any person to whom the notice of appeal was
required to be given, not later than the third day preceding the day fixed BA 1976,
for the hearing of the appeal (disregarding any Saturday, Sunday or s.3(10); SI
bank holiday in England and Wales). 1987/299

Judge's action on allowing appeal

23–018 Where:

(1) the prosecutor successfully appeals a grant of bail by the magistrates' court the judge must stipulate a date (within the powers
of the magistrates under MCA 1980, ss.128, 128A and 129) as
a remand date on which the accused is to be brought before the
magistrates' court (*R. v Manchester MC Ex p. Szakal* [2000] 1
Cr. App. R. 248);

(2) the accused successfully appeals, and is admitted to
bail by reason of the expiry of the custody time limit,
the judge's powers to impose conditions on the grant are
restricted.

There is no power to require a surety for his surrender, or power to require the accused to give security for his surrender under BA 1976, s.3(4), (5). He may be required, however, after (not before) his release, to comply with any other conditions of bail appropriate under s.3(6).

Notes

24. DANGEROUS OFFENDERS; PROTECTIVE SENTENCES

Quick guide

1. Introduction

General

24–001 "Protective" sentences which exceed the normal determinate sentence of imprisonment are provided by both PCC(S)A 2000 and CJA 2003, for both dangerous and persistent offenders. The provisions of PCC(S)A 2000, which now apply only to offences committed before April 4, 2005 have been overtaken by the provisions of CJA 2003, and are no longer dealt with in this work.

Amendments tabled by the Justice Secretary in the last days of October to the Legal Aid etc. Bill 2011 now before Parliament propose the repeal of the existing sentences for dangerous offenders and their replacement by new forms of sentence.

CJA 2003, ss.224–229

24–002 Specified violent or sexual offences committed on or after April 4, 2005, attract the provisions of CJA 2003, ss.224 to 229, as modified by CJIA 2008, Pt 2, namely.

(1) a sentence of life imprisonment;
(2) imprisonment (or in the case of a juvenile, detention) for public protection; or
(3) an extended sentence.

A sentence of imprisonment or detention for public protection is essentially concerned with future risk and public protection; although punitive in its effect, strictly speaking it does not represent punishment for past offending,

The assessment of future risk must necessarily be based on the information available to the judge, who, once he has evaluated it, must direct his decision not to the past, but to the future, and future protection of the public (*R. v Johnson* [2006] EWCA Crim 2486, [2007] 1 Cr. App. R. (S.) 112; *Att Gen's Reference (No. 55 of 2008)* [2008] EWCA Crim 2790, [2009] 2 Cr. App. R. (S.) 22).

CJIA 2008, Pt 2, substantially reduces the potency of the original provisions by making most of the powers discretionary rather than mandatory, by inserting new conditions to be met and by removing the presumption of "dangerousness". Authorities pre-dating the 2008 Act need to be read in the light of these amendments.

Note that:

(a) if, in relation to a dangerous offender, the requirements of MHA 1983 are satisfied, the judge may dispose of the case by means of a hospital order under ibid. s.37 (see MENTALLY DISORDERED OFFENDERS)

(b) where an offender is to be sentenced for several offences, only some of which are "specified", the judge who imposes an indeterminate sentence under ss.225 or 226 or an extended sentence under ss.227 or 228, for the principal offences should generally impose shorter concurrent sentences for the other offences; in the case of a specified offence where there is a risk of serious harm, the sentence for such other offence must be an extended sentence where the principal offence is a "serious" offence (s.227(2)).

As to the "protective" sentences under PCC(S)A 2000, reference may be made to the 2007 edition.

As to offences spanning the commencement date of the 2003 provisions, see 24–003 below. As to consecutive sentences, see 24–004.

Offences spanning the commencement date

24–003 Where an offender falls to be sentenced for offences committed both before and after April 4, 2005, it will generally be preferable to pass sentence on the later offences by reference to the 2003 regime, imposing determinate sentences on the earlier offences, but this may not be possible if the later offences are less serious than the earlier ones.

Note that:

(1) where a count spans the commencement date, the provisions of CJA 2003, Pt 12, Ch.5 should not be applied unless the count specifies that at least one offence was committed after the qualifying date;

(2) care should be taken to ensure that a continuing offence which, as initially indicted, straddled April 4, 2005, is indicted, if necessary by amendment, so that sentence can properly be passed by reference to the 2003 and/or the pre-2003 regime as appropriate (see *R. v Harries* [2007] EWCA Crim 1622, [2008] 1 Cr. App. R. (S.) 47);

(3) even where the judge is unsure if a qualifying offence was committed after the 2003 commencement date, offences before that date do not cease to be relevant, and may have some bearing on the question of "dangerousness" and on the minimum term to be specified: *R. v Harries* (above) following *R. v Howe* [2006] EWCA Crim 3147, [2007] 2 Cr. App. R. (S.) 11.

Consecutive sentences

24–004 Although there is no statutory prohibition on the imposition of:

(1) consecutive indeterminate sentences;

(2) an indeterminate or extended sentence consecutive to another period of imprisonment; or

(3) sentences of life imprisonment and consecutive sentences of detention for life or for public protection,

judges should try to avoid such consecutive sentences if at all possible and adjust the custodial term or minimum period within concurrent sentences to reflect the overall criminality if that is possible within other sentencing constraints.

Where consecutive sentences are considered appropriate or necessary:

(a) if one or more of those sentences are determinate sentences, the determinate sentences should be imposed first, and the extended sentence(s) expressed to be consecutive;

(b) in shaping the overall sentence, there is no obligation for the sentences to be expressed in historical date order; nothing prevents the sentence for the first offence in point of time being served consecutively to a sentence or sentences imposed for any later offence(s).

(*R. v O'Brien* [2006] EWCA Crim 1741, [2007] 1 Cr. App. R. (S.) 75, *Att Gen's Reference (No.55 of 2008)* (above) where the legislation and the authorities are reviewed.)

2.   Adult offenders

Powers under CJA 2003, s.225

24–005   Where an offender aged 18 or over is convicted of a serious offence offence (see 24–017 below) committed on or after April 4, 2005, and the judge is of the opinion that there is a significant risk to members of the public (see 24–020 et seq.) of serious harm occasioned by the commission by him of further specified offences (see 24–015) then if:

CJA 2003, s.225

(1) (a) the offence is one in respect of which the offender would, apart from s.225, be liable to imprisonment for life; and

(b) the judge considers that the seriousness of the offence, or of the offence and one or more offences associated with it, is such as to justify the imposition of a sentence of imprisonment for life, he must impose a sentence of imprisonment for life (as to which see LIFE SENTENCES);

(2) otherwise, i.e. in a case not falling within (1) the judge may impose a sentence of imprisonment, (or, in the case of an of an offender aged at least 18 but under 21, a sentence of detention in a young offender institution, for public protection), provided either of the following conditions is met, namely:

(a) at the time the offence was committed, the offender had had been convicted of an offence specified in CJA 2003, Sch.15A ("condition 3A"); or

(b) "the notional minimum term" is at least four years ("condition 3B").

R. v Olawaiye [2009] EWCA Crim 1925, [2010] 1 Cr. App. R. (S.) 100, makes it clear that as a matter of principle a discretionary life sentence under s.225 should be reserved for offences of the utmost gravity.

The provisions of s.225 are mirrored in s.226 in relation to offenders under 18 at the time of conviction (see 24–014 below).

The "road maps" in relation to protective sentences at 24–013 in relation to adults and at 24–016 in relation to offenders under 18 may be found useful.

The notional minimum term

24–006 A sentence imposed for public protection is imposed for the offence(s) committed after the commencement date and is assessed by reference to the dangerousness of the offender at the date of sentence. The calculation of the minimum term is arrived at by taking into account the whole of the offending behaviour reflected in any other offences before the court including those which occurred before April 4, 2005.

"The notional minimum term" referred to in (2)(b) of 24–005 is:

(1) that part of the sentence that the judge would specify under PCC(S)A 2000, s.82A(2) (determination of the tariff) if he imposed a sentence of imprisonment for public protection, (or in the case of an offender aged at least 18 but under 21, a sentence of detention in a young offender institution); but

(2) was required to disregard any credit for periods of remand (see DEALING WITH AN OFFENDER).

As to fixing the minimum term, see 24–007 below.

Consideration of the statutory provisions led CACD, in *R. v O'Brien* (above) and *R. v O'Halloran* [2006] EWCA Crim. 3148 to conclude that the combined totality of the previous offending should be reflected in the assessment of the notional term for the purposes of condition 3B. There is no indication of change in the 2008 Act. Thus:

(a) if the offender's overall criminality requires a sentence in excess of the minimum laid down in condition 3B, and the judge is satisfied of the necessary risk, it would be illogical for the protective powers inherent in imprisonment for public protection to be unavailable;

(b) condition 3B may be established notwithstanding the absence of an individual offence for which a 4 year term would be appropriate.

Section 225(3) excludes any deduction for the purposes of time spent on remand from the calculation of the minimum term for the purposes of condition 3B.

Appropriate determinate sentence should be imposed in respect of the pre-April 4, 2005 offences to indicate the judge's view of the appropriate sentence, but those sentences will inevitably be subsumed in the determination of the appropriate minimum term (24–007 below) when the entire criminality falls to be considered (*R. v Stannard* [2008] EWCA Crim 2789, [2009] 2 Cr. App. R. (S.) 21).

As to offences spanning the commencement date of the 2003 provisions, see 24–003 above.

An offence the sentence for which is imposed under s.225 is not to be regarded as an offence the sentence for which is fixed by law.

Fixing the minimum term

24–007   The procedure for fixing a minimum term in relation to offences dealt with under s.225 should be that which, before the 2003 Act, related to discretionary and automatic life sentences.

The judge, taking into account the seriousness of the offence or the combination of the offence and one or more offences associated with it should:

(1) identify the "notional determinate sentence" (24–006) which would have been imposed if a life sentence or imprisonment for public protection had not been required (not exceeding the maximum permitted for the offence); and

(2) normally, in the case of a single offences, take half that term; and

(3) from this, deduct time spent in custody or on remand (see IMPRISONMENT).

(*R. v Lang* [2005] EWCA Crim 2564, [2006] 2 Cr. App. R. (S.) 3; *R. v Delucca* [2010] EWCA Crim 710, [2011] 1 Cr. App. R. (S.) 7.)

There will be exceptional cases where more than half (see (2) above) may be appropriate (see *R. v Szczerba* [2002] EWCA Crim 2864, [2002] 2 Cr. App. R. (S.) 387, paras 31–34).

The judge is:

(a) imposing an indeterminate sentence to reflect the risk of serious harm from the offender in the future, and

(b) imposing a notional minimum term to take into account the totality of the offender's offending.

In the case of (b) a notional minimum term which takes into account ALL the offences, before the court, may exceed the statutory maximum for the offence in respect of which the offender is given the indeterminate sentence.

In approaching sentence in such a case:

(i) step 1 is to decide what determinate sentence he would have imposed for the offence if the need to protect the public had not required him to pass an indeterminate sentence; and then,

(ii) step 2 is generally to take half of that sentence as the specified part of the indeterminate sentence, although in certain cases he may exceed the half (see *R. v Hayward* [2000] 2 Cr. App. R. (S.) 418; *R. v Szczerba* (above); *R. v Delucca*, above).

In calculating the minimum term, an appropriate reduction should be allowed for a plea of guilty (see DISCOUNTS ON SENTENCE) and care should be taken not to incorporate in the notional determinate sentence an element for risk which is already covered by the indeterminate sentence (*R. v Lang,* above).

Approach to pre- conditions 3A and 3B

24–008   In relation to the preconditions stated in s.225 (see 24–005), condition 3A is self-explanatory. The significant difference introduced by the 2008 amendment is that the list of offences specified in CJIA 2008, Sch.15A is much shorter than the list of "specified offences" in CJA 2003, Sch.15, and is effectively confined to very grave offences indeed.
Thus:

(1) where the offender's previous convictions include one of the offences now specified in Sch.15A,
(2) a sentence of imprisonment for public protection becomes available irrespective of the seriousness of the latest offence, provided always that the judge is satisfied that the public is at "significant risk" as specified in s.225(1)(b).

Condition 3A stands distinct from condition 3B which requires that the "notional minimum term" (24–006) should be at least 4 years' imprisonment (or appropriate custodial order for a young offender).
That condition does not form part of condition 3A.
Accordingly:

(a) if condition 3A is established, a sentence of imprisonment for public protection may be imposed if the over-arching consideration is established, whether or not such a notional minimum term would be appropriate; but
(b) unless condition 3A is established, a sentence of imprisonment for public protection may not be imposed under condition 3B unless the offence justifies the specified "notional minimum term", even if there is a significant risk of serious harm.
(*Att Gen's Reference (No.55 of 2008),* above).

Note that:

(i) is it not proper to impose longer than appropriate sentences in order to avoid the restriction created by condition 3;
(ii) CJA 2003, s.153(2) remains in force, and any custodial sentence must be for the shortest term (not exceeding the permitted maximum) that in the judge's opinion is commensurate with the seriousness of the offence, or the combination of the offence and one or more offences associated with it. *Att Gen's Reference (No.55 of 2008);*
(iii) where the offender has been convicted of, or has admitted, a number of offences, the length of the minimum term is governed by PCC(S)A 2000, s.82A(3)(a), namely that the determination of the "tariff should reflect "the seriousness of the offence, or the combination of the offence and one or more offences associated

with it", but disregarding the credit which would normally be due for time already spent in custody.

Extended sentence under s.227

CJA 2003, s.227

24–009   Where:

(1) a person aged 18 or over is convicted of a specified offence committed after April 4, 2005 and the judge considers that there is a significant risk to members of the public of serious harm occasioned by the commission by the offender of further specified offences, but
(2) the court is not required by s.225(2) to impose a sentence of imprisonment for life, or (in the case of an offender aged at least 18 but under 21 a sentence of custody for life),

the judge **may** impose on the offender an extended sentence of imprisonment, (or, in the case of an offender aged 18 but under 21 an extended sentence of detention in a young offender institution), if either of the following conditions is met, namely:

(a) at the time the offence was committed, the offender had been convicted of an offence specified in CJA 2003, Sch.15A (inserted by CJIA 2008); or
(b) if the judge were to impose an extended sentence of imprisonment, the term that he would specify as the appropriate custodial term (taking into account any discount for plea – *R. v Fazli* [2009] EWHC Crim 939, 73 J.C.L. 463) would be at least four years.

The appropriate custodial term here means a term of imprisonment (not exceeding the maximum term permitted for the offence) which is the term that would (apart from this section) be imposed in compliance with s.153(2), or where the term that would be so imposed is a term of less than 12 months, is a term of 12 months.

The provisions of s.227 are mirrored in s.228 in relation to offenders under 18 at the time of conviction (see 24–014 below).

In passing sentences the judge should bear in mind that if he wrongly imposes an extended sentence in respect of a serious offence, CACD has no power to substitute an indeterminate sentence under ss.225 or 226 (*R. v Reynolds* [2007] EWCA Crim 538, [2007] 2 Cr. App. R. (S.) 87).

He must take care to identify the offence or offences to which the extended sentence is intended to apply (*R. v Pepper* [2005] EWCA Crim 1181, [2006] 1 Cr. App. R. (S.) 20).

The principle in *R. v O'Brien* (24–004 above) in relation to indeterminate sentences applies also to extended sentences. Where the offender is to be sentenced for a number of associated offences none of which, individually, would justify an extended sentence, the judge may nevertheless aggregate the proposed sentences together in relation to one offence for the purpose of passing an extended sentence on that offence and passing concurrent sentences for the associated offences (assuming the other statutory conditions are met) (*R. v Pinnell* [2010] EWCA Crim 2848, [2011] 2 Cr. App. R. (S.) 30).

(As to the length of the extended term, see 24–010 below.)

Length of extended term

24–010 An extended sentence of imprisonment (or in the case of an offender aged 18 but under 21, an extended sentence of detention in a young offender institution), is a sentence of imprisonment (or detention), the term of which is equal to the aggregate of:

(1) the appropriate custodial term; and
(2) a further period ("the extension period") for which the offender is to be subject to a licence, and which is of such length as the judge considers necessary for the purpose of protecting members of the public from serious harm occasioned by the commission by him of further specified offences.

The extension period must not exceed;

(a) 5 years in the case of a specified violent offence; and
(b) 8 years in the case of a specified sexual offence.

The term of the extended sentence passed under s.227 in respect of an offence must not exceed the maximum term permitted for the offence (see *R. v Oldfield* [2011] EWCA Crim 2314).

The most important change introduced by the 2008 Act is that the extended sentence is no longer limited to "specified offences" which are not also "serious", that is offences punishable with a maximum of less than 10 years' imprisonment. Where the offence is indeed a "serious specified offence", the options of both imprisonment for public protection and an extended sentence are now available.

Nature of extended term

24–011 The custodial term must be the shortest term commensurate with the seriousness of the offence or the offence and other offences associated with it (s.153(2)), save that, if the commensurate term would be less than 12 months, 12 months must be imposed (s.227(3)(b)).

Also:

(1) the extension period must be of such length as the judge considers necessary to protect the public from serious harm by the commission of further specified offences (s.227(2)(b)) but must not exceed 5 years for a violent offence or eight years for a sexual offence;
(2) the extended sentence must not exceed the maximum term permissible for the offence (s.227(4) and (5));
(3) it will not usually be appropriate to impose consecutive extended sentences, whether the principal offence is serious or merely specified (cf. *R. v Nelson* [2001] EWCA Crim 2264, [2002] 1 Cr. App. R.(S.) 134).

It is to be noted that, in contrast to an extended sentence under PCC(S)A 2000, s.85 (which is repealed by the CJA 2003, Sch.37, Pt 7) the sentence under CJA 2003, s.227 does not apply to offences punishable with 10 years or more. This means that most sexual offences under SOA 2003 are without these provisions.

Until CJCSA 2000, s.74 is brought into force, applying imprisonment to those aged 18 or over, the sentence for 18 to 20 year olds should
continue to be expressed as "custody for life" or "detention in a young
offender institution".

The three stage approach to an extended term

24–012   Some parts of the judgment in *R. v Nelson* (above) may continue to be helpful, though the judgment must be read in the light of the
2008 provisions.

It was said in that case that the judge should approach the imposition
of an extended sentence in three stages:

(1) decide on the sentence which would be commensurate with the
offence;
(2) consider whether a longer period in custody was necessary to
protect the public from serious harm from the offender; and
(3) consider whether the sentence was adequate to protect the public
from the commission of further offences by the offender and
impose an extended sentence.

It is not appropriate to reduce the custodial term because an extended
licence period is imposed.

In *R. v Pinnell* (above) CACD issued guidance based upon existing
authorities where an offender is convicted of multiple offences:

(a) if, on ordinary principles, no single offence justifies a four-
year custodial term, the seriousness of the aggregate offending must be considered;
(b) if a four-year custodial term results from aggregating the
shortest terms commensurate with the seriousness of each
offence, then that four-year term may be imposed in relation
to the specified offence;
(c) if there is more than one specified offence, that aggregate
term should be passed for the lead specified offence, or,
if appropriate, concurrently on more than one specified
offence;
(d) if appropriate, a concurrent determinate term may be
imposed for other offences;
(e) there is no objection to imposing an extended sentence
consecutive to another sentence, or (since the amendments
made to the release provisions for extended sentences by the
CJIA 2008) to imposing consecutive extended sentences,
although this should be done only where there is a particular
reason for doing so;
(f) the extension periods in the case of consecutive extended
sentences will themselves be consecutive;
(g) in a case of consecutive extended sentences, each offence
must justify a custodial term of at least four years; and
it is not possible to pass separate sentences of less than
four years to meet this condition for the imposition of an
extended sentence, even if their total is more than four
years.

DANGEROUS OFFENDERS; PROTECTIVE SENTENCES

A recommended road-map: (A) 18 and over

24–013 In the case of an offender aged 18 years or over, the following approach may be recommended if a protective sentence is contemplated;

(1) the offender must have been convicted of one of those "specified offences" listed in CJA 2003, s.15; if he has not been, he is liable to a determinate sentence only; if he has been, go to step (2);

(2) there must be, in the judge's opinion, a significant risk of serious harm from future "specified" offences likely to be committed by the offender; if that significant risk does not exist, he is liable to a determinate sentence only; if it does exist then go to (3);

(3) if the offence is punishable with life imprisonment, the judge needs to consider whether the seriousness of the offence committed justifies such a sentence, if it does, the ordinary rules as to life sentences (see LIFE SENTENCES) apply; if it does not, go to (4);

(4) the crucial question then is whether the offence is a "serious offence", i.e. an offence punishable with 10 years imprisonment or more; if:

    (a) it is not a "serious offence" then a subsidiary question arises – whether at the time the offence was committed, the offender has been convicted of an offence listed in CJA 2003, Sch.15A if:

        (i) he has been, then step (6) applies;

        (ii) he has not been, then the judge must consider whether the offence justifies a sentence of at least four years, in which case step (5) applies;

    (b) it is a "serious offence" the question again arises, whether at the time the offence was committed, the offender has been convicted of an offence listed in CJA 2003, Sch.15A; if he has not been, then unless the offence would justify a sentence of at least 4 years, an appropriate determinate sentence, or a community sentence, should be imposed; if the offence would justify at least 4 years, then step (6) applies;

(5) in this situation the following sentences are available—a community order, a commensurate determinate sentence, or an extended sentence of imprisonment (the custodial term being of any length, but of at least 12 months under (a)(i) above, or 4 years under (a)(ii) or (b);

(6) if the offence is a "serious offence" AND the offender has been convicted of an offence listed in Sch.15A AND the offence would justify a sentence of at least four years, then in addition to the penalties mentioned in (5) above, a sentence of imprisonment for public protection may be passed, the minimum term being for at least two years before the deduction of any time spent in custody on remand.

In considering whether a sentence of imprisonment for public protection should be passed, the judge should have in mind all the alternative and cumulative methods of providing the necessary public protection against any risk posed by the individual offender. There will be cases where a determinate sentence, or an extended sentence with appropriate conditions attached, might form part of the "total protection sentencing package" without imprisonment under s.225 being imposed (*Att-Gen's Reference (No.55 of 2008)* [2008] EWCA Crim 2790, [2009] 2 Cr. App. R. (S.) 22).

3.   Offenders under 18

Detention for life or detention for public protection
24–014   Where:

CJA 2003, s.226

(1) an offender aged under 18 is convicted of a serious offence committed after April 4, 2005; and
(2) the judge is of opinion that there is a significant risk to members of the public of serious harm occasioned by the commission by the offender of further specified offences, then if;
    (a) the offence is one in respect of which the offender would apart from this section be liable to a sentence of detention for life under PCC(S)A 2000, s.91 and the judge considers that the seriousness of the offence, or of the offence and one or more offences associated with it, is such as to justify the imposition of a sentence of detention for life, he must impose a sentence of detention for life under that section; but
    (b) the case does not come within (a), the judge may impose a sentence of detention for public protection, if the "notional minimum term" is at least 2 years.

An offence the sentence for which is imposed under this provision is not to be regarded as an offence the sentence for which is fixed by law.

Extended sentence for certain violent or sexual offences
24–015   Where:

CJA 2003, s.228

(1) a person aged under 18 is convicted of a specified offence committed after April 4, 2005; and
(2) the judge considers:
    (a) that there is a significant risk to members of the public of serious harm occasioned by the commission by the offender of further specified offences; and
    (b) where the specified offence is a serious offence, that the case is not one in which the judge is required by CJA 2003, s.226(2) to impose a sentence of detention for life under PCC(S)A 2000, s.91,

he may impose on the offender an extended sentence of detention, provided that if the he were to impose an extended sentence of detention, the term that it would specify as the appropriate custodial term would be at least 4 years.

"The appropriate custodial term" means such term as the judge considers appropriate, which must, however, be at least 12 months, and must not exceed the maximum term of imprisonment permitted for the offence.

Similar provisions as to the length and nature of such a sentence apply as they apply to the sentence in respect of an adult, see 24–010 and 24–011 above.

The term of an extended sentence of detention passed under this section in respect of an offence must not exceed the maximum term of imprisonment permitted for the offence. A reference to the maximum term of imprisonment permitted for an offence is a reference to the maximum term of imprisonment that is, apart from s.225, permitted for the offence in the case of a person aged 18 or over.

In passing sentences the judge should bear in mind that if he wrongly imposes an extended sentence in respect of a serious offence, CACD has no power to substitute an indeterminate sentence under ss.225 or 226 (*R. v Reynolds* [2007] EWCA Crim 538, [2007] 2 Cr. App. R. (S.) 27). He must also take care to identify the offence or offences to which the extended sentence is intended to apply (*R. v Pepper* [2005] EWCA Crim 118, [2006] 1 Cr. App. R. (S.) 20).

As to the suggested three stage approach to this sentence, see 24–012 above.

Road map: (B) offenders under 18

24–016   The judge may approach the matter in this way:

(1) Was the offender aged under 18 when convicted of the current offence? If the answer is: "No", go to route "A" above at 24–013, if the answer is "Yes", take step (2);

(2) Is the current offence, of which the offender has been convicted, a specified offence under Sch.15? If the answer is:
  (a) "No", the judge should impose either;
     (i)   a youth rehabilitation order with appropriate requirements; or
     (ii) an appropriate determinate sentence of detention;

(3) Is the judge of the opinion that there is "a significant risk of serious harm" caused, in the future, from further specified offence(s) being committed by the offender? If the answer is:
  (a) "No", the judge should pass a sentence as in (2)(a)(i) or (ii) above;
  (b) "Yes", take step (4);

(4) Is the current specified offence punishable with:
  (a) life imprisonment; or
  (b) imprisonment of at least 10 years; or
  (c) imprisonment under 10 years,?
  if the answer is (a), go to step (5), if the answer is (b), go to step (6) below, if the answer is (c), go to step (7)(ii) below;

(5) Taking into account the seriousness of the offence, does the judge consider that a sentence of detention for life is justified? If the answer is:
  (a) "No", go to step (6) below;
  (b) "Yes", a sentence of detention for life must be passed, and a minimum term under PCC(S)A 2000, s.82A fixed;

(6) Where the current offence is a "serious specified offence" (i.e. punishable with 10 years or more), has the offender been

previously convicted of a specified offence under Sch.15A? Whether the answer is "Yes" or "No", go to step (7);

(7) Would a sentence of at least 4 years be justified for the current offence? If the answer is:

   (a) "No", resort to:

      (i) a youth rehabilitation order with appropriate requirements; or

      (ii) an appropriate and commensurate determinate sentence of detention;

   (b) "Yes", there are two options:

      (i) where the current offence is a serious specified offence, the following sentences are available:

- a sentence under (i) or (ii) above; or
- an extended sentence (with a custodial term of at least 4 years); or
- detention for public protection (with a minimum notional term of at least two years, before time spent in custody on remand is deducted);

      (ii) where the current offence is not a serious specified offence, the following sentences are available:

- a youth rehabilitation order with appropriate requirements; or
- commensurate sentence of detention under PCC(S)A 2000, s.91; or
- a detention and training order; or
- an extended sentence of detention (with a custodial term of at least four years).

4. Definitions and approach

24–017   For the purposes of CJA 2003, Pt 12, Ch.5 an offence is: CJA 2003, s.224

(1) a **"specified offence"** if: it is:

   (a) a specified violent offence, that is an offence specified in CJA 2003, Sch.15, Pt 1;

   (b) a specified sexual offence, that is an offence specified in CJA 2003, Sch.15, Pt 2.

(2) a **"serious offence"** if, and only if, it is:

   (a) a "specified offence"; and

   (b) apart from s.225, punishable in the case of a person aged 18 or over with imprisonment for life or imprisonment for a determinate period of 10 years or more (or in the case of an offender aged 18 but under 21 custody for life).

"**A**ssociated offences:" CJA 2003, s.305(1) (adopting PCC(S)A 2000, s.161(1)) provides that an offence is associated with another if:

      (i) the offender is convicted of it in proceedings in which he is convicted of the other offence, or (although convicted of it in earlier proceedings), is sentenced for it at the same time as he is sentenced for that offence; or

   (ii) the offender admits the commission of it in the pro-
        ceedings in which he is sentenced for the other offence
        and requests the judge to take it into consideration
        when sentencing him for that offence.

"**Serious harm**" means death or serious personal injury, whether physical or psychological.

This is a concept familiar since CJA 1991, s.2(2)(b) and pre-2004
decisions of CACD continue to be relevant to its assessment. In *R. v
Bowler* (1994) 15 Cr. App. R. (S.) 78 it was said sexual assaults which
are relatively minor physically may lead to serious psychological
injury; and downloading indecent images of children may cause serious
psychological injury to a child arising not only from what the child has
been forced to do but also from the knowledge that others will see what
they were doing (see for instance *R. v Collard* [2004] EWCA Crim
1664, [2005] 1 Cr. App. R. (S.) 34; *R. v Lang* [2005] EWCA Crim
2664, [2006] 2 Cr. App. R. (S.) 3).

"Specified offences" as "serious" offences

24–018   A "specified" offence may or may not be a "serious" offence"
(s.224). It will be "serious" if it is punishable, in the case of a person
aged 18 or over, with 10 years' imprisonment or more (s.224(2)(b)).
   If serious, it may attract:

(1) life imprisonment; or
(2) imprisonment for public protection for an adult (s.225) or deten-
    tion for life or detention for public protection for an offender
    under 18 on the day of conviction (s.225).

It will attract such a sentence if the judge is of opinion that there is a
"significant risk" to members of the public of serious harm by the commission of further specified offences (ss.225(1), 226(1)). Indeterminate
sentences should not be imposed for the commission of relatively minor
offences.

"**Members of the public**" seems to be an all-embracing term. It is
wider than "others", which would exclude the offender himself.

In *R. v Lang* (above), CACD saw no reason to construe it so as to
exclude any particular group, for example:

(a) prison officers or staff at mental hospitals, all of whom, like
    the offender, are members of the public;
(b) in some cases, particular members of the public may be
    more at risk than members of the public generally, e.g.
    when an offender has a history of violence to cohabitees or
    of sexually abusing children of cohabitees, or, where the
    offender has a particular problem in relation to a particular
    woman.

This provision requires the judge to look beyond the instant offence
(and any offences associated with it) in order to see whether there are
aggravating factors which he should have in mind when assessing the
seriousness of that instant offence.

When considering the seriousness of an offence CJA 2003, s.143 requires the judge:

> (i) where an offender has previous convictions to treat each previous conviction as an aggravating factor if, in the case of that previous conviction, he considers that it can reasonably be so treated, having regard in particular to the nature of the offence to which the conviction relates and its relevance to the current conviction and the time that has elapsed since the conviction;
>
> (ii) to treat the commission of an offence on bail as an aggravating factor, when considering the seriousness of that.

"Dangerousness" and its assessment

24–019 Where a person has been convicted of a "serious offence" the judge has to assess under any of ss.225–228 whether there is a "significant risk" to members of the public of serious harm occasioned by the commission by the offender of further such offences.

The first question which arises for decision is whether the court is of that opinion. Absent such risk, no question of imprisonment for public protection arises.

In making his assessment, the judge:

> (1) must take into account all such information as is available to him about the nature and circumstances of the offence;
>
> (2) may take into account all such information as is available to him about the nature and circumstances of any other offences of which the offender has been convicted by a court anywhere in the world; and
>
> (3) may take into account any information which is before him about any pattern of behaviour of which any of the offences mentioned in (1) or (2) forms part; and
>
> (4) may take into account any information about the offender which is before him.

The reference in (2) to a conviction by a court includes a reference to a finding of guilt in service disciplinary proceeding and a conviction of a service offence within the meaning of the Armed Forces Act 2006 ("conviction" here including anything that under s.376(1) and (2) of that Act is to be treated as a conviction).

"**Information**" is not restricted to evidence; information bearing on the assessment of dangerousness which discloses previous offences committed by the offender may be considered even where the offender has not been charged or convicted of the offences (*R. v Considine* [2007] EWCA Crim 1166, [2008] 1 Cr. App. R. (S.) 41; *R. v Lavery* [2008] EWCA Crim 2499, [2009] 3 All E.R. 295).

The section provides statutory direction on the approach to "dangerousness" which should be adopted by the judge, after taking into account all relevant matters. The word is intended as a convenient form of shorthand to describe the words in ss.224—229, i.e. "a significant risk to members of the public of serious harm occasioned by the commission of further specified offences" (s.229(2)).

375

"Significant risk"

24–020 Significant risk must be shown in relation to:

(1) the commission of further specified, but not necessarily serious, offences; and
(2) the causing thereby of serious harm to members of the public.

If there is a significant risk of both, either a life sentence or indeterminate imprisonment for public protection must be imposed on an adult (s.225(2), (3)), which must be:

(a) a life sentence if the offence is one for which the offender is liable to life imprisonment and the seriousness of the offence, or of the offence and one or more offences associated with it, is such as to justify imprisonment for life (s.225(2)); or
(b) imprisonment for public protection (s.225(3)).

The issue is the risk to the public, not simply what the offender desired or intended. A reckless offender, or one with little or no insight into the consequences of his actions, may represent a significant risk to the public, and an order of imprisonment for public protection may be fully justified notwithstanding that, in the broadest sense, the offender did not intend or desire the outcome of his actions. If the harm consequent on any individual offence was not intended or desired by the offender, then, in the context of condition 3B, a determinate sentence of four years or more imprisonment is less likely to be appropriate. On the other hand, a relatively minor offence may well re-ignite concern about the element of public danger posed by a defendant who has already committed one of the very serious offences identified in condition 3A. These considerations are all relevant to the judge's decision (*Att-Gen's Reference (No.55 of 2008)* [2008] EWCA Crim 2790, [2009] 2 Cr. App. R. (S.) 22).

In relation to those under 18, there are similar provisions in relation to detention for life and detention for public protection subject, in the latter case, to an additional criterion by reference to the adequacy of an extended sentence under ss.228 (s.226(2)–(3)). For all practical purposes, imprisonment and detention for public protection are exactly the same as a life sentence, though there may be exceptional cases where the offence itself is so serious that an indeterminate sentence is justified by the seriousness of the offence irrespective of the risk to the public (PD 2004, IV.47) and imprisonment or detention for public protection.

Factors in the assessment of dangerousness: R. v Lang

24–021 In *R. v Lang* (above) also in *R. v Pedley* [2009] EWCA Crim 846, [2010] 1 Cr. App. R. (S.) 24, CACD considered that the following factors should be borne in mind where a judge is assessing significant risk:

(1) the risk identified must be significant, this is a higher threshold than mere possibility of occurrence and can be taken to mean "noteworthy, of considerable amount or importance";
(2) in assessing the risk of further offences being committed, the judge should take into account:

(a) the nature and circumstances of the current offence;

(b) the offender's history of offending, including not just the kind of offence but its circumstances and the sentence passed, details of which the prosecution must have available;

(c) whether the offending demonstrates any pattern; social and economic factors in relation to the offender including accommodation, employability, education, associates, relationships and drug or alcohol abuse; and the offender's thinking, attitude towards offending and supervision and emotional state;

(d) any pre-sentence or medical report which he calls for, which, together with the antecedents and any medical report, will provide information on the matters mentioned in (c) above.

Further guidance was given in *R. v Johnson* [2006] EWCA Crim 2486, [2007] 1 Cr. App. R. (S.) 112 (p.674). It is clear from the Sentencing Guidelines Council's paper on dangerous offenders and from decisions of the court such as *R. v G* [2006] EWCA Crim 3277, [2007] 2 Cr. App. R. (S.) 32 (p.185); *R. v Dee* [2006] EWCA Crim 1635 and *R. v Puckey* [2008] EWCA Crim 2326 that a court must apply with particular care the dangerousness provisions (*R. v Beesley* [2011] EWCA Crim 1021, [2011] Crim. L.R. 668).

The risk may arise out of a single set of convictions of an offender of previous good character where the offending was otherwise inexplicable (*R. v Troninas (Att-Gen.'s Reference (No.5 of 2011))*) [2011] EWCA Crim 1244, [2011] Crim. L.R. 730.

Where a judge has to assess future risk, in the great majority of cases he will be assisted in doing so by as much background as it is possible to have and by the kind of discussion about behaviour and offending which a probation officer might have with an offender (see *R. v Lang*; *Att Gen's Ref (No.73 of 2010)* [2011] Crim. L.R. 571. But cf. *Att Gen's Ref (No.5 of 2011)* [2011] EWCA Crim 1244; [2011] Crim. L.R. 730). An assessment of dangerousness is a judicial responsibility based on a consideration of all the available information. Psychological assessments are not essential, and a finding of dangerousness may be made in appropriate circumstances even though the offender has no previous convictions.

The judge has an obligation under CJA 2003, s.156(3) to obtain such a report unless of opinion that it is not necessary to do so (see, e.g. *Att-Gen's Reference (No.145 of 2006), The Times*, March 20, 2007).

In relation to a particularly young offender, an indeterminate sentence may be inappropriate even where a serious offence has been committed and there is a significant risk of serious harm from further offences (see *R. v D* [2005] EWCA Crim 2292, [2006] 1 Cr. App. R. (S.) 104).

Pre-sentence and other reports

24–022   A pre-sentence report should usually be obtained before any sentence is passed which is based on significant risk of serious harm. The judge should guard against assuming there is a significant risk of serious harm merely because the foreseen specified offence is serious.

The judge:

(1) will be guided, but not bound by, the assessment of risk in any reports;

(2) if he contemplates differing from the assessment in such a report he should give both advocates the opportunity of addressing the point;

(3) will only in the rarest cases allow cross-examination of the author of the report (*R. v S* [2005] EWCA Crim 3616, [2006] 2 Cr. App. R. (S.) 35).

In a small number of cases, where the circumstances of the current offence or the history of the offender suggest mental abnormality on his part, a medical report may be necessary before risk can properly be assessed. If one is asked for the must address the risk of serious harm posed by the offender (above).

As to the relevance of previous conviction, and the judge's duty to give reasons, see 24–023, below.

Relevance of previous convictions

24–023 It is not a prerequisite to a finding of dangerousness that the offender should have previous convictions The judge may come to the conclusion that an offender with previous convictions, even for specified offences, does not necessarily satisfy the requirements of dangerousness.

Note that:

(1) previous offences, not in fact specified for the purposes of s.229 are not disqualified from consideration; a pattern of minor previous offences of gradually escalating seriousness may be significant;

(2) the fact that no harm was actually caused both in the current and in any specified offence when examined for the purposes of s.229 (see, e.g. *R. v Isa* [2005] EWCA Crim 3330, [2006] 2 Cr. App. R. (S.) 29) may be fortuitous; it does not follow from the absence of actual harm caused by the offender to date, that the risk that he will cause serious harm in the future is negligible (*R. v Shaffi* [2006] EWCA 418, [2006] 2 Cr. App. R. (S.) 92 does not suggest the contrary);

(3) inadequacy, suggestibility or vulnerability may mitigate the offender's culpability; they may also serve to reinforce the conclusion that he is dangerous.

It is desirable, if not always practicable, for the prosecutor to give the facts of previous specified offences, but there is no reason why his failure to comply with good practice should render an adjournment obligatory or preclude the imposition of sentence; the defence advocate should have instructions sufficient to explain the circumstances, and if the prosecutor is unable to challenge those instructions, the judge may proceed to sentence on such information as he has (*R. v Lang* (above); *R. v Johnson* [2006] EWCA Crim 2486, [2007] 1 Cr. App. R.(S.) 112).

Spelling it out

24–024 The judge should usually, and in accordance with CJA 2003, s.174(1)(a), give reasons for all his conclusions, in particular:

(1) whether there is or is not a significant risk of further offences or serious harm; and

(2) for not imposing an extended sentence under ss.227 and 228.

He should, in giving reasons, briefly identify the information which he has taken into account.

The judge:

    (a) does not need (*R. v Johnson*, above) to spell out all the details of the previous offences; but

    (b) should not rely on a disputed fact in reaching a finding of dangerousness, unless the dispute can fairly be resolved adversely to the offender;

    (c) should explain in his sentencing remarks the reasoning which has led him to his conclusion.

5.   Rectification of errors

General

24–025   The regime for dangerous offenders requires the judge to carry out a careful step by step evaluation of the sentencing consequences of:

(1) the type of offence;

(2) the age of the offender; and

(3) the assessment of his dangerousness.

A common mistake is the failure to appreciate that a "specified" offence is a "serious" offence.

Rectification by the Crown Court

24–026   Where a mistake is made:

(1) if it is identified quickly enough, the Crown Court may exercise the power under PCC(S)A 2000, s.155(1) to vary the sentence within the period of 56 days beginning on the day on which the sentence or other order was imposed:

    (a) the power would be properly exercised if the mistake was that the sentencing judge had failed to appreciate, e.g. that the specified offence was a "serious offence" and that the mandatory provisions of CJA 2003, ss.225 or 227 required an indeterminate sentence as opposed to an extended sentence;

    (b) equally the power could be exercised where the mistake was a failure to recognise the offence as a "specified" offence, as a result of which an ordinary determinate sentence or other disposal had been imposed;

(2) if the mistake is identified within the 56-day period, but for whatever reason the sentencing court is either:

    (a) unable to deal with the matter by way of variation within 56 days; or

    (b) considers that sentencing should be delayed beyond the 56-day period, the sentencing judge should rescind the sentence; the sentencing court then being in the same position as it was at the time that the original sentence was imposed and accordingly having all the powers it had at that time, including the jurisdiction to adjourn sentence, if the justice of the case so required.

The Crown Court has power, after rescinding all or part of its original order, to adjourn the final sentence to a later date (*R. v Stillwell* (1992) 13 Cr. App. R. (S.) 253 not followed).

Rectification by CACD
24–027 Where:

(1) the sentencing court has not exercised its power under s.155, and has, by mistake, imposed an indeterminate sentence for a "specified" but not "serious" offence, the matter may be put right on appeal;

(2) the judge concluded that an offender met the criteria of dangerousness, but has in some other way misunderstood or misapplied that consequence to the offender's disadvantage, again the matter may be put right on appeal;

(3) the Attorney-General seeks a reference under CJA 1988, s.36, CACD has the power to put right any mistake.

Difficulties arise where an error in favour of the offender emerges as a result of an appeal by him.

If it becomes apparent during the course of the appeal that the sentencing judge has failed to appreciate that a mandatory sentence should have been imposed, or alternatively that an indeterminate sentence should have been passed as opposed to an extended sentence, the sentence is an unlawful sentence, but CAA 1968, s.11(3) precludes CACD from interfering with such a sentence (*R. v Reynolds* [2007] EWCA Crim 538, [2007] 2 Cr. App. R. (S.) 87).

25. DEALING WITH AN OFFENDER

Quick guide

General

25–001   Some general principles governing the sentencing of offenders and the various sentencing options available are, for convenience, set out below in a single composite section which takes the form of a **"road map" of sentencing** which may assist those not entirely familiar with criminal practice or who may use it as a checklist.

1.   Some pre-sentencing requirements

Presence of offender

25–002   As a general rule the offender must be physically present in court where:

(1) he is sentenced to a custodial sentence; or
(2) a driving disqualification is imposed on him, unless, in this latter case:
    (a) the court has adjourned after conviction; and
    (b) he has been notified of the time and place for the resumption of the hearing, and the reason for the adjournment, and he fails to appear.

Where several offenders fall to be sentenced, it is desirable that they should all be sentenced by the same court. Where one pleads not guilty and his case is adjourned for trial, sentences on those who plead guilty should be adjourned to the conclusion of his trial (*R. v Weekes* (1982) 74 Cr. App. R. 161).

Care must be taken in dealing with a number of co-offenders to differentiate between them according to the mitigating or aggravating factors affecting each one of them.

DEALING WITH AN OFFENDER

Remittal, adjournment, deferment

25–003 An offender need not be dealt with on the very day of conviction, nor in every case by the judge before whom he appeared or was convicted.

There is:

(1) a duty in certain circumstances to remit a juvenile offender to the appropriate youth court in (see CHILDREN AND YOUNG PERSONS);

(2) a power to transfer an offender's case, administratively, from one court, or from one circuit, to another, where sentence or another trial is pending, in that court;

(3) a common law power to adjourn, which may be appropriate for:
    (a) the making of enquiries;
    (b) the provision of reports;
    (c) consolidating other outstanding charges, or other co-accused; or
    (d) the making of reparation by the offender (see COMPENSATION ORDERS);

(4) a statutory power to adjourn for the production of a driving licence (see DRIVING DISQUALIFICATIONS);

(5) certain statutory powers under MHA ss.35, 36 to remand to hospital for a medical examination and report (see MENTALLY DISORDERED OFFENDERS);

(6) power to postpone the making of a confiscation order under POCA 2002, ss.14, 15 (see CONFISCATION ORDERS); and

(7) a statutory power to defer passing sentence for a fixed period, (see DEFERRING SENTENCE).

Outstanding indictments or offences

25–004 An accused who has a number of indictments, or counts, outstanding against him, should be sentenced on one occasion at the conclusion of all matters on which the Crown intend to proceed. Only in this way will consistency of sentencing be achieved. The problems caused by doing otherwise are obvious (*R. v Bennet* (1980) 2 Cr. App. R(S). 96).

In particular, where one offender has undertaken, after pleading guilty, to give evidence at the trial of his co-accused or other criminal confederates, while it is a matter for the judge to decide whether to sentence him before he gives evidence (*R. v Payne* (1950) 30 Cr. App. R. 43), it is generally more sensible to wait until he has given his evidence at the trial of the others (*R. v Weekes*, above).

Reports; representation

25–005 In some cases a pre-sentence report may be required by statute (see REPORTS); in other cases the judge may derive assistance from:

(1) a pre-sentence, or other report;
(2) a medical or psychiatric report;

as to which see REPORTS.

The latter may be mandatory where the judge has a mental health disposal in contemplation (see MENTALLY DISORDERED OFFENDERS).

It is unsafe to proceed to sentence unless the offender is represented (25–007, below).

Adjournment for reports—R. v Gillam: a potential trap

25–006 Where the judge adjourns for enquiries to be made or reports to be provided, he should be careful to observe the rules laid down in *R. v Gillam* [1980] 2 Cr. App. R. (S.) 267, and the numerous cases which have followed it.

The judge:

(1) must be careful not to say or do anything which might reasonably create in the offender's mind any expectation that he will adopt a particular option if the reports are favourable; and
(2) should state expressly that:
    (a) he is "keeping his options open"; and
    (b) that the grant of bail pending the preparation of a report is no indication of the nature of any sentence which he has in mind (*R. v Renan* (1994) 15 Cr. App. R. (S.) 722),

otherwise CACD has indicated that a sense of injustice, "real or imagined," may be created in the offender's mind, though failure to warn the offender that the court is considering a custodial sentence does not vitiate any subsequent sentence (*R. v Woodin* (1994) 15 Cr. App. R. (S.) 307).

Need for legal representation

25–007 A judge must not, on conviction on indictment, or on committal for sentence:

(1) pass an immediate sentence of imprisonment (other than a committal for contempt or any kindred offence) on an offender who has not previously been sentenced to such imprisonment by a court in the United Kingdom; or
(2) pass a sentence of detention on a young offender under PCC(S)A 2000, ss.90, 91 or 96; or
(3) make a detention and training order, unless the offender has had the assistance of counsel or a solicitor to represent him in the proceedings at some time after he is found guilty and before sentence, except where:
    (a) he was granted a right to representation out of public but the right has been withdrawn because of his conduct, or because it appeared that his financial resources were such that he was not eligible to be granted such a right; or
    (b) having been informed of his right to apply for a representation order and having had the opportunity to do so, he refused or failed to apply; or
    (c) he applied for such representation and the application was refused because it appeared that his financial resources were such that he was not eligible to be granted a right to it.

DEALING WITH AN OFFENDER

A breach of these provisions renders any subsequent sentence unlawful, and a nullity (*R. v Wilson* (1995) 16 Cr. App. R. (S.) 997).

Difficulties arise where an offender "sacks" his solicitor and/or counsel, or they withdraw between conviction and sentence. Under the representation order, an offender has the right to be represented by solicitor and counsel of his choice and who are willing to act, unless and until that order is withdrawn (*R. v Kirk* (1983) 76 Cr. App. R. 194; *R. v Harris* [1985] Crim. L.R. 244; *R. v Dimech* [1991] Crim. L.R. 846; *R. v Stowell* [2006] EWCA Crim 27, [2006] Crim. L.R. 760).

Faced with a recalcitrant offender, the proper course is for the judge to revoke the representation order before proceeding to sentence (*R. v Wilson,* above). (See also LEGAL AID; PUBLIC FUNDING).

Antecedents

25–008 Immediately following the proceedings in the magistrates' court court resulting in a case being sent for trial, or committed for sentence to the Crown Court or upon receipt of a notice of appeal from the magistrates' court the police will:
PD 2004, III.27.1–4

(1) prepare the antecedents of the offender (in the form set out in PD 2004, III.27.3);
(2) provide brief details of the circumstances of the last three similar convictions and/or of convictions likely to be of interest to the judge, the latter being judged on a case by case basis, being provided separately and attached to the antecedents;
(3) where the current alleged offence might constitute a breach of an existing order, and it is known that that order is still in force, to enable the judge to consider the possibility of revoking the order, details of the circumstances of the offence leading to its imposition.

Seven copies of the antecedents will be prepared in respect of each accused. Two copies are provided to the CPS direct, the remaining five being sent to the Crown Court. The appropriate officer will send one copy to the defence and one to the Probation Service. Where, following conviction a custodial order is made, one of the court's copies will be attached to the order sent to the prison.
PD 2004, III.27.4–7

Note that:

(a) the antecedents must be provided within 21 days of the case being sent to the Crown Court;
(b) any points arising from them must be raised with the police by the defence solicitor as soon as possible and, if there is time, at least seven days before the hearing date so that that the matter can be resolved prior to the hearing;
(c) seven days before the hearing date, the police must check the record of convictions; details of any additional convictions must be provided, using the standard form, and attached to the documents already supplied. Details of any additional outstanding cases must also be provided at this stage.

The antecedents should include dates of release from prior sentences and sentence expiry dates (*R. v Egan* [2004] EWCA Crim 6303, *The Times,* March 9, 2004).

Bail or custody on adjournment

25–009 There is no general presumption in favour of bail after conviction, though it may be granted (subject to CJPOA 1994, s.25, see BAIL) where:

(1) the offender's case is adjourned for the purpose of enabling enquiries and a report to be made, to assist the court in dealing with him for the offence; or

(2) the offender appears or is brought before the court to be dealt with for breach of the requirements of a community order.

Where an offender's case is adjourned for enquiries or reports, and the offence, or one of the offences, of which he is convicted in the proceedings is punishable with imprisonment, he need not be granted bail if it appears that it would be impracticable to complete the enquiries or to make the report without keeping him in custody.

2. The statutory purposes of sentencing

Adult offenders

25–010 A judge dealing with an offender aged 18 or over in respect of his offence must, in every case, have regard to the following purposes of sentencing: CJA 2003, s.142

(1) the punishment of offenders,

(2) the reduction of crime (including its reduction by deterrence),

(3) the reform and rehabilitation of offenders,

(4) the protection of the public, and

(5) the making of reparation by offenders to persons affected by their offences.

The foundation of any sentence is CJA 2003, s.142(1). The section, which is mandatory in effect, makes clear that whilst the punishment of an offender is one purpose of any sentence, it is not the only purpose. The rehabilitation of offenders and the protection of the public are other purposes to which the judge must have regard when considering sentence (*R. v Rakib* [2011] EWCA Crim 870, [2011] Crim. L.R. 570).

But as a matter of sentencing reality, whenever a gun is made available for use, as well as when a gun is used, public protection is the paramount consideration. Deterrent and punitive sentences are required and should be imposed (*R. v Olawaiye* [2009] EWCA Crim 1925, [2010] 1 Cr. App. R. (S.) 100).

This provision does not apply:

(a) in relation to an offender who is aged under 18 (as to which CJA 2003, s.142A, will apply as and when brought into force);

(b) to an offence the sentence for which is fixed by law;

(c) to an offence the sentence for which falls to be imposed FA 1968, s.51A(2) (minimum sentence for certain firearms offences), under PCC(S)A 2000, ss.110(2) or 111(2) (required custodial sentences) or under CJA 2003, ss.225(2) or 226(2) (dangerous offenders); or

     (d) in relation to the making, under MHA 1983, Pt 3, of a hospital order (with or without a restriction order), an interim hospital order, a hospital direction or a limitation direction.

"Sentence", in relation to an offence, includes any order made by a court when dealing with an offender in respect of his offence; and "sentencing" is to be construed accordingly. (See APPEALS FROM THE CROWN COURT).

As to those aged under 18, and children and young persons, see CHILDREN AND YOUNG PERSONS.

3. A "road-map" of sentencing

25–011 For those steeped in criminal practice, much of the machinery of sentence will be well-known, if not instinctive. For those coming from other disciplines, common law, commercial or family law, may find themselves assisted by the following "road map" useful in approaching the current maze of sentencing provisions, and deciding where the balance lies between the declared purposes of sentencing set out in 25–010, above.

Once the decision has been made to proceed to sentence and not to remit the offender to another court or judge for sentence (see 25–012, below), the following "step by step" approach may be useful for assessing:

    (1) the seriousness of the offence;
    (2) the culpability of the offender; and
    (3) the level of actual, intended or foreseeable harm,

thus arriving at a proper and just disposal of the case.

The sentencing decision does not represent a mathematical exercise, nor does it result from an arithmetical calculation; the reality is that the judge must balance all the circumstances of the case to reach an appropriate sentence (*R. v Martin* [2006] EWCA Crim 1035, [2007] 1 Cr. App. R. (S.) 3).

There is nothing to prevent the judge from showing leniency in passing sentence provided that in his sentencing remarks he indicates that he is being merciful in the circumstances of the case and gives his reasons for being so.

The suggested steps, or stages, may be spelt out in brief as follows:

Step 1—The factual basis for sentence
Step 2—Choice of disposal
Step 3—Aggravating and mitigating features
Step 4—TIC's
Step 5—Discounts
Step 6—Credit of remand periods
Step 7—Other factors
Step 8—Following sentencing guidelines
Step 9—Ancillary orders
Step 10—Spelling it out

Special considerations apply in relation to cases of corporate manslaughter and health and safety offences causing death, as to which see SGC 2010, para.37.

4.   Step 1—The factual basis for sentence

General

25–012   As far as possible an offender should be sentenced on a basis which accurately reflects the facts of the individual case; a different set of circumstances is likely to arise depending upon whether there has been a trial or sentence follows a plea of guilty. A factual basis for sentence, (holding a Newton hearing where necessary—see GUILTY PLEAS) must be established, and also, in particular:

(1) the offender's age—generally crucial to the sentencing process (see 25–048, below and AGE OF OFFENDER); in general 18 is the watershed though, in the case of young offenders; a further breakdown may be necessary (see DETENTION OF YOUNG OFFENDERS);

(2) the date of the commission of the offence—also crucial: SI 2005/643 brought into force most of the sentencing provisions of CJA 2003 and these apply to offences committed on or after April 4, 2005. Sentences for offences committed before that date continue to be governed by PCC(S)A 2000; certain specific orders are available only after certain stated dates;

(3) the number of offences to be dealt with—an offender may be sentenced only on the basis of the offences proved against him by admission or verdict, or which he has asked to be taken into consideration (see 25–042—25–045 below) (*R. v Canavan* [1988] 1 Cr. App. R. (S.) 243; *R. v Tovey* [2005] EWCA Crim 530, [2005] 2 Cr. App. R. (S.) 100);

(4) the seriousness of the offence(s) (25–024, below);

(5) the culpability of the offender; and

(6) the harm caused to individuals, to the community or other types of harm (see, as to victims' views, VICTIM IMPACT STATEMENTS);

(7) the prevalence of the offence(s) being dealt with (see 25–052, below);

(8) any mental health considerations (25–034, below).

Crown's obligation to state facts in open court

25–013   To enable the public and the press to know the circumstances of an offence of which the accused has been convicted and for which he is being sentenced, in relation to each offence to which the offender has pleaded guilty, the prosecution must state the facts in open court before sentence is passed.

While he is not obliged to pass sentence on the least serious version of the facts (*R. v Solomon* (1984) 6 Cr. App. R. (S.) 120), the judge should give the offender the benefit of any doubt (see *R. v Stosiek* (1982) 4 Cr. App. R. (S.) 205). Other than in a case of murder reduced to manslaughter (see *R. v Frankum* (1983) 5 Cr. App. R. (S.) 259) it is inappropriate for the judge to take a "special verdict" (*R. v Larkin* [1943] K.B. 174).

At this stage, or immediately before sentence, the offender may ask for other admitted offences, not the subject of the indictment, or of committal from the magistrates' court, to be taken into consideration on sentence. As to the procedure for TIC's, see 25–045 below.

Facts emerging following plea of guilty

25–014   Where sentence is passed following a plea of guilty, the basis for the sentence is to be derived from the prosecution case, which includes the facts disclosed in the witness statements of the prosecution and the facts outlined by the prosecution advocate, unless the plea is tendered and accepted on an agreed basis. As to the procedure in such a case, see GUILTY PLEAS.

Facts emerging following trial

25–015   Where an offender is convicted after a trial:

(1) the factual basis for sentence may be derived from the evidence called at the trial; but
(2) the judge must be careful to sentence only for those offences:
    (a) to which the offender has pleaded guilty; or
    (b) of which the offender has been convicted at the trial, or any other trial where sentence is pending and falls to be dealt with; or
    (c) which the offender formally asks to be taken into consideration (as to which see 25–042—25–045 below).

Where an issue arises as to sentence on which no evidence was called at the trial, the judge may hold a Newton hearing (see GUILTY PLEAS) to determine the matter (*R. v Finch* (1993) 14 Cr. App. R. (S.) 226).

Clearly, where the prosecution does not proceed on a count, the judge must pass sentence on the basis that the offender is not guilty of it.

Interpreting the verdict

25–016   Problems may arise in interpreting the jury's verdict. In particular:

(1) if the verdict can be explained only on one view of the facts the judge must adopt that view as the basis for sentence;
(2) if more than one view of the facts is consistent with the verdict, the judge may form his own view in the light of the evidence given;
(3) if the verdict leaves open an important issue which may affect sentence, the judge must decide where the truth lies.

(*R. v Solomon* (1984) 6 Cr. App. R. (S.) 120; *R. v McGlade* (1991) 12 Cr. App. R. (S.) 105; *R. v Martin* [2006] EWCA Crim 1035, [2007] 1 Cr. App. R. (S.) 3.)

5.   Step 2—Choice of disposal

General
25–017   The form of sentence imposed on an offender will depend
upon the factors outlined above, and the objective which the judge has
in view, bearing in mind any restrictions placed upon his discretion, in
particular by PCC(S)A 2000, as amended by CJA 2003.

Where the judge seeks:

(1) to punish, the appropriate custodial sentence, be it imprisonment
or one of those forms of detention provided for young offenders,
as the case may be, will be apposite, or a financial penalty;
(2) merely to mark the conviction, and no more, an absolute discharge may be appropriate;
(3) to encourage the offender not to offend again, there are available
four forms of preventive or conditional sentences:
(a) a bind-over under JPA 1361, where breach involves forfeiture of a specific sum;
(b) a common law bind-over, the breach of which may also
involve a fresh sentence; and
(c) a conditional discharge, which permits a court to act on
a breach, but does not involve a specific sentence on the
breach; and
(d) a suspended sentence of imprisonment;
(4) to rehabilitate the offender, he is likely to go for a community
order to which a whole range of requirements may be added;
Note that a detention and training order (see DETENTION OF
YOUNG OFFENDERS), though punitive, is intended to have
a regime which is, at the same time, "constructive", with an
emphasis on discipline and education;
(5) to deal with a person who requires treatment for a specified
mental disorder, hospital and guardianship orders under MHA
1983 may be made, or treatment requirements may be added to
a community order;
(6) to keep dangerous offenders out of circulation, the appropriate
provisions of PCC(S)A 2000 and CJA 2003 will be appropriate.

A good working rule is not to mix sentences which fall into established
and different categories (*R. v McElhorne* [1983] Crim. L.R. 487).

Mandatory or discretionary?
25–018   The judge needs to know whether he is obliged by law or
whether the choice lies in his discretion.

Certain sentences are fixed, or prescribed by law, thus:

(1) a life sentence (see LIFE SENTENCES);
(2) sentences for dangerous offenders, CJA 2003, s.225 and following (see DANGEROUS OFFENDERS; PROTECTIVE
SENTENCES);
(3) "automatic" life sentences for 2nd serious offence (PCC(S)A 2000,
s.109 may still be available in rare cases (see IMPRISONMENT);
(4) third time domestic burglary (PCC(S)A 2000, s.111) carries a 3
year required minimum sentence (see IMPRISONMENT);

(5) third time drug trafficking offence, (PCC(S)A 2000, s.110) carries a required minimum sentence of seven years (see IMPRISONMENT);

(6) certain offences regarding prohibited weapons (FA 1968, s.51A) carry a required minimum sentence of five years (see IMP-RISONMENT; DETENTION OF YOUNG OFFENDERS); and

(7) minimum terms a prescribed in certain cases of using a person to mind a weapon (VCRA 2006, s.29(4) or (6)), (see IMPRISONMENT).

Dangerous offenders

25–019 In relation to offenders sentenced after July 14, 2008, for offences committed after April 4, 2005, who qualify as "dangerous" offenders under CJA 2003, ss.225–228, amended by CJIA 2008, ss.13–18, the judge may impose:

(1) a mandatory sentence of life imprisonment (or custody for life in the case of an offender under 18);

(2) a discretionary sentence of imprisonment (or detention in the case of an offender under 18) for public protection (IPP/DPP);

(3) a discretionary extended sentence of imprisonment (or in the case of an offender under 18 detention) (EPP).

Where the offender does not qualify for (1)–(3) above, a determinate sentence or a community penalty may be imposed.

Both imprisonment or detention for public protection, for a serious specified offence and an extended sentence for a specified offence (not necessarily a "serious" specified offence), are conditional upon:

(a) the offender having been previously convicted of an offence contained in Sch.15A; or

(b) the projected determinate custodial term being at least four years (making the specified notional sentence at least two years before deducting time spent on remand—see IMPRISONMENT).

There will be cases where the offences before the court have been committed both before and after April 4, 2005. For those committed before that date, the relevant sentencing provisions are contained in a number of statutes, of which PCC(S)A 2000, is the most important (though see also, in relation to sexual offences, SOA 1956 and SOA 2003). In relation to offences committed before April 4, 2005, neither a sentence of imprisonment for public protection (IPP) nor an extended sentence (EPP) under the CJA 2003 can be imposed (for further detail of which see DANGEROUS OFFENDERS; PROTECTIVE SENTENCES).

Thresholds

25–020 In considering the nature of the sentence to be imposed, it is necessary for the judge to consider whether:

(1) the case is "so serious" that it crosses the "custody threshold?" (25–022, below);

(2) if the case crosses the custody threshold, immediate custody is required;

(3) there are realistic alternatives to a custodial sentence, e.g. deferring sentence (see DEFERRING SENTENCE);

(4) if custody is not appropriate, the case is "serious enough" to cross the "community sentence" threshold (see 25–033), below);

(5) if it is a case for a community sentence penalty, which requirements should be attached to the order (see COMMUNITY SENTENCES in the case of an adult, YOUTH REHABILITATION ORDERS in the case of young offenders);

(6) if the community sentence threshold is not reached, a lesser sentence is appropriate, e.g. a fine (FINES AND ENFORCE-MENT), a compensation order (see COMPENSATION ORDERS), a conditional discharge (see DISCHARGE: CONDITIONAL AND ABSOLUTE) or a bind over (see BIND OVER);

(7) orders for deprivation or forfeiture of property (see FORFEITURE) or restitution (see RESTITUTION ORDERS) are appropriate;

(8) a confiscation order under POCA 2002 is appropriate? (see CONFISCATION ORDERS);

(9) any other ancillary order is called for (see ANCILLARY ORDERS);

(10) orders for prosecution and/or defence costs are appropriate (see COSTS AND ASSESSMENT).

Discretionary custodial sentences

25–021 Custodial sentences, for the purposes of PCC(S)A 2000, Pt V, are, in relation to an offender:

PCC(S)A 2000, s.76(1)(2)

(1) **imprisonment** (other than a committal or attachment for contempt of court or any kindred offence), as to which see PCC(S)A 2000, s.89(1)(a);

(2) **detention for public protection** under CJA 2003, s.226 in relation to offences committed on or after April 4, 2005;

(3) **detention** under **CJA 2003, s.228,** in relation to offences committed on or after April 4, 2005;

(4) **detention in a young offender institution** under PCC(S)A 2000, s.96;

(5) **detention** under **PCC(S)A 2000, s.90 or 91;** or

(6) **detention and training orde**r under PCC(S)A 2000, s.100.

Different considerations govern different types of custodial sentence, but the imposition of any of them is subject to:

(a) the offence(s) "qualifying" for a custodial sentence (see 25–022, below);

(b) the offender's age (see AGE OF OFFENDER);

(c) unless unnecessary, the availability of a pre-sentence report (see REPORTS); and

(d) in general, the offender being legally represented (see 25–007 above).

So complex are many of the interlocking provisions governing the question of custodial sentences, that it is in this field particularly, that judges should not be slow to invite assistance from prosecuting counsel", nor should they be "affronted" where the latter offers such assistance on the relevant provisions and authorities (*Att-Gen's Reference (No.7 of 1997*) [1998] 1 Cr. App. R. (S.) 268).

Threshold for custodial sentences

25–022   Where a person is convicted of an offence committed on or after April 4, 2005, punishable with a custodial sentence, other than one: CJA 2003, s.152

- fixed by law, or
- under FA 1968, s.51A (firearms),
- under PCC(S)A 2000, ss.109 where still appropriate, ss.110(2) or 111(2), (repeat offences), or
- under any of CJA 2003, ss.225–228 (dangerous offenders), or
- under VCRA 2006, s.29(4) or (6) (minding dangerous weapons),

the judge must not pass a custodial sentence on the offender unless he is of the opinion that the offence, or the combination of the offence, and one or more offences "associated" with it (25–023) is "so serious" (25–024) that neither a fine alone nor a community sentence can be justified for it.

Nothing, however, prevents the judge from passing a custodial sentence on an offender who fails to express his willingness to comply with a requirement which it is proposed to include in a community order, and which requires an expression of such willingness.

"Associated offences" for the purposes of CJA 2003, s.152

25–023   "Associated" in relation to an offence is to be read in accordance with PCC(S)A 2000, s.161(1) (CJA 2003, s.305). Under that section an offence is said to be "associated" with another for this purpose if:

(1) the offender is convicted of it in the proceedings in which he is convicted of the other offence, or, (although convicted of it in earlier proceedings) he is sentenced for it at the same time as he is sentenced for the other offence; or

(2) he admits the commission of it in the proceedings for which he is sentenced for that other offence and asks the judge to take it into consideration (see 25–044) in sentencing him for that offence.

It follows that:

(a) an offence in respect of which a suspended sentence was passed (*R. v Crawford* (1993) 14 Cr. App. R. (S.) 782), or a conditional discharge was made (*R. v Godfrey* (1993) 14 Cr. App. R. 804) on a previous occasion; or

(b) an uncharged offence, not represented by a sample count, and not taken into consideration on sentence,

are not "associated" offences.

"Seriousness" for the purposes of CJA 2003 s.152

25–024   CJA 2003 is silent as to when an offence is so "serious" that only a custodial sentence is justified; it is a subjective test. Obviously a crime which is deliberate and premeditated, and causes personal or mental injury, is usually more serious than one which is spontaneous and unpremeditated, causing only financial loss. Lawton L.J.'s approach in *R. v Bradbourn* (1987) 7 Cr. App. R. (S.) 180 in respect of the previous legislation was deprecated by CACD in *R. v Howells* [1999] 1 Cr. App. R. (S.) 335. Of course:

(1) the judge is not bound to impose a custodial sentence just because the offence "qualifies"; he is still required to consider whether, having regard to mitigating circumstances, such a sentence is appropriate;
(2) the fact that a court imposed a community sentence for an offence, does not prevent it "qualifying" for a custodial sentence if the offender is in breach of the order (*R. v Bray* (1991) 12 Cr. App. R. (S.) 705; *R. v Webster* (1990) 12 Cr. App. R. (S.) 760; *R. v Oliver* (1993) 96 Cr. App. R. 426).

In considering the seriousness of an offence, the judge:

(a) may take into account the offender's previous convictions, and/or any failure of his to respond to previous sentences;
(b) may take into account the prevalence of offences of a particular class, and public concern about them (*R. v Cunningham* (1992) Cr. App. R. (S.) 444; *R. v Cox* (1993) 96 Cr. App. R. 464); and
(c) **must** treat as aggravating factors those matters stated at 25–037—25–039.

Custodial sentences: length – suspension

25–025 Where the judge decides on a custodial sentence he will need to consider:

(1) How long that sentence should be? (25–026, below) (as to joint conviction with juvenile see *R. v Tyre* (1984) 6 Cr. App. R. (S.) 247);
(2) Whether the sentence should be suspended? (see 25–027 below) and if so whether:
(a) for offences committed before April 4, 2005, there are "exceptional circumstances" justifying a suspended sentence?
(b) for offences committed after April 4, 2005, a suspended sentence order is appropriate?

(See IMPRISONMENT.)

Length of discretionary sentence

25–026 In the case of a custodial sentence other than one fixed by law or be imposed under CJA 2003, s.225 or 226, for an offence committed on or after April 4, 2005, then, subject to:

(1) FA 1968, s.51A (firearms);
(2) PCC(S)A 2000, ss.109 where still appropriate, 110(2) and 111(2) (required sentences for certain repeat offences); and

(3) CJA 2003, ss.227(2) and 228(2) (dangerous offenders); or

(4) VCRA 2006, s.29(4) or (6) (minding dangerous weapons),

the custodial sentence must be for the shortest time (not exceeding the permitted maximum) that is, in the judge's opinion commensurate with the seriousness of the offence, or the combination of the offence and one or more offences associated with it.

Suspending a sentence of imprisonment

25–027   A judge passing a sentence of imprisonment, or, in the case of an offender aged at least 18 but under 21, detention in a young offender institution, for a term of at least 14 days but not more than 12 months in respect of an offence committed on or after April 4, 2005, in accordance with CJA 2003, s.181, may order:

(1) the offender to comply during a specified supervision period with one or more of the requirements falling within s.190(1) and specified in the order; and

(2) that the sentence of imprisonment will not take effect unless:

    (a) during the supervision period the offender fails to comply with a requirement imposed under (1) above; or

    (b) during the "operational period" specified in the order, the offender commits in Great Britain another offence (whether or not punishable with imprisonment). (See IMPRISONMENT.)

Offences not qualifying for custodial sentence

25–028   If none of the offences with which he is dealing qualifies for a custodial sentence in this sense, the judge can impose only a **financial penalty** or a **community sentence**. Where the offences with which he is dealing are of differing gravity, some "qualifying", others not:

(1) he is not prevented from passing custodial sentences in respect of the offences not qualifying (*R. v Mussell* (1990) 12 Cr. App. R. (S.) 607; *R. v Oliver* (1993) 6 Cr. App. R. 426); but

(2) he ought not, in general, to pass consecutive sentences for such offences, or make the overall sentence longer by reference to them (*R. v Oliver,* above).

Financial penalties

25–029   Where a person is convicted on indictment of any offence other than an offence:

(1) for which the sentence is fixed by law; or

(2) falls to be imposed under PCC(S)A 2000, ss.109 where still appropriate, 110(2) or 111(2) (required sentence for certain repeat offences); or

(3) falls to be imposed under any of the sections CJA 2003, ss.225–228 (dangerous offenders),

the judge, if not precluded from sentencing an offender by his exercise of some other power, may impose a fine:

    (a) instead of; or

(b) in addition to,

dealing with him in any other way in which he has power to deal with him, subject to any enactment requiring the offender to be dealt with in a particular way. As to surcharges, see FINES AND ENFORCEMENT.

While judges may be reluctant to impose a fine, since fines are often not properly enforced by the magistrates' courts, recent statutory enactments have provided for a more rigorous approach to enforcement. If these prove to be effective, where an offender has means, a heavy fine may often be an adequate and appropriate punishment. If this is the case, CJA 2003 requires a fine to be imposed rather than a community sentence (*R. v Seed* [2007] EWCA Crim 254, [2007] 2 Cr. App. R. (S.) 69).

Proper approach to financial penalty

25–030　The amount of any fine fixed must be such as, in the judge's opinion, reflects the seriousness of the offence, but in fixing the amount, he must:

(1) in the case of an individual offender, inquire into his financial circumstances; and

(2) whether the offender is an individual or other person, take into account the circumstances of the case including, amongst other things, the financial circumstances of the offender, so far as they are known, or appear to him,

and (2) above applies whether it has the effect of increasing or reducing the amount of the fine.

The judge may, before sentencing, make a financial circumstances order under CJA 2003, s.162, and where the offender fails to comply or otherwise fails to co-operate in an enquiry into his financial circumstances, the judge may make such order as he thinks fit.

Community sentences

25–031　Community sentences, for the purposes of CJA 2003, Pt 12 are, in relation to an offence committed on or after April 4, 2005, those which consist of:

(1) a community order, as defined by s.177 (see COMMUNITY SENTENCES); or

(2) a youth rehabilitation order under CJIA 2008, see YOUTH REHABILITATION ORDERS).

A number of individual requirements may be added to such orders.

Community sentences for offences committed before April 4, 2005, are dealt with under PCC(S)A 2000, and consist principally of a community rehabilitation order, a community punishment order and the combination of the two, to which additional requirements may be added (see COMMUNITY SENTENCES).

No community sentence where sentence fixed by law, etc.

25–032　No community order or youth community order may be made in respect of an offence committed on or after April 4, 2005, for which the sentence;

(1) is fixed by law;
(2) falls to be imposed under FA 1968, s.51A (required sentences for certain firearms offences);
(3) falls to be imposed under PCC(S)A 2000, s.109 where still appropriate, or ss.110(2) or 111(2) (required sentences for certain repeat);
(4) falls to be imposed under any of CJA 2003, ss.225–228 (custodial sentences for dangerous offenders); or
(5) falls to be imposed under VCRA 2006, s.29(4) or (6) (required custodial sentence for minding a weapon).

General restrictions on imposing community sentences

25–033   In relation to offences committed on or after April 4, 2005, the judge may not pass a community sentence on an offender unless he is of opinion that, subject to CJA 2003 s.151(2), the offence, or the combination of the offence and one or more offences associated with it, was serious enough to warrant such a sentence, and where he does pass such a sentence:

(1) the particular requirement or requirements forming part of the community order must be such as in his opinion is, or taken together are, the most suitable for the offender; and
(2) subject to CJA 2003 s.134(2), the restrictions on liberty imposed by the order must be such as in his opinion are commensurate with the seriousness of the offence, or the combination of the offence and the one or more offences associated with it.

Where the judge passes a community sentence which consists of or includes one or more youth community orders:

(a) the particular order or orders forming part of the sentence must be such as in his opinion is, or taken together are, the most suitable for the offender; and
(b) the restrictions on liberty imposed by the order or orders must be such as in his opinion are commensurate with the seriousness of the offence, or the combination of the offence and the one or more offences associated with it.

As to the recommended approach to such an order see COMMUNITY SENTENCES.

Where an offender falls to be sentenced for two or more offences, one or more of which were committed before and some after, April 4, 2005, sentences on the differing counts fall to be passed under different provisions and take differing forms, e.g. where the offender is to be sentenced for two such offences, one pre- and one post-commencement, and the judge seeks to deal with him by means of a community punishment order under the old law, he will need to make in respect of the post commencement offence, a community order under CJA 2003 with a requirement for unpaid work.

Mental health disposal

25–034   In the case of an offender who is not so mentally disordered as to be absolved from criminal responsibility for his actions, but is nevertheless in need of psychiatric treatment, a judge may, in certain circumstances, remand to hospital for treatment accused persons who are waiting to be tried, as well as those waiting to be sentenced. Those who have been convicted may be:

(1) sent to a hospital under an interim hospital order, or a hospital order;
(2) made the subject of a guardianship order; or
(3) made the subject of a community order with a mental health treatment requirement.

As to the procedure to a verdict of not guilty by reason of insanity or a finding of disability, see UNFITNESS TO PLEAD/INSANITY.

The judge in considering whether to make a hospital order or an interim hospital order, may ask the Regional Health Authority to assist in identifying an appropriate hospital for a particular offender. In some cases a hospital order may be made in conjunction with a restriction order (see generally MENTALLY DISORDERED OFFENDERS).

6. Step 3—Determining seriousness; aggravating and mitigating features

Judge's approach
25–035 In approaching the nature or length of any sentence; the judge should:

(1) first determine the order, or the length of the custodial term which he has in mind; and
(2) then adjust it in the light of any mitigating (or aggravating) factors.

(*R. v Fraser* (1982) 4 Cr. App. R. (S.) 254.)

Previous convictions and offences committed whilst on bail are treated as aggravating factors under CJA 2003, s.143 (see 25–036 below). Other aggravating and mitigating factors are dealt with from 25–037—25–041 below.

CJA 2003, s.143;
25–036 The judge must (CJA 2003, s.143(1)–(3)) in relation to all offences whether committed before or after April 4, 2005:

(1) consider the offender's culpability in committing the offence and any harm which the offence caused, was intended to cause or might foreseeably have caused; and
(2) when considering the seriousness of:
  (a) the current offence committed by an offender who has one or more **previous convictions,** to treat each previous conviction as an aggravating factor if, in the case of that conviction, he considers that it can reasonably be so treated having regard to the nature of the offence to which the conviction relates and its relevance to the current offence, and the time that has elapsed since the conviction;
  (b) an offence committed while the offender was **on bail,** to

treat the fact that it was committed whilst he was on bail as an aggravating factor.

A "previous conviction" here, refers to one by a court in the United Kingdom, and a previous finding of guilt in service disciplinary proceedings, but the judge is not prevented from treating a previous conviction by a court outside the United Kingdom as an aggravating feature in any case where he considers it appropriate to do so.

Additional aggravating features

25–037   The nature and length of the sentence may be enhanced not only by the facts of the case but by aggravating features in addition to those mentioned in 25–036 above, such as:

(1) the number of offences;
(2) the period of offending;
(3) any racial or religious element in the offence (25–038), below);
(4) hostility based on the victim's sexual orientation or disability (20–039, below);
(5) the impact of the offences on the community;
(6) planning and sophistication;
(7) offence(s) committed while the offender was subject to a community order (see BREACH, AMENDMENT AND REVOCATION);
(8) offence(s) committed in contravention of other court orders (see BREACH, AMENDMENT AND REVOCATION).

The effect of having offences taken into consideration (TICs) may being either aggravating or mitigating (see 25–042 below)

Increase racial or religious aggravation

25–038   In considering the seriousness of an offence, whether committed before or after April 4, 2005, other than one under CDA 1998, ss.29 to 32 (racially or religiously aggravated assaults, criminal damage, public order offences and harassment) if the offence was racially or religiously aggravated (within the meaning of CDA 1998, s.28) the judge must treat that as a factor which increases the seriousness of the offence, and must state in open court: CJA 2003 s.145

(1) that it was so aggravated:
    (a) identifying the sentence which would have been appropriate in the absence of racial aggravation; and
    (b) adding an appropriate amount to reflect the element of racial aggravation; and
(2) indicating by how much the sentence has been enhanced to reflect the racial aggravation.

(See *R. v Kelly* [2001] EWCA Crim 1751, [2002] 1 Cr. App. R. (S.) 85); *R. v Saunders* [2000] 1 Cr. App. R. (S.) 71, considered in *R. v Kelly* [2001] EWCA Crim 1751, [2001] 2 Cr. App. R. (S.) 73, though there may be cases where such an approach is inappropriate, see e.g. *R. v O'Brien* [2003] EWCA Crim 302, [2003] 2 Cr. App. R.(S.) 66, *R. v Fitzgerald* [2003] EWCA Crim 2875, [2004] 1 Cr. App. R.(S.) 74.

The amount of the enhancement will depend on the circumstances of the particular case (*R. v Morrison* [2001] 1 Cr. App. R. (S.) 5).

As to what amounts to "racial" aggravation, contrast the cases of *R. v White* [2001] EWCA Crim 216, [2001] Crim. L.R. 576 and *DPP v Pal* [2000] Crim. L.R. 756. As to where it is not possible to identify which member of a group shouted racist slogans, see *R. v Davies* [2003] EWCA Crim 3700, [2004] 2 Cr. App. R. (S.) 29.

It is not open to the judge to sentence on the basis of racial aggravation unless the offender has been convicted on that basis (*R. v O'Callaghan* [2005] EWCA Crim 317, [2005] 2 Cr. App. R. (S.) 83; *R. v McGillivray* [2005] EWCA Crim 604, [2005] 2 Cr. App. R. (S.) 60), though in *R. v Lester* (1976) 63 Cr. App. R. 144 the prosecutor was allowed to adduce evidence of such aggravation, which was not adduced at the trial, in the course of a Newton hearing.

The judge should be careful not to draw any inference that the offence was so aggravated unless he gives notice to the offender and permits him to challenge the inference.

Aggravation related to disability or sexual orientation

25–039   Where the judge is considering the seriousness of an offence   CJA 2003, s.146 committed on or after April 4, 2005, in any of the following circumstances, namely that, at the time of committing the offence, or immediately before or after doing so, the offender demonstrated towards the victim of the offence hostility based on:

(1) the sexual orientation (or presumed sexual orientation) of the victim; or
(2) a disability (or presumed disability) of the victim; or
(3) a motivation (wholly or partly) by hostility towards persons who:
    (a) are of a particular sexual orientation, or
    (b) have a disability or a particular disability, the judge must:
        (i) treat the fact that the offence was committed in any of those circumstances as an aggravating factor; and
        (ii) state in open court that the offence was committed in such circumstances.

It is immaterial for the purposes of (1) to (3) above whether or not the offender's hostility is also based, to any extent, on any other factor. "Disability" means any physical or mental impairment.

Where the prosecutor seeks to adduce evidence of such aggravation, which was not adduced at the trial, the evidence should be adduced after verdict at a Newton hearing. The judge should be careful not to draw any inference that the offence was so aggravated unless he gives notice to the offender and permits him to challenge the inference (see *R. v Lester*, above). The same approach to sentence will apply as in 25–038.

Mitigating factors

25–040   The nature and length of the sentence may be reduced by mitigating factors such as:

(1)   positive good character or lack of previous convictions;

DEALING WITH AN OFFENDER

(2) a plea of guilty and the application of the reduction principles (see DISCOUNTS ON SENTENCE, GUILTY PLEAS);
(3) the level of the offender's responsibility for the offence(s);
(4) whether the offender acted under pressure from others;
(5) clear evidence of contrition and remorse;
(6) the offender cooperating with the prosecutor (see DISCOUNTS ON SENTENCE);
(7) lapse of time between the commission of the offence and the date of sentence;
(8) credit of any remand period (see IMPRISONMENT);
(9) the offender's conduct during any remand period; and
(10) restorative justice factors (see *R. v Collins* [2003] EWCA Crim 1687; *R. v Bard* [2003] EWCA Crim 2816), and factors such as compensation (see COMPENSATION ORDERS).

Statutory saving for mitigation

25–041   In so far as offences committed on or after April 4, 2005 are concerned nothing in relation to: CJA 2003, s.166(1)(3)

(1) imposing community sentences (CJA 2003, s.148 or CJIA 2008, s.151(2));
(2) imposing custodial sentences (CJA 2003, ss.152,153 or 157);
(3) pre-sentence reports and other requirements (CJA 2003, s.164);
(4) the fixing of fines (CJA 2003, s.164);
(5) youth rehabilitation orders with intensive supervision and surveillance (CJIA 2008, Sch.1, para.3); or
(6) youth rehabilitation with fostering (CJIA 2008, Sch.1, para.41),

prevents the judge from mitigating an offender's sentence by taking into account any such matters as, in his opinion, are relevant in mitigation of sentence, including his power to mitigate:

(a) any penalty included in the offender's sentence by taking into account any other penalty included in that sentence; and
(b) the sentence of an offender convicted of one or more other offences, by applying the "totality principle" (see IMPRISONMENT).

In particular:

(i) CJA 2003, s.152, does not prevent the judge, after taking into account such matters, from passing a community sentence, even though he is of opinion that the offence, or the combination of the offence and one or more offences associated with it, was so serious that a community sentence could not normally be justified for the offence (CJA 2003, s.166(2)); and
(ii) in the case of a person suffering from a mental disorder within the meaning of MHA 1983, nothing mentioned in the sections referred to in (1)–(4) above is to be taken as requiring the judge to pass a custodial sentence, or any CJA 2003, s.166(5)(6)

particular custodial sentence, or as restricting any power (whether under MHA 1983 or otherwise) which enables the judge to deal with an offender in the manner he considers to be most appropriate in all the circumstances.

7. Step 4—TICs

TICs

25–042   There is a convention, although it has no statutory authority, that where the judge, when passing sentence upon an offender for an offence:

(1) is informed that there are outstanding charges against the offender; and
(2) the offender admits each of them and asks for them to be taken into consideration,

he may formally take them into consideration, and pass a longer sentence than he would if he were dealing only with the counts on the indictment (*R. v Batchelor* (1952) 36 Cr. App. R. 64). Any sentence imposed is intended to reflect an offender's overall criminality *(R. v Miles,* [2006] EWCA Crim 256, *The Times*, April 10, 2006);

There is no reason, therefore, in principle why an offence to be taken into consideration which is of a more serious nature than the one before the court should not result in a higher sentence than would otherwise have been the case (*R. v Lavery* [2008] EWCA Crim 2499, [2009] 3 All E.R. 295) provided that the maximum term for these offences is not exceeded.

As with other aspects of sentencing, the way in which the judge deals with such offences will depend on context. They may add nothing, or nothing very much, to the sentence he would otherwise have imposed. They may aggravate the sentence and lead to a substantial increase, particularly where the offences show a pattern of criminal activity which suggests careful planning, or if the offences were committed on bail after an earlier arrest. On the other hand, when assessing their significance, the judge is likely to attach weight to the demonstrable fact that the offender has assisted the police. Such co-operative behaviour may provide its own early indication of guilt and will usually mean that no further proceedings need to be started (*R. v Miles*, above).

Taking offences into consideration does not, technically, amount to a conviction of those offences, nor does the procedure found a subsequent plea of autre fois convict. It is perfectly feasible "as a matter of theoretical jurisprudence" to charge an offender with offences which have been taken into consideration. By convention it is not done, and where, perhaps in error, it is done, the judge dealing with the offences on the second occasion should see to it, without any doubt whatever, that no additional punishment is imposed on the offender on account of those offences.

Ancillary orders

25–043   Where an offence is formally taken into consideration in this manner, ancillary orders such as:

DEALING WITH AN OFFENDER

(1) a compensation order (PCC(S)A 2000, s.130); (see COMPENSATION ORDERS); and

(2) a restitution order under PCC(S)A 2000, s.148 (see RESTITUTION ORDERS),

may be made in respect of them.

Approach to taking offences into consideration

25–044 In general, offences taken into consideration should be offences similar to that, or those, for which the judge is passing sentence on the indictment. The judge should not take an offence into consideration without the consent of the prosecutor; the public interest may require investigation, and a trial of that offence (*R. v McLean* (1912) 6 Cr. App. R. 26). Nor should the judge taken into consideration;

(1) offences which he would have no jurisdiction to try (*R. v Simons* (1953) 37 Cr. App. R. 120);

(2) offences which, though triable in the Crown Court, involve RT disqualification (*R. v Simons*, above), unless the offender is liable to such an order under offences of which he has been convicted (*R. v Collins* (1948) 32 Cr. App. R. 27; *R. v Jones* (1971) 55 Cr. App. R. 32);

(3) the breach of conditional discharge or a community order (*R. v Webb* (1953) 37 Cr. App. R. 82), which should be dealt with in the way prescribed for dealing with the breach of such orders (see BREACH, AMENDMENT AND REVOCATION);

(4) offences committed outside the jurisdiction of the criminal courts of England and Wales, e.g. offences of a purely military disciplinary nature (*R. v Anderson* (1958) 42 Cr. App. R. 91) or offences committed in Scotland (see *Hilson v Easson* 1914 S.C. (J.) 99).

Where offences committed by a member of the armed forces are civil offences under service legislation, there is nothing to prevent their being taken into consideration (*R. v Anderson*, above).

Procedure

25–045 The procedure involves an offender, convicted of one or more offences, being punished for other offences for which he has never been arraigned, tried or convicted and to which he has never pleaded guilty.

It is essential, therefore, if justice is to be done, that the judge is satisfied in respect of each offence that the offender admits it, and wishes it to be taken into consideration. In practice the police prepare a list of such offences, serving it, with the consent of his legal advisors, upon the offender and obtaining his signature to it, striking through such offences as are not admitted.

Thus, before being sentenced:

(1) the offender (not his advocate) should be asked in open court, whether he has received the list, and if so, whether:
(a) he admits each of the offences (not struck out); and
(b) whether he wishes each of them to be taken into consideration;

(2) on a committal for sentence, the fact that the magistrates indicate that they have taken certain offences into consideration, does not

relieve the trial judge from ensuring that the accused still wishes them to be taken into consideration;

(3) if there is a lengthy schedule of offences, it is not normally necessary to take the accused through the document page by page; but

(4) if there is any doubt as to which offences the offender admits and wishes to have taken into consideration, the issue must be resolved in open court;

(5) if the judge is not satisfied that the offender has had time to consider the list in detail, it may be necessary to adjourn (*R. v Marquis* (1951) 35 Cr. App. R. 33; *DPP v Anderson* (1978) 67 Cr. App. R. 185; *R. v Nelson* (1967) 51 Cr. App. R. 98; *R. v Davies* (1981) 72 Cr. App. R. 262).

As to compensation orders made in relation to offences taken into consideration, see COMPENSATION ORDERS.

8.   Step 5—"Discounts" on sentence

25–046   A tract of cases developed by the CACD has given an offender the right to expect a discount on the otherwise appropriate sentence, where:

(1) he pleads guilty to the indictment (*R. v Barnes* (1983) 5 Cr. App. R. (S.) 368); the position is now governed by statute (see DISCOUNTS ON SENTENCE);

(2) the judge considers that the offence would not have been committed but for the activities of an informer (*R. v Beaumont* (1987) 9 Cr. App. R. (S.) 342; *R. v Chapman* (1989) 11 Cr. App. R. (S.) 222; *R. v Tonnessen* [1998] 2 Cr. App. R. (S.) 328; *R. v Underhill* [1979] 1 Cr. App. R. (S.) 270);

(3) the accused co-operates with the prosecuting authorities, not only by pleading guilty, but by giving information early enough for it to be potentially useful; this is also now covered by statute (see DISCOUNTS ON SENTENCE).

Such a discount should reflect the seriousness of the offence, the importance of the information, and the effect, where the informant gives evidence, on his future circumstances (*R. v Wood* [1996] Crim. L.R. 916) and the circumstances of the entrapment or other factors should be expressly mentioned in the judge's sentencing remarks (*R. v Mackey* (1993) 14 Cr. App. R. (S.) 53) save, obviously, in cases where the judge receives a "confidential text".

9.   Step 6—Credit of remand periods

25--047   In relation to determinate sentences of imprisonment and detention, where an offender is sentenced to imprisonment for a term in respect of an offence committed on or after April 4, 2005, the judge must, in computing the length of the sentence, order that any time spent on remand in custody, or on bail with certain restrictive conditions, count towards the sentence imposed (see IMPRISONMENT).

10.   Step 7—Other factors affecting sentence

Age

25–048   The age of the offender ought to be taken into account on sentence. In relation to a young offender, in addition to the distinctive range of penalties available for such, there is an expectation that, generally, he will be dealt with less severely than an adult, although this distinction diminishes as he approaches the age of 18.

Young people are unlikely to have the same experience and capacity as adults to realise the effect of their actions on other people or to appreciate the pain and distress caused and because a young person is likely to be less able to resist temptation, especially where peer pressure is exerted (SGC(Y) 3.1) but:

(1) where deterrence may be a factor in the case of an adult, it is necessary to balance that aspect against the youth of the offender (*R. v Marriott* (1995) 16 Cr. App. R. (S.) 428); but

(2) in the case of very serious offences, however, the room for reduction is limited, indeed there may be none at all (*R. v Dodds, The Times*, January 28, 1997).

See generally AGE OF OFFENDER.

As to offenders of advanced age, see *R. v W (Sentencing; Age of defendant), The Times*, October 26, 2000.

Offender's ill-health

25–049   Questions of an offender's life expectancy or risks of his deterioration in prison will usually be a matter for the administrative authorities, thus:

(1) if the offender is HIV positive or has otherwise a reduced life expectancy, this should not generally affect the sentence;

(2) the fact that the offender has a serious medical condition and is not easily treatable in prison does not automatically entitle him to a shorter sentence; but

(3) that does not, however, mean that a judge in sentencing must ignore the impact of ill- health on a man of a certain age.

(*R. v Bernard* [1997] 1 Cr. App. R. (S.) 135; *R. v Price* [2009] EWCA Crim 2918, [2010] 2 Cr. App. R. (S.) 44.)

As to the wholly exceptional case in which it is claimed that the very fact of imprisonment may create a breach of ECHR art.3, see *R. v Qazi* [2010] EWCA Crim 2579, [2011] 2 Cr. App. R. (S.) 8.

Cultural background

25–050   The cultural background of an offender is not necessarily relevant to sentence (*Att-Gen's Reference (No.1 of 2011) The Times*, April 11, 2011).

Foreign jurisdictions; deportation, etc.

25–051   The level of sentence which might be imposed in other jurisdictions is irrelevant: *R. v Maguire* [1997] 1 Cr. App. R. (S.) 130.

The fact that the offender will eventually be deported is not a matter which goes to reducing the length of a sentence of imprisonment.

There are procedures at the end of a sentence for considering whether the Home Secretary will adopt a recommendation to deport: *R. v Chen (Siao Bing), The Times*, April 17, 2001.

As to foreign offenders serving sentences in English prisons, that is a comparatively small consideration where deterrent sentences are merited.

Prevalence of offence
25–052   The prevalence of offences of a particular class, and public concern about them, is relevant to the seriousness of an offence before the court (*R. v Cunningham* (1993) 96 Cr. App. R. 452; *R. v Cox* (1993) 14 Cr. App. R. (S.) 479).

Amount and purity of drugs
25–053   With regard to assessing the amount and purity of drugs in reference to sentences for drugs offences, see *R. v Morris* [2001] 1 Cr. App. R. 25.

Views of victim
25–054   As to the relevance of the views of victims of crime, see VICTIM IMPACT STATEMENTS.

11.   Step 8—Following sentencing guidelines

General
25–055   The judge, in considering sentence is obliged to have regard to:

(1) any guideline judgment of CACD;
(2) any guidelines or advice from the SGC set up under CJA 2003, s.167, or its successor SCEW, set up under CorJA 2009, s.255;
(3) any helpful indications from other reported cases, relevant to sentencing the offender.

There is a statutory obligation on the judge, in sentencing an offender, to follow any sentencing guidelines issued under (2) above, which are relevant to the offender's case, and he must, in exercising any other function relating to the sentencing of offenders, follow any sentencing guidelines which are relevant to the exercise of that function, unless he is satisfied that it would be contrary to the interests of justice to do so. CorJA 2009, s.125(1)(6)(7)

The obligation is hedged around with savings in relation e.g. to statutory restrictions on custodial sentences and the imposition of mandatory sentences, for which reference needs to be made to CorJA 2009, s.225. There is a saving for mentally disordered offenders.

From March 11, 2011 the judge is required, when sentencing an offender for an offence committed **before April 6, 2010,** to have regard to and explain decisions by reference to sentencing guidelines issued by SCEW under CorJA 2008, s.120 as well as to guidelines under CJA 2003, s.170 (SI 2011/722).

Proposals of the Sentencing Advisory Panel do not, of themselves, constitute guidance to judges serving to displace, amend or in any way undermine the authority of the guidance issued in guideline decisions of CACD (*R. v Valentas* [2010] EWCA Crim 200, [2010] 2 Cr. App. R. (S.) 73).

The jurisdiction of CACD to amplify and explain definitive sentencing guidelines, or to offer a definitive sentencing guideline of its own, is undiminished: *Att Gen's References (Nos 73, 75 and 3 of 2010)* [2011] EWCA Crim 633; [2011] 2 Cr. App. R. (S.) 100.

Approach to guidelines.

25–056 The obligation is to have regard to a relevant guideline applying at the time of sentence even if it did not apply at the time of conviction, and even if the offender might have received a more lenient sentence under pre-guideline sentencing authorities (*R. v Bao* [2007] EWCA Crim 278, [2008] 2 Cr. App. R. (S.) 10).

Note that:

(1) a "guideline" is no more than a guideline. It does not affect the judge's powers as set out in the legislation, it merely indicates how those powers might be exercised. It does not alter the law (*R. v Peters* [2005] Crim. L.R. 407);

(2) there will be cases where there is good reason to depart from a guideline; justice may require a more merciful sentence than a guideline level might indicate, sometimes a more severe one; sometimes the individual case will not fit into the structure of any definitive guideline (*Att-Gen's Reference (No.8 of 2007)* [2007] EWCA Crim 922, [2008] 1 Cr. App. R. (S.) 1; *Att-Gen's References (Nos 8, 9 and 10 of 2009)* [2009] EWCA Crim 1636, [2010] 1 Cr. App. R. (S.) 66);

(3) where the judge decides not to apply a relevant sentencing guideline, he must (r.42.1) explain why he has not done so when he explains the sentence he has passed. See also Sentencing—Form of Words (25–062 below).

Role of prosecutor

25–057 The advocate for the Crown ought not to be prevented from advising the judge on the legal aspects of any sentence that he might be contemplating, whether at the judge's invitation or otherwise. He should be immediately familiar with the maximum sentences for the offence(s) which are being dealt with, and with the preconditions for any form of sentence which the judge proposes to impose (see generally *Att-Gen's Reference (No.7 of 1997)* [1998] 1 Cr. App. R. (S.) 268; *R. (Inner London Probation Service) v Tower Bridge MC* [2001] EWHC 401 (Admin), [2002] 1 Cr. App. R. (S.) 43). In particular he must bring to the judge's attention:

(1) any matters of law relating to sentence; and

(2) any sentencing guideline cases, making copies available to the judge.

(See *R. v Pepper* [2005] EWCA Crim 1181, [2006] 1 Cr. App. R. (S.) 29 where the authorities are reviewed).

He also has functions in relation to disputed issues of fact (see GUILTY PLEAS) and as to the acceptance or otherwise of pleas, (see GOODYEAR INDICATION).

If the judge makes an error in sentencing, particularly in relation to his powers, the advocate, whether for the Crown or for the defence, should be alive to the possibility of rectifying the sentence under the slip rule (PCC(S)A 2000, s.155 (see VARIATION OF SENTENCE)).

The DPP, on February 22, 2010, issued an updated edition of the Code for Crown Prosecutors.

12. Step 9—Ancillary orders

25–058 Consider whether any other additional ancillary order should be attached to the sentence, see ANCILLARY ORDERS.

13. Step 10—Spelling it out

General
25–059 Apart from those offences for which the sentence is fixed by law (provision for which is made in CJA 2003, s.270), or falls to be imposed under FA 1968, s.51A (minimum sentences for firearms), or under PCC(S)A 2000, ss.109, where still appropriate, 110(2), 111(2) (required sentences for certain repeated offences) or under VCRA 2006, s.29(4) or (6) (minding dangerous weapons), the judge, in passing sentence on an offender, must:

(1) state in open court, in ordinary language and in general terms, his reasons for deciding on the sentence passed; and
(2) explain to the offender in ordinary language;
    (a) the effect of the sentence;
    (b) where the offender is required to comply with any order forming part of the sentence, the effects of non-compliance with the order;
    (c) any power, on the application of the offender or any other person, to vary or review any order forming part of the sentence; and
    (d) where the sentence consists of or includes a fine, the effects of failure to pay that fine.

(CJA 2003, s.174(1).)

Where the judge reduces his reasoning to writing, he must read it out in open court, and not leave it to be promulgated later behind closed doors (*Att-Gen's Reference (No.96 of 2009) (Sentencing reasons)* [2010] EWCA Crim 350, *The Times*, April 17, 2010).

Particular cases
25–060 In particular, the judge must (CJA 20203, s.174(2)):

(1) identify any relevant definitive sentencing guidelines and explain how he has discharged his duty to follow, or depart from, them;
(2) if he did not follow any relevant sentencing guidelines, state why he was of the opinion that it was it was contrary to the interests of justice for him to do so;
(3) in relation to a custodial sentence, where the duty in CJA 2003, s.152(2) is not excluded by subs.(1)(a) or (b) or (3), state that he is of the opinion referred to in s.152(2) and why he is of that opinion;

(4) in relation to a community sentence other than one consisting of, or including, a youth rehabilitation order with intensive supervision and surveillance or fostering, if the case does not fall within s.151(2) state that he is of opinion that s.148(1) applies and why he is of that opinion;

(5) where the sentence consists of or, includes, a youth rehabilitation order with intensive supervision and surveillance and the case does not fall within CJIA 2008, Sch.1, para.5(2) state that he is of the opinion that section 1(4)(a) to (c) of that Act and CJA 2003, s.148(1) apply and why he is of that opinion;

(6) where the sentence consists of or, includes, a youth rehabilitation order with fostering, state that he is of the opinion that CJIA 2008, s 1(4)(a) to (c) and CJA 2003, s.148(1) apply and why he is of that opinion;

(7) where as a result of taking into account any matter referred to in s.144(1), he imposes a punishment on the offender which is less severe than the punishment he would otherwise have imposed, state that fact; and

(8) in any case, mention any aggravating or mitigating factors which he has regarded as being of particular importance.

Where:

(a) the judge passes a custodial sentence in respect of an offence on an offender who is aged under 18; and

(b) the circumstances are such that the court must make the statement to the effect that only a custodial sentence is justified, that statement must include:

  (i) a statement by the judge that he is of the opinion that a sentence consisting of or including a youth rehabilitation order with intensive supervision and surveillance or fostering cannot be justified for the offence; and

  (ii) a statement why he is of that opinion.

(CJA 2003, s.174(2).)

Effect of custodial sentences

25–061 The judge must in passing a custodial sentence, explain the practical effect of the statutory provisions governing the particular term, and ensure that it is understood not only by the offender, but also by any victim and by any member of the public present in court, or "who reads a full report of the proceedings" (see *R. v Hennessey* [2000] Crim. L.R. 602).

PD 2004 makes it clear that the judge:

(1) may give the explanation in terms of his own choosing—no form of words is prescribed; but

(2) must ensure that the explanation is clear and accurate; and

(3) must, in any event, continue to give such explanations:

(a) as are required in other respects by statute; and

(b) as he considers necessary, of any ancillary orders relating to matters such as disqualification, confiscation, compensation and costs, etc. and should bear in mind that where terms imposed are consecutive, or wholly or partly concurrent, they are to be treated as a single term (see PD 2004, I.7).

As to the general requirement to spell out the effect of an accused's plea of guilty, see DISCOUNTS ON SENTENCE.

Forms of words

25–062   In complying with CJA 2003, s.174 25-059-060, above) and CJA 1991, s.51(2) forms of words are suggested both in PD 2004, Annex C and in Sentencing—Forms of Words issued by the former JSB in the Crown Court Bench Book, the last edition of which is was dated January 2006 and applied to pre-CJA 2003 sentences.

It covered:

(1) short term prisoner not subject to licence (total term less than 12 months);
(2) short term prisoner subject to licence (total term of 12 months and less than four years);
(3) long term prisoner (total term of four years or more); and
(4) discretionary life sentence.

14.   Procedure after sentence

Suspending sentence pending appeal

25–063   There is no obligation on a court to suspend the operation of any sentence or order where an offender gives notice of appeal, but:

(1) it is the usual practice not to enforce a fine pending the result of any appeal;
(2) there is a power, but no obligation, to suspend a driving disqualification (RTA 1988, s.39; MCA 1980, s.113(1));
(3) there is a power but no obligation, to grant bail to a person sentenced to a custodial term (see APPEALS FROM THE CROWN COURT).

A compensation order (see COMPENSATION ORDERS), and in certain cases, a restitution order (see RESTITUTION ORDERS), are suspended until the expiration of the time for appeal has expired, or, where notice is given, until the determination of the appeal.

Rescission and alteration

25–064   Ordinarily, a sentence imposed or other order made by the Crown Court when dealing with an offender, takes effect from the beginning of the day on which it is imposed, unless the judge otherwise directs, but:

(1) as a court of record, the Crown Court has an inherent jurisdiction to rectify mistakes in its record (*R. v Saville* [1981] Q.B. 12); and, more importantly
(2) a sentence or order may be varied or rescinded under PCC(S)A 2000, s.151(1), (2), (3), within the 56 day statutory time limit (PCC(S) A 2000, s.155); and
(3) a reduced sentence passed in pursuance of an offender's agreement to give information to the authorities may be reviewed under SOCPA 2005, s.74 (see VARIATION OF SENTENCE).

Notes

26. DEFERRING SENTENCE

Introduction

26–001   The judge may defer passing sentence on an offender until such date as he may specify, not being more than six months after the date of deferment is announced, for the purpose of enabling the court, or any other court to which it falls to deal with him, to have regard in dealing with him, to:

PCC(S)A 2000, s.1(1), (3), (4)

(1) his conduct after conviction (including, where appropriate, his making reparation for his offence); or
(2) any change in his circumstances,

but the power to defer is exercisable only:

(a) where the offender consents;
(b) the judge is satisfied, having regard to the nature of the offence and the character and circumstances of the offender, that it would be in the interests of justice to exercise the power; and
(c) in relation to offences committed **on or after April 4, 2005** the offender undertakes to comply with any requirements as to his conduct during the period of the deferment that the judge considers it appropriate to impose.

The requirements may be activities such as reparation to the community.

PCC(S)A 2000, s.1(3)

The court dealing with sentence on the due date may take into consideration the extent to which the offender has complied with any requirements imposed under (c) above.

Nothing in these provisions affects the judge's power:

(i) to bind over an offender to come up for judgment (see BIND OVER); or
(ii) to defer passing sentence for any other purpose for which he may lawfully do so.

PCC(S)A 2000, s.1(8)

26–002   Where the passing of sentence is deferred under these provisions, it may not be deferred again under the same provisions, though where sentence has been deferred in respect of one or more offences and the magistrates' court deals with the offender by committing him to the Crown Court under PCC(S)A 2000, s.3, the judge's power to deal with him includes the same power of deferring sentence on him as if he had just been convicted of the offence or offences on indictment.

Deferment does not imply that the offence or offences were "not so serious that a non-custodial sentence cannot be justified". The judge may consider that a custodial sentence is justified, and yet defer, having regard to the offender's circumstances (*R. v Bray* (1991) 12 Cr. App. R. (S.) 705).

PCC(S)A 2000, ss.1(4), 1D(3)

DEFERRING SENTENCE

Approach to sentence

26–003   SGC 3, 1.2.6 suggests that a deferred sentence is likely to be used in very limited circumstances.

It does, however, enable the judge:

(1) to review the conduct of the offender before passing sentence,
(2) having first prescribed certain requirements; and

it also provides several opportunities for an offender to have some influence over the sentence passed on him, as it:

- tests his commitment not to re-offend;
- gives him an opportunity to do something where progress can be shown within a short period; and
- provides him with an opportunity to behave or refrain from behaving in a particular way that will be relevant to his sentence.

Given the power to require undertakings and the ability to enforce those undertakings before the end of the period of deferral, SGC 3, 1.2.7 recommends that the decision to defer sentence should be reserved predominantly for a small group of cases at either the custody threshold or the community sentence threshold where the judge considers that there would be particular value in giving the offender the opportunities listed because, if the offender complies with the requirements, a different sentence will be justified at the end of the deferment period, i.e. a community sentence instead of a custodial sentence or a fine or discharge instead of a community sentence.

A deferment of sentence involves the message that compliance with whatever is required of the offender during the period of deferment will lead to a lesser category of sentence; it is appropriate only if such a sentence is a proper and realistic possibility on the facts of the case (*Att-Gen's Reference (No.10 of 2006) (R. v P)* [2006] EWCA Crim 3335).

The above guidance, though given in regard to adults, applies equally to young offenders.

The judge may impose any conditions during the period of deferment that he considers appropriate. These may be:

(a) specific requirements as set out in the provisions for community sentences (see COMMUNITY SENTENCES); or
(b) requirements that are drawn more widely.

The latter should be specific, measurable conditions so that the offender knows exactly what is required and the court can assess compliance; the restriction on liberty should be limited to ensure that the offender has a reasonable expectation of being able to comply whilst maintaining his or her social responsibilities (SGC 3, 1.2.8).

The requirements which may be imposed by virtue of (c) above include requirements as to the offender's residence during the whole or any part of the period of deferment.
PCC(S)A 2000, s.1A(1)

Appointment of supervisor

26–004   Where an offender has agreed to comply with any such requirements, as are mentioned in (c) above, the judge may appoint:
PCC(S)A 2000, s.1A(2)–(4)

(1) a probation officer; or

(2) any other person whom the court thinks appropriate in relation to him, to act as a supervisor, provided that that person consents.

The supervisor's duty is to:

(a) monitor the offender's compliance with the requirements; and

(b) provide the court to which it falls to deal with the offender in respect of the offence in question with such information as the court may require relating to the offender's compliance with the requirements.

Administrative provisions

26–005 Where sentence is deferred under these provisions the appropriate officer will forthwith give a copy of the order, setting out any requirements imposed: PCC(S)A 2000, s.1(5)

(1) to the offender;

(2) where a probation officer has been appointed to act as his supervisor, to that board; and

(3) where any other person has been appointed to act as his supervisor, to that person.

The procedure

26–006 In order to avoid the problems that often arise from the exercise of the power to defer sentence the judge should note that:

(1) if he intends to exercise his power under s.1 he should use the word "defer", while if he intends to impose, e.g. a common law bind over, or merely to adjourn, he should avoid the use of the expression "defer" altogether (*R. v Fairhead* (1975) 61 Cr. App. R. 102);

(2) sentence may be deferred only with the offender's consent; the judge should therefore ask him expressly if he consents to the deferment, and undertakes to comply with such requirements as are proposed (*R. v McQuaide* (1974) 60 Cr. App. R. 239).

Spelling it out

26–007 Given the need for clarity in the mind of the offender and the possibility of sentence by another court, the judge should: SGG 2, 2.2.9–2.2.10

(1) give a clear indication of the sentence he would be minded to impose if he had not decided to defer sentence;

(2) ensure that the offender understands the consequences of failure to comply with the requirements during the deferral period;

(3) make clear the consequence of not complying with any requirements; and

(4) indicate the type of sentence he would be minded to impose,

though under the pre-2003 provisions it was said that only a judge who is sure that he will deal with the case on the date to which sentence is deferred should give any hint as to the probable outcome of the case (*R. v Johnson* (1981) 145 J.P. 491).

DEFERRING SENTENCE

A judge who sits regularly at a particular location should reserve to himself the duty of dealing with the case on the date to which it is deferred, otherwise he ought to leave a note of his reasoning, or arrange for a transcript to be available at the point of sentence (*R. v Jacobs* (1976) 62 Cr. App. R. 116).

Ancillary orders; RT disqualification

26–008 Deferment being, in effect, a species of adjournment, there is no power to make any other order, other than:

(1) a restitution order; or
(2) a road traffic disqualification (see below).

(*R. v Dwyer* (1974) 60 Cr. App. R. 39.)

No power to remand: process

26–009 No question of remand arises and therefore no question of bail. Where the passing of sentence is deferred, and it is proposed to deal with him on the date originally specified, then, if the offender does not appear on the day, a summons may be issued requiring him to appear before the court at a time and place specified, or a warrant may be issued to arrest him and bring him before the court at a time and place specified in the warrant.

PCC(S)A 2000, s.1(16)(7)

Appeal and review

26–010 Deferment of sentence ranks as a "sentence" for the purposes of CAA 1968, s.50 (*Att-Gen's Reference (No.22 of 1992)* [1993] 14 Cr. App. R. (S.) 435; *Att-Gen's References (Nos 36 and 38)* [1999] Crim. L.R. 236). As such it may be referred to CACD by the Attorney-General for review (see APPEALS FROM THE CROWN COURT) under CJA 1988, s.36(10) if it appears to him to be unduly lenient (see *Att-Gen's Reference (No.22 of 1992)* above).

Breach of undertakings; sentence on due date

General

26–011 This topic is dealt with at BREACH, AMENDMENT AND DEVOCATION.

27. DEPORTATION

Automatic deportation – UK Borders Act 2007

27–001   UKBA 2007 introduces the concept of mandatory automatic deportation for "foreign criminals" (i.e. offenders who are not British citizens but are convicted in the UK of an offence) to whom one of the two conditions set out in s.32 (see below) apply and who are not then covered by the exceptions set out in s.33.

The:

(1) prosecutor is responsible for informing the judge at the stage of sentence that the offender is liable to automatic deportation;
(2) Crown Court officer is responsible for informing both the prison and the UK Borders and Immigration Agency whenever an order is made resulting in the offender being liable to automatic deportation;
(3) executive will also seek to deport offenders who are sentenced to a custodial sentence for a drug or gun offence, even where the conditions in s.32 are not fulfilled, i.e. where the sentence is for less than 12 months.

Where (3) applies, the Borders and Immigration Agency will need to be informed so that the Secretary of State's powers may be exercised.

The judge retains the power under IA 1971, s.6, to recommend deportation only where the conditions in UKBA 2007, s.33 are not fulfilled

Requisite conditions s.32

27–002   Automatic deportation applies where;

(1) an adult offender is sentenced to an immediate term of imprisonment of at least 12 months for a single offence (i.e. not a totality of shorter consecutive sentences); or
(2) the offence is one specified under the Nationality, Immigration and Asylum Act 2007, s.72(4)(a) and the offender is sentenced to a term of imprisonment.

A suspended sentence of imprisonment, when passed does not attract automatic deportation, but will if a court subsequently orders the suspended to take effect.

A reference to a person sentenced to a term of imprisonment of at least 12 months includes a reference to an offender who is sentenced to:

(a) detention, or ordered or directed to be detained, in an institution other than a prison (including in particular in a hospital or an institution for young offenders) for at least 12 months; and
(b) imprisonment or detention, or ordered or directed to be detained, for an indeterminate period (provided that it may last for 12 months).

415

DEPORTATION

The power of the Secretary of State to make the deportation order derives from IA 1971, s.5(1) which provides that he may make such order where, *inter alia,* it is conducive to the public good. UKBA 2007, s.32(4) provides that for the purposes of the 1971 Act deportation of a "foreign criminal" is conducive to the public good.

Exceptions under s.33
27–003   Automatic deportation under s.32 does not apply where;

(1) the offender falls within IA 1971, ss.7 and 8 (Commonwealth or Irish citizens, crew and other exemptions);
(2) removal would breach a person's Convention rights or the UK's obligations under the Refugee Convention;
(3) removal would breach the foreign criminal's rights under the Community Treaties;
(4) the offender was under 18 on the date of conviction;
(5) the offender is subject to proceedings under the Extradition Act 2003; or
(6) the offender is subject to an order under MHA 1983, or the relevant Scottish legislation.

As a matter of principle, it is wrong to reduce an otherwise appropriate sentence so as to avoid liability for automatic deportation. Deportation is not part of the sentence but a consequence of it, see *R. v Mintchev* [2011] EWCA Crim 499; see also *R v. Hakimazdeh* [2009] EWCA Crim 959, [2010] 1 Cr. App. R. (S.) 10.

In view of the above, it is no longer appropriate for a judge to recommend the deportation of a "foreign criminal" to whom s.33 applies; the Secretary of State is required by statute to make an order (*R. v Kluxen* [2010] EWCA Crim 1081, [2011] 1 Cr. App. R. (S.) 39). There is no need for the judge to be involved in the process at all, nor is it necessary for him, in sentencing a "foreign criminal", to explain during his sentencing remarks that because the 2007 Act applied, he is not making a recommendation.

Where recommendation appropriate
27–004   UKBA 2007, s.33(7) makes it clear that an offender to whom that Act does not apply may still be deported under existing legislation, an important factor of which is the power of a judge to recommend deportation in a proper case. Subject to certain limitations (see below) the judge, in sentencing an offender to whom UKBA 2007, s.33 does not apply, may, in relation to an offender:

(1) aged 17 or over;
(2) who is not a British citizen within the meaning of the British Nationality Act 1981;
(3) for an offence punishable with imprisonment,

may impose, as part of the sentence, but ancillary to any other principal sentence, a recommendation to the Secretary of State that the offender be deported from the United Kingdom.

Preconditions for order

27–005   Before making a recommendation in an appropriate case the judge must be satisfied that:

(1) the offender is not a British citizen and has no right of abode;
(2) the offender is 17 or over;
(3) the offence is punishable with imprisonment;
(4) the offender has been given not less than seven days clear notice in writing of the court's intention.

The fact that the offender has no right of abode does not mean that it is obligatory to make a recommendation for deportation upon completion of a custodial sentence; it must always depend upon the circumstances (*R. v Wong* [2005] EWCA Crim 296).

There are technical differences between the approach to the deportation of EU citizens and non-EU citizens, evidenced by the authorities. The judge should apply the tests laid down in *R. v Nazari* ((1980) 71 Cr. App. R. 87, (i.e. whether the offender's continued presence in the United Kingdom was to its detriment) and *R. v Bouchereau* (1978) 66 Cr. App. R. 202, whether the offender's conduct constitutes a genuine and sufficiently serious threat to the requirements of public policy affecting one of the fundamental interests of society; there being no practical difference between those two tests.

Commonwealth citizens

27–006   A British citizen, or any citizen who has a "right of abode" in the United Kingdom (IA 1971, s.2), may not be the subject of a recommendation for deportation, nor may a citizen of a Commonwealth country or of the Republic of Ireland, where the judge is satisfied that the offender:

(1) was such at the coming into force of the Act on January 1, 1973; and
(2) was ordinarily resident in this country at that time; and
(3) has been ordinarily resident here for the five years immediately preceding his conviction; although
(4) any part of that five years during which he was undergoing imprisonment or detention by virtue of a sentence passed on conviction in the United Kingdom, Channel Islands or the Isle of Man, and for which he was imprisoned or detained for six months or more, is excluded from the period.

Note that:

(a) "ordinary residence" is a matter of fact and degree; mere temporary absence will not create a gap in "ordinary" residence; and
(b) illegal residence *ab initio* cannot amount to "ordinary residence" (*R. v Bangoo* [1976] Crim. L.R. 746).

EU nationals

27–007   The Immigration (European Economic Area) Regulations SI 2006/1003) transpose into UK domestic law the requirements of the

DEPORTATION

Citizens Directive 2004/38/EEC (OJ June 29, 2004 L229/35).These apply to any nationals of the European Economic Area who have been admitted to or have a right to reside in the UK.

Such a person may be deported only where;

    (1) there are serious grounds of public policy (reg.21(2)), threatening one of the fundamental interests of society (reg.21(5)(c)); and

    (2) expulsion is proportionate (reg.21(6)).

Protecting members of society from violent crime is clearly such a fundamental interest, though there does not appear to be any direct guidance on the question of what suffices; to make threatened future criminal conduct "serious" in the sense of the 2006 Regulations and the Directive. No attempt had been made to lay down rules or guidelines at Community level as to the necessary level of violence, and the member state is therefore given a certain amount of judgment in deciding what its law-abiding citizens must put up with: see *Van Duyn v Home Office* [1975] 3 All E.R. 190 and see *B (Netherlands) v Secretary of State for the Home Department* [2008] EWCA Civ 806; [2009] Q.B. 536.

Approach to expulsion of EU citizens

27–008 The provisions of the Treaty, Council Directive 64/221 EC made under it, and certain rulings of the Court of Justice (see, e.g. (1980) 2 C.M.L.R. 208) oblige a court considering such a recommendation to note, *inter alia,* that:

    (1) no recommendation should be made without full enquiry (*R. v Kraus* (1982) 4 Cr. App. R. (S.) 113);

    (2) the judge may act where the offender's record, taken together with the offence committed, indicates it is likely that he will offend again this is a very important consideration (*R. v Compassi* (1987) Cr. App. R. (S.) 270; *R. v Spura* (1988) 10 Cr. App. R. (S.) 376);

    (3) the existence of a previous conviction is not, in itself, a basis for making a recommendation;

    (4) the judge must be satisfied that the offender's continued presence in the United Kingdom represents "a genuine and sufficiently serious threat to the requirements of public policy affecting one of the fundamental interests of society" (*R. v Escauriaza* (1987) 9 Cr. App. R. (S.) 542; *R. v Soura* (1988) 10 Cr. App. R. (S.) 376) which indicates that the requirements of EU law are not substantially different from the principles enunciated in *R. v Nazari* (see below);

    (5) reasons for the recommendation must be given both to the Secretary of state and to the offender (*Ex p. Dannenberg* [1984] 2 All E.R. 481; *R. v Frank* (1992) 13 Cr. App. R. 500; *R. v Bozat* [1997] 1 Cr. App. R. (S.) 270).

Non-EU nationals

27–009 The question of making a recommendation in relation to an offender who is not an EU national, must be decided independently of the offender's status under IA 1971 (*R. v Nunu* (1991) 12 Cr. App. R. (S.) 752). *R. v Benabbas* [2005] EWCA Crim 2113; [2006] 1 Cr. App. R. (S) 94, reaffirms the distinction drawn between immigration-related cases, and cases where offences are committed by a person unlawfully in the country (see below).

The judge must consider only whether the offence committed justifies the conclusion that the offender's continued presence in the country is contrary (i.e. a "detriment") to the public interest (*R. v Carmona* [2006] EWCA Crim 508; [2006] 2 Cr. App. R. (S.) 102).

R. v Nazari (above, 27–005) still provides the classic test, namely that in examining "detriment" the judge should consider:

(1) the nature and seriousness of the offence, which is generally indicated by the sentence imposed (*R. v Carmona*, above);
(2) the likelihood of its being repeated, or of other offences being committed;
(3) the broad picture and such evidence as is available.

The mere fact that the offender is living on social security benefits is not a reason for regarding his continued presence as a detriment (*R. v Serry* (1980) 2 Cr. App. R. (S.) 336).

The judge may not take into account the human rights of the offender, the political situation in the country to which he might be deported, the effect that a recommendation might have on innocent persons not before the court, or the provisions of art.28 of Council Directive 2004/38/EC or the Immigration (European Economic Area) Regulations (SI 2006/1003), as those governed only a decision of the Secretary of State to deport, not a recommendation by the court (see *R. v Carmona,* above; *R. v Altawel* (1981) 3 Cr. App. R. (S.) 28). The judge is not equipped to undertake such an assessment, which is a matter for the Secretary of State, or for the Asylum and Immigration Tribunal if a deportation order is made.

Relevance of immigration status

27–010   *R. v Benabbas* [2005] EWCA Crim 2113; [2006] 1 Cr. App. R. (S.) 94 reviewed the cases in detail and restated the principle that where the offender's presence on this country:

(1) is lawful and regular, the *Nazari* approach (above) involves a relatively straightforward exercise, i.e. balancing the aggravation of the offender's wrong-doing, present, past and potential against any mitigation which may be put forward;
(2) is illegal or irregular, the position may be more complicated, varying from:
(a) a lawful entrant who overstays his permit;
(b) an unlawful entrant who gains entry by fraudulent means; and also because the illegality or irregularity may be either:
(i) the essence of the offence; or
(ii) entirely irrelevant to it.

While a recommendation ought not to be made simply because of the irregularity or illegality of status, rather than on the *Nazari* principle, it is justified where, e.g. entry is by the use of a forged passport, since there is a detriment to the public interest which undermines confidence in the system (see also *R. v Brown (Romeka)* [2010] EWCA Crim 1807, [2011] 1 Cr. App. R. (S.) 482(79)). As to "sham" marriages for the purpose of establishing a right of abode, see *R. v Ahemed* [2006] 1 Cr. App. R. (S.) 78, distinguishing *R. v Aziz* [2004] EWCA Crim 1700.

Giving reasons

27–011 The recommendation is part of the sentence and CJA 2003, s.174 applies to it, requiring the judge to give, in general terms, and in ordinary language the reasons for his decision, the bald statement "that your continued presence in this country is contrary to the public interest" without giving reasons, may not be sufficient (see *R. v Mohammed Ahsan* [2006] EWCA Crim 826).

28. DETENTION OF YOUNG OFFENDERS

Quick guide

1. Available custodial sentences (28–003)
2. Detention in Young Offender Institution (28–005)
3. Detention and training order (28–009)
4. Detention during HM Pleasure (28–018)
5. Offenders under 18 – certain grave offences – s.91 (28–019)
6. Dangerous offenders; protective sentences (28–024)

Introduction

28–001   An offender under 18 years of age may not be sentenced to imprisonment nor may he be committed to prison for any reason other than that of:

(1) remanding him in custody;
(2) committing him in custody for sentence; or
(3) sending him for trial under CDA 1998, s.51 and following.

Note that:

(a) an offender's age is deemed to be that which it appears to the court to be on the date of conviction (*R. v Danga* (1992) 13 Cr. App. R. (S.) 408) after considering any available evidence (see AGE OF OFFENDER);
(b) it is not proper to adjourn after conviction for the purpose only of the offender reaching the age of 18 before being sentenced (*Arthur v Stringer* (1987) 84 Cr. App. R. 361);
(c) where an offender is convicted on a date before reaching a birthday relevant to his sentence, and is then sentenced on another date, after that "milestone" birthday has passed, he falls to be sentenced as if he were still under that age (*R. v Danga* (1992) 94 Cr. App. R. 252; *R. v Robinson* (1993) 14 Cr. App. R. (S.) 448); and
(d) a sentence will not be invalidated because it is later discovered that the offender is of a different age (*R. v Brown* (1989) 11 Cr. App. R. (S.) 263).

CACD has said that CYPA 1933, ss.44(1) and 107(1) (regarding the welfare of the child) does not prevent the judge from considering other matters, such as general deterrence, but that a deterrent sentence should not be passed upon a juvenile unless the court has weighed most carefully in the balance, deterrence on one side and individual treatment for the rehabilitation of the offender on the other.

Interval between date of offence and sentence

28–002   Where, between the date of:

(1) the commission of the offence; and

(2) conviction;

the offender has crossed a relevant age threshold, the starting point in considering sentence is the sentence that he would have been likely to have received at the time of the commission of the offence. Whilst other factors may need to be considered, there would need to be good reason for departing from that starting point, although clearly, particularly where a long interval has elapsed between points (1) and (2) above, circumstances may have changed significantly, e.g. the offender may have revealed himself to be a dangerous criminal, or the tariff may have been increased.

The judge is entitled to take such factors into account and:

(a) may impose a sentence higher than that which would have been imposed at the date of the offence; but

(b) will seldom need to consider passing a sentence beyond the maximum which he could have passed on the date of the commission of the offence.

(*R. v Ghafoor* [2003] 1 Cr. App. R. (S.) 84; *R. v L M* [2002] EWCA Crim 3047, [2003] 2 Cr. App. R. (S.) 26.)

1. Available custodial sentences

28–003 Custodial sentences for this age group, recognised and governed by PCC(S)A 2000, Pt V, Ch.2 as amended by CJCSA 2000 and CJA 2003, Pt 12, Ch.5 are six in number, namely:

(1) for offenders aged 18–20, the normal sentence in lieu of imprisonment is **detention in a young offender institution** under PCC(S)A 2000, s.96;

(2) for offenders under 18, the normal sentence is a **detention and training order** under PCC(S)A 2000, s.100;

(3) for offenders under 18 convicted of certain grave crimes, **detention** under PCC(S)A 2000, s.91;

(4) protective sentences for **dangerous offenders** under 18, in relation to **offences committed on or after April 4, 2005**, detention for life or for public protection under CJA 2003, s.226;

(5) protective sentences for offenders under 18, for specified violent or sexual **offences committed on or after April 4, 2005**, an **extended sentence** under CJA 2003, s.228;

(6) in the case of a person under 18 convicted of murder, **detention during HM Pleasure** under PCC(S)A 2000, s.90; and

different considerations govern different types of custodial sentence, but the imposition of any of them is subject, like any other custodial sentence:

(a) to the offence(s) "qualifying" for a custodial sentence (see DEALING WITH AN OFFENDER);

(b) to the offender's age (see AGE OF OFFENDER);

(c) unless unnecessary, to the availability of a pre-sentence report (see DEALING WITH AN OFFENDER); and

(d) the offender being legally represented (see DEALING WITH AN OFFENDER).

Custody for life and detention of defaulters and contemnors aged 18–20 under PCC(S)A 2000, s.108, were abolished by CJCSA 2000, s.75, Sch.8, from a date to be appointed; this date has not yet been appointed.

Those defaulters, etc. who would previously have been detained under PCC(S)A 2000, s.108 are now likely to be made the subject of an attendance centre order (see COMMUNITY SENTENCES).

Spelling it out

28–004 Special care needs to be taken, in the case of young offenders, to indicate at the point of sentence the exact provisions which are being applied. In such cases, one of the most common reasons for appeals against sentence being allowed is the judge's failure to specify exactly what powers he is exercising (see *R. v Venison* (1993) 15 Cr. App. R. (S.) 624; *R. v Edgell* (1994) 15 Cr. App. R. (S.) 509; *R. v Anderson* (1991) 13 Cr. App. R. (S.) 325).

2. Detention in Young Offender Institution

28–005 The ordinary custodial sentence (i.e. leaving aside ss.90, 91, and 93) for an offender **aged at least 18 but under 21**:

PCC(S)A 2000, s.96

(1) who is convicted of an offence punishable with imprisonment in the case of a person aged 21 or over; and
(2) where the prerequisites for a custodial sentence (see DEALING WITH AN OFFENDER), are present,

is detention in a young offender institution.

Sections 96–98 are to be repealed by CJCSA 2000, s.75, Sch.8 (no day has yet been appointed).

Length of term

28–006 As far as the length of the term is concerned:

PCC(S)A 2000 s.97(1), (2), (3)

(1) the maximum term is the same as the maximum term of imprisonment which the judge may impose for the offence; and
(2) the minimum term which may be ordered is 21 days, applying not to the totality, but to each separate sentence (*R. v Kent YC Ex p. K (a Minor)* [1999] Crim. L.R. 168).

The authorities show that what has become the customary discount for a plea of guilty (see DISCOUNTS ON SENTENCE) should be given under the provisions (*R. v Stewart* (1983) 5 Cr. App. R. (S.) 320; *R. v George* (1993) 14 Cr. App. R. (S.) 12) and the maximum should not be imposed on a plea of guilty unless the offender had no realistic defence to the charge (*R. v Bright* (1987) 9 Cr. App. R. (S.) 329).

As to prescribed minimum sentences for certain firearms offences, see 28–022, below and IMPRISONMENT.

DETENTION OF YOUNG OFFENDERS

Consecutive sentences

28–007   Subject to the statutory maxima set out above, a young offender: PCC(S)A 2000, s.97(4)

(1) convicted of more than one offence for which he is liable to such a term; or
(2) serving such a term, and convicted of one or more further offences for which he is so liable,

may be sentenced to consecutive terms, as if they were sentences of imprisonment.

In the case of consecutive sentences, each term must comply in terms of length, with s.101, but the total sentence need not be one of those terms (*R. v Norris* [2001] 1 Cr. App. R. (S.) 401; cf. *R. v C* [2009] EWCA Crim 446).

If he is: PCC(S)A 2000, s.97(5)

(a) serving such a term; and
(b) is aged 21 or over; and
(c) is convicted of one or more further offences for which he is liable to imprisonment,

he may be sentenced, subject to PCC(S)A 2000, s.84 (restrictions on consecutive sentences for released prisoners) to imprisonment to run consecutively to the term(s) of detention.

Suspending a term

28–008   Although not possible under PCC(S)A 2000, CJA 2003, ss.189–194, (as implemented by SI 2005/950) allows, in respect of **offences committed on or after April 4, 2005**, a term of detention of at least 14 days but not more than 12 months to be suspended in the case of an offender aged 18–21, provided it contains a community requirement. Suspension does not apply in the case of pre-commencement offences.

See generally IMPRISONMENT.

3.   Detention and training order

28–009   The ordinary custodial sentence (subject to PCC(S)A 2000, ss.90 and 91, and CJA 2003, ss.226 and 228) to be passed on a offender **aged under 18** where: PCC(S)A 2000, ss.100(1), (2), (3) 102103

(1) he is convicted of an offence which is punishable with imprisonment in the case of a person aged 21 or over; and
(2) the judge is of opinion that CJA 2003, s.152(2) (the general restriction on custodial sentences) applies, or the case falls within CJA 2003, s.152(3) (persistent offender, see below),

is a detention and training order, which provides a period of detention and training, followed by a period of supervision.

The judge must not make such an order in the case of an offender:

(a) under the age of 15 at the time of his conviction, unless he is of opinion that he is a persistent offender;
(b) under the age of 12 at that time, unless:

(i) he is of opinion that only a custodial sentence would be adequate to protect the public from his further offending; and

(ii) the offence was committed on or after such date as the Secretary of State may appoint.

The judge is entitled (by virtue of CYPA 1963, s.29(1)) to impose a detention and training order on an offender who was aged 17 at the date he committed an offence, even though he has attained the age of 18 by the date on which sentence is imposed (*Aldis v DPP* [2002] EWHC 403 (Admin), [2002] 2 Cr. App. R. (S.) 88 L.R. 434). A young person aged 15 at the time of conviction may be sentenced to a detention and training order even though he was 14 at the time of the commission of the offence (*R. v BR (Sentencing; Extended Licences)* [2003] EWCA 2199, [2004] 1 Cr. App. R. (S.) 59).

There is no power to impose an extended sentence under PCC(S)A 2000, s.85 with a detention and training order—there is no licence period (*R. v B* [2005] EWCA Crim 312; [2005] 2 Cr. App. R. (S.) 87).

What amounts to a "persistent offender"

28–010 "Persistent offender" is not defined in the Act, nor is it to be interpreted by reference to the government circular *Tackling Delays in the Youth Justice System* (*R. v Thomas* [2001] 1 Cr. App. R. (S.) 415). The currently understood meaning of the words should be applied to the facts of the case: *R. v S (A)* [2001] 1 Cr. App. R. (S.) 18 (a series of offences over two days).

Their application is best left to the good sense of the judge (*R. v Dexter* [2001] 1 Cr. App. R. (S.) 389).

Note that it is not necessary to come within the definition that:

(1) the offender should have previous convictions (*R. v Smith* [2001] 1 Cr. App. R. (S.) 62); or

(2) he should have committed a string of offences, either of the same or a similar character (*R. v BR*, above); or

(3) his failure to address his offending behaviour arises by his failure to comply with previous orders (*ibid.*); and

PCC(S)A 2000, s.101(8); CJIA 2008, s.22(6)

account may be taken of offences in respect of which he has been formally cautioned (*R. v D* [2001] Crim. L.R. 864), (and no doubt, reprimanded under CDA 1998, s.65) and of offences committed after the offence for which the offender is being sentenced (*R. v B* [2001] 1 Cr. App. R. (S.) 389 and see *R. v C* [2001] 1 Cr. App. R. (S.) 415).

Term of order

28–011 The term of an order must:

PCC(S)A 2000, s.101(1), (2), (3), (5), (8)

(1) be for 4, 6, 8, 10, 12, 18 or 24 months; and

(2) not exceed 24 months, taking into account any period for which the offender has been remanded in custody in connection with the offence, or any other offence the charge for which was founded on the same facts or evidence; and

(3) not exceed the maximum term of imprisonment that the judge could, in the cases of an offender aged 21 or over, impose for the offence.

Consecutive terms may be imposed, each for one of the terms set out in (1) above, though the aggregate does not amount to one of those specified (*R. v Norris* [2001] 1 Cr. App. R. (S.) 116), but it is not permissible to pass a number of shorter terms and aggregate them into a term of four months (*R. v Kent YC Ex p. Kingwell* [1999] 1 Cr. App. R. (S.) 263).

Where the offence is a summary offence, and the maximum term of imprisonment that a court could (in the case of an offender aged 18 or over) impose for the offence is 51 weeks (see IMPRISONMENT) the term of detention and training must not exceed six months.

Discount for plea

28–012   When reflecting a plea of guilty (see DISCOUNTS ON SENTENCE) in the sentence, it is appropriate for the judge, where the offender is: PCC(S)A 2000,
s.101(2A)

- (1) not liable to a term of detention under PCC(S)A 2000, s.91, to reduce the term of the detention and training order below the maximum available term, unless there are proper grounds for not allowing a discount (*R. v Kelly* [2002] 1 Cr. App. R. (S.) 11, [2001] EWCA Crim 1030; *R. v Marley* [2001] EWCA Crim 2779, [2002] 2 Cr. App. R. (S.) 21); and
- (2) liable to such a term, the discount may properly be reflected by imposing a detention and training order for the maximum term (*R. v March* [2002] 2 Cr. App. R. (S.) 98).

Time spent in custody

28–013   The judge must, in fixing the term of the order, take into account time spent

- (1) in custody; or
- (2) on bail subject to a qualifying curfew condition and a qualifying electronic monitoring condition within the meaning of CJA 2003, s.240A (see IMPRISONMENT).

He should indicate his intention to make such an order, so that he can be informed of any period spent in custody or on remand before considering the length of term (*R. v Haringey YC Ex p. A, The Times*, May 30, 2000; *R. v Davis, The Times*, December 20, 2000).

In relation to this type of order:

- (a) the judge is not bound to reflect mathematically all such time in the sentence passed;
- (b) it is neither appropriate nor desirable in determining the period of such an order that a precise reflection should be given for a day or two spent in custody (*R. v ILCC Ex p. N* [2001] 1 Cr. App. R. 323); but
- (c) if a significant time has been spent in custody, a matter of weeks or months, the proper approach is to reduce the otherwise appropriate term to reflect that period;
- (d) how the judge reflects *longer* periods in custody will depend on the circumstances, including:
  - (i) the apparent impact, if any, of the period of custody on the offender;

    (ii) the length of time spent in custody; and

    (iii) the relationship between the period spent in custody and the period of detention and training contemplated (*R. v Fieldhouse* [2001] 1 Cr. App. R. (S.) 104).

In the case of adult offenders (see IMPRISONMENT) time on remand is taken from time to be served rather than from the determinate sentence. To ensure in dealing with a young offender that he does not face a harsher regime than an adult, the judge should:

- double the time spent on remand and subtract this from the nominal term considered to be appropriate; and
- if the result does not equate to one of the periods specified in s.101(1), adopt the nearest permissible period (not necessarily the next lowest).

(*R. v Eagles* [2006] EWCA Crim 2366, [2002] 1 Cr. App. R. (S.) 99.)

References to "remand in custody"

28–014   The reference in s.101(8) to an offender being remanded in custody, is a reference to his being held in a police station, his being remanded in or committed to custody by an order of the court, his being remanded or committed to local authority accommodation under CYPA 1969, s.23, and placed and kept in secure accommodation or detained in a secure training centre or being remanded, admitted or removed to hospital under MHA 1983, ss.35, 36, 38 or 48.

    A person is in "police detention" for the purposes of s.23(7) where he is in police detention at any time under PACE 1984, or at any time when he is detained under the Prevention of Terrorism (Temporary Provisions) Act 1989, s.14.

PCC(S)A 2000, s.101(11), (12)

Consecutive terms

28–015   Where the offender:

PCC(S)A 2000, s.101(3), (7)

(1) is convicted of more than one offence for which he is liable to an order; or

(2) is already subject to such an order and is convicted of one or more further offences for which he is liable to an order,

the judge has the same power to pass consecutive terms as if they were sentences of imprisonment, save that, while there is no requirement that the total term add up to one of the periods specified in s.101(1) (*R. v Norris* [2001] 1 Cr. App. R. (S.) 116):

    (a) an order must not be made in respect of an offender the effect of which would be that he would be subject to detention and training orders for an aggregate which exceeds 24 months; and

    (b) if the aggregate term to which he would otherwise be subject, does exceed 24 months, the excess will be treated as remitted.

The judge may, when imposing consecutive detention and training orders, whose individual terms are taken from the list in subs.(1), agree to an aggregate term taken from the list, i.e. any even number of months between four and 24. This gives him some measure of discretion in arriving at terms which reflect the varying culpability of different offenders involved in the same case (*R. v B* [2001] Crim. L.R. 80).

By statute a detention and training order may be ordered to take effect consecutively to a term of detention under PCC(S)A 2000, s. 91 (cf. *R. v H (Grant) (A juvenile)* [2001] Cr. App. R. (S.) 31).

PCC(S)A 2000,
s.106A

Improper combinations

28–016   A detention and training order may not be imposed to run concurrently with a term of detention under PCC(S)A 2000, s.91: *R. v Hayward* [2001] 2 Cr. App. R. (S.) 31; and the converse also applies (*R. v Lang* [2001] 2 Cr. App. R. (S.) 39).

New offences during currency of the order

28–017   Where:

PCC(S)A 2000,
s.105

(1) after his release and before the date on which the term of the order ends, the offender commits an offence punishable with imprisonment in the case of a person aged 21 or over; and
(2) whether before or after that date he is convicted of that "new offence" the judge of the court by or before which he is convicted may, whether or not the judge passes any other sentence on him, order him to be detained in such secure accommodation as the Secretary of State may determine for the whole or any part of the period which:
   (a) begins with the date of the judge's order; and
   (b) is equal in length to the period between the date on which the new offence was committed, or the last of the days if it was committed over several, and the date on which the order would end.

The term will, as the judge directs, be served either before and be followed by, or concurrently with, any sentence imposed for the offence, and in either case will be disregarded in determining the appropriate length of that sentence.

4.   Detention during HM Pleasure

28–018   Where a person convicted of murder, or of any other offence the sentence for which is fixed by law, as life imprisonment, appears to the court to have been under 18 at the time the offence was committed, the judge must (notwithstanding anything in PCC(S)A 2000 or any other Act) sentence him to be detained during Her Majesty's Pleasure.
   See LIFE SENTENCES.

PCC(S)A 2000,
ss.82A, 90

5.   Offenders under 18—certain grave offences—s.91

28–019   Where:

PCC(S)A 2000,
s.91

(1) an offender under 18 is convicted on indictment of an offence:
   (a) punishable in the case of a person aged 21 or over with

imprisonment for 14 years or more, not being an offence the sentence for which is fixed by law;

(b) under SOA 2003, s.3 (sexual assault); or

(c) under SOA 2003, s.13 (child sex offences committed by children or young persons); or

(d) under SOA 2003, s.25 (sexual activity with a child family member); or

(e) under SOA 2003, s.26 (inciting a child or family member to engage in sexual activity); or

(2) (a) an offender under 18 is convicted on indictment of an offence under the FA 1968 that is listed in s.51A(1A)(b), (e) or (f) of that Act and was committed in respect of a firearm or ammunition specified in s.5(1)(a), (ab), (aba), (ac), (ad), (ae), (af) or (c) or s 5(1A)(a);

(b) the offence was committed after the commencement of VCRA 2006, s.30, and for the purposes of FA 1968, s.51A(3) at a time when he was aged 16 or over; and

(c) the judge is of the opinion mentioned in FA 1968, s.51A(2);

(3) (a) an offender under 18 is convicted of an offence under VCRA 2006, s.28 (using someone to mind a weapon);

(b) s.29(3) of that Act applies (minimum sentences in certain cases); and

(c) the judge is of the opinion mentioned in s.29(6) (exceptional circumstances which justify not imposing the minimum sentence);

(4) an offender aged at least 14 but under 18 is convicted of an offence under:

(a) RTA 1988, s.1 (causing death by dangerous driving); or

(b) RTA 1988, s.3A (causing death by careless driving while under the influence of drink or drugs); and

(5) the judge is of the opinion that neither a youth rehabilitation order nor a detention and training order is suitable,

he may, subject to the general restrictions on passing custodial sentences set out in CJA 2003, ss.152 and 153, sentence the offender to be detained for such period as he may specify, not exceeding the maximum term of imprisonment with which the offence is punishable in the case of a person aged 21 or over.

In general:

(i) unless the offence merits a sentence *longer than two years*, and the criteria under s.91 are met, a term of detention and training should be imposed; and

(ii) if such is not permitted, then a non-custodial sentence should be passed (*R. (W) v Thetford YC* [2002] EWHC 1252 (Admin), [2003] 1 Cr. App. R. (S.) 67).

Where FA 1968, s.51A(2) or VCRA 2006, s.29(6) requires the imposition of a sentence of detention for a minimum term the sentence must be for the offender to be detained for at least the term so provided for, but not exceeding the maximum term of imprisonment with which the offence is punishable in the case of a person aged 21 or over.

Such an offender is liable to be detained in such place as the Secretary of State may direct or arrange.

Guideline cases

28–020   An order is primarily applicable to cases where the judge contemplates a sentence of at least two years; anything less than that should be dealt with by a detention and training order.

If the 24-month limit on detention and training orders is intended to ensure that offenders under 18 are not sentenced to lengthy periods of detention where this can be avoided, the judge ought to think long and hard before passing a sentence which exceeds this limit. However, the co-existence of the powers contained in s.91 recognise the "unwelcome but undoubted fact" that some crimes committed by offenders of this age merit sentences of detention in excess of 24 months.

The following principles are to be deduced from *Fairhurst* (1987) 84 Cr. App. R. 19; *R. v Wainfur* [1997] 1 Cr. App. R. (S.) 43; *R. v Mills* [1998] 1 Cr. App. R. 43; and *R. v Manchester City YC* [2001] EWHC (Admin) 860; [2002] 1 Cr. App. R. (S.) 135:

(1) a sentence of detention under s.91 should not be passed simply because a 24-months' term seems to be on the low side for the particular offence; the 24-month limit should not be exceeded unless the offence is clearly one calling for a longer sentence;

(2) if the judge is minded to impose a sentence of, e.g. four years under s.91, but is persuaded by mitigation that the circumstances justify a significant reduction, to e.g. 2 1/2 years:

(a) while he ought not to exceed the 24-month limit without careful thought;

(b) if he concludes that a longer sentence, even if not a much longer sentence, is called for, he should impose what he considers the appropriate period under s.91;

(3) if, on a plea of guilty to an offence falling within s.91, the judge imposes a sentence of 24-months under s.100, where, but for the plea, detention under s.91 for a longer period would have been ordered, he should state this fact expressly.

CACD has said that where an offender is convicted of a number of offences, for some of which detention under s.91 is available but for others it is not, the judge should sentence under s.91 where available and make the rather dubious order of "no separate penalty" (really a magistrates' courts order) in respect of those offences not qualifying (*R. v Carroll,* [2004] EWCA Crim 1367, [2005] 1 Cr. App. R. (S.) 10), but see now DANGEROUS OFFENDERS; PROTECTIVE SENTENCES.

Length of sentence

28–021   The offender may be sentenced to be detained for a determinate period not exceeding the maximum term of imprisonment with which the offence is punishable in the case of an offender of 21 or over, as may be specified in the order.

Note that:

Thank you for purchasing Crown Court Index 2012.

 Don't miss important updates

So that you have all the latest information, **Crown Court Index 2012** is published annually. Sign up today for a Standing Order to ensure you receive the updating copies as soon as they publish. Setting up a Standing Order with Sweet & Maxwell is hassle-free, simply tick, complete and return this FREEPOST card and we'll do the rest.

You may cancel your Standing Order at any time by writing to us at Sweet & Maxwell, PO Box 2000, Andover, SP10 9AH stating the Standing Order you wish to cancel.

Alternatively, if you have purchased your copy of **Crown Court Index** from a bookshop or other trade supplier, please ask your supplier to ensure that you are registered to receive the new editions.

All goods are subject to our 30 day Satisfaction Guarantee (applicable to EU customers only)

Yes, please send me new editions of **Crown Court Index** to be invoiced on publication, until I cancel the standing order in writing.

☐ All new editions

Title .... Name ....

Organisation ....

Job title ....

Address ....

....

Postcode ....

Telephone ....

Email ....

S&M account number (if known) ....

PO number ....

All orders are accepted subject to the terms of this order form and our Terms of Trading. (see www.sweetandmaxwell.co.uk). By submitting this order form I confirm that I accept these terms and I am authorised to sign on behalf of the customer.

Signed .... Job Title ....

Print Name .... Date ....

UK VAT Number: GB 900 5487 43. Irish VAT Number: IE 9513874E. For customers in an EU member state (except UK & Ireland) please supply your VAT Number. VAT No [   ]

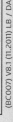
(BC007) V8.1 (11.2011) LB / DA

Delivery charges are not made for titles supplied to mainland UK. Non-mainland UK please add £4/€5 per delivery. Europe - please add £10/€13 for first item, £2.50/€3 for each additional item. Rest of World - please add £30/€38 for first item, £15/€19 for each additional item. For deliveries outside Europe please add £30/€42 for first item, £15/€21 for each additional item.

Goods will normally be dispatched within 3-5 working days of availability. The price charged to customers, irrespective of any prices quoted, will be the price specified in our price list current at the time of dispatch of the goods, as published on our website, unless the order is subject to a specific offer or discount in which case special terms may apply.

UK VAT is charged on all applicable sales at the prevailing rate except in the case of sales to Ireland where Irish VAT will be charged at the prevailing rate. Customers outside the EU will not be charged UK VAT.

Thomson Reuters (Professional) UK Limited – Legal Business (Company No. 1679046). 100 Avenue Road, Swiss Cottage, London NW3 3PF. Registered in England and Wales. Registered office: Aldgate House, 33 Aldgate High Street, London EC3N 1DL. Trades using various trading names, a list of which is posted on its website at sweetandmaxwell.co.uk

"Thomson Reuters" and the Thomson Reuters logo are trademarks of Thomson Reuters and its affiliated companies.

SWEET & MAXWELL   THOMSON REUTERS

SWEET & MAXWELL

FREEPOST

PO BOX 2000

ANDOVER

SP10 9AH

UNITED KINGDOM

(1) the judge will need to have in mind the period during which danger is capable of arising from the offender's activities, without imposing a term which leaves the offender without hope (*R. v Storey* (1973) 57 Cr. App. R. 840; *R. v Bryson* (1974) 58 Cr. App. R. 464);

(2) if the offence carries life imprisonment in the case of an offender of 21, and the doctors cannot indicate the period required, protection of the public should be secured by custody for life under s.94 (*R. v Nightingale* (1984) 6 Cr. App. R. (S.) 65).

The term should not exceed that which would be passed on an offender over 18, or over 21, for the same offence(s) (*R. v Burrowes* (1985) 7 Cr. App. R. (S.) 106).

In *R. v AM* [1998] 2 Cr. App. R. 57, CACD upheld a single sentence of detention under s.91 in respect of one offence, making the length commensurate with the gravity of all the offences, and passing no separate penalty (a doubtful practice) for the other offences.

Prescribed minimum sentences for certain firearms offences

28–022 Where a person is convicted of certain offences under FA 1968, s.5, **committed on or after April 4, 2005**, the judge must impose in the case of an offender aged under 18 when convicted, a sentence of detention under s.91 for at least three years (with or without a fine), unless he is of opinion that there are exceptional circumstances relating to the offence or to the offender which justify his not doing so.

FA 1968, s.51A

Where an offence is found to have been committed over a period of two or more days, or at some time during a period of two or more days, it is to be taken to have been committed on the last of those days.

Combination of sentences

28–023 It is generally undesirable that sentences of detention under s.91 and secure training orders under s.100, be imposed, either consecutively to, or concurrently with, each other (*R. v Gaskin* (1985) 7 Cr. App. R. (S.) 28; *R. v McKenna* (1985) 7 Cr. App. R. (S.) 348).

However, it is not always possible to avoid this. Thus:

(1) terms of detention under s.91, and those under s.100, may be served in different establishments and it is generally undesirable to impose terms *concurrent* under both sections;

(2) the judge minded to impose *concurrent* terms under the two sections, should make sure that no administrative difficulty will result before doing so;

(3) where some of the offences fall within s.91 and others are "associated" but do not fall within the section, it will usually be preferable to impose a term under s.91 which takes account of the associated offence or offences, and to impose "no separate penalty" for the lesser offences; and

(4) there is no power to order a detention and training order to run consecutively to a sentence under s.91 (*R. v H (Grant) (A juvenile)* [2001] 2 Cr. App. R. (S.) 31).

Detention of Young
Offenders

6.   Dangerous offenders; protective sentences

28–024   The sentences created under CJA 2003, ss.224–228 are dealt with in DANGEROUS OFFENDERS; PROTECTIVE SENTENCES.

29. DISCHARGE; ABSOLUTE AND CONDITIONAL

General

29–001   A discharge, whether absolute or conditional, may be appropriate:

> PCC(S)A 2000, s.12(1)

(1) generally, for any age of offender, provided the offence is not one for which the sentence is fixed by law, or falls to be imposed under PCC(S)A 2000, ss.109, 110(2), 111(2) (required custodial sentences for certain repeat offences), FA 1968, s.51A(2) (minimum sentences for certain firearms offences) CJA 2003, ss.225(2), 226 (sentences for public prosecution) and (2) or VCRA 2006, s.29(4) or (6) (minimum sentences for using person to mind a weapon); and

(2) specifically, where the nature of the offence and the character of the offender make the infliction of punishment inexpedient.

> CJIA 2008, s.148, Sch.26, Pt 2, para.41

A discharge is not a "community order" in terms of CJA 2003, s.177.

Absolute discharge

29–002   An absolute discharge is appropriate where the judge considers no action is required beyond the mere finding of guilt, reflecting:

(1) the triviality of the offence (*R. v King* [1977] Crim. L.R. 627);
(2) the circumstances in which it came to be prosecuted (*Smedleys Ltd v Breed* [1974] Crim L.R. 309); or
(3) factors relating to the offender (*R. v O'Toole* (1971) 55 Cr. App. R. 206).

It is not an order likely to be made frequently in the Crown Court.

Conditional discharge

29–003   The effect of an order is to discharge an offender subject to a *single condition* that he commit no offence during the "operational period" specified in the order, which may not exceed three years.

> PCC(S)A 2000, s.12(3)

An order may **not** be made:

(1) where a person has been warned by a constable under CDA, s.65 and is convicted of an offence within two years of that warning, save in exceptional circumstances which the judge must spell out in open court;

> CDA 1998, ss.1(11), 65, 66F, 66(4) CJIA 2008, s.48, Sch.9, para.3

(2) where a person has been given a youth conditional caution and is convicted of an offence committed within two years of the giving of that caution, unless the judge is of the opinion that there are exceptional circumstances relating to the offence or the offender which justify his doing so, and he states in open court why he is of that opinion;
(3) on the breach of a sexual offences prevention order (see BREACH, AMENDMENT AND REVOCATION OF ORDERS);
(4) on the breach of an anti-social behaviour order (see BREACH, AMENDMENT AND REVOCATION OF ORDERS).

DISCHARGE; ABSOLUTE AND CONDITIONAL

The judge should explain that:

(a) in view of the nature of the offence and any mitigating factors (including a plea of guilty) he does not propose to *punish* the offender;

(b) instead he proposes to discharge the offender conditionally for x months or years on condition that he commit no further offence during the period;

(c) if he stays out of trouble for that period he will not be punished for the instant offence, but if he does commit another offence he may be brought back and sentenced in a different way, which might include a custodial sentence as well as being dealt with for the fresh offence.

Combining other orders

29–004   Since the whole basis for the imposition of a conditional discharge is that punishment is inexpedient, a punitive order such as a **fine** (*R. v Sanck* (1990) 12 Cr. App. R. (S.)262) or a **confiscation order** under PCA 2002 (*R. v Clarke* [2009] EWCA Crim 1074; [2010] 1 Cr. App. R. (S.) 48, *R. v Magro* [2010] EWCA Crim 1575, [2010] 2 Cr. App. R. 25) may not be combined with it. There is, however, nothing to prevent the judge combining with it such ancillary orders as are set out in 29–005 below.

PCC(S)A 2000, S.12(7)

Ancillary orders

29–005   On making an order for discharge, the judge may:

PCC(S)A 2000, s.12(6)(7); PD 2004, III.31.18

(1) in the case of a conditional discharge, if he thinks it expedient for the purpose of the offender's reformation, allow any person who consents to do so, to give **security for the offender's good behaviour**; specifying the type of conduct from which the offender is to refrain; (as to which, see PD 2004, III.31.18);

(2) when discharging an offender absolutely or conditionally in respect of an offence, make an order for **costs** against him, or make a **compensation order** under PCC(S)A 2000, s.130, a **deprivation order** under s.143 or a **restitution order** under s.148; and

(3) where still appropriate make a recommendation for **deportation** (IA 1971, s.6(3); PCC(S)A 2000, s.14(1));

(4) when discharging an offender conditionally, make:

   (a) an **anti-social behaviour order** (see ANTI-SOCIAL BEHAVIOUR ORDERS AND ISOs);

   (b) a **football banning order** (see FOOTBALL BANNING ORDERS);

   (c) a **drinking banning order** (see DRINKING BANNING ORDERS); or

   (d) a **serious crime prevention order** (see SERIOUS CRIME PREVENTION ORDERS).

In an appropriate case, the judge must:

(a) give his reasons for not making a compensation order where personal injury, loss or damage is involved;

(b) discharge any duty under RTOA 1988, s.46(1) to **disqualify** a road traffic offender, or to order the **endorsement** of his licence.

Effect of discharge

29–006 A conviction of an offence for which an absolute or conditional discharge is made is deemed not to be a conviction for any purpose other than the purposes of the proceedings in which the order was made, or of any subsequent proceedings taken against the offender under *ibid.* s.13 for a breach (see, e.g. *R. v Longworth* [2006] UKHL 1, [2006] 2 Cr. App. R. (S.) 62, where the imposition of a conditional discharge was held not to activate the notification procedures of SOA 1997), though: PCC(S)A 2000, s.14

(1) where the offender was aged 18 or over at the time of his conviction of the offence in question, and is subsequently sentenced under s.13, this provision ceases to apply;
(2) the "deeming" provision does not affect:
   (a) any right of the offender to rely on his conviction in bar of any subsequent proceedings for the same offence;
   (b) the restoration of any property in consequence of his conviction; or
   (c) the operation in relation to him, of any enactment or instrument in force on July 1, 1974, which is expressed to extend to persons dealt with under POA 1907, s.1(1) as well as to convicted persons, and
(3) in any event, the conviction is to be disregarded for the purposes of an enactment or instrument which imposes any disqualification or disability on convicted persons, or authorises or requires the imposition of such; and
(4) the deeming provisions have effect subject to CAA 1968, s.50(1A) and MCA 1980, s.108(1A), and do not prevent an appeal against conviction, or otherwise.

Conviction of further offence

29–007 An offender convicted in any part of Great Britain of an offence committed during the "operational period" of a conditional discharge, and who is dealt with in respect of that further offence, is liable to be dealt with for the offence for which he was made the subject of the order. PCC(S)A 2000, s.13

Where the original order was made by:

(1) the Crown Court, and the subsequent conviction is in a magistrates' court, the latter may commit him to the Crown Court, a judge of which, if satisfied of the breach, may deal with him for the offence for which the order was made in any way in which he could deal with him if he had just been convicted before him of that offence;
(2) the Crown Court, as is the subsequent conviction, a judge may deal with the offender as if he had just been convicted before him of the original offence; and
(3) a magistrates' court, and the subsequent conviction is in the Crown Court, or the offender is dealt with in the Crown Court after committal under (1) above:

435

    (a) the judge's powers are limited to dealing with the offender in a manner in which the lower court could have dealt with him had he just been convicted before it; unless

    (b) the original order was made when the offender was under 18, in respect of an offence triable only on indictment in the case of an adult, in which case the judge's powers in dealing with the original offence extend to a fine not exceeding £5,000, or the lower court's powers in relation to an offence punishable with imprisonment for a term not exceeding six months (see COMMITTALS FOR SENTENCE).

The relevant date for considering the appropriate sentencing option on the commission of a further offence is the date of subsequent sentence (*R. v Keelan* (1975) 61 Cr. App. R. 212).

Orders made on appeal

29–008   Where an order for conditional discharge has been made on appeal, for the purposes of s.13 above, it is deemed: PCC(S)A 2000, s.15(1)

    (1) if it was made on an appeal brought from a magistrates' court, to have been made by that magistrates' court; and

    (2) if it was made on an appeal brought from the Crown Court or from CACD, to have been made by the Crown Court.

Procedure on the breach

29–009   In dealing with the alleged commission of a further offence during the operational period of a conditional discharge, the accused must be asked in terms whether: PCC(S)A 2003, s.15(3)

    (1) on the date specified he was convicted of the offence and made the subject of a conditional discharge;

    (2) he admits that his subsequent conviction was within the operational period of that order; and

    (3) he realises that he is liable to be dealt with for the origin-al offence.

Should he dispute (1) or (2) above, the issue falls to be determined by the judge, not by the verdict of a jury.

While there is no statutory obligation to deal with an offender for breach of the order, failure to do so, save for good reason, renders the making of the original order pointless.

Generally there should be a sentence which is more than nominal, though there is nothing to prevent the judge dealing with the breach by a fresh conditional discharge where the circumstances are exceptional and such a course is justified.

Termination of the order

29–010   If a person conditionally discharged under s.12, is sentenced for the offence in respect of which the order was made, the order ceases to have effect though a compensation order made when the original order was made remains in force (*R. v Evans* (1961) 45 Cr. App. R. 59).   PCC(S)A 2000, s.12(5)

30. DISCLOSURE

Quick guide

A.   General

Introduction

30–001   While it is vital that obligations of disclosure are properly discharged by both the prosecution and the defence, the judge's active hands-on oversight of the process is an important safeguard against any potential miscarriages of justice.

The judge needs to have clearly in mind that:

(1) consideration of irrelevant unused material may consume wholly unjustifiable and disproportionate amounts of time and public resources, undermining the overall performance and efficiency of the criminal justice system; and

(2) unused prosecution material falls to be disclosed if, and only if, it satisfies the test for the disclosure regime applicable to the proceedings in question, subject to any overriding public interest considerations.

A prosecutor is required to disclose material and the formalities relating to defence statements, the time limits applicable to defence disclosure being set out in SI 1997/684.

Regard must be had to the Attorney-General's Guidelines on disclosure (April 2005), though they do not have the force of law (*R. v Brown* [1995] 1 Cr. App. R. 191); see also *Disclosure: A Protocol for the Control and Management of Unused Material in the Crown Court,* issued by the Court of Appeal in 2006, in the light of which the text in this section has been updated. This is referred to in the text merely as The Protocol.

CPR 2011, Pt 1 sets out the procedures to be followed in applying to the court in relation to both sensitive and non- sensitive unused material. Pt 3 is relevant in respect of the judge's general case management powers, as is PD 2004.

The Attorney-General has issued guidelines on disclosure of digitally-stored material. They supplement the 2005 guidelines on the disclosure of unused material to the defence, specifically para. 27 (responsibilities of a disclosure officer when examining material retained by the investigator). The objective is to set out how digital material satisfying the test for disclosure can best be identified and disclosed to the defence without imposing unrealistic or disproportionate demands on the investigator or prosecutor. For the full text of the guidelines, see http://www.ago.gov.uk.

Lord Justice Gross, at the request of the Lord Chief Justice, has published a review of the disclosure regime in criminal cases.

Application of regime

30–002   The regime applicable to the case will depend on the date on which the particular criminal investigation started, thus where it commenced:

(1) before April 1, 1997, the common law applies, as set out in *R. v Keane* (1994) 99 Cr. App. R. 1;

(2) on or after April 1, 1997, but before April 4, 2005, the test under CPIA 1997, before its amendment by CJA 2003, applies, with separate tests for disclosure of unused prosecution material at the primary and secondary stages (the latter following service of a defence statement by the accused), supported by the Code of Practice (SI 1999/1033) issued under CPIA 1996, s.23(1);

(3) on or after April 4, 2005, the "enhanced" provisions test set out in CPIA 1996, (as amended by CJA 2003, Pt V) apply, providing a single test for the disclosure of unused material, supported by the 2005 Code of Practice (SI 2005/985).

There may be circumstances where an investigation is commenced before April 4, 2005 and further offences are committed after that date. In such a situation the original disclosure scheme under the Act will apply to the original investigation and the enhanced provisions to the fresh offences.

The provisions of the Act, the Code of Practice and the Guidelines of 2005, although expressed in a domestic context, make clear the prosecutor's obligation to pursue reasonable lines of enquiry in relation to material which might be held overseas, outside the European Union *(R. v Flook* [2009] EWCA Crim 682; [2010] 1 Cr. App. R. 30).

As to the duties of the parties, and the prosecutor's approach, see *R. v Olu* [2010] EWCA Crim 2795, [2011] 1 Cr. App. R.

The concept of fairness

30–003   The concept of fairness recognises that:

(1) there are interests other than those of the accused that need to be protected, including those of victims and witnesses who might otherwise be exposed to harm; the scheme of CPIA 1996 seeks to protect those interests;

(2) where there are fears for the safety of a prosecution witness, the prosecutor may be justified in not providing the defence with

copies of audio and video tapes, but instead providing transcripts of the tapes and confining them to inspection of the tapes under controlled conditions (*R. v DPP Ex p. J.* [2000] 1 All E.R.183DC);

(3) material should not be disclosed which over-burdens the participants in the trial process, diverts attention from the relevant issues, leads to unjustifiable delay, and is wasteful of resources;

(4) disclosure is a continuing process throughout the proceedings, up to the stage when any final appeal is determined.

In order to facilitate the extent of such disclosure, and to narrow the issues in respect of which it is necessary to call evidence, the accused is required to make advance disclosure of the general nature of his defence (30–018—30–024) and of any expert evidence (30-025) upon which he proposes to rely.

The "equality of arms" principle in ECHR requires close attention to the appropriate rules: see, e.g. *Dowsett v UK* [2003] Crim. L.R. 890; *Edwards v UK* [2003] Crim. L.R. 891.

B.   The application of the common law

30–004   The common law rules on disclosure as set out in *R. v Keane* (1994) 99 Cr. App. R. 1:

(1) continue to apply where a case does not fall within CPIA 1996;

(2) govern disclosure prior to the stage when the Act applies, i.e. to cases where the criminal investigation started before April 1, 1997 (30-002); and

(3) govern the judge's decision in relation to disclosure of sensitive material for which public interest immunity is claimed (30-000).

CPR 2011, r. 22 governs the procedure to be followed when an application is made for non-disclosure on the grounds of public interest immunity (see 30–037). Insofar as ECHR is concerned, *Rowe v UK* [2000] Crim.L.R. 584 did not criticise the procedure used in PII applications, which was approved by CACD in *R. v Davis; R. v Rowe; R. v Johnson* (1997) 97 Cr. App. R. 110.

C.   The Criminal Procedure and Investigations Act 1996

Application of the Act

30–005   CPIA 1996 applies to cases reaching the Crown Court by any of the recognised channels set out in *ibid.* s.1(2), i.e.

- committal under MCA 1980, ss.6(1) or 6(2);
- transfer under CJA 1987, s.4 or CJA 1991, s.53;
- documents containing evidence served on the accused in accordance with SI 2005/90;
- where the matter has been sent to the Crown Court pursuant to CDA 1998, ss.51 or 51A;
- where a matter has been added to the indictment in accordance with CJA 1988, s.40 or;

- where a voluntary bill has been preferred under AJ(MP)A 1933,s.2(2)(b) or POA 1985, s.22B(3)(a).

Initial duty of prosecutor to disclose

30–006 In relation to cases in which a criminal investigation began **after April 4, 2005,** CJA 2003, Pt 5, replaces the previous two-stage test with a new objective single test for the disclosure of unused prosecution material to the defence.

The former duty of secondary disclosure by the prosecutor is replaced with a revised continuing duty to disclose material that meets the new test, and he is specifically required to review the prosecution material on receipt of the defence statement, and to make further disclosure as required under his continuing duty. In relation to criminal investigations begun before April 4, 2005, the former two-tier procedure applies.

Under the new provisions the prosecutor is required to:

(1) disclose to the defence any prosecution material which has not previously been disclosed and which might reasonably be considered as capable of undermining the case for the prosecution against the accused, or of assisting the case for the accused; or

(2) give the accused a written statement that there is no such material, informing the Crown Court officer that he has done so.

"Prosecution material" for the purposes of both primary and secondary disclosure by the prosecution is defined as material which:

(a) is in the prosecutor's possession and came into his possession in connection with the case for the prosecution against the accused; or

(b) in pursuance of the Code of Practice, he has inspected in connection with the case for the prosecution against the accused.

Information affecting credibility of defence witness

30–007 At common law, information affecting only the credibility of a defence witness did not need to be disclosed (*R. v Brown* [1995] 1 Cr. App. R. 191) unless it also contained evidence favourable to the accused (*R. v Mills* [1998] 1 Cr. App. R. 43). See as to the disclosure of previous convictions *R. v Vasilou* [2000] Crim.L.R. 845; the fact that a witness giving evidence can expect to receive a reward at the conclusion of the trial ought to be disclosed (*R. v Allan* [2004] EWCA Crim 2236, [2005] Crim. L.R. 716).

Time within which prosecutor must act

30–008 Although no specific time limit is prescribed, the prosecutor must act under this provision as soon as is "reasonably practicable" after the: CPIA 1996, s.13(1)

(1) accused pleads not guilty;

(2) accused is committed or transferred for trial;

(3) accused is sent for trial under CDA 1998, s.51;

(4) court includes a count in the indictment; or

(5) bill of indictment is preferred,

depending on the manner in which the matter comes before the Crown Court.

When a case is sent to the Crown Court under CDA 1998, s.51, the rules (SI 2000/3305) allow the prosecutor 70 days from the date on which the case was sent (50 days where the accused is in custody) within which to serve the evidence on which the charge or charges are based. These time limits may be extended or varied at the court's direction.

Where the prosecutor acts under s.3 above and before doing so he was given a document in pursuance of a provision included by virtue of s.24(3) in a Code operative under Pt II of the Act, he must give that document to the accused at the same time as he acts under s.3.

CPIA 1996, s.4

Case management; enforcement of scheme

30–009 The Protocol (see 30–001, above) makes it clear that the judge has a duty to enforce the statutory scheme. He needs to consider at any preliminary hearing whether it is practicable for the prosecution to comply with primary or initial disclosure at the same time as service of the s.51 papers, or whether disclosure ought to take place after a certain interval but before the matter is listed for a PCMH.

It is important if the listing of the PCMH is to be an effective one, that the defence have a proper opportunity to read the case papers and to consider the initial or primary disclosure, with a view to the timely drafting of a defence case statement (where the matter is to be contested) before the matter is listed for a PCMH.

If the nature of the case does not allow service of the evidence and initial or primary disclosure within the 70, or if applicable 50, days (or such other period as directed by the magistrates' court):

(1) the prosecution advocate at the preliminary Crown Court hearing, or further hearing prior to the PCMH, must be made aware of the problems, why and how the position has arisen so as to be able to assist the judge as to what revised time limits are realistic;
(2) the prosecution advocate should make any foreseeable difficulties clear as soon as possible at the Crown Court preliminary hearing (where there is one); or
(3) failing this, where such difficulties arise or have come to light after directions for service of case papers and disclosure have been made, the prosecution should notify the court and the defence promptly, in advance of the PCMH date, and prior to the date set by the judge for the service of the material.

In order to ensure that the listing of the PCMH is appropriate, the judge should not impose time limits for service of case papers or initial/primary disclosure unless and until he is confident that the prosecution advocate has taken the requisite instructions from those who are actually going to do the work specified. It is better to impose a realistic timetable from the outset than to set unachievable limits. Reference should be made to CPR 2011, Pt 3 and the PD 2004 in this respect.

disclosure

DISCLOSURE

Timetable; directions and further directions

30–010 The provisions set out in the preceding paragraph are likewise appropriate where directions, or further directions, are made in relation to prosecution or defence disclosure at the PCMH. Failure to consider whether the timetable is practicable may dislocate the court timetable and can even imperil trial dates.

Thus:

(1) at the PCMH all the advocates must be fully instructed about any difficulties the parties may have in complying with their respective disclosure obligations, and must be in a position to put forward a reasonable timetable for resolution of them;

(2) where the judge gives directions in the light of such inquiry, extensions of time should not be given lightly or as a matter of course. If extensions are sought, then an appropriately detailed explanation must be given;

(3) as part of any timetabling exercise the judge should set a date by which any application by the defence for disclosure, if there is to be one, should be made and should require the defence to indicate in advance of the cut-off date what documents they are interested in and from what source; in appropriate cases, the judge should require justification of any request.

Default by parties

30-011 It is not sufficient merely for the prosecutor to say that the papers have been delivered late by the police or other investigator; the judge will need to know why they have been delivered late.

Likewise, where the accused has been dilatory in serving a defence statement after the prosecutor has complied with his duty to make primary or initial disclosure, or has purported to do so, it is not sufficient for the defence to say that insufficient instructions have been taken for service of this within the 14-day time limit: the judge will need to know why sufficient instructions have not been taken, and what arrangements have been made for the taking of such instructions; delays and failures by the defence are as damaging to the timely, fair and efficient hearing of the case as delays and failures by the prosecution, and judges should identify and deal with all such failures firmly and fairly.

Questions of disclosure for prosecutor

30-012 Questions of disclosure must be decided by the prosecutor, and the judge's assistance should only be sought if a question can properly be decided by him, most obviously where questions of public interest immunity are involved (*R. v B* [2000] Crim. L.R. 500).

It follows that:

(1) the judge should not allow the prosecutor to abdicate his statutory responsibility for reviewing the unused material by the expedient of allowing the defence to inspect (or providing the defence with copies of) everything on the schedules of non-sensitive unused prosecution material, irrespective of whether that material, or all of, satisfies the relevant test for disclosure.

(2) where the test is satisfied it is for the prosecutor to decide the form in which disclosure is made; disclosure need not be in the same form as that in which the information was recorded.

Guidance on case management issues relating to this point was given by Rose L.J. in *R. v CPS (Interlocutory Application under sections 35/36 CPIA)* [2005] EWCA Crim 2342, and see CASE MANAGEMENT

In *R. v Olu,* above, CACD observed that disclosure under the CPIA 1996 regime must be carried our 'thinkingly' and not as a 'box-ticking exercise'. It is the task of a prosecution lawyer to identify the issues in the case and for a police officer who is not trained in that skill to act under the guidance of the prosecutor.

The statement must be given during the period which, by virtue of s.12, is the "relevant period" for this section.

Compulsory disclosure by accused: (1) general

30–013   In relation to criminal investigations begun after April 4, 2005, CJA 2003, Pt 5, requires the accused to provide a more detailed defence statement than the previous legislation required.

CPIA 1996
s.5(1),(5)

Where the prosecutor has complied, or purported to comply, with the initial duty on him, the accused is required to give a defence statement both to the court and to the prosecutor:

(1) setting out the nature of his defence (but see *R. v Tibbs* [2000] 2 Cr. App. R. 309; *R. v Wheeler* [2001] 1 Cr. App. R. 10);
(2) indicating the matters on which he takes issue with the prosecutor; and
(3) setting out, in respect of each such matter, the reason why he takes issue with the prosecutor.

As to the contents of such a statement, see 30–018, below. It must be served, in the form shown in PD 2004, Annex D, on the court officer and on the prosecutor (r.22.4).

Compulsory disclosure by accused: (2) time limits

30–014   Service of the defence statement is a critical stage in the disclosure process, and timely service of the statement will allow for the proper consideration of disclosure issues well in advance of the trial date.

In relation to cases begun after **February 28, 2011,** defence disclosure must be made in accordance with DTLR 2011. Cases that begin before that date are governed by DTLR 1997 (as to which see previous editions of this work).

Defence disclosure must be:

(1) made within 28 days of the date upon which the prosecutor complies, or purports to comply, with the requirements of initial disclosure; and
(2) extended, if the judge so orders, by as many days as he (entirely at his own discretion) specifies.

There may be cases where it is not possible to serve a proper defence case statement within the 28 day time limit; well founded defence applications for an extension of time under (2) above may be granted in a proper case. It may be proper to put the PCMH back by a week or so, to enable a sufficient defence case statement to be filed and considered by the prosecutor. As to the contents of such a statement, see 30–018, below.

The judge may extend the period only if an application is made by the accused before the end of that period which: DTLR 2011, regs1,2(2)

(a) states that the accused believes, on reasonable grounds, that it is not possible for him to give a defence statement under ss.5 or 6 of the Act during the limitation period;
(b) specifies the grounds for so believing; and
(c) specifies the number of days by which he wishes the period to be extended.

Where the relevant period would end on a weekend, or on Christmas Day, Good Friday or a bank holiday, it is to be treated as expiring on the next day that is not one of those days. DTLR 2011, reg.2(4)

Compulsory disclosure by accused: (3) grant of extension

30–015 The judge may order an extension (or further extension) of as many days as he thinks appropriate. DTLR 2011, reg.3

An extension may be ordered only on an application made by the accused, and only if the judge is satisfied that it would be unreasonable to require the accused to give a defence statement under ss.5 or 6, or a notice under s.6C, within the relevant period.

An application must:

(1) be made within the relevant period,
(2) specify the grounds on which it is made and
(3) specify the number of days by which it is sought to have the period extended.

There is no limit on the number of applications that may be made.

Compulsory disclosure by accused: (4) prosecutor's representations

30–016 The prosecutor may make representations to the court concerning the application in writing within 14 days of the service of the defence notice. Where such representations are received, or on the expiration of 14 days from service of the defence notice, the judge will consider the application to extend the defence time limit and may do so on the papers or at a hearing.

If a hearing is held, the:

(1) court must give notice of it to the prosecutor and to the applicant;
(2) hearing is with notice; and
(3) prosecutor and the applicant are entitled to make representations to the court.

A copy of any order made by the court must be served on the prosecutor and the applicant. Before the extension order has expired, the judge may, on application by the accused (following the same procedure), further extend the period at his discretion. There is no limit to the number of times this procedure may be repeated.

Voluntary disclosure by accused

30–017　Where the prosecutor complies with his duty of initial disclosure under s.3 above, or purports to comply with it, the accused may give a defence statement to the prosecutor, and if he does so, must give one to the court.

If the accused gives such a statement, he must give it during the period which is, by virtue of s.12 the relevant period.

CPIA 1996, s.6, Sch.25, Pt 2, paras 20, 26

Contents of defence statement

30–018　A purported defence case statement which is little more than reiteration of the accused's plea, i.e., an assertion that he is not guilty, is not a defence statement under the Act. A defence statements must comply with the requisite formalities set out in CPIA 1996, ss 5(6) and (7) or s.6A as applicable (*R. v Bryant (Patrick)* [2005] EWCA Crim.2079 (per Judge L.J. at para.12).

Where the pre-April 2005 regime applies under CPIA 1996, the accused must, in his defence statement, set out the nature of his defence in general terms, indicating the matters upon which he takes issue with the prosecutor and setting out, in relation to each matter, why issue is taken. Any alibi defence relied upon must comply with the formalities in s.5(7)(a) and (b).

Where the enhanced requirements for defence disclosure apply under s.6A of the Act, i.e. where the case involves a criminal investigation commencing on or after April 4, 2005, the defence statement must spell out in detail:

(1) the nature of the accused's defence, including any particular defences on which he intends to rely;

(2) the matters of fact on which he takes issue with the prosecution;

(3) where the criminal investigation commenced after November 3, 2008 the particulars of the matters of fact on which he intends to rely for the purposes of his defence (CJIA 2008, s.60; S.I. 2008/2712);

(4) in the case of each such matter, why he takes issue with the prosecution; and

(5) any point of law (including any point as to the admissibility of evidence) or abuse of process which he wishes to take, and any authority on which he intends to rely for that purpose.

Where an accused has no positive case to advance but declines to plead guilty, he is under no obligation to put into the statement an admission of guilt or a refusal to give instructions. However, the statement must say that

(a) the accused does not admit the offence or relevant part of it; and

(b) calls on the prosecutor to prove it. advancing no positive case,

because if he did advance a positive case he would have to give notice of it and it would have to appear in the statement *(R. v Rochford* [2010] EWCA Crim 1928, [2011] 1 Cr. App. R. 11 and see *R. v Malcolm* [2011] EWCA Crim 2069).

DISCLOSURE

A defence statement purporting to be given under s.5, 6 or 8B above or a statement of the kind mentioned in s.6B(4) on behalf of an accused by his solicitor will, unless the contrary is proved, be deemed to be given with the authority of the accused.

CPIA 1996,
s. 6A

Preparation of defence statements

30-019   Guidance on the preparation of defence statements were issued by the Standards Committee of the Bar Standards Board with effect from January 2011.

In *R. v G* [2010] EWCA Crim 1928 CACD said of the requirements of the contents of defence statements under s.6A:

(1) the accused is not required to advance a positive case if he simply intends to put the prosecutor to proof, but the defence statement must say so;

(2) the accused is not required to breach his rights to legal professional privilege or to incriminate himself;

(3) the obligation to file a defence statement is a statutory obligation on the accused;

(4) if the accused refuses to plead but advances no positive case, his lawyer should go no further than to explain the nature and extent of the statutory obligation and to advise of the consequences of disobedience.

Alibi defence

30–020   Where an alibi defence is relied upon:

(1) in relation to the pre-April 4, 2005 regime, the particulars must comply with s.5(7) (a) and (b) of the Act;

CPIA 1996,
s.6A

(2) and the enhanced provisions apply under s.6A, the particulars given must comply with s.6(2)(a) of the Act, and the defence statement must give particulars which include:

(a) the name, address and date of birth of any witness the accused believes is able to give evidence in support of the alibi, or as many of those details as are known to the accused when the statement is given;

(b) any information in the accused's possession which might be of material assistance in identifying or finding any such witness in whose case any of the details mentioned in paragraph (a) are not known to the accused when the statement is given,

These latter provisions (i.e. (2) above) do not apply in relation to offences in to which the criminal investigation began before July 15, 2005.

In *R. (on the application of Tinnion) v Reading CC* [2009] EWHC 2930 (Admin.); [2010] Crim. L.R. 733, it was said obiter that breach of this provision does not render the evidence of a witness inadmissible; the appropriate sanction is not that such a witness should not be called, but that adverse comment may be made pursuant to CPIA 1996, s.11, and the court or jury may draw such inferences as appear proper from the failure to comply.

"Evidence in support of an alibi"; definition

30-021 "Evidence in support of an alibi" is evidence tending to show that by reason of the presence of the accused at a particular place or in a particular area at a particular time he was not, or was unlikely to have been, at the place where the offence is alleged to have been committed at the time of its alleged commission.

Insofar as an alibi defence is concerned, if, at trial the accused:

(1) raised the issue of location, said that he was located somewhere else at the material time, or called evidence from somewhere else that he was e.g. not the driver, he will have failed to comply if no notification has been given; but

(2) was going to make no positive case at all, nor raise the issue of his location elsewhere and simply put the prosecutor to proof, there will be no failure to comply.

The judge's role

30–022 The Protocol (see 30–001, above) makes it clear that where there are disclosure failings on the party of the defence or the prosecution, the judge should, in exercising appropriate oversight, pose searching questions to the parties and, having done so and having explored the reasons for default, should give clear directions to ensure that such failings are addressed and remedied well in advance of the trial date.

The judge must insist that the defence case statement is served by the due date, and he should then examine it with care to ensure that it complies with the formalities required by the Act (see 30–013, 30–014, above) bearing in mind that:

(1) if the material does not weaken the prosecution case or strengthen that of the accused, there is no requirement to disclose it;

(2) for this purpose the parties' respective cases should not be restrictively analysed, but they must be carefully analysed, to ascertain the specific facts the prosecution seek to establish and the specific grounds on which the charges are resisted;

(3) the trial process is not well served if the defence are permitted to make general and unspecified allegations and then seek far-reaching disclosure in the hope that material may turn up to make them good;

(4) neutral material or material damaging to the accused need not be disclosed and should not be brought to the attention of the court.

(*R. v H* [2004] UKHL 3, [2004] 2 Cr. App. R. 10 HL).
Where:

(a) no defence case statement, or no sufficient case statement, has been served by the date of the PCMH, the judge should make a full investigation of the reasons for this failure to comply with the mandatory obligation under CPIA 1996, s.5(5);

(b) there is no, or no sufficient, defence statement by the date of the PCMH, or any pre-trial hearing where the matter falls to be considered, the judge must consider whether the defence should be warned, pursuant to CPIA 1996, s.6E(2) (see below), that an adverse inference may be drawn at the trial.

DISCLOSURE

In the usual case, where s.6E(2) applies and there is no justification for the deficiency, such a warning as in (b) should be given.

Section 6E(2) referred to in (b) above provides that in relation to a criminal investigation begun after April 4, 2005, if it appears to the judge at a pre-trial hearing that an accused has failed to comply fully with ss.5, 6B or 6C, so that there is a possibility of comment being made or inferences drawn under s.11(5), he must warn the accused accordingly. This is the ultimate sanction for a failure in disclosure by the accused.

Any order by the judge to comply with the requirements of ss.5(5) and 6A of the Act to serve a defence statement in the required form, is no more than an articulation of the provisions of the Act; he cannot not invest himself with an extrastatutory power to punish non-compliance as a contempt of court. The sanctions are explicit in s.11 (*R. v Rochford*, above).

The defence statement and legal privilege

30-023   The judge is entitled to ask, but not to require, the defence advocate, before the trial commences, to reveal his instructions, if no positive case is going to be made, but fundamental rights of legal professional privilege and the accused's privilege against self incrimination are not taken away by s.6A. The accused is required by that section to disclose what will happen at trial, but not his confidential discussions with his advocate, nor is he obliged to incriminate himself.

A lawyer is not permitted to advise an accused not to file a defence statement, or to omit from it something required by s.6A. The obligation to file is a statutory one on the accused, and it is not open to a lawyer to disobey his client's statutory obligation. If it were otherwise, it would be open to any accused at trial to put in evidence that he had been so advised, therefore resulting in no adverse comment, depriving s.5(5) of any effect.

The lawyer's duty is to explain the statutory obligation and the consequences that follow from disobedience of it (*R v Rochford,* above).

The judge must, of course, be alert to ensure that accused persons do not suffer because of the faults and failings of their lawyers, but there must be a clear indication to the professions that if justice is to be done, and if disclosure is to be dealt with fairly in accordance with the law, a full and careful defence case statement is essential.

Notification of intention to call defence witnesses

30–024   In relation to cases reaching the Crown Court (see 30-005) on or after Feb 28, 2011, an accused is required to serve, on the court and on the prosecutor, before the trial, details of any witnesses (other than himself) whom he intends to call, and also details of all experts instructed, including those not called to give evidence. A Code of Practice governs police interviews with the defence witnesses disclosed.

CPIA 1996, s.6C; DTLR 2011, regs. 1,2(2)

Where under s.6C of the 1996 Act, the accused gives a defence witness notice, he must serve such notice (in the form shown in PD 2004, Annex D) on the court officer and on the prosecutor

R.22.4

For cases before that date the former rules in CPIA 1996 (Notification of Intention to Call Defence Witnesses) (Time Limits) Regulations 2010 (S.I. 2010 No. 214) still apply (see previous editions).

The notice must indicate, subject to the extent to which such details have already been given under s.6(2), whether he intends to give or call any evidence at trial and, if so:

(1) giving the name, address and date of birth of each proposed witness (other than the accused himself), or as many of those details as are known to the accused when the notice is given; and

(2) providing any information in the accused's possession which might be of material assistance in identifying or finding any proposed witness in whose case any of the details mentioned in (1) are not known to the accused when the notice is given.

Details do not have to be given under this provision to the extent that they have already been given under s.6A(2), above.

The relevant period for the giving of notice is 28 days from the day on which the prosecutor complies or purports to comply with s.3 of the Act. A judge may extend, or further extend (there is no limit the number of applications which may be made) any application by the accused within the period, specifying the grounds on which it is made and the number of days by which the accused wishes the period to be extended. *DTLR 2011 Regs.1,2(2)*

The judge may order an extension (or further extension) of as many days as he thinks appropriate. An extension may be ordered only on an application made by the accused, and only if the judge is satisfied that it would be unreasonable to require the accused to give a defence statement under section 5 or 6, or a notice under section 6C, within the relevant period. *DTLR 2011, reg. 3*

An application must:

(a) be made within the relevant period
(b) specify the grounds on which it is made, and
(c) specify the number of days by which it is sought to have the period extended

There is no limit on the number of applications that may be made.

Service of expert evidence

30–025 A party (not just the accused) who wants to adduce expert evidence must serve it on the Crown Court officer and on each other party: *R.33.4*

(1) as soon as possible; and
(2) in any event with any application in support of which a party relies on that evidence, and
(3) if another party so requires, give that party a copy of, or a reasonable opportunity to inspect:
   (a) a record of any examination, measurement, test or experiment on which the expert's findings and opinion are based or that were carried out in the course of reaching those findings and opinion; and

(b) anything on which any such examination, measurement, test or experiment was based.

A party may not adduce expert evidence if it has not complied with r.33.4 unless every other party agrees or the judge gives leave

Note that the provisions of CPIA 1996, s.6S (inserted by CJA 2003, s.35) have never been brought into force. CPR 2005, r.24 as originally enacted has been revoked and its provisions are absorbed into CPR 2011, r.33.4.

The effect of CPR 2011, Parts 1.2 and 3.3 together is that it is incumbent upon both the prosecutor and the defence, if it is intended or may be intended, to adduce such evidence, to alert the court and the other side at the earliest practical moment, if possible at a PCMH. If it cannot be done then it must be done as soon as the possibility becomes live. The nearer the start of the trial, the greater the urgency in informing the court and other side so that appropriate steps can be taken to manage the expert evidence in an efficient way (R. *(DPP) v Chorley JJ* [2006] EWHC (Admin.) 1795; *R. v Ensor* [2009] EWCA Crim 2519; [2010] 1 Cr. App. R. 18).

As to the court's case management powers in relation to expert evidence, see r.33.6-9 and CASE MANAGEMENT.

Disclosure by accused: copies to jury

30–026   The judge in a trial before a judge and jury:

CPII 1996, s. 6E (4),(5).(6)

(1) may, whether of his own motion or on application of a party, and where he is of opinion that seeing a copy of the defence statement would help the jury to understand the case or to resolve any issue in the case, direct that the jury be given a copy of any defence statement; and
(2) if he does so, may direct that it be edited so as not include references to matters evidence of which would be inadmissible.

The reference here, to "a defence statement" is a reference, where the accused has given:

(a) only an initial defence statement (that is, a defence statement given under ss.5 or 6), to that statement;
(b) both an initial defence statement and an updated defence statement (that is, a defence statement given under s.6B), to the updated defence statement;
(c) both an initial defence statement and a statement of the kind mentioned in s.6B(4), to the initial defence statement.

These provisions do not affect an alleged offence into which a criminal investigation has not begun before July 15, 2005.

Continuing duty of prosecutor to disclose

30–027   At all times in relation to an alleged offence into which a criminal investigation has begun on or after July 15, 2005:

CPIA 1996, s.7A

(1) after the prosecutor has complied with s.3, or purported to comply with it; and
(2) before the accused is acquitted or, convicted, or the prosecutor decides not to proceed with the case concerned.

the prosecutor must keep under review the question whether at any given time taking into account the state of affairs at that time (including the case for the prosecution as it stands at that time and, in particular, following the giving of a defence statement), there is prosecution material which:

    (a) might reasonably be considered capable of undermining the case for the prosecution against the accused or of assisting the case for the accused; and

    (b) has not been disclosed to the accused,

he must disclose it to the accused as soon as is reasonably practicable (or within the period mentioned in subs.(5)(a), where that applies).

For the purposes of these provisions "prosecution material" is material which is in the prosecutor's possession and came into his possession in connection with the case for the prosecution against the accused, or which, in pursuance of a code operative under Pt 2 of the Act, he has inspected in connection with the case for the prosecution against the accused.

Where the accused gives a defence statement under ss.5, 6 or 6B, and if as a result of that statement:

    (i) the prosecutor is required by this section to make any disclosure, or further disclosure, he must do so during the relevant period under s.12; but

    (ii) he should only disclose material in response to such a request if the material meets the appropriate test for disclosure and if declines to make disclosure he will during that period give to the accused a written statement to that effect, and the matter must proceed to a formal hearing under s.8 (see below, 30–028).

Subsections (3) to (5) of s.3 (method by which prosecutor discloses) apply for the purposes of this section as they apply for the purposes of that.

Material must not be disclosed under this section to the extent that the court, on an application by the prosecutor, concludes it is not in the public interest to disclose it and orders accordingly, or to the extent that it is material the disclosure of which is prohibited by RIPA 2000, s.17.

Application by accused for disclosure: (1) notice

30–028   Where the accused has given a defence statement under ss.5, 6 or 6B and the prosecutor has complied with s.7A(5) or has purported to comply with it or has failed to comply with it, if the accused has at any time reasonable cause to believe that:

    (1) there is prosecution material which is required to be disclosed under s.7A to be disclosed to him; and

    (2) that material has not been disclosed to him,

he may apply to the court for an order requiring the prosecutor to disclose such material to him. The accused must serve notice on the Crown Court officer and on the prosecutor:

CPIA 1996, s.7

    (a) describing the material that he wants the prosecutor to disclose;

    (b) explaining why he thinks there is reasonable cause to believe that;

       (i) the prosecutor has that material; and

       (ii) it is material which CPIA 1996 requires the prosecutor to disclose; and

    (c) asking for a hearing, if he wants one, and explaining why it is needed.

CJA 2003, s.38 above has no effect in relation to alleged offences into which a criminal investigation began before July 15, 2005.

Application by accused: (2) dealing with the application

30–029 The judge may determine any such an application at a hearing, in public or in private or without a hearing, but must not require the prosecutor to disclose material unless the prosecutor is present, or has had at least 14 days in which to make representations.   R.22.5(4),(5)

On an application by the prosecutor, the judge may give leave for the matter to be determined in the absence of the accused and his legal representative

Note that:

(1) not being a "question of law" under CJA 1987, s.9, such an application does not fall to be decided within the scope of a preparatory hearing, although nothing prevents it being dealt with in parallel proceedings (see CASE MANAGEMENT) on the occasion of a preparatory hearing; and

(2) no interlocutory appeal lies, of course, under s.9(11) of the 1987 Act. (*R. v H (Interlocutory application; Disclosure)* [2007] UKHL 7, [2007] 2 Cr. App. R. 6).

The consideration of detailed defence requests for specific disclosure (so-called "shopping lists") otherwise than in accordance with r.22.6, is wholly improper. Likewise, defence requests for specific disclosure of unused prosecution material in purported pursuance of CPIA 1996, s.8 and r.22.6, which are not referable to any issue in the case identified by the defence case statement, should be rejected.

The judge should require an application to be made under s.8 and in compliance with r.25.6 before considering any order for further disclosure. Any practice of making a blanket order for disclosure is inconsistent with the statutory framework laid down by the Act (*R. v H* (above)).

A copy of any order made by the judge must be served on the prosecutor and the applicant.

Methods of disclosure

30–030 Where disclosure by the prosecutor is required, and: CPIA 1996, ss.3(3)(4)(5), 5,7(4)

(1) the material consists of information which has been recorded in any form:

    (a) the prosecutor discloses it by securing that a copy is made of it and that the copy is given to the accused; or

(b) if, in the prosecutor's opinion, that is not practicable or is not desirable, by allowing the accused to inspect it at a reasonable time and a reasonable place, or by taking steps to secure that he is allowed to do so, and a copy may be in such form as the prosecutor thinks fit and need not be in the same form as that in which the information has already been recorded;

(2) the material consists of information which has not been recorded, the prosecutor discloses it by securing that it is recorded in such form as he thinks fit and taking either of the disclosure steps set out in (a) and (b) above;

(3) the material does not consist of information, the prosecutor discloses it by allowing the accused to inspect it at a reasonable time and a reasonable place or by taking steps to secure that he is allowed to do so.

The above provisions, i.e. CPIA 1996, s.3(3)–(5) do not apply in relation to disclosure required by ss.3, 7 or 9, of the Sexual Offences (Protected Material) Act 1997. S.3(1) applies in relation to that disclosure (s.9(2)).

Where material has been seized and retained by the police, but not examined by the disclosure officer or the prosecutor, the Attorney General's guidelines require that a s.9 statement must be included in the sensitive schedule describing the material in general terms and justifying its not having been examined. Permission must be given to the defence to inspect the material. *CPIA 1996, s.3(6),(7)*

Material must not be disclosed under these provisions to the extent that it is:

(i) material the disclosure of which is prohibited by RIPA 2000, s.17; or

(ii) a judge, on the application of the prosecutor, decides that it is not in the public interest to disclose it (see 30–037 and following) and orders accordingly.

Prosecutor's failure to observe time limits
30–031 The prosecutor's failure to act: *CPIA 1996, s.10*

(1) where he purports to act under s.3 after the end of the period which, by virtue of s.12 is the relevant period for ss.3, or 12;

(2) where he purports to act under s.7A(5) after the end of the period which by virtue of s.12 is the relevant period for s.7A,

does not, on its own, constitute grounds for staying the proceedings for abuse of process (see ABUSE OF PROCESS), but his failure may constitute such grounds if it involves such delay by him that the accused is denied a fair trial.

Faults in disclosure by accused; comment
30–032 The trial judge or any other party may make such comment as appears appropriate, and the judge or jury may draw such inferences as appear proper, in deciding whether the accused is guilty of the offence concerned, in three different sets of circumstances (set out in the next three paragraphs). *CPIA 1996, s.11*

DISCLOSURE

The first set of circumstances

30-033 The first set of circumstances in which comments may be made is where the accused:

(1) fails to give an initial defence statement;
(2) gives an initial defence statement, but does so after the end of the period which is the relevant period for s.5 by virtue of s.12;
(3) is required by s.6B to give an updated statement or a statement of the kind mentioned in s.6B(4), but fails to do so;
(4) gives an updated statement, or a statement of the kind mentioned in s.6B(4), but does so after the end of the period which is the relevant period for s.6B by virtue of s.12;
(5) sets out inconsistent defences in his defence statement;
(6) at his trial:
    (a) puts forward a defence which was not mentioned in his defence statement or is different from any defence set out in that statement;
    (b) relies on matter which, in breach of the requirements imposed by or under s.6A, was not mentioned in his defence statement;
    (c) adduces evidence in support of an alibi without having given particulars of the alibi in his defence statement; or
    (d) calls a witness to give evidence in support of an alibi without having complied with s.6A(2)(a) or (b).

The second set of circumstances

30–034 The second of circumstances in which comment may be made is where s.6 applies, that is where the accused gives an initial defence statement, but:

(1) gives the initial defence statement after the end of the period which, by virtue of s.12, is the relevant period for s.6; or
(2) does any of the things mentioned in paras (3) to (6) in 30-030 above.

The third set of circumstances

30-035 The third set of circumstances in which comment may be made is, and here any comment by another party under subs.(5)(a) party may be made only with the leave of the court, is where the accused: SI.2010/1183

(1) gives a witness notice but does so after the end of the period which, by virtue of s.12, is the relevant period for s.6C; or
(2) at his trial calls a witness not included, or not adequately identified, in a witness notice.

Where the accused puts forward a defence which is different from any defence set out in his defence statement, then in doing anything under subs.(5) or in deciding whether to do anything under it, the judge must have regard in taking, or deciding whether to take, either of the above courses of action to:

    (a) the extent of the difference in the defences; and
    (b) whether there is any justification for it.

A person may not be convicted of an offence solely on an inference drawn under subs.(5). Where the accused calls a witness whom he has failed to include, or to identify adequately, in a witness notice, in doing anything under subsection (5) or in deciding whether to do anything under it, the judge must have regard to whether there is any justification for the failure.

Interpretation

30–036 In these provisions:

- "initial defence statement" means a defence statement given under s.5 or 6;
- "updated defence statement" means a defence statement given under s.6B;
- a reference simply to an accused's "defence statement" is a reference:
  - (a) where he has given only an initial defence statement, to that statement;
  - (b) both an initial and an updated defence statement, to the updated defence statement;
  - (c) both an initial statement and a statement of the kind mentioned in s.6B(4), to the initial defence statement.
- a reference to evidence in support of an alibi must be construed in accordance with s.5;
- "witness notice" means a notice given under s.6C.

D. Public interest immunity (PII)

(1) General

Introduction

30–037 There is provision in the Code of Practice for the police "disclosure officer" to list on a sensitive schedule any material which he believes it is not in the public interest to disclose, and the reasons for that belief. The schedule must include a statement that the disclosure officer believes the material is sensitive.

Examples are material:

(1) relating to national security;
(2) received from the intelligence and security agencies;
(3) relating to intelligence from foreign sources which reveals sensitive intelligence gathering methods, given in confidence;
(4) relating to the use of a telephone system and which is supplied to an investigator for intelligence purposes only;
(5) relating to the identity or activities of informants, or undercover police officers or other persons supplying information to the police who may be in danger if their identities are revealed;
(6) revealing the location of any premises or other place used for police surveillance or the identity of any person allowing a police officer to use them for surveillance;
(7) revealing, directly or indirectly, techniques and methods relied on by a police officer in the course of a criminal investigation, e.g. covert surveillance techniques or other methods of detecting crime;

(8)   disclosure of which might facilitate the commission of other offences or hinder the prevention and detection of crime;

(9)   comprising internal police communications such as management minutes;

(10)   upon the strength of which search warrants were obtained;

(11)   containing details of persons taking part in identification parades;

(12)   supplied to an investigator during a criminal investigation which has been generated by an official of a body concerned with the regulation or supervision of bodies corporate or of persons engaged in financial activities, or which has been generated by a person retained by such a body; or

(13)   supplied to an investigator during a criminal investigation which relates to a child or young person and which has been generated by a local authority social services department, an Area Child Protection Committee or other party contacted by an investigator during the investigation.

Disclosure to prosecutor

30–038   In exceptional circumstances, where an investigator considers that material is so sensitive that its revelation to the prosecutor by means of an entry on the sensitive schedule is inappropriate, as where the material would be likely to lead directly to the loss of life, or directly threaten national security, the existence of the material must be revealed to the prosecutor separately.

In such circumstances:

(1)   the responsibility for informing the prosecutor lies with the investigator who knows the detail of the sensitive material;

(2)   the investigator should act as soon as reasonably practicable after the file containing the prosecution case is sent to the prosecutor; and

(3)   he must ensure that the prosecutor is able to inspect the material so that he can assess whether it needs to be brought before a court for a ruling on disclosure.

The judge's role

30–039   The judge:

(1)   must give detailed consideration to the material sought to be withheld in the context of the prosecution and defence cases;

(2)   must identify the public interest in question and assess the prejudice claimed to ensure that any derogation from the full disclosure rule was the minimum necessary to secure the required protection;

(3)   may (CPIA 1996, ss.3(6), 7(5), 8(5), 9(8)) order that it is not in the public interest to disclose material, and if he does so, the material must not be disclosed by the prosecutor (the common law rules as to whether disclosure is in the public interest, summarised in the cases set out below, continue to apply);

(4)   must (CPIA 1996, s.15(3), (4); CJA 2003, s.331, Sch.36, Pt 3, para.31) without need of any application by the accused, throughout the trial keep under review the question whether,

at any given time, it is still not in the public interest to disclose material affected by his order; and

(5) must, in making his decision, undertake a balancing exercise between the competing interests of non-disclosure in the public interest and fairness to the accused.

If the disputed material may prove the accused's innocence or avoid a miscarriage of justice, then the balance comes down resoundingly in favour of disclosing it (*R. v Keane*, (1994) 99 Cr. App. R.1.) The cases were reviewed in *R. v H, R. v C* [2004] UKHL 3, [2004] 2 Cr. App. R. 10.

The interests of justice include allowing an accused to put forward a tenable case in its best light (*R. v Agar* (1990) 90 Cr. App. R. 318).

Material damaging to the accused is not disclosable and should not be brought to the judge's attention.

Prosecutor's application for public interest hearing
30–040   Where: R.22.1

- without a court order, the prosecutor would have to disclose material; and
- the prosecutor wants the judge to decide whether it would be in the public interest to disclose it,

the procedure is governed by r.22.

The application
30-041   The prosecutor:

(1) must apply in writing, serving the application on the court officer, on any person who the prosecutor thinks would be directly affected by disclosure of the material and on the accused (but only to the extent that serving it on the accused would not disclose what the prosecutor thinks ought not be disclosed);

(2) the application must:
  (a) describe the material, and explain why the prosecutor thinks that:
    (i) it is material that the prosecutor would have to disclose,
    (ii) it would not be in the public interest to disclose that material, and
    (iii) no measure such as the prosecutor's admission of any fact, or disclosure by summary, extract or edited copy, would adequately protect both the public interest and the accused's right to a fair trial;
  (b) omit from any part of the application that is served on the accused anything that would disclose what the prosecutor thinks ought not be disclosed, in which case, he must mark the other part, to show that it is only for the court; and in that other part, explain why the prosecutor has withheld it from the accused;.
  (c) explain why, if no part of the application is served on the accused; unless already done, the judge may direct the prosecutor to serve an application on the accused or any other person whom the judge considers material.

DISCLOSURE

The hearing

30-042   The judge will determine the application at a hearing which will be in private, unless he otherwise directs; and, if he so directs, may take place, wholly or in part, in the absence of the accused.

At the hearing, at which the accused is present, the general rule is that the judge will receive, in the following sequence

(1) representations by the prosecutor and by any other person served with the application, and then
(2) by the accused, in the presence of them all, and then
(3) any further representations by the prosecutor and any such other person in the absence of the accused, but

the judge may direct other arrangements.

The judge will only determine the application if satisfied that he has been able to take adequate account of such rights of confidentiality as apply to the material; and the accused's right to a fair trial.

Unless the judge otherwise directs, the Crown Court officer will not give notice to anyone other than the prosecutor of the hearing of an application unless the prosecutor served the application on that person, or of the judge's decision on the application, but may keep a written application or representations, or arrange for the whole or any part to be kept by some other appropriate person, subject to any conditions that the judge imposes.

The approach to disclosure

30–043   When any issue of derogation from the golden rule to diclose arises, the judge must address a series of questions:

(1) What is the nature of the material which the prosecution seek to withhold? He must consider this in detail.
(2) Is the material such as may weaken the prosecution case or strengthen the defence? If "No", disclosure should not be ordered. If "Yes", disclosure should be ordered in full.
(3) Is there a chance of serious prejudice to an important public interest? If so, what, if any, disclosure of the material should be ordered? If not, full disclosure should be ordered.
(4) If the answer to (2) and (3) is "Yes", can the accused's interests be protected without disclosure, or should disclosure be ordered to an extent which will give adequate protection to the public interest in question and also afford adequate protection to the interests of the defence?
(5) Do the measures proposed in answer to (4) represent a derogation necessary to protect the public interest, or should he order such greater disclosure as will represent the minimum derogation from the golden rule of full disclosure? If limited disclosure is ordered pursuant to (4) or (5), may the effect be to render the trial process, viewed as a whole, unfair to the accused?
(6) If "Yes", then fuller disclosure should be ordered even if this leads, or may lead, the prosecution to discontinue the proceedings so as to avoid having to make disclosure.
(7) If the answer to (6) when first given is "No", does that remain the correct situation once evidence is adduced and the defence

458

advanced? It is important that the answer to (6) should not be treated as final, but as a provisional, answer which the judge must keep under review (*R. v H, R. v C* above).

It is the virtually inevitable rule that the same judge that determines the public interest immunity application will continue to act as trial judge and keep the situation under review. There is no obligation on the judge to recuse himself from presiding at the trial because of knowledge acquired during the PII hearing, but he is entitled to do so if he considers that the interests of justice so require (*R. v Dawson* [2007] EWCA Crim 822).

Appointment of special advocate
30–044   In *R. v H, R. v C.* (above) HL suggested that the power of the judge to appoint a special advocate to represent the accused on an application should be used only in exceptional cases where it might be necessary in the "interests of justice". Such an appointment ought not be ordered unless and until the judge was satisfied that no other course would adequately meet the overriding requirement of fairness to the accused.

Other persons claiming interest
30–045   Where an application is made by the prosecutor under ss.7A(8) or 8(5), 14(2) or 15(4) and a person claiming to have an interest in the material: CPIA 1996, s.16

(1) applies to be heard by the court; and
(2) shows that he was involved (whether alone or with others) in the prosecutor's attention being brought to the material,

the judge must not make an order unless that person has been given an opportunity to be heard. Where the prosecutor has reason to believe that a person who was involved (whether alone or with others and whether directly or indirectly) in the prosecutor's attention being brought to any material to which an application relates may claim to have an interest in that material, he must give notice in writing to:

(a) the person concerned in the application; and
(b) the Crown Court officer or, as the case may require, the judge, of his belief and the grounds for it.

Emergence of new situation
30–046   It was not suggested that the procedure set out in *Davis, Johnson & Rowe* (30–004 above) offended ECHR Art. 6(1), but it was made clear that where competing interests, including the safety of witnesses, arise, only such measures restricting the rights of the defence (including the principle of equality of arms) "which are strictly necessary" are permissible. See *Jasper v UK; Fitt v UK* [2000] Crim. L.R. 584), also *PG and JH v UK* [2002] Crim. L.R. 308.

Public interest; review
30–047   After a judge has made an order as above, the trial judge must keep under review, until the accused is acquitted or the prosecutor decides not to proceed with the case, the question whether, at any given

time, it is still not in the public interest to disclose material affected by the order.

There is no need for any application, but the accused may apply to the judge for a review of the question if at any time the judge considers that it is in the public interest to disclose material to any extent, he will so order, and take steps to inform the prosecutor of his order.

Review; (1) procedure on application
30–048   R.22.6 applies where:

(1) the judge has ordered that it is not in the public interest to disclose material that the prosecutor otherwise would have to disclose, and
(2) the accused wants the judge to review that decision, or the judge reviews that decision on his own initiative.

Where the accused wants the court to review that decision:

(a) he must serve an application on the Crown Court officer, and on the prosecutor, and in that application must describe the material that he wants the prosecutor to disclose, and explain why he thinks it is no longer in the public interest for the prosecutor not to disclose it;
(b) the prosecutor must serve any such application on any person who he thinks would be directly affected if that material were disclosed, and the prosecutor, and any such person, must serve any representations on the Crown Court officer, and on the accused unless to do so would in effect reveal something that either thinks ought not be disclosed.

The judge may direct the prosecutor to serve any such application on any person who the judge considers would be directly affected if that material were disclosed, and may direct the prosecutor and any such person to serve any representations on the accused.

Review: (2) the hearing
30-049   The judge will review a decision to which the rule applies at a hearing which will be in private, unless he otherwise directs, and if he does so direct, may take place, wholly or in part, in the accused's absence.

At a hearing at which the accused is present the general rule is that the judge will receive, in the following sequence:

(1) representations first by the accused, and then by the prosecutor and any other person served with the application, in the presence of them all, and then
(2) further representations by the prosecutor and any such other person in the accused absence;

but the judge may direct other arrangements for the hearing.

The judge may only conclude a review if satisfied that it has been able to take adequate account of such rights of confidentiality as apply to the material; and the accused's right to a fair trial.

(2)   Material held by other agencies

General

30–050   There is no specific procedure for the disclosure of unused material held by third parties in criminal proceedings, although the procedure under CP(AW)A 1965, s.2, MCA 1980, s.97 is often used in order to effect such disclosure. The test applied under both Acts, however, is not the test to be applied under the CPIA 1996, whether in the original or enhanced form.

These two provisions require that the material in question is material evidence, i.e. immediately admissible in evidence in the proceedings (see *R. v Reading JJ. Ex p. Berkshire CC* [1996] 1 Cr.App.R. 239; *R. v Derby MC Ex p. B* [1996] 1 Cr. App. R. 385 and *R. v Alibhai and Others* [2004] EWCA Crim. 681) (Disclosure Protocol, see 30–001).

Material held by other government departments or Crown agencies is not prosecution material for the purposes of CPIA 1996, ss.3(2) or 8(4) but under the Attorney-General's updated guidelines (paras 51 and following) where it is suspected that a non-government agency or other third party has material which might be disclosable if it were in the possession of the prosecution and it is appropriate to seek access to that material, the prosecution should take steps to obtain it. If a request for access by the prosecution is refused by the third party and if the requirements of CP(AW)A 1965, s.2 are complied with, the prosecutor should apply for a witness summons requiring a representative of the third party to produce the material to the court.

Social services files

30–051   Where material is held by a third party such as a local authority, hospital or business, the prosecutor may seek to make arrangements to inspect the material with a view to applying the relevant test for disclosure to it and determining whether any or all of the material should be retained, recorded and, in due course, disclosed to the accused. In considering the latter, the investigators and the prosecution will establish whether the holder of the material wishes to raise PII issues, as a result of which the material may have to be placed before the court.

CPIA 1996, s.16 gives such a party a right to make representations to the court.

Where the third party in question declines to allow inspection of the material, or requires the prosecution to obtain an order before handing over copies of the material, the prosecutor will need to consider whether it is appropriate to obtain a witness summons under CP(AW)A 1965, s.2, where the statutory requirements are satisfied, and where the prosecutor considers that the material may satisfy the test for disclosure. *R. v Alibhai,* above, makes it clear that the prosecutor has a "margin of consideration" in this regard (Disclosure Protocol, paras 53–55, see above 30–001).

Objections by third party

30–052   The third party may have a duty to assert confidentiality, or the right to privacy under art.8 of the ECHR, where requests for disclosure are made by the prosecution, or anyone else.

DISCLOSURE

Where issues are raised in relation to allegedly relevant third party material, the judge must:

(1) ascertain whether inquiries with the third party are likely to be appropriate, and, if so, identify who is going to make the request, what material is to be sought, from whom is the material to be sought and within what time scale must the matter be resolved;

(2) consider what action would be appropriate in the light of the third party failing or refusing to comply with a request, including inviting the defence to make the request on its own behalf and, if necessary, to make an application for a witness summons.

The judge should be aware that a summons can only be issued where the document(s) sought would be admissible in evidence.

While it may be that the material in question may be admissible in evidence as a result of the hearsay provisions of CJA 2003, ss.114 to 120, it is this that determines whether an order for production of the material is appropriate, rather than the wider considerations applicable to disclosure in criminal proceedings (see *R. v Reading JJ.* (above); *R. v Derby MC* (above 30–050)).

Any directions made (for instance, the date by which an application for a witness summons with supporting affidavit under CP(AW)A 1965, s.2 should be served) should be put into writing at the time. Any failure to comply with the timetable must immediately be referred back to the court for further directions, although a hearing will not always be necessary.

Where the prosecution do not consider it appropriate to seek such a summons, the defence should consider doing so, where they are of the view (notwithstanding the prosecution assessment) that the third party may hold material which might undermine the prosecution case or assist that for the accused, and the material would be likely to be "material evidence" for the purposes of the 1965 Act.

The judge at the PCMH should specifically enquire whether any such application is to be made by the defence and set out a clear timetable.

Relevance and use of material

30–053   The court, by issuing a witness summons to produce the documents, can only require disclosure of relevant or "material" documents.
On the authorities:

(1) to be material such documents must not only be relevant to the issues arising in the criminal proceedings, but also admissible in evidence;

(2) documents desired merely for the purpose of cross- examination are not admissible in evidence;

(3) the applicant must satisfy the court that there is a real possibility that the documents are likely to be material; and

(4) the procedure is not to be used as a fishing expedition (*R. v Reading JJ.,* above 30–050; *R. v Derby MC*, above 30–050).

It is then for the judge, doing a balancing exercise, to decide whether the public interest in maintaining the confidentiality of those documents and the public interest in seeing that justice is done, requires the documents to be disclosed or withheld (*R. v Higgins* [1996] 1 F.L.R. 137).

Such documents are ordinarily to be used only for the purposes of taking instructions and putting matters contained within them to witnesses in the course of cross- examination; they are generally subject to public interest immunity, and the rights both of social services and of the persons who are the subject of the documentation must be respected;

The judge's order for disclosure does not, therefore, entitle either party to use the documents in any other way; where it is considered necessary by either party that wider use be made of the documentation or information, an application must be made to the judge to extend the use to which it may be put, so that the balance between the respective interests can properly be considered, *R. v J* [2010] 3 Archbold Review 2, CA.

Procedure

30–054   An application must identify the documents sought and why they are said to be material evidence, particularly where attempts are made to access the medical reports of those who allege that they are victims of crime. Victims do not waive the confidentiality of their medical records, or their right to privacy under art.8 of the ECHR, by the mere fact of making a complaint against the accused.

The procedure is as follows:

(1) the possessor of the documents must first decide whether or not they are relevant;

(2) the assistance of the judge should only be sought if a question can properly be decided by him, most obviously where questions of public interest immunity are involved: *R. v B* [2000] Crim. L.R. 50;

(3) if the judge is to be involved, it will be for him either to accept the assertion of the possessor or to look at the document himself. That decision is to be taken at his discretion, judicially exercised;

(4) the judge should be alert to balance the rights of victims against the real and proven needs of the defence. As a public authority, he must ensure that any interference with the ECHR art.8 rights of those entitled to privacy is in accordance with the law and necessary in pursuit of a legitimate public interest; general and unspecified requests to trawl through such records should be refused;

(5) if the possessors' claim that the documents are irrelevant suspect or implausible, the judge will no doubt look at them himself, or he may regard assistance from an independent and competent member of the Bar as being sufficient;

(6) a verbatim record must be kept of any ex parte application (*R. v Turner* (1995) 2 Cr. App. R. 94).

If material is held by any person in relation to family proceedings (e.g. where there have been care proceedings in relation to a child, who has also complained to the police of sexual or other abuse) then an application has to be made by that person to the family court for leave to disclose that material to a third party (see Family Procedure Rules 2010, Pt 7). This would permit, for instance, a local authority, in receipt of such material, to disclose it to the police for the purpose of a criminal investigation, or to the CPS, in order for the latter to discharge any obligations under CPIA 1996 (Protocol, para.62, 30–001, above).

Costs

30–055 There is power to award costs in favour of local authorities out of public funds only where the court orders under CP(AWA) 1965, s.2C that the witness summons shall be of no effect (see WITNESS SUMMONSES AND WARRANTS).

E. Confidentiality

General

30–056 If an accused is given, or allowed to inspect, a document or other object under CPIA 1996, ss.3,4, 7A,14 or 15, he must not disclose it, or any information recorded in it, except: CPIA 1996, s.17

(1) in connection with the proceedings for whose purposes he was given the object or document, or allowed to inspect it; or
(2) with a view to the taking of further criminal proceedings (e.g. by way of appeal) in connection with those proceedings.

The accused may use or disclose;

(a) an object to the extent to which it has been displayed to the public in open court; or
(b) information to the extent to which it has been communicated to the public in open court; or
(c) to an object and information, with permission of the court, for the purpose, and to the extent specified by the judge.

Where an accused wants the court's permission to use disclosed prosecution material otherwise than in connection with the case in which it was disclosed, or beyond the extent to which it was displayed or communicated publicly at a hearing, he must proceed under r.22.7.

Contravention

30–057 Any contravention by the accused of the restrictions on use or disclosure is a contempt of court, punishable in the Crown Court by imprisonment not exceeding two years or a fine or both.

Where a person is accused of using disclosed prosecution material in contravention CPIA 1996, s.17, any party who wants the court to exercise its power to punish that person for contempt of court must comply with the rules in r.62 (see CONTEMPT OF COURT).   R.22.8

An applicant wanting the judge to exercise that power must comply with r.62.

The judge must not exercise his power to forfeit material used in contempt of court unless: R.22.8

(1) the prosecutor, and
(2) any other person directly affected by the disclosure of the material, is present, or has had at least 14 days in which to make representations.

31. DISCOUNTS ON SENTENCE

Quick Guide

1. General (31–001)
2. Reduction in sentence for a guilty plea (31–002)
3. Informers (31–008)
4. Co-operation by the accused
   (1) At common Law (31–009)
   (2) Statutory Agreements under SOCPA 2005 (31–010)
5. Information given after sentence (31–013)
6. Referral back to court (31–014)

1.   General

31–001   Both at common law and by statute the judge must give an offender the right to expect a discount on the otherwise appropriate sentence, where:

- (1) he pleads guilty timeously to the indictment (*R. v Barnes* (1983) 5 Cr.App.R.(S.) 368); the position is now governed by CJA 2003, s.144 (and for offences committed before April 4, 2005, by PCC(S)A 2000, s. 152(2)) (see 31–002, below);
- (2) the judge considers that the offence would not have been committed but for the activities of an informer (*R. v Beaumont* (1987) 9 Cr. App. R.(S.) 342; *R. v Chapman* (1989) 11 Cr. App. R. (S.) 222; *R. v Tonnessen* [1998] 2 Cr. App. R. (S.) 328; *R. v Underhill* [1979] 1 Cr. App. R. (S.) 270) (see 31-009 below); or
- (3) the accused co-operates with the prosecutor, not only by pleading guilty, but by giving information early enough for it to be potentially useful; this is now partially covered by SOCPA 2005, Pt 5 (see 31–010, 31–011, below).

2.   Reduction in sentence for a guilty plea

Statutory provisions
31–002   By CJA 2003, s.144(1) (and for offences committed before April 4, 2005, PCC(S)A 2000, s.152(2)), in determining the sentence to be passed on an offender who has pleaded guilty to an offence, the judge must take into account:

- (1) the stage in the proceedings at which the offender indicated his intention to plead guilty (and see *R. v Hussain* [2002] Crim. L.R. 327); and
- (2) the circumstances in which this indication was given (and see *R. v Fearon* [1996] 2 Cr. App. R.(S.) 25; *R. v Aroride* [1999] 2 Cr. App. R. (S.) 406).

DISCOUNTS ON SENTENCE

If the judge imposes a punishment on the offender which is less severe than he would otherwise have imposed, he must state in open court that he has done so (*R. v Hastings* [1996] 1 Cr. App. R. (S.) 167); if he withholds a discount he must explain why.

As to the attitude of the CACD where the judge fails to state that he has taken the plea into consideration, see *R. v Wharton* [2001] EWCA Crim 622, *The Times*, March 27, 2001, considering *R. v Bishop* [2000] 1 Cr. App. R. (S.) 432.

But note that —

> (a) In the case of an offence the sentence for which falls to be imposed under PCC(S)A 2000, ss.110(2) or 111(2) (required minimum sentences for certain repeat offences) nothing in that subsection prevents the judge, after taking into account any matter referred to in (1) and (2) above, from imposing any sentence which is not less than 80 per cent of that specified in those subsections, e.g. in the case of s.110 (minimum 7 years for drug trafficking), five years seven months (see *R. v Gray* [2007] 2 Cr. App R(S) 494). SGC Guidelines do not apply (*Att-Gen's Reference (No. 6 of 2006)* [2006] EWCA Crim 1043; [2007] 1 Cr. App. R. (S) 58.
> (b) No reduction for a guilty plea is permissible in relation to minimum sentences for firearms offences committed under FA 1968, s.51A.

(*R. v Jordan* [2004] EWCA Crim 3291 [2005] 2 Cr. App. R. (S.) 44). Any reduction can only come from a finding of 'exceptional circumstances' (see further IMPRISONMENT).

SGC Guideline

31–003   SGC issued guidelines on July 23, 2007, (SGC 1), *Reduction in Sentence for a Guilty Plea* making a statement of purpose, and stating a recommended approach to the application of the principle, guidance on determining the level of reduction in an individual case and guidance on whether to withhold a reduction.

The content of this guideline is also intended to assist judges when arriving at the appropriate minimum term for the offence of murder, applying CJA 2003, Sch.21, para.12 (see LIFE SENTENCES).

SGC: Statement of Purpose

31–004   A reduction in sentence is appropriate because a guilty plea:

(1) avoids the need for a trial (thus enabling other cases to be disposed of more expeditiously);
(2) shortens the gap between charge and sentence;
(3) saves considerable cost; and,
(4) in the case of an early plea, saves victims and witnesses from the concern about having to give evidence.

For the procedure to be followed in taking pleas of guilty, see GUILTY PLEAS.

It is a separate issue from aggravation and mitigation generally.

SGC suggests that the judge, in deciding the most appropriate length of sentence and before calculating the reduction for the guilty plea, should:

(a) address separately the issue of remorse, together with any other mitigating features; similarly, assistance to the prosecuting or enforcement authorities is a separate issue which may attract a reduction in sentence under other procedures;

(b) reflect in the sentence the implications of any other offences that the offender asks to be taken into consideration on sentence.

The reduction should be applied only to the punitive elements of the sentence; it has no impact on decisions in relation to ancillary orders.

Where an offence crosses the threshold for the imposition of a community or custodial sentence, application of the reduction principle may properly form the basis for imposing a fine or discharge, rather than a community sentence, or an alternative to an immediate custodial sentence. Where the reduction is applied in this way, the actual sentence imposed incorporates the reduction.

SGC: Application of the reduction principle

31–005   SGC 1, 3.1., recommends that the judge should:

(1) decide the sentence for the offence(s), taking into account any other offences which have been formally admitted (see DEALING WITH OFFENDERS);

(2) select the amount of the reduction by reference to a prescribed sliding scale;

(3) apply that reduction to the sentence he has decided on; and

(4) state, when pronouncing sentence, what the sentence would have been if there had been no such reduction.

SGC: Determining the level of deduction

31–006   SGC 1, 4.1, and 2, recommends that the level of reduction should be:

(1) a proportion of the total sentence imposed, with the proportion calculated by reference to the circumstances in which the guilty plea was indicated, in particular the stage of the proceedings; the greatest reduction ought to be given where the plea was indicated at the "first reasonable opportunity";

(2) save where CJA 2003, s.144(2) (or, PCC(S)A 2000, s. 152(3)) applies, (i.e. required minimum sentences) the level of the reduction is to be gauged on a sliding scale generally ranging from:

(a) a maximum of one third (where the guilty plea was entered at the first reasonable opportunity in relation to the offence for which sentence is being imposed);

(b) reducing to one quarter (where a trial date has been set), and to one tenth (for a guilty plea entered at the "door of the court" or after the trial has begun).

Decisions on sentence do not and should not, however, involve a mathematical exercise resulting from arithmetical calculations. (see *R. v Martin* [2006] EWCA Crim 1035; [2007] 1 Cr. App. R. (S.) 3).

The level of reduction should reflect the stage at which the offender indicated a willingness to admit guilt to the offence for which he is eventually sentenced:

> (i) the largest recommended reduction should not normally be given unless the offender indicated willingness to admit guilt at the first reasonable opportunity; when this occurs will vary from case to case;
>
> (ii) where the admission of guilt comes later than the first reasonable opportunity, the reduction for a guilty plea will normally be less than one third;
>
> (iii) where the plea of guilty comes very late, it is still appropriate to give some reduction;
>
> (iv) if, after pleading guilty there is a Newton hearing and the offender's version of the circumstances of the offence is rejected, this should be taken into account in determining the level of reduction;
>
> (v) if a not guilty plea was entered and maintained for tactical reasons (such as to retain privileges whilst on remand), a late guilty plea should attract very little, if any, discount.

When the judge is considering credit for plea, the question is not the propriety of the actions of the lawyers, or whether the case is ready for trial, but when the accused has properly confronted his own guilt. He is entitled to explore the accuracy of the scientific evidence and invite the possibility of independent scientific evidence, but he will not, thereafter, ordinarily gain full credit for a plea (*A-G's Reference (No.79 of 2009) The Times*, March 17, 2010).

Where one of two accused pleads guilty, e.g. at a PCMH, and the second six weeks later, the latter cannot expect the same discount as the former (*R. v McDonald* [2001] EWCA Crim 2496 [2002] 1 Cr. App. R. (S.) 138).

SGC: Withholding a reduction

31–007 The guideline addresses certain special cases recommending, e.g.:

> (1) where a sentence for a **dangerous** offence is imposed under CJA 2003, whether the sentence requires the calculation of a minimum term or is an extended sentence, the approach should be the same as for any other determinate sentence;
>
> (2) where the **prosecution case is overwhelming** it may not be appropriate to give the full reduction that would -otherwise be given; while there is a presumption in favour of the full reduction being given where a plea was indicated at the first reasonable opportunity, the fact that the prosecution case is overwhelming without relying on admissions by the offender may be a reasonable justifying departure from the guideline; a recommended reduction of 20 per cent is likely to be appropriate;

(3) **maximum penalty thought to be too low**—the judge is bound to sentence for the offence with which the offender has been charged, and to which he has pleaded guilty; he cannot remedy perceived defects (e.g. an inadequate charge or maximum penalty) by refusal of the appropriate discount.

Note also that in the case of:

(a) two or more summary only offences, where the maximum sentence available is six months imprisonment and the sentence for each offence should be reduced to reflect the guilty plea, it may be appropriate for the sentences to be ordered to run consecutively to each other. The overall sentence would not undermine the general principle that the maximum sentence should not be imposed following a guilty plea, since the decision whether or not to make the individual sentences concurrent or consecutive will follow the normal principles that apply to that decision;

(b) an offender under 18 where the offence is one which would, but for the plea, have attracted a sentence of long-term detention in excess of 24 months under PCC(S)A 2000, s.91, a detention and training order of 24 months might be imposed.

3. Informers

31–008 Where the judge takes the view that the offence would not have been committed save for the activities of an informer, he may, if he thinks fit, give a discount on sentence (*R. v Beaumont* (1987) 9 Cr. App. R.(S.) 342; *R. v Chapman* (1989) 11 Cr. App. R.(S.) 222; *R. v Tonnessen*, [1998] 2 Cr. App. R.(S.) 328; *R. v Underhill* [1979] 1 Cr. App. R.(S.) 270).

Using test letters to establish the guilt of postal employees suspected of theft of mail does not come within this principle (*R. v Ramen* (1988) 10 Cr. App. R.(S.) 334); nor does the use of test purchases by undercover officers in relation to drug dealing (*R. v Springer* [1999] 1 Cr. App. R.(S.) 217; *R. v Mayeri* [1999] 1 Cr. App. R.(S.) 304).

4. Co-operation by the accused

(1) At common law

General

31–009 Offenders need to know that it is worth their while disclosing the criminal activities of others (*R. v Sivan* (1988) 10 Cr. App. R.(S.) 282). To this end, and within the time limits specified below, the judge will need to tailor any sentence on any offender who has given such assistance to the authorities, punishing him for his offences, while at the same time rewarding him as far as is possible for the help he has given.

DISCOUNTS ON SENTENCE

Information relevant to the offender's assistance should be put before the judge in the form of a document from a senior member of the police or other law-enforcement agency. A document of this kind although supplied by a police officer is supplied at the request of the accused. It follows that the judge must rely very heavily on the greatest possible care being taken in compiling such a document. Where the common law principles apply, i.e. where both the offence and the sentencing process took place before the coming into force of SOCPA 2005, pt 2, Ch.2, the common law procedure as set out below applies (see *R. v Z* [2007] EWCA Crim 1473; [2008] 1 Cr. App. R.(S) 60).

Thus:

(1) except in very unusual circumstances, it will not be necessary or desirable for a document of this kind to contain details which will attract a public interest immunity application;

(2) if such a document does contain information which attracts a public interest immunity consideration, the usual rules about the conduct of such an application apply. It will be a case in which the defence could and should be told of the public interest immunity application;

(3) in the absence of any consideration of public interest immunity, a document of this kind should be shown to the defence, who will discuss its contents with the offender. On general principles, an offender is entitled to see documents put before the sentencing judge. There should not normally be any question of evidence being given or of an issue being tried on the question of the extent of the information provided;

(4) if the offender wishes to disagree with the contents of such a document, it is not appropriate for there to be cross-examination of the police officer. The officer is not a Crown witness. It will be possible in an appropriate case for an offender to ask for an adjournment to allow further consideration to be given to the preparation of the document. Otherwise, his remedy is not to rely on the document;

(5) the judge will normally disregard such a document if asked by the offender to do so. In such a case he will not be minded to entertain any submission that the offender has given valuable assistance to the police;

(6) if the judge does take the documents into consideration, he should say no more than that he has taken into consideration all the information about the defendant with which he had been provided.

(*R. v X* [1999] 2 Cr. App. R. 125.).

Information relevant to the agreement between the prosecutor, and such assistance given by the offender in pursuance of it, should be put before the judge in the form of a written document from the specified prosecutor's staff. There should be no need to see the judge in chambers.

Any discount should reflect the seriousness of the offence, the importance of the information, and the effect, where the informant gives evidence, on his future circumstances (*R. v Wood* [1996] Crim. L.R. 916) and the circumstances of the entrapment or other factors should

470

be expressly mentioned in the judge's sentencing remarks (*R. v Mackey & Shaw* (1993) 14 Cr. App. R.(S.) 53).

(2) Statutory Agreements under SOCPA 2005

General

31–010 Under SOCPA 2005, Pt 2, Ch.2, where an offender:

(1) following a plea of guilty;
(2) is either convicted of an offence in proceedings in the Crown Court or is committed to the Crown Court for sentence; and
(3) has, pursuant to a written agreement made with a specified prosecutor (within the meaning of s.71(4)), assisted, or offered to assist the investigator or prosecutor in relation to that or any other offence,

the judge may, in determining what sentence to pass on the offender, take into account the extent and nature of the assistance given or offered.

If he passes a sentence which is less than it would have passed but for the assistance given or offered, the judge:

(a) must state in open court:
    (i) that he has passed a lesser sentence than he would otherwise have passed; and
    (ii) what the greater sentence would have been, but
(b) need not do so if he thinks that it would not be in the public interest to disclose that the sentence has been discounted; but in such a case he must give written notice of the matters specified in (i) and (ii) above to both the prosecutor and the offender.

If s.73(3) does not apply by virtue of s.73(4) (i.e. the judge thinks it would not be in the public interest to disclose that the discount on the sentence), then CJA 2003, ss.174(1)(a) and 270 (requirement to explain reasons for sentence or other order) do not apply to the extent that the explanation will disclose that a sentence has been discounted in pursuance of this provision.

Note that in this provision:

- a reference to a sentence includes, in the case of a sentence which is fixed by law, a reference to the minimum period an offender is required to serve, and a reference to a lesser sentence must be construed accordingly;
- a reference to imprisonment includes a reference to any other custodial sentence within the meaning of PCC(S)A 2000, s.76.

Each of the following is a specified prosecutor: the DPP, the DRCP, the DSFO, the DPP for Northern Ireland, and any prosecutor designated for the purpose by one of those.

An agreement with a specified prosecutor may provide for assistance to be given to that prosecutor or to any other prosecutor (s.73(9)).

31-011 Nothing in any enactment which:

(1) requires that a minimum sentence be passed in respect of any offence or an offence of any description, or by reference to the

circumstances of any offender (whether or not the enactment also permits the court to pass a lesser sentence in particular circumstances); or

(2) in the case of a sentence which is fixed by law, requires the court to take into account certain matters for the purposes of making an order which determines or has the effect of determining the minimum period of imprisonment which the offender must serve (whether or not the enactment also permits the court to fix a lesser period in particular circumstances),

affects the power of a court to act under this provision.

If, in determining what sentence to pass on the offender, the judge takes into account the extent and nature of the assistance given or offered as mentioned above, that does not prevent the court from also taking account of any other matter which it is entitled by virtue of any other enactment to take account of for the purposes of determining, the sentence, or in the case of a sentence which is fixed by law, any minimum period of imprisonment which an offender must serve.

The essential feature of the new statutory framework is that the offender must publicly admit the full extent of his own criminality and must agree to participate in a formalised process. The legislation has not, however, abolished a well-understood feature of the sentencing process and there will be occasions when an offender has provided assistance to the police which does not fall within the new arrangements, and in particular the written agreement. He is not thereby deprived of whatever consequent benefit he should receive. *R. v P, R. v Blackburn* [2007] EWCA Crim 2290; [2008] 2 Cr. App. R(S) 5.

Extent of Discount

31–012   The extent of the discount given will ordinarily depend on the value of the help given. Non-compliance with the written agreement is not a separate crime, nor an aggravating feature of the original offence; the penalty is that the offender is deprived of the reduction of sentence which would have been allowed if he had complied with the agreement. Unlike the common law arrangements by which discounts for a guilty plea should normally be reflective of the time when it was tendered, for the purposes of a review any discount should continue to reflect the extent and nature of the assistance given or offered (*R. v P. R. v Blackburn*, above). Value is a function of quality and quantity. In dealing with such a case the judge must balance, on the information before him:

(1) the nature and effect of the assistance given; if the information is:
  (a) unreliable, vague, lacking in practical utility or already known to the authorities, no identifiable discount need be given or, if given, may be minimal;
  (b) is accurate, particularised, useful in practice and hitherto unknown to the authorities, enabling serious criminal activity to be stopped and serious criminals brought to book, the discount may be substantial;
(2) the degree of assistance provided, e.g. whether the offender is prepared to back up his information by testifying or expressing

willingness to testify, or making a witness statement incriminating a co-accused, particularly where such conduct leads to the co-accused's conviction on his plea of guilty (see *R. v D* [2010] EWCA Crim 1485; [2011] 1 Cr. App. R. (S.) 69);

(3) the degree of risk to which the offender exposes himself or his family to personal jeopardy.

Note that:

(a) there is no automatic entitlement, where an offender provides information of significant value and fulfils his side of the agreement to a "normal" discount of between 50 and 66 per cent of the sentence that would have been passed after a trial;

(b) what the offender has earned by participating in the written agreement system under s.73 is an appropriate reward for the assistance provided to the administration of justice, and that is, in the end, fact-specific;

(c) when it applies, the discount for a guilty plea is separate from, and additional to, the appropriate reduction for assistance provided by the offender.

Accordingly, the best course to adopt is to:

(i)   go back to the starting point before any allowance is made for plea, then

(ii) discount that by the appropriate amount for the assistance given; and then

(iii) apply any discount for a plea of guilty of guilty to the resulting figure.

(*R. v P; R. v Blackburn* (above) *R. v Newman* [2010] 7 *Archbold Review* 3 CA).

Only in the most exceptional case will the appropriate level of reduction exceed three-quarters of the total sentence which would otherwise be passed, and the normal level continues, as before, to be a reduction of somewhere between one half and two thirds of that sentence (*R. v P, R. v Blackburn, above*).

R. v. Dougall [2010] EWCA Crim 1048 [2011] 1 Cr. App. R. (S.) 227(37), C.A. is not to be taken as laying down a principle that anyone who enters into a section 73 agreement is entitled to expect a discount of 50 per cent from the sentence that would otherwise be correct after allowance for guilty plea (*R. v Ford* [2011] EWCA Crim 473 [2011] 2 Cr. App. R. (S.) 371(64)).

5.   Information given after sentence

31–013   The 2005 Act does not abolish the former common law procedure which may still be appropriate in certain circumstances (*R. v. H.* [2009] EWCA Crim 2485; [2010] 2 Cr. App. R. (S.) 18 Crim. L.R. 246). It does not apply however for instance where information is given AFTER sentence which is covered by the provisions of the Act. See *R. v A* [1999] 1 Cr. App. R. (S.) 52.

DISCOUNTS ON SENTENCE

In the absence of a statutory agreement under the Act the former system obtains. Credit for information provided after sentence will be given by the CACD only in certain circumstances, as where, for one reason or another, the material was not put before the sentencing judge. An offender who, after sentence, seeks to provide information must either adopt the statutory agreement or seek to persuade the secretary Justice to exercise prerogative powers in his favour (*R. v Chaudhury* above).

6. Referral back to Court

31–014 An offender receiving such a discounted sentence, and who either fails to any extent to give assistance in accordance with the agreement; or, having given the assistance in accordance with the agreement, in pursuance of another written agreement, gives or agrees to give further assistance, may have his sentence referred back to court, see VARIATION OF SENTENCE.

32. DRINKING BANNING ORDERS

These orders brought into effect in specified local justice areas by SI 2010/469 and SI 2010/2641. They are **not yet in force** in the Crown Court.

VCRA 2006, s.2

General
32–001   Where:

(1) a person aged 16 or over is convicted of an offence; and
(2) at the time he committed the offence, he was under the influence of alcohol,

VCRA 2006, ss.6, 7: SI 2009/1840

then, the judge *must* consider whether a drinking banning order under VCRA 2006 is necessary to protect other persons from further conduct by him of criminal or disorderly behaviour while he is under the influence of alcohol. The provision will apply equally to cases where the offender is convicted before the Crown Court, as to cases where he is committed to the Crown Court for sentence (s.7(11)).

Procedure is governed by r.50 (Civil behaviour orders after verdict or finding) as to which see ANTI-SOCIAL BEHAVIOUR ORDERS.

For the purpose of deciding whether to make an order the judge may consider evidence led by the prosecution and/or by the defence, and it is immaterial whether that evidence would have been admissible in the proceedings in which the offender was convicted.

If the judge decides that it is, he may make an order. If he does not make an order, he must give his reasons for not doing so in open court.

An order does not stand alone; it must be made:

(a) in addition to a sentence imposed in respect of the offence; or
(b) in addition to an order discharging the offender conditionally.

The judge may adjourn any proceedings in relation to a drinking banning order even after sentencing the offender. If the offender does not appear for any adjourned proceedings, the judge may further adjourn the proceedings or may issue a warrant for his arrest, though a warrant may not be issued if the judge is satisfied that the offender has had adequate notice of the time and place of the adjourned proceedings.

An order takes effect on the day on which it is made; or if on that day the offender is detained in legal custody, the day on which he is released from that custody.

Nature of order
32–002   A drinking banning order is an order that prohibits the individual against whom it is made from doing the things described in the order. Such an order may impose any prohibition on the offender which is necessary for the purpose of protecting other persons from criminal or disorderly conduct by him while he is under the influence of alcohol. This order must include such prohibitions as the judge making the order considers necessary, for that purpose, on the subject's entering:

VCRA 2006, s.1

(1) premises in respect of which there is a premises licence authorising the use of the premises for the sale of alcohol by retail; and

(2) premises in respect of which there is a club premises certificate authorising the use of the premises for the supply of alcohol to members or guests, but

an order may not impose a prohibition on the offender that prevents him from:

(a) having access to a place where he resides;

(b) attending at any place which he is required to attend for the purposes of any employment of his or of any contract of services to which he is a party;

(c) attending at any place which he is expected to attend during the period for which the order has effect for the purposes of education or training or for the purpose of receiving medical treatment; or

(d) attending at any place which he is required to attend by any obligation imposed on him by or under an enactment or by the order of a court or tribunal.

(Expressions used in subs.(3) and in the Licensing Act 2003 or in a Part of that Act have the same meanings in that subsection as in that Act or Part.)

Duration of order

32–003 An order has effect for the period specified in the order ("the specified period") which must be not less than two months and not more than two years. It may, however, provide that different prohibitions contained in it have effect for different periods; but, in each case, the period ("the prohibition period") must be not less than two months and not more than two years.

The order may include provision for the order, or a prohibition contained in it, to cease to have effect before the end of the specified period or the prohibition period if the offender satisfactorily completes the approved course specified in the order (see SI 2009/1839) but such a provision must fix the time at which the order or the prohibition will cease to have effect if the offender satisfactorily completes the specified approved course at whichever is the later of:

(1) the time specified in the order, being a time after the expiry of at least half the specified period, or as the case may be, the prohibition period; and

(2) the time when he does satisfactorily complete that course. Such a provision may be included in the order only if:

(a) the judge is satisfied that a place on a specified approved course will be available for the offender; and

(b) the offender has agreed to the inclusion of the provision in question in the order.

Before making such a provision the court must inform the subject in ordinary language (whether in writing or otherwise) about:

(i)   the effect of including the provision in the order;
(ii) what, in general terms, attendance on the course will involve if he undertakes it;
(iii) any fees he will be required to pay for the course if he undertakes it; and
(iv) when he will have to pay any such fees.

Where the judge makes an order which does *not* include such a provision he must give his reasons for not including it in open court.

Publicity in relation to juveniles

32–004   Insofar as proceedings relate to the making of an order against a young person:

(1) CYPA 1933, s.49 (restrictions on reports of proceedings in which children and young persons are concerned) does not apply in respect of the young person against whom the order is made; but

(2) CYPA 1933, s.39 (power to prohibit publication of certain matters) does apply.

VCRA 2006, s.7(8), (9)

Variation or discharge of orders made on conviction

32–005   An order made on conviction may be varied or discharged on the application of:

VCRA 2006, ss.8, 14(1)

(1) the offender;
(2) the DPP; or
(3) a relevant authority, i.e. a chief officer of police, the Chief Constable of the British Transport Police or a local authority,

provided that an order may not be varied so as to extend the specified period to more than two years.

If the offender makes such an application, he must also send notice of his application to the DPP; if the DPP or a relevant authority makes such an application, he or it must also send notice of the application to the offender.

An order may not be discharged on such an application unless:

(a) it is discharged from a time after the end of the period that is half the duration of the specified period; or
(b) the DPP has consented to its earlier discharge.

Procedure on revocation and discharge is governed by r.50.5 as amended by SI 2010/1921, as to which see BREACH, AMENDMENT AND REVOCATION, under Anti-Social Behaviour Orders.

Breach of order

32–006   If an offender, subject to a drinking banning order does, without reasonable excuse, anything that he is prohibited from doing by the order, he is guilty of an offence, and is liable on summary conviction to a fine not exceeding level 4 on the standard scale (see FINES AND ENFORCEMENT). He may not be made the subject of a conditional discharge.

VCRA 2006, s.11

Notes

33. DRIVING DISQUALIFICATION

Quick guide

1. Introduction

General

33–001   An offender convicted of certain offences may be disqualified from driving a mechanically propelled vehicle and from holding or obtaining a driving licence. Disqualification:

(1) to some extent serves a basic public protection purpose, where the offender's conduct has proved a danger to other road users; and

(2) in most cases, is intended to punish misuse, or careless use of vehicles and to deter both the offender and others from indulging in it.

Disqualification is part of the basic penalty imposed by the court for the offence, but it is an ancillary order and must be attached to the sentence; it cannot stand alone (but see 33–011, below).

Where the judge decides not to order, where he can, the offender's disqualification from driving for the usual minimum period or at all, or to order the endorsement of his driving record, he must explain why he has not done so, when he explains the sentence that he has passed.

Length of disqualification

33–002   The law provides no limit to the length of a disqualification beyond any minimum prescribed period, but: R.42

(1) very long periods should be avoided unless the offender is a menace to other road users (*R. v Rickeard* [1975] R.T.R. 104; *R. v Davitt* [1974] Crim. L.R. 719), since such offenders are particularly likely to commit offences of driving while disqualified which they might not, were the term shorter;

(2) RTOA 1988, s.35A permits the discretionary period of disqualification imposed on an offender sentenced to a custodial

sentence to be extended for the prescribed period (see 33-023 below);

(3) as to disqualification for life, see *R. v Buckley* (1994) 15 Cr.App.R.(S.) 695.

Disqualifications run from the date of imposition, and will ordinarily be concurrent; as to extension periods in custody cases, see 33–023.

The references in the text in bold type emphasise matters found by CACD to be ignored or not sufficiently appreciated in the Crown Court (see, in particular, *R. v Kent* (1983) 77 Cr.App.R. 120).

Situations in which disqualification arises

33–003   An offender may be disqualified:

(1) where a vehicle has been used for the purpose of crime (see 33–008)

(2) on conviction of any offence (33–011)

(3) on conviction of an RT offence attracting discretionary disqualification (33–033);

(4) on conviction of an RT offence attracting discretionary disqualification (33–027); and

(5) where RT disqualification is obligatory owing to the accumulation of penalty points for a series of offences (33–028), in addition to dealing with him in any other way, see 33–011, below.

PCC(S)A 2000, s.147; RTOA 1988, ss.34, 35; RTA 1991, s.29, Sch.4, para.95; AVTA 1992, s.3(2)

The various systems of disqualification run parallel to each other and are not mutually exclusive (see *Jones v West Mercia Chief Constable* [2001] R.T.R.8).

A magistrates' court, as part of its procedures for enforcing the payment of fines and other financial penalties may, under CJA 2003, s.30, instead of issuing a warrant of commitment, or proceeding under MCA 1980, s.81, order a defaulter to be disqualified for a period not exceeding 12 months.

The provisions of C(IC)A 2003, Pt 3, govern the recognition and enforcement of disqualifications imposed on persons normally resident in the United Kingdom by courts in EU member states.

Endorsement

33–004   The particulars of all offences involving obligatory or discretionary disqualification must be endorsed on the offender's licence, where he holds one, unless there are special reasons for not doing so. This is irrespective of whether he is disqualified or not. In the case of an offender who does not hold a licence, or a foreign driver, the court ordering endorsement with any particulars or penalty points must send notice of the order to the Secretary of State for endorsement of the offender's "driving record."

For reasons essentially connected with the imposition of fixed penalties (which cannot be issued to non-GB drivers), RSA 2006 introduces the concept of a "driving record" (defined in RTOA 1988, s.97A, inserted by RSA 2006, s.8) held by the Secretary of State.

RTOA 1988, ss.44, 44A

The first stage of this procedure is introduced by s.9 and Sch.2 in relation to unlicensed and foreign drivers. At this stage there is no change as regards EU and Northern Ireland licence holders who fall to be dealt with in the same way as GB licence holders. The second stage, to be introduced later (s.10 and Sch.3) will introduce the new system of endorsement of driving records for all drivers, after which the "counterpart" of a licence will have no further function.

As to applications for removal of an endorsement, see RTOA 1988, s.45.

Conditional and absolute discharge

33–005 Where the judge makes an order of conditional or absolute discharge in respect of an offence carrying obligatory or discretionary disqualification, he may also on that occasion exercise any power conferred, and must also exercise any duty imposed, on the court by RTOA, 1988, ss.34, 35, 36 or 44.

RTOA 1988, s.46(1)

Mechanics of disqualification: interim disqualification

33–006 In order to decide whether or not to exercise his power of disqualification, the judge may take into consideration particulars of any previous conviction or disqualification endorsed on the offender's licence.

RTOA 1988, ss.29, 31 RTOA 1988, s.26;

While, in general, a disqualification will be imposed at the time sentence is pronounced, which will normally follow upon conviction:

(1) there is nothing to prevent the judge from dealing with the substantive part of the sentence on the day of conviction and postponing ancillary questions of endorsement and disqualification until the licence is produced, and any other relevant information is to hand (*R. v Annesley* (1976) 62 Cr. App. R. 113);

(2) a judge who:
  (a) defers sentence in respect of an offence carrying obligatory or discretionary disqualification; or
  (b) adjourns after convicting an offender of such an offence, before dealing with him; may order him to be disqualified until he has been dealt with for the offence.

An order under (2) ceases to have effect on the expiry of six months from the date it is made, if the offender has not been dealt with before that and, when the court comes to deal with the offender, it is precluded from disqualifying him further in respect of the same offence or any offence in respect of which an order could have been made at the time the first order was made. Where the judge proposes to disqualify, he should draw this to the attention of counsel, so that the latter may deal with the point specifically (*R. v Powell* (1984) 6 Cr. App. R. (S.) 354).

Production of licence: suspension

33–007 Before making an order the court *must require* the offender, if he is the holder of a licence, (including an EU licence) to produce it, and if he has not caused it to be delivered to the court, or he does not produce it:

RTA 1988, s.27(1), (3), (4);

(1) he may be guilty of an offence; and

(2) the licence *must* be suspended until it is produced,

and the obligation imposed on him in respect of the licence also applies in relation to the counterpart.

2. Vehicle used for the purpose of crime

33–008 Where a person is convicted in the Crown Court or, having been convicted in the magistrates' court, is committed to the Crown Court for sentence under PCC(S)A 2000, s.3:

(1) for an offence punishable with imprisonment for not less than two years on indictment; or

PCC(S)A 2000, s.147

(2) having been convicted in a magistrates' court of such an offence was committed to the Crown Court for sentence; or

(3) is convicted by or before any court of common assault, or for any other offence involving an assault, including the aiding, abetting or procuring of such an offence, or

(4) the judge is satisfied that a vehicle was used by that person, or by anyone else, for the purpose of committing or facilitating the commission of the offence, including the taking of any steps after it was committed for the purposes of disposing of any property to which it related, or of avoiding apprehension or detection, or that the assault was committed by driving a motor vehicle,

he may disqualify that person for such period as he thinks fit. As to the appropriate mandatory extension in custody cases, under PCC(S)A 2000, s.147A, see 33–023.

The "offence" must be that, or one of those, of which he is convicted (*R. v Parrington* (1985) 7 Cr. App. R.(S.) 18).

Important considerations

33–009 A number of points needs to be noted in respect of the exercise, and the effect of exercising, this power:

(1) the power under PCC(S)A 2000, s.147 is exercisable even though the offence committed does not attract endorsement under RTOA 1988;

(2) if the driving is only incidental to the offence, the power of disqualification under s.147 should not be used (*R. v Wilmot, The Times*, January 24, 1985);

(3) the fact that the offender did not himself drive the vehicle in the course of committing the offence does not protect him from disqualification; if one of several offenders uses a vehicle for the purposes of an offence, all or any of them may be disqualified (*R. v Wilmot*, above);

(4) the power should not be exercised without first giving the defence advocate an opportunity of dealing with it (*R. v Powell* (1984) 6 Cr. App. R.(S.) 354; *R. v Lake* (1986) 8 Cr. App. R. (S.) 69; *R. v Money* [1988] Crim. L.R. 626);

(5) the judge, in imposing a disqualification under s.147, should take account of the effect on the offender's employment prospects on his release (*R. v Wright* (1979) 1 Cr. App. R.(S.) 82; *R. v Davegun* (1985) 7 Cr. App. R.(S.) 110; *R. v Liddey* (1999) 2 Cr. App. R.(S.) 122);

(6) where a custodial sentence is imposed the length of disqualification should be equal to or slightly in excess of the period the offender will spend in custody (*R. v Bowling* [2008] EWCA Crim 1148; [2009] 1 Cr. App. R. (S.) 23; long periods are undesirable (*R. v Fazal* [1999] 1 Cr. App. R.(S.) 152);

(7) endorsement under s.147 does not "wipe the slate clean" of penalty points previously accumulated on the licence; nor is there any power, if the court declines to disqualify under s.147, to impose penalty points under RTOA 1988; and

(8) there is no power to order a re-test under s.147 (*R. v Rajesh Patel* (1995) 16 Cr. App. R.(S.) 756).

Obligation to produce licence

33–010   A judge ordering a disqualification under s.147 must require the offender to produce:

(1) any licence (defined in s.146(5));

(2) in the case where he holds a Northern Ireland licence, that licence; and

(3) in the case of a person holding an EU licence (as defined in RTA 1988, Pt III), his community licence.

3.   Disqualification for any offence

33–011   The court before which a person is convicted of any offence committed after December 31, 1997 may:

(1) provided the judge has been notified that he has that power;

(2) instead of (unless the sentence is fixed by law or is one which falls to be imposed under PCC(S)A 2000, ss.110(2) or 111(2) (minimum sentences for certain repeat offences), FA 1968, s.51A(2) (minimum sentences for certain firearms offences), CJA 2003, ss.225(2) or 226(2) (dangerous offenders) or VCRA 2006, s.29(4) or (6) (minimum sentences in certain cases of using a person to mind a weapon)); or

(3) in addition to, dealing with him in any other way,

PCC(S)A 2000, s.146(1)–(3)

order him to be disqualified for such period as he thinks fit, for holding or obtaining a driving licence.

As to the appropriate mandatory extension period in custody cases, under PCC(S)A 2000, s.147A, see 33–023.

This power is wide-ranging; it is not limited to any particular offence, nor is it necessary that the offence be connected in any way with the use of a motor vehicle (*R. v Cliff* [2004] EWCA Crim 3139; [2005] 2 Cr. App. R.(S.) 22; see also *R. v Skitt* [2004] EWCA Crim 3141; [2005] 2 Cr. App. R.(S.) 22).

DRIVING DISQUALIFICATION

Obligation to produce licence

33–012   A judge ordering a disqualification under s.146 must require the offender to produce:

PCC(S)A 2000, s.146(4)

(1) any licence (defined in s.146(5));

(2) in the case where he holds a Northern Ireland licence, that licence; and

(3) in the case of a person holding an EU licence (as defined in RTA 1988, Pt III), his EU licence.

4.   Obligatory disqualification for serious RT offences

33–013   An offender *must* be disqualified, in the absence of special reasons (see below) for at least the minimum prescribed period, on conviction of any one of the following offences:

(1) manslaughter by the driver of a mechanically propelled vehicle (DD60) (indictment only—common law);

(2) causing death by dangerous driving (RTA 1988, s.1; RTA 1991, s.1 (DD70));

(3) causing death by careless driving when under the influence of drink or drugs (RTA 1988, s.3A; RTA 1991, s.3) unfit through drink, (CD40); unfit through drugs, (CD50); excess alcohol, (CD60); failure to provide specimen, (CD70); fails without reasonable excuse to give permission for specimen of blood to be taken under RTA 1988, s.7A);

(4) causing death by careless or inconsiderate driving (CD 80) (RTA 1988, s.2B; RSA 2006, s.20);

(5) causing death by driving unlicensed, disqualified or uninsured drivers (CD 90) (RTA 1988, s.3ZA; RSA 2006, s.21);

(6) dangerous driving (RTA 1988, s.2; RTA 1991, s.l) (DD40);

(7) driving or attempting to drive while unfit through drink or drugs (RTA 1988, s.4(l)) (through drink (DR20), through drugs (DR 80));

(8) driving or attempting to drive with excess alcohol concentration (RTA 1988, s.5(l)(a)) (DR 10);

(9) failing without reasonable excuse to supply an evidential specimen, when driving or attempting to drive (RTA 1988, s.7(6)) (DR30);

(10)   motor racing or speed trials on the highway (RTA 1988,s.12) (MS50); and

(11)   aggravated vehicle taking (TA 1968, s.12; AVTA 1992, s.3).

33–014   On conviction of any of the offences under (1) to (9) above, the offender must be disqualified for such period as the court thinks fit, for *not less than*:

(1) two years in the case of (1), (2) and (3), or 12 months in the case of (4) to (9) above; or

(2) three years, if the offender is convicted of an offence under (3), (5), (6), or (7) and was in the 10 years immediately preceding the commission of that offence convicted of a like offence;

unless for special reasons (see below) the court thinks fit to order him:

(a) *not* to be disqualified; or

(b) to order him to be disqualified for a shorter period.

RTOA 1988,
s.36

As to the appropriate mandatory extension period under RTOA 1988, s.35A, see 33–023.

In such a case the grounds for that decision must be stated in open court (RTOA 1988, s.47(10)).

On conviction of any of the offences under (1), (2) and (4) a re-test *must* be ordered and the offender remains disqualified until he has passed the appropriate driving test, which in these circumstances is an extended driving test (RTOA 1988, s.36; RTA 1991, s.32).

If on conviction of any of the offences under (1) to (9) inclusive, the court finds special reasons and does not disqualify, the licence must be endorsed with 3–11 penalty points.

Sentencing: offences under ss.1, 2B and 3A

33–015   The maximum period of imprisonment for causing death by dangerous driving and causing death by careless driving while under the influence of drink or drugs was increased to 14 years' imprisonment with the coming into force of CJA 2003, s.285, on February 27, 2004 (SI 2004/81). Sentencing thresholds (33–019 below), as set out below (*R. v Cooksley*, below) needed to be adjusted accordingly. This increase in the maximum sentence affects not only the gravest cases but leads to an increase in sentences below that level of gravity, continuing down the scale to cases where there are no aggravating features (*R. v Richardson*, [2006] EWCA Crim 3186; [2007] 2 Cr. App. R. (S.) 36). CACD made adjustments to the sentencing thresholds (at 33–019, below).

Whilst offences under ss.1 and 3A were regarded in *Cooksley*, for sentencing purposes, on an equal basis, once the new offence under RTA 1988, s.2B, inserted by RSA 2006, s.20 of causing death by careless or inconsiderate driving simpliciter (i.e. without having consumed alcohol) comes into force, it will be critical to a fair and balanced sentencing practice for the difference to be understood and acknowledged (as above).

R. v Cooksley

33–016   In *R. v Cooksley* [2003] EWCA Crim 996; [2003] 2 Cr. App. R. 18, CACD made the following points;

(1) it would ordinarily be obvious to an offender that his driving was dangerous, and he deserved to be punished accordingly;

(2) where death resulted this could justify a higher sentence than if it did not;

(3) the impact on the family of the victim could reasonably be taken into account;

(4) though causing death by dangerous driving was invariably a serious crime, culpability must be the dominant factor when assessing where, in the level of serious crime, the facts of the particular case came.

Aggravating features

33–017 CACD adopted the recommendations of the Sentencing Panel, that aggravating features included:

Highly culpable standard of driving at the time of the offence

(1) The consumption of alcohol or drugs (including legal medication known to cause drowsiness), ranging from a couple of drinks to a "motorised pub crawl".

(2) Competitive driving against another vehicle; greatly excessive speed; showing off.

(3) Disregard of warnings from passengers.

(4) A prolonged, persistent and deliberate course of bad driving.

(5) Aggressive driving (such as driving too close to the vehicle in front), persistent, inappropriate attempts to overtake, cutting in after overtaking.

(6) Driving whilst driver's attention is avoidably distracted, e.g. by use of mobile phone (especially when hand-held).

(7) Driving when knowingly suffering from a medical condition which significantly impairs offender's driving skills.

(8) Driving when knowingly deprived of adequate sleep or rest.

(9) Driving a poorly maintained or dangerously loaded vehicle (especially when the driver is motivated by commercial considerations).

(10) Committing the offence while on bail.

Driving habitually below careful standard

(1) Other offences committed at the same time and related offences, e.g. driving without ever having had a licence; driving while disqualified; driving with no insurance, while a learner driver driving without a supervisor and so on.

(2) Previous convictions for motoring offences, particularly offences which involve bad driving or the consumption of excessive alcohol before driving—in other words the man who demonstrates that he is determined to continue driving badly despite past experience.

(3) Driving after having taken a vehicle without consent or in a stolen vehicle.

Outcome of offence

(1) Where more than one person has been killed as a result of the offence (especially if the offender knowingly put more than one person at risk, or the occurrence of multiple deaths was foreseeable).

(2) Severely injuring more than one victim in addition.

Irresponsible behaviour at the scene of the offence

(1) Failing to stop or, even more reprehensible, trying to blame the victim for causing the collision, throwing the victim off the bonnet of the car by swerving in order to escape.

(2) Causing death in the course of dangerous driving in an attempt to avoid detection or apprehension.

Mitigating features

33–018   The offence might be mitigated by the following features:

(1) a good driving record;
(2) absence of previous convictions;
(3) a timely plea of guilty;
(4) genuine shock or remorse, which may be greater where the victim was either a close relative or friend of the offender;
(5) the offender's age (but only in cases where lack of driving experience has contributed to the commission of the offence);
(6) offender also severely injured as a result of the accident caused by his dangerous driving.

Sentencing thresholds

33–019   In *R. v Cooksley* (above) CACD, basing its opinions on a 10-year maximum (increased to 14 years' imprisonment after the coming into force of CJA 2003, s.285, February 27, 2004), set out four "starting points" in sentencing such offenders. These were adjusted by CACD in *R. v Richardson* (above) as follows:

(1) no aggravating features: two years' custodial sentence;
(2) intermediate culpability: two to four years' custodial sentence;
(3) higher culpability: four to seven years' custodial sentence;
(4) most serious: 7–14 years' custodial sentence.

Young persons

33–020   Where an offender aged at least 14, but under 18, is convicted of an offence:

PCC(S)A 2000,
s.91(2), (3)

(1) of causing death by dangerous driving (RTA 1988, s.l); or
(2) of causing death by careless driving while under the influence of drink or drugs (RTA 1988, s.3A);

and the judge is of opinion that none of the other methods in which the case may be legally dealt with is suitable, he may sentence the offender to the same maximum term of 10 years as applies to an adult.

Manslaughter involving use of a motor vehicle

33–021   The maximum sentence for manslaughter is life imprisonment. The sentence for manslaughter involving the use of a motor vehicle, which involves an element of hostility, cannot be equated with other offences of causing death by driving, such as causing death by dangerous driving and causing death by careless driving, having consumed alcohol so as to be over the prescribed limit. The maximum sentence for these two offences has always corresponded and was increased from February 27, 2004 to 14 years.

RTOA 1988,
s.34A

Reduced disqualification for offender attending course

33–022   Where a person is convicted by or before a court of a relevant drink offence, or a specified offence, and the court makes an order under RTOA 1988, s.34 disqualifying him for a period of not less than 12 months, it may order that the period of disqualification be reduced if, by a specified date, the offender satisfactorily completes an approved course specified in the order.

A "relevant drink offence" is an offence under the following provisions of RTA 1988:

- s.3A(1)(a)—causing death by careless driving when unfit to drive, etc.;
- s.3A(1)(b)—causing death by careless driving with excess alcohol;
- s.3A(1)(c)—failing to provide a specimen where required in connection with drink or the consumption of alcohol;
- s.4—driving or being in charge when under the influence of drink, committed by of unfitness through drink;
- s.5(1) —driving or being in charge with excess alcohol;
- s.7(6)—failing to provide a specimen committed in the course of an investigation into an offence within any of the above offences;
- s.7A(6)—failing to allow a specimen to be subjected to a laboratory test in the course of an investigation into an offence within any of the above.

A "specified offence" means an offence under:

- RTA 1988, s.3—careless and inconsiderate driving;
- RTA 1988, s.36—failing to comply with a traffic sign;
- RTRA 1984, s.17(4)—misuse of special road;
- RTRA 1984, s.89(1)—excess speed.

An order must not be made in the case of an offender convicted of a **specified offence** if the offender has, during the period of three years ending with the date on which the offence was committed, committed a specified offence and successfully completed an approved course (either under s.34A or under s.30A (totting up procedure), or the specified offence was committed during his probationary period (i.e. under Road Traffic (New Drivers) Act 1995, s.1)).

The court may make such an order only where:

(1) the offender appears to be 17 or over;
(2) it is satisfied that a place on a course is available for the offender;
(3) it informs the offender (orally or in writing and in ordinary language) of the effect of the order, and the fees payable and when they must be paid; and
(4) the offender agrees to the order being made.

Note that:

(a) the reduction must be of not less than three months nor more than one-quarter of the unreduced period (thus nine months in the case of a 12-month disqualification which is the usual period for a drink-driving offence, but, of course, it may be higher according to the alcohol level);
(b) the offender disqualified for two years, as is the case under RTA 1988, s.3A, will be eligible for a six-month reduction; and

(c) the date specified as the latest date for the completion of the course must be at least two months before the last day of the period of disqualification as reduced by the order.

Custody cases; extension period

33–023   Where a person is convicted of an offence for which the judge imposes a custodial sentence, other than a suspended sentence, and orders that person to be disqualified under RTOA 1988, ss.34 or 35, or PCC(S)A 2000, ss.146 or 147 the order **must** provide for the offender to be disqualified for:

RTOA 1988, s.35A

(1) the discretionary disqualification period; being the period for which the judge would have imposed in the absence of s.35A; **and**
(2) an appropriate extension period, being where:
   (a) a **life sentence tariff determination** is made under PCC(S)A 2000, 82A(2), a period equal to the part of the sentence specified in that order;
   (b) a **detention and training order** is made under PCC(S)A 2000, s 100, a period equal to half the term of that order;
   (c) a prison **sentence of less than 12 months** is imposed under CJA 2003, s.181 a period equal to custodial period specified (s.181(3)(a) less any relevant discount, see below);
   (d) CJA 2003, s.227 (**extended sentence**; persons **18 or over**) applies in relation to the custodial sentence, a period equal to half the term imposed (pursuant to *ibid*. s.227(2C)(a)) calculated after that term has been reduced by any relevant discount (see below);
   (e) CJA 2003, s.228 (**extended sentence** for certain violent or sexual offences against the persons **under 18**) applies in relation to a custodial sentence, a period equal to half the term imposed (pursuant to *ibid* s.228(2B)(a)) calculated after that term has been reduced by any relevant discount (see below);
   (f) an order under CJA 2003, s.269(2) (determination of minimum term in relation to **mandatory life sentence; early release**) is made in relation to the custodial term, a period equal to the part of the sentence specified in the order.

In any other case, the appropriate extension period is a period equal to half the custodial sentence imposed, calculated after that sentence has been reduced by any relevant discount (see 33–024 below).

If a period determined under subs.(4) includes a fraction of a day, that period is to be rounded up to the nearest number of whole days.

"Relevant discount" defined

33–024   The "relevant discount" referred to above, is the total number of days to count as time served by virtue of an order under;

RTOA 1988, s.35A

    (1) CJA 2003, s 240 (crediting periods of remand, in custody); or

    (2) CJA 2003, s.240A (crediting periods of remand on bail).

Excluded sentences

33–025   The above provisions do not apply where the judge has made an order:

    (1) under CJA 2003, s 269(4) (determination of minimum term) in relation to a **mandatory life sentence; no early release** in relation to a custodial sentence; or

    (2) under PCC(S)A 2000, s.82A(4) (determination of minimum term in relation to **discretionary life sentence no early release;** in relation to the custodial sentence.

[margin: RTOA 1988, s.35A(6); CorJA 2009, s.137, Sch.16, paras 2, 5,]

Effect of custodial sentence in other cases

33–-026   Where a person is convicted of an offence for which a judge proposes to order the person to be disqualified under s.34 or 35, or under PCC(S)A 2000, ss.146 or 147, and

[margin: RTOA 1988, s.35B; CorJA 2009, s.137,Sch. 16, paras 2, 5]

    (1) the judge proposes to impose on the person a custodial sentence, (other than a suspended sentence) for another offence, or

    (2) at the time of sentencing for the offence, a custodial sentence imposed on the person on an earlier occasion has not expired,

the judge must have regard, in determining the period for which the person is to be disqualified under s.34 or 35, to the consideration below if and to the extent that it is appropriate to do so. That consideration is the diminished effect of disqualification as a distinct punishment if the person who is disqualified is also detained in pursuance of a custodial sentence.

    If the judge proposes to order the person to be disqualified under s.34 or 35, and to impose a custodial sentence for the same offence, he may not in relation to that disqualification take that custodial sentence into account for the purposes of the first paragraph above.

5.   Offences carrying discretionary disqualification

33–027   Discretionary disqualification and obligatory endorsement apply to road traffic offences which are not, like those carrying obligatory disqualification, invariably grave matters, but which may still be serious enough to justify a period of disqualification. Where the court does not exercise its power of disqualification it *must*, in the absence of special reasons, endorse the licence with the appropriate number of penalty points.

    These offences are (as amended by CJA 2003, ss.281, 282 and 286 and RSA 2006, ss.15, 22, 23, 24, 26, 27 and 39 when these sections come into force):

Provision creating offence	General nature of offence	Maximum penalty	Disqualification	Penalty points	Code
RTRA 1984, s.16(1)	Contravention of temporary prohibition or restriction	Level 3	Discretionary in respect of speed restriction	3–6 or 3 (fixed penalty)	MW10
RTRA 1984, s.17(4)	Traffic regulation on special roads	Level 4	Discretionary in certain circumstances; obligatory in respect of speed restriction	2–6 or fixed penalty in respect of speed limit, 3 in any other case	MW10
RTRA 1984, s.25(5)	Contravention of pedestrian crossing regulations	Level 3	Discretionary if committed in respect of motor vehicle	3	PC10
RTRA 1984, s.28(3)	Not stopping at school crossing	Level 3	Discretionary if committed in respect of motor vehicle	3	TS60
RTRA 1984, s.29(3)	Contravention of order relating to street playground	Level 3	Discretionary if committed in respect of motor vehicle	2	MS30
RTRA 1984, s.89(1)	Exceeding speed limit	Level 3	Discretionary	3–6 or fixed penalty	SP10
Common law	Manslaughter or culpable homicide by driver of motor vehicle	14 years on indictment			DD60
RTA 1988, s.1	Causing death by dangerous driving	(a) summarily: 6 months or the statutory maximum or both (b) on indictment: 2 years or a fine or both	Obligatory	3–11	DD70
RTA 1988, s.2	Dangerous driving		Obligatory	3–11	DD40
RTA 1988, s.2B	Causing death by careless or inconsiderate driving	(a) summarily: 12 months or the statutory maximum or both (b) on indictment: 5 years or a fine or both	Obligatory	3–11	CD80

Provision creating offence	General nature of offence	Maximum penalty	Disqualification	Penalty points	Code
RTA 1988, s.3	Careless and inconsiderate driving	Level 5	Discretionary	3–9	CD10 CD20 CD30
RTA 1988, s.3A	Causing death by careless driving when under the influence of drink or drugs	14 years or a fine or both	Obligatory	3–9	CD40 CD50 CD60 CD70 CD71
RTA 1988, s.3ZB	Causing death by driving unlicensed, disqualified or uninsured drivers	(a) summarily: 12 months or the statutory maximum or both (b) on indictment: 2 years or a fine or both	Obligatory	3–11	CD90
RTA 1988, s.4(1)	Driving or attempting to drive when unfit to drive through drink or drugs	6 months or a fine on level 5 or both	Obligatory	3–11	DR20 DR80
RTA 1988, s.4(2)	Being in charge of a mechanically propelled vehicle when unfit to drive through drink or drugs	3 months or level 4 or both	Discretionary	10	DR50
RTA 1988, s.5(1)(a)	Driving or attempting to drive with excess alcohol in breath, blood or urine	6 months or level 5 or both	Obligatory	3–11	DR10
RTA 1988, s.5(1)(b)	Being in a charge of a motor vehicle with excess alcohol in breath, blood or urine	3 months or level 4 or both	Discretionary	10	DR40
RTA 1988, s.6(4)	Failing to co-operate with preliminary test	Level 3	Discretionary	4	DR70

Statute	Offence	Details	Disqualification	Period (years)	Code
RTA 1988, s.7	Failing to provide specimen for analysis or laboratory test	Where specimen required to ascertain ability to drive at the time offender was driving or attempting to drive, 6 months or level 5 or both	Obligatory	3–11	DR30 DR60
		In any other case, 3 months or level 4 or both	Discretionary	10	
RTA 1988, s.7A	Failing to allow specimen to be subjected to laboratory test	(a) Where the test would be for ascertaining ability to drive or proportion of alcohol at the time offender was driving or attempting to drive, 6 months or level 5 or both	Obligatory	3–11	
		(b) in any other case, 3 months or level 4 or both	Discretionary	10	
RTA 1988, s.12	Motor racing and speed trials on public ways	Level 4	Obligatory	3–11	MS50
RTA 1988, s.22	Leaving vehicle in dangerous position	Level 3	Discretionary if committed in respect of motor vehicle	3	MS10
RTA 1988, s.23	Carrying passenger on motor cycle contrary to s.23	Level 3	Discretionary	3	MS20

Provision creating offence	General nature of offence	Maximum penalty	Disqualification	Penalty points	Code
RTA 1988, s.35	Failing to comply with traffic directions	Level 3	Discretionary if committed in respect of a motor vehicle by failure to comply with direction of constable or traffic warden	3	TS10 TS20 TS30 TS40 TS50
RTA 1988, s.36	Failure to comply with traffic sign	Level 3	Discretionary if committed in respect of a motor vehicle by failure to comply with signs specified in the regulations	3	
RTA 1988, s.40A	Using vehicle in dangerous condition	Level 3 if committed in respect of a goods vehicle or vehicle adapted to carry more than 8 passengers Level 4 in any other case	Obligatory if committed within 3 years of a previous conviction of the offender under s.40A Discretionary in any other case	3	CU20
RTA 1988, s.41A	Defective brakes, steering gear or tyres	Level 5 if committed in respect of goods vehicles or a vehicle adapted to carry more than 8 passengers Level 4 in any other case	Discretionary	3	CU10 CU30 CU40
RTA 1998, s.41B	Breach of requirement as to weight, goods and passengers				CU50 CU60

Statute	Offence	Maximum penalty	Disqualification	Penalty points	Code
RTA 1988, s.87(1)	Driving otherwise than in accordance with licence	Level 3	Discretionary in a case where the offender's driving would not have been in accordance with any licence that could have been granted to him	3–6	TS40 TS50 LC10
RTA 1988, s.92(10)	Driving after making false declaration as to physical fitness	Level 4	Discretionary	3–6	LC30
RTA 1988, s.94(3A)	Driving after failing to notify SofS of onset of or deterioration in, relevant or prospective disability	Level 3	Discretionary	3–6	LC40
RTA 1988, s.94A	Driving after refusal, revocation etc. of licence	6 months or level 4 or both	Discretionary	3–6	LC50
RTA 1988, s.96	Driving with uncorrected defective eyesight etc.	Level 3	Discretionary	3	MS40
RTA 1988, s.103(1)(b)	Driving whilst disqualified	6 months or level 5 or both	Discretionary	6	BA10 BA20
RTA 1988, s.143	Using uninsured	Level 5	Discretionary	6–8	IN10
RTA 1988, s.170(4)	Failing to stop, report, after accident	6 months or level 5 or both	Discretionary	5–10	AC10 AC20 AC30

Provision creating offence	General nature of offence	Maximum penalty	Disqualification	Penalty points	Code
RTA 1988, s.173	Failure of keeper of vehicle to give information	Level 3	Discretionary if committed otherwise than by virtue of subs. (5) or (11)	3	MS90
OAPA 1861, s.35	Furious driving		Discretionary	3–9	DD90
	Stealing or attempting to steal a motor vehicle		Discretionary		UT20
TA 1968, s.12	Offence or attempt of taking conveyance etc		Discretionary		UT10
TA 1968, s.25	Going equipped etc. committed with reference to the theft or taking of motor vehicles		Discretionary		UT30

The use of a compulsory admission under RTA 1988, s.172(2)(b) of having been the driver of a vehicle at the time of the commission of a road traffic offence does not infringe an accused's privilege against self-incrimination or his right to a fair trial under the European Convention, art.6: *DPP v Wilson* [2002] R.T.R. 6, cf. *Brown v Procurator Fiscal, The Times*, February 1, 2000.

6.   Repeated offences – penalty points

General

33–028   Under the penalty points system, an offender who commits a series of offences within a period of three years *must* be disqualified because of his repeated offending, whether or not the particular offence before the court would, in itself, justify disqualification.

RTOA 1988,
ss.28–31, 35;

It should be noted that:

(1) the system applies only to offences carrying obligatory disqualification in respect of an order made under RTOA 1988, s.34, as amended by RTA 1991, Sch.4, para.95 or to discretionary disqualification and obligatory endorsement as set out above;

(2) it applies in relation to an offence committed by aiding and abetting, etc. the commission of an offence such as is described in (1) above as if the offence involved discretionary disqualification;

(3) **if the court disqualifies the offender for his offence,** *no penalty points* **fall to be endorsed on his licence**; if he is not disqualified they are, unless there are special reasons for not doing so; where a driver is disqualified under RTOA 1988, s.34 and has to be dealt with on the same occasion for another road traffic offence carrying an obligatory endorsement, the endorsement under s.44 should be limited to the particulars of the conviction and should not include particulars of the offence or the penalty points attributable to the offence (*Martin v DPP* [2000] 2 Cr. App. R.(S.) 18);

(4) if the offender is convicted, whether on the same occasion or not, of two or more offences committed on the same occasion and involving obligatory endorsement, **the total number of penalty points to be attributed to them is the number that would be attributed on a conviction for one of them (the most serious).** Thus if the convictions are on separate occasions, the number to be attributed on later occasions is thereby restricted; but if (4) would ordinarily apply to two or more offences, the judge may still, if he thinks fit, decide that it will not apply to the offences, but must state his reasons for so doing in open court and enter those reasons in the record;

(5) once an offender is disqualified, the "slate is wiped clean" of all penalty points accumulated up to the time of disqualification (see *R. v Brentwood JJ. Ex p Richardson* (1992) 95 Cr. App. R. 187).

The references in the text in bold type emphasise matters found by CACD to be ignored or not sufficiently appreciated in the Crown Court (see, in particular, *R. v Kent* (1983) 77 Cr. App. R. 120).

Reduced penalty points for attendance on course

33–029   Where a person is convicted of certain specified offences (see below); and:

RTOA 1988,
s.30A

(1) penalty points are to be attributed to the offence and the court does not order him to be disqualified; and

(2) at least seven but no more than 11 penalty points are to be taken into account on the occasion of the conviction,

the court may order that three of the penalty points attributed to the offence (or all of them if three or fewer are so attributed) shall not be taken into account under s.29(1)(b) on the occasion of any conviction of an offence after the end of the period of 12 months beginning with the date of the order, if, by the relevant date, the offender completes an approved course.

The specified offences are those under RTA 1988, s.3 (careless or inconsiderate driving), RTA 1988, s.36 (failing to comply with a traffic sign), RTRA 1984, s.17(4) (use of special roads) and RTRA 1984, s.89(1) (excess speed).

Repeated offences; disqualification

33–030 Disqualification under the penalty points system arises where the offender has, as a result of an offence committed within the three-year period, accumulated a total of 12 or more penalty points, including those to be endorsed on the instant occasion: *(RTOA 1988, s.35)*

(1) if, taking the current offence into account, but disregarding any offence for which he is disqualified under RTOA 1988, s.34, the number of penalty points over the three-year period comes to 12 points or more, the disqualification is obligatory unless there are "mitigating circumstances";

(2) the qualifying date for both the earlier and the current offences is the *date of the offence*, not the date of conviction;

(3) where the offender is convicted on *the same occasion* of more than one offence involving obligatory or discretionary disqualification, **not more than one "totting up" disqualification may be imposed, and it must be allocated to a single offence**;

(4) the *minimum period* for which such a person is to be disqualified varies according to whether he has been previously disqualified during the three years preceding the commission of the latest offence in respect of which penalty points are being taken into account. If:

    (a) there are no such disqualifications, the minimum period is *six months*;

    (b) if there is one—*12 months*; and

    (c) if there are two or more, the minimum period is *two years*.

As to the appropriate mandatory extension period under RTOA 1988, s.35A, inserted by CorJa 2009, s.120, see 33–023 above). *(RTOA 1988, s.36)*

Disqualifications by the Crown Court under PCC(S)A 2000, s.147 or interim disqualifications by a magistrates' court pending committal to the Crown Court (RTOA 1988, s.26), are not included (PCC(S)A 2000, s.147).

Mitigating circumstances

33–031 The judge may disqualify such an offender under the totting up provisions for a period below the minimum required under the system, or may decide not to disqualify at all, where he is satisfied that there are, **and states, the grounds** for mitigating the normal consequences of conviction, but may *not* do so where the offence is one carrying obligatory disqualification (see also *R. v Thomas* (1984) 78 Cr. App. R. 55).

"Mitigating circumstances" are not to be equated with "special reasons" (see below). The former will, in the ordinary way, be largely circumstances pertaining to the offender, and concerned not with the gravity of the offence, but with the repetition of offences within a comparatively short period.

The statute expressly excludes from consideration any circumstances:

(1) that are alleged to make the offence(s) not serious; or
(2) that show hardship, short of "exceptional hardship"; or
(3) which have been taken into consideration already on another occasion within the three years immediately preceding the conviction.

The test of "exceptional hardship" is not the same as that for "special reasons". The judge does not need to hear sworn evidence, although obviously it will usually be desirable to do so (*Owen v Jones* [1988] R.T.R. 102). Where an offender seeks to contend that mitigating grounds which he is putting forward are other and different from those put forward to some other court within the three-year period, it is for him to prove that they are different, by reference to that court's record or by calling evidence (*R. v Sandbach JJ. Ex p. Pescud* (1983) 5 Cr. App. R.(S.) 177).

Where no mitigating circumstances exist the offender must be disqualified

33–032   The references in the text in bold type emphasise matters found by CACD to be ignored or not sufficiently appreciated in the Crown Court (see, in particular, *R. v Kent* (1983) 77 Cr. App. R. 120).

Discretionary disqualification and totting up

33–033   Where an offender commits a motoring offence which attracts discretionary disqualification when he may also be liable for obligatory disqualification under the totting up provisions, the judge should use his discretion to consider:

(1) whether the offence itself should attract discretionary disqualification, in the light of the offender's whole record, for the repetition is an aspect of the offence, as are the facts of the case before him;
(2) whether he should have a longer disqualification than the Act provides, then the judge may, instead of disqualifying him on the offence, add the appropriate points to his licence, thus leading to a totting up disqualification under s.34: *Jones v DPP* [2001] RTR 8.

7. Driving test order

General

33–034 Where:

RTOA 1988,
s.36

(1) an offender:
(a) is disqualified on conviction of manslaughter, or of an offence under RTA 1988, ss.1 or 2; or
(b) is disqualified under s.3A (death by careless driving whilst under the influence of drink or drugs) where the offence is committed on or after January 31, 2002; or
(c) is disqualified under RTA 1988, ss.34 or 35; or
(d) is convicted of such other offence involving obligatory disqualification as the Secretary of State may prescribe,

the judge must (whether or not the offender has previously passed a test (*R. v Miller* (1994) 15 Cr. App. R.(S.) 505)) order him to be disqualified until he passes the "appropriate driving test";

(2) persons have been convicted of any other offence involving obligatory *endorsement* the court *may* make such an order (whether or not he has previously passed any test).

An "appropriate driving test" means:

(a) in such circumstances as the Secretary of State may prescribe, an extended driving test; and
(b) otherwise, a test of competence to drive which is not an extended driving test.

The judge is bound, in deciding whether to make an order, to have regard to the safety of other road users.

Such a disqualification does not expire until proof of the passing of the test is delivered to the Secretary of State.

The superior courts have emphasised on a number of occasions (the most recent of which are *R. v Peat* (1984) 6 Cr. App. R.(S.) 311 and *R. v Lazzari* (1984) 6 Cr. App. R.(S.) 83), that such an order is *not* intended as a punishment, but to protect the public against incompetent drivers including those not having regard for other road users (*R. v Bannister* (1990-91) 12 Cr. App. R.(S.) 314).

Unless obligatory, the power should be exercised only where there is reason to doubt the offender's competence to drive, whether through age, infirmity or the circumstances of the offence.

When sentencing for aggravated vehicle taking it is inappropriate to order a passenger to take an extended driving test at the end of a period of disqualification (see *R. v Bradshaw* [2001] R.T.R.4).

Notification of disability

33–035 Where, in any proceedings for an offence committed in respect of a motor vehicle, it appears to the judge that the accused may be suffering from any relevant disability, or prospective disability, within the meaning of RTA 1988, Pt III, he must notify the Secretary of State.

If there is evidence that an offender is liable to recurring bouts of an illness, such as hypomania, but is otherwise competent to drive, this is the course to take rather than to make a driving test order (*Hughes v Challes* (1983) 5 Cr. App. R.(S.) 374).

8.   Proceedings after disqualification; suspension; removal

General
33–036   The giving of notice of appeal does not operate to suspend the order of disqualification. If the order is to be suspended, it must be done by judicial act.

If an offender gives notice of appeal, or of his intention to apply for judicial review:

(1) the judge may, if he thinks fit, suspend any disqualification pending appeal;
(2) any disqualification, whether obligatory or discretionary, may be suspended:
   (a) by the Crown Court, where the offender appeals to it against conviction or sentence;
   (b) by CACD where the offender appeals, or applies for leave to appeal, against conviction or sentence;
   (c) by the High Court, where the offender applies to the magistrates to state a case under MCA 1980, s.87; or
   (d) by the High Court, where the offender applies, or applies for leave to apply, for a quashing order in respect of the proceedings before the magistrates' court.

Removal; procedure
33–037   A person disqualified by order of the court may apply to the court which made the order to remove it, provided that: *RTOA 1988, s.48*

(1) two years have elapsed, if the disqualification was for less than four years; or
(2) half the period has elapsed, if the disqualification was for not less than four and not more than 10 years; or
(3) five years have elapsed in any other case.

The judge, as he thinks fit, having regard to the character of the applicant and his subsequent conduct, the nature of the offence and any other circumstances:

(a) may, by order, remove the disqualification from such date as he may specify; or
(b) may refuse the application; but
(c) must *not* add to it any conditions or additional requirements (*R. v Bentham* (1981) 3 Cr. App. R.(S.) 229).

Application should be made to the location of the Crown Court where   *R.55.1*
the order of disqualification was made. An offender who wants the court to exercise the power of removal must apply in writing, no earlier than the date on which the court can exercise the power, serving the application on the Crown Court officer, specifying the disqualification that he

wants the court to remove, and explaining why. The Crown Court officer will serve a copy of the application on the chief officer of police for the local justice area.

There is no power in removing a disqualification, to remove a driving test order.

If the application is granted, the applicant may be ordered to pay the whole or any part of the costs. Where the application is refused, a further three months must elapse before another is entertained.

These provisions do not differentiate between discretionary and obligatory disqualification, and there is nothing in law to prevent the court removing an obligatory disqualification although, if it thinks fit, the court may regard it as one which it is somewhat less ready to remove than a discretionary disqualification (*Damer v Davison* (1975) 61 Cr. App. R. 232).

9. Special reasons

General

33–038   Before the court can justify, for special reasons, not disqualifying for an offence where it is otherwise obligatory, or disqualifying for a period shorter than the statutory minimum, or for not ordering endorsement, four conditions must be fulfilled. These are that the facts advanced:

(1) must amount to mitigating or extenuating circumstances;
(2) must *not* amount to a defence to the charge;
(3) must be directly connected with the commission of the offence; and
(4) must be matters which can properly be taken into account when imposing punishment (*R. v Wickens* (1958) 42 Cr. App. R. 236; *Myles v DPP* [2004] EWHC 594 (Admin); [2004] 2 All E.R. 902).

The judge **must state openly** any grounds for finding that special reasons exist for mitigating the statutory penalty.

Note that:

(a) the mere fact that the circumstances disclose a special reason does not, of itself, mean that the offender is entitled, as a matter of course, to escape disqualification; there is a serious burden on a court to decide, in its discretion, whether to refrain from disqualifying (*Taylor v Rajan* (1974) 59 Cr App. R. 11) and that discretion should be exercised only in clear and compelling circumstances (*Vaughan v Dunn* [1984] R.T.R. 376; *DPP v Bristow* [1998] R.T.R. 100);
(b) even where the above conditions are fulfilled, there may be some over-riding factor which precludes the court from regarding as "special reasons" some circumstance which at first appeared to fall within the scope of the four preconditions (*Delaroy-Hall v Tadman* (1969) 53 Cr. App. R. 143).

In an excess alcohol case where the court found special reasons, and where it was not suggested that the actual driving undertaken or even attempted could have posed any appreciable risk of danger to anyone it would be hard to justify a period of disqualification in excess of the mandatory 12 months (*R. v St Albans Crown Court Ex p. O'Donovan* [2000] 1 Cr. App. R.(S.) 344, DC).

The court is concerned not with the special reason that caused the offender to take his car onto the road, but with the special reason for not disqualifying or for imposing a lesser disqualification.

Special to the offence

33–039   The need for the facts to be directly connected with the commission of the offence, means that the facts put forward as a special reason must be "special", in contrast with those that are general, and special to the *offence* rather than to the offender. It is because of this that special reasons are not to be found in the following circumstances (for example), that:

(1) the offender is a professional driver (*Whittal v Kirby* (1947) 111 J.P. 1), or has been driving for many years without complaint (*Lines v Hersom* [1951] 2 All ER 650), or is a careful person who would never have risked driving had he realised his condition (*Newnham v Trigg* [1970] R.T.R. 107);

(2) the offender is disabled and had no other means of getting home (*Mullarkey v Prescott* [1970] R.T.R. 296), or relies on his vehicle for transport (*R. v Jackson, R. v Hart* (1969) 53 Cr. App. R. 341), or that disqualification will cause him serious hardship and/or hardship to his family (*Rennison v Knowler* [1947] 1 All ER 302; *Taylor v Austin* [1969] 1 All ER 544; *Reynolds v Roche* [1972] R.T.R. 282; *East v Bladen* (1986) 8 Cr App R.(S.) 186);

(3) the offender is a doctor, and the medical services in his area will deteriorate by reason of his being unable to drive (*Holroyd v Berry* [1973] R.T.R. 145), or a soldier on active service who must be in a position to drive (*Gordon v Smith* [1971] R.T.R. 52), or that the offender is a detective engaged in "undercover" activities which involve visiting public houses (*Vaughan v Dunn* [1984] R.T.R. 376);

(4) the offender has an idiosyncratic medical condition or diabetes (*R. v Wickins* (1958) 42 Cr. App. R. 236; *R. v Jackson, R. v Hart* (above); *Jarvis v DPP* (2001) 165 JP 15);

(5) the offender has to drive because of his domestic situation (*Reynolds v Roche* [1972] R.T.R. 282).

Even less is it any sort of special reason that the court considers the penalty of disqualification too severe (*Williamson v Wilson* [1947] 1 All E.R. 306) or unfair (*Boliston v Gibbons* (1984) 6 Cr. App. R.(S.) 134). The fact that the offence is a trivial one is not a special reason for not *endorsing*, but the court is always entitled to take account of the minor nature of the offence, and the fact that any breach was unintentional (*Hawkins v Roots, Hawkins v Smith* [1976] R.T.R. 49). An incorrect statement by a police officer to the effect that failing to provide a specimen of blood or urine would not necessarily result in disqualification which misled the defendant into refusing to supply such a specimen, can amount to a special reason (*Bobin v DPP* [1999] R.T.R. 375).

Excess alcohol offences

33–040   The vast majority of cases in which offenders seek to put forward special reasons, are those relating to excess alcohol. In deciding whether special reasons exist and whether to exercise discretion the court should consider what would a sober, reasonable and responsible friend of the defendant advise: drive or not? Discretion should be exercised in favour of the driver only if there was a real possibility rather than a mere off-chance that the friend would advise the driver to drive (*DPP v Bristow*, [1998] R.T.R. 100). The views of the superior courts over a number of years, when analysed, are that in relation to such offences:

(1) in a case under RTA 1988, ss.4, 5 and 7(6), it must be borne in mind that a person who deliberately drives, knowing that he has consumed a considerable quantity of alcohol, presents a potential danger to the public, which no private crisis can lightly excuse;

(2) in a case under s.5, the amount of excess, however small, is not capable of amounting to a special reason—the Act lays down the prescribed statutory limit (*Delaroy Hall v Tadman*, above);

(3) the effect of lack of food, or the effect of drink on an empty stomach, is not capable of amounting to a special reason, whether under s.4 or s.5 (*Archer v Woodward* [1959] Crim. L.R. 461; *Knight v Baxter* [1971] R.T.R. 270; *Kinsella v DPP* [2002] EWHC 545 (Admin));

(4) the fact that an offender, unknown to him, was suffering from a disease which produced a greater degree of unfitness than would be present in a normal person, might amount to a special reason under s.4 (*R. v Wickins* (1958) 42 Cr. App. R. 236, but see *DPP v Jowle* (1999) 163 JP 85), as might the fact that he had inhaled industrial fumes at work (*Brewer v MPC* (1969) 53 Cr. App. R. 157), but such factors are irrelevant on a conviction under s.5 (*Goldsmith v Laver* [1970] R.T.R. 162); see also *DPP v Jowle* (above) (mouthwash containing 26.9 per cent alcohol); cf. *R. v Cambridge MC Ex p Wong* [1992] R.T.R. 382; a motorist has a duty to enquire what he is drinking (*Robinson v DPP* [2003] EWHC 2718 (Admin); [2004] Crim. L.R. 670);

(5) the court should rarely, if ever, exercise its discretion in favour of an offender where the alcohol content exceeded 100 mg per 100 ml of blood (*Taylor v. Rajan* (1974) 59 Cr. App. R. 11, 15; *Vaughan v Dunn* [1984] R.T.R. 376);

(6) the fact that the offender offered a specimen of urine when blood was required of him cannot be taken into account as a special reason (*Grix v Chief Constable of Kent* [1987] R.T.R. 193); and

(7) it is difficult to conceive of a special reason in relation to a contravention of s.7(6) (*R. v Jackson, R. v Hart* (1969) 53 Cr. App. R. 341, but see *DPP v Kinnersley* (1993) 14 Cr. App. R.(S.) 516 (genuine fear of contracting AIDS by blowing into machine)).

A gloss on (4) above is provided by the cases of *Woolfe v DPP* [2006] EWHC 1497 (Admin) where the offender suffered from a medical condition whereby alcohol was regurgitated from his stomach into his mouth, thereby making it possible that the reading was erroneous, and *O Sang Ng v DPP* [2007] EWHC 36 (Admin); [2007] RTR 35, where the reading may have been affected by belching.

Sudden emergencies

33–041   A sudden emergency may amount to a special reason in cases under ss.4 and 5, as where an unexpected situation arises in which a person who has been drinking but not intending to drive, is impelled to do so by a sudden medical necessity, or in answering an emergency call (*Aichroth v Cottee* [1954] 2 All ER 856; *Brown v Dyerson* (1968) 52 Cr. App. R. 630; *R. v Lundt-Smith* (1964) 128 J.P. 534; *R. v O'Toole* (1971) 55 Cr. App. R. 206).

A burglary at club premises where the driver was a keyholder has been held to be an emergency sufficient to justify a finding of special reasons (*DPP v Cox* [1996] R.T.R. 123, DC).

A threat by a woman to accuse a man of rape unless he drove to a cash point in order to give her money and then drove her home, amounted to special reasons (*DPP v Enston* [1996] R.T.R. 324). See also *DPP v Upchurch* [1994] R.T.R. 366; *DPP v Knight* [1994] R.T.R. 374; *DPP v Whittle* [1996] R.T.R. 154.

In dealing with such cases, the superior courts have said that the whole of the circumstances should be considered, including the nature and degree of the crisis or emergency which caused the offender to take his car onto the road, and:

(1) whether the emergency was sufficiently acute to justify the offender taking out his car;
(2) whether there were alternative means of transport available, or alternative means of dealing with the crisis;
(3) the manner of the offender's driving, the commission of traffic offences may be a consideration telling against exercise of the court's discretion; and
(4) whether the offender otherwise acted responsibly and reasonably.

These matters need to be considered objectively (*Taylor v Rajan* (1974) 59 Cr. App. R. 11, 15; *DPP v Bristow* [1998] R.T.R. 100), and it is not for the court to put itself into the offender's position in assessing "reasonableness". A driver complaining of dizziness and blurred vision did not constitute a medical emergency sufficient to justify a finding of special reasons where the passenger, her husband, who was affected by drink, decided to take over the driving (*DPP v Whittle* [1996] R.T.R. 154, DC). There is a difference in a situation presented to a driver on the outward journey and that on the homeward journey after the emergency has been dealt with (*DPP v Waller* [1989] R.T.R. 112).

It is unlikely that merely travelling to a near relative because of some emotional need will ever be able to amount to a special reason (*Thompson v Diamond* [1985] R.T.R. 316).

DRIVING DISQUALIFICATION

"Laced drinks" case

33–042 It is often put forward in excess alcohol cases that the offender's drink had been "laced" by a third party, in order to found a special reason on the ground that the drink which the offender consumed was stronger or more potent than he had anticipated. It is not enough to show that the drink was stronger than he thought.

To be capable of amounting to a special reason:

(1) there must be an element of intervention or misleading by a third party, whereby the offender was induced to take stronger drink than he would normally have done by someone who misled him, or gave him false information;

(2) it must be shown (*Pugsley v Hunter* [1973] R.T.R. 284; *Smith v Geraghty* [1986] R.T.R. 222) and the burden is on the offender to show, that the quantity of alcohol in his blood in excess of the prescribed limit:

   (a) is attributable to additional drink; and

   (b) was put into his glass without his knowledge—this will inevitably involve scientific evidence.

The judge must decide:

   (i) whether the facts are capable of amounting to a special reason; and

   (ii) additionally, whether the offender should have realised, when he came to drive, that he was not fit to do so by reason of the alcohol present in his body (*Pridige v Grant* [1985] R.T.R. 196; *DPP v Barker* [1990] R.T.R. 1; *Donahue v DPP* [1993] R.T.R. 156). See also *DPP v Connor* [1992] R.T.R. 66.

It is undesirable for the court to let itself be drawn into detailed scientific calculations, even where these are put before it by expert witnesses (*Smith v Geraghty* [1986] R.T.R. 222).

Factors to be considered

33–043 It was suggested in *Chatters v Burke* (1986) 8 Cr. App. R. (S.) 222 that there were seven factors to be considered and taken into account when deciding whether there were special reasons for mitigating the normal consequences of a conviction, namely:

(1) how far was the vehicle driven?;

(2) in what manner was it driven?;

(3) the state of the vehicle;

(4) whether it was the offender's intention to go further;

(5) the conditions of road and traffic prevailing;

(6) the reason for the car being driven; and

(7) most importantly of all, whether there was a danger of the offender's coming into contact with pedestrians or other road users.

The mere fact that the offence occurred late at night, at a time and place where there were not many people about, or that the offender was merely re-parking, is not of itself capable of amounting to a special reason for not disqualifying. It might, however, amount to a special reason to show that the offender drove only a few yards in circumstances where his manoeuvres were unlikely to bring him into contact with other road users (*Mullarkey v Prescott* [1970] R.T.R. 296; *Coombs v Kehoe* [1972] 1 W.L.R. 797; and cf. *Haime v Walklett* (1983) 5 Cr. App. R.(S.) 165) but cf. *DPP v Humphries* [2000] R.T.R. 52, where the offender's intention was to drive some distance had he not been apprehended; see also *DPP v Conroy* [2003] EWHC 1674 [2004] 1 Cr. App. R.(S.) 37).

Proof of special reasons

33–044   The burden of proving circumstances amounting to a special reason lies upon the offender; the standard is that of a "balance of probabilities". The court should take into account, any:

(1) relevant admissible evidence, given on oath;
(2) any admissions made in accordance with CJA 1967, s.10;
(3) any "expert reports" tendered and admissible by virtue of CJA 1988, s.30; and
(4) any submissions made by the Crown and/or defence counsel, but evidence from the offender as to what he has heard since the incident, does not qualify (*James v Morgan* [1988] R.T.R. 85).

10.   New drivers

General

33–045   The Road Traffic (New Drivers) Act 1995 provides for the revocation of the driving licences of new drivers who accumulate six or more penalty points within a probationary period of two years after the driver first qualified. A driver whose licence is thus revoked must pass a further test to regain his entitlement to drive.

Notes

34. EUROPEAN COURT

34–001   Under the EEC Treaty, art.177, the European Court of Justice has jurisdiction, among other things, to give preliminary rulings concerning the interpretation of the Treaty, the validity or interpretation of Acts of the institutions of the Community, and the interpretation of the statutes of bodies established by an act of the Council, where these statutes so provide.

Where a question of such nature is raised before any court or tribunal of a member state, then it may, if it considers that a decision on a question of law is necessary to enable it to give judgment, request the Court of Justice to give a ruling.

The Crown Court is a "court or tribunal" falling within art.177, and a judge of the Crown Court has a discretion to refer a question if he considers it "necessary" to enable him to give judgment.

Courses open to the court
34–002   The European Communities Act 1972 requires Community law to be treated as a question of law, not one of fact which requires proof by a skilled witness. It is ordinarily applied like any domestic law. If a question of interpretation arises, and the judge is satisfied that there is a real doubt as to the law, which must be settled before the case is decided, three courses are open to him:

(1) usually, particularly in trials on indictment, he may decide the question himself, leaving an appellate court to refer any question to the European Court;

(2) in an appeal from a magistrates' court, he may state a case for the opinion of the High Court, leaving that court to refer any question to the European Court; or

(3) he may refer the matter himself to the European Court.

This last option, which is likely to be impracticable in most cases in the Crown Court, is not an appeal. The European Court does not decide the case; it gives a ruling, binding on all courts in the Community.

Approach to reference
34–003   Ordinarily, a court should exercise considerable caution before referring a question of Community law, and should certainly not do so before all the evidence has been called, and there is no possibility of an acquittal on the facts. It is better for the judge to form his own view, and if his decision is questioned, the appellate court will usually be in a better position to assess the appropriateness of, and to formulate, the question to be referred (*R. v Plymouth JJ. Ex p. Rogers* [1982] Q.B. 863).

Procedure
34–004   An order submitting a request for a preliminary ruling may be made by the judge on application by a party, or on his own initiative,

R.75

and he may give directions for the preparation of the terms of such a request.

The following matters must be included in such a request:

    (i)   the identity of the court making the request,

    (ii) the parties' identities,

    (iii) a statement of whether a party is in custody,

    (iv) a succinct statement of the question on which the judge seeks the ruling of the European Court,

    (v) a succinct statement of any opinion on the answer that he may have expressed in any judgment that he has delivered,

    (vi) a summary of the nature and history of the proceedings, including the salient facts and an indication of whether those facts are proved, admitted or assumed,

    (vii) the relevant rules of national law,

    (viii) a summary of the relevant contentions of the parties,

    (ix) an indication of the provisions of European Union law that the European Court is asked to interpret, and

    (x) an explanation of why a ruling of the European Court is requested.

The request should be expressed in terms that can be translated readily into other languages, and should be set out in a schedule to the order.

The Crown Court officer will serve the order for the submission of the request on the Senior Master of the QBD, who will submit the request to the European Court. Unless the court otherwise directs, he will postpone the submission of the request until the time for any appeal against the order has expired, and any appeal against the order has been determined.

Where the judge orders the submission of a request, the general rule is that he will adjourn or postpone any further hearing, but he may otherwise direct.

See also *Practice Direction (ECJ reference procedure)* [1999] 1 Cr. App. R. 452 and PD 2004, I.10.).

35. FINANCIAL REPORTING ORDERS

Introduction

35–001 Where a person is convicted in the Crown Court of certain specified offences the judge may make a financial reporting order in respect of him, but only if he is satisfied that the risk of that person committing another such offence is sufficiently high to justify doing so.

SOCPA 2005, ss.76(1)–(3)

An order may not be made for the purposes of facilitating the enforcement of a confiscation order, but only if there is a risk of the offender committing further specified offences (*R. v Wright* [2009] 2 Cr. App. R.(S.) 45).

The specified offences are:

- an offence under either of the following provisions of Fr A 2006:
    s.1 (fraud); or
    s.11 (obtaining services dishonestly);

SOCPA 2005, ss.76(1)–(3)

- a common law offence of conspiracy to defraud;
- an offence under TA 1968, s.17 (false accounting);
- any offences specified in POCA 2002, Sch.2 ("lifestyle offences");
- a common law offence of bribery;
- an offence under the Public Bodies Corrupt Practices Act 1889, s.1 (corruption in office);
- the first two offences under the Prevention of Corruption Act 1906, s.1 (bribes obtained by or given to agents);
- an offence under any of the following provisions of CJA 1988:
    s.93A (assisting another to retain the benefit of criminal conduct);
    s.93B (acquisition, possession or use of proceeds of criminal conduct);
    s.93C (concealing or transferring proceeds of criminal conduct);
- an offence under any of the following provisions of DTA 1994:
    s.49 (concealing or transferring proceeds of drug trafficking);
    s.50 (assisting another person to retain the benefit of drug trafficking);
    s.51 (acquisition, possession or use of proceeds of drug trafficking);
- an offence under any of the following provisions of TerrA 2000:
    s.15 (fund-raising for purposes of terrorism);
    s.16 (use and possession of money etc. for purposes of terrorism);
    s.17 (funding arrangements for purposes of terrorism);
    s.18 (money laundering in connection with terrorism);
- an offence under POCA 2002, s.329 (acquisition, use and possession of criminal property);
- a common law offence of cheating in relation to the public revenue;

- an offence, under CEMA 1989, s.170 (fraudulent evasion of duty);
- an offence under VATA 1994, s.72 (offences relating to VAT);
- an offence under the Finance Act 2000, s.144 (fraudulent evasion of income tax);
- an offence under the Tax Credits Act 2002, s.35 (tax credit fraud);
- an offence of attempting, conspiring in or inciting the commission of the above;
- an offence of aiding, abetting, counselling or procuring the commission of an offence mentioned above.

Effect of order

35–002   A person in relation to whom an order is made must:

  (1) make a report, in respect of:

    (a) the period of a specified length beginning with the date on which the order comes into force; and

    (b) each subsequent period of that length beginning immediately after the end of the previous period;

  (2) set out in each report, in the specified manner, such particulars of his financial affairs relating to the period in question as may be specified;

  (3) include any specified documents with each report;

  (4) make each report within the specified number of days after the end of the period in question;

  (5) make each report to the specified person.

Rules may provide for the maximum length of the periods which may be specified; "specified" means specified by the court in the order.

The making of an order may be appealed under CAA 1968, s.9(1) (*R. v Adams* [2008] EWCA Crim 914; [2008] 4 All E.R. 574).

A person who without reasonable excuse includes false or misleading information in a report, or otherwise fails to comply with any requirement of this section, is guilty of an offence.

[margin: SOCPA 2005, ss.79(1)–(6), 79(7) (8)]

[margin: SOCPA 2008, s.79(10)]

Variation and revocation of order

35–003   An application for variation or revocation of an order may be made by either the person in respect of whom it was made, or the specified person to whom reports are to be made under it. The application must be made to the court which made the order, but if the order was made on appeal, the application must be made to the court which originally convicted the person in respect of whom the order was made. If (in either case) that court was a magistrates' court, the application may be made to any magistrates' court acting in the same local justice area as that court.

[margin: SOCPA 2005, s.80]

Verification and disclosure

35–004   SOCPA 2005, s.81 provides for the specified person, i.e. the person to whom reports under a financial reporting order are to be made, to verify the accuracy of any report made.

36. FINES AND ENFORCEMENT

Introduction
36–001 Financial penalties may be said to be three in number, namely: a fine, a compensation order, and an order to pay the costs of the prosecution. Although fines and other financial penalties do not restrict the offender's liberty in quite the same way as a community or custodial sentence, they deprive the offender of money and therefore the ability to spend that money in other ways.

The general power
36–002 Where a person is convicted on indictment of any offence other than an offence:

    CJA 2003, s.163

  (1) for which the sentence is fixed by law; or
  (2) falls to be imposed under PCC(S)A 2000, ss.109, where still appropriate, 110(2) or 111(2); (minimum required sentence) or
  (3) falls to be imposed under CJA 2003, ss.225(2), 226(2) (dangerous offender).

the judge, if not precluded from sentencing an offender by his exercise of some other power, may impose a fine:

  (a) instead of; or
  (b) in addition to,

dealing with him in any other way in which he has power to deal with him, subject to any enactment requiring the offender to be dealt with in a particular way.

On appeal from a magistrates' court, the powers of the Crown Court are those of the magistrates.

    CJA 1981, s.4(1)(b)

A person guilty of attempting to commit an offence is liable on conviction on indictment to any penalty to which he would have been liable on conviction for the full offence.

Duty to order payment of surcharge
36–003 The judge, in dealing with an offender, other than by means of an absolute discharge or an order under MHA 1983, for one or more offences committed on or after the April 1, 2007 *must also*, where he:

    CJA 2003, ss.163A, 163B

  (1) imposes a fine, whether or not in addition to a costs order; or
  (2) imposes a fine and makes a compensation order under PCC(S)A, s.130, whether or not in addition to a costs order,

order him to pay a surcharge in the prescribed amount. That amount is presently (SI 2007/707) £15.

Where the judge considers that:

  (a) it would be appropriate to make a compensation order; but

513

(b) the offender has insufficient means to pay both the surcharge and appropriate compensation,

the surcharge must be reduced accordingly, if necessary to nil.

The standard scale

36–004 Where reference is made to the "standard scale" of fines, the standard scale is as follows: CJA 1982, .s37

Level on the scale	Amount of fine
1	£200
2	£500
3	£1,000
4	£2,500
5	£5,000

Proper approach to financial penalty

36–005 The amount of any fine fixed must be such as, in the judge's opinion, reflects the seriousness of the offence, but in fixing the amount, he must: CJA 2003, ss.164(3), (4)

(1) in the case of an individual offender, inquire into his financial circumstances; and
(2) whether the offender is an individual or other person, take into account the circumstances of the case including, amongst other things, the financial circumstances of the offender, so far as they are known, or appear to him,

and (2) above applies whether it has the effect of increasing or reducing the amount.

It is wrong to impose a fine upon an offender of substantial means for an offence for which one of lesser means would go to prison (*R. v Lewis* [1965] Crim. L.R. 121); conversely it is wrong to imprison an offender because he is unable to pay a substantial fine (*R. v Reeves* (1972) 56 Cr. App. R. 366).

In applying subs.(3), the judge must not reduce the amount of a fine on account of any surcharge he orders the offender to pay under CJA 2003, s.161A, except to the extent that he has insufficient means to pay both.   CJA 2003, s.164(4A)

Ability to pay; means

36–006 The overriding principle in relation to the imposition of a fine is that the fine imposed should be within the offender's ability to pay.

It should be remembered that:

(1) it is wrong to scale up a fine in the case of an unusually affluent offender (*R. v Fairbairn* (1980) 2 Cr. App. R.(S.) 315);
(2) it may be necessary to scale down an otherwise appropriate fine if the sum is more than the offender can be fairly required to pay within a reasonable time; and
(3) despite a number of pronouncements to the contrary, CACD in *R. v Olliver* (1989) 11 Cr. App. R.(S.) 10, said that there was no

reason in principle why an order to pay a fine by monthly instalments should not extend for two or even three years.

Clearly, unless the circumstances warrant it, an offender should not be fined more heavily merely because he has elected trial by jury; this is a matter which can be dealt with by an order for costs (*R. v Jamieson* (1974) 60 Cr. App. R. 318).

A fine should not, of course, be imposed on the basis that someone other than the offender is going to pay it on his behalf (*R. v Baxter* [1974] Crim. L.R. 611) let alone on the basis that the public should be reimbursed for any possible claim made on the Criminal Injuries Compensation Board (*R. v Roberts* (1980) 2 Cr. App. R.(S.) 121).

Corporations; health and safety legislation

36–007 Fines imposed on large **corporations,** particularly in relation to breach of health and safety legislation where death or serious injury results, are in a class of their own. In such a case the fine needs to be large enough to bring the message home not only to those that manage the corporation but also to its shareholders (*R. v Rimac Ltd* [2000] 1 Cr. App. R.(S.) 468). The fine may reflect public disquiet at the unnecessary loss of life.

In relation to offences of corporate manslaughter and health and safety offences causing death, see the Definitive Guidelines at SGC 2010. As to the approach to environmental pollution, see *Re Thames Water* [2010] 3 All E.R. 47.

SGC 2010 makes the following points (paras 22–26):

There will inevitably be a broad range of fines because of the range of seriousness involved and the differences in the circumstances of the defendants. Fines must be punitive and sufficient to have an impact on the defendant.

Fines cannot and do not attempt to value a human life in money. Civil compensation will be payable separately. The fine is designed to punish the offender and is therefore tailored not only to what it has done but also to its individual circumstances.

The offence of corporate manslaughter, because it requires gross breach at a senior level, will ordinarily involve a level of seriousness significantly greater than a health and safety offence. The appropriate fine will seldom be less than £500,000 and may be measured in millions of pounds.

The range of seriousness involved in health and safety offences is greater than for corporate manslaughter. However, where the offence is shown to have caused death, the appropriate fine will seldom be less than £100,000 and may be measured in hundreds of thousands of pounds or more.

A plea of guilty should be recognised by the appropriate reduction.

SGC 2010 (para.24 suggests that observations in *Friskies Petcare (UK) Ltd* [2000] EWCA Crim 95; [2000] 2 Cr. App. R. (S.) 401 notwithstanding, it is no longer the case that fines of £500,000 are reserved for major public disasters.

The court should require what is known as "a Friskies Schedule" from the prosecutor setting out any aggravating features which may include resulting death or serious injury, failure to heed prior warnings or deliberate breaches with a view to cost-cutting or profit. Mitigating factors, which may include a good safety record, and remedying of any defects, ought also to be provided (see *R. v F Howe & Sons (Engineers) Ltd* (1999) 2 Cr. App. R.(S.) 37).

As to the approach to calculating the fine, see SGC 2010, and as to the financial information the judge may expect to be provided, see ibid Annex A.

Any award of costs may include the costs of the prosecuting authority's investigations (*R. v Associated Octel Ltd* [1997] 1 Cr. App. R.(S.) 435). Also SGC 2010, para.29.

There is no tariff. The principles and the authorities are reviewed in *R. v Bodycote HIP* [2010] EWCA Crim 802, [2011] 1 Cr. App. R.(S.) 6.

Financial circumstances order

36–008 Where an individual offender is convicted of an offence, the judge may, before sentencing him, make a financial circumstances order, requiring him to give to the court, within a specified period, such statement of his financial circumstances as the judge may require. Failure to comply is an offence. [CJA 2003, s.162]

Parents and guardians

36–009 For the enforcement of fines in respect of juvenile offenders against parents and guardians, see CHILDREN AND YOUNG PERSONS.

Time to pay: instalments

36–010 Where the judge imposes a fine he may make an order: [PCC(S)A 2000, s.139(1)]

(1) allowing time for the payment of the amount of the fine;
(2) directing payment of that amount by instalments of such amounts and on such dates as may be specified in the order,

and he must fix a term of imprisonment in default of payment, but no person may on the occasion when a fine is imposed on him by the Crown Court be committed to prison or detention unless:

(a) in the case of an offence punishable with imprisonment, he appears to the court to have sufficient means to pay forthwith;
(b) it appears to the judge that he is unlikely to remain long enough at a place of abode in the United Kingdom to enable the payment of the fine to be enforced by other methods; or
(c) on the occasion when the fine is imposed, the judge sentences him to an immediate prison sentence, custody for life, or detention in a young offender institution for that or another offence, or so sentences him for an offence in addition to forfeiting his recognisance, or he is already serving a sentence of custody for life or a term of imprisonment or detention.

Approach to order

36–011 When imposing a fine payable by instalments, with imprisonment in default, the proper course is for the judge to:

(1) impose the fine;

(2) fix an appropriate term in default of the *whole* amount; and

(3) make such an instalment order as he thinks fit (*R. v Cooper* (1982) 4 Cr. App. R.(S.) 55; *R. v Power* (1986) 8 Cr. App. R. (S.) 8).

Maximum terms in default

36–012   The maximum periods of imprisonment or detention under s.108, are:

PCC(S)A 2000, s.139(4)

An amount not exceeding £200	7 days
An amount exceeding £200 but not exceeding £500	14 days
An amount exceeding £500 but not exceeding £1,000	28 days
An amount exceeding £1,000 but not exceeding £2,500	45 days
An amount exceeding £2,500 but not exceeding £5,000	3 months
An amount exceeding £5,000 but not exceeding £10,000	6 months
An amount exceeding £10,000 but not exceeding £20,000	12 months
An amount exceeding £20,000 but not exceeding £50,000	18 months
An amount exceeding £50,000 but not exceeding £100,000	2 years
An amount exceeding £100,000 but not exceeding £250,000	3 years
An amount exceeding £250,000 but not exceeding £1 million	5 years
An amount exceeding £1 million	10 years

Custodial sentence and default terms

36–013   Where a person liable for the payment of a fine is sentenced to, or is serving, or is otherwise liable to, serve a term of imprisonment, the judge may order that any default term shall not begin to run until after the end of the first-mentioned term, nor is this power restricted by any enactment authorising the Crown Court to deal with an offender in any way the magistrates might have dealt with him or could deal with him.

PCC(S)A 2000, s.139(5), (7)

Where both the maximum sentence of imprisonment and a fine have been imposed for an offence, a further sentence of imprisonment may be imposed for default in payment of the fine (*R. v Carver* (1955) 39 Cr. App. R. 27).

Improper combinations

36–014   A fine may be imposed in addition to any other penalty except that a fine may not be imposed for the same offence as that on which the court makes an order for conditional or absolute discharge (see DISCHARGE: ABSOLUTE AND CONDITIONAL).

FINES AND ENFORCEMENT

Coupling a fine with a custodial sentence

36–015 Insofar as combining an immediate custodial sentence with a fine is concerned, while this may be permissible:

(1) it must be clear that the offender has the resources to arrange for payment even though he is to be in custody (*R. v Fairbairn* (1980) 2 Cr. App. R.(S.) 315);

(2) if this is not clear, then a fine ought not to be added (*R. v Maund* (1980) 2 Cr. App. R.(S.) 289); and

(3) it is appropriate if the general circumstances of the case show that the offender will continue to have access to the proceeds of his crime (*R. v Benmore* (1983) 5 Cr. App. R.(S.) 468).

Coupling a fine with an order for costs

36–016 The judge may both impose a fine and order the offender to pay the costs of the prosecution in an appropriate case. The principles governing such an order were reviewed in *R. v Northallerton MC Ex p. Dove* [2000] 1 Cr. App. R. (S.) 136.

(1) The judge must have regard to the means of the offender, and it is quite wrong to impose a very small fine and a very heavy order for costs—the two must go in step (*R. v Whalley* (1972) 56 Cr. App. R. 304; and see *R. v Firmston* (1984) 6 Cr. App. R.(S.) 189, *R. v Nottingham JJ Ex p. Fohmann* (1987) 84 Cr. App. R. 316; *R. v Jones* (1988) 10 Cr. App. R.(S.) 95, cf. *R. v Boyle* (1995) 16 Cr .App. R.(S.) 927).

(2) While there is no requirement that the costs should stand in any arithmetical relationship to the fine, the costs should not in the ordinary way be grossly disproportionate to the fine.

Personal search of offender

36–017 A judge of the Crown Court may, where:
PCC(S)A 2000, s.142

(1) any person has been fined, or has had a recognisance forfeited;

(2) any person is made the subject of an order for costs, or compensation;

(3) a parent or guardian is ordered to pay a fine, costs or compensation;

(4) the Crown Court orders any person to pay a surcharge under CJA 2003, s.151A (see 36–003, above); or

(5) an appellant from the magistrates' court is liable to pay any sum by virtue of an order made by the Crown Court or the magistrates' court,

order that person, if before him, to be searched, and any money found on him may be applied towards the payment of any sum owing, the balance being returned.

Enforcement by magistrates' court

36–018 The enforcement of Crown Court fines is a matter for the appropriate magistrates' court.
PCC(S)A 2000, s.140

37. FOOTBALL BANNING ORDERS

Introduction

37–001 Under FSA 1989, as amended by PCrA 2009, a judge of the Crown Court may, in dealing with an offender convicted of certain types of offence, make a banning order, by which the offender is:

(1) in relation to regulated football matches in the United Kingdom prohibited from entering into any premises for the purpose of attending such matches; and

(2) in relation to regulated football matches outside the United Kingdom is required to report himself to a designated police station at a time when a specified match is taking place.

The police station specified may be in England, Wales, Scotland or Northern Ireland. FSA 1989,
ss.14, 14A

As to the compatibility of such an order with ECHR, art.7, see *Gough v Derbyshire Chief Constable,* [2002] EWCA Civ 351; [2002] 2 All E.R. 985.

Where an offender is:

(a) convicted before the Crown Court of a "relevant" offence (defined in Sch.1); or

(b) committed to the Crown Court for sentence for such an offence, the judge may, in addition to:

    (i) imposing a sentence in respect of the relevant offence; or

    (ii) discharging him conditionally (in spite of the provisions of PCC(S)A 2000, ss.12 and 14),

make a banning order in relation to him, and *must* make such an order if satisfied that there are reasonable grounds to believe that making a banning order would help to prevent violence or disorder (both of which expressions are defined in s.14C) at or in connection with any regulated football matches.

Procedure is governed by r.50 (Civil behaviour orders after verdict or finding as to which see ANTI-SOCIAL BEHAVIOUR ORDERS).

For the purpose of deciding whether to make an order the judge may consider evidence led by the prosecution and the defence, and it is immaterial whether such evidence would have been admissible in the proceedings in which the offender was convicted.

If he is not so satisfied he must state that fact in open court, and give his reasons.

Appeals

37–002 The prosecution has a right of appeal to Civil Division of the Court of Appeal (*R v. Boggild* [2011] EWCA Crim 1928, *The Times*, Spetember 5, 2011) against a failure by the judge to make a banning order though only where CACD gives permission or the judge who decided not to make an order grants a certificate that his decision is fit for appeal. FSA 1989,
s.14(5A), (5B)

FOOTBALL BANNING ORDERS

An order made on appeal under this section (other than one directing that an application be re-heard by the court from which the appeal was brought) is to be treated for the purposes of this Part as if it were an order of the court from which the appeal was brought.

Remand; bail
37–003 If the proceedings are adjourned, or further adjourned, the judge may remand the offender, who may be required by the conditions of his bail:

    (a) not to leave England and Wales before his appearance before the court; and

    (b) if the control period relates to a regulated football match outside the United Kingdom or to an external tournament which includes such matches, to surrender his passport to a police constable if he has not already done so.

FSA 1989,
s.14A(4BA),
(4BB)

Declaration of relevance
37–004 Before making an order, the judge must make a "declaration of relevance", by determining in relation to any offence under the provisions of Sch.l, whether it is "relevant" in the sense that it is related to football. An offence committed on a train while returning from a football match was held not to be "relevant" to the match in *R. v O'Keefe* [2003] EWCA Crim 2629; [2004] 1 Cr. App. R.(S.) 67, but see *DPP v Beaumont* [2008] EWHC 523 (Admin); [2008] 2 Cr. App. R.(S.) 98. "Relevant to football matches" does not mean "relating to a football match" (ibid).

FSA1989, s.23

The fact that the offender has no history of misconduct in connection with football matches or the act is an isolated incident does not prevent an order being made. The potential deterrent effect of the order on other spectators may be taken into account (*R. (on the application of White) v Blackfriars Crown Court* [2008] EWHC 510 (Admin); [2008] 2 Cr. App. R.(S.) 97); *AG's Reference (No.14 of 2009 (R. v Morgan))* [2010] 1 Cr. App. R.(S.) 93).

CACD has said that it is instructive to identify the spark which caused the violence and whether it could be said to be wholly unrelated to the football, A fight between rival supporters may still relate to football even where their teams have not played against one another in a match – see *R. v Parkes* [2010] EWCA Crim 2803; 175 J.P.33.

Ordinarily the judge is not entitled to make a declaration unless it is shown that the prosecutor gave notice to the offender at least five days before the first day of the trial that it proposed to relate the offence to football matches, to a particular football match or to particular football matches. However, in any particular case, he may make a declaration notwithstanding the fact that notice was not given as required provided the accused consents to waive that notice; or the judge is satisfied that the interests of justice do not require more notice to be given.

The making of a declaration ought to involve an express statement announced in open court and recorded in the memorandum of conviction (though failure in this regard will not invalidate the order provided it is shown that judge considered the matter (*DPP v Beaumont, above*).

Appeal lies to CACD against the making of a declaration of relevance, and if the declaration is reversed, the banning order will be quashed.

Surrender of passport

37–005   In making a banning order the judge *must* impose a requirement as to the surrender, in accordance with the Act, in connection with regulated football matches outside the United Kingdom, of the offender's passport. This requirement is now mandatory. VCRA 2006 removes the judge's discretion.

FSA 1989,
s.14A(3)(4)

Effect of banning order

37–006   The judge must, on making an order, explain the effect of it in ordinary language to the offender, the effect being that:

FSA 1989,
s.14E

(1) he report initially to the police station specified in the order within five days, beginning on the day the order is made (special rules apply where he is in custody, see ss.14E(5), (6) above);
(2) he surrender his passport in an appropriate case; and
(3) subject to any exemption, he report on the occasion of any "regulated" football matches when required to do so, to the police station so specified at the time, or between the times, specified in the notice by which the requirement is imposed.

The order must also require the offender to give notification of certain events to the enforcing authority, being:

(a) a change of any of his names;
(b) the first use by him after the making of the order of a name for himself that was not disclosed by him at the time of the making of the order;
(c) a change of his home address;
(d) his acquisition of a temporary address, that is an address, other than his home address, at which he intends to reside or has resided for a period of at least four weeks;
(e) a change of his temporary address or his ceasing to have one;
(f) his becoming aware of the loss (including theft or destruction) of his travel authorisation (i.e. passport);
(g) receipt by him of a new (or replacement) travel authorisation;
(h) an appeal made by him in relation to the order;
(i) an application made by him under s.14H(2) for termination of the order;
(j) an appeal made by him under s.23(3) against the making of a declaration of relevance in respect of an offence of which he has been convicted.

Any notification thus required must be given before the end of the period of seven days beginning with the day on which the event in question occurs and:

FSA 1989,
ss.14G, 21C

(i) in the case of a change of a name or address or the acquisition of a temporary address, must specify the new name or address;

(ii) in the case of a first use of a previously undisclosed name, must specify that name; and

(iii) in the case of a receipt of a new travel authorisation, must give details of that travel authorisation.

Failure, without reasonable excuse, to report or to comply with conditions is a summary offence punishable with a fine not exceeding level 5 on the standard scale, or 51 weeks imprisonment, or both. The judge may, if he thinks fit, impose additional requirements.

Offences committed under the comparable provisions of the Scottish legislation (Police, Public Order and Criminal Justice (Scotland) Act, 2006 ss.68(1)(a) or (c)) may be dealt with in England, carrying the same punishment (PCrA 2009, s.106).

Such an order is not inconsistent with art.27 of Directive 2004/3 8/ EC (freedom of movement of EEC citizens) (*R. (on the application of White) v Blackfriars CC, above*) (see 37–004).

Period of ban

37–007   A banning order has effect for a period beginning with the day it is made, being neither more than the maximum nor less than the minimum. Where: | FSA 1989, s.14F

(1) it is made under s.14A in addition to a sentence of imprisonment taking immediate effect, the maximum is 10 years and the minimum six years;

(2) in any other case where it is made under s.14A, the maximum period five years and the minimum three; and

(3) it is made on complaint to the magistrates' court under s.14B, the maximum is three years and the minimum two years.

Administrative provisions

37–008   The order will specify the police station at which the offender is to report initially and the Crown Court officer will:

(1) give a copy of the order to the offender and, as soon as reasonably practicable, send a copy to the enforcing authority and the officer responsible for the police station at which the offender is to report initially; and | FSA 1989, s.18(1), (2)

(2) if the offender is sentenced to or is serving a custodial sentence, send a copy to the governor of the prison or other person to whose custody he is committed.

Application to terminate

37–009   The offender may apply to the court by which it was made to terminate it. On such an application the judge may:

(1) having regard to: | FSA 1989, s.14H
  (a) the offender's character;
  (b) his conduct since the order was made;
  (c) the nature of the offence which led to it; and
  (d) any other circumstances,
  either terminate the order from a specified date or refuse the application; and

(2) order the offender to pay all or any part of the costs of the application. Where an application is refused, no further application in respect of the order, may be made within a period of six months beginning with the date of the refusal.

Notes

38. FORFEITURE ORDERS

Quick guide

1. Deprivation order, PCC(S)A 2000 s.143

Introduction

38-001   The scope of a deprivation order under PCC(S)A 2000, s.143, which applies to all criminal offences, overlaps the narrower scope of specific orders available under other criminal statutes, to which reference should be made where appropriate.

There were 59,500 forfeiture orders made at all courts in 2008, a rise of 29 per cent from 2007. This was made up of 14,500 at the Crown Court, a rise of 40 per cent, and 45,000 at magistrates' courts, a rise of 25 per cent. At both the Crown Court and magistrates' courts, the highest proportions of forfeiture orders were for drug offences (60 and 71 per cent respectively).

The general power

38–002   Subject to certain restrictions (see below) a general power is given to deprive an offender of his rights in property where he is convicted of an offence, and:

> PCC(S)A 2000, s.143

(1) the judge is satisfied that any property which:
  (a) has been lawfully seized from him; or
  (b) was in his possession, or under his control at the time when he was apprehended for the offence, or when the summons in respect of it was issued,
    (i) has been used for the purpose of committing, or facilitating the commission of, any offence; or
    (ii) was intended by him for that purpose; or
(2) the offence (or an offence which the court has taken into consideration) consists of unlawful possession of property which:
  (a) has been lawfully seized from him; or
  (b) was in his possession, or under his control, at the time when he was apprehended for the offence, or when the summons in respect of it was issued.

FORFEITURE ORDERS

"Facilitating the commission of an offence" includes, for this purpose, the taking of any steps after it has been committed, for the purpose of disposing of any property to which it relates or of avoiding apprehension or detection.

PCC(S)A 2000, s.143(8)

Such an order may be made whether or not the judge also deals with the offender in any other way in respect of the offence of which he has been convicted, and without regard to any restrictions on forfeiture in any enactment contained in an Act passed before July 29, 1988.

PCC(S)A 2000, s.143(4)

Order only in straightforward cases

38–003 An order should be made only in the most straightforward of cases, and only upon the offender's admission, or on a specific finding by the court (*R. v Troth* (1980) 71 Cr. App. R. 1, *R. v Kearney* [2011] EWCA Crim 826; [2011] Crim. L.R. 567; [2011] 2 Cr. App. R.(S.) 106). The offender may be deprived only of such interest as he has in the property (ibid —motor vehicle encumbered by hire purchase). There may be cases where the order will have a disproportionately severe effect on an offender and should not be made (*R. v Tavernor* [1976] R.T.R. 242) and see *R v Townsend-Johnson* [2010] EWCA Crim 1027.

Where a number of offenders are equally guilty, it is wrong to make an order in relation to one accused only (*R. v Ottey* (1984) 6 Cr. App. R.(S.) 163) but it may be fair and proper to reflect the differing levels of participation (*R. v Burgess* [2001] 2 Cr. App. R.(S.) 2).

It is desirable that the judge, on making such an order, should make an express finding on the basis on which it is made (*R. v Ranasinghe* [1999] 2 Cr. App. R.(S.) 366).The judge must not make an order unless, prior to sentencing, he has made an enquiry as to the likely financial and other effects that the order is likely to have on the offender (*R. v Highbury Corner Magistrates Court Ex p. Di Matteo* (1991) 92 Cr. App. R. 263).

Serious road traffic offences

38–004 Where a person commits an offence:

PCC(S)A 2000, s.143(6), (7), (7A)

(1) under RTA 1988 which is punishable with imprisonment; or

(2) of manslaughter; or

(3) under OPA 1861, s.35 (furious or wanton driving),

and the offence consists of:

(a) driving, attempting to drive or being in charge of a vehicle; or

(b) certain breathalyser offences; or

(c) failing, as the driver of a vehicle, to comply with RTA 1988, s.170(2) and (3) (duty to stop and give information or to report accident),

the vehicle is said to be regarded for the purposes of s.143(1), above, and s.144(1)(b), below, as used for the purpose of committing the offence, and for committing any offence of aiding, abetting, counselling or procuring the commission of the offence.

As to the power of a constable to seize and dispose of vehicles driven without a licence or insurance, see RTA 1988, ss.165A, 165B, inserted by SOCA 2005, s.152.

Effect of order

38–005 The effect of an order is that, apart from depriving the offender of his rights, if any, in the property, it enables the property to be taken into the custody of the police, if not already in their possession, and the Police (Property) Act 1897, s.69 then applies, with certain modifications, leaving any third party or other claimant to make a claim within the six months under the Act.

PCC(S)A 2000,
ss.143(4), 144

Restrictions on use of section 143

38–006 As forfeited property has some financial value, the judge must, in considering whether to make an order, have regard to:

PCC(S)A 2000,
s.143(5)

(1) the value of the property; and
(2) the likely financial and other effects on the offender (taken together with any other order the court contemplates making).

Note also that:

(a) the power is applicable to all offences, including those to which a narrower specific statutory power applies (e.g. drugs and firearms, as to which see below) (*R. v O'Farrell* (1988) 10 Cr. App. R.(S.) 74);
(b) the power does not extend to depriving an offender of his rights in real property (*R. v Khan* (1983) 76 Cr. App. R. 29);
(c) the order is confined to the use, etc. of the property by the offender, not, e.g. by a person to whom drugs are supplied (*R. v Slater* (1986) 83 Cr. App. R. 265);
(d) the order is punitive in nature, and must be looked on as part of the sentence. The "totality principle" is therefore appropriate and it may be necessary to adjust other parts of the sentence (*R. v Priestley* [1996] Crim. L.R. 356).

Procedure and evidence

38–007 An order may be made only:

(1) where the Prosecutor proves that the requirements of the section are fulfilled (*R. v Kingston-upon-Hull JJ. Ex p. Hartung* (1981) 72 Cr. App. R. 26; *R. v Pemberton* (1982) 4 Cr. App. R.(S.) 328); or
(2) on an admission by the accused or a precise finding of fact by the judge (*R. v Troth* (above); *R. v Ball* [2002] EWCA Crim 2777; [2003] 2 Cr. App. R.(S.) 18);
(3) in the most straightforward cases, where the judge has given a warning of his intention, and a prior opportunity is given for representations to be made (*R. v Powell* (1984) 6 Cr. App. R.(S.) 354; *R. v Ball*, above); and
(4) in the case of a number of joint offenders, against all rather than against one only (*R. v Ottey* (1984) 6 Cr. App. R.(S.) 163).

Application for benefit of victim

38–008 Where the judge makes an order in a case where:

PCC(S)A 2000,
s.145

(1) the offender has been convicted of an offence which has resulted in a person suffering personal injury, loss or damage; or

(2) any such offence is taken into consideration on sentence; and

(3) but for the inadequacy of the offender's means he would have made a compensation order under which he would have been required to pay not less than a specified amount,

SOA 2003, s.60A

he may also order that any proceeds which arise from the disposal of the property and which do not exceed a sum he specifies, shall be paid to that person.

An order of this kind is not effective:

(a) before the end of the period specified in s.144(1)(a);

(b) if a successful application under the Police (Property) Act 1897, s.1(1) has been made.

2. Firearms offences, FA 1968, s.52 (1)

38–009 An order as to the forfeiture or disposal of a firearm or ammunition found in the possession of an offender may be made, where the offender:

FA 1968, s.52(1); CJIA 2008, s.6, Sch.4, para.7

(1) is convicted of an offence under FA 1968 (other than one under s.23(3) or an offence relating specifically to air weapons); or

(2) is convicted of an offence for which he is sentenced to imprisonment or detention in a young offender institution; or

(3) has been ordered to enter into a recognisance to keep the peace and/or be of good behaviour, a condition of which was that he should not carry a firearm; or

(4) is subject to a community order containing a requirement that he shall not possess, use or carry a firearm.

A "community order" means a community order within CJA 2003, Pt 12, made in England and Wales, or a youth rehabilitation order within the meaning CJIA 2008, Pt 1.

FA 1968, s.52(3)

Where a firearm is forfeited, it may be seized and detained by a constable.

3. Drugs offences, MDA 1971, s.27

38–010 Where a person is convicted of an offence:

MDA 1971, s.27(1), (2)

(1) under MDA 1971; or

(2) an offence specified in POCA 2002, Sch.2, para.1 (drug trafficking offences); or

(3) so far as it relates to that paragraph, Sch.2, para.10,

and anything is shown to the satisfaction of the judge to relate to the offence, the judge may order it to be forfeited and either destroyed or dealt with in such other manner as he may order. If a person claiming to be the owner, or to be otherwise interested in the property, applies to be heard, an order must not be made unless an opportunity is given to him to be heard.

A number of broad principles were laid down in the cases of *R. v Cuthbertson* (1980) 71 Cr. App. R. 148; *R. v Ribeyre* (1982) 4 Cr. App.

R.(S.) 165; *R. v Marland* (1986) 82 Cr. App. R. 134; *R. v Churcher* (1986) 8 Cr. App. R.(S.) 94; *R. v Cox* (1986) 8 Cr. App. R.(S.) 384; *R. v Llewellyn* (1985) 7 Cr. App. R.(S.) 225, thus:

(a) the order is concerned with forfeiture and not with restitution, compensation or the redress of unlawful enrichment;
(b) the order is apt to deal only with things which are tangible in the sense that physical possession may be taken of them by order of the court; "anything" includes money (*R. v Beard* [1974] 1 W.L.R. 1549);
(c) it is necessary to connect the specific thing forfeited with a particular offence to which it relates (and see *R. v Morgan* [1977] Crim. L.R. 488); working capital for future deals may be forfeited under the general power in PCC(S)A 2000, s.143 (*R. v O'Farrell* (1988) 10 Cr. App. R.(S.) 74); and
(d) the offender ought to be permitted to adduce any material tending to show that the thing in question is not related to the offence.

4. Public Order Act 1986 ss.25, 33

38–011 A court by which a person is convicted of an offence under ss.19, 21, 23, 29B, 29C, 29E or 29F of the Act in relation to racial or religious hatred, or s.18 relating to the display of racially offensive written material, must order to be forfeited any written material or recording (as defined in s.29) produced and shown to be written material or a recording to which the offence relates. *POrA 1986, ss.25, 33*

The order does not take effect until the ordinary time for appeal has expired, or, if an appeal is initiated, until it is finally determined or abandoned.

5. Protection of Children Act 1978

38–012 A Schedule to the Act, inserted by PJA 2006, s.39, Sch.11, makes provision for the forfeiture of photographs and pseudo-photographs under the 1978 Act.

6. SOA 2003; forfeiture of land vehicle, ship or aircraft

38–013 Where a person is convicted on indictment of an offence under SOA 2003, ss.57 to 59, the judge may order the forfeiture of:

(1) a land vehicle used or intended to be used in connection with the offence if the convicted person:
(a) owned the vehicle at the time the offence was committed;
(b) was at that time a director, secretary or manager of a company which owned the vehicle;
(c) was at that time in possession of the vehicle under a hire-purchase agreement;

   (d) was at that time a director, secretary or manager of a company which was in possession of the vehicle under a hire-purchase agreement; or

   (e) was driving the vehicle in the course of the commission of the offence;

  (2) a ship or aircraft used or intended to be used in connection with the offence if the convicted person:

   (a) owned the ship or aircraft at the time the offence was committed;

   (b) was at that time a director, secretary or manager of a company which owned the ship or aircraft;

   (c) was at that time in possession of the ship or aircraft under a hire-purchase agreement;

   (d) was at that time a director, secretary or manager of a company which was in possession of the ship or aircraft under a hire-purchase agreement;

   (e) was at that time a charterer of the ship or aircraft; or

   (f) committed the offence while acting as captain of the ship or aircraft.

But in a case to which (2)(a) or (b) above does *not* apply, forfeiture may be ordered only, in the case of a ship, if (i) or (ii) below applies, or in the case of an aircraft, if (i) or (iii) below applies:

   (i) applies where a person who, at the time the offence was committed, owned the ship or aircraft or was a director, secretary or manager of a company which owned it, knew or ought to have known of the intention to use it in the course of the commission of an offence under SOA 2003, ss.57 to 59;

   (ii) applies where a ship's gross tonnage is less than 500 tons;

   (iii) applies where the maximum weight at which an aircraft (which is not a hovercraft) may take off in accordance with its certificate of airworthiness is less than 5,700 kg.

Where a person who claims to have an interest in a land vehicle, ship or aircraft applies to the judge to make representations on the question of forfeiture, an order may not be made under this provision in respect of the vehicle, ship or aircraft, unless the person has been given an opportunity to make representations.   SOA 2003, 60C

 In both this section and in s.60B below, unless the contrary intention appears, "aircraft" includes hovercraft; "captain" means master (of a ship) or commander (of an aircraft); "land vehicle" means any vehicle other than a ship or aircraft; and "ship" includes every description of vessel used in navigation.

Release of seized vehicle, etc.

38–014 Where a land vehicle, ship or aircraft has been provisionally seized by a constable under SOA 2003, or senior immigration officer under the provisions of SOA 2003, s.60, a person (other than the arrested person) may apply to the appropriate court for it on the grounds that: SOA 2003, s.60B

(a) he owns the vehicle, ship or aircraft;

(b) he was, immediately before its detention, in possession of it under a hire-purchase agreement; or

(c) he is a charterer of the ship or aircraft.

The appropriate court will be, if the arrested person has not been charged, or he has been charged but proceedings for the offence have not begun to be heard, a magistrates' court, or, if he has been charged and proceedings for the offence are being heard, then the court hearing the proceedings.

The court to which an application is made may, on such security or surety being tendered as it considers satisfactory, release the vehicle, ship or aircraft on condition that it is made available to the court if the arrested person is convicted and an order for its forfeiture is made under s.60A.

7.   Game Act 1831

38–015   CJPOA 1994, Sch.9, para.4 contains provisions for forfeiting vehicles in the possession or under the control of poachers.

8.   Confiscation orders

38–016   These are governed by the provisions of PCA 2002, see CONFISCATION ORDERS.

9.   Forfeiture of seized cash

38–017   As to forfeiture of seized cash, see above CONFISCATION ORDERS.

Notes

39. GOODYEAR INDICATION

Introduction
39–001   A judge dealing with a case:

(1) may be asked by the accused to give, and
(2) if asked is entitled to give,

an indication, which should ordinarily be confined to the maximum sentence he would pass on the accused if a plea of guilty were to be tendered at the stage **at which the indication is sough**t (*R. v Goodyear* [2005] EWCA Crim 888; [2005] 2 Cr. App. R. 20; *R. v Patel* [2009] EWCA Crim 67; [2009] 2 Cr. App. R.(S.) 16).

Synopsis of Goodyear
39–002   The following are the important points to be gleaned from *Goodyear:*

(1)   The process of seeking an advance indication of sentence should be **initiated by the defence;** the defence advocate should have written instructions from the accused.
(2)   An indication should not be sought while there is any uncertainty about an acceptable plea or the **factual basis** of sentencing.
(3)   The judge should not give an advance indication unless one is sought by the accused.
(4)   Hearings relating to such advance indications should normally take place in **open court.**
(5)   The judge should *not* become **involved in discussions** which link the acceptable plea to the sentence which is likely to be imposed.
(6)   Advance indications should not be given on **alternative bases.**
(7)   The judge may give an advance indication of the **maximum sentence** which he would impose if a guilty plea was to be tendered at the stage the indication is sought.
(8)   Once an advance indication of sentence is given, it is **binding** on the judge and any other judge who becomes responsible for the case.
(9)   If the accused does not plead guilty within a reasonable time after the advance indication has been given, the indication **ceases to have effect** (*R. v Patel* above).
(10)   The judge may **reserve his position** until he feels able to give an advance indication, for instance where reports on the accused are expected.
(11)   The judge retains an **unfettered discretion to refuse** to give an advance indication.
(12)   The right of the **Attorney General** to refer a sentence to CACD on that it is unduly lenient is not affected by the giving of an advance indication of sentence.

GOODYEAR INDICATION

The rules set out in *Goodyear* are quite specific. Deviation from these rules is likely to cause problems, see e.g. *R. v Omole* [2011] EWCA Crim 1428; [2011] Crim. L.R. 804.

General provisions

39–003   The hearing will normally take place in open court, in the presence of the accused, with both sides represented and the proceedings being recorded in full.

In particular:

(1) there should be no prosecution opening at this stage, nor any mitigation plea by the defence – these should be postponed until after the accused has pleaded guilty;

(2) the judge should not give an advance indication of sentence unless one has been sought by the accused, though he is always entitled, in an appropriate case, to remind the defence advocate that the accused is entitled to seek an advance indication of sentence;

(3) where appropriate, there must be an agreed, written basis of plea; unless there is, the judge should refuse to give an indication – otherwise he may become inappropriately involved in negotiations about the acceptance of pleas, and any agreed basis of plea;

(4) there should be little need for the judge to involve himself in discussions with the advocates, although he may wish to seek better information on any aspect of the case which is troubling him;

(5) since the case may yet proceed as a trial, and if it does, no reference may be made to the request for a sentence indication, reporting restrictions should normally be imposed, to be lifted if and when the accused pleads or is found guilty,

(see further REPORTING AND ACCESS RESTRICTIONS).

Even where the judge gives an indication the Attorney-General may refer the sentence to CACD as too lenient.

Indication to be sought at earliest opportunity

39–004   A sentence indication should normally be sought at the plea and case management hearing. In cases "sent" to the Crown Court under CDA 1998, s.51, or transferred under CJA 1987, s.4 or CJA 1991, s.53, this is usually the first opportunity for the accused to plead guilty and therefore the moment when the maximum discount for the guilty plea will be available to him.

This does not, however, rule out the accused's entitlement to seek an indication at a later stage, or even, in a rare case, during the course of the trial itself.

Since the judge is most unlikely to be able to give an indication, even if it is sought, in a complicated or difficult case, unless issues between the prosecution and the defence have been addressed and resolved, in such a case:

(1) no less than seven days' notice in writing of an intention to seek an indication should normally be given in writing to the prosecutor, and to the court;

(2) if an application is made without notice when notice should have been given, the judge may conclude that any inevitable adjournment ought to have been avoided and that the discount for the guilty plea should be reduced accordingly.

The fact that notice has been given, and any reference to a request for a sentence indication, or the circumstances in which it was sought, is inadmissible in any subsequent trial.

Limits on practice

39–005   Subject to the judge's power to give an appropriate reminder to the advocate for the accused:

(1) the process of seeking a sentence indication should normally be started by the accused;

(2) whether or not the judge has given an appropriate reminder, the accused's advocate should not seek an indication without written authority, signed by his client, indicating that he wishes to seek an indication;

(3) an unrepresented accused is entitled to seek a sentence indication of his own initiative.

There will be difficulties in (3) in either the judge or the prosecuting advocate taking any initiative and informing an unrepresented accused of this right. That might too readily be interpreted as, or subsequently argued, to have been improper pressure.

It must be understood that any indication given by the judge:

(a) reflects the situation at the time when it is given, and that if a "guilty plea" is not tendered in the light of that indication the indication will cease to have effect;

(b) relates only to the matters about which an indication is sought; certain steps, like confiscation proceedings, follow automatically, and the judge cannot dispense with them, nor, by giving an indication of sentence, create an expectation that they will be dispensed with; and

(c) remains subject to the right of the Attorney-General, where it arises, to refer an unduly lenient sentence to CACD.

The accused's right to apply for leave to appeal against sentence if, for example, insufficient allowance has been made for matters of genuine mitigation, remains unaffected.

R. v Goodyear makes it clear that:

• any advance indication of sentence should normally be confined to the maximum sentence if a plea of guilty were tendered at the stage that the indication was sought, and

• that a judge should treat a request for a sentence indication, in whatever form it reached him, as if he were being asked to indicate the maximum sentence on the accused at that stage;

• the only other type of indication envisaged in *Goodyear,* should the judge see fit to give it, is an indication that the sentence or type of sentence to be imposed on the accused would be the same whether the case proceeded as a plea of guilty or went to trial; but

535

Goodyear recognises that such an indication would be unusual; finally,

• the judge retains an unfettered discretion to refuse to give an indication at all or to reserve his position until a later stage, if he thinks it appropriate to do so.

(R. v Omole [2011] 7 Archbold Review 3, C.A).

No plea bargaining
39–006 The defence should not seek an indication while there is any uncertainty between the prosecution and the defence about:

(1) an acceptable plea or pleas to the indictment; or
(2) any factual basis relating to the plea.

Any agreed basis should be reduced into writing before an indication is sought. Where there is a dispute about a particular fact which counsel for the accused believes to be effectively material to the sentencing decision, the difference should be recorded, so that the judge can make up his own mind.

There should be no question of the judge giving a preliminary indication, followed by comments on it by the prosecution advocate, with the judge then reconsidering his indication, and perhaps raising it to a higher level, with the defence advocate then making further submissions to persuade the judge, after all, to reduce his indication.

The judge should not:

(a) be invited to give an indication on the basis of what would be, or what would appear to be, a "plea bargain";
(b) be asked or become involved in discussions linking the acceptability to the prosecution of a plea; or
(c) asked to indicate levels of sentence which he may have in mind depending on possible alternative pleas;
(d) indicate the nature of any sentence he might pass if the accused were convicted after a trial (see *R. v Patel*, above).

Discretion to refuse indication
39–007 The judge retains an unfettered discretion to refuse to give an indication: It may inappropriate. He may consider:

(1) that if he were to give an indication at the stage when it is sought, he would not properly be able to judge the true culpability of the accused, or the differing levels of responsibility between accused; this is a very important consideration;
(2) that, for a variety of reasons, the accused is already under pressure (perhaps from a co-accused), or is vulnerable, and that to give the requested indication, even in answer to a request, might create additional pressure;
(3) that the particular accused may not fully have appreciated that he should not plead guilty unless in fact he is guilty;
(4) in a case involving a number of accused, that an indication given to one, may itself create pressure on another;
(5) that the application is nothing less than a "try on" by an accused

who intends or is likely to plead guilty in any event, seeking to take a tactical advantage; in such a case he will probably refuse to say anything at all, and indeed, it may strike him as a plea tendered later than the first reasonable opportunity for doing so, with a consequent reduction in the discount for the guilty plea.

The judge may, instead of refusing to give an indication, reserve his position until such time as he feels able to give one, e.g. until a pre-sentence report is available. There will be cases where a psychiatric or other report may provide valuable insight into the level of risk posed by the accused, and if so, he may justifiably feel disinclined to give an indication at the stage when it is sought.

Again, the judge may not be sufficiently familiar with the case to give an informed indication, and if so, he may defer doing so until he is.

Special considerations apply to dangerous offenders cases, see 39–008 below.

"Dangerous offenders" cases
39–008 It is not necessarily inappropriate to give an indication merely because the accused is charged with a specified offence which attracts the mandatory dangerous offender provisions of CJA 2003, but there are dangers in doing so.

At the time when an indication is sought, the judge may not be in possession of the information necessary to enable him to make the assessment of risk required by the Act. Pre-sentence and other reports will not be available. In such cases it is a matter for the judge's discretion whether it is appropriate to give an indication; he is under no obligation to do so.

If the judge decides to give an indication:

(1) the prosecutor must make it clear that the offence is a specified offence to which the mandatory dangerous offender provisions apply, that the information necessary to make an assessment of dangerousness is not available;
(2) if the accused is later assessed not to be dangerous, the indication will relate to the maximum determinate sentence which will be imposed;
(3) if the accused is later assessed as dangerous, the indication can relate only to the notional determinate term which will be used in the calculation of the minimum term to be served in conjunction with a sentence of life imprisonment or imprisonment for public protection, or the custodial term of an extended sentence (which could never be less than twelve months).

(R. v Kulah [2007] EWCA Crim 1701, [2008] 1 Cr. App. R.(S) 85; *R. v Seddon* [2009] EWCA Crim 3022, [2008] 2 Cr. App. R.(S.) 3.)

Giving reasons
39–009 In a case:

(1) of an outright refusal, the judge will probably conclude that it is inappropriate to give his reasons;

(2) where he has in mind to defer any indication, he may choose to explain his reasons, and further indicate the circumstances in which, and when, he would be prepared to respond to a request for a sentence indication.

If at any stage the judge refuses to give an indication (as opposed to deferring it) it remains open to the accused to seek a further indication at a later stage. Once the judge has refused to give an indication, however, he should not normally initiate the process, except, where it arises, to indicate that the circumstances had changed sufficiently for him to be prepared to consider a renewed application for an indication.

Binding effect of indication

39–010   An indication, once given, is binding ("as far as it goes" — *R. v Newman* [2010] EWCA Crim 1566; [2011] 1Cr. App. R.(S.) 68), and:

(1) remains binding on the judge who has given it; and
(2) binds any other judge who becomes responsible for the case.

If, after a reasonable opportunity to consider his position in the light of the indication, the accused does not plead guilty, the indication ceases to have effect (see *R. v Patel,* above).

In straightforward cases, once an indication has been sought and given, there should not be an adjournment for the plea to be taken on another day, but:

(a) the judge who has given an indication, should, wherever possible, deal with the case immediately;
(b) if that is not possible, any subsequent hearings should be listed before him;
(c) if that is not possible, and another judge deals with the case, while he has his own sentencing responsibilities, judicial comity as well as the expectation aroused in the accused that he will not receive a sentence in excess of that which the first judge indicated, requires that the subsequent judge should not exceed the earlier indication.

As to the judge rectifying an error, see *R. v Newman,* above.

The role of the Prosecutor

39–011   If an indication is sought, the prosecution advocate should ensure that the judge is in possession of, or has had access to, all the evidence relied on by the prosecution, including the antecedents and any personal impact statement from the victim of the crime (see VICTIM IMPACT STATEMENTS, etc.).

He may also need:

(1) to draw the judge's attention to any minimum or mandatory statutory sentencing requirements;
(2) to offer assistance with relevant guideline cases, or the views of the SGC, or to invite the judge to allow him to do so; and
(3) where applicable, to remind the judge that the position of the

Attorney-General to refer any eventual sentencing decision as unduly lenient is not affected.

If there has been no final agreement about the plea(s) or the basis of the plea(s), and the defence nevertheless seek an indication, which the judge appears minded to give, the prosecuting advocate ought to remind the judge of the guidance given in the preceding paragraphs that an indication of sentence should not normally be given until the basis of the plea has been agreed, or the judge has concluded that he can properly deal with the case without the need for a Newton hearing.

The prosecuting advocate should not say anything which may create the impression that the sentence indication has the support or approval of the Crown.

As to the acceptance of pleas by the Crown, see CCP 2004, para.19, *Att-Gen's Guidelines on the Acceptance of Pleas,* updated to October 21, 2005 and the *Attorney-General's Guidelines on Plea Discussions in Cases of Serious and Complex Fraud* (unreported) which came into force on May 5, 2009.

Effect on reference under CJA 1988, s.36

39–012   If the prosecution advocate has addressed his responsibilities, the discretion of the Attorney-General to refer a sentence to CACD as unduly lenient will be wholly unaffected by the advance sentence indication process.

In particular:

(1) if a sentence indication has been given in accordance with these guidelines, before referring the eventual sentencing decision to CACD, the Attorney-General's decision will no doubt reflect that the accused had indeed pleaded guilty in response to the sentence indication, properly sought and given by the judge;

(2) if the prosecuting advocate, contrary to the above guidance, has said or done anything which may indicate or convey support for, or approval of, the sentence indicated, the question whether the sentence should be referred to CACD as unduly lenient, and the decision of CACD whether to interfere with and increase it, will be examined on a case by case basis, in the light of everything said and done by the advocate for the Crown.

(See *Att-Gen's Refs (Nos 80 and 81 of 1999) (R. v Thompson and Rodgers)* [2000] 2 Cr. App. R.(S.) 138; *Att-Gen's Refs (Nos 86 and 87 of 1999) (R. v Webb)* [2001] 1 Cr. App. R.(S) 141; *R. v Mohammed)* [2002] EWCA Crim 1607, [2003] 1 Cr. App. R.(S.) 57; but *cf. Att-Gen's Ref (No.19 of 2004)* [2005] 1 Cr.App.R.(S.) 18).

Notes

40. GUILTY PLEAS

Quick Guide

1. Introduction (40–001)
2. Plea of guilty on the basis of the prosecution case (40–003)
3. Plea of guilty on agreed basis of plea (40–004)
4. Cases/involving serious or complex fraud (40–007)
5. "Goodyear indication" (40–012)
6. Newton hearings (40–013)
7. Interpretation of jury's verdict (40–020)
8. Change of plea (40–021)

1. Introduction

40–001   The following overarching principles apply to guilty pleas;

PD 2004. IV.45

(1) advocates must be free to perform their duty namely to give the accused the best advice possible and, if need be, in strong terms;
(2) that advice will often include advice that, in accordance with the relevant authorities and sentencing guidelines, the judge will normally reduce a sentence as a result of a guilty plea (see DISCOUNTS ON SENTENCE), and that the level of reduction will reflect the stage in the proceedings at which willingness to admit guilt was indicated;
(3) the advocate will, of course, emphasise that the accused must not plead guilty unless he is guilty of the offence(s) charged;
(4) the accused, having considered the advocate's advice, must have complete freedom of choice whether to plead guilty or not guilty.

There must be freedom of access between advocate and judge; but any discussion must be between the judge and the advocates on both sides. If an advocate is instructed by a solicitor who is in court, he, too, should be allowed to attend the discussion.

PD 2004, IV.45

This freedom of access is important because there may be matters calling for communication or discussion of such a nature that the advocate cannot, in the client's interest, mention them in open court, e.g. the advocate, by way of mitigation, may wish to tell the judge that reliable medical evidence shows that the accused is suffering from a terminal illness and may not have long to live.

Note that:

(a) it is imperative that, so far as possible, justice be administered in open court;
(b) advocates should, therefore, only ask to see the judge when it is felt to be really necessary; and
(c) the judge must be careful only to treat such communications as private where, in the interests of justice, this is necessary.

GUILTY PLEAS

Where any such discussion takes place it should be recorded either by a tape recorder or a shorthand writer.

Three routes

40–002   PD 2004 IV.45 outlines the three routes by which a plea of guilty may be put forward in the Crown Court;

PD 2004, IV.45.4

(1) a plea of guilty to all or some of the charges on the basis of the prosecution case set out in the papers (40–003 below);
(2) a plea of guilty upon a basis of plea agreed by the prosecution and defence, or upon a basis of plea put forward by the defence and not contested by the prosecutor (40–004 below); and
(3) in cases involving serious or complex fraud conducted in accordance with PD 2004, IV.45.16 to IV.45.28, a plea of guilty upon a basis of plea agreed by the prosecution and the defence, accompanied by joint submissions as to sentence (40–007 below).

2.   Plea of guilty on the basis of the prosecution case

Procedure

40–003   In many cases, an accused wishing to plead guilty will simply plead guilty to all charges on the basis of the facts as alleged and opened by the prosecutor, with no dispute as to the factual basis and extent of offending alleged by the prosecutor. (2008 statistics show 68% of accused pleading guilty to all counts). Alternatively he may plead guilty to some of the charges brought. As to the position where the accused offers a plea to a lesser offence which is refused by the prosecutor, see *R. v Birt* [2011] EWCA Crim 2823; [2011] 2 Cr. App. R.(S.) 14, and *R. v Rainford* [2010] EWCA Crim 3220; [2011] 2 Cr. App. R.(S.) 15.

PD 2004, IV.45.5-9

When an accused pleads guilty as set out above, the judge will consider whether that plea represents a proper plea on the basis of the facts set out in the papers. Where the judge is satisfied that the plea is properly grounded, sentencing may take place.

Where the prosecution advocate is considering whether to accept a plea to a lesser charge:

(1) he may invite the judge to approve the proposed course of action, in which circumstances, the advocate must abide by the judge's decision;
(2) if he does not invite the judge to approve the acceptance by the prosecution of a lesser charge, it is open to the judge to express his dissent with the course proposed and invite the advocate to reconsider the matter with those instructing him.

In any proceedings, where the judge is of the opinion that the course proposed by the advocate may lead to serious injustice, the proceedings may be adjourned to allow the following procedure to be followed:

(a) as a preliminary step, the prosecution advocate must discuss the judge's observations with the Chief Crown Prosecutor or the senior prosecutor of the relevant prosecuting authority, as appropriate, in an attempt to resolve the issue; or

(b) where the issue remains un resolved, the DPP or the Director of the relevant prosecuting authority should be consulted; or

(c) in extreme circumstances the judge may decline to proceed with the case until the prosecuting authority has consulted with the Attorney-General as may be appropriate.

Prior to entering a plea of guilty, an accused may seek a "Goodyear Indication" from the judge (see GOODYEAR INDICATION). PD 2004, IV.45.9

3. Plea of guilty upon an agreed basis of plea

Principles

40–004 The prosecution may reach an agreement with an accused as to the factual basis on which the latter will plead guilty, often known as an "agreed basis of plea"; it is always subject to the approval of the judge who will consider whether it is fair and in the interests of justice. *R. v Underwood* [2004] EWCA Crim 2256; [2005] 1 Cr. App. R. 13 outlines the principles to be applied where the accused admits that he is guilty, but disputes the basis of offending alleged by the prosecution. PD 2004 IV.45.10-15

In such a case:

(1) the prosecutor may accept and agree the accused's account of the disputed facts or reject it in its entirety;

(2) if the prosecutor accepts the accused's basis of plea, he must ensure that the basis of plea is factually accurate and that it enables the judge to impose a sentence which appropriately reflects the justice of the case;

(3) in resolving any disputed factual matters, the prosecutor must consider his primary duty to the court and must not agree with, or acquiesce, in an agreement which contains material factual disputes;

(4) if the prosecutor accepts the accused's basis of plea, it must be reduced to writing, be signed by the advocates for both sides, and made available to the judge prior to the prosecutor's opening;

(5) an agreed basis of plea which has been reached between the parties must not contain any matters which are in dispute;

(6) where the prosecutor lacks the evidence positively to dispute the accused's account, as where, e.g. the accused asserts a matter outside the knowledge of the prosecution, it does not mean that those assertions should be agreed; in such a case, the prosecutor should test the accused's evidence and submissions by requesting a Newton hearing (see 40-013) following the procedure set out in PD 2004 IV.45.13;

(7) if it is not possible for the parties to resolve a factual dispute when attempting to reach a plea agreement under this procedure, it is the responsibility of the prosecutor to consider whether the matter should proceed to trial, or to invite the judge to hold a Newton hearing as necessary;

(8) subject to PD 2004 IV.45.12, where: the prosecutor has not invited the judge to hold a Newton hearing, and the factual dispute between the prosecution and the defence is likely to have

a material impact on sentence, and the defence does not invite the judge to hold a Newton hearing, the judge is entitled to reach his own conclusion on the facts on the evidence before him.

Judge not bound by agreement

40–005   *R. v Underwood* makes it clear that, whether or not pleas have been "agreed", the judge is not bound by any such agreement and is entitled of his own motion to insist that any evidence relevant to the facts in dispute, or upon which the judge requires further evidence for whatever reason, should be called. Any view formed by the prosecutor on a proposed basis of plea is deemed to be conditional on the judge's acceptance of the basis of plea.

PD 2004
IV.45.11

Procedure

40–006   Where the accused pleads guilty, but disputes the basis of offending alleged by the prosecutor, the following procedure should be followed:

PD 2004
IV.45.13

(1) the accused's basis of plea must be set out in writing, identifying what is in dispute;
(2) the judge may invite the parties to make representations about whether the dispute is material to sentence; and if the judge decides that it is a material dispute, he will invite such further representations or evidence as he may require and decide the dispute at a Newton hearing (40-013).

Where the disputed issue arises from facts which are within the exclusive knowledge of the accused and he is willing to give evidence in support of his case, the defence advocate should be prepared to call the accused. If the accused is not willing to testify, and subject to any explanation which may be given, the judge may draw such inferences as appear appropriate. Paragraphs 6 to 10 of *Underwood* provide additional guidance regarding the Newton hearing procedure.

PD 2004
IV.45.14

The judge must always, if he does not accept the accused's version, inform him of that fact before proceeding to sentence, so that the accused may decide how to proceed (*R. v Lucien* [2009] EWCA Crim 2004, *The Times*, July 13, 2009).

The Attorney General has issued guidance for prosecutors regarding their duties when accepting pleas and during the sentencing exercise entitled *Attorney General's Guidelines on the Acceptance of Pleas and the Prosecutor's Role in the Sentencing Exercise.*

PD 2004.
IV.45.15

4.   Cases involving serious or complex fraud

General; definitions

40–007   This section applies when the prosecutor and the accused in a case involving allegations of serious or complex fraud have agreed a basis of plea and seek to make submissions regarding sentence.

PD 2004
IV.45,16, 17,-18

Guidance for prosecutors regarding the operation of this procedure is set out in the Attorney-General's *Guidelines on Plea*

Discussions in Cases of Serious or Complex Fraud, published on March 18, 2000.

Note that:

(1) "a plea agreement" here means a written basis of plea agreed between the prosecutor and the accused in accordance with the principles set out in *R. v Underwood* (above) supported by admissible documentary evidence or admissions under CJA 1967, s.10;

(2) "a sentencing submission" means sentencing submissions made jointly by the prosecutor and the defence as to the appropriate sentencing authorities and applicable sentencing range in the relevant sentencing guideline relating to the plea agreement;

(3) "serious or complex fraud" includes, but is not limited to, allegations of fraud where two or more of the following are present:

(a) the amount obtained, or intended to be obtained, exceeded £500,000;

(b) there is a significant international dimension; the case requires specialised knowledge of financial, commercial, fiscal or regulatory matters such as the operation of markets, banking systems, trusts or tax regimes;

(c) the case involves allegations of fraudulent activity against numerous victims;

(d) the case involves an allegation of substantial and significant fraud on a public body;

(e) the case is likely to be of widespread public concern; or

(f) the alleged misconduct endangered the economic well-being of the United Kingdom, e.g. by undermining confidence in financial markets.

Procedure

40–008 The procedure regarding agreed bases of plea outlined in 40–005—40–006 above, applies with equal rigour to the acceptance of pleas under this procedure. However, because under this procedure the parties will have been discussing the plea agreement and the charges from a much earlier stage, it is vital that the judge is fully informed of all relevant background to the discussions, the charges and the eventual basis of plea.

PD 2004
IV.45.19, 22

Where the accused:

(1) has not yet appeared before the Crown Court, the prosecutor must send full details of the plea agreement and sentencing submission(s) to the court, at least seven days in advance of the accused's first appearance;

(2) has already appeared before the Crown Court, the prosecutor must notify the court as soon as is reasonably practicable that a plea agreement and sentencing submissions under the Attorney-General's Plea Discussion Guidelines are to be submitted. The court should set a date for the matter to be heard, and the prosecutor must send full details of the plea agreement and sentencing submission(s) to the court as soon as practicable, or in accordance with the directions of the court.

GUILTY PLEAS

Sufficiency of material

40–009 The provision of full details of the plea agreement requires sufficient information to be provided to allow the judge to understand the facts of the case and the history of the plea discussions, to assess whether the plea agreement is fair and in the interests of of justice, and to decide the appropriate sentence. PD 2004, IV.45.21, 22

The material must include, but is not limited to:

(1) the plea agreement;
(2) the sentencing submission(s);
(3) all of the material provided by the prosecutor to the accused in the course of the plea discussions;
(4) relevant material provided by the accused, e.g. documents relating to personal mitigation; and n.p. (5) the minutes of any meetings between the parties and any correspondence generated in the plea discussions.

The parties should be prepared to provide additional material at the request of the court.

The judge should have regard to the:

(a) length of time that has elapsed since the date of the occurrence of the events giving rise to the plea discussions;
(b) the time taken to interview the accused;
(c) the date of charge and the prospective trial date (if the matter were to proceed to trial),

so as to ensure that his consideration of the plea agreement and sentencing submissions does not cause any unnecessary further delay.

Status of plea agreement and joint sentencing submissions

40–010 Where a plea agreement and joint sentencing submissions are submitted, it remains entirely a matter for the judge how to decide how to deal with the case. He retains an absolute discretion to refuse to accept the plea agreement, and sentence otherwise than in accordance with the sentencing submissions made under the Attorney-General's Plea Discussion Guidelines. PD 2004, IV.45.23

Note that:

(1) sentencing submissions should draw the judge's attention to any applicable range in any relevant guideline, and to any ancillary orders that may be applicable; they should not include a specific sentence or agreed range other than the ranges set out in sentencing guidelines; PD 2004, IV.45.25, 26
(2) prior to pleading guilty in accordance with the plea agreement the accused may apply to the judge for a Goodyear indication under the procedure set out in 40–012 and following, below;
(3) in the event of the judge indicating a sentence or passing a sentence which is not within the submissions made on sentencing, the plea agreement remains binding.

Accused not pleading guilty, or withdrawing plea

40-011 If the accused:

(1) does not plead guilty in accordance with the plea agreement; or

(2) having pleaded guilty in accordance with a plea agreement successfully applies to withdraw his plea under r.39.3: then

    (a) the signed plea agreement may be treated as confession evidence, and may be used against him at a later stage in these or any other proceedings; and

    (b) any credit for a timely guilty plea may be lost.

PD 2004, IV.45.27,28

The judge may, however, exercise his discretion under PACE 1984, s.78 to exclude any such evidence if it appears to him that, having regard to all the circumstances, including the circumstances in which the evidence was obtained, the admission of the evidence would have such an adverse effect on the fairness of the proceedings that the court ought not to admit it.

Where an accused has failed to plead guilty in accordance with a plea agreement, e.g. in the circumstances set out above, the case is unlikely to be ready for trial immediately. The prosecution may have been commenced earlier than it otherwise would have been, in reliance upon the accused's agreement to plead guilty. This is likely to be a relevant consideration for the judge in deciding whether or not to grant an application to adjourn or stay the proceedings to allow the matter to be prepared for trial in accordance with the protocol on the *Control and Management of Heavy Fraud and other Complex Criminal Cases* (see CASE MANAGEMENT), or as required.

6. "Goodyear Indication"

Right to seek indication

40–012 Prior to pleading guilty by any of the above routes, it is open to an accused to request from the judge an indication of the maximum sentence likely to be imposed if a guilty plea is tendered at that stage in the proceedings, in accordance with the guidance in *R. v Goodyear* [2005] EWCA Crim 888; [2005] 2 Cr. App. R. 20; [2006] 1 Cr. App. R.(S.) 6 (see GOODYEAR INDICATION).

PD 2004, IV.45.29 33

During the sentence indication process and during the actual sentencing hearing, the prosecution advocate is expected to assist the court in sentencing by providing, where appropriate, references to the relevant statutory powers of the court, relevant sentencing guidelines and authorities, and such assistance as the court is likely to require.

Whether to give such an indication is a matter for the discretion of the judge, to be exercised in accordance with the principles outlined in *Goodyear*. Such indications should normally not be given if there is a dispute as to the basis of plea unless the judge concludes that he can properly deal with the case without the need for a Newton hearing.

In cases where a dispute arises, the procedure in *R. v Underwood* should be followed prior to the court considering a sentencing indication further, as set out in PD 2004 IV.45.1.

Following an indication of sentence, if an accused does not plead guilty, the indication will not bind the court.

6. Newton Hearing

General

40–013 A Newton hearing (*R. v. Newton* (1982) 77 Cr. App. R. 13) is the appropriate procedure by which a judge determines disputed issues of fact affecting sentence, where evidence of such facts was not called at a trial, or cannot be said to have been decided by a jury.

The most common occasion for such a hearing is where, on a plea of guilty, there is a dispute as to the facts; it may also be an appropriate procedure after a jury trial, for the purpose of interpreting a jury's verdict (see 40-020 below). ,

Plea of guilty

40–014 Where an offender pleads guilty, the prosecution must state the facts in open court before sentence is passed. While he is not obliged to pass sentence on the least serious version of the facts (*R. v Solomon* (1984) 6 Cr. App. R.(S.) 120), the judge should give the offender the benefit of any doubt (see *R. v Stosiek* (1982) 4 Cr. App. R.(S.) 205).

Unless a disputed fact is proved by the prosecution to the satisfaction of the judge, it ought not to count in passing sentence (*R. v Kerrigan* (1993) 14 Cr. App. R.(S.) 179). The judge will need to direct himself that the offender's account must be accepted unless it is proved to be untrue (*R. v Ahmed* (1984) 6 Cr. App. R.(S.)391).

In *R. v Underwood* [2004] EWCA Crim 2256; [2005] 1 Cr. App. R. 13, CACD re-stated the principles, and gave general guidance.

The court recognised three common scenarios, namely that the prosecutor might:

(1) accept and agree the offender's account of the disputed facts;
(2) reject the offender's version; or
(3) lack the evidence to dispute positively the offender's version.

Where there is a difference between the prosecution evidence and the factual basis on which the offender intends to plead guilty, responsibility for taking the initiative and alerting the prosecutor to the disputed areas rests with the defence. It will generally be sensible for the judge to agree to a request for a hearing when asked for one by any advocate, and not to indicate any provisional view formed on the papers.

Judge acting of his own motion

40–015 The judge is entitled, of his own motion, on a plea of guilty, to make known any concerns he may have about any matter revealed by the state of the evidence before him, and to insist on holding a Newton hearing to determine any disputed facts notwithstanding prior agreement between the prosecutor and the defence as to the facts (*R. v Beswick* [1996] 2 Cr. App. R. 427).

Where appropriate, he may:

(1) decline to accept the plea, and in an appropriate case, direct trial by a jury; or

(2) hear submissions, and then form his own view of the facts, in which case, if there is a substantial conflict, he is bound to accept the version given by the accused; or

(3) if he is not prepared to sentence on the accused's version, conduct a hearing, and after considering the evidence on both sides, if tendered, come to his own decision on the facts.

Where the judge considers the basis of the plea tendered by the accused to be "absurd or manifestly untenable" in the light of evidence given during a trial of a co-accused, he may resolve the issue against the accused without holding a hearing, provided he remains of the same view after hearing submissions from both sides, and gives a reasoned judgment (*R. v Taylor* [2006] EWCA Crim 3132; [2007] 2 Cr. App. R.(S.) 24).

The judge is not entitled to make findings of fact and pass sentence on a basis that is inconsistent with pleas to counts already approved by the court; particular care is needed in relation to a multi-count indictment involving one accused or an indictment involving a number of accused where there was joint enterprise. The judge, while reflecting the individual basis of pleas, must bear in mind the seriousness of the joint enterprise in which all were involved;

Where procedure inappropriate
40–016   There will be occasions when a Newton hearing will be inappropriate, as where:

(1) some issues, particularly where the accused denies committing a specific offence, will require a jury's verdict;

(2) the sentence would be the same whatever version of the facts the judge adopted - in such a case there is no need to hold a hearing (*R. v Bent* (1986) 8 Cr. App. R.(S.)19);

(3) the accused's account is manifestly false or implausible – in such a case the judge is not obliged to hold a hearing (*R. v Hawkins* (1985) 7 Cr. App. R.(S.) 351; *R. v Bilinski* (1988) 86 Cr. App. R.(S.) 146; *R. v Walton* (1987) 9 Cr. App. R.(S.) 107; *R. v Mudd* (1988) 10 Cr. App. R.(S.) 22; *R. v Palmer* (1993) Cr. App. R.(S.) 123; cf. *R v Satchell* [1996] 2 Cr. App. R.(S.) 258);

(4) it is sought to determine whether the accused has committed offences other than those to which he has pleaded guilty or has had taken into consideration (*R. v Huchison* (1972) 56 Cr.App. R. 307) or which were not included in the indictment (*R. v Eubank* [2001] EWCA Crim 891; [2002]1 Cr. App. R.(S.) 4).

Matters of mitigation are not normally dealt with by way of a Newton hearing but it is always open to the judge to allow an offender to give evidence as to matters of mitigation (*R. v Underwood*, above).

Conduct of the hearing
40–017   After submissions, the judge must decide how to proceed; he is not bound by any agreement as to the plea, and is entitled to insist that

any evidence relevant to the facts in dispute be called. Whatever view may be formed by the prosecutor on any proposed basis of the plea is conditional on the judge agreeing to it (*R. v Underwood*, above, 40–014).

The judge is entitled to expect the prosecuting advocate to assist him in reaching the true facts by testing the evidence and the prosecution is not bound by any agreement reached with the other side, which is merely conditional until it receives the judge's approval.

A decision to hold a hearing does not give rise to a ground for the offender to change his plea. Special provisions apply to committals for sentence (see 40–019 below).

Where necessary:

(1) relevant evidence should be called by the prosecution and by the defence (particularly where the issue arises from facts which are within the offender's exclusive knowledge);

(2) where the offender does not give evidence, then, subject to any explanation offered, the judge may draw such inference as he sees fit;

(3) the judge is entitled to take into account evidence which he has heard in the separate trials of co-accused (*R. v Smith* (1988) 87 Cr. App. R. 393) but should bear in mind that that evidence was not the subject of cross- examination by the accused who pleaded guilty (*R. v Winter* [1997] 1 Cr. App. R.(S.) 331);

(4) the judge is not obliged to accept the version given by the accused and indeed he may draw adverse inferences from his conduct (*R. v Ghandi* (1986) 8 Cr. App. R.(S.) 391);

(5) in coming to his decision he may have regard to the accused's previous convictions (*R. v Walton* (1987) 9 Cr. App. R.(S.) 107).

The judge may reject the evidence called by the prosecution or by the accused or his witnesses, even if the prosecution has not called contradictory evidence; but his reasons should be explained in a judgment (*R. v Underwood above*). Where the hearing involves the assessment of identification evidence, the judge must direct himself in accordance with the Turnbull guidelines. The criminal burden and standard of proof apply (*R v. Ahmed* (1984) 80 Cr. App. R. 295).

The judge needs to make it clear in his sentencing remarks what facts he is accepting (*R. v Gillespie* [1998] Crim. L.R.13).

Effect on credit for guilty plea
40–018   If:

(1) the issues at the hearing are resolved entirely in the offender's favour, credit for his guilty plea should not be reduced;

(2) the offender is disbelieved, having required prosecution witnesses to be called (see e.g. *R. v Stevens,* below), or if he shows no insight into the consequences of his offence and no genuine remorse, the discount may be reduced.

There may be exceptional circumstances in which the entitlement to credit for his plea may be entirely dissipated as a result of a hearing, and in such a case the judge should explain why (*R. v Underwood above*). He is entitled to withhold the full credit he might otherwise have given for a plea of guilty where the offender insists on a hearing and the victim of a sexual assault is compelled to give evidence (*R. v Stevens* (1986) 8 Cr.App.R.(S.) 297), but it is wrong for him to give the offender no credit at all for his plea (*R. v Hassall* [2000] 1Cr.App.R.(S.) 67).

Committals for sentence

40-019 While a judge at the Crown Court has jurisdiction to hold a Newton hearing in the case of an offender committed for sentence, where it is in the interest of fairness and justice to do so, he should not necessarily accede to an application to do so in a case where it is apparent that the magistrates have already conducted such a hearing and made clear findings of fact as part of the decision-making process with regard to committing the offender for sentence.

The matter is one for the discretion of the judge, in the proper exercise of which he must be fully mindful of his obligation to carry out a proper inquiry into the circumstances of the case.

In the ordinary way, he ought not to exercise his discretion in favour of allowing an offender to reopen the magistrates' findings of fact unless the offender is able to point to some significant development or matter, such as the discovery of important further evidence having occurred since the lower court reached its decision on the facts (*Gillian v DPP* [2007] EWHC (Admin) 380, [2007] 2 Cr. App. R. 12).

7. Interpretation of jury's verdict

40-020 Where a Newton hearing is held after a jury trial, for the purpose of interpreting a jury's verdict (see 40–013), the following points should be noted:

(1) if the verdict can be explained only on one view of the facts, the judge must adopt that view as the basis for sentence;
(2) if more than one view of the facts is consistent with the verdict the judge may form his own view in the light of the evidence given;
(3) if the verdict leaves open an important issue which may affect sentence, the judge must decide where the truth lies.

(*R. v Solomon* (1984) 6 Cr. App. R.(S.) 120; *R. v McGlade* (1991) 12 Cr. App. R.(S.) 105; *R. v Martin* [2002] 2 Cr. App. R.(S.) 34).

Other than in a case of murder reduced to manslaughter (see *R. v Frankum* (1983) 5 Cr. App. R.(S.) 1259) it is inappropriate for the judge to take a "special verdict" (*R. v Larkin* (1944) 29 Cr. App. R. 18).

8. Change of Plea

40-021 A plea of guilty may be changed, with leave of the judge, up to the moment of sentence (*R (an infant) v Manchester City Recorder* [1969] 3 All E.R. 230).

An accused must apply as soon as practicable after becoming aware of the grounds for making an application to change a plea of guilty, and may only do so before the final disposal of the case, by sentence or otherwise. R. 39.3

Guilty Pleas

GUILTY PLEAS

Unless the judge otherwise directs, the application must be in writing and it must:

(1) set out the reasons why it would be unjust for the guilty plea to remain unchanged;
(2) indicate what, if any, evidence the defendant wishes to call;
(3) identify any proposed witness; and
(4) indicate whether legal professional privilege is waived, specifying any material name and date. The accused must serve the written application on the Crown Court officer; and the prosecutor.

41. IMPRISONMENT

Quick guide

1. General

Introduction

41–001 Immediate custody is the most commonly used disposal in relation to persons convicted of indictable offences at the Crown Court.

Before a sentence of imprisonment may be imposed;

(1) the offence must be punishable at common law or by statute by imprisonment;
(2) the offender must (save in the case of a public protection sentence), be aged 21 or over;
(3) the circumstances of the offence must have crossed the threshold for custodial offences; and
(4) the offender must have been represented, or have had the opportunity to be represented, between conviction and sentence (see generally DEALING WITH AN OFFENDER).

As to suspended sentences of imprisonment, see 41-044 below. As to custodial sentences for young offenders, see DETENTION OF YOUNG OFFENDERS As to imprisonment (IPP) and extended sentences (EPP), for public protection, see DANGEROUS OFFENDERS; PROTECTIVE SENTENCES; As to life sentences, see LIFE SENTENCES.

As to the nature of the term, see 41-003-005; as to the length, 41-007 and following.

Custody threshold

41–002 Apart from those cases where the sentence is fixed by law, or falls to be imposed under PCC(S)A 2000, ss.110(2) or 111(2) (required minimum sentences for certain offenders, see 41–032), or any of

CJA 2003, s.152

IMPRISONMENT

CJA 2003, ss.225–228 (IPP), (see DANGEROUS OFFENDERS; PROTECTIVE SENTENCES;), an offender may not be sentenced to a term of imprisonment unless the judge is of the opinion that:

(1) the offence; or
(2) the combination of the offence and one or more offences "associated" with it,

is "so serious" that neither a fine alone, nor a community sentence, can be justified for it.

Nevertheless, nothing prevents the judge from passing a custodial sentence on an offender who fails to:

(a) express his willingness to comply with a requirement which it is proposed to include in a community order, and which requires an expression of such willingness; or
(b) comply with an order under CJA 2003, s.161(2) (pre-sentence drug testing), when that provision comes into force.

The definition of "imprisonment" in CJA 2003, ss.195 (interpretation), 237 and 257 (fixed-term prisoners) excludes sentences of imprisonment passed in respect of a summary conviction for a bail offence under BA 1976, s.6(1) or (2).

As to offenders under 21, see DETENTION OF YOUNG OFFENDERS. As to the need for a pre-sentence or medical report, and for legal representation, see DEALING WITH AN OFFENDER.

2. Nature of term

Date of commission of offence

41–003 The nature of a determinate sentence of imprisonment will depend crucially on whether the offence for which it is to be imposed was **committed before, or on or after, April 4, 2005;** in relation to life sentences (see LIFE SENTENCES) and minimum sentences for firearms offences (41-040) other dates may be crucial.

Categories of sentence

41–004 A sentence if imprisonment may be:

(1) a normal determinate sentence;
(2) a sentence fixed by law;
(3) a life sentence (see LIFE SENTENCES);
(4) a required minimum sentence under PCC(S)A 2000, ss.110(2) or 111(2) (41-034), or under FA 1968, s.51A (41-040); or
(5) a public protection sentence under CJA 2003.

The "intermittent custody order", introduced under CJA 2003, ss.183-188, ran as a pilot from January 2004 to November 2006 but was not proceeded with. The "custody plus order", introduced by CJA 2003, ss.151, 182, attaching community activities to a short term of imprisonment, has never been brought into effect. As to the restricted power under PCC(S)A 2000, s 116 to return to prison a prisoner on licence, see 41-056.

What may be termed public protection sentences fall to be imposed on dangerous offenders, in relation to offences committed on or after April 4, 2005, those sentences being:

(i) an indefinite term for the protection of the public (IPP), under CJA 2003, s.225 (41–031, below) in respect of a dangerous offender; and

(ii) an extended term under CJA 2003, s.228 in respect of "violent" or "sexual" offences,

as to which, see DANGEROUS OFFENDERS; PROTECTIVE SENTENCES.

A number of general topics in relation to sentence of imprisonment are dealt with in DEALING WITH AN OFFENDER.

Length of term served relevance to sentence

41–005 CJA 1991, ss.32–39 abolished remission, and replaced it with a system under which all prisoners released before the end of their sentences remained at risk of having their sentences re-activated if they offended again. It replaced parole with a system of discretionary early release for those serving four years or more. It restricted an offender's liberty throughout the entire term imposed by the court to ensure that:

(1) at least half of that term was served in custody; and

(2) offenders sentenced to 12 months or more were supervised by a probation officer, whether or not they were granted parole.

CJA 2003 repealed CJA 1991, ss.32–51, and substituted for the division into sentences of less and those of more than four years, a division between those of less than 12 months, and those of 12 months and over. *CJA 2003, ss. 244,245*

With effect from **April 4, 2005**, CJA 2003, Pt 12, makes a distinction between:

(a) a fixed term prisoner sentenced to a determinate sentence of imprisonment for a term of 12 months or more (or a determinate sentence of detention under PCC(S)A 2000, s.91); he qualifies for release automatically after half his sentence has been served, (unless he misbehaves in prison), and serves the remainder of his sentence in the community; he is liable to recall to custody throughout the whole period;

(b) an offender serving a sentence of imprisonment for a term of less than 12 months qualifies for release at the end of the "custodial period" (expressed in weeks) stated by the judge;

(c) an offender serving two or more concurrent sentences, is governed by rules under CJA 2003, ss.263(2) and 264(2);

(d) an offender classified as a "dangerous offender" by the judge imposing the sentence is released only on a direction by the Parole Board (i.e. when it is safe to do so);

(e) an offender serving an extended sentence under CJA 2003, ss.227, 228 qualifies for release automatically at the end of onehalf of the "appropriate custodial term", if the Parole Board has not authorised his earlier release.

IMPRISONMENT

For the special rules governing life sentences, see LIFE SENTENCES.

SGC 3, 2.1.2 points out that under this new framework, the impact of a custodial sentence will be more severe, since the period in custody and under supervision will be for the whole of the sentence term imposed by the judge. These requirements will be set shortly before release by the Secretary of State (with advice from the probation authorities) but the judge may, (41-027 below) make recommendations at the sentencing stage on the content of those requirements (SGC 3, 2.1.3). The conditions that the Secretary of State may attach to a licence are to be prescribed by order.

Commencement of sentence

41–006 Any sentence imposed, or other order made, by the Crown Court when dealing with an offender, takes effect from the beginning of the day on which it is imposed unless the judge otherwise directs. *PCC(S)A 2000. ss.154,155*

Note that:

(1) a sentence, or other order, varied under SCA 1981, s.47 (see VARIATION OF SENTENCE), takes effect from the beginning of the day on which it was originally imposed unless the judge otherwise directs; but

(2) the judge has no power under that section, or otherwise, to ante-date the commencement of the sentence (*R. v Gilbert* (1974) 60 Cr. App. R. 220; *R. v Whitfield* [2001] EWCA Crim 3043, [2002] 2 Cr. App. R.(S.) 44).

3. Length of term: discretionary sentences

Approach to custodial sentence

41–007 Where a custodial sentence is appropriate:

(1) it is a general principle that the offender may be sentenced only in respect of offences:
  (a) proved against him, whether by a plea of guilty, or by a guilty verdict on indictment; or
  (b) admitted by him, where he asks for them to be taken into consideration on sentence (see DEALING WITH AN OFFENDER) and see *R. v Ganavar* [1998] 1 Cr. App. R. 79 (specimen or sample counts);

(2) apart from a case in which the sentence is fixed by law,or falls to be imposed under PCC(S)A 2000, ss.110–111 (required minimum sentences for certain repeat offence), under CJA 2003, s.225 (dangerous offenders), or under FA 1968, s.51A (minimum sentences for certain firearms offences), **the sentence must be commensurate with the seriousness of the offence;** but *CJA 2003, s.153*

(3) in the case of a "violent" or "sexual" offence, the sentence may be extended as to its licence period under PCC(S)A 2000, s.85, or CJA 2003, s.227, as the case may be (see DANGEROUS OFFENDERS; PROTECTIVE SENTENCES,

(4) in the case of a sentence of less than 12 months, the term must be expressed in weeks, and must be:
    (a) for at least 28 weeks; and
    (b) not more than 51 weeks in respect of any one offence; and

the judge **must** pay due regard to the statutory maxima (41–008, below), the regularly expressed views of CACD, and of the Sentencing Guidelines Council (SGC) established under CJA 2003, s.167 or the Sentencing Council to England and Wales (SCEW) established by CorJA 2009.

Where a judge passes a custodial sentence other than one of those mentioned in (2) above, **the custodial term must be for the shortest term** (not exceeding the permitted maximum, see below) that in the judge's opinion is commensurate with the seriousness of the offence, or the combination of the offence and one or more offences associated with it.

CJA 2003,
s.152(2)

Statutory maximum

41–008   The maximum term provided by statute for a particular offence ought to be reserved for the most serious type of case (*R. v Byrne* (1975) 62 Cr. App. R. 159), and should not be imposed where there is substantial mitigation (*R. v Markus* (1975) 61 Cr. App. R. 58; *R. v Thompson* [1980] 2 Cr. App. R.(S.) 242; *R. v Cade* (1984) 6 Cr. App. R.(S.) 28), and

(1) where the statutory maximum is altered by a provision taking effect:
    (a) after the commission of the offence, but
    (b) before sentence, the former maximum should govern the sentence unless there is a clear indication to the contrary (*R. v Penwith Ex p. Hay* (1979) 1 Cr. App. R.(S.) 265; *R. v Cairns* [1998] Crim. L.R. 141; *R. v Hobbs* [2002] EWCA Crim 387, [2002] 2 Cr. App. R.(S.) 22); (*R. v Harris* [2007] EWCA Crim 1622, [2008] 1 Cr. App. R.(S.) 47), although if the case has been conducted on the basis that the offence was committed after the date on which the increase came into effect, the new maximum may be applied (*R. v Lewis* (1993) Cr. App. R.(S.) 744);
(2) where the facts of the offence of which the offender has been been convicted fall clearly within the definition of another offence with a lesser maximum, it may be appropriate to approach the sentence with the lower maximum in view— this is particularly apposite in dealing with sexual offences (see, e.g. *R. v Quayle* (1993) 14 Cr. App. R.(S.) 726; *R. v Blair* [1996] 1 Cr. App. R.(S.) 336);
(3) the judge is always entitled to take into account prevalence and public concern (*R. v Cunningham* (1993) 14 Cr. App. R.(S.) 444).

The maximum sentence should not normally be imposed on an offender who has pleaded guilty (see DEALING WITH AN OFFENDER).

4. Concurrent or consecutive

41–009 In passing sentence, the judge:

(1) must pass a separate sentence on each count of the indictment; it is wrong to impose a comprehensive sentence covering all of them together;

(2) has a general power to order that sentences run concurrently (*R. v Torr* (1966) 50 Cr. App. R. 73); and

(3) may, (subject to PCC(S)A 2000, s.84 as to **prisoners released on licence** (41-010 below) order one term to commence at the expiration of a previous sentence imposed by any court in England and Wales, and this is so whether the sentences are passed in respect of separate counts contained in one indictment, or of counts in different indictments (*R. v Greenberg* (1944) 29 Cr. App. R. 51,

(4) ought not to order one sentence to run *partly* concurrently and *partly* consecutively to another (*R. v Salmon* [2002] EWCA Crim 2088, [2003] 1 Cr. App. R.(S.) 85).

In relation to the release of prisoners, and their eligibility for home detention curfew, administrative problems may arise where one or more of the component sentences falls to be treated under the release provisions of CJA 1991 and one or more under the provisions of CJA 2003 (see 43-000). The problem is highlighted in a note from the Senior Presiding Judge of March 16, 2009. See also *R v Round* [2009] EWCA Crim 2667, [2010] 2 Cr.App.R.(S.) 94.

Special considerations apply to the combination of fixed term and extended sentences, see DANGEROUS OFFENDERS; PROTECTIVE SENTENCES;

Restriction on consecutive sentences for released prisoners

41–010 Questions of release on licence and recall to prison are within the jurisdiction of the executive. The power of a judge of the Crown Court to return a prisoner on licence to custody under PCC(S)A 2000, s. 116 was abolished by CJA 2003, though partially saved in respect of certain offences, (see 41-056) by SI 2005/950.

A judge sentencing a person to a term of imprisonment, including:

(1) a term of imprisonment for an offence committed **before** 4 **April 2005**; or   CJA 2003, s.265

(2) a term of imprisonment of less than 12 months for an offence committed **on or after that date,** may not now order or direct that the term is to commence on the expiry of any other sentence of imprisonment from which he has been released under:

(a) CJA 2003, Ch 6; or

(b) CJA 1991, Pt 2.

Nor may the judge evade this prohibition by increasing a new concurrent sentence beyond what the offence merits (in terms of CJA 2003, s.153, (see 41-007 at para (2)) in order to ensure a sensible increase in the overall term (*R. v Costello* [2010] EWCA Crim 371, [2010] 2 Cr. App. R.(S.) 94 where the history and complexity of the section is considered).

"Sentence of imprisonment" here includes a sentence of detention under PCC(S)A 2000, s.91 or CJA 2003, s.228 or a sentence of detention in a young offender institution under PCC(S)A 2000, s.96 or under CJA 2003, s.227.

General points

41–011   A number of general points may be made in respect of consecutive sentences:

(1) consecutive sentences should not ordinarily be imposed:
   (a) in respect of offences which arise out of a single incident (*R. v Jones* (1980) 2 Cr. App. R.(S.) 152), though there may be exceptional circumstances (see *R. v Wheatley* (1983) 5 Cr. App. R.(S.) 417; *R. v Dillon* (1983) 5 Cr. App. R.(S.) 439; *R. v Lawrence* (1989)11 Cr. App. R.(S.) 580; *R v. Ralphs* [2009] EWCA Crim 2555, [2010] Crim L.R.318); or
   (b) where offences form part of a series committed against the same victim over a short period of time;
(2) where there are convictions on two or more indictments, it is bad practice to make part of a sentence on the second indictment consecutive to a sentence on the first (*R. vMills* (1969) 53 Cr. App. R. 294);
(3) where a very long sentence is passed, no useful purpose is generally served by imposing a short consecutive sentence for a different offence (*R. v Smith* (1981) 3 Cr. App. R.(S.) 201).
(4) the judge should, in all cases, have regard to the totality of the sentence

to be served (*R v Watts* [2000] 1 Cr. App. R.(S.) 460).
Special considerations apply in the case of consecutive minimum terms, see 41-032 below, and the cases mentioned there.

Otherwise, see generally DEALING WITH AN OFFENDER.

Spelling it out

41–012   Where he passes on an offender more than one term of imprisonment,the judge should state in the presence of the offender whether the terms are to be concurrent or consecutive. Should this not be done, the court officer should ask the judge, before the offender leaves court, to do so.   PD 2004, I.8.1

If the offender is at the time of sentence, already serving two or more consecutive terms of imprisonment, and the judge intends to increase the total period, he should use the expression "consecutive to the total period of imprisonment to which you are already subject".   PD 2004, I.8.2

Particular cases

41–013   CACD has indicated that;

- where an offender commits **further offences while on bail** awaiting trial or sentence for earlier offences, the sentences for the subsequent offences ought to be **consecutive** to those for the earlier offences (*R. v Young* (unreported) March 16, 1973; *R. v Hunnybun* (unreported) November 23, 1979);

- where an offender is convicted of a substantive offence and also of an **assault upon an officer** - if the assault is part and parcel of the substantive offence it may be treated as aggravating that offence and concurrent sentences may be passed (*R. v Kastercum* (1972) 56 Cr. App. R. 298; *R. v Wellington* (1988) 10 Cr. App. R.(S.) 384); but if the assault is in the course of an effort to escape, the offender should be sentenced for the substantive offence independently, a consecutive term being imposed for the assault (*R. v Kastercum*, above; *R.v Gormley* [1973] R.T.R. 483; *R. v Fitter* (1983) 5 Cr. App. R.(S.) 168);

- where an offender **burgles** with intent to steal, and in the course of the offence **uses violence on an occupant** who interrupts him, the offences do not form part of the same transaction and a **consecutive** term ought to be imposed for the assault (*R. v Bunch* (unreported) November 6, 1971; *R. v Jones*, December 15, 1975);

- where an offender is sentenced to a custodial term for an offence, a sentence for **attempting to pervert the course of justice** in relation to that offence ought normally to be made **consecutive** (*Att-Gen's Ref (No. 1 of 1990)* (1990) 12 Cr. App. R.(S.) 245);

- where an offender **carries a firearm** with intent when pursuing his criminal activities, a **consecutive** sentence should be imposed in respect of the firearm (*R. v Jaffier* [2004] 2 Cr. App. R.(S.) 41);

- **a drug dealer** who is prepared to resort to violence and **keeps weapons** for that purpose must expect any sentence imposed to be **significantly increased** to reflect that fact, and that should normally be emphasised by the imposition of **consecutive** sentences (*R. v Hawkes, The Times*, December 11 2007);

- in imposing a **life sentence**, it is **pointless** to make it consecutive to a fixed term which the offender is serving (*Jones v DPP* (1962) 46 Cr. App. R. 129); a determinate sentence cannot be made consecutive to a life term (*R. v Foy* (1962) 46 Cr. App. R. 290);

- where **serious offences are committed in prison** a sentence **consecutive** to that which the prisoner is already serving should be imposed;

- there may be other **exceptional circumstances** where a consecutive sentence is justified e.g. indecent assault and threats to kill arising from the same circumstances (*R. v Fletcher* [2002] EWCA Crim 834, [2002] 2 Cr. App. R.(S.) 127).

The totality principle

41–014   Wherever consecutive sentences are imposed, while there is nothing to prevent the aggregate from exceeding the maximum for any one of them (*R. v Blake* (1961) 45 Cr. App. R. 292) it is the final duty of the judge to ensure (particularly in the case of young offenders - *R. v Morgan* (1972) 56 Cr. App. R. 181) that the totality of the terms is not:

(1) excessive or unjust in relation to the types of offence committed; or

(2) unsuitable to the offender (*R. v Bocskei* (1970) 54 Cr. App. R. 519).

(See also *R. v Reeves* (1980) 2 Cr. App. R.(S.) 35; *R. v Millen* [1980] 2 Cr. App. R.(S.) 357; *R. v Stevens* [1997] 2 Cr. App. R.(S.) 180; *R. v Cooper* (1984) 5 Cr. App. R.(S.) 295); *R v Ralphs* [2009] EWCA Crim 2555, [2010] Crim. L.R.313).

The totality principle still applies where an offender is sentenced for a number of offences one of which is is subject to a mandatory or required sentence.

The judge must:

(a) consider whether the aggregate of consecutive sentences produces a term which is disproportionate to the overall criminality of the offender's conduct; but

(b) apply the principle in such a way that it does not reduce substantially an otherwise appropriate consecutive sentence for another offence, so as to render nugatory the effect of the mandatory minimum term: *R. v Raza* [2009] EWCA Crim 1413, [2010] 1 Cr. App. R.(S.) 56.

5. Credit of remand periods

General

41–015 In relation to determinate sentences of imprisonment and detention, where an offender is sentenced to imprisonment for a term in respect of an offence committed on or after April 4 2005, the judge must, in computing the length of the sentence, order that any time spent on remand in custody, or on bail with certain restrictive conditions, count towards the sentence imposed.

CJA 2003. s.240, 240A

A "sentence of imprisonment" does not include a committal in default of payment of any sum of money, other than one adjudged to be paid on conviction. As to the application of the provisions to suspended sentences, see 41-022 below; as to concurrent and consecutive terms, see 41-023. As to community sentences, see COMMUNITY SENTENCES.

Without a specific order no deduction can be made (*R. v Gordon* [2007] EWCA Crim 167, [2007] 2 Cr. App. R.(S.) 66).

There is a clear distinction between the application of this provision to a community order, on the one hand, and a suspended sentence order on the other (*R. v Rakib* [2011] EWCA Crim 870; [2011] Crim. L.R. 570).

Application of provisions

41–016 The above provision applies where the offender has been either CJA 2003, s.240(1):

(1) "remanded in custody" (see 41-017) below) in connection with the offence or a "related offence", that is to say any other offence, the charge for which was founded on the same facts or evidence, (whether or not he has also been remanded in custody

in connection with other offences or has also been detained in connection with other matters); or

(2) remanded on bail by a court in the course of, or in connection with proceedings for the offence, (or for any related offence after November 3, 2008), and his bail was subject to a qualifying curfew condition and an electronic monitoring condition ("the relevant conditions") (*R. v Barrett*, [2009] EWCA Crim 2213; [2010] 1 Cr. App. R.(S.) 87).

Where this situation arises the judge must direct:

(a) in respect of (1) that the number of days for which the offender was remanded in connection with the offence, or a related offence; and

(b) in respect of (2) that the "credit period" (as defined in 41-019 below), count as time served as part of the sentence, unless and to the extent that:

    (i) any rules made by the Secretary of State provide otherwise (see 41-021), or

    (ii) the judge is of the opinion that it is just (*R.v Whitehouse* [2010] EWCA Crim 1927, [2011] 1 Cr. App. (S.) 95) in all the circumstances of the case not to give a direction (41-021 below),

in which circumstances he may give a direction to the effect that a period of days which is less than the credit period is to count as time served by the offender as part of the sentence.

In respect of (2) above (bail cases), in considering whether to take such a course the judge must, in particular, take into account whether or not the offender has, at any time whilst on bail subject to the relevant conditions, broken either or both of them. CJA 2003, s.40A(7)

Meaning of "remanded in custody"

41–017 In relation to para (1) above (custody cases), references in CJA 2003, ss.240 and 241 to an offender's being "remanded in custody" are references to his being: CJA 2003, s.242(2)

(a) remanded in, or committed to, custody by an order of a court;

(b) remanded or committed to local authority accommodation under CYPA 1969, s.23 (see CHILDREN AND YOUNG PERSONS) and placed and kept in secure accommodation or detained in a secure training centre pursuant to arrangements under CYPA 1969, s.23(7A); or

(c) remanded, admitted or removed to hospital under MHA 1983, ss.35, 36, 38 or 48 (see MENTALLY DISORDERED OFFENDERS).

The periods for which an offender is in the custody of the court for the orderly and efficient conduct of the trial are not to be credited (*Burgess v S of S* [2001] 1 W.L.R. 93).

Special rules apply to detention and training orders (see DETENTION OF YOUNG OFFENDERS).

Bail conditions

41–018   In relation to 41-016 para (2) (bail cases) the following defini- ·   CJA 2003,
tions need to be noted   s.240A(12)

- **"electronic monitoring condition"** means any electronic monitoring requirements imposed under BA 1976, s.3(6ZAA) for
  the purpose of securing the electronic monitoring of a person's
  compliance with a qualifying curfew condition;
- **"qualifying curfew condition"** means a condition of bail which
  requires the person granted bail to remain at one or more specified places for a total of not less than 9 hours in any given day.

The "credit period" defined for bail cases

41–019   The "credit period" for the purposes of bail cases, ie 41-016   CJA 2003,
para (2), is the number of days represented by: s.240A(12)

(1) half of the sum of the day on which the offender's bail was first
    subject to conditions that, had they applied throughout the day
    in question, would have been "relevant conditions" (see 41-016
    para (2) above); and
(2) the number of other days on which the offender's bail was
    subject to those conditions (excluding the last day on which it
    was so subject), rounded up to the nearest whole number.

Note that the provisions

(a) do not apply to a period spent on bail subject to such condi-
    tions prior to Nov 3, 2008; but
(b) do apply to a period spent on bail subject to those conditions,
    after that date, even if the accused was initially remanded
    on bail subject to those conditions before that date and there
    has been no further court order since that date (*R. v Barrett*,
    (above),

Although a judge might, in his discretion, give a modest period of credit
for time spent on bail subject to such a condition before Nov 3, 2008, or
time spent on bail before or after that date subject to conditions falling
just short of the qualifying curfew (see *R. v Sherif* [2009] EWCA Crim
2653 [2009] 2 Cr. App. R.(S.) 235) no reduction in sentence should normally be given for a period spent on night time curfew (*R. v Monaghan*
[2009] EWCA Crim 2699; [2010] 2 Cr. App. R.(S.) 50).

Spelling it out

41–020   Where the judge: CJA 2003,
    ss.240(5),
(1) gives a direction he must state in open court: 240A(8)
    (a) the number of days for which the offender was remanded in
        custody, or the number of days on which he was subject to
        the "relevant conditions", as the case may be; and
    (b) the number of days in relation to which the direction is
        given;
(2) does not give a direction or gives such number of days less than   CJA 2003, ss.
    that for which the offender was remanded in custody he must   240(6), 240A(9)
    state in open court that:

563

    (a) his decision is in accordance with the Rules; or

    (b) he is of the opinion mentioned in 41-016 para (2)(a)(ii) above, stating what the circumstances are.

Where the judge is minded to give a direction for such number of days less than that for which the offender was remanded, he ought to raise the matter with the defence advocate, who may wish to make representations (*R. v Barber* 2006] EWCA Crim 162, [2006] 2 Cr. App. R.(S.) 81; *R. v Metcalfe* [2009] EWCA Crim 374; [2009] 2 Cr. App. R.(S.) 85).

    Where the judge omits to give a direction, it is the responsibility of the advocates to bring the matter to his attention. Where that does not occur the same procedural mechanism as set out in (2) above, should be used to correct the mistake.

Disapplying the credit period

41–021   If the judge wishes to disapply the period (41-016 (2)(b)(ii)) he must give reasons for so doing (*R. v Norman* [2008] EWCA Crim 1810]; [2009] 1 Cr. App. R.213.).

    Note that it was held not to be a good reason for disapplying the period that;

    (1) the offender persisted in denying his guilt up to a certain point (*R. v Vaughan* [2008] EWCA Crim 1613; [2009] 1 Cr. App. R.(S.) 65,

    (2) the offender breached his bail and had to be arrested on a bench warrant, and having been released again failed to attend on the probation officer for the purposes of preparing a report (*R. v Floriman* [2009] EWCA Crim 2237; [2010] 1 Cr. App. R.(S.) 96, or

    (3) when a suspended sentence fell to be activated, the offender had already spent a period of custody on remand that was almost the equivalent of the period of detention to be activated with the effect that he was likely to be instantly released (*R. v Shariff* [2009] EWCA Crim 2687; [2010] 2 Cr. App. R.(S.) 39).

Care must be taken in the case of young offenders to note that, if a detention and training order has intervened between arrest and sentence, the 2011 Rules do not apply (see DETENTION OF YOUNG OFFENDERS).

    The Remand in Custody (Effect of Concurrent and Consecutive Sentences of Imprisonment) Rules 2005/108 are important. They provide that:

    (a) no direction should be made if, while on remand, the offender was also serving another sentence of imprisonment and was not released on licence;

    (b) no direction is to be made where the judge imposes a sentence to be served consecutively to a sentence to which CJA 1967, s.67 applies. These Rules ensure that the courts will not inadvertently make a direction whose effect is that the same remand day counts towards sentence twice.

Application to suspended sentences

41–022 A suspended sentence under CJA 2003, and in relation to bail cases a sentence to which an order under PCC(S)A 2000, s 118 (suspended sentence) relates, it to be treated as a sentence of imprisonment:

CJA 2003, s. 240(7)

(1) when it takes effect under CJA 2003,Sch.12, paras 8(2)(a) or (b), (see BREACH, AMENDMENT AND REVOCATION OF ORDERS)

(2) not when it is first imposed (see *R. v Fairbrother* [2007] EWCA Crim 3280 [2008] 2 Cr. App. R.(S.) 43, *R. v Whitehouse* above).

When a judge imposes a suspended sentence he should not normally give credit for days spent on remand when fixing the term to be suspended. Days spent on remand should normally be taken into account by the judge activating the suspended sentence who should, in the usual way, give a s. 240 direction specifying the number of days, unless it would be unjust to do so. It follows that:

(a) if the judge imposing the suspended sentence extraordinarily considered that there were good reasons for taking days on remand into account when fixing the term to be suspended, he must make that clear, and his reasons for doing so.

(b) a judge activating a suspended sentence should not assume that days spent on remand have been taken into account by the sentencing judge unless it is clear and obvious that the sentencing judge has done so. If it was clear and obvious, the judge activating the suspended sentence should not make a direction under s, 240 since it would be unjust for the defendant to obtain double credit for those days.

Although the sentencing judge should not normally give credit for days spent on remand, it is important that he is informed as to the number of days so spent, because if the offender had already spent longer on remand than he would serve under a custodial sentence merited by the offence, a suspended sentence would usually be inappropriate.

(*R v. Hewitt* [2011] EWCA Crim 885, [2011] Cr. App. R.(S.) 111). See also *R v. Barrett* [2009] EWCA Crim 2213) (above); *R v Shariff* [2010] 1 Cr. App. R.(S.) 87.

It is not appropriate to impose a suspended sentence when a sentence of immediate custody would have resulted in the offender getting the benefit of a substantial period spent on remand. In those circumstances the sentence should not be suspended but should be constructed in such a way as to give the appellant the benefit of the time spent on remand (*R. v Maughan* [2011] EWCA Crim 787; [2011] Crim. L.R. 569; see also *McCabe* (1988) 10 Cr. App. R. (S.) 134; [1988] Crim. L.R. 469 CA (Crim Div), and *Peppard* (1990) 12 Cr. App. R.(S.) 88; *Barrett* [2009] EWCA Crim 2213; [2010] 1 Cr. App. R.(S.) 87).

Concurrent and consecutive terms

41–023 For the purposes of the reference (in 41-016) to the term of imprisonment to which an offender has been sentenced (that is to say,

CJA 2003, s.240(8)

the reference to his 'sentence"), consecutive terms and terms which are wholly or partly concurrent are to be treated as a single term if:

(1) the sentences were passed on the same occasion; or
(2) where they were passed on different occasions, the person has not been released under CJA 2003 Ch.6 at any time during the period beginning with the first and ending with the last of those occasions.

Where an offence is found to have been committed over a period of two or more days days, or at some time during a period of two or more days, it shall be taken for the purposes or of subs.(1) to have been committed on the last of those days. **CJA 2003, s.240(8)(9)**

This section applies to a determinate sentence of detention under PCC(S)A 2000, s.91, or CJA 2003, s.228 as it applies to an equivalent sentence of imprisonment. **CJA 2003, s.240(10)**

Number of days: correction and amendment

41–024 In *R. v Norman* (above) pointed out that it is vital that the judge is provided with accurate information as to the number of days which are said to have been spent on remand. A record of "electronic monitoring of curfew bail" should accompany an accused from court to court. If an accused is on bail before the Crown Court and there is no form, the court officer needs to ask the magistrates' court for clarification and obtain the form if it exists (*R. v Irving* [2010] EWCA Crim 189, [2010] 2 Cr. App. R.(S.) 75).

Where:

(1) the information provided subsequently turns out to be incorrect, the sentencing court can only correct the mistake within 56 days, unless the judge's order has identified the period in question but the order as drafted has simply miscalculated the number of days, in which case the court record may be amended;
(2) the period for which the direction has been given is wrong, and both parties agree, but more than 56 days have elapsed since the sentence was imposed, any application for leave to appeal should so state, in which event, on receipt of confirmation of that agreement from both the prosecution and the defence, the matter will be remitted by the Registrar direct to the court for it to correct the mistake.

Judges should adopt the following formula suggested in *R. v Gordon* (above), see also *R v Nnaji* [2009] EWCA Crim 468; [2009] 2 Cr. App. R.(S.) 107:

"The accused will receive full credit for the full period of time spent in custody on remand and half the time spent under curfew if the curfew qualified under the provisions of section 240 [of the Criminal Justice Act 2003]. On the information before me the total period is . . . days but if this period is mistaken, this court will order an amendment of the record for the correct period to be recorded"

so that errors may be corrected in the court office (see also *R. v Irving* (above). That formula may be adapted to apply to s.240A, as inserted by CJIA 2008, s.21 as it applies to s.240.

Additional guidance is given in *R. v Boutell.* EWCA Crim 2054 174 J.P. 546 [2009].

If an error cannot be corrected administratively, and requires correction by the court, the court must be constituted as it was originally (*R. v McKenzie* [2010] EWCA Crim 2441).

Pre-2005 principles

41–025   Certain general principles were enunciated before the enactment of CJA 2003. Thus;

(1) the same remand period cannot be taken into account twice in relation to separate periods of imprisonment imposed on different occasions for different offences which are not ordered to run concurrently or consecutively (*R. v Home Secretary Ex p. Kitaya,* The Times, January 20, 1988);

(2) where an offender is remanded at the same time for related offences, which are subsequently tried and he is sentenced separately, time spent on remand not credited against the first sentence may be credited against the second (*R. v Governor of Haverigg Prison Ex p. McMahon,* The Times, September 24, 1997);

(3) time on remand in relation to offences for which the sentences are later quashed on appeal does not count towards a later sentence for a different offence for which the accused was on remand at the same time (*R. v Governor of Wandsworth Prison Ex p. Sorhaindo*, The Times, January 5, 1999).

In respect of young offenders, *see R. v M (Young Offender: Time Spent in Custody)* [1999] 1 W.L.R 485; *R. v Home Secretary Ex p. Furber* [1998] 1 Cr. App. R. (S.) 208).

6.   Ancillary orders

Custodial sentence combined with fine

41–026   It may be appropriate to combine a financial penalty with an immediate custodial sentence where:

(1) there is reason to believe that the offender has assets which he has not disclosed (*R. v Michel* (1984) 6 Cr. App. R.(S.) 379; *R. v Benmore* (1983) 5 Cr. App. R.(S.) 468);

(2) there is reason to believe that a substantial amount of stolen property remains available for the offender's benefit on release (*R. v Chatt* (1984) 6 Cr. App. R.(S.) 75); and

(3) exceptionally, the maximum custodial term is not an adequate penalty (*R. v Garner* (1986) 82 Cr. App. R.27).

7.   Recommending licence conditions

General

41–027   In respect of offences **committed after April 4, 2005**, save in the case of a sentence of: CJA 2003, s.238

(1) detention for juveniles under PCC(S)A 2000, s.91; or

(2) a term under CJA 2003, s.228 (dangerous offenders), the judge who sentences an offender to a term of imprisonment for **12 months or more** in respect of an offence, may, when passing sentence, recommend to the Secretary of State (who is bound to have regard to such a recommendation), particular conditions which, in his view, should be included in any licence granted to the offender on his release. Such a recommendation is not part of the sentence.

The conditions which may be recommended are those which impose on an offender:

(a) a requirement that he reside at a certain place;
(b) a requirement relating to his making or maintaining contact with a person;
(c) a restriction relating to his making or maintaining contact with a person;
(d) a restriction on his participation in, or undertaking of, any activity;
(e) a requirement that he participate in, or co-operate with, a programme, or set of activities, designed to further one or more of the purposes referred to in s.250(8) of the Act;
(f) a requirement that he comply with a curfew arrangement;
(g) a restriction on his freedom of movement (which is not a requirement referred to in subpara.(f));
(h) a requirement relating to his supervision in the community by a responsible officer.

Guidance as to licence conditions

41–028   In practice the judge is not likely to know with any certainty at the point of sentence:

(1) to what extent the offender's behaviour may have been addressed in custody; or
(2) what the offender's health and other personal circumstances may be on release,

so that it will be difficult, especially in the case of longer custodial sentences, for him to make an informed judgment about the most appropriate licence conditions to be imposed on release.

SGC (at 3, 2.1.1-14) considered that it might be helpful for the judge to:

(a) indicate any areas of an offender's behaviour about which he has the most concern; and
(b) make suggestions about the types of intervention whether this, in practice, will take place in prison or in the community.

A curfew, exclusion requirement or prohibited activity requirement might be suitable conditions to recommend for the licence period. The judge might also wish to suggest that the offender should complete a rehabilitation programme, e.g. for drug abuse, anger management, or improving skills such as literacy and could recommend that this should be considered as a licence requirement if the programme has not been undertaken or completed in custody.

The probation authorities need to have due regard to any such recommendations and the final decision on licence conditions will need to build upon any interventions during the custodial period and any other changes in the offender's circumstances.

The involvement of the probation authorities at the pre-sentence stage will clearly be pivotal. A recommendation on the likely post-release requirements included in a pre-sentence report will assist the judge in making his decision on the overall length of the sentence although any recommendation would still have to be open to review when release is being considered.

8. Sentences of 12 months or more

Length of term

41–029 Judges need to be aware that: SGC 3, 2.1.7.

- (1) a fixed term custodial sentence of 12 months or more under the 2003 framework (41–005, above) will increase the sentence actually served, whether in custody or in the community, by up to one-third; and
- (2) SGC recommends that in order to maintain consistency between the lengths of sentence under the former framework and the 2003, the judge imposing a fixed term custodial sentence of 12 months or more for an offence **committed on or after April 4, 2005**, should consider reducing the overall length of the sentence that would have been imposed under the former provisions, by no more than one quarter).

Spelling it out

41–030 The changes in the nature of custodial sentences for offences **committed on or after April 4, 2005**, required changes in the way the sentence was pronounced (see DEALING WITH AN OFFENDER).

The judge in imposing such a sentence (other than for a "dangerous offender" (see 41–045 and following) needs to spell out the practical implications of the sentence being imposed, so that offenders, victims and the public alike all understand).

He should state clearly, at the point of sentence:

- (1) the way in which the sentence has been calculated;
- (2) how it will be served;
- (3) that the sentence is in two parts, one in custody and one under supervision in the community.
- (4) that the sentence does not end when the offender is released from custody;
- (5) that non-compliance with licence requirements imposed in the second half of the sentence is likely to result in a return to custody.

9.   Dangerous offenders; CJA 2003, Pt 12

Introduction

41–031   "Protective" sentences, or sentences for public protection, which exceed the normal determinate sentence of imprisonment are provided by both by PCC(S)A 2005 and CJA 2003, for both dangerous and persistent offenders. The former, which now apply only to offences committed **before April 4, 2005** have been overtaken by the latter, and are no longer dealt with in this work. They are dealt with at DANGEROUS OFFENDERS; PROTECTIVE SENTENCES;

Amendments tabled by the Justice Secretary in the last days of October to the Legal Aid Etc Bill 2011 now before Parliament propose the repeal of the existing sentences for dangerous offenders and their replacement by new forms of sentence.

10.   Mandatory minimum sentences

Introduction

41–032   PCC(S)A 2000 introduced mandatory minimum sentences of:

(1) Seven years for a third Class A drug trafficking committed since 30 September 1997;

(2) Three years for a third domestic burglary committed since 30 November 1999;

(3) automatic life sentence for a second serious offence committed since 30 September 1997. This section has subsequently been replaced from 4 April 005 by indeterminate sentences for public protection.

CJA 2003 introduced a mandatory minimum sentence of five years (three years in the case of those aged 16 or 17) for certain offences under section 5 of the Firearms Act 1968.

(1)   Automatic life sentence

General

41–033   PCC(S)A 2003 introduced minimum terms for offenders who committed:

(1) a second serious offence (mandatory or "automatic" life life sentence);

(2) a third class A drug trafficking offence (minimum of seven years); and

(3) a third domestic burglary (minimum of three years).

The **automatic life sentence** under (1) applied only to offences committed **after October 1, 1997 and before April 4, 2005**, and has been overtaken by the provisions of CJA 2003. It is no longer dealt with in this work, and reference should be made to the 2007 edition. Those sentence under (2) and (3) are dealt with below.

(2) Minimum seven years for third Class A drug trafficking offence

General
41–034 Where:

PCC(S)A 2000
s.110(1)(2)(5)

(1) an offender is convicted of a Class A drug trafficking offence committed **after October 1, 1997**; and

(1) at the time the offence was committed, the offender was 18 or over and had been convicted in any part of the United Kingdom of two other Class A drug trafficking offences; and

(2) one of those had been committed after he had been convicted of the other, the judge **must** impose upon an offender an appropriate custodial sentence for a term of **at least seven years**, that is, in the case of:

(a) an offender who is 21 or over, a sentence of at least seven years' imprisonment; or in the case of

(b) an offender under 21, a sentence of at least seven years' detention in a young offender institution,

unless he is of opinion that there are particular circumstances relating to any of the offences or to the offender, which would make that sentence unjust in all the circumstances.

A hospital order may be made in respect of a mentally disordered offender as an alternative to such a sentence, or a hospital direction under MHA 1983, s.45A (inserted by CSA 1997, s.46) and see MENTALLY DISORDERED OFFENDERS.

MHA 1983,
s.82(1)

Definitions
41–035 "Class A drug trafficking offences", as the term implies, means a drug trafficking offence committed in respect of a Class A drug, and for this purpose "Class A drug" has the same meaning as in MDA 1971; "drug trafficking offence" means an offence which is specified in:

PCC(S)A 2000,
s.110(5)

(1) POCA 2002, Sch.2, para.1; or

(2) so far as it relates to that paragraph, para.10 of that Schedule.

The approach to "unjust"
41–036 In *R. v Harvey* [2000] 1 Cr. App. R.(S.) 368, the CACD rejected an approach to the section based on the contention that a sentence passed under the section which was manifestly excessive on the facts of the case was "unjust." Section 110 is intended to have a deterrent effect. The Guidelines issued by SGC on the seriousness of offences do not apply (*Att-Gen's Reference (No.6 of 2006) (Michael Farish)* [2006] EWCA Crim 1043, [2007] 1 Cr. App. R.(S.) 12).

As to the application of the "totality principle" (see 41-014) to consecutive sentences, see 41-039 below.

Discount for plea
41–037 Nothing prevents the judge under this section, after taking into account any matters referred to in PCC(S)A 2000, s.152, from imposing a sentence which is not less than 80 per cent of the minimum

mandatory sentence (see *R. v Brown* [2000] 2 Cr. App. R.(S.) 435; *R. v Hickson* [2002] 1 Cr. App. R.(S.) 298).In *R. v Darling* [2009] EWCA Crim 1610, [2010] 1 Cr. App. R.(S.) 63 CACD said that the discount was not restricted to the 20% allowed by s.144(2).

Section 110 is intended to have a deterrent effect. The Guidelines issued by SGC on the seriousness of offences do not apply (*Att-Gen's Reference (No.6 of 2006 (Michael Farish)* above.)

(3) Minimum three years for third domestic burglary

General
41–038 Where:

(1) an offender is convicted of a domestic burglary (i.e. a burglary committed in respect of a building or part of a building which is a dwelling) committed **after November 30, 1999;** and   PCC(S)A 2000, s.111(1)(2)(5)(6)

(2) at the time when that burglary was committed, he was 18 or over and has been convicted in England or Wales of two other domestic burglaries; and

(3) one of those other burglaries was committed after he had been convicted of the other and both of them were committed after November 30, 1999, the judge must impose a sentence of imprisonment for a term of at least three years, except where he is of opinion that there are particular circumstances which:

  (a) relate to any of the offences or to the offender, and

  (b) would make it unjust to do so in all the circumstances.   PCC(S)A 2000, s.115

Where an offence is found to have been committed over a period of two or more days, or at some time during a period of two or more days, it will be taken for the purposes of ss.110–111 to have been committed on the last of those days. As to persons convicted of corresponding offences under Service Law, see PCC(S)A 2000, s.114.

In *R. v Stephens* [2000] 2 Cr. App. R.(S.) 320 failure to warn the offender of his liability to these provisions was held to be capable of amounting to an "exceptional circumstance".

The indictment must make clear that the building is a "dwelling" to found a sentence under this provision (*R v Miller* [2010] EWCA Crim 809, [2011] 1 Cr.App.R.(S.) 12).

Attempted burglary is not burglary (*R. v Maguire* [2002] EWCA Crim 2689, [2003] 2 Cr. App. R.(S.) 10). As to conspiracy cases, see *A-G's Reference (Nos. 48 & 49 of 2010)* [2011] Crim L.R.169.

Prescribed sequence
41–039 The sequence of events required before an offender qualifies for such a sentence is as follows:

(1) he must have committed a first offence of burglary;

(2) he must have been convicted of that offence; then

(3) he must have committed a second offence of burglary; and then

(4) he must have been convicted of that second offence; then

(5) he must have committed a third offence of burglary.

(*R. v Hoare* [2004] EWCA Crim 191, [2005] 2 Cr. App. R.(S.) 50).

As to the necessity of applying the "totality principle" (see 41-014), and the construction of the sentences to achieve this result, see *R. v. Raza* [2009] EWCA Crim 1413; [2010] 1 Cr. App. R. (S.) 56, *R. v. Sparkes* [2011] EWCA Crim 880, [2011] Crim. L.R. 654.

A person convicted under Service Law, where the corresponding civil offence qualifies under ss.110–111, these provisions apply as if he had been convicted in England and Wales of the corresponding civil offence; See as to a *Gilham* situation *R. v Gibson* [2004] EWCA Crim 593, [2004] 2 Cr. App. R.(S.) 84.

PCC(S)A 2000, s.114

In respect of qualifying offences, a certificate from the sentencing court is sufficient proof.

PCC(S)A 2000, s.113

11. Prescribed minimum sentences for certain firearms offences

FA 1968, s.51A

41–040   Where a person **aged 21 or over** is convicted of:

(1) an offence under FA 1968, s.51(a), (ab), (aba), (ac), (ae), s.51A (af) or (c); or

FA 1968, s.51A

(2) an offence under FA 1968, s.5(1A)(a); or

(3) an offence committed **on or after April 6, 2007** in respect of a firearm or ammunition specified in s.5(1)(a) under any provisions of FA 1968, listed in (1) above, being ss.16, 16A, 17, 18, 19 and 20(1); and

the offence was committed at a time when he was aged 16 or over, the judge **must** impose a sentence of imprisonment, for at least a minimum term (with or without a fine) of five years unless he is of opinion that there are exceptional circumstances relating to the offence or to the offender which justify his not doing so.

The offence must have been charged in the indictment; mere evidence of possession, without a count in the indictment is not enough (*Att-Gen's Reference (No. 114 of 2004)* [2004] EWCA Crim, 2954, [2005] 2 Cr. App. R.(S.) 6).

Where an offence is found to have been committed over a period of two or more days, or at some time during a period of two or more days, it is to be taken to have been committed on the last of those days.

Gun crime; the approach to the section

41–041   The theme that that emerges from the judgments in *R. v Jordan* [2004] EWCA Crim 3291, [2005] 2 Cr. App. R.(S.) 44); *R. v Rehman* [2005] EWCA Crim 2056, [2006] 1 Cr. App. R.(S.) 77 and *R. v Olawaiye* [2009] EWCA Crim 1925, [2010] 1 Cr. App. R.(S.) 100, is that the gravity of gun crime cannot be exaggerated. Guns kill and maim, terrorise and intimidate; that is why criminals want them: that is why they use them: and that is why they organise their importation and manufacture, supply and distribution.

Sentencing courts must address the fact that too many lethal weapons are too readily available, too many are carried, too many are used, always with devastating effect on individual victims and with insidious corrosive impact on the wellbeing of the local community.

In regard to sentencing, the judge needs to bear in mind that:

(1) possession of a firearm, without more, and without any aggravating features beyond the fact of such possession, is, of itself, a grave crime, and should be dealt with accordingly;

(2) Parliament intended that, for protection of the public against the dangers arising from the unlawful possession of firearms, considerations of retribution and deterrence should be given greater emphasis, and the personal circumstances of the offender less than would normally be the case (per Lord Nimmo Smith in the Scots case of *HMA v McGovern*, 2007 HCJA 21) unless these pass the "exceptional" threshold to which the section relates;

(3) the Act, (unlike PCC(S)A 2000, ss.110, 111) does not permit of a discount on the minimum sentence for a plea of guilty, unless the judge identifies "exceptional" circumstances.

Guidance in sentencing gun crime is to be found in *R. v Avis* [1998] 1 Cr. App. R.120 updated by *R. v Olawaiye,* (above). The minimum term provisions of FA 1951 are harsh, even Draconian, however their purpose is clear; it is to deter people from possessing firearms (*R v Moses* [2009] EWCA Crim 2820).

"Exceptional circumstances"

41–042 If the judge identifies "exceptional circumstances" :

(1) the sentence is then at large, and the prescribed minimum sentence will be a factor which he can take into account (as he will the guideline case of *R. v Avis* (above) and all available mitigation);

(2) he will then, but only then, take into account not only the "exceptional circumstances" themselves but also good character and any timely plea of guilt;

It is not appropriate for him to look at each circumstance separately and to conclude that it does not amount to an exceptional circumstance; a holistic approach is necessary. There will be cases where there is one single striking feature which relates either to the offence or to the offender, which causes the case to fall within the requirement of "exceptional circumstances". There will be other cases where no single factor by itself will amount to "exceptional" circumstance but the collective impact of all the relevant circumstances makes the case exceptional.

Cases in which exceptional circumstances can be said to arise are likely to be rare (*R. v Jordan* (above); *R. v McEneaney* [2005] EWCA Crim 431, [2005] Cr. App. R.(S.) 86; *Evans v The Queen* [2005] ECWA Crim 811; *R v. Lashari* [2010] EWCA Crim 1504 [2011] 1 Cr. App. R.(S.) 72; but see *R. v Blackall* [2005] EWCA Crim 1128, [2006] 1 Cr. App. R.(S.) 22 (paraplegic offender); *R. v Mehmet* [2005] EWCA Crim 2074; [2006] 1 Cr. App. R.(S.) 75 (early plea, good character, no criminal intention, no ammunition) and *R. v Rehman* (above) (early plea, good character, cooperation with the authorities, public employment).

The circumstances are "exceptional" for the purposes of s.51A(2) if the minimum five-year term would be an arbitrary and disproportionate sentence (*R. v Rehman*, above). In *R v. Edwards (Michelle Marie)* [2006] EWCA Crim 2833, [2007] 1 Cr. App. R.(S.) 111, CACD emphasized that strong personal mitigation on its own is unlikely to be sufficient to amount to "exceptional circumstances". See also *R v Ocran* [2010] EWCA Crim 1209; [2011] 1 Cr. App. R(S.) 225(6) [2011] EWCA Crim 861; *R. v Boateng* [2011] *Att.-Gen.'s Reference (No. 64 of 2010) (R. v Brunt)* [2011] 2 Cr. App. R.(S.) 135(25), C.A. [2011] 2 Cr. App. R.(S.) 104, *R. v Shaw* [2011] 2 Cr. App. R.(S.) 376 (offender's poor health, age, guilty plea, lack of convictions, no evidence weapons used in the commission of any crime, low risk of re-offending).

The judge ought to accept the accused's account unless he is sure that it is not true (*R v. Lashari* above).

Using someone to mind a weapon

41–043   Where an offender is guilty of an offence under VCRA 2006, s.28 (using someone to mind a weapon) and:

VCRA 2006 ss. 28,29

(1) at the time of the offence, the offender was aged 16 or over; and
(2) the dangerous weapon in respect of which the offence was committed was a a firearm mentioned in FA 1968, s.5(1)(a)–(f) or (c) or FA 1968, s.51A (possession of a firearm which attracts a minimum sentence),

the judge **must** impose (with or without a fine) where the offender is:

(a) aged 18 or over at the time of conviction, a term of imprisonment of not less than five years;
(b) under 18 at the time of conviction, a term of detention under PCC(S)A 2000, s.91 of not less than three years,

unless, in either case he is of the opinion that there are "exceptional circumstances" relating to the offence which justify his not doing so.

In respect of (a), until such time as CJCSA 2000, Sch.7, para.180 comes into force, the reference to a sentence of imprisonment in relation to an offender under 21 at the time of conviction is to be read as a reference to a sentence of detention in a young offender institution.

Where:

(i) the judge is considering for the purposes of sentencing the seriousness of an offence under s.28; and
(ii) at the time of the offence the offender was aged 18 or over and the person used to look after, hide or transport the weapon was not,

he must treat the fact that that person was under the age of 18 at that time as an aggravating factor (that is to say, a factor increasing the seriousness of the offence), and must state in open court that the offence was so aggravated.

Where an offence under s.28 of using another person for a particular purpose is found to have involved that other person's having possession of a weapon, or being able to make it available, over a period of two or more days, or at some time during a period of two or more days, and on any day in that period, an age requirement was satisfied, the question whether s.29(3) applies or (as the case may be) the question whether the offence was aggravated under this section is to be determined as if the offence had been committed on that day.

12. Suspending a sentence

If the Legal Aid Etc. Bill 2011, now going through Parliament, is enacted in its present form, it will make substantial changes to this section.

Statutory provisions

41–044   A judge passing a sentence of imprisonment (or in the case of a person aged at 18 but under 21, detention in a young offender institution) a term of **at least 14 days but not more than 12 months** for an offence committed on or after April 4, 2005, may order:

CJA 2003, s.!89(1)(2)(7)

(1) the offender to comply during a specified supervision period with one or more of the requirements falling within s. 190(1) and specified in the order; and
(2) that the sentence of imprisonment (or detention in a young offender institution) is not to take effect unless:
   (a) during the supervision period the offender fails to comply with a requirement imposed under (1) above; or
   (b) during the "operational period" specified in the order, the offender commits in Great Britain another offence (whether or not punishable with imprisonment).

Where two or more sentences imposed on the same occasion are to be served consecutively, the power conferred by subs.(l) is not exercisable in relation to any of them unless the aggregate of the terms of the sentences does not exceed 65 weeks.

There is no need for "exceptional circumstances" as contained in PCC(S)A 2000 ss.l18-124 unless sentence is being passed in respect of a pre-commce-ment offence. In respect of pre-commencement offences, the aggregate of the terms may be up to two years instead of 12 months.

The position in relation to offences committed before April 4 2005 under the provisions of PCC(S)A 2000, ss.l18-124; is no longer dealt with in this work, and reference will need to be made to the 2008 edition.

Additional provisions

41–045   Several matters need to be borne in mind, namely:

(1) a suspended sentence order under s.l 89 must include at least one of the community requirements under CJA 2003, s.190(1) and must not be for longer than 12 month;
(2) the judge must specify not only the operational period of the sentence, but also the supervision period for the purpose of the community requirements; these may not be the same (*R. v Lees Wolfenden* [2006] EWCA Crim 3068; [2007] 1 Cr. App. R.(S.) 119);

(3) where the judge feels able to take a merciful course and not imposean immediate and substantial custodial sentence, it may be moresensible to impose a community sentence rather than a suspended sentence of imprisonment kept artificially low, since on the breach of;

    (a) a suspended sentence, the judge is restricted to activating the term of the suspended sentence, or a lesser term (Sch.12, para.8); while

    (b) a community order, the offender may be dealt with in any manner originally available to the sentencing court had a community order not been made (Sch.8 para.l0) and *R. v Phipps* [2007] EWCA Crim 2923; [2008] 2 Cr. App. R. (S.) 20).

Subject to any provision to the contrary contained in CJA 1967, PCC(S)A 2000 or any other enactment passed or instrument made under any enactment after December 31, 1967, a suspended sentence which has not taken effect under CJA 2003, Sch.12, para.8 is to be treated as a sentence of imprisonment for the purposes of all enactments and instruments made under enactments (CJA 2003, s.l 89(6); SI 2005/643).

Pre-conditions to suspension

41–046   There are similarities between a suspended sentence under CJA 2003 and a community sentence. In both cases, requirements may be imposed during the supervision period, and the judge may respond to a breach by imposing a custodial sentence. The crucial difference is that the suspended sentence is aentence of imprisonment; it is appropriate only for an offence that passes the custody threshold and for which imprisonment is the only option. A community sentence may be imposed for an offence that passes the custody threshold where the court considers that to be appropriate.   *SGC 3,2.2.10*

It follows that the judge, if minded to impose a suspended sentence;

(1) must already have decided that a prison sentence is justified; and

(2) should also have decided the length of sentence that would be the shortest term commensurate with the seriousness of the offence if it were to be imposed immediately;

(1) should not, having decided to suspend the sentence, impose a longer term than he would have if the sentence were to take effect immediately. SGC has recommended that the judge ask himself whether: *SGC 3, 2.2.12*

    (a) the custody threshold has been passed;

    (b) if so, is is unavoidable that a custodial sentence be imposed;   *SGC 3, 2.2.11*

    (c) if so, that sentence can be suspended,

if not, the judge should impose a sentence which takes immediate effect for the term commensurate with the seriousness of the offence.

It is not appropriate to impose a suspended sentence when a sentence of immediate custody would have resulted in the offender getting the benefit of a substantial period spent on remand. In such circumstances the sentence should not be suspended but should be constructed in such a way as to give the appellant the benefit of the time spent on remand, see the authorities cited at 41-002 above.

IMPRISONMENT

Length of term

41–047   A prison sentence which is suspended should be for the same term which would have applied if the offender were being sentenced to immediate custody, and in assessing the length of the operational period, the judge should have in mind:

(1) the relatively short length of the sentence being suspended; and
(2) the advantages to be gained by retaining the opportunity to extend the operational period at a later stage (see BREACH, AMENDMENT AND REVOCATION OF ORDERS).

The operational period of a suspended sentence should reflect the length of the sentence being suspended. As an approximate guide an operational period of up to:

(a) 12 months might normally be appropriate for a suspended sentence of up to six months; and
(b) 18 months might normally be appropriate for a suspended sentence of up to 12 months.

SGC 3, 2.2.10-13

The ordinary rules as to crediting time spent in custody on remand (see DEALING WITH AN OFFENDER) apply to suspended sentences, but a suspended sentence is treated as a sentence of imprisonment when it takes effect under s.1 19 and is "imposed" by the order under which it takes effect.

Consecutive or concurrent

41–048   Under the pre-2003 legislation it was for the judge suspending the sentence to decide whether one or more terms are to run concurrently or consecutively *(Practice Direction* (1962) 46 Cr. App. R. 119). A suspended sentence passed could not be made consecutive to another suspended sentence which was not brought into effect *(R. v Blakeway* (1969) 53 Cr.App.R.498).

Imposition of requirements by suspended sentence order

41–049   The requirements which may be imposed under s.190(1)(2) are those numbered (1)-(13) in COMMUNITY SENTENCES) subject to the restrictions of ss.150 and 218 and the provisions as to particular requirements stated in that paragraph.

CJA 2003, s. 190(1)(2)

The particular requirement(s) will need to ensure that they properly address those factors that are most likely to reduce the risk of re-offending.
Whilst:

SGC 3, 2.2.14

(1) the offence for which a suspended sentence is imposed is generally likely to be more serious than one for which a community sentence is imposed;
(2) the imposition of the custodial sentence is a clear punishment and deterrent. Because of the very clear deterrent threat involved in a suspended sentence:
   (a) requirements imposed as part of that sentence should generally be less onerous than those imposed as part of a community sentence; and

(b) a judge who seeks to impose onerous or intensive requirements on an offender should reconsider his decision to suspend a term of imprisonment and consider whether a community sentence might be more appropriate.

Before making a suspended sentence order imposing two or more different requirements falling within subs.(l), the judge must consider whether, in the circumstances of the case, the requirements are compatible with each other.

The judge's powers to make an electronic monitoring requirement when imposing a suspended sentence are the same as where he makes a community order, as to which see COMMUNITY SENTENCES.

Where the judge feels able to take a merciful course and not impose an immediate and substantial custodial sentence, it may be more sensible for him to impose a community sentence rather than a suspended sentence kept artifi cially low, for

(i) on the breach of a suspended sentence the court is restricted to activating the term of the suspended sentence, or a lesser term (Sch.12, para.8); while

(ii) on the breach of a community order the offender may be dealt with in any manner originally available to the sentencing court had a community order not been made (Sch.8 para. 10). *(R. v Phipps* (above)).

Combinations of other custodial sentences

43–050   Since the whole purpose of suspending a sentence of imprisonment is to avoid sending an offender to prison, it is bad sentencing practice to impose:

(1) on the same occasion, an immediate term in respect of one offence and a suspended term in respect of another *(R. v Sapiano* (1968) 52 Cr. App. R. 674);

(2) a suspended sentence on an offender already serving an immediate term for another offence *(R. v Hammond* [1969] Crim. L.R. 500).

Attaching community requirement

41–051   In its modified form, s.198 provides that the judge who passes a sentence of imprisonment (or, in the case of a person aged at least 18 but under 21, detention in a young offender institution), for a term of at least 14 days but not more than 12 months **must** *(R. v Lees-Wolfenden* [2006] EWCA Crim 3068, [2007] Cr. App. R.(S.) 119) order:

(1) the offender to comply during the supervision period with one or more requirements falling within s.190(1) and specified in the order, and

(2) that the sentence of imprisonment or (detention in a young offender institution is not to take effect unless either:

(a) during the supervision period the offender fails to comply with a requirement imposed under (1); or

(b) during the operational period of the sentence the offender commits in the United Kingdom another offence (whether or not punishable with imprisonment), and, in either case, a court having power to do so subsequently orders, under para.8 of Sch.12 that the original sentence take effect.

Where two or more sentences imposed on the same occasion are to be served consecutively, the power conferred by (1) is not exercisable in relation to any of them unless the aggregate of the terms of the sentences does not exceed 65 weeks).

Note that:

    (i) the supervision period and the operational period must each be a period of not less than six months and not more than two years beginning with the date of the order;

    (ii) the supervision period must not end later than the operational period.

A judge passing a suspended sentence on any person for an offence may not impose a community sentence in his case in respect of that offence or any other offence of which he is convicted by or before the court or for which he is dealt with by the court.

The judge must specify not only the operational period of the sentence, but also the supervision period for the purpose of the community requirement(s); these may not be the same (above).

Where the judge imposes a requirement in connection with a suspended sentence, the court officer will notify the appropriate persons of those matters set out in r.42.2. (see COMMUNITY SENTENCES).

Breach, amendment and revocation

41–052   Breach, amendment and revocation of the order is ealt with under CJA 2003, Sch.12, for which see BREACH, AMENDMENT AND REVOCATION OF ORDERS. As to transfer to Scotland and Northern Ireland, see CJA 2003, Sch.13.

Power to provide for review of suspended sentence order

41-053 A suspended sentence order may:

CJA 2003, s.!91(l)(2) (3)(5)

    (1) provide for the order to be reviewed periodically at specified intervals;

    (2) provide for each review to be made, subject to s.173(3), at a review hearing held for the purpose by the judge;

    (3) require the offender to attend each review hearing; and

    (4) provide for the responsible officer to make to "the court responsible for the order", before each review, a report on the offender's progress in complying with the community requirements of the order.

This provision does not apply in the case of an order imposing a drug rehabilitation requirement, provision for such a requirement to be subject to review being made by CJA 2003, s.210.

"The court responsible for a suspended sentence order" is:

    (a) where a court is specified in the order in accordance with subs.(4), that court;

    (b) in any other case, it is the court by which the order is made.

A suspended sentence order made on an appeal brought from the Crown Court or from CACD is deemed for this purpose to have been made by the Crown Court.

Powers on periodic review

41–054   At a review hearing the judge may, after considering the responsible officer's report, amend the community requirements, or any provision of the order, which relates to those requirements, but:

CJA 2003, s. 192(1)-(3)

(1) may not amend the community requirements of the order so as to impose a requirement of a different kind unless the offender **consents** to that requirement;

(2) may not amend a mental health treatment requirement, a drug rehabilitation requirement or an alcohol treatment requirement unless the offender **consents** to comply with the amended requirement;

(3) may amend the supervision period only if the period as amended complies with s.189(3) and (4);

(4) may not amend the operational period of the suspended sentence; and

(5) may not except with the offender's consent, amend the order while the order is being appealed.

For the purposes of s.192(2)(a) a community requirement falling within any paragraph of s.190(1) is of the same kind as another community requirement if they fall within the same paragraph of s.190(1), and an electronic monitoring requirement is a community requirement of the same kind as any requirement falling within s.190(1) to which it relates.

Conduct of review hearing
41-055 If:

(1) before a review hearing is held the judge, after considering the responsible officer's report, is of the opinion that the offender's progress in complying with the community requirements of the order is satisfactory, he may order that no review hearing be held at that review; and

CJA 2003,s.102(4)(8)

(2) before a review hearing is held, or at a hearing, the judge, after considering that report, is of that opinion, he may amend the suspended sentence order so as to provide for each subsequent review to be held without a hearing. If:

CJA 2003, s. 175(6)-(8)

(a) at a review held without a hearing ,the judge, after considering the responsible officer's report, is of the opinion that the offender's progress under the order is no longer satisfactory, he may require the offender to attend a hearing at a specified time and place;

(b) at a review hearing, the judge is of the opinion that the offender has without reasonable excuse failed to comply with any of the community requirements of the order, he may adjourn the hearing for the purpose of dealing with the case under CJA 2003, Sch.12, para. 8 (see BREACH, AMENDMENT AND REVOCATION OF ORDERS);

(c) at a review hearing the judge may amend the suspended sentence order so as to vary the intervals specified under S.191(1) (periodic reviews).

13.   Return to prison: PCC(S)A 2000: s: 116

A restricted power

41–056   The repeal by CJA 2003 of PCC(S)A 2000, s.116 and its partial saving by SI2005/950, have severely restricted the operation of the section . However it is still the case that where an offender, (in relation to an offence committed before April 4 2005):

(1) has been serving;
 (a) a determinate sentence of imprisonment (other than a committal for contempt or any kindred offence);
 (b) a determinate sentence of detention under s.91; or
 (c) a sentence of detention in a young offender institution, which he began serving **on or after October 1, 1992;** and
(2) he was released on licence under any provision of CJA 1991, Pt II (other than s.33(1)(a)); and
 (a) commits, before the date on which he would, but for his release, have served his sentence, an offence punishable with imprisonment; and
 (b) is convicted, whether before or after that date, of the new offence before the Crown Court, or is committed to the Crown court by a magistrates' court (whether under s.116(3)(b) or otherwise (*R. v Stephenson* [1999] 1 Cr. App. R.(S.) 177),

then, whether or not the judge passes any other sentence on him, he may order him to be returned to prison for the whole or any part of the period which:

(i) begins with the date of the judge's order; and
(ii) is equal in length to the period between the date on which the new offence was committed and the date on which he would otherwise have served his sentence in full.

Where the judge makes an order in respect of several offences each must begin on that date and must accordingly run concurrently with each other (*R. v Divers* [1999] 2 Cr. App. R.(S.) 421).

The judge may order the period for which the offender is returned to prison to be served before and be followed by, or concurrently with, the sentence for the new offence. The sentence for the return and that for the new offence constitute a single term (*R. v Taylor* [1998] 1 Cr. App. R.(S.) 312). As to juvenile offenders, see *R. v Foran* [1996] 1 Cr. App. R.(S.)149; *R. v F & S* [2000] 1 Cr. App. R.(S.) 519

Special provisions apply to sentences imposed in Scotland, see PCC(S)A 2000, s.16.

Explanations

41–057   The difficulties of applying this section are well known and regard may be had to *R. v Howell* [2006] EWCA Crim 860, [2006] 2 Cr.

App. R.(S.) 115; *R. v Jesson* [2007] EWCA Crim 1399, [2007] Crim. LR 810; *R. v Booker* [2009] EWCA Crim 311, [2009] 2 Cr. App. R.(S.) 18; *R. v Whittle* [2009] EWCA Crim 580, [2009] 2 Cr. App. R.(S.) 102). Note that:

(1) the power is available in respect of a prisoner released on licence, not in respect of an offence committed by an escaped prisoner (*R. v Mathews & Jacobs* [2002] EWCA Crim 677; [2002] 2 Cr. App. R.(S.) 103) or an offence committed by a prisoner still serving his sentence (*R. v Qureshi (Sajid)* [2001] EWCA Crim 1807, [2002] 1 Cr. App. R. 33);

(2) the fact that the prisoner has been recalled to prison on revocation of his licence is no bar to an order (*R. v Sharkey* [2000] 1 Cr. App. R. 409; *R. v Cawthorn* [2001] 1 Cr. App. R.(S.) 130);

(3) more than one order may be made in respect of the same sentence, as where an offender commits a further offence after a s.116 order has been made (*R. v Pick & Anor* [2005] EWCA Crim 1853, [2006] 1 Cr. App. R.(S.) 61);

(4) where the new offence was committed over a period of two or more days, or at some time during a period of two or more days, it is to be taken as committed on the last of those days.

Approach to an order

41–058   The judge, in contemplating a s.116 order, will need to establish:

(1) the period of the sentence originally imposed; and

(2) the date on which the offender was released on licence, in order to determine whether the new offence was committed within the term of the original sentence; and

(3) the *quantum* remaining from the original sentence on the day the new offence was committed.

Once he has established that he has power to make an order under s.116, he must, in deciding whether to exercise that power:

(a) decide what is the appropriate sentence for the *new* offence— the possibility of an order under s.116 being disregarded at this stage; then

(b) in deciding whether an order under s.116 should be made, have regard to:
  (i) any progress made by the offender since his release on licence (*R. v Taylor* [1998] 1 Cr. App. R.(S.) 312); and
  (ii) the nature and gravity of the new offence, and whether it calls for a custodial sentence; and finally,

(c) having regard to the *totality* of the sentence, decide:
  (i) whether he should make an order under s.116;
  (ii) whether the term imposed under s.116 should be served concurrently with the sentence for the new offence(s); and
  (iii) if the term under s.116 is to be served *before* the sentence(s) for the new offence(s), how long it should be (*R. v Taylor*, above).

42. INDICTMENTS

Quick guide

1. General

Introduction

42–001 Trial on indictment may be before a judge and jury, or before a judge without a jury under CJA 2003 or under DVA 2004. Specialties referring to the latter are to be found in TRIAL WITHOUT A JURY.

The statutory basis for the preferment, form and contents of the indictment is IA 1915, AJ(MP)A 1933, CPR 2011, r.14, supplemented by PD 2004.

A valid indictment, not withdrawn, stayed or quashed, must be disposed of by the verdict(s) of a jury, or by the order of a judge, either entering a verdict of not guilty or by allowing it to lie on the file not to be proceeded with save with the leave of the court or CACD.

Where the sole accused named in an indictment is proved before trial to have died, it is the practice for the judge to order the indictment to be endorsed "deceased".

Indictments Act 1915

42–002 IA 1915, s.3 provides for a statement of the offence or offences with which the accused is charged "together with such particulars as may be necessary for giving reasonable information as to the nature of the charge". The section further provides that an indictment would not be open to an objection if it were framed in accordance with the rules made under the 1915 Act.

Rules were contained in a schedule to the act which was repealed by the Indictment Rules 1971 which have been in turn replaced by CPR 2011 r.14, supplemented by PD 2004.

The present position

42–003 The current form of indictment is required to set out the matters alleged by the prosecution to justify the conviction of the accused. Draft indictments (or "bills" as they were formerly called) presented to the Crown Court are drawn by the CPS, or sometimes by counsel, based upon specimens contained in the leading textbooks. Practice is far from systematic. For many offences, there are no standard particulars. Among the existing forms, there is considerable variation, ranging from forms which are little more than recitals of the legal elements of the offence, to others which are more fully particularised. In many cases, there is no discernable principle even within the count to explain the inclusion or exclusion of allegations corresponding to an element of the offence.

Duty of prosecutor

42–004 Where a case is to be tried on indictment, the prosecutor will need to present a draft indictment, though in cases of difficulty or where more than ordinary care is required in drafting it, counsel should be instructed (see *R. v Follett* (1989) 88 Cr. App. R.310). In the case of a private prosecution, the indictment will always need to be drafted by counsel. The draft remains a "bill" until the proper officer of the Crown Court has signed it, when it becomes an "indictment" (see *R. v Morais* (1988) 87 Cr. App. R.9; *R. v Clarke* [2008] UKHL 8, [2008] 2 Cr. App. R. 18).

The responsibility for the final correctness of the indictment at the trial rests on the prosecuting advocate (*R. v Newland* 87 Cr. App. R. 118; *R. v Moss* [1995] Crim. LR 828).

The prosecuting advocate at the trial may not be the same person who has had charge of the case at earlier stages. The indictment should be carefully scrutinised at the plea and case management hearing and preferably before arraignment of the accused. At all stages the prosecutor will need to check the indictment for the accuracy of the charges, their proper form, and potential overloading.

Duty of the prosecuting advocate

42–005 While he remains instructed, it is for the prosecuting advocate to take all necessary decisions in the presentation and general conduct of the case. In general:

(1) it is for him to decide whether to offer no evidence on a particular count, or on the indictment as a whole, and whether to accept pleas to a lesser count or counts; though

(2) when it comes to offering no evidence on the indictment, or on a particular count, or the acceptance of pleas to lesser counts it is his duty to consult those instructing him, and

(3) in the rare case where he and those instructing him are unable to agree on a matter of policy, he should apply for an adjournment if instructed so to do.

The role of the judge

42–006   As part of his case management duties the judge should scrutinise the indictment before trial. All too often, defects in the indictment, which have gone unnoticed by the prosecutor, result in "cracked" trials.

It is sensible for him, before the start of the trial, to check that:

(1) the indictment has been signed by the appropriate officer of the Crown Court;
(2) if there is a time limit within which the prosecution must be brought, that it has not expired;
(3) if consent to prosecution is required, that consent has been obtained; and
(4) the indictment is not overloaded, in that it contains too many counts;
(5) in the case of a multi-count indictment, whether one or more counts ought to be tried separately; and that
(6) it is not an appropriate case for the indictment, or some of the counts in the indictment, to be tried without a jury (see TRIAL WITHOUT A JURY).

2.   The requirements of a valid indictment

General

42–007   Every indictment must contain, and is sufficient if it contains, a statement of the specific offence or offences with which the accused person s.3 is charged, together with such particulars as may be necessary for giving reasonable information as to the nature of the charge).   IA 1915

An indictment may be preferred only if:

(1) the person charged has been committed for trial for the offence; or
(2) the person charged has been sent for trial for the offence under CDA 1998, s. (no committal proceedings for indictable-only offences);
(3) the bill is preferred by the direction of CACD or by the direction or with the consent of a judge of the High Court (a "voluntary bill");
(4) the bill is preferred under POA 1985, s.22B(3)(a) (reinstitution of proceedings);

provided that where the person charged has been committed or sent for trial, the bill of indictment against him may include, either in substitution for, or in addition to, any count charging an offence for which he was committed or sent for trial, any counts founded on material which was served on the person charged, being counts which may lawfully be joined in the same indictment.   AJ(MP)A1933, s.2(2)

Form of Indictment

42–008   The Rules prescribe as follows: R.14.2

(1) An indictment must be in be in the forms set out in PD 2004, Annex D and must contain, in a paragraph (a 'count'):
    (a) a statement of the offence charged that:
        (i) describes the offence in ordinary language; and
        (ii) identifies any legislation that creates it; and
    (b) such particulars of the conduct constituting the commission of the offence as to make clear what the prosecutor alleges against the accused.
(2) More than one incident of the commission of the offence may be included in a count if those incidents taken together amount to a course of conduct having regard to the time, place or purpose of commission.
(3) An indictment may contain more than one count if all the offences charged—
    (a) are founded on the same facts; or
    (b) form, or are a part of, a series of offences of the same or a similar character.
(4) The counts must be numbered consecutively.
(5) An indictment may contain—
    (a) any count charging substantially the same offence as one;
        (i) specified in the notice of the offence or offences for which the defendant was sent for trial;
        (ii) on which the defendant was committed for trial; or
        (iii) specified in the notice of transfer given by the prosecutor; and
    (b) any other count based on the prosecution evidence already served which the Crown Court may try.

Valid indictment

42–009   Thus a valid indictment must:

(1) be a single indictment; an offender may not be tried on more than one indictment at a time; where several indictments are in existence, the prosecutor is compelled to elect on which he will proceed – any others will then by stayed until the conclusion of the one tried;
(2) be properly preferred by the by the Crown Court officer and validated by him in the proper manner;
(3) be founded on a judicial proceeding, whether the act of a magistrates' court, or of a High Court judge, granting a voluntary bill;
(4) include one or more counts, justiciable within the territorial and offence jurisdiction of the Crown Court, and based on the judicial proceedings on which it is founded or any other offences arising;
(5) be restricted to offences triable on indictment only or triable either way, save where the inclusion of summary offences is permitted by statute, such offences being offences known to the law;
(6) be free from any suggestion of abuse of process.

The remedy for defects in requirements (1) to (5) is by means of a motion to quash the indictment as a whole, or a count of the indictment;

the remedy for (6) is to apply for a stay of the proceedings (see ABUSE OF PROCESS).

Multiple indictments
42–010   There is no rule of law or practice which prohibits two indictments being in existence at the same time for the same offence against the same person on the same facts, but the court will not allow the prosecution to proceed on both such indictments (PD 2004, IV 34.2). Two or more indictments may be founded on a single committal (*R. v Follett* 88 Cr. App. R. 310); and there may be two indictments outstanding against an accused at any one time (*Poole v The Queen* [1960] 3 All ER 398). They cannot, however, be tried together and the court will insist that the prosecutor elect the one on which the trial shall proceed.

Where different persons have been separately committed for trial for offences which can lawfully be charged in the same indictment it is permissible to join in one indictment the counts founded on the separate committals despite the fact that an indictment in respect of one of those committals has already been signed. Where necessary the court should be invited to exercise its powers of amendment under IA 1915, s. 5 (see 42-036).

Time limits and service
42-011   The prosecutor must serve a draft indictment on the Crown Court officer not more than 28 days after: R.14.1,

(1) service on the accused and on the Crown Court officer of copies of the documents containing the evidence on which the charge or charges are based, in a case where the accused is sent for trial;
(2) a High Court judge gives permission to serve a draft indictment;
(3) CACD orders a retrial; or
(4) the committal or transfer of the accused for trial.

The Crown Court may extend the time limit, even after it has expired. Unless the Crown Court otherwise directs, the court officer must:

(a) sign, and add the date of receipt on, the indictment; and
(b) serve a copy of the indictment on all parties.

Signature
42–012   By AJ(MP)A, s.2(1) and (6ZA) (as amended by CorJA 2009) a bill of indictment becomes an indictment once it is preferred before the Crown Court (appearing to remove the previous requirement that its validity derived from its signature by the Crown Court officer, without which the indictment was a nullity – see *R v. Clarke* [2008] UKHL 8, [2008] 2 Cr. App. R. 2 18). The position now is that an indictment must be signed but, if it is not, no objection may be taken to non-compliance with the rules and the indictment may still be signed, presumably even after the trial had begun (see r. 14.1(3)). It now seems unlikely that a technical objection to an indictment remaining unsigned (as in *R v. Leeks* [2009] EWCA Crim 1612; [2010] 1 Cr. App. R. 5) would succeed.

Where the prosecutor intends to include in the draft indictment counts which differ materially from, or are additional to, those on which the   PD 2004, IV.34.1

accused defendant was sent or committed for trial then the defendant should be given as much notice as possible, usually by service of a draft indictment, or a provisional draft indictment, at the earliest possible opportunity.

3. Structure of the indictment

General

42–013 Whilst responsibility for the form and structure of the indictment is for the prosecutor, the judge has an inherent right to regulate the proceedings before him in the interests of justice and for case management purposes. Thus he may, in relation to an indictment, or counts in an indictment:

(1) stay them;
(2) split them;
(3) order separate trials of them;
(4) sever counts or accused; or
(5) join counts and accused.

Matters of practice and procedure may be dealt with by the judge, on his own initiative and as part of the case management, as in the case of:

(a) joinder of counts (see 42–016, below);
(b) joinder of accused (see 42–019, below);
(c) splitting of counts (see 42–000, below);
(d) sample or specimen counts (see 42–025, below);
(e) multiple offending counts (see 42–021—43–024, below);
(f) preventing overloaded or unnecessarily complex indictments, (see 42–024, below); or
(g) ordering additional particulars (see 42–029).

Minor or trivial offences

42–014 It is good drafting practice:

(1) for the most serious offence disclosed on the papers to be charged in the indictment; e.g. wounding with intent to do grievous bodily harm rather than unlawful wounding;
(2) where the papers disclose evidence which is strong in respect of one offence and weak on another, for the offence in respect of which there is strong evidence only to be included in the indictment; and
(3) where a serious offence is included in the indictment, for trivial, or comparatively minor offences to be omitted; where an accused is indicted for murder, there is little point in including a count for resisting arrest.

No purpose is served by charging trivial offences. "Those who draft indictments should use common sense and should not put in to indictments charges which are of a trivial nature. Not only is it unfair, but it also tends to impede the doing of justice on more important aspects of the indictment" and "it is not fair to throw at an accused man, 'everything except the kitchen sink'." (per Lawton LJ in *R* v *Ambrose* (1973) 57 Cr. App. R. 538, at p 540).

Length and complexity
42–015　It is undesirable that a large number of counts should be contained in one indictment.

A good working rule for the prosecutor is:

(1) not to include counts trivial in themselves, which merely detract from the really serious nature of the case, and add nothing to it (see *R. v Ambrose* above);

(2) to charge a single count where the alleged criminality involved can be embraced satisfactorily in it *(R. v O' Meara* (1989) *The Times,* December 15);

(3) it is not appropriate to include more counts than are necessary to encourage an accused to plead guilty to one or more. Equally it is not appropriate to include a more serious count in the hope that this will encourage the accused to plead guilty to a less serious count;

(4) in a case where there are a number of accused and there are complicated issues, for there to be separate trials, dividing the case into smaller parts by drafting two or more indictments and preparing two or more Crown Court packages.

4.　Joinder of Counts

42–016　An indictment may contain more than one count if all the offences charged are founded on the same facts or form or are a part of a series of offences of the same or a similar character.　　R,14.2(3)

As to offences:

(1) founded on the same facts - the test is not to be interpreted too narrowly; the test being whether they have a common factual origin (*R. v Barrell* (1979) 69 Cr. App. R. 250).

(2) of the same or a similar character - the test was settled in *Ludlow v Metropolitan Police Commissioner* 54 Cr. App. R. 233.

Note that:

(a) two offences may constitute a "series"; but

(b) the offences must display a nexus between them explained as "a feature of similarity which in all the circumstances enables the offences to be described as a series". The similarity may arise due to the same victim (*R. v C The Times,* 4 February 1993), similar facts (*R. v Baird* [1993] 97 Crim App. R. 308), but a gap of 19 years between the alleged offences may be too great (*R. v O'Brien* [2000] Crim. L.R. 863).

5.　Joinder of summary offences

42–017　The Prosecution may include within the indictment a count charging certain offences otherwise triable only summarily under CJA 1988,s.40 if the charge:　　CJA 1988 s.40

Indictments

(1) is founded on the same facts or evidence as a count charging an indictable offence; or

(2) is part of a series of offences of the same of a similar character as an indictable offence charged,

but only if the facts or evidence relating to the offence have been disclosed to the accused.

Section 40 applies to the following offences:

(a) common assault;

(b) assaulting a prisoner custody officer (CJA 1991, s. 90(1));

(c) assaulting a secure training centre officer (CJPOA 1994, s.13(1));

(d) taking a motor vehicle without authority (TA 1968, s.12(1));

(e) driving whilst disqualified (RTA 1988, s.103(1)(b));

(f) criminal damage where triable only summarily;

(g) any further offences as may be specified by statutory instrument.

Any such offence included in an indictment may be tried as if it were an indictable offence save that the Crown Court only has the same sentencing powers as would be available to a magistrates' court.

Note that s. 40 does not permit the prosecution otherwise to add any other summary only charge to an indictment as an alternative count to a count already included (for example to enable the accused to plead guilty to a lesser charge, see *R. v. Hill* [2010] EWCA Crim 2999).

(See further SENDING ETC FOR TRIAL.)

42–018   Further, where a magistrates' court commits a person to the Crown Court for an offence, or offences, triable either way, it may also commit him in relation to any connected summary only offences for which the Crown Court may try him following conviction on the indictment (but without a jury) but its powers of sentence are only those as would be available to a magistrates' court.   CJA 1988 s.41

Such charges are attached to the indictment, but do not form part of it. Section 41 will be repealed when CJA 2003, sch.3, para.60(8) and sch. 37, part 4 comes into effect. The result will be that magistrates will be able to send to the Crown Court for trial a summary only offence, related to an indictable or either-way offence, so long as it is punishable with imprisonment or disqualification from driving (see, further, SENDING ETC FOR TRIAL).

6.   Joinder of accused

42–019   Two or more accused may be joined in the same indictment or in the same individual count. However the trial judge has an inherent discretion to order separate trials of accused who have properly been joined in an indictment. Where more than one accused is sent for trial for one or more offences, and there is no joint count, the prosecutor must show some nexus disclosed in the papers related by time and other factors before they or any of them can be joined in the same indictment or count. (See, further, severance of counts, 42–025 below).

As to joining a new co-accused in an indictment on a retrial ordered by CACD, see CAA 1968, s.7, also *R v Hemmings* [2000] 1 Cr. App. R. 360; *R v Booker* [2011] EWCA Crim 7, [2011] 1 Cr. App. R. 26.

7. Specimen Counts

42–020 Where a number of similar acts on different occasions is to be alleged, it is not open to the prosecution to charge one offence only as being representative of the whole course of conduct, in order for the court to sentence for the whole of that course of conduct. The judge may sentence only on those offences in respect of which the accused has been convicted, or which he has asked to be taken into consideration on sentence (*R. v Canavan,* [1998] 1 Cr. App. R.79).

In *R. v Hartley* [2011] EWCA Crim 1299); [2011] Crim. L.R. 726 CACD indicated three ways of dealing with this situation:

(1) to frame the counts in a form which complied with Rule 14.2(2),which permits a count to allege a course of conduct; where this is done, it will often be appropriate to include both a "course of conduct" count and a "single instance" count in relation to the same period; or

(2) to take advantage of DVA 2004, ss.17-19, which, subject to strict conditions, permits trial by judge alone on outstanding allegations following conviction on representative counts; or

(3) to include sufficient counts so that the judge was enabled to impose sentence on a basis which sufficiently represented what had actually happened but care was needed so as not to overload the indictment.

In drafting the indictment, a balance needs to be struck between including sufficient counts to give the court sufficient sentencing power, and overloading it.

Where the prosecutor includes specimen count(s) in an indictment he must take care that the samples reveal to the defence:

(1) the case that the accused has to meet *(R. v Evans* [1995] Crim. LR 245);

(2) "with as much particularity as the circumstances admit" *R. v Rackham* [1997] Crim. L.R. 592.

(And see also multiple offending counts below).

8. Multiple offending counts: more than one incident

42–021 More than one incident of the commission of an alleged offence may be included in a single count in certain circumstances. Each incident must be of the same offence.

A multiple offending count may be appropriate where:

R.14, 2(2); PD 2004, IV. 34)

(1) the victim on each occasion was the same, or there was no identifiable victim (for example, a case of the unlawful importation
of controlled drugs or of money laundering);
(2) the alleged incidents involved a marked degree of repetition in
the method employed or in their location, or both;
(3) the alleged incidents took place over a clearly defined period,
typically (but not necessarily) up to about a year;
(4) in any event, the defence is such as to apply to every alleged
incident without differentiation.

Using a multiple offending count may preferable to using specimen
counts in some cases where repeated sexual or physical abuse is alleged.
The choice of count will depend on the circumstances of the case but
the implications for sentencing set out in *R v Canavan* above should be
borne in mind.

In some cases a complainant may be able to testify to a series of
similar incidents without being able to specify when, or the precise
circumstances in which, they occurred. In such cases, a multiple
offending count may be desirable. If, however, the complainant is able
to identify particular incidents by reference to a date or other specific
event, but alleges that there were also other incidents which cannot
be specified, then it may be desirable to include (1) separate counts
for the identified incidents and a (2) a 'multiple incidents' count, or
counts, alleging that incidents of the same offence occurred 'many'
times.

42–022 Note that:

(1) Where what is in issue differs between different incidents, a
single count will not be appropriate, though two or more counts
may be appropriate, according to the circumstances and to the
issues raised by the defence. *PD 2004, IV.34.10*
(2) For some offences, particularly sexual offences, the penalty for
the offence may have changed during the period over which the
alleged incidents took place. In such a case, additional 'multiple
incidents' counts should be used so that each count only alleges
incidents to which the same maximum penalty applies). *PD 2004, IV.34.12*
(3) There may be occasions on which a multiple offending count may
be appropriate but the prosecutor chooses not to use such a count,
in order to bring the case within POCA 2002, s. 75(3)(a) (criminal
lifestyle established by conviction of three or more offences in
the same proceedings). Such a course may be unobjectionable,
subject to the general principles of overloading and complexity
set out in paragraph PD 2004 IV.34.13 (see 42–024 below). *PD 2004, IV.34.11*
(4) In some cases, such as money laundering or theft, there will
be documented evidence of individual incidents but the sheer
number of these will make it desirable to cover them in a single
count. Where the indictment contains a multiple offending count,
and during the course of the trial it becomes clear that the jury may
bring in a verdict in relation to a lesser amount than that alleged
by the prosecution, it will normally be desirable to direct them to
return a partial verdict with reference to that lesser amount). *PD 2004, IV.34.13*

9. Multiple Offending Counts: trial by jury and then by judge alone

42–023   In the case of a large number of separate offences where the judge exercises the powers in the DVA 2004, ss.17-21, to direct a trial by a jury and then by a judge alone the procedure directed in PD 2004 IV.34.4-34.9 should be followed (see TRIAL WITHOUT A JURY).

10.   Overloaded and complex indictments

42–024   Where the indictment contains substantive counts and one or more one or more related conspiracy counts: PD 2004, IV.34.13

(1) the prosecutor may be required to justify the joinder;
(2) joinder is 'justified' for this purpose if the judge considers that the interests of justice demand it;
(3) failing justification he may be required to elect whether to proceed on the substantive counts or the conspiracy counts;
(4) in either event, if there is a conviction, the other count(s) may remain on the file marked 'Not to be proceeded with without leave of the court or of CACD'. Should such conviction(s) be quashed, the others may be tried;
(5) an indictment may be split, some counts being put into another indictment.

If the trial is not estimated to be within a manageable length, the judge will consider what steps should be taken to reduce its length, though he must ensure that the prosecutor has the opportunity of placing the full criminality before the court.

He may be assisted by:

(a) the lead advocate for the prosecution explaining why he has rejected a shorter way of proceedings; the judge may invite him to divide the case into sections of evidence and explaining the scope of each section and the need for each section;
(b) the lead advocates for the prosecution and for the defence putting forward in writing, if requested, ways in which a case estimated to last more than three months can be shortened, including possible severance of counts or accused, exclusions of sections of the case or of evidence or areas of the case where admissions can be made.

The judge may consider pruning the indictment, but must not usurp the function of the prosecution. He may seek to persuade the prosecutor that it is not worthwhile pursuing certain counts and/or certain accused. The aim is to achieve fairness to all parties and to meet the overriding objective in the CPR 2011.

11. Severance of Counts

Indictments Act 1915, s.5

42–025 Where, before trial, or at any stage of a trial, the judge is of IA 1915, s.5 opinion that:

(1) a person accused may be prejudiced or embarrassed in his defence by reason of being charged with more than one offence in the same indictment, or that

(2) for any other reason it is desirable to direct that the person should be tried separately for any one or more offences charged in an indictment, he may order a separate trial of any count or counts of such indictment, and

(3) that the postponement of the trial of a person accused is expedient as a consequence of the exercise of any power to amend an indictment or to order a separate trial of a count, the judge must make such order as to the postponement of the trial as appears necessary.

Where an order is made under IA 1915, s.5, for the postponement of a trial:

(a) if such an order is made during a trial the judge may discharge the jury from giving a verdict on the count or counts the trial of which is postponed or on the indictment, as the case may be; and

(b) the procedure on the separate trial of a count will be the same in all respects as if the count had been found in a separate indictment, and the procedure on the postponed trial will be the same in all respects (if the jury has been discharged under paragraph (a) above) as if the trial had not commenced; and

(c) the judge may make such order as to granting the accused person bail and as to the enlargement of recognisances and otherwise as he thinks fit.

The power contained in s.5(3) to sever an indictment was held to apply only to valid indictments in *R. v Newland*, above. But see, *R. v Smith* [1997] 1 Cr. App. R. 390 and *R. v Lockley* [1997] Crim. L.R. 455.

The intention of the Act

42–26 The manifest intention of IA 1915, s.5, is that:

(1) charges founded on the same facts or related to a series of offences of the same or a similar character properly can, and normally should be, joined in one indictment and a joint trial of the charges will normally follow, although the judge has a discretionary power to direct separate trials under section 5(3);

(2) the judge has no duty to direct separate trials under section 5(3) unless in his opinion there is some special feature of the case which would make a joint trial of the several counts prejudicial or embarrassing to the accused and separate trials are required in the interests of justice.

In some cases the offences charged may be too numerous and complicated, or too difficult to disentangle, so that a joint trial of all the counts is likely to cause confusion and the defence may be embarrassed or prejudiced. As to the number and/or complexity of the counts in the trial of counts for sexual offences, see *DPP v Boardman* 60 Cr. App. R.. 1165; *R. v Scarroti* 65 Cr. App. R. 225. The fact that co-accused are running "cut throat" defences will not generally be a good ground for severance (*R. v Miah* [2011] EWCA Crim 945 [2011] Crim L.R. 662).

In other cases objection may be taken to the inclusion of a count on the ground that it is of a scandalous nature and likely to arouse in the minds of the jury hostile feelings against the accused *(Ludlow v MPC* 54 Cr. App. R. 233). As to the scandalous nature of the evidence, see *R. v Laycock* [2003] Crim L.R. 803.

Where there is a multi-count indictment for some other type of offence, the principles in *Ludlow v MPC* (above) apply. See also *DPP v P* 93 Cr. App. R. 267; *R. v Christou* [1996] 2 Cr. App. R. 360; *R. v Cannan* (1991) 92 Cr. App. R. 16.

The fact that the accused wishes to give evidence in his own defence on one of the counts but not on the others is not, in the normal case, a sufficient reason for severance, even though non-severance will oblige him to choose between not testifying at all and exposing himself to cross-examination about all the charges *(R. v Phillips* (1987) 86 Cr. App. R. 18).

In exercising his discretion, the trial judge should seek to achieve a fair resolution of the issues. This requires fairness to the accused but also to the prosecution.

An application to sever the indictment may be made on more than one occasion, as where it is made at a preliminary hearing and, being refused, is made again at the trial. The question for any subsequent judge will be whether there has been a sufficient change to justify reopening the question. If there has not, he is not obliged to hear the same point argued again (*R. v Wright* (1989) 90 Cr. App. R. 325).

12. Separate trial of accused

42–027 The trial judge has an inherent discretion to order separate trials of accused who have properly been joined in an indictment in accordance with the principles stated in *Ludlow v MPC* (above) - see *R. v Assim* [1966] 50 Cr. App. R. 224. The manner in which the discretion is exercised does not ordinarily provide a successful ground of appeal. Guidance may, however, be drawn from the authorities, as follows:

(1) where the accused are charged in a joint count, the arguments in favour of a joint trial are very strong (see *R. v Lake* (1976) 64 Cr. App. R. 172; *R. v Josephs* (1977) 65 Cr. App. R. 253) and separate trials will not be ordered unless here is good reason for it. Thus:

    (a) severance will necessitate much or all of the prosecution evidence being given twice before different juries and increase the risk of inconsistent verdicts;

    (b) even if the accused are expected to blame each other for the offence, the interests of the prosecution and the public in a single trial will generally outweigh the interests of the defence in not having to call each accused before the same jury to give evidence for himself which will incriminate the others (see *R. v Grondkowski* [1946] KB 369, *R. v Moghal* (1977) 65 Cr. App. R 56, *R. v. Edwards* [1998] Crim LR 756 and *R. v Crawford* [1998] 1 Cr. App. R. 338).

(2) Where the prosecution case against one accused includes evidence that is admissible against him but not against his co-accused, there is no obligation to order severance simply because the evidence in question might prejudice the jury against the latter. However the judge should balance the advantages of a single trial against the possible prejudice to the second accused and should consider especially how far an appropriate direction to the jury is really likely to ensure that they take into account the evidence only for its proper purpose of proving the case against the first (see *R. v Lake* (1976) 64 Cr App R 172 and *R. v B* [2004] EWCA Crim 1254).

42–028   This ground for separate trials is linked to the rule against overloading indictments (see 42–024) above. Where a joint trial of numerous accused would lead to a very long and complicated trial, the judge should consider whether a number of shorter trials, each involving only some of the accused, might make for a fairer and more efficient disposition of the issues. There may be a distinction to be drawn between cases where the accused are jointly charged in a single count and those where they are alleged to have committed separate offences which were nonetheless sufficiently linked to be put in one indictment. In the latter situation, the cases against the accused are unlikely to be as closely intertwined as when a joint offence is alleged, and the public interest argument in favour of a single trial is correspondingly less strong.

13.   Ordering additional particulars

42–029   It is open to the defence to ask for additional particulars of a count. One of the purposes of doing so is to anchor the prosecutor to a particular means by which the charge may be made out (See e.g., *R. v Landy* 72 Cr. App. R. 237; *R. v Hancock* [1996] 2 Cr App R 554).

It may be helpful to the defence, and good practice, for the Prosecution to be required to provide the defence, and also the jury, if appropriate, with a separate document in the form of a guide to the indictment or a summary of the allegations in each count.

14.   Objections to the indictment

The need for action
42–030   Issues arising from the preferment and form of the indictment may be raised by the advocates on either side, or the judge may, in an appropriate case, act of his own initiative.

The means by which defects in the indictment may be cured, or otherwise disposed of are by:

(1) demurrer (in theory), or plea to the jurisdiction;

(2) motion to quash; or

(3) application to amend.

The time for action

42–031 The time for raising objections to the indictment, or to individual counts of the indictment is properly before arraignment. Provided that advocates on either side have done their work properly, the grounds for objection should be properly crystallised at the time of the PCMH.

Note that;

(1) the rules of disclosure (see DISCLOSURE) require the accused in his defence statement to indicate where he joins issue with the prosecutor; and

(2) the rules require such matters to be raised in the course of the PCMH.

There will always be matters which are overlooked, or which first surface at a later stage of the trial, in which case only the interests of prevents them being raised at the stage they arise.

CACD Guidance: R v Gleeson

42–032 In *R. v Gleeson* [2003] EWCA Crim 3357; [2004] 1 Cr. App. R.29 the defence advocate chose to reserve until the close of the prosecution case a fundamental objection to the indictment.

On appeal, a number of points were made by CACD:

(1) the defence should have drawn attention to the proposed legal challenge at the PCMH and in the defence statement served under the discovery provisions of CPIA 1996; had they done so they could have had no valid objection to the prosecutor correcting his error at that stage or certainly by the commencement of the trial;

(2) the proper determination of such difficulties when they arise was often fact-sensitive; it might not always be possible for amendments to be permitted with fairness to the accused at so late a stage, wherever the fault lay;

(3) just as an accused should not be penalized for errors by his legal representatives made in the course of the defence, so also a prosecution should not be frustrated by errors of the prosecutor unless such an error made a fair trial for the accused impossible;

(4) for a defence advocate to seek to take advantage of such errors by deliberately delaying identification of an issue of fact or law in the case until the last possible moment is no longer acceptable given the legislative and procedural changes to the criminal justice process in recent years; it is contrary to the requirement on an accused under CPIA 1996, s. 5(6)(b) to indicate the matters on which he takes issue with the prosecutor, and to his professional duty to the court, and is not in the legitimate interests of the accused;

(5) the fact that an accused may prefer as a matter of tactics to keep his case close to his chest was not a valid reason to for preventing a full and fair hearing on the issues canvassed at the trial;

Indictments

(6) requiring an accused to indicate in advance what he disputed about the prosecution case offended neither the principle that the prosecutor had to prove his case nor that an accused was not obliged to inculpate himself.

15.   Demurrer and plea to the jurisdiction

42–033.   If demurrer still survives it is most unlikely that it will arise at the present day. It had long been supposed to be obsolete, supplanted by a motion to quash the indictment or a motion in arrest of judgment, but made a brief re-appearance in *R. v ILQS Ex p. MPC* 54 Cr. App. R. 49, cf. *R v. Cumberworth* [1989] Crim. L.R 591.

Demurrer was a plea in bar of trial, being an objection to the form or substance of the indictment, apparent on its face. The plea, like other pleas in bar had to be tendered in writing by or on behalf of the accused, and lodged with the Crown Office, a copy being served on the prosecutor, preferably prior to arraignment. The issue was decided by the judge, who is not entitled to refer to the depositions or other committal statements for the purpose. If demurrer failed, as in the case of autrefois acquit and convict, the accused was entitled to plead over to the indictment (CLA 1967, s.6(1)).

Similar principles apply in the case of a plea to the jurisdiction. If the plea fails, the indictment will be put and the accused is entitled to plead not guilty to the general issue (CLA 1967, s.6(1)).

Pleas to the jurisdiction are probably obsolete. Objections to jurisdiction clear from the face of the indictment are better taken by a motion to quash or a simple plea to the indictment.

16.   Motion to quash

Defence motion
42–034.   A motion to quash may be brought where the indictment:

(1) is bad on its face (e.g., for duplicity or because the particulars of a count do not disclose an offence known to law);

(2) (or a count thereof) has been preferred otherwise than in accordance with the provisions AD(MP)A 1933, s.2; such an indictment must be quashed because it is preferred without authority (see *R. v Lombardi* 88 Cr. App. R. 179);

(3) contains a count for an offence in respect of which the accused was not committed for trial and the committal documents do not disclose a case to answer for that offence *(R. v Jones* (1974) 59 Cr. App. R. 120 'but see *R. v Thompson [2011] EWCA Crim 102;* [2011] 4 All E.R. 408 where a new count was added based on a notice of additional evidence'.).

(4) there is divergence or departure, the matter may be dealt with at that stage of the trial at which evidence in support of it emerges, or at the close of the prosecutor's case, when an application may be made to split the count.

In (3) but only in (3) the judge is entitled to consider the prosecution evidence foreshadowed in the documents (see *R. v Jones* above). Where the indictment follows the committal charges and is properly drafted on its face, the defence cannot invite the judge to quash on the basis that the committal evidence did not in fact disclose a case to answer and the accused was wrongly committed for trial (*R. v London County QS ex fane Downes* (1903) 37 Cr. App. R. 148). Where, however, the indictment contains a count on which the accused was not committed the normal rule has to be relaxed in respect of that count, because otherwise the accused would be put on trial for the offence without any prior opportunity of arguing that the evidence is insufficient.

Failure to apply at trial may show that there was no miscarriage of justice (see, e.g., *R. v Donnelly* [1995] Crim L.R 131). As to the time when a motion should be made, see 42–039 below.

The prosecutor may apply under IA 1915, s.5(1) (see below) to amend a count held to be duplicitous, by splitting the count into two separate counts.

Prosecutor's motion
42–035 The prosecutor may seek to quash his own indictment, or counts in it, where he realises that the indictment is defective or invalid. The effect of a successful application to quash is that the accused may not be tried on the indictment (or particular count to which the motion relates). However, this does not mean that the accused is thereby acquitted.

Although the quashing of the indictment exhausts the effect of the committal proceedings on which it was founded (*R. v Thompson* (1975) 61 Cr. App. R. 108; *R. v Newlands*, above) the prosecution are not prevented from instituting fresh committal proceedings or applying for a voluntary bill.

The better course will usually be to ask the judge to stay (but not quash) the defective indictment and at the same time prefer a fresh indictment correcting the error in the original draft (see *R. v Fallet* (1989) 98 Cr. App. R. 310). Care should be taken to arraign the accused on the fresh indictment before the original indictment is stayed.

17.   Amending the indictment

Statutory provisions
42–036 Where, before trial, or at any stage of the trial it appears to the judge that the indictment is defective, he must make such order or amendment of the indictment as he thinks necessary to meet the circumstances of the case, unless, having regard to the merits of the case, the required amendment cannot be made without injustice.   IA 1915 s.5

The power to amend may be exercised both:

(1) in respect of formal defects in the wording of a count, for example when the statement of offence fails to specify the statute contravened or when the particulars do not disclose an essential element of the offence; and

(2) in respect of substantial defects such as divergences between the

allegations in the count and the evidence foreshadowed in the witness statements or called at trial.

Any alteration in matters of description, and probably in many other respects, may be made in order to meet the evidence in the case so long as the amendment causes no injustice to the accused (*R. v Pople* [1950] 34 Cr. App. R. 168). An indictment may be defective if it merely fails to allege an offence disclosed by the witness statements. 'Defective', in the context of s. 5(1), is not restricted to defects in form, but 'has got a very much wider meaning' (*R. v Radley* (1973) 58 Cr App R 394).

The power to amend may be exercised in respect of voluntary bills of indictment preferred on the direction of a High Court judge (see 42-041 below) just as it may be exercised in respect of other indictments (*R. v Alcock* (1999) 1 Cr. App. R. 227; *R. v Wells* [1995] 2 Cr. App. R. 417; *R v Walters* (1979) 69 Cr. App. R. 115).

Limitation on power to amend

42–037   If the indictment is so defective as to be a nullity, it is not capable of amendment and there is a mistrial. An indictment is invalid from the outset in this way where, for example, it alleges an offence unknown to law. Where a count describes a known offence inaccurately, however, it is capable of amendment, subject to the usual considerations of prejudice to the defendant *(R. v McVitie* (1960) 44 Cr. App. R. 201, applied in *R. v Tyler* (1992) 96 Cr. App. R. 332).

Insertion of a new count

42–038   As well as enabling amendments to be made to existing counts, s. 5(1) permits the insertion of an entirely new count into an indictment, whether in addition to or in substitution for the original counts (*R. v Johal* 56 Cr. App. R. 348). Where the addition is made after arraignment, it will be necessary to put the new counts to the accused for him to plead to them.

The amendment to an indictment may be so extensive that the question arises whether it amounts to the substitution of a fresh indictment (see *R. v Fyffe* [1992] Crim. L. R. 442).

As to whether it is necessary for the amendment to be founded on facts or evidence disclosed to the examining justices at committal, cf. *R. v Osieh* [1996] 2 Cr. App. R. 144; *R. v Dixon* (1991) 92 Cr. App. R. 43 and *R. v Hall* (1968) 52 Cr. App. R. 528, granted that there was power to amend, the question is really "whether the amendment asked for and granted was supported by evidence given at the committal proceedings" *(R. v. Hall,* above).

In *R. v Thompson [2011] EWCA Crim 102;* [2011] 4 All E.R. 408, a new count was properly added where it was based on a notice of additional evidence.

Timing of amendment; risk of injustice

42–039   IA 1915, s.5(1), makes clear that an indictment may be amended at any stage of a trial, whether before or after arraignment - see *R. v Johal* (1972) 56 Cr. App. R. 348 (after arraignment but before empanelling the jury); *R. v Pople* (above), (after the close of the prosecution case); *R v Collison* (1980) 71 Cr. App. R. 249 (after the jury had been out considering their verdict for over three hours). See also *Teong Sun Chuah* [1991] Crim. L. R. 463.

The later the amendment, the greater the risk of its causing injustice and therefore the less likely it ought to be allowed. However, an indictment may be amended even at the stage of retrial, provided that no injustice is done *(R v. Swaine* [2001] Crim LR 166).

The principal consideration for the judge in deciding whether to allow an amendment is the risk of injustice. If the amendment cannot be made without injustice, it must not be made (IA 1915, s. 5(1)). The timing of the amendment is a major factor in determining whether there will be injustice, see *R. v Gregory* (1972) 56 Cr. App. R. 441 (late amendment to the particulars by the deletion of the allegation as to ownership where that was the central issue in the case); *R. v O'Connor* [1997] Crim. L. R. 516, (amendment made at the close of the prosecution case allowing the prosecutor to shift his ground significantly).

When amendment is allowed, a note of the order must be endorsed on the indictment (IA 1915, s.5(2)).

If necessary, an adjournment may be granted to allow the parties (in particular the defence) to deal with the altered position (s.5(4)). Where the amendment comes during the course of a trial, there is power to discharge the jury from giving a verdict and to order a retrial on the indictment (ibid).

18. Cases of serious fraud

42–040 The Protocol for the Control and Management of Heavy Fraud and other Complex Criminal Cases 2005 [2005] 2 All ER 429 governs serious fraud and complex cases which are expected to last more than eight weeks, in conjunction with the CPR. In respect of matters concerning the indictment:

(1) One course the judge may consider is pruning the indictment by omitting certain charges and/or by omitting certain accused. The judge must not usurp the function of the prosecution in this regard, and he must bear in mind that he will, at the outset, know less about the case than the advocates. The aim is to achieve fairness to all parties.

(2) The judge has two methods of pruning available for use in appropriate circumstances:
    (a) persuading the prosecution that it is not worthwhile pursuing certain charges and/or certain accused;
    (b) severing the indictment. Severance for reasons of case management alone is perfectly proper, although the judge should have regard to any representations made by the prosecution that severance would weaken their case.

Before using what may be seen as a blunt instrument, the judge should insist on seeing full defence statements of all affected defendants. Severance may be unfair to the prosecution if, for example, there is a cut-throat defence in prospect. For example, the defence of the principal defendant may be that he relied on the advice of his accountant or solicitor that what was happening was acceptable. The defence of the professional may be that he gave no such advice. Against that background, it might be unfair to the prosecution to order separate trials of the two defendants (See, further, CASE MANAGEMENT).

19. Applying for voluntary bill

General

42–041   AJ(MP)A 1933, s.2(2)(b) allows the preferment of a bill of indictment by the direction or with the consent of a judge of the High Court.

PD 2004
IV.35.1-35.6

In such rare cases as the prosecutor will now need to apply for such consent, he must not only comply with each paragraph of I(P)R 1971, but the application must also be accompanied by the proper documents as specified by PD 2004, para.IV.35.2, in relation to each accused named in the indictment for which consent is sought, whether or not it is proposed to prefer any new count against him.

The preferment of a voluntary bill is an exceptional procedure. Consent will only be granted where good reason to depart from the normal procedure is clearly shown and only where the interests of justice, rather than considerations of administrative convenience, require it (PD 2004, para.IV.35.3).

Procedure

42–042   The prosecuting authorities for England and Wales have issued guidance to prosecutors on the procedures to be adopted in seeking judicial consent to the preferment of voluntary bills. These procedures direct prosecutors (PD 2004, para.IV.35.5):

(a) on the making of application for consent to preferment of a voluntary bill, forthwith to give notice to the prospective accused that such application has been made;

(b) at about the same time, to serve on the prospective accused a copy of all the documents delivered to the judge (save to the extent that these have already been served on him); and

(c) to inform the prospective accused that he may make submissions in writing to the judge, provided that he does so within nine working days of the giving of notice under (a) above.

Judges should not give leave to dispense unless good grounds are shown.

A judge to whom application for consent to the preferment of a voluntary bill is made, will (PD 2004, para.IV.35.6), of course, wish to consider carefully the documents submitted by the prosecutor and any written submissions timeously made by the prospective accused, and may properly seek any necessary amplification. The judge may invite oral submissions from either party, or accede to a request for an opportunity to make such oral submissions, if the judge considers it necessary or desirable to receive such oral submissions in order to make a sound and fair decision on the application. Any such oral submissions should be made on notice to the other party, who should be allowed to attend.

43. JURISDICTION

General

43–001   The Crown Court is part of the Senior Courts (that is the pre-2007 Supreme Court). It is a superior court of record. Its jurisdiction is exercisable by:

SCA 1981,
ss.1(1), 8(1),
45(1)

(1) any judge of the High Court;

(2) any Circuit Judge or Recorder; and

(3) subject to, and in accordance with, the provisions of SCA 1981, ss.74 and 75(2), a judge of the High Court, a Circuit Judge, a Recorder or, a District Judge (Magistrates' Courts), sitting with not more than four lay magistrates,

and any such persons, when exercising the jurisdiction of the Crown Court, are judges of the Crown Court.

CA 2003,
s.24(5)

Note that:

(a) during the period of his appointment, a Deputy District Judge (Magistrates' Courts) is be treated for judicial purposes as if he were a District Judge (Magistrates' Courts);

SCA 1981,
s.8(2)

(b) when the Crown Court sits in the City of London it is known as the Central Criminal Court, and the Lord Mayor of the City and any alderman of the City is entitled to sit as a judge of the Central Criminal Court and any judge of the High Court, or any Circuit Judge or Recorder;

SCA 1981,
s.8(2).

(c) a lay magistrate is not disqualified from acting as a judge of the Crown Court for the reason only that proceedings are not at a place within the area for which he was appointed, or because the proceedings are not related to that area in any way.

Judges, etc. as justices of the peace

43–002   A Circuit judge, a Deputy Circuit Judge, a Deputy Judge of the High Court, a Judge of the High Court, and a Recorder have the powers of a justice of the peace who is a District Judge (Magistrates' Courts) in relation to criminal causes and matters. Each of the holders of such office is qualified to sit as a member of a youth court.

CA 2003,
s.66(2), (3)

From the explanatory notes to s.66 it was clearly envisaged that the power was intended to enable a judge of the Crown Court to deal with a summary offence attached. The power is clearly wider than that and has been used by judges in the Crown Court to rectify errors of procedure. See, e.g. *R. v Ashton* [2006] 2 Cr.App.R. 15 where a judge acting as a District Judge (Magistrates' Courts) e.g. quite properly (a) conducted mode of trial proceedings where these had been omitted, and (b) committed an accused to the Crown Court for sentence where that was appropriate. In the latter case, it was held that there was no statutory impediment prevent him in his capacity as a judge of the Crown Court from passing sentence on an accused so committed.

Jurisdiction

Any matter required under r.6.1 to be recorded in the magistrates' court's register, should be recorded by the clerk in the Crown Court records, ensuring that there is an accurate and accessible record of any decision or other important feature of the proceedings (*R. v Ashton*).

In *R. v Ashton* (above) CACD stressed that in most instances when there has been a procedural failure, it will be unnecessary for s.66 to be used to carry out a process of rectification. Instead, the matter should be approached on the principles set out in *Soneji* and *Knights* (see above, 13–011) which will normally obviate the need to go through such procedural steps.

See also *R. v Miller* [2010] EWCA Crim 809, [2011] 1 Cr. App. R.(S.) 12 where the accused was wrongly committed for sentence.

General jurisdiction

43–003   Subject to the provisions of SCA 1981, the Crown Court exercises:

SCA 1981, s.45(2), (3)

(1) all such appellate and other jurisdiction as is conferred upon it by that or any other Act; and
(2) all such jurisdiction as was exercisable by it immediately before the commencement of that Act (i.e. January 1, 1972);

and its jurisdiction includes all such powers and duties as were exercisable by it, or fell to be performed by it, immediately before that date.

SCA 1981, s.45(4)

The Crown Court is a creature of statute, it lacks inherent jurisdiction (see e.g. *R. (Trinity Mirror Plc) v Croydon CC* [2008] EWCA Crim 50; [2008] 2 Cr. App. R. 1).

CA 1971, s.8 and Sch.1 conferred on the Crown Court all appellate and other jurisdictions conferred on courts of quarter session, or on any committees of such courts.

Subject to CP(AW)A 1965, s.8, the Crown Court has, in relation to the attendance and examination of witnesses, any contempt of court, the enforcement of its orders and all other matters incidental to its jurisdiction, the like powers, rights, privileges and authority of the High Court. As to the meaning of "incidental" see *R. (Trinity Mirror Plc)* above.

Jurisdiction on indictment; practice and procedure

43–004   All proceedings on indictment are brought before the Crown Court, and its jurisdiction with respect to such proceedings includes jurisdiction:

SCA 1981, s.46(1)

(1) in proceedings on indictment in England and Wales for offences wherever committed, and in particular;
(2) in proceedings on indictment for offences within the jurisdiction of the Admiralty of England.

The rules as to service and signature of the indictment are contained in r.14, but note that the amendments effected by SI 2009/2087 imply that a signature is no longer required to convert a draft indictment into an indictment. see generally INDICTMENTS.

SCA 1981 continues in effect all enactments and rules relating to procedure in connection with indictable offences, and in particular preserves:

SCA 1981, s.79(1), (2)

(a) the practice by which, on any one indictment, the taking of pleas, the trial by jury and the pronouncement of judgment may respectively be by or before different judges;

(b) the release, after respite of judgment, of a convicted person on recognisance to come up for judgment if called on, but meanwhile to be of good behaviour;

(c) the manner of trying any question relating to the breach of a recognisance; and

(d) the manner of execution of any sentence on conviction, or the manner in which any other judgment or order given in connection with trial on indictment may be enforced.

The provisions of the Act relating to the Crown Court's appellate jurisdiction are dealt with under APPELLATE JURISDICTION. The court's powers to grant bail are dealt with under BAIL.

Sittings of the Crown Court

SCA 1971, s.78

43–005   In relation to the business of the Crown Court:

(1) any business may be conducted at any place in England or Wales, and the sittings of the court at any place may be continuous or intermittent or occasional;

(2) judges may sit simultaneously to take any number of different cases in the same or different places, and may adjourn cases from time to time; and

(3) the places at which the court sits and the days and times at which the court sits at any place are matters to be determined in accordance with directions given by the Lord Chief Justice.

The Crown Court is a single court and those who sit in it sit merely from time to time as judges of the court. There is nothing which prevents a case which is part-heard at one location or before one judge, from being adjourned to a later date in contemplation of its being reheard before a different court. There is no principle which retains a case within the so-called "seisin" of an individual judge (*R. v Dudley CC Ex p. Smith* (1974) 58 Cr. App. R. 184).

Composition of the Crown Court

43–006   All proceedings in the Crown Court are heard and disposed of before a single judge of the court, except in relation to courts -comprising lay magistrates. Where a judge of the High Court, a Circuit Judge, a Recorder or a District Judge (Magistrates' Courts), sits with lay magistrates, he presides, and:

SCA 1981, s.73(1), (3)

(1) the decision of the Crown Court may be by a majority; and

(2) if the members of the court are equally divided, the presiding judge, Recorder, etc. has a second and casting vote.

Where a situation arises during the course of the proceedings which involves an interlocutory decision, it must be dealt with by the court as then constituted, i.e. including the magistrates.

On a question of law the magistrates will obviously defer to the views of the presiding judge (*R. v Orpin* (1974) 59 Cr.App.R. 231). See generally APPELLATE JURISDICTION.

R.16.11

JURISDICTION

Business in chambers

43–007   A judge of the Crown Court may exercise the following jurisdiction, sitting in chambers:

(1) hearing applications for bail;
(2) issuing a summons or warrant;
(3) hearing any application relating to procedural matters preliminary or incidental to criminal proceedings in the Crown Court,
including applications relating to CDS funding;
(4) jurisdiction under:
   (a) r.12.2 (listing first appearance of accused sent for trial);
   (b) r.28.3 (application for witness summons);
   (c) r.63.2(5) (extending time for appeal against decision of
      magistrates' court);
   (d) r.64.6 (application to state a case for consideration of High
      Court);
(5) hearing an application under YJCA 1999, s.41(2) (evidence of
complainant's sexual history);
(6) hearing applications under POA 1985, s.22(3) (extension or
further extension of a custody time limit);
(7) hearing an appeal brought by an accused under POA 1985,
s.22(7) against a decision of the magistrates' court to extend or
further extend a time limit, or by the prosecution under s.22(8)
against the magistrates' refusal to extend or further extend such
a limit;
(8) hearing an appeal under B(A)A 1993, s.1 (against grant of bail   R.19
by the magistrates' court;
(9) hearing appeals under CJA 2003, s.16, (against condition of bail
imposed by magistrates' court.

Note that in relation to applications for bail, except in the case of
an application made by the prosecutor or a constable under BA 1976,
s.3(8), the applicant is not entitled to be present on the hearing of the
application unless the Crown Court gives him leave to be present.

An application to vary the place of trial (see ALLOCATION AND
DISTRIBUTION OF BUSINESS) must be heard in open court.

Hearings in camera

43–008   If in any proceedings, a prosecutor or accused has served   R.16.9
notice under r.16.10 of his intention to apply for an order that all or part
of a trial be held in camera, an application relating to a witness in those
proceedings need not identify the witness by name and date of birth.

Application to hold trial in camera

43–009   Where a prosecutor or an accused intends to apply for an order   R.16.10(1), (2)s
that all or part of a trial be held in camera for reasons of national security
or for the protection of the identity of a witness or any other person, he
must, not less than seven days before the date on which the trial is
expected to begin, serve a notice in writing to that effect on the Crown
Court officer and the prosecutor or the accused as the case may be. On
receiving such notice, the court officer will forthwith cause a copy to be
displayed in a prominent place within the precincts of the Court.

An application by a prosecutor or an accused who has served such a notice:

R.16.10(3)

(1) must, unless the judge orders otherwise, be made in camera; and
(2) if an order is made, the trial must be adjourned until whichever of the following is appropriate:
    (a) 24 hours after the making of the order, where no application for leave to appeal from the order is made; or
    (b) after the determination of an application for leave to appeal, where the application is dismissed; or
    (c) after the determination of the appeal, where leave to appeal is granted.

Jurisdiction

44. JURY MANAGEMENT

General

44–001   CJA 2003, s.321 and Sch.33 made considerable amendments to the Juries Act 1974, in relation to the qualifications for jury service in s.1, and other matters. Mentally disordered persons and persons disqualified from service are listed in JA 1974, Sch.1, substituted by CJA 2003, s.321, Sch.33, para.15.

A number of matters arise in relation to the management of the jury, and of potential jurors.

These are:

1. Excusal from jury service (44–002);
2. Challenges (44–007);
3. Difficulties during the trial; bias, friction (44–019);
4. Discharge and appeal therefrom (44–021);
5. Access to material outside court; the internet (44–024)

1.   Excusal and deferment of attendance

44–002   A person summoned for jury service may, subject to s.9A(1A) below, show to the satisfaction of the Crown Court officer that there is good reason: JA 1974, ss.9(2), 9A

(1) why he should be excused from attending, in which case the Crown Court officer may excuse him; or
(2) why his attendance should be deferred, in which case that officer may defer his attendance,

though in a case under (2), if an application has been granted or refused, the powers may not be exercised again in respect of the same summons. Special provisions apply under ss.9(2A) and 9(2B) to serving naval, military or air force personnel, both in relation to excusal and deferment.

Where it appears to the Crown Court officer that a juror attending may be unable to act as such on account of physical disability or of insufficient knowledge of English, he may refer the matter to a judge (JA 1974, s.9B and see *R. v Osman* [1996] 1 Cr. App. R. 126).

Reasons for excusal

44–003   There will be circumstances in which a juror should be excused, as for instance:

(1) where he or she is personally concerned with the facts of the particular case, or is closely connected with a party or prospective witness; or PD 2004, IV.42.3
(2) on grounds of personal hardship or conscientious objection to jury service.

Any person who appeals to the court against a refusal by the appropriate officer to excuse him from service must be given an opportunity to make representations in support of his appeal.

A conscientious objection arising from religious beliefs is unlikely, by itself, to amount to a good reason for excusal unless, possibly, it would prevent the potential juror from properly fulfilling his duties (see *R. v Guildford CC Ex p. Siderfin* (1990) 90 Cr. App. R. 192).

As to prospective jurors who are, or have been, police officers, prison officers or members of the prosecuting authority, see *R. v Adroiko* UKHL 37, [2008] 1 Cr. App. R. 21; *R v Khan* [2008] EWCA Crim 531, [2008] 2 Cr. App. R. 13; *R v. GC* [2008] Crim. L.R.984. Each case is fact-specific (*R. v LL* [2010] EWCA Crim 65, [2011] 1 Cr. App. R. 27 (conviction quashed where jury included two police officers (one retired) and an employee of CPS). It is essential that the trial judge be informed at the stage of jury selection whether any juror in waiting falls within this category (*R. v Khan*, above).

Effect of CJA 2003, s.321

44–004   The effect of CJA 2003, s.321 was to remove certain categories of persons from those previously ineligible for jury service (the judiciary and others concerned with the administration of justice) and certain other categories ceased to be eligible for excusal as of right (such as Members of Parliament and medical professionals).

PD 2004, IV.42.1–3 (as amended by [2005] 1 W.L.R. 1361) while emphasising that jury service is an important public duty which individual members of the public are chosen at random to undertake, and that normal presumption is that everyone, unless mentally disordered or disqualified, will be required to serve when summoned to do so, point out, however, that:

(1) the legislative change has meant an increase in the number of jurors with professional and public service commitments; and the trial judge must continue to be alert to the need to exercise his discretion to adjourn a trial, excuse or discharge a juror should the need arise;

(2) whether or not an application has already been made to the jury summoning officer for deferral or excusal it is also open to the person summoned to apply to the court to be excused; such applications must be considered with common sense and according to the interests of justice. An explanation should be required for an application being much later than necessary;

(3) where a juror appears on a jury panel, it may be appropriate for a judge to excuse the juror from that particular case where the potential juror is personally concerned with the facts of the particular case or is closely connected with a prospective witness;

(4) where the length of the trial is estimated to be significantly longer than the normal period of jury service, it is good practice for the trial judge to enquire whether the potential jurors on the jury panel foresee any difficulties with the length and if the judge is satisfied that the jurors' concerns are justified he may say that they are not required for that particular jury; this does not mean

that the judge must excuse the juror from sitting at that court altogether as it may well be possible for the juror to sit on a shorter trial at the same court.

Excusal in the course of the trial

44–005   Where a juror unexpectedly finds himself in difficult professional or personal circumstances during the course of the trial, jurors should be encouraged to raise such problems with the trial judge. This might apply, for example, to a parent whose childcare arrangements unexpectedly fail or a worker who is engaged in the provision of services the need for which can be critical or a Member of Parliament who has deferred his jury service to an apparently more convenient time, but is unexpectedly called back to work for a very important reason. Such difficulties would normally be raised through a jury note in the normal manner.

In such circumstances:

(1) the judge must exercise his discretion according to the interests of justice and the requirements of each individual case;

(2) the judge must decide for himself whether the juror has presented a sufficient reason to interfere with the course of the trial; if the juror has presented a sufficient reason, in longer trials it may well be possible to adjourn for a short period in order to allow the juror to overcome the difficulty. In shorter cases it may be more appropriate to discharge the juror and to continue the trial with a reduced number of jurors. The power to do this is implicit in JA 1974, s.16(1);

(3) in unusual cases (such as an unexpected emergency arising overnight) a juror need not be discharged in open court.

PD 2004,
IV.42.3

The good administration of justice depends on the co-operation of jurors who perform an essential public service. All applications for excusal should be dealt with sensitively and sympathetically and the trial judge should always seek to meet the interests of justice without unduly inconveniencing any juror.

Appeal to the judge

44–006   A person summoned for jury service may appeal in accordance with the provisions of r.39.2 (as amended by SI 2006/353), against any refusal of the Crown Court officer to excuse him or to defer his attendance. The appeal is commenced by the appellant's giving notice in writing of the appeal to the Crown Court officer, specifying the matters upon which the appellant relies as providing good reason why he should be excused from attending in pursuance of the summons or why his attendance should be deferred.

R.39.2

The judge may not dismiss such an appeal unless the appellant has been given an opportunity of making representations.

Where the appeal is decided in the absence of the appellant, the appropriate court officer of the will notify him of the decision without delay.

2. Challenges
Principle of a Random Jury

44–007 The residual discretion of a judge at common law to discharge a juror in order to ensure a fair trial has never been held to include a discretion to influence the overall composition of the jury, as by discharging a jury drawn from a particular section of the community (see *R. v Tarrant*, [1990] Crim. L.R. 342). Fairness, in relation to this aspect of the trial, is achieved by the principle of random selection. That residual discretion may be exercised:

(1) even in the absence of objection by either party;
(2) on grounds that would found a challenge for cause;
(3) for instance, where a juror is not likely to be able or willing to perform his duties; and
(4) for instance, where the juror is infirm, hard of hearing, or whose attendance at a long trial would be burdensome (*R. v Mason* (1980) 71 Cr. App. R. 157).

That common law discretion has now been confirmed by JA 1974, s.10 (see also PD 2004 IV.42) expressly providing for excusal, at the judge's discretion, on grounds of "personal hardship or conscientious objection to jury service."

This discretion does not envisage excusal on more general grounds such as race, religion, political beliefs or occupation.

Racial, etc. cases
44–008 Applications are sometimes made to the trial judge where the case involves an accused of a particular racial or ethnic group, and where it is suggested that the jury should consist, either wholly or partly, of that same particular racial or ethnic group. The trial judge has no discretion to interfere in that way with the composition of the panel, or of an individual jury (see *R. v Danvers* [1982] Crim. L.R. 680; *R. v Broderick* [1970] Crim. L.R. 155; *R. v Ford* (1989) 89 Cr. App. R. 278).
Note that:

(1) the mere fact that a juror is, for instance, of a particular race, or holds a particular religious belief, cannot be made the basis for a challenge for cause on the ground of bias, or on any other ground;
(2) there is no principle of the criminal law that a jury should be racially balanced (*R. v McCalla* [1986] Crim. L.R. 335);
(3) the trial judge's inherent discretion, in the absence of any challenge, to exclude from the jury a person who is obviously incompetent to act (*R. v Mason,* above), is not to be exercised so as to undermine the random nature of the jury, or to influence its overall composition (*R. v Ford*, above).

Challenge for cause
44–009 A challenge may be made for cause, to the panel or part panel, or, more usually, to an individual juror. The judge should require the — CJA 1988, s.118(2)

advocate to make plain immediately which form of challenge he is pursuing, and must decide whether to hear the challenge in chambers, *in camera*, or in open court.

A record should be made of all proceedings, and in every case the fact of the challenge and the court's decision on it should be entered in the court record.

Challenge to panel or part panel

44–010   An advocate seeking to challenge the panel or part panel on the basis of its composition, should submit his written grounds for the challenge, before any jurors in waiting are called into court—these grounds should be put on the court record. The judge should ensure that counsel understands the position, namely that:

(1) the composition of the panel is the responsibility of the Lord Chancellor; and
(2) challenge will only be entertained if the summoning officer has acted consciously and deliberately in breach of his duty to summon the panel on a random basis.

If the right is not immediately exercised, it is lost.

Prima facie grounds

44–011   If it appears to the judge that there are prima facie grounds on which the challenge could be supported, the summoning officer should be asked to appear and answer the challenge. If the grounds are contested, the judge must determine, after hearing evidence, whether it is borne out, the burden is on the challenger to satisfy the court on a balance of probabilities.

Result of determination
44–012   If the challenge is:

(1) overruled, the jury should be called into court in the normal way, and the judge should make no further reference to the challenge; or
(2) upheld, the trial should be adjourned until a new panel can be produced.

Challenge to individual juror
44–013   Challenges are made when 12 jurors have been called into the box:

(1) at the time when the juror is sworn (*R. v Morris* (1991) 93 Cr. App. R. 102); but
(2) before he is sworn.

The accused should be informed of his right of challenge.

Indication of challenge
44–014   If a challenge is indicated and the advocate can state the grounds of challenge without prejudicing his client in the eyes of the jury or embarrassing the juror concerned, the judge may be able to deal with the matter in open court, briefly and informally.

If the challenge succeeds, another juror will be called from the panel. Subsequent challenges will be dealt with in the same manner. All 12 jurors will then be sworn in the presence of each other.

Need for hearing
44–015 Where it is not possible to deal with the matter informally, the sworn jurors should be asked to retire to their room in the charge of the jury bailiff, and the remainder of the panel should be asked to leave court for the time being; the challenged juror should be kept outside, in the care of an usher, but close by in case it is necessary to question him.

The judge will decide whether:

(1) to hear the challenge in open court; or
(2) to exclude the public and press.

If the grounds of the challenge make it desirable in the interests of justice, and of the challenged juror, to close the court, the judge should announce that that court will sit "as in chambers" and the public and press should be asked to leave the court.

Challenges should not be heard in the judge's room.

Hearing the challenge
44–016 If the ground of challenge appears prima facie valid and the facts are contested, the judge must decide the facts. The burden of proof is on the party challenging, on a balance of probabilities.

The judge may:

(1) hear evidence on the voir dire;
(2) question the juror; and
(3) permit advocates to ask questions directed to the particular ground of challenge alleged.

Before there can be any right under (3) to question a juror, a prima facie foundation of fact must be laid (*R. v Chandler (No. 2)* (1964) 48 Cr. App. R. 143; *R. v Broderick* [1970] Crim. L.R. 155. cf. *R. v Kray* (1969) 53 Cr. App. R. 412).

The questioning of jurors, whether orally or in a witness questionnaire, where there is no suggestion that they might have an interest in the case, should be avoided save in the most exceptional circumstances (*R. v Andrews* [1999] Crim. L.R. 156). Speculative questions, seeking to establish the basis for challenge on different grounds, are not permissible.

Decision on the facts
44–017 If the challenge is:

(1) allowed, the juror should be discharged and a fresh juror called to take his place when the remainder of the jury return; or
(2) disallowed, the judge should caution the juror not to disclose to the others any of the matters considered at the hearing of the challenge, and not to allow the fact of the challenge to influence him in any way.

Order under CCA 1981, s.4(2)

44–018 Where matters raised in the challenge might prejudice the trial, the judge should consider making an order under CCA 1981, s.4(2), restricting publication.

3. Difficulties during the trial; bias, friction, etc.

Guidance to jurors

44–019 PD 2004 IV.42.5, 6 makes it clear that the judge should ensure that the jury is alerted to the need to bring any concerns about fellow jurors to his attention at the time, and not to wait until the case is concluded. At the same time, it is undesirable to encourage inappropriate criticism of fellow jurors, or to threaten jurors with contempt of court. *(PD 2004, IV.42.7, 8)*

Therefore:

(1) the judge should take the opportunity, when warning the jury of the importance of not discussing the case with anyone outside the jury, to add a further warning, which should be tailored to the case, and to the phraseology used in the usual warning;

(2) the effect of the further warning should be that it is the duty of jurors to bring to the judge's attention, promptly, any behaviour among the jurors or by others affecting the jurors, that causes concern;

(3) the point should be made that, unless that is done while the case is continuing, it may be impossible to put matters right;

(4) the judge should consider, particularly in a longer trial, whether a reminder on the lines of the further warning is appropriate prior to the retirement of the jury.

In the event that such an incident does occur, the judge should have regard to the words of Lord Hope in *R. v Mirza* [2004] UKHL 2, [2004] 2 Cr. App. R. 8 and consider the desirability of preparing a statement that could be used in any appeal arising from the incident (PD 2004, IV.42.9; see also *Practice Direction (Guidance to Jurors)* [2004] 2 cr. App. R. 1 and *R. v. Thompson* [2010] EWCA Crim 1623) [2010] 2 Cr. App. R. 27.

Discharge of juror(s)

(JA 1974, s.16)

44–020 The trial judge has an inherent discretion to discharge a juror or jurors in the course of the trial:

(1) through illness or incapacity of continuing to act, provided the number of jurors does not fall below 9 (see *R. v Hambery* (1977) 65 Cr. App. R. 233; *R. v S* [2009] EWCA Crim.104);

(2) in a case where, after enquiry, it is shown that a juror has been approached (*R. v Blackwell* [1995] 2 Cr. App. R. 625; *R. v Oke* [1997] Crim. L.R. 898, *R. v Appiah* [1998] Crim. L.R. 134);

(3) where it is alleged that dissension is being caused in the jury room (*R. v Orgles* (1994) 98 Cr. App. R. 185; *R. v Farooq* [1995] Crim. L.R. 169).

Where it is alleged that a juror or jurors is or are unable to fulfil their duty, the particular juror may be questioned without the presence of the jury as a whole, but where dissension is alleged, and therefore the inability of the jury as a whole to fulfil their duty, the whole jury ought to be present.

While discharge is a matter within the discretion of the judge, it is sensible, and good practice, to canvass their views on the matter (*R. v Richardson* (1979) 69 Cr. App. R. 235, and *R. v Bryan* [2001] EWCA Crim 2550, [2002] Crim. L.R. 240).

Where a member of the jury is discharged at any stage of the trial it is not incumbent on the judge to direct the remaining members to ignore any views expressed by the discharged juror (*R. v Carter, The Times,* February 22, 2010).

As to the judge's duties, see *R. v Azam* [2006] EWCA Crim 161, [2006] Crim. L.R. 776.

4. Discharge of jury as a whole

General

44–021 The trial judge has a discretion to discharge the whole jury from giving a verdict. This position may be reached in a number of ways:

(1) where it clear that the jury is not able to arrive at a verdict;
(2) where there is a "real danger", from anything said or done in the course of the trial, that the jury may be prejudiced against the accused (*R. v Sawyer* (1980) 71 Cr. App. R. 283; *R. v Spencer* (1986) 83 Cr. App. R. 277; *R. v Gough* (1992) 95 Cr. App. R. 433);
(3) in the case of an irregularity as where:
   (a) an accused's bad character is inadvertently disclosed (cf. *R. v Weaver* (1967) 51 Cr. App. R. 77; *R. v Blackford* (1989) 89 Cr. App. R. 239);
   (b) where one accused pleads guilty and the prosecution propose to continue the trial of co-accused (*R. v Fredrick* (1990) Crim. L.R. 403); or
   (c) the judge deals with a recalcitrant witness for contempt before the trial is completed (*R. v Maguire* [1997] 1 Cr. App. R. 61);
(4) in the case of misconduct by a juror; or
(5) where a juror's personal knowledge of the accused emerges in the course of the trial (*R. v Hood* (1968) 52 Cr. App. R. 265).

As to the position where the contempt is by the accused in a deliberate attempt to abort the trial, see *R. v Russell* [2006] EWCA Crim 470, [2006] Crim. L.R. 862.

Separation of jury during consideration of verdict

44–022 CJPOA 1994, s.43 amends JA 1974, s.13 by permitting the jury, if the court thinks fit and so permits, to separate at any time, whether before or after they have been directed to consider their verdict.

This gives the judge unfettered discretion to allow the jury to separate at any time.

A direction along the following lines should be given to a jury if they are allowed to separate during consideration of their verdict:

(1) they must decide the case on the evidence and arguments they have seen and heard in court and not on anything they may have seen or heard or may see or hear outside the court;

(2) that the evidence has been completed and it would be wrong for any juror to seek for or receive further evidence or information of any sort about the case;

(3) that they must not talk to anyone about the case save to other members of the jury and then only when they are deliberating in the jury room; and that they must not allow anyone to talk to them about the case unless that person is a juror and he or she is in the jury room deliberating about the case; and

(4) that when they leave court they should try to set the case they are trying on one side until they return to court and retire to their jury room to resume their deliberations.

(*R. v Oliver* [1996] 2 Cr. App. R. 514; *R. v Hunt* [1998] Crim. L.R. 343)

Where the jury separates in contravention of the judge's order, the judge should ask both the court clerk and the usher who has witnessed any incident to 'articulate in open court in front of the accused and the advocates precisely what has transpired in order that he might receive informed submissions as to the approach to be adopted with the jury (*R. v B* [2011] EWCA Crim 1183).

Enquiry into verdict

44–023 Where there has been no ambiguity, procedural defect or dissent at the time when the verdict is delivered, an inquiry into that verdict will not be authorised on the basis, e.g. of a subsequent allegation by one of the jurors that the verdict was not in fact unanimous: *R. v Lewis*, *The Times*, April 26, 2001 (*Gregory v UK* (1997) 25 E.H.R.R. 577 and *Sanders v UK* (2000) 8 B.H.R.C. 279 distinguished). The court will not inquire as to what went on in the jury room (CCA 1981, s.8(1); *R. v Miah and Akhbar* [1997] 2 Cr. App. R. 12; followed in, *R. v Qureshi* [2001] EWCA Crim 1807, [2002] 1 Cr. App. R. 33). See also *R. v Thompson* [2010] EWCA Crim. 1623, [2010] Cr. App. R. 27.

The authorities establishing this principle are not affected by the implementation of HRA 1998 (*R. v Young* [1995] 2 Cr. App. R. 379; *R. v Ellis and Deheer* [1922] 2 K.B. 113; *Nanan v Trinidad & Tobago* (1986) 83 Cr. App. R. 292; *R. v Lewis* [2001] EWCA Crim 749 considered).

In dealing with such a matter;

(1) the judge must apply his mind to the correct principles laid down by European authority;

(2) to accept what the jurors say without determining whether it is correct, or hearing the accused's account which disputes the jurors' account, is a failure to ascertain the circumstances and to consider whether a fair-minded observer would conclude that there was a real possibility of bias.

(*R. v Brown (Robert Clifford)* [2001] EWCA Crim 2828, [2002] Crim.
L.R. 409, following *R. v Medicaments (No.2)* [2001] 1 W.L.R. 700).

5. Access to material outside court; the internet

44–024 The rule against any investigation or inquiry into jury deliberations is a rule of admissibility (*R. v Mirza* [2004] UKHL 2, [2004] 2
Cr. App. R. and, evidence about the deliberations of a jury is therefore
inadmissible, subject to two narrow exceptions;

(1) where there are serious grounds for believing a complete repu-
    diation of the oath taken by the jurors to try the case on the evi-
    dence (as by resorting to use of a Ouija board) has taken place,
    the court will inquire into it; or
(2) where extraneous material has been introduced into the jury
    deliberations; (e.g. papers mistakenly admitted to the jury room,
    discussions with outsiders and, more recently, information
    derived from research on the internet).Where it appears that a
    juror may be misconducting himself, this must immediately be
    drawn to the attention of the judge by the other jurors; trial judges
    should underline unequivocally the collective responsibility of
    jurors for their own conduct; jurors should understand that any
    irregularity must be brought to the attention of the judge imme-
    diately, since precisely because of confidentiality and collective
    responsibility for the verdict, it will be too late to do so after the
    end of the trial.

In relation to the use of the internet, jurors should be given a clear direction that, although it may be a part of their daily lives, the case must not
be researched or discussed there, any more than it can be researched
with, or discussed amongst friends and family; a direction on this issue
should be given at the outset of the trial and it should be given not in
terms of a polite request but in terms of an order given for the purposes
of ensuring a fair trial (*R. v. Thompson*; [2010] EWCA Crim 1623,
[2010] 2 Cr. App. R. 27.

Where the judge enquires into such a matter he must ask himself
whether there is reason to think that the jury might be influenced to
reach a decision otherwise than on the evidence in the case, considering:

(1) most importantly, the material itself;
(2) the fact that private researches were carried out contrary to
    judge's directions;
(3) what, if any, other material may have been viewed that poten-
    tially affected the jury's decision;
(4) whether there is a risk that the conduct will be repeated; and
(5) what, if any, steps can be taken by him to remedy the position.
    It is necessary to have regard not simply to the logical relevance
    of the material but also to the possibility that the jury may have
    been adversely influenced by information that was not logically
    probative, but nonetheless potentially prejudicial.

(See *R. v McDonnell* [2010] EWCA Crim 2352, [2011] 1 Cr. App. R. 28.)

Power to rectify mistake in verdict

44–025   Where the jury have made a mistake, and the interests of justice so require, the trial judge has a discretion to set aside the discharge of the jury before they have separated or seen or heard anything which they should not have seen or heard, in order to let them deliberate further. This is provided that the mistake is brought to his notice without delay. See *Igwemma v Chief Constable of Greater Manchester*, [2001] EWCA Civ 9531[2001] 4 All E.R. 751; cf. *R. v Tantram* [2001] EWCA Crim 1364, [2001] Crim. L.R. 824.

45 LEGAL AID; PUBLIC FUNDING

Quick guide

1. Introduction

SI 2009/3328, reg.4,

45–001 Following the enactment of the Criminal Defence (Contribution Orders) Regulations, 2009 (S.I. 2009/3328), funding for "relevant proceedings" that is criminal proceedings:

(1) in respect of an offence for which a person may be, or has been committed or sent by a magistrates' court for trial at the Crown Court;

(2) which may be, or have been, transferred from a magistrates' court for trial at the Crown Court;

(3) in respect of which a bill of indictment has been preferred by virtue of AJ(MP)A 1933, s.2(2)(b); or

(4) which are to be heard in the Crown Court following an order of CACD for a retrial,

is initially dealt with in the appropriate **magistrates' court** where applications will be subjected to a means test in accordance with the regulations. The Crown Court will no longer be empowered to grant funding in respect of those proceedings.

Persons accused in "either way" proceedings, and not eligible for funding for the magistrates' court proceedings, will be granted a representation order only after the case has been sent, committed or transferred to the Crown Court.

Special arrangements are made for dealing with persons who appear unrepresented at the Crown Court.Since there seems to be a widely perceived lack of appreciation of the term "CDS funding" amongst users of this work, the editors have gone back to the widely used term "legal aid" to identify the topic, adding "public funding" for good measure. It should be noted that if the Legal Aid Etc Bill 2011, now going through Parliament, is enacted in its present form, it will make substantial changes to this section.

Crown Court powers

45–002 The Crown Court retains power to make a representation order in proceedings for:

(1) contempt of court (see AJA 12(2)(f)); and

(2) breaches of court orders);

where an application will need to meet the "interests of justice" test, but will not be subject to a means test.

In any proceedings for contempt committed, or alleged to have been committed, by an individual in the face of the court, a judge may order that the person concerned be granted representation for the purposes of the proceedings, if it appears desirable in the interests of justice.

As to the apportionment of costs by a judge of the Crown Court see 45–008 below.

The Crown Court may also deal with a number of matters in relation to the transfer and amendment etc. of orders as to advocates (see 45–015).

Applying to the magistrates' court

45–003   An application for a representation order in respect of proceedings in The Crown Court must be made in writing to the representation authority at the relevant magistrates' court, being:

GR 2001, reg.9; SI 2009/2876

(1) the court in which the proceedings are to be, or are being, heard;

(2) in the case of a court enquiring into the offence as examining justices or sending for trial under CDA 1998, s.51, that court;

(3) the court from which the applicant has been committed or sent for trial at the Crown Court;

(4) in the case of a voluntary bill of indictment, the magistrates' court in which the proceedings had been heard or in which they would have been heard;

(5) in the case of an appeal to the Crown Court from a magistrates' court, that court; and

(6) in the case of a retrial ordered by CACD, a magistrate's court sitting in the local justice area of Camden and Islington.

Extent of representation order

45–004   A representation order which is granted to a person while the proceedings are in a magistrates' court includes representation in the Crown if the proceedings continue there, except where they do so by way of appeal.

ROCR 2006, reg.4; S.I. 2009/ 3331

A representation order which is granted to a person includes representation in any proceedings incidental to the proceedings, but proceedings dealing with a person who has failed to comply with an order of the court are not to be regarded as incidental to the proceedings in which the order was made.

Proceedings in the Crown Court alone

45–005   Where a person applies for a representation order for proceedings in a magistrates' court and, should they continue there, the Crown Court, and either:

ROCR 2006, reg.4A; S.I. 2009/ 3331

(1) that person is not financially eligible for such an order for the proceedings in the magistrates' court; or

(2) the representation authority considers that the interests of justice do not require him to be represented in such proceedings; and

(3) the proceedings continue to the Crown Court,

the representation authority must grant a representation order to that person for the proceedings in the Crown Court.

The "interests of justice" criteria

45–006 The "interests of justice" criteria are considered to be met in cases (1) and (3) of 45–001 but will need to be considered by the magistrates' court in relation to (2).

S.I. 2009/2875, regs.1,2

In deciding what the interests of justice are in relation to any individual, the following factors must be taken into account, namely whether:

(1) the applicant would, if any matter arising in the proceedings is decided against him, be likely to lose his liberty or livelihood or suffer serious damage to his reputation;
(2) the determination of any matter arising in the proceedings may involve consideration of a substantial question of law;
(3) the applicant may be unable to understand the proceedings or to state his case;
(4) the proceedings may involve the tracing, interviewing or expert cross-examination of witnesses (not the cross-examination of expert witnesses *R. v Liverpool City Magistrates Ex p. McGhee*, [1993] Crim. L.R. 609) on his behalf; or
(5) it is in the interests of another person that the applicant be represented.

In considering whether an applicant is likely to lose his liberty, it is not the fact that the offence carries a custodial penalty that is important, but whether on the facts alleged by the prosecutor, a custodial sentence might be imposed (*R. v Highgate JJ. Ex p. Lewis* [1977] Crim. L.R. 611). A community punishment order is not to be regarded as depriving the applicant of his liberty (*R. v Liverpool City Magistrates Ex p. McGhee* above).

As to the cross-examination of police witnesses, see *R. v Scunthorpe JJ. Ex p. S (The Times,* March 5, 1998).

2. Trials

General

45–007 An accused person facing trial in the Crown Court will be granted a representation order in the relevant magistrates' court for the purpose of those proceedings, provided he has submitted a completed application form, providing the required information as to his income and capital for the purpose of a means test being conducted.

The result of that means test will determine whether the applicant is:

(1) entitled to free legal representation;
(2) exempt from paying income contributions;
(3) required to pay income contributions;
(4) required to pay income contributions and is liable, if convicted, to pay a contribution from capital towards some or all of his defence costs.

Applicants who do not provide the required supporting evidence of income and capital will still be granted a representation order, but will need to provide the necessary evidence within 14 days of the representation order being made or the committal etc. whichever is the later, or face a sanction.

Apportionment by a judge of the Crown Court

45–008   Where an offender is convicted of:

S.I. 2009/3328, reg.21

(1) one or more; but
(2) not all the offences,

with which he is indicted he may apply to the Crown Court under reg.21 for an order that he pay a proportion of the costs of his legal aid representation on the grounds that it would be manifestly unreasonable for him to pay the whole amount, .

Such an application must be made in the prescribed form:

(a) within 21 days of sentence,
(b) stating the ground on which it is made; and
(c) stating the proportion (as a percentage) of the costs that would be reasonable.

The trial judge, or when he is not available, a judge nominated by the Resident Judge, will consider the application and grant or refuse it. Where it is granted the judge will state on the order the percentage of costs payable. The order must not require any co-accused to pay any part of the applicant's costs.

The order will be recorded as appropriate and a copy will be sent to the applicant and to the Legal Services Litigator Fee Team.

There is no appeal from the judge's order.

Approach to apportionment

45–009   As a general principle, a decision to apportion an offender's costs should not be made solely on the basis of any concerns the trial judge may have about the prosecution's conduct of the case, but should be a fair reflection of the outcome for the offender. A situation may, however, arise where, at the end of the trial process, the judge is satisfied that the prosecution's conduct of the case has contributed significantly to an unfair financial outcome for the offender. If, having taken all the factors of the trial process into account, the judge reaches such a conclusion, it may inform his decision about whether apportionment is appropriate.

The taxing authorities point out that:

(1) cases can and do change following sending etc. to the Crown Court, for a variety of reasons, e.g. a review of the evidence based on subsequent developments; a reluctance of a witness to appear; or the willingness of the victim to agree at a late stage to a plea to a lesser charge;
(2) the judge may consider that the offender's own conduct during the investigation contributed to the framing of particular charges, and that it was reasonable for the prosecution to continue to pursue those charges, until events took a different turn;

(3) the judge may be satisfied that, notwithstanding a conviction on some, but not all, counts that it was reasonable to consider the counts on which the accused was acquitted to be a proper part of the case as a whole, that it was manifestly unreasonable for the offender to be required to contribute the sum originally ordered, rather than succeeding in an application for apportionment.

If, after consideration, the judge is satisfied that apportionment is the reasonable way forward, then the amount that is considered appropriate should be expressed as a percentage of the total amount payable under the terms of a contribution order, rather than a defined amount of money.

Under Reg. 11 where a trial judge considers there are exceptional circumstances, an acquitted defendant may nevertheless be required to make a contribution to his defence costs. While this Regulation deals with acquitted rather than part-convicted defendants, its provisions, and those of Reg. 21, emphasise the need for the judge to be satisfied that, in the individual circumstances of the defendant's case, either a contribution should be payable or apportionment should apply.

3.   Appeals to the Crown Court

General

45–010   Applications for representation in respect of appeals to the Crown Court must, unlike the case of a trial (see 45–007), satisfy the interests of justice criteria, as to which see 45–006. Applicants who do not satisfy the criteria will not be granted representation. As to reconsideration by a judge of the Crown Court, see 45–011 below. GR 2001, reg.15; S.I. 2009/2876

An applicant must, as part of his application, provide information (and supporting evidence) about his income so that a means test may be conducted. The means assessment will determine whether the applicant is: S.I. 2009/3328, reg.31

(1) entitled to free legal representation; or
(2) required to pay a contribution towards his defence costs if his appeal is dismissed or abandoned.

An applicant serving an immediate custodial sentence and therefore unable to access the necessary supporting evidence, may make a declaration of truth as to his financial circumstances so that representation may be granted expeditiously.

Where a judge of the Crown Court reconsiders the magistrates' determination of the "interests of justice" criteria, and determines that the case does satisfy the criteria, the Crown Court officer will inform the legal aid team at the relevant magistrates' court, which will then grant the application.

Reconsideration by the Crown Court

45–011   A person whose application for the grant of a representation order for an appeal to the Crown Court has been refused on the grounds that the interests of justice do not require such an order to be granted S.I. 2006/2494, reg.6; S.I. 2009/3329, regs1, 4

may appeal to the appropriate officer of the Crown Court against the refusal.

The appropriate officer may refer the appeal to a judge, and either the appropriate officer, or the judge, may decide that it would be in the interests of justice for an order to be granted, or refuse the appeal.

Where a decision is made in favour of the applicant, he may apply to the magistrates' court for a representation order.

4. Committals for sentence

45–012 In the case of committals to the Crown Court for sentence or to be dealt with, the "interests of justice" criteria are taken to be met. Applicants who previously failed the means test will not be able to re-submit their applications after conviction and applicants who did not submit an application for the magistrates' court proceedings will be subject to a means test assessment.

The magistrates' court means test will extend to cover the sentence hearing at the Crown Court, and will determine whether the applicant is eligible for funding or not.

Special rules apply in relation to persons who are deemed capable of paying privately, and for those who have failed the means test but may be unable to meet the costs of proceedings on committal for sentence.

5. Crown Court powers to grant

General
45–013 The Crown Court retains power:

(1) to make a representation order in proceedings for:
   (a) contempt of court (see AJA 12(2)(f)); and
   (b) breaches of court orders) where an application will need to meet the "interests of justice" test, but will not be subject to a means test; and
(2) to amend the representation order made by the magistrates' court, in appropriate circumstances (see below).

An application to the Crown Court will not be subject to a means test but it will need to satisfy the interests of justice test.

In any proceedings for contempt committed, or alleged to have been committed by an individual, in the face of the court, a judge may order that the person concerned be granted representation for the purposes of the proceedings, if it appears desirable in the interests of justice.

Representation by advocate alone
45–014 Notwithstanding Reg.9 which requires application to the relevant magistrates' court, the Crown Court may grant a representation order for representation by an advocate alone in any proceedings to which reg.8 applies, that is to say, proceedings in the Crown Court:

(1) as are referred to in AJA 12(2)(f);
(2) arise out of an alleged failure to comply with an order of the

Crown Court where it appears to the court that there is no time to instruct a litigator; or

(3) where a person is brought before the court in pursuance of warrant issued under SCA 1981, s.81.

6. Crown Court's power of amendment, transfer, withdrawal etc

Transfer of representation

45–015 Where, on an application, which must be made to the Crown Court, a judge allows a change of representation, a copy of the notice of transfer will, additionally, be sent to the legal aid team at the relevant magistrates' court.

Withdrawal of representation

45–016 Where:

(1) an accused no longer wishes to be represented under CDS funding he must notify the appropriate magistrates' court who will withdraw representation and inform the Crown Court;

(2) a judge of the Crown Court withdraws representation, as where legal representatives are unable to continue to represent the accused, the Crown Court will inform the legal aid team at the magistrates' court, so that the collection of contributions may be stopped.

Note that;

(a) accused persons who are subject to contribution orders will be liable for defence costs incurred prior to withdrawal;

(b) representation orders will not be withdrawn where an accused fails to pay his required contributions.

If legal representatives withdraw during the trial, fresh solicitors and advocate must be assigned unless the order is revoked (*R. v Harris* [1985] Crim. L.R. 244; *R. v Chambers* [1989] Crim. L.R. 367; *R. v Dimech* [1991] Crim. L.R. 846). In some circumstances, the judge may have to conduct an enquiry as to why an accused has dispensed with his legal representatives (*R. v Scale* [1997] Crim. L.R. 899 and see *R. v Iqbal*, [2011] EWCA Crim 1294; [2011] 2 Cr. App. R. 19).

Withdrawal of representation order

45–017 An individual whose representation order has been withdrawn may on one occasion apply to the person who, or the body which, withdrew the order, to set aside the withdrawal.

ROA 2006, reg.7 S.I. 2009/3329

Where the application is made to the appropriate officer of the Crown Court, the officer may set aside the withdrawal or refer the application to a judge, who may set aside the withdrawal or refuse the application.

Application for a Q.C. alone or more than one advocate

45–018 An application made otherwise than in the course of:

- a trial;
- a preliminary hearing;
- a pre-trial review; or
- a plea and case management hearing held by the judge presiding at that trial or hearing,

for representation by a Q.C. alone, or by more than one advocate, will be placed before the Resident Judge of the court (or in his absence, a judge nominated for that purpose by a Presiding Judge, for determination), save that, where the application relates to a case which is to be heard before a named High Court Judge or a named Circuit Judge, he should refer the application to that named judge for determination (PD 2004, IV.38.1, 2). In the event of any doubt as to the proper application of this direction, reference should be made by the judge concerned to a Presiding Judge, who will give such directions as he thinks fit.

Assignment of two or more advocates

45–019 A representation order may be amended to provide for the services of Queen's Counsel, or of more than one advocate, in any of the following terms:

GR 2001,reg.
S.I. 2009/2876

Queen's Counsel alone (reg.14(2)(a)):

- where two advocates are required;
- Queen's Counsel with junior counsel (reg.14(2)(b)(i));
- Queen's Counsel with noting junior counsel (reg.14(2)(b)(ii));
- two junior advocates (reg.14(2)(b)(iii));
- junior advocate with noting junior advocate (reg.14(2)(b)(iv));
- where three advocates are required;
- in any of the terms provided for above plus an extra junior advocate (reg.14(2)(c)(i)); or
- in any terms provided for above, plus a noting junior (reg.14(2)(c)(ii)).

An amendment under the terms of:

(1) reg.14(2)(a) above, may be made if, and only if;
  (a) in the court's opinion the case for the assisted person involves substantial, novel or complex issues of law or fact which could not be adequately presented except by Queen's Counsel; and
  (b) either:
    (i) Queen's Counsel or Senior Treasury Counsel has been instructed on behalf of the prosecution; or
    (ii) the case for the assisted person is exceptional compared with the generality of cases involving similar offences;
(2) para.2(b)(iii) or (iv) above, may be made if and only if:
  (a) in the court's opinion the case for the assisted person involves substantial, novel or complex issues of law or fact which could not be adequately presented by a single advocate; and
  (b) either:
    (i) two or more advocates have been instructed on behalf of the prosecution;

    (ii) the case for the assisted person is exceptional compared with the generality of cases involving similar offences;

    (iii) the number of prosecution witnesses exceeds 80; or

    (iv) the number of pages of prosecution evidence, including the witness statements, documentary and pictorial exhibits, and records of interview with the assisted person and other accused, forming part of the committal documents or included in any notice of additional evidence, exceeds 1000;

(3) para.2(b)(i) or (ii) above, may be made if and only if:

  (a) the court is of opinion that the case for the assisted person involves substantial novel or complex issues of law or fact which could not be adequately presented except by Queen's Counsel assisted by a junior advocate; and

  (b) either:

    (i) the case for the assisted person is exceptional compared with the generality of cases involving similar offences; or

    (ii) Queen's Counsel or Senior Treasury Counsel has been instructed on behalf of the prosecution and one of the conditions in reg.4(b)(i)(iii) or (iv) (above) is satisfied.

(4) para.(2)(c) above, may be made if and only if:

  (a) the proceedings arise from a prosecution brought by the Serious Fraud Office;

  (b) the court making the order considers that three advocates are required; and

  (c) in the case of proceedings in the Crown Court, the conditions in reg.12(4) and (5) (see above) are satisfied.

The fact that a Queen's Counsel has been, or is proposed to be, assigned under this regulation is not by itself a reason for making an order in any of the terms provided for by reg.14 (2) (b) or (c).

The "equality of arms" principle embodied in the European Convention, art.6 is not breached by the refusal to allow representation by Queen's Counsel where the Crown is so represented (*Att-Gen's Reference (No. 82 of 2000)* [2002] 2 Cr. App. R. 342).

Restrictions on grant

45–020 No order may be amended in the terms of resolution 14:

- 2(b), where two advocates are required, unless the court making the amendment is of the opinion that the assisted person could not be adequately represented under para.2(a), namely by Queen's Counsel alone;
- 2(b)(i) (Queen's Counsel with junior counsel), unless the court amending the order is of the opinion that the assisted person could not be adequately represented under an order in the terms of para.2(b)(ii),(iii) or (iv) (Queen's Counsel with a noting junior, or two junior counsel or junior counsel with a noting counsel);

- 2(b)(ii) (Queen's Counsel with a noting junior), unless the court amending the order is of the opinion that the assisted person could not be adequately represented under an order in the terms of para.2(b)(iii) or (iv) (two junior counsel or junior counsel with a noting junior);
- 2(b)(iii) (two junior counsel), unless the court amending the order is of the opinion that the assisted person could not be adequately represented under an order in the terms of para.2(b)(iv) (junior counsel with a noting junior);
- (2)(c)(i), unless the court making the amendment is of the opinion that the assisted person could not be adequately represented under an order in the terms under para.(2)(c)(ii).

Every application for an amendment in any of the terms provided for by reg.14(2), (above) must be in writing specifying:

(a) the terms of the amendment sought and the grounds of the application; and
(b) which of the conditions in paras (3), (4), (5), (6) and (9) is relied upon in support of the amendment sought, and on what grounds it is contended that each condition is fulfilled.

Before amending an order under para.(15) the court may require from any advocate already assigned to the applicant written advice on the question of what representation is needed in the proceedings. The court making a decision whether to amend an order under para.(2) must make annotations to the written application, stating whether each of the conditions relied upon in support of the order made or sought is fulfilled.

Apart from the grant of Queen's Counsel by the magistrates' court, the decision to amend, a representation order to allow for Queen's Counsel, or more than one advocate, may only be made:

(i) in the course of the trial;
(ii) at a preliminary hearing;
(iii) at a pre-trial review; or
(iv) at a plea and directions hearing,

by the judge presiding at that trial or hearing; otherwise, where the proceedings are in the Crown Court, by a High Court judge, the Resident Judge of the Crown Court or (in the absence of the Resident Judge) a judge nominated for the purpose by the presiding judge of the circuit.

Duties of advocates

45–021 Where a representation order is amended to allow representation by:

GR 2001, regs 14(16)(11); S.I. 2009/2876

(1) Queen's Counsel with a junior;
(2) Queen's Counsel with a noting junior;
(3) two junior advocates; or
(4) junior advocate with a noting junior,

under GR 2001, reg. 14(2)(b), and where three advocates are required under para.(2)(c), it is the duty of:

(a) each representative:
  (i) to keep under review the need for more than one advocate to be present in court or otherwise providing services; and
  (ii) to consider whether the representation order should be amended under para.(15) (above);
(b) Queen's Counsel, where the services of Queen's Counsel are provided, to keep under review the question whether he could act alone.

If representatives are of opinion that the representation order should be amended as provided for under the regulations, it is their duty to notify that opinion in writing to the other representatives for the assisted person and to the court, and the court must, after considering the opinion and any representations made by any other representatives for the assisted person, determine whether and in what manner the order should be amended.

Change of representatives

45–022 The Crown Court may grant or refuse an application for a change of representative. The application may be made to the court before which proceedings are being heard to select a representative in place of a representative previously selected. The application must state the grounds on which it is made.

GR 2001, reg.16

The application may be granted where:

(1) the representative considers himself under a duty to withdraw from the case in accordance with his professional rules of conduct and, in such a case, the representative must provide details of the nature of such duty;
(2) there is a breakdown in the relationship between the assisted person and the representative such that effective representation can no longer be provided and, in such a case, the representative must provide details of the nature of the breakdown;
(3) through circumstances beyond his control, the representative is no longer able to represent the assisted person; or
(4) some other substantial compelling reason exists.

Selection of representative by two or more accused

45–023 Where an individual who is:

GR 2001, reg.16A

(1) granted a right to representation is one of two or more co-accused whose cases are to be heard together; or
(2) provisionally granted a right to representation is one of two or more persons involved in an investigation whose cases, if proceedings were to result from the investigation, would be likely to be heard together,

that individual must select the same litigator as a co-accused, unless there is or is likely to be a conflict of interest.

7.   Miscellaneous

Authorisation of expenditure

45–024   Where it appears necessary for the proper conduct of pro-   GR 2001, reg.19
ceedings in the Crown Court for costs to be incurred under a representation order by taking any of the following steps:

(1) obtaining the written report of one or more experts;
(2) employing any other person to provide a written report or
    opinion (otherwise than as an expert);
(3) obtaining any transcripts or recordings; or
(4) doing anything which is unusual in its nature or requires unusu-
    ally large expenditure,

the solicitor may apply to the Costs Committee appointed by the Legal
Services Commission for prior authority to do so.

Travelling and accommodation expenses

45–025   A representative assigned to an assisted person in the Crown   GR 2001, reg.20
Court may apply to the Crown Court for prior authority for the incurring
of travelling and accommodation expenses in order to attend at the trial
or other main hearing in those proceedings.

Transfer of documents

45–026   Where an accused is committed or sent for trial by a   GR 2001, reg.21
lower court to a higher court, or appeals or applies for leave to appeal
from a lower court to a higher court, the appropriate officer of
the lower court must send to the appropriate officer of the higher
court:

(1) a copy of any representation order previously made in respect of
    the same proceedings; and
(2) a copy of any application for a representation order which has
    been refused.

Notification of very high costs cases

45–027   Any solicitor who has conduct of a funded very high cost case   GR 2001, reg.23
must notify the Commission as soon as practicable. If he fails to do so
without good reason, and as a result there is a loss to public funds, the
court or the Commission, as appropriate, may refuse payment of his
costs up to the extent of such loss. However, such payment must not be
refused without the solicitor being given a reasonable opportunity to
show why it should not be refused.

Duty to report abuse

45–028   Where a representative for an applicant or assisted person   GR 2001, reg.24
knows or suspects that that person:

(1) has intentionally failed to comply with any provision of regula-
    tions made under the AJA 1999 concerning the information to
    be provided by him; or
(2) in furnishing such information, has knowingly made a false
    statement or false representation,

the representative must immediately report the circumstances to the Commission.

This duty applies notwithstanding the relationship between, or rights of, a representative and client or any privilege arising out of such a relationship.

Recovery of defence costs order (RDCO)

45–029   The introduction of the new contribution regulations will phase out the recovery of defence costs scheme under RDCOR 2001. An order may not be made under that scheme where an assessment has been made under the new regulations.

RDCOR,2001, reg.4(5); S.I.2009/3352

Licensed Premises
Exclusion Order

46. LICENSED PREMISES EXCLUSION ORDER

46–001   Where any court by or before which a person is convicted of an offence committed on licensed premises is satisfied that in committing that offence he resorted to violence, or offered or threatened to resort to violence, the judge *may in addition* to:

LP(E)A 1980, s.1

(1) any sentence which is imposed in respect of the offence of which he is convicted; and
(2) a community order, or an order discharging him conditionally or absolutely,

make an **exclusion order** prohibiting him from entering those premises or any other licensed premises which the court may specify by name and address without the express consent of the licensee, his servant or agent, for such period, of not less than three months or more than two years, as may be specified. Such an order cannot stand alone.

The order continues in force for the period specified unless it is terminated earlier.

Note that:

(a) the order is designed for those who make a nuisance of themselves in public houses, to the annoyance of other customers and the danger of the landlord, not for persons of otherwise clean record (*R. v Grady* (1990) 12 Cr. App. R.(S.) 152);
(b) there is no need for an application to be made; the trial judge may make an order of his own motion;
(c) if there is to be an application it is undesirable that it should be made by a person who is not a victim or a party in the case. An interested third party ought to make an approach to the prosecuting authority (*R. v Penn* (1996) 2 Cr. App. R.(S.) 214);
(d) the name of each appropriate premises should be included in the same order; there is no need for a separate order in respect of each premises (ibid).

Penalties for non-compliance

46–002   A person who enters premises in breach of such an order commits an offence and is liable on summary conviction to a fine of £1,000 or to imprisonment for 51 weeks or both. A court before which a person is so convicted must consider whether the order should continue in force and may, if it thinks fit, terminate the order, or vary it by deleting the name of any specified premises, but the order is not otherwise affected by a person's conviction for such an offence.

LP(E)A 1980, ss.2, 3

The licensee of any premises is entitled to expel a person under the Act.

47. LIFE SENTENCES

Life sentence—meaning

47–001 A life sentence means:

CJA 2003, s.277

(1) a sentence of imprisonment for life;
(2) a sentence of detention during HM Pleasure; and
(3) a sentence of custody for life passed before the commencement of CJCSA 2000, s.61(1) (which abolishes that sentence).

Where appropriate

47–002 Life imprisonment is appropriate in three different circumstances. It is:

(1) **a mandatory life sentence**, the sentence fixed by law (in the case of an offender aged 21 or over convicted of murder);
(2) **the maximum discretionary sentence** which the judge may impose where there is evidence that the offender is likely to commit grave offences in the future (*R. v Bellamy* [2001] 1 Cr. App. R.(S.) 34); and
(3) **the maximum discretionary sentence** which the judge may impose for public protection under CJA 2003, s.226 in relation to offences committed **on or after April 4, 2005**.

It is unsuitable to impose on an offender:

(a) already serving a custodial term, a life sentence to commence on the expiry of that term—it should take effect immediately (*R. v Jones* (1962) 46 Cr. App. R. 129);
(b) disproportionate fixed terms for other offences, to run concurrently with a life sentence, thus restricting the chances of the offender's release (*R. v Nugent* (1984) 6 Cr. App. R.(S.) 93; *R. v Daniels* (1984) 6 Cr. App. R.(S.) 8);
(c) a determinate sentence to run consecutively to a life sentence (*R. v Foy* (1962) 46 Cr. App. R. 290).

Automatic life sentences under PCC(S)A 2000, s.109 will be abolished by CJA 2003, s.332, Sch.37, Pt 7 when that repeal is brought into force.

Amendments tabled by the Justice Secretary in the last days of October to the Legal Aid Etc Bill 2011 now before Parliament propose the repeal of the existing sentences for dangerous offenders and their replacement by new forms of sentence. One of these is a mandatory life sentence for a second listed offence.

Mandatory or discretionary

47–003 On conviction for murder, an offender aged

(1) 21 years or over *must* be sentenced to **life imprisonment**,
(2) 18–20 *must*, (until the abolition of that sentence comes into effect), be sentenced to **custody for life**, and

(3) 18 or under at the date of the offence *must* be sentenced to **detention at Her Majesty's pleasure**.

In appropriate circumstances, a judge *may* pass a **discretionary life sentence**.

Since November 30, 2000, the minimum term under (3) has been set by the trial judge, as it was, and is, for adults subject to a discretionary life sentence, by virtue of PCC(S)A 2000, s.82A.

The court vis à vis the Parole Board

47–004   The release of a prisoner serving a life sentence is a matter for the Parole Board; there is a clear division of functions in relation to such sentences. Thus:

(1) the judge specifies the period which the offender should serve by way of punishment and deterrence; and

(2) the Parole Board decides whether the offender continues to represent a danger to the public.

CJA 2003, Pt 12, Ch. 7, already in force, empowers the judge, rather than the executive, as formerly, to set the minimum term to be served by a person convicted of murder, determined by reference to a new statutory framework set out in Sch.21. Once the minimum term has expired, the Parole Board will consider the offender's suitability for release and, if appropriate, direct his release. See generally *R. v Sullivan,* [2004] EWCA Crim 1762, [2004] 1 Cr. App. R. 3.

A.   Mandatory life sentences

47–005   CJA 2003, s.269, together with other relevant sections relating to life sentences, apply to murders committed from **December 18, 2003**, when those sections came into force.

In dealing with murders committed **prior to December 18, 2003**, care must be taken to ensure that the transitional arrangements applying to offences committed before that date are followed; these are set out in PD 2004, IV.49, below, and apply to murders committed **after May 31, 2002** and **before December 18, 2003** (see 47–015, below). **Before May 31, 2002**, the minimum term was fixed by the Home Secretary, as to which see Lord Bingham's letter at 47–016, below.

(1)   Setting the minimum term

The practice direction

47–006   Since December 18, 2003, when CJA 2003, s.269 came into force, a judge passing a mandatory life sentence must either announce in open court: PD 2004, IV.49.2

(1) the minimum term the offender must serve before the Parole Board may consider release on licence under the provisions of CSA 1997, s.28 (as amended by CJA 2003, s.275); or

(2) **a "whole life order"** in that the seriousness of the offence is so exceptionally high that the early release provisions should not apply at all.

In setting the minimum term the judge must set the term he considers appropriate taking into account:

PD 2004, IV.49.3

    (a) the seriousness of the offence; and

    (b) the effect of any direction which he would have given under CJA 2003, s.240 (crediting periods of remand in custody) or 240A (crediting periods of remand on bail spent subject to certain types of conditions) see DEALING WITH AN OFFENDER) if he had sentenced him to a term of imprisonment.

The judge must have regard to the guidance in Sch.21 but each case will depend on its own facts. Where he concludes that it is appropriate to follow a course that does not appear to reflect the guidance he should explain his reasons for this (*Re Jones (Setting of Minimum Term)* [2005] EWCA Crim 3115; [2006] 2 Cr. App. R.(S.) 19).

As to reduction in sentence for a guilty plea, see 47–028, below.

CJA 2003, s.269(4)

Where the offender was 21 or over when he committed the offence and the judge is of opinion that, because of the seriousness of the offence (or of the combination of the offence and one or more offences associated with it), that the offender should spend the rest of his life in prison, he must order that the early release provisions are not to apply to the offender.

Transitional provisions

47–007 In relation to an offence committed before December 18, 2003, when s.269 came into force, where it falls to a judge to pass a mandatory life sentence, he may not make an order:

    (1) under s.269(2), specifying a minimum term which, in his opinion, is greater than the Secretary of State would have been likely to notify under the previous practice (as mentioned in Sch.22, para.2(a)); and

    (2) under s.269(4), unless he is of opinion that under the previous practice the Secretary of State would have been likely to give a notification falling within Sch.22, para.2(b).

Duty to give reasons

47–008 In making an order under the above provisions, the judge must state in open court, in ordinary language, his reasons for deciding on the order made, and in giving his reasons must, in particular state:

    (1) which of the starting points in CJA 2003, Sch.21 (below) he has chosen, and his reason for doing so; and

    (2) his reasons for any departure from that starting point.

Life Sentences

LIFE SENTENCES

Starting points

47–009 The "minimum term", in relation to a mandatory life sentence, means the part of the sentence to be specified in an order under s.269(2) (see Transitional Provisions, para.(1)).

CJA 2003, Sch.21, para 5

1. A **whole life order**, where the early release provisions should not apply, that is an order under s.269(4), (see Transitional Provisions para.(2)) will be appropriate where:
(1) the judge considers that the seriousness of the offence, (or the combination of the offence and one or more offences associated with it) is exceptionally high; and
(2) the offender was aged 21 or over when he committed the offence.

Cases that would normally fall within (Sch.21, para.4) include:

   (a) the murder of two or more persons, where each murder involves any of the following:
       (i)   a substantial degree of premeditation or planning;
       (ii) the abduction of the victim; or
       (iii) sexual or sadistic conduct;
   (b) the murder of a child (i.e. under 18) if involving the abduction of the child or sexual or sadistic motivation;
   (c) a murder done for the purpose of advancing a political, religious, racial or ideological cause; or
   (d) a murder by an offender previously convicted of murder,but the judge must consider all the material facts before concluding that a very lengthy finite term is not a sufficiently severe penalty (*R. v Jones,* above).

2. **30 years** will be the appropriate starting point where:
(1) the case does not fall within (1) above, but the judge considers that the seriousness of the offence or the combination of the offence and one or more offences associated with it is particularly high; and
(2) the offender was aged 18 or over when he committed the offence.

The standard of proof that the judge should apply when deciding whether aggravating features exist for lifting the starting point from 15 to 30 years is the same as that to be applied by a jury when reaching its verdict (*R. v Davies (Gareth)*, [2008] EWCA Crim 1055, [2009] 1 Cr. App. R.(S.) 15).

Cases that (if not falling within Sch.21 para.4(1) above) would normally fall within para.2 include:

   (a) the murder of a police officer or prison officer in the course of his duty;
   (b) a murder involving the use of a firearm or explosive;
   (c) a murder done for gain (such as a murder done in the course or furtherance of robbery or burglary, done for payment or done in the expectation of gain as a result of the death);
   (d) a murder intended to obstruct or interfere with the course of justice;
   (e) a murder involving sexual or sadistic conduct;
   (f) the murder of two or more persons;

    (g) a murder that is racially or religiously aggravated (CDA 1998, s.28) or aggravated by sexual orientation (CJA 2003, s.146(2)(a)(i),(b)(i)); or

    (h) a murder falling within para.1 committed by an offender who was aged under 21 when he committed the offence (Sch.21, para.5).

As to what amounts to sadism, see *R. v Bonellie* [2008] EWCA Crim 1417, [2009] 1 Cr. App. R. (S.) 55.

Sadism need not be sexual to justify a 30-year term (*Att-Gen's Reference (Nos 108 and 109 of 2005)* [2006] EWCA Crim 513; [2006] 2 Cr. App. R.(S.) 80). See also *R. v Davies* (above).

The above criteria, suggesting a starting point of 30 years, are not exhaustive of the cases which fall into that category, and do not exclude the possibility that in some cases, probably rare, the seriousness may be such as to justify a 30 year starting point even when the express criteria normally required for that purpose and set out above are absent (*R. v Height* [2005] EWCA Crim 2500 [2009] 1 Cr. App. R.(S.) 117); *R. v Herbert* [2008] EWCA Crim 2501, [2009] 2 Cr. App. R.(S.) 9). *CJA 2003, Sch. 21, para 5A; SI 2010/197*

3.   The difficulties arising from the interpretation of this section were examined in *R. v Kelly (Marlon)* [2011] EWCA Crim 1462 [2011] Crim L.R. 806. CACD pointing out that its application was not confined to murders committed with the use of a knife which had been taken out and used in public; a murder committed with a knife in the home of the offender or victim could might still engage para.5A if the knife had been brought to the property for that purpose. Problems would always arise in the context of defining what was meant by "the scene".

4.   **25 years** will ordinarily be the appropriate starting point where the case does not fall within 1 or 2 (above) but the murder was committed **after March 2, 2010**, the offender was aged 18 or over when the murder was committed, and he took a knife or other weapon to the scene intending:
    (a) to commit any offence; or
    (b) have it available as a weapon, and used that knife or weapon in committing the murder.

5.   **15 years** will be the appropriate starting point where the offender was aged 18 or over when he committed the offence and the case does not fall within paras1 or 2 above (Sch.21, para.6);

6.   **12 years** is the appropriate starting point where the offender was aged under 18 when he committed the offence (Sch.21, para.7).

Aggravating and mitigating factors

47–010   Having chosen a starting point, the judge must take into account any aggravating or mitigating factors, to the extent that he has not allowed for them in his choice of starting point. *CJA 2003, s.269(5), Sch.21, paras 8, 9, 10*

The starting points (2)–(4) provide the judge with guidance as to the range within which the sentence is likely to fall having regard to the salient features of the case. It will often be impossible to divorce the choice of starting point from a consideration of aggravating and mitigating circumstances. Detailed consideration of these circumstances may result in a minimum term of *any* length (whatever the starting point) or in the making of a whole life order.

Aggravating factors (additional to those mentioned in Sch.21, paras 4(2) and 5(2)) that may be relevant to the offence of murder include:

(1) a significant degree of planning or premeditation;
(2) the fact that the victim was particularly vulnerable because of age or disability;
(3) mental or physical suffering inflicted on the victim before death;
(4) the abuse of a position of trust;
(5) the use of duress or threats against another person to facilitate the commission of the offence;
(6) the fact that the victim was providing a public service or performing a public duty; and
(7) concealment, destruction or dismemberment of the body.

Mitigating factors that may be relevant to the offence of murder include:

(1) an intention to cause serious bodily harm rather than to kill;
(2) lack of premeditation;
(3) the fact that the offender suffered from any mental disorder or mental disability which (although not falling within MHA 1959, s.2(1), lowered his degree of culpability;
(4) the fact that the offender was provoked (for example, by prolonged stress) in a way not amounting to a defence of provocation;
(5) the fact that the offender acted to any extent in self-defence;
(6) a belief by the offender that the murder was an act of mercy; and
(7) the offender's age.

Nothing in these provisions restricts the application of CJA 2003,

(a) s.143(2) (previous convictions);
(b) s.143(3) (bail); or
(c) s.144 (guilty plea).

Application of s.269 and Sch.21; (1) the first step

47–011   Where the offender is 21 or over, the first step is to choose one of three starting points, viz., "whole life", 30 years or 15 years. Where the 15 year starting point is chosen, the judge must have in mind that this starting point encompasses a very broad range of murders. It should not be assumed (*R. v Sullivan*, 47–004, above) that Parliament intended to raise all minimum terms that would previously have had a starting point of less than 15 years.
  Where:

CJA 2003,
s.269(5),
Sch.21, paras
11, 12
PD 2004
IV.49.4

PD 2004,
IV.49.5

(1) the offender was 21 or over at the time of the offence, and the judge takes the view that the murder is so grave that the offender ought to spend the rest of his life in prison, the appropriate starting point is a "whole life order", the effect of which is that the early release provisions of CSA 1997, s.28 will not apply; such

an order should only be specified where the judge considers that the seriousness of the offence (or the combination of the offence and one or more other offences associated with it) is exceptionally high. Sch. 21, para.4(2) (above) sets out examples of cases where it will normally be appropriate to take the "whole life order" as the appropriate starting point; PD 2004, IV.49.6

(2) the offender is aged 18 to 20 and commits a murder that is so serious that it would require a whole life order if committed by an offender aged 21 or over, the appropriate starting point will be 30 years; PD 2004, IV.49.7

(3) a case is not so serious as to require a "whole life order" but where the seriousness of the offence is particularly high and the offender was aged 18 or over when he committed the offence the appropriate starting point, is 30 years. Schedule 21, para.5(2) (above) sets out examples of cases where a 30 year starting point will normally be appropriate if they do not require a "whole life order"; PD 2004, IV.49.8

(4) the offender was aged 18 or over when he committed the offence and the case does not fall within Sch.21, paras 4(1) or 5(1) the appropriate starting point is 15 years. PD 2004, IV.49.9

Note that:

(a) 18 to 20 year olds are only the subject of the 30 year and 15 year starting points;

(b) the appropriate starting point when setting a sentence of detention during HM Pleasure for an offender under 18 when he committed the offence is 12 years, but the actual sentence remains fact-specific and may be well below or well above the defined starting point (*Att-Gen's Reference (No. 126 of 2006)* [2007] EWCA Crim 53; [2007] Cr. App. R.(S.) 59); PD 2004, IV.49.10

(c) where two offenders commit a murder jointly, and one is aged just over 18 and the other just under, the judge should adopt the starting point appropriate to each age and then move to a position where any disparity between the two is no more than a reflection of the age difference between them (*R. v Brown and Carty* [2007] EWCA Crim 1245; [2008] 1 Cr. App. R.(S.) 28). PD 2004, IV.49.11

(2) the second step

47–012 After choosing a starting point, the second step is to take account of any aggravating or mitigating factors which would justify a departure from the starting point. Additional aggravating factors (other than those specified in paras 4(1) and 5(1)) are listed at Sch.21, para.10 (above). Examples of mitigating factors are listed at ibid., para.11. Taking into account the aggravating and mitigating features the judge may add to or subtract from the starting point to arrive at the appropriate punitive period.

(3) the third step

47–013 The third step is to consider the effect of:

LIFE SENTENCES

(1) CJA 2003, s.143(2) in relation to previous convictions;
(2) CJA 2003, s.143(3) where the offence was committed whilst on bail; and
(3) CJA 2003, s.144 where the offender has pleaded guilty.

PD 2004, IV.49.12

The judge should then take into account what credit the offender would have received for a remand in custody under CJA 2003, s.240 or 240A, but for the fact that the mandatory sentence is one of life imprisonment. Where the offender has been remanded in custody in connection with the offence or a related offence the judge should have in mind that no credit will otherwise be given for this time when the offender will be considered for early release. The appropriate time to take it into account is when setting the minimum term. The court should normally subtract the time for which the offender was remanded in custody in connection with the offence or a related offence from the punitive period it would otherwise impose in order to reach the minimum term.

As to reduction in sentence for a guilty plea, see 47–028, below.

Conclusion

47–014 Following these calculations the judge should have arrived at the appropriate minimum term to be announced in open court. As para.9 of Sch.21 makes clear, the judge retains ultimate discretion and may arrive at any minimum term from any starting point. The minimum term is subject to appeal by the offender under CJA 2003, s.271 and to review on a reference by the Attorney-General under CJA 2003, s.272.

PD 2004, IV.49.13

(2) Transitional arrangements; offences committed before December 18, 2003 (For the position in relation to murders committed after 31 May 2002, see (3) below.)

A fourth step

47–015 Where the judge passes a sentence of mandatory life imprisonment for an offence committed before December 18, 2003, he should take a fourth step in determining the minimum term in accordance with s.276 and Sch.2.

PD 2004, IV.49.14

Before setting the minimum term he must check whether the proposed term is greater than that which the Home Secretary would probably have notified under the practice before September 2002.

R. v Sullivan (see 47-004, above):

(1) gives detailed guidance as to the correct approach to this practice and a judge passing a mandatory life sentence where the murder was committed prior to December 18, 2003 is advised by PD 2004, IV.49.16 to read that judgment before proceeding;

PD 2004, IV.49.15

(2) indicates that where the murder was committed before May 31, 2002, the best guide to what would have been the practice of the Home Secretary is the letter sent to judges by Lord Bingham on February 10, 1997 (the relevant parts of which are set out below).

PD 2004, IV.49.17

Lord Bingham:

PD 2004, IV.49.20

(a) stated that the fact that an offender was under the influence of drink or drugs at the time of the killing, is so common that he would regard it as neutral. But not in the not unfamiliar case in which a married couple, or two derelicts, or two homosexuals, inflamed by drink, indulge in a violent quarrel in which one dies, often against a background of longstanding drunken violence, when he would tend to recommend a term somewhat below the norm; and

(b) said that given the intent necessary for proof of murder, the consequences of taking life and the understandable reaction of relatives of the deceased, a substantial term will almost always be called for, save perhaps in a truly venial case of mercy killing. While a recommendation of a punitive term longer than, say, 30 years will be very rare indeed, there should not be any upper limit. Some crimes will certainly call for terms very well in excess of the norm.

PD 2004, IV.49.21

PD 2004, IV.49.18

Lord Bingham's practice

47–016 The practice of Lord Bingham C.J. (as set out in his letter of February 10, 1997) was to take 14 years as the period actually to be served for the "average", "normal" or "unexceptional" murder. Examples of factors he outlined as capable, in appropriate cases of mitigating the normal penalty were:

(1) youth;
(2) age (where relevant to physical capacity on release or the likelihood of the offender dying in prison);
(3) subnormality or mental abnormality;
(4) provocation (in a non-technical sense), or an excessive response to a personal threat;
(5) the absence of an intention to kill;
(6) spontaneity and lack of premeditation (beyond that necessary to constitute the offence: e.g. a sudden response to family pressure or to prolonged and eventually insupportable stress);
(7) mercy killing; and
(8) a plea of guilty or hard evidence of remorse or contrition.

PD 2004, IV.49.19

He then listed the following factors as likely to call for a sentence more severe than the norm:

(1) evidence of a planned, professional, revenge or contract killing;
(2) the killing of a child or a very old or otherwise vulnerable victim;
(3) evidence of sadism, gratuitous violence, or sexual maltreatment, humiliation or degradation before the killing;
(4) killing for gain (in the course of burglary, robbery, blackmail, insurance fraud, etc.);
(5) multiple killings;

Life Sentences

(6) the killing of a witness or potential witness to defeat the ends of justice;

(7) the killing of those doing their public duty (policemen, prison officers, postmasters, firemen, judges, etc.);

(8) terrorist or politically motivated killings;

(9) the use of firearms or other dangerous weapons, whether carried for defensive or offensive reasons;

(10) a substantial record of serious violence; and

(11) macabre attempts to dismember or conceal the body.

(3) Murder committed after May 31, 2002 and before December 18, 2003

47–017 For the purpose of a sentence where the murder was committed after May 31, 2002 and before December 18, 2003, the judge should apply the Practice Statement handed down on May 31, 2002 reproduced at PD 2004 IV.49.23–33, below. This statement replaces the single normal tariff of 14 years by a higher and a normal starting point of respectively 16 (comparable to 32 years) and 12 years (comparable to 24 years). These starting points have then to be increased or reduced because of aggravating or mitigating factors such as those below. It is emphasised that they were no more than a starting point. PD 2004, IV.49.22 PD 2004, IV.49.23

The normal starting point of 12 years
47–018 Cases falling within this starting point will normally involve the killing of the victim, arising from a quarrel or loss of temper between two people known to each other. It will not have the characteristics referred to in para.49.26. Exceptionally, the starting point may be reduced because of the sort of circumstances described in the next paragraph. PD 2004, IV.49.24

The normal starting point may be reduced because the murder is one where the offender's culpability is significantly reduced, for example, because:

(a) the case came close to the borderline between murder and manslaughter; or PD 2004, IV.49.25

(b) the offender suffered from mental disorder, or from a mental disability which lowered the degree of his criminal responsibility for the killing although not affording a defence of diminished responsibility;

(c) the offender was provoked (in a non-technical sense), such as by prolonged and eventually unsupportable stress; or

(d) the case involved an overreaction in self-defence; or

(e) the offence was a mercy killing.

These factors could justify a reduction to 8/9 years (equivalent to 16/18 years).

The higher starting point of 15/16 years

47–019 The higher starting point will apply to cases where the offender's culpability was exceptionally high or the victim was in a particularly vulnerable position. Such cases will be characterised by a feature which makes the crime especially serious, such as: PD 2004, IV.49.26

   (a) the killing was "professional" or a contract killing;
   (b) the killing was politically motivated;
   (c) the killing was done for gain (in the course of a burglary, etc.);
   (d) the killing was intended to defeat the ends of justice (as in the killing of a witness or potential witness);
   (e) the victim was providing a public service;
   (f) the victim was a child or was otherwise vulnerable;
   (g) the killing was racially aggravated;
   (h) the victim was deliberately targeted because of his or her religion or sexual orientation;
   (i) there was evidence of sadism, gratuitous violence or sexual maltreatment, humiliation or degradation of the victim before the killing;
   (j) extensive and/or multiple injuries were inflicted on the victim before the killing;
   (k) the offender committed multiple murders.

Variation of the starting point

47–020 Whichever starting point is selected in a particular case, it may be appropriate for the trial judge to vary the starting point upwards or downwards, to take aggravating or mitigating factors which relate to either the offence or the offender in the particular case, into account. PD 2004, IV.49.27

Aggravating factors relating to the offence can include:

   (a) the fact that the killing was planned;
   (b) the use of a firearm; PD 2004, IV.49.28
   (c) arming with a weapon in advance;
   (d) concealment of the body, destruction of the crime scene and/or dismemberment of the body;
   (e) particularly in domestic violence cases, the fact that the murder was the culmination of cruel and violent behaviour by the offender. PD 2004, IV.49.29

Aggravating factors relating to the offender will include the offender's previous record and failures to respond to previous sentences, to the extent that this is relevant to culpability rather than to risk.

Mitigating factors relating to the offence will include: PD 2004, IV.49.30

   (a) an intention to cause grievous bodily harm, rather than to an intent to kill;
   (b) spontaneity and lack of pre-meditation. PD 2004, IV.49.31

Mitigating factors relating to the offender may include:

   (a) the offender's age;
   (b) clear evidence of remorse or contrition;

Life Sentences

(c) a timely plea of guilty (see 47–028, below).

Very serious cases

47–021 A substantial upward adjustment may be appropriate in the most serious cases, for example, those involving a substantial number of murders, or if there are several factors identified as attracting the higher starting point present. Thus;

(1) in suitable cases the result might even be a minimum term of 30 years (equivalent to 60 years) which would offer little or no hope of the offender's eventual release;
(2) in cases of exceptional gravity, the judge, rather than setting a whole life minimum term, may state that there is no minimum period which could properly be set in that particular case;
(3) among the categories of case referred to in PD 2004 IV.49.26 (at 47–019 above) some offences may be especially grave; these include cases in which the victim was performing his duties as a prison officer at the time of the crime or the offence was a terrorist or sexual or sadistic murder or involved a young child—in such a case, a term of 20 years and upwards might be appropriate.

In following this guidance, judges should bear in mind the conclusion of CACD in *Sullivan* (see 47–015) that the general effect of both these statements is the same. While Lord Bingham does not identify as many starting points, it is open to the judge to come to exactly the same decision irrespective of which was followed. Both pieces of guidance give the judge a considerable degree of discretion.

(4) Announcing the minimum term

47–022 Having gone through the three (or four) steps outlined above, the judge then has a duty under CJA 2003, s.270, to state in open court, in ordinary language, his reasons for deciding on the minimum term or for passing a whole life order. PD 2004, IV.49.35

In order to comply with this duty he should state clearly the minimum term he has determined.

In doing so, he must:

(1) state which of the starting points he has chosen and his reasons for doing so; PD 2004, IV.49.36
(2) where he has departed from that starting point due to mitigating or aggravating features state the reasons for that departure and any aggravating or mitigating features which have led to that departure;
(3) at that point also declare how much, if any, time is being deducted for time spent in custody;
(4) then explain that the minimum term is the minimum amount of time the prisoner will spend in prison, from the date of sentence, before the Parole Board can order early release. If it remains necessary for the protection of the public, the prisoner will continue to be detained after that date;

(5) state that where the prisoner has served the minimum term and the Parole Board has decided to direct release, he will remain on licence for the rest of his life and may be recalled to prison.

Where the offender was 21 or over when he committed the offence and the judge considers that the seriousness of the offence is so exceptionally high that a "whole life order" is appropriate, he should state clearly his reasons for reaching this conclusion. He should also explain that the early release provisions will not apply.

(B) Discretionary life sentences: criteria

47–023   The criteria governing the imposition of a *discretionary* life sentence are essentially the same whether the form of such a sentence is one of imprisonment, custody for life under PCC(S)A 2000 s.93 or detention for life under s.91 (*R. v Turton* (1986) 8 Cr. App. R.(S.) 174; *R. v Hall* (1986) 8 Cr. App. R.(S.) 458; *R. v Kelly* (1987) 9 Cr. App. R.(S.) 181; *R. v Silson* (1987) 9 Cr. App. R. (S.) 282; *R. v Powell* (1989) 11 Cr. App. R.(S.) 113), or, presumably, CJA 2003, ss.225 and 226; (and see PD 2004, para.IV.47.1–6, below).

The sentence is imposed only in the most exceptional circumstances (*R. v Wilkinson* (1983) 5 Cr. App. R.(S.) 105), particularly in cases where the offender is subject, in a marked degree, to mental instability. With few exceptions, it is reserved for offenders:

(1) who satisfy the criteria of PCC(S)A 2000, s.80(2)(b) as being in a mental state which makes them dangerous to the public (*R. v Picker* (1970) 54 Cr. App. R. 330; *R. v Headley* (1979) 1 Cr. App. R.(S.) 158; *R. v Meek* (1995) 16 Cr. App. R.(S.) 1003); but

(2) who cannot be dealt with under the provisions of MHA 1983 (see MENTALLY DISORDERED OFFENDERS).

For these reasons a life sentence is appropriate where:

(a) the offence or offences of which the offender stands convicted are, in themselves, grave enough to warrant a very long sentence; or

(b) the nature of the offences or the offender's history show that he is a person of unstable character likely to commit such offences again in the future; *and*

(c) his *mental instability or psychiatric illness* is of a kind that requires constant supervision and reassessment; and

(d) if such offences, particularly the major sexual offences or offences of violence, are committed in the future, the consequences to others may be specially injurious.

(*R. v Hodgson* (1968) 52 Cr. App. R. 113; *R. v Wilkinson* (1983) 5 Cr. App. R.(S.) 105; *Att-Gen's Reference (No.34 of 1992 (Oxford))* [1994] 15 Cr. App. R.(S.) 167; *Att-Gen's Reference (No.32 of 1996 (Whittaker))* [1997] 1 Cr. App. R.(S.) 261; *R. v Chapman* [2000] 1 Cr. App. R. 77.) In the case of a personality, rather than a mental, disorder, a long determinate sentence may be appropriate (cf. *R. v Chapman* (1994)

15 Cr. App. R.(S.) 844; *R. v Spear* (1995) 16 Cr. App. R.(S.) 242; *R. v Trowbridge* [2001] EWCA Crim 2984 [2002] 2 Cr. App. R.(S.) 38).

Wherever a life sentence is contemplated, counsel should be asked to address the judge on the question (*R. v Mac Dougall* (1983) 5 Cr. App. R.(S.) 78; *R. v J* (1992) 14 Cr. App. R.(S.) 506).

Medical evidence

47–024   As to the matters raised in paras (b)–(d) above, there should be a medical report (*R. v De Havilland* (1983) 5 Cr. App. R.(S.) 109), but since the judge must ultimately decide the sentence, there may be cases where a report is not necessary (*R. v Birch* (1987) 9 Cr. App. R.(S.) 509; *Att-Gen's Reference (No. 32 of 1996)* [1997] 1 Cr. App. R.(S.) 261; *R. v Cobb* [2001] EWCA Crim 1228, [2002] 1 Cr. App. R.(S) 19; *R. v Powell* [2001] EWCA Crim 1362; [2002] 1 Cr. App. R(S) 48). As to persistent paedophiles, see *R. v Hatch* [1997] 1 Cr. App. R.(S.) 22.

Offender eligible for hospital order

47–025   Where the pre-conditions for a hospital order (see MENTALLY DISORDERED OFFENDERS) are satisfied, and a bed is available in a secure hospital, the judge should make a hospital order instead of imposing a discretionary life sentence (*R. v Mitchell* [1997] 1 Cr. App. R.(S.) 90) (*R. v Fleming* (1993) 14 Cr. App. R.(S.) 151 to be disregarded), unless, in *abnormal circumstances* the judge decides to impose a life sentence in such a case, where he considers the offender's culpability so great that a hospital order cannot be justified (*R. v Fairhurst* [1996] 1 Cr. App. R.(S.) 242. It is not proper to impose a life sentence merely to frustrate the offender's premature release by a Mental Health Review Tribunal.

For a recent example, see *R. v IA* [2005] EWCA Crim 2077; [2006] 1 Cr. App. R.(S.) 91.

The minimum term

47–026   PCC(S)A 2000, s.82A empowers the judge when passing a sentence of life imprisonment, where such a sentence is *not fixed by law*, to specify the period which must be served before the offender may require the Secretary of State to refer his case to the Parole Board. The discretionary life sentence therefore falls into two parts:

(1) that period which consists of the period of detention imposed for punishment and deterrence, taking into account the seriousness of the offence; and

(2) the remaining part of the sentence, during which the offender's detention will be governed by considerations of risk to the public.

The judge is not obliged by statute to make use of this provision when passing a discretionary life sentence, but he should do so, save in the very exceptional case (under s.82A(14)) where he considers that the offence is so serious that the offender should spend the rest of his life in prison, irrespective of the risk to the public. In such a case, the judge should make that clear in open court when passing sentence.

PD 2004, IV.47.1–3

When fixing the minimum term under section 82A the judge should reduce the term by any time spent in custody on remand if a direction in respect of that amount of time would have been given under CJA 2003, s.240 had the offender been sentenced to a determinate term; such is the effect of section 82A(3)(b): *R. v McKenzie* [2011] L.S. Gazette, October 13, 19, C.A.

Approach to the minimum term

PD 2004, IV.47.4

47–027 In cases where the judge must specify the relevant period under s.82A, he should allow the accused's advocate to address him as to the appropriate length of the period. Where he proposes not to specify such a period, the accused's advocate should be allowed to address him as to the appropriateness of that course of action.

PD 2004, IV.47.5

In specifying the relevant part of the sentence, the judge should have regard to the specific terms of s.82A and should indicate the reasons for reaching his decision as to the length of the relevant period. He is not obliged to, though there is no reason why he should not, have regard to the provisions of CJA 2003, Sch.21 (above 47–009) in relation to the tariff in respect of mandatory life sentences (*R. v McNee* [2007] EWCA Crim 1529 [2008] 1 Cr. App. R.(S.) 24).

PD 2004, IV.47.6

Whether or not the judge orders that s.82A should apply, he must not, following the imposition of a discretionary life-sentence, make a written report to the Secretary of State through the Lord Chief Justice as was the practice until February 8, 1993.

Reduction for plea of guilty

47–028 There are important differences between the usual fixed term sentence and the minimum term set following the imposition of the mandatory life sentence for murder. The most significant of these is that a reduction for a plea of guilty in the case of murder will have double the effect on time served in custody when compared with a determinate sentence. This is because:

(1) a determinate sentence provides, in most circumstances, for the release of the offender on licence half way through the total sentence; whereas
(2) in the case of murder, a minimum term is the period in custody before consideration is given by the Parole Board to whether release is appropriate.

SGC 1,6.4,6.5

Given this difference, the special characteristic of the offence of murder and the unique statutory provision of starting points, careful consideration needs to be given to:

(a) the extent of any reduction; and
(b) the need to ensure that the minimum term properly reflects the seriousness of the offence.

Whilst the general principles continue to apply (both that a guilty plea should be encouraged and that the extent of any reduction should reduce if the indication of plea is later than the first reasonable opportunity), the process of determining the level of reduction is different. (See *R. v Last*

[2005] EWCA Crim 106, [2005] 2 Cr App R(S) 64; *R. v Peters* [2005] 2 Cr. App. R.(S.) 101 [2005] EWCA Crim 605).

CJA 2003, ss.240 and 240A (crediting periods of remand in custody or of remand on bail subject to certain types of condition, see DEALING WITH AN OFFENDER), apply to the sentence, and the judge should ordinarily give full credit for the period spent by the offender on remand in accordance with those provisions (*R. v Marklew* [1999] 1 Cr. App. R.(S.) 60) where appropriate, the period specified being based on accurate information provided by the prison authorities, and not being "rounded up or down" (*R. v McStay* [2002] EWCA Crim 1449, [2003] 1 Cr. App. R.(S.) 176).

Approach to reduction

47–029   SGC 1, 6.5 recommends the following approach:

(1) Where the judge determines that there should be a *whole life* minimum term, there will be no reduction for a guilty plea; however, the judge should bear in mind the fact that offender has pleaded guilty when deciding whether it is appropriate to order a whole life term—this applies also to other matters of mitigation (*R. v Jones* [2005] EWCA Crim 3115 [2006] 2 Cr. App. R.(S.) 19);

(2) in other circumstances:

  (a) the judge must weigh carefully the overall length of the minimum term taking into account other reductions for which offenders may be eligible so as to avoid a combination leading to an inappropriately short sentence;

  (b) where it is appropriate to reduce the minimum term having regard to a plea of guilty, the maximum reduction will be one sixth and should never exceed five years;

  (c) the sliding scale will apply so that, where it is appropriate to reduce the minimum term on account of a guilty plea, the recommended reduction (one sixth or five years whichever is the less) is only available where there has been an indication of willingness to plead guilty at the first reasonable opportunity, with a maximum of five per cent for a late guilty plea;

  (d) the judge should then review the sentence to ensure that the amended term accurately reflects the seriousness of the offence taking account of the statutory starting point, all aggravating and mitigating factors and any guilty plea entered.

Announcing the minimum term

47–030   When a judge gives in public his decision as to the minimum term a prisoner is required to serve, he should:

PD 2004, Annex C

(1) make clear how that term is calculated;

(2) normally commence by indicating what he considers would be the appropriate determinate sentence suitable for punishment and deterrence;

(3) then explain that it is necessary to calculate a minimum term so

that it will be known when the prisoner's case should be referred to the Parole Board; and finally;

(4) explain that if a prisoner is released on licence, still, for the remainder of his life, he can be recalled to prison if he does not comply with the terms of his licence.

48. LIVE LINKS

Quick guide

1. CJA 2003; witnesses other than the accused (48–002)
2. CJA 1988; witnesses outside United Kingdom (48–010)
3. CDA 1998; Pt 3A; Accused's attendance at certain preliminary and sentencing hearings (48–012)
4. YJCEA 1999; evidence of vulnerable accused (48–016)

Nature of live link

48–001 A "live link" enables a person to give evidence, usually be means of CCTV from a place outside the court building instead of having to attend court in the usual manner. It needs to be distinguished from recordings of evidence given as a witness's examination-in-chief.

Provision is made for this procedure to be adopted in a number of different situations under various statutes:

(1) by a witness, under YCJEA 1999, s.24 by means of a special measures direction (see SPECIAL MEASURES DIRECTIONS);
(2) by a witness other than the accused under CJA 2003, ss.51–56;
(3) by a witness other than the accused who is outside the United Kingdom, under CJA 1988, s.32;
(4) under CDA 1998, ss.57B, 57D and 57E (inserted by PJA 2006, s.45) permitting the presence of the accused at preliminary hearings and in relation to sentencing hearings by means of live link; and
(5) in relation to a vulnerable accused under YJCEA 1999, ss.33A and 33B (inserted by PJA 2006, s.47).

A "live link" must enable the person in relation to whom a direction is made to see and hear a person at the place where the proceedings are being held and to be seen and heard by the accused, where appropriate, the judge and the jury (if there is one), legal representatives acting in the proceedings, and any interpreter or other person appointed by the court to assist the witness, disregarding for this purpose the extent (if any) to which such a person is unable to see or hear by reason of any impairment of eyesight or hearing.

Nothing in the statutory provisions is to be regarded as affecting any power of a judge:

(a) to make an order, give directions or give leave of any description in relation to any witness (including the accused); or
(b) to exclude evidence at his discretion (whether by preventing questions being put or otherwise).

657

1. CJA 2003; witnesses other than the accused

General

48–002 A witness (other than the accused) may, if the judge so directs, give evidence through a live link in:

CJA 2003,
s.51(1)–(5) SI
2010/1183

(1) an appeal to the Crown Court arising out of a summary trial;
(2) a trial on indictment; and
(3) a hearing before the Crown Court which is held after the accused has entered a plea of guilty; and

the judge may give such a direction either on an application by a party to the proceedings, or of his own motion, but may authorise such a course only where:

(a) he is satisfied that it is in the interests of the efficient or effective administration of justice for the witness to give evidence in the proceedings through a live link, e.g. from his place of work;
(b) he has been notified that suitable facilities are available in the area in which it appears that the proceedings will take place.

The responsibility for ensuring that facilities are in place is that of the prosecutor. The withdrawal of any such a notification will not affect a direction given under this provision before that withdrawal.

The specified offences are;

- an offence under SOA 2003, Pt 1 (rape, assault by penetration, sexual assault, etc.),
- rape or burglary with intent to rape,
- an offence under any of SOA 1956, ss.2 to 12 and 14 to 17 (unlawful intercourse, indecent assault, forcible abduction, etc.),
- an offence under MHA 1959, s.128 (unlawful intercourse with person receiving treatment for mental disorder by member of hospital staff, etc.),
- an offence the Indecency with Children Act 1960, s.1 (indecent conduct towards child under 14), and
- an offence under CLA 1977, s.54 (incitement of child under 16 to commit incest).

The procedure applies notwithstanding that the proceedings also relate to an offence that is not listed above.

Exercise of court's powers

48–003 The judge may decide whether to give or discharge a live link direction:

R.29.23; SI
2010/1921

(1) at a hearing, in public or in private, or without a hearing;
(2) in a party's absence, if that party:
  (a) applied for the direction or discharge, or
  (b) has had at least 14 days in which to make representations.

Content of application

48–004   An applicant for a live link direction must:

R.29.24; SI
2010/1921

(1) unless the judge otherwise directs, identify the place from which the witness will give evidence;

(2) if that place is in the United Kingdom, explain why it would be in the interests of the efficient or effective administration of justice for the witness to give evidence by live link;

(3) if the applicant wants the witness to be accompanied by another person while giving evidence:

    (a) name that person, if possible, and

    (b) explain why it is appropriate for the witness to be accompanied;

(4) ask for a hearing, if the applicant wants one, and explain why it is needed.

A form of application is set out in Annex D to PD 2004.

(The procedure under r.29.24 applies equally to cases under CJA 1988, s.32, see 48–016 below), but not to cases under YJCEA 1999, s.24 as to which see SPECIAL MEASURES DIRECTIONS.

Representations in response

48–005   Where a party wants to make representations about:

R.29.26;SI
2010/1921

(1) an application for a live link direction;

(2) an application for the discharge of such a direction; or

(3) a direction or discharge that the court proposes on its own initiative, he must;

    (a) serve the representations on:

      (i)   the Crown Court officer, and

      (ii) each other party; and

    (b) do so not more than 14 days after, as applicable;

      (i)   service of the application; or

      (ii) notice of the direction or discharge that the judge proposes; and

    (c) ask for a hearing, if that party wants one, and explain why it is needed.

Representations against a direction or discharge must explain, as applicable, why the conditions prescribed by CJA 1988 (or CJA 2003) are not met.

48–006   In deciding whether to give a direction, the judge must consider all the circumstances of the case, some of the more important being:

CJA 2003,
s.51(6)–(8)

(1) the availability of the witness;

(2) the need for the witness to attend in person;

(3) the importance of the witness's evidence to the proceedings;

(4) the views of the witness;

(5) the suitability of the facilities at the place where the witness would give evidence through a live link; and

(6) whether a direction might tend to inhibit any party to the proceedings from effectively testing the witness's evidence.

The judge must state in open court his reasons for refusing an application for a direction under the section.

Application to discharge a live link direction

48–007 A party who wants the judge to discharge a live link direction must:

(1) apply in writing, as soon as reasonably practicable after becoming aware of the grounds for doing so; and
(2) serve the application on:
   (a) the Crown Court officer, and
   (b) each other party, and. must:
      (i) explain what material circumstances have changed since the direction was given;
      (ii) explain why it is in the interests of justice to discharge the direction; and
      (iii) ask for a hearing, if the applicant wants one, and explain why it is needed.

Effect of direction; rescission

48–008 Where the judge gives a direction for a witness to give evidence through a live link, the witness must give all his evidence through the live link unless the direction is rescinded. The judge may rescind a direction if it appears to him to be in the interests of justice to do so, on an application by a party to the proceedings, or of his own motion, but no application may be made by a party unless there has been a material change of circumstances since the direction was given, e.g. where problems arise with the technology after a direction has been given. *[CJA 2003, s.52(1), (2)]*

Where the judge does rescind the order, the witness ceases to be able to give evidence through the live link, but this does not prevent the judge from giving a further direction under s.51 in relation to him.

The judge must state in open court his reasons for rescinding a direction, or for refusing an application to do so.

Warning to jury

48–009 Where, as a result of a direction under s.51, evidence has been given through a live link, the judge may give the jury (if there is one) such directions as he thinks necessary to ensure that the jury give the same weight to the evidence as if it had been given by the witness in the courtroom or other place where the proceedings were held. *[CJA 2003, s.54]*

2. CJA 1988; witnesses outside the United Kingdom

General

48–010 With the leave of the judge, a person other than the accused, who is outside the United Kingdom, may, in a trial on indictment for certain specified proceedings, give evidence through a live television link. *[CJA 1988, s.32; SI 1990/2084]*

A statement made on oath by a witness outside the United Kingdom

and given in evidence through such a link is treated for the purposes of
s.1 of the Perjury Act 1911 as having been made in the proceedings in
which it is given in evidence.

The proceedings to which such procedure applies are:

(1) proceedings for murder, manslaughter or any other offence consisting of the killing of any person;
(2) proceedings being conducted by the Director of the Serious
Fraud Office under CJA 1987, s.1(5); and
(3) proceedings (other than those falling within (2)) in which a
notice of transfer has been given CJA 1987, s.4 by any of the
designated authorities.

Overseas witness giving evidence in the Crown Court

48–011 Any party may apply for leave under CJA 1988, s.32(1) for R.31
evidence to be given through a live television link by a witness who is
outside the United Kingdom.

Such an application, and any matter relating to it, which, by virtue
of the following provisions, falls to be determined by the Crown Court,
may be dealt with in chambers by any judge of the Crown Court.

An application is made:

(1) by giving notice in writing, in form set out in PD 2004, Appendix
D, within 28 days after the date of the committal of the accused
or, as the case may be, of the giving of a notice of transfer under
CJA 1987, s.4(1)(c), or of the service of copies of the documents;
(2) containing the evidence on which the charge or charges are based
under CDA 1998, Sched.3, para.1, or of the preferring of a bill
of indictment in relation to the case,

although the period of 28 days may be extended by the Crown Court,
either before or after it expires, on an application made in writing,
specifying the grounds of the application.

The Crown Court officer will notify all the parties of the decision
of the Crown Court. That notice or any application must be sent to the
Crown Court officer and at the same time a copy will be sent by the
applicant to every other party to the proceedings.

A party who receives a copy of a notice must, within 28 days of the
date of the notice, notify the applicant and the Crown Court officer, in
writing:

(a) whether or not he opposes the application, giving his reasons
for any such opposition; and
(b) whether or not he wishes to be represented at any hearing of
the application.

After the expiry of that period the Crown Court will determine
whether the application is to be dealt with without a hearing; or at a
hearing at which the applicant and such other party or parties as the
court may direct may be represented; and the Crown Court officer will
notify the applicant and, where necessary, the other party or parties, of
the time and place of any such hearing.

The Crown Court officer will notify all the parties of the decision

Live Links

of the Crown Court in relation to the application and, where leave is granted, the notification will state the country in which the witness will give evidence, and if known, the place where the witness will give evidence, the location of the Crown Court at which the trial should take place, and any conditions specified by the Crown Court in accordance with the provisions below.

Where the witness is to give evidence on behalf of the prosecutor, or where disclosure is required by CPIA 1996, s.5(7) (alibi) or by rules under PACE 1984, s.81 (expert evidence), the name of the witness will be notified.

The Crown Court dealing such an application may specify that as a condition of the grant of leave the witness should give the evidence in the presence of a specified person who is able and willing to answer under oath or affirmation any questions the trial judge may put as to the circumstances in which the evidence is given, including questions about any persons who are present when the evidence is given and any matters which may affect the giving of the evidence.

3.   CDA 1998, Pt 3A: Accused's attendance at certain preliminary and sentencing hearings

Introduction

48–012   CDA 1998, Pt 3A applies to preliminary hearings and sentencing hearings in the course of proceedings for an offence and enforcement proceedings relating to confiscation orders, enabling the judge, in the circumstances provided for by ss.57B, 57C, and 57E (and a magistrates' court under s.57F), to direct the use of a live link for securing the accused's attendance at a hearing to which it applies. The accused is treated as present in court when, by virtue of such a live link direction, he attends the hearing through a live link.

CDA 1998, s.57A CorJA 2009, s.109

"Confiscation order" here means an order made under CJA 1988, s.71, an order made under DTA 1994, s.2, or an order made under POCA 2002, s.6.

Preliminary hearings

48–013   In relation to a preliminary hearing, where the accused is in custody and it appears to the judge before which the preliminary hearing is to take place that the accused is likely to be held in custody during the hearing, he may give a live link direction in relation to the attendance of the accused at the hearing, but he must not give (or rescind) such a direction (whether at a hearing or otherwise) unless he has given the parties to the proceeding an opportunity to make representations.

CDA 1998, s.57B

Note that:

(1) such a direction is a direction requiring the accused, if he is being held in custody during the hearing, to attend it through a live link from the place at which he is being held;

(2) if a hearing takes place in relation to the giving or rescinding of such a direction, the judge may require or permit a person attending the hearing to do so through a live link.

Continued use at sentencing hearing

48–014   Where a live link under s.57B or 57C is in force and:

CDA 1998, s.57D; Cor JA 2009, s.106

(1) the accused is convicted of the offence in the course of that hearing (whether by virtue of a guilty plea or an indication of an intention to plead guilty); and

(2) the judge proposes to continue the hearing as a sentencing hearing in relation to the offence,

the accused may continue to attend through the live link by virtue of the direction if:

(a) the hearing is continued as a sentencing hearing in relation to the offence;

(b) the judge is satisfied that the accused continuing to attend through the live link is not contrary to the interests of justice.

The accused may not, however, give oral evidence through the live link during the continued hearing unless the judge is satisfied that it is not contrary to the interests of justice for him to give it in that way.

Use of live link in sentencing hearings

48–015   If it appears to the judge by or before whom the accused is convicted that it is likely that the accused will be held in custody during any sentencing hearing for the offence, he may give a live link direction in relation to that hearing, being a direction requiring the accused, if he is being held in custody during the hearing, to attend it a through a live link from the place at which he is being held.

CDA 1998, 57E; Cor JA 2009, s.106

Such a direction may be given:

(1) by the judge of his own motion or on an application by a party; and

(2) in relation to all subsequent sentencing hearings before the court or to such hearing or hearings as may be specified or described in the direction, but,

the judge may not give such a direction unless he is satisfied that it is not contrary to the interests of justice to give the direction.

The judge may rescind such a direction at any time before or during a hearing to which it relates if it appears to him to be in the interests of justice to do so (but this does not affect his power to give a further live link direction in relation to the offender).

The judge may exercise his power of his own motion or on an application by a party.

The court must state in open court its reasons for refusing an application for, or for the rescission of, a live link direction under this section.

The offender may not give oral evidence while attending a hearing through such a live link unless the judge is satisfied that it is not contrary to the interests of justice for him to give it in that way.

This section applies to hearings in proceedings relating to a reference under SOCPA 2005, s.74 (see above 71–008) as it applies to sentencing hearings (PJA 2006, Sch.15, para.62).

4.   YJCEA 1999; evidence of vulnerable accused

General

48–016   In any proceedings against a person for an offence the judge may, on the application of the accused, give a live link direction if he is satisfied: YJCEA 1999, ss.33A–33C

(1) that specified conditions (below) are met in relation to the accused; and

(2) that it is in the interests of justice for the accused to give evidence through a live link.

Such a direction is a direction that any oral evidence to be given before the court by the accused is to be given through a live link.

The specified conditions are that, in the case of an accused who:

(a) is aged under 18 when the application is made, and:
   (i) his ability to participate effectively in the proceedings as a witness giving oral evidence in court is compromised by his level of intellectual ability or social functioning; and
   (ii) use of a live link would enable him to participate more effectively in the proceedings as a witness (whether by improving the quality of his evidence or otherwise);
(b) has attained the age of 18 at that time, and:
   (i) he suffers from a mental disorder (within the meaning of MHA 1983) or otherwise has a significant impairment of intelligence and social function;
   (ii) he is for that reason unable to participate effectively in the proceedings as a witness giving oral evidence in court; and
   (iii) use of a live link would enable him to participate more effectively in the proceedings as a witness (whether by improving the quality of his evidence or otherwise).

While a live link direction has effect, the accused may not give oral evidence before the court in the proceedings otherwise than through a live link.

The judge may discharge a live link direction at any time before ordering any hearing to which it applies if it appears to him to be in the interests of justice to do so (but this does not affect the power to give a further live link direction in relation to the accused).

The judge may exercise his power of his own motion or on an application by a party, and must state in open court its reasons for:

• giving or discharging a live link direction; or
• refusing an application for or for the discharge of a live link direction.

Interpretation

48–017   For the purposes of these provisions a "live link" means an arrangement by which the accused, while absent from the place where the proceedings are being held, is able to see and hear a person there, and to be seen and heard by the persons mentioned below (and for this purpose any impairment of eyesight or hearing is to be disregarded) being:

(1) the judge and the jury (if there is one);
(2) where there are two or more accused in the proceedings, each of the other accused;
(3) legal representatives acting in the proceedings; and
(4) any interpreter or other person appointed by the court to assist the accused.

Nothing in these provisions affects:

(a) any power of a court to make an order, give directions or give leave of any description in relation to any witness (including an accused), or
(b) the operation of any rule of law relating to evidence in criminal proceedings.

Definitions
48–018 Note that:

- "custody" includes local authority accommodation to which a person is remanded or committed by virtue of s.23 of the CYPA 1969, but does not include police detention;
- "live link" means an arrangement by which a person (when not in the place where the hearing is being held) is able to see and hear, and to be seen and heard by, the court during a hearing (and for this purpose any impairment of eyesight or hearing is to be disregarded);
- "police detention" has the meaning given by PACE 1984, s.118(2);
- "preliminary hearing" means a hearing in the proceedings held before the start of the trial (within the meaning of subs (11A) or (11B) of s.22 of POA 1985) including, in the case of proceedings in the Crown Court, a preparatory hearing held under CJA 1987, s.7 (cases of serious or complex fraud); or CPIA 1996, s.29 (other serious, complex or lengthy cases);
- "sentencing hearing" means any hearing following conviction which is held for the purpose of proceedings relating to the giving or rescinding of a direction under s.57 and sentencing the offender or determining how the court should deal with him in respect of the offence.

49. MAJORITY VERDICT

Judge's direction

49–001 It is important that all those trying indictable offences should so far as possible adopt a uniform practice when complying with JA 1974, s.17, both in directing the jury in summing-up and also in receiving the verdict or giving further directions after retirement. So far as the summing-up is concerned, it is inadvisable for the judge, or indeed for advocates, to attempt an explanation of the section for fear that the jury will be confused. Before the jury retire, however, the judge should direct them in some such words as the following:

> *"As you may know, the law permits me, in certain circumstances, to accept a verdict which is not the verdict of you all. Those circumstances have not as yet arisen, so that when you retire I must ask you to reach a verdict upon which each one of you is agreed. Should, however, the time come when it is possible for me to accept a majority verdict, I will give you a further direction."*

PD 2004, IV.46.1

Taking the verdict

49–002 It is not generally desirable that the jury be told the actual time which must elapse before they may return a majority verdict (*R. v Porter* [1996] Crim. L.R. 126). Thereafter the practice should be as follows:

PD 2004, IV.46.2–8

(1) Should the jury return BEFORE two hours and 10 minutes since the last member of the jury left the jury box to go to the jury room (or such longer time as the judge thinks reasonable) has elapsed (see s.17(4)), they should be asked, in respect of each count separately:
   (a) "Have you reached a verdict upon which you are all agreed? Please answer 'yes' or 'no'."
   (b) (i) if unanimous, or on those counts where it is unanimous, this verdict to be accepted;
       (ii) if not unanimous, or on those counts where not unanimous, the jury should be sent out again for further deliberation with a further direction to arrive, if possible, at a unanimous verdict.

(2) Should the jury return, (whether for the first time or subsequently) or be sent for AFTER the two hours and 10 minutes (or the longer period) has elapsed then questions (a) and (b) above should be put to them, and if it appears that they are not unanimous, they should be asked to retire once more and told that they should continue to endeavour to reach a unanimous verdict but that, if they cannot, the judge will accept a majority verdict (as in s.17(4)), i.e. the verdict on which at least 10 out of 12, or 10 out of 11, or 9 out of 10 jurors are agreed.

(3) When the jury FINALLY return, they should be asked, separately on each count:

(i) "Have at least 10 (or 9 as the case may be) of you agreed upon your verdict?"

(ii) If "yes", "What is your verdict? Please answer only 'Guilty' or 'Not Guilty'."

(iii) If "Not Guilty", accept the verdict without more ado;

(iv) If "Guilty", "is that the verdict of you all, or by a majority?"

(v) If "Guilty by a majority", "How many of you agreed to the verdict and how many dissented?"

Where the clerk goes wrong when taking the verdict it is better for the advocates to interrupt and ask him to start again, thus avoiding unnecessary excursions to CACD (*R. v Stringfellow* [2008] EWCA Crim 2825, [2008], *The Times*, November 14).

Recording the time; further deliberations

49–003   At whatever stage the jury return, before question (a) above, is asked, the senior Crown Court officer present will state in open court, for each period when the jury was out of court for the purpose of considering their verdict(s), the time at which the last member of the jury left the jury box to go to the jury room, and the time of their return to the jury box, and will additionally state in open court the totals of such periods.   *PD 2004, IV.46.5*

If there is an error in procedure, e.g. in timing, the judge has a discretion to correct that error by a further direction (*R. v Shields* [1997] Crim. L.R. 758).

If the jury is not able to agree on a verdict by the requisite majority, the judge, in his discretion, may either ask them to deliberate further or discharge them from giving a verdict.

Multiple count indictment

49–004   Where there are several counts (or alternative verdicts) left to the jury the above practice will, of course, need to be adapted to the circumstances.   *PD 2004, IV.46.7*

Thus:

(1) the procedure will have to be repeated in respect of each count (or alternative verdict);

(2) the verdict being accepted in those cases where the jury is unanimous; and

(3) the further direction in PD 2004, 46.3 being given in cases in which it is not unanimous;

(4) should the jury in the end be unable to agree on a verdict by the required majority (i.e. if the answer to the question in para.46.4(a) be in the negative) the judge in his discretion will either ask them to deliberate further or discharge them. See *R. v Noah* (2004) S.J. 1249.

Application to other verdicts

49–005   JA 1974, s.17 applies also to verdicts other than "Guilty" or "Not Guilty", e.g. to:

(1) special verdicts under the CP(I)A 1964;   *PD 2004, IV.46.8*
(2) special verdicts on findings of fact.

Accordingly in such cases the questions to jurors will have to be suitably adjusted.

A majority verdict which does not comply with the statutory language is not a proper majority verdict (*R. v Bateson* (1970) 54 Cr. App. R. 11; *R. v Barry* (1975) 61 Cr. App. R. 172; *R. v Austin* [2003] Crim. L.R. 426).

50. MENTALLY DISORDERED OFFENDERS

Introduction

50–001 Faced with an accused or an offender who is not so mentally disordered as to be absolved from criminal responsibility for his actions, but is nevertheless in need of treatment, a judge has power:

(1) for the purpose of informing his sentencing decision, to remand that person to hospital for a medical report (50–004), or treatment (50–006) or to make an interim hospital order (50–007);

(2) to divert the offender from punishment by ordering treatment in a hospital instead of in prison (50–009 and following); or

(3) to combine hospital treatment with a prison sentence, by making a hospital direction (50–020);

(4) to make an offender the subject of a guardianship order (50–021); or

(5) to make an offender the subject of a community order, or a youth rehabilitation order, with a requirement that he undergo psychiatric treatment (50–026).

Where appropriate, a hospital order may be made in conjunction with a restriction order (see 50–012).

Although offenders do receive treatment in prison, the judge has no control over the allocation of offenders to prisons which are able to provide treatment, nor is it correct sentencing practice to pass a sentence of imprisonment on the assumption that the offender will receive psychiatric treatment in prison.

The position in relation the judge's powers on a special verdict being returned that the accused is not guilty by reason of insanity, or findings being recorded that the accused is under a disability and that he did the act or made the omission charged against him, are dealt with under UNFITNESS TO PLEAD/INSANITY.

General

50–002 It should be noted that:

(1) the psychiatric facilities which the courts may use for their purposes are the same as those provided by the NHS for treatment of non-offender patients;

(2) with the exception of those "medical hospitals" which provide treatment in conditions of the highest security, any given psychiatric hospital will, as a general rule, admit patients only from a particular catchment area, from which each prospective patient must come, or with which he must have some connection;

(3) different hospitals specialise in the treatment of different forms of mental disorder, so that in respect of any one catchment area there are likely to be at least two hospitals, one providing treatment for mental illness, and one providing treatment for mental

handicap; for this reason the consent of the hospital is required before the judge may order admission; and

(4) where the judge has in mind making a hospital order or an interim hospital order, the Primary Care Trust (or the Local Health Board in Wales for the area in which the offender resides) is required to assist in identifying an appropriate hospital for a particular offender.

Definition of "mental disorder"

50–003 "Mental disorder" means any disorder or disability of the mind; and "mentally disordered" is to be construed accordingly. MHA 2007 substitutes this single test for the four categories contained in the 1983 Act.

A person with learning disability is not to be considered by reason of that disability to be suffering from mental disorder for the purposes of those orders dealt with in this section (i.e. orders under ss.35–38, 45A, 47, 48 and 51) unless that disability is associated with abnormally aggressive or seriously irresponsible conduct on his part.

A person is not to be treated under mental health powers *solely* on grounds of dependence on alcohol, though a person dependent on alcohol is not excluded where he suffers from another mental disorder, even if that other mental disorder is associated with alcohol or drug abuse (MHA 2007, s.3).

Quick Guide

1. Remand for reports (50–004)
2. The sentencing stage (50–008)
3. Hospital orders (50–009)
4. Restriction orders (50–012)
5. Hospital directions (50–020)
6. Guardianship orders (50–021)
7. Miscellaneous (50–022)

1.   Remand for Reports, etc.

Remand to hospital for reports

50–004 The judge may remand to hospital, for a report on his mental condition, a person who:

MHA 1983, s.35(1)(2)

(1) is awaiting trial for an offence punishable with imprisonment; or
(2) has been arraigned for such an offence but has not yet been sentenced or otherwise dealt with for that offence provided that this power is not to be exercised in the case of an offender convicted of an offence for which the sentence is fixed by law.

Before doing so, however, the judge must:

(a) be satisfied on the written or oral evidence of an approved clinician, that there is reason to suspect that the person is suffering from mental disorder (see 50–010); and

MHA 1983, s.35(3)(4)

(b) be of the opinion that it would be impracticable for a report

MENTALLY DISORDERED OFFENDERS

on his mental condition to be made if he were remanded on bail; and

(c) be satisfied on the oral or written evidence of the approved clinician who would be responsible for making the report (or of some other person representing the managers of the hospital) that arrangements have been made for his admission to that hospital within the seven days beginning with the date of the remand.

The judge may ask for evidence of the availability of age-appropriate hospital facilities for offenders under the age of 18.

Remand conditions; absconding

50–005 When a person is remanded to hospital under these provisions:

(MHA 1983, s.35(7))

(1) the remand, or further remand, must be for not more than 28 days at a time, or for more than 12 weeks in all, and the Crown Court may terminate the remand at any time if it appears appropriate to do so;

(2) the Crown Court may further remand, beyond the 28 days, if it appears, on the written or oral evidence of the approved clinician, that a further remand is warranted;

(MHA 1983, s.35(5))

(3) such further remand may be granted without the need for the patient to be brought before the court, provided he is represented by an advocate who is given an opportunity of being heard; and

(MHA 1983, s.35(6))

(4) the patient is entitled to obtain, at his own expense, a independent medical report, and to apply to the judge, on the basis of it, for his remand to be terminated.

(MHA 1983, s.35(7))

If a person absconds from a hospital to which he has been remanded, or while being conveyed to or from that hospital, he may be arrested and brought before the court that remanded him. A judge may thereupon terminate the remand and deal with him in any way in which he would have dealt with him if he had not been remanded.

Remand to hospital for treatment

50–006 The judge may, instead of remanding in custody:

(MHA 1983, ss.36(1)–(3), 54)

(1) a person in custody awaiting trial before the court for an offence punishable with imprisonment (other than an offence for which the sentence is fixed by law); or

(2) a person who, at any time before sentence, is in custody in the course of a trial before that court for such an offence,

remand him to a specified hospital if he is satisfied, on the written or oral evidence:

(a) of two registered medical practitioners that he is suffering from mental disorder of a nature or degree which makes it appropriate for him to be detained in a hospital for medical treatment, and that appropriate medical treatment is available for him;

673

(b) of the approved clinician who would have overall responsibility for his case or a representative of the hospital managers, that arrangements have been made for his admission within a period of seven days beginning with the date of the remand.

It should be noted that:

    MHA 1983, s.36(4)

  (i) where the judge has remanded under these provisions, he may further remand if it appears on the written or oral evidence of the responsible clinician that a further remand is warranted;

  (ii) the power of further remand may be exercised without that person being brought before the court, provided he is represented by an advocate who is given an opportunity of being heard;

    MHA 1983, s.36(5)

  (iii) a person must not be remanded, or further remanded under these provisions, for more than 28 days at a time, or for more than 12 weeks in all; a judge may at any time terminate the remand if it appears appropriate to do so; and

    MHA 1983, s.36(6)

  (iv) a person remanded under these provisions is entitled to obtain, at his own expense, an independent medical report from a medical practitioner (or an approved clinician) chosen by him, and to apply to the court on the basis of it, for his remand to be terminated.

    MHA 1983, s.36(7)

As with a remand for reports, the judge requires evidence of arrangements to admit the person to hospital within seven days of the remand. That evidence may come from the approved clinician who would have overall responsibility for his case, or anyone representing the hospital managers. If the judge does not have the requisite evidence to make a remand for treatment under s.36, an alternative is to remand in custody and rely on the Secretary of State to use his power under s.48 to direct the accused's transfer to hospital.

The same provisions in relation to an absconder apply as they do under s.35(9) and (10) above.

Interim hospital order

50–007 Where a person is convicted before the Crown Court of an offence punishable with imprisonment (other than an offence the sentence for which is fixed by law), and the judge is satisfied, on the written or oral evidence of two registered medical practitioners, at least one of whom is employed at the hospital which is to be specified in the order that:

    MHA 1983, ss.38(1)(3)(4), 54(1)

(1) the offender is suffering from mental disorder (see 50–003); and

(2) there is reason to suppose that the mental disorder from which the offender is suffering is such that it may be appropriate for a hospital order to be made in his case; and

(3) the judge is satisfied on the written or oral evidence of the approved clinician who would have overall responsibility for his case, or of some other representative of the hospital managers,

that arrangements have been made for his admission within the period of 28 days beginning with the date of the order,

he may, before making a hospital order, or dealing with him in some other way, make an interim hospital order authorising the offender's admission to such hospital as is specified and his detention there.

An interim hospital order remains in force for such period not exceeding 12 weeks as the judge may specify in making the order, but may be renewed for further periods of not more than 28 days at a time, if it appears, on the written or oral evidence of the responsible clinician, that such continuation is warranted. No order may continue in force for more than 12 months in all, and the judge must terminate the order:

(a) if he makes a full hospital order in respect of the offender; or
(b) after considering the written or oral evidence of the responsible medical officer, he decides to deal with the offender in some other way.

The power of renewing an interim hospital order may be exercised without the offender being brought before the court if he is represented by counsel who is given an opportunity of being heard. The same provisions apply in relation to persons absconding from hospital, etc. as apply in the case of ss.35 and 36 (see above).

As to obtaining information from health authorities as to the availability of places, see 50–023, below.

2. The sentencing stage

Approach to sentence

50–008 The judge, at the sentencing stage, unless he makes a guardianship order, is faced with the choice of:

(1) passing an appropriate sentence of imprisonment and either;
  (a) relying on the Secretary of State's power to direct transfer to hospital for treatment; or
  (b) exercising his own power to direct treatment by adding a hospital direction (50–020); or
(2) diverting the offender from punishment by making a hospital order (50–009), and if he does so:
  (a) delegating decisions on management and discharge to the care team, based on clinical criteria, by means of an unrestricted hospital order under MHA 1983, s.37 (50–009); or
  (b) requiring the Secretary of State to oversee the risk management of the case in the interests of protection of the public, by means of a restriction order under MHA 1983, s.41 (50–012); or
(3) where appropriate, making a community order (50–026), or, if the offender is under 18, a youth rehabilitation order (50–026) with a treatment requirement.

CACD has said that in approaching sentence in a case involving a degree of mental disorder the judge should take the following steps (*R. v Birch* (1990) 90 Cr. App. R. 78, at p.87):

- if a period of compulsory detention is not, or may not, be apposite, he should consider the possibility of a community order, or a youth rehabilitation order, with a requirement of in- or out-patient treatment;
- otherwise, he will need to satisfy himself that the preconditions for making a hospital order are satisfied; here he acts on the evidence of the doctors, and if left in doubt may use the provisions of ss.38 and 39 to make an interim order;
- if he is satisfied that the preconditions for a hospital order are made out, he will have to decide whether to make such an order or whether "the most suitable way of disposing of the case" is to impose a sentence of imprisonment (see 50–019, below);
- he must then consider whether the further condition imposed by s.41 (see 50–012, below and Pt 5, restriction order) is satisfied, in which case he may make a restriction order; he is not obliged to do so, and may again -consider sending the offender to prison, either for life or for a fixed term (*R. v Speake* (1957) 41 Cr. App. R. 222);
- if he decides to make a restriction order, he must make one without limit of time; and
- he must choose between an order without restriction, which may enable the author of a serious act of violence to be at liberty within months of the making of the order, and a restriction order which may lead to the offender being detained, in some cases, for a longer period than if he had been given a custodial sentence; it is, moreover, a choice which depends upon the prognosis, the ultimate responsibility for which is left to the judge.

The decision whether to make a hospital order instead of imposing a sentence of imprisonment is discretionary, and fulfilment of the preconditions in s.37 does not give rise to a presumption that an order will be made. Whilst the welfare of the offender is an important matter to be taken into consideration, it must be assessed in the light of the seriousness of the offence. Where there are other co-offenders, it is not wrong to take account of parity of sentencing (*R. v Khelifi* [2006] EWCA Crim. 770 [2006] 2 Cr. App. R.(S.) 100).

The gravity of the offence committed is not material save that it may indicate a need for special treatment (*R. v Eaton* [1976] Crim. L.R. 390).

An offender should always be represented where the court is contemplating such an order (*R. v Blackwood* (1974) 59 Cr. App. R. 170).

3. Hospital order

General

50–009 Where a person is convicted before the Crown Court of an offence punishable with imprisonment, other than an offence for which the sentence is fixed by law, the judge may make a hospital order authorising his admission to, and detention in, a specified hospital. In the case of an offence the sentence for which would otherwise fall to be imposed under:

MHA 1893,
s.37(1) CJIA
2008, s.148,
Sch.26, para.8

(1) FA 1968, s.51A(2) (minimum term for certain firearms offences); or
(2) PCC(S)A 2000, ss.109 where still appropriate, 110(2) or 111(2) (minimum term for certain repeat offences); or
(3) CJA 2003, ss.225(2), 226(2) (dangerous offenders); or
(4) VRCA 2006, s.29(4) or (6) (minimum sentences in certain cases of using someone to mind a weapon),

CJIA 2008, s.148, Sch.26, para.8

(read in accordance with CJA 2003, s.305(4)) there is nothing to prevent the judge from making a hospital order.

As to the effect of such an order, see 50–011 below.

Preconditions for hospital order

50–010 Before a hospital order may be made, the judge must be:

(1) dealing with an offender for an imprisonable offence;
(2) satisfied on the written or oral evidence of two medical practitioners (at least one of whom is approved for the purposes of s.12 of the 1983 Act) that:
   (a) the offender is suffering from mental disorder (see below); and
   (b) the mental disorder from which the offender is suffering is of a nature or degree which makes it appropriate for him to be detained in a hospital for medical treatment and appropriate treatment is available for him;
(3) satisfied, on the written or oral evidence of the approved clinician who would have overall responsibility for the offender's case or of some other person representing the managers of the hospital, that arrangements have been made for his admission within 28 days;
(4) of the opinion, having regard to all the circumstances, including the nature of the offence and the character and antecedents of the offender, and to other available methods of dealing with him, that the most suitable method of disposing of the case is by means of a hospital order (see, e.g. *R. v I A* [2005] EWCA Crim 2077 [2006] 1 Cr. App. R.(S.) 91).

As to the improper combination of such a sentence with other orders, see 50–022, below.

In view of (4), even where the other criteria are met, the judge has a duty to decide whether a hospital order is the most suitable method of disposing of the case, or whether there ought to be a custodial sentence, see 50–019, below.

Effect of order

50–011 Once the offender is admitted to hospital pursuant to such an order, unless it is accompanied by a restriction order under s.41, his position is almost exactly the same as if he were a civil patient. In effect he passes out of the penal system and into the hospital regime; neither the judge nor the Secretary of State has any say in his disposal. Thus:

(1) he becomes a patient to be managed at the discretion of his responsible clinician;

(2) he can be discharged at any time by the responsible clinician, the question informing the decision to discharge being whether his disorder, and the risk arising from it, justifies his continuing detention for medical treatment;

(3) the order will lapse after six months, if it has not already been discharged, unless renewed by the responsible clinician;

(4) from the point where renewal is made, the patient is entitled to seek review of his detention by the Mental Health Review Tribunal, as is his nearest relative;

(5) the responsible clinician may discharge him into the community subject to conditions, under a community treatment order, which will include conditions that the patient be available to his care team as directed to ensure that he receives the treatment he requires, or for purposes of assessment; he may be recalled to hospital by the responsible clinician if that becomes necessary, to ensure that he receives the treatment he needs, for his own health and safety or for the protection of others.

The community treatment order lapses after six months unless renewed, and can be lifted at any time by the responsible clinician or the Tribunal. Unless a community treatment order is made, discharge from hospital signals the end of any obligation on the patient to accept treatment. His responsible clinician, or the Tribunal, can discharge him absolutely at any time. He can also apply for a discharge by the hospital managers. These reviews are in practice delegated to volunteers who may have no legal or clinical knowledge, but are nonetheless empowered to override the opinion of the responsible clinician.

It is thus essential, where doubt in relation to future risk exists at the time of sentencing, for the judge to make a restriction order, since otherwise a patient under a hospital order may be discharged without regard to the criteria which his clinical supervisor would have to apply.

The Tribunal has discretion to discharge the patient from hospital even where the criteria for detention are met, and must do so if it is not satisfied that he remains mentally disordered to a nature or degree which justifies his continuing detention in hospital for medical treatment; or if it is not satisfied that his detention is not necessary for his own health or safety or for the protection of others. It has no power to discharge subject to a community treatment order, thus a discharge by the tribunal invariably terminates an unrestricted hospital order absolutely.

4.   Restriction order: s.41

General

HO 1990

50–012   A restriction order is an order which accompanies a hospital order in cases where the judge considers that for the protection of the public from serious harm, the offender should not be released from hospital without careful consideration by either the Secretary of State or by the Tribunal. The order prevents the offender from being discharged, granted leave of absence or transferred to another hospital without the approval of the Secretary of State. In certain circumstances a restricted patient may be discharged by the Tribunal.

Preconditions

50–013   The judge may, where he makes a hospital order in respect   MHA 1983, s.14
of an offender, also make a restriction order, ordering that the offender
be subject to special restrictions, provided that:

(1) having regard to the nature of the offence, the antecedents of the
offender, and the risk of his committing offences if set at large,
he considers it necessary for the protection of the public from
serious harm to do so; and
(2) at least one of the medical practitioners whose evidence is taken
into account has given evidence orally before the court.

Under the amendments effected by MHA 2007, all restriction orders
are now to be made without limit of time. In the ordinary case,
where punishment as such is not intended and the object is that
the offender should receive treatment and be at large again as soon
as he can safely be discharged, a restriction order is not appropriate
(*R. v Morris* (1961) 45 Cr. App. R. 185); but a restriction order ought
to be made, where the judge considers that the public needs to be
protected:

(a) in cases of violence or the more serious sexual offences,
particularly if the offender has a record of involving violent
behaviour (*R. v Gardiner* (1967) 51 Cr. App. R. 187; *R. v
Birch* (1989) 11 Cr. App. R.(S.) 202);
(b) in the case of the anti-social pest who requires treatment
under a hospital order (*R.v Toland* (1974) 58 Cr. App. R.
453; *R. v Royse* (1981) 3 Cr. App. R.(S.) 58); and
(c) where doubt in relation to future risk exists at the time of
sentencing.

The section places the responsibility of making a restriction order on the
judge if, in his opinion, it is necessary for the protection of the public;
the fact that all the medical witnesses advise against it does not mean
that it is wrong in principle, but there must be evidence on which to base
such an order (*R. v Courtney* (1987) 9 Cr. App. R.(S.) 404).

In certain, circumstances, as an alternative to recommending a
restriction order under s.41, the responsible medical officer may make a
"supervision application" to the Health Authority under s.25A (inserted
by s.1 of the Mental Health (Patients in the Community) Act 1995)
which provides limited "teeth", including recall to hospital.

Effect of restriction order

50–014   In marked contrast with the regime under the ordinary hospital order, is an order coupled with a restriction on discharge pursuant
to s.41. Such an order is not a separate means of disposal; it has no
existence independently of the hospital order to which it relates. It does,
however, fundamentally affect the circumstances in which the patient
is detained.

Where the judge imposes a restriction order, he is still ordering
treatment as a substitute for punishment. The distinction from the
unrestricted order is that he has concluded, in the light of the circumstances of the offender and the offence, that decisions on liberty should

not be left to clinical discretion. The patient's management will still be determined by clinical assessment of his mental disorder and the risks arising from it, but the Secretary of State for Justice becomes responsible for the risk assessment informing decisions to grant greater liberty and, consequently for taking those decisions. The making of a restriction order has a number of significant effects on the hospital order. Thus:

(1) it converts it into an order of indefinite duration; it does not require regular renewal to prevent it from lapsing, but remains in force indefinitely until it is discharged by the responsible clinician with the agreement of the Secretary of State under s.23, or s.42 or by the Tribunal under ss.73 or 75;

(2) nearest relatives have no powers in respect of restricted patients; nor can a restricted patient be discharged by hospital managers, unless the Secretary of State for Justice agrees;

(3) restrictions relieve the responsible clinician of ultimate responsibility for protecting the public from further harm, by requiring him to obtain the Secretary of State's agreement to certain decisions; his agreement is required before the patient can be given leave in the community, can be transferred to a different hospital or discharged into the community;

(4) a restricted patient may be, and usually is, discharged into the community subject to conditions; this is to ensure that the patient continues to receive the medical treatment he needs, and to protect the public; he may be made subject to supervision by social and psychiatric supervisors, charged with keeping the Secretary of State informed of the patient's progress and behaviour in the community;

(5) the patient may be recalled to hospital by the Secretary of State at any time if he decides it is necessary for the protection of the public, and provided he has current medical evidence of mental disorder;

(6) the conditionally discharged patient remains liable to detention in hospital, and consequently to recall, unless and until the Secretary of State lifts his restrictions under s.42(1), or the Tribunal orders absolute discharge from his restrictions under s.75.

The Tribunal is required to order the discharge of a patient if not satisfied that the nature or degree of his disorder, on the day of the hearing, justifies his liability to detention in hospital. It cannot sanction continuing detention of the patient simply because he is dangerous. A restricted hospital order will be absolutely discharged in the great majority of cases well within the offender's lifetime, when his mental disorder is assessed as insufficiently serious to justify continuing liability to detention. Unlike the life or indeterminate sentence, a restricted -hospital order is not, therefore, a device which can invariably protect the public from further harm for the offender's lifetime. Restrictions can, however, remain in place for as long as all parties, including the Tribunal, assess that they are necessary in the light of risk arising from the offender's mental disorder.

Approach to restriction order

50–015 The judge is required to assess not the seriousness of the risk that the accused will re-offend, but the risk that if he does so the public will suffer serious harm. In *R. v Birch* (above) where the principles were reviewed, CACD was of the opinion that:

(1) the harm need not be limited to personal injury;

(2) the harm need not relate to the public in general, it suffices if a single person or category of persons is at risk; and

(3) the potential harm must however be serious; a high possibility of a recurrence of minor offences is not enough.

The decision whether to make an order is one for the judge; he may make an order even where the medical witnesses do not advise it (*R. v Royse* (1981) 3 Cr. App. R.(S.) 58; cf. *R. v Reynolds, The Times,* November 1, 2000). The seriousness of the offence is only one of the factors which he is required to take into consideration.

A minor offence by an offender who is shown to be mentally disordered and dangerous may be the subject of a restriction order; conversely, a serious offence committed by an offender adjudged to have a low risk of re-offending may lead to a restriction order being made (*R. v Courtney* (1987) 9 Cr. App. R.(S.) 404; *R. v Khan* (1987) 9 Cr. App. R.(S.) 455).

A restriction order should not be imposed merely to mark the gravity of the offence (though this is a factor in the assessment of risk), or as a means of punishment, since a hospital order is not intended for that purpose.

Restriction order after committal by magistrates

50–016 Where an offender is committed to the Crown Court by a magistrates' court, with a view to a restriction order being made, the judge must enquire into the circumstances of the case, and:

MHA 1981, s.43(1)(2)

(1) if he has power under s.41 to do so, and the offence is punishable on summary conviction with imprisonment, he may make a hospital order with or without a restriction order (see *R. v Avbunudje* (1999) 2 Cr. App. R.(S.) 189); or

(2) if he does not make such an order, he may deal with the offender in any other manner in which the magistrates could have dealt with him.

The Crown Court has the same powers to make orders under ss.35, 36 and 38 as in the case of a person convicted before it.

Restriction order: naming a hospital unit

50–017 Where the judge makes a restriction order, he may direct that the patient be detained in hospital at a level of security that he deems necessary to ensure protection of the public; he may do the same in the case of a hospital direction.

MHA 1983, s.43(1)(3);

The majority of hospital trusts manage accommodation ranging from medium secure to locked wards or unlocked wards. A hospital order directing admission to a Primary Care Trust or an NHS Trust in Wales or a major psychiatric hospital, will give to the hospital

681

managers a discretion over the level of security under which the patient is detained. The judge may wish to specify a level of security if the offender has been found to present a risk of serious harm to others, where he presents a serious escape or absconding risk, or where his hospital admission is attached to a life, or indeterminate sentence under a hospital direction.

Note that:

(1) naming a hospital unit allows the judge to require that the patient be detained under the level of security he deems appropriate;
(2) the unit named may be any unit of an individual hospital which the judge chooses to name;
(3) the intention is that it should be a ward or secure unit which offers a specific level of security, so that in naming it, the judge is directing the offender's detention under that category of security; if the judge does not have adequate knowledge of the levels of security available in the hospital to which it wishes to order admission, MHA 1983, s.39 (see 50–023 below) may serve to acquire that information;
(4) while clinicians who will be responsible for the patient's care are likely to be ready to advise the judge on the naming of hospital units, the discretion lies with the judge;
(5) the practical effect of naming a hospital unit is that the Secretary of State's authority is required to move the offender to a different level of security, whether in a different hospital or the one to which the offender was admitted.

The Secretary of State may agree, in due course, to remove the requirement to detain within a named unit, allowing the offender to be managed more flexibly within the hospital. This would happen after a risk assessment had concluded that the offender's management could safely be managed without the constraints of a named unit.

Restriction order; ancillary provisions

50–018 Where a restriction order is made, the judge should ascertain that the hospital to which the offender is to be admitted has the facilities for his safe custody (*R. v Cox* (1968) 52 Cr. App. R. 106).

In addition:

(1) arrangements may be made for his admission to hospital in any part of the country where a vacancy exists; and
(2) the judge may give such directions as he thinks fit for his conveyance to a place of safety and his detention there, pending his admission to hospital within 28 days (*R. v Marsden* (1968) 52 Cr. App. R. 301).

Custodial sentence as an alternative

50–019 The choice of a custodial sentence as an alternative to a hospital order coupled with a restriction order may arise where:

(1) the offender is dangerous and no suitable secure hospital accommodation is available;
(2) the judge is of the opinion that notwithstanding the offender's

mental disorder, there was an element of culpability in the offence deserving of punishment, as where there is no connection between his disorder and the offence, or his responsibility, though diminished, is not extinguished, though even where a custodial sentence may not be appropriate (see, e.g. *R. v Mbatha* (1985) 7 Cr. App. R.(S.) 373).

A sentenced prisoner can be transferred to hospital for treatment by warrant of the Secretary of State at any time during sentence, if two medical reports confirm that he is suffering from mental disorder and that detention in hospital for treatment is appropriate. A prison sentence does not, therefore, automatically deprive the offender of treatment during his sentence (see also the power to combine a prison sentence with hospital treatment, 50–020, below).

Decisions on the release of the transferred prisoner will continue to be governed by his tariff. The Tribunal can only recommend discharge, and not order it, until the prisoner reaches his release date. The result of a Tribunal recommendation for discharge before release date will usually be a return to prison to complete the sentence. The responsible clinician can recommend to the Secretary of State that the prisoner no longer needs detention in hospital for treatment. The Secretary of State will normally then use his power under MHA 1983, s.50 to return the prisoner to prison to complete his sentence.

5. Hospital directions

General

50–020 Where an offender convicted of an offence before the Crown Court, the sentence for which is not fixed by law, and the judge:

MHA 1983, s.45A

(1) considers making a hospital order in respect of him before deciding to impose a sentence of imprisonment ("the relevant sentence");
(2) is satisfied, on the written or oral evidence of two registered medical practitioners, that:
   (a) the offender is suffering from a mental disorder;
   (b) that the mental disorder is of a nature or degree which makes it appropriate for him to be detained in a hospital for medical treatment; and
   (c) such medical treatment is available for him,

he may give both of the following directions:

   (i) a hospital direction that the offender, instead of being removed to and detained in prison, be removed to and detained in a specified hospital, and
   (ii) a limitation direction, that the offender be subject to the special restrictions imposed by s.41,

but the latter direction should not be given unless one of the medical practitioners has given oral evidence before the court. Similar provisions as to admission, etc. apply as in the case of a hospital order.

These directions must not be given unless the judge is satisfied on the oral or written evidence of the approved clinician who would have overall responsibility for his case, or of some other person representing the hospital managers, that arrangements have been made for the patient's admission within 28 days.

A hospital direction enables the judge to combine the effects of an order for treatment in hospital with the tariff associated with a prison sentence. Under the 1997 Act, a hospital direction could only be made for offenders categorised as psychopathically disordered; under the 2007 Act, there is no sub-categorisation of mental disorder, and a hospital direction is available in respect of any offender who receives a prison sentence, except where the sentence is fixed by law.

A prisoner subject to a hospital direction will subsequently be managed exactly as if he had been transferred to hospital after sentence by the Secretary of State. He may be transferred to prison at any time, on the responsible clinician's advice that his detention in hospital for treatment is inappropriate. His release will be determined by his sentence, as if no hospital direction had been made. The Tribunal may recommend, but cannot order, his discharge, under s 74. If his sentence is determinate, he may be detained in hospital as if a civil patient, if he is still there after his release date. If he has an indeterminate sentence, his release will be determined by the Parole Board once his tariff is served. He will be released on life licence and subject to recall to prison.

HO 1990

6. Guardianship order

50–021 An alternative to a community order under CJA 2003, Pt 12, or a youth rehabilitation order within the meaning of CJIA 2008, Pt 1, with a requirement of treatment may be, in some cases, a guardianship order which places the offender under the guardianship either of the local authority social services department, or of some person approved by the local authority (such as a relative). The conditions for the making of a guardianship order are essentially the same as those for a hospital order.

MHA 1983, s.37(1)(2)(6)

The judge will need to be satisfied:

(1) in the case of an offender who has attained the age of 16, that the mental disorder is of a nature or degree which warrants his reception into guardianship; and

(2) that the local authority or other person is willing to receive him into guardianship.

The order gives the guardian power to require the offender to live at a specified place, to attend specified places at specified times for treatment, occupation, education or training, and to allow access to any doctor, approved social worker or other person specified. The disadvantage is that there is no sanction available to the court in the event of non-compliance as there is in the case of a community order, or a youth rehabilitation order.

For a consideration by the CACD of the power under s.45A see *R. v. Cooper* [2010] EWCA Crim 2335.

7. Miscellaneous

Improper combination of sentence

MHA 1983, s.37(8)

50–022   When making a hospital or guardianship order, the judge may not, in addition:

(1) pass a sentence of imprisonment, impose a fine, or make a community order within the meaning of CJA 2003, Pt l2, or a youth rehabilitation order within the meaning of CJIA 2008, Pt 1; or

(2) make an order under PCC(S)A 2000, s.150, binding over the parent or guardian of a juvenile offender; or

(3) if the order is a hospital order, make a referral order within the meaning of PCC(S)A 2000, in respect of the offence.

Information from Health Authorities

MHA 1983, s.39

50–023   Where a court is minded to make a hospital order, or an interim hospital order, in respect of any person, it may request the Health Authority for the region in which that person resides or last resided, or any other Health Authority that seems to the court to be appropriate to furnish the court with such information as it has, or can reasonably obtain, with respect to the hospital or hospitals in its region or elsewhere at which arrangements could be made for the admission of that person.

In the case of a person who has not attained the age of 18, this provision has effect as if reference to the making of a hospital order included a remand under ss 35 or 36, or the making of an order s.44. In the case of such a person, the information which may be requested may include information about the availability of age-appropriate accommodation or facilities.

In Wales, such a request should be addressed to the Secretary of State.

Adding a restraining order: SOA 1997

SOA 1997, s.5A

50–024   Where the judge:

(1) imposes a sentence of imprisonment, makes a hospital order or makes a guardianship order in respect of a person convicted of a sexual offence to which SOA 1997, Pt I applies; or

(2) orders that a person who has been found not guilty of such an offence by reason of insanity, or to be under disability, and to have done the act charged against him in respect of the offence, be admitted to hospital, or makes a guardianship order against him,

he may, if satisfied that it is necessary to do so in order to protect the public in general, or any particular members of the public, make a restraining order in respect of that person, prohibiting him from doing anything prescribed in it.

The person subjected to the order may, if he was convicted of the offence, appeal against it as if it were a sentence passed for the offence, and in the other circumstances, as if he had been convicted of the offence and the order were a sentence passed on that conviction. The order may be varied or discharged by the Crown Court.

Reports by medical practitioners

50–025   The registered practitioner whose evidence is taken into account under s.35(3)(a) and at least one of the registered medical practitioners whose evidence is taken into account under ss.36(1), 37(2)(a), 38(1), 45A(2) and 51(6)(a) and whose reports are taken into consideration under ss 47(1) and 48(1) must be a practitioner approved for the purpose by the Secretary of State as having special expertise in the diagnosis or treatment of mental disorder.

MHA 1983, s.54(1)(2)(2a) (3)

Where, for the purposes of provision of this Part of MHA 1983, under which a judge may act on the written evidence of any person, a report in writing purporting to be signed by that person may be received in evidence without proof of:

(1) the signature of that person, or

(2) of his having the requisite qualifications or approval or authority or of being of the requisite description to give the report,

but the judge may require the signatory of any such report to attend and give oral evidence.

Where, in pursuance of a direction of the court, any such report is tendered in evidence otherwise than by or on behalf of the person who is the subject of the report then:

(a) if that person is represented by an advocate or solicitor, a copy of the report must be given to that advocate or solicitor;

(b) if that person is not represented, the substance of the report must be disclosed to him or, if he is a child or young person, to his parent or guardian if present in court; and

(c) except where the report relates only to his admission to hospital, that person may require the signatory of the report to be called to give oral evidence and evidence to rebut that contained in the report may be called by or on behalf of that person.

As to the expenses of any such practitioner see COSTS AND ASSESSMENT.

Community order with medical treatment requirement

50–026   Where imprisonment is inexpedient, the court may consider making a community order with a requirement of medical treatment (see COMMUNITY SENTENCES), or a youth rehabilitation order with a similar requirement (see YOUTH REHABILITATION ORDERS). Where the judge:

R. 42.8

(1) requests a medical examination of the accused and a report; or

(2) requires information about the arrangements that could be made for the accused where he is considering:

(a) a hospital order; or

(b) a guardianship order,

unless the judge otherwise directs, the court officer must, as soon as practicable, serve on each person from whom a report or information is sought a note that:

    (i) specifies the power exercised by the court;

    (ii) explains why the court seeks a report or information from that person; and

    (iii) sets out or summarises any relevant information available to the court.

Information to be supplied on admission to hospital or guardianship

50–027   Where the judge: R. 42.9

(1) orders the accused's detention and treatment in hospital; or

(2) makes a guardianship order,

unless the judge otherwise directs, the court officer will, as soon as practicable, serve on (as applicable) the hospital or the guardian:

    (a) a record of the court's order;

    (b) such information as the court has received thatappears likely to assist in treating or otherwise dealing with the accused, including information about:

        (i)   the accused's mental condition;

        (ii) his other circumstances; and

        (iii) the circumstances of the offence.

51. MITIGATION: DEROGATORY ASSERTIONS

General
CPIA 1996, s.58

51–001 Where:

(1) a person has been convicted of an offence, and a speech in mitigation is made by him or on his behalf before a judge of the Crown Court determining what sentence should be passed on him in respect of the offence; or

(2) sentence has been passed on a person in respect of an offence and a submission relating to the sentence is made by him or on his behalf, before the Crown Court hearing an appeal against the sentence, and

there are substantial grounds for believing:

(a) that an assertion forming part of the speech or submission is derogatory to a person's character (for instance because it suggests that his conduct is, or has been, criminal, immoral or improper); and

(b) that the assertion is false, or that the facts asserted are irrelevant to the sentence; and

(c) that the assertion was not made at the trial at which the person was convicted of the offence, or during any other proceedings relating to the offence,

the court may, as soon as is reasonably practicable after making the determination on sentence, make an order under s.58(8), in relation to the assertion, prohibiting its publication. Where it appears to the court that there is a real possibility of such an order being necessary this order may be made before the court has made its determination on sentence, under s.58(7).

Orders under s.58(8) and s.58(7)
51–002 An order under s.58(7), made in anticipation of an order under s.58(8) being made, may be revoked at any time, and in any event ceases to have effect when the court makes a determination with regard to sentencing. An order under s.58(8) may be made whether or not one under s.58(7) was made. An order under s.58(8) may also be revoked at any time, and in any event ceases to have effect at the end of a period of 12 months beginning with the day on which it was made.

Appeal
51–003 Appeal lies in respect of making such an order where a person has been convicted on indictment (see APPEALS FROM THE CROWN COURT).

52. OATHS AND FORMALITIES

Quick guide

1. Legal requirements (52–001)
2. The effect of the oath or affirmation (52–002)
3. Children and Young Persons (52-003—52–004)
4. Jurors (52–005)
5. Oaths and Formalities: wording (52–006)

1.   Oaths and Affirmations

Legal requirements

52–001   An oath is taken or an affirmation made by a witness prior to giving evidence and by a juror following empanelment. If an oath is taken, it may be taken in the manner, and with the effect, prescribed by the Oaths Act 1978, ss.1-6:

(1) the person swearing shall hold the New Testament, or, in the case of a Jew, the Old Testament in his uplifted hand and shall say or repeat after the officer administering the oath the words 'I swear by Almighty God that . . .' followed by the words of the oath prescribed by law;

(2) unless the person to be sworn objects, or is incapable of taking the oath, it shall be administered as in (a) above;

(3) in the case of a person who is neither a Christian nor a Jew, the oath shall be administered in any lawful manner; it is for the person swearing to specify the holy book on which, or the manner by which, he wishes to be sworn;

(4) any person who objects to taking an oath may instead make a solemn affirmation which has the same force and effect as an oath. The form is 'I [name] do solemnly sincerely and truly declare and affirm that ';

(5) any person desiring to swear with uplifted hand, in the form and manner used in Scotland, is permitted to do so;

(6) where an oath has been taken the fact that the person taking it had, at the time, no religious belief, does not affect the validity of the oath.

Where an oath is to be taken by a child or young person, for the words the Oaths Act 1978, s.1 has effect as if the words 'I promise before Almighty God' are used instead of the words 'I swear by Almighty God'. The oath taken in either form is deemed to have been duly taken (CYPA 1963, s. 28(1)). (And see further 52-006 below)

It is customary for Sikhs and Muslims to be sworn on vernacular editions of their own Books. Jews may require to cover their heads while taking the oath, Muslims to perform ritual ablutions before coming to the Book. Where swearing a Muslim in the name of Allah, it is better practice to precede the oath with the words: 'There is no God but Allah and Muhammad is His Prophet'.

The effect of the oath or affirmation

52–002 Failure to comply with the words prescribed in the Oaths Act 1978 will not necessarily invalidate the oath or affirmation, so long as it was taken, or made, in such a way as was binding, and intended to be binding on the conscience of the taker (*R. v Chapman* [1980] Crim L.R. 42 (where the witness failed to take the testament in his hand). Similarly, the lawfulness of an oath depends not on the intricacies of the witness's religion but on whether (a) the oath taken appeared to the court to be binding on the conscience of the witness and (b) the witness himself considers his conscience to be bound (*R. v. Kemble* (1990) 91 Cr. App. R. 178). A witness may not, generally, be questioned as to the form of his oath but where a witness desires to affirm when he is reasonably expected to take the oath on a holy book, see *R. v Mehrban* [2001] EWCA Crim 2627 [2002] 1 Cr. App. R. 40.

Children and Young Persons

52–003 No witness in criminal proceedings may be sworn unless –

(1) he has attained the age of 14 years and
(2) he has a sufficient appreciation of the solemnity of the occasion and of the particular responsibility to tell the truth which is involved in taking an oath.

A person, if he is able to give intelligible testimony, is presumed to have a sufficient appreciation of those things unless any party adduces evidence to show the contrary and, if such evidence is adduced, the burden is on the party seeking to have the witness sworn to prove the matters in (1) and (2) above.

A person is able to give intelligible testimony if he is able to –

(a) understand questions put to him as a witness, and
(b) give answers to them which can be understood (YJCEA 1999, s.55).

If, by virtue of YJCEA 1999, s.55(2), a person is not permitted to be sworn for the purpose of giving evidence on oath his evidence shall be given unsworn. No conviction, verdict or finding in proceedings in which such a person gave evidence may be taken as unsafe for the purposes of the Criminal Appeals Act 1968, ss.2(1), 13(1) and 16(1) YJCEA 1999, s.56(1), (2) and (5).

Children under 14

52–004 It is good practice before a child under the age of 14 gives evidence for the judge to address him with words such as 'Tell us all you can remember of what happened. Don't make anything up or leave anything out. This is very important'.

Where a child is aged 14 or over and his evidence has been admitted by means of a pre-recorded interview under YJCEA 1999, s. 27 (see SPECIAL MEASURES), he should take the oath prior to cross-examination (*R. v Simmonds* [1996] Crim. L.R. 816).

For the evidence of children generally see CHILDREN AND YOUNG PERSONS.

Jurors

52–005 The wording of the oath to be taken, or affirmation to be made, by jurors is set out in PD 2004, IV.42.5 (see 52–006 below).

2. Oaths and Formalities: wording

52–006 The following are commonly used forms of wording.

(1) Arraignment

"A . . . . . B . . . . . you stand indicted for that you, on the . . . . day of. . . . (e.g. stole) . . . . . How say you A . . . . B . . . . . are you guilty or not guilty?"

(2) Challenge to jurors

"A . . . . . B . . . . . , the names that you are about to hear called are the names of the jurors who will try you. If, therefore, you wish to object to them, or to any of them, you must do so as they come to the Book to be sworn and before they are sworn, and your objection shall be heard."

(3) Jurors' oath or affirmation

(a) On trial

The oath to be taken by jurors is:

(i) "I swear by Almighty God that I will faithfully try the defendant(s), and give a true verdict according to the evidence."

Any person who objects to being sworn will be permitted to make his solemn affirmation instead. The words of the affirmation are:

(ii) "I do solemnly, sincerely and truly declare that I will faithfully try the defendant(s), and give a true verdict according to the evidence."

(b) Defendant standing mute

"I swear by Almighty God (or I solemnly, sincerely and truly declare and affirm) that I will well and truly try whether A . . . . B . . . . . , the defendant, who stands charged with . . . . . is mute of malice (or will not answer directly to the indictment wilfully and of malice), or by the Visitation of God, and a true verdict give according to the evidence."

(4) Charge to the jury

"Members of the Jury, the defendant A . . . . . B . . . . . stands indicted for that he, on the . . . . day of . . . . (e.g. stole) . . . .To this indictment he has pleaded not guilty, and it is your charge to say, having heard the evidence, whether he be guilty or not guilty."

(5) Witness' oath or affirmation

"I swear by Almighty God (or I solemnly, sincerely and truly declare and affirm) that the evidence I shall give shall be the truth, the whole truth, and nothing but the truth."

Oaths and Formalities

(6) Witness under 18

"I promise before Almighty God to tell the truth, the whole truth, and nothing but the truth."

(7) Interpreter's oath or affirmation

"I swear by Almighty God (or I solemnly, sincerely and truly declare and affirm) that I will well and faithfully interpret, and true explanation make, of all such matters and things as shall be required of me, according to the best of my skill and understanding."

(For the form of the oath in Welsh, see Welsh Courts (Oaths & Interpreters) Rules 1943 S R & O, 1943 No.683, as amended by SI 1959/1507, SI 1972/97).

(8) Jury retiring: bailiff's oath

"I shall keep this jury together in some private and convenient place; I shall suffer none to speak to them, neither shall I speak to them myself, touching the trial held here this day, without leave of the court, unless it be to ask them if they are agreed upon their verdict."

Note: CJPOA 1994, s.43, amending JA 1974, s.13, allows the jury, if the judge thinks fit and so permits, to separate at any time, whether before or after they have been directed to consider their verdict.

(9) Voir dire

"I swear by Almighty God (or I solemnly, sincerely and truly declare and affirm) that I will true answer make to all such questions as may be asked of me."

(10) Intermediary declaration

"I solemnly, sincerely and truly declare that I will well and faithfully communicate questions and answers and make true explanation of all matters and things as shall be required of me according to the best of my skill and understanding."

(See further SPECIAL MEASURES DIRECTIONS).

(11) Person accompanying witness into Live Link TV room

"I swear by almighty God to adhere to the instructions given by the learned judge and to observe them fully."

(For procedure see SPECIAL MEASURES DIRECTIONS).

As to the use of the Welsh language in courts in Wales, see PD 2004, IV.22 and IV.23 (and see further WELSH LANGUAGE CASES).

53. PARENTING ORDERS

General

53–001   A parenting order is an order requiring the parent or guardian of a young offender:

CDA 1998,
s.8(1)(c),(2).

(1) to comply, for a period not exceeding 12 months, with such requirements as the judge considers desirable in the interests of preventing the repetition or commission of any offence, as are specified in the order; and
(2) to attend, for a concurrent period not exceeding three months and not more than once in any week, such counselling or guidance sessions as may be specified in directions given by the "responsible officer".

The "responsible officer" will be an officer of a provider of probation services, a local authority or a member of a youth offending team.

Discretionary order

53–001   An order; may be made in respect of the offender's parent or guardian in any court proceedings where a child or young person is convicted of an offence, (except in a case where s.8A applies or in certain other situations), provided that:

(1) the judge is satisfied that such an order would be desirable in the interests of preventing the commission of any further offence by the offender; and
(2) the court has been notified by the Secretary of State that arrangements for implementing such orders are available in the area in which the parent resides or is to reside,

though a requirement under (2) need not be included where an order has been made in respect of that parent or guardian on a previous occasion.

The Act requires that any requirements included should, as far as is practicable, avoid conflict with a parent's religious beliefs, and interference with the times, if any, at which the offender normally works or attends an educational establishment.

Where directions under an order are to be given by an officer of provider of probation services that officer must be one appointed for or assigned to the local justice area within which it appears the child or, as the case may be, the parent or guardian, resides or will reside.

Procedure is governed by r.50 (Civil behaviour orders after verdict or finding) as to which see ANTI-SOCIAL BEHAVIOUR ORDERS.

Mandatory orders

53–003   An order **must** be made in the case of a person under the age of 16 where:

CDA 1998,
s.9(1)(2)

(1) the offender is convicted of an offence, other than an offence under CDA 1988, s.l(10) (breach of anti-social behaviour order); or,

(2) the judge is satisfied, after obtaining and considering information about the offender's family circumstances and the likely effect of an order on those circumstances, he is satisfied that condition (1) in 53-001 is fulfilled; if he is not so satisfied, he must state in open court that he is not so satisfied and why;

(3) (**once CSA 2010, s.40 comes into force**) the offender is convicted of an offence under CDA 1988, s.l(10) of breaching an anti-social behaviour order, unless the judge is of opinion that there are exceptional circumstances which would make an order inappropriate; again, if he does not make an order on that ground, the judge must state in open court, his opinion, and what such circumstances were.

An order made under (3) above must specify such requirements as the judge considers would be desirable in the interests of preventing:

(a) any repetition of the kind of behaviour which led to the ASBO being made; or

(b) the commission of any further offence by the offender

Explaining the effects of the order; review

53–004 Whichever the section under which the order is made. The judge has a duty, before making it, to explain to the parent or guardian in ordinary language:

CDA 1998,ss.8A,9

(1) the effect of the order and of the requirements proposed to be included in it;

(2) the consequences which may follow under s.9(7) (i.e. a possible fine on level 3) if he fails to comply with any of the requirements; and

(3) the power of the court to review the order on the application either of the responsible officer or of the parent (see BREACH, AMENDMENT AND REVOCATION OF ORDERS).

Non-compliance with requirements

53–005 If, while an order is in force, a parent fails to comply with any requirement included in it or specified directions given by the responsible officer, he or she is liable on summary conviction to a fine not exceeding level 3 on the standard scale.

CDA 1998, ss.8A(6),

54. PRODUCTION AND ACCESS ORDERS; SEARCH WARRANTS

Quick guide

A. The Police and Criminal Evidence Act 1884
B. Proceeds of Crime Act 2002

54–001 A judge of the Crown Court may grant a production order or a search warrant under PACE 1984, and a number of orders under POCA 2002. He may grant access to bankers' books under BBEA 1879, and may issue Letters of Request under CJA 1988. As to proceedings under C(IC)A 2003, ss.13–15, for the taking of evidence for overseas proceedings, see 61–034, below.

A. The Police and Criminal Evidence Act 1984

54–002 Jurisdiction is conferred upon a Circuit Judge, but not upon the Crown Court (thus a Recorder has no such jurisdiction (*R. v CCC Ex p. Francis & Francis* (1989) 88 Cr. App. R. 213), to entertain an application by an investigating officer to gain access to special-procedure and excluded material (it makes no provision for access to legally privileged material, as to which see *R. v ILCC Ex p. Baines* (1988) 87 Cr. App. R. 111 and *R. v CCC Ex p. Francis* (above)). See also *Hallinan Blackburn Gittings & Nott (A Firm) v Middlesex Guildhall CC* [2004] EWHC 2726 (Admin); [2005] 1 W.L.R. 766. He may, if he thinks fit, hear the application in chambers (*R. v CCC Ex p. DPP The Times*, April 1, 1988).

An application under PACE 1984 (as opposed to one under POCA 2002 (see 54–011, below) is appropriate where production of the material is sought for criminal investigation purposes, to determine whether an offence has been committed, and, if so, to provide evidence of it (*R. v Southwark CC* [1996] Cr. App. R. 436).

1. Production order

54–003   If, on an application made by a constable or a designated member of SOCA, a judge is satisfied that one or other of the sets of access conditions set out below is fulfilled, he may make an order that the person who appears to be in possession of the material to which the application relates:

PACE 1984, Sch.2

(1) produce it to a constable or a member of SOCA for him to take away; or
(2) give him access to it,

not later than the end of the period of seven days from the making of the order, or such longer period as he may specify. Special rules apply under Sch.2, para.5, as amended by CJPA 2001, Sch.2, para.14, in relation to material stored in any electronic form.

A computer and its hard disk are within the definition of "material" in PACE 1984, s.8(1) (*R. (Barclay) v Lord Chancellor and S of S for Justice etc* [2008] EWCA Civ 1319; [2009] 2 W.L.R. 1205).

A person who fails to comply with an order may be dealt with by a judge as if he had committed a contempt of the Crown Court, and enactments relating to contempt of that court have effect in relation to the matter.

Inter partes application

54–004   The preferred method of proceeding should always be by way of an inter partes order under para.4, after notice of application served under para.8 (*R. v Maidstone CC Ex p. Waitt* [1988] Crim. L.R. 384).

The application:

(1) must be accompanied by a document or documents containing a description of the material for which discovery is sought (*R. v CCC Ex p. Adegbesan* (1987) 84 Cr. App. R. 219), though there may be occasions on which oral information is sufficient (*R. v Manchester CC Ex p. Taylor* (1988) 87 Cr. App. R. 358);
(2) must state the general nature of the offence under investigation, though it is not necessary to state the precise section of any enactment (*R. v Manchester CC Ex p. Taylor* (above));
(3) may be served on the person concerned by leaving it at his proper address, or by posting it to him in a registered letter or by recorded delivery;
(4) may be served on one of the partners of a firm, or on the secretary, clerk, etc. of a corporation;
(5) must state the address of the premises where the material is alleged to be (*R. v CCC Ex p. Carr*, *The Independent*, March 5, May 13, 1987); and
(6) when served, prohibits the concealment, destruction, alteration or disposal of the material until the application has been dismissed or abandoned, or an order has been complied with.

Whatever material is given to the judge must be served upon the party against whom the order is sought; statements which have no substance, and which are to the prejudice of the party against whom the order is sought, ought to be ruled out by the judge (*R. v ILCC Ex p. Baines & Baines* (1988) 87 Cr. App. R. 111).

The Act does not require the suspect to be given notice when the evidence sought is in the hands of a third party (*R. v Leicester CC Ex p. DPP* (1988) 86 Cr. App. R. 254).

The "access conditions"

54–005   Before granting an order, the judge must himself be satisfied that one or other of the access conditions contained in paras 2 and 3 of the Schedule are made out; it is not enough that the applicant believes them to be satisfied (*R. v CCC* [2002] Crim. L.R. 65). Although the strict rules of evidence do not apply to a hearing there must be evidence that the relevant set of access conditions has been fulfilled. The Act sets out two sets of "access conditions." *(PACE 1984, s.11)*

54–006   **"The first set of access conditions"** is fulfilled if:

(1) there are reasonable grounds for believing:
  (a) that a serious arrestable offence (as defined in Sch.5 to the Act) has been committed;
  (b) that there is material which consists of special procedure material as defined under s.14 or includes special procedure material and does not also include excluded material on premises specified in the application;
  (c) that the material is likely to be of substantial value (whether by itself or together with other material) to the investigation in connection with which the application is made; and
  (d) that the material is likely to be relevant evidence;
(2) other methods of obtaining the material:
  (a) have been tried without success; or
  (b) have not been tried because it appeared that they were bound to fail; and
(3) it is in the public interest, having regard:
  (a) to the benefit likely to accrue to the investigation if the material is obtained; and
  (b) to the circumstances under which the person in possession of the material holds it,that it should be produced or that access should be given to it.

54–007   **"The second set of access conditions"** is fulfilled if: *(PACE 1984, s.9, Sch.1, paras 12–15)*

(1) there are reasonable grounds for believing that there is material which consists of or includes excluded material or special procedure material on premises specified in the application;
(2) but for s.9(2) of the Act a search of the premises for that material could have been authorised by the issue of a warrant to a constable under an enactment; and
(3) the issue of such a warrant would have been appropriate.

Definitions

54–008   The following expressions are defined in the Act:
"Excluded material" as:

(1) personal records which a person has acquired or created in the course of any trade, business, profession or other occupation or for the purposes of any paid or unpaid office and which he holds in confidence; and

(2) human tissue or tissue fluid which has been taken for the purpose of diagnosis or medical treatment and which a person holds in confidence; and

(3) journalistic material which a person holds in confidence and which consists of:

    (a) documents; or

    (b) records other than documents.

A person holds material other than journalistic material in confidence for these purposes if he holds it subject:

    (a) to an express or implied understanding to hold it in confidence; or

    (b) to a restriction on disclosure or an obligation of secrecy contained in any enactment, including an enactment contained in an Act passed after PACE 1984.

A person holds journalistic material in confidence for those purposes if:

    (i) he holds it subject to such an undertaking, restriction or obligation; and

    (ii) it has been continuously held (by one or more persons) subject to such an undertaking, restriction or obligation since it was first acquired or created for the purposes of journalism.

Where the first set of access conditions is made out, the judge may make a production order even where it might infringe the privilege against self-incrimination (*R. v CCC Ex p. Bright* [2001] 2 All E.R. 244). Though in exercising his discretion, he should consider the implications of self-incrimination.

2. Search warrant

54–009 There will be cases where a production access order is likely to be obstructed, where only a search warrant will be appropriate, but an application under PACE 1984 Sch.2, para.12 must not become a matter of common form, and where such a search is authorised the High Court has said that the reason for authorising it ought to be made clear (*R. v Maidstone CC, Ex p. Waitt* [1988] Crim. L.R. 384); *R. v Leeds CC Ex p. Switalski* [1991] Crim. L.R. 559). Nevertheless, if, on application made by a constable or a designated member of SOCA, a Circuit Judge is satisfied that:

(1) either set of the access conditions set out above is fulfilled (see 54–006, 54–007, above); and

(2) that:

    (a) it is not practicable to communicate with any person entitled to grant entry to the premises to which the application relates;

    (b) it is practicable to communicate with such person, but not with any person entitled to grant access to the material;

    (c) the material contains information subject to a restriction or obligation of confidentiality (defined in s.11(2)(b) of the Act) and which is likely to be disclosed in breach of it if a warrant is not issued; or

    (d) that service of a notice of application for an access order might seriously prejudice the investigation,

he may issue a warrant authorising entry to and search of the premises under that warrant; anything for which a search has been authorised may be seized and retained.

The authorities emphasise the importance of strictly adhering to the proper procedure by which a warrant is obtained, see e.g. *R. v Lewes CC Ex p Hill* (1991) 93 Cr. App. R. 60; *Wood v North Avon MC* [2009] EWCH 3614 (Admin); (2010) 174 JP 157; *G v MPC* [2011] EWHC (Admin) (not yet reported).

As to the situation where a search warrant is sought in respect of solicitors, (see *R. Barclay v Lord Chancellor and S of S for Justice etc* (above)).

Approach to application

54–010   An application is made *ex parte*. The authorities show that since the issue of a warrant is a very serious interference with the liberty of the subject:

    (1) it should be issued only after the "most mature careful consideration of all the facts of the case" (*Williams v Summerfield* (1972) 56 Cr. App. R. 597);

    (2) the responsibility for ensuring that the procedure is not abused lies with the judge, who should be scrupulous in discharging that responsibility (*R. v Maidstone CC Ex p. Waitt*, above);

    (3) in a case of complexity, it should not go through "on the nod", but the judge ought to give his reasons for granting the warrant, showing that he has taken the appropriate matters into account (*R. v Southwark CC Ex p. Sorsky Defries* [1996] C.O.D. 117).

B.   Proceeds of Crime Act 2002

54–011   Under POCA 2002, as amended by CorJA 2009, s.66, a judge entitled to exercise Crown Court jurisdiction may be called upon, in relation to confiscation, laundering and detained cash proceedings, to make orders as follows: R.62.3

    (1) a production order (ss.345 to 351) requiring a person to produce any relevant material which is in his possession or under his control;

    (2) a search and seizure warrant (ss.352 to 356) where a production order is not complied with or the requirements for the issue of a production order are not available;

(3) a disclosure order (ss.357 to 362) requiring persons to give the appropriate person any relevant information;

(4) a customer information order (ss.363 to 369) requiring a financial institution to provide information relating to the affairs of a customer;

(5) an account monitoring order (ss.370 to 375) requiring a financial institution to provide details of transactions on a particular account over a specified period of time;

(6) Letters of Request (s.376) requesting assistance relating to evidence arising outside the UK.

As to the Codes of Practice issued by the Home Secretary under POCA 2002, s.377, see The Proceeds of Crime Act 2002 (Investigations in England, Wales and Northern Ireland: Code of Practice) Order 2008, SI 2008/946 and The Proceeds of Crime Act 2002 (Cash Searches: Code of Practice) Order 2008, SI 2008/947.

Application may be made under r.6.22 to punish for contempt of court a person accused of disobeying a production order or an account monitoring order (SI 2009/2087).

In relation to applications for the purpose of a civil recovery investigation or a detained cash investigation, jurisdiction is reserved to a judge of the High Court.

It was said under the previous legislation that applications under these provisions are to be contrasted with those under PACE 1984, s.9 since they are essentially appropriate where the dominant purpose of the application is to determine, in respect of a criminal offence, whether, and, if so to what extent, a person has benefited from it, or the whereabouts of any proceeds *(R. v Guildford CC, Ex p. Bowles* [1997] Cr, App. R. 436).

Proof of identity and accreditation

54–012   In relation to order under POCA 2002, where an appropriate officer applies for

(1) a production order (s.345);

(2) a customer information order (s.363);

(3) an account monitoring order (s.370),

R.62.3

for the purposes of a confiscation investigation or a money laundering investigation, then, subject to s.449 which provides for members of the staff of SOCA or the relevant Director to use pseudonyms, he must provide the judge with proof of his identity and, if he is a financial investigator, his accreditation under POCA 2002, s.3.

1.   Production order

54–013   A production order is an order either requiring:

(1) the person the application for the order specifies as appearing to be in possession or control of material to produce it to an appropriate officer for him to take away; or

POCA 2002, s.345(4)

(2) the person to give an appropriate officer access to the material, within the period stated in the order.

A judge exercising the jurisdiction of the Crown Court may, on an application made to him by an appropriate officer, make a production order if he is satisfied that each of the requirements for the making of the order (set out at 54–014, below) is fulfilled.

An application for an order is made under rr.6.14,15. As to information to be withheld from the respondent or other, see r.6.21. An application for variation or discharge is made under r.6.20.

POCA 2002, s.345(1)

An application for a production order (or an order to grant entry) may be made ex parte in chambers. A specimen application and a draft production order are included in the Code of Practice, issued under s.337, see SI 2003/334.

POCA 2002, s.345(3)

The application must state that a specified person is subject to a confiscation investigation (or a money laundering investigation), or that money specified in the application is subject to a civil recovery investigation or a detained cash investigation, and must also state that:

(a) the order is sought for the purposes of the investigation;
(b) the order is sought in relation to material, or material of a description, specified in the application; and
(c) a person specified in the application appears to be in possession or control of the material.

POCA 2002, s.345(5)

As to proof of the identity and accreditation of the applicant, see 54–012, above.

The period stated in the order will be a period of seven days beginning with the day on which it is made, unless it appears to the judge by whom it is made that a longer or shorter period would be appropriate in the particular circumstances.

Requirements for making an order

54–014   Before making an order the judge must be satisfied that there are reasonable grounds for:

POCA 2002, s.346(2)

(1) suspecting that:
(a) in the case of a confiscation investigation, the person the application for the order specifies as being subject to the investigation has benefited from his criminal conduct;
(b) in the case of a money laundering investigation, the person the application for the order specifies as being subject to the investigation has committed a money laundering offence;
(c) in the case of a detained cash investigation into the derivation of cash, the property the application for the order specifies as being subject to the investigation, or part of it, is recoverable property;
(d) in the case of a detained cash investigation into the intended use of cash, the property the application specifies as being subject to the investigation or part of it, is intended to be used by any person in unlawful conduct, and

(2) believing that the person the application specifies as appearing to be in possession or control of the material so specified is in possession or control of it;

(3) believing that the material is likely to be of substantial value (whether or not by itself) to the investigation for the purposes of which the order is sought;

(4) believing that it is in the public interest for the material to be produced or for access to it to be given, having regard to:

    (a) the benefit likely to accrue to the investigation if the material is obtained;

    (b) the circumstances under which the person the application specifies as appearing to be in possession or control of the material holds it.

Order granting entry

54–015 Where the judge makes a production order requiring a person to give an appropriate officer access to material on any premises, he may, on an application made to him by an appropriate officer and specifying the premises, make an order to grant entry in relation to the premises.

POCA 2002, s.347

Such an order requires any person who appears to an appropriate officer to be entitled to grant entry to the premises to allow him to enter the premises to obtain access to the material.

An application for an order is made under rr.6.14,16. As to information to be withheld from the respondent or other, see r.6.21. An application for variation or discharge is made under r.6.20.

Privileged material

54–016 A production order:

POCA 2002, s.348(1)–(3)

(1) does not require a person to produce, or give access to, privileged material, i.e. material which the person would be entitled to refuse to produce on grounds of legal professional privilege in proceedings in the High Court;

(2) does not require a person to produce, or give access to, excluded material;

(3) has effect in spite of any restriction on the disclosure of information (however imposed).

Retention of material

54–017 An appropriate officer (see 54–020, below) may take copies of any material which is produced, or to which access is given, in compliance with the order and material produced in compliance with the order may be retained for so long as it is necessary to retain it (as opposed to copies of it) in connection with the investigation for the purposes of which the order was made, but if an appropriate officer has reasonable grounds for believing that:

POCA 2002, s.348(5)–(7)

(1) the material may need to be produced for the purposes of any legal proceedings; and

(2) it might otherwise be unavailable for those purposes,

it may be retained until the proceedings are concluded.

Special cases

54–018   Special provisions apply under s.349 to computer information, and under s.350 to government departments.

Discharge and variation

54–019   An application to discharge or vary a production order or an order to grant entry may be made to a judge of the Crown Court by:

POCA 2002,
s.351(3)–(6) Cor
JA 2009, s.66(5)

(1) the person who applied for the order;
(2) any person affected by the order and the judge may discharge or vary the order.

The procedure is under r.56.4

POCA 2002,
s.352(1)

If an accredited financial investigator, a member of SOCA's staff, a constable or a customs officer applies for an order an application to discharge or vary the order need not be by the same accredited financial investigator, constable or customs officer.

2.   Search and seizure warrants

General

54–020   A judge may, on an application made to him by an appropriate officer (below) issue a search and seizure warrant if he is satisfied that either of the requirements for the issuing of the warrant is fulfilled, these are that a production order made in relation to material has not been complied with and there are reasonable grounds for believing that the material is on the premises specified in the application for the warrant, or that s.353 is satisfied in relation to the warrant.

POCA 2002,
s.352(3)

An application for such a warrant must state that a person specified in the application is subject to a confiscation investigation or a money laundering investigation, or property specified in the application is subject to a detained cash investigation.

The application must also state that the warrant is sought;

(1) for the purposes of the investigation, or that the property specified in the application is subject to a detained cash investigation;
(2) in relation to the premises specified in the application;
(3) in relation to material specified in the application, or that there are reasonable grounds for believing that there is material falling within ss.353(6), (7) or (8) on the premises.

POCA 2002,
s.352(4)

A search and seizure warrant is a *warrant* authorising an appropriate person to enter and search the premises specified in the application for the warrant, and to seize and retain any *material* found there which is likely to be of substantial value (whether or not by itself) to the investigation for the purposes of which the application is made.

A specimen application and a draft form of search and seizure warrant are included in the Code of Practice issued under s.377, see SI 2003/334.

PRODUCTION AND ACCESS ORDERS; SEARCH WARRANTS

"An appropriate officer" is, for the purposes of confiscation, money laundering or detained cash investigations, a constable, an accredited financial investigator or a customs officer.

Requirements where production order not available

54–021 A search and seizure warrant may be issued where there are reasonable grounds or suspecting that:

(1) in the case of a confiscation investigation, the person specified in the application for the warrant has benefited from his criminal conduct; or

POCA 2002,
s.353(1)(2)

(2) in the case of a money laundering investigation, the person specified in the application for the warrant has committed a money laundering offence; and

(3) in the case of a detained cash investigation into the derivation of cash, the property the application for the order specifies as being subject to the investigation, or part of it, is recoverable property;

(4) in the case of a detained cash investigation into the intended use of cash, the property the application specified as being subject to the investigation or part of it, is intended to be used by any person in unlawful conduct; and

(5) either the first or the second set of conditions is complied with.

54–022 **The first set of conditions** is that there are reasonable grounds for believing that:

POCA 2002,
s.353(3)(4)

   (a) any material on the premises specified in the application for the warrant is likely to be of substantial value (whether or not by itself) to the investigation for the purposes of which the warrant is sought,

   (b) it is in the public interest for the material to be obtained, having regard to the benefit likely to accrue to the investigation if the material is obtained; and

   (c) it would not be appropriate to make a production order for any one or more of the following:

      (i) that it is not practicable to communicate with any person against whom the production order could be made;

      (ii) that it is not practicable to communicate with any person who would be required to comply with an order to grant entry to the premises;

      (iii) that the investigation might be seriously prejudiced unless an appropriate person is able to secure immediate access to the material.

54–023 **The second set of conditions** is that:

POCA 2002,
s.353(5)

(1) there are reasonable grounds for believing that there is material on the premises specified in the application for the warrant and that the material falls within subss.(6), (7) or (8),

(2) there are reasonable grounds for believing that it is in the public interest for the material to be obtained, having regard to the benefit likely to accrue to the investigation if the material is obtained, and

(3) any one or more of the requirements in subs.(9) is met, i.e.:

    (a) that it is not practicable to communicate with any person entitled to grant entry to the premises;

    (b) that entry to the premises will not be granted unless a warrant is produced;

    (c) that the investigation might be seriously prejudiced unless an appropriate person arriving at the premises is able to secure immediate entry to them.

POCA 2002, s.353(7)

In the case of a confiscation investigation, material falls within this provision if it cannot be identified at the time of the application but it relates to the person specified in the application, and the question whether he has benefited from his criminal conduct or any question as to the extent or whereabouts of his benefit from his criminal conduct, and is likely to be of substantial value (whether or not by itself) to the investigation for the purposes of which the warrant is sought.

In the case of a money laundering investigation, material falls within this provision if it cannot be identified at the time of the application but it relates to the person specified in the application or the question whether he has committed a money laundering offence, and is likely to be of substantial value (whether or not by itself) to the investigation for the purposes of which the warrant is sought.

POCA 2002, s.353(8)

In the case of a detained cash investigation into the derivation of cash, material falls within this subsection if it cannot be identified at the time of the application but it:

POCA 2002, s. 353(5)

    (a) relates to the property specified in the application, the question whether the property, or a part of it, is recoverable property or any other question as to its derivation; and

    (b) is likely to be of substantial value (whether or not by itself) to the investigation for the purposes of which the warrant is sought.

In the case of a detained cash investigation into the intended use of cash, material falls within this subsection if it cannot be identified at the time of the application but it:

    (i) relates to the property specified in the application or the question whether the property, or a part of it, is intended by any person to be used in unlawful conduct; and

    (ii) is likely to be of substantial value (whether or not by itself) to the investigation for the purposes of which the warrant is sought.

POCA 2002, s.353(10)

An "appropriate person" is, if the warrant is sought for the purposes of a confiscation investigation or a money laundering investigation, a constable, an accredited financial investigator or a customs officer.

3. Disclosure orders

General

POCA 2002, s.357

54–024 A judge may, on the application of the relevant authority, make a disclosure order if he is satisfied that each of the requirements for the making of the order is fulfilled, save that no application for a disclosure order may be made in relation to a money laundering investigation.

An application for an order is made under rr.6.14,17. As to information to be withheld from the respondent or other, see r.6.21. An application for variation or discharge is made under r.6.20.

The application must state that:

(1) a person specified is subject to a confiscation investigation which is being carried out by the relevant authority and the order is sought for the purposes of the investigation; or
(2) property specified is subject to a civil recovery investigation and the order is sought for the purposes of the investigation.

The relevant authority may only make an application for a disclosure order in relation to a confiscation investigation if the relevant authority is in receipt of a request from an appropriate officer.

A disclosure order is an order authorising an appropriate officer to give to any person he considers has relevant information notice in writing requiring him, with respect to any matter relevant to the investigation for the purposes of which the order is sought, to:

(a) answer questions, either at a time specified in the notice or at once, at a place so specified;
(b) provide information specified in the notice, by a time and in a manner so specified;
(c) produce documents, or documents of a description, specified in the notice, either at or by a time so specified or at once, and in a manner so specified.

"Relevant authority" means in relation to a confiscation investigation, a prosecutor; and in relation to a civil recovery investigation, a member of SOCA's staff or the relevant Director.

A prosecutor for this purpose is:—

(i) in relation to a confiscation investigation carried out by a member of SOCA's staff, the relevant Director or any specified person;
(ii) in relation to a confiscation investigation carried out by an accredited financial investigator, the DPP or any specified person;
(iii) in relation to a confiscation investigation carried out by a constable, the DPP, the DSFO or any specified person; and
(iv) in relation to a confiscation investigation carried out by an officer of Revenue and Customs, the Director of Revenue and Customs Prosecutions, or any specified person.

"Specified person" means any person specified, or falling within a description specified, by an order of the Secretary of State.

As to proof of the identity and accreditation of the applicant, see 54–012, above.

Requirements for making order

54–025 For the making of a disclosure order there must be reasonable grounds for suspecting that in the case of a confiscation investigation, the person specified in the application for the order has benefited from his criminal conduct.

POCA 2002, s.358

There must be reasonable grounds for believing that information which may be provided in compliance with a requirement imposed under the order is likely to be of substantial value (whether or not, by itself) to the investigation for the purpose for which the order is sought.

There must be reasonable grounds for believing that it is in the public interest for the information to be provided, having regard to the benefit likely to accrue to the investigation if the information is obtained.

The order takers effect in spite of any restrictions on the disclosure of information, however imposed (s.351(6)); as to matters of legal privilege and excluded material, see ss.361(l)-(5). Restrictions are imposed on the use of such statements, by s.360.

Procedure

54–026 An application for a disclosure order may be made ex parte to a judge in chambers.

POCA 2002, s.362

An application to discharge or vary an order may be made to a judge by the prosecutor or by any person affected by it.

4. Customer information order

Nature of order; application

54–027 A judge may, on the application of an appropriate officer (above, 54–020) make a customer information order if he is satisfied that each of the requirements for the making of the order is fulfilled.

POCA 2002, s.363; R.62.2

Such an order is an order that a financial institution covered by the application for the order must, on being required to do so by notice in writing given by an appropriate officer, provide any such customer information (as defined in POCA 2002, s.364) as it has relating to the person specified in the application. A financial institution which is required to provide information under a customer information order must provide the information to an appropriate officer in such manner, and at or by such time, as an appropriate officer requires.

An application for an order is made under rr.6.14,18. As to information to be withheld from the respondent or other, see r.6.21. An application for variation or discharge is made under POCA 2002, s.369 and r.6.20 (SI 2009/2087).

An application for a customer information order:

(1) *must* state that:
   (a) a person specified in the application is subject to a confiscation investigation or a money laundering investigation;
   (b) the order is sought for the purposes of the investigation; or
   (c) the order is sought against the financial institution or financial institutions specified in the application;
(2) *may* specify:

Production and Access Orders; Search Warrants

(a) all financial institutions;

(b) a particular description, or particular descriptions, of financial institutions; or

(c) a particular financial institution or particular financial institutions.

POCA 2002, s.365

A specimen application, a draft customer information order and a specimen notice in writing, are included in the Code of Practice issued under s.377. See SI 2003/334.

Requirements for making order

54–028 For the making of a disclosure order there must be reasonable grounds for suspecting that in the case of a confiscation investigation, the person specified in the application for the order has benefited from his criminal conduct.

POCA 2002, s.370

There must be reasonable grounds for believing that information which may be provided in compliance with a requirement imposed under the order is likely to be of substantial value (whether or not, by itself) to the investigation for the purposes for which the order is sought.

There must be reasonable grounds for believing that it is in the public interest for the information to be provided, having regard to the benefit likely to accrue to the investigation if the information is obtained.

The order takes effect in spite of any restrictions on the disclosure of information, however imposed (s.368). Restrictions are imposed on the use of such statements, by s.367.

As to proof of the identity and accreditation of the applicant, see 54–012, above.

If a member of SOCA's staff or a person falling within a description of persons specified by virtue of section 357(9) applies for a disclosure order, an application to discharge or vary the order need not be by the same member of SOCA's staff or (as the case may be) the same person falling within that description. References to a person who applied for a disclosure order must be construed accordingly.

5. Account monitoring order

54–029 A judge may, on an application made to him by an appropriate officer (54–020, above) make an account monitoring order if he is satisfied that each of the requirements set out below is fulfilled.

POCA 2002, s.370(5)

An account monitoring order is an order that the financial institution specified in the application for the order must, for the period stated in the order, provide account information of the description specified in the order to an appropriate officer in the manner, and at or by the time or times, stated in the order. The period stated in an account monitoring order must not exceed the period of 90 days beginning with the day on which the order is made.

The application for an order (as to procedure see r.62.1) must state that:

(1) a person specified in the application is subject to a confiscation investigation or a money laundering investigation; or

(2) property specified in the application is subject to a civil recovery investigation and a person specified in the application appears to hold the property; and

(3) that the order is sought for the purposes of the investigation, or is sought against the financial institution specified in the application in relation to account information of the description specified.

A specimen application and a draft account monitoring order are included in the Code of Practice issued under s.377, see SI 2003/334.

"Account information" is information relating to an account or accounts held at the financial institution specified in the application by the person specified (whether solely or jointly with another).

The application may specify information relating to:

(a) all accounts held by the person specified in the application for the order at the financial institution so specified;

(b) a particular description, or particular descriptions, of accounts so held; or

(c) a particular account, or particular accounts, so held.

A copy of any order made will be given by the Crown Court officer to the financial institution specified in the application.

Requirements for making the order

54–030   In the case of:

POCA 2002, s.371

(1) a confiscation investigation, there must be reasonable grounds for suspecting that the person specified in the application for the order has benefited from his criminal conduct;

(2) a money laundering investigation, there must be reasonable grounds for suspecting that the person specified in the application for the order has committed a money laundering offence.

C(IC)A 2008, ss.113–115, Sch.1

There must be reasonable grounds for believing that information which may be provided in compliance with a requirement imposed under the order is likely to be of substantial value (whether or not by itself) to the investigation for the purposes of which the order is sought.

There must be reasonable grounds for believing that it is in the public interest for the information to be provided, having regard to the benefit likely to accrue to the investigation if the information is obtained.

An application for an order is made under rr.6.14,19. As to information to be withheld from the respondent or other, see r.6.21. An application for variation or discharge is made under r.6.20.

As to proof of the identity and accreditation of the applicant, see 54–012, above.

The order takes effect in spite of any restrictions on the -disclosure of information, however imposed (s.374). As to applications to vary or discharge, see s.375 and rr.6.21(2), (3).

C.   Bankers' Books Evidence Act 1879

54–031   A judge may, on the application of any party to legal proceed-   BBEA 1879, s.7
ings, order that such a party be at liberty to inspect and take copies of
any entry in a banker's book for any of the purposes of such proceedings. That order may be made with or without summoning the bank or
other party, and must be served on the bank three clear days before the
order is to be obeyed, unless the judge otherwise orders.

Note that:

(1) before making the order the judge should satisfy himself that
the application is not solely a "fishing expedition" to find material on which to hang a charge, but should consider whether the
prosecution, who normally make such an application, have in
their possession other evidence against the accused (*Williams v
Summerfield* (1972) 56 Cr. App. R. 597);

(2) the order ought to be limited to a certain specific period, and
ought not to be oppressive (*Ex p. Simpson* (1980) 70 Cr. App. R.
291); and

(3) the mere fact that the accused has given notice of intention
to plead guilty is not a reason for refusing an order (*Owen v
Sambrook* [1981] Crim. L.R. 329).

D.   Letters of request

54–032   Where, on an application made to him, it appears to a judge   C(IC)A 2003,
s.7
that:

(1) an offence has been committed or that there are reasonable
grounds for suspecting that an offence has been committed;
and

(2) proceedings in respect of the offence have been or that the
offence is being investigated,

he may request assistance in obtaining outside the United Kingdom
any evidence specified in his request for use in the proceedings or
investigation.

Applying for letters of request

54–033   Notice under s.3(1) is given to the Crown Court officer. It   R.32
must:

(1) be made in writing, save that the court may in exceptional circumstances dispense with the need for notice;

(2) state the particulars of the offence which it is alleged has been
committed or the grounds upon which it is suspected that an
offence has been committed;

(3) state whether proceedings in respect of the offence have been
instituted or the offence is being investigated; and

(4) include particulars of the assistance requested in the form of a
draft letter of request.

The application is heard ex parte, and in addition and without prejudice to any other powers of the court to hear proceedings in camera,

the court may, when hearing the application, if it thinks it necessary in the interests of justice, direct that the public be excluded from the court.

No such form of application is contained in CPR 2011.

E.   Evidence for use overseas

54–034   Where a request, under the Crime (International Co-operation) Act 2003, for assistance in obtaining evidence in England and Wales is received, and the Secretary of State nominates the Crown Court to receive any evidence to which the request relates which appears appropriate to that court for the purpose of giving effect to the request or part, the following provisions apply, and:

(1) the judge has the like powers for securing the attendance of a witness as he has for the purposes of other proceedings before the court (see WITNESS SUMMONS AND WARRANTS);

(2) the court may take evidence on oath;

(3) rule 32.4 makes provision in respect of the persons entitled to appear or take part in the proceedings and for excluding the public from the proceedings; and r.32.5–9 make provision for other miscellaneous matters, such as record, interpretation, TV and telephone links;

(4) in relation to the privilege of witnesses:

(a) a person cannot be compelled to give any evidence which he could not be compelled to give:

(i) in criminal proceedings in England and Wales; or

(ii) in criminal proceedings in the country from which the request for the evidence has come, provided his claim to be exempt from giving the evidence is conceded by the court or authority which made the request; if it is not, he may be required to give the evidence to which the claim relates, but the evidence may not be forwarded to the court or authority which requested it, if a court in the country in question, on the matter being referred to it, upholds the claim;

(b) a person cannot be compelled to give any evidence if his doing so would be prejudicial to the security of the United Kingdom (a certificate signed by or on behalf of the Secretary of State is conclusive);

(c) a person cannot be compelled to give any evidence in his capacity as an officer or servant of the Crown;

(5) the evidence received by the court must be given to the court or authority that made the request or to the Secretary of State for forwarding to the court or authority that made the request; so far as may be necessary in order to comply with the request, where the evidence consists of:

(a) a document, the original or a copy must be provided;

(b) any other article, the article itself, or a description, photograph or other representation of it, must be provided;

(6) BBEA 1879 (above) applies to the proceedings as it applies to other proceedings before the court;

(7) no order for costs may be made.

"Evidence" is not confined to direct evidence for use at trial, and may extend to information which might lead to the discovery of evidence (*R. v Home Secretary Ex p. Fininvest Spa* [1997] 1 Cr. App. R. 257) (a decision under the 1990 Act). As to references to the DFFO, see *R. (Evans) v DSFO* [2002] EWHC 2304 (Admin); [2003] W.L.R. 299 as to the application of "section 2 notices" (under CJA 1988, s.2).

C(IC)A 2003, ss.43, 46

F. Requests for information about banking transactions for use in the United Kingdom

Information about a person's bank account

C(IC)A 2003, ss.43, 46

54–035   A judge entitled to exercise the jurisdiction of the Crown Court may, on an application made by a specified prosecuting authority if satisfied that:

(1) a person is subject to an investigation in the United Kingdom into serious criminal conduct;

(2) the person holds, or may hold, an account at a bank which is situated in a participating country; and

(3) the information which the applicant seeks to obtain is likely to be of substantial value for the purposes of the investigation, request assistance in obtaining from a participating country:

(a) information as to whether the person in question holds any accounts at any banks situated in the participating country;

(b) details of any such accounts;

(c) details of transactions carried out in any period specified in the request, in respect of any such accounts.

Any request must:

(i) state the grounds on which the authority making the request thinks that the person in question may hold any account at a bank which is situated in a participating country and (if possible) specify the bank or banks in question;

(ii) state the grounds on which the authority making the request considers that the information sought to be obtained is likely to be of substantial value for the purposes of the investigation; and

(iii) include any information which may facilitate compliance with the request.

For the purposes of s.43, a person holds an account if the account is in his name or is held for his benefit, or he has a power of attorney in respect of the account.

Monitoring banking transactions

54–036 A judge entitled to exercise the jurisdiction of the Crown Court may, on an application made by a specified prosecuting authority, if satisfied that the information which the applicant seeks to obtain is relevant to an investigation in the United Kingdom into criminal conduct, request any assistance in obtaining from a participating country details of transactions to be carried out in any period specified in the request in any accounts at banks situated in that country.

C(IC)A 2003, ss.44, 46

Sending requests for assistance

54–037 A request for assistance under ss.43 or 44 is sent to the Secretary of State for forwarding to a court specified in the request and exercising jurisdiction in the place where the -information is to be obtained or to any authority recognised by the participating country in question as the appropriate authority for receiving requests for assistance of the kind to which this section applies, though in cases of urgency the request may be sent to the court itself.

C(IC)A 2003, ss.45, 46

55. REPORTING AND ACCESS RESTRICTIONS

1. Approach to reporting restrictions

The principle of open justice

55–001   The general rule is that:

(1) the administration of justice must be done in public; and
(2) the media have a right to attend all court hearings and are entitled to report those proceedings fully and contemporaneously.

The public has the right to know what takes place in the criminal courts and the media in court act as the eyes and ears of the public enabling it to follow court proceedings and to be better informed about criminal justice issues.

ECHR jurisprudence requires any restriction on the public's right to attend court proceedings and the media's ability to report them must be necessary, proportionate and convincingly established.

The requirements of open justice are ordinarily satisfied if proceedings are held in public and fair and accurate media reporting of the proceedings is not prevented by any action of the court (*R (Guardian News Etc) v Westminster MC* [2010] EWHC 3376 (Admin), [2011] 1 Cr. App. R. 36. Nothing in CPR 2011 extends the principle of open justice to a right to public or press to inspect documents or other exhibits placed before the court (ibid).

The effect

55–002   The effect of the general rule stated in 55–001 is that:

(1) proceedings must be heard in public;
(2) evidence must be communicated publicly;
(3) fair, accurate and contemporaneous media reporting of proceedings should not be prevented by any action of the court unless,

unless there are exceptional circumstances laid down by statute or the common law.

A judge must not, therefore:

(a) order or allow the exclusion of the press or public from court for any part of the proceedings;
(b) permit the withholding of information from the open court proceedings;
(c) impose a permanent or temporary ban on the reporting of the proceedings or any part of them, including anything that prevents the proper identification, by name and address, of those appearing or mentioned in the course of the proceedings.

Particular rights are given to the press to give effect to the open justice principle, so that they can report court proceedings to the wider public, even if the public is excluded.

If a judge is asked to exclude the media or prevent them from reporting anything, however informally, he should not agree to do so without:

> (i) first checking whether the law permits him to do so;
> (ii) considering whether he ought to do so;
> (iii) inviting submissions from the media or their legal representatives.

The prime concern is the interests of justice.

Checking the legal basis

55–003 In checking the legal basis for any proposed restriction, the judge needs to:

(1) check whether there is there any statutory power which allows departure from the open justice principle;
(2) check the precise wording of the statute;
(3) decide whether the terms of the statute are relevant to the particular case; and
(4) determine, where it is suggested that the power for the requested departure from the open justice principle is derived from common law and the court's inherent jurisdiction to regulate its own proceedings, if the authorities support that contention.

The interests of justice

55–004 The judge needs to decide whether action is necessary in the interests of justice. Thus:

(1) automatic statutory restrictions upon reporting may already apply; or
(2) there may be restrictions on reporting imposed by the media's own codes, or as a result of an agreed approach.

Further questions are whether:

(a) the applicant has adduced the factual evidence necessary for the judge's assessment of his case, which the law requires; and
(b) any derogation from the open justice principle is really necessary.

If there are less restrictive alternatives available, these should be considered.

Reporting restrictions must be proportionate. The judge should always check whether the same objective may be achieved by a more narrowly tailored restriction.

Judges powers

55–005 Where the judge can   R. 16.4

(1) impose a restriction on:
  (a) reporting what takes place at a public hearing; or
  (b) public access to what otherwise would be a public hearing,
(2) withhold information from the public during a public hearing,

he may do so: on application by a party or on his own initiative.

A party who wants the judge to do so must apply as soon as reasonably practicable, notifying each other party, and specifying the proposed terms of the order, and for how long it should last.

He must explain what power the judge has to make the order, and why an order in the terms proposed is necessary.

Where the application is for a reporting direction in respect of a witness under YCJEA 1999, s.46 (see SPECIAL MEASURES DIRECTIONS) he must explain how the witness is eligible for assistance, and why a reporting direction would be likely to improve the quality of the witness evidence, or the level of co-operation the witness gives the applicant in connection with the preparation of the applicant's case.

Varying or removing restrictions

55–006   Where the judge can vary or remove a reporting or access restriction he may do so on application by a party or person directly affected; or on his own initiative. | R.16.5.

A party or person who wants the judge to do so must, in the same way as above, apply as soon as reasonably practicable, notifying each other party, and such other person (if any) as the judge directs, specifying the restriction and explaining, as appropriate, why it should be varied or removed.

CPR 2011, r 16

55–007   CPR 2011 emphasise that when exercising any power under the judge r.16 must have regard to the importance of dealing with criminal cases in public and allowing a public hearing to be reported to the public. | R.16.2

He may determine an application at a hearing, in public or in private or without a hearing, but he must not exercise a power to which the rule applies unless each party and any other person directly affected:

(1) is present; or
(2) has had an opportunity to attend, or to make representations.

Judge's general power to vary requirements

55–008   The judge has general powers to: | R. 16.3

(1) shorten or extend (even after it has expired) a time limit;
(2) require an application to be made in writing instead of orally;
(3) consider an application or representations made orally instead of in writing;
(4) dispense with a requirement to give notice, or to serve a written application.

Someone who wants an extension of time must apply when making the application or representations for which it is needed, and explain the delay.

Media representations

55–009   Where relevant, the judge should invite:

(1) oral or written representations by the media or their representatives;

(2) legal submissions on the applicable law from the prosecutor,

in addition to any legal submissions and any evidence which the law may require in support of an application for reporting restrictions from a party.

He should:

    (a) invite media representations at the time he is first considering an order; and,

    (b) if an order is imposed, hear media representations as to whether any restriction imposed should be lifted or varied.

In his Instructions to Prosecution Advocates, the DPP highlights the role of the prosecutor in respect of safeguarding open justice, including opposition to restrictive applications, where appropriate.

Committing the order to writing

55–010 If an order is made, the judge should make it clear in open court that a formal order has been made and its precise terms. It may be helpful to suggest at the same time that the judge would be prepared to discuss any problems arising from the order with the media in open court, if they are raised by written note.

The order should be in precise terms, stating;

(1) its legal basis;

(2) its precise scope;

(3) its duration and when it will cease to have effect if appropriate. The reasons for making the order should always be recorded in the court record.

Review of order

55–011 The judge should exercise his discretion to hear media representations against the imposition of any order under consideration or as to the lifting or variation of any reporting restriction as soon as possible.

2.   Hearings from which the public are excluded

General

55–012 The public are generally excluded from proceedings held in private (in camera) and from those held in chambers under r.16.11.

(a)   Proceedings in private (in camera)

General

55–013 The court has an inherent power to regulate its own proceeding and may hear a case in secret in exceptional circumstances.

Note that:

(1) the only exception to the open justice principle at common law

justifying hearings in camera is where the hearing of the case in public would frustrate or render impracticable the administration of justice (*A-G v Leveller Magazine* (1979) 68 Cr. App. R. 342);

(2) the test is one of necessity.

The necessity test requires that even where the judge concludes that part of a case should be heard in camera, he must give careful consideration as to whether other parts of the same case can be heard in public and adjourn into open court as soon as exclusion of the public ceases to be necessary.

Alternative measures

55–014   Since hearing a case in secret has a severe impact upon the public's right to know about court proceedings, permanently depriving it of the information heard in secret, it follows that if the judge can prevent the anticipated prejudice to the trial process by adopting a lesser measure he should adopt that course.

Such measures may include:

(1) a discretionary reporting restriction such as a postponement order under CCA 1981, s.4(2) (see below);
(2) allowing a witness to give evidence from behind a screen; (see SPECIAL MEASURES DIRECTIONS); or
(3) ordering that a witness shall be identified by a pseudonym (such as by a letter of the alphabet) and prohibiting publication of the witness's true name by an anonymity order under CCA 1981, s.11,

thus removing the need to exclude the public.

Where only a small part of the witness's evidence is sensitive, is permissible to allow that part to be written down and not shown to the public or media in court.

However, measures such as these are also exceptional and stringent tests must be satisfied before they are adopted.

Circumstances justifying proceedings in private

55–015   Circumstances which may justify hearing a case in camera include situations where the nature of the offence, if made public, would cause harm to national security, e.g. by:

(1) disclosing sensitive operational techniques; or
(2) identifying a person whose identity for strong public interest reasons should be protected, such as an undercover police officer.

Any application to proceed in camera should be supported by relevant evidence and the test to be applied in all cases is whether proceeding in private is necessary to avoid the administration of justice from being frustrated or rendered impracticable.

Disorder in court may also justify an order that the public gallery be cleared. Again the exceptional measure should be no greater than necessary. Representatives of the media (who are unlikely to have participated in the disorder) should normally be allowed to remain.

REPORTING AND ACCESS RESTRICTIONS

Procedure

55–016   Where the judge can order a trial in private, a party who wants   R.. 16.6
the court to do so must;

   (1) apply in writing not less than 5 business days before the trial is
       due to begin, serving the application on the Crown Court officer,
       and on each other party, explaining the reasons for the applica-
       tion, how much of the trial the applicant proposes should be in
       private; and
   (2) explaining why no measures other than trial in private will
       suffice, such as:
       (a) reporting restrictions,
       (b) an admission of facts,
       (c) the introduction of hearsay evidence,
       (d) a direction for a special measure under YJCEA, 1999, s. 19;
       (e) a witness anonymity order CorJA 2009,s.86 (see SPECIAL
           MEASURES DIRECTIONS), or
       (f) arrangements for the protection of a witness.

Where the application includes information that the applicant thinks
ought not be revealed to another party, the applicant must omit that
information from the part of the application that is served on that other
party, mark the other part to show that, unless the judge otherwise
directs, it is only for the court and in that other part, explain why the
applicant has withheld that information from that other party.

   The Crown Court officer will at once display a notice of the application somewhere prominent in the vicinity of the courtroom, and will
give notice of the application to reporters by such other arrangements
as the Lord Chancellor directs.

Determination at a hearing

55–017   The application will be determined at a hearing which will be   R.. 16.6
in private, unless the judge otherwise directs. If he so directs it may
be,wholly or in part, in the absence of a party from whom information
has been withheld and must be **after the accused is arraigned** but
before the jury is sworn.

   At the hearing of the application, the judge will generally receive:

   (1) representations first by the applicant and then by each other
       party, in all the parties' presence; and then
   (2) further representations by the applicant, in the absence of a party
       from whom information has been withheld; but

the judge may direct other arrangements for the hearing.

   The trial in private will not be held until the business day after the
day on which such trial is ordered, or the disposal of any appeal against,
or review of, any such order, if later.

Representations in response

55–018   Where a party, or person directly affected, wants to make   R.16.7
representations about an application, he must serve the representations
on the Crown Court officer, the applicant, each other party, and such
other person (if any) as the judge directs, and do so as soon as

reasonably practicable after notice of the application, asking for a hearing, if that party or person wants one, and explaining why it is needed, specifying any alternative terms proposed.

Order about restriction or trial in private

55-019 Where the judge orders, varies or removes a reporting or access-restriction or orders a trial in private, the Crown Court officer will:

R. 6.8

(1) record the court's reasons for the decision; and
(2) as soon as reasonably practicable, arrange for a notice of the decision to be displayed somewhere prominent in the vicinity of the courtroom, and communicated to reporters by such other arrangements as the Lord Chancellor directs.

If an order is made, the proceedings must be adjourned for a short period to allow for an appeal to CACD under CJA 1988, s.159 (see APPEALS FROM THE CROWN COURT).

(b)   Youth Court proceedings

Proceedings emanating from youth courts

55–020   In so far as proceedings in the Crown Court are concerned:

CYPA 1933, s.49

(1) on appeal from a youth court; or
(2) in proceedings on appeal from a magistrates' court under CJIA 2008, Sch.2, (proceedings for breach, revocation or amendment of youth rehabilitation orders);

no report may be published which reveals the name, address or school of any child or young person concerned in the proceedings, whether as the subject of those proceedings or as a witness, or which includes any particulars likely to lead to his identification (a similar ban applies to pictures) and it is the duty of the judge to announce in the course of the proceedings that this prohibition applies (otherwise it does not).

These automatic reporting restrictions may be lifted in three specific circumstances, i.e. where:

(1) the judge is satisfied that it is appropriate to do so for avoiding injustice to the child or young person;
(2) to assist in the search for a missing, convicted or alleged young offender who has been charged with, or convicted of, a violent or sexual offence (or one punishable with a prison sentence of 14 years or more in the case of a 21-year-old offender who is unlawfully at large); and
(3) in relation to a child or young person who has been convicted, if the court is satisfied that it is in the public interest to do so.

The judge must offer the parties an opportunity to make representations and take these into account before lifting the restrictions.

As to the differing emphasis in this section and CYPA 1933 (s.39) (55–025) below see *R. v Lee (A Minor)*, 96 Cr. App. R. 188.

YJCEA 1999, s.44 (not yet in force) creates an automatic reporting restriction that prohibits the publication of any matter likely to identify a child or young person who is the subject of a criminal investigation and which lasts until the commencement of proceedings. The Act also makes a number of amendments to CYPA 1933, s.49.

(c) Special measures and other directions

55–021 The publication of any matter relating to: YJCEA 1999, s.47

(1) the use of a live link for an accused (s.19) and directions prohibiting an accused from cross-examining a witness in person (ss.33A and 36) an order discharging, or in the case of an order under s.19, varying such a direction; or

(2) proceedings:

    (a) on an application for such a direction or order; or

    (b) where a judge acts of his own motion to determine whether to give or make any such order or direction,

may not be reported before they are determined, either by conviction or otherwise, or are abandoned.

These automatic restrictions may, however, be lifted by the judge and lapse automatically when proceedings against the accused are determined or abandoned.

(d) Indecent material calculated to injure public morals

55–022 The Judicial Proceedings (Regulation of Reports) Act 1926, s.1 prohibits the publication in relation to any judicial proceedings of any indecent medical, surgical or physiological details which would be calculated to injure public morals.

3. Discretionary reporting restrictions

(a) Approach

General

55–023 Before imposing a discretionary reporting restriction, the judge should check that no automatic reporting restriction already applies which would make a discretionary restriction unnecessary.

The following are the principal discretionary restrictions:

(1) in the case of a **child under 18** concerned as an accused, witness or victim;

    (a) good reason for ordering that child not be identified;

    (b) on the facts of the case good reason welfare of child outweighs strong public interest in open justice;

    (c) proposed restriction is necessary and terms of order proportionate; an order may be made not to disclose name, address, school, picture or any detail likely to lead to child being identified as being concerned in the proceedings (CYPA 1933, s.39);

(2) in the case of an **adult** witness (other than the accused) concerned in the proceedings whose evidence or co-operation with the preparation of the case is likely to be diminished by reason of fear or distress in connection with being identified:

    (a) on the facts of the case the interests of justice favour the making of an order;

    (b) the order does not impose a substantial and unreasonable restriction on the reporting of the proceedings taking into account the open justice principle; and

    (c) the restriction are necessary and the terms of the proposed order proportionate,

the media may be ordered not to publish any matter relating to the witness during his lifetime if it is likely to lead members of the public to identify him as being a witness in the proceedings (YJCEA 1999, s.46).

Procedural safeguards

55–024 Where automatic reporting restrictions *already* provide protection it is generally not necessary to impose additional discretionary restrictions, but note that:

- care must be taken to ensure that the statutory conditions for imposing a discretionary reporting restriction are met;
- where the statutory conditions are met, the judge must balance the need for the reporting restriction against the public interest in open justice and freedom of expression;
- the need for an order must be convincingly established and the terms of it must be proportionate, going no further than is necessary to meet the statutory objective;
- the media should be given an opportunity to make representations about an discretionary reporting restriction;
- the order should be put in writing as soon as possible; and
- the media should be put on notice as to the existence and terms of the order.

(b) Protection of under-18s

55–025 The judge may, in relation to any proceedings in the Crown Court, direct that: no newspaper report of the proceedings in the Crown Court shall:

CYPA 1933, s.39

(1) reveal the name, address or school; or

(2) include any particulars calculated to lead to the identification of any child or young person concerned in the proceedings, either as being the person by or against or in respect of whom the proceedings are taken, or as being a witness, nor shall any picture be published, except in so far, if at all, as the judge permits.

There must be good reason, apart from age alone, for making such an order and the onus is on the applicant to show cause for restricting publicity (*R. v CCC Ex p. W, B, & C* [2001] 1 Cr. App. R. 2). There is a clear distinction between the automatic ban on identification in matters emanating from the youth court (s.49 at 55–020 above) and the discretion to impose a ban under s.39.

In deciding whether to make an order under s.39 the judge must balance the interests of the public in the full reporting of criminal proceedings against the desirability of not causing harm to a child. Where the child is an accused the judge should give considerable weight to the age of the offender and the potential damage to any young person of public identification as a criminal before having the burden or benefit of adulthood (*R. v ILCC ex p* Bornes [1996] COD 17).

The judge has complete discretion as to who to hear on any application (*R. v CCC ex p Crook* [1995] 2 Cr. App. R. 212, and see *Re R. (a Minor) (Wardship) Restrictions on Publication* [1994] 2 F.L.R. 637).

In *Ex p Crook* (above) it was suggested that:

(a) the judge should make it clear what the terms of his order are, clearly identifying the relevant children where necessary;

(b) a written copy of the order should be drawn up as soon as possible and made available for press representatives to inspect; and

(c) the fact that an order has been made should be communicated to those who were not present when it was made, perhaps a short notice might be included in the Daily List.

The order must, of course, be strictly in accordance with the terms of s.39 (*Ex p. Godwin* (1992) 94 Cr. App. R. 34), and its details must be clear and precise (*Briffett and Another v DPP* (2002) 166 J.P. 66). It must also comply with Article 10 ECHR in that it must be necessary, proportionate and there must be a pressing social need for it. Age alone is not sufficient to justify imposing an order as very young children cannot be harmed by publicity of which they will be unaware and s.39 orders are therefore unnecessary.

An order may be reviewed at any time. Judges are frequently invited to do so where an accused named in an order has been convicted at trial. In considering whether to lift an order:

(i) the welfare of the child must be taken into account; but

(ii) the weight to be given to that interest changes where there has been a conviction,

particularly in a serious case; there is a legitimate public interest in knowing the outcome of proceedings in court and the potential deterrent effect in respect of the conduct of others in the disgrace accompanying the identification of those guilty of serious crimes.

(c)   YJCEA 1999, s.45 (not yet in force)

55–026   Once YJCEA 1999, s.45 as amended by CA 2003, s.109(1), Sch.8 comes into force, the judge in any criminal proceedings (other than one to which CYPA 1933, s.49 applies (see 55–020, above)) will be able, having regard to the welfare of the person concerned, to:

(1) direct that no matter relating to any person concerned in the proceedings, that is:

(a) a person against whom or in respect of whom the proceedings are taken; or

(b) (in particular) a witness in the proceedings be, while he is under the age of 18, included in any publication if it is likely to lead members of the public to identify him as a person concerned in the proceedings;

(2) (or an appellate court will be able) by an "excepting direction" dispense to any extent specified in the direction with the restrictions imposed by (1) above if satisfied that:

(a) it is necessary to do so in the interests of justice; or

(b) that their effect is to impose a substantial and unreasonable restriction on the reporting of proceedings; or

(c) that it is in the public interest to remove or relax that restriction,

but no excepting direction may be given under (b) and (c) by reason only of the fact that the proceedings have been determined in any way or have been abandoned.

The excepting direction may be given at the time the direction under (1) is given, or subsequently, and may be varied or revoked by the judge or by an appellate court.

(d)   Protection of adult witnesses

55–027   The judge may, as a form of special measures direction, prohibit the the publication of matters likely to identify an adult witness in criminal proceedings (other than the accused during his lifetime).   YJCEA 1999, s.46

He must:

(1) be satisfied that the quality of the witness' evidence or his co-operation with the preparation of the case is likely to be diminished by reason of fear or distress in connection with his identification by the public as a witness; and.

(2) in exercising his discretion, balance the interests of justice against the public interest in not imposing a substantial and unreasonable restriction on reporting of the proceedings.

Excepting directions may be given, or the order revoked or varied at any stage of the proceedings, or written consent to identification may be given by the subject or, if under 16, by their parent or guardian.

The topic is dealt with in detail at SPECIAL MEASURES DIRECTIONS.

(e)   Witholding names and other matters

55–028   Where the judge exercises his power to allow a name or any other matter to be withheld from the public in criminal proceedings, he may make such directions as are necessary under CCA 1981, s.11 prohibiting the publication of that name or matter in connection with the proceedings. Section 11 does not itself give the judge power to withhold matters from the public. The power to do this must exist either at common law or by statute   CCA 1981, s.11

Reporting and Access
Restrictions

It will ordinarily be necessary for an application under s.11 to be made *in camera* (*R. v Tower Bridge MC, ex p Osbourne* (1989) 88 Cr. App. R. 28).

Section 11 may be invoked only where the judge allows a name or matter to be withheld from being mentioned in open court. It follows that there is no power to prohibit publication of any name or other matter which has been given in open court in the proceedings. An order should be made only where the nature or circumstances of the proceedings are such that hearing all the evidence in open court would frustrate or render impracticable the administration of justice.

It is not appropriate to invoke s.11 to withhold matters, e.g.:

(1) for the benefit of an accused's feelings;
(2) to comfort or to prevent financial damage or damage to reputation resulting from proceedings concerning a person's business;
(3) to prevent identification and embarrassment of the accused's children, because of his public profile,

but is properly employed to safeguard the identity of children and young persons, complainants in rape cases, witnesses who might later be exposed to violence or blackmail, or the revelation of whose identity might prejudice national security.

Where the ground for seeking a s.11 order is that the identification of a witness will expose that person to a risk to his life engaging the state's duty to protect life under art.2 ECHR, the court ought to take into consideration that person's subjective fears and the extent to which those fears are objectively justified.

The judge has a discretion to hear representations from the media about making an order and should wherever possible give the media the opportunity to do so. In cases of urgency, a temporary order should be made and the media should be invited to attend on the next convenient date.

The media have a right of appeal against a s.11 order made in the Crown Court (see APPEALS FROM THE CROWN COURT), under s.159 CJA.

(f) Postponement of fair and accurate reports

55–029 In respect of any legal proceedings held in public, the judge may, where it appears to be necessary for avoiding a substantial risk of prejudice to the administration of justice in;
CCA 1981,
s.4(2)

(1) those proceedings; or
(2) any proceedings pending or imminent,

order the publication of a fair, accurate good faith and contemporaneous report of the proceedings or any part of the proceedings be postponed for such period as he thinks necessary for the purpose.

'The order, which must be put into writing must be formulated in precise terms, and must be communicated to the press. It must include;

(a) the order's precise scope;

(b) the time at which the order will cease to have effect; and

(c) the specific purpose for which it is made.   PD 2004, I.3.3.

The judge must balance the competing interests of ensuring a fair trial and open justice. He should approach the matter in three stages:

(i) whether the reporting of the proceeding would give rise to a substantial risk of prejudice of the administration of justice; if not that is an end of the matter;

(ii) if there is a substantial risk, whether an order would eliminate that risk; if not there can be no necessity for an order;

(iii) even if satisfied that the order would achieve the objective consider whether the risk can be overcome by less restrictive means; and

If he is satisfied that an order is necessary he has a discretion and must balance the competing public interests between protecting the administration of justice and ensuring open justice and fullest possible reporting of criminal trials (*Ex parte The Telegraph plc* (1993) 98 Cr. App. R. 91).

In Re MGN Ltd [2011] EWCA Crim 100, [2011]1 Cr. App. R. 31 it was said that an order under s.4(2) should be regarded as a last resort. Applying *R. (on the application of Telegraph Group Plc) v Sherwood* [2001] EWCA Crim 1075, [2001] 1 W.L.R. 1983 the following approach was suggested:

(1) would the reporting give rise to a not insubstantial risk of prejudice to the administration of justice?;

(2) would an order under s.4(2) eliminate that risk? If not, there would be no necessity to impose such a ban and that would be the end of the matter;

(3) if, an order would achieve the objective, the judge still had to consider whether the risk could satisfactorily be overcome by less restrictive measures;

(4) even if there was no other way of eliminating the perceived risk of prejudice, it still did not follow necessarily that an order had to be made; that required a value judgement.

CACD added that the use of s.4(2) for the purposes of alleviating the difficulties of giving evidence, even if evidence had to be given in more than one trial, was rarely appropriate. If the conditions for an order under s.4(2) were established in the case of a particular witness or witnesses so that the order was justified in accordance with principle, then the order should be made; but in essence the protection of witnesses was more appropriately secured by statutory measures designed for that purpose, such as CYPA 1933, s. 39 or YJCEA 1999 s.23-s.30, or any further legislation designed to enable witnesses to give of their best.

In order to comply with ECHR, art.10, an order must be proportionate and should be limited to those specific matters that create a substantial risk of prejudice to the administration of justice if published contemporaneously.

The procedure is regularly invoked in cases involving sequential trials. The aim in those cases is to postpone the reporting of specific parts of the evidence in the first trial to prevent prejudice to the accused in the second trial. It is generally not appropriate to invoke this power in relation to matters that form part of the evidence in both trials because in those cases prejudice is unlikely to arise.

(g)   Quashing of acquittal and retrial

55–030   Under CJA 2003, s.82, CACD, if necessary in the interests of justice, may make an order to prevent the inclusion of any matter in a publication which appears to give rise to a substantial risk of prejudice to the administration of justice in a retrial. Before the prosecution has given notice of its application for an acquittal to be quashed and a case to be retried, such an order may only be made on the application of the DPP and where an investigation has commenced.

After such notice has been given, the order may be made either on the application of the DPP, or of the CACD's own motion. The order may apply to a matter which has been included in a publication published before the order takes effect, but such an order applies only to the later inclusion of the matter in a publication (whether directly or by inclusion of the earlier publication), and does not otherwise affect the earlier publication.

Unless an earlier time is specified, the order will automatically lapse when there is no longer any step that could be taken which would lead to the acquitted person being tried pursuant to an order made on the application, or, if he is so tried, at the conclusion of the trial.

(h)   Postponement of derogatory remarks in mitigation

55–031   CPIA 1996, s.58 gives the judge the power to postpone reports of certain assertions about named or identified persons that have been made in mitigation. In such a case:

(1) The judge must have substantial grounds for believing that the assertion is derogatory and false or that the facts asserted are irrelevant to the sentence.
(2) An order must not be made in relation to assertions that were made during the trial or any other proceedings relating to the offence.

(i)   Anti-social behaviour orders

55–032   In criminal proceedings specifically for breach of an ASBO or proceedings in so far as they relate to making an ASBO order after conviction in the youth court (not the preceding criminal proceedings or other youth court proceedings), the normal rule prohibiting the identification of under-18s in the youth court does not apply. The youth court retains a discretion to impose such an order under CYPA 1933, s.39. However/ there must be a good reason for such an order and Home Office guidance emphasises the importance of publicising the identity of persons subject to ASBOs.

5. Miscellaneous

(a) Unauthorised recording of court proceedings

55–033 Unauthorised tape recording of proceedings in court is a contempt of court. However, the court may in its discretion permit journalists
to record proceedings in court as an aide memoire. The recording must not
be broadcast or used to brief witnesses: see *Practice Direction (Criminal
Proceedings: Consolidation)* [2002] 1 W.L.R. 2870 para.1.2. It is an
offence to take photographs or make sketches (with a view to publication)
or attempt do so in court, in respect of a judge, a juror, witness or party if
in the court room, court building or court precincts including the cell area.
The court may issue guidance on the extent of the precincts of the court
buildings, e.g. by way of a map. The prohibition on the taking of photographs includes taking pictures on a mobile phone, video recordings,
photographs on conventional cameras or by any other means.

CCA 1981, s.19

(b) Jury's deliberations

55–034 It is a contempt of court disclose or solicit any details of statements made, opinions expressed, arguments advanced or votes cast by
members of a jury in their course of their deliberations in any legal
proceedings. The prohibition on disclosure binds both jurors themselves and the media in relation to the publication of any such
disclosure.

CCA 1981, s.58

Jury deliberations are confidential; except with the authority of the
trial judge during the trial, or the Court of Appeal after the verdict,
inquiries into jury deliberations are "forbidden territory" (*R. v Adams*
[2007] EWCA Crim 1; [2007] 1 Cr. App. R. 449(34), C.A; the rule
against any investigation or inquiry into jury deliberations is a rule of
admissibility (*R. v Mirza* [2004] UKHL 2 [2004] 2 Cr. App. R. 8; [2004]
1 A.C. 1118, H.L.), and evidence about the deliberations of a jury is
therefore inadmissible, subject to two narrow exceptions:

(1) where there has been a complete repudiation of the oath taken by
the jurors to try the case on the evidence (as by resorting to use
of a ouija board); if there are serious grounds for believing such
a repudiation of the oath has taken place, CACD will inquire into
it, and may hear evidence *de bene esse*, including from the jurors
themselves, to decide whether it has happened;

(2) where extraneous material has been introduced into the jury
deliberations; examples include papers mistakenly admitted to
the jury room, discussions with outsiders and, more recently,
information derived from research on the internet; where this
has occurred, CACD will examine the evidence to ascertain the
facts.

R. v Thompson [2010] EWCA Crim 1623; [2010] 2 Cr. App. R. 27

56. REPORTS

Pre-sentence report: (1) need for

56–001   For the purposes of forming any such opinion as is, mentioned in CJA 2003, ss.148(l) or (2)(b), 152(2), 153(2), or CJIA 2008, s.s.14(b) or (c) the judge is obliged to take into account all such information as is available to him about the circumstances of the offence, and the offence or offences associated with it including any aggravating or mitigating factors. In forming such opinion as is mentioned in CJA 2003, s.148(2)(a), he may take into account any information about the offender which is before him.

CJA 2003
156(1)(2); CJIA
2008, s.6, Sch.4,
Pt 1, para.77

He must, unless in the circumstances of the case he is of the opinion that it is unnecessary to do so, obtain and consider a pre-sentence report before:

(1) in the case of a custodial sentence, forming any such opinion as is mentioned in CJA 2003, ss. 152(2), 153(2), 225(1)(b), 226(1)(b), 227(1)(b) or 228(1)(b)(i); or

CJA 2003,
s.156(3)(4);
CJIA 2008,
s.6, Sch.4, Pt 1,
para.77

(2) in the case of a community sentence, forming any such opinion as is mentioned in CJA 2003, ss.148(1) or (2)(b) or CJIA 2008, s.14(b) or (c) or any opinion as to the suitability for the offender of the particular requirement or requirements to be imposed by the community order or youth rehabilitation order.

Offenders under 18

56–002   In a case where:

CJA 2003,
s.156(4), (5)

(1) an offender is aged under 18; and
(2) the offence is not triable only on indictment; and
(3) there is no other offence associated with it which is triable on indictment only, the judge is not entitled to say it is unnecessary to obtain a report, unless:
   (a) there exists a previous report, or reports; and
   (b) he considers the information contained in that report or the most recent, if there is more than one.

In *R. v Atkins*, [2001] EWCA Crim 2004 *The Times*, January 14, 2002, it was suggested that it might be desirable to require a pre-sentence report in all cases involving young offenders, even if a custodial sentence was inevitable.

Basic considerations

56–003   Quite apart from statute, in all cases where a judge is contemplating sending an offender to prison for the first time, other than perhaps for an extremely short period of time, it should be the invariable practice that a pre-sentence report be obtained. *R. v Gillette, The Times*, December 3, 1999 suggests that is always necessary, but in *R. v Armsaramah* [2001] 1 Cr. App. R.(S.) 133, CACD disagreed and see

R. v ILCC Ex p. Mentesh [2001] Cr. App. R.(S.) 467. *Gillette* does not need to be followed in every case.

No report; effect

56–004 A custodial sentence is not invalidated by a breach of the provisions, but any court dealing with an appeal will need to obtain and consider a report if one were not obtained in the court below unless it is satisfied that the lower court was justified in finding it unnecessary, or itself finds it unnecessary to do so. CJA 2003, s.156(6), (7)

The same caveat applies in relation offenders under 18 (CJA 2003, s.159, below) respecting disclosure of pre-sentence reports, applies.

Pre-sentence report: (2) adequacy and availability

56–005 It is for the judge to decide whether a report available to him is adequate for sentencing purposes, and constitutes compliance with PCC(S)A 2000, s.162, and if he considers a further report necessary he may call for one (see *R. v Okinikan* (1993) 96 Cr. App. R. 431).

A degree of care needs to be taken in the assessment of pre-sentence reports, since great importance is likely to be given to them, especially by inexperienced judges. Much of the material contained in them offends the cardinal rules of criminal evidence.

There is a deal of self-serving information contributed by the offender and his family, frequent hearsay drawn from former reports by other officers and other material on the file, and opinion evidence contributed by persons not necessarily qualifying as "experts" on the required level. There tends to be a bias towards non-custodial recommendations, and sometimes there is prejudice created by incompatibility between the officer reporting and the offender.

National guidelines seek to correct a frequently found lack of objectivity (see, e.g. *R. v James* (1981) 3 Cr. App. R.(S.) 233).

Note that:

(1) the judge is not obliged to ensure that every detail advanced by the defence is checked and confirmed; CJA 2003, s.157

(2) where "fresh and highly relevant" material is raised for the first time in the report, the judge ought to discuss the implications with both parties (*R. v Cunnah* [1996] 1 Cr. App. R.(S.) 393), and there may be need for a Newton hearing (see GUILTY PLEAS).

Mentally disordered offenders

56–006 Before sentencing an offender who is, or appears to be, mentally disordered within the meaning of MHA 1983, to a custodial sentence, other than one fixed by law, the judge must, in addition to the requirements as to pre-sentence reports:

(1) obtain and consider a medical report, made orally or in writing by a medical practitioner approved for the purpose under MHA 1983, s.12, unless he is of opinion that it is unnecessary to do so; and

(2) consider any information before the court relating to his mental condition (whether given in a medical report, a pre-sentence

report or otherwise), and the likely effect of such a sentence on that condition and on any treatment which may be available for it.

Nothing in CJA 2003, ss.148, 152, 153 or 157, 156 or 164:

CJA 2003, s.166(1), (5), (6)

(a) requires the judge to pass a custodial sentence, or any particular custodial sentence, on a mentally disordered offender; or

(b) restricts his power to deal with such an offender in a more appropriate way under MHA 1983 or otherwise, to deal with such an offender in the manner he considers to be the most appropriate in all the circumstances.

Disclosure of pre-sentence reports

56–007 A "pre-sentence report" is defined by statute, and differs from other reports, such as those of providers of probation services and members of youth offending teams. The term is restricted to reports which:

CJA 2003, s.158

(1) are made or submitted by an appropriate officer (as defined), with a view to assisting the court in determining the most suitable method of dealing with the offender; and

(2) contain information as to such matters as may be prescribed by Rules.

A pre-sentence report that:

(a) relates to an offender aged under 18; and

(b) is required to be obtained and considered before the court forms an opinion mentioned in s.156(3)(a), must be in writing.

Otherwise, subject to any rules made under the section, the judge may accept a pre-sentence report given orally in open court.

CJA 2003, s.159(1), (2)

Where the court obtains a pre-sentence report, other than a report given orally in court, a copy must be given to:

(a) the offender or his advocate or solicitor; and

(b) any parent or guardian of an offender under 18, who is present in court; and

(c) to the prosecutor, that is to say, the person having conduct of the proceedings in respect of the offence.

Note that:

CJA 2003, s.159(4)

(i) if the offender is aged under 18 and it appears to the judge that the disclosure to the offender or to any parent or guardian of his of any information contained in the report would be likely to create a risk of significant harm to the offender, a complete copy of the report need not be given to the offender or, as the case may be, to that parent or guardian;

CJA 2003, s.159(5)

(ii) if the prosecutor is not of a description prescribed by order made by the Secretary of State (below), a copy of

735

the report need not be given to him if the judge considers that it would be inappropriate for him to be given it;

(iii) in relation to an offender aged under 18 for whom a local authority has parental responsibility and who is in its care, or is provided with accommodation by it in the exercise of any social services functions, references to his parent or guardian are to be read as references to the authority.

CJA 2003, s.159(6)

The Pre-Sentence Report Disclosure (Prescription of Prosecutors) Order 1998 (SI 1998/191) prescribes a Crown Prosecutor, any other person acting on behalf of the Crown Prosecution Service or a person acting on behalf of the Commissioners of Revenue and Customs, the Secretary of State for Social Security, and the Director of the Serious Fraud Office.

Other reports

56–008 Where a report by an officer of a provider of probation services or a member of a youth offending team is made to any court (other than to a youth court) with a view to assisting the court in determining the most suitable method of dealing with any person in respect of an offence, and the report does not qualify as a pre-sentence report, a copy of the report must be given:

CJA 2003, s.160

(1) to the offender or his counsel or solicitor; and
(2) if the offender is aged under 18, to any parent or guardian of his who is present in court.

In relation to:

(a) an offender aged under 18, where it appears to the judge that disclosure to the offender or to any parent or guardian of his of any information contained in the report would be likely to create a risk of significant harm to the offender, a complete copy of the report need not be given to the offender, or as the case may be, to that parent or guardian;

(b) an offender aged under 18 for whom a local authority have parental responsibility and who is in their care, or is provided with accommodation by them in the exercise of any social services functions, references in this section to his parent or guardian are to be read as references to the authority.

57. RESTITUTION ORDERS

General

57–001 A restitution order should be made only where the title to property is abundantly clear; in any other case an applicant should be left to seek his remedies under the Police (Property) Act 1897, or in the civil courts (*R. v Ferguson* (1970) 54 Cr. App. R. 410).

PCC(S)A 2000, s.148(1), (2), (10), (11)

An order may, however, be made where:

(1) goods have been stolen and a person is convicted with reference to the theft (whether or not stealing is the gist of the offence); or

(2) the court takes such an offence into consideration on determining sentence.

The words "stolen" and "theft" refer also to offences of obtaining property by deception, blackmail, and handling property obtained by deception and blackmail.

"Goods" includes, unless the context otherwise requires, all kinds of property within the meaning of TA 1968 except land, and includes things severed from the land by stealing.

An order may be made in respect of money owed by the Crown.

Nature of order

57–002 Whether or not the passing of sentence is deferred in other respects, the judge may make an order:

(1) ordering any person having possession of the goods to restore them to a person entitled to recover them from him;

PCC(S)A 2000, ss.148(2), 149(2)

(2) on the application of a person entitled to recover from the offender any other goods, directly or indirectly representing those in (1) above, as being the proceeds of any disposal or realisation of the whole or part, or of goods representing them, that those other goods be delivered or transferred to the applicant; and

(3) ordering that a sum not exceeding the value of the goods in (1) above be paid out of any money of the offender, taken out of his possession on apprehension, to any person who, if the goods were in the possession of the offender, would be entitled to recover them from him.

Orders under (2) and (3) above may be combined provided the person in whose favour the orders are made does thereby recover more than the value of the goods.

PCC(S)A 2000, s.148(4)

Where an order is made under (1) above, and it appears that the offender has sold the goods to another who acted in good faith, or has borrowed money from that other on their security, the court may order to be paid to that person, out of the money of the offender taken from his possession on apprehension, a sum not exceeding the price paid or the amount owed. No application is necessary.

737

RESTITUTION ORDERS

Note that in relation to (3) above:

(a) money found in the offender's possession after his arrest may be seized (*R. v Ferguson* (above)); but
(b) not money found on him before his arrest (*R. v Hinde* (1977) 64 Cr. App. R. 213).

It is not necessary to show that the money was the proceeds of the crime, only that it belonged to the offender (*R. v Lewis* [1975] Crim. L.R. 353). The magistrates have no power to make a restitution order when committing an offender to the Crown Court for sentence (*R. v Blackpool JJ. Ex p. Charlson* (1972) 56 Cr. App. R. 823).

Procedure

57–003   A person who wants the court to exercise that power if the accused is convicted must apply in writing as soon as practicable (without waiting for the verdict), serving the application on the Crown Court officer, identifying the goods, and explaining why the applicant is entitled to them. The Crown Court officer will serve a copy of the application on each party. The judge will not determine the application unless the applicant and each party has had an opportunity to make representations at a hearing (whether or not each in fact attends). The judge may extend (even after it has expired) the above time limit and may allow an application to be made orally. r.42.7

No order should be made unless, in the judge's opinion, the relevant facts appear from:

(1) evidence given at the trial, or the "available documents"; together with PCC(S)A 2000, s.148(5), (6)
(2) any admissions made by or on behalf of any person, in connection with the proposed exercise of the court's powers.

The "available documents" include any written statements or admissions which were made for use, and would have been admissible, as evidence at the trial, and such documents as were served on the offender in pursuance of regulations made under CDA 1998, Sch.3, para.1 (sending for trial).

Evidence given after sentence is not "evidence given at the trial" (*R. v Church* (1971) 55 Cr. App. R. 65).

A representation order ought to be made where complex matters of restitution fall to be decided.

58. RESTRAINING ORDER

Making of order on conviction

PHA 1997, s.5

58–001 A judge sentencing or otherwise dealing with an offender convicted of an offence may:

(1) as well as sentencing him or dealing with him in any other way;
(2) make a restraining order, for the purpose of protecting the victim of the offence, or any other person mentioned in the order, from further conduct which amounts to harassment, or will cause fear of violence,

by preventing him from doing anything described in the order, for a specified period or until further order. There is no reason in principle why a restraining order should not be made to protect a company or a group of persons from harassment (*R v Buxton* [2010] EWCA Crim 2925; [2011] 2 Cr. App. R.(S.) 23).

Both the prosecution and the defence may lead, as further evidence, any evidence that would be admissible in proceedings for an injunction under PHA 1997, s.3. Any person mentioned in the order is entitled to be heard.

Procedure is governed by r.50 (Civil behaviour orders after verdict or finding) as to which see ANTI-SOCIAL BEHAVIOUR ORDERS.

A court dealing with a person for an offence may vary or discharge the order by further order. Procedure on revocation and discharge is governed by r.50.5 as amended by SI 2010/1921, as to which see BREACH, AMENDMENT AND REVOCATION (under Anti-Social Behaviour Orders).

Breach of the order without reasonable excuse is an offence punishable on conviction on indictment with five years' imprisonment.

Order following acquittal

58–002 Section 5A(1) was inserted to deal with those cases where there was:

(1) clear evidence that the victim needed protection; but
(2) insufficient evidence to convict of the particular charges before the court.

The fact that a jury is not sure that the conduct alleged amounted to harassment is not necessarily a ground for concluding that there is no risk of harassment in the future. The section is silent as to the standard of proof required but the order is a civil order so the ordinary civil standard of proof applied.

The evidence does not have to establish on the balance of probabilities that there had been harassment; it is enough if the evidence establishes conduct which falls short of harassment but which might well, if repeated in the future, amount to harassment and so make an order necessary. *(R v Major* [2010] EWCA Crim 3016; [2011] 1 Cr.

RESTRAINING ORDER

App. R. 25; see also *R. v Thompson* [2010] EWCA Crim 2955 [2011] 2 Cr. App. R.(S.) 131(24), C.A).

Requirements of order

58–003   In making an order the judge should:

(1) bear in mind that the purposes of an order is to prohibit particular conduct with a view to protecting the victim(s) of the offence and preventing further offences under ss.2 or 4 of the Act;

(2) ensure that the order is expressed and drawn up in clear and precise terms so that there is no doubt as to what the offender is prohibited from doing; and

(3) in including terms in the order have regard to considerations of proportionality, i.e. whether any term is proportionate and necessary to achieve the aim set out in (1).

(*R. v Debnath* [2005] EWCA Crim 3472; [2006] 2 Cr. App. R.(S.) 25).

The judge is required to identify the factual basis for imposing an order (*R v Major; R v Buxton* above).

In the case of a group of persons the group must be sufficiently defined so that that they know who they are and those against whom the order is made also know which persons are included and which are not (*R v Buxton,* above).

Breach and sentence

58–004   In sentencing for such a breach, the judge should consider:

(1) whether there is a history of disobedience to court orders;

(2) the seriousness of the particular conduct proved, (which may range from violence, to threats, to letters of affection);

(3) whether there has been persistent misconduct or merely a solitary instance of misbehaviour;

(4) the effect on the victim;

(5) the degree of future risk and whether the victim requires protection;

(6) the offender's mental health; and

(7) any plea of guilty, remorse shown, etc.

(*R. v Liddle* [2000] 1 Cr. App. R.(S.) 131).

Where a breach is alleged, and any issue of reasonable excuse is raised, the burden of proving absence of reasonable excuse is on the prosecutor (*R. v Evans (Dorothy)* [2004] EWCA Crim 3102; [2005] 1 Cr. App. R. 32. See also *R. v Hunt* (1987) 84 Cr. App. R. 163; *R. v Nicholas* [2006] 2 Cr. App. R. 30 and *R. v Charles,* [2009] EWCA Crim 1570; [2010] 1 Cr. App. R. 2).

Order on acquittal

58–005   An order may be made even where an accused is acquitted of   PHA 1997, s.5A
an offence if the judge considers that it is necessary to do so to protect a person from harassment by him, and in such a case, both prosecution and defence may lead further evidence.

Where CACD allows an appeal against conviction, it has power to remit the case to the Crown Court to consider whether an order ought to be made.

Where the judge indicates that he is considering the making of such an order, he should, of his own initiative, consider adjourning the hearing in order:

(1) to enable the parties to serve notice in writing identifying any evidence they wish the court to take account of, in compliance with rule 50.4(2); and

(2) to enable compliance with the rules relating to hearsay (rr.50.6 and 50.7).

even if he is minded to exercise the discretion open to him under rule 50.9 (which allows the court to shorten or extend a time limit, and allow a notice or application to be given in a different form, or presented orally),

His judgment has to bear in mind the fundamental principle underlying CPR 2011, Part 50, namely that any person faced with the possible imposition of a restraining order should be given proper notice of what is sought and the evidential basis for the application and, in addition, should be allowed a proper opportunity to address the evidence and make informed representations as to the appropriateness of such an order.

Where the judge is contemplating making an order immediately following a trial, provided the accused's representative has had an opportunity to address all relevant issues, consideration can properly be given to exercising the discretion contained in rule 50.9. (*R. v K* [2011] EWCA Crim 1843; (2011) 175 J.P. 378).

An appeal against such an order lies as if the person made subject to it had been convicted of the offence in question by the court which made the order, and the order had been made under s.5 above.

59. RESTRAINT ORDERS; RECEIVERS

Quick guide

A. Restraint orders

General

59–001 A restraint order under POCA 2002 prohibits a specified person from dealing with any realisable property held by him. "Dealing with property" includes removing it from England and Wales. The order is analogous to a *Mareva* injunction, (now known as a "freezing" order). The object of the order, like that of a *Mareva* injunction is to strike a balance at an interlocutory stage between: *(PD 2004, Annex F)*

(1) keeping assets available to satisfy a final order, if and when one is made; and
(2) meeting the reasonable requirements of their owner in the meantime.

(*Peters, Re* [1988] 3 All E.R. 46 per Nourse L.J. at 51), preventing the dissipation of realisable property which may become subject to a confiscation order.

Where dishonesty is charged there will usually be reason to fear that assets will be dissipated (*Jennings v CPS* [2008] UKHL 29; [2008] 2 Cr. App. R. 29) but see *Re B (Restraint Order)* [2008] EWCA Crim 1374; [2009] 1 Cr. App. R. 14 where there was no such evidence.

Applications for restraint orders should be determined by the Resident Judge, or a judge nominated by the Resident Judge, at the Crown Court location at which they are lodged. In cases of great complexity they should be listed before a judge with sufficient time to read and absorb the papers and with sufficient time to conduct a proper hearing) *Windsor v CPS* [2011] EWCA Crim 143; [2011] 2 Cr. App. R. 7.

Applications to:

(1) vary or discharge restraint orders;
(2) appoint management receivers; or
(3) commit the accused or an affected third party for contempt of court in respect of an alleged breach of the order,

should, where possible, be heard by the judge who made the restraint order(s).

Jurisdiction to make restraint orders (and to appoint receivers) was transferred by POCA 2002 from the High Court to the Crown Court. Where complicated issues of beneficial interest and equitable charges arise, consideration should be given to adjourning the proceedings to a specialist Chancery Circuit Judge or to a judge of the Chancery Division, or at least to listing the case in the Crown Court before a judge with the relevant expertise and experience (*SFO v Lexi Holdings Plc etc* [2008] EWCA (Crim) 1443; [2009] 1 Cr. App. R. 23).

The enforcement in England and Wales of restraint and receivership proceedings from Scotland and Northern Ireland, is governed by SI 2002/ 3133.

Where an accused in criminal proceedings is said to have breached a restraint order made under POCA 2002, by making prohibited transactions, a judge of the Crown Court has jurisdiction to try an application made by the prosecutor for the accused to be committed for contempt (*R. v M* [2008] EWCA Crim 1901; [2008] EWCA Crim 1901; [2009] 1 Cr. App. R. 17). As to sentence, see *R. v. Baird* [2011] EWCA Crim 459; [2011] 2 Cr. App. R.(S.) 78.

Nature of order

59–002 A restraint order, unlike a confiscation order (see CONFISCATION ORDERS) is not a final order made on conviction of an offender; it is pre-emptive and provisional in operation, and is intended to prevent the dissipation of assets until the court is in a position, if satisfied that it is right so to do, to make a confiscation order.

Thus:

(1) provided one of the conditions set out in POCA 2002, s.40 is satisfied, an order it may be made at a stage before there has been any determination of whether or not the person in respect of whose property it is made has been guilty of criminal conduct, let alone whether or not he has benefited from such conduct;

(2) the judge is concerned solely with the preservation of assets at a time when it cannot be known whether an accused will be convicted or not, thus he must seek to strike the balance referred to in 59–001 above;

(3) it need not be shown that the respondent has property rights in the property to be restrained; any of the fraudsters in a fraudulent scheme has a beneficial interest in money retained in the execution of the fraud (*R. v S* [2008] EWCA 2919);

(4) the grant of an order is discretionary; the judge must proceed on the basis of statements made *ex parte* on behalf of the prosecutor; he cannot assume that a confiscation order under the Act will be made in due course;

(5) the order takes effect immediately it is made, before intimation to the specified person.

Where there are several accused it may be appropriate to make orders in respect of each to protect, as against each other, the whole sum which is said to represent the proceeds of the offence(s) (*Peters, Re, above, R. v Jennings* (above)).

The application

59–003   An order may be made on an ex parte application made in chambers by the prosecutor or by an accredited financial investigator (accredited in accordance with POCA 2002, s.3).

POCA 2002, s.43(1)(2) R.59.1

Application is made without notice, but must be made in writing and must be supported by a witness statement giving the grounds for the application, and:

(1) to the best of the witness's ability full details of the realisable property in respect of which the applicant is seeking the order, specifying the person holding that property;
(2) the grounds for, and full details of any application for any ancillary order under s.41(7) for the purpose of ensuring that the restraint is effective; and
(3) where the application is made by an accredited financial investigator (see below), a statement that he has been authorised under POCA 2002, s.68 to make the application.

An application for the appointment of a management receiver or an enforcement receiver under r.60.1 may be joined with an application for a restraint order, or an application for the conferral of powers on a receiver.

Making an order

R.61.2

59–004   An order may be made where any of the following preconditions is satisfied, namely:

(1) a criminal investigation has been started in England and Wales with regard to an offence that has taken place after March 24, 2008 and there is reasonable cause to believe that the alleged offender has benefited from his criminal conduct; or
(2) proceedings for an offence have been started in England and Wales and not concluded, and there is reasonable cause to believe that the alleged offender has benefited from his criminal conduct; or

POCA 2002, s.40

(3) an application by the prosecutor for subsequent reconsideration of an order which has been made under ss.19, 20, 27 or 28 of the Act and not concluded, or the judge believes that such an application is to be made, and there is reasonable cause to believe that the offender has benefited from his criminal conduct; or
(4) an application by the prosecutor has been made under s.21 for reconsideration of the benefit and not concluded, or the judge believes that such an application is to be made, and there is reasonable cause to believe that the court will decide under that section that the amount found under the new calculation of the offender's benefit exceeds the relevant amount (as defined in that section); or
(5) an application by the prosecutor has been made under s.22 for a

reconsideration of the available amount, and not concluded, or the judge believes that such an application is to be made, and there is reasonable cause to believe that the court will decide under that section that the amount found under the new calculation the available amount exceeds the relevant amount (as defined in that section).

Note that condition (2) is not satisfied if the judge believes that there has been undue delay in continuing the proceedings, or that the prosecutor does not intend to proceed, and the same applies if an application as mentioned in conditions (3), (4) and (5) has been made.

If condition (1) is satisfied:

(a) references here to the defendant (or offender) are to the "alleged" offender;
(b) references to the "prosecutor" are to the person the judge believes is to have conduct of any proceedings for the offence;
(c) s.77(9) has effect as if proceedings for the offence had been started against the offender when the investigation was started.

The judge should examine whether there is any real risk of dissipation of assets by the accused or anyone else prior to satisfaction of a confiscation order, should a restraint order not be made. There will rarely be direct evidence of the risk, but he may infer such risk from the circumstances *(Re B, 59-001 above)*.

POCA 2002, s.41(6)(7)

If:

(i) a judge makes a restraint order; and
(ii) the applicant for the order applies to the judge for him to do so, (whether as part of the application for the restraint order or at any time afterwards),

the judge may make such order as he believes to be appropriate for the purpose of ensuring that the restraint order is effective POCA 2002, (see *DPP v Scarlett* [2000] 1 W.L.R. 515).

Particularities of the order

59–005   The order may:

POCA 2002, s.41(2)

(1) provide that it applies to;
    (a) all realisable property held by the specified person whether or not the property is described in the order;
    (b) realisable property transferred to the specified person after the order is made;

POCA 2002, s.41(3), (6)

(2) be made subject to exceptions, and an exception may in particular;
    (a) make provision for reasonable living expenses and reasonable legal expenses (see 59–009, below);
    (b) make provision for the purpose of enabling any person to carry on any trade, business, profession or occupation;
    (c) be made subject to conditions, but an exception to a restraint order must not make provision for any legal expenses which;

(i) relate to an offence which falls within subsection (5); R.59.2
and

(ii) are incurred by the defendant or by a recipient of a
tainted gift.

An order must include a statement that disobedience of the order,
either by a person to whom it is addressed, or by any other person, may
be contempt of court, and details of the possible consequences of being
held in contempt must be included. It is the duty of the applicant to serve
copies of the order and of the witness statement made in support, on
the defendant and any person prohibited from dealing with realisable
property by the order, and to notify any person whom he knows to be
affected by the order, of its terms.

Charges; seizure

59–006   Charging orders are abolished by POCA 2002, but s.41(8)
provides that a restraint order is not to affect property for the time being
subject to a charge under:

- DTA 1986, s.9;
- CJA 1988, s.78;
- CJ(Confiscation) (NI) Order 1990 (SI 1990/2588 (N.I. 17)),   POCA 2002,
  art.14;   s.45
- DTA 1984, s.27;
- Proceeds of Crime (NI) Order 1996 (SI 1996/1299 (N.I. 9)), art.
  32.

Where a restraint order is in force a constable, an accredited financial
investigator or a customs officer may seize any realisable property
to which it applies to prevent its removal from England and Wales.
Property so seized will be dealt with in accordance with the directions
of the court which made the order.

Restraint orders: power to retain seized property etc.

59–007   A restraint order may include provision authorizing the   POCA 2002,
detention of the detention of any property to which it applies if the   s.41A
property:

(1) is seized by an appropriate officer under a relevant seizure
    power, or
(2) is produced to an appropriate officer in compliance with a pro-
    duction order under s. 345.

In particular such provision may relate to:

(a) specified property, to property of a specified description or
    to all property to which the restraint order applies;
(b) property that has already been seized or produced or to prop-
    erty that may be seized or produced in future.

"Appropriate officer" here means an accredited financial investigator; a constable, an officer of Revenue and Customs. a member of
staff of SOCA or a member of staff of the relevant director (within
the meaning of s.352(5A)). "Relevant seizure power" means a power

to seize property which is conferred by, or by virtue of, s.47C, s.352, or Pt 2 or 3 of PACE 1984, (including as applied by order under *ibid.* s.114(2)).

Order subject to exceptions

59–008   The judge may make a restraint order subject to exceptions   R.59.(2) (1)-(3)
including, but not limited to exceptions for:

(1) reasonable living expenses; and

(2) reasonable legal expenses; and

(3) the purpose of enabling any person to carry on any trade, business or occupation,

but must not make an exception for legal expenses where this is prohibited by POCA 2002, s.41(4) (see, e.g. *S v C&E Commrs.* [2004] EWCA Crim 2374; [2005] 1 Cr. App. R. 17, also *R v. AP* [2007] EWCA Civ 3128; [2008] 1 Cr.App.R. 39; cf. *HMRC v Robert William Briggs-Price* [2007] EWCA Civ 568).

An exception to a restraint order may be made subject to conditions.

It is suggested that the terms of any exception need careful consideration, since an order may cause serious hardship to the subject of it. Save in exceptional cases its terms should not go beyond what is required to prevent dissipation of the assets; the order does not, and properly does not, prevent the meeting of ordinary and reasonable expenditure (*Peters, Re*, above).

The civil courts have generally insisted upon adequate provision being made in the order for the specified person's reasonable living expenses (see s.41(3)(a) in the preceding paragraph). See also *Peters, Re*, above.

In relation to reasonable living expenses:

(a) an order ought, ordinarily, from the moment it is granted on the ex parte application, to contain a provision for such expenses unless good reason is shown why this should not be done in the particular case;

(b) it may be convenient for the prosecutor, when applying for the order, to insert such an exception into the draft order sought; or, if he does not, he should come before the judge prepared to explain why, in the circumstances of the case, it would be inappropriate to include such a provision; and the circumstances relied upon ought to be set out in the application.

In a case where it is known that the specified person carries on a trade, business, profession or occupation, a similar approach should be taken, in line with the provisions in s.41(3)(b) of the Act.

Approach to living and legal expenses

59–009   In a case on the similar Scottish provisions of the Act (*HMA v WMM for a Restraint Order*, September 22, 2005) a number of points were made in relation to "reasonable living expenses":

(1) it will generally be appropriate to put a limit in the order;

(2) consistent with the principle that a person not convicted of any

offence should not unreasonably be made to incur expenditure in coming to court, the limit should err on the side of generosity, though at the ex parte stage it may not be possible to fix the appropriate limit with any accuracy;

(3) the applicant may, of course, once the order is granted, attempt to reach agreement with the specified person as to the appropriate level of expenditure to be permitted by the exception to the order; if agreement is reached, the order may be varied by consent; if not, either party may apply to the court;

(4) the expression "reasonable living expenses" may cover the payment of ordinary debts as they fall due, though a separate exception may be required here; if there is any uncertainty about this, an application may be made to the court.

As to policing the exception, s.41(3)(c) permits the judge to impose conditions. He might require the specified person, as a condition of making an exception allowing payment of -reasonable living expenses, to take certain steps designed to enable the prosecutor to be aware of the level and type of -expenditure and apply to the court if he considers that it goes beyond what is permissible. There might be a condition to require the specified person to identify the accounts from which he habitually makes payment of his ordinary living expenses. There may be other appropriate conditions. Alternatively, the specified person might be required to establish a separate account into which certain sums can be paid and from which payments can be made consistent with the order.

In relation to costs, i.e. reasonable legal expenses (see s.41(3)(a)), the judge is not entitled (see s.41(4)) to make an exception to allow the specified person to pay the legal expenses of defending the criminal case brought against him, but he may, in making a restraint order, include an exception allowing the specified person to incur legal expenses in connection with the restraint order itself.

See *CPS v Campbell* [2009] EWCA (Crim) 997; [2010] 1 W.L.R. 650.

General procedural provisions

59–010 A number of general provisions contained in CPR 2011 may be noticed in relation to restraint and receivership proceedings: R.61.3, 4

(1) applications in restraint and receivership proceedings are dealt with without a hearing, unless the judge orders otherwise; (see below); proceedings may be heard in chambers;

(2) as far as evidence in the proceedings is concerned: R.61.5

    (a) the judge may control it by giving directions as to the issues on which he requires evidence, the nature of that evidence and the way in which it is to be placed before him; he may exclude evidence that would otherwise be admissible, and may limit cross-examination; R.61.6

    (b) any fact which needs to be proved by the evidence of a witness may be proved, unless the judge orders otherwise, by his evidence in writing; a party may apply for leave to cross-examine, and if it is granted and the witness fails to R.61.7

attend, his evidence may not be used without the judge's permission;

(c) a party may apply to the court to issue a witness summons requiring a witness to attend or to produce documents to the court; r.28.3 applies;

R.61.8

(d) hearsay evidence may be admitted without the duty to give notice required by CEA 1995, s.2(1).

A hearing may be required if:

PD 2004 Annex F 9.1

(i) the application is unusually complex or sensitive;
(ii) it is appropriate that the application be made on notice to the accused and/or affected third parties; or
(iii) for any other reason, the judge considers it appropriate that a hearing should take place.

As to costs in such proceedings, see r.61.19–61.22.

Hearsay evidence

59–011   Evidence must not be excluded in restraint proceedings on the ground that it is hearsay (of whatever degree); CEA 1995, ss.2 to 4 apply in relation to them as those sections apply in relation to civil proceedings.

POCA 2002, s.46

Note that for the purposes of this section:

(1) "restraint proceedings" are proceedings for a restraint order; for the discharge or variation of such an order; and on an appeal under ss.43 or 44;
(2) "hearsay" is a statement which is made otherwise than by a person while giving oral evidence in the proceedings and which is tendered as evidence of the matters stated.

Nothing in s.46 affects the admissibility of evidence which is admissible apart from that section.

Obligations in relation to exercise of powers

59–012   In relation to the powers conferred on a judge by ss.41 to 60 and 62 to 67, below and to the powers of a receiver appointed under ss.48, 50 or 52, there is a general obligation to exercise them:

POCA 2002, s.69(1)–(3)

(1) with a view to the value for the time being of realisable property being made available (by the property's realisation) for satisfying any confiscation order that has been or may be made against a defendant;
(2) in a case where a confiscation order has not been made, with a view to securing that there is no diminution in the value of such property;
(3) without taking account of any obligation of the defendant or a recipient of a tainted gift, if the obligation conflicts with the object of satisfying any confiscation order that has been or may be made against the defendant;

and they may be exercised in respect of a debt owed by the Crown, subject to the following rules:

(a) the powers must be exercised with a view to allowing a person other than the defendant or a recipient of a tainted gift to retain or recover the value of any interest held by him;

(b) in the case of realisable property held by a recipient of a tainted gift, the powers must be exercised with a view to realising no more than the value or the time being of the gift;

(c) in a case where a confiscation order has not been made against the defendant, property must not be sold if the judge so orders.

POCA 2002, s.69(4), (5)

The judge may order it not to be sold, if, on an application by the defendant, or by the recipient of a tainted gift, he decides that the property cannot be replaced. Such an order may be revoked or varied.

The provisions set out in (2) and (3) above are different from those under the pre-2002 legislation (cf. *Re X (Restraint Order; Variation)* [2004] EWCA 861(Admin); [2004] 3 All ER 1071) allowing for variation and discharge not only where there is an existing confiscation order but also where one might be made in the future. As to the position where it is sought to pay from the restrained assets a debt to a third party creditor, see *SFO v Lexi Holdings Plc etc.* [2008] EWCA Crim 1443; [2009] 1 Cr. App. R. 23.

Discharge and variation

59–013 An application to discharge or vary a restraint order or an order under s.41(7) may be made to the Crown Court in accordance with s.59.3 or 59.4 by the person who applied for the order, or by any person affected by it, and on such application the court may discharge the order, or vary it.

POCA 2002, s.42(2)–(7)

Where the condition in s.40 which was satisfied was that:

(1) proceedings were started or an application was made, the judge must discharge the order on the conclusion of the proceedings or of the application (as the case may be);

(2) an investigation was started or an application was to be made, the judge must discharge the order if within a reasonable time proceedings for the offence are not started or the application is not made, as the case may be.

Application for:

(a) discharge or variation by a person affected by the order is made in terms of r.59.3;

(b) variation of the order by the person who applied for the order is made in terms of r.59.4; and

(c) discharge of the order by the person who applied for it in terms of r.59.5.

Appeal to CACD

59–014 There is no appeal against the making of a restraint order. A person dissatisfied with the making of an order must apply to the Crown Court for its variation or discharge.

POCA 2002, ss.43, 44

RESTRAINT ORDERS; RECEIVERS

Appeal does, however, lie to CACD where:

(1) on an application for a restraint order the court decides not to make one, by the person who applied for the order, against that decision;

(2) an application is made under s.42(3) in relation to a restraint order or an order under s.41(7), by the person who applied for the order or any person affected by it in respect of the Crown Court's decision on the application,

and CACD may either confirm the order or make such order as it believes appropriate. Leave is required, and leave will be given only where CACD considers that the appeal would have a real prospect of success or there is some other compelling reason why the appeal should be heard. An order giving leave may limit the issues to be heard and may be made subject to conditions (r.73.1). See further APPEALS FROM THE CROWN COURT.

Detention of property pending appeal
59–015   Where a restraint order

POCA 2002, s.44

(1) includes provision under s. 41 authorising the detention of property, and the restraint order is discharged under s.42(5) or 43(3)(b); or

(2) includes provision under s.41A authorising the detention of property, and the restraint order is varied under s.42(5) or 43(3)(b) so as to omit any such provision,

the property may be detained until there is no further possibility of an appeal against the decision to discharge or vary the restraint order, or any decision made on an appeal against that decision.

POCA 2002, s.190A

Where a restraint order includes:

(a) provision under s.190A authorising the detention of property, and the restraint order is discharged under s.91(5) or 192(3)(b); or

(b) provision under section 190A authorising the detention of property, and the restraint order is varied under s.191(5) or 192(3)(b) so as to omit any such provision,

the property may be detained until there is no further possibility of an appeal against the decision to discharge or vary the restraint order, or any decision made on an appeal against that decision.

POCA 2002, s.47(1)–(3)

Registration
59–016   The Registration Acts, as defined in s.48(2) apply in relation to:

(1) restraint orders as they apply in relation to orders which affect land and are made by the court for the purpose of enforcing judgments or recognisances;

(2) applications for restraint orders as they apply in relation to other pending land actions,

but no notice may be entered in the register of title under the Land Registration Act 2002 in respect of a restraint order.

The person applying for a restraint order is treated for the purposes of s.57 of the Land Registration Act 1925 (inhibitions) as a person interested in relation to any registered land to which the application relates, or a restraint order made in pursuance of which the application relates.

POCA 2002, s.47(4)

B.   Receivers

59–017   A judge of the Crown Court is empowered under the provisions of POCA 2002, to appoint receivers of property in three instances.

Receivers perform two quite different functions under the Act:

(1) "**management receivers**" manage property pending a defendant's conviction (and sometimes afterwards);
(2) "**enforcement receivers**" dispose of such property to satisfy a confiscation order.

The appointment of a receiver before trial is essentially to safeguard the defendant's assets rather than to maximise the amount which may be available to meet any future confiscation order (*Peters, Re*, [1988] 3 All E.R. 46).

A receiver is entitled to be recompensed in respect of his costs, expenses and remuneration out of the assets in his hands as receiver (and r.69.7 cannot override this position) (*Capewell v C&E Commissioners* [2007] UKHL2; [2007] 2 All ER 370).

1.   Management receivers

59–018   Where:

(1) a restraint order is made; and
(2) the applicant for that order applies to a judge for an order (whether as part of the application for the restraint order or at any time afterwards),

POCA 2002, ss.48(1), (2), 49(1), (2)

the judge may by order appoint a receiver in respect of any realisable property to which the restraint order applies, and on the application of the person who applied for the restraint order, may confer on him, in relation to any such property to which the restraint order applies, powers to:

(a) take possession of the property;
(b) manage or otherwise deal with it;
(c) commence, carry on or defend any legal proceedings in respect of it; and
(d) realise so much of it as is necessary to meet the receiver's remuneration and expenses,

provided the property is not for the time being subject to a charge under any of those provisions mentioned above and may further (s.49(3)(4)) by order confer on the receiver power to enter any premises in England and Wales and to:

   (i) search for or inspect anything authorised by the judge;

   (ii) make or obtain a copy, photograph or other record so authorised; and

   (iii) remove anything which the receiver is required or authorised to take possession of in pursuance of a court order.

As to procedure, see rr. 60.1, 60.2 at 59–022, below.

The judge may also by order authorise the receiver, for the purpose of the exercise of his functions, to hold property, enter into contracts, sue and be sued, employ agents, execute powers of attorney, deeds or other instruments and take any other steps the judge thinks appropriate.

An application to appoint a management receiver should, where possible, be heard by the judge who made the restraint order(s).

Persons having possession of realisable property

59––019 The judge may order any person who has possession of realisable property to which the restraint order applies to give possession of it to the receiver.   *POCA 2002, ss.51(6), (7)*

The judge may:

 (1) order a person holding an interest in realisable property to which the restraint order applies to make to the receiver such payment as the court specifies in respect of a beneficial interest held by the defendant or the recipient of a tainted gift; and   *POCA 2002, s.49(5), (6), (7)*

 (2) may (on payment being made) by order transfer, grant or extinguish any interest in the property,

provided that the property is not for the time being subject to a charge under any of those provisions mentioned at 59–006, above.   *POCA 2002, s.49(8)(9)*

The judge must not:

 (a) confer the power to manage the property under s.49(2)(b) or to realise property to meet the receiver's expenses under s.49(2)(d); or

 (b) exercise the power conferred on it under (1) above in respect of property,

unless he gives persons holding interests in the property a reasonable opportunity to make representations to it. The judge may order that any power conferred under this section be subject to such conditions and exceptions as he specifies but this does not apply to property which is perishable, or ought to be disposed of before its value diminishes.   *POCA 2002, s.49(10)*

"Managing or otherwise dealing with property" includes:

   (i) selling it, or any part of it or interest in it;

   (ii) carrying on or arranging for another person to carry on any trade or business the assets of which are or are part of the property;

   (iii) incurring capital expenditure in respect of the property.

2. Enforcement receivers

59–020 In the case of a confiscation order made but not satisfied, and not subject to appeal, (e.g. an order falling to be enforced in the magistrates' court) a judge may, on the application of the prosecutor, appoint a receiver in respect of realisable property, and if he does so, he may, on the prosecutor's application, by order, confer on the receiver:

POCA 2002, ss.50, 51(1), (2), (3)

(1) in relation to the realisable property, the powers to:
    (a) take possession of it;
    (b) manage or otherwise deal with it;
    (c) realise it in such manner as the judge may specify; and
    (d) commence, carry on or defend any legal proceedings in respect of it; provided it is not for the time being subject to a charge under any of the enactments set out at 59–006, above;
(2) the power to enter any premises in England and Wales and:
    (a) search for or inspect anything authorised by the judge;
    (b) make or obtain a copy, photograph or other record of anything so authorised; and
    (c) remove anything which the receiver is required or authorised to take possession of in pursuance of a court order.

The judge may also authorise the receiver, for the purpose of the exercise of his functions to hold property, enter into contracts, use and be used, employ agents, execute powers of attorney, deeds or other instruments and take any other steps the court thinks appropriate.

POCA 2002, s.51(4), (5)

"Managing or otherwise dealing with property" includes:

POCA 2002, s.51(10)

    (i) selling the property or any part of it or interest in it;
    (ii) carrying on or arranging for another person to carry on any trade or business the assets of which are or are part of the property;
    (iii) incurring capital expenditure in respect of the property.

As to procedure, see rr. 60.1, 60.2 at 59–022, below.

Persons having possession of realisable property
59–021 The judge may order any person who has possession of realisable property to give possession of it to the receiver; and may:

(1) order a person holding an interest in realisable property to make to the receiver such payment as he specifies in respect of a beneficial interest held by the defendant or the recipient of a tainted gift;
(2) (on payment being made) by order transfer, grant or extinguish any interest in the property, unless the property is for the time being subject to a charge under any of the enactments set out at 59–006.

The judge must not:

POCA 2002, ss.51(8), (9)

    (a) confer the power to manage or to realise property; or

(b) exercise the power conferred on him by (1) and (2) above, in respect of property,

unless he gives persons holding interests in the property a reasonable opportunity to make representations. He is not obliged to do that where the property is perishable, or ought to be disposed of before its value diminishes. He may order that a power conferred by an order under this section is subject to such conditions and exceptions as he specifies.

3. Procedure

Appointment of receiver

59–022   An application for the appointment of a management receiver   R.60(1)
under s.48(1) or an enforcement receiver under s.50(1) is made as follows under r.60.1.

The application may be made without notice if:

(1) the application is joined with an application for a restraint order under r.59.1;
(2) the application is urgent; or
(3) there are reasonable grounds for believing that giving notice would cause the dissipation of realisable property which is the subject of the application.

It must be in writing and must be supported by a witness statement giving:

(a) the grounds for the application;
(b) full details of the proposed receiver;
(c) to the best of the witness's ability, full details of the realisable property in respect of which the applicant is seeking the order, and specifying the person holding that realisable property;
(d) where the application is made by an accredited financial investigator, a statement that he has been authorised to make the application under s.68; and
(e) if the proposed receiver is not a member of staff of SOCA, the CPS, or the Revenue and Customs Prosecution Office and the applicant is asking the court to allow the receiver to act;
    (i) without giving security; or
    (ii) before he has given security or satisfied the court that he has security in place, explain the reasons why that is necessary.

Where the application is for the appointment of an enforcement receiver, the applicant must provide the Crown Court with a copy of the confiscation order made against the defendant.

The application and witness statement must be lodged with the Crown Court, and except where notice of the application is not required to be served, the application and witness statement must be lodged with the Crown Court and served on the defendant, any person who holds realisable property to which the application relates; and any other person whom the applicant knows to be affected by the application, at least seven days before the date fixed by the court for hearing the application, unless the Crown Court specifies a shorter period.

If the court makes an order for the appointment of a receiver, the applicant must serve copies of the order and of the witness statement made in support of the application on such persons.

Confessal of powers

59–023 An application to the court for the conferral of powers on a management receiver under s.49(1), or an enforcement receiver under s.51(1), is made as follows under the procedure in r.60.2. The application may be made without notice if the application is to give the receiver power to take possession of property and: R.60.2

(1) the application is joined with an application for a restraint order under r.59.1;
(2) the application is urgent; or
(3) there are reasonable grounds for believing that giving notice would cause the dissipation of the property which is the subject of the application.

The application must be made in writing and supported by a witness statement which must:

(a) give the grounds for the application;
(b) give full details of the realisable property in respect of which the applicant is seeking the order and specifying the person holding that realisable property; and
(c) where the application is made by an accredited financial investigator, include a statement that he has been authorised to make the application under s.68.

Where the application is for the conferral of powers on an enforcement receiver, the applicant must provide the Crown Court with a copy of the confiscation order made against the defendant.

The application and witness statement must be lodged with the Crown Court, and except where notice of the application is not required to be served, the application and witness statement must be served on the defendant; any person who holds realisable property in respect of which a receiver has been appointed or in respect of which an application for a receiver has been made, any other person whom the applicant knows to be affected by the application, and the receiver (if one has already been appointed), at least seven days before the date fixed by the court for hearing the application, unless the Crown Court specifies a shorter period.

If the judge makes an order for the conferral of powers on a receiver, the applicant must serve copies of the order on those persons.

Miscellaneous

59–024 As to the giving of security by a receiver see r.60.5; as to non-compliance by receiver; see r.28, as to distress and forfeiture, see r.29.

4. Application of sums received

By enforcement receivers

59–025 Sums in the hands of an enforcement receiver (s.50), being the proceeds of the realisation of property (under s.51), or sums other than those in which the defendant holds an interest, are applied:

POCA 2002, s.54(1)–(5)

(1) in payment of such expenses incurred by a person acting as an insolvency practitioner as are payable by virtue of s.432;
(2) in making any payments directed by the Crown Court; and
(3) on the defendant's behalf towards satisfaction of the -confiscation order.

If the amount payable under the confiscation order has been fully paid and any sums remain in the receiver's hands he will distribute them among such persons who held, or hold, interests in the property concerned (i.e. the proceeds of realisation and other sums mentioned above), as the Crown Court directs, and in such proportions as it directs.

Before making any direction the judge must give persons who held, or hold interests in the property concerned a reasonable opportunity to make representations.

The receiver will apply sums as mentioned in (3) above by paying them to the designated officer of the magistrates' court responsible for enforcing the confiscation order as if the amount ordered to be paid were a fine on account of the amount payable under the order.

By the magistrates' court

59--026 Where the designated officer of the magistrates' court receives sums on account of the amount payable under a confiscation order (whether the sums are received under s.54 or otherwise), receipt reduces the amount payable under the order, but he must apply them in payment of such expenses incurred by a person acting as an insolvency practitioner as are payable under s.432, and are not already paid under s.54(2)(a).

POCA 2002, s.55

If he received the sums under s.54 he must next apply them in payment of the remuneration and expenses of:

(1) any management receiver (s.48), to the extent that they have not been met by virtue of the exercise by that receiver of a power conferred under s.49(2)(d); and
(2) the enforcement receiver appointed under s.50,

unless the receiver is a member of the staff of the CPS or of the Commissioners for Revenue & Customs, it being immaterial whether he is a permanent or temporary member or he is on secondment from else-where. If a direction was made (under s.13(6), see COMPENSATION) for an amount of compensation to be paid out of sums recovered under the confiscation order, he will next apply the sums in payment of that amount.

If any amount remains after he makes those payments, the amount will be treated for the purposes of JPA 1997, s.60 as if it were a fine imposed by a magistrates' court.

Seized money

59–027 Where money is held by a person;   POCA 2002, s.67

(1) in an account maintained by him with a bank or a building society; or

(2) which has been seized by a constable under PACE 1984, s.19 and is held in an account maintained by a police force with a bank or a building society; or

(3) which has been seized by an officer of revenue and customs under PACE 1984, s.19 as applied by an order made under s.114(2) of that Act, and is held in an account maintained by the Commissioners for Revenue & Customs with a bank or a building society; and

    (a) a restraint order has effect in relation to the property; or

    (b) a confiscation order is made against the person by whom the money is held; or

    (c) a receiver has not been appointed under s.50 in relation to the money;

    (d) any period allowed under s.11 for payment of the amount ordered to be paid under the confiscation order has ended.

A magistrates' court may order the bank or building society to pay the money to the designated officer of the magistrates' court on account of the amount payable under the confiscation order. The procedure is under r.58.12.

Failure to comply with an order may result in the defaulting bank or building society being fined; for the purposes of MCA 1980, the sum will be treated as adjudged to be paid by a conviction of the court.

5. Applications for directions

59–028 A receiver appointed under ss.48 or 50 may apply to a judge   POCA 2002,
of the Crown Court for an order giving directions as to the exercise of   s.62
his powers, as may any person affected by action taken by the receiver
and any person who may be affected by action the receiver proposes to
take. On such an application the judge may make such order as he
believes is appropriate.

The procedure on such an application (and on applications under
s.63(1) for the discharge or variation of orders relating to receivers) is
as follows.

The application must be made in writing and lodged with the Crown
Court. It must also be served on the following persons (except where
they are the person making the application):

(1) the person who applied for appointment of the receiver;

(2) the defendant;

(3) any person who holds realisable property in respect of which the receiver has been appointed;

(4) the receiver; and

(5) any other person whom the applicant knows to be affected by the application,

at least seven days before the date fixed by the court for hearing the application, unless the Crown Court specifies a shorter period.

If the judge makes an order for the discharge or variation of an order relating to a receiver under s.63(2), the applicant must serve copies of the order on any persons whom he knows to be affected by the order.

6. Discharge and variation

Variation and discharge of orders

59–029   The following persons may apply to a judge of the Crown Court to vary or discharge an order made under any of ss.48 to 51:

POCA 2002, s.63

(1) the receiver;
(2) the person who applied for the order;
(3) any person affected by the order.

The procedure is under r.60.3

On such application the judge may discharge or vary the order, but in the case of an order under ss.48 or 49 in relation to management receivers:

(a) if the condition in s.40 which was satisfied was that proceedings were started or an application was made, the judge must discharge the order on the conclusion of the proceedings or of the application (as the case may be);
(b) if the condition which was satisfied was that an investigation was started or an application was to be made, the court must discharge the order if within a reasonable time proceedings for the offence are not started or the application is not made (as the case may be).

As to when applications and other proceedings are commenced or concluded, see CONFISCATION ORDERS.

Management receivers: discharge

59–030   Where:

POCA 2002, s.64

(1) a management receiver stands appointed under s.48 in respect of realisable property; and
(2) a judge appoints an enforcement receiver under s.50,

he will order the management receiver to transfer to the other receiver all property held by him by virtue of the powers conferred on him by s.49, other than that which he holds by virtue of the exercise by him of his power under s.49(2)(d).

Where the management receiver complies with the order he is discharged from his appointment under s.48, and from any obligation under the Act arising from his appointment.

Where this section applies the judge may make such a consequential or incidental order as he believes appropriate.

Where the amount payable under a confiscation order has been fully paid, the receiver must make an application to the court under r.68.4 as to any sums still in his hands.

7. Restrictions on dealing with property

Restraint orders

59–031 Where a restraint order is made:

POCA 2002, s.58

(1) no distress may be levied against any realisable property to which the order applies except with the leave of a judge of the Crown Court and subject to any terms he may impose;

(2) if the order applies to a tenancy of any premises, no landlord or other person to whom rent is payable may exercise any right of forfeiture by peaceable re-entry in relation to the premises in respect of any failure by the tenant to comply with any term or condition of the tenancy, except with the leave of a judge and subject to any terms he may impose;

(3) if any court in which proceedings are pending in respect of any property is satisfied that a restraint order has been applied for or made in respect of the property, that court may either stay the proceedings or allow them to continue on any terms it thinks fit, provided it gives an opportunity to be heard to the applicant for the restraint order, and any receiver appointed in respect of the property under ss.48 or 50.

Enforcement receivers

59–032 Where an enforcement receiver is appointed under s.50 in respect of any realisable property:

POCA 2002, s.59

(1) no distress may be levied against any realisable property to which the order applies except with the leave of a judge of the Crown Court and subject to any terms he may impose;

(2) if the order applies to a tenancy of any premises, no landlord or other person to whom rent is payable may exercise any right of forfeiture by peaceable re-entry in relation to the premises in respect of any failure by the tenant to comply with any term or condition of the tenancy, except with the leave of a judge and subject to any terms he may impose;

(3) if any court in which proceedings are pending in respect of any property is satisfied that an order under s.50 appointing a receiver in respect of the property has been applied for or made, the judge may either stay the proceedings or allow them to continue on any terms he thinks fit, but before exercising any such power must give an opportunity to be heard to the prosecutor, and the receiver (if the order under s.50 has been made).

C. Appealing restraint orders, etc.

Appeal to CACD

59–033 There is no appeal against the making of a restraint order. A person dissatisfied with the making of an order must apply to the Crown Court for its variation or discharge.

POCA 2002, ss.43, 44

Appeal does, however, lie to CACD where:

(1) on an application for a restraint order the court decides not to make one, by the person who applied for the order, against that decision;

(2) an application is made under s.42(3) in relation to a restraint order or an order under s.41(7), by the person who applied for the order or any person affected by it in respect of the Crown Court's decision on the application,

and CACD may either confirm the order or make such order as it believes appropriate.

Leave is required, and leave will be given only where CACD considers that the appeal would have a real prospect of success or there is some other compelling reason why the appeal should be heard. An order giving leave may limit the issues to be heard and may be made subject to conditions.

R.73.1

On an appeal against the making of restraint and receivership orders under POCA 2002, Part 2 CACD has power to suspend the effect of its final order. *Windsor v CPP* (see 59–001 above).

See further APPEALS FROM THE CROWN COURT.

Financial investigators; applications and appeals

59–034 In relation to applications under ss.41, 42, 48, 49 or 63, or appeals under ss.43, 44, 65 or 66, an accredited financial investigator must not make such an application or bring such an appeal unless he is one of the following, or is authorised for the purpose by one of the following:

POCA 2002, s.68

(1) a police officer who is not below the rank of superintendent;

(2) an officer of Revenue & Customs who is not below such grade as is designated by the Commissioners for Revenue & Customs as equivalent to that rank;

(3) an accredited financial investigator who falls within a description specified in an order made for the purposes of this paragraph by the Secretary of State under s.453.

If such an application is made or appeal brought by an accredited financial investigator any subsequent step in the application or appeal or any further application or appeal relating to the same matter may be taken, made or brought by a different accredited financial investigator who falls within subs.(3).

If:

(a) an application for a restraint order is made by an accredited financial investigator; and

(b) a court is required under s.58(6) to give the applicant for the order an opportunity to be heard, the court may give the opportunity to a different accredited financial investigator who falls within subs.(3).

Definitions

59–035 A reference to the offence (or offences) concerned must be construed in accordance with s.6(9).

A "criminal investigation" is an investigation which police officers or other persons have a duty to conduct with a view to it being ascertained whether a person should be charged with an offence.

A "defendant" is a person against whom proceedings for an offence have been started (whether or not he has been convicted).

A reference to "sentencing the defendant for an offence" includes a reference to dealing with him otherwise in respect of the offence.

D.   External Requests

The legislation

59–036 POCA 2002 (External Requests and Orders) Order 2005 (SI 2005/3181), and in regard to the former law, CJ(IC)A 1990 (Enforcement of Overseas Forfeiture Orders) Order 2005 (SI 2005/3180) make provision for "restraint orders" on dealing with property situated in England and Wales specified in a request by an overseas authority.

POCA 2002, s.88

Articles 6,7 and 8 of the POCA 2002 (External Requests and Orders) Order 2005, provide a scheme to make a restraint order in response to an external request only in respect of property in England and Wales.

There is no power to make such an order in respect of property outside the jurisdiction, e.g. in Scotland (*King v SFO* [2008] W.L.R. (D) 147).

Such a request is channelled through the Secretary of State to the "relevant Director" being the DPP or DRC, or in certain circumstances the DSFO.

The scheme

59–037 The procedure under both orders is similar. On an application by a relevant Director, a judge of the Crown Court, on being satisfied that:

(1) a relevant property in England and Wales is identified in the request (other than property already subject to a charge);

(2) a criminal investigation or proceedings for an offence have been started in the country from which the request is made; and

(3) it appears to the judge that there are reasonable grounds for believing that as a result of the investigation or those proceedings an external forfeiture order may be made against the person named in the request,

may make a restraint order, prohibiting any specified person from dealing with relevant property which is identified in the request and specified in the order, other than property subject to a charge (see above 59–006).

The order may be made subject to exceptions (see above 59–005)

RESTRAINT ORDERS; RECEIVERS

and be made subject to conditions When the judge makes an order, and the applicant applies to him either then or afterwards, he may also make such further orders for the purpose of ensuring that the restraint order is effective. There is also power, on application, to discharge or vary a restraint order, a right of appeal by either side to CA and SC, and a power to appoint a management receiver.

Procedure

59–038   CPR 2011, rr.59–61 and 71 apply with the necessary modifications to proceedings under SI 2005/3181 as they apply to corresponding proceedings under POCA 2002 (r.57.15).

60. RETRIALS

General
60–001 Certain specialties of evidence and procedure apply to retrials ordered under:

(1) CAA 1968 s.7; and
(2) CJA 2003, Pt 10.

A. Retrial under CAA 1968, s.7

Arraignment

60–002 In a case where CACD has ordered that an appellant should be re-tried:

(1) The appellant must be arraigned on a new indictment, preferred at the direction of CACD within the time limit specified by that court, being within two months of the order; see CAA 1968, s.8.
(2) The Registrar will write to the court manager of the Crown Court immediately a re-trial has been ordered and send with the letter a copy of the draft judgment; his letter is copied to the prosecuting authority and the defence.
(3) The Registrar will send a copy of the approve judgment of the court as soon as it is available.

CACD will normally order that the venue of the re-trial be determined by the Presiding Judge of the circuit where the original trial took place. The court manager or listing officer should therefore contact the regional listing coordinator immediately so that the Presiding Judge can make the decision as to venue.

Immediately after the decision of the Presiding Judge as to the location of the trial is made the listing officer of the court nominated by the Presiding Judge, or the listing officer's staff, should:

(a) contact the prosecutor to ask when the indictment will be delivered; and
(b) list the case for arraignment as soon as possible within the time period directed by the Court of Appeal.

These cases must be given sufficient priority so that the case is listed for arraignment in the period between receipt of the indictment and expiry of the time limit. In cases where a retrial is ordered by CACD the custody time limit is 112 days starting from the date that the new indictment is preferred, i.e. from the date that the indictment is delivered to the Crown Court (PD 2004, Annex F,4.6).

As to bail pending retrial, see Criminal Appeal Rules 1968, rr.3, 4.

As to joining a new co-accused see CAA 1968, s.7, also *R. v Hemmings* [2000] 1 Cr. App. R. 360; *R. v Booker* [2011] EWCA Crim 7, [2011] 1 Cr. App. R. 26. Special rules apply in relation to persons subject to mental health procedures (see CAA 1968, s.8(3), (3A)).

765

CACD may make orders as to the custody of the exhibits pending the retrial.

After the end of two months from the date of the order, such person:

(1) may not be arraigned on an indictment preferred in pursuance of such a direction unless CACD gives leave; and
(2) such person is entitled to apply to CACD to set aside the order and to direct the trial court to enter a judgment of acquittal of the offence for which he was ordered to be retried.

While there is no rule of law which forbids a prosecutor from seeking a second retrial, where two juries have been unable to agree, a second retrial should be confined to the small number of cases in which:

(a) the jury are being invited to address a crime of extreme gravity;
(b) which has undoubtedly occurred; and
(c) in relation to which the evidence that the accused committed the crime remains powerful.

Ultimately it is for the trial judge to decide whether the interests of justice (which require a fair trial that is neither oppressive nor unjust) justify a third trial (*R. v Bell* [2010] EWCA Crim 3; [2010] 1 Cr. App. R. 27.

In dealing with an application, whether under (1) or under (2) CACD may either grant leave to arraign or set aside the order for retrial and direct a judgment and verdict of acquittal.

The procedure is provided by r.68.31.

CACD will not give leave to arraign in these circumstances unless satisfied that:

(a) the prosecution has acted with all due expedition (*R. v Coleman* (1992) 95 Cr. App. R. 345; [1992] Crim. L.R. 305; *R. v Horne, The Times*, February 27, 1992); and
(b) that there is good and sufficient cause for a retrial in spite of the lapse of time since the order under s.7 was made.

The words "with all due expedition" are not to be equated with "all due diligence and expedition" required under POA 1985 (see CUSTODY TIME LIMITS); the former is a less exacting test (*R. v Jones* [2002] EWCA Crim 2284, [2003] 1 Cr. App. R. 20).

Whilst it is impermissible at a retrial to amend the indictment to put the accused in a worse position than he was at the original trial (*R. v Hemmings* [2000] 1 Cr. App. R. 360) it is not necessarily an abuse of process to add a hitherto untried co-conspirator to the indictment on a retrial for conspiracy (*R. v Booker* [2011] EWCA Crim 7, [2011] 1 Cr. App. R. 26).

Evidence

60–003 Evidence at a retrial must be given orally if it was given orally at the original trial, unless:

CAA 1968, Sch.2, paras 1, 1A

(1) all the parties to the retrial agree otherwise;

(2) CJA 2003, s.116 applies (admissibility of hearsay evidence where a witness is unavailable); or

(3) the witness is unavailable to give evidence, otherwise than as mentioned in s.116(2) and CJA 2003, s.114(1)(d) applies (admission of hearsay evidence under residual discretion).

CDA 1998, Sch.3, para.5 (use of depositions) does not apply at a retrial to a deposition read as evidence at the original trial.

The prosecution may be permitted to adduce evidence on a retrial of statements made on oath by the accused at the original trial, to show that he had lied (*R. v Binham* [1991] Crim. L.R. 774).

Sentence

60–004 Where a person ordered to be retried is again convicted on retrial, the judge may pass in respect of the offence any sentence authorised by law:

CAA 1968,
Sch.2, para.2

(1) not being a sentence of greater severity than that passed on the original conviction; and

(2) notwithstanding that, on the date of conviction on retrial, the offender has ceased to be of an age at which such a sentence could otherwise be passed.

Where imprisonment or other detention is imposed in such a case, the sentence begins to run from the time when a like sentence passed at the original trial would have begun to run; but in computing the term of his sentence or the period for which he may be detained thereunder, the judge must have regard to any time:

(a) before the offender's conviction on retrial which would have been disregarded in computing that term or period if the sentence had been passed at the original trial and the original conviction had not been quashed; and

(b) during which he was released on bail under CAA 1968, s.8(2).

CJA 2003, ss.240 and 240A (crediting of periods of remand in custody or on bail subject to certain types of condition) apply to the sentence (see DEALING WITH AN OFFENDER).

B.   Retrial for serious offences under CJA 2003, Pt 10

60–005 CJA 2003, Pt 10 provides a limited exception to the common law double jeopardy rule by permitting retrials in respect of a number of specified very serious offences, whenever committed, where there has been an acquittal and new and compelling evidence comes to light. The police are empowered to re-investigate the case, and the prosecutor is enabled to apply to CACD for the acquittal to be quashed and for a retrial to take place.

The legislative arrangements which abrogate the double jeopardy principle make no distinction between an acquittal following a prosecution by the Crown, or an acquittal following a private prosecution (*R. v Dobson* [2011] EWCA Crim 1256; [2011] 2 Cr. App. R. 8).

The Act sets out measures relating to the re-investigation of such offences, provisions as to arrest, charge and bail and custody; and the procedure for making applications to CACD for retrial. See also the Criminal Justice Act 2003 (Retrial for Serious Offences) Rules 2005 (SI 2005/679) in relation to procedure in CACD.

General

60–006 Where:

CJA 2003, ss.76, 77

(1) a person has been acquitted, whether before or after the passing of CJA 2003:
   (a) of a "qualifying offence" in proceedings:
      (i) on indictment in England and Wales;
      (ii) on appeal against conviction, verdict or finding on indictment in England and Wales; or
      (iii) on appeal from a decision of such an appeal; or
   (b) in proceedings elsewhere than in the United Kingdom of an offence under the law of the place where the proceedings were held, if the commission of the offence as alleged would have amounted to, or included, the commission in the United Kingdom or elsewhere of a "qualifying offence"; and
(2) there is new and compelling evidence, within the meaning of s.78 that that person is guilty of the qualifying offence; and
(3) in all the circumstances it is in the interests of justice for such an order to be made, then, with the written consent of the DPP, the prosecutor may apply to CACD, in the case of (1) for an order quashing that person's acquittal in England and Wales and ordering his retrial for the qualifying offence, and in the case of (2) for a determination whether the acquittal is a bar to that person being retried in England and Wales for the offence, and if it is, for an order that it should not be a bar.

Not more than one application may be made in relation an acquittal.

Definitions

60–007 A person acquitted of an offence in proceedings under the above provisions is treated for the purposes of that provision as also acquitted of any qualifying offence of which he could have been convicted in the proceedings because of the first-mentioned offence being charged in the indictment, except an offence:

CJA 2003, s.75(2)

(1) of which he has been convicted; or
(2) of which he has been found not guilty by reason of insanity; or

CJA 2003, s.75(3), (8)

(3) in respect of which, in proceedings where he has been found to be under a disability (as defined by CP(I)A 1964, s.4), a finding has been made that he did the act or made the omission charged against him.

CJA 2003, s.75(5)

"Qualifying offences" are those set out in CJA 2003, Sch.5, Pt 1, but do not include references to an offence which, at the time of the acquittal was the subject of an order under ss.77(1) or (3) above.

Conduct punishable under the law in force elsewhere than in the United Kingdom is an offence under that law for the purposes of s.62(4) however it is described in that law.

Consent of DPP

60–008 The written consent of the DPP is required before any application may be made to CACD. He may give his consent only if satisfied that:

CJA 2003, s.76(3), (4)

(1) there is evidence as respects which the requirements of s.65 (as to new and compelling evidence) appear to be met; and
(2) it is in the public interest (within the meaning of s.65) for the application to proceed.

Determination by CACD

60–009 A retrial will be ordered only where CACD is satisfied that the requirements of:

CJA 2003, s.77

(1) s.78 as to new and compelling evidence; and
(2) s.79 as to the interests of justice,

are met, otherwise the application will be dismissed.

Where CACD determines that the acquittal is a bar to the person being tried for the qualifying offence, it must, if satisfied that the provisions of ss.78 and 79 are met, make the order applied for, or otherwise make a declaration to the effect that the acquittal is a bar to the person being tried for the offence.

Where CACD determines that the acquittal is not a bar to the person being tried for the qualifying offence, it will make a -declaration to that effect (see, e.g. *R. v Dunlop,* [2006] EWCA Crim 1354, [2007] 1 Cr. App. R.(S.) 8).

"New and compelling" evidence

60–010 The quashing of an acquittal is an exceptional step and can only be ordered if the statutory requirement in relation to the reliability of the new evidence is clearly established, in relation to "new and compelling" evidence that the acquitted person is guilty of the qualifying offence:

CJA 2003, s.78(1), (2), (3)

(1) evidence is "new" if it was not adduced in the proceedings in which the person was acquitted (nor, if those were appeal proceedings, in earlier proceedings to which the appeal related);
(2) evidence is "compelling" if:
    (a) it is reliable (see, e.g. *R. v Miell* [2007] EWCA 3130; [2008] 1 Cr. App. R. 23);
    (b) it is substantial; and
    (c) in the context of the outstanding issues, it appears highly probative of the case against the acquitted person.

CJA 2003, s.78(4), (5) (6), (7)

To be "compelling" evidence does not have to be irresistible, nor is absolute proof of guilt required (*R. v Dobson*, above applying *R. v G (G)* [2009] EWCA Crim 1207, [2009] Crim. L.R. 738). The legislative structure does not suggest that availability of a realistic defence argument, which might serve to undermine the reliability or probative value of the new evidence, precludes an order quashing the acquittal. Provided the new evidence is reliable, substantial and appears to be highly probative, then for the purposes of s.78, it is "compelling".

(See further as to these requirements *R. v B (J)* [2009] EWCA Crim

1036, [2009] Crim. L.R. 736; *R. v G (G) & B (S)* [2009] EWCA Crim 120, [2009] Crim. L.R. 738 and *R. v A* [2008] EWCA Crim 2908; [2009]1 Cr. App. R. 25.)

Note that:

    (i) "the outstanding issues" are the issues in dispute in the proceedings in which the person was acquitted and, if those were appeal proceedings;

    (ii) any other issues remaining in dispute from earlier proceedings against the acquitted person;

    (iii) for the purpose of this provision, it is irrelevant whether any evidence would have been admissible in earlier proceedings against the acquitted person.

The "interests of justice"

60–011 The "interests of justice" for the purposes of these provisions,   CJA 2003, s.79
are to be determined having regard, in particular, to:

    (1) whether existing circumstances make a fair trial unlikely;

    (2) for the purposes of that question and otherwise, the length of time since the qualifying offence was allegedly committed;

    (3) whether it is likely that the new evidence would have been adduced in the earlier proceedings against the acquitted person but for a failure by an officer or a prosecutor to act with due diligence; and

    (4) whether, since those proceedings or, if later, since the commencement of CJA 2003, Pt 10, any officer or prosecutor has failed to act with due diligence or expedition.

The interests of justice test contained in s.79 require attention to be focused on the express statutory criteria provided in that section. Those criteria, however, whilst wide ranging, are not exhaustive. However compelling the new evidence, it is elementary that any second trial should be a fair one (*R. v Dobson*, above).

A reference to an "officer or prosecutor" includes a reference to a person charged with corresponding duties under the law in force elsewhere than in England and Wales, and where the earlier prosecution was conducted by a person other than officer or prosecutor, (3) above applies in relation to that person as well as in relation to a prosecutor.

Application by the prosecutor

60–012 The prosecutor may apply under s.76(1) for the quashing of an acquittal in England and Wales, or under s.76(2) in the case of a person acquitted elsewhere than in the United Kingdom, for a determination that that acquittal is no bar to a trial in England and Wales, or if it is, for an order that it should not be such a bar.

The double jeopardy bar does not ordinarily apply to cases which have been discontinued for reasons other than acquittal.

A prosecutor seeking to make a s.76 application must serve notice of   R.41.2
that application in the form set out PD 2004, Annex D on the Registrar and the acquitted person and that notice must be accompanied, where practicable by:

(1) relevant witness statements which are relied upon as forming new and compelling evidence of guilt of the acquitted person as well as any relevant witness statements from the original trial;

(2) any unused statements which might reasonably be considered capable of undermining the application or of assisting an acquitted person's application to oppose that application (under r.41.3);

(3) a copy of the indictment and paper exhibits from the original trial;

(4) copies of the transcript of the summing up and any other relevant transcripts from the original trial; and

(5) any other documents relied upon to support the application,   R.41.16

and file with the Registrar a witness statement or certificate of service which exhibits a copy of that notice.

An application may be abandoned by the prosecutor before the hearing by serving notice in the form set out in the Practice Direction on the Registrar and the acquitted person.

Response of the acquitted person

60–013   An acquitted person seeking to oppose a s.76 application   R.41.3 must serve a response in the form set out in PD 2004, Annex D on the Registrar and the prosecutor which:

(1) indicates if he is also seeking an order under s.80(6) of the Criminal Justice Act 2003 for:
  (a) the production of any document, exhibit or other thing, or
  (b) a witness to attend for examination and to be examined before CACD; and

(2) exhibits any relevant documents.

The acquitted person must serve that response not more than 28 days after receiving notice under r.41.2, although CACD may extend the period for service under para.(2), either before or after that period expires.

Examination of witnesses or evidence by the CACD

60–014   An application may be made to CACD by a party at least 14   R.41.4 days before the day of the hearing of the s.76 application, in the form set out in PD 2004, Annex D for an order under s.80(6) for:

(1) the production of any document, exhibit or other thing; or

(2) a witness to attend for examination and to be examined before CACD,

sending it to the Registrar with a copy sent to each party to the application.

Such application will need to set out the reasons why the order was not sought from the Court when;

  (a) the notice was served on the Registrar under r.41.2, if the application is made by the prosecutor; or

(b) the response was served on the Registrar under r.41.3, if the application is made by the acquitted person.

If CACD makes an order under s.80(6) of its own motion or on application from the prosecutor, it will serve notice and reasons for that order on all parties to the s.76 application.

Reporting restrictions

60–015   CJA 2003, ss.59 and 70 provide for restrictions on reporting anything done under ss.62–68, and create offences in respect of infringements of those proceedings. See, e.g. *R. v D (Acquitted person: Retrial)* [2006] EWCA Crim 828; [2006] 2 Cr. App. R. 18.

Effect of determination

60–016   Where CACD:

(1) quashes an acquittal under CJA 2003, s.77(1); or
(2) declares an acquittal to be no bar to a prosecution, under CJA 2003, s.77(3),

any subsequent trial will be on an indictment preferred by direction of CACD, and arraignment must take place within two months from the date of the order, unless CACD allows a longer period.

CACD will not extend the period unless satisfied that:

(a) the Crown has acted with due expedition (see above in relation to retrial under CAA 1968, s.7); and — CJA 2003, s.84(1), (2), (3)
(b) there is good and sufficient cause for trial despite the lapse of time since the order under s.77 was made.

The determination of the application may be given at the conclusion of the hearing, or may be reserved. Notice will be given by the Registrar to the parties. Where CACD orders a retrial, the Registrar will serve notice on the Crown Court officer of the appropriate court. — R.41.13

Where the accused is not arraigned within the time limits, he may apply to CACD in the form set out in the Practice Direction, to set aside the order and:

(i) for any direction required for restoring an earlier judgment and verdict of acquittal of the qualifying offence; or — CJA 2003, s.84(4); R.41.14
(ii) in the case of a person acquitted elsewhere than in the United Kingdom, for a declaration to the effect that the acquittal is a bar to his being tried for the qualifying offence. — CJA 2003, s.84(5)

The prosecutor must ensure that arraignment takes place within two months of the date which CACD ordered a retrial. If the acquitted person has not been arraigned before the end of two months after that date, the prosecutor may apply, by serving the form set out in PD 2004. Annex D on the Registrar, for leave to arraign (r.41.5). The acquitted person may apply to CACD to set aside the order.

An indictment under (1) or (2) may relate to more than one offence, or more than one person, and may relate to an offence which, or a person who, is not the subject of an order or declaration under s.77. — CJA 2003, s.84(6), (7)

Evidence on retrial

60–017   The trial will take account of all the evidence in the case. The evidence given must be given orally if it was given orally at the original trial, unless:

(1) all the parties to the trial agree otherwise;
(2) CJA 2003, s.116 (witness unavailable) applies; or
(3) the witness is unavailable to give evidence, otherwise than as mentioned in CJA 2003, s.116(2), and s.114(1)(d) (interests of justice).

At a trial pursuant to an order under s.77(1), CDA 1998, Sch.3, para.5 (use of depositions) does not apply to a deposition read as evidence at the original trial.

The prosecution may be permitted to adduce evidence on a retrial of statements made on oath by the accused at the original trial, to show that he had lied (*R. v Binham* [1991] Crim. L.R. 77).

C.   Bail under CJA 2003, Pt 10

Bail and custody before application

CJA 2003, s.88(4), (5)

60–018   The Act recognises that it may take some time for the police and the Crown to formulate the case for CACD, but this time should not be disproportionate. The power to remand in custody or on bail is given to the Crown Court.

Where a person appears or is brought before the Crown Court in accordance with s.88(1) or (2), the judge may either:

(1) grant bail for him to appear, if notice of application is served on him under s.80(2), before CACD at the hearing of that application; or
(2) remand him in custody to be brought before the Crown Court under s.89(2).

Where bail is granted under this provision, it may be revoked, and the person may be remanded in custody as referred to in (2) above.

If, at the end of the "relevant period" that is:

CJA 2003, s.88(6), (7)

(a) the period of 42 days beginning with the day on which he is granted bail or remanded in custody; or
(b) that period as extended or further extended under s.88(8) below,

no notice of application under CJA 2003, s.76(1) or (2) in relation to that person has been given under s.80(1), that person:

(i)   if on bail subject to a duty to appear, ceases to be under that duty and to any conditions of that bail; or
(ii) if in custody on remand under ss.88(4)(b) or (5) must be released immediately without bail.

As to applications for bail, see r.41.7.

Procedure; hearing in the Crown Court

R.41.5

60–019   Where a person is to appear, or be brought, before the Crown Court pursuant to CJA 2003, ss.88 or 89, rr.19.18, 19.22 and 19.23 (see

BAIL) apply as if there were an application for bail under r.19.18(1) but with the substitution for r.18 of a requirement that the prosecutor serve notice of the need for such a hearing on the Crown Court officer.

Where a person is to appear or be brought before the Crown Court pursuant to s.88 or 89 the judge may order that the person shall be released from custody on entering into a recognisance, with or without sureties, or giving other security before the Crown Court officer, or any other person authorised by virtue of MCA 1980, s.119(1) to take a recognisance where a magistrates' court having power to take the recognisance has, instead of taking it, fixed the amount in which the principal and his sureties, if any, are to be bound.

The court officer will forward a copy of any record made in pursuance of BA 1976, s.5(1) to the Registrar.

Extension of the "relevant period"

60–020 A judge may, on the application of the prosecutor, extend or further extend the "relevant period" until a specified date, but only where he is satisfied that:

R.41.5

(1) the need for the extension is due to some good and sufficient cause; and
(2) the prosecutor has acted with all due diligence and expedition.

(As to "good and sufficient cause" and "diligence and expedition" see ABUSE OF PROCESS.)

R.41.6

Further provisions regarding bail and custody in the Crown Court.

The prosecutor may only apply to extend or further extend the relevant period before it expires and that application must be served on the Crown Court officer and the acquitted person.

Bail and custody before hearing

60–021 Where notice of application is given under CJA 2003, s.80(1), then in relation to the person to whom that application relates, if he:

CJA 2003, s.89(1), (2), (3) (4), (5)

(1) is in custody under s.88(4)(b) or (5) he must be brought before a judge of the Crown Court as soon as practicable and, in any event within 48 hours after the notice is given;
(2) is not in custody under s.88(4)(b) or (5) the Crown Court may, on application by the prosecutor, issue:
   (a) a summons requiring him to appear before CACD at the hearing of the application; or
   (b) a warrant for his arrest,

and a warrant may be issued at any time even though a summons has previously been issued.

The summons, or a subsequent direction of the Crown Court, may specify the time and place at which that person must appear, and the time and place may be varied from time to time by a direction of the Crown Court.

A prosecutor's application for a summons or a warrant under s.89(3) (a) or (b) must be served on the court officer and the acquitted person (r.41.6(2)).

Appearance before the Crown Court

60–022   A person arrested under a warrant under s.89(3)(b) must be brought before a judge of the Crown Court as soon as practicable and in any event within 48 hours after his arrest (and SCA 1981, s.81(5) giving the magistrates' court as an alternative, does not apply).

The judge must, where a person is brought before him under either s.89(2) or (6) either:

CJA 2003, s.89(6), (7)(8), (9)

(1) remand him in custody to be brought before CACD at the hearing of the application; or

(2) grant bail for him to appear before the CACD at the hearing.

Bail granted by the Crown Court may be revoked, and the person remanded in custody in accordance with s.89(7)(b).

Revocation of bail

60–023   Where bail is revoked under CJA 2003, Pt 10, and the person concerned is not before the Crown Court when his bail is revoked, a judge must order him to surrender himself forthwith to the custody of the court, and where he surrenders in compliance with that order, the judge must remand him in custody.

CJA 2003, s.91(1), (2)

Procedure in CACD

60–024   The procedure in CACD is governed by rr.41.7–41.12. As to applications by the DPP under CJA 2003, s.82, to restrict publication, see rr.41.8–41.9.

61. SENDING ETC. FOR TRIAL

Quick guide

General

61–001 Until CJA 2003, Sch.3 comes into force, cases are moved from the magistrates' courts to the Crown Court for trial in four ways, namely in the case of:

(1) offences triable either way, by committal proceedings under MCA 1980, s.6;
(2) certain offences involving children, by notice of transfer under CJA 1991, s.53, Sch.3;
(3) serious fraud cases, by notice of transfer under CJA 1987, s.4;
(4) indictable-only offences, under the provisions of CDA 1998, ss.51 and following.

A judge of the Crown Court may be required to deal with applications for dismissal in cases arising under (2)–(4) above.

A.   Committal for trial of summary offences: s.41

61–002 Where a magistrates' court commits a person to the Crown Court for trial for an offence triable either way, or a number of such offences, it may also (on the same occasion—*R. v Dodson* [2009] EWCA Crim 1830, [2010] Crim. L.R. 230) commit to the Crown Court for trial proceedings against that person for any summary offence with which he is also charged, and which: *CJA 1988, s.41(1)(3)*

(1) is punishable with imprisonment or carries obligatory or discretionary RT disqualification; and
(2) arises out of circumstances that appear to be the same as, or connected with, those giving rise to the either-way offence(s),

whether or not evidence relating to the summary offence(s) appears on the papers. (In the magistrates' court the information charging the summary offence(s) will be treated as if it had been adjourned under MCA 1980, s.10 *sine die*.)

Committal for trial cannot be challenged in the Crown Court, but judicial review will lie in an appropriate case (see *R. v Miall* (1992) 94 Cr App R 258).

Notice under s.41

61–003 The magistrates' court will give notice both to the accused and to the Crown Court stating which of the either-way offences appears to arise out of circumstances which are the same as, or connected with, those giving rise to the summary offence(s).

CJA 1988, s.41(2)

Crown Court procedure

61–004 Liability to be dealt with for a s.41 offence does not arise unless the accused is convicted of the either-way offence. If he is not convicted, or the Crown offers no evidence on the either-way offence, he cannot be required to answer the summary offence(s).

CJA 1988, s.41(2)

A s.41 offence is not put to the accused unless he is convicted on the indictment of the either-way offence.

If he is convicted:

(1) the judge considers whether the preconditions for committal of the summary offence(s) are made out;

(2) if the judge is satisfied as to (1), the substance of the summary offence(s) is put to the accused and he is called upon to plead;

(3) if the accused pleads guilty to the summary offence(s) he may be dealt with in any manner in which the magistrates could have dealt with him for the offence(s) (see *R. v Avbunudje* [1999] 2 Cr. App. R. (S.) 189);

(4) if the accused does not plead guilty to the summary offence(s), any powers of the Crown Court to deal with the accused in respect of the summary offence(s) cease; and

(5) if the Crown indicates that it does not wish to submit evidence on a summary offence the judge will dismiss it.

The magistrates' court will be informed of the outcome of the proceedings (CJA 1988, s.41(10)).

B.   Notice of transfer procedure

(1)   General

Effect of notice

61–005 The effect of a notice of transfer, whether given under CJA 1991, s.53 or under CJA 1987, s.4 is to:

CJA 1987, s.5(6), (7)

(1) deprive the magistrates' court of its jurisdiction to conduct a preliminary enquiry into the facts of the case;

(2) restrict the powers of the magistrates' court in dealing with applications for bail, public funding, enlargement of recognisances and the making of witness orders; and

(3) impose on the Crown Court the management of the case.

The notice will specify the proposed place of trial and the charge(s) to which it relates.

Remand, necessity for appearance

61–006 Matters of remand and bail are dealt with in the magistrates' court, but where a notice is given after the person to whom it relates has been remanded on bail to appear before a magistrates' court on an appointed day:

(1) the requirement that he appear ceases on the giving of the notice, unless the notice states that it shall continue;

(2) if the requirement ceases, it is his duty to appear before the Crown Court at the place specified in the notice as the proposed place of trial, or at any place substituted for it by a direction under SCA 1981, s.76 (see ALLOCATION AND DISTRIBUTION OF CASES);

(3) if the notice states that the requirement is to continue, then where the person to whom the notice relates appears before the magistrates' court, that court may grant bail, and enlarge the recognisances of any surety, so that the surety is bound to secure the appearance of the person charged before the Crown Court.

An application for dismissal of the charge or charges is made to a judge of the Crown Court under r.13.1 (see 61–027, below).

(2) Certain cases involving children

General

61–007 If a person has been charged with an offence to which CJA 1988, s.32(2) applies (sexual offences and offences involving violence or cruelty), and the DPP is of opinion that:

CJA 1991, s.53(1)–(4), Sch.3, para.1

(1) the evidence of the offence would be sufficient for proceedings against a person charged to be transferred for trial;

(2) a child who is alleged:

  (a) to be the person against whom the offence was committed; or

  (b) to have witnessed the commission of the offence, will be called as a witness at the trial; and

(3) for the purpose of avoiding any prejudice to the welfare of the child the case should be taken over and proceeded with without delay by the Crown Court;

notice of transfer certifying that opinion, and specifying the charge or charges to which it relates, and any other requisite information, may be served by or on behalf of the DPP on the magistrates' court in whose jurisdiction the offence has been charged.

This must happen not later than the time at which the DPP would be required to serve a notice of the prosecution's case under MCA 1980, s.5, and the functions of the magistrates' court cease except for the making of ancillary orders. The decision is not subject to appeal.

SENDING ETC. FOR TRIAL

Definition of "child"

61–008 For the purposes of s.53, "child" means, in the case of an offence falling within:

CJA 1987, s.4(1)(c)

(1) CJA 1988, s.32(2)(a) or (b), under 14 years of age, or if he was under that age when a video recording (under s.32A(2) of that Act) was made in respect of him, under 15;

CJA 1991, s.53(6)(7)

(2) CJA 1988, s.32(2)(c), under 17, or if under that age when the recording was made, under 18.

References to such offences include offences of attempting or conspiring to commit them, or aiding, abetting, etc. their commission.

In *R. v T & K* [2001] 1 Cr. App. R. 446, CACD stated that notices of transfer should not be given in the case of an accused under 18 unless the DPP concluded that the justices would be likely to commit on account of the seriousness of the charge (MCA 1980, s.24(1)) and that a statement to that effect should be included in the notice.

Application for dismissal

61–009 Where notice of transfer has been given, any person to whom it relates, may, at any time before he is arraigned (and whether or not an indictment has been preferred against him), apply, orally or in writing, to the Crown Court sitting at the place specified by the notice of transfer as the proposed place of trial, for the charge, or any of the charges in the case, to be dismissed.

CJA 1991, Sch.6, paras5(1)–(6)

The judge must dismiss a charge, and accordingly quash a count relating to it in any indictment preferred against the applicant, if it appears to him that the evidence against the applicant would not be sufficient for a jury properly to convict him.

Dismissal of a charge against the applicant has the same effect as a refusal by examining justices to commit, save that *no* further proceedings may be brought on the dismissed charge except by means of the preferment of a voluntary bill of indictment.

Note that:

(1) an oral application for dismissal may not be made unless the applicant has given written notice of his intention to do so to the Crown Court at the place specified by the notice of transfer as the proposed place of trial; and

(2) oral evidence may be given on an application only with the leave of the judge or by his order, and the judge will give leave only if it appears to him, having regard to any matters stated in the application, that the interests of justice require him to do so. If he does give leave or make an order permitting or requiring a person to give oral evidence, and that person does not do so, the judge may disregard any document indicating the evidence that he might have given.

As to procedure, see r.13, at 16–027 and following, below.

Reporting restrictions

61–010 As to reporting restrictions, see REPORTING AND ACCESS RESTRICTIONS.

CJA 1991, Sch.6, para.5(1)–(3)

(3) Serious fraud cases

Giving of notice

61–011 A notice of transfer may be given to a magistrates' court, other than in a case to which CDA 1998, s.48 applies, where: CJA 1987, s.4

(1) a person has been charged with an indictable offence;
(2) in the opinion of a "designated authority" or one of its officers the evidence of the offence would be sufficient for the person charged to be committed to the Crown Court; and
(3) it reveals a case of such seriousness or complexity, that it is appropriate that the management of the case be taken over by the Crown Court without delay.

A "designated authority" includes the DPP, the DSFO, the DRCP and the Secretary of State. The decision to give notice of transfer is not subject to appeal, or liable to be questioned in any court (CJA 1987, s.4(3)).

The notice must be given not later than the time at which the authority would be required to serve a notice of the prosecution case under MCA 1980, s.5, and that court's functions then cease in relation to the case except as provided by CJA 1987, ss.5(3), 5(7A) and (8), and by AJA 1999 (public funding).

The notice will specify:

(a) the proposed place of trial; and
(b) the charge(s) to which it relates.

CJA 1987, s.5(1)(2)

As to the places of trial for such offences, see ALLOCATION AND DISTRIBUTION OF BUSINESS.

Dismissal of transferred charge(s)

61–012 Where notice of transfer has been given, any person to whom it relates, at any time before he is arraigned (and whether or not an indictment has been preferred against him), may apply, orally or in writing, to the Crown Court sitting at the place specified by the notice of transfer as the proposed place of trial, for the charge, or any of the charges in the case, to be dismissed. CJA 1987, s.6

The judge may dismiss a charge, and quash a count relating to it in any indictment preferred against the applicant, if it appears to him that the evidence against the applicant would not be sufficient for a jury properly to convict him.

As to procedure, see r.13, at 16–027 and following, below. CJA 1987, s.6

Dismissal of the charge(s) against the applicant has the same effect as a refusal by examining justices to commit, save that no further proceedings may be brought on a dismissed charge except by means of the preferment of a voluntary bill of indictment.

Oral application

61–013 An oral application for dismissal may not be made unless the applicant has given written notice in the prescribed form to the Crown Court at the place specified by the notice of transfer as the proposed place of trial. CJA 1987, s.6(2)

As to procedure, see r.13, at 16–027 and following, below.

Oral evidence

61–014   Oral evidence may be given on an application for dismissal only with the leave of the judge or by his order, and he will give leave or make an order only if it appears to him having regard to any matters stated in the application for leave, that the interests of justice require him to do so.

CJA 1987, s.6(3), (4)

If he does give leave, or make an order, permitting or requiring a person to give oral evidence and that person does not do so, the judge may disregard any document indicating the evidence that he might have given.

C.   Sending for trial CDA 1998, s.51
(1)   Introduction

General

61–015   Where:

(1) a person aged 18 or over, appears or is brought before a magistrate's court, charged with an offence triable only on indictment, the court must send him immediately to the Crown Court for trial for:

CDA 1998, s.51(1)–(6), (12)

   (a) that offence; and
   (b) any either-way or summary offence with which he is charged, and which appears to be related to the indictable-only offence, and in the case of a summary offence, is punishable with imprisonment or involves obligatory or discretionary RT disqualification;
(2) such a person, who has been sent for trial, is subsequently brought before a magistrates' court charged with an either-way or summary offence which fulfils those conditions, he may be sent forthwith to the Crown Court;
(3) another person aged 18 or over appears or is brought before the magistrates' court on the same occasion, charged jointly with him with an either-way offence, and that offence appears to be related to the indictable-only offence, that person may be sent to the Crown Court with him;
(4) the magistrates send a person aged 18 or over to the Crown Court in either of the above circumstances, they may send with him, any child or young person brought before them on the same occasion, charged jointly with the adult in the indictable-only offence and on any summary or either-way offence which fulfils the requisite conditions.

An either-way offence is "related to" an indictable-only offence if the charge for the either-way offence could be joined in the same indictment as the indictable-only offence. A summary offence is "related to" an indictable-only offence if it arises out of circumstances which are connected with those giving rise to the indictable-only offence.

Listing of first Crown Court appearance

61–016 A Crown Court officer to whom notice has been given under CDA 1998, s.51(7) will list the first appearance in the Crown Court of the person to whom the notice relates in accordance with any directions given by the magistrates' court.

R.12.2

Where a surety has entered into a recognizance in the magistrates' court in respect of a case committed or sent to the Crown Court and where the bail order or recognizance refers to attendance at the first hearing in the Crown Court, the accused will be reminded by the listing officer that the surety should attend the first hearing in the Crown Court in order to provide further recognizance. The court should also notify sureties of the dates of the hearing at the Crown Court at which the accused is ordered to appear in as far in advance as possible (see the observations of Parker L.J. in *R. v Reading CC Ex p. Bello* (1991) 92 Cr. App. R. 303).

PD 2004, Annex F, 8.4

(2)   Application for dismissal

General

61–017 A person sent for trial in such circumstances, on any charge or charges may, at any time:

CDA 1998, s.52(6), Sch.3, para.2(1)(2)(3)

(1) after he has been served with copies of the documents containing the evidence on which the charge or charges are based; and
(2) before he is arraigned (and whether or not the indictment has been preferred against him),

apply orally, or in writing, to the Crown Court sitting at the place specified in the notice served upon him (under s.48(5)) for the charge, or any of the charges in the case to be dismissed.

Procedure on application

61–018 No oral application may be made unless the applicant has given written notice to the court of his intention to make the application. Note that:

CDA 1998, s.52(6),Sch.3, para.2(4)(5)

(1) notice in writing of intention to apply orally or any written application must be served:
   (a) on the court no later than 14 days after service of the documents containing the prosecution case; and
   (b) on the prosecution and any co-accused;
(2) application to extend the time limit in (1) may be made before or after it has expired, in writing to the court, specifying the grounds, a copy being sent to the prosecutor and to any joint accused;
(3) any written application to dismiss must be accompanied by a copy of any statement or other document, and must identify any article on which the applicant relies, a copy being given to the prosecutor and to any joint accused;
(4) a notice of application to dismiss must specify the charge or charges to which it relates and state whether the leave of the judge is sought to adduce oral evidence, indicating what witnesses it is proposed to call at the hearing;

(5) the prosecutor may, within seven days of service by the defence of the notice in (4) make similar applications to call oral evidence, or to have an oral hearing where a written application has been made;

(6) oral evidence may be given on the application only with the leave of the judge, or by his order; he will give leave, or make an order, only if it appears to him, having regard to any matters stated in the application for leave, that the interests of justice require him to do so;

(7) if the judge does give leave, or make an order requiring a person to give evidence, and that person does not do so, the judge may disregard any document indicating the evidence he might have given;

CDA 1998, s.57(6), Sch. 3, para.2(2)(6)

The judge will dismiss a charge (and accordingly quash any count relating to it in any indictment preferred against the applicant), which is the subject of the application, if it appears to him that the evidence against the applicant would not be sufficient for a jury properly to convict him.

Reporting restrictions
61–019 Reporting restrictions similar to those imposed on committal proceedings are imposed in such a case.

As to reporting restrictions, see REPORTING AND ACCESS RESTRICTIONS

CDA 1998, s.52(6), Sch.3, para.3

(3) Dealing with summary offences

General
61–020 Where the magistrates' court has sent a person for trial under s.42 for offences which include a summary offence, the procedure at the Crown Court is as follows:

CDA 1998, s.52(6), Sch.3, para.6

(1) if that person is convicted on indictment, the judge will consider whether the summary offence is "related" (see above) to the offence or offences triable only on indictment;

(2) if he finds that it is, the substance of the offence will be put to the accused and he will be asked to plead it;

(3) if the accused pleads guilty, he will be convicted, the judge's powers of sentencing being limited to those of the magistrates' court;

(4) if the accused does not plead guilty, the Crown Court ceases to have powers in the matter, unless the prosecution inform the judge that they do not wish to offer any evidence on the charge, when he may dismiss it.

Summary offences under CJA 1988, s.40
61–021 If the summary offence is one to which s.40 applies, the Crown Court may exercise in relation to it, the powers conferred by that section, but where the accused is tried on indictment for such an offence, the functions of the court under this paragraph cease.

CDA 1998, s.52(6), Sch.3, para.6(8)

Section 40 does not permit the prosecutor to add a summary-only charge to an indictment as an alternative count (*R. v. Hill* [2010] EWCA Crim 2999).

No indictable-only offence remaining

61–022 Where a person has been sent for trial in this manner, but has not been arraigned, and is charged on an indictment which, as a result of amendment, or a successful application to dismiss or for any other reason, no longer includes any offence triable on indictment only, the court will proceed as follows:

CDA 1998,
s.52(6), Sch.3,
paras7, 8, 9

(1) each count of the indictment charging an offence triable either-way, will be read to the accused;
(2) he will be informed in ordinary language, that in relation to each of those offences he may indicate whether, if it were to proceed to trial, he would plead guilty or not guilty, and that if he pleads guilty he will be treated as if he had pleaded guilty on arraignment;
(3) he will then be asked whether, if the offence in question were to proceed to trial, he would plead guilty or not guilty;
(4) if he indicates that he would plead guilty, the court will proceed as if had been arraigned on the count in question and had pleaded guilty;
(5) if he indicates that he would plead not guilty, or fails to indicate how he would plead, the judge will consider whether the offence is more suitable for summary trial or for trial on indictment.

Where, in the exceptional case, the judge considers that because of his disorderly conduct before the court, it is not practicable for the proceedings to be conducted in the presence of the accused, and he considers that the proceedings should be conducted in his absence:

(a) provided that the accused is legally represented;
(b) the judge will cause each count of the indictment charging an either-way offence to be read to the representative; and
(c) that representative will be asked whether, if the offence were to proceed to trial the accused would plead guilty or not guilty;
(d) depending on the representative's reply, the ordinary procedure (outlined above) will apply.

Whether more suitable for trial summarily or on indictment

61–023 In considering the question whether an offence is more suitable for summary trial or for trial on indictment, the judge must:

CDA 1998,
s.52(6), Sch.3,
para.9

(1) first afford the prosecutor, and then the accused, an opportunity to make representations as to which mode of trial would be more suitable; and
(2) in considering the question, have regard to:
    (a) any representations so made;
    (b) the nature of the case, and whether the circumstances make it one of a serious character;
    (c) whether the punishment which a magistrates' court would have power to impose for it would be adequate;

(d) any other circumstances which appear to the judge to make it more suitable for the case to be dealt with in one way rather than the other.

Special provisions apply (see Sch.3, para.14) in the case of "schedule offences".

61–024 Where:

(1) the judge considers that such an offence is more suitable for summary trial, he will:

    (a) explain to the accused in ordinary language that it appears to him more suitable that he be tried summarily for the offence, and that he can either consent to be so tried, or if he wishes, be tried by a jury; and

    (b) explain that if he is tried summarily and convicted, he may still be committed for sentence to the Crown Court (under MCA 1980, s.38) if the lower court is of such opinion as is mentioned in s.38(2); and

    (c) ask the accused whether he wishes to be tried summarily or by a jury;

    (d) remit him for trial to a magistrates' court acting for the place from which he was sent for trial, if the accused indicates that he wishes to be tried summarily. If the accused does not give such an indication, the Crown will retain its functions and proceed accordingly;

(2) the judge considers that the offence is more suitable for trial on indictment he will tell the accused that he has so decided and the Crown Court will retain its functions and proceed accordingly.

CDA 1998, s.52(6), Sch.3, para.11

Powers of Law Officers

61–025 Where the prosecution is being carried on by the Attorney General, the Solicitor-General or the DPP, and he applies for an offence which may be tried on indictment to be so tried, the Crown Court will retain its functions in any event. The power of the DPP under this provision is not to be exercised except with the consent of the Attorney-General.

CDA 1998, s.52(6), Sch.3, para.12

Power to proceed in absence of accused

61–026 The judge may deal with any of the procedures under Sch. 3, paras 9–14 in the absence of the accused, provided he is legally represented by a representative who signifies to the court the accused's consent to such a course, and the judge is satisfied that there is good reason for proceeding in the accused's absence. In such a case, any explanations and questions to, and any consents to be given by, the accused will be given to and answered by the legal representative.

CDA 1998, s.52(6), Sch.3, para.15

(4)   Application for dismissal; procedure

General

61–027   CPR 2011, r.13 governs the procedure in all cases where: R.13.1

(1) notice of transfer has been given under CJA 1987 or CJA 1991; or

(2) a person has been sent for trial under CDA 1998;

and the person concerned proposes to apply orally under:

  (a) CJA 1987, s.6(1);
  (b) CJA 1991, Sch.6, para.5(1); or
  (c) CDA 1998, Sch.3, para.2(1),

for any charge in the case to be dismissed.
  Note that:

  (i) "notice of transfer" means a notice referred to in CJA 1987, s.4(1) or CJA 1991, s.53(1); and
  (ii) "the prosecution" means the authority by or on behalf of whom notice of transfer was given under the Acts or the authority by or on behalf of whom documents were served under CDA 1998, Sch.3, para.1.

Requirement of notice

61–028   Such person must give notice of his intention in writing to the   R.13.2.(1)
Crown Court officer at the place specified by the notice of transfer under
the 1987 or 1991 Acts or the notice given under s.51(7) of the 1998 Act
as the proposed place of trial. Notice of intention to make an application
under the 1987 or 1991 Acts must be in the forms prescribed in PD
2004, Annex D.
  Notice of intention to make an application must be given in the case
of an application to dismiss charges:

(1) transferred under the 1987 Act, not later than 28 days after the day on which notice of transfer was given;

(2) transferred under the 1991 Act, not later than 14 days after the   R.13.2(2)
day on which notice of transfer was given; and

(3) sent under the 1998 Act, not later than 14 days after the day on which the documents were served under para.1 of Sch.3 to that Act,

and a copy of the notice must be given at the same time to the prosecu-   R.12.2(3), (4)
tion and to any person to whom the notice of transfer relates or with
whom the applicant for dismissal is jointly charged.

Extension of time

61–029   The time for giving notice may be extended, before it expires,   R.13.2(5)
by the Crown Court, on an application in writing, specifying the
grounds for it, and sent to the Crown Court officer, a copy being given
at the same time to the prosecution and to any other person to whom the
notice of transfer relates or with whom the applicant for dismissal is
jointly charged.
  Notice will be given by the Crown Court to all parties, in the form   R.13.2(6)

prescribed in PD 2004, Annex D as appropriate, of the judge's decision as to an extension of time.

Notice of intention to make an oral application for dismissal under any of the Acts mentioned above must be accompanied by a copy of any material on which the applicant relies, and the notice must:

(1) specify the charge or charges to which it relates; and
(2) state whether leave is sought to adduce oral evidence on the application, indicating the witnesses it is proposed to call; and
(3) in the case of a transfer under CJA 1991 (certain offences involving children) confirm in relation to each witness that he is not a child to whom Sch.6, para.5(5) of the Act applies.   R.13.2(7), (8)

The Crown Court officer will give notice in the same form, as appropriate, of the judge's decision as to oral evidence being given, and indicating what witnesses are to be called, if applicable, and the appropriate officer will list the application for hearing.

Written application

61–030 An application may be made for dismissal under: R.13.3(1)–(3)

(1) CJA 1987, s.6(1);
(2) CJA 1991, Sch.6, para.5(1); or
(3) CDA 1998, Sch.3, para.2(1),

and may be made without an oral hearing. It must be made in writing in the form at PD 2004, Annex D and sent to the Crown Court officer, accompanied by a copy of any statement or other document, and identifying any article, on which the applicant relies. A copy of the application, and of any accompanying documents must be given, at the same   R.13.3(4) time, to the prosecution and to any other person to whom the notice of transfer relates, or with whom the applicant is jointly charged.

Such application must be made not later than:

(a) 28 days after the day on which notice of transfer was given under (1) above;
(b) 14 days after the day on which notice of transfer was given under (2) above; or
(c) 14 days after the day on which documents required by CDA   R.13.4(1), (2) 1998, Sch.3 were served,

unless the time for making the application is extended, either before or after it expires, by the Crown Court, in which case rr.13.2(4) and (5) (see 16–029, above) apply as if references to giving notice of intention to make an oral application were references to making a written one.

Prosecution reply

61–031 The prosecution may apply to the Crown Court under CJA 1987, s.6(3), CJA 1991, Sch.6, para.5(4), or CDA 1998, Sch.3, para.2(4):

(1) not later than seven days from the date of service of notice of intention to apply orally for the dismissal of any charge contained in a notice of transfer or based on documents served under

CDA 1998, Sch.3, para.1, the prosecution may apply for leave to adduce oral evidence at the hearing of the application, indicating what witnesses it proposes to call; and

(2) not later than seven days from the date of receiving a copy of an application for dismissal under r.13.3, for an oral hearing of the application.

Such applications must be served on the Crown Court officer in writing in the form prescribed in PD 2004, Annex D and, in the case of (1) above must state whether the leave of the judge is sought to adduce oral evidence and, if so, must indicate what witnesses it is proposed to call.   `R.13.4(5)`

Where, having received the material specified (in r.13.2 or, as the case may be, r.13.3), the prosecution proposes to adduce in reply, any written comments or any further evidence, they must serve on the Crown Court officer:

(a) any such comments, copies of the statements or other documents outlining the evidence of any proposed witnesses;

(b) copies of any further documents; and

(c) in the case of an application to dismiss charges transferred under the 1991 Act, copies of any video recordings which it is proposed to tender in evidence,

not later than 14 days from the date of receiving the material, and must, at the same time serve copies on the applicant for dismissal and any other person to whom the notice of transfer relates or with whom the applicant is jointly charged. In the case of a defendant acting in person, copies of video recordings need not be served but must be made available for viewing by him.

Leave to adduce oral evidence

61–032   Where leave is sought to adduce oral evidence under CJA 1991, Sch.6, para.5(4), the application should confirm in relation to each such witness that he is not a child to whom CJA 1991, Sch.6, para.5(5) applies. In proceedings under the 1987 or 1991 Acts, such an application must be in the form set out in PD 2004, Annex D.   `Rr.13.4(1)–(3)`

Notice of the judge's determination, indicating what witnesses, if any, are to be called will be served in writing by the Crown Court officer on in the form set out at PD 2004, Annex D: `R.13.4(4)`

(1) the prosecution;

(2) the applicant for dismissal; and

(3) any other party to whom the notice of transfer relates or with whom the applicant for dismissal is jointly charged. In proceedings under the 1987 or 1991 Acts.

Extension of time

61–033   The time for: `R.13.4(6), (7)`

(1) making an application in pursuance of r.13;

(2) serving any material on the Crown Court officer,

may be extended, either before or after it expires, by the Crown Court, on application. Such application must be made in writing and must be served on the Crown Court officer, a copy being served at the same time on the applicant for dismissal and on any other person to whom the notice of transfer relates or with whom the applicant for dismissal is jointly charged. In proceedings under the 1987 or 1991 Acts an application must be in the form set out in PD 2004, Annex D.

Determination of applications; supplementary

61–034   Note that:

(1) a judge may grant leave for a witness to give oral evidence on an application for dismissal notwithstanding that notice of intention to call the witness has not been given in accordance with r.13.5(1); and

(2) where an application for dismissal is determined otherwise than at an oral hearing, the Crown Court officer will, as soon as practicable, send to all the parties to the case written notice of the outcome of the application. In proceedings under the 1987 and 1991 Acts the notice will be in the form prescribed in PD 2004, Annex D.

As to reporting restrictions, see REPORTING AND ACCESS RESTRICTIONS.

62. SERIOUS CRIME PREVENTION ORDERS

Powers

62–001   Where a judge of the Crown Court is dealing with a person aged 18 or over (see 62–009 below) who:

SCA 2007, s,2(1)-(3)

(1) has been convicted by or before a magistrates' court of having committed a serious offence in England and Wales and has been committed to the Crown Court to be dealt with; or

(2) has been convicted by or before the Crown Court of having committed a serious offence in England and Wales,

he may, in addition to dealing with that person in relation to the offence, to make an SPO if he has reasonable grounds to believe that the order would protect the public by preventing, restricting or disrupting involvement by that person in serious crime in England and Wales.

SCA 2007, ss.19(1)(2)(7)(8); SI 2008/755

Such an order is ancillary and may be made only:

(a) in addition to a sentence imposed in respect of the offence concerned; or

(b) in addition to an order discharging the person conditionally.

The order may contain such prohibitions, restrictions or requirements, and such other terms, as the judge considers appropriate see 62–007 for the purpose of protecting the public in the manner set out above, subject to the safeguards set out below at 62–009—62–012. As to a form of application by the prosecutor, see PD 2004, Annex D.

Procedure is governed by r.50 (civil behaviour orders after verdict or finding) as to which see ANTI-SOCIAL BEHAVIOUR ORDERS.

General

62–002   When considering making such an order, the judge is concerned with future risk. There must be a real, or significant, risk (not a bare possibility) that the offender will commit further serious offences. The principles set out in *R. v Mee* [2004] EWCA Crim 629, [2004] 2 Cr. App. R. (S.) 81 in relation to travel restriction orders under CJPOA 2001, s.31 (see TRAVEL RESTRICTION ORDERS) apply, namely that;

(1) such orders can be made only for the purpose for which the power is given by statute; and

(2) they must be proportionate.

The latter requirement follows from the requirements of ECHR, art.8 (see *EB (Kosovo) v Home Secretary* [2008] UKHL 41, [2008] 4 All E.R. 28). It is not enough that the order may have some public benefit in preventing, restricting or disrupting the offender's involvement in serious crime, the interference which it would create with his freedom of action must be justified by the order and must be commensurate with the risk (*R. v Hancox* [2010] EWCA Crim 102; [2010] 2 Cr. App. R. (S.) 74).

SERIOUS CRIME PREVENTION ORDERS

Failure to comply

62–003   A person who, without reasonable excuse, fails to comply with an order, commits an offence, punishable:

SCA 2007, ss.25, 26

(1) on summary conviction, with imprisonment for a term not exceeding 12 months or to a fine not exceeding the statutory maximum or to both; and

(2) on conviction on indictment, to imprisonment for a term not exceeding five years or to a fine or to both; and

the court before which a person is convicted of such an offence may order the forfeiture of anything in his possession at the time of the offence which the judge considers to have been involved in the offence, provided that before making such an order he gives an opportunity to make representations to any person (in addition to the convicted person) who claims to be the owner of that thing or otherwise to have an interest in it.

Where a forfeiture order is made it may include such other provisions as the judge considers necessary for giving effect to the forfeiture, including provision relating to the retention, handling, destruction or other disposal of what is forfeited.

The forfeiture order must not be made so as to come into force before there is no further possibility (ignoring any right to appeal out of time) of the order being varied or set aside on appeal.

"Involvement in serious crime"

62–004   For the purposes of SCA 2007, a person has been involved in serious crime in England and Wales if he:

(1) has committed a serious offence in England and Wales;

(2) has facilitated the commission by another person of a serious offence in England and Wales; or

(3) has conducted himself in a way that was likely to facilitate the commission by himself or another person of a serious offence in England and Wales (whether or not such an offence was committed).

"A serious offence in England and Wales" means an offence under the law of England and Wales which, at the time when the court is considering the matter in question:

(a) is specified, or falls within a description specified, in Pt 1 of Sch.1 of the Act; or

(b) is one which, in the particular circumstances of the case, the judge considers to be sufficiently serious to be treated for the purposes of the application or matter as if it were so specified.

An order is not restricted to violent or sexual crimes and may be imposed on a single offender operating alone (fraud) (*R. v. Hancox*, above); the test is clear, and depends on whether there are reasonable grounds to believe that an order would prevent, restrict or disrupt involvement in serious crime (which by virtue of the 2007 Act, Sch.1, para.7, is defined as including fraud).

"Involvement in serious crime in England and Wales" is any one or more of the following:

(i) the commission of a serious offence in England and Wales;
(ii) conduct which facilitates the commission by another person of a serious offence in England and Wales;
(iii) conduct which is likely to facilitate the commission, by the person whose conduct it is or another person, of a serious offence in England and Wales (whether or not such an offence is committed).

"Serious crime elsewhere than in England and Wales"

62–005   A person has been involved in serious crime elsewhere than in England and Wales if he:

SCA 2007, s.2(4)(5)(7)

(1) has committed a serious offence in a country outside England and Wales;
(2) has facilitated the commission by another person of a serious offence in a country outside England and Wales; or
(3) has conducted himself in a way that was likely to facilitate the commission by himself or another person of a serious offence in a country outside England and Wales (whether or not such an offence was committed).

"A serious offence in a country outside England and Wales" means an offence under the law of a country outside England and Wales which, at the time when the court is considering the matter in question:

(a) would be an offence under the law of England and Wales if committed in or as regards England and Wales; and
(b) either:
 (i) would be an offence which is specified, or falls within a description specified, in Pt 1 of Sch.1 if committed in or as regards England and Wales; or
 (ii) is conduct which, in the particular circumstances of the case, the judge considers to be sufficiently serious to be treated for the purposes of the application or matter as if it meets the test in sub-paragraph (i).

An act punishable under the law of a country outside the United Kingdom constitutes an offence under that law for the purposes of subsection (5), however it is described in that law.

Proof of involvement

62–006   In considering whether a person has committed a serious offence, the judge *must* decide that the person has committed the offence if he has been convicted of it and the conviction has not been quashed on appeal nor has the person been pardoned of the offence; but not otherwise.

SCA 2007, s.4

In deciding whether a person ("the respondent"):

(1) facilitates the commission by another person of a serious offence; or

(2) conducts himself in a way that is likely to facilitate the commission by himself or another person of a serious offence (whether or not such an offence is committed), the judge must ignore:

    (a) any act that the respondent can show to be reasonable in the circumstances; and

    (b) subject to this, his intentions, or any other aspect of his mental state, at the time of the act in question.

This, apparently, according to the "Explanatory Notes" means that it does not matter if the accused did not e.g., intend to facilitate the commission of a serious offence, or had no knowledge that he was conducting himself in a way that was likely to facilitate serious crime.

Types of provision that may be made

62–007 The Act sets out examples of the type of provision that may be made by an order, but does not limit the type of provision that may be made. The examples of prohibitions, restrictions or requirements that may be imposed by such orders include prohibitions, restrictions or requirements in relation to places other than England and Wales.

SCA 2007, s.5

Examples of prohibitions, etc. that may be imposed on:

(1) individuals (including partners in a partnership) by an order, include prohibitions or restrictions on, or requirements in relation to:

    (a) an individual's financial, property or business dealings or holdings;

    (b) an individual's working arrangements;

    (c) the means by which an individual communicates or associates with others, or the persons with whom he communicates or associates;

    (d) the premises to which an individual has access;

    (e) the use of any premises or item by an individual;

    (f) an individual's travel (whether within the United Kingdom, between the United Kingdom and other places or otherwise);

(2) bodies corporate, partnerships and unincorporated associations by an order include prohibitions or restrictions on, or requirements in relation to;

    (a) financial, property or business dealings or holdings of such persons;

    (b) the types of agreements to which such persons may be a party;

    (c) the provision of goods or services by such persons;

    (d) the premises to which such persons have access;

    (e) the use of any premises or item by such persons;

    (f) the employment of staff by such persons.

Any provision must be proportionate to the risk foreseen (see 62–002 above). The provisions must be expressed in terms which the offender and any officer contemplating arrest or other means of enforcement can readily know what he may or may not do (*R. v Hancox,* above).

Further requirements

62–008 Examples of requirements that may be imposed on any persons by an order include:

SCA 2007, s.5(5)(6)(7)

(1) a requirement on a person to answer questions, or provide information, specified or described in an order:
   (a) at a time, within a period or at a frequency;
   (b) at a place;
   (c) in a form and manner; and
   (d) to a law enforcement officer or description of law enforcement officer;

notified to the person by a law enforcement officer specified or described in the order;

(2) a requirement on a person to produce documents specified or described in an order;
   (a) at a time, within a period or at a frequency;
   (b) at a place;
   (c) in a manner; and
   (d) to a law enforcement officer or description of law enforcement officer;

notified to the person by a law enforcement officer specified or described in the order.

The prohibitions, etc. that may be imposed on individuals by an order include prohibitions, restrictions or requirements in relation to an individual's private dwelling (including, for example, prohibitions or restrictions on, or requirements in relation to, where an individual may reside).

Note that:

"document" means anything in which information of any description is recorded (whether or not in legible form); "a law enforcement officer" means:

(i) a constable;
(ii) a member of the staff of SOCA who is for the time being designated under SOCA 2005, s.43;
(iii) an officer of Revenue and Customs; or
(iv) a member of the SFO; and

"premises" includes any land, vehicle, vessel, aircraft or hovercraft.

General safeguards in relation to orders

62–009 An individual under the age of 18 may not be the subject of an order, (nor may a person be the subject of an order if he falls within a description specified by order of the Secretary of State).

SCA 2007, s.14

An order may be made only on an application by:

(1) the DPP;
(2) the DRCP; or
(3) the DSFO.

A judge must, on an application by a person, give the person an opportunity to make representations in the proceedings before him arising by virtue of ss.19, 20 or 21 if he considers that the making or variation of the order concerned (or a decision not to vary it) would be likely to have a significant adverse effect on that person.

Any court considering an appeal in relation to an order must, on an application by a person, give the person an opportunity to make representations in the proceedings if that person was given an opportunity to make representations in the proceedings which are the subject of the appeal.

Notice requirements

62–010   The subject of an order is bound by it (or a variation of it) only if: SCA 2007, s.10

  (1) he is represented (whether in person or otherwise) at the proceedings at which the order or, as the case may be, the variation is made; or
  (2) a notice setting out the terms of the order or, as the case may be, the variation has been served on him.

The notice may be served on him by delivering it to him in person; or sending it by recorded delivery to him at his last-known address (whether residential or otherwise).

For the purposes of delivering such a notice to him in person, a constable or a person authorised for the purpose by the relevant applicant authority (see 62–008, above) may, if necessary by force, enter any premises where he has reasonable grounds for believing the person to be and search those premises for him.

Information safeguards

62–011   An order may not require: SCA 2007, ss.11, 12

  (1) a person to answer questions, or provide information, orally.
  (2) a person:
    (a) to answer any privileged question;
    (b) to provide any privileged information; or
    (c) to produce any privileged document.

A "privileged question" is defined as a question which the person would be entitled to refuse to answer on grounds of legal professional privilege in proceedings in the High Court; "privileged information" being information which the person would be entitled to refuse to provide on grounds of legal professional privilege in such proceedings. A "privileged document" is a document which the person would be entitled to refuse to produce on grounds of legal professional privilege in such proceedings.

But the above provision does not prevent an order from requiring a lawyer to provide the name and address of a client of his.

Excluded material and banking information

62–012   An order may not require a person: SCA 2007, s.13

  (1) to produce any excluded material as defined by PACE 1984, s.11;
  (2) to disclose any information or produce any document in respect

of which he owes an obligation of confidence by virtue of carrying on a banking business unless one of two conditions is met,
namely:

(a) the person to whom the obligation of confidence is owed
consents to the disclosure or production; or
(b) the order contains a requirement:
  (i) to disclose information, or produce documents, of this
  kind; or
  (ii) to disclose specified information which is of this kind
  or to produce specified documents which are of this
  kind.

Restrictions relating to other enactments

62–013   An order may not require a person: SCA 2007, ss.6,
                                                                     7, 9

(1) to answer any question;
(2) to provide any information; or
(3) to produce any document;

if the disclosure concerned is prohibited under any other enactment, as
defined.

Duration of orders

62–014   An order must specify when it is to come into force and when   SCA 2007, s.16
it is to cease to be in force. It is **not to be in force for more than five
years** beginning with its coming into force. It may specify different
times for the coming into force, or ceasing to be in force, of different
provisions of the order.

Where an order specifies different times, it:

(1) must specify when each provision is to come into force and cease
to be in force; and
(2) is not to be in force for more than five years beginning with the
coming into force of the first provision of the order to come into
force.

The fact that an order, or any provision of an order, ceases to be in
force does not prevent the court from making a new order to the same
or similar effect. A new order may be made in anticipation of an earlier
order or provision ceasing to be in force.

Power to vary order on conviction

62–015   Where a judge is dealing with a person who:

(1) has been convicted by or before a magistrates' court of having   SCA 2007, s.20
committed a serious offence in England and Wales and has been
committed to the Crown Court to be dealt with; or
(2) has been convicted by or before the Crown Court of having committed a serious offence in England and Wales,

he may in the case of a person who is the subject of a serious crime
prevention order in England and Wales, and in addition to dealing with
the person in relation to the offence, vary the order if he has reasonable
grounds to believe that the terms of the order as varied would protect

the public by preventing, restricting or disrupting involvement by the person in serious crime in England and Wales, but a variation may be made only on an application by the relevant applicant authority (see 62–016, below), and, as in the case of an original order, only:

    (a) in addition to a sentence imposed in respect of the offence concerned; or

    (b) in addition to an order discharging the person conditionally.

A variation may include an extension of the period during which the order, or any provision of it, is in force (subject to the original limits imposed on the order by ss.16(2) and (4)(b) (see 62–014, above)).

Power to vary orders on breach

62–016   Where a judge is dealing with a person who: SCA 2007, s.21

    (1) has been convicted by or before a magistrates' court of having committed an offence under SCA 2007, s.25 in relation to a serious crime prevention order and has been committed to the Crown Court to be dealt with; or

    (2) has been convicted by or before the Crown Court of having committed an offence under s.25 in relation to a serious crime prevention order,

he may, in addition to dealing with that person in relation to the offence, vary the order, if he has reasonable grounds to believe that the terms of the order as varied would protect the public by preventing, restricting or disrupting involvement by that person in serious crime in England and Wales.

A variation under this section may be made only on an application by the relevant applicant authority, and only:

    (a) in addition to a sentence imposed in respect of the offence concerned; or

    (b) in addition to an order discharging the person conditionally.

A variation may include an extension of the period during which the order, or any provision of it, is in force (subject to the original limits imposed on the order by ss.16(2) and (4)(b).

Procedure on revocation and discharge is governed by r.50.5 as amended by SI 2010/1921, as to which see BREACH, AMENDMENT AND REVOCATION.

Inter-relationship between different types of orders

62–017   Serious crime prevention orders may also be made, on appli-   SCA 2007, s.22
cation, by the High Court. It should be noted that:

    (1) the fact that an order has been made or varied by the High Court does not prevent it from being varied by the Crown Court in accordance with this Part;

    (2) the fact that an order has been made or varied by the Crown Court does not prevent it from being varied or discharged by the High Court in accordance with this Part;

    (3) a decision by the Crown Court not to make an order does not

prevent a subsequent application to the High Court for an order under s.1 in consequence of the same offence;

(4) a decision by the Crown Court not to vary an order under ss.20 or 21 does not prevent a subsequent application to the High Court for a variation of the order in consequence of the same offence.

Nature of proceedings

62–018   Proceedings before the Crown Court arising by virtue of ss.19, 20 or 21 are civil proceedings. This has three consequences:

SCA 2007, s.36

(1) the standard of proof to be applied in such proceedings is the civil standard of proof;
(2) the court is not restricted to considering evidence that would have been admissible in the criminal proceedings in which the person concerned was convicted; and
(3) the judge may adjourn any proceedings in relation to an order even after sentencing the person concerned.

The Crown Court, when exercising its jurisdiction under this Part of the Act, remains a criminal court for the purposes of CA 2003, Pt 7, in relation to procedure rules and practice directions.

Note also that:

(a) an order may be made as mentioned in SCA 2007, s.19(7)(b) in spite of anything in PCC(S)A 2000, ss.12 and 14 which relate to orders discharging a person absolutely or conditionally and their effect; and
(b) a variation of an order may be made as mentioned in s.20(6)(b) or 21(6)(b) in spite of anything in those sections of PCC(S)A 2000.

Procedure is governed by r.50 (civil behaviour orders after verdict or finding) as to which see ANTI-SOCIAL BEHAVIOUR ORDERS.

Appeals to CACD

62–019   An appeal against a decision of the Crown Court in relation to a serious crime prevention order may be made to the CACD by:

SCA 2007, s.24(1)-(4)

(1) the person who is the subject of the order; or
(2) the relevant applicant authority (see 60–009, above).

In addition, an appeal may be made to the CACD in relation to a decision of the Crown Court:

(a) to make an order; or
(b) to vary, or not to vary, such an order;

by any person who was given an opportunity to make representations in the proceedings concerned by virtue of s.9(4).

Appeal lies only with the leave of CACD, or without such leave, where the judge who made the decision grants a certificate that the decision is fit for appeal.

The procedure is set out in Pt 1 of the Serious Crimes Act 2007 (Appeals under Section 24) Order 2008 (SI 2008/1863).

Notes

63. SERVICE OF DOCUMENTS

Application of CPR 2011, Pt 4

Rr.4.1, 12

63–001   CPR 2011, Pt 4 applies to the service of every document in a case to which the Rules apply, subject to any special rules in other legislation (including other Parts of the Rules or in PD 2004). R.4.12

The court may treat a document as served if the addressee responds to it even if it was not served in accordance with the rules in Pt 4.

The court may specify the time as well as the date by which a document must be; R.4.11

(1) served under r.4.3 or r.4.8; or
(2) transmitted by fax, e-mail or other electronic means if it is served under r.4.6.

The person who serves a document may prove that by signing a certificate explaining how and when it was served.

As to date of service, see 63–010 below.

As to pagination and indexing of evidence served on the Crown Court, see 63–011 below.

Methods of service

63–002   A document may be served by any of the methods described in r.4.3 to 4.6, below (subject to r.4.7), or in r.4.8, these being: R.4.2

(1) by handing over a document (r.4.3);
(2) by leaving or posting a document (r.4.4);
(3) through a DX (r.4.5);
(4) by fax, email or other electronic means (r.4.6);
(5) by persons in custody (r.4.8); or
(6) by other methods (r.4.9).

Where a document may be served by electronic means, the general rule is that the person serving it will use that method. Rule 4.7 restricts the method of service in the case of certain specified documents.

Handing over a document

R.4.3

63–003   A document may be served on:

(a) an individual by handing it to him or her;
(b) a corporation by handing it to a person holding a senior position in that corporation;
(c) an individual or corporation who is legally represented in the case by handing it to that representative;
(d) the prosecution by handing it to the prosecutor or to the prosecution representative;
(e) the court officer by handing it to a court officer with authority to accept it at the relevant court office; and
(f) the Registrar of Criminal Appeals by handing it to a court officer with authority to accept it at the Criminal Appeal Office.

801

SERVICE OF DOCUMENTS

If an individual is 17 or under, a copy of a document served under paragraph (a) must be handed to his or her parent, or another appropriate adult, unless no such person is readily available.

[*Note. Certain legislation treats a body that is not a corporation as if it were one for the purposes of rules about service of documents. See, e.g. the Adoption and Children Act 2002, s.143*].

Leaving or posting a document

63–004 A document may be served by leaving it at the appropriate address for service under this rule or by sending it to that address by first class post or by the equivalent of first class post.

R.4.4

The address for service on:

    (a) an individual, is an address where it is reasonably believed that he or she will receive it;

    (b) a corporation, is its principal office in England and Wales, and if there is no readily identifiable principal office then any place in England and Wales where it carries on its activities or business;

    (c) an individual or corporation who is legally represented in the case, is that representative's office;

    (d) the prosecution, is the prosecutor's office;

    (e) the court officer, is the relevant court office; and

    (f) the Registrar of Criminal Appeals is the Criminal Appeal Office, Royal Courts of Justice, Strand, London WC2A 2LL.

Service through a document exchange

63–005 A document may be served by document exchange (DX) where:

R.4.5

(1) the person to be served:
    (a) has given a DX box number; and
    (b) has not refused to accept service by DX; or
(2) the person to be served is legally represented in the case and the representative has given a DX box number.

Service by electronic means

63–006 A document may be served by electronic means where:

R.4.6

(1) the person to be served:
    (a) has given an electronic address; and
    (b) has not refused to accept service by that method; or
(2) the person to be served is legally represented in the case and the representative has given an electronic address.

Where a document is served under this rule the person serving it need not provide a paper copy as well.

Documents that must be served by specified methods

63–007 The documents listed below may be served:

R. 4.7

(1) on an individual, only under r.4.3(1)(a) (handing over) or rule 4.4(1) and (2)(a) (leaving or posting); and

(2) on a corporation, only under r.4.3(1)(b) (handing over) or r.4.4(1) and (2)(b) (leaving or posting).

The documents are:

- (a) a summons, requisition or witness summons;
- (b) notice of an order under RTOA 1988, s.25;
- (c) a notice of registration under RTOA 1988, s.71(6);
- (d) notice of a hearing to review the postponement of the issue of a warrant of detention or imprisonment under MCA 1980, s.77(6);
- (e) notice under MCA 1980, s.86 of a revised date to attend a means inquiry;
- (f) any notice or document served under r.9 (Bail);
- (g) notice under r.37.15(a) of when and where an adjourned hearing will resume;
- (h) notice under r.42.5(3) of an application to vary or discharge a compensation order;
- (i) notice under r.42.10(2)(c) of the location of the sentencing or enforcing court;
- (j) a collection order, or notice requiring payment, served Under r.52.2(a).

An application or written statement, and notice, under r.62. alleging contempt of court may be served—

- (i) on an individual, only under r.4.3(1)(a) (by handing it to him or her);
- (ii) on a corporation, only under r.4.3(1)(b) (by handing it to a person holding a senior position in that corporation).

Service by person in custody

63–008   A person in custody may serve a document by handing it to   R.4.8
the custodian addressed to the person to be served.

Such custodian must then:

- (a) endorse it with the time and date of receipt;
- (b) record its receipt; and
- (c) forward it promptly to the addressee.

Service by another method

63–009   The court may allow service of a document by a method: R.4.9

(1) other than those described in rr.4.3 to 4.6 and in r.4.8;

(2) other than one specified by r.4.7, where that rule applies.

An order allowing service by another method must specify:

- (a) the method to be used; and
- (b) the date on which the document will be served.

Date of service

63–010   A document served under r.4.3 or r.4.8 is served on the day it   R.4.10
is handed over. Unless something different is shown, a document served
on a person by any other method is served:

(a) in the case of a document left at an address, on the next business day after the day on which it was left;

(b) in the case of a document sent by first class post or by the equivalent of first class post, on the second business day after the day on which it was posted or despatched;

(c) in the case of a document served by document exchange, on the second business day after the day on which it was left at the addressee's DX or at a correspondent DX;

(d) in the case of a document transmitted by fax, email or other electronic means, on the next business day after it was transmitted; and

(e) in any case, on the day on which the addressee responds to it if that is earlier.

Unless something different is shown, a document produced by a court computer system is to be taken as having been sent by first class post or by the equivalent of first class post to the addressee on the business day after the day on which it was produced.

In this Part "business day" means any day except Saturday, Sunday, R.2 Christmas Day, Boxing Day, Good Friday, Easter Monday or a bank holiday. Where a document is served on or by the court officer, "business day" does not include a day on which the court office is closed.

Pagination and indexing of served evidence
63–011 Where:

PD 2004,
IV.41.12, 13

(1) the prosecutor serves evidence in committal proceedings;

(2) there is an application to prefer a bill of indictment in relation to a case;

(3) there is service of notice of transfer under CJA 1987, s.4(1) or CJA 1991, s.53(1) (notice of transfer in certain cases involving children);

(4) a person is sent for trial under CDA 1998, s.51; or

(5) an accused wishes to serve evidence,

a party who serves documentary evidence in the Crown Court should:

(a) paginate each page in any bundle of statements and exhibits sequentially;

(b) provide a tabulated index to each bundle of statements produced including the following information:
   - the name of the case;
   - the author of each statement;
   - the start page number of the witness statement;
   - the end page number of the witness statement;

(c) provide a tabulated index to each bundle of documentary and pictorial exhibits produced, including the following information:
   - the name of the case;
   - the exhibit reference;
   - a short description of the exhibit;
   - the start page number of the exhibit;
   - the end page number of the exhibit;

PD 2004,
IV.41.14

- where possible, the name of the person producing the exhibit should be added.

Where additional documentary evidence is served, a party should paginate following on from the last page of the previous bundle or in a logical and sequential manner. A party should also provide notification of service of any amended index.

The prosecution must ensure that the running total of the pages of prosecution evidence is easily identifiable on the most recent served bundle of prosecution evidence.

For the purposes of these directions, the number of pages of prosecution evidence served on the court includes all:

(i) witness statements;
(ii) documentary and pictorial exhibits;
(iii) records of interviews with the accused; and
(iv) records of interviews with other accused,

which form part of the committal or served prosecution documents or which are included in any notice of additional evidence, but does not include any document provided on CD-ROM or by other means of electronic communication.

PD 2004, IV.41.16

Notes

64. SEX OFFENDER ORDERS

Introduction
64–001   SOA 2003:

(1) repealed SOA 1997, Pt I relating to the registration of sex offenders;

(2) abolished restraining orders under SOA 1997, s.5A;

(3) abolished sex offender orders under CDA 1998, but retained the "disqualification from working with children order" under CJCSA 2000, Pt 2. That order is abolished by the Vulnerable Groups Act 2006.

A judge of the Crown Court is now left with;

(a) a duty to certify the facts in relation to a certificate under the notification provisions of SOA 2003, Pt 2;

(b) the power to make a sexual offences prevention order; and

(c) (during the transitional period) the obligation to disqualify him from working with children, under CJCSA 2000, s.28 (*R. v Cooper, The Times*, September 9, 2011, reversing the decision in *Att Gen's Reference (No.18 of 2011)* [2011] EWCA Crim 1300, [2011] Crim. L.R. 721); and

(d) the obligation to notify an offender in certain circumstances that he will be barred from working with children or vulnerable adults by the Independent Safeguarding Authority established under the 2006 Act.

Where, on a conviction, sentence or order, legislation requires an offender: R.42.3

(1) to notify information to the police; or

(2) to be included in a barred list,

the judge must tell him that such requirements apply, and under what legislation.

A.   Certification

64–002   For the purposes of the notification requirements in SOA 2003, Pt 2, a certificate is required in the case of any person: SOA 2003, s.113(3)

(1) convicted of an offence listed in Sch.3; or

(2) found not guilty of such an offence by reason of insanity; or

(3) found to be under a disability and to have done the act charged against him, in respect of such an offence.

The judge should certify those facts in open court, either at the time of sentence or subsequently that:

(a) on that date he was convicted, found not guilty as in (2)

807

above, or found to be under a disability in the circumstances
stated in (3) above;
(b) that the offence in question is an offence listed in Sch.3; and
(c) that he is so certifying (*R. v G (Sex Offender) (Registration)*,
[2002] 2 Cr. App. R. (S.) 79), so that the certificate may
be used as evidence in later proceedings (see also *R. v
Rawlinson, The Times*, October 14, 1999).

The imposition of a conditional or absolute discharge is not a "conviction" for these purposes and does not activate the procedure under
s.92 (*R. v Longworth*, [2006] UKHL 1, [2006] 2 Cr. App. R. (S.) 62).

B. Sexual offences prevention order (SOPO)

General

64–003   A SOPO replaces both the sex offender order and the restraining order under the previous legislation.
Where the judge:

(1) deals with an offender, in respect of an offence listed in SOA
2003, Schs 3 or 5; or
(2) deals with an accused in respect of a finding that he is:
(a) not guilty of an offence listed in Sch.3 or 5 by reason of
insanity; or
(b) under a disability and has done the act charged against him
in respect of such an offence; and
(3) is satisfied that it is **necessary** to make such an order, for the
purpose of protecting the public, or any particular members of
the public from serious sexual harm from the offender, he may
make a SOPO prohibiting the offender from doing those things
prescribed in the order. The judge must not make an order unless
he considers it "necessary". The fact that it is "appropriate" is not
sufficient (*R. v Halloren* [2004] EWCA Crim 233, [2004] 2 Cr.
App. R. (S.) 57).

The making of an order is not restricted to cases in which a determinate sentence of more than 12 months is imposed (*R. v Terrell* [2007]
EWCA Crim 3079, [2008] 2 Cr. App. R. (S.) 49).

Breach of the order is an offence carrying five years on indictment
(s.113(2)); the Act expressly excludes the making of a conditional discharge (s.113(3)).

The effect of such an order on the notification provisions of SOA
2003, is set out at s.107(2), (4). Where a sexual offences prevention
order is made in relation to a person already subject to such an order
(whether made by that court or another), the earlier order ceases to
have effect.

A SOPO imposed under SOA 2003, s.104 to protect the public
from serious sexual harm is not governed by the provisions relating to
"dangerousness" in CJA 2003, s.227. The schemes under the two Acts
were intended to be, and are, distinct. It follows that it is not a pre-
condition for imposing a SOPO that the offender should also qualify for

an extended sentence or life imprisonment or imprisonment for public protection under CJA 2003: *R. v Richards* [2006] EWCA Crim 2549; [2007] 1 Cr. App. R. (S.) 120; *R. v Rampley* [2006] EWCA Crim 2203, [2007] 1 Cr. App. R. (S.) 87.

"Necessary" and "proportionate"

64–004   Both the order and the restrictions and prohibitions contained in it must be necessary and proportionate. (*R. v R* [2010] EWCA Crim 907). The fact that an order is "appropriate" is not sufficient *(R. v Halloren*, above).

The conduct against which protection is necessary is defined in s.106(3). The protection required is against "serious sexual harm". The focus of s 104 is the risk of future offences; the judge must, therefore, conduct a risk assessment and consider the likelihood of the offender committing further Sch.3 offences *(R. v D* [2004] EWCA Crim 3660, [2006] 2 Cr. App. R. (S.) 32).

Section 107(2) states in terms that the only prohibitions that may be included in the order are those necessary for the purpose of protecting the public or any particular members of the public from serious sexual harm from the defendant. No order should be drawn wider than is necessary to achieve its stated purpose. In the absence of evidence or inference which can properly be drawn, normal activities should not be prohibited or restrained (*R. v Buchanan* [2010] EWCA Crim 1316). Each prohibition must be necessary and proportionate (*R. v Mortimer* [2010] EWCA Crim 1303).

In *R. v Hensley* [2010] EWCA Crim 225, [2010] 3 All E.R. 965, it was said that an order must be:

(1) clear on its face;
(2) capable of being complied with without unreasonable difficulty or the assistance of a third party; and
(3) free of the real risk of an unintentional breach.

Duration of order

64–005   The order has effect for a specified fixed period (of not less than five years) or until further notice (s.107(1)(2)). Any order made for a period less than 5 years is therefore unlawful (*R. v R* [2010] EWCA Crim 907). The duration of the order should be aligned with the length of the notification requirements (*R. v Hammond* [2008] EWCA Crim 1358; *R. v Smith* [2009] EWCA Crim 1795).

Procedure

64–006   Procedure is governed by r.50 (civil behaviour orders after verdict or finding) as to which see ANTI-SOCIAL BEHAVIOUR ORDERS.

If a person is convicted of a qualifying offence and presents a significant risk of harm to children:

(1) the defence advocate should be alert to the possibility, if not the likelihood, of such an order being made when sentence is finally passed; and

(2) the prosecutor should be in a position, when asked by the court, to submit draft proposals for incorporation into the order both to the court and to the defence in good time for the hearing.

If the judge takes the initiative and prepares a proposed draft order, or alters one submitted by the Crown, that is effectively a discussion document. If there is insufficient time for the defence advocate and the offender to consider the contents or terms of such proposed order because of late service, application should be made to the judge for the hearing to be put back in order for instructions to be taken (*R. v Buchanan, above*).

Where the judge has formed a provisional view as to the imposition of order (subject, of course, to the assessment of risk), it will be helpful, where he directs the preparation of a pre-sentence report and a consideration of the assessment of dangerousness, to invite the Probation Service to consider whether the management of the risk could be assisted by the imposition of an order and, if so, the restrictions which might be appropriate.

In deciding whether the facts alleged require an order, it is desirable that the standard of proof, though theoretically the civil standard, should be the equivalent of the criminal standard (*Cleveland Chief Constable v Haggas* (unreported, November 20, 2009, QBD applying *R. (McCann) v Manchester CC* [2002] UKHL 39; [2003] 1 Cr. App. R. 27).

Orders in relation to siblings

64–007 Where the judge is considering making a sexual offences prevention order to protect from abuse within the family, particularly a sibling of the abused person and it might be desirable, to draft the order in terms that provide a link with the court's family jurisdiction.

CJCSA 2000, ss.28, 29

Where the victim has a sibling living in the same family, the judge must conduct a risk assessment and consider:

(1) the likelihood of the offender committing a further Sch.3 offence; and
(2) the sibling being caused serious physical or psychological harm as a result, even if the offence was not directed against him.

Where the judge considers that there is a risk that the offender will in future commit one or more Sch.3 offences which, unless the sibling is protected by a SOPO, will cause him to suffer serious psychological harm it is necessary to make such an order. Under s.108 the persons who may apply for the SOPO to be varied do not include a sibling or anyone acting on his behalf. There may be occasions when a SOPO is made to protect a child of the offender where the family court's jurisdiction should be reflected in the order because of the additional flexibility that it provides. The judge has jurisdiction to make a SOPO in the following terms: "[the offender] shall not, without the order of a judge exercising jurisdiction under the *Children Act 1989*, communicate or seek to communicate, whether directly or indirectly with [the sibling] whilst he remains under the age of 16 years". In that way the child's interest in a possibly changing situation can better be met than through the blunt instrument of the SOPO alone (*R. v D, above*).

Variation, revocation and discharge

64–008 An offender may:
SOA 2003, s.108(1)

(1) apply to the Crown Court to vary an SOPO made by the Crown Court;

(2) on the hearing of such an application the Crown Court may make an order varying, renewing or discharging the order;
SOA 2003, s.108(4)

(3) an order refusing to vary an order is an order made by a court when dealing with an offender, and is therefore a 'sentence' for the purposes of CAA Act 1968, s50(1);
SOA 2003, s.110(3).

(4) the offender may appeal to CACD against the refusal of the Crown Court judge to make an order, including a variation; and
CAA 1968, s.11(3)

(5) on such an appeal CACD may quash the order and make another appropriate order (since it is an appeal against sentence) *(R. v Hoath* [2011] EWCA Crim 274, [2011] 4 All E.R. 306).

The procedure on revocation and discharge is governed by r.50, as to which See BREACH, AMENDMENT AND REVOCATION OF ORDERS.

C.   Disqualification from working with children

General

64–009   The power of a judge of the Crown Court to make an order under CJCSA 2000, s.29A (as amended by CJA 2003, Sch.30, para.2) disqualifying an offender from working with children, ceased on the coming into force of the Safeguarding Vulnerable Groups Act 2006. That Act set up an Independent Safeguarding Authority (known as the ISA) responsible for establishing and maintaining a "children's barred list" and an "adult barred list".

The result is that the judge, in such a case need no longer make a s.28, disqualification order under the PCC(S) 2000. Instead where;

(1) formerly he would have had power to make such an order; or

(2) where the offender is convicted of an offence involving harm or risk of harm to children or vulnerable adults (the offences are specified in the legislation),

he should tell the offender, as required by PCC(S)A 2000, Sch.3, para.25, that he will be included by the ISA on the barred list (in much the same way as the court informs an offender as to notification requirements under the SOA 2003 *(Att-Gen's Reference (No.18 of 2011)* [2011] EWCA Crim 1300).

D.   Sexual Offences Act 2003: certification

64–010   For the purposes of the notification requirements set out in SOA 2003, Pt 2, a certificate is required in the case of a person:

(1) convicted of an offence listed in Sch.3; or

(2) found not guilty of such an offence by reason of insanity; or

(3) found to be under a disability and to have done the act charged against him, in respect of such an offence.

The judge should state in open court, that:

(a) on that date he was convicted, found not guilty as in (2) above, or found to be under a disability in the circumstances stated in (3) above;

(b) that the offence in question is an offence listed in Sch.3; and

(c) that he is so certifying (*R. v G (Sex Offender): Registration,* above)

and should certify those facts, whether at the time or subsequently, so that the certificate may be used as evidence in later proceedings (see also *R. v Rawlinson,* above). (SOA 2003, s.92).

The court officer will give notice (in form Annex C) to the offender of the requirement to register with the police, and of the duration of such requirement, which, in the case of:

(i) custodial sentences of:
30 months or more, runs for life
6–30 months, runs for 10 years
6 months or less, runs for 7 years

(ii) no custody, runs for five years

(iii) a hospital order runs for seven years, or where a restriction order is imposed, indefinitely
though adjustments will be made where there are two or more notification requirements in existence.

If the offender is under 18 the periods are halved.

65. SHERIFF'S AWARDS; COMMENDATIONS

65–001 A judge of the Crown Court may, where a person appears to CLA 1826, s.28 have been active in or towards the apprehension of a person later charged with an *indictable* offence, order the sheriff of the county in which the offence was committed, to pay a reward of such sums as seem to him to be just and reasonable.

This is an important power and the Senior Master has recently commented as follows:

(1) there are no fetters on this power; any suggestions that there is no money in the budget etc. ought to be discounted; the 1826 Act does not allow for such intervention by the executive;

(2) an award is not intended to be compensatory but to be sufficient to reflect the public's appreciation of the recipient's bravery;

(3) many of the awards made are, in the light of modern day standards, extremely mean; it is suggested that a sum of £350 might be the bottom line save for small children, and that an award of £500 would not be over-generous;

(4) once an award is made, a cheque is drawn by the Crown Court officer and sent to the High Sheriff for presentation.

The Crown Court also issues from time to time a certificate of commendation, where the judge identifies a person who has merited commendation for conduct not coming within CLA 1826. Such certificates are intended to supplement the existing system.

Notes

66. SPECIAL MEASURES DIRECTIONS

Quick guide

1. General procedure in relation to special measures (66–001)
2. Special measures directions under YJCEA 1999 (66–002)
3. Reporting direction: adult witnesses (66–025)
4. Witness anonymity (66–039)
5. Witness preparation (66–055)
6. Restraint (handcuffing of accused) (66–057)

1. General procedure in relation to special measures

General procedural rules

66–001   CPR 2011 r.29.2–29.21 provides general procedural rules for   R.29.2
those topics numbered 1–3 in the guide above. These general rules
provide that:

(1) a party wishing the court to exercise its powers to give a direction   R.29.4
or order must apply in writing as soon as reasonably practicable,
and in any event within 14 days after the defendant pleads not
guilty, serving the application on the court officer and each other
party;

(2) a party wanting to introduce the evidence of a witness who is the   R.29.4
subject of an application, direction or order must inform the
witness of the court's decision as soon as reasonably practicable,
explaining to the witness the arrangements that as a result will be
made for him to give evidence.

The judge will announce at a hearing in public, before the witness gives
evidence, the reasons for his decision to give, vary or discharge any
direction or order or his refusal to do so.

The judge has a general power to: R.29.5

(a) shorten or extend (even after it has expired) any time limits
under r.29;

(b) allow any application or representation to be made in a different form to one set out in the Annex to PD 2004, or to be
made orally.

A person wanting an extension of time must apply when serving the   R.29.8
application or representation for which it is needed, explaining the
delay.

The judge may decide whether to give, vary or discharge a special
measures direction at a hearing in public or in private, or without a
hearing, and in a party's absence if that party applied for the direction,
variation or discharge, or has had at least 14 days in which to make
representations.

2. Special measures directions under YJCEA 1999

Eligible witnesses

66–002   A witness is eligible for a special measures direction under YJCEA 1999 if, at the time the judge makes a determination, that witness: *(YJCEA 1999, s.16(4))*

(1) is under 18 (i.e. a "child witness" or a "qualifying witness"); or
(2) the judge considers the quality of the evidence given by the witness is likely to be diminished by reason of the fact that the witness:
    (a) suffers from mental disorder within the meaning of MHA 1983 (see MENTALLY DISORDERED OFFENDERS); or *(YJCEA 1999, s.18(2))*
    (b) otherwise has a significant impairment of intelligence and social functioning; or *(YJCEA 1999, s.16(5))*
    (c) has a physical disability or is suffering from a physical disorder.

In determining whether a witness falls within (2) above, any views expressed by the witness must be considered.

Once it is established that a witness is eligible for assistance by way of special measures, s.19(2) of the Act provides that:

    (i) it is for the trial judge to determine whether any of the special measures available would be likely to improve the quality of the evidence given by a witness; and *(YJCEA 1999, s.17(1))*

    (ii) if the judge so concludes, it is for him to decide which of the special measures, or which combination of them, would be likely to maximise so far as practicable the quality of the particular witness's evidence. *(YJCEA 1999, s.164)*

In deciding this matter the judge is required by s.19(3) to consider all the circumstances of the case including any view expressed by the witness and whether the measure or measures might inhibit the effective testing of the evidence on behalf of the defendant (*R. v Davies* [2011] EWCA Crim 1177, [2011] Crim. L.R. 732).

Throughout these provisions references to the "quality" of a witness's evidence are to its quality in terms of completeness, coherence and accuracy, and for this purpose "coherence" refers to a witness's ability in giving evidence to give answers which address the questions put to him and can be understood both individually and collectively.

Witness in fear or distress

66–003   A witness other than the accused is also eligible for assistance if the judge is satisfied that the quality of evidence (see 66–002 above) given by the witness is likely to be diminished by reason of fear or distress on his part in connection with giving evidence in the proceedings. *(YJCEA 1999, s.17(2))*

In making his determination as to whether a witness is so eligible, the judge must take into account, in particular:

(a) the nature and alleged circumstances of the offence;
(b) the age of the witness;
(c) his/her social and cultural background, and ethnic origins;
(d) his/her domestic and employment circumstances;

(e) his/her religious beliefs or political opinions;

(f) any behaviour towards the witness on the part of the accused or his associates or members of his family, or of any other person likely to be an accused or witness in the proceedings,

to the extent that these matters appear to him to be relevant, and he must also, in determining the question, consider any views expressed by the witness.

It is open to the judge to determine the issue on (a) above, alone, and he may do so notwithstanding the fact that the witness is neither young nor particularly vulnerable (*R. v Brown* [2004] Crim. L.R. 1034).

Complainant in sexual case

66–004   Where the complainant in respect of a sexual offence is a witness in proceedings relating to that offence (or to that offence and any other offences) the witness is eligible for assistance in relation to those offences unless the witness has informed the court of his/her wish not to be eligible.

YJCEA 1999, s.17(4)

Offences involving weapons

66–005   A witness in proceedings relating to an offence involving weapons listed in CorJA 2009, Sch.1A, (or to such an offence and any other offences) is eligible for assistance in relation to those proceedings unless the witness has informed the court of his/her wish not to be so eligible.

YJCEA 1999, s.17(5)(6); CorJA 2009, s.99

Available special measures

66–006   The measures set out below may be adopted only where the court has been notified by the Secretary of State that relevant arrangements may be made available in the area in which the proceedings will take place, but see *R. v R (S A)* [2008] 2 Cr. App. R. 16.

The following are "special measures":

(1) screening the witness from the accused (s.23);

(2) evidence by live link (s.24);

(3) permitting evidence to be given in private (s.25);

(4) removal of wigs and gowns (s.26);

(5) video recorded evidence in chief (s.27);

(6) video recorded cross-examination and re-examination (s.28 **not in force**);

(7) examination of witness through intermediary (s.29);

(8) aids to communication (any appropriate device to assist in overcoming communication problems due to a witness's disability, disorder or impairment.

Duty of applicant

66–007   A party who wants to introduce the evidence of a 'child' or "qualifying" witness (66–002) must, as soon as reasonably practicable:

(1) notify the court that the witness is eligible for assistance;

Rr.29.9,11

(2) provide the court with any information that it may need to assess the witness' views, if he not want the primary rule to apply; and

(3) serve any recorded evidence on the Crown Court officer and each other party.

The contents of any application are stated in r.29.10 and an appropriate form is to be found in PD 2004, Annex D.

Where the application is for variation or discharge of a direction, the applicant must;

(a) explain what material circumstances have changed since the direction was given (or last varied);

(b) explain why the direction should be varied or discharged; and

(c) ask for a hearing, if he wants one, and explain why it is needed.

Application containing information withheld from another party

66–008 Where an applicant serves an application for a direction (or for its variation or discharge) and the application includes information that he thinks should not be revealed to another party, he must: R.29.12

(1) omit that information from the part of the application that is served on that other party;

(2) mark the other part to show that, unless the judge otherwise directs, it is only for the court; and

(3) in that part, explain why he has withheld that information from that other party.

Any hearing must be in private unless the judge otherwise directs, and if he so directs may be wholly or in part in the absence of a party from which the information has been withheld. In general, on a hearing the judge will receive in sequence:

(a) representations first by the applicant and then by each other party, in all the parties presence; and then

(b) further representations by the applicant in the absence of a party from whom information has been withheld; but the judge may direct other arrangements.

Representations in response

66–009 Where a party wishes to make representations in respect of an application for a direction, (its variation or discharge) or a direction (variation or discharge) that the judge proposes to make of his own initiative, he must: R.29.13

(1) serve the representations on the Crown Court officer and each other party;

(2) do so not more than 14 days after the service of the application, or notice of the direction (variation or discharge) which the judge proposes; and

(3) ask for a hearing if he wants one and explain why it is needed.

Where representations include information that the person making them thinks ought not to be revealed to another party, he must take the steps indicated in 66–008 above.

Representations against a direction must explain:

(a) why the witness is not eligible for assistance; or
(b) if he is eligible; why
    (i) no special direction would be liable to improve the quality of his evidence;
    (ii) the proposed measure(s) would not be likely to so far as practicable to maximise the quality of his evidence; or
    (iii) the proposed measure(s) might tend to inhibit the effective testing of that evidence.

Representations against the variation or discharge of a direction must explain why it should not be varied or discharged.

Judge's determination

66–010 Where the judge determines that a witness is eligible for assistance by virtue of either s.16 or s.17 he must then determine: *YJCEA 1999, s.19(2)*

(1) whether any of the special measures available in relation to the witness (or any combination of them) would, in his opinion, be likely to improve the quality (see 66–002) of the evidence given by the witness; and
(2) if so:
    (a) determine which would in his opinion be likely to maximise as far as is practicable, the quality of such evidence; and
    (b) give a direction for the measure or measures to apply to the evidence given by the witness.

Witnesses under 18, or those who suffer from disabilities or disorders may be eligible for all the measures set out in 66–006, those suffering from fear or distress may be considered only for those numbered (1)–(6) in that paragraph.

Status of directions; reasons

66–011 A special measure direction is binding until the proceedings are determined or abandoned in relation to each accused. A direction may be varied or discharged in the interests of justice, by the judge of his own initiative, or on application by a party where there has been a material change of circumstances.   *YJCEA 1999, s.20(1)(2)*

The judge must state in open court the reasons for all his determinations relating to special measures directions.   *YJCEA 1999, s.20(5)*

Child witnesses: (1) general

66–012 A witness under 18 is a "child witness" for the purposes of these provisions whether or not he is eligible for special measures under any other provisions of the Act.   *YJCEA 1999. s.21(1)(2); CorJA. 2009, s.98(1)(2) (3),100(1)-(3)*

Where the judge in making a determination under s.19(2) (see 66–010 above) determines that a witness is a child witness, he must:

SPECIAL MEASURES DIRECTIONS

(1) first have regard to s.21(3) to (4C) below; and
(2) then have regard to s.19(2) (66–010 above),

and for the purposes of s.19(2), as it then applies to the witness, any special measures required to be applied to him are treated as if they were determined, pursuant to ss.19(2)(a) and (b)(i), to be ones that (whether on their own or with any other special measures) would be likely to maximise so far as practicable the quality of his evidence.

Child witnesses: (2) the primary rule

66–013 The primary rule in the case of a child witness or a "qualifying witness" (66–002 above), is that the judge **must** give a direction in relation to the witness which provides for his evidence being admitted:

YJCEA 1999, s.21(3)(4)

(1) under s.27 by means of a video of an interview with the witness in place of his examination-in-chief); and
(2) after that evidence which is not given by means of a video recording, whether in chief or otherwise) by means of a live link in accordance with s.24; or
(3) when CorJA 2009 s.100, comes into force, if one or both of those measures is not taken, for the witness when giving evidence to be screened from seeing the defendant,

unless:

(a) (once CorJA 2009 s.100, comes into force) the witness does not want the rule to apply and the judge is satisfied that to omit a measure usually required would not diminish the quality of the witness's evidence; or
(b) the judge is satisfied that compliance with it would not be likely to maximise the quality of the witness's evidence.

Child witnesses: (3) limitations on primary rule

66–014 There are limitations on the primary rule, namely:

YJCEA 1999, s.21(4)

(1) the requirement in (1) of 66–010 is subject to the availability of the special measure in question;
(2) the requirement in (1) of 66–010 is subject to s.27(2), i.e. that a special measure may not provide for a video recording,- or part of it, to be admitted, if the judge is of opinion that, in all the circumstances of the case, in the interests of justice, that recording, or part of it, should not be admitted;
(3) if the witness informs the judge of his wish that the rule should not apply or should apply only in part, the rule does not apply to the extent that the judge is satisfied that not complying with the rule would not diminish the quality of the witness's evidence; and
(4) the primary rule does not apply to the extent that the judge is satisfied that compliance with it would not maximise the quality of the witness's evidence so far as practicable (whether because any other special measure available would have that effect or otherwise).

In making his decisions under the above provisions, the judge must take into account (together with any other factors he considers relevant):

(a) the age and maturity of the witness;
(b) the ability of the witness to understand the consequences of giving evidence otherwise than in accordance with the primary rule;
(c) the relationship (if any) between the witness and the accused;
(d) the witness's social and cultural background and ethnic origins; and
(e) the nature and alleged circumstances of the offence to which the proceedings relate.

The above provisions (s.21) are extended to witnesses other than the accused who do not qualify as child witnesses at the time of the hearing, but were under 18 when a relevant recording was made. The provisions of s.21(2)–(4) and (4C) so far as relating to the giving of a direction complying with the requirement contained in s.21(3)(a), apply to a qualifying witness in respect of the relevant recording as they apply to a child witness (within the meaning of that section). `YJCEA 1999, s.22`

Consequences of disapplication

66–015 Where, as a consequence of all or part of the primary rule stated in the preceding paragraph being disapplied under (c), a witness's evidence or any part of it would fall to be given as testimony in court, the judge must give a special measures direction making such provision as is described in s.23 for the evidence or that part of it. `YJCEA 1999, s.21(4B), (4C)`

The requirement in subs.(4A) is subject to the following limitations:

(1) if the witness informs the court of his wish that the requirement in subs.(4A) should not apply, the requirement does not apply to the extent that the judge is satisfied that not complying with it would not diminish the quality of the witness's evidence; and
(2) the requirement does not apply to the extent that the court is satisfied that making such a provision would not be likely to maximise the quality of the witness's evidence so far as practicable (whether because the application to that evidence of one or more other special measures available in relation to the witness would have that result or for any other reason).

In making either decision (i.e. one under (4)(ba) or (4B)(a)) the judge must take into account the following factors (and any others he considers relevant):

(a) the age and maturity of the witness;
(b) the ability of the witness to understand the consequences of giving evidence otherwise than in accordance with the requirements in sub(3) or (as the case may be) in accordance with the requirement in subs.(4A);
(c) the relationship (if any) between the witness and the accused;

(d) the witness's social and cultural background and ethnic origins;

(e) the nature and alleged circumstances of the offence to which the proceedings relate.

Special provisions relating to sexual offences

66–016 Where in criminal proceedings in the Crown Court relating to a sexual offence (or to a sexual offence and other offences): YJCEA 1999, s.22A

(1) the complainant in respect of that offence is a witness in the proceedings; and

(2) is not an eligible witness by reason of s.16(1)(a) (whether or not he is an eligible witness by reason of any other provision of s.16 or 17),

then, if a party to the proceedings makes an application under s.19(1)(a) for a special measures direction in relation to the complainant, the party may request that the direction provide for any relevant recording to be admitted under s.27 (video recorded evidence in chief).

If:

(a) a party to the proceedings makes a request under subsection (4) with respect to the complainant; and

(b) the judge determines for the purposes of s.19(2) that the complainant is eligible for assistance by virtue of s.16(1)(b) or 17,

the judge must firstly have regard to subss.(7) to (9), and then have regard to s.19(2); and for the purposes of s.19(2), as it then applies to the complainant, any special measure required to be applied in relation to him by virtue of this section is to be treated as if it were a measure determined by the judge pursuant to s.19(2)(a) and (b)(i), to be one that (whether on its own or with any other special measures) would be likely to maximise, so far as practicable, the quality of the complainant's evidence.

Subject to s.27(2) the judge must give a special measures direction in relation to the complainant that provides for any relevant recording to be admitted under s.27, except that that requirement does not apply to the extent that the judge is satisfied that compliance with it would not be likely to maximise the quality of the complainant's evidence so far as practicable (whether because the application to that evidence of one or more other special measures available in relation to the complainant would have that result or for any other reason).

A "relevant recording" in relation to a complainant, is a video recording of an interview of him made with a view to its admission as the evidence in chief of the complainant."

Evidence by live link

66–017 A special measures direction may provide for the witness to give evidence by means of a live link (see LIVE LINKS). Such a direction may also provide for a specified person to accompany the witness while the witness is giving evidence by live link. In determining who that person is the judge will have regard to the wishes of the witness. YJCEA 1999, s.24

Where a direction provides for a witness to give evidence by that means he may not give evidence in any other way without the permission of the judge, which permission may be given if it appears to the judge to be in the interests of justice to do so, in which case he may do so:

(1) on the application of a party to the proceedings if there has been a material change of circumstances since the time the direction was made, or since any previous application; or
(2) on his own initiative.

Such a direction may also provide for a specified person to accompany the witness while he is giving his evidence by live link. In determining who that person is the judge must have regard to the wishes of the witness.

Evidence given in private
66–018   In a case where:

(1) the proceedings relate to a sexual offence; or
(2) it appears to the judge that there are reasonable grounds for any person (other than the accused) has sought to, or will, intimidate the witness in connection with testifying in the proceedings,

YJCEA 1999, s.25

a special measures direction may provide for the exclusion from the court during the giving of the witness's evidence, of persons specified in it, provided that the persons excluded do not include the accused, legal representatives acting in the proceedings or any interpreter or other person appointed in pursuance of the direction to assist the witness. Special provisions are made in s.25(3) for the press.

Video recorded evidence-in-chief
66–019   A special measure direction may provide for a video recording of an interview of a witness to be admitted as evidence-in-chief of that witness, unless the judge is of the opinion, having regard to all the circumstances of the case, that in the interests of justice the recording, or that part of it should not be so admitted.

YJCEA 1999, s.27

In determining that question, the judge:

(1) must consider whether any prejudice to the accused which might result from that part being admitted is outweighed by the desirability of showing the whole or substantially the whole of the recording; and.
(2) may, if he gives such a direction, subsequently direct that it is not to be admitted if;
   (a) the witness will not be available for cross-examination (whether conducted in the ordinary way or in accordance any such direction); or
   (b) the parties to the proceedings have not agreed that there is no need for the witness to attend; or
   (c) CPR requiring disclosure of the circumstances in which the recording was made have not been complied with.

Giving evidence is not a memory test and the speculative possibility that a witness might say something when giving live evidence in chief which is different from what she said in a pre-recorded interview and, thereby, deprive the defence of the opportunity of cross-examining on those differences is not, in itself, an adequate reason for refusing to allow the playing of an interview (*R. v Davies* [2011] EWCA Crim 1177, [2011] Crim. L.R. 732).

Where a recording, or part of a recording, is admitted, the witness must be called by the party tendering it in evidence unless either a direction provides for his cross-examination to be given otherwise than by testimony in court, or the parties have agreed that there is no need for him to be available. The witness may not, without the permission of the judge, give evidence-in-chief otherwise than by means of the recording, as to any matter which in the judge's opinion, is dealt with in the witness's recorded testimony.

The judge may give such permission, either on the application of a party, if there has been a change of circumstances, or on his own initiative, if it appears to him to be in the interests of justice to do so. In giving such permission, the judge may direct that evidence in question be given by the witness by means of a live link, in which case s.24(5)–(7) will apply.

Examination of witness through intermediary

66–020 A special measures direction may provide for any examination of a witness (however and wherever conducted) to be conducted through an intermediary, that is an interpreter or other person approved for the purpose by the judge (see, e.g. *R. v Watts* [2010] EWCA Crim 1824, [2011] Crim L.R. 68).

YJCEA 1999, s.29, r.29

The intermediary's function is to communicate to the witness questions put to him, and to the person asking such questions the answers given by the witness in reply, and to explain those questions and answers so far as is necessary to enable them to be understood by the witness or person in question.

Any such examination of the witness must take place in the presence of such persons as the Rules, or the judge's direction, may provide, but in such circumstances in which:

(1) the judge and legal representatives acting in the proceedings are able to see and hear the examination of the witness and to communicate with the intermediary; and

(2) (except in the case of a video recorded examination) the jury (if there is one) are able to see and hear the examination of the witness.

Where two or more legal representatives are acting for a party to the proceedings (2) above is to be regarded as satisfied in relation to those representatives, if at all material times it is satisfied in relation at least one of them.

The intermediary must not act in a particular case except after making the appropriate statutory declaration, (see OATHS AND FORMALITIES).

Note that these provisions do not apply to an interview of the witness which was recorded by means of a video recording (see 66–016 above) with a view to its admission as the witness's evidence-in-chief, although a special measures direction may provide for such a recording to be admitted under s.27 if that interview was conducted through an intermediary, provided that;

    (a) the intermediary made the statutory declaration before the interview began; and

    (b) the judge's approval for the purposes of these provisions (i.e. s.29) is given before the direction is given.

Examination of accused through intermediary (not in force)

66–021   When CorJA 2009, s.104, which inserts new ss.33BA and 33BB into YJCEA 1999, is brought into force an accused will be able to give evidence through an intermediary. The judge will be able, on the application of the accused, if he is satisfied.

    (1) in the case of an accused aged under 18 when the application is made that his ability to participate effectively in the proceedings as a witness giving oral evidence in court is compromised by his level of intellectual ability or social functioning; or

    (2) in the case of an accused who has attained the age of 18 when the application is made that he suffers from a mental disorder (within the meaning of MHA 1983) or otherwise has a significant impairment of intelligence and social function, and is for that reason unable to participate effectively in the proceedings as a witness giving oral evidence in court; and

    (3) that making such a direction is necessary in order to ensure that the accused receives a fair trial,

to give a direction that provides for any examination of the accused to be conducted through an interpreter or other person approved by the judge for the purpose, known as "an intermediary". His function is to communicate to the accused, questions put to the accused, and to any person asking such questions, the answers given by the accused in reply to them, and to explain such questions or answers so far as necessary to enable them to be understood by the accused or the person in question.

    Any such examination of the accused must take place in the presence of such persons as the Rules, or the judge's direction, may provide and in circumstances in which:

    (a) the judge and legal representatives acting in the proceedings are able to see and hear the examination of the accused and to communicate with the intermediary;

    (b) the jury (if there is one) are able to see and hear the examination of the accused; and

    (c) where there are two or more accused in the proceedings, each of the other accused is able to see and hear the examination of the accused,

disregarding for this purpose any impairment of eyesight or hearing.

    Where two or more legal representatives are acting for a party to the proceedings, (a) above is to be regarded as satisfied in relation to those representatives if at all material times it is satisfied in relation to at least one of them.

SPECIAL MEASURES DIRECTIONS

A person may not act as an intermediary in a particular case except after making a declaration, in such form as may be prescribed by the Rules, (see OATHS AND FORMALITIES) that the person will faithfully perform the function of an intermediary.

The Perjury Act 1911, s.1 applies in relation to a person acting as an intermediary as it applies in relation to a person lawfully sworn as an interpreter in a judicial proceeding.

In *SC v UK,* (2005) 40 E.H.R.R. 226 it was said that the duty to provide an intermediary for a vulnerable accused applies not only during the proceedings (as provided for above) but also beforehand as the child and his lawyers prepare for trial.

Examination of accused through intermediary: further provisions

66–022   The judge may discharge a direction given under s.33BA above at any time before or during the proceedings to which it applies if it appears to him that the direction is no longer necessary in order to ensure that the accused receives a fair trial (but his does not affect the power to give a further direction under the section in relation to the accused). The judge may also vary (or further vary) a direction given under the section at any time before or during the proceedings to which it applies if it appears to him that it is necessary for the direction to be varied in order to ensure that the accused receives a fair trial. He may exercise these powers of its own motion or on an application by a party.   YJCEA 1999, s.33BB

The judge must state in open court his reasons for giving, varying or discharging any such direction or for refusing an application for, or for the variation or discharge of, any such direction.

Aids to communication

66–023   A special measures direction may provide for a witness while giving evidence (whether in testimony in court or otherwise) to be provided with such as the judge considers appropriate with a view to enabling questions or answers to be communicated to or by the witness despite any disability or disorder or other impairment which he has or suffers from.   YJCEA 1999, s.30

Status and weight of statements made; jury warning

66–024   Where a statement may by a witness is not, in accordance with a special measures direction, made in direct oral testimony in court but forms part of the witness's evidence in the proceedings, that statement is to be treated as if made by the witness in direct oral testimony, and accordingly: YJCEA 1999, s.31

(1) it is admissible evidence of any fact of which such testimony from the witness would be admissible; but

(2) is not capable of corroborating any other evidence given by the witness,

and this provision applies to a statement admitted under s.27 (66–019) which is not made on oath even of it would have been required to be given on oath if made by the witness in direct oral testimony in court.   YJCEA 1999, s.32

In estimating the weight, if any, to be attached to such a statement, the judge must have regard to all the circumstances from which an inference can reasonably be drawn as to the accuracy of the statement or otherwise.

Where, in a trial on indictment with a jury, a statement has been given in accordance with a special measures direction, the judge must give the jury, such warning, if any, as he considers necessary to ensure that the fact that the direction was given to the witness does not prejudice the accused.

When the judge tells the jury that he will deal with a particular set of criticisms, it is important that he does so, especially when he has made countervailing points for the other side (*R. v Davies* [2011] EWCA Crim 1177, [2011] Crim. L.R. 733).

3. Reporting direction: adult witnesses

General

66–025 The judge may on the application of any party to the proceedings, make a reporting direction in respect of any witness in the proceedings, other than the accused, who has attained the age of 18, where he determines that:

YJCEA 1999, s.46(1)–(5), (8), (12)

(1) the witness is eligible for protection; and
(2) giving a reporting direction in relation to him is likely to improve:
   (a) the quality of his evidence; or
   (b) the level of co-operation given by him to any party to the proceedings in connection with that party's preparation of its case.

"Quality" refers to the quality of the evidence in completeness, coherence and accuracy, and for this purpose, "coherence" refers to the witness's ability, in giving evidence, to give answers which address the questions put to him and can be understood both individually and collectively.

References to a party's preparation of the case include, in the case of the prosecutor, the carrying out of investigations into any offence at any time charged in the proceedings.

For the purposes of this provision a witness is "eligible for protection" if the judge is satisfied that:

YJCEA 1999, s.46(7)

(i) the quality of evidence given by the witness; or
(ii) the level of co-operation given by the witness to any party to the proceedings in connection with that party's preparation of its case,

is likely to be diminished by reason of fear or distress on the part of the witness in connection with being identified by members of the public as a witness in the proceedings.

In determining whether a witness is eligible for protection the judge must take into account, in particular:

- the nature and alleged circumstances of the offence to which the proceedings relate;
- the age of the witness;
- such of the following matters as appear to the court to be relevant, namely:

- the social and cultural background and ethnic origins of the witness;
- the domestic and employment circumstances of the witness; and
- any religious beliefs or political opinions of the witness;
- any behaviour towards the witness on the part of:
  - the accused, members of the family or associates of the accused; or
  - any other person who is likely to be an accused or a witness in the proceedings, and,

in determining that question the judge, must in addition, consider any views expressed by the witness.

In determining whether to give a reporting direction the judge must consider whether it would be in the interests of justice to do so, and the public interest in avoiding the imposition of a substantial and unreasonable restriction on the reporting of the proceedings.

Effect of reporting direction

66–026 A reporting direction of this nature is a direction that no matter relating to the witness may, during the witness's lifetime, be included in any publication if it is likely to lead members of the public to identify him as being a witness in the proceedings.

The matters in relation to which the restrictions imposed by a reporting direction apply if their inclusion in any publication is likely to have that result include in particular:

(1) the witness's name;
(2) the witness's address;
(3) the identity of any educational establishment attended by him;
(4) the identity of any place of work; and
(5) any still or moving picture of him.

Exception, revocation

66–027 The judge, or an appellate court, may, by an excepting direction, dispense to any extent specified in the excepting direction, with the restrictions imposed by a reporting direction if:

YJCEA 1999, ss.46(9)–(11)

(1) he is satisfied that it is necessary in the interests of justice to do so; or
(2) he is satisfied that:
  (a) the effect of those restrictions is to impose a substantial and unreasonable restriction on the reporting of the proceedings; and
  (b) it is in the public interest to remove or relax that restriction,

but no excepting direction may be given under (2) by reason only of the fact that the proceedings have been determined in any way or have been abandoned.

A reporting direction may be revoked by the judge (or by an appellate court). An excepting direction may be given at the time the reporting direction is given or subsequently; and may be varied or revoked by the judge (or by an appellate court).

Procedure

66–028   An application for a reporting direction in relation to a witness is made in the form set out at PD 2004, Annex D, or orally under r.16.3. If in writing it must be sent to the court officer, and copies must be sent at the same time to every other party to the proceedings. R.16.1

If the application is in writing any party to the proceedings wishing to oppose that application must notify the applicant, and the court officer, in writing of his opposition, giving for it, within five business days of the date the application was served on him (unless an extension of time is granted under r.16.6 below), stating whether he disputes that:

(1) the witness is eligible for protection under s.46; or   R. 16.2

(2) the granting of protection would be likely to improve the quality of the evidence given by the witness or the level of co-operation given by the witness to any party to the proceedings in connection with that party's preparation of its case.

Urgent action

66–029   A judge may give a reporting direction under s.46 of the Act in relation to a witness in those proceedings, notwithstanding that the five business days specified in r.16.2(3) have not expired if: Rr.16.3(2), (3)

(1) an application is made to him it for the purpose; and

(2) he is satisfied that, due to exceptional circumstances, it is appropriate to do so.

Any party to the proceedings may make such an application, whether or not an application has already been made under 16.1, and the application may be made orally or in writing. If it is made orally, the judge may hear and take into account any representations made to him by a person who in his view has a legitimate interest in the application (r.16.3(4)). The application must specify the exceptional circumstances on which the applicant relies (r.16.3(5)).

Excepting direction

66–030   An application for an excepting direction under s.46(9) (dispensing with restrictions imposed by a reporting direction) may be made by: R.16.4(1), (2)

(1) any party to the proceedings; or

(2) any person who, although not a party to the proceedings, is directly affected by a reporting direction given in relation to a witness in the proceedings,

stating why:

(a) the effect of a reporting direction places a substantial and unreasonable restriction on the reporting of the proceedings; and Rr.16.4(3), (4)

(b) it is in the public interest to remove or relax those restrictions.

The application may be made in writing in the form set out in the Practice Direction at any time after the commencement of the proceedings in the court or orally at a hearing of an application for a reporting R.16.4(5), (6) direction. The written application must be sent to the Crown Court officer and copies must be sent at the same time to every party to the proceedings.

Any person served with a copy of an application for an excepting direction who wishes to oppose it, must notify the applicant and the court officer in writing of his opposition and give reasons for it, within five business days of the date the application was served on him (unless an extension of time is granted under r.16.6). Rr.16.5(1)–(4)

Variation or revocation

66–031 An application to:

(1) revoke a reporting direction; or
(2) vary or revoke an excepting direction,

may be made to a judge at any time after the commencement of the proceedings in the court, by:

(a) a party to the proceedings in which the direction was issued; or
(b) a person who, although not a party to those proceedings, is in the judge's opinion directly affected by the direction.

It must be made in writing, and the applicant must send the application to the officer of the court in which the proceedings commenced, and at the same time copies of the application must be sent to every party or, as the case may be, every party to the proceedings, setting out in his application the reasons why he seeks to have the direction varied or, as the case may be, revoked. R.16.5(5), (6)

A person served with a copy of an application who wishes to oppose it, must notify the applicant and the appropriate officer in writing within five business days of the date the application was served on him (unless an extension of time is granted under r.16.6 below), of his opposition and give reasons for it.

Application for an extension of time

66–032 An application may be made in writing to extend the period of time for notification under r.16.2(3), 16.4(6) or 16.5(6) before that period has expired. It must be accompanied by a statement setting out the reasons why the applicant is unable to give notification within the period, and must be sent to the Crown Court officer and a copy of the application must be sent at the same time to the applicant. R.16.7

Decisions of the court

66–033 The judge may:

(1) determine any application made under r.16.1 and 16.3–16.6 without a hearing; or
(2) direct a hearing of any application.

The judge may hear and take into account representations made to him by any person who in his view has a legitimate interest in the application.

The court officer will notify all the parties of the judge's decision as soon as reasonably practicable. If a hearing of an application is to take place, the appropriate officer will notify each party to the proceedings of the time and place of the hearing.

Transfer of magistrates' courts proceedings to the Crown Court

66–034 Where proceedings are sent or transferred from a magistrates' court to the Crown Court, in which reporting directions or excepting directions have been ordered, the magistrates' court officer is under a duty to forward copies of all relevant directions to the Crown Court officer at the place to which those proceedings are sent or transferred. R.16.8

Restrictions on cross-examination of witness

66–035 Where an accused is prevented from cross-examining a witness in person by virtue of YJCEA 1999, ss.34, 35 or 36: R.31.1

(1) the judge must explain to the accused, as early in the proceedings as is reasonably practicable, that he is prevented from cross-examining a witness in person; and should arrange for a legal representative to act for him for the purpose of cross-examining the witness;

(2) the accused must then notify the court officer in writing, within seven days of the judge giving his explanation, or within such other period as the judge may in any particular case allow, of the action, if any, that he has taken;

(3) where the judge gives his explanation to the accused, either within seven days of the day set for the commencement of any hearing at which a witness in respect of whom a prohibition under ss.34, 35 or 36 applies may be cross-examined, or after such a hearing has commenced, the period of seven days will be reduced in accordance with any directions issued by the judge;

(4) where the accused has arranged for a legal representative to act for him, the notification must include details of the name and address of the representative, and the Crown Court officer will notify all other parties to the proceedings of the name and address of the person, if any, appointed to act for the accused;

(5) where at the end of the period of seven days or such other period as the judge has allowed, the court has received no notification from the accused, it may grant the accused an extension of time, for such period as is considered appropriate in the circumstances of the case, whether on its own motion or on the application of the accused. Before granting of an extension, the judge may hold a hearing, at which all parties to the proceedings may attend and be heard.

Any decision as to the grant of an extension of time will be notified to the parties by the Crown Court officer.

Appointment of legal representative

66–036 Where the court decides in accordance with YJCEA 1999, s.38(4) to appoint a qualified legal representative, the Crown Court officer will notify all parties to the proceedings of the name and address R.31.2

of the representative. Such an appointment, except to the extent as the judge may in a particular case determine, terminates at the conclusion of the cross-examination of the relevant witness or witnesses.

The accused may arrange for the legal representative appointed by the court to be appointed to act for him for the purpose of cross-examining any witness in respect of whom a prohibition applies.

Where such an appointment is made:

(1) both the accused and the legal representative appointed must notify the court of the appointment; and

(2) the legal representative must, from the time of his appointment, act for the accused as though the arrangement had been made under YJCEA 1999, s.38(2)(a) and will cease to be the representative of the court under s.38(4);

(3) where the court receives notification of the appointment, either from the legal representative or from the accused, but not from both, it will investigate whether the appointment has been made, and if it concludes that the appointment has not been made, the representative will continue as if appointed by the court.

An accused may, notwithstanding an appointment by the court under YJCEA 1999, s.38(4), arrange for a legal representative to act for him for the purpose of cross-examining any witness in respect of whom a prohibition under s.34, 35 or 36 applies. Where the accused arranges for, or informs the court of his intention to arrange for, a legal representative to act for him, he must notify the court, within such period as the court may allow, of the name and address of any person appointed to act for him. **R.31.3**

The required notifications will be made to the parties by the court officer.

Prosecutor's application

66–037 An application by the prosecutor for the court to give a direction under YJCEA 1999, s.36 in relation to any witness must: **R.31.4(1)–(4)**

(1) be sent to the Crown Court officer and, at the same time, a copy must be sent by the applicant to every other party to the proceedings;

(2) must state why, in the prosecutor's opinion;

(a) the evidence given by the witness is likely to be diminished if cross-examination is undertaken by the accused in person;

(b) the evidence would be improved if a direction were given under s.36(2); and

(c) it would not be contrary to the interests of justice to give such a direction.

On receipt of the application, the Crown Court officer will refer it if the trial has started, to the trial judge, or if the trial has not started when the application is received, to the judge who has been designated to conduct the trial, or if no judge has been designated for that purpose, to such judge who may be designated for the purposes of hearing that application.

Where a copy of the application is received by a party to the proceedings more than 14 days before the date set for the trial to begin, that party may make observations in writing on the application to the Crown Court officer, but any such observations must be made within 14 days of the receipt of the application and be copied to the other parties to the proceedings.

Party seeking to oppose order

66–038   A party to whom such an application is sent, who wishes to oppose the application, must give his reasons for doing so to the Crown Court officer and the other parties to the proceedings. Those reasons must be notified:

R.31.4(5)–(12)

(1) within 14 days of the date the application was served on him, if that date is more than 14 days before the date set for the trial to begin;
(2) if the trial has begun, in accordance with any directions issued by the trial judge; or
(3) if neither para.(1) or (2) applies, before the date set for the trial to begin.

Where the application is made before the date set for the trial to begin and it:

(a) is not contested by any party to the proceedings, the court may determine the application without a hearing;
(b) is contested by a party to the proceedings, the court must direct a hearing of the application.

Where the application is made after the trial has begun, the application may be made orally giving reasons why the application was not made before the trial commenced; and providing the court with the information set out in 66–032 above, and the trial judge may give such directions as he considers appropriate to deal with the application.

Where a hearing is to take place, the court officer will notify each party to the proceedings of the time and place of the hearing, and a party notified in accordance may be present at the hearing and be heard.

The court officer will, as soon as possible after the determination of the application, give notice of the decision and the reasons for it to all the parties to the proceedings.

4.   Witness anonymity

General

66–039   CE(WA)A 2008 enacted new provisions in relation to witness anonymity orders. While the Act abolished the rules of the common law, it remains a fundamental principle that, save in the exceptional circumstances permitted by the new legislation, an accused person is entitled to know the identity of witnesses who incriminate him. The legislation seeks to preserve the balance between the accused's rights, including his entitlement to a fair trial and a public hearing and to examine the witnesses against him (*R. v Mayers* [2008] EWCA Crim 2899 [2009] 1 Cr. App. R. 30). With the coming into force of CorJA Pt

3, Ch.2 2009, the provisions of CE(WA)A 2008, ss.1 to 9 and 14 have ceased to have effect.

While anonymous witnesses ought not to be called as a matter of routine, now that witness intimidation has become a feature of contemporary life, orders should not be confined to cases of terrorism and gangland killings (*R. v Powar* [2009] EWCA Crim 594; [2009] 2 Cr. App. R. 8).

Nothing in the legislation diminishes the overriding responsibility of the trial judge to ensure that the proceedings are conducted fairly.

An "anonymity order" is to be regarded as "the special measure of last resort"; witness protection and relocation can only be a practical alternative in the rarest of circumstances and if, in effect, forced on a witness, will itself engage his or her right to a private life.

CorJA 2009, s.95

Nothing in the provisions affects the common law rules as to the withholding of information on the grounds of public interest immunity. The common law principles relating to PII are expressly preserved (*R. v H* [2004] UKHL 3, [2004] 2 Cr. App. R. 10 remains authoritative). Disclosure must be complete, in accordance with the Attorney-general's guidelines and other guidance.

Thus:

(1) the prosecutor must comply with his duties in relation to full and frank disclosure, and must be proactive, focussing closely on the credibility of the anonymous witness and the interests of justice; and

(2) defence statements complying with CJIA 2008, s.60, providing for broader identification by the defence of the issues, are crucial.

The obligations of the prosecutor in the context of witness anonymity go much further than the ordinary duties of disclosure.

Where the judge entertains reservations about the good faith of the efforts made by the prosecution investigation into any relevant consideration bearing on the question of witness anonymity, an application for an order is likely to be met with a blank refusal (*R. v Mayers*, above).

Nature of order

66–040 A "witness anonymity order" is an order made by a court that requires such measures as may be specified in the order to be taken in relation to a witness in criminal proceeding, as the judge considers appropriate to ensure that the identity of the witness is not disclosed in, or in connection with, the proceedings.

COrJA 2009, s.86

The kinds of measures that may be required to be taken in relation to a witness include (but is not limited to) measures for securing one or more of the following:

(1) that the witness's name and other identifying details may be:
    (a) withheld;
    (b) removed from materials disclosed to any party to the proceedings;

PD 2004, I.15.3

(2) that the witness may use a pseudonym;
(3) that the witness is not asked questions of any specified description that might lead to the identification of the witness;

(4) that the witness is screened to any specified extent;

(5) that the witness's voice is subjected to modulation to any specified extent, although,

nothing in this provision authorises the judge to require the witness to be screened to such an extent that the witness cannot be seen by the judge or other members of the court (if any), or the jury (if there is one); nor the witness's voice to be modulated to such an extent that the witness's natural voice cannot be heard by such persons.

Case management; service

66–041   Where such an application is proposed, with the parties' active assistance the court should set a realistic timetable, in accordance with the duties imposed by rr.3.2 and 3.3 (see CASE MANAGEMENT). Where possible, the trial judge should determine the application, and any hearing should be attended by the parties' trial advocates.

PD 2004, I.15.2

Where the prosecutor proposes an application for such an order, it is not necessary for the application to have been determined before the proposed evidence is served. In most cases an early indication of what that evidence will be if an order is made will be consistent with a party's duties under rr.1.2 and 3.3.

The prosecutor should serve with the other prosecution evidence a witness statement setting out the proposed evidence, redacted in such a way as to prevent disclosure of the witness' identity, (as permitted by s.87(4)). Likewise the prosecutor should serve with other prosecution material disclosed under CPIA 1996 any such material appertaining to the witness, similarly redacted.

Making an application

66–042   An application for a witness anonymity order to be made in relation to a witness in criminal proceedings may be made to the court by the prosecutor or by the accused.

COrJA 2009, s.87

Where an application is made:

(1) by the prosecutor, he:
- (a) must (unless the court directs otherwise) inform the court of the identity of the witness; but
- (b) is not required to disclose in connection with the application:
  - (i) the identity of the witness; or
  - (ii) any information that might enable the witness to be identified, to any other party to the proceedings or his or her legal representatives;

(2) by the accused, he:
- (a) must inform the court and the prosecutor of the identity of the witness; but
- (b) (if there is more than one accused) is not required to disclose in connection with the application;
  - (i) the identity of the witness; or
  - (ii) any information that might enable the witness to be identified, to any other accused or his legal representatives.

Accordingly, where the prosecutor or the accused proposes to make an application under this section in respect of a witness, any relevant material which is disclosed by or on behalf of that party before the determination of the application may be disclosed in such a way as to prevent the identity of the witness, or any information that might enable the witness to be identified, from being disclosed except as required above. "Relevant material" in this context, means any document or other material which falls to be disclosed, or is sought to be relied on, by or on behalf of the party concerned in connection with the proceedings or proceedings preliminary to them.

The judge must give every party to the proceedings the opportunity to be heard on an application under this section, he is not prevented from hearing one or more parties in the absence of an accused and his or her legal representatives, if it appears to him to be appropriate to do so in the circumstances of the case. R.29.21

The Crown Court officer will notify the DPP of an application, unless the prosecutor is, or acts on behalf of, a public authority.

Content and conduct of application

66–043 An applicant for a witness anonymity order must include in the application nothing that might reveal the witness' identity, but must describe the measures proposed by the applicant, and explain how the proposed order meets the conditions prescribed by CorJA 2009, s.88 and explain why no measures other than those proposed will suffice, such as: R.29.19(1)

(1) an admission of the facts that would be proved by the witness;
(2) an order restricting public access to the trial;
(3) reporting restrictions, in particular under YJCEA 1999, s.46 or under CYPA 1933, s.39;
(4) a direction for a special measure under YJCE 1999; s.19;
(5) introduction of the witness's written statement as hearsay evidence under CJA 2003, s.116; or
(6) arrangements for the protection of the witness.

The applicant must also attach to the application:

(a) a witness statement setting out the proposed evidence, edited in such a way as not to reveal the witness' identity;
(b) where the prosecutor is the applicant, any further prosecution evidence to be served, and any further prosecution material to be disclosed under CPIA 1996, similarly edited; and
(c) any defence statement that has been served, or as much information as may be available to the applicant that gives particulars of the defence; and

must ask for a hearing, if he wants one.

Representations in response

66–044 All parties must have an opportunity to make oral representations to the judge on an application for an order: s.87(6). A party upon whom an application for an order is served must serve a response on the PD 2004, I.15.8,9 other parties and on the court. To avoid the risk of injustice a respondent must actively assist the court. If not already done, a respondent defendant should serve a defence statement under CPIA 1996, ss.5 or 6 (see DISCLOSURE) so that the judge is fully informed of what is in issue. The prosecutor's continuing duty to disclose material (under CPIA 1996, s.7A) may be engaged by a defendant's application for a witness anonymity order. Therefore a prosecutor's response should include confirmation that that duty has been considered.

Nothing disclosed under the 1996 Act by a respondent prosecutor to a respondent defendant should contain anything that might reveal the witness' identity. A respondent prosecutor must provide an applicant defendant and the court with all available information relevant to the considerations to which the Act requires a court to have regard, whether or not that information falls to be disclosed under the 1996 Act. R.29.22

Where a party or, where the case is over, a witness, wants to make such representations about:

(1) an application for a witness anonymity order;
(2) an application for the variation or discharge of such an order; or
(3) a variation or discharge the judge proposes on his own initiative.

He must serve the representations on the Crown Court officer, and on each other party; and do so not more than 14 days after, as applicable, service of the application, or notice of the variation or discharge that the court proposes; asking for a hearing, if that party or witness wants one.

Where representations include information that the person making them thinks might reveal the witness' identity, that person must:

(a) omit that information from the representations served on an accused;
(b) mark the information to show that it is only for the court (and for the prosecutor, if relevant); and
(c) with that information include an explanation of why it has been withheld.

Representations against a witness anonymity order must explain why the conditions for making the order are not met, and representations against the variation or discharge of such an order must explain why it would not be appropriate to vary or discharge it, taking account of the conditions for making an order.

A prosecutor's representations in response to an application by an accused must include all information available to the prosecutor that is relevant to the conditions and considerations specified by CorJA 2009, ss.88 and 89.

Conditions for making order

66–045   Where an application is made for a witness anonymity order to be made in relation to a witness in criminal proceedings, the judge may make such an order only if he is satisfied that the following conditions, A to C, are met. CorJA 2009, s.88

(1) **Condition A is** that the proposed order is necessary in order to:

    (a) protect the safety of the witness or another person or to prevent any serious damage to property; or

    (b) prevent real harm to the public interest (whether affecting the carrying on of any activities in the public interest or the safety of a person involved in carrying on such activities, or otherwise).

(2) **Condition B** is that, having regard to all the circumstances, the effect of the proposed order would be consistent with the accused receiving a fair trial.

(3) **Condition C** is that the importance of the witness's testimony is such that in the interests of justice the witness ought to testify and:

    (a) the witness would not testify if the proposed order were not made; or

    (b) there would be real harm to the public interest if the witness were to testify without the proposed order being made.

In determining whether the proposed order is "necessary" for the purpose mentioned in (1) above, the judge must have regard (in particular) to any reasonable fear on the part of the witness, that he or another person would suffer death or injury, or that there would be serious damage to property, if the witness were to be identified.

No order may be made unless all three of the above conditions are satisfied. The fact that a witness provides the sole or decisive evidence against the accused is not, of itself, conclusive as to whether conditions (1) to (3) are met. Condition (3) (interests of justice) should be considered first. In relation to condition (1) (safety of witness) it matters not whether the risk to the safety of the witness is attributable to the actions of the accused personally; it may be established if and when the safety of the witness is under threat from any source. Condition (2) (fair trial) is fact-specific (*R. v Mayers,* above).

Relevant considerations

66–046   When deciding whether Conditions A to C in para.66–045 above are met in the case of an application for a witness anonymity order, the judge must have regard to the considerations mentioned below, and such other matters as he considers relevant.   *CorJA 2009, s.89*

The considerations are:

(1) the general right of a person accused in criminal proceedings to know the identity of a witness in the proceedings;

(2) the extent to which the credibility of the witness concerned would be a relevant factor when the weight of his or her evidence comes to be assessed;

(3) whether evidence given by the witness might be the sole or decisive evidence implicating the accused;

(4) whether the witness's evidence could be properly tested (whether on grounds of credibility or otherwise) without his or her identity being disclosed;

(5) whether there is any reason to believe that the witness:

    (a) has a tendency to be dishonest; or

    (b) has any motive to be dishonest in the circumstances of the witness and to any relationship between the witness and the accused or any associates of the accused; and

(6) whether it would be reasonably practicable to protect the witness by any means other than by making a witness anonymity order specifying the measures that are under consideration by the court.

This list is not to be seen as being in any order of priority. None of them is conclusive of whether the accused can have a fair trial (and that applies to the question whether the evidence is the sole or decisive evidence against the accused) (*R. v Mayers,* above).

Evaluation of evidence

66–047 The judge should examine whether the anonymous evidence is supported extraneously, or whether there were a number of witnesses who incriminated the accused. If numerous witnesses are to give evidence anonymously it will be advisable to investigate any link between them, although there is no corroboration requirement.

Witnesses who come forward before there would be an opportunity to manufacture a case incriminating the accused are likely to be treated with less suspicion than witnesses who come forward later out of the blue.

In relation to police witnesses, particularly those working undercover, it may be accepted that there are often sound reasons for maintaining their anonymity. The judge will normally be entitled to follow the unequivocal assertion by such a witness that without an anonymity order, he would not be prepared to testify *(R. v Mayers,* above).

The need for a hearing

66–048 The judge may decide whether to make, vary or discharge an order at a hearing (which will be in private, unless he otherwise directs), or without a hearing (unless any party asks for one) and in the absence of an accused.

R.29.18

A hearing may not be needed if none is sought: r.29.18(1)(a). Where, for example:

PD 2004, I.15.10

(1) the witness is an investigator who is recognisable by the defendant but known only by an assumed name, and there is no likelihood that the witness' credibility will be in issue, then the judge may indicate a provisional decision and invite representations within a defined period, usually 14 days, including representations about whether there should be a hearing; in such a case, where the parties do not object the judge may make an order without a hearing; or
(2) where the judge provisionally considers an application to be misconceived, an applicant may choose to withdraw it without requiring a hearing.

Where the judge directs a hearing of the application then he should allow adequate time for service of the representations in response. Nothing in the statute permits the giving of hearsay evidence from an anonymous witness (*R. v Ford* [2010] EWCA Crim 2250, [2011] Crim. L.R. 475).

SPECIAL MEASURES DIRECTIONS

Determination of the application

66–049 The judge must not exercise his power to make, vary or discharge such an order, or to refuse to do so: R.29.18

(1) before or during the trial, unless each party has had an opportunity to make representations;
(2) on an appeal by the accused to which r.63 (appeal to the Crown Court), unless in each party's case that party has had an opportunity to make representations, or the appeal court is satisfied that it is not reasonably practicable to communicate with that party;
(3) after the trial and any such appeal are over, unless in the case of each party and the witness, each has had an opportunity to make representations, or the court is satisfied that it is not reasonably practicable to communicate with that party or witness.

At the hearing, the general rule is that the judge will receive, in the following sequence: R.29.19(3)

(a) representations, first by the applicant and then by each other party in all the parties' presence; and then
(b) information withheld from the defendant, and further representations by the applicant, in the absence of any, or any other defendant, but the judge may direct other arrangements.   PD 2004, I.15.16

During the last stage of the hearing it is essential that the judge test thoroughly the information supplied in confidence in order to satisfy himself that the conditions prescribed by the Act (see 66–046 above) are met. At that stage, if the judge concludes that this is the only way in which he can satisfy himself as to a relevant condition or consideration, exceptionally he may invite the applicant to present the proposed witness to be questioned by him. Any such questioning should be carried out at such a time, and the witness brought to the court in such a way, as to prevent disclosure of his or her identity.   R.29.19(4)

Before the witness gives evidence, the applicant must identify the witness to the judge, if not already done, and without revealing his name, to any other party or person, unless, at the prosecutor's request the judge orders otherwise.   PD 2004, I.15.15

On a prosecutor's application, the court is likely to be assisted by the attendance of a senior investigator or other person of comparable authority who is familiar with the case.   PD 2004, I.15.17

Appointment of special counsel

66–50 The judge may ask the Attorney-General to appoint special counsel to assist. However, it must be kept in mind that, "Such an appointment will always be exceptional, never automatic; a course of last and never first resort. It should not be ordered unless and until the trial judge is satisfied that no other course will adequately meet the overriding requirement of fairness to the defendant": *R. v H* (above) at [22]. Whether to accede to such a request is a matter for the Attorney-General, and adequate time should be allowed for the consideration of such a request.

Nature and announcement of order

66–051   Where the court makes a witness anonymity order it is essential that the measures to be taken are clearly specified in a written record of the order approved by the judge and issued on his behalf. The written record of the order must not disclose the identity of the witness to whom it applies, however, it is essential that there be maintained some means of establishing a clear correlation between witness and order, and especially where in the same proceedings witness anonymity orders are made in respect of more than one witness, specifying different measures in respect of each.

PD 2004,
I.15.19,20

Careful preservation of the application for the order, including any confidential information presented to the court, ordinarily will suffice for this purpose.

PD 2004,
I.15.18

The judge should announce his decision on an application in the parties' presence and in public. He should give such reasons as it is possible to give without revealing the witness's identity. He will be conscious that reasons given in public may be reported and reach the jury. Consequently, he should ensure that nothing in his decision or his reasons can undermine any warning he may give to jurors under s.90(2) of the Act (see 66–054 below). The announcement of those reasons will be recorded.

Recording the proceedings

66–052   A recording of the proceedings will be made, in accordance with r.66.8(2). The Crown Court officer must treat such a recording in the same way as the recording of an application for a public interest ruling. It must be kept in secure conditions, and the arrangements made by the Crown Court officer for any transcription must impose restrictions that correspond with those under r.66.9(2)(a).

Discharge or variation of the order

66–053   The judge may discharge or vary a witness anonymity order on application, if there has been a material change of circumstances since the order was made, or since any previous variation of it; or on his own initiative. Rule 29.21 allows the parties to apply for the variation of a pre-trial direction where circumstances have changed.

CorJA 2009,
s.91; r.29

The judge should keep under review the question of whether the conditions for making an order are met. In addition, consistently with the parties' duties under duties under rr.1.2 and 3.3, (see CASE MANAGEMENT) it is incumbent on each and in particular on the applicant for the order, to keep the need for it under review.

PD 2004,
I.15.22

R.29.22

A party who wants the court to vary or discharge a witness anonymity order, or a witness who wants the court to do so when the case is over, must apply in writing, as soon as reasonably practicable after becoming aware of the grounds for doing so; and serve the application on the Crown Court officer, and on each other party.

(1) explaining what material circumstances have changed since the order was made (or last varied, if applicable);

(2) explaining why the order should be varied or discharged, taking account of the conditions for making an order; and

(3) asking for a hearing, if the applicant wants one.

Where an application includes information that the applicant thinks might reveal the witness' identity, the applicant must:

(a) omit that information from the application that is served on an accused;

(b) mark the information to show that it is only for the court and the prosecutor (if the prosecutor is not the applicant); and

(c) with that information include an explanation of why it has been withheld.

Where a party applies to vary or discharge an order after the trial and any appeal are over, the party who introduced the witness's evidence must serve the application on the witness.

Discharge or variation after proceedings

66–054 If:

CorJA 2009, s.92

(1) a court has made a witness anonymity order in relation to a witness in criminal proceedings ("the old proceedings"), and

(2) the old proceedings have come to an end,

the court that made the order may discharge or vary (or further vary) the order if it appears to the judge to be appropriate to do so in view of:

(a) the provisions that apply to the making of a witness anonymity order; and

(b) such other matters as the judge considers relevant.

The court may do so on an application made by a party to the old proceedings if there has been a material change of circumstances since the relevant time, or on an application made by the witness if there has been a material change of circumstances since the relevant time. A judge may not, determine such an application unless in the case of each of the parties to the old proceedings and the witness, he has given the person the opportunity to be heard, or he is satisfied that it is not reasonably practicable to communicate with the person.

These provisions do not prevent the court hearing one or more of the persons mentioned above in the absence of a person who was an accused in the old proceedings and that person's legal representatives, if it appears to be appropriate to do so in the circumstances of the case.

The "relevant time" means the time when the old proceedings came to an end, or, if a previous application has been made the time when the application (or the last application) was made.

Warning to jury

66–055 Where, on a trial on indictment with a jury, any evidence has been given by a witness at a time when a witness anonymity order applied to the witness, the judge must give the jury such warning as the judge considers appropriate to ensure that the fact that the order was made in relation to the witness does not prejudice the accused.

CorJA 2009, s.90

5. Witness preparation

General
66–056 There is a dramatic difference between:

(1) witness training or coaching; and
(2) witness familiarisation.

The training or coaching of witnesses in criminal proceedings, whether for the prosecution or the defence, is not permitted. Such a rule:

(a) minimises the risk inherent in witness training, that a witness may tailor his evidence in the light of what someone else said; and, equally
(b) avoids any unfounded perception that he may have done so.

That is so even where the training takes place one-to-one with someone completely remote from the facts of the case; the witness may come, even unconsciously, to appreciate which aspects of his evidence are perhaps not quite consistent with what others are saying, or indeed not quite what is required of him.

But this principle does not extend to preclude pre-trial arrangements to familiarise witnesses with:

(i) the layout of the court;
(ii) the likely sequence of events when the witness is giving evidence; and
(iii) a balanced appraisal of the different responsibilities of the various participants.

Such arrangements are to be welcomed. Nor does the principle prohibit the training of expert and similar witnesses in, for example, the technique of giving comprehensive evidence of a specialist kind to a jury, or the developing of the ability to resist the inevitable pressure of going further in evidence than matters covered by the witness's specific expertise (*R. v Momodou* [2005] EWCA Crim 177, [2005] 2 Cr. App. R. 6).

Guidance from CACD
66–057 CACD (in *R. v Momodou*, above) stated that if arrangements are made for familiarisation with outside agencies rather than the witness service then the following guidance should be followed:

(1) in relation to prosecution witnesses, the CPS should be informed in advance of any proposal for familiarisation; if appropriate after obtaining police input, they should be invited to comment in advance on the proposals;
(2) if relevant information comes to the police, the police should inform the CPS; the proposals for the intended familiarisation programme should be reduced into writing, rather than left to informal conversations; if, having examined them, the CPS suggest that the programme may be breaching the permitted limits, it should be amended; if the defence engage in the process, it would be wise for counsel's advice to be sought, again

in advance, and again with written information about the nature and extent of the training;

(3) in any event, it is a matter of professional duty on counsel and solicitors to ensure that the judge is informed of any familiarisation process organised by the defence using outside agencies, and it will follow that the prosecution will be made aware of what has happened;

(4) the familiarisation process should normally be supervised or conducted by a criminal justice process, and preferably by an organisation accredited for the purpose by the Bar Council and Law Society;

(5) none of those involved should have any personal knowledge of the matters in issue;

(6) records should be maintained of all those present and the identity of those responsible for the familiarisation process, whenever it takes place; the programme should be retained, together with all the written material (or appropriate copies) used during the familiarisation sessions; none of the material should bear any similarity whatsoever to the issues in the proceedings to be attended by the witnesses, and nothing in it should play on or trigger the witness's recollection of events;

(7) if discussion of the instant criminal proceedings begins, as it almost inevitably will, it must be stopped, and advice given about precisely why it is impermissible, with a warning against the danger of evidence contamination and the risk that the course of justice may be perverted; a note should be made if and when any such warning is given;

(8) all documents used in the process should be retained, and if relevant to prosecution witnesses, handed to the CPS as a matter of course, and in relation to defence witnesses, produced to the court; none should be destroyed; it should be a matter of professional obligation for lawyers involved in these processes, or indeed the trial itself, to see that the guidance is followed.

On December 20, 2004 the Attorney-General issued a report in which he signalled his decision to permit prosecutors to speak to prosecution witnesses. In the light of the judgment in *Momodou* the Professional Standards Committee of the Bar Council set up a working group to examine, as a matter of urgency the implications for barristers involved in training witnesses.

6. Restraint (handcuffing of accused)

66–058 Unless there is sufficient reason (which usually means a real risk of violence or escape) an accused ought not to be visibly restrained by handcuffs or otherwise in the dock or in the witness box. Even if there is some relevant risk, alternative forms of avoiding it ought to be investigated before resort is made to visible restraint; thus

(1) a secure dock;

(2) the interposition of prison officers between accused or on either side of a particular accused;

(3) police officers inside or outside the courtroom; or

(4) in an extreme case, authorisation from the Senior Presiding Judge for armed officers to be in the court building,

are alternatives which are routinely employed.

The jury must be free to decide on the guilt or otherwise of an accused without the risk of being influenced against him by the sight of restraint which, in their minds, suggests that he is regarded, with good cause, as a dangerous criminal (*R. v Horden* [2009] EWCA Crim 388; [2009] 2 Cr. App. R. 24).

Special Measures
Directions

Notes

67. SPENT CONVICTIONS

67–001   Where a person has been convicted of an offence and certain conditions are satisfied, he is, after the applicable rehabilitation period has expired, treated for the purposes of the Rehabilitation of Offenders Act 1974 as a "rehabilitated person" in respect of that conviction, and the conviction is treated as "spent".

Effect of rehabilitation

67–002   The effect of ROA 1974, s.4(1) is that a person who has become a rehabilitated person for the purpose of the Act in respect of a conviction (known as a "spent" conviction) must be treated for all purposes in law as a person who has not committed, been charged with, prosecuted for, convicted of or sentenced for the offence or offences which were the subject of that conviction.

Section 4(1) does not apply, however, to evidence given in criminal proceedings (see s.7(2)(a)). Convictions are often disclosed in such criminal proceedings. When the Bill was before the House of Commons on June 28, 1974 the hope was expressed that the Lord Chief Justice would issue a practice direction for the guidance of the Crown Court with a view to reducing disclosure of spent convictions to a minimum and securing uniformity of approach.

PD 2004, I.6.2

The direction is set out in the following paragraphs:

PD 2004, I.16.3–7

(1) During the trial of a criminal charge, reference to previous convictions (and therefore to spent convictions) can arise in a number of ways. The most common is when the character of the accused or a witness is sought to be attacked by reference to his criminal record, but there are, of course, cases where previous convictions are relevant and admissible as, for instance, to prove system.

(2) It is not possible to give general directions which will govern all these different situations, but it is recommended that both court and advocates should give effect to the general intention of Parliament by never referring to a spent conviction when such reference can reasonably be avoided.

(3) After a verdict of guilty the judge must be provided with a statement of the offender's record for the purposes of sentence. The record supplied should contain all previous convictions, but those which are spent should, so far as practicable, be marked as such.

(4) No one should refer in open court to a spent conviction without the authority of the judge, who should not give it unless the interests of justice require.

(5) When announcing sentence the court should make no reference to a spent conviction unless it is necessary to do so for the purpose of explaining the sentence to be passed.

SPENT CONVICTIONS

Convictions excluded from rehabilitation

67–003   The following are excluded from rehabilitation,

(1) sentences of imprisonment for life;

(2) sentences of imprisonment, youth custody, detention in a young offender institution or corrective training for a period exceeding 30 months;

(3) sentences of preventive detention, detention during HM Pleasure or for life under PCC(S)A 2000, ss.90 or 91, or under the Armed Forces Act 2006, ss.209 or 218, or under the Criminal Procedure (Scotland) Act 1975;

(4) a sentence of detention for a term exceeding 30 months passed under CYPA 1933, s.53 or under PCC(S)A 2000, s.91 or CJA 2006, s.209;

(5) a sentence of custody for life, a sentence of imprisonment for public protection under CJA 2003, s.225;

(6) a sentence of detention for public protection under ibid, s.226, or an extended sentence under *ibid.*, ss.227 or 228 or a youth rehabilitation order under CJIA 2008, Pt 1.

Special provisions apply to spent cautions under ROA 1974, ss.8A, 9A and Sch.2, as inserted by CJIA 2008, s.49, Sch.10 and as to orders under s.1(2)(a) of the Street Offences Act 1959, see the Policing and Crime Act 2009, s.18 (SI 2010/507).

67–004   Table

Where the sentence imposed on conviction is:	The rehabilitation period begins on conviction and lasts for:	ROA 1974
Imprisonment, detention in a young offender institution, youth custody, corrective training, 6–30 months	10 years*	s.5(2) Table A
Imprisonment, detention in a young offender institution, youth custody, not exceeding 6 months	7 years*	
Fine, or any other order not specified in Table B	5 years*	
Borstal training	7 years	s.5(2) Table B
Detention PCC(S)A 2000, s.91, for a term of 6–30 months	5 years	
Detention CYPA 1933, s.53, PCC(S)A 2000, s.91, for not more than 6 months	3 years	
Detention in a detention centre	3 years	
Community punishment order, or community punishment and rehabilitation in case of: (a) offender aged 18 or over at date of conviction; (b) offender under 18 at date of conviction	5 years 2½ years from conviction, or a period beginning with the date of conviction and ending when the order ceases to have effect (whichever is the longer)	CJPOA 1994, Sch.9, para.11; CJA 2003, s.304, Sch.32, para.18
Community rehabilitation (sentenced before Feb 3, 1995) community rehabilitation order (sentenced on or after Feb 3, 1995), community order under CJA 2003, s.177	Date order ceases or 1 year, whichever is the longer, 5 years for an adult, 2½ for a juvenile	
Detention and training order, PCC(S)A 2000, s.100	In the case of an offender: (a) 15 or over at date of conviction, 5 years if it was, 3½ years if it was not, for period exceeding 6 months; (b) under 15, a period beginning with date of conviction and ending 1 year after date on which order ceases to have effect	s.5(6A)

Secure training order, CJPOA 1994, s.1, conditional discharge, bind over, care order CYPA 1933, s.57, a youth rehabilitation order under CJIA 2008, Pt 1, supervision order under PCC(S)A 2000, s.63(1), supervision order CYPA 1933 or CYPA 1963	Duration of order + 1 year	s.5(4), (5)
Committal to remand home CYPA 1933, s.54, committal to approved school CYPA 1933, s.57, attendance at an attendance centre	Duration of order + 1 year	s.5(6)
Hospital order with or without restriction order	5 years or duration of the order + 2 years (whichever is the longer)	s.5(7)
Disqualification, disability, prohibition or other penalty	Duration of the order	s.5(8)
Absolute discharge	6 months	s.5(3)

* Subject to a reduction by half for an offender under 18.

68. TRAVEL RESTRICTION ORDERS

General

68–001   Where:

CJPA 2001, s.33

(1) an offender is convicted of a drug trafficking offence; committed on or after April 1, 2002; and

(2) the judge determines that it appropriate to impose a sentence of imprisonment for that offence; and

(3) the term of imprisonment which he considers appropriate is a term of 4 years or more, the judge **must** in sentencing the offender consider whether it would be more appropriate for such sentence to include a travel restriction order.

If he:

(a) considers that it is appropriate to make such an order in all the circumstances (including any other convictions of the offender for drug trafficking offences in respect of which he is also passing sentence), he should make such an order in relation to him; or

(b) determines that it is not so appropriate he must state his reasons for not making an order. The term in (3) above R.42.1 refers to a single sentence of 4 years for a drug offence, and not a combination of consecutive sentences making a total of 4 years in all (*R. v Alexander* [2011] EWCA Crim 89, [2011] 2 Cr. App. R. 287(52)).

Where the judge decides not to make an order, he must explain why he has not done so when he explains the sentence he has passed.

Such an order prohibits the offender from leaving the United Kingdom at any time in the period which:

(i) begins with release from custody; and

(ii) continues after that time for such period of not less than two years as may be specified in the order.

The order cannot be made retrospectively or, in the case of offences added by statutory order under s.34(1)(c), in respect of an offence committed on or after the date of the coming into force of the relevant order.

There is no statutory maximum; the general presumption is that the travel ban should escalate based on the level of the sentence. It is for the judge to weigh the respective lengths of the term of imprisonment and the travel restriction order in any given case.

The provisions of the order do not prevent deportation, extradition or other statutory removal action, see 68–008, below.

Approach to order

68–002   In approaching the making of an order, the judge needs to bear in mind that:

(1) the section confers a discretion in broad terms;
(2) that discretion must be exercised for the purpose granted, i.e. the reduction of risk of re-offending after release, and must be proportionate;
(3) whilst the power to make such an order is not confined to important cases, the judge has a duty to consider the making of such an order, and if he makes an order must give his reasons for so doing including the reasons for the chosen length;
(4) the mere fact that the offender has been convicted of an offence of importation does not give rise to an inference that he will do it again on release; but
(5) if, on an assessment of all the circumstances, a risk does arise such as to require an order, proportionality is required as to length.

Freedom to travel is a significant aspect of modern life. In restricting a person's freedom in that respect there is a need for balance; the length of any order should be restricted to that which is necessary to protect the public. The drug trade being truly international, the Act does not contemplate an order being made in relation to certain parts of the world only (*R. v Mee* [2004] EWCA Crim 629; [2004] 2 Cr. App. R. (S.) 81).

Direction to deliver up passport

68–003 The order may contain a direction to the offender to deliver up, or cause to be delivered up to the court, any UK passport held by him. Where such a direction is given, the court will send any passport delivered to the Secretary of State (in practice to the nearest Passport Office), who (without prejudice to any other power or duty of his to retain the passport) may retain it for so long as the prohibition imposed by the order applies to the offender, and is not for the time being suspended, and will not return the passport after the prohibition has ceased to apply, or when it is suspended, except when the passport has not expired and an application for its return is made to him by the offender. *CJPA 2001, s.33(5)*

Definitions

68–004 "Drug trafficking offence" has the same meaning as under the DTA 1994, s.1(3) except that it includes any such offence under the MDA 1971 as may be designated by an order made by the Secretary of State under s.34(1)(c). *CJPA 2001, s.34(1), (2)*

"UK passport" means a UK passport within the meaning of IA 1971. This includes a current or expired UK passport. The passports of foreign nationals and the non-British passports of those with dual nationality, whatever their domicile, remain the property of the issuing government. The court should record details of non-British passports. *CJPA 2001, s.33(8)*

"Release from custody" refers to an offender's first release from custody after the imposition of the travel restriction order, which is neither: *CJPA 2001, s.33(7)*

(1) a release on bail; nor
(2) a temporary release for a fixed period.

Revocation and suspension

CJPA 2001, s.35

68–005 An offender who has had a travel restriction order made against him may apply to the court which made the order, for the order to be either revoked or suspended subject to the following:

(1) on an application for revocation made by that person at any time which is:
   (a) after the end of the minimum period; and
   (b) not within three months after the making of any previous application for the revocation of the prohibition, revoke the prohibition imposed by the order with effect from such date as the court may determine; or
(2) on an application made by that person at any time after the making of the order, suspend the prohibition imposed by the order for such period as the court may determine.

The judge must not:

(a) revoke the prohibition unless he considers it appropriate to do so in all the circumstances of the case and having regard, in particular, to:
   (i) that person's character;
   (ii) his conduct since the making of the order; and
   (iii) the offences of which he was convicted on the occasion on which the order was made;
(b) suspend a prohibition for any period unless he is satisfied that there are exceptional circumstances in that person's case that justify the suspension of the prohibition on compassionate grounds for that period.

When determining an application to suspend the judge must have regard to the same three requirements for revocation, mentioned above under (i), (ii) and (iii) and to any other circumstances of the case that he considers relevant.

CJPA 2001, s.35(5)

Effect of suspension

CJPA 2001, s.35(6)

68–006 Where the prohibition is suspended, the person who is the subject of the suspension must:

(1) be in the United Kingdom when the period of suspension ends; and
(2) if the order contains a direction under s.33(4) above, surrender, before the end of that period any passport returned or issued to him in respect of that suspension by the Secretary of State.

A passport that is required to be surrendered under (2) above, must be surrendered to the Secretary of State in such manner, or by being to such address, as he may direct at the time when he returns or issues it.

Where the prohibition imposed on any person by a travel restriction order is suspended for any period under this section, the end of the period of the prohibition imposed by the order is treated (except for the purposes of subs.(7) below) as postponed or, if there has been one or more previous suspensions further postponed, by the length of the period of suspension.

Travel Restriction Orders

"The minimum period" means:

CJPA 2001, s.35(7)

(a) in the case of a travel restriction order imposing a prohibition for a period of four years or less, the period of two years beginning at the time when the period of prohibition began;

(b) in the case of a travel restriction order imposing a prohibition of more than four but less than 10 years, the period of four years beginning at that time; and

(c) in any other case, the period of five years beginning at that time.

Contravention of order

68–007 A person commits an offence who:

CJPA 2001, s.36

(1) leaves the United Kingdom at a time when he is prohibited from doing so by a travel restriction order; and

(2) is not in the United Kingdom at the end of the period during which a prohibition imposed on him by such an order has been suspended.

For each of these offences, the offender is liable, on summary conviction, to up to six months' imprisonment or to a fine not exceeding the statutory maximum, or both and, on indictment to up to five years' imprisonment, and an unlimited fine, or both.

A person who fails to comply with a direction contained in a travel restriction order to deliver up, or cause to be delivered up, a passport to a court, commits an offence and is liable on summary conviction to up to six months' imprisonment or to a fine not exceeding level 5 (£5,000) on the standard scale, or to both.

Removal powers

68–008 Special savings and provisions in relation to travel restriction orders are made in respect of the Secretary of State's prescribed removal powers.

CJPA 2001, s.37

69. TRIAL WITHOUT A JURY

69–001   CJA 2003, Pt 7, makes provision for trial on indictment without a jury:

(1) in certain fraud cases of a serious or complex nature; and
(2) where there is a real and present danger of jury tampering.

CJA 2003,
s.48(1), (2), (3)

As to the trial by jury and then by judge alone, under DVA 2004, ss.17–21, see 69–009 and following, below.

The provisions for fraud cases (69–002) **are not yet in force**; the provisions in relation to jury tampering (68–003, below) were brought into force on July 24, 2006 (SI 2006/1835).

The effect of an order under CJA 2003, ss.43, 44, or 46(5) is that the trial to which the order relates is *conducted* without a jury, the effect of an order under s.46(3) is that the trial to which the order relates is *continued* without a jury. Where a trial is conducted or continued without a jury, the court has all the powers, authorities and jurisdiction which it would have had if the trial had been conducted or continued with a jury (including power to determine any question and to make any finding which would be required to be determined or made by a jury).

CJA 2003,
s.48(4)

Note that:

(a) except where the context otherwise requires, any reference in an enactment to a jury, the verdict of a jury or the finding of a jury is to be read, in relation to a trial conducted or continued without a jury, as a reference to the court, the verdict of the court or the finding of the court;
(b) where a trial is conducted or continued without a jury and the court convicts an accused, the judge must give a judgment which states the reasons for the conviction at, or as soon as reasonably practicable after, the time of the conviction.

CJA 2003,
s.48(5)(1)

See the observations of the Lord Chief Justice on the justification for holding trials without a jury in *R. v Twomey* [2011] EWCA Crim 8, [2011] 1 Cr. App. R. 29.

Fraud cases (not yet in force)

69–002   Where one or more accused are to be tried on indictment at the Crown Court for one or more offences, and notice has been given under CJA 1987, s.4 (notices in serious fraud cases) in respect of that offence or those offences, the prosecutor may apply to a judge for the trial to be conducted without a jury.

CJA 2003,
s.43(1), (2), (3),
(4), (5)

On such an application the judge may order the case to be tried without a jury where he is satisfied that:

(1) the complexity of the trial, or the length of the trial (or both) is likely to make the trial so burdensome to the members of the jury hearing it;

(2) that the interests of justice require that serious consideration should be given to the question of whether the trial should be conducted without a jury,

otherwise he must refuse the application.

CJA 2003, s.43(6), (7)

An order requires the approval of the Lord Chief Justice or a judge nominated by him.

In deciding whether to make an order, the judge must consider whether there are any steps which might reasonably be taken to reduce the complexity or length of the trial. Particularly relevant will be the provisions made for the preparatory hearing procedure (see CASE MANAGEMENT). The judge is not, however, to regard as reasonable any measures which would significantly disadvantage the prosecution (as by severing an indictment or excluding relevant and important evidence).

Danger of jury tampering

69–003   Where one **or more** accused are to be tried on indictment for one or more offences, the prosecution may apply to a judge of the Crown Court for the trial to be conducted without a jury where there is said to be a real and present danger of the jury being tampered with.

CJA 2003, ss.44(1)–(5)

The judge must make an order that the trial is to be conducted without a jury where he is satisfied that:

(1) there is a real and present danger that jury tampering would take place; and

(2) notwithstanding any steps (including the provision of police protection) which might reasonably be taken to prevent jury tampering, the likelihood that it would take place would be so substantial as to make it necessary in the interests of justice for the trial to be conducted without a jury,

CJA 2003, s.44(6)

otherwise he must refuse the application. He should not grant an application unless he is sure, to the criminal standard of proof, that both conditions are fulfilled (*R. v Twomey,* above*),* as to evidence see 69–004 below.

(1) and (2) above are distinct, and must both be established before an order for trial by judge alone can be made, the context and nature of the threat of jury tampering fall for examination when subs.(5) and the reasonableness of proposed protective steps are being considered; any proposed protective measures must be proportionate to the threat; unduly alarmist proposals (in terms of the likely adverse impact on the jury and on precious police resources) should be resisted: *R. v KS* [2010] EWCA Crim 2377, [2010] 1 Cr. App. R. 285.

As to *continuing* a trial without a jury after the sitting jury has been discharged, see CJA 2003, s.46, below.

The Act gives examples of cases where there may be evidence of a "real and present danger" that jury tampering would take place, namely a case where:

(a) the trial is a retrial and the jury in the previous trial was discharged because jury tampering had taken place;

   (b) jury tampering has taken place in previous criminal proceedings involving the accused or any of the accused;

   (c) there has been intimidation, or attempted intimidation of any person who is likely to be a witness at the trial.

Trial without a jury, remains a decision of last resort, only to be ordered when the judge is sure (and not when he entertains doubts, suspicions or reservations) that the statutory conditions are fulfilled, except in extreme cases, where the necessary protective measures would constitute an unreasonable intrusion into the lives of the jurors (where, for example, there might be a constant police presence in or near their homes, day and night and at the weekends, or police protection, which meant that at all times when they are out of their homes, they are accompanied or overseen by police officers, with its consequent impact on the availability of police officers to carry out their ordinary duties). The confident expectation must be that the jury will perform their duties with their customary determination to do justice (*R. v J* [2010] EWCA Crim 1755, [2011] 1 Cr. App. R. 5).

There will be cases where it will be quite inappropriate for the particular judge to continue to try the case alone, as where his knowledge of the accused's antecedents and his personal involvement in a series of trials which were directly concerned with a fraud in which the accused was said to have been a central figure (*R. v Twomey*, above). See *R. v KS*, above.

Procedure for applications under ss.43, 44

69–004   An application under s.43 or 44 must be determined at a preparatory hearing (see CASE MANAGEMENT) the parties to such preparatory hearing being given an opportunity to make representations with respect to the -application.

CJA 2003, s.45(1)–(3)

Rule 15.1 relating to preparatory hearings (see CASE MANAGEMENT) applies to such applications.

CJA 1987, s.7(1) (which sets out the purposes of preparatory hearings) is modified for this purpose in that for paras (a) to (c) there are substituted:

   (a) identifying issues which are likely to be material to determinations and findings which are likely to be required during the trial;

   (b) if there is to be a jury, assisting their comprehension of those issues and expediting the proceedings before them;

   (c) determining an application to which CJA 2003, s.45 applies.

The evidence which may demonstrate the statutory danger is not confined to evidence which would be admissible at the trial of the accused. The second condition in s.44 requires that:

   (a) after making due allowance for any reasonable steps which might address and minimise the danger of jury tampering,

   (b) the judge should be sure that there would be a sufficiently high likelihood of jury tampering to make a judge alone trial necessary.

In *R. v Twomey*, above, CACD approved the approach taken in *R. v Mackle* [2008] NI 183 where attention was drawn to "the feasibility of measures, the cost of providing them, the logistical difficulties that they may give rise to, and the anticipated duration of any necessary precautions" as well as whether the level of protection appropriate to protect the integrity of the jury might "affect unfavourably the way in which the jury approached its task. If a misguided perception was created in the minds of the jury by the provision of high level protection this would plainly sound on the reasonableness of such a step".

In *R. v Twomey*, CACD examined the likely impact of possible measures on the ordinary lives of the jurors and considered whether even the most intensive protective measures for individual jurors would be sufficient to prevent the improper exercise of pressure on them through members of their families who would not fall within the ambit of the protective measures.

Section 45(3) requires the judge to permit representations to be made by the accused when an application is being made. There will be cases, however, where the evidence to demonstrate the risk of jury tampering will be so sensitive that it can only be addressed under public immunity interest principles. The evidence should be disclosed to the fullest extent possible, but it would be contrary to the legislative purpose to make an order for disclosure which would, in effect, bring the prosecution to an end, and enable those who had been involved in jury tampering to derail the trial and avoid the consequences prescribed by statute, trial by judge alone (*R. v Twomey*, above).

Trials under way: discharge of jury because of tampering

69–005   Where a trial on indictment is under way, and the judge is minded to discharge the jury because jury tampering appears to have taken place, he must, before taking any steps to discharge the jury:

CJA 2003,
ss.46(1)–(7)

(1) notify the parties that he is minded to discharge the jury;
(2) inform the parties of the grounds on which he is so minded; and
(3) allow the parties an opportunity to make representations, and

where, after considering any such representations, he discharges the jury, he may make an order that the trial is to continue without a jury if, but only if, he is satisfied:

(a) that jury tampering has taken place; and
(b) that to continue the trial without a jury would be fair to the accused, but

must if he considers that it is necessary in the interests of justice for the trial to be terminated, terminate it, and where he does so, he may make an order that any new trial which is to take place be conducted without a jury if he is satisfied in respect of the new trial that both of the conditions set out in s.44 are likely to be fulfilled.

If, during the course of the trial, attempts are made to tamper with the jury to the extent that the judge feels it necessary to discharge the jury, it should be clearly understood that the judge may continue with the trial and deliver a judgment and verdict on his own; the principle of trial by jury is precious, but any accused who is responsible for abusing this

TRIAL WITHOUT A JURY

principle by attempting to subvert the process has no justified complaint that he has been deprived of a right which, by his own actions, he himself has spurned (*R. v J* [2010] EWCA Crim 1755, [2011] 1 Cr. App. R. 5).

This provision is without prejudice to any other power that the judge may have on terminating the trial, nor does anything in it affect the application of s.43 or 44, above, in relation to any new trial which takes place following the termination of the trial.

The fact that the judge, in ruling on jury tampering and discharge, heard material about that conduct does not mean that he will be unable to exclude inadmissible material from his consideration of whether or not the accused is guilty (*R. v Guthrie* [2011] EWCA Crim 1338, [2011] 2 Cr. App. R. 20) but there will be cases, as where his knowledge of the accused's antecedents or the ramifications of a series of trials, where it will be appropriate for him to recuse himself, see *R. v Twomey*, above, *R. v KS*, above.

Appeal
69–006   Part 7 provides a right of appeal to CACD by the accused or the prosecutor from an order under s.46(3) or (5) but only with the leave of the judge or CACD, and the order from which the appeal lies is not to take effect before the expiration of the period for bringing the appeal, or, if such an appeal is brought, before it is finally disposed of.

CJA 2003, s.47

Effect of order
69–007   Where an order is made:

CJA 2003, ss.48(1)–(3)

(1) under ss.43, 44 or 46(5), the trial to which the order relates is then conducted without a jury; and
(2) under s.46(3), the trial is continued without a jury.

In either case the trial will proceed in the usual way, the judge having all the powers, authority and jurisdiction which the court would have had if the trial had been with a jury (including power to determine any question and to make any finding which would be required to be determined or made by a jury).

Except where the context otherwise requires, any reference in an enactment to a jury, the verdict of a jury or the finding of a jury, is to be read, in relation to a trial conducted or continued without a jury, as a reference to the court, the verdict of the court or the finding of the court.

CJA 2003, s.42(5)

Where a trial is conducted or continued without a jury and the judge convicts an accused, he must give a judgment which states the reasons for the conviction at, or as soon as reasonably practicable after, the time of the conviction.

CJA 2003, ss.48(4), (6)

The reference in CAA 1968, s.18(2) (notice of appeal or of application for leave to appeal to be given within 28 days from date of conviction, etc.) to the date of the conviction is to read as a reference to the date of that judgment.

Trial of part of indictment without a jury (not yet in force)
69–008   The prosecution may apply to a judge of the Crown Court for a trial to take place on the basis that the trial of some, but not all, of the counts included in an indictment be conducted without a jury where:

DVA 2004, ss.17–21; SI 2006/3423

859

(1) the number of counts in the indictment is such that a trial by jury involving all of them would be impracticable;

(2) each count or group of counts which would be tried by jury if such an order was made, can be regarded as a sample of counts which could accordingly be tried without a jury; and

(3) it is in the interests of justice to do so,

though these provisions have no effect in relation to cases where one of the following events has occurred before the January 8, 2007:

(a) the accused has been committed for trial;

(b) notice of transfer was given under CJA 1987, s.4 (serious or complex fraud);

(c) notice of transfer was given under CJA 1991, s.53 (cases involving children); or

(d) the prosecution evidence has been served on the accused in a case sent for trial under CDA 1988, s.51.

A "sample count" is to be regarded as a sample of other counts where:

(i) the accused in respect of each count is the same;

(ii) the evidence in respect of each count is admissible at the trial of the sample count; and

(iii) the judge considers that the sample count is a sample of the other counts.

Procedure under DVA 2004, ss.17–21

69–009 The use of the powers under these sections is likely to be appropriate where justice cannot be done without charging a large number of separate offences and the allegations against the accused appear to fall into distinct groups by:

PD 2004, IV.34.4–7

(1) reference to the identity of the victim;

(2) reference to the dates of the offences; or

(3) some other distinction in the nature of the offending conduct alleged.

In such a case it is essential to make clear from the outset the association asserted by the prosecutor between those counts to be tried by a jury and those counts which it is proposed should be tried by judge alone, if the jury convict on the former. A special form of indictment is prescribed in PD 2004, Annex D for this purpose.

An order for such a trial may be made only at a preparatory hearing, to which r.15.1 applies (see CASE MANAGEMENT). It follows that where the prosecutor intends to invite the court to order such a trial it will normally be appropriate to proceed as follows:

(a) the draft indictment served under CPR 2011, r.14.1(1) should be in the form appropriate to such a trial;

(b) the indictment should be accompanied by an application under r.15.1 for a preparatory hearing;

(c) on receipt of such a draft indictment, Crown Court staff should not sign it before consulting a judge, who is likely to direct under r.14.1(3) that it should not be signed before the prosecutor's application is heard. This will ensure that the defendant is aware at the earliest possible opportunity of what the prosecution propose and of the proposed association of counts in the indictment.

It is undesirable for a draft indictment in the usual form to be served where the prosecutor expects to apply for a two stage trial and hence, of necessity, for permission to amend the indictment at a later stage in order that it may be in the special form.

If the judge allows the prosecutor's application for a two-stage trial then he will direct the Crown Court officer to sign the draft indictment accordingly. If the court refuses the application then it will give such directions for the preparation and signature of an indictment as may be appropriate.

Effect of order

69–010   The effect of an order under DVA 2004, s.17 is that where an accused is found guilty by a jury of a count which is a "sample" of other counts to be tried in those proceedings, those other counts may be tried without a jury in those proceedings (DVA 2004, s.19).

Notes

70. UNFITNESS TO PLEAD/INSANITY

General

70–001 Where, on the trial of any person, the question arises, at the instance of the defence or otherwise, whether the accused is under a disability such that, apart from CP(I)A 1964 (as amended by CP(IUP)A 1991), would constitute a bar to his being tried, then, though ordinarily such a question falls to be determined as soon as it arises:

CP(I)A 1964, ss.4(1)–(4)

(1) if, having regard to the nature of the supposed disability, the judge is of the opinion that it is inexpedient to do so, he may postpone consideration of the question of fitness to be tried, until any time up to the opening of the case for the defence; and

(2) if, before the question of fitness to be tried falls to be determined, the jury return a verdict of acquittal on all or each of the counts on which the accused is being tried, that question shall not be determined.

CP(I)A 1964, s.4(5), (6)

Where one of several accused becomes unfit after a jury has been empanelled, there is nothing to prevent the same jury from considering whether that accused has committed the *actus reus* although the question of guilt would be removed. *A fortiori,* in a case of several accused, where the principal is found unfit to stand trial by reason of mental illness, and a second as a result of a stroke, there is nothing to prevent a single jury once empanelled, proceeding to consider whether the principal accused committed the actus reus while looking, in the case of the other fit accused to both actus reus and mens rea (*R. v B* [2008] EWCA Crim 1997; [2009] 1 Cr. App. R. 19); it is not "inescapable" that separate trials should take place.

Proceedings under ss.4 and 4A do not offend against the provisions of ECHR art.6; they are not "criminal proceedings". See *R. v Kerr, Kerr and H* [2002] EWCA Crim 2374; [2002] 1 W.L.R. 824 and the cases considered there.

The test

70–002 The classic test for fitness to plead was set out *R. v Pritchard* (1836) 7 Car. & P. 303 shows that there are three points to be enquired into:

(1) whether the accused is mute of malice or not;

(2) whether he can plead to the indictment or not;

(3) whether he is of sufficient intellect to comprehend the course of the proceedings in the trial so as to make a proper defence – to know that he might challenge any of the jury to whom he might object – and to comprehend the details of the evidence.

That test was reaffirmed in *R. v Podola* (1959) 43 Cr. App. R. 220. The word "comprehend" being considered to go no further in meaning than the word "understand". See also *R. v Robertson* (1968) 52 Cr. App. R. 690; *R. v Berry* (1978) 66 Cr. App. R. 156, where the court emphasised that although a person was highly abnormal, it did not mean that he was incapable of doing those things set out in *Pritchard*.

Determination by the judge; evidence

70–003 The accused's legal representatives are the persons best placed to decide whether to raise the issue of fitness to plead, and indeed to seek medical assistance to resolve the problem. There is, however, a separate and distinct responsibility in the judge to oversee the process so that if there is any question of the accused's fitness to plead, he can raise it directly with his legal advisers (*R. v Erskine* [2009] EWCA Crim 1425, [2010] 2 Cr. App. R. 29). CP(I)A 1964, s.4(5), (6)

If the question of fitness to be tried is raised it is determined by the judge. He must not make such a determination (before plea – *R. v Ghalam* [2009] EWCA Crim 2285, [2010] 1 Cr. App. R. 12) except on the written evidence of two registered medical practitioners at least one of whom is duly approved (see also *R. v Borkan* [2004] EWCA Crim 1642, [2004] M.H.L.R.216). There is no need for oral evidence (cf. MHA 1983, s.41(2)): *Narey v C & E Commrs.* [2005] EWHC 759 (Admin), [2005] M.H.L.R. 194.

The purpose of CP(I)A 1964, s. 4A is to prevent a person from being detained unless he would have been found guilty at a criminal trial. It is imperative, therefore, that the same rules of evidence be applied to proceedings under s. 4A as to those that would have applied if the trial were a criminal trial in the strict sense. The judge is entitled to admit a witness statement as hearsay evidence in accordance with the present practice (*R. v Chad* [2007] EWCA Crim 2647, [2008] 1 Cr. App. R. 18, followed in *R. v Creed* [2011] EWCA Crim 144, [2011] Crim. L.R. 644).

Save in clear cases, the judge must rigorously examine evidence of psychiatrists adduced before him and subject that evidence to careful analysis against the *Pritchard* criteria as interpreted in *Podola*. Unless the unfitness is clear, the fact that psychiatrists agree is not sufficient (*R. v Walls* [2011] EWCA Crim 443, [2011] 2 Cr. App. R. 6).

Finding that the accused did the act, etc.

70–004 Where the judge determines that the accused is under a disability, the trial will not proceed further, but a jury must then determine whether: CP(I)A 1964, s.4A

(1) on the evidence, if any, already given at the trial; or
(2) on such evidence as may be adduced or further adduced by the prosecutor or by such person appointed by the court to put the case for the accused,

it is satisfied, as respects each of the counts on which he was to be, or is being tried, that he did the act or made the omission charged against him as the offence.

Care needs to be taken to ensure that the act to be proved is accurately particularised – see *R v. McKenzie* [2011] 2 Cr. App. R. 381(27).

If, as respects that or any of the counts, the jury are:

(a) so satisfied, they must make a finding that he did the act or made the omission charged against him; or

    (b) not so satisfied, they must return a verdict of acquittal, as if, on that count the trial had proceeded to a conclusion.

At this stage it is necessary to ensure very careful case management to ensure that full information is provided for the judge without delay. The judge has a duty under s. 4A(2) to consider carefully who is the best person to be appointed to put the case for the defence at this stage: Note that:

    (a) the duty is personal to the judge, who must consider afresh who is the best person for this difficult task, and he may need time to consider the matter;

    (b) the person appointed will not necessarily be the same person who has represented the accused up to that stage;

    (c) the responsibility placed upon the person appointed is quite different from that placed on an advocate, who can take instructions from a client, and this is underlined by the fact that he is remunerated out of central funds and not through legal aid funding;

(*R. v Norman, The Times*, August 21, 2008).

    Under the present legislation CACD, should it consider the resulting verdict unsafe or unsatisfactory, cannot order a retrial save in certain very limited circumstances (see *R. v Norman*):

    (i) where the question of disability is determined after arraignment, the question of whether or not the accused did the act or made the omission charged is to be determined by the jury by whom the accused is being tried;

    (ii) in the exceptional case, where despite the original finding of disability, at a later hearing the accused is found to be fit to be tried, the procedure under ss.4A and 5 are inapplicable. The proper course is for the judge to hold a second s.4 hearing, and if the accused is found fit to plead to order his arraignment (*R. (Hasani) v Blackfriars CC* [2005] EWHC 3016 (Admin); [2006] 1 Cr. App. R. 27).

Disposal after special verdict of finding a disability

70–005 Where a special verdict is returned that the accused is not guilty by reason of insanity, or findings have been made that the accused is under a disability and that he did the act or made the omission charged against him the judge's powers of sentencing in relation to a case where the accused was arraigned on or after March 31, 2005 are limited to making:

    CP(I)A 1964, s.5

    (1) a hospital order (with or without a restriction order);

    (2) a supervision order within the meaning of CP(I)A 1964, Sch.1A, Pt 1 as added by DVA 2004, s.24, Sch.2; or

    (3) an order for absolute discharge.

    DVA 2004 abolishes admission orders. Two important changes introduced by DVA 2004 are that the Secretary of State no longer has a role in deciding whether or not the accused is admitted to hospital, and the judge is no longer able to order the accused's admission to a psychiatric hospital without hearing any medical evidence.

CP(I)A 1964, Sch.1A, para.5

Where an accused is acquitted of all counts of the indictment, save a summary offence attached to it by virtue of CJA 1988, s.40, the judge is restricted to magistrates' powers; there is no finding of guilt, as such, and the accused is not therefore an offender (*R. v Southwark CC Ex p. Koncar* [1998] 1 Cr. App. R. 321).

Supervision order; CP(I)A 1964, Sch.1A

70–006 The supervision order introduced by DVA 2004 where arraignment was on or after March 31, 2005 is an order which requires the person in respect of whom it is made ("the supervised person") to be under the supervision of a social worker or an officer of a local probation board ("the supervising officer") for a period specified in the order of not more than two years. It may require the supervised person to submit, during the whole of that period, or such part of it as may be specified in the order, to treatment by or under the direction of a registered medical practitioner (CP(I)A 1964, para.1(1)).

CP(I)A 1964, s.5A, Sch.1A, para.1(1)

The judge must not make a supervision order unless he is satisfied that:

(1) having regard to all the circumstances of the case, the making of such an order is the most suitable means of dealing with the accused or appellant; and
(2) the supervising officer intended to be specified in the order is willing to undertake the supervision; and
(3) arrangements have been made for the treatment intended to be specified in the order.

The order must either:

(a) specify the local social services authority area in which the supervised person resides or will reside, and require him to be under the supervision of a social worker of the local social services authority for that area; or
(b) specify the local justice area in which that person resides or will reside, and require him to be under the supervision of a probation officer appointed for or assigned to that area.

Before making such an order, the judge must explain to the supervised person in ordinary language the effect of the order (including any requirements proposed to be included in it) and that a magistrates' court has power to review the order on the application either of the supervised person or of the supervising officer (CP(I)A 1964, paras 2, 3(1)–(3)).

The offender has a duty to keep in touch with the supervising officer in accordance with instructions given to him and to notify him, of any change of address (CP(I)A 1964, para.3(5)).

Administrative provisions

70–007 After making an order, the Crown Court officer will give copies of the order to a probation officer assigned to the court, and also to the supervised person, and to the supervising officer.

CP(I)A 1964, Sch.1A, para.3(4)

The officer will also send to the designated officer for the local justice area in which the supervised person resides or will reside a copy of the order; and such documents and information relating to the case as it considers likely to be of assistance to a court acting for that area in the exercise of its functions in relation to the order.

Requirement as to medical treatment

70–008 An order may, if the judge is satisfied as mentioned below, include a requirement that the supervised person submit, during the whole of the period specified in the order or during such part of that period as may be so specified, to treatment by or under the direction of a registered medical practitioner with a view to the improvement of his mental condition.

CP(I)A 1964, Sch.1A, paras 4(1)–(4)

The judge must however be satisfied on the written or oral evidence of two or more registered medical practitioners, at least one of whom is duly registered, that the mental condition of the supervised person:

(1) is such as requires and may be susceptible to treatment; but
(2) is not such as to warrant the making of a hospital order within the meaning of the MHA 1983.

The treatment required by the order must be one of the following kinds of treatment, specified in the order, that is to say:

(a) treatment as a non-resident patient at such institution or place as may be specified in the order; and
(b) treatment by or under the direction of such registered medical practitioner as may be so specified,

but the nature of the treatment must not be specified in the order except as mentioned in para.(a) or (b) above.

Treatment by a medical practitioner

70–009 Where the judge is satisfied on the written or oral evidence of two or more registered medical practitioners that, because of his medical condition, other than his mental condition, the supervised person is likely to pose a risk to himself or others, and the condition may be susceptible to treatment:

(1) the order may (whether or not it includes a requirement under para.4) include a requirement that the supervised person submit, during the whole of the period specified in the order, or during such part of that period as may be so specified, to treatment by or under the direction of a registered medical practitioner with a view to the improvement of the condition;
(2) the treatment required by any such order must be such one of the following as may be specified in the order:
(a) treatment as a non-resident patient at such institution or place as may be specified in the order; and
(b) treatment by or under the direction of such registered medical practitioner, but

the treatment must not be specified in the order except as mentioned in para.(a) or (b) above.

Where the medical practitioner by whom, or under whose direction, the supervised person is being treated in pursuance of a requirement is of the opinion that part of the treatment can be better or more conveniently be given in, or at, an institution or place which is not specified in the order, and is one in, or at, which the treatment of the supervised person will be given by or under the direction of a registered medical practitioner, he may, with the consent of the supervised person, make arrangements for him to be treated accordingly. Such arrangements may provide for the supervised person to receive part of his treatment as a resident patient in an institution or place of any description.

CP(I)A 1964,
Sch.1A, para.5

Where any such arrangements are made for the treatment of a supervised person, the medical practitioner by whom the arrangements are made must give notice in writing to the supervising officer, specifying the institution or place, in or at, which the treatment is to be carried out; and the treatment provided for by the arrangements will be deemed to be treatment to which he is required to submit in pursuance of the supervision order.

CP(I)A 1964,
Sch.1A, para.7

While the supervised person is under treatment as a resident patient in pursuance of arrangements under para.6 above, the supervising officer will carry out the supervision to such extent only as may be necessary for the purpose of the revocation or amendment of the order.

Requirements as to residence

70–010   A supervision order may include requirements as to the residence of the supervised person, but before making such an order containing any such requirement, the judge must consider the home surroundings of the supervised person.

CP(I)A 1964,
Sch.1A, para.8

Appeal against order

70–011   In a case where arraignment took place on or after March 31, 2005, a person in whose case a judge of the Crown Court makes:

CAA 1968,
s.16A

(1) a hospital order or interim hospital order by virtue of CP(I)A 1964, ss.5 or 5A; or
(2) a supervision order under s.5,

may appeal to CACD against the order, but only:

(a) with the leave of CACD; or
(b) if the judge of the court of trial grants a certificate that the case is fit for appeal.

If, on such an appeal, CACD considers that the appellant should be dealt with differently from the way in which the court below dealt with him it may quash any order which is the subject of the appeal and may make such order, whether by substitution for the original order or by variation of or addition to it, as it thinks appropriate for the case and as the court below had power to make. CACD may not order a retrial of the facts should it quash a finding that the accused did the act (*R. v McKenzie* [2011] EWCA Crim 1550).

Note that in relation to cases where arraignment was on or after March 31, 2005:

(i) the fact that an appeal is pending against an interim hospital order under MHA 1983 does not affect the power of the Crown Court to renew or terminate the order or deal with the appellant on its termination;

(ii) where CACD makes an interim hospital order by virtue of these provisions, the power of renewing or terminating it and of dealing with the appellant on its termination is exercisable by the Crown Court and not by CACD, and the Crown Court is treated for the purposes of *ibid.*, s.38(7) (absconding offenders) as the court that made the order;

(iii) the fact that an appeal is pending against a supervision order under CP(I)A 1964, s.5 does not affect the power of the Crown Court to revoke the order.

Where CACD makes a supervision order the power of revoking or amending it is exercised as if the order had been made by the Crown Court. CAA 1968, s.16B

Compatibility with ECHR

70–012 Proceedings under s.4 determine whether the accused is fit to plead: it is not a criminal charge. In proceedings under s.4A:

(1) if an accused is found to have committed the act, the verdict is not one of guilty, but a finding that he did the act or made the omission charged against him;

(2) the finding of the jury that an accused has committed the act lacks a finding as to intent and is not, therefore, a finding of guilty of the offence;

(3) the criminal charge provisions of ECHR, art.6 do not apply to proceedings which cannot result in a conviction;

(4) proceedings under ss.4 and 4A comply with the requirements of art.6.

The submission that a person who is unfit to plead cannot have the fair trial required by art.6 because he cannot sufficiently understand the proceedings or give proper instructions and may therefore be unable to give evidence, is to confuse the rights assured by art.6 with the enjoyment of those rights. Persons under mental disabilities, whose condition does not prevent their being fit to plead to a criminal charge, may well be under a disadvantage in legal proceedings, whether civil or criminal. A judge should do his best to minimise that disadvantage, but might be unable to remove it totally.

A trial in civil or criminal proceedings where the disadvantage has been minimised could be "fair": *R. v Kerr* (above 70-001), considering *T v United Kingdom* [2000] Crim. L.R. 187; *Brown v Stott* [2001] 2 All E.R.97; *R. v Antoine* [1999] 2 Cr. App. R. 225.

Notes

71. VARIATION OF SENTENCE

Introduction

71–001   Ordinarily, a sentence imposed, or other order made, by the Crown Court when dealing with an offender, takes effect from the beginning of the day on which it is imposed, unless the judge otherwise directs but:

(1) as a court of record, the Crown Court has an inherent jurisdiction to rectify mistakes in its record (*R. v Saville* (1980) 70 Cr. App. R. 204); and, more importantly;

(2) a sentence or order may be varied or rescinded under the provisions of PCC(S)A 2000, s.155(1), (2), (3), see below; and

(3) a "discounted" sentence passed upon an offender in view of an undertaking to assist the authorities, may be subsequently reviewed (under SOCPA 2005, s.74) where it is shown that such assistance is not forthcoming;

(4) special rules apply in relation to adjusting a sentence in subsequent proceedings under POCA 2002, see CONFISCATION ORDERS.

1. Variation of sentence: PCC(S)A 2000, ss.154, 155; CJIA 2008, s.149, Sch.8, Pt 3

General

71–002   A sentence or other order may be varied or rescinded:

(1) within, and only within (*R. v Menocal* (1979) 69 Cr. App. R. 148; *R. v Hart* (1983) 5 Cr. App. R. (S.) 25; *R. v Stillwell* (1992) 94 Cr. App. R. 65; *R. v Bukhari* [2009] Crim. L.R. 300), the period of 56 days beginning with the day on which the sentence was imposed or other order was made;

(2) in open court (*R. v Dowling* (1989) 88 Cr. App. R. 88) in the presence of the offender (*R. v Hussein* [2000] 1 Cr. App. R. (S.) 181) and after his representatives have had an opportunity to make submissions on the alteration;

(3) by the court constituted as it was when sentence was passed or any other order was made or, where the Crown Court comprised one or more justices, a court so constituted save for the omission of any one or more of those justices.

In *R. v Gordon* [2007] EWCA Crim 165, [2007] 2 Cr. App. R. (S.) 66 CACD pointed out that the correction of an error, notwithstanding the expiry of the 56 day period, was permitted in *R. v Saville* [1980] 2 Cr. App. R. (S.) 26, where an inchoate order was simply adjusted in such a way that the sentence or other orders were unaffected, and followed in *R. v Michael* [1976] 1 All E.R. 629 upholding the inherent jurisdiction of the court to correct an order properly to reflect the decision pronounced in court. Section 155 allows a small degree of latitude and the

56 day limit does not prohibit what is in effect a later curing of a mere procedural irregularity in the way in which the order of the court was recorded, or a later procedural step to complete an inchoate order, but without affecting what has already been announced, *R. v Nnaji* [2009] EWCA Crim 468, [2009] 2 Cr. App. R. (S.) 107 (the calculation of days spent on remand, which would have no effect on the recorded sentence passed) but it is otherwise in a matter of substance (*R. v Hudson* [2011] EWCA Crim 906, [2011] 2 Cr. App. R. (S.) 116).

In relation to (2) above, there may be cases where it is proper to proceed in the absence of the offender, as where he has clearly waived his right to be present, either expressly or by implication, as by absconding, but this ought to be an exceptional course (see *R. v May* (1981) 3 Cr. App. R. (S.) 165; *R. v Cleere* (1983) 5 Cr. App. R. (S.) 465; *R. v McLean* (1988) 10 Cr. App. R. (S.) 18; *R. v Hussein,* (above).

Where the original sentence is rescinded within the 56 day period, there is nothing to prevent the judge from exercising his common law powers of adjournment to hear further argument, and passing a fresh sentence, more than 28 days after the original sentence was imposed (*R. v Reynolds* EWCA Crim 538, [2007] 2 Cr. App. R. (S.), cf. *R. v Dunham* [1996] 1 Cr. App. R. (S.) 438).

The sentence or order as varied takes effect from the beginning of the day on which it was originally imposed or made, unless the court otherwise directs.

"Order", "sentence" defined

71–003 "Order" does not include a contribution order under AJA 1999, s.17(2) (CDS funding); it was held under the previous law to include a confiscation order under DTA 1994 (*R. v Miller* (1991) 92 Cr. App. R. 191), and thus, probably, a confiscation order under POCA 2002.

A "sentence" includes a recommendation for deportation, also a forfeiture order made in consequence of a conviction (*R. v Menocal,* above).

"Variation" defined

71–004 The word "varied" is an ordinary English word and bears its dictionary meaning (*R. v Sodhi* (1978) 66 Cr. App. R. 260). The provisions empower the judge, in an appropriate case, to:

(1) correct minor errors made in sentencing;
(2) change the nature of the sentence where necessary (e.g. *R. v Grice* (1978) 66 Cr. App. R. 167 (imprisonment varied to hospital order);
(3) reduce the sentence imposed if, after further reflection, it appears too severe; and
(4) increase the sentence originally passed, but only in exceptional cases (*R. v Newsome* (1970) 54 Cr. App. R. 485 under previous legislation); cf. *R. v Grice,* above) where, e.g.:
   (a) additional material is put before the judge (*R. v Reilly* (1982) 75 Cr. App. R. 266); or
   (b) it is clear that the original sentence was passed on an

incorrect factual basis (*R. v Hart* (1983) 5 Cr. App. R. (S.) 25; *R. v McLean* (1988) 10 Cr. App. R. (S.) 18; *R. v Hadley* (1995) 16 Cr. App. R. (S.) 358), cf. *R. v Woop* [2002] EWCA Crim 58; [2002] 2 Cr. App. R.(S.) 65).

As to the problems caused by "rescinding" rather than varying a sentence, see *R. v Smith* (1995) 16 Cr. App. R. (S.) 974, and *R. v Dunham* [1996] 1 Cr. App. R. (S.) 438. Where the judge, in imposing consecutive sentences for two offences, has properly had regard to the totality principle but in imposing one of the sentences has exceeded the maximum, he may vary the sentence under s.47(2), so as to reduce the unlawful sentence and increase the other, provided the total is not increased: *R. v Lees* [1999] 1 Cr. App. R. (S.) 194, cf. *R. v Evans* (1992) 13 Cr. App. R. (S.) 377.

Procedure

71–005   Rule 42.4 applies where the Crown Court can vary or rescind a sentence or order; and authorises a judge, in addition to his other powers, to do so within the period of 56 days beginning with another accused's acquittal or sentencing where:

(1) accused persons are tried separately in the Crown Court on the same or related facts alleged in one or more indictments; and
(2) one is sentenced before another is acquitted or sentenced.

A judge may exercise his power:

(a) on application by a party; or
(b) on his own initiative.

A party who wants a judge to exercise that power must:

(a) apply in writing as soon as reasonably practicable after:
   (i) the sentence or order that that party wants the court to vary or rescind; or
   (ii) where paragraph (2) above applies, the other accused's acquittal or sentencing;
(b) serving the application on the Crown Court officer, and each other party; and
(c) in the application, explaining why the sentence should b varied or rescinded;
(d) specifying the variation that the applicant proposes, and if the application is late, explaining why.

The judge will not exercise his power in the accused's absence unless either he makes a variation proposed by the accused, or the accused has had an opportunity to make representations at a hearing (whether or not he in fact attends).

The judge may extend (even after it has expired) the time limit unless the court's power to vary or rescind the sentence cannot be exercised; and he may allow an application to be made orally.

VARIATION OF SENTENCE

Ancillary orders

71–006 Where the judge is contemplating making an ancillary order, such as a compensation order or a confiscation order, which requires consideration of further evidence as to the amount, etc., he ought to state that he is postponing that question at the time he passes the substantive sentence. He cannot otherwise make, for example, a compensation order after the expiration of the 56 day period: see *R. v Dorrian* [2001] 1 Cr. App. R. (S.) 135.

Rectification of errors in relation to dangerous offenders

71–007 As to the rectification of errors in sentencing under the regime for dangerous offenders enacted in CJA 2003, see DANGEROUS OFFENDERS; PROTECTIVE SENTENCES.

2. Review of discounted sentence under SOCA 2005

General

71–008 Where a judge of the Crown Court has passed a sentence on a person in respect of an offence, and that person receives:

SOCPA 2005, s.74, (1)–(3), 13

(1) a discounted sentence in consequence of his having offered in pursuance of a written agreement to give assistance to the prosecutor or investigator of an offence; and
   (a) knowingly fails to any extent to give assistance in accordance with the agreement; or
   (b) having given the assistance in accordance with the agreement, in pursuance of another written agreement gives or agrees to give further assistance; or
(2) a sentence which is not discounted, and in pursuance of a written agreement he subsequently gives or offers to give assistance to the prosecutor or investigator of an offence,

a specified prosecutor (i.e. the DPP, the DRCP, the DSFO, the DPP for Northern Ireland, or a prosecutor designated for the purposes of this section by one of those), may at any time refer the case back to the court by which the sentence was passed, if that person is still serving his sentence, and the specified prosecutor thinks it is in the interests of justice to do so.

A person does not fall within this provision if he was convicted of an offence for which the sentence is fixed by law, and he did not plead guilty to the offence for which he was sentenced.

The hearing

71–009 A case referred as above must, if possible, be heard by the judge who passed the sentence to which the referral relates.

SOCPA 2005, s.74(4)–(7)

Where that judge is satisfied that the person concerned (under 71–008, (1)(a), above) knowingly failed to give the assistance, he may substitute for the sentence to which the referral relates such greater sentence (not exceeding that which the original judge would have passed but for the agreement to give assistance) as he thinks appropriate.

Note that:

(1) in a case of a person who falls within (1)(b) or (2) of 71–008 above, the judge may take into account the extent and nature of the assistance given or offered; and substitute for the sentence to which the referral relates such lesser sentence as he thinks appropriate;

(2) any part of the sentence to which the referral relates which the person has already served must be taken into account in determining when a greater or lesser sentence imposed by s.71(5) or (6) has been served;

(3) the duty (CJA 2003, s.174(1)(a) or s.270 as the case may be) applies to a sentence substituted under this provision above unless the Judge thinks that it is not in the public interest to disclose that the person falls within s.74(2)(a).

The public may be excluded in relation to such proceedings.

Appeal

71–010 A person in respect of whom a reference is made under s.74(3), and the specified prosecutor, are each given the right, subject to the leave of CACD, to appeal against the decision of the judge of the Crown Court, CAA 1968, s.33(3) (limitation on appeal from CACD) does not prevent a further appeal to the Supreme Court.

SOCPA 2005, s.75

SOCPA 2005, s.74(8)(9)

Procedure on such an appeal is governed by r.68. As to live links, see LIVE LINKS.

3. Reduction and amendment of sentence on subsequent proceedings under POCA 2002

71–011 Where a judge varies a confiscation order under POCA 2002, ss.21, 22, 23, 29, 32 or 33, the effect of the variation is to vary the maximum period applicable in relation to the order under PCC(S)A 2000, s.139(4) and:

POCA 2002, s.39

(1) if the result is that that maximum period is less than the term of imprisonment or detention fixed in respect of the order under PCC(S)A 2000, s.139(2), the judge must fix a reduced term of imprisonment or detention in respect of the confiscation order under s.139(2) in place of the term previously fixed; or

(2) if (1) is not the case, the judge may amend the term of imprisonment or detention fixed in respect of the confiscation order under PCC(S)A 2000, s.139(2).

See generally CONFISCATION ORDERS.

Notes

72. VICTIM IMPACT STATEMENTS

Views on sentence

72–001   The damaging and distressing effects of a crime on the victim clearly represent an important factor in the sentencing decision, and those effects may include the anguish and emotional suffering of the victim or, in a case of death, the surviving close family (*R. v Nunn* [1996] Crim. L.R. 210), but:

    (1) the sentence imposed by the court cannot *depend* upon the views of the victim of the offence; it is for the judge to assess the impact of the offence(s) on the particular victim though where:

        (a) the sentence passed may actually aggravate the victim's distress, this may be a consideration; and

        (b) the victim's forgiveness may be treated as showing that the harm done by the offender is less than would otherwise be the case (see *R. v Roche* [1999] Crim. L.R. 339);

    (2) the judge needs to balance the victim's views with the nature of the offence and the particular facts of the case (*R. v Nunn*, above *R. v Hayes, The Times,* April 5, 1999, *R. v Roche,* above); and

    (3) the judge is entitled to receive evidence of the psychological effects of the offence on the victim.

SGC Guidelines on domestic violence (Archbold 2012, Appendix K-82 et seq.) emphasise that (1) is particularly important in such cases; the victim's feelings of being responsible for the offender's incarceration being a familiar consequence of controlling and intimidating behaviour.

Personal statements

72–002   A victim's personal statement given to the prosecutor may help to identify whether the victim has a particular need for information, support or protection. The judge may take the statement into account when determining sentence. As to the Victims' Advocate Scheme, see below.

PD 2004, III.28.1, 2

If the judge is presented with a victim's personal statement the following approach should be adopted:

    (1) the statement and any evidence in support should be considered and taken into account prior to passing sentence;

    (2) evidence of the effects of an offence on the victim, contained in the victim's personal statement or any other statement, must be in proper form, that is made in the form of a witness statement made under CJA 1967, s.9, or as an expert's report, and served upon the accused's solicitor or on the accused if he is not represented, prior to sentence;

    (3) except where inferences can properly be drawn from the nature of the offence, or the circumstances surrounding it, the judge

ought not to make assumptions unsupported by evidence about the effects of an offence on the victim;

(4) the judge should pass what he considers to be the appropriate sentence having regard to the circumstances of the offence and of the offender, taking into account, so far as he considers it appropriate, the consequences to the victim; and

(5) the judge should consider whether it is desirable in pronouncing the sentence to refer to the evidence provided on behalf of the victim.

The opinions of the victim or the victim's close relatives as to what the sentence should be are therefore not relevant, unlike the consequence of the offence on them. Victims should be advised of this. If, despite the advice, opinions as to sentence are included in the statement, the judge should pay no attention to them. There are two recognised exceptions to this rule, namely where:

(a) the sentence passed may actually aggravate the victim's distress; and

(b) the victim's forgiveness may be treated as evidence that the damage done by the offender is less than would normally be the case (see the cases reviewed in *R. v Roche*, above.

Advocate Scheme

72–003 In respect of cases of murder and manslaughter (excluding death by dangerous driving) charged on or after April 24, 2006, a Protocol issued by the President of the QBD on May 3, 2006 provides for a scheme which allows the family of the victim an opportunity to make a "family impact statement" (FIS) in open court after the offender's conviction and before the judge proceeds to sentence about the effect of the crime on the family. PD 2004, III.28.1.2 (at 72–002, above) continues to apply.

The family is entitled to choose whether that statement is made by:

(1) a CPS prosecutor;

(2) an independent advocate (at public expense); or

(3) a lay "friend"; and,

may choose whether the statement be in the form of:

(a) a written document put before the judge;

(b) oral testimony by the maker; or

(c) a statement read out in court by any of those persons in (1)–(3) above.

The contents of the statement must be brought to the attention of the accused.

In so far as procedure is concerned, the prosecutor will serve the FIS at the PMCH together with the preferred mode of presentation.

In relation to procedure:

(i) a decision should ordinarily be taken at the PCMH as to the method by which the victim's family prefers to present the statement though, where appropriate, that choice may be changed at a later stage with the judge's leave;

(ii) the judge will ordinarily accede to the family's choice unless there are good reasons for not doing so; where there is a disagreement between family members as to who will make the statement, the judge will decide;

(iii) where a written statement is made the judge will need to indicate that he has received and read it;

(iv) where an oral statement is made it is given by a witness from the witness box, that witness:

- will be examined by the CPS, independent advocate or lay friend;
- may be cross-examined, where appropriate, on behalf of the offender.

The judge will intervene to prevent questions which go beyond the effect of the murder/manslaughter on the victim's family.

Notes

73. VIEW BY JURY

General

73–001 A view or inspection of real evidence may take place in the course of a trial. Where that view takes the form of a view of the *locus in quo*, it may be of two kinds:

(1) *informal*, for there is nothing to prevent an individual juror, the judge or counsel from informally viewing premises or a location for the purposes of familiarising himself with the place or surroundings concerned; or

(2) *formal*, at which witnesses give demonstrations, distances are measured off and, in effect, evidence is given.

In relation to the first kind of view, no rules can apply since such an informal inspection is no part of the trial. The judge may not, however, send one or more jurors to view the scene and report back to the others: *R. v Gurney* [1976] Crim. L.R. 567.

Formal view with jury

73–002 The trial judge, in his discretion, may permit the jury to view the *locus* at any stage of the trial up to retirement of the jury (*R. v Whalley* (1847) 2 C. & K. 376). In relation to a formal view, it is essential to bear in mind that it is part of the evidence given at the trial and certain basic principles apply. There is almost no relevant authority in England and Wales as to the procedure to be adopted at a formal view, and many of those held bristle with impropriety.

JA 1974, s.14, provides for rules to be made, though none have been. It is submitted that the practice adopted in the courts of many former British overseas territories, where views were frequent, is of assistance here.

Thus, since a formal view is part of the evidence:

(1) judge, jury, prosecuting counsel, the accused and defence counsel, proceed to the *locus* together, with any relevant witnesses, accompanied by the clerk and a shorthand writer or logger;

(2) at the scene the witnesses point out such places or things as are relevant, and distances are measured, stepped off or otherwise arrived at;

(3) the court then re-assembles and those persons who took a material part in the view testify formally as to the part they played at the scene; and

(4) any opposing party then has the opportunity to cross-examine.

(See also the Privy Council cases of *Karamat v The Queen* (1956) 40 Cr. App. R. 13, *Tameshwar v The Queen* (1957) 41 Cr. App. R. 161, and *Goold v Evans* [1951] 2 T.L.R. 1189.)

The absence of the judge, who has a duty to prevent improper communications being made to the jurors (*R. v Martin and Webb* (1872)

L.R. 1 C.C.R. 378), is a fatal flaw (*R. v Hunter* (1985) 81 Cr. App. R. 40) even where no witnesses are present. The presence of the accused is as necessary at the view as in the courtroom. He may be able to point out matters of which his counsel is unaware or about which others attending the view are mistaken (*R. v Ely JJ. Ex p Burgess* [1992] Crim. L.R. 888).

No view after jury retire

73–003   Since a formal view is part of the evidence in the case, it follows that, as is the case where it is sought to introduce any new evidence, it must not infringe the general rule preventing the introduction of such once the jury has retired (see *R. v Davis* (1976) 62 Cr. App. R. 194, 210; *R. v Lawrence* (1968) 52 Cr. App. R. 163; cf. *R. v Nixon* (1968) 52 Cr. App. R. 218).

74. VULNERABLE ACCUSED

Introduction

74–001   Special rules apply to proceedings on the trial, sentencing or appeal of:

PD 2004, III.30.1

(1) children and young persons under 18; or
(2) adults who suffer from a mental disorder within the meaning of MHA 1983 or who have any other significant impairment of intelligence and social function (see YJCEA 1999, s.33A; PJA 2006, s.47),

referred to collectively in PD 2004, Pt III as "vulnerable defendants".

The purpose of the direction in PD 2004, III.30 is to extend to proceedings in relation to such persons in the adult courts procedures analogous to those in use in youth courts.

The steps which should be taken to comply with the overriding principle set out in PD 2004, III.30.3 are to be judged, in any given case, taking account of the age, maturity and development (intellectual, social and emotional) of the accused concerned and all other circumstances of the case.

PD 2004, III.30.3

The overriding principle

74–002   An accused may be young and immature or may have a mental disorder within the meaning of MHA 1983, or some other significant impairment of intelligence and social function such as to inhibit his understanding of and participation in the proceedings. The purpose of criminal proceedings being to determine guilt, if that is in issue, and decide on the appropriate sentence if the accused pleads guilty or is convicted, all possible steps should be taken to assist a vulnerable accused to understand and participate in those proceedings. The ordinary trial process should, therefore, so far as is necessary, be adapted to meet those ends.

PD 2004, III.30.3

Regard should be had to the welfare of a young accused as required by CYPA 1933, s.44, and generally to CPR 2011, Pts 1 and 3 (the overriding objective and the court's powers of case management).

Where a judge is called upon to exercise his discretion in relation to any procedural matter falling within the scope of PD 2004, III.30, but not the subject of specific reference, such discretion should be exercised having regard to the principles in this paragraph.

PD 2004, III.30.18

Before the trial, sentencing or appeal

74–003   Where a vulnerable accused, especially one who is young, is to be tried jointly with one who is not the judge should consider at the plea and case management hearing, whether the vulnerable accused should be tried on his own and should so order unless of the opinion that a joint trial would be in accordance with r.1 (the overriding objective) and in the interests of justice.

PD 2004, III.30.4, 30.5

If a vulnerable accused is tried jointly with one who is not, the judge should consider whether any of the modifications set out in PD 2004, III.30 should apply in the circumstances of the joint trial and so far as practicable make orders to give effect to any such modifications.

At the plea and case management hearing, the judge should consider and so far as practicable give directions on the matters covered in PD 2004 III.30.9 to III.30.18 (below).

It may be appropriate to arrange that a vulnerable accused should visit, out of court hours and before the trial, sentencing or appeal hearing, the courtroom in which that hearing is to take place so that he can familiarise himself with it.

PD 2004, III.30.6

If any case against a vulnerable accused has attracted, or may attract, widespread public or media interest, the assistance of the police should be enlisted to try and ensure that the accused is not, when attending the court, exposed to intimidation, vilification or abuse. CJA 1925, s.41 prohibits the taking of photographs of the accused and witnesses (among others) in the court building or in its precincts, or when entering or leaving those precincts. A direction informing media representatives that the prohibition will be enforced may be appropriate.

PD 2004, III.30.7

The judge should be ready at this stage, if he has not already done so, where relevant, to make a reporting restriction under CYPA 1933, s.39 or, on an appeal from a youth court, to remind media representatives of the application of CYPA 1933, s.49. Any such order, once made, should be reduced to writing and copies should on request be made available to anyone affected or potentially affected by it.

The trial, sentencing or appeal hearing

74–004 To avoid an atmosphere of intimidation where a vulnerable accused is on trial:

(1) subject to the need for appropriate security arrangements the proceedings should, if practicable, be held in a **courtroom** in which all the participants are on the same or almost the same level;

PD 2004, III.30.9

(2) a vulnerable accused, especially if he is young, should normally, if he wishes, be free to sit with members of his **family** or others in a like relationship, and with some other suitable **supporting adult** such as a social worker, and in a place which permits easy, informal communication with his **legal representatives;** the judge should ensure that a suitable supporting adult is available throughout the course of the proceedings;

PD 2004, III.30.10

(3) at the beginning of the proceedings the judge should ensure that what is to take place has been **explained** to a vulnerable accused in terms he can understand, ensuring in particular, at a trial, that the role of the jury has been explained; he should remind those representing him, and the supporting adult of their responsibility to explain each step as it takes place, and at a trial to explain the possible consequences of a guilty verdict. Throughout the trial the judge should continue to ensure, by any appropriate means, that the accused understands what is happening and what has been said by those on the bench, the advocates and witnesses;

PD 2004, III.30.11

(4) a trial should be conducted according to a **timetable** which takes full account of a vulnerable accused's ability to concentrate; frequent and regular breaks will often be appropriate. The judge should ensure, so far as practicable, that the trial is conducted in simple, clear language that the accused can understand and that cross-examination is conducted by questions which are short and clear; PD 2004, III.30.12

(5) a vulnerable accused who wishes to give evidence by **live link** in accordance with YJCEA 1999, s.33A, may apply for a direction to that effect; before making such a direction the judge must be satisfied that it is in the interests of justice to do so, and that the use of a live link would enable the accused to participate more effectively as a witness in the proceedings. The direction will need to deal with the practical arrangements to be made, including the room from which the accused will give evidence, the identity of the person or persons who will accompany him, and how it will be arranged for him to be seen and heard by the court; PD 2004, III.30.13

(6) **robes and wigs** should not be worn unless the judge for good reason orders that they should; it may be appropriate for the judge to be robed for sentencing in a grave case even though he has sat without robes for the trial. It is generally desirable that those responsible for the security of a vulnerable accused who is in custody, especially if he is young, should not be in uniform, and that there should be no recognisable police presence in the courtroom save for good reason; PD 2004, III.30.14

(7) the judge should be prepared to restrict **attendance** by members of the public in the court room to a small number, perhaps limited to those with an immediate and direct interest in the outcome; the judge should rule on any challenged claim to attend. PD 2004, III.30.15

Facilities for reporting

74–005   Facilities for reporting the proceedings (subject to any restrictions under CYPA 1933, ss.39 or 49) must be provided, but the judge court may restrict the number of reporters attending in the courtroom to such number as is judged practicable and desirable. In ruling on any challenged claim to attend in the court room for the purpose of reporting the court should be mindful of the public's general right to be informed about the administration of justice. PD 2004, III.30.16, 30.17

Where it has been decided to limit access to the courtroom, whether by reporters or generally, arrangements should be made for the proceedings to be relayed, audibly and if possible visually, to another room in the same court complex to which the media and the public have access if it appears that there will be a need for such additional facilities. Those making use of such a facility should be reminded that it is to be treated as an extension of the court room and that they are required to conduct themselves accordingly.

Attendance of parent or guardian

74–006   Where a child or young person is charged with an offence or is, for any other reason brought before a court, the court: CYPA 1933, s.34A

VULNERABLE ACCUSED

(1) *may*, in any case; and

(2) *must* in the case of a young person under the age of 16,

require a parent or guardian to attend during all stages of the proceedings, unless and to the extent that the judge is satisfied that it would be unreasonable to do so, having regard to the circumstances of the case.

Reference to a "parent" or "guardian" is a reference to a local authority where the child or young person is in its care, or is provided with accommodation by it in the exercise of its functions referred to its social services committee under the AJA 1970, and to any person with whom he is allowed to live.

75. WELSH LANGUAGE CASES

Introduction

75–001   Section 22(1) of the Welsh Language Act 1993 provides that in any legal proceedings in Wales the Welsh language may be spoken by any party, witness or other person who desires to use it, subject in the case of proceedings in a court other than a magistrates' court, to such prior notice as may be required by rules of court; and any necessary provision for interpretation shall be made accordingly.

A number of matters, mainly administrative, peculiar to Wales, have been dealt with by means of practice directions and protocols, the principal of which are;

(1) the Practice Direction issued by the Lord Chief Justice in 1998;
(2) a supplementary Practice Direction issued by the Presiding Judges on the February 28, 2000;
(3) a Practice Direction issued by the Presiding Judges in May 2001 on appeals from magistrates' courts against conviction; and
(4) a Protocol for the Listing of Cases where the Welsh language is used, issued by the Presiding Judges in December 2005.

See now PD 2004 III.22 and 23.

The purpose of all these Directions may be said to ensure that in the administration of justice in Wales the English and Welsh languages should be treated on a basis of equality.

The Directions provide for a Liaison Judge, and if any question or problem arises concerning the implementation of the above directions, contact should be made in the first place with him.

General

75–002   The 1998 Practice Direction makes it the responsibility of the legal representatives in every case in which the Welsh language may be used by any witnesses or party, or in any document which may be placed before the court, to inform the Crown Court of that fact so that appropriate arrangements can be made for the listing of the case. In particular:

(1) if the possible use of the Welsh language is known at the time of committal, transfer or appeal to the Crown Court, the court should be informed immediately after committal or transfer, or when the notice of appeal is lodged; otherwise, the court should be informed as soon as the possible use of the Welsh language becomes known;
(2) if costs are incurred as a result of failure to comply with these Directions, a wasted costs order may be made against the defaulting party and/or his legal representatives.

An advocate in a case in which the Welsh language may be used must raise that matter at the PCMH and endorse details of it on the Judge's Questionnaire, so that appropriate directions may be given for the progress of the case.

WELSH LANGUAGE CASES

Listing

75–003 The listing officer, in consultation with the Resident Judge, should ensure that a case in which the Welsh language may be used is listed, wherever practicable, before a Welsh speaking judge; and in a court in Wales with simultaneous translation facilities.

It follows that all cases involving evidence to be given in the Welsh language should wherever practicable be heard in Wales. If for any reason any such case committed for trial or sentence or transferred from a magistrates' court in Wales cannot be heard in Wales, the Supplementary Practice Direction of the February 28, 2000 applicable to cases originating from North Wales provides that the case must be referred to one of the Presiding Judges. No hearing or trial in that case may take place in a court outside Wales without the express consent of one of them.

For this purpose the Presiding Judges must be provided with:

(1) detailed information about the case;
(2) the scope of the intended use of the Welsh language;
(3) information about the views of the prosecution and defence about the hearing/trial and the use of Welsh; and
(4) the name of the judge who is to hear the case.

Consent to the hearing of a case outside Wales will be on the basis that it is heard by the judge specifically nominated for that case; no other judge may hear that case without a further reference being made to one of the Presiding Judges.

No judge other than a judge designated as approved to try cases in the Welsh language may try any case involving the use of the Welsh language, unless the consent of one of the Presiding Judges or the Liaison Judge for the Welsh language has been specifically obtained.

Interpreters

75–004 Whenever an interpreter is needed to translate evidence from English into Welsh of from Welsh into English, the court manager in whose court the case is to be heard shall ensure that the attendance is secured of an interpreter whose name is included in the list of approved court interpreters.

Jurors

75–005 The law does not permit the selection of jurors in a manner which enables the court to discover whether a juror does or does not speak Welsh, or to secure a jury whose members are bilingual, to try a case in which the Welsh language may be used.

The Jury Bailiff when addressing the jurors at the start of their period of jury service must inform them that each may take an oath, or affirm, in Welsh or English as he or she wishes, and after the jury has been selected to try a case, and before it is sworn, the court officer swearing-in the jury must inform the jurors in open court that each may take an Oath or affirm in Welsh or English as he or she wishes.

Witnesses

75–006 When each witness is called the court officer administering the oath or affirmation must inform the witness that he or she may be sworn or affirm in Welsh or English as he or she wishes.

Appeals from the magistrates' court against conviction

75–007 A Practice Direction issued by the Presiding Judges in May 2001 on appeals from magistrates' courts against conviction (heard at Newport, Cardiff, Swansea, Carmarthen, Merthyr Tydfil and Haverfordwest), provided that;

(1) The Crown Court will, on receipt of a notice of appeal against conviction, send a copy of the notice of appeal by facsimile or direct computer link to the CPS;

(2) As soon as possible, and in any event within a maximum of two working days of the sending of the copy of the notice of appeal by the Crown Court, the CPS will advise the Crown Court Liaison Officer for the relevant police area of the names of the witnesses in the case. The list of witnesses will identify separately (a) those who gave oral evidence in the magistrates' court and (6) those whose statements were read;

(3) As soon as possible, and in any event within a maximum of four working days of the receipt of the list of witnesses, the necessary enquiries to ascertain witness availability will be completed by the relevant police area;

(4) Prior to the listing of the case, the Crown Court will contact the Crown Court Liaison Officer of the relevant police area and ascertain the details of the availability of the witnesses in the case. In cases where the accused is on bail, a period of seven days notice will be given before the case is listed. In cases where the accused is in custody seven days notice will be provided wherever possible.

The Resident Judge or his deputy may abridge any of the time limits in any case where expedition is required.

1. Protocol for listing cases where the Welsh language is used

General right to use the Welsh language

75–008 An individual who wishes to use Welsh in the proceedings, has the right to do so and should not be required to justify or limit the extent to which he does so. The fact that the individual is bilingual and is competent in English does not affect or limit his right to use the Welsh language. Having regard to the principle of equality, it is essential that the use of Welsh does not result in any disadvantage to any of the parties or the witnesses by reason of delay in listing or deficiencies in the arrangements made for interpretation.

The following guidance should be followed when the court is informed that a party or any of the witnesses wishes to use Welsh during any part of the proceedings.

WELSH LANGUAGE CASES

Protocol to be followed:

75–009 On receiving information that a case is likely to involve the use of Welsh:

(1) the listing officer should immediately contact one of the two Liaison Judges;

(2) the PCMH should be listed before one of the Liaison Judges or a Welsh-speaking judge; if it is not known, prior to the hearing that the accused wishes to speak Welsh, the case should either be listed for sentence or mention (as soon as is practicable) before a Welsh speaking judge;

(3) at the PCMH or mention, the judge will need to give directions about the arrangements for translation; it is therefore essential that accurate information is obtained, as soon as possible, about the identity and number of accused and/or witnesses (particularly any child or vulnerable witness) who wish to use the Welsh language. It is also helpful to identify whether trial advocates are Welsh speaking. (CPS has agreed to ensure that the prosecution advocate will be Welsh speaking in such cases);

(4) the listing officer should ascertain the availability of a Welsh-speaking judge before fixing the date of trial or sentence. A Liaison Judge must be informed immediately if there is any difficulty in doing so;

(5) on receipt of any Allocation Questionnaire and/or Listing Questionnaire (pre trial checklist) the listing clerk must ensure that the question as to language preference has been answered and the necessary action taken if Welsh is to be used during the proceedings; it is also helpful to identify whether the trial advocates are Welsh speaking – if not, or only one is Welsh speaking, two-way translation will be required;

(6) the case should be listed before a Welsh-speaking judge. If there is any difficulty in doing so a Liaison Judge must be informed immediately;

(7) the judge should give consideration (in particular where special measures are adopted) as to whether a Welsh-speaking usher/clerk is required for the hearing.

Interpreters

75–010 Where any individual chooses to testify in Welsh, any questions put in English must be translated into Welsh for his benefit. When there is a need for translation into English and Welsh, it is essential to have two interpreters present. Even in those cases, when the case only requires translation into one language (e.g. when both advocates speak Welsh), two interpreters are required for any hearing when the interpreter would have to translate for any length of time so that the interpreters have regular and frequent breaks without delaying or extending the length of the hearing unnecessarily.

Note that:

(1) Only interpreters on the approved list may be used; they should be selected, wherever possible, on a rotation basis, so as to

ensure that they have an equal opportunity to gain experience
and maintain their courtroom skills;

(2) in certain exceptional cases when there are child witnesses or
issues of unusual complexity for example, and it would be desirable to have especially skilled and experienced interpreters, one
of the Liaison Judges should be consulted as to the choice;

(3) an interpreter should be given every assistance in preparing
for the hearing and allowed access to, or be given copies of,
the witness statements and copies of the indictment before the
hearing to allow him time to prepare and to note any unusual or
specialist terminology which may be used during the hearing;

(4) the Welsh version of the interpreter's oath/affirmation must be
available in the courtroom.

Pre-recorded video evidence and video link

75–011   When a child or vulnerable witness has been interviewed on
video in Welsh, the court will give directions for adding sub-titles in
English to the video; it is essential that these directions are given at the
earliest opportunity so as to avoid delay.

Translation equipment

75–012   The equipment used for translation should be tested at least
seven days before the hearing to allow time to obtain any additional
equipment or, if necessary, the services of an engineer. In particular,
the court must ensure that there are sufficient headsets (40 will normally
be required for a jury trial). There must be a special enclosed headset
for witnesses who will be questioned by English speaking advocates or
by video link.

The equipment should be checked to ensure that two separate channels work with the headsets and that both languages are recorded
separately.

Particular care should be taken in relation to any child or vulnerable
witness who gives evidence by video link, e.g. the witness should not
be expected to wear a bulky headset. Appropriate equipment must be
installed in the video link room which will transmit only the Welsh
translation of any question asked of the witness. The witness must not
hear any background noise or the English version of the question.

Welsh Language Cases

Notes

76. WITNESS SUMMONSES AND WARRANTS

76–001   A bench warrant may be issued at the Crown Court for the arrest of a person: BA 1976, s.7(1), (2)

(1) released on bail in criminal proceedings, and thus under a duty to surrender to the custody of the court, who:
   (a) fails to surrender at the appointed time and place; or
   (b) having surrendered, absents himself at any time and before the court is ready to begin or resume the hearing of the proceedings,

unless he is absent in accordance with leave given by or on behalf of the court; or SCA 1981, s.80(2)

(2) where an indictment has been signed but the person charged has not been sent for trial, where a summons is inappropriate.

A warrant may, in an appropriate case, be backed for bail.

There is no express requirement that a warrant for arrest issued under BA 1976, s.7 following failure to surrender to bail must state on its face the statutory source of its authority. Lords Wilberforce and Diplock in *IRC v Rossminster Ltd* [1980] A.C. 952, HL (suggesting that a warrant should state its statutory authority upon its face), were making a statement of what would be good practice in such circumstances; *R. (Bromley) v Secretary of State for Justice* [2010] A.C.D. 43, DC.

As to the terms and contents of a warrant, see CPR 2011, Pt 18.

Contempt by witness

76–002   A person who, without just excuse, disobeys a witness order or witness summons requiring him to attend before the Crown Court is guilty of contempt and may be punished summarily as if his contempt had been in the face of the court (see CONTEMPT OF COURT). The maximum term of imprisonment is three months. For sentencing principles, see *R. v Montgomery* [1995] 2 Cr. App. R. 23. CP(AW)A 1965, s.3

Obviously, the witness must have notice of the summons before he can be found in contempt, even though he may have rendered service impracticable, e.g. by changing his address (see e.g. *R. v Noble* [2008] EWCA Crim 1473; *The Times*, July 21, 2008).

Witness summons

76–003   In criminal proceedings a judge may issue a summons:

(1) on application, under the Rules, where he is satisfied that: CP(AW)A 1965, ss.2(1), (2), (3)
   (a) a person is likely to be able to give evidence likely to be material evidence or to produce any document or thing likely to be material evidence, for the purpose of any criminal proceedings before the Crown Court; and
   (b) it is in the interests of justice to issue a summons to secure

           the attendance of that person to give evidence or to produce
           the document or thing; or

(2) of his own motion,

in which circumstances a summons will be issued directing the person
concerned to attend at a specified time and place and to give the evidence or produce the document, or produce it for inspection. Under (1)
a summons may be refused if any requirement relating to the application
is not fulfilled. The procedure is set out in r.28.3 (below).   CP(AW)A 1965, s.2D

    The judge may issue (or withdraw) a witness summons, warrant or
order with or without a hearing. If there is a hearing it must be in private
unless the court otherwise directs. The procedure (which applies also to
applications under BBEA 1879, s.7, see PRODUCTION AND ACCESS
ORDERS; SEARCH WARRANTS) is set out in r.28.3 and following,
below.   Rr.28.1, 28.2, 28.8

    The judge may shorten or extend (even after it has expired) a time
limit under CPR 2011, Pt 4; he may also allow an application required
to be in writing under the Rules to be given orally.

Application for summons etc.; general rule

76–004   A party wishing the judge to issue a summons, warrant or
order must apply as soon as practicable after becoming aware of the
grounds for doing so: Rr.28.3, 28.4, 28.8

(1) identifying the proposed witness; and
(2) explaining:
    (a) what evidence the proposed witness can give or produce;
    (b) why it is likely to be material evidence; and
    (c) why it would be in the interests of justice to issue such
        process.

The application may be made orally unless r.28.5 applies or the judge
otherwise directs.

    Where someone wishes the judge to allow an application to be made
orally, he must give as much notice as the urgency of his application
permits to those on whom he would otherwise have served the application in writing, and in doing so, explain the reasons for the application
and for wishing the judge to consider it orally.

    Where it is in writing it must be in the form set out in PD 2004,
Annex D containing the same declaration of truth as a witness statement. The party applying must serve the application in every case on
the court officer and as directed by the judge, and as required by r.28.5
(see below) if that rule applies.

Summons to produce document etc.

76–005   Where (apart from an application under BBEA 1879, s.7) the
witness summons requires a proposed witness: R.28.5

(1) to produce in evidence a document or thing; or
(2) to give evidence about information apparently held in confi-
    dence, that relates to another person, the application must be in
    writing in the form required in r.28 and the party applying must
    serve it:

(a) on the proposed witness, unless the judge otherwise directs; and

(b) if the judge so directs, on a person to whom the proposed evidence relates, or another party.

Where this rule applies, a witness summons must not be issued unless:

    (i) everyone served has had at least 14 days in which to make representations including representations about whether there should be a hearing before the summons is issued; and

    (ii) the judge is satisfied that he has been able to take account of the rights and duties, including rights of confidentiality, of the proposed witness and of any person to whom the evidence relates (see, e.g. *R. (B) v Stafford Combined Court* [2006] EWHC 1645 (Admin); [2006] 2 Cr. App. R. 34 DC in relation to a patient's medical records).

Assessment of relevance and confidentiality

76–006 Where a person served with an application for a witness summons requiring him to produce in evidence a document or thing objects to its production on the ground either that:

R.28.6

(1) it is not likely to be material evidence; or

(2) even if it is likely to be material evidence, the duties or rights, including rights of confidentiality, of the proposed witness or of any person to whom the document or thing relates outweigh the reasons for issuing a summons, the judge may:

    (a) require the proposed witness to make the document or thing available for the objection to be assessed; and

    (b) may invite the proposed witness or any representative of his, or a person to whom the document or thing relates or any representative of his, to help him assess the objection.

Application to withdraw summons etc.

76–007 The judge may withdraw a witness summons, warrant or order on the application of any of the following:

R.28.7

(1) a party who applied for it on the ground that it is no longer needed;

(2) the witness, on the grounds that:

    (a) he was not aware of any application for it; and

    (b) he cannot give or produce evidence likely to be material evidence;

    (c) even if he can, his duties or rights, including rights of confidentiality, or those of any person to whom the evidence relates outweigh the reasons for the issue of the summons etc.;

(3) any person to whom the evidence relates, on the grounds that;

    (a) he was not aware of the application for it; and

    (b) that evidence is not likely to be material evidence; or

    (c) even if it is, his duties or rights, including rights of

Witness Summonses and Warrants

confidentiality or those of the witness outweigh the reasons for the issue of the summons, etc.

Any application must be made in writing as soon as practicable after the person making it becomes aware of the grounds for doing so, explaining why he wishes the summons etc. to be withdrawn, and must be served by that person on the court officer and, as appropriate, on the witness, the person who applied for the summons etc., and any other person known to have been served with the application. Rule 28.6 (above) applies.

The general principles are that material required to be produced on a summons:

(a) must be *prima facie* admissible (*R. v Cheltenham JJ. Ex p. SoS for Trade and Industry* [1977] 1 All E.R. 460; see also *R. v Derby MC Ex p. B* [1996] 1 Cr. App. R. 385; *R. v H(L)* [1997] 1 Cr. App. R. 176); and   CP(AW)A 1965, s.4(1)

(b) must be material, i.e. relevant to an issue in the case (*R. v Reading JJ. Ex p. Berkshire CC* [1996] 1 Cr. App. R. 239);   CP(AW)A 1965, s.2C(2)

(c) must *not* be subject to public interest immunity (*R. v Cheltenham JJ.*, above; *R. v K (Trevor Douglas)* (1993) 97 Cr. App. R. 342).

It is immaterial for these purposes whether the Rule requires such a person to be served with notice of the application or enables such a person to be present or represented at the hearing of the application to issue the summons.   CP(AW)A 1965, ss.2C(4), 2E(2)

The judge may refuse to make such a direction if any requirement relating to it under the Rules is not fulfilled.

Costs

76–008   Where a summons is issued on application by a party and the court later makes a direction that it shall be of no effect, the person on whose application the summons was issued may be ordered to pay the whole or any part of the costs of the application under this section, to be taxed by the Crown Court officer.   CP(AWA) 1965, s.2C(8), (9)

The issue of a purely speculative summons may well amount to an "improper, unreasonable or negligent act" capable of being the subject of a wasted costs order (*R. v Cheltenham JJ.*, above; also *Re Ronald A Prior & Co (Solicitors)* [1996] 1 Cr. App. R. 248).

Witness warrant

76–009   A warrant may be issued for the arrest of a witness who: CP(AW)A 1965, s.4(2)

(1) is required by virtue of a witness order or a witness summons to give evidence; or

(2) fails to attend in compliance with a summons or order,

provided the prosecutor proves that notice has been given (*R. v Abdulaziz* [1989] Crim. L.R. 717).

The judge may:

(a) cause notice to be served on the witness requiring him to attend forthwith or at a specified time; or

(b) if he is satisfied there are reasonable grounds for believing that there is no just excuse for the witness's failure to attend, or he has already failed to comply with a notice under (a), he may issue a warrant.

CP(AW)A 1965, s.4(3)

Culpable forgetfulness is not a "reasonable excuse" (*R. v Lennock* (1993) 97 Cr. App. R. 228).

A witness brought before the court in pursuance of the warrant may be remanded in custody or on bail, with or without sureties, until such time as the court appoints for receiving his evidence or otherwise dealing with him. The power to remand in custody under s.4(5) is to remand until such time as the witness is released from further attendance at court (*R.(H) v. Wood Green CC* [2006] EWHC 2683 (Admin); [2007] Crim. L.R. 727).

In order to avoid a witness who fails to appear in response to a summons having to be locked up overnight or for longer, it is better practice either:

  (i) for the warrant to be backed for bail; or

  (ii) for the officers to be directed not to execute the warrant, except at the Crown Court, if satisfied that the witness is going to attend voluntarily or is going to accompany them.

(*R. v Popat* [2008] EWCA Crim 1927, (2009) 172 J.P. 24.)

Service outside the United Kingdom

76–010   A summons or order requiring a person to attend before the court for the purpose of giving evidence in criminal proceedings may be issued or made notwithstanding that the person in question is outside the United Kingdom, and may be served outside the United Kingdom in accordance with arrangements made by the Secretary of State.

CJ(IC)A 1990, s.2

Such service does not impose any obligation under the law of England and Wales to comply with it, so that failure to do so does not constitute contempt of court, nor is it a ground for issuing a warrant, unless that person is subsequently served in the United Kingdom.

Where a witness summons is issued or a witness order is made by the Crown Court in such circumstances, it is sent to the Secretary of State with a view to its being served in accordance with arrangements made by him.

Warrant of arrest

76–011   A judge of the Crown Court, if satisfied on oath that a witness in respect of whom a witness summons or order is in force is unlikely to comply with it, may issue a warrant for his arrest provided that in the case of a witness subject to a witness summons, he is satisfied that the witness is likely to be able to give material evidence or produce a document or thing likely to be material evidence in the proceedings.

R.32

"Unlikely to attend" may include a situation where the witness is willing but because of factors outside his control he is unable to attend (*R. v Sokolovics* [1981] Crim. L.R. 788).

Notes

77. YOUTH REHABILITATION ORDERS

Quick guide

1. General (77–001)
2. The available requirements (77–003)
3. Duties of officers (77–008)
4. Requirements to be included in orders (77–011)
5. Individual requirements (77–015)
6. Miscellaneous (77–036))
7. Administrative (77–038)

1. General

General

77–001 CJIA 2008 provides for a single community sentence (the youth rehabilitation order) within which the judge may include one or more requirements variously designed to provide for punishment, protection of the public, reducing reoffending and for reparation.

A youth rehabilitation order with intensive supervision and surveillance or with fostering is also provided but may be imposed only where a custodial sentence otherwise would have been appropriate (see 77–004 below).

The order replaces curfew orders, exclusion orders, supervision orders and action plan orders. The orders replaced will continue in force in relation to offences committed before November 30, 2009; the new order will apply to offences committed on or after that date.

The commencement order expressly saves attendance centre orders, which may, it seems, be made in respect of offenders aged 16 or 17.

In practice, many of the new requirements do not differ substantially from the former orders, save that there is no action plan requirement, though a judge will probably be able achieve the same result by the inclusion of other available requirements, such as an activity requirement or a prohibited activity requirement or a combination of both.

It is important to note that the making of a youth rehabilitation order is not subject to CJA 2003, s.150A (see 16–004), so that unlike an adult community order **it is not dependent on the offence being punishable with imprisonment,** unless there is included a requirement of intensive supervision and surveillance; otherwise it may be made in respect of any offence.

CJIA 2008, Sch.2 makes provision about failure to comply with the requirements of such an order and about its revocation and amendment. CJIA 2008, Sch.3 makes provision about the transfer of such an order to Northern Ireland.

Power to make order

77–002 Where a person aged under 18 is convicted of an offence, the court before which he is convicted may, subject to CJA 2003, ss.148   CJIA 2008, s.1

and 150, make a youth rehabilitation order in relation to him, imposing on him any one or more of the requirements set out 77–003 below.

The statutory restrictions referred to above require before imposing an order the judge must be satisfied that offence "is serious enough", and in determining the content and length of the order that it be commensurate with the seriousness of the offence, and its requirements are the most suitable for the offender.

SGC(Y) 10.7, 10.8 suggest that where the judge is considering sentence for an offence for which a custodial sentence is justified, a guilty plea may be one of the factors that persuades him that he can properly impose a youth rehabilitation order instead and no further adjustment to the sentence needs to be made to fulfil the obligation to give credit for that plea. Where the provisional sentence is already a youth rehabilitation order, the necessary reduction for a guilty plea should apply to those requirements within the order that are primarily punitive, rather than to those which are primarily rehabilitative.

Before making a youth rehabilitation order the judge must obtain and consider information about the offender's family circumstances and the likely effect of such an order on those circumstances.

Before making:

(1) a youth rehabilitation order imposing two or more requirements; or
(2) two or more youth rehabilitation orders in respect of associated offences,

the judge must consider whether, in the circumstances of the case, the requirements to be imposed by the order, or orders, are compatible with each other.

The judge must ensure, as far as practicable, that any requirement imposed by a youth rehabilitation order is such as to avoid:

(a) any conflict with the offender's religious beliefs;
(b) any interference with the times, if any, at which the offender normally works or attends school or any other educational establishment; and
(c) any conflict with the requirements of any other youth rehabilitation order to which the offender may be subject.

Where the judge imposes a requirement in connection with a youth rehabilitation order, the Crown Court officer will notify the appropriate persons of those matters set out in r 42.2 (as to which, see COMMUNITY SENTENCES).

CJIA 2008, s.1, Sch.1, Pt 3, para.28
CJIA 2008, s.1, Sch.1, Pt 3, para.29

2. The available requirements

77–003   The requirements which may be imposed under Sch.1 are:

- an **activity requirement** (paras 6 to 8),
- a **supervision requirement** (para.9),
- in a case where the offender is aged 16 or 17 at the time of the conviction, an **unpaid work requirement** (para.10),
- a **programme requirement** (para.11),
- an **attendance centre requirement** (para.12),

- a **prohibited activity requirement** (para.13),
- a **curfew requirement** (para.14),
- an **exclusion requirement** (para.15),
- a **residence requirement** (para.16),
- a **local authority residence requirement** (para.17),
- a **mental health treatment requirement** (para.20),
- a **drug treatment requirement** (para.22),
- a **drug testing requirement** (para.23),
- an **intoxicating substance treatment requirement** (para.24), and
- an **education requirement** (para.25).

The order:

(1) **may** also impose an **electronic monitoring requirement** (para.26), and

(2) **must** do so if para.2 of Sch.1 so requires.

Intensive supervision, surveillance and fostering

77–004   An order may be:

(1) a youth rehabilitation order **with intensive supervision and surveillance** (para.3); or

(2) a youth rehabilitation order **with fostering** (para.4) but such orders may only be made where:

   (a) the judge is dealing with the offender for an offence which is punishable with imprisonment;

   (b) the judge is of the opinion that the offence, or the combination of the offence and one or more offences associated with it, is so serious that, but for paras 3 or 4, a custodial sentence would be appropriate (or, if the offender is aged under 12 at the time of conviction, would be appropriate if the offender had been aged 12); and

   (c) the offender is aged under 15 at the time of conviction and the judge is of opinion that the offender is a persistent offender (see DENTENTION OF YOUNG OFFENDERS).

Approach to determining nature and extent of requirements

77–005   SGC(Y) (10.9, 10.10) suggest that in determining the nature and extent of requirements to be included within an order and the length of that order, the key factors are;

(1) the assessment of the seriousness of the offence;

(2) the objective(s) the judge seeks to achieve;

(3) the risk of re-offending;

(4) the ability of the offender to comply; and

(5) the availability of requirements in the local area.

Since the Judge must determine that the offence (or combination of offences) is "serious enough" to justify such an order, he will be able to determine the nature and extent of the requirements within the order primarily by reference to the likelihood of the young person re-offending and to the risk of the offender causing serious harm.

YOUTH REHABILITATION ORDERS

Before making an order the judge will need to consider a pre-sentence report.

SGC(Y) (10.22) suggests that the judge should ask himself the following questions:

   (a) What requirements are most suitable for offender?
   (b) What overall period is necessary to ensure that all requirements may be satisfactorily completed?
   (c) Are the restrictions on liberty that result from those requirements commensurate with the seriousness of the offence?

CJIA 2008, Sch.1, para.32(1)

Length of order

77–006   When imposing a youth rehabilitation order, the court must fix a period within which the requirements of the order are to be completed:

   (1) this must not be more than 3 years from the date on which the order comes into effect; though
   (2) where the order contains two or more requirements, the order may specify an earlier date for any of those requirements.

CJIA 2008, Sch.1, para.30

The period specified as the overall period for the order will ordinarily commence on the day the order is made but, where the offender is already subject to a detention and training order, the judge may specify that the youth rehabilitation order will take effect either on the day that supervision begins in relation to the detention and training order or on the expiry of the term of that order.

CJIA 2008, Sch.1, para.30(4)

It is not possible to make a youth rehabilitation order where the offender is already subject to another youth rehabilitation order or to a reparation order unless the judge revokes those orders.

SGC(Y) (10.20) points out that the overall length of an order has three main consequences:

   (a) where a supervision requirement is included, the obligation to attend appointments as directed by the responsible officer continues for the whole period;
   (b) where an offender is in breach of an order, one of the sanctions available to a court is to amend the order by including within it any requirement that it would have had power to include when the order was made; but that new requirement must be capable of being complied with before the expiry of the overall period;
   (c) an offender is liable to be re-sentenced for the offence(s) for which the order was made if convicted of another offence whilst the order is in force.

In determining the length of an order, SGC(Y) (10.21) suggests that the judge should allow sufficient time for the order as a whole to be complied with, recognising that the offender is at risk of further sanction throughout the whole of the period, but allowing sufficient flexibility should a sanction need to be imposed for breach of the order.

Where appropriate, an application for early discharge may be made.

Order with intensive supervision and surveillance

77–007   A youth rehabilitation order with intensive supervision and surveillance is an order that contains an "extended activity require-ment", that is, an activity requirement with a maximum of 180 days. As a result, there are further obligations to include a supervision requirement (para.9) and a curfew requirement (para.14). Where appropriate, such an order may also include additional requirements, although the order as a whole must comply with the obligation that the requirements must be those most suitable for the offender and that any restrictions on liberty must be commensurate with the seriousness of the offence.

SGC(Y) (10.27) suggests that when imposing such an order, the judge must ensure that the requirements are not so onerous as to make the likelihood of breach almost inevitable.

As to a fostering requirement, 77–029 below.

3.   Duties of officers

Meaning of "the responsible officer"

77–008   "The responsible officer", in relation to an offender to whom a youth rehabilitation order relates, means: CJIA 2008, s.4(1)

(1) in a case where the order:
  (a) imposes a curfew requirement or an exclusion require-ment but no other requirement mentioned in 77–003, above; and
  (b) imposes an electronic monitoring requirement, the person who is (under para.26(4)) responsible for the electronic monitoring required by the order;
(2) in a case where the only requirement imposed by the order is an attendance centre requirement, the officer in charge of the centre in question;
(3) in any other case, the "qualifying officer" who, as respects the offender, is for the time being responsible for discharging the functions conferred on the responsible officer (77–009, below).   CJIA 2008, s.4(2)

Meaning of "qualifying officer"

77–009   "Qualifying officer", in relation to a youth rehabilitation order means:

(1) a member of a youth offending team established by a local authority for the time being specified in the order for the pur-poses of this section; or
(2) an officer of a local probation board appointed for or assigned to the local justice area for the time being so specified or (as the case may be) an officer of a provider of probation services acting in the local justice area for the time being so specified.

An order under may, in particular, provide for the court to determine which of two or more descriptions of responsible officer is to apply in relation to any youth rehabilitation order.

Duties of responsible officer and offender in relation to the other

77–010   Where a youth rehabilitation order has effect, it is the duty of the responsible officer:

CJIA 2008, s.5

(1) to make any arrangements that are necessary in connection with the requirements imposed by the order;

(2) to promote the offender's compliance with those requirements; and

(3) where appropriate, to take steps to enforce those requirements, unless he is merely the person responsible for supervising electronic monitoring.

He must ensure, as far as practicable, that any instruction given is such as to avoid;

(a) any conflict with the offender's religious beliefs;

(b) any interference with the times, if any, at which the offender normally works or attends school, or any other educational establishment; and

(c) any conflict with the requirements of any other youth reahbilitation order to which the offender may be subject.

An offender in respect of whom a youth rehabilitation order is in force:

(i) must keep in touch with the responsible officer in accordance with such instructions as he may from time to time be given by that officer; and

(ii) must notify the responsible officer of any change of address, such obligations being enforceable as if they were requirements imposed by the order.

4.   Requirements to be included in orders

Imposition of requirements

77–011   Section 1(1) has effect subject to the following paragraphs of Sch.1, Pt 2 which relate to particular requirements:

CJIA 2008,
s.1, Sch.1, Pt 1,
para.1

- activity requirement (77–015),
- supervision requirement (77–019),
- unpaid work requirement (77–020),
- programme requirement (77–021),
- attendance centre requirement (77–022),
- prohibited activity requirement (77–023),
- curfew requirement (77–024),
- exclusion requirement (77–025),
- residence requirement (77–026),
- local authority residence requirement (77–027),
- fostering requirement (77–029),
- mental health treatment requirement (77–030),
- drug treatment requirement (77–032),
- intoxicating substance treatment requirement (77–033),
- education requirement (77–034) and
- electronic monitoring requirement (77–035).

Electronic monitoring requirement

77–012   Where a youth rehabilitation order:

CJIA 2008, s.1, Sch.1, Pt 1, para.2

(1) imposes a curfew requirement (whether by virtue of para.3(4)(b) or otherwise); or

(2) imposes an exclusion requirement,

the order must also impose an electronic monitoring requirement unless the judge:

(a) in the particular circumstances of the case, considers it inappropriate for the order to do so; or

(b) is prevented by para.26(3) or (6) (see 77–035, below) from including such a requirement in the order.

Subsection (2)(a) of s.1 has effect subject to paragraph 26(3) and (6) (see 77–035, below).

The duty of notification by the Crown Court officer under r.42 2(3) is the same as in the case of a community order (see COMMODITY SENTENCES).

Intensive supervision and surveillance

77–013   Where paragraphs (a) to (c) of section 1(4) are satisfied, the judge, if he makes a youth rehabilitation order which imposes an activity requirement, may specify in relation to that requirement a number of days, being more than 90 but not more than 180.

CJIA 2008, s.1, Sch.1, Pt 1, para.3

Such an activity requirement is referred to as "an extended activity requirement".

A youth rehabilitation order which imposes an extended activity requirement **must** also impose:

(1) a supervision requirement; and

(2) a curfew requirement (and, accordingly, if so required by para.2 (77–035) an electronic monitoring requirement).

An order which imposes an extended activity requirement (and other requirements in accordance with (1) and (2)) is referred to as "a youth rehabilitation order with intensive supervision and surveillance" (whether or not it also imposes any other requirement mentioned in 77–011, above).

Youth rehabilitation order with fostering

77–014   Where paras (a) to (c) of s.1(4) (77–029) are met, and the judge is satisfied:

CJIA 2008, s.1, Sch.1, Pt 1, para.4

(1) that the behaviour which constituted the offence was due to a significant extent to the circumstances in which the offender was living; and

(2) that the imposition of a fostering requirement (see para.18) would assist in the offender's rehabilitation,

he may make an which imposes a fostering requirement, but he may not impose such a requirement unless:

(a) he has consulted the offender's parents or guardians (unless it is impracticable to do so); and

(b) he has consulted the local authority which is to place the offender with a local authority foster parent.

An order which imposes a fostering requirement must also impose a supervision requirement.

This paragraph has effect subject to paras 18(7) and 19 (pre-conditions to imposing fostering requirement), as to which see 77–029 below.

An order which imposes a fostering requirement is referred to "a youth rehabilitation order with fostering" (whatever other requirements mentioned in 77–011 it imposes).

CJIA 2008,
s.1, Sch.1, Pt 1,
para.5

An order with intensive supervision and surveillance may not impose a fostering requirement.

Nothing in—

(i) s.1(4)(b); or
(ii) CJA 2003, s.148(1) or (2)(b) (restrictions on imposing community sentences);

prevents the judge from making a youth rehabilitation order with intensive supervision and surveillance in respect of an offender if the offender fails to comply with an order under CJA 2003, s.161(2) (pre-sentence drug testing).

5. Individual requirements

(1) Activity requirements

General

77–015 An "activity requirement" is a requirement that the offender do any or all of the following:

CJIA 2008,
s.1, Sch.1, Pt 2,
para.6

(1) participate, on such number of days as may be specified in the order, in activities at a specified place, or places;
(2) participate in a specified activity, or activities, on a specified number of days;
(3) participate in one or more residential exercises for a continuous period, or periods comprising such number or numbers of days as may be specified in the order;
(4) in accordance with paragraph 7, engage in activities in accordance with instructions of the responsible officer on such number of days as may be specified in the order.

Subject to 77–013 the number of days specified in an order must not, in aggregate, be more than 90.

A requirement such as is mentioned in (1) or (2) above operates to require the offender, in accordance with instructions given by the responsible officer, on the number of days specified in the order in relation to the requirement, in the case of a requirement such as is mentioned in:

(a) (1) above to present himself or herself at a place specified in the order to a person of a description so specified; or
(b) (2) above to participate in an activity specified in the order, and, on each such day, to comply with instructions given by,

or under the authority of, the person in charge of the place or the activity (as the case may be).

As to consultation and reports, see 77–018, below.

Residential exercise

77–016 Where the order requires the offender to participate in a residential exercise, it must specify, in relation to the exercise;

(1) a place; or
(2) an activity.

A requirement to participate in a residential exercise operates to require the offender, in accordance with instructions given by the responsible officer:

(a) if a place is specified as above:
    (i) to present himself or herself at the beginning of the period specified in the order in relation to the exercise, at the place so specified to a person of a description specified in the instructions; and
    (ii) to reside there for that period;
(b) if an activity is specified under sub-paragraph (4)(b), to participate, for the period specified in the order in relation to the exercise, in the activity so specified,

and, during that period, to comply with instructions given by, or under the authority of, the person in charge of the place or the activity (as the case may be).

Instructions of responsible officer under paragraph 6(1)(d)

77–017 Subject to 77–013, instructions under (4) in 77–015 above relating to any day must require the offender to do either of the following:

CJIA 2008, s.1, Sch.1, Pt 2, para.7

(1) present himself or herself to a person or persons of a description specified in the instructions at a place so specified;
(2) participate in an activity specified in the instructions.

Such instructions operate to require the offender, on that day or while participating in that activity, to comply with instructions given by, or under the authority of, the person in charge of the place or, as the case may be, the activity.

If the order so provides, such instructions may require the offender to participate in a residential exercise for a period comprising not more than seven days, and, for that purpose:

(a) to present himself or herself at the beginning of that period to a person of a description specified in the instructions at a place so specified and to reside there for that period; or
(b) to participate for that period in an activity specified in the instructions.

Instructions of this nature:

    (i) may not be given except with the consent of a parent or guardian of the offender; and

(ii) operate to require the offender, during the period specified, to comply with instructions given by, or under the authority of, the person in charge of the place or activity specified.

Further provisions

77–018 Instructions given by, or under the authority of, a person in charge of any place under any of the above provisions may require the offender to engage in activities otherwise than at that place. CJIA 2008,
s.1, Sch.1, Pt 2,
para.8

An activity specified under (2) or (4) of 77–015 above may consist of or include an activity whose purpose is that of reparation, such as an activity involving contact between an offender and persons affected by the offences in respect of which the order was made.

The judge may not include an activity requirement in a youth rehabilitation order unless:

(1) he has consulted a member of a youth offending team, an officer of a local probation board or an officer of a provider of probation services;
(2) he is satisfied that it is feasible to secure compliance with the requirement; and
(3) he is satisfied that provision for the offender to participate in the activities proposed to be specified in the order can be made under the arrangements for persons to participate in such activities which exist in the local justice area in which the offender resides or is to reside.

The judge may not include an activity requirement in a youth rehabilitation order if compliance with that requirement would involve the cooperation of a person other than the offender and the responsible officer, unless that other person consents to its inclusion.

(2) Supervision requirement

77–019 A "supervision requirement", in relation to a youth rehabilitation order, means a requirement that, during the period for which the order remains in force, the offender must attend appointments with the responsible officer or another person determined by the responsible officer, at such times and places as may be determined by the responsible officer. CJIA 2008,
s.1, Sch.1, Pt 2,
para.9

(3) Unpaid work requirement

77–020 An "unpaid work requirement" is a requirement that the offender perform unpaid work in accordance with para.10. CJIA 2008, s.1,
Sch.1, para.10

The number of hours which a person may be required to work under such a requirement must be specified in the order and must be, in aggregate:

(1) not less than 40; and
(2) not more than 240.

The judge may not impose such a requirement in respect of an offender unless:

(a) after hearing (if he thinks necessary) an appropriate officer, he is satisfied that the offender is a suitable person to perform work under such a requirement; and

(b) he is satisfied that provision for the offender to work under such a requirement can be made under the arrangements for persons to perform work under such a requirement which exist in the local justice area in which the offender resides or is to reside.

"An appropriate officer" in (a) means a member of a youth offending team, an officer of a local probation board or an officer of a provider of probation services.

An offender in respect of whom an unpaid work requirement of a youth rehabilitation order is in force must perform for the number of hours specified in the order such work at such times as the responsible officer may specify in instructions.

Subject to Sch.2, para.17 (extension of unpaid work requirement, see BREACH, AMENDMENT AND REVOCATION, etc.) the work required to be performed under such a requirement must be performed during the period of 12 months beginning with the day on which the order takes effect. Unless revoked, a youth rehabilitation order imposing an unpaid work requirement remains in force until the offender has worked under it for the number of hours specified in it.

(4)   Programme requirement

77–021   A "programme requirement", is a requirement that the offender participate in a systematic set of activities ("a programme") specified in the order at a place or places so specified on a specified number of days.

CJIA 2008, s.1, Sch.1 n Pt 2, para.11

Such a requirement may require the offender to reside at any place specified in the order for a specified period if it is necessary for him to reside there for that period in order to participate in the programme.

A programme requirement may not be specified in an order unless:

(1) the programme which the judge proposes to specify in the order has been recommended by:
   (a) a member of a youth offending team;
   (b) an officer of a local probation board; or
   (c) an officer of a provider of probation services, as being suitable for the offender; and

(2) the judge is satisfied that the programme is available at the place or places proposed to be specified.

A programme requirement may not be included if compliance with that requirement would involve the cooperation of a person other than the offender and the offender's responsible officer, unless that other person consents to its inclusion.

A requirement to participate in a programme operates to require the offender:

> (i) in accordance with instructions given by the responsible officer to participate in the programme at the place or places specified in the order on the number of days so specified; and
>
> (ii) while at any of those places, to comply with instructions given by, or under the authority of, the person in charge of the programme.

(5) Attendance centre requirement

77–022 The commencement order (see 77–001) expressly saves attendance centre orders under PCC(S)A 2000, s.50 which remain available in the case of offenders aged 16 and 17, in respect of offences committed before November 9, 2009 (see AGE OF OFFENDER). An "attendance centre requirement" is a requirement that the offender attend at an attendance centre specified in the order for such number of hours as may be specified.   *CJA 2008, s.1, Sch.1, Pt 2, para.12*

The aggregate number of hours for which the offender may be required to attend at the centre:

(1) if the offender is aged 16 or over at the time of conviction, must be;
  (a) not less than 12; and
  (b) not more than 36;
(2) if the offender is aged 14 or over but under 16 at the time of conviction, must be;
  (a) not less than 12; and
  (b) not more than 24;
(3) if the offender is aged under 14 at the time of conviction, must not be more than 12.

An attendance centre requirement may not be included in a youth rehabilitation order unless the court:

(a) has been notified by the Secretary of State that:
  (i) an attendance centre is available for persons of the offender's description; and
  (ii) provision can be made at the centre for the offender; and
(b) is satisfied that the centre proposed to be specified is reasonably accessible to the offender, having regard to the means of access available to the offender and any other circumstances.

The first time at which the offender is required to attend at the centre will be a time notified to the offender by the responsible officer. The subsequent hours will be fixed by the officer in charge of the centre, in accordance with arrangements made by the responsible officer, having regard to the offender's circumstances.

An offender may not be required under this requirement to attend at an attendance centre on more than one occasion on any day, or for more than three hours on any occasion.

A requirement to attend at the centre for any period on any occasion operates as a requirement to attend at the centre at the beginning of the period and during that period, to engage in occupation, or receive instruction, under the supervision of and in accordance with instructions given by, or under the authority of, the officer in charge, whether at the centre or elsewhere.

(6) Prohibited activity requirement

77–023 A "prohibited activity requirement", means a requirement that the offender refrain from participating in activities specified in the order, on a specified day or days or during a specified period.

CJIA 2008, s.1, Sch.1, Pt 2, para.13

Such a requirement may not be included in an order unless the judge has consulted;

(1) a member of a youth offending team;
(2) an officer of a local probation board; or
(3) an officer of a provider of probation services.

The requirements that may by virtue of this paragraph be included in a youth rehabilitation order include a requirement that the offender does not possess, use or carry a firearm within the meaning of the FA 1968.

(7) Curfew requirement

77–024 A "curfew requirement", is a requirement that the offender remain, for periods specified in the order, at a specified place.

CJIA 2008, s.1, Sch.1, Pt 2, para.14

An order imposing such a requirement may specify different places or different periods for different days, but may not specify periods which amount to less than two hours or more than 12 hours in any day, nor may it specify periods which fall outside the period of six months beginning with the day on which the requirement first takes effect.

Before making a youth rehabilitation order imposing a curfew requirement, the judge must obtain and consider information about the place proposed to be specified in the order (including information as to the attitude of persons likely to be affected by the enforced presence there of the offender).

(8) Exclusion requirement

77–025 An "exclusion requirement" is a provision prohibiting the offender from entering a place specified in the order for a specified period.

CJIA 2008, s.1, Sch.1, Pt 2, para.15

The period specified must not be more than three months An exclusion requirement may:

(1) provide for the prohibition to operate only during the periods specified in the order; and
(2) may specify different places for different periods or days.

"Place" includes an area.

(9) Residence requirement

77–026 A "residence requirement" is a requirement that, during the period specified in the order, the offender reside: CJIA 2008, s.1, Sch.1, Pt 2, para.16

(1) with an individual; or

(2) at a place,

specified in the order.

Before making a youth rehabilitation order containing a place of residence requirement, the judge must consider the offender's home surroundings.

A requirement under (1) may not be included unless that individual has consented to the requirement.

An order under (2) is referred to as "a place of residence requirement," and may not be included unless the offender was aged 16 or over at the time of conviction.

If the order so provides, a place of residence requirement does not prohibit the offender from residing, with the prior approval of the responsible officer, at a place other than that specified in the order.

The judge may not specify a hostel or other institution as the place where an offender must reside except on the recommendation of:

(a) a member of a youth offending team;

(b) an officer of a local probation board;

(c) an officer of a provider of probation services; or

(d) a social worker of a local authority.

(10) Local authority residence requirement

General

77–027 A "local authority residence requirement" is a requirement that, during the period specified in the order, the offender reside in accommodation provided by or on behalf of a local authority specified in the order for the purposes of the requirement. CJIA 2008, s.1, Sch.1, Pt 2, para.17

An order which imposes such a requirement may also stipulate that the offender is *not* to reside with a person specified in the order.

A local authority residence requirement may not be included in an order made in respect of an offence unless the judge is satisfied that:

(1) the behaviour which constituted the offence was due to a significant extent to the circumstances in which the offender was living; and

(2) the imposition of that requirement will assist in the offender's rehabilitation.

The judge may not include such a requirement in an order unless he has consulted;

(a) a parent or guardian of the offender (unless it is impracticable to consult such a person); and

(b) the local authority which is to receive the offender.

The order must specify, as the local authority which is to receive the offender, the local authority in whose area the offender resides or is to reside.

Any period specified in the order as a period for which the offender must reside in accommodation provided by or on behalf of a local authority must not be longer than six months, and must not include any period after the offender has reached the age of 18.

Pre-conditions: local authority residence requirement or fostering requirement

77–028 The judge may not include a local authority residence requirement (or a fostering requirement, see below) in an order in respect of an offender unless:

CJIA 2008, s.1, Sch.1, Pt 2, para.19

(1) the offender was legally represented at the relevant time in court; or
(2) either of the following conditions is satisfied, namely that:
    (a) the offender was granted a right to representation funded by the Legal Services Commission as part of the Criminal Defence Service for the purposes of the proceedings but the right was withdrawn because of the offender's conduct; or
    (b) the offender has been informed of the right to apply for such representation for the purposes of the proceedings and has had the opportunity to do so, but nevertheless refused or failed to apply.

"The proceedings" here means the whole proceedings, or that part of the proceedings relating to the imposition of the local authority residence requirement or the fostering requirement. The "relevant time" means the time when the court is considering whether to impose that requirement.

(11)   Fostering requirement

77–029 A "fostering requirement" is a requirement that, for a period specified in the order, the offender reside with a local authority foster parent. The preconditions set out in 77–028 above apply.

CJIA 2008, s.1, Sch.1, Pt 2, para.18

A period specified as a period for which the offender must reside with a local authority foster parent must:

(1) end no later than the end of the period of 12 months beginning with the date on which the requirement first has effect (but subject to extension or new periods permitted by Sch.2, paras 6(9), 8(9) and 16(2) as to which see BREACH AMENDMENT AND REVOCATION); and
(2) not include any period after the offender has reached the age of 18.

An order imposing such a requirement must specify the local authority which is to place the offender with a local authority foster parent (CA 1989, s.23(2)(a)), and the authority specified must be the local authority in whose area the offender resides or is to reside.

If at any time during the period specified the responsible officer notifies the offender that no suitable local authority foster parent is available, and that the responsible officer has applied or proposes to apply under Sch.2, Pts 3 or 4 for the revocation or amendment of the order (see BREACH, AMENDMENT AND REVOCATION), the fostering requirement is, until the determination of the application, to be taken to require the offender to reside in accommodation provided by or on behalf of a local authority.

A fostering requirement may not be included in a youth rehabilitation order unless the court has been notified by the Secretary of State that arrangements for implementing such a requirement are available in the area of the local authority which is to place the offender with a local authority foster parent.

(12)   Mental health treatment requirement

General

77–030   A "mental health treatment requirement" is a requirement that the offender submit, during a period or periods specified in the order, to treatment by or under the direction of a registered medical practitioner or a chartered psychologist, (or both, for different periods) with a view to the improvement of the offender's mental condition.

CJIA 2008, s.1, Sch.1, Pt 2, para.20

The treatment required during a specified period must be such one of the following kinds of treatment as may be specified in the order:

(1) treatment as a resident patient in an independent hospital or care home within the meaning of the Care Standards Act 2000 or a hospital within the meaning of MHA 1983, but not in hospital premises where high security psychiatric services within the meaning of that Act are provided;

(2) treatment as a non-resident patient at such institution or place as may be specified in the order;

(3) treatment by or under the direction of such registered medical practitioner or chartered psychologist (or both) as may be so specified;

but the order must not otherwise specify the nature of the -treatment.

Such a requirement may not be included in a youth rehabilitation order unless:

(a) the judge is satisfied, on the evidence of a registered medical practitioner approved for the purposes of MHA 1983, s.12, that the mental condition of the offender;

   (i) is such as requires and may be susceptible to treatment; but

   (ii) is not such as to warrant the making of a hospital order or guardianship order within the meaning of that Act;

(b) the judge is also satisfied that arrangements have been or can be made for the treatment intended to be specified in the order (including, where the offender is to be required to submit to treatment as a resident patient, arrangements for the reception of the offender); and

(c) the offender has expressed willingness to comply with the requirement.

MHA 1983, s.54 (2) and (3) have effect with respect to proof of an offender's mental condition for the purposes of (a) above as they have effect with respect to proof of an offender's mental condition for the purposes of a hospital order (see MENTALLY DISORDERED OFFENDERS).

A "chartered psychologist" means a person for the time being listed in the British Psychological Society's Register of Chartered Psychologists.

While the offender is under treatment as a resident patient in pursuance of such a requirement, the responsible officer will carry out the supervision of the offender to such extent only as may be necessary for the purpose of the revocation or amendment of the order.

Treatment at place other than that specified in order

77–031 Where the registered medical practitioner or chartered psychologist by whom or under whose direction an offender is being treated in pursuance of such a requirement is of the opinion that part of the treatment can be better or more conveniently given in or at an institution or place which;

CJIA 2008, s.1, Sch.1, Pt 2, para.21

(1) is not specified in the youth rehabilitation order; and
(2) is one in or at which the treatment of the offender will be given by or under the direction of a registered medical practitioner or chartered psychologist,

the medical practitioner or psychologist may make arrangements for the offender to be treated accordingly, but such arrangements may only be made if the offender has expressed willingness for the treatment to be given.

These arrangements may provide for part of the treatment to be provided to the offender as a resident patient in an institution or place notwithstanding that the institution or place is not one which could have been specified for that purpose in the youth rehabilitation order.

Where any such arrangements are made for the treatment of an offender:

(a) the registered medical practitioner or chartered psychologist by whom the arrangements are made must give notice in writing to the offender's responsible officer, specifying the institution or place in or at which the treatment is to be carried out; and
(b) the treatment provided for by the arrangements is deemed to be treatment to which the offender is required to submit in pursuance of the youth rehabilitation order.

(13) Drug treatment requirement

77–032 A "drug treatment requirement" is a requirement that the offender submit, during a period or periods specified in the order, to

CJIA 2008, s.1, Sch.1, Pt 2, para.22

treatment, by or under the direction of a specified person having the necessary qualifications or experience ("the treatment provider"), with a view to the reduction or elimination of the offender's dependency on, or propensity to misuse, drugs.

Such a requirement may not be included in an order unless the judge is satisfied that:

(1) the offender is dependent on, or has a propensity to misuse, drugs; and

(2) the offender's dependency or propensity is such as requires and may be susceptible to treatment.

The treatment required must be such one of the following kinds of treatment as may be specified in the order, namely:

(a) treatment as a resident in such institution or place as may be specified in the order; or

(b) treatment as a non-resident at such institution or place, and at such intervals, as may be so specified,

but the order must not otherwise specify the nature of the treatment.

A requirement may not be included unless:

(i) the court has been notified by the Secretary of State that arrangements for implementing drug treatment requirements are in force in the local justice area in which the offender resides or is to reside;

(ii) the judge is satisfied that arrangements have been or can be made for the treatment intended to be specified in the order (including, where the offender is to be required to submit to treatment as a resident, and arrangements for his reception);

(iii) the requirement has been recommended as suitable for the offender by a member of a youth offending team, an officer of a local probation board or an officer of a provider of probation services; and

(iv) the offender has expressed willingness to comply with the requirement.

"Drug" means a controlled drug as defined by MDA 1971, s.2.

(14) Intoxicating substance treatment requirement

77–033 An "intoxicating substance treatment requirement" is a requirement that the offender submit, during a period or periods specified in the order, to treatment by or under the direction of a specified person having the necessary qualifications or experience, with a view to the reduction or elimination of the offender's dependency on, or propensity to misuse, intoxicating substances. CJIA 2008, s.1, Sch.1, Pt 2, para.24

Such a requirement may not be included in an order unless the judge is satisfied that:

(1) the offender is dependent on, or has a propensity to misuse, intoxicating substances; and

(2) the offender's dependency or propensity is such as requires and may be susceptible to treatment.

The treatment required must be such one of the following kinds of treatment as may be specified in the order:

(a) treatment as a resident in such institution or place as may be specified; or

(b) treatment as a non-resident at such institution or place, and at such intervals, as may be specified,

but the order must not otherwise specify the nature of the treatment.

Again, such a requirement may not be included unless:

(i) the judge is satisfied that arrangements have been or can be made for the treatment intended to be specified in the order (including, where the offender is to be required to submit to treatment as a resident, arrangements for his reception);

(ii) the requirement has been recommended as suitable for the offender by a member of a youth offending team, an officer of a local probation board or an officer of a provider of probation services; and

(iii) the offender has expressed willingness to comply with the requirement.

"Intoxicating substance" means here alcohol, or any other substance or product (other than a drug) which is, or the fumes of which are, capable of being inhaled or otherwise used for the purpose of causing intoxication.

"Drug" means a controlled drug as defined by MDA 1971, s.2.

(15) Education requirement

77–034 An "education requirement" is a requirement that the offender comply, during a period or periods specified in the order, with approved education arrangements, which for this means arrangements for the offender's education; CJIA 2008, s.1, Sch.1, Pt 2, para.25

(1) made for the time being by the offender's parent or guardian; and

(2) approved by the local education authority specified in the order.

The specified local education authority be the local education authority for the area in which the offender resides or is to reside.

Such a requirement may not be included in an order unless:

(a) the court has consulted the local education authority proposed to be specified in the order with regard to the proposal to include the requirement; and

(b) the judge is satisfied:

(i) that, in the view of that local education authority, arrangements exist for the offender to receive efficient full time education suitable to the offender's age, ability, aptitude and special educational needs (if any); and

(ii) that, having regard to the circumstances of the case, the inclusion of the education requirement is necessary for securing the good conduct of the offender or for preventing the commission of further offences.

Any period specified in a youth rehabilitation order as a period during which an offender must comply with approved education arrangements must not include any period after the offender has ceased to be of compulsory school age.

"Local education authority" here, and "parent", have the same meanings as in the Education Act 1996.

(16)   Electronic monitoring requirement

77–035   An "electronic monitoring requirement" is a requirement for securing the electronic monitoring of the offender's compliance with other requirements imposed by the order during a period specified in the order or determined by the responsible officer in accordance with the order.

CJIA 2008, s.1, Sch.1, Pt 2, para.26

Where:

(1) it is proposed to include an electronic monitoring requirement in a youth rehabilitation order; but

(2) there is a person (other than the offender) without whose cooperation it will not be practicable to secure that the monitoring takes place,

such requirement may not be included in the order without that person's consent.

Where an electronic monitoring requirement is required to take effect during a period determined by the responsible officer in accordance with the youth rehabilitation order, the responsible officer must, before the beginning of that period, notify:

(a) the offender;

(b) the person responsible for the monitoring; and

(c) any person falling within (b) above,

of the time when the period is to begin.

An order which imposes such a requirement must include provision for making a person responsible for the monitoring, and that person must be of a description specified in an order made by the Secretary of State.

An electronic monitoring requirement may not be included in an order unless:

(a) the court has been notified by the Home Secretary that arrangements for electronic monitoring of offenders are available:

(i) in the local justice area proposed to be specified in the order; and

(ii) for each requirement mentioned in the first column of the Table in sub-paragraph (7) which the court proposes to include in the order, in the area in which the relevant place is situated; and

(b) the judge is satisfied that the necessary provision can be made under the arrangements currently available.

6. Miscellaneous

Date of taking effect and other existing orders

77–036 A youth rehabilitation order ordinarily takes effect on the day after the order is made; but if a detention and training order is in force in respect of an offender, the judge making a youth rehabilitation order in respect of the offender may order that it is to take effect instead:

CJIA 2008,
s.1, Sch.1, Pt 3,
para.30

(a) when the period of supervision begins in relation to the detention and training order (PCC(S)A 2000, s.103(1)(a); or

(b) on the expiry of the term of the detention and training order.

A youth rehabilitation order must not be made in respect of an offender at a time when:

(a) another youth rehabilitation order; or

(b) a reparation order made under PCC(S)A 2000, s.73(1),

is in force in respect of the offender, unless when the order is made the earlier order is revoked.

Where the earlier order is revoked, para.24 of Sch.2 (provision of copies of orders) applies to the revocation as it applies to the revocation of a youth rehabilitation order.

Concurrent and consecutive orders

77–037 Where the court is dealing with an offender who has been convicted of two or more associated offences, and in respect of one of the offences, the court makes an order of any of the following kinds:

CJIA 2008,
s.1, Sch.1, Pt 3,
para.31

(a) a youth rehabilitation order with intensive supervision and surveillance;

(b) a youth rehabilitation order with fostering; or

(c) any other youth rehabilitation order,

the judge may not make an order of any other of those kinds in respect of the other offence, or any of the other offences.

If the court makes two or more youth rehabilitation orders with intensive supervision and surveillance, or with fostering, both or all of the orders must take effect at the same time (para.30, above).

Where the requirements of the same kind are included in two or more youth rehabilitation orders, the judge must direct, in relation to each requirement of that kind, whether;

(a) it is to be concurrent with the other requirement or requirements of that kind, or any of them; or

(b) it and the other requirement or requirements of that kind, or any of them, are to be consecutive; but he may not direct that two or more fostering requirements are to be consecutive.

If the judge directs that two or more requirements of the same kind are to be consecutive:

(a) the number of hours, days or months specified in relation to one of them is additional to the number of hours, days, or months specified in relation to the other or others; but

(b) the aggregate number of hours, days or months specified in relation to both or all of them must not exceed the maximum number which may be specified in relation to any one of them.

Requirements are "of the same kind" if they fall within the same paragraph of Pt 2 of Sch.1.

7. Administrative

Date for compliance with requirements to be specified in order

77–038 A youth rehabilitation order must specify a date, not more than three years after the date on which the order takes effect, by which time all the requirements in it must have been complied with.

CJIA 2008, s.1, Sch.1, Pt 4, para.33

A youth rehabilitation order which imposes two or more different requirements falling within Pt 2 of Sch.1 may also specify an earlier date or dates in relation to compliance with any one or more of them.

In the case of a youth rehabilitation order with intensive supervision and surveillance, the date specified for the purposes of sub-paragraph (1) must not be earlier than six months after the date on which the order takes effect.

Local justice area to be specified in order

77–039 A youth rehabilitation order must specify the local justice area in which the offender resides or will reside.

CJIA 2008, s.1, Sch.1, Pt 4, para.33

Provision of copies of orders

77–040 The court by which any youth rehabilitation order is made must forthwith provide copies of the order:

CJIA 2008, s.1, Sch.1, Pt 4, para.34

(a) to the offender;

(b) if the offender is aged under 14, to the offender's parent or guardian; and

(c) to a member of a youth offending team assigned to the court, to an officer of a local probation board assigned to the court or to an officer of a provider of probation services.

Where a youth rehabilitation order is made by the Crown Court, the court making the order must:

(a) provide to the magistrates' court acting in the local justice area specified in the order;

(i) a copy of the order, and

(ii) such documents and information relating to the case as

it considers likely to be of assistance to a court acting in that area in the exercise of its functions in relation to the order; and

(b) provide a copy of the order to the local probation board acting for that area or (as the case may be) a provider of probation services operating in that area.

Where a youth rehabilitation order imposes any requirement specified in the first column of the following Table set out in Sch.1, Pt 4, para.34, the court by which the order is made must also forthwith provide the person specified in relation to that requirement in the second column of that Table with a copy of so much of the order as relates to that requirement.

Direction in relation to further proceedings

77–041 Where the Crown Court makes a youth rehabilitation order, it may include in the order a direction that further proceedings relating to the order be in a youth court or other magistrates' court (subject to para.7 of Sch.2).

CJIA 2008, s.1, Sch.1, Pt 4, para.36

"Further proceedings", in relation to a youth rehabilitation order, means proceedings:

(1) for any failure to comply with the order within the meaning given by para.1(2)(b) of Sch.2; or
(2) on any application for amendment or revocation of the order under Pt 3 or 4 of that Schedule.

Notes

SUBJECT INDEX

An Index of material, such as this work is, should not require a further Subject Index. There may, however, be matters included in a wider-ranging, "catch-all" section which may need to be identified. A selection of these is set out below.

SUBJECT INDEX

2012

	January					
M		2	9	16	23	30
T		3	10	17	24	31
W		4	11	18	25	
T		5	12	19	26	
F		6	13	20	27	
S		7	14	21	28	
S	1	8	15	22	29	

	February				
M		6	13	20	27
T		7	14	21	28
W	1	8	15	22	29
T	2	9	16	23	
F	3	10	17	24	
S	4	11	18	25	
S	5	12	19	26	

	March				
M		5	12	19	26
T		6	13	20	27
W		7	14	21	28
T	1	8	15	22	29
F	2	9	16	23	30
S	3	10	17	24	31
S	4	11	18	25	

	April					
M		2	9	16	23	30
T		3	10	17	24	
W		4	11	18	25	
T		5	12	19	26	
F		6	13	20	27	
S		7	14	21	28	
S	1	8	15	22	29	

	May				
M		7	14	21	28
T	1	8	15	22	29
W	2	9	16	23	30
T	3	10	17	24	31
F	4	11	18	25	
S	5	12	19	26	
S	6	13	20	27	

	June				
M		4	11	18	25
T		5	12	19	26
W		6	13	20	27
T		7	14	21	28
F	1	8	15	22	29
S	2	9	16	23	30
S	3	10	17	24	

	July					
M		2	9	16	23	30
T		3	10	17	24	31
W		4	11	18	25	
T		5	12	19	26	
F		6	13	20	27	
S		7	14	21	28	
S	1	8	15	22	29	

	August				
M		6	13	20	27
T		7	14	21	28
W	1	8	15	22	29
T	2	9	16	23	30
F	3	10	17	24	31
S	4	11	18	25	
S	5	12	19	26	

	September				
M		3	10	17	24
T		4	11	18	25
W		5	12	19	26
T		6	13	20	27
F		7	14	21	28
S	1	8	15	22	29
S	2	9	16	23	30

	October				
M	1	8	15	22	29
T	2	9	16	23	30
W	3	10	17	24	31
T	4	11	18	25	
F	5	12	19	26	
S	6	13	20	27	
S	7	14	21	28	

	November				
M		5	12	19	26
T		6	13	20	27
W		7	14	21	28
T	1	8	15	22	29
F	2	9	16	23	30
S	3	10	17	24	
S	4	11	18	25	

	December					
M		3	10	17	24	31
T		4	11	18	25	
W		5	12	19	26	
T		6	13	20	27	
F		7	14	21	28	
S	1	8	15	22	29	
S	2	9	16	23	30	